THE LETTERS OF
T. S. ELIOT
VOLUME 7

By T. S. Eliot

THE POEMS OF T. S. ELIOT
Volume 1: Collected and Uncollected Poems
Volume 2: Practical Cats and Further Verses
edited by Christopher Ricks and Jim McCue

COLLECTED POEMS 1909–1962
PRUFROCK AND OTHER OBSERVATIONS
THE WASTE LAND AND OTHER POEMS
FOUR QUARTETS
SELECTED POEMS
THE WASTE LAND:
A Facsimile and Transcript of the Original Drafts
edited by Valerie Eliot
INVENTIONS OF THE MARCH HARE:
Poems 1909–1917
edited by Christopher Ricks
THE ARIEL POEMS
THE WASTE LAND
Anniversary Edition
OLD POSSUM'S BOOK OF PRACTICAL CATS
THE COMPLETE POEMS AND PLAYS

plays
MURDER IN THE CATHEDRAL
THE FAMILY REUNION
THE COCKTAIL PARTY
THE CONFIDENTIAL CLERK
THE ELDER STATESMAN

literary criticism
THE SACRED WOOD
SELECTED ESSAYS
THE USE OF POETRY AND THE USE OF CRITICISM
THE VARIETIES OF METAPHYSICAL POETRY
edited by Ronald Schuchard
TO CRITICIZE THE CRITIC
ON POETRY AND POETS
FOR LANCELOT ANDREWES
SELECTED PROSE OF T. S. ELIOT
edited by Frank Kermode
THE COMPLETE PROSE OF T. S. ELIOT: THE CRITICAL EDITION
Volume 1: Apprentice Years, 1905–1918
edited by Jewel Spears Brooker and Ronald Schuchard
Volume 2: The Perfect Critic, 1919–1926
edited by Anthony Cuda and Ronald Schuchard
Volume 3: Literature, Politics, Belief, 1927–1929
edited by Frances Dickey, Jennifer Formichelli, Ronald Schuchard
Volume 4: English Lion, 1930–1933
edited by Jason Harding and Ronald Schuchard

social criticism
THE IDEA OF A CHRISTIAN SOCIETY
NOTES TOWARDS THE DEFINITION OF CULTURE

letters
THE LETTERS OF T. S. ELIOT
Volume 1: 1898–1922; Volume 2: 1923–1925
edited by Valerie Eliot and Hugh Haughton
Volume 3: 1926–1927; Volume 4: 1928–1929;
Volume 5: 1930–1931; Volume 6: 1932–1933
edited by Valerie Eliot and John Haffenden

THE LETTERS OF
T. S. Eliot

EDITED BY
VALERIE ELIOT

AND

JOHN HAFFENDEN

VOLUME 7
1934–1935

ff

FABER & FABER

First published in 2017
by Faber & Faber Ltd, Bloomsbury House,
74–77 Great Russell Street, London WC1B 3DA

Typeset by Donald Sommerville
Printed in England by T. J. International,
Padstow, Cornwall

A CIP record for this book is available from the British Library

ISBN 978–0–571–31636–6

For letters omitted from this and the previous volumes of T. S. Eliot's correspondence,
please visit www.tseliot.com

2 4 6 8 10 9 7 5 3 1

CONTENTS

ILLUSTRATIONS

ACKNOWLEDGEMENTS

For help and advice in many capacities, including copyright permissions, the publishers and editors would like to thank the following individuals and institutions. (Sadly, a number of those named below are now deceased, but we wish still to put on record our gratitude to them.) Dr Donald Adamson; Barry Ahearn; Ruth M. (Beth) Alvarez; The American Jewish Archives, Cincinnati, Ohio; Dr Norma Aubertin-Potter; Camilla Bagg; Buona Barnes; Joan Bailey; Ruth Baker; Susan Bank, Secretary to Rev. Carl Scovel, Minister, King's Chapel, Boston, Massachusetts; Owen Barfield; Tansy Barton, Special Collections Administrator, Senate House Library, University of London; H. Baugh; BBC Written Archives Centre; Denison Beach; T. O. Beachcroft; Anne Olivier Bell; Mrs W. J. Bender; Joanne Bentley; Robert J. Bertholf, Curator, The Poetry/Rare Books Collection, University Libraries, State University of New York at Buffalo; Bibliothèque Nationale, Paris; Kevin Birmingham; Kenneth Blackwell, Mills Memorial Library, McMaster University; Michael Harry Blechner, McFarlin Library, University of Tulsa; Mary Boccaccio, McKeldin Library, University of Maryland; Maxwell Bodenheim; John Bodley; William H. Bond; University of Bonn Library; J. M. L. Booker, Archivist, Lloyds Bank; Michael Borrie, Manuscript Collections, British Library; Ann Bowden, Harry Ransom Humanities Research Center, University of Texas at Austin; David Bradshaw; The British Library; Valerie Brokenshire; Jewel Spears Brooker; Robert Brown, Archivist, Faber & Faber Ltd; Sally Brown; Richard Buckle; Penelope Bulloch, Balliol College Library; Dr R. W. Burchfield; Roland Burke Savage, SJ, Clongowes Wood College; Professor P. H. Butter; William R. Cagle and Saundra Taylor, Lilly Library; Herbert Cahoon, The Pierpont Morgan Library; Anne Caiger, Manuscripts Librarian, University of California, Los Angeles; Douglas Campbell; Kathleen Cann, Department of Manuscripts and University Archives, Cambridge University Library; Humphrey Carpenter; François Chapon, Bibliothèque Littéraire Jacques Doucet; Mrs Charlton; Christopher M. Cherry; Joseph Chiari; David E. Chinitz; Mary Clapinson, Keeper of Western Manuscripts, Bodleian Library; Alexander P. Clark, Firestone Library, Princeton University; Alan Clodd; Librarian in Charge, Codrington Library, All Souls College, Oxford; Marguerite Cohn;

Dorothy Collins; Henri Colliot, Fondation Saint-John Perse; John Constable; Alistair Cooke; Bonnie Costello; Joyce Crick; Peter Croft; Arthur Crook; Tanya Crothers; Anthony Cuda; Charles T. Cullen, President and Librarian, The Newberry Library; Rexi Culpin; Helen Davies, Librarian, Royal Central School of Speech and Drama; Dr Robin Darwall-Smith, Archivist, University College, Oxford; Roy L. Davids; Carolyn A. Davis, Reader Services Librarian, The George Arents Research Library for Special Collections, Syracuse University Library; Dr A. Deiss, General Secretariat, Swiss Medical Institutions; Giles de la Mare; the Literary Trustees of Walter de la Mare; Rodney G. Dennis; Herbert Dieckmann; Valentine Dobrée; E. R. Dodds; David Doughan, Fawcett Library; Kenneth W. Duckett, Morris Library, Southern Illinois University at Carbondale; Ellen S. Dunlap, Harry Ransom Humanities Research Center; Jackie DuPont; Peter du Sautoy; Donald D. Eddy, Department of Rare Books, Cornell University Library; Professor Charles W. Eliot; Sarah Ethier, University of Wisconsin-Milwaukee Libraries; Matthew Evans; Sir Richard Faber, KCVO; Toby Faber; Tom Faber; Elizabeth A. Falsey; Patricia Fanshawe; Christopher Farley; David Farmer, Harry Ransom Humanities Research Center (and Warren Roberts, Mary Hirth, Sally Leach, and many other members of staff); Donald Farren, University of Maryland Libraries; Barbara Fehse, Secretary in Manuscripts, University of Virginia Library; Anton Felton, Continuum Ltd; Dominique Fernandez; James Fergusson Books and Manuscripts; Mrs Harry Fine; Mrs Burnham Finney; Christopher Fletcher; Barbara Floyd, Director of the Ward M. Canaday Center for Special Collections, University of Toledo; Angel Flores; Henri Fluchère; Fondren Library; Jennifer Formichelli; Robert Fraser; Donald Gallup; Special Collections, Isabella Stewart Gardner Museum, Boston, Mass.; K. C. Gay, Lockwood Memorial Library, State University of New York, Buffalo; Herbert Gerwing, University of Victoria; Mrs Ghika; Catherine Gide; M. A. M. Gilbert; Robert Giroux; Dr Peter Godman; Emile Goichot; Estate of Enid Goldsmith; Adrian M. Goodman; Philip Goodman; Christian Goodwillie, Director and Curator, Special Collections, Burke Library, Hamilton College, Clinton, New York; Lyndall Gordon; Warwick Gould; Nicollette Gray; Herbert T. Greene; Ernest G. Griffin; J. C. Hall; Dr Michael Halls; Susan Halpert; Saskia Hamilton; Bonnie Hardwick, Manuscripts Division, The Bancroft Library, University of California, Berkeley; Sir Rupert Hart-Davis; Harvard University Archives; Professor E. N. Hartley, Institute Archives, MIT; Michael Hastings; The Library, Haverford College; Lilace Hatayama, Manuscripts Division, University Research Library, University of

California; Desmond Hawkins; Cathy Henderson, Research Librarian, Harry Ransom Humanities Research Center; Robert Henderson; David Higham Associates Ltd; Roger Highfield; Robert W. Hill, New York Public Library; Aurelia Bolliger Hodgson; Michael Hofmann; Michael Holroyd; Hornbake Library, University of Maryland (Beth Alvarez, Ann L. Hudak); Lélia Howard; Penelope Hughes-Hallett; J. W. Hunt, Royal Military Academy, Sandhurst; Jeremy Hutchinson; Lord Hutchinson; Elizabeth Inglis (Special Collections, The Library, University of Sussex); Carol Jackson, Chipping Campden History Society; Robin Jackson, The British Academy; William A. Jackson, Houghton Library; Carolyn Jakeman; P. D. James; Revd Martin Jarrett-Kerr, CR; Dorothy O. Johansen, Reed College, Portland, Oregon; Gregory A. Johnson, Alderman Library, University of Virginia; William Jovanovich; William L. Joyce, Princeton University Library; Michael Kammen; Paul Keegan; Ann M. Kenne, Head of Special Collections Department/University Archivist, University of St Thomas, St Paul, Minnesota; Professor John Kelly; Dr Paul Kelly, National Library of Scotland; Mary Kiffer, Assistant Secretary, John Simon Guggenheim Memorial Foundation, New York; Modern Archives Centre, King's College, Cambridge; Monique Kuntz, Bibliothèque Municipale, Vichy; Dr L. R. Leavis; Major N. Aylward Leete; Mrs Dorothy Milburn Léger; Paul Levy; Lockwood Memorial Library; Kenneth A. Lohf, Librarian for Rare Books and MSS, Butler Library, Columbia University; London Library; Pat Lowe; Richard Luckett; Richard M. Ludwig, and Howard C. Rice Jr., Princeton University Library; Charles Madge; Lady Marshall; Jay Martin; Jim McCue; Mary C. McGreenery, Harvard Alumni Records; Patricia McGuire, Archivist, and Peter Monteith, Assistant Archivist, King's College, Cambridge; Ed Maggs; Professor R. B. Martin; Professor B. K. Matilal; Francis O. Mattson, Berg Collection, New York Public Library; R. Russell Maylone, Special Collections Department, Northwestern University Library; Robert Medley; Bernard Meehan, Keeper of Manuscripts, Trinity College Dublin; Ed Mendelson; Erik Mesterton; Wim van Mierlo; Prof. Andrew M. Miller; Marvin A. Miller, Director of Libraries, University of Arkansas; Mrs Edward S. Mills; University Library, Missouri History Museum; Joe Mitchenson; Kate Mole, Librarian/Archivist, The British Academy; Glen E. Morgan; Frank Vigor Morley; J. D. I. Morley; Leslie A. Morris, Houghton Library, Harvard University; Lewis Morris; Tim Munby; Katherine Middleton Murry; Mary Middleton Murry; Richard Murry; Ben Nelson; The Bursar, New College, Oxford; Jeanne T. Newlin, Harvard Theatre Collection; Anne Oakley, Archivist, Cathedral, City and Diocesan

Record Office, Canterbury; Richard Ollard; Richard D. Olson, Curator of Rare Books and Special Collections, The University Library, Northwestern University; Jessie Orage; Dr James Marshall Osborn; Anne Owen; Martin Page; Stephen Page; Stephen R. Parks, Curator, The James Marshall and Marie-Louise Osborn Collection, Yale University; Alasdair Paterson, University of Exeter Library; Fondation Saint-John Perse; C. G. Petter, Archivist Librarian, Special Collections, University of Victoria; Robert Phillips; Sir Charles Pickthorn Bt; Charles E. Pierce, Jr., Director, The Pierpont Morgan Library; Jean F. Preston, Princeton University Library; Lord Quinton; Mary de Rachewiltz; Craig Raine; Lawrence S. Rainey; Wanda M. Randall; Benedict Read; Special Collections, Reading University; Real Academia de la Historia; Dr R. T. H. Redpath; Joseph Regenstein Library, University of Chicago; Stanley Revell; Howard C. Rice, Jr., Associate Librarian for Rare Books & Special Collections, Princeton University Library; Glyn Richards; I. A. and Dorothea Richards; Canon Pierre Riches; Christopher Ricks; Helene Ritzerfeld; Alain Rivière; Professor A. D. Roberts; Sir Adam Roberts; Judith Robinson-Valéry; Ruth R. Rogers, Special Collections Librarian, Margaret Clapp Library, Wellesley College; Galleria Nazionale d'Arte Moderna, Rome; Rosenbach Museum & Library, Philadelphia, PA; Anthony Rota; Bertram Rota; Mme Agathe Rouart-Valéry; Carol Z. Rothkopf; A. L. Rowse; Oliver Rowse; Royal Literary Fund; Lord Russell; Mrs N. Ryan; Professor Alfred W. Satterthwaite; Marcia Satterthwaite; Sean Sayers; Schiller-National-museum, Marbach am Neckar; Gerd Schmidt; David E. Schoonover, Yale University Library; Susan Schreibman; Revd Karl Schroeder, SJ.; Ronald Schuchard; Grace Schulman; Timothy and Marian Seldes; Miranda Seymour; Christopher Sheppard, Brotherton Collection, Leeds University; Ethel C. Simpson, Trustee, John Gould Fletcher Literary Estate; G. Singh; Samuel A. Sizer, Curator, Special Collections, University Libraries, University of Arkansas; Wilma R. Slaight, Archivist, Wellesley College; Janet Adam Smith; Theodora Eliot Smith; Virginia L. Smyers, Harvard University Archives; Revd Charles Smyth; Natasha Spender; Sir Stephen Spender; Martha Sprackland; Tom Staley; Jayme Stayer; Dom Julian Stead; Alix Strachey; James Strachey; Jenny Stratford; Kendon L. Stubbs, University of Virginia Library; Barbara Sturtevant; University of Sussex Library; Michael Sutton; Dorothy L. Swerdlove, Curator, The Billy Rose Theatre Collection, New York Public Library; Lola L. Szladits, Berg Collection, New York Public Library; Allen Tate; Elizabeth Stege Teleky, The Joseph Regenstein Library, University of Chicago; David S. Thatcher, University of Victoria, British Columbia; Alan G Thomas; Dr Richard

Thompson; Willard Thorp; Dr Michael J. Tilby; Kathleen Tillotson; Trinity College, Cambridge; Francois Valéry; The Paul Valéry Collection, Bibliothèque Nationale, Paris; Julian Vinogradoff; University of Virginia Library; Rebecca Volk, Archivist, Jesuits in Britain Archives; Graham Wallas and Angela Raspin, London School of Economics; Michael J. Walsh, Heythrop College; Mrs Antonia Warren; J. Waterlow; Dr George Watson; John Weightman; John Wells, Cambridge University Library; Richard Wendorf; Gretchen Wheen; James White, National Gallery of Ireland; Brooke Whiting, Department of Special Collections, University Research Library, University of California, Los Angeles; Widener Library, Harvard University; Helen Willard; David G. Williams; Dr Charlotte Williamson; George Williamson; Julia Ross Williamson; Patricia C. Willis, Beinecke Rare Book and Manuscript Library, Yale University; Joan H. Winterkorn; Melanie Wisner; Harriet Harvey Wood; Woodson Research Center, Rice University; Dr Daniel H. Woodward, Huntington Library; C. J. Wright; Yale University Archives; Michael Yeats; Mrs E. D. Yeo, Assistant Keeper, National Library of Scotland.

For permission to quote from unpublished letters and other material, we thank the following estates and individuals. W. H. Auden: by permission of Edward Mendelson, the Estate of W. H. Auden. George Barker: by permission of Elspeth Barker. Ernest Bird: by permission of the trustees of the Estate of Sir Ernest Bird. E. Martin Browne: by permission of Denis Browne. Quotations by Emily Holmes Coleman are copyright © 2017 by Estate of Emily Holmes Coleman. Alistair Cooke: by permission of Colin Webb. F. Scott Fitzgerald: by permission of Harold Ober Associates, Inc., for the Estate of F. Scott Fitzgerald. Sir Victor Gollancz: by permission of Livia Gollancz. Bryan Guinness: by permission of Rosaleen Mulji. Ralph Hodgson: courtesy of the Ralph Hodgson and Aurelia Bolliger Hodgson Papers, Special Collections Department, Bryn Mawr College Library. James Laughlin: copyright © 2017 by the New Directions Ownership Trust. Reprinted by permission of New Directions Publishing Corp. F. R. Leavis: by permission of Dr Robin Leavis. Henry Miller: by permission of the Estate of Henry Miller. Harriet Monroe: by permission of Ann Monroe. Lady Ottoline Morrell: by permission of Adrian Goodman and the Estate of Ottoline Morrell. Sylvia Pankhurst: by permission of Dr Helen Pankhurst. Ezra Pound: by permission of New Directions Publishers acting as agent, copyright © 2017 by Mary de Rachewiltz and the Estate of Omar S. Pound. Reprinted by permission of New Directions Publishing Corp. Frederic Prokosch: by permission of Jack Bady. Michael

Roberts: by permission of Sir Adam Roberts and Professor A. D. Roberts. Stephen Spender, by permission of Matthew and Lizzie Spender.

Special thanks go to Judith Hooper and Clare Reihill, trustees of the Estate of T. S. Eliot, for their generous support, faith and friendship; Matthew Hollis of Faber & Faber Ltd; Nancy Fulford, Project Archivist – T. S. Eliot Collection; Donald Sommerville for expert copy-editing and typesetting; Iman Javadi for swift, authoritative help with translations; Sara Ayad for her resourceful picture research; David Wilson for proof-reading; Douglas Matthews for indexing; Mrs Valerie Eliot's assistant Debbie Whitfield for her commitment and long hard work; and the Institute of English Studies, University of London, for hosting the T. S. Eliot Editorial Project funded by the Arts and Humanities Research Council. John Haffenden is grateful above all to Jemma Walton for her good humour, love and kindness.

The editors and publishers apologise if any person or estate has been overlooked. They would be grateful to be informed if any copyright notice has been omitted, or if there have been any changes of ownership or location.

PREFACE

'A dark green blotting paper wall paper, & books rather meagre, stood on top of each other; bookcases with shelves missing . . . Nothing nice to look at. Purple covers. Respectable china . . . A pallid very cold experience . . . A large faced pale faced man – our great poet.' Having sought in 1933 to secure a formal separation from his wife Vivien, T. S. Eliot chose from 1934 to live a reclusive life in a Kensington presbytery-house run by the local vicar, Eric Cheetham. It was more than a year later that Virginia Woolf penned her sorry account of the austere conditions which the celebrated author was to inhabit for several years. Recognising Eliot as a devout, dependable parishioner, Cheetham appointed him Vicar's Warden; and the poet stuck to this task for a quarter of a century.

Understandably, as often as he could get away from his professional and church duties, and from his dour lodgings, Eliot was the complete weekender. He enjoyed visiting friends such as Geoffrey and Polly Tandy and their young family in Hampton-on-Thames; his Faber colleague Frank Morley and family in Surrey; and for at least one week each year he stayed with the Fabers at their vacation home in Wales. And most of all during this period he loved to spend days with his intimate American friend Emily Hale in the old market town of Chipping Campden, Gloucestershire, where she was staying for several weeks in the summer of 1934, and again in 1935, in a house rented by her elderly uncle and aunt, the Revd and Mrs John Carroll Perkins (visiting from Boston).

But Eliot's sojourns at Stamford House were not as idyllic as he must have hoped. The Perkinses, who admired him and his work, and who encouraged their gentleman caller and his care for their ward, got on his nerves. In particular, he conceived an especial antipathy to the lady of the house; and uncharacteristically – he was by nature a big-hearted man – he spelt out to one of his American cousins, in a letter, the compound faults of 'Aunt Edith': 'Mrs Perkins strikes me as one of those gentle, stupid, kind, tyrannous, prejudiced, oppressive and tremendously powerful personalities who blight everyone about them . . . I may be completely wrong. But she makes my hair bristle; and confound it one can't help trusting that bristle. Dr Perkins is a very lovable, lazy-minded, muddleheaded man who is completely dominated by his wife, and who is really happier in Emily's company than he is with Mrs Perkins, but he doesn't know it.' All the same, in the face of such startling dislike, he felt he had to keep up appearances, if only because the Perkinses gave him access to lengthy spells in Emily's company. The degree to which it went against the grain for him to have to pay court to Mrs Perkins is manifest in this constrainedly Jamesian letter of thanks: 'I should like to formulate, if not express, my appreciation of a delightful weekend in a lovely household . . . I shall not try to trace the ramifications of gratefulness in detail; but my perceptions are at least superior to my power of expression, and I think exceed the need of it.' The root of the problem, it would seem, was not simply his aversion to the woman's conduct and personality, but jealousy. Edith Perkins expected Emily to pay her much attention, and Emily – whether by instinct or inveterate training – willingly afforded her the attention she claimed. Eliot came to resent Emily's subservience to her aunt; but whether or not he felt that Emily should be paying much more attention to himself is not so evident. On 12 April 1935 he wrote to a sympathetic confidante, Jeanette McPherrin (a friend of Emily's), of his vexation: 'It is difficult enough to cope with Emily's sense of duty at any time . . . One can only try cautiously to affect her (a) behaviour (b) attitude towards her relatives, to whom she seems to me exasperatingly respectful. But as I was once put in my place for commenting not too favourably about the behaviour-towards-her of a relative of hers not nearly so closely related as these, I am very careful . . . In a way, I think it is as much her fault as theirs that they have such a repressive effect on her and make her so depressingly humble.' One irony of the situation was that the friends of the poet to whom he introduced Emily commonly found her grim and prim – 'like a Sergeant Major', said Lady Ottoline Morrell – and bossy towards him.

Ways of escape from the Perkinses included long walks in the Cotswold countryside; and it was on one such ramble that they chanced upon the 'third-rate manor house' of Burnt Norton, whose rose garden and empty ponds took possession of the poet's imagination. The poem 'Burnt Norton' was begun the following year. Some friends of Eliot, and some biographers, have understandably speculated about the larger meaning of the poet's experience: possibly the poet and his friend consummated their love in the deserted garden? But in truth that would seem to have been most unlikely: the experience in the garden and the experience of the poem are not to be equated, and at this stage of his life Eliot still considered celibacy 'the highest ideal'. The poet and his dear friend may have kissed, and even come to an understanding; but, given the character and convictions of the poet, sexual intercourse was not a likelihood.

Back in London, he was ever-anxious to avoid running into Vivien, who refused to accept that her husband had left her. The privacy-loving poet was forced to go to law to retrieve his books and papers. Following a prolonged legal to-and-fro, Vivien's flat was raided by bailiffs – to her strained horror. (She purported to have been unaware that she had been served with a court order for the restoration of her husband's property.) In truth, her mind seems to have been so far askew that she was never able to comprehend why her husband should not simply resume cohabitation with the wife from whom he had separated himself; at times, she left the door open for him. She stalked Eliot at the offices of Faber & Faber; begged him to come home to her; sought to accost and embarrass him. She haunted the Mercury Theatre in London – attending performances of *Sweeney Agonistes*, and of *Murder in the Cathedral* – in a quest to confront him. Ultimately, she did succeed in tracking him down, in November 1935, at the *Sunday Times* book exhibition at Dorland Hall where he was giving a lecture. Just as his talk finished, she rushed up to the podium (dressed in her Fascist uniform), unleashing her dog and letting it leap up at Eliot, and she asked her estranged husband, 'Will you come home with me?' 'I cannot speak to you now,' he told her curtly (while frantically signing the copies of three of his books that she had placed before him), before making smartly for the exit. Bizarrely and pitifully, Vivien proceeded forthwith to advise her solicitors that her husband had reclaimed her: she wished to put her affairs back into his hands. (When she told the same thing to her mother and aunt, they froze, knowing the falsehood she was retailing.) Her desperate bid to seize the initiative did not survive examination. At other times, she persuaded herself that her husband had been kidnapped, or was being bullied by colleagues, or blackmailed: that he needed to be rescued. A notable bonus of this volume of Eliot's correspondence is that it draws upon Vivien Eliot's letters and diaries to provide a picture of her mental state and her way of life – and to enable the reader to appreciate her thoughts and feelings.

'That play represents a period of four months' consistent hard work. I devoted six mornings a week to the writing of *Murder in the Cathedral*, mornings that were relentlessly filched from one hundred other activities.' Eliot always claimed that he was a playwright not by instinct but by dint of sheer hard work. His modesty is belied by his extraordinarily successful career as a stage dramatist as it gathers pace through the fascinating letters of this volume.

Following his early experimentation with the fast-paced and jazzy – though regrettably unfinished – dark comedy *Sweeney Agonistes: An Aristophanic Melodrama*, the poet was invited to compose all the words for an ambitious scenario sketched by the producer-director E. Martin Browne (who was to direct all of Eliot's plays), for a grand pageant called *The Rock* (1934) – 'a kind of Play', as Eliot correctly styled it – drawing on the resources of several London parishes and mounted at Sadler's Wells Theatre, with twenty-two scene changes and over 300 amateur performers (including the Bishop of London), and with the proceeds going to fund a push for church-building in the suburbs.

Eliot told a friend, the historian A. L. Rowse, at the end of the ten-day run: 'I often felt, while working on the pageant, that I had bitten off more than I could chew. I hope at least that it will put an end to the nonsense about "intellectualism" and "obscurity". I am anything but an intellectual; more nearly a pure *émotif*. And nobody with anything to say wants to be obscure. But one isn't naturally simple or lucid; it takes work and experience to get there. One has to shed a great deal, or work out a lot of poison; and perhaps simplicity only comes through a gradual mastery of one's own emotions.'

The capacious pageant form enabled Eliot to experiment with a variety of devices, in both verse and prose, ranging from historical vignettes to contemporary comedy, and including a scene of savage satire targeting plutocrats and demagogues: one passage is unsparingly antagonistic towards Sir Oswald Mosley and the Fascists. Above all, this venture pushed forward Eliot's enthusiasm for writing choral verses of varyingly inventive kinds, including solo voices in succession adding up to a crescendo of sound and meaning, as well as striking antiphonal passages. Indeed, the poet was so pleased with the choruses that he considered them fit to be weighed with his best work in poetry – at least for scale. He wrote to his New York publisher: 'the choruses do represent a new verse experiment on my part; and taken together, make a sequence of verses about twice the length of *The Waste Land*'.

The applause and attention attracted by *The Rock* led George Bell, Bishop of Chichester, to invite Eliot to write a play entirely of his own devising for the Canterbury Festival. The commission, which Eliot grasped to himself with passionate commitment, resulted in the writing of a triumph of modern verse drama, *Murder in the Cathedral*. *Murder* was first staged in June 1935 in the acoustically challenged confines of the Chapter House at Canterbury and subsequently brought to the London stage – where it ran at the Mercury Theatre for 108 performances and was seen by

20,000 people – and so to the world stage, as a huge commercial success. A quasi-liturgical masterpiece of dramatic writing, it remains in repertoire after eighty years. In one way, the play represents an ambitious, risky endeavour to compose verse for the modern theatre – 'good ranting stuff' Eliot called it – to invent an idiom to enable the import of a momentous historical occasion to speak to the twentieth century. More profoundly, it was the expression of Eliot's efforts to seize and clutch and penetrate to spiritual truths in his own life. He told Charles Williams (a fellow striver): 'It is surprising how few people seem to have any awareness of other than material realities, or of Good and Evil as having anything to do with the nature of things – as anything more than codes of conduct. I suppose it is because there is something so terrifying, like a blast from the North Pole, in spiritual reality that just natural cowardice and laziness makes us all try to evade it as much of the time as we can.' This volume of letters documents in full rewarding detail the writing and producing of Eliot's first major play.

Even while absorbed in time-consuming theatre work, Eliot was untiring in his other professional and public undertakings. He went to great lengths to cultivate over this period a considerable number of young writers including Charles Madge, Hugh Sykes Davies, D. G. Bridson, Rayner Heppenstall, A. L. Morton, Dilys Powell, Basil Bunting, James Hanley, Janet Adam Smith, F. T. Prince, Bernard Blackstone, Kenneth Allott, Henry Miller and Ronald Bottrall. (He commented *inter alia*: 'There seems to me good solid work in [Bottrall's poetry], nothing flashy, and at least greater maturity than in the Oxford Group.') He promoted the work of George Barker; telling Barker on 1 June, 'An advance on a book of poems by an author who has not hitherto received general publicity is not, of course, economically justifiable but we are making the offer because we believe in the future of your work and are ready to back it.' He remarked to Walter de la Mare: 'I believe [Barker] to have unusual imaginative and emotional gifts, and a deeper feeling for rhythm than most of the younger poets.' (His commitment to the unemployed young poet extended to setting up a private charitable fund to support him and his family for two years.) He made efforts, ultimately without success, to secure the first publication in the UK of Joyce's *Ulysses*. He brought on the work of Louis MacNeice and Marianne Moore; Djuna Barnes (his initial reading of passages from her novel *Nightwood* led him to think it 'incredibly tortured and tedious'); and Michael Roberts (the production of *The Faber Book of Modern Verse* is one of the signal publishing achievements of this period). In addition, Eliot worked assiduously for the Christian Church he had espoused, serving the Church Literature Association (for several months as secretary), and creating at Faber & Faber a list that extended to books on liturgy and witness. One such work which spoke to Eliot's own convictions was a testimony by a Methodist minister, T. S. Gregory, entitled *The Unfinished Universe* (1935), for which Eliot wrote this blurb: 'This book is the record of a passionate and sincere pursuit of spiritual conviction, of the journey of one human mind.'

In January 1935 Eliot rehearsed his chief activities and commitments, in a letter to his brother: 'I have a hard three months ahead of me, as I have a play to write in the next three months, which means abstaining from all weekends, from as many evening engagements as possible. Correspondence with, and interviews with solicitors have not lightened the burden . . . Vivienne by a policy of inaction . . . has given me the maximum of trouble and legal expense in getting my property . . . Apparently, I can dismiss from mind the fear of her molesting me. With what I provide, she now should still have an income of nearly £600 a year . . . but my chief fear is that she will get into financial difficulties . . . I have to entertain a lot of young writers to lunch, etc. occasionally help them out with a five pound note, and that sort of thing; as well as sometimes reciprocating the hospitality of people richer than myself. Also, the sort of reputation that I have gained, involves being asked to do all sorts of worthy things which don't bring in any money . . . One can't do everything one is asked to, but one must do some of it. I am sometimes asked to give a lecture, or a poetry reading, on behalf of some excellent charity. And so on. I am not grumbling about this, but it is pleasant to yarn on about it . . . When I envisaged a celibate life, I thought that I should have an infinity of leisure for writing letters; but I have found that the more time you have the more duties come to fill it, and things which were impossible become obligations.'

Despite the air of reluctance there, Eliot fulfilled his many obligations with entire good grace. And he did find time to write hundreds of letters – more than he had written in any previous year, and more than can be accommodated in a volume of this scope. Happily, all of the letters omitted from this printed volume, along with the letters omitted from the earlier volumes in the series, are now to be found, fully annotated, on the official website of the Eliot Estate: tseliot.com.

JOHN HAFFENDEN

2017

BIOGRAPHICAL COMMENTARY

1934–1935

1934 JANUARY – TSE serves on the Council of the Church Literature Association. 2 JANUARY – F. Scott Fitzgerald expresses a desire to have his new novel, *Tender is the Night*, published by Faber & Faber, but finds he is tied by contract to Chatto & Windus. 'I would much prefer to have you publish it,' he tells TSE. 4 JANUARY – TSE's solicitors inform Vivien Eliot's solicitors: 'She should long since have been convinced that under no circumstances will Mr Eliot go back to her.' TSE publishes 'Personality and Demonic Possession' in *Virginia Quarterly Review*. 5 JANUARY – approaches Marianne Moore with the wish that F&F might publish her poems. Seeks to find ways to publish James Joyce's *Ulysses* without fear of prosecution. Geoffrey Faber consults Donald Somervell (Solicitor General) about legal possibilities. TSE and Frank Morley interview an Assistant Secretary at the Home Office. But nothing avails: Faber & Faber is too cautious, and the book falls to Allen Lane at the Bodley Head. 17 JANUARY – publishes in the *Criterion* 'Four Poems' by Louis MacNeice. 30 JANUARY – dines with Leonard and Virginia Woolf. TSE works 'by fits & starts' on the text of his pageant *The Rock* – 'a kind of Play', as he styles it (with a scenario by E. Martin Browne) – to be produced in May. FEBRUARY – finds lodging in two rooms ('a furnished flat'), with use of shared bathroom – 'excellent servants, and meals served in my rooms' – of the clergy-house at 9 Grenville Place, South Kensington, presided over by the Revd Eric Cheetham, vicar of St Stephen's, Gloucester Road. The sculptor Donald Hastings creates 'a very good likeness' of TSE. 9 FEBRUARY – TSE tells the American theatre producer Hallie Flanagan that he hopes to 'start something new of the same kind' as *Sweeney Agonistes* as soon as *The Rock* is over and done with. 19 FEBRUARY – tells Herbert Read, 'the fascist and the royalist ideology are incompatible'. He makes a second visit to the Society of the Sacred Mission at Kelham. 23 FEBRUARY – publishes 'Le Morte Darthur' (a review of *Le Morte Darthur, Reduced into Englisshe by Sir Thomas Malory*), in the *Spectator*. 22 FEBRUARY – publishes *After Strange Gods: A Primer of Modern Heresy: The Page-Barbour Lectures at the University* *of Virginia*: 3,000 copies (with a second impression of 1,500 in Dec. 1934). The blurb has it that TSE 'maintains that the weakness of modern literature, indicative of the weakness of the modern world in general, is a religious weakness; and that all our social problems including those of literature and criticism, begin and end in the religious problem.' (However, TSE concedes to A. L. Rowse on 11 May 1934: 'I am particularly ashamed of . . . the greater part of my output while I was in America.') 27 FEBRUARY – invites Sylvia Pankhurst to submit her translations of stories by the Roumanian author Mihail Eminescu. Seeks to find a publisher for an article by the young Alistair Cooke entitled 'Salvation and Eugene O'Neill'. TSE is elected a Corresponding Honorary Member of the *Institut Littéraire et Artistique de France*. MARCH – publishes 'Tradition and Orthodoxy' in *American Review*. He begins a critical conversation with Serge Bolshakoff – 'this curious Russian' – about a proposal to establish an International Academy of Christian Sociologists. 'One feels instinctively that this is a rather pretentious Russian nonsense.' (To Christopher Dawson, 4 June 1935, he expresses grave misgivings about Bolshakoff's 'apparent flirtations with real or so called fascist organizations, particularly in the Far East'.) TSE enjoys tea in London with Hallie Flanagan, who writes: 'We have had the most crazy and amusing times, and we talk entirely in Sweeney-ese. Eliot thinks [her production of *Sweeney Agonistes* at Vassar College in 1933] the best play he ever saw, and of course this makes me think him very discerning'. 6 MARCH – TSE advises Spender: 'In general I like to keep the poetry in the *Criterion* for people who are unknown or only beginning to be known.' He publishes 'Shakespearian Criticism I: From Dryden to Coleridge' in *A Companion to Shakespeare Studies*, ed. Harley Granville-Barker and G. B. Harrison. His lecture 'Religion and Literature' (given in the parish hall of St John-the-Divine, Richmond, Surrey) comes out in *Faith That Illuminates*, ed. V. A. Demant: 'the whole of modern literature is corrupted by what I call Secularism.' 7 MARCH – writes an 81-word postcard biography of Samuel Taylor Coleridge, for a series put out by the National Portrait Gallery: published in May 1934. 8 MARCH – discusses with Gabriel Hebert, SSM, the prospect of a book eventually published as *Liturgy and Society* (F&F, 1935): 'we aim to reach the many people who are sympathetic to the Christian faith, and whose minds are frequently concerned with it; but who have no conviction and who are not active members of the Church'. 10 MARCH – visits I. A. Richards and his wife in Cambridge, where he sees a production of *Antony and Cleopatra*; meets the historian G. G. Coulton (author of *Five Centuries of Religion*), whom he finds 'charming'. 12 MARCH – warns

Ezra Pound: 'Rabbit I don't mind much what you do so long as you don't go involve yourself with that Mosley' – leader of the British Union of Fascists. (TSE writes to the *New English Weekly*, 21 Mar. 1935: 'I have at hand a book containing statements by Sir Oswald Mosley, which anyone with the merest smattering of theology can recognise to be not only puerile but anathema.') 15 MARCH – publishes in the *New English Weekly* a letter headed 'Mr Eliot's Virginian Lectures' (in reply to a harsh review by Ezra Pound of *ASG*). Thereafter TSE engages in a running disputation with Pound. 20 MARCH – turns down an 'interesting essay on Rilke' by Maurice Bowra. 21 MARCH – Ottoline Morrell remarks of Eliot: 'I believe his Church views were first started by his feeling against Bertie [Russell] – he said so in a letter to me once that he thought B was definitely Evil & that converted him to being a Christian . . . Tom is an orthodox Churchman . . . He is a man who is timid & needs the backing & Safety of the Church – He loves order.' 29 MARCH – TSE publishes 'The Theology of Economics' in *New English Weekly*. He supports the Group Theatre in its bid to set up a full-time working retreat, and offers practical, commonsensical advice. 'I feel a little worried by the responsibility of appearing to encourage people to throw up jobs (i.e. like Auden) for an indefinite future . . . I don't want any responsibility for 20 young people living miserably and half fed.' Tells his former student, Hugh Wade (who will become a publisher): 'Through a good many years of a man's career, and for more years with some than with others, the main thing is to get people to read his works, and not attempt serious criticism until they have done so.' Entertains Dylan Thomas to tea at his office at 24 Russell Square: he admired 'Light breaks where no sun shines' just published in the *Listener*. (He will tell Pound, 28 Dec. 1934: 'I think Dylan Thomas has some punch behind the fist.') 2 APRIL – Appointed Vicar's Warden of St Stephen's (a High Anglican parish): he will serve in this senior lay position – duties include supervision of financial matters – until 1959. TSE goes for confession to Father Philip Bacon at St Simon's, Kentish Town, in north London. Following Bacon's death, his confessor is Frank Hillier, who remarks upon Eliot's 'truly child-like heart'. Another priest, Father Nicholson, notes of TSE: 'It was a spiritual experience to administer the Bread and the Wine to so devout a worshipper.' TSE becomes a lay member of the Society of Retreat Conductors. 4 APRIL – signs a letter published in *The Times* (co-signatories include Aldous Huxley and Edwin Muir) advocating 'a thorough and public examination of some scheme of National Credit' – specifically the Social Credit scheme devised by Major C. H. Douglas. 5 APRIL – TSE advises Louis MacNeice, 'I am confident that I shall be able to recommend your poems to my firm.' 12 APRIL – G. S. Street, in his report to the Lord Chamberlain's Office, writes of *The Rock*: 'The author's religious view and the auspices of the Bishop of London guarantee the reverence of the religious portions of the pageant ... I think Mr Eliot goes out of his way to exaggerate the views of "The Blackshirts", if he means the followers of Sir Oswald Mosley and this introduction of political animus seems a great pity. I should be inclined at least to suggest to the author the excision of these passages.' The Lord Chamberlain overrules the recommendation: 'I hardly think any interference necessary.' The Revd Vincent Howson, a quondam professional actor who is to play the part of 'Bert' the builder, objects to TSE's draft speeches as 'not true cockney' and undertakes to rewrite them: TSE, who will remain friends with 'Bert', happily credits him as co-author of the amended speeches. 17 APRIL – explains to W. H. Auden – with reference to certain remarks in *ASG* which might be taken to be anti-semitic: 'On the whole I don't regret those remarks because I don't think one should be entirely muzzled by the fear of being misunderstood or made use of for purposes one does not approve. Furthermore having said this much I propose to make other remarks in future to discourage such people from claiming me as a friend.' 19 APRIL – publication day of US edition of *After Strange Gods*. TSE visits Virginia Woolf's flat to talk over the work with John Maynard Keynes, who is sympathetic to TSE's religious values. TSE writes to Harriet Monroe about Pound's latest Canto: 'I have so much admiration for the technical merits of the remaining Cantos that I should certainly be inclined to take it on faith ... As for his letters, I hope that you don't take the violence of his style too seriously; I am completely habituated to it myself.' Publishes George Barker's poem 'Daedalus' in the *Criterion*. 3 MAY – publishes 'Modern Heresies' (letter), *New English Weekly*. 15 MAY – advises David Gascoyne on his poems: 'They seem to me quite good ... but I feel that you will do still better before long, and I should like to wait for the next stage before printing anything.' 18 MAY – to Barker: 'What I have in mind to lay before my firm is to offer you a small advance on the Poems (something we have never done before, and something I have never had myself)'. On 1 June he offers Barker an advance of £25. TSE lunches with Ernst Robert Curtius. 24 MAY – dress rehearsal of Part I of *The Rock*. 25 MAY – rehearsal of Part II. 26 MAY – full rehearsal. 27 MAY – Browne recalls, 'Some detailed polishing was done on Sunday (then a practice much frowned upon).' 29 MAY–9 JUNE – *The Rock: A Pageant Play* written ... on behalf of the forty-five Churches Fund of the Diocese of London, has a successful run at Sadler's Wells

Theatre. The production involves 22 scene changes, an elaborate lighting scheme, and a cast of more than 300 (mostly amateur performers from suburban churches including the Bishop of London).' TSE tells his brother, 'the run was well attended and they made several hundred pounds'. Vivien Eliot goes to the first night, but fails to catch sight of her husband; she also goes to the last performance, but again fails to spot TSE. 31 MAY – *The Rock: A Pageant Play: Book of Words* is published by F&F; 2,000 copies. 4 JUNE – lunches with Bernard Iddings Bell, Canon of Providence, Rhode Island. Attends Encaenia Day in Oxford: at lunch at All Souls College, TSE meets Nevill Coghill: they talk about *Sweeney Agonistes*. 'Who is Sweeney?' asks Coghill. TSE replies, presumably with teasing inventiveness: 'I think of him as a man who in younger days was perhaps a professional pugilist, mildly successful; who then grew older and retired to keep a pub.' 6 JUNE – TSE begins contributing to the *New English Weekly* a series of occasional articles, 'Views and Reviews', mostly on matters of Church doctrine and ethics. Reviews in the *Criterion* three books: *The Oxford Handbook of Religious Knowledge*; *The Mystical Doctrine of St John of the Cross*; *A Christian Sociology for To-day*, by Maurice B. Reckitt. 20 JUNE – writes to Paul Elmer More ('for whom I have a warm affection,' as he says elsewhere): 'I am painfully aware that I need a much more extensive and profound knowledge of theology, for the sort of prose work that I should like to do – for pure literary criticism has ceased to interest me . . . And I am not a systematic thinker . . . I depend upon intuitions and perceptions; and although I may have some skill in the barren game of controversy, have little capacity for sustained, exact, and closely knit argument and reasoning.' Confides in Alida Monro: 'The matter at the moment on my mind is the question whether Vivienne is really going to move out of Clarence Gate on the June Quarter Day. If she doesn't, it may become unpleasant, as I shall be responsible to the landlord for her vacating.' 23 JUNE – TSE lets it be known to his brother-in-law Maurice: 'I hear . . . that V[ivien] has taken on the same flat in her own name.' 30 JUNE – attends Commemoration Day at King's School, Rochester, to distribute prizes. EARLY JULY – entertains the poet Horace Gregory and his wife to lunch in London. Long afterwards, Gregory was to recall: 'Eliot . . . seemed younger than when I had first met him in New York – more sensitive, more volatile, more alert.' 11 JULY – tells Herbert Read: 'I don't think my poetry is any good; not *The Rock*, anyway, it isn't; nothing but a brilliant future behind me.' He interviews Laurence Whistler with a view to helping him find a job. MID-JULY – visits Emily Hale at Stamford House, Chipping Campden, Gloucestershire, where she is staying with her uncle and aunt, the Revd Dr John Carroll Perkins – retired Minister of King's Chapel, First Unitarian Church of Boston (the oldest church in the USA) – and his wife Edith. Jeanette McPherrin – a friend of Emily's – meets TSE there: she later tells Valerie Eliot: 'He was so unpretentiously kind and generous to me when I came to England as a young student on my way to a French university. The summer in Chipping Campden, in a household presided over by Emily's mean old aunt and her lecherous old uncle, would have been a misery without his visits . . . Most gratefully I remember our talks about literature on walks to Willersey and Broadway.' (On 30 May 1935 TSE will confide to McPherrin: 'Mrs P[erkins] is a type of stupid woman that I have come across before, and I know that the only way to save oneself from them in the long run is to run away. She is terrifically powerful . . . This type has a gentle relentlessness that no one can stand up to.') SECOND WEEK OF JULY – TSE is visited for two months by his sister Marian and niece Dorothea ('Dodo'). 16 JULY – tells Mary Hutchinson, 'it is difficult to know what to do with the combination of a sister considerably older than myself and a niece considerably younger, both very nice but with no pronounced tastes.' 17 JULY – takes Marian and Theodora to tea with Morrell, and subsequently writes to her (20 JULY): 'My sister has suffered from youth from the conviction that she was the most ill-favoured and least intelligent of the family, and is rather tied up in consequence.' Meets the young American poet and publisher James Laughlin. 23 JULY – Virginia Woolf notes, at a dinner party: 'Tom read Mr Barker's poems, chanting, intoning. Barker has some strange gift he thinks & dimly through a tangle of words ideas emerge. He thinks there is some melody some rhythm some emotion lacking in the Audens, & Spenders.' 25 JULY – publishes 'In Sincerity and Earnestness: New Britain As I See It', in *New Britain: A Weekly Organ of National Renaissance*: 'The Churches . . . should denounce any political form which is either hostile to or subversive of the Christian Life. Nothing accordingly need be said about the necessary Christian attitude towards Communism, except to repeat the obvious warning against accepting any other form simply because it is anti-Communistic. As for Fascism, we have been told by its English exponent that it "synthesizes" the Nietzschean and the Christian doctrines. The Christian ought to know what to think about a doctrine which "synthesizes" Christianity with something else. And the Christian cannot possibly agree that any simply political reorganization can be "the greatest cause and the greatest impulse in the world".' 26 JULY – completes poem 'Mr Pugstyles: The Elegant Pig'. Publishes 'John Marston' (a review of *The Plays of John Marston*) in the

TLS. Samuel Beckett writes a notice of J. B. Leishman's translation of Rilke's Poems for the *Criterion*. (TSE and Beckett do not meet.) 27 JULY – TSE considers applying for a writ to recover his books and papers from Vivien. 1 AUGUST – TSE writes to Henry S. Canby: 'I prefer to avoid reading contemporary poetry as much as I can.' (On 24 Aug. TSE remarks likewise to Clare Leiser, 'I never know what I think about my contemporaries anyway; and reading their work is only disturbing, more so if it is good.') 3 AUGUST – leaves for a two-week break in the country, taking Marian and Dodo to the Cotswolds. (He writes on 5 Sept.: 'The summer . . . is always a broken period for me; and this year I was confined for the better part of two months by the happy duty of entertaining a sister and a niece from America.') 20 AUGUST – writes to F. O. Matthiessen about his pioneering monograph *The Achievement of T. S. Eliot*: 'I haven't been allowed to see it, but both of the directors who had read it, speak of it with the highest praise. In the second place, I raised very strong objections to our publishing a book about myself, however good. This is not pure modesty, but the belief that it would be better all round, and much better publicity for me, if some other firm undertook it. Your first version is now, I understand, in the hands of the Oxford University Press, and I have heard from a friend of mine whom they asked to report on it, that he has recommended them to publish it. If they do not want it, I dare say we shall in spite of my personal protests.' Takes on a book of personal witness entitled *The Unfinished Universe* by a Methodist minister, T. S. Gregory. 29 AUGUST – Rejects poems by A. L. Rowse: 'The matter of the poems seems to me to exist, but the poems don't seem to me to be written yet.' END OF AUGUST – visits the Faber family for a week at their holiday home in south Wales. TSE tells Enid Faber (19 Sept.): 'I slept particularly well, and felt singularly remote from anxieties of every kind - which helps me to face with equanimity the possibility of an action [against his wife] in the King's Bench division of the High Court, or whatever it is.' 30 AUGUST – Marian and Dodo return to the USA. SEPTEMBER – arranges and publishes *Make It New: Essays by Ezra Pound*. 7 SEPTEMBER – turns down translations of plays by Jean Cocteau: 'Our experience with translations of French works which are likely to appeal only to the more fastidious public is that those who wish to read them at all will always prefer to read them in French.' (TSE will tell Pound, 4 Apr. 1935: 'I dont think Cocteau much of a poet myself but I Wish I had a 3/8 1/8 a fraction of his theatrical ability.') In company with Emily Hale, he visits the garden of the manor house of Burnt Norton. (The poem 'Burnt Norton' is begun in the autumn of 1935.) Laurence Irving entertains TSE to lunch: 'I was empowered to offer the poet a commission of £150 to write the play, with performance guaranteed [at the Canterbury Festival 1935], which really meant more to them [*sic*] than anything else. We spent the morning in the Cathedral and I showed him the stage [built in the Chapter House] and everything. I said: "Does this suggest any idea to you for a play?" "Oh, yes, I think I'd like to write about Thomas à Becket." Of course I was utterly dismayed. I thought "worn-out Thomas à Becket", but then I realised that he'd make something entirely new, as he did."' 19 SEPTEMBER – TSE proceeds with a writ to recover his property from his wife. 24 SEPTEMBER – 'Words for Music' ('New Virginia', 'Hampshire') is published in *The Best Poems of 1934*, selected by Thomas Moult. 26 SEPTEMBER – TSE to F. R. Leavis: 'I take the liberty of congratulating you on the work you are doing in *Scrutiny* in stirring up examination of educational realities and probabilities. In the long run this seems to me as important and as neglected a problem as any we have.' 28 SEPTEMBER – encourages George Santayana's disciple and literary executor George Cory to submit an essay on his 'philosophy with particular reference to its latest developments'. Spends an evening with Charles Williams and was to recall much later, 'Those who met Charles Williams would not at first have been impressed by a plain, spectacled man of rather frail physique, who made no attempt to impress anybody. But when he began to speak, they would be struck by several qualities: his liveliness, his intelligence and his amiability. And if they were alert and sensitive, they would begin to notice, behind the intelligence, a kind of extra perceptiveness. Williams had an extended spiritual sense: he was like a man who can notice shades of colour, or hear tones, beyond the ordinary range. Those would could perceive this in him, would also begin to notice that behind the amiability, behind the evident modesty and simplicity, was that much rarer gift – humility.' (For his part, Williams told Mary Butts, 21 Feb. 1935: 'It may amuse you to know that Eliot has been reading the novels during the last year or so and wrote the other week after I had sent him *The Greater Trumps* to say that he did not like that as much as the others – like you, and you are both quite right – but that he simply ate them up and asked for more. I have always liked Eliot but for a moment I felt he was much more bright and good than I had supposed.') TSE publishes 'The Problem of Education' in the *Harvard Advocate* (Freshman Number 1934). EARLY OCTOBER – Rowse proposes to TSE that they share a flat – 'Two celibates like you & me ought to be able to get on without too much noise', but TSE declines the offer: 'I am now engaged in litigation, which at present is private and I hope will remain so, with my wife, for the possession of my books and a number of objects of sentimental value which remain in her flat. I don't know how expensive this is going to be; and of course one feels very unsettled while such a business is going on. I am expecting a pretty large bill from one firm of lawyers for settling my arrears of Income Tax – the taxes are paid, I sweated in America to do that, hence the poor quality of the lectures; and I shall get another from my regular lawyers for this miserable business.' 4 OCTOBER – publishes *Elizabethan Essays* (Faber Library No. 24). To F. S. Flint: 'I could not publish a pro-fascist article because people might think the *Criterion* was going fascist; but I could publish a pro-communist article because nobody would imagine that the *Criterion* was becoming communist; I can publish things by people I am known to be in substantial agreement with or by people with whom I am known to be in emphatic disagreement.' 5 OCTOBER – contracts for poems by Louis MacNeice: 'the book seems to me to show a vast improvement over last year's. It seems to me that the new poems are quite the best that you have done.' Writes to Marianne Moore about his introduction to her *Selected Poems*: 'I feel more than ever diffident and miserable about this puny Introduction. It seems to me to fall very far short of doing you justice, at best.' 6 OCTOBER – publishes 'Religious Drama and the Church', in *REP* (magazine of the Westminster and Croydon Repertory Theatre). 9 OCTOBER – accepts Dylan Thomas's story 'The Visitor' for the *Criterion* (Jan. 1935). Takes a positive interest in work by the young Robert Waller: 'it shows very considerable ability, and is, at least, a remarkable tour de force for a boy of 20'. 11 OCTOBER – Vivien notes in her diary, 'I feel sure & more sure, that if all is as it is said to be, the poor fellow [TSE] was, & has been for 2 years . . . under some delusion which makes him not understand that we here are his friends & true champions & loyal to the death, & that we still wait for him with open arms.' 12 OCTOBER – TSE publishes a letter, 'Our Mr Eliot', in the *Church Times*. 18 OCTOBER – lectures at Leeds University on 'Literature and the Modern World'. 19 OCTOBER – Frank Morley reports that the sale of Eliot's collected *Poems* is 'round about 10,000'. TSE publishes 'What Does the Church Stand For?' in the *Spectator*. MID-OCTOBER – takes an interest in the fiction of James Hanley. Dines with Theodore Spencer, visiting from Harvard. 3 NOVEMBER – invites himself to tea with Virginia Woolf, along with 'an American friend [Emily Hale] who greatly admires your works as they all do'. 5 NOVEMBER – TSE just misses out on the opportunity to publish the poems of Dylan Thomas: even as he deliberates, the *Sunday Referee* presses Thomas for a decision. Contracts with W. H. Auden for a play called *The Chase* – it will in due course become *The Dog Beneath the Skin* (*Dogskin*). 6 NOVEMBER – publishes *Homage to Sextus Propertius* by Ezra Pound. Rejects the poems of David Gascoyne: 'While they seem to me to have considerable merit and perhaps excessive fluency, I feel that your stuff ought to simmer for a good bit longer before it boils down into a proper book.' 7 NOVEMBER – at Robert Sencourt's request, the Egyptian Minister of Education invites TSE to spend the winter in Cairo: TSE is unable to accept – nor was he at all expecting such a sudden invitation. 9 NOVEMBER – TSE informs his brother-in-law: 'I want to put the seriousness of the situation as clearly and forcibly to you as possible, because it is inconceivable that [Vivien] should continue to behave as she is doing, if she realised herself how serious the matter is, and is likely to be for her. I wish to implore you, by every means in your power, and in cooperation with your mother if you think best, to induce Vivienne to agree to the inevitable, in her own interest.' 10 NOVEMBER – visits Geoffrey and Polly Tandy. MID-NOVEMBER – attends the Aquinas Society to hear a talk on 'The Mysticism of St John of the Cross' by the Very Revd Fr Vincent McNabb, OP, STM. 11 NOVEMBER – attends a private performance, with Aldous Huxley as his guest, of *Sweeney Agonistes*, produced by Rupert Doone at the Group Theatre Rooms in London. John Hayward reports: 'Eliot . . . was satisfied with it all . . . He admits, however, that Sweeney himself was conceived after a different plan from the one he imagined. If he really looked like Crippen, as Eliot says he did, then he is not the same never-to-be-forgotten apenecked Sweeney of the early poems.' TSE wrote: 'This production was completely the reverse of what I meant.' (To W. B. Yeats, 6 Dec.: 'I must say that, although the presentation was in important respects entirely alien to my intentions, I was very much pleased with the skill and intelligence of the production.' To Auden, 6 Dec.: 'I was really very pleasantly surprised by Doone's skill in presentation in these circumstances, and the general level of intelligence. I think that they put their backs into it. I am still uncertain whether the company are up to a play which will make such heavy claims upon them as yours.' Yeats sees the production of *Sweeney* on 16 Dec. Brecht sees it too; so do Ottoline Morrell and Virginia Woolf.) 14 NOVEMBER – encourages the Irish writer Blánaid Salkeld. 15 NOVEMBER – pays tribute in the *New English Weekly* to A. R. Orage, and writes a longer memorial essay for the *Criterion*: 'He was that necessary and rare person, the moralist in criticism.' 16 NOVEMBER – visits Hull University to give a talk. 19 NOVEMBER – dines with Woolf, who notes: 'Sits very solid – large shoulders – in his chair, & talks easily but with authority. Is a great man, in a way, now: self confident, didactic. But to me, still, a dear old ass.' MID-NOVEMBER – visits Kelham for the Dedication Festival. 26 NOVEMBER – gives a charity reading at the Fulham Skilled Apprenticeship Committee. 30 NOVEMBER – TSE, Dr and Mrs Perkins, and Emily Hale visit Chichester Cathedral. Faber & Faber publishes Bhagwan Shri Hamsa's *The Holy Mountain: The Story of a Pilgrimage to Lake Manas and of Initiation on Mount Kailas in Tibet*, trans. Shri Purohit Swami, with an introduction by W. B. Yeats, and a blurb by TSE. Publishes Spender's poem *Vienna*. DECEMBER – Matthiessen's *The Achievement of T. S. Eliot* is published by OUP (London) and Houghton Mifflin (New York). EARLY DECEMBER – Hale leaves England for Italy: she will visit Florence and spend the winter with Dr and Mrs Perkins in Rome. TSE introduces her to Marguerite Caetani as 'one of my nearest friends'. 4 DECEMBER – TSE is advised by his solicitor, 'we have obtained a writ enabling the Sheriff to enter your Wife's flat for the purpose of obtaining your effects. It now appears that, contrary to the opinion previously expressed to you, the Sheriff to whom the writ will be delivered is not entitled to break down the door but must seize an opportunity of entering peacably [*sic*].' TSE sets up a fund – with contributions from Bryan Guinness, Victor Rothschild, Walter de la Mare, Mary Hutchinson, Siegfried Sassoon, and himself – to support George Barker and his family: they will receive twenty-five shillings a week for a year. TSE to Sassoon: 'I hope that [Barker] may gain in time enough reputation to make it possible for him to live as a writer, but at best there is no telling how long this may take.' 11 DECEMBER – bailiffs enter Vivien's flat and seize TSE's books and papers, but not without shock and melodrama. It turns out that VHE has taken the precaution of depositing some of TSE's possessions in two separate banks. (Vivien tells the District Bank, 9 Jan. 1935: 'It was only by Brute Force that his things were snatched from me.' To her solicitors, Aug. 1935: 'If my husband is free, and in his right mind, why should he go to the vast expense of employing hired men to force an entry into my flat to get hold of some old papers when he has had access to the flat the whole time?') 15 DECEMBER – TSE spends the weekend with Browne and his wife at their home in Rottingdean: TSE is a weary, silent guest. They see an experimental play called 'The Revolving Year: a drama in verse and prose', by Mona Swann – who 'had evolved a method of making plays from the words of the King James version of the Bible, using the Psalms as a medium of community expression', and making use of choral devices and folk melodies in ways which impress TSE. 21 DECEMBER – TSE visits Francis Underhill at Rochester. CHRISTMAS – a *Criterion* party at the offices of Faber & Faber brings together Geoffrey Faber,

Rayner Heppenstall, Rowse, Babette Deutsch, E. W. F. Tomlin, William Empson (who rapidly gets drunk), and Dylan Thomas (who arrives drunk and becomes reportedly 'foul-mouthed'). According to Tomlin, TSE was 'the most commanding figure there' – despite his quiet demeanour. 28 DECEMBER – TSE declares to GCF: 'I am, by temperament but not in doctrine, an old-style hellfire calvinist.' END OF DECEMBER – Henry Miller asks TSE to publish in the *Criterion* an extract from his book on D. H. Lawrence. TSE responds by asking to see *Tropic of Cancer*. 31 DECEMBER –visits the Morleys for the New Year, 'with a proper haggis and pre-war whisky (Christina being Scotch) as well as roast duck and champagne'.

1935 JANUARY – TSE lunches with W. H. Auden. 6 JANUARY – to Virginia Woolf: 'I have . . . got to make a Speech on the 30th as Secretary of the Standing Committee of the Book Committee of the Joint Council of the Book & Tract Committees of the Church Literature Association [and] the MSS. submitted to Faber & Faber multiply, increase in geometrical ratio, as they say.' 7 JANUARY – Vivien tells Elizabeth Wentworth, 'I keep this HOME still for Tom, & keep it as nicely as I can in the circumstances . . . I leave the Door open every evening, & at certain hours, always, for Tom, & . . . I wrote & told him it is so. So that he has no excuse to lead a life without the very necessary protection of a wife. It is indeed a tragedy.' He lectures for the Shakespeare Association on 'Shakespeare and the Modern Stage'. 12 JANUARY – T. S. Gregory notifies TSE that the Methodist authorities – as a consequence of his decision to publish *The Unfinished Universe* – have told him to tender his resignation. TSE takes pains to help find him a suitable job. MID-JANUARY – TSE has lunch in London with Pound's mistress Olga Rudge. 24 JANUARY – advises I. A. Richards that the *New English Weekly* 'is being edited chiefly by Philip Mairet, who, I think, is quite the best man available for the job, and I have promised to help in an advisory way . . . We are anxious to strengthen the non-political and non-economic side of the paper . . . I do hope you can help.' Mairet was to recall, of TSE at editorial committee meetings of *New English Weekly* – on which TSE served for a decade – 'He gave his complete attention to what was submitted to him; and you knew it, though his comments were usually brief, even laconic. His words were not subject to the usual discount for politeness or the desire to be encouraging.' In 'Notes on the Way', *Time and Tide* (12 Jan.), TSE challenges A. A. Milne's book *Peace with Honour* 'as an instance of . . . a frequent type of confused and insufficient thinking about war . . . I do not see how you can condemn War in the abstract unless you assert (a) that there is no higher value than Peace; (b) that there is nothing worth fighting for; and (c) that a war in which one side is right and the other wrong is inconceivable.' He argues too: 'a soldiers' war is the outcome of an economic war; I suggested that we ought to enquire more closely into the economic causes of war and try to stop them.' 1 FEBRUARY – TSE sends Martin Browne 'the first 396 lines of the Archbishop . . . about half of Act I'. 4 FEBRUARY – tea with Leonard and Virginia Woolf: 'A religious soul: an unhappy man, a lonely very sensitive man, all wrapt up in fibres of self torture, doubt, conceit, desire for warmth & intimacy. And I'm very fond of him . . .' 12 FEBRUARY – to Browne: 'I have completely re-written my dull dialogue after the first choral part, and have shown it to Doone, who likes it much better than the first version. It is much more formalised, with no attempt at realism, and more in the mode of Everyman or a Morality play . . . Also, Doone and other people think it would be very much pleasanter to have the murder take place actually on the stage.' 13 FEBRUARY – warns an American cousin about Oswald Mosley: 'Politically, the man is at present pretty well discredited. His political philosophy is clap-trap. He has no economic or financial theory . . . [A]nti-Semitism is not, and cannot be, a serious political issue in England, nor does it seem to be a very practical way of inflaming popular passion. Mosley's movement has been on the decline since a disgraceful meeting at a big public hall last year, at which interrupters seem to have been treated with considerable barbarity.' 14 FEBRUARY – vexed by the ineffectual findings of the Church Commission on Unemployment, TSE urges in the *New English Weekly* that 'the Church commit itself to the assertion that the present situation is intolerable and unreasonable, and that it devolved upon the temporal authorities to recognise the present situation for what it is and do something about it.' 15 FEBRUARY – to Richards: 'I simply dare not break the thread of my typing until I have killed the Archbishop.' Henry Moore expresses interest in designing the masks and costumes, if he can find the time; but it is not to be. TSE seeks to persuade Auden that Christopher Isherwood should not be credited as joint author of *Dogskin*: he might well be mentioned in a preface. Auden insists otherwise. 20 FEBRUARY – TSE submits works by Spender for consideration for the King's Medal for Poetry. Frederic Prokosch prints twenty copies of *Words for Music* (1934) – comprising 'New Hampshire' and 'Virginia' – as a Butterfly Book: TSE is pleased with the venture. TSE completes Act I of his play. He feels that 'The Archbishop Murder Case' will not do as title: it seems 'too flippant'. 21 FEBRUARY – To his brother: 'I have only about five weeks to finish my play about the murder of St Thomas à Becket, which is to be produced in London in May (with plays by Yeats and Auden) and at Canterbury in June; so I have to avoid all possible engagements in order to work.' TSE makes this overture to Michael Roberts: 'My firm has conceived the idea that there is room for another anthology of modern verse, and we wonder whether you would consider editing a collection for us.' *The Faber Book of Modern Verse* is soon under way. 22 FEBRUARY – feeling undecided about the work of F. T. Prince, he asks for Herbert Read's assessment. Publishes 'Literature and the Modern World' (a shortened version of a lecture given at Leeds and at Hull) in the *Teaching Church Review*. 25 FEBRUARY – sends Browne the revised text of Act I of *Murder in the Cathedral*. 26 FEBRUARY – attends the funeral of his friend Frederic Manning (d. 22 Feb.). 28 FEBRUARY – gives a reading of his poetry at the Albert Hall on behalf of the Pivot Club. 8 MARCH – turns down a proposal from Spender to publish his translation, co-authored with Edwin Muir, of poems by Friedrich Hölderlin: 'for sales purposes he is so little known in this country that his name gives no advantage over a poet completely unknown'. Balks at writing a piece on Gerard Manley Hopkins for *New Verse*: 'I am not, after all, one of those who know Hopkins most intimately, or one of those to whom he means most.' (To Edouard Roditi, 18 March, of Hopkins: 'there is something, to my mind, extremely insular about the spirit which informs the poetry'.) Turns down a submission by Randall Swingler: 'The unity or continuity of the pieces is not sufficiently obvious to establish itself in the mind of the ordinary reader.' Vivien seeks to surprise TSE by calling at 24 Russell Square. 'They said he was not there & that he is very erratic. Tom never was erratic. He was the most regular of men, liking his meals at home, his Church, his club very seldom, & a most sweet & homely man. It is not right of Tom to refuse to come home & it is cruel, anti-social, anti-religious, anti-economic, untidy, stupid, un-moral, & in NO way excusable.' 9 MARCH – TSE dines with Michael Roberts and Janet Adam Smith: the primary topic of conversation is the *Faber Book of Modern Verse*. (To Roberts, 17 May 1935: 'if the somewhat larger payments to Pound exhaust the resources, I should prefer to help by forgoing part or all of my own fees rather than have you raid your editorial fee.') 13 MARCH – Vivien calls again at Faber & Faber: 'I saw Miss Swan who first said he was there. So I waited in the waiting room, & made up how I should be very quiet & gentle with him. Then Miss Swan be-thought her that she had not seen him come back after lunch. She offered to get the Secretary down again, & so she did. This time the Secretary, Miss O'Donovan, looked rather sick. I said, so Mr Eliot is not always here for the Board Meetings?

Then I said of course you know I shall have to keep on coming here – & she said "Of course it is for you to decide" & I said loudly "it is too absurd, I have been frightened away too long. I am his wife["] – so then I left.' 16 MARCH – TSE takes tea with Virginia Woolf; Spender is another guest: TSE (said Woolf) was 'very easy & honest & kind to Stephen'. 18 MARCH – TSE suggests to A. Desmond Hawkins, with regard to a projected review of Ezra Pound and Marianne Moore: 'I . . . feel that they are not poets whom anyone should review unless he is fundamentally an admirer of their work. I don't mean that it is necessary to admire these particular Cantos, but I do feel that unless one has a general admiration for Pound's work one has not got the right angle from which to criticise these poems, even in the most damaging way.' 19 MARCH – TSE finishes a draft of Part II of his play; a complete draft is done by the end of the month. 20 MARCH – Rupert Doone resiles from the idea of putting on an Eliot–Auden–Yeats season at the Mercury Theatre in the spring. (The designer Robert Medley recalls: 'However much respect Eliot and Yeats had for each other, there were disagreements. Eliot told Rupert after one meeting that he felt like "kicking Yeats downstairs".') 21 MARCH – publishes 'The Church and Society' (letter), *New English Weekly*. Accepts invitation from Bishop George Bell to join the Advisory Council of the 1937 World Conference on Church, Community & State. 28 MARCH – finally relinquishes all of the terrible provisional titles – 'Fear in the Way', 'Doom on the Archishop', 'The Archbishop Murder Case' – in favour of 'Murder in the Cathedral': Henzie Raeburn (Browne's wife) has come up with the winning suggestion. TSE to Geoffrey Faber: 'when you read the text, you see there isn't any "case" about it'. 30 MARCH – entertains Virginia Woolf and Alida Monro to tea at his lodgings: they squat in chill discomfort before a gas fire in his angular sitting room overlooking the District Line railway. 3 APRIL – TSE tells his brother, of the new play: 'I have no illusions about its dramatic importance, but I think some of the verse, which is largely choral, is good ranting stuff . . . I don't think that this play is even suitable for an ordinary London audience, though it is not "religious drama" in the usual sense.' 4 APRIL – publication of Barker's *Poems*. TSE takes an interest in the case of a forty-year-old Russian exile named N. M. Iovetz-Tereshchenko, who has endured hardship, and who has written a study entitled *Friendship-Love in Adolescence*, based on his doctoral dissertation in experimental psychology (it is to be published by Allen & Unwin in 1936). TSE finds him sympathetic, and seeks at every turn to assist the man and his family. (On 15 May, TSE writes to H. M. Spalding: 'this book directly challenges . . . Freud's fundamental assumptions ... Dr. Tereshchenko's main thesis is one, I think, of the greatest importance in the difference between traditional Christianity and the new psychology; and his book ought to be of great support to Christian apologists.') 9 APRIL – *Selected Poems* by Marianne Moore (with Introduction by TSE) is published by Macmillan, New York. TSE attends a meeting of Bolshakoff's International Academy of Christian Sociologists: elected an Associate Member. 11 APRIL – *Selected Poems* by Marianne Moore (Faber & Faber): 1,000 copies. 15 APRIL – W. B. Yeats reports to his wife: 'Elliots [*sic*] play is about murder of Becket, half play half religious service as spoken poetry exceedingly impressive ... It will require magnificent speaking, its oratory is swift & powerful.' 25 APRIL – TSE joins a committee of friends of Yeats, headed by John Masefield, to honour the poet's seventieth birthday. MAY – further meeting with Emily Hale. 2 MAY – confides in John Hayward (who has encouraged him to move to a flat above his own at Swan Court, South Kensington): 'I have not yet got over the feeling of being hunted [by Vivien]: in my sleep I am pursued like Orestes, though I feel with less reason than that hero. Where I am I feel relatively safe. My status there is highly respectable, they know who I am, they know my circumstances, and if I was ever tracked down and molested I should be in a strong position. Anywhere else, I should be merely an ordinary tenant; I should be more accessible & vulnerable; and if I was tracked down & a disturbance followed I might simply be invited to leave.' 9 MAY – tells Spender: 'I think and hope that I have overcome any desire to write Great Poetry, or to compete with anybody. One has got at the same time to unite oneself with humanity, and to isolate oneself completely; and to be equally indifferent to the "audience" and to oneself as one's own audience. So that humility and freedom are the same thing.' 10 MAY – publication of *Murder in the Cathedral: Acting Edition for the Festival of the Friends of Canterbury Cathedral*: 750 copies. Publishes William Saroyan's book of stories, *The Daring Young Man on the Flying Trapeze*. 11 MAY – TSE reports to Susie Hinkley: 'Emily has been up to town, and seen the King & Queen . . . I encourage her to come up as often as she can afford to. Between ourselves, I find the Perkins's, with all their amiability, very trying.' 17 MAY – seeks to commission the memoirs of the artist Walter Sickert – unavailingly. Contacts Henry Miller with a view to publishing his study of D. H. Lawrence, and possibly his novel *Black Spring*. 22 MAY – visits Morrell, who introduces him to the Irish novelist and poet James Stephens and his wife 'Cynthia'. 25 MAY – departs for Inverness: he visits Neil and Jessie Gunn, and George and Ellie Blake: they go motoring in the highlands. (TSE in 1961: 'Neil Gunn taught me how to educate my palate to the best whisky. In consequence I am a very temperate drinker, for whisky is the only spirit to which I am addicted.') 28 MAY – enquires of George Malcolm Thomson why he is so reluctant to 'come out as a [Scottish] nationalist'. Starts negotiating with the Portuguese for the right to publish an English translation of *Salazar: Portugal and her Leader* by António Ferro (it will appear in 1939). 30 MAY – publishes *The Dog Beneath the Skin* by Auden and Isherwood: 'I feel confident of its success, which it fully deserves,' he tells Auden (4 June). 1 JUNE – spends a weekend with the Tandy family. Becomes a committee member of the Sadler's Wells Society. 3 JUNE – requests from Harper & Row the proofs of Frederic Prokosch's novel *The Asiatics*, with a view to publishing it in the UK. (Prokosch to TSE, 17 May: 'I personally am frantically eager to have Faber and no one else.') 3 JUNE – TSE is charmed to be told that T. E. Lawrence (Lawrence of Arabia) had written of him in 1925 as 'the most important poet alive'. 6 JUNE – visits Chipping Campden to celebrate Dr Perkins's birthday; writes a poem for the occasion entitled 'The Anniversary'. 13 JUNE – Faber & Faber publishes *Murder in the Cathedral*: 3,000 copies. Seventieth birthday of W. B. Yeats, whom TSE applauds in the *Criterion*: 'It should be apparent at least that Mr Yeats has been and is the greatest poet of his time.' Starts negotiations to publish *The Book of Margery Kempe*. Writes to Henry Miller, '*Tropic of Cancer* seems to me a very remarkable book . . . a rather magnificent piece of work. There is writing in it as good as any I have seen for a long time.' 15 JUNE – *Murder in the Cathedral* opens at Canterbury Cathedral: the production runs until 29 June. 17 JUNE – TSE attends the anniversary dinner for the Harvard Class of 1910, at the Grill Room of the Victoria Hotel, London. Contributes autobiography to *Harvard College Class of 1910: Seventh Report*. Elected an honorary member of Phi Beta Kappa. 28 JUNE – Vivien Eliot writes to TSE, 'Come to this hotel [Hotel Cecil, Paris] & fetch me away on July 13th (or before). Votre femme – your wife Vivienne Haigh Eliot.' END OF JUNE – at Faber's invitation, TSE goes to Encaenia lunch at All Souls College. Meets Isaiah Berlin – 'whom I liked'. 9 JULY – reads a paper at the inaugural meeting of the *Green Quarterly* Luncheon Club – 'Should there by a Censorship of Books? – published in *The New Green Quarterly* (Aut. 1935). 10 JULY – Vivien calls again at 24 Russell Square, where Ethel Swan tells her that 'Tom does not go there often now, & that has deeply upset me.' The following day, Vivien notes in her diary: 'My belief is that he wants to get back to me, & is in chains.' 12 JULY – TSE is notified that Prokosch has committed his novel to Chatto. TSE accepts invitation to contribute an introduction to a reissue of the Nelson Classics edition of Tennyson's early poems. 13 JULY – encourages C. A. Siepmann to consider becoming organising secretary of the new National Book League. 14–15 JULY – spends weekend with the Tandys. 15 JULY – second visit to Vivien's flat by Sheriff's officers. (James & James to Vivien, 22 Aug. 1935: 'In reply to our letter asking for the return of the articles belonging to you which were wrongfully taken away by the Sherriff's officers we are now informed by Messrs Bird & Bird that those things which were found not to belong to Mr T. S. Eliot have been returned to your flat. We trust the matter may now be considered as closed.') MID-JULY – spends weekend with Mr and Mrs Bruce Richmond (editor of the *TLS*). Publishes W. B. Yeats's 'Mandookya Upanishad' in the *Criterion*. LAST WEEK OF JULY – visits Chipping Campden again, keeping company with Emily Hale: 'a very happy and unforgettable week'. 28 JULY – Vivien takes a day trip to Oxford, where she reminisces about Scofield Thayer and punting, and about visiting TSE at Merton College in 1915. TSE publishes 'A Commentary' (*Criterion*) on W. B. Yeats. AUGUST – publishes *Poems* by Louis MacNeice, with this blurb by TSE: 'The most original Irish poet of his generation, dour without sentimentality, intensely serious without political enthusiasm, his work is intelligible but unpopular, and has the pride and modesty of things that endure.' TSE is approached by the BBC with an offer of £20 for a radio broadcast of *Murder in the Cathedral*; after representations by TSE, the offer is raised to £30. Holidays with the Faber family. 11 AUGUST – to Enid Faber, 'I have never had a week's visit of more unadulterated pleasure.' 27 AUGUST – pays another visit to Chipping Campden: Willard and Margaret Thorp, from Princeton, visit there for two days – Margaret is an old schoolfriend of Emily's. LATE AUGUST – TSE spends a weekend with the Tandys at their holiday home in Newhaven, Sussex. 4 SEPTEMBER – TSE dines at Schmidt's, Charlotte Street, London, as the guest of William Empson, with Sir George and Lady Katharine Sansom. Empson: 'There was some dinner including a charming diplomat's wife, who remarked to Eliot that she too was very fond of reading. She didn't get much time, but she was always reading in bed, biographies and things. "With pen in hand?" inquired Mr Eliot, in a voice that contrived to form a question without leaving its lowest note of gloom. There was a rather fluttered disclaimer, and he went on: "It is the chief penalty of becoming a professional literary man that one can no longer read anything with pleasure".' 5 SEPTEMBER – lunches with John Gielgud at the Langham Hotel, London. 7 SEPTEMBER – Vivien writes to her brother: 'I consider that, ever since July 1933, you have treated me with almost insane cruelty and casualness.' 10 SEPTEMBER – TSE dines with Kenneth Murdock and his wife (visiting from Harvard). 17 SEPTEMBER – Faber & Faber turns down Roger Fry's translation of Stéphane Mallarmé's poems. 19 SEPTEMBER – *Murder in the Cathedral* published by Harcourt, Brace and Company, New York: 1,500 copies. 21–3 SEPTEMBER – TSE visits the Woolfs at Monks House, Sussex. Woolf notes, 'he is more masterly; tells a story like one who has the right; is broader & bonier & more wild eyed – long almond shaped eyes – that he means to write modern verse plays . . . A very nice man, Tom: I'm very fond of Tom.' 23 SEPTEMBER – TSE dines in London with Herbert Read and his wife. 24 SEPTEMBER – lunches with the Revd M. C. D'Arcy, SJ, at the Oxford & Cambridge Club. 26 SEPTEMBER – celebrates his forty-seventh birthday with Hale at Chipping Campden. 'I was in Gloucestershire and ran away from a Bull down a hill into some blackberry bushes.' 28 SEPTEMBER – Edwin Muir recommends some passages (made available by Emily Holmes Coleman) from a novel-in-progress by Djuna Barnes. 29 SEPTEMBER – TSE writes complimentary verses, 'Forbidding Mourning: to the Lady of the House', to Edith Perkins – 'the happiest birthday party I have had since I was a boy . . . I had come to feel "at home" at Campden in a way in which I had not felt at home for some twenty-one years, anywhere.' 2 OCTOBER – 'setting off fireworks to amuse Auden and Hayward'. *Sweeney Agonistes* is staged for two weeks, in a double bill with Auden's *The Dance of Death*, in a season directed by Rupert Doone at the Westminster Theatre. Geoffrey Faber notes: 'Monstrous perversion of *Sweeney Agonistes* – as TSE admitted afterwards . . . As produced it was unrecognizable by the author!' TSE receives a royalty of £8. 6s. od. Vivien Eliot goes to the play: 'I sat in the front row of the stalls. Close up, it was a terrible ordeal. How I contrived not to faint I do not know. The absolute horror of the thing. And the awful Homicidal Maniac walking down from the stage, right on top of me, & seeming to be telling me his hideous, plausible, perishing wheeze. A terrible little man, in spectacles, with an earnest manner, & a tale to tell indeed . . . What a marvellous brain Tom has.' TSE publishes 'Early Poems and Extracts' by Gerard Manley Hopkins in the *Criterion*. 3 OCTOBER – begins discussing with Geoffrey Grigson a publishing idea that will come to pass as *New Verse: An Anthology* (1939). 9 OCTOBER, 11 OCTOBER – Vivien goes to the Westminster Theatre again. 'The play Sweeney Agonistes touches me very much. But of course no-one wld. see how pitiful it is, but me.' 11 OCTOBER – TSE lunches with Wyndham Lewis. 13 OCTOBER – gives first reading of his poetry at Student Movement House, where Mary Trevelyan (the Warden) notes: 'He read *The Waste Land* and *The Hollow Men* . . . with his head on one side, a harsh voice, and a face of acute agony.' 17 OCTOBER – gives opening address at the Lincoln Diocesan Conference, on 'The right observance of Sunday'. 20 OCTOBER – takes Emily Hale to a service at St George's Chapel, Windsor: Ottoline Morrell (whom they happen to meet) sees Emily as the 'dominating efficient Hales'. 23 OCTOBER – TSE is lay preacher at the Kelham Reunion held at Church House, London. 24 OCTOBER – At Morrell's tea party: '[TSE] brought that awful American Woman Miss Hales [*sic*] with him – She is like a Sergeant Major quite Intolerable – How can Tom take her about everywhere.' 27 OCTOBER – TSE is godfather at the christening of Anthea Margaret Crane Tandy. 28 OCTOBER – a further visit to Kelham. 29 OCTOBER – chairs a lecture by Jacques Maritain – 'Science et Sagesse' – at the Warburg Institute. TSE gives his first response to the untitled novel (*Nightwood*) by Djuna Barnes, in a letter to Coleman: 'I admit that the extracts which Mr Muir sent me did not seem to me promising as parts of a novel, and the style struck me as incredibly tortured and tedious. I should doubt whether anyone would have the endurance to read through a novel written in this style . . . As you put the matter, however, I shall be quite willing to look at the whole manuscript and have it read.' LATE OCTOBER – puts in a word with Richard Jennings (leader writer of the *Daily Mirror*) to secure a job for Charles Madge. Goes to Thanksgiving Party at the Morleys. 31 OCTOBER – publishes a letter on 'Pacifism' in *New English Weekly*. 1 NOVEMBER – *Murder in the Cathedral* opens at the Mercury Theatre, London (seating 136), with Speaight as Becket, Browne as Fourth Knight, and chorus trained by Elsie Fogerty: the production will run for 255 performances before going on tour and transferring to the West End. Yeats tells his wife, 'It is to my great surprise a powerful religious play.' 6 NOVEMBER – TSE participates in a discussion of foreign affairs (including the question of Collective Security) at the Chandos Club. 7 NOVEMBER – meets Dame Ethel Smythe at tea with Morrell. 'I have a special passion for merry old ladies and fiery old gentlemen and I should love to add [Smythe] to my collection as one of its most distinguished items.' 8 NOVEMBER – visits I. A. Richards in Cambridge, where he is introduced to the scholar Enid Welsford. 12 NOVEMBER – Virginia Woolf writes to Julian Bell, of *Murder in the Cathedral*: 'I had almost to carry Leonard out, shrieking. What was odd was how much better it reads than acts; the tightness, chillness, deadness and general worship of the decay and skeleton made one near sickness.' 14 NOVEMBER – TSE recruits subscribers for a second year of the George Barker fund (Lady Gerald Wellesley makes a contribution). 21 NOVEMBER – gives a lunchtime talk on 'The Christian in the

Modern State', at Christ Church Vicarage, Westminster. Dines with Lady Maclagan and Francis Underhill. 26 NOVEMBER – takes Emily to tea with Virginia Woolf, who finds Hale 'a dull impeccable Bostonian lady'. 18 NOVEMBER – gives a lecture at the third *Sunday Times* Book Exhibition held at Dorland Hall. Vivien turns up, wearing her Fascist uniform, and asks him afterwards to go home with her. He replies 'I cannot talk to you now.' Bizarrely and pitifully, Vivien subsequently tells her solicitors that she has been 'claimed' by her husband. 27 NOVEMBER – gives a poetry reading for the Fitzroy Unemployed Women's Club. 28 NOVEMBER – takes the chair at the Tomorrow Club for a talk by Spender. Publishes 'Literature and the Modern World', in *American Prefaces* I. 15 DECEMBER – writes a kind of testimony, an essay on 'Audiences, Producers, Plays, Poets', for *New Verse*: 'the poet who starts to write plays, to-day, should not expect to turn himself into a very good playwright. He must learn to work hard at an unfamiliar task for which he probably has no native gift, and to learn when (as well as when not) to be guided by those who know the theatre better than he does . . . The play should have form: it needs more form than an ordinary conversation piece; it must have "dramatic form" and also the musical pattern which can be obtained only by verse; and the two forms must be one.'

ABBREVIATIONS AND SOURCES

PUBLISHED WORKS BY T. S. ELIOT

ASG	*After Strange Gods* (London: Faber & Faber, 1934)
AVP	*Ara Vos Prec* (London: The Ovid Press, 1920)
CP	*The Cocktail Party* (London: Faber & Faber, 1950)
CPP	*The Complete Poems and Plays of T. S. Eliot* (London: Faber & Faber, 1969)
EE	*Elizabethan Essays* (London: Faber & Faber, 1934)
FLA	*For Lancelot Andrewes: Essays on Style and Order* (London: Faber & Gwyer, 1928)
FR	*The Family Reunion* (London: Faber & Faber, 1939)
Gallup	Donald Gallup, *T. S. Eliot: A Bibliography* (London: Faber & Faber, 1969)
HJD	*Homage to John Dryden: Three Essays on Poetry of the Seventeenth Century* (London: The Hogarth Press, 1924)
IMH	*Inventions of the March Hare: Poems 1909–1917*, ed. Christopher Ricks (London: Faber & Faber, 1996)
KEPB	*Knowledge and Experience in the Philosophy of F. H. Bradley* (London: Faber & Faber, 1964; New York: Farrar, Straus & Company, 1964)
L	*Letters of T. S. Eliot* (London: Faber & Faber, Vol. 1 [rev. edn], 2009; Vol. 2, 2009; Vol. 3, 2012; Vol. 4, 2013; Vol. 5, 2014)
MiC	*Murder in the Cathedral* (London: Faber & Faber, 1935)
OPP	*On Poetry and Poets* (London: Faber & Faber, 1957; New York: Farrar, Straus & Cudahy, 1957)
P	*Poems* (London: The Hogarth Press, 1919)
P 1909–1925	*Poems 1909–1925* (London: Faber & Gwyer, 1925)

Poems	*The Poems of T. S. Eliot*, ed. Christopher Ricks & Jim McCue (London: Faber & Faber, 2015)
POO	*Prufrock and Other Observations* (London: The Egoist Press, 1917)
SA	*Sweeney Agonistes: Fragments of an Aristophanic Melodrama* (London: Faber & Faber, 1932)
SE	*Selected Essays: 1917–1932* (London: Faber & Faber, 1932; 3rd English edn, London and Boston: Faber & Faber, 1951)
SW	*The Sacred Wood: Essays on Poetry and Criticism* (London: Methuen & Co., 1920)
TCC	*To Criticise the Critic* (London: Faber & Faber, 1965; New York: Farrar, Straus & Giroux, 1965)
TUPUC	*The Use of Poetry and the Use of Criticism: Studies in the Relation of Criticism to Poetry in England* (London: Faber & Faber, 1933)
TWL	*The Waste Land* (1922, 1923)
TWL: Facs	*The Waste Land: A Facsimile and Transcript of the Original Drafts*, ed. Valerie Eliot (London: Faber & Faber, 1971; New York: Harcourt, Brace Jovanovich, 1971; reissued, with corrections, 2011)
VMP	*The Varieties of Metaphysical Poetry*, ed. Ronald Schuchard (London: Faber & Faber, 1993; New York: Harcourt Brace, 1994)

PERIODICALS AND PUBLISHERS

A.	*The Athenaeum* (see also *N&A*)
C.	*The Criterion*
F&F	Faber & Faber (publishers)
F&G	Faber & Gwyer (publishers)
MC	*The Monthly Criterion*
N.	*The Nation*
N&A	*The Nation & The Athenaeum*
NC	*New Criterion*
NEW	*New English Weekly*
NRF	*La Nouvelle Revue Française*
NS	*New Statesman*
NS&N	*New Statesman and Nation*
TLS	*Times Literary Supplement*

PERSONS

CA	Conrad Aiken
RA	Richard Aldington
WHA	W. H. Auden
RC-S	Richard Cobden-Sanderson
RdlM	Richard de la Mare
BD	Bonamy Dobrée
CWE	Charlotte Ware Eliot, TSE's mother
EVE	(Esmé) Valerie Eliot
HWE	Henry Ware Eliot (TSE's brother)
TSE	T. S. Eliot
VHE	Vivien (Haigh-Wood) Eliot
GCF	Geoffrey (Cust) Faber
MHW	Maurice Haigh-Wood
JDH	John Davy Hayward
MH	Mary Hutchinson
AH	Aldous Huxley
JJ	James Joyce
GWK	G. Wilson Knight
DHL	D. H. Lawrence
FRL	F. R. Leavis
WL	Wyndham Lewis
HM	Harold Monro
FVM	Frank (Vigor) Morley
OM	Ottoline Morrell
JMM	John Middleton Murry
EP	Ezra Pound
HR	Herbert Read
IAR	I. A. Richards
BLR	Bruce Richmond
ALR	A. L. Rowse
BR	Bertrand Russell
ES	Edith Sitwell
SS	Stephen Spender
WFS	William Force Stead
CW	Charles Whibley
OW	Orlo Williams
LW	Leonard Woolf
VW	Virginia Woolf
WBY	W. B. Yeats

Arkansas	Special Collections, University Libraries, University of Arkansas
BBC	BBC Written Archives, Caversham
Beinecke	The Beinecke Rare Book and Manuscript Library, Yale University
Berg	Henry W. and Albert A. Berg Collection of English and American Literature, the New York Public Library
Bodleian	The Bodleian Library, Oxford University
BL	The British Library
Brotherton	The Brotherton Collection, Leeds University Library
Buffalo	Poetry Collection, Lockwood Memorial Library, State University of New York, Buffalo
Butler	Rare Books and Manuscripts Division, Butler Library, Columbia University, New York
Caetani	Fondazione Camillo Caetani
Cambridge	Cambridge University Library
Colby College	Special Collections, Colby College, Waterville, Maine
Cornell	Department of Rare Books, Olin Library, Cornell University
Bib Jacques Doucet	Bibliothèque littéraire Jacques Doucet, Paris
Exeter	Exeter University Library
Faber	Faber & Faber Archive, London
Harcourt Brace	Harcourt Brace & Company
Harvard	University Archives, Harvard University
Hornbake Library	Hornbake Library, University of Maryland
Houghton	The Houghton Library, Harvard University
House of Books	House of Books, New York
Howard	Lelia Howard
Huntington	Huntington Library, San Marino, California
King's	Modern Archive Centre, King's College, Cambridge
Lambeth	Lambeth Palace Library
Lilly	Lilly Library, Indiana University, Bloomington
Magdalene	Old Library, Magdalene College, Cambridge
Marshall	Marshall Library, University of Cambridge
Morgan	Pierpont Morgan Library, New York

National Gallery of Ireland	National Gallery of Ireland, Dublin
NHM	Natural History Museum Archives
Northwestern	Special Collections Department, Northwestern University Library, Evanston, Illinois
Princeton	Department of Rare Books and Special Collections, Princeton University Library
Reading	Special Collections, University of Reading
Renishaw	Sitwell Papers, Renishaw Hall, Derbyshire
Rosenbach	Rosenbach Museum and Library, Philadelphia, PA
Southern Illinois	Southern Illinois University Library, Carbondale
Sussex	Manuscript Collections, University of Sussex Library
Syracuse	Syracuse University Library, Syracuse, New York
TCD	The Library, Trinity College, Dublin
Templeman	Templeman Library, University of Kent at Canterbury
Texas	The Harry Ransom Humanities Research Center, University of Texas at Austin
UCLA	University of California at Los Angeles
VE Papers	Vivien Eliot Papers, Bodleian Library, Oxford
Victoria	Special Collections, McPherson Library, University of Victoria, British Columbia
Wellesley	Wellesley College Library
Williamson	Mrs M. H. Williamson (Dr Charlotte Williamson)
Wyoming	University of Wyoming

CHRONOLOGY OF *THE CRITERION*

The Criterion

Vol. 1. No. 1. 1–103, Oct. 1922; No. 2. 105–201, Jan. 1923;
  No. 3. 203–313, Apr. 1923; No. 4. 315–427, July 1923.

Vol. 2. No. 5. 1–113, Oct. 1923; No. 6. 115–229, Feb. 1924;
  No. 7 231–369, Apr. 1924; No. 8 371–503, July 1924.

Vol. 3. No. 9. 1–159, Oct. 1924; No. 10. 161–340, Jan. 1925;
  No. 11 341–483, Apr. 1925; No. 12. 485–606, July 1925.

The New Criterion

Vol. 4. No. 1. 1–220, Jan. 1926; No. 2. 221–415, Apr. 1926;
  No. 3. 417–626, June 1926; No. 4. 627–814, Oct. 1926.

Vol. 5. No. 1. 1–186, Jan. 1927.

The Monthly Criterion

Vol. 5. No. 2. 187–282, May 1927; No. 3. 283–374, June 1927.

Vol. 6. No. 1. 1–96, July 1927; No. 2. 97–192, Aug. 1927; No. 3.
  193–288, Sept. 1927; No. 4. 289–384, Oct. 1927; No. 5. 385–480,
  Nov. 1927; No. 6. 481–584, Dec. 1927.

Vol. 7. No. 1. 1–96, Jan. 1928; No. 2. 97–192, Feb. 1928;
  No. 3. 193–288, Mar. 1928.

The Criterion

Vol. 7. No. 4. 289–464, June 1928.

Vol. 8. No. 30. 1–183, Sept. 1928; No. 31. 185–376, Dec. 1928;
  No. 32. 377–573, Apr. 1929; No. 33. 575–772, July 1929.

Vol. 9. No. 34. 1–178, Oct. 1929; No. 35, 181–380, Jan. 1930;
  No. 36, 381–585, Apr. 1930; No. 37, 587–787, July 1930.

Vol. 10. No. 38. 1–209, Oct. 1930; No. 39. 211–391, Jan. 1931;
  No. 40. 393–592, Apr. 1931; No. 41. 593–792, July 1931.

Vol. 11. No. 42. 1–182, Oct. 1931; No. 43. 183–374, Jan 1932;
  No. 44. 375–579, Apr. 1932; No. 45. 581–775, July 1932.

Vol. 12. No. 46. 1–174, Oct. 1932; No. 47. 175–338, Jan. 1933;
No. 48. 339–548, Apr. 1933; No. 49. 549–722, July 1933.

Vol. 13. No. 50. 1–178, Oct. 1933; No. 51. 179–352, Jan. 1934;
No. 52. 353–536, Apr. 1934; No. 53. 537–716, July 1934.

Vol. 14. No. 54. 1–180, Oct. 1934; No. 55. 181–350, Jan. 1935;
No. 56. 351–546, Apr. 1935; No. 57. 547–730, July 1935.

Vol. 15. No. 58. 1–182, Oct. 1935; No. 59. 183–378, Jan. 1936;
No. 60. 379–578, Apr. 1938; No. 61, 579–780. July 1936.

Vol. 16. No. 62. 1–204, Oct. 1936; No. 63, 205–404, Jan. 1937;
No. 64. 405–584, Apr. 1937; No 65. 585–772, July 1937.

Vol. 17. No. 66. 1–204, Oct. 1937; No. 67. 205–402, Jan. 1938;
No. 68. 403–602, Apr. 1938; No. 69. 603–799, July 1938.

Vol. 18. No. 70. 1–178, Oct. 1938; No. 71. 179–413, Jan. 1939.

Ceased publication.

EDITORIAL NOTES

The source of each letter is indicated at the top right. CC indicates a carbon copy. Where no other source is shown it may be assumed that the original or carbon copy is in the Valerie Eliot collection or at the Faber Archive.

del.   deleted

MS   manuscript

n. d.   no date

PC   postcard

sc.   *scilicet*: namely

TS   typescript

< >   indicates a word or words brought in from another part of the letter.

Place of publication is London, unless otherwise stated.

Some obvious typing or manuscript errors, and slips of grammar and spelling, have been silently corrected.

Dates have been standardised.

Some words and figures which were abbreviated have been expanded.

Punctuation has been occasionally adjusted.

Editorial insertions are indicated by square brackets.

Words both italicised and underlined signify double underlining in the original copy.

Where possible a biographical note accompanies the first letter to or from a correspondent. Where appropriate this brief initial note will also refer the reader to the Biographical Register at the end of the text.

Vivienne Eliot liked her husband and friends to spell her name Vivien; but as there is no consistency it is printed as written.

'Not in Gallup' means that the item in question is not recorded in Donald Gallup, *T. S. Eliot: A Bibliography* (1969).

THE LETTERS
1934–1935

For letters omitted from this and the previous volumes of T. S. Eliot's
correspondence, please visit www.tseliot.com

1934

1 January 1934   *The Criterion*, 24 Russell Square,
                                        London w.c.1.

My dear Mary,

Your beautiful handkerchiefs arrived this morning – or at least, were here this morning, as I have been laid up for several days they may have arrived sooner. I have taken so little notice of Christmas this year – after despatching 180 cards to people who had entertained me in America I was sickened by the thought of sending more – that I am all the more pleased by being remembered. Living in a suspended vacuum, as I have been, one expects to be forgotten. The last handkerchief you gave me – and a tie of year before last – are still very active. I am very happy to have these and the thought.

I am at the moment considerably worried by the lack of progress, and by letters from V. ignoring the reality and begging me to return to 'be protected'. When this is settled, I hope to be more sociable. I suppose that you will both have your hands full – with Jeremy's holidays, perhaps, and with Barbara's affairs – so I shall not bother you. But if you ever feel like a Shakespeare play or a ballet, do come with me.

                          Ever affectionately,
And with very best wishes for the New Year for Mary & Jack,
                          Tom

1–Mary Hutchinson (1889–1977), a half-cousin of Lytton Strachey; prominent hostess, author: see Biographical Register.

TO *P. W. G. McCormick*[1]

2 January 1934   [Faber & Faber Ltd,
                                                   24 Russell Square,
                                                   London w.c.1.]

Dear Mr McCormick,

Thank you for your letter of the 1st.[2] I have not yet designed the scene which your people have undertaken to carry out, and I will certainly keep in mind your suggestion about the homeless taking shelter in the crypt. I cannot say definitely yet whether I can use it or not, because the whole scene is in the melting pot. The idea of introducing an air raid, reminiscent of the late War, was not mine, and I am decidedly averse to it. Only last week I had some correspondence on this point with the Master of the Temple, who is of the same opinion.[3] I do not know what stage I shall have reached by the 9th of February, but I shall be delighted to talk over the whole matter with you then.

I have also received your kind invitation to lunch on that date after the reading. I shall be most happy to accept. I shall be very much obliged to you if you would in the meanwhile ask your secretary to inform me where the reading is to be held, and where I should present myself at the appointed time.

                                   With many thanks for your letter,
                                   Yours sincerely,
                                   [T. S. Eliot]

1 – The Revd P. W. G. 'Pat' McCormick (1877–1940), Vicar of St Martin-in-the-Fields, Trafalgar Square, London, 1927–40; Chaplain to the King from 1928.
2 – 'With regard to this Pageant . . . I understand that the scene that St Martin's have undertaken to do is an air-raid and people take shelter in the crypt, would it be possible, if you have not already gone too far with the arrangements to give a much more practical demonstration of what the Church is doing by having a scene depicting the homeless men taking shelter in the Crypt as they have done every night since the middle of the war. This is an entirely unique aspect of the work of the Church which is not undertaken elsewhere . . . [P]ersonally I am not frightfully keen on resurrecting the horrors of the War . . .'
   (TSE was to give a poetry reading at St Martin's on 9 Feb. 1934.)
3 – S. C. Carpenter, MA, DD (1877–1959): Master of the Temple, London, 1930–5; Chaplain to the King, 1929–35; Dean of Exeter, 1935–50. His works include *The Anglican Tradition* (1928). Carpenter – having been apprised that the episode in *The Rock* proposed for St Martin's was to take the topic 'During an Air Raid' – wrote on 23 Dec. 1933: '[T]o me alas it seems very unfortunate . . . Such a scene would call up many bitter anti-German war memories, from which the British people have for the most part escaped, & it could [arouse] the young people who take part in the acting to represent emotions of terror & panic which seem at the least unnecessary.
   'There are plenty of other things done at St Martin's which might serve, e.g. their Christmas tree, or even the nightly dossing of the down and out.'

2 January 1934   [*The Criterion*]

Dear John,

I was very glad to get your letter of the 10th December, and to have some news of you. First of all, I should be much pleased to have the Russian Chronicle in time for the March issue, that is to say, by the 1st February. Could you let me have it by then? Don't feel cramped for space if you find a good deal to say, because it is so long since we have had the Russian Chronicle, that it will be very welcome.[2]

I must apologise about your son's story. The fact is that I was living a rather nomadic life during this summer, with the result that I still have bundles of papers and manuscripts in hopeless confusion. I am trying to sort them out now, and will look for Alfred's story. I am extremely glad to hear that he is in touch at Harvard with Matthiessen, who is an extremely likeable fellow, is, I believe, a good tutor, and takes a keen interest in his best students. If he is working in English, I don't think that he could be under a better man.[3]

I do hope that you will get over to Europe next year, and be able to drink your whisky in my company.[4] But remember, as I warned you in my last letter, I have not yet had anything from the Guggenheim people.

Best wishes to you and Mrs Cournos for the new year.

Yours ever,

[T. S. Eliot]

1–John Cournos (1881–1966): poet, novelist, essayist, translator: see Biographical Register L6.

2–'Russian Periodicals', C. 13 (Apr. 1934), 529–36.

3–'I am particularly anxious', wrote Cournos, 'to hear if you like the story I gave you by my son, Alfred Satterthwaite. It is called "The Quick and the Dead" . . . [Alfred] is now at Harvard, where he immediately seems to have attracted Matthiesen's interest by his critical papers on poetry . . . It may interest you to know that Matthiesen speaks very highly of you to his students.' Satterthwaite (1915?–87), Cournos's stepson, read Comparative Literature at Harvard, and went on to teach in Vermont and at St John's College, Annapolis, Maryland, before joining Haverford College in 1956: he was made full professor in 1968. During WW2 he served in US Army Intelligence as a French interpreter, and after VE Day worked for the Air Corps Intelligence: his novel *Evasion Line* (1972) drew on wartime experiences. Other works include *Spenser, Ronsard and DuBellay: A Renaissance Comparison* (1960). See too Satterthwaite, 'John Cournos and "H.D."', *Twentieth Century Literature* 22: 4 (Dec. 1976), 394–410.

4–'Repeal came in a few days ago, and the sight of Martell, Haig and Haig, Chambertin, etc., visible in the shop windows, is the most tempting sight I have seen in a long time . . . but these things come high, double of what they are in England, and the empty purse rather than virtue dictates that I put them behind me . . . But the rich Yale students are ordering whole cases . . .'

TO *T. O. Beachcroft*[1]

2 January 1934   [*The Criterion*]

My dear Beachcroft,

I am look forward to seeing you tomorrow evening, but I think that your letter of the 27th needs a written as well as a verbal reply.[2]

All the stories of yours which I have seen have pleased me very much indeed. I am sorry that we are not publishing your book, and I hope that you may have more stories before long to supply to the *Criterion*. That is to say that I would as soon preface a volume of your short stories than anybody's, but upon thinking your suggestion over carefully, I believe that it would be better for me not to appear in such a role.

I am leaving out of account my belief that such introductions do very little for a book in any case. That, after all, is for you to decide for your own book. I am only taking into account my point of view, and not that of the author. In the first place, I never write introductions to volumes of contemporary poetry, partly for the reason that if I did so for one person, it would be very difficult to refuse a dozen others; and partly because the whole theory seems to me bad. But my reason for not wanting to introduce a volume of short stories, or for that matter one long story, is different. I have never read short stories except as an ordinary reader, with no special attention to technique, and it is rather late in the day for me to set up as an expert. It would seem to me in fact as much of an impertinence as for me to introduce a volume of economics. In fact rather more so, because everybody would know that I know nothing about economics, so that I should do no harm; but people might be persuaded that I did know something about short stories.

And finally, I think it is much better that a person like myself should abstain altogether from this form of publicity. I hope that I can do more in other ways for books that I like. Of course I do take a genuine interest in short stories, and particularly in yours, and I should be very glad to have

---

1 – T. O. Beachcroft (1902–88), author and critic. A graduate of Balliol College, Oxford, he joined the BBC in 1924 but then worked for Unilevers Advertising Service until 1941. He was Chief Overseas Publicity Officer, BBC, 1941–61; General Editor of the British Council series 'Writers and Their Work', 1949–54. Works include *Collected Stories* (1946).
2 – Beachcroft was to publish a volume of stories with the firm of Boriswood, and asked if TSE would write an introduction to the volume setting out his views of the short story as a genre.

the opportunity of discussing the subject in conversation. And I want to hear about progress of the Herbert book.

Yours ever,
[T. S. Eliot]

TO *John Simon Guggenheim Memorial Foundation*[1]

TS Guggenheim Foundation

5 January 1934   *The Criterion*

I do not know Mr Lowenfels[2] personally, and have no knowledge of his background and history. I do not remember what I said about him before. He has from time to time sent me poems, which have always been too long for THE CRITERION. His scheme sounds very interesting, certainly. I have never quite made up my mind about his quality as a poet. His work sometimes seems to me brilliant, and sometimes diffuse and prolix with a Jewish facility. But he is far from being negligible.[3]

T. S. Eliot. Publisher. 24, Russell Square London W.C.1.

TO *Marianne Moore*[4]

TS Rosenbach Museum & Library

5 January 1934   Faber & Faber Ltd

Dear Miss Moore,

Thank you very much for your letter of Christmas Day. I do not quite know where to address this letter; I think possibly it is safest to send it to your Brooklyn address.[5]

Your review of the *Cantos* has gone to the printer, and I look forward to reading it in proof.[6]

My real reason for writing now has nothing to do with your letter, however. I have thought for some time that your poems ought to be

---

1 – Henry Allen Moe, John Simon Guggenheim Memorial Foundation, had asked on 27 Nov. 1933 for TSE's 'present opinion of the quality of Mr Lowenfels' writings'. (TSE submitted to the Guggenheim Foundation, early in 1934, statements concerning Horace Gregory, John Cournos and Walter Lowenfels. He had also supported Lowenfels's application in 1929.)

2 – Walter Lowenfels (1897–1976): American poet, activist; member of the Communist Party; see letter to him, 20 Mar. 1934, below.

3 – Lowenfels's application was not successful.

4 – Marianne Moore (1887–1972), American poet and critic: see Biographical Register.

5 – Moore had been staying, together with her mother, in the mountains of Pennsylvania – to help look after a friend who had been injured in a motor accident.

6 – Moore, review of EP's *A Draft of XXX Cantos* (F&F, 1933): C. 13 (Apr. 1934), 482–5.

collected, or at any rate selected, and put upon the London market again. Miss Weaver's book was, of course, very small, and furthermore she was not in the position as a publisher to do very much about getting books advertised and reviewed.[1] We have discussed the matter, and would very much like to have the honour of publishing your poems. I very much hope this suggestion will not be unwelcome to you, and that you will accept in principle. There is not, of course, very much money in poetry for anybody, but we should like to add your name to our small and, I think, fairly select list of poets. A 10% royalty is what we have always given. Do please write to me about this as soon as you can, and, if you do accept, tell me when you could have the material ready, and about how much of it there would be.[2]

With all best wishes for the new year,

Yours sincerely,
T. S. Eliot

TO *Harriet Weaver*[3]   TS National Gallery of Ireland

5 January 1934   Faber & Faber Ltd

Dear Miss Weaver,

The question of the publication of *Ulysses* in this country has again arisen, and I am anxious to supplement my meagre knowledge of the early facts in the case with a possible view to discussing the matter with a high official. My impression is that the reason why *Ulysses* was not printed in this country was simply that you were unable to find a reputable printer to undertake it. I believe that after that you had an edition of 500 copies printed in France with the imprint of the *Egoist Press*, London, and that 499 of these were the consignment which was seized at Folkestone. I should like to know if this is correct, and furthermore anything that you could tell me about the circumstances of the seizure: by what authorities, and if possible through what channel the book was drawn to the notice of these authorities. The question of the legal position is at present rather obscure.

1–Moore, *Poems* (The Egoist Press, 1921).
2–Two volumes of Moore's poetry had been published: *Poems* (1921) and *Observations* (1924). See Charles Molesworth, *Marianne Moore: A Literary Life* (1990), 267–8: 'Eliot's enthusiasm must have meant a great deal to Moore, for she admired not only his poetry, but his adopted Englishness and his spiritual "weight". Moore had read "The Rock", and shared it with her mother.'
3–Harriet Shaw Weaver (1876–1961), English editor and publisher: see Biographical Register, *L* 4, 5.

If and when you are in town, it would be a pleasure to me to see you again, and no doubt it would be easier to discuss these matters in conversation than by letter. But if you are at present in the country, I should be very grateful for all the information that you care to give me in a letter.

With all best wishes for the new year,[1]

Yours sincerely,
T. S. Eliot

FROM *Geoffrey Faber*[2] *to Donald Somervell*[3] CC

5 January 1934 [Faber & Faber Ltd]

My dear Donald,

I want your advice[4] – if possible your help – in an obscure matter, not without its importance for English letters. I don't really know if it falls within the Solicitor-General's province; if it doesn't I feel sure you will tell me what authority we ought to approach, and perhaps even give us a line of introduction.

The question I am raising is that of the publication of James Joyce's *Ulysses* in England. As I expect you know, this book was originally published – and is still published – in Paris. Arrangements were made for a part of the original Paris edition to be published in London by a small firm called THE EGOIST PRESS (whose publications we took over some time ago, but after the Ulysses affair). Practically the whole of the consignment from Paris to the London publishers was seized by the Customs – I suppose by instructions from the Home Office – as 'obscene'.

1 – Weaver replied, 7 Jan.: 'I will gladly give you any information I can as to the early facts of the attempt to publish *Ulysses* in this country. And . . . I will ring up tomorrow afternoon to try to make an appointment with you.' See Jane Lidderdale and Mary Nicolson, *Dear Miss Weaver: Harriet Shaw Weaver 1876–1961* (1970), 330: 'On 9th January . . . Harriet went to see him at his own request to tell him about her own adventures in publishing *Ulysses*. But by then James Joyce had lost patience. He had received an offer to publish from The Bodley Head and gave Faber five more days in which to make up their minds. It was not long enough for them and *Ulysses* went to The Bodley Head.' Lidderdale and Nicolson note too: 'Progress had, however, hardly been encouraged by James Joyce's refusal to answer letters from the firm for six months.'
2 – Geoffrey Faber (1889–1961), publisher and poet: see Biographical Register.
3 – Sir Donald Somervell, KC, MP (1889–1960), barrister, judge and Conservative Party politician, served as Solicitor General, 1933–6.
4 – GCF noted in his diary, 5 Jan.: 'A crisis over James Joyce's Ulysses – someone else has offered to publish it here.'

Copies imported from Paris are still liable to be seized, though they have always been obtainable quite easily from London booksellers. They can, in fact, now be bought at little more than one would have to pay in Paris.

Whatever the legal definition of obscenity may be, it has always been felt by most competent English critics that the term could not intelligently be applied to *Ulysses*, which is certainly a work of genius and, in the opinion of many, much the most important literary work of art produced in English during the present century. The fact that it should have been classed by the police or the Home Office or the Customs authorities with pornographic literature has seemed, to those who hold the opinion I have suggested, to constitute a considerable slur on the intelligence of the authorities.

Sooner or later the publication of *Ulysses* in England is inevitable; and the question has now been raised in an acute form by its open publication in the U.S.A.

The position in the U.S.A. has been not dissimilar from that in this country. That is, the Customs seized all copies which came into their hands. Their action in doing so has recently been made the subject of a test case, heard by Judge Woolsey. The Judge gave a remarkable, and extremely intelligent judgement, to the effect that *Ulysses* was not an obscene book and might be admitted into the United States. As the result of this judgement, the book will shortly be published in the U.S.A.

Naturally this decision has encouraged Mr Joyce and his advisers to hope for English as well as American publication. My firm is particularly interested in this situation, because we are now Mr Joyce's official publishers in England – we have issued parts of his unfinished book WORK IN PROGRESS and shall publish the book when it is finished. For some time Mr Joyce has been pressing us to publish *Ulysses*, and matters have now come to a head because (as we have just heard) another London firm has made him an offer to publish *Ulysses* in the form of a six months' option.

I had intended to sound out official opinion in this country before long, but this communication obliges me to act more quickly than I had intended. We are, in fact, asked for an immediate reply in the form of a definite offer. That is, of course, of no interest to the English authorities, but it will explain to you why I am writing to you personally and informally in the matter. For any opinion or assistance you can give us I should be exceedingly grateful.

I have to go down to Wales this afternoon, and shall be away for ten days or so – whereas our answer to Joyce's agent cannot be delayed for more than two or three days. But in my absence the matter will be handled here by two of my directors – Mr T. S. Eliot (of whom you know) and Mr F. V. Morley. Is it asking too much of you to say that I should be very grateful if you could give Eliot and Morley an opportunity to see you for a quarter of an hour? They know the contents of this letter, and are – if anything – more familiar with the facts than I am myself. Either of them can be got on the telephone here on Monday morning.

Yours ever,
[Geoffrey Faber]

P.S. I enclose a copy of the American *Saturday Review of Literature* containing Judge Woolsey's judgement.

FROM *Donald Somervell*   Faber

6 January 1934   11 Cornwall Terrace,
                                      Regent's Park, N.W.1

Dear Eliot,

I have had a letter from Geoffrey re *Ulysses* & he has asked me to write or see you. As I am just off for a week or so I am afraid that I can't see you so write – I have been on to the Home Office & if you or Geoffrey would write or telephone to J. F. Henderson of the Home Office he would see you & give any assistance he can. He is in charge of that department. In case there is a muddle Mr Hacking's (The Under Sec) Private Sec told me that he would let Henderson know & that H would be glad to see you & give you any help he could.

I daresay they may not be able to be very helpful and I am not sure even if they were definitely prepared to say they would not move whether they could in fact stop a private person instituting a prosecution or whether they have any control outside the London area. These anyhow are points which he could tell you. I am very vague about the initiation of prosecutions, though I expect I ought to know about it; but I expect the Home Office could not as a matter of practical politics prevent or undertake to prevent the case going to the Court if there was a demand for having it so tested. However Henderson should be able to let you know the general position.[1]

Donald Somervell

1 – The only record of TSE and FVM's otherwise off-the-record interview with J. F. Henderson, Assistant Secretary at the Home Office, Whitehall, is a memo by Henderson

himself written on 7 Oct. 1936 – at the time when John Lane had chosen to publish at the Bodley Head an edition of *Ulysses* without seeking permission from the Home Office. Henderson noted: 'The last time the book was discussed in H. O. was in Jan. 1934 when Mr T. S. Eliot and Mr Morley of Faber & Faber came to see me, being introduced by the present A. G. [Donald Somervell]. It was then decided to await developments, and to consider what action shd. be taken if & when the book was published here and if there were any protests.' (National Archives, Kew: HO 144/20071)

Evidently the Home Office gave no ruling: merely the fudgy, temporising advice that they would wait and see if anyone did publish the book and whether complaints would ensue.

TSE was taken aback by the absurd and potentially imperilling predicament with which he and FVM were presented by the Home Office. Some time later, in a talk given at a *Green Quarterly* luncheon club (9 July 1935), he rehearsed the briefing, and the implicit warning, given by Henderson: 'Let me put a hypothetical case. Let us suppose that there was a book which I regarded as a great work of art which any publisher should feel honoured to have his imprint upon, and that this book contained certain words not commonly used in middle-class company of both sexes, and contained passages dealing with subjects not usually addressed in such company. Let us suppose also, in order to illustrate a further complication, that this book had been previously published in another country, and that any copies of the foreign edition brought into this country had been ordered to be confiscated by the Customs. Let us suppose that with the lapse of time this book had come to be recognized as a great work of art; and that so many copies had been smuggled into this country that no person with any pretence to literary knowledge and taste could admit, without shame, that he had not read it. I go to the Home Office, the official custodian of morals, to ask whether I may or may not publish the book in England. I am told, with all courtesy, that I am perfectly free to publish it. There was never anything to prevent me from publishing it. As for the Custom House, that is, in some way which I do not understand, independent of the Home Office: the Customs may confiscate books, but they cannot forbid their publication in England. But, of course, if I publish the book, I must understand that I do so at my own risk. The Home Office cannot prevent, and has no desire to prevent me from publishing it; but neither has it the power to protect me when I have published it. I am at the mercy of any Briton who sends a marker copy to a magistrate, if the magistrate agrees with the informant that the book is obscene. Being still perfectly free, I have the opportunity to appeal. But unless I have a couple of thousand pounds or more which I can spare for the purpose – and a publisher's capital is usually fully employed – I shall not risk an appeal. For my appeal will be to legal authorities who, however eminent on the bench, however distinguished for learning and for integrity, will not necessarily be moral theologians or sages. In the present state of affairs, it is safer to publish the book which makes vice attractive, than the book that makes it repulsive. And in publishing a book which I believe to be highly moral but which offends the prejudices of a magistrate, I get the worst of it, I cannot even be sure in advance what the penalty may be. I may only suffer the cost of printing the book, or I may have a fine imposed, or I may, perhaps, go to gaol. And what is still worse, if I publish a book which I fear may be condemned, I am never safe. There is no statute of limitations. It is nobody's business to prosecute me for publishing the book, but it is *anybody's* business.' ('Should there be a Censorship of Books?', *The New Green Quarterly* I: 4 [Aut. 1935], 197–200.) Not in Gallup.

TO *Ezra Pound*[1]   TS Beinecke

7 January 1934 A.D.   Faber & Faber Ltd

NO, Podesta,[2] I may be laughter-loving, as the squamish would say and as I gladly admit – but so was Aphrodite – but I am Not COARSE. If I am, as my old friend Winthrop Sprague Brooks[3] used to say, I'll be horse-fucked.

I was just thinkin of taking out a subscription to the *Adelphi* for you, but if you have that queasey stomach you cant pass water with Murry or Leavis, thats no use – what about havin a friendly wipe at *New Verse* and its editor. Young Grigson has elements of good in him, which might be better elicited if he had his ears beat down a bit, and he dont know how to box yet – witness his passes with Edith Sitwell recently.

Shall I send you a copy of *Basic Rules of Reason* by Richards[4] for your digestion. Its a small book.

Anyway, if you just fire away and write Enough in the *N.E.W.* you will sooner or later say somefin foolish what I can take advantage of if it comes at the right time, only make it after the end of the present month if you can. You did say somethin some time ago about defining religion which I failed to take up; but the trouble is good boxin is wasted on a audience like that Yours etc.

Tp

[Enclosed with letter to EP]

COME, Glorious Rabbitt, how long wilt thou slumber,
    lying supine or prone in luxurious lair.
Shaking the sleep from besotted eyes, spring a sur-
    prise, do something to make 'em all stare,
Sturdy of hoof and long in the toof, Thunderer, grasp
    hard the bastards by the short hair.
Not once, or twice, shalt thou bugger 'em, in our
    rough island story,

1–Ezra Pound (1885–1972), American poet and critic: see Biographical Register.
2–Podesta: *Podestà* (*Ital.*): a holder of public office such as governor, mayor, magistrate, or other municipal officer.
3–Winthrop Sprague Brooks (1887–1965), TSE's contemporary at Milton and Harvard, collector and zoologist, was for some years Curator of Birds at the Boston Society of Natural History; custodian of birds' eggs and nests at the Harvard Museum of Comparative Zoology, 1929–34.
4–I. A. Richards, *Basic Rules of Reason* (1933).

But again and again and again and again, leaving their
 arseholes all gory;
And when I say, again and again, I mean repeatedly, I
 mean continually, I mean in fact many times,
Chaunting a one-way song in mellifluous proses and
 rugged tempestuous lines I mean rhymes.
Lord of a hundred battles, a cauliflower ear and 1000
 hardwon scars,
Proclaim aloud to the morning that a r s e spells arse.[1]

TO *Ernest Bird, Messrs Bird & Bird*[2]   CC

8 January 1934   [Faber & Faber Ltd]

My dear Bird,

Thank you for your letter of the 4th instant with enclosure. I am writing to tell you that your letter of that date to Messrs James & James has my full approval.[3]

In writing a letter of condolence to Mr James I suggested that in the circumstances it might be in everyone's interest to transfer my income tax papers to your office. In a letter which I have this morning he says that

---

1 – Beinecke: Ezra Pound Papers YCAL MSS 43, Box 15, folder 664. See *Poems*, ed. Ricks and McCue (2015), II, 287–8.

2 – Ernest Bird (1877–1945), solicitor.

3 – TSE's solicitors Bird & Bird wrote to James & James, 4 Jan. 1934: 'We desire to take this opportunity of repeating the expressions of deep regret that we have already tendered to you through the telephone on the death of Mr Shapcott whose loss after so long an association will, we are sure, be not only a great sorrow but also a source of much inconvenience to you . . .

'Mr Leigh-Hunt was on the same day good enough to inform Mr Ernest Bird on the telephone of what had passed at his recent interview with Mrs Eliot. We gathered in effect that she demands her Husband returns to her, that she consequently declines to sign any deed of separation and that, in any event, she requires an allowance of £2 per day. She should long since have been convinced that under no circumstances will Mr Eliot go back to her and we can only describe the suggested weekly payment as ridiculous. The time has now arrived when this matter must be brought to a conclusion. We must therefore say quite definitely that, as stated by Mr Bird to Mr [Alfred E.] James on the telephone today, in default of Mrs Eliot executing forthwith the separation deed in the form in which it was finally agreed between us we must on our client's behalf give effect to the conditions it contains. In other words, our client's provision for his Wife will be restricted to a payment of £5 per week, plus the rent and other outgoings payable in respect of the flat.

'We ought perhaps to add that if Mrs Eliot desires to take proceedings against her Husband for restitution of conjugal rights – which we gather is in her mind – it is, of course, open to her so to do.'

Mr Cumming in his office, whom I do not know, is conversant with these affairs, and he further thinks that it would be better not to transfer the business at this stage. I presume that I had best accede to his suggestion in this matter. Of course when my tax for the current year is settled, my business with James and James will be completed.[1]

Yours sincerely,
[T. S. Eliot]

TO *James Joyce*[2]

TS National Gallery of Ireland

9 January 1934   *The Criterion*

Dear Joyce,

Morley will have written today to Léon,[3] but here is the matter as things seem to be at the moment.

---

1 – TSE's tax affairs were to be transferred to Bird & Bird at the close of the current tax year.

2 – James Joyce (1882–1941), Irish novelist, playwright, poet: see Biographical Register.

3 – Paul Léon, né Paul Léopoldovich (1893–1942?): cultured multilingual Jewish émigré from the Bolshevik revolution who had settled in Paris; he met JJ in 1928, when JJ was forty-seven and Léon thirty-five. He became JJ's unpaid assistant and amanuensis from 1930, and protected his papers even after the Nazis took over Paris. Léon was eventually seized by the German authorities and despatched to a camp where he died in unknown circumstances. See *The James Joyce–Paul Léon Papers in the National Gallery of Ireland: A Catalogue*, compiled by Catherine Fahy (1992); John Naughton, 'Arm in arm with a literary legend' (interview with Alexis Léon), the *Observer*, 13 Jan. 1991.

Léon had advised TSE and FVM, 3 Jan. 1934: 'An offer in writing has been handed to me today by a representative of an English publishing firm for the publication of an edition of Mr Joyce's ULYSSES in Great Britain.

'This offer provides for a certain advance on the royalties part of which is to be paid immediately and to constitute an option for the eventual publication and the balance payable on publication.

'The option will last for six months and is given with the special purpose to allow negotiations with the British authorities, it will be subject to extension by *mutual* agreement in case proof is given that the negotiations are actually started and their protraction is not attributable to the publishers' fault.

'Mr Joyce has empowered me to deal with this matter and I would like to know if you are prepared to make a similar or better offer. As I am bound by a certain date to give my reply your counter-offer, if any, should reach me within five days.'

FVM wrote to Léon, 9 Jan. 1934: 'It was obvious, when we began to study the ULYSSES problem in November, that two things were vital. First, legal preparations adequate not merely to fight but to win a case. Second, the interest of people in power, sufficient to keep the Home Office out of the matter. These remain vital because premature publication might easily result in a court decision against ULYSSES, which would kill the present chances.

'As you know, there are three ways in which ULYSSES may be damaged: a customs ban, a magistrate's decision, and action by the Home Office. At the moment you have the first against you; by publication in England, you risk the others.

I think it was understood when we saw you in Paris that Faber & Faber were prepared to publish *Ulysses* as soon as publication proved feasible.

—

'The customs ban is not, I understand, being very strictly enforced at the moment. It would, I take it, be removed if one fought and won a court action; but probably the English publisher would then wish it enforced for another reason – to protect his edition from the competition of imported copies.

'A magistrate's decision, on an edition printed in England, could result from any hostile individual laying an information against ULYSSES; on which, if there seemed to the magistrate a prime facie case against it, he could inflict penalties. There could be appeals, first to quarter sessions, eventually (if necessary) to the House of Lords.

'A Home Office action might result from the publication being brought to the Home Secretary's attention either by a common informer or, say, by a question in the House of Commons . . .

'Until ULYSSES is actually published in England, it is impossible to know what will happen. But since we discussed the matter in Paris, Mr Eliot and I have made it our business to collect opinions from the kind of people who will be concerned. We soon found that too many people are interested for there to be any chance of publishing ULYSSES unobserved. We learned that several publishers had written to the Home Office for information; in that case there could be no harm in our finding out the private opinions of the people in power there. We found the private opinions. They are less encouraging than you hope.

'We are only giving our estimate, and I hope we are wrong; but for what that estimate is worth, there is little likelihood of publishing ULYSSES without a court action, and little hope of winning that action this year.

'We were unwilling to come to this opinion, and had not intended to admit it without exploring all possible information. That was why we were disturbed when you asked for an immediate answer. But thinking over what we have learned, we doubt whether six months would materially alter it. If so, there is less point in making a counter-offer, as you suggest, for a six months option.

'We don't think successful publication is possible in England in 1934. If we are wrong, and any rival can be successful in 1934, more power to him. But if he isn't successful, and in six months time merely comes to the position at which we have already arrived, we should regret it if we didn't have another chance. I hope that chance will come. If our report of our investigation is accurate, it would be unfortunate if we were penalised for having got to work promptly. We think we are in as close touch with the changing temper of England as anybody; and I needn't stress the obvious fact that we want ULYSSES as well as WORK IN PROGRESS [*Finnegans Wake*]. So if you accept the rival offer for the option, and if that option should lapse when the problem is investigated, we want to have the chance of cutting in.'

GCF regretted in his preface to *A Publisher Speaking* (1934), 11: 'James Joyce's *Ulysses*, though now officially admitted into the land of the stars and stripes, is excluded from this land of hope and glory. The argument against the censorship has, therefore, a permanent relevance.'

John Bodley of F&F wrote in an undated, unpublished essay, 'Faber and Ireland', that Geoffrey Faber 'was an extremely cautious man, and he insisted that the firm took legal advice at the highest level, from the Solicitor-General. Meanwhile John Lane bravely made an offer direct to Joyce to publish it at The Bodley Head. Joyce then gave Fabers five days to make a counter offer, but Fabers hung back and lost this great book to The Bodley Head.' Peter du Sautoy, in 'Editing Ulysses: A Personal Account', *James Joyce Quarterly* 27: 1 (Fall 1989), 69–76, confirmed that F&F 'lost' *Ulysses* to Allen Lane 'through failure to act quickly enough'.

We had of course been pursuing enquiries when Léon's letter of the other day arrived, asking for a decision within five days. My own enquiries might, in one direction, have proceeded quicker if I had thought to ask you to instruct Monro, Saw to let us have any information in their possession about the history of the case. Perhaps they have none, but they did take a long time to reply that they had no authority from you to communicate with us. I doubt whether this matters much, because I gather from Miss Weaver that nobody knows much about the confiscation at Folkestone, except for what little Rodker may know, and I have not yet been able to see him.

But the history of the case, although we want as full a chronicle as possible, is not the main line of investigation. It is impossible to get any positive statement from the Home Office, and nobody else will have any more success in that than we; but what can be done, and [it] is a slow and delicate business, is to take the official temperature. We speeded things up as much as possible in order to be able to make some reply by the time that Léon wanted it; but our enquiries are not complete, and could not be completed within that time.

While I appreciate your desire that *Ulysses* should be available before *WIP* appears, and of course agree as to the desirability, I do not feel that it is so vital as you may think. I learn that copies come through constantly from Paris, and so far I have not heard of a single instance of confiscation. The effect of publishing *Ulysses* here of course will be to open up a new public; but I am convinced that there is a very large public indeed familiar with the book – though only in part in possession of it – which is quite ready for *WIP* the moment it appears.

My impressions are that the general atmosphere is steadily becoming more favourable. Now, if there were *no* symptoms of change, I should say: as well try the book now as any time. But I believe that there will be much better chances of success in six months or a year's time. What I have in mind is, that public opinion can change and is changing; but a decision of a high court is a different matter; and I am afraid that premature attempts might actually delay the general availability of the book. I say a *high* court, because it would be bad for both publisher and book, if a publisher undertook to publish it without being ready to go on fighting for it. If it were published, and the publisher then lay down tamely under a mere magistrate's decision, the effect would be bad. But if on the other hand the magistrate's decision were sustained, there would be a legal precedent difficult to break for a long time.

I do not think that the other publisher will be able to gather any more assurance than we, or will be able to find out any more than we are finding. If he succeeds, I shall be as delighted as anybody. But if he abandons the attempt, we should like, when his option expires, to have an option for the following period, or periodically until the way is clear.

I should have written before, during this time, had I thought that I had enough information to bother you with. As soon as I have any further news, I will write to you at once.

Yours ever sincerely,
T. S. Eliot

TO *Laurence Pollinger*[1]   CC

12 January 1934   [Faber & Faber Ltd]

Dear Pollinger,

I think that you have already learned from Morley what our views on the subject of Pound's JEFFERSON/MUSSOLINI are. It seems to me that it is a problem for New York rather than for London, and I don't see what I could do with any part of it in the *Criterion*.

I am therefore returning it to you.

Yours sincerely,
[T. S. Eliot]

TO *Ezra Pound*   TS Beinecke

12 January 1934   *The Criterion*

Exmo Respmo Santmo Bullcat,

Numerous letter & points to answer, probabbly shall not succeed in getting them all dealt with.

First, re *Propertius*. My own idea is rather this: regular or x3/that is it 7/6 edition the keys are rubbed off of your SElected Poems is now out of print & superseded by People's Edition at 3s.6d. What I suggest is bringing out an edition not SElected but your own selection that is All you care to Preserve of your work up to Cantos, including what I left out & of course *Propert*. We should want to be able to consider this 'the standard text for many years to come'. Produce this at 7/6 if possible, it might cost more. Retain 3/6 edition as it stands for beginners. Seems to me much

---

1 – Laurence Pollinger (d. 1976?), literary agent with the firm of Curtis Brown.

more sensible than reprinting *Prop.* separately. No introduction to new edition, unless you feel you really must do one yourself.[1]

I have not yet put this to my co-directors, thinking it best to sound your feelings first.

Lowwenfels called yesterday. I am sorry he's no better than that, but there it is. I believe Bridson coming to London soon and will see him. His Poem in A. A. much better than anything he has sent me.[2]

SECOND. We are ready for next batch of cantos, assuming that that particular section is to appear by itself because *you* think that it is capable of so doing. I suggest that they should appear in the autumn at the same time as *Selected Essays*.[3] New York can't do them any sooner, unless they have them already in hand: but if they came out SIMULTANEOUS that ought to do for you. We are ready to produce contract as soon as you say so.[4]

If you were the sort of guy what ever admitted anything you would admit that Faber & Faber are good publishers.[5]

At any rate you are not an Irishman. I admit it ungrudgingly.

I never see the Harvard Periodical, but I shant mind much, whatever you said.[6]

1–EP responded, 14 Jan.: 'Wdn't the incidence on the whatever is the Ersatz fer crikikul consciounsiousness of Britain be sharper if the Propertius were printed alone/ fer ONCE at least/ and not giving the BASTUDS the excuse of divagating on the already familiar; or treatink the woik as a reprint of the Selected. ???' In the event, *Homage to Sextus Propertius* was to be reprinted by F&F in a separate edition on 8 Nov. 1934.

2–EP, 14 Jan.: 'Bridson I believe to be a good ROOT and worth cultivating. they will never make a bloomsbuggah of him.'

3–EP, 12 Jan.: 'I spose the Cantos XXXI/XLI of the most interest to youze guys?? wot HO?!' EP, 14 Jan.: 'Date fer Cantos <XXXI–XL> and Essays SAZISFAKORY. What I was fussing over was to get a CLEAR statement, so'z either to git the job <of essays> OUT of this room NOW / or shed it; and do something else.

'THE SOONER you and F/V. [Morley] come to definite decision re exact contents even re/ Contemporary Mentality . . . the sooner old EZ can soaRRRR into Cantos XLI/L.'

This new volume of putative 'Selected Essays' was ultimately to appear as *Make It New: Essays by Ezra Pound* (F&F, 1934; Yale University Press, 1935).

4–*Eleven New Cantos: XXXI–XLI* was to be published by Farrar & Rinehart, NY, in Oct. 1934; then by F&F as *A Draft of Cantos XXXI–XLI* on 14 Mar. 1935, with this flat blurb (probably by TSE): 'Mr Pound's *A Draft of XXX Cantos* was described in the *Morning Post* as an "immense and already famous work" and "magnificent". These eleven cantos are a further instalment.'

5–EP, 14 Jan.: 'The due, and requested tribute to you and F/V/ in yr/ hypostasis Fab/ Fab wuz rendered in epistle of a few days ago/ handing it tu YUH!! For having busted the BeaverRother and circumvented the mangy remnants of the Squirarchy and McFarty [Desmond MacCarthy].'

6–EP, 'Ignite! Ignite!', *Harvard Advocate* 120: 3 (Dec. 1933), 3–5. EP explained further on 14 Jan.: 'You seem to have misunderstood my allusion to the Advocate. They headlined me

Not quite clear what you mean about starting things. I dont suppose my paragraph about Winston is going to raise a revolution, but I do what I can.[1] See my next book. For God's sake dont be so indirect. What old gang am I supporting?

THIRD. I dont see WHAT I can do with Jeff-Muss in the *Criterion*. Serialisation is No Good in a Quarterly, its worse than a waste of powder and shot. Much better that you should write something else, or occasionally the same in a different form, I mean at a proper length and Without cryptic allusions. How can you expect Britons to get excited about Martin V. Buren[2] and Biddle?[3] They dont know who Jefferson[4] was and never heard of John Quincy[5] etc. You might as well talk to Tammany Hall about the foreign policy of Castlereagh. Partly that the human Mind never connects anything, but partly quite justifiable ignorance. If they put anything in their minds at all, they wouldnt even then begin on the Adams.[6] The Essay Outht Ought I mean to be published in New York, and NOT serially but in one lump as a book.[7]

---

with an article labled IGNITE . . . Specifically that no man who had sat pretty thru the era of shit/ past 40 years was FIT to educate the next generation.

'In that periodical or Hoot/ there appeared some undergrad/ scorn of yr/ sacred person /// [by Case] FER WHICH I am NOT responsible. Anymore than [Cyrus] SUlzbergers bullshit apropos ME.

'The Hoot in Nov. carried a long and solemn article called "The Absolute and Utter Farce of American Univ. Edderkashun <by EZ>."

1 – While TSE praised Winston Churchill – in his 'Commentary', C. 13 (Jan. 1934), 270 – as 'an honester historian than Macaulay', and with sound judgement, he considered his prose style 'second-rate' to the point of being 'dead': 'The historical style, as developed by Mr Churchill and others . . . is the style of a man accustomed to public speaking – to oratory, an art largely concerned with evoking stock emotional responses. It is sometimes maintained that practice in speech is excellent preparation for writing; this may be so, but . . . no kind of speaking is without its dangers as well as its benefits. In a style formed by oratory, we must never expect intimacy; we must never expect the author to address us as individual readers, but always as members of a mob.'

2 – Martin Van Buren (1782–1862), 8th President of the USA.

3 – Nicholas Biddle (1786–1844), American financier; president of Second National Bank from 1822; antagonist of Jackson in the war against the banks.

4 – Thomas J. Jefferson (1743–1826), 3rd President of the USA, 1801–9; wrote the Declaration of Independence.

5 – John Quincy Adams (1767–1848). *The Memoirs of John Quincy Adams*, 12 vols, 1874–1877, ed. Charles Francis Adams.

6 – See further David Ten Eyck, *Ezra Pound's Adams Cantos* (2012); A. David Moody, *Ezra Pound: Poet: A Portrait of the Man and His Work*, II: *The Epic Years 1921–1939* (2014).

7 – EP, 25 Dec. 1933: 'Pol/ reps/ Jeff/Muss delivered to you. I think the Criterion must be able to use at least some of it. Leaving the cuts to you/ and to simult with the American serialization if that damm mag starts.

'Otherwise an eventual Faber vol// WHEN F. V. [Morley] thinks the time is ripe.'

What the little Txt book?[1] As we are carrying most of your stuff, we are just entitled to information about the rest. <If it works in in any way: advertising etc. Not jealousy.>

Question of *Active Anthology* must I think wait till we see a little better how much we lose on this.[2]

Your wishes re review copies have been carried out.

The Hoot is or was better than anything at Harvard. But it was run by an Able Jew who is now setting at the foot of Maynard Keynes, so I dont knowwhats become of either it or him.

The root idea in your Morley review is of course absolutely sound.

The CONTRACT for Essays has been awaiting cast off of cost & price of book – i.e. its a fine matter & we want to give you the best terms possible which depends on what book costs us and what we sell it at. I am on to that at once.

PROGRAMME.

Autumn. SELECTED ESSAYS and NEXT CANTOS.
Question of another Active held over for the moment.
SPRING 1935: COMPLETE PRECANTO POETICAL WORKS.

I think copy of best up to date photograph of the author ought to be in possession of our advertising dept. in case.[3]

Will write in few days time about essays & Contract.

Basil Blackwell wrote to GCF, 19 Dec. 1933: 'I have had a rather odd letter from a young man, who professes to write on behalf of Ezra Pound, concerning a political tract, which he wishes to have published by us, and entitled "Jefferson or Mussolini". Isn't Ezra Pound your bird? My correspondent hints at trouble of some kind. In fact, he seems to have a persecution complex.' GCF drafted his reply at the foot of Blackwell's letter: 'We turned the Jefferson tract down. It's good Pound, all right; but we didn't think it meat for English readers.'

1 – *ABC of Reading* (1934). EP, 12 Jan.: 'The li'l tex book wiff Routledge ought to do scout woik [for] the essays . . .' 14 Jan.: 'Langdon Davies told Routledge they ought to bring out a text book by me on econ/ or lit/ they said "lit" // and have now got the "How to Read" thesis or Anschauung, in the form of a school book. Sent it on choosday/ and they ought to be answering SOON. They have signed a contract, but what is that among Englishmen.'

2 – EP, 12 Jan.: 'A kid at Oxon/ suggests periodical pubctn/ I have said I wd edit/ an annual Active Anth/ . . . but that the thing must be offered to F/F . . . Idea being rather to use NEW writers than to have same gang each year . . .'

3 – EP replied, 14 Jan.: 'Will look for some purty pixchoors. Of EZ. In his latest beach pyjamaZ . . . What about that photo of ALL england star team of potes visiting Wilfrid Blunt and thereby twistin the lion's proboscis in 1914 ?? . . . Ole Blunt/ Yeats, Sturge Moose, Plarr / Ez / Flint/ Ricardo Aldingtongio (minus capa y spada) . . . (sign on Blunt's front gate: "Belligerents will please use kitchen entrance" does NOT appear in the photo.' 16 Jan.: 'remitted pixchoors oggi'.

And in virtue of the authority given to me as a Director of this firm, I give you my blessing for 1934, expiring on Dec. 31st.[1]

T.

TO *Mario Praz*[2] TS Galleria Nazionale d'Arte Moderna, Rome

12 January 1934   Faber & Faber Ltd

My dear Praz,

Many thanks for your letter of the 30th December.[3] I will let you know if and when I arrange to go to Rome, though it does not look as if you would be there and I imagine that you will have to be too busy to want to see me when you are in London.

Thank you very much for sending me *Circoli*, with your translation of *The Waste Land*.[4] To me, it seems extremely good, and indeed very much better than I should have thought possible. <You know, however, that I am far from knowing the language well enough to appreciate the translation fully.> *A priori*, I should have said that *The Waste Land* was much more difficult to translate into Italian than *Ash Wednesday*. Your notes are perfectly legitimate and helpful. I shall look forward with curiosity to your translation of the Agon.[5] But I must tell you that Jean de Menasce, who was by far the best translator that I ever had into French, had to abandon the attempt, finding it untranslatable. I do hope, however, that it can be done.

With all best wishes for the new year, and for your prospects for the future,

Yours sincerely,
T. S. Eliot

1 – EP would write to James Laughlin, 17 Jan. 1934, that TSE 'proposes that Faber continue, and get out collected essays / Cantos to XLI, and collected poems inserting what he (T. S.) fer Victoria's sake forebore, and omittin' his shoehorn.

'Very firm on its being no use to tell England America was there in 1830 [. . .]' (*Ezra Pound and James Laughlin: Selected Letters*, ed. David M. Gordon [1994], 15–16).

2 – Mario Praz (1896–1982), scholar of English life and literature: see Biographical Register.

3 – Praz was due to be married in London by the end of March, but he and his wife would not be going to live in Rome until the end of June, at the close of the academic session in Manchester.

4 – Praz had sent TSE his own copy of 'La Terra Desolata', *Circoli* (Genoa), 2 (July/Aug. 1932), 27–57. 'I have also translated yr *Fragment of an Agon*, wch will be published some time. My notes to *The Waste Land* are a bit fuller than yours: I wonder what you'll think of the additions.'

5 – Praz, 'Frammento di un Agone', *Letteratura* 1: 2 (Apr. 1937), 97–102.

TO *Hugh Mason Wade*[1]   CC

13 January 1934   [*The Criterion*]

Dear Wade,[2]

Sulzberger was right; the only difficulty is of time. I have a difficult piece of work on hand of a theatrical nature, and I don't know how much time it is going to take.[3] I hope that the hardest part of my work with it will be over by March; if so I can let you have something in time for the May number. All I can promise is to do it as soon as possible, and then you use it when convenient.

I wish you would send me a copy with Pound's outburst.[4] Of course I can't be so outspoken as he can – biting the hands that fed me, etc. As for Auden etc. I don't know; my principle has been to let the boys have a fair chance with the public first, and do my criticising privately in conversation. I can't be impresario and critic at once; perhaps when I retire from publishing etc. If the public cant discriminate (and it cant) I cant help it. But I *might* make a few mild remarks about the educational system – esp. teaching of English; England just as diseased but the pustules have not appeared yet. I suppose I shall get round to subscribing to the *Advocate* eventually, but I flinch from the physical labour of writing cheques.

1–Hugh Mason Wade (1913–86), whom TSE had taught at Harvard in 1932–3 (Wade would graduate in 1936), was to become an editor with Harcourt, Brace; then a university professor.

2–Wade, as editor of the *Harvard Advocate*, wrote on 19 Dec. 1933: 'My predecessor, Cy [Cyrus] Sulzberger, has informed me that you have promised us an article. We have adopted a policy of running one article each issue by some prominent *Advocate* or Harvard man. We have already had an article by Pound (a ringer, of course) and will have others by Roosevelt, Lippman, MacLeish, Dos Passos, Cummings, etc.

'As to subject, a paper on your year at Harvard would be admirable, if you cared to do it. Pound on this in the last issue: "Eliot, picked as a safe man, perhaps the only safe man among educated writers under fifty, was not on speaking terms with former President Lowell; & dear ole Binyon has been called on to correct the too advanced and too dangerous daring of Eliot. My gorrd wotter country . . ."' (Laurence Binyon, TSE's successor, lectured on Oriental Art.)

Wade went on: 'Or perhaps something on Auden, Spender, Day Lewis, et al., in whom there is great interest here now and about whom very little is known. Of course you could use this elsewhere, as we would waive copyright . . .

'P.S. Called at Russell Sq. this August & was sorry to miss you.'

3–*The Rock*.

4–EP, 'Ignite! Ignite!', *Harvard Advocate* 120: 3 (Dec. 1933), 3–5.

I was very sorry to miss you in August – I was out of town until November – another year you are much more likely to find me in Russell Square in August.

With best wishes,
Yours always sincerely,
[T. S. Eliot]

TO *Leonard Woolf*[1]   TS University of Sussex Library

13 January 1934   *The Criterion*

Dear Leonard,

Many thanks for the New Year greetings and for the photograph. The look of rapt imbecility worries me; it is a warning of how I shall look in my dotage. I dare say I am doting already.

I should like to come in to see you & Virginia, afternoon, after dinner, or at any time.[2]

Yrs.
T. S. E.

TO *Alida Monro*[3]   TS BL

13 January 1934   *The Criterion*

Dear Alida,

I don't believe in formal introductions except for getting rid of people – not, at any rate, to people I know well. I am writing to my brother &

1 – Leonard Woolf (1880–1969), writer and publisher: see Biographical Register.
2 – TSE dined with the Woolfs, in company with Stephen Tomlin (1901–37) – bisexual artist and sculptor intimately associated with the Bloomsbury Group – on Tues., 30 Jan.
3 – Alida Klementaski (1892–1969) married Harold Monro on 27 Mar. 1920, having fallen in love with him in 1913. F. S. Flint wrote in 1933, of Alida: 'She was a young and beautiful woman who was earnestly bent on doing some good in the world, and who, to an equal degree with Harold, had a passion for poetry. She wanted to be a doctor, and to spend her life rescuing prostitutes; but Harold Monro persuaded her that, if she worked in the Poetry Bookshop, she would be doing as great a piece of social work as she would by the practice of medicine . . . She had an incisive mind and a keen sense of the ridiculous. Before the laughter in her cool, clear eyes, many of Harold Monro's phantasms and romantic illusions must have vanished, never to return again . . . For the rest of his life, Alida Klemantaski was at his side in the Bookshop, his chief help, assistant and guide. He himself said that, without her, he could not have carried on.'

my sister anyway, and will notify them of your arrival.[1] I suggest in the places you mention:

Chicago: Mrs James F. Porter (a cousin)
                 1085 Sheridan Avenue,
                 Hubbard Woods, near Chicago.

Pittsburgh: Prof. & Mrs Samuel Eliot
                 I don't know his address, but ask Henry for it.
                 The wife is German, and intelligent.[2]

Brooklyn: Marianne Moore,
                 260 Cumberland Street.
                 One of the most intelligent of women. You hardly need any introduction, as she is a poet.

Minneapolis: The Revd & Mrs Frederick Eliot,[3]
                 807 Fairmont Avenue, *ST PAUL*.
                 Interesting specimen of the best that Unitarianism can do in the way of clergy. There are also some pleasant cousins named Furness, but I forget their address.

Buffalo: Prof. & Mrs Henry Ten Eyck Perry,[4]
                 15 Arlington Place
                 These are merely the people that I stayed with; I hardly can be said to know them.

I am so sorry I don't know Cummings.[5] Edmund Wilson is worth knowing, but I can't find his address.

I will write to Frederick too. The Porters are rich, nice, but boring.

---

1 – Monro, who was soon to leave for a two-month tour of the USA, giving lectures, asked on 12 Jan.: 'Can I just go and see your brother and sister or will you give me a letter to them?'

2 – TSE's cousin Samuel Ely Eliot (1882–1976), born in Oregon – son of the Revd Thomas Lamb Eliot (who had founded, with his father William Greenleaf Eliot, Washington University in St Louis) – worked as Resident Director of the Woods Run Settlement House (a community centre), Pittsburgh. His wife was Elsa von Manderscheid (1880–1978) of San Francisco.

3 – The Revd Frederick May Eliot (1889–1958) was Minister of Unity Church, St Paul, Minnesota, 1917–37. For a fuller biography see TSE's letter to him, 9 Jan. 1935.

4 – Henry Ten Eyck Perry (1890–1973).

5 – E. E. Cummings (1894–1962), poet, prose writer, playwright, artist. Alida Monro had requested: 'I would like to meet E. E. Cummings if you know him and could give me a note to him.' In 1913 TSE had played Lord Bantock to Cummings's Second Footman in a play called *Fanny and the Servant Problem* (letter to Eleanor Hinkley, 3 Jan. 1915). TSE to Henry Sherek, 25 May 1960: 'In the play in which E. E. Cummings was the second footman, I played a charming young man, of course, but in the lowest order of the peerage. I was merely Lord Bantock and a Jerome K. Jerome peer at that.' For his part, Cummings, who

With every good wish,

Yours

Tom

Don't be too confident! 3 lectures a week is a *good deal*. It isn't the lecturing that wears you out, but the *people*.[1]

Be careful what you *eat*. Avoid salads. Ice cream is safe.

It would be worth your while to buy a cheap fur coat in New York. One must dress lightly *indoors*. You will need American galoshes.

My sister-in-law will gladly help about shopping etc.

TO *Stephen Spender*[2]   TS Northwestern

13 January 1934   *The Criterion*

My dear Spender,

I have been thinking about your problem, and wondering whether, if you have to produce books for Cape or for us or for anyone else in order to raise money, you have made the best choice, either from your point of view or from that of the publisher.[3] I think that now a prose book

---

was at Harvard with TSE, remembered that the hero had been brilliantly played by a 'cold and aloof' person.

TSE was to tell Charles Norman, 13 Sept. 1957: 'I have a very high opinion of Mr Cummings as a poet, in spite of my dislike of his typography.'

See too 'The Londoner's Diary', *Evening Standard*, 4 Sept. 1962, 6: 'Mr T. S. Eliot gave me today an unusual recollection of E. E. Cummings, the 67-year-old American poet who died yesterday.

'"I am very grieved indeed," he said. "Although I did not always agree with his spelling. I think he was a genuine poet who made a real contribution.

'"I knew him only very slightly, but long ago, before either of us was known to the public. We acted together in some amateur theatricals."'

1 – 'I don't think that as I am not a celebrity I shall be so hard worked. I seem only to have an average of two or three lectures a week and not so far apart in distance either.'

2 – Stephen Spender (1909–95), poet and critic: see Biographical Register.

3 – SS had written to FVM, 2 Jan.: 'I think you know that I am doing Henry James for Cape.

'I ought also to tell you that I think I shall almost certainly have to bind myself, if it is possible for me to do so, to that or some other publisher in the next few days. The reason is that, without doing so, I cant get on with my James book as I have to keep interrupting it by earning little bits of money by reviewing.

'So have Faber any objection to my promising a book of short stories, and a third book, away from them? That is, if I can get the contract. I sent one of the stories to Eliot for the *Criterion*, but it was twice too long. I wrote to Faber to tell him about the other story, The Burning Cactus, which appeared in the summer no. of the *Oxford Outlook*, & which will also appear in the *Hound & Horn*. I mention these two, because they are specimens, so that you may be able to gauge what sort of a book it would be.

by you might have a fair chance, though I had rather you did not do one unless compelled by necessity; but I think that you might do better than by a volume of short stories. A single narrative would have much better prospects. It seems to us that you have a special gift for a form which we may call the 'diary': indeed it seems to me that the story you showed me is merely a bit of diary, and that it would have, in such a context, a significance which it lacks as a complete shape by itself; lacking the point or the *clou* of a short story. It seems to me that you have the diarist's ability of reproducing dialogue, and (as notably in the suppressed book[1]) a gift of mordant (that's a journalistic word, I know) portraiture of people with great economy of strokes. In some cases you seem to me to be stimulated into this exactness in the degree to which people irritate you – at any rate, what remain most clearly in my mind both of the story and of the book are the light sketches of dislikeable people. Not that I want to encourage you to dislikes! but anything one does well helps to show one what one can do. And you may reflect upon the great superiority of the second version of 'The Temple' to the first. You know that on intrinsic merit we should have been glad to have published that.

I am anxious to keep you out of bookmaking if possible. I know quite well the horrid slavery of reviewing; but that has the spiritual advantage over some kinds of book-writing of being wholly ephemeral and irresponsible; whereas one can never escape from the consequences of a book one has published. I have been pretty cautious, but there are things I would give a tooth to be able to suppress.

Please think it over and – assuming that you *must* write a book – consider whether you can produce something of this sort which we could publish.[2]

Yours,
T. S. Eliot

'The third book would be reportage: a short biography of a soldier in the regular army. This would simply aim at being a true social document.

'I would be very sorry to break away from Faber, & I hope that even if I do so, the doors will be open for my return, when I have got over this stupid bother about my overdraft.'

1 – SS's autobiographical novel *The Temple* was to be published only in 1988.

2 – John Sutherland observes: 'Faber accepted the proposed volume of short stories "of the diary kind" in January. It would eventually be published as *The Burning Cactus* [1936]' (*Stephen Spender: The Authorized Biography* [2004], 157).

TO *Henry Eliot*[1]   TS Houghton

13 January 1934   *The Criterion*

My dear Henry,

First to thank you for the beautiful linen handkerchiefs, the finest I have ever had. I was very much pleased to get them; and they will be used on best occasions.

Second to thank you for your long letter.[2] I am glad to know that for the moment at least you are less harrassed by financial worries; and I am glad to have the news you give. When is Chardy's baby due, I wonder? and will she have it in New York, or go to Boston.

Third, to tell you that Alida Monro, widow of my friend the poet Harold Monro, is sailing for New York in a few days and will be making a lecture tour. I have asked her to try to see you and Theresa.[3] She has been a very good friend, and knows a good deal about my affairs and knows V. pretty well. I should be grateful for anything you could do for her.

I am still in a boarding house in South Kensington. My affairs have not progressed, as it seems impossible to get V. to sign any agreement. So the financial terms of the agreement are to be put in force. If she does not like that she can sue for Restitution of Conjugal Rights (or Rites. I am not sure which); my lawyer says that that would be all to the good, as it would mean a judicial recognition of the separation and terms certainly no more generous than I am offering and probably not so good.

Meanwhile I go on with my daily tasks, seeing a few people, and have just finished preparing my Virginia lectures, which will be published in February,[4] and working by fits & starts on the text which I have to produce for a pageant in May.[5]

1 – Henry Ware Eliot, Jr (1879–1947), TSE's elder brother: see Biographical Register.
2 – Not traced.
3 – Theresa Garrett Eliot (1884–1981), HWE's wife. Born in Louisville, Kentucky, she studied at St Louis School of Fine Arts where she received the Wayman Crowe Scholarship; at the Art Institute of Chicago; at Beaux Arts in Paris; and at Art Students League of New York. She had her own studio in Chicago for many years and did commercial illustrating and decorative design, as well as exhibiting etchings, portraits and paintings in Chicago, New York and Boston. She also designed dossal and cross, and altar vases and candlesticks, for Groton School.
4 – *After Strange Gods: A Primer of Modern Heresy* was to be published by F&F on 22 Feb.; in New York by Harcourt, Brace & Company on 18 Apr.
5 – See Browne, *The Making of T. S. Eliot's Plays* (1969, 1970), ch. 1: 'The Rock', 1–33. TSE had accepted the invitation to fill out Browne's scenario of the pageant by 6 Oct. 1933. He wrote in a later year: 'To be, at such a moment, commissioned to write something which, good or bad, must be delivered by a certain date, may have the effect that vigorous cranking

Frank Morley, my colleague here, will also be in New York in a month or so, and he will look you up. He is superior to Christopher in every way.[1] He and his wife have been very good friends to me; I do not know how I should have managed without them this summer. They found me the lodgings near them, and I took supper with them every night, so that I have got to know them intimately. You will find him exceptionally intelligent and perceptive.

Ever affectionately your brother
Tom

FROM *Geoffrey Faber* TO *Vivien Eliot*[2] ᴍꜱ Valerie Eliot

13 January 1934   Ty Glyn Aeron, Ciliau Aeron,
                                   Cardiganshire

My dear Vivienne

I am afraid from your letter that you may be making things more difficult and painful both for yourself and Tom than they need be. I write simply as an outsider and a friend of you both, and it is impertinent of me to say anything, especially as there is nothing – so far as I know – which I can explain to you, that you don't know far better already.

I don't think I am breaking my determination not to intervene in any way in the private affairs of others, if I say what follows in this letter. I am only telling you how it all looks to me, and giving you my opinion for what it may be worth, because it may be of some help to you to have it. More than this I cannot and will not do, except that I will ask Tom if he cannot see you again. (I say again, because I understood that he had seen you at his solicitor's since his return.)

There seem to me to be two fundamental facts, which you are *hurting yourself* by your refusal to face. The first is (and you must forgive me for saying this so plainly) that you and Tom have for years been getting on each other's nerves until the strain of living together was having a very serious effect upon you both. This has been obvious to Enid & to me, and

---

sometimes has upon a motor car when the battery is run down. The task was clearly laid out: I had only to write the words of prose dialogue for scenes of the usual historical pageant pattern, for which I had been given a scenario' ('The Three Voices of Poetry', *OPP* [1957], 91).

1 – Christopher Morley (1890–1957) – FVM's elder brother – journalist, novelist, essayist and poet; co-founder and contributing editor of the *Saturday Review of Literature*.

2 – Vivien Eliot, née Haigh-Wood (1888–1947), estranged wife of TSE: see Biographical Register.

I have no doubt to others. As soon as Tom went off to America we were struck by the remarkable improvement in your own health and looks. It seemed as if the relaxation of the strain – whether you were conscious of it or not – had done you good. It wasn't until you began to worry about getting him back that you became ill again. The conclusion which I draw myself is that your real chance of health and happiness lies in accepting, instead of uselessly and hopelessly resisting, a separation which is as much in your interest as in his; and in living your *own* life, instead of his.

The second fundamental fact is that Tom is irrevocably determined upon a separation. He has told me this himself, and he has also told me that he would not see you until the terms of the separation were finally settled. Now, dear Vivienne, I know no more than this; but I am *perfectly certain* that this is so. I have refrained from asking him what has been happening, and I had supposed – until I received your letter this morning – that the necessary legal formalities were either completed or about to be completed. But you say: '*I* cannot sign my own death warrant, nor agree to what I think wrong.' Does this mean that you will not agree to the terms of the deed of separation? If so, then I very much fear that you are adopting a quite impossible position. You cannot prevent the separation – that is a matter of fact. All that you can do is to prevent your husband from *undertaking* to contribute to your support. You can – it is true – sue him for the restitution of conjugal rights (if that is the correct legal phrase). It is some time since I studied law, but I am a qualified barrister and I know this much: that, if you did sue him, you would accomplish nothing that would not be much more advantageously settled by a voluntary deed of separation. The Court cannot compel your husband to come back to you; it can only compel him to contribute to your support. And as the Court would be told that you had refused to agree to the terms of a separation there can be no doubt that the terms of its award would not be very favourable to you – probably much less favourable than the terms which Tom has proposed, whatever they may be.

I advise you, most earnestly, *in your own interest*, to look these facts in the face, and to come to a proper arrangement with Tom. And that, dear Vivienne, is all I or Enid could possibly say to you.[1]

Yours ever, affectionately
Geoffrey Faber

1 – VHE noted in her diary, 23 Jan.: '*Rude* letter from Faber.' On 30 Jan. she referred to what she called 'Faber's rather libelous argument' (Bodleian MS Eng. misc. e. 877).

P.S. Of course we shall be very glad to see you when we are back in London.[1]

TO *F. Scott Fitzgerald*[2]   TS Princeton

15 January 1934   Faber & Faber Ltd

Dear Fitzgerald,

I am glad to have your letter of January 2nd.[3] I had had a little correspondence with Wheelock a short time ago, and was wondering

---

1 – VHE saw the Fabers at home a few weeks later, and recorded in her diary, 20 Mar.: 'The Fabers have moved to 1 Oak Hill Park, a *smaller* house, & not so grand, but *very* nice & homelike. I was *happy* to see them again, & Enid looked *charming*. Tom's name was never once mentioned among us, that, we had agreed to beforehand. So we had a quiet but happy evening & I got back, by bus, after 11. But feeling saner.' GCF's diary records: 'Vivienne Eliot to dinner.'

VHE's diary, 26 Mar.: 'Then I rang up Faber & Faber, & found that Tom *had* been there, & does go every day. A great relief to me – I cried for joy. Poor, silly boy. His *poor, hot, stubborn head*.'

2 – F. Scott Fitzgerald (1896–1940): American novelist and short-story writer.

3 – 'Dear T. S. Eliot: / Wheelock of Scribner's wrote me that you are interested in my novel, Tender is the Night. It is my first since The Great Gatsby, very much longer and much more ambitious in scope.

'I think an English publisher would have more luck with it than did either Collins with This Side of Paradise and Beautiful and Damned, my first attempts, or Chatto & Windus with The Great Gatsby. However, the first thing is to see whether or not I am bound to Chatto & Windus, a matter which I shall take up immediately. I would much rather come under your aegis. I am tremendously grateful to you for your interest . . .

'With most cordial best wishes including one that I will see you and talk to you soon, I am as ever, / F Scott Fitzgerald.'

Fitzgerald wrote to Chatto & Windus, 24 Jan. 1934: 'My novel "Tender is the Night", the very dilatory successor to "The Great Gatsby", will be issued by Scribner's late in March. It is a long book, which is to say about 110,000 words, and you might have better luck with it than with "Gatsby". Mr T. S. Eliot of Faber and Faber is interested and for that reason could I ask you to make your approximate decision from the first half which appears in the January and February numbers of Scribner's magazine. They are indicative of the tone and scope of the book. This is in order to obtain, if possible, simultaneous publications in England and here. Another question to be considered is that the book contains certain episodes which Scribner's have found not advisable to print in the magazine, in general would you say that what will get by the censors in book form here will get by the censors in England? Such things are very much liberalized here, for instance, the unexpurgated "Ulysses" is permitted. Do you know whether Hemingway's "Farewell to Arms" was published in England exactly as it was here? So consider in making your decision whether you would be using Scribner's plates or setting up the whole thing from a faintly expurgated text in London. I may tell you that the book is getting an extraordinary response here.'

On a copy of that last letter forwarded to TSE, Fitzgerald wrote by hand: 'Dear Eliot: They seem to have an option on the book. I would much prefer to have you publish it.'

how soon the novel would be ready. I await your further news with much interest. Chatto and Windus is a good firm, and it would in any case be contrary to publishing ethics to attempt to seduce you away from them, but of course if you are quite free in the matter, it is up to you to send the manuscript first to whatever firm you elect. In any event, I look forward with much interest to reading the book.

If and when you and Mrs Fitzgerald are returning to Europe, I hope that you will come by way of London, so that I may have the pleasure of seeing you again.

Yours ever sincerely,
T. S. Eliot

TO *Ezra Pound*   TS Beinecke

16 January 1934   Faber & Faber Ltd

Ex. Podesta Possum I mean Rabet,

Re Cantos: You can consider 83m I mean 'em a standing order I mean release them in chunks according to your own sense of time and consuitability. But I think this autumn will be appropriate time for next chunk you have bit off.

Re Essays: FVM & Myself think best you send Introduction & Supplementaty Matter as soon as it is ready: then we figger out cost of production on size of book and send on agreement. Were you wanting to produce Introduction only at last moment? If so I will let you know what is the last moment, but there wont be so much time to spare as you might Think what with proof correcting mistakes in foreign quotations and attempts of British printers to improve your grammar & syntax I mean syntax, accidence and style. You might as well also send a FINAL list of contents and alterations of text in the volumes we have on hand: it is verree difficult to contain all of Hon. Sahib's correspondence in poor servant's mind. Re your ltr. of 12th inst. FVM is going to visit New York very presently and can do a good deal in quiet way of conversation.[1] So will remain yours etc.

T. S. E.

1 – EP responded, 18 Jan.: 'F. V. [Morley] sure cd/ blow N. Y. out of the harbour . . . What Morely OUGHT to place in the U.S. is the ABC ECON REVISED . . . and the Jeff/Muss. I mean ef he wants my love an respect.'

TO *Louis MacNeice*[1]   CC

17 January 1934   [Faber & Faber Ltd]

Dear Mr MacNeice,

I have been having some correspondence lately with Tom Burns about the possibility of publishing your volume of 45 poems, and have given a good deal of thought to the matter. I have for a long time had in view the prospect of eventually being able to offer to publish a volume of your poems. While I still have that hope, and while, so far as I can remember, the present volume seems to me to be a more satisfactory arrangement than the previous manuscript which I had, I still feel obstinately, without perhaps being able to give a satisfactory reason for the feeling, that even this volume is not quite ripe for publication. I think that my feeling is largely a practical and tactical one. I think that a first volume ought, if possible, to be able to start off with one or two longish poems which will arrest the attention of the reader at once, and these, if possible, should be among the poet's most recent work. It seems to me that this book could be very much improved by re-arrangement, and by making it shorter; but I am not sure that it yet contains the poems that we want to start off with. I know that it is rather a tax upon your patience, but I have the feeling that if these suggestions strike you as having any value, the book may turn into something much more effective in six months' time.

I must admit, however, that I believe there are other publishers who would be ready to publish it as it stands, but whether you agree with me or not, and whether you alter the book or not, and whether you write in the mean time any more poems that you want to include or not, I should be very glad to consider it again if you would let me see it in the autumn.

                                    Yours very sincerely,
                                    [T. S. Eliot]

TO *Stephen Spender*   TS Northwestern

22 January 1934   Faber & Faber Ltd

Dear Spender,

I have your letter of the 21st. The scheme you suggest seems to us possible.[2] Perhaps it would be best if you could come in and have a talk

1–Louis MacNeice (1907–63), poet and BBC producer: see Biographical Register.
2–'I had a letter from my bank – the letter – saying that they wont let me have any more money and threatening also not to cash the cheques with which I have paid for my rent,

about it. Tomorrow, for instance, any time from 4:15 to closing time – if not tomorrow best to ring up and fix a time ahead.

God damb it I can't find the carbon of the letter I wrote to you, but I did not MEAN to say anything about a novel. I agree with what you say about novel writing and for this reason and other suggested a book of the *diary* kind, in which you have already shown your abilities.[1] But we can clear this up when we meet.

I should very much like to see the chapters of the Army Life book which are ready.[2] I would read them at once so as not to hold them up from publication elsewhere.

Yours ever,
T. S. E.

TO *Eric Cheetham*[3]   CC

23 January 1934   [Faber & Faber Ltd]

Dear Father Cheetham,

I ought to have written to you before, but preparation for, and execution

---

electricity etc . . . I wondered therefore, if Fabers would be a party to a mild ruse which will enable me to force their hands.

'I have the right to make a will. I therefore thought that I might leave either all or one of the directors of Faber £100. This will cover the faint possibility of my dying within a year if you would guarantee my overdraft to that extent for a year. Could you let me know soon about this before I am left in the dark, in the cold, and evicted?'

1 – 'I should certainly like to do a novel. My difficulty is though that my experiences and my whole view of experience – in a theatrical sense – is so thin . . . The advantage of writing poetry is that one can make as much out of one's limitations as out of what one has. In fact the limitation, the knowing that one doesn't know all about certain human relationships, becomes an approach to them. For that reason I never care very much because I know so little about the whole of people's lives, so long as my clear realization of the small foreground, makes me realize that there is also the vast background behind. But you cannot impose such boundaries on a novel.'

2 – Late in 1933 Spender had fallen in love with a Welsh former guardsman, Tony Hyndman (1911–80) – depicted as Jimmy Younger in Spender's candid autobiography *World within World* (1951) – and lived with him until Sept. 1936. 'Tony Hyndman has done about 50pp of his reminiscences of his life in the army. Is it all right for us to submit a selection from the first two chapters to *Life & Letters*. Or would you care to "consider" them for *The Criterion?*'

3 – See TSE, 'Fr Cheetham Retires from Gloucester Road', *Church Times* 139: 4,856 (9 Mar. 1956), 12: 'On February 29 there took effect the resignation of the Rev. Eric Samuel Cheetham, Prebendary of St Paul's, from the living of St Stephen's, Gloucester-road, in the sixty-fourth year of his age and the thirty-ninth year of his service in that parish . . . The

achievement of Fr Cheetham at St Stephen's may be summed up by saying that he made it a centre of Evangelical Catholicism: truly Catholic and truly wholly Anglican.'

Fr Eric Cheetham (1892–1957) had been appointed in 1917 to a curacy under the Revd Lord Victor Seymour: he succeeded Lord Victor in 1929.

See TSE's tribute, 'The Panegyric', *St Stephen's Magazine*, May 1959: 'It was in the autumn of 1933 that I first attended Mass at St Stephen's. I had returned from a year of lecturing in America; and while looking about for a more permanent abode, was stopping at a boarding house in Courtfield Gardens [see Sencourt, *T. S. Eliot*, 129]. I think that Father Cheetham came to dinner there one night, for he knew the lady [Freda Bevan] who was the proprietor. In this way or some other, I became known to him as a new member of his congregation; and not very long afterwards he offered me rooms, which had become vacant, in his presbytery in Grenville Place. My circumstances at the time were somewhat unusual, and I shall not forget the sympathy and understanding with which he responded to my explanation. I remained his Paying Guest for seven years, first in Grenville Place and then in Emperor's Gate, in a house of which he had rented the two top stories. We only parted in the autumn of 1940: the furniture was stored, I retired to friends in the country and to my office in Bloomsbury, and Father Cheetham found shelter in what always seemed to me a characteristic choice of abode – the basement of the Albert Hall . . . There are others who have known him longer than I: I think of two who are probably here today. There must be many who have known him not so long as I, but who have known him in different contexts and seen other aspects of his character than those which I have seen. I only speak as one who lodged with him for seven years, and who was his Warden from 1934 – just twenty-five years ago – throughout the rest of his incumbency. It is characteristic of his ways, that I was never elected formally, but merely appointed by him, no objections being raised at the Vestry. Years later, when I discovered this irregularity, I suggested to the Archdeacon that I should have an act of indemnity for everything that I had done in the capacity of Warden; but he thought it unnecessary. I only mention this trifling fact because it throws a tiny ray of light on the character of a man who was the most modest, the most diffident, the humblest-minded autocrat whom I have ever known.

'Eric Cheetham came to St Stephen's, as curate to Lord Victor Seymour, in 1917. He was himself a son of the vicarage, in Lancashire: he remained a Lancastrian, even to taking an occasional holiday at Blackpool. But after St Chad's he went, I think, to an East End Parish before he came to us. [Cheetham had passed two years as Curate of St Luke's, Burdett Road, to the south of Mile End – in the working-class district of the East End of London.] It is not every young priest who can be equally successful in the East End and in Kensington. I know nothing of Fr Cheetham's earlier career: but I feel sure, from my knowledge of his character, that he would have been as distinguished and successful as a vicar in East London, as he was here.

'Eric Cheetham possessed several gifts invaluable to a priest. To mention a small matter first – or what may seem a small matter – he had the gift of being able to edit a parish magazine – or to adapt a parish magazine to his peculiar talents. For his parish magazine was certainly original. How he found the time to edit it – I was about to say, write it – I do not know. His own contributions were composed in a very individual style, in which dashes often seemed to do duty for more conventional punctuation marks. It reminded me of his conversation; and perhaps that was one reason for the magazine being read, as I believe it was, by many former parishioners who liked to keep in touch with St Stephen's. Then again, he had a great love of the theatre, and had in him just enough, but not too much, of the showman. A moment ago I suggested that it seemed appropriate that he should have made his abode in the Albert Hall during the bombing: I was reminded of a pageant which he put on there, I think on behalf of the Mothers' Union, at rather short notice. It was an impressive pageant: and in such enterprises Fr Cheetham showed great resourcefulness – for he could, at a pinch, make bricks without straw. His theatrical gifts were always under his control; and his liturgical sense of accuracy and precision was combined with good taste and discretion. As a preacher, too, he was very effective: his sermons had a beginning, a middle and an end. They always gave the impression of having been thought out for that particular congregation and for that particular occasion; and one always had the feeling of being the man in the pew – the man or woman – to whom he was talking. With devotion to Catholic doctrine and Catholic observance, he combined true evangelical zeal. He had a strong sense of pastoral responsibility, and I suspect that he often helped those who were in need of help, in ways which exceeded the bounds of ordinary pastoral activity.

'At the time of Fr Cheetham's resignation, when he was a very sick man with not long to live, I wrote an appreciation of his ministry in which I made some of the same points that I have just repeated. In any such piece of writing, about a man whom one has known and loved, one is always most conscious, especially after the man is dead, of the things that one has failed to say. I can at least add a word now about Fr Cheetham's war service, at the time when he slept, so far as sleep was possible, in the depths of the Albert Hall. I don't think that Fr Cheetham was any more impassive or insensitive to danger than the rest of us. But at no time was St Stephen's closed or the offices unsaid: he and Fr Alderson, who was then his curate, said their daily masses through the worst of the bombardment. This was not all: Fr Cheetham made himself, one might say, almost priest-in-charge of the Gloucester Road Tube Station platform, and gave much attention to the needs of the people who came to spend their nights there.

'But a recital of gifts, accomplishments and achievements never can be enough in itself to account for the impression that such as man as Fr Cheetham makes upon those who come in close contact with him. It can do everything, perhaps, but one thing – explain why the man was lovable and loved. When we really love a person, we love the weaknesses and foibles of that person. Eric Cheetham was very lovable, and was also, at times, extremely irritating; and one loved him the more for the irritation he caused. There was more than one occasion on which my fellow warden and I, having gone by appointment to discuss some problem with him, were obliged finally to leave in a state of exhaustion and frustration, because Fr Cheetham had done all the talking and had not given us the opportunity to say what we had come to say or to ask the questions to which we needed answers. Again, there was in the man a mixture of shrewdness and simplicity, of business sense and confusion, of order and disorder. I suppose we all present some contradictions, to the eyes of those who know us best: in Eric Cheetham's case I think they were aggravated by the fact that he tried to do too many things and to respond to too many appeals. He pushed himself too hard, and his health, always uncertain because of early illnesses, suffered accordingly. We recognised in him qualities of integrity, generosity, and natural goodness developed by Christian discipline; we recognised the strength and depth of his faith: but in the end the quality of which one is most aware in people one loves is simply – their loveableness.

'A generation or two passes, and the name of such a man means nothing to the world. Those who come to worship here after the lapse of time will know only that a man of that name was there as curate and vicar for thirty-nine years. May this figure of St Stephen, erected in his memory, at least remind the worshippers who will follow us that a priest named Eric Samuel Cheetham was loved and honoured by all those who came under his care.'

The Minutes of the Annual Parochial Church Meeting held in St Stephen's Vestry on Easter Monday, 2 Apr. 1934, record: 'The Vicar then expressed his appreciation of the work of the retiring Churchwardens (Messrs W. G. H. Rawlinson & G. Badger-Clark), and asked the Meeting to approve his appointment of Mr T. S. Eliot as Vicar's Warden. This was accepted. On the proposal of Sir Henry Johnson, seconded by Mr [Arthur Edward] Wood, Captain A. A. West was appointed the other Warden.'

It was only in 1956 that TSE confessed to the Archdeacon of Middlesex his own anomalous position: that his appointment had not been ratified throughout all of the twenty-two years of his service: 'the Parochial Church Council took no part in my appointment' (18 Apr. 1956); 'It would seem, then . . . that St Stephen's has been without a Vicar's Warden since 1934' (2 July 1956) The technicality was set aside by the Archdeacon.

See too 'Inside of the Week', *Church Times*, 8 Jan. 1965: 'In a note written for this paper some years ago Fr Cheetham (who died in 1957) paid a striking tribute to Eliot as Churchman:

'When I asked him to be churchwarden, I was in an *impasse*. I wrote to him to ask him to consider it, and he sent me a list of all the reasons why he was unsuitable. He concluded by saying that "of course, if you need me, and are in any sort of fix, then here I am, use me." That has been his stand all along, and he has been invaluable.

'His previous experience in the City means that he has a very good head for business, etc. Like most authors he is a very shrewd judge of character, and frequently amazes me by summing up people he has only met once or twice in the most surprisingly accurate way. You wouldn't find a more amazing contrast than the two us.

'I am only just a passman, and yet the very fact that he backs me up at St Stephen's and all these years has worshipped here and listened to my simplicity makes me feel that God must indeed have sent him to me to make up in some strange way for what I lacked. I remember sending him up my script for the Mothers' Union pageant which I wrote and produced for two weeks at the Albert Hall in 1936. Mine was the art of the circus in the arena of the Albert Hall, and I was, as it were, playing the big drum, while his play Family Reunion, produced at the Westminster some time after, was the direct opposite.

'I suppose it is because we are such opposites, and yet bound together in a very real faith, the Catholic Faith, in its daily practical interpretation, that we work together as we do. He never misses any of the ceremonies if he can possibly help it, in Holy Week following everything, using all the liturgical ways of the Church. Before the war, when he lived with me so close to church, he was, practically, a daily communicant.

'Whenever there has been any very adverse criticism of his work in the paper I have found him most amused, but he is very sensitive to the sorrows and agonies of others, and again and again I have found him helping quiet, individual cases in such a way that the left hand would never know what the right hand did. To me he has been like a spiritual big brother – just sent by God for this impossible task of being Vicar of a parish like this.'

Valerie Eliot told Helen Gardner on 24 July 1973: 'I think [Tom] was at Courtfield Road in 1934 for a matter of months only, or at most a year. He told me that the owner prided herself on having only public school men!' The 'owner' was actually an eccentric character named William Edward Scott-Hall, who had been ordained a bishop in the 'Old Catholic' Church; but the real proprietor of the boarding house, which lay quite near the Gloucester Road tube station, was a Miss Freda Bevan, who was to recall of TSE: 'He would come in and sit in the garden listlessly. "I wonder," he would keep repeating, "I wonder."' (Robert Sencourt)

According to Sencourt, Father Nicholson related, of TSE at his devotions: 'It was a spiritual experience to administer the Bread and the Wine to so devout a worshipper. At such a sacred moment the officiating priest could not but be aware that he was in the presence of a sublime spiritual reality.'

See also *St Stephen's Church, Gloucester Road 1867–1967* (n.d.), 28–33.

Eric Cheetham wrote to TSE, 1 May 1935: 'I am always so grateful for what you are doing for S. Stephen's and for me'; and on 27 Dec. 1935, 'This is so kind of you: my only

of, an arduous weekend at Kelham (reading a paper, interviews etc.)[1]

My only hesitation has been over the District Railway, but I have decided to risk that! as it is only mechanical noise. I could come about the end of *next* week.[2] I suggest that I should pay a month's rent in advance.

Let us recapitulate the terms. I should have the set of two rooms that I saw, furnished, with use of bathroom, and 7 breakfasts and 7 dinners a week served in my room, for £3 : 3 : 0 a week. There would be no deduction for odd meals out (though I would of course notify the housekeeper in reasonable time) or for weekends, but for as much as a week's continuous absence there would be some deduction to be arranged. On the other hand, if I found the arrangement satisfactory enough to make a protracted stay, and was used to the District, I would hope to be able to offer say three and a half guineas as soon as my financial affairs reach a settled state.

Will you let me know whether this arrangement is satisfactory to you, and whether you think of any other points to be discussed?[3]

Yours very sincerely,
[T. S. Eliot]

---

bottle of whiskey this Christmas, and I am more than grateful. I wish I could thank you adequately for all you have done for me during the past year. I do, however, remember you very regularly.

'My blessing.'

Fr Cheetham is memorialised at St Stephen's Church (which was consecrated by Bishop Tait) in words that may have been drafted by TSE:

> A devoted parish priest, a wise counsellor
> Fearless in his guardianship of the Faith
> A master of pageantry, and a compassionate
> And generous-hearted friend.

1 – Norman Hester wrote from Kelham, 22 Feb.: 'I am returning with this your lecture-notes. I have made a copy for myself and one or two others who were interested.' Hester thanked TSE too for sending the college a copy of *ASG*. 'I have read it myself and enjoyed it; I wish, in some ways, you had been able to bring in some of the more pungent remarks in your lecture here. But perhaps it would not do to declare to the world that Pound is an "eminent Confucian dissenter".'

2 – The 'Emperor's curve' of the District Line underground railway, running between Notting Hill Gate to the north and Gloucester Road, swept around the foot of the building at Grenville Place. (It might almost have been the site of a key scene in the Conan Doyle story 'The Adventure of the Bruce-Partington Plans' – as TSE would have been aware.)

3 – TSE paid in advance the sum of twelve guineas (£12.12.0d) for the four weeks 12 Feb. to 12 Mar. 1934. For the period 5 Mar. to 2 Apr. he paid fourteen guineas (£14. 14. 0d). TSE's eldest sister Ada Sheffield wrote on 4 Mar. 1934: 'Do insist on plenty of good food from your vicar. I haven't confidence in ecclesiastical diet. No more moor-fowls! You see Mr Morley told us that this prolific creature is not edible. One would think that an ingenious Burbank might cross-breed him (and her) into tastiness.' (Moor fowl is perhaps better known as red grouse.)

TO *Ezra Pound*   TS Beinecke

25 January 1934   *The Criterion*

Au Lapin[1] Agile, Chieftain Coney[2] of the Isles & of other Septs:[3]

Podesta, the young & enterprisin firm of Faber & Faber is forchnite in having secured the services of Mr T. S. Eliot, at a salary named in five or six figgers (in milreis, lei etc.) After 12 years with the Federation of British Industries Mr Eliot is probly better qualified than any other Big Executive to cope with the task for which he has been engaged, which is to superintend the department devoted to correspondence with Mr Ezra Pound. In our rotogravure secture our readers will find to-day a portrait of the celebrated condottiere, beneath the palmettoes of his native Rappaloo in conversation with Gen. Goering. This photograph, for the authenticity of which we vouch, will give our readers some idea of the magnitude of the job which Mr Eliot has undertaken. When interviewed on the subject Mr Eliot observed to our representative: 'I rose from nothing – and I stop at nothing.'

I will arise & go NOW, & go to Rappaloo,
Where the Ink is mostly Green, & the pencils mostly Blue . . . [4]

Etc. Of course theres Lots more to be said, but for sake of Brevity I Couch it in this way.

Hurrah! Let's begin again on another typewriter. There thats better. HELL is being set up.[5] Britain aint bounded by Berwick on Tweed you poor sap but by the Arctic Ocean.[6] Some say England is bounded by the Scottish Frontier but I hold as it stops further South than that. Now as to putting in Contemp. Mentality I am only ADVISING you only TELLING you FOR YOUR OWN GOOD from those who have to keep their paw on the pulse etc. or starve. If you WILL have it in thats for you to say BUT

1 – Lapin: rabbit.
2 – Coney: rabbit.
3 – Sept: 'A division of a nation or tribe; a clan' (*OED*)
4 – This couplet parodies W. B. Yeats, 'The Lake Isle of Innisfree':
    I will arise and go now, and go to Innisfree,
    And a small cabin build there, of clay and wattles made . . .'
5 – EP, 'Hell' – on Laurence Binyon, *Dante's Inferno translated into English Triple Rhyme* – C. 13 (Apr. 1934), 382–96.
6 – EP wrote on 18 Jan.: 'Bloody Britons ever will be slaves and congenitally incapable of learning the world ain't bounded on the south by Dover channel, on the narth by Berrick on Tweed and on the west by the Curragh of Kinsale.'

I think youd better look it over again in Cold blood I await your permission to send (registered?)[1]

Now *Propertius* allright we are ready to publish separately in the autumn a-part all by itself. Exact dates of *Prop.* and Cant. publication to be fixed. Straight 10?%%%%, thats it ½ ½ ½ ½ %%%% royalty. THAT means three (3) books in autumn and the Thames rising every day.

Fixtures[2] beauuutifulll o lovely

I don't know that anything has happened except as that some lads who began reading our worx before they had time to be corrupted are now growing up and there are on the whole more of them than the others e.g. Grigson[3] in *Morning Post* formerly great anti-cyclone centre, <Jennings[4] on *Daily Mirror*>, Derek Verschoyle[5] who runs literary dept. of *Spectator* is well disposed and has been received at Court i.e. at one of the evening carousses at 24, Russell Sq. The Present Generation does not change get that straight

But I think that in time we may even do something to the Educational system

And Perhapps I can move somethink under the Bishop of Kensington[6] I dont kno

Yours etc.

Thats enough subjectmatter for one letter.

T.P.

Enc.

1 –EP, 18 Jan.: 'I want decision re/ Contemporary Mentality. I personally want it IN. But think (much as it wd. bore me) I had possibly or not better see IT again and see if there is chance of cut it. I don't believe so / I mean it cant in the natr of IT, be made into a cameo.'
2 –Pictures (photographs).
3 –Geoffrey Grigson. See TSE to him, 26 April 1934, below.
4 –Richard Jennings (1881–1952), literary editor of the *Daily Mirror*.
5 –Derek Verschoyle (1911–73): literary editor of the *Spectator*, 1932–40.
6 –Dr Bertram F. Simpson (1883–1971), Bishop of Kensington, 1932–42.

TO *Martin Shaw*[1]   TS Houghton

25 January 1934   Faber & Faber Ltd

Dear Shaw,

Here is the revised song, with apologies for the delay in getting it to you.[2] You will observe that I have made two versions for your choice; in both I have stretched or shortened the stanzas so that they are all of equal length. I prefer version 2 myself, but you may choose which you like best. If they are both unsatisfactory for your purpose, will you please let me know?

Yours sincerely,
T. S. Eliot

TO *Dorothy Richards*[3]   TS Magdalene

25 January 1934   Faber & Faber Ltd

Dear Mrs Richards,

Thank you for your card. I am afraid that I shall be too busy to come down on Friday night, but I shall be very glad to take the 11.50 on

---

1–Martin Shaw (1875–1958), composer of stage works, choral pieces and recital ballads; associate of Edward Gordon Craig, Ralph Vaughan Williams and Percy Dearmer (with whom he put together *The English Carol Book* [1913]); Director of Music, Diocese of Chelmsford, 1935–44. Other works include *Anglican Folk Mass* (1918); *Songs of Praise* (co-ed., 1925); *The Oxford Book of Carols* (co-ed., 1928). He was writing the music for TSE's *The Rock* (1934). See obituary in *Musical Times*, Dec. 1958.

2–Shaw wrote, 9 Jan. 1934: 'The Dean of Chichester & his Society for Peace (I can't remember its name) clamour for an outline or Scenario. They are very keen & will run the whole thing I think but they feel at present too much in the dark. Could you sketch them out something?

'Either send to me or to the Dean direct at
    The Deanery
    Chichester
I believe you know him.

'Once they get this the ball can be set a-rolling.'

See *The Builders: Song from 'The Rock'* (1934) – no. 107 in Cramer's Library of Unison and Part-Songs by Modern Composers, ed. Martin Shaw – published on about 25 May 1934: see Gallup, 353. (See too score for tenor solo, double choir, and organ, from part of Chorus X: *The Greater Light Anthem* (1966.)

3–Dorothy Richards, *née* Pilley (1894–1986), journalist and climber, worked as a reporter (for a few years at the *Daily Express*) before marrying IAR in 1926. She and IAR scaled mountains all over the world. *Climbing Days* (1935) recounts some of their ascents in the Alps, notably including the North Ridge of the Dent Blanche. See further Dan Richards, *Climbing Days* (2016).

Saturday morning, the 10th, and reach you in time for lunch. I don't know that there is anyone in particular that I want to see, except yourselves, and I will leave that entirely to you.[1]

Yours sincerely,
T. S. Eliot

TO *K. de B. Codrington*[2]   CC

26 January 1934   [*The Criterion*]

Dear Codrington,

Many thanks for your note enclosing the interesting statement about the teaching of history in German schools. Do you want it back immediately, or may I keep it for a bit? I might possibly make some use of it in a Commentary. The present difficulty in mentioning the subject at all is that I have a German contributor in the next number, and I have reason to believe that a German contributing to any periodical which at the same time comments unfavourably upon the Government of Germany, is likely to get into hot water. I have not made up my mind, indeed, whether it is necessary or desirable for the *Criterion* to take up such a subject at all. The only positive and pressing reason that could be imagined is that the *Criterion* has more or less some attitude to Communism, and it might at some point be desirable to make clear that it is not a Fascist organ either. What do you think?

Yours sincerely,
[T. S. Eliot]

1–Richards Diary (primarily penned by Dorothy Richards), Sat., 10 Feb. 1934: 'T. S. Eliot . . . Talking partly about English teaching & then about T. S.'s "play". He is enjoying working to a set task – having to make, as a craftsman, verses of the right kind with an immediate popular appeal & taking the opportunity to learn about the theatre. Said he would have been too lazy, otherwise, to write more poetry . . .

'Sun., 11 Feb. . . . 3.15 off to Ely. D & I perched in the dickey . . . Cathedral . . . Eliot better than most, but bows to the High Altar every time he goes by . . . Eliot very annoyed at having been caught at the Church with only a shilling which he had to put in the Collecting Box for the Codex. After Hall, very interesting talk about Belief & Politics. Instead of making T. S. E. miserable he came back glowing. Drank several whiskies with gusto. Types all his writings direct (except verse) hates writing even a cheque, says he gets writers cramp. Said he once diagnosed a man as being in an emotional upheaval from his handwriting who killed himself soon after. Didn't want to go to bed 1.0. Said he could make up sleep next night. Very easy guest.'

2–Kenneth de Burgh Codrington (1899–1986) worked in the India Section, Victoria & Albert Museum; later as a professor of Indian Archaeology. His writings include *An Introduction to the Study of Mediaeval Indian Sculpture* (1929), and *Cricket in the Grass* (reminiscences, 1959).

26 January 1934   [Faber & Faber Ltd]

Dear Mr Cooke,

I was glad to get your letter of the 7th January, but I am sorry to hear of your difficulties in getting the right photographs.² I do not think, however, that for such a book it is essential to get exactly the right photographs.

I shall be very glad to give you any help I can in getting your article published.³ I should think from what you say that the *Spectator* might be a suitable vehicle, as I know Verschoyle, the literary editor, who is very well disposed.⁴ But possibly it is too long for a weekly, and that makes it a very difficult question. I would, however, try *Life & Letters*, which is again to be a monthly. If I can't do anything with it, I understand that you authorise me to choose any agent that seems best.

I am glad of your bits of news. I had heard from other sources that *Bartholomew Fair* was successful.⁵

Yours sincerely,

[T. S. Eliot]

1 – Alistair (Alfred) Cooke (1908–2004), broadcaster and writer: see Biographical Register.

2 – 'The Hollywood people are very slow in supplying photographs . . .'

3 – Cooke had written a long article, 'Salvation and Eugene O'Neill' – out of 'concern and anger' – discussing *Ah, Wilderness* and other plays by O'Neill, and was intending to offer it to a British magazine – perhaps the *New Statesman* or *The Spectator* – or even the *Daily Mail*.

4 – Verschoyle (*Spectator*) sent it on to TSE on 21 Feb. 1934.

5 – Cooke reported that Theodore Spencer had put on in Cambridge, Mass., 'a splendid "Bartholomew Fair" . . . rollicking, irreverent, dishevelled'.

TO *Francis Underhill*[1]

30 January 1934   [Faber & Faber Ltd]

Dear Father Underhill,

Thank you for your letter suggesting my co-operation in the volume you are to edit.[2] To begin with, however, I can't possibly take on any more work of any kind until this Forty-Five Churches business is over, which will be in the middle of June. That, I imagine, would exclude me from your book automatically, although you do not say when you propose to publish the volume.

Secondly, I am extremely diffident, as an ordinary and not very well educated layman, in attempting to express in such a way my views on such a vast subject. I am sure that all the others on your list will know very much better what they want to say than I do. Furthermore, I should not be at all happy at the prospect of appearing in a volume on this subject in the company of my old friend Middleton Murry,[3] with whose views I should have no patience whatever. I feel sure in any case that whatever I did would give me great dissatisfaction. Even though I am rarely satisfied with anything I do in retrospect, yet it is a help in writing to be able to believe that one may be able to satisfy oneself.

I hope that you will not think me cowardly in the matter, but I simply quail at a prospect like this.

> With many regrets and apologies,
> Yours very sincerely,
> [T. S. Eliot]

1–Revd Francis Underhill, DD (1878–1943) – TSE's spiritual counsellor – Anglican priest and author; Warden of Liddon House and priest in charge of Grosvenor Chapel, Mayfair, London, 1925–32; Dean of Rochester, 1932–7; and Bishop of Bath and Wells from 1937. Works include *The Catholic Faith in Practice* (1918) and *Prayer in Modern Life* (1928). TSE would notify the Revd D. V. Reed, 30 Mar. 1961, that he 'continued to be a penitent of Father Underhill during his period as Dean of the Cathedral [Rochester]'. TSE went to Underhill for his weekly confession, on Fridays.
2–Underhill was editing, with Henry Brinton, a volume of twelve essays entitled 'What I mean by Christianity', and he invited TSE to contribute a 4,000-word essay. Contributors included JMM, the Revd C. Martindale, Evelyn Underhill and George Lansbury.
3–John Middleton Murry (1889–1957), English writer, critic and editor: see Biographical Register.

30 January 1934.   [Faber & Faber Ltd]
Charles King & Martyr[1]

Sir,

The letter of Fr Pierce-Butler in your issue of Jan 26. seems to me to express an attitude towards Fascism, on the part of pious Christians, which is likely to spread, and which therefore deserves close examination.[2]

I am perfectly ready to accept Fr Pierce-Butler's testimony gathered amongst the young people of his acquaintance, and I am very glad to hear it. But with all due respect, I believe that he misses the point. The point is whether a large number of people, with or without the inspiration

1–Published as 'The Blackshirts', *Church Times* 111: 3706 (2 Feb. 1934), 116.

2–The *Church Times* reported on 19 Jan. 1934, 59: 'The Liberal and Labour newspapers profess to be vastly amused by the manifesto printed in the *Daily Mail* on Tuesday, with the catch-title, "Hurrah for the Black Shirts!" in which Lord Rothermere pledged his support to the Fascist movement in England . . . Lord Rothermere may not be a serious politician . . . But he is a shrewd man of affairs, and it is most unlikely that he would have nailed the black shirt to his mast unless he had precise information concerning the progress of Fascism in England. We have several times lately drawn attention to the large increase in the number of Sir Oswald Mosley's followers; and we find Lord Rothermere's article the proof of the accuracy of our information. We hold strongly that everywhere Fascism is necessarily a danger to the Christian religion.'

R. Pierce-Butler, 'Fascism and Christianity' (letter), *Church Times*, 26 Jan. 1934, 84: 'May a humble priest, of intensely and even extremist Catholic views, say a word in reply to your Summary on Lord Rothermere's article on Fascism? . . . The article did make very clear which of the various bodies was referred to, and gave the address of the British Union of Fascists for the benefit of inquirers . . . But where I do most definitely join issue with the writer of the Summary is at the statement that "everywhere Fascism is necessarily a danger to the Christian religion." I am not concerned with foreign countries, though personal experience of Italy is in flat contradiction to these words. An intimate knowledge of British Fascism, as expounded and lived by the followers of Sir Oswald Mosley, utterly disproves this very sweeping remark. The branch of the B.U.F. to which I belong asked me to act as their chaplain. Of their own initiative they further asked that I should hold an initiative service and give an address on Sunday afternoons. This is attended both by Anglicans and Roman Catholics . . .

'A prominent young officer from Headquarters told me that he was first brought to appreciate the glory of the Catholic Faith through Fascism. And, indeed, the teaching of utter self-sacrifice and service on behalf of others, which is the basis of British Fascism, and which I can assure you is lived by our active members, is no bad foundation on which to build the Catholic ideals.

'Day by day I am among these young enthusiasts; I know their staff officers and the "Leader", and never once have I heard or seen a word or act of opposition to real religion.'

and example of Sir Oswald Mosley[1] and Lord Rothermere,[2] are both zealous Fascists and devout Christians. The human mind is capable of containing the most contradictory ideas at once, especially when in a state of emotional excitement. The point is, not what some people at the moment actually maintain, but whether the Christian and Catholic idea and the Fascist idea are in themselves compatible. I am not answering this question, but putting it; for it is a question which Fr Pierce-Butler does not answer.

The most authoritative statement of Fascist principle, I suppose, should be the one statement which Signor Mussolini has made, which he contributed to the *Enciclopedia Italiana*, and which is published by the Hogarth Press for a shilling under the title of *The Political and Social Doctrine of Fascism*. From it I extract the following propositions, which are relevant to the present enquiry:

1. 'War alone brings up to its highest tension all human energy and puts the stamp of nobility upon the peoples who have the courage to meet it.'

2. 'Absolute monarchy has been, and can never return, any more than blind acceptance of ecclesiastical authority.'

(N.B. The question here is that of the differentiation between acceptance, and *blind* acceptance, of ecclesiastical authority; and how this difference differs from the difference between acceptance, and *blind* acceptance, of temporal authority).

3. 'Fascism conceives of the State as an Absolute.'

4. 'Peoples which are rising, or rising again after a period of decadence, are always imperialist.'

---

1 – Sir Oswald Mosley, 6th Bt. (1896–1980), founder in 1932 of the British Union of Fascists. In 1954 TSE's German translator Countess Nora Purtcher-Wydenbruck (1894–1959) mentioned in a letter that a correspondent of hers had suggested there might have been some sort of connection in the 1930s between TSE and Mosley. TSE replied, 11 May 1954: 'Will you please disclaim any connection between myself and Sir Oswald Mosley. I am sure that at no time did I ever have any correspondence with him, and have never met him personally. I was never in agreement with his views, and I once refered to him <by implication> in print as a kind of "Catiline". As for what I thought of him in the Thirties, there is some evidence in the Pageant Play, *The Rock*, which was produced and published in 1934. This has been long out of print, but there are copies in existence . . . In this Pageant, I had a scene lampooning the British fascists as well as the communists, and indeed, as somebody got hold of a text and mentioned it in a newspaper before the Pageant was produced, we were in some apprehension lest there might be a demonstration on the opening night. I have no sympathy with Sir Oswald Mosley's attitude towards the Jews.'
2 – Harold Sidney Harmsworth, first Viscount Rothermere (1868–1940): newspaper proprietor.

I am not taking upon myself to criticise these assertions; I only suggest that every Catholic who inclines to sympathise with Fascist politics should make it his business to meditate upon them. In conclusion, I should like to call attention to the excellent article by Mr Christopher Dawson in the current issue of *Theology*.[1]

> I am,
> Your obedient servant,
> [T. S. Eliot]

TO *Gabriel Hebert*[2] CC

30 January 1934 [Faber & Faber Ltd]
Charles King & Martyr

Dear Father Gabriel,

I am writing to let you know that I have spoken to my Board – without your permission – about your suggestion of writing a book on the Liturgical Revival, and found them most keenly interested.[3] They would not be very enthusiastic about a book by a Roman, considering that such a book could be better handled by Sheed & Ward, if not Burns & Oates; but in a book by an Anglican authority like yourself (one who knows and is able to render account of what is going on in the Roman Communion also) they are very much interested. So I write to let you know that unless you have very definite reasons for preferring some other house, we should very much like to have the opportunity. When you get to the point of being able to draw up a brief synopsis of the book, that would be useful. It seems to me, too, that a few photographs illustrating the architectural and

1–Christopher Dawson, 'Civilization and the Faith', *Theology: A Monthly Journal of Historical Christianity* 28: 164 (Feb. 1934), 67–77. '[T]he true social function of religion is not to busy itself with economic or political reforms, but to save civilization from itself by revealing to men the true end of life and the true nature of reality. In other words, religion must be religious. That is the unum necessarium. If Christianity can generate a truly religious faith, it can transform culture; if not, it is powerless to help the world' (p. 76).

2–Fr Arthur Gabriel Hebert (1886–1963), Society of the Sacred Mission, Kelham Theological College, Newark, Notts.; theologian. See Christopher Irvine, *Worship, Church and Society: An exposition of the work of Arthur Gabriel Hebert to mark the Centenary of the Society of the Sacred Mission (Kelham), of which he was a member* (1993).

3–See A. G. Hebert, *Liturgy and Society* (F&F, 1935); Andrew Scott Bishop, *Eucharist Shaping: Church, Mission and Personhood in Gabriel Hebert's 'Liturgy and Society'* (PhD thesis, King's College London, 2013).

sculptural side of the movement, such as those you showed me of Maria Laach, would be very desirable too.[1]

So I very much hope that I may hear more about your book from you.

With all good wishes,
I am,
Yours very sincerely,
[T. S. Eliot]
(Director, Faber & Faber Ltd.)

TO *Robert Sencourt*[2]   CC

30 January 1934   [Faber & Faber Ltd]

My dear Robert,

I wired in reply to your letter of the 10th as quickly as possible, and I hope that you received the telegram, and will receive this letter.[3] 'The Pyramids' seems an impossible address for anybody. I may mention that the Post Office would not accept it for the telegram, and I had to add the word 'Cairo'.

I very much appreciate your kindness in getting me this invitation to lecture in Cairo. It was all the more tempting as I had been dallying with another attractive invitation to lecture in Rome. I could have combined the two engagements, and the prospect was most pleasing. Both, however, were out of the question. Apart from the difficulty of preparing three solid lectures within the time assigned, this month of March would be absolutely the most impossible time for me to get away from London. For one thing, one of my colleagues is just leaving for a brief visit to New York, and will not be back until the end of March. For another thing, I am working on a Pageant for the London Diocese, and my text has got to be completed by the beginning of April. I can only do this by devoting all the time I can spare to the task.

1 – The Benedictine Abbey of Maria Laach (founded 1093), near Andernach in the Eifel region of the Rhineland-Palatinate, is a magnificent example of German Romanesque architecture.
2 – Robert Sencourt – originally Robert Esmonde Gordon George – (1890–1969): critic, historian, biographer: see Biographical Register.
3 – Sencourt invited TSE 'to come out here in February or March and give a few lectures. I should suggest 5 or 6. The Government of Egypt would give you £250 in all, out of which you would have to pay your fare which you should do comfortably for £70 first class: so it works out at something like £30 a lecture: and I should suggest you should give 2 a week, and stay here as my guest . . . All I want is a definite yes (or, if it must be, *no*) by deferred cable . . .'

May I make bold to say that if the invitation could be repeated sufficiently far ahead, no holiday could give me greater pleasure, especially with the prospect of being your guest. But to make it possible to do a job like this, prepare the lectures satisfactorily, and get ten days or a fortnight off, I ought to have about six months' notice if possible.

Thank you very much also for the cheque, which I am obliged to return, as you will observe that you have dated it 1933.

Do let me know whether there is any prospect of your coming to England, or even to France, during the summer. I will try to write you a more personal letter than this as soon as I can.

> Again with grateful thanks,
> Yours affectionately,
> [Tom]

TO *Ezra Pound*

TS Beinecke

30 January 1934:   *The Criterion*
Charles King & Martyr

Dear Rabet. Yes I see the point about *Propertius* that's an Idea about printin same type as eventual Complete Juvenilia[1] Now where can I get a copy being separated From my books etc. have not either *Personae* or *Quia Pauper*[2] latter more suitable for purpose I would be willing to pay for it but there Seems to be no more about Here one Point does the *Quia Pauper* text of *Prop.* stand intact if so we cd. begin setting up at any time Now please give us a Guess When will the 10 next cantotos be ready the Earlier the better that's what.

Re Contempment I think I had better send text Out for you to look At and see whether you still agree or Not which I will do.

1–EP, 27 Jan.: 'Re/ Propertius/ Wot I mean is dew yew GIT me? The POINT of seperate pubctn/ ?? an does yr/ astuteness approve? Seems to me it wd/ get more publicity, for wot thet is worth and in no way interfere with subsequet Collected. In fact the collected moight be tipographically planned So that the plates of the Propertius wd/ serve for Collected when the time kum??'

2–*Quia Pauper Amavi* (1919), which included the text of 'Homage to Sextus Propertius', was reviewed by TSE in the *Athenaeum*, 23 Oct. 1919, 1065–6: '[*Homage*] is one of the best things Mr Pound has done. It is a new persona, a creation of a new character, recreating Propertius in himself, and himself in Propertius . . . It is impossible, of course, to employ the words "translation", "original", or "derivative" in dealing with a poem like this. Certainly, there is no other poet living who could justify such a method; but we believe that Mr Pound has succeeded.'

Am inclined to agree we better Go a head with your list and see how many pages that Makes then add on extensions as needed to fill 454 pp.[1] am Doubtful whether suggestion in middle of p.1 of your letter of Jan. 27[2] I wonder do you keep copies of your letters and If so where do you keep them might not result in public indigestion too Much to assissimilate at Once?

Esqre I have heard of thats All.[3] This is leaving two previous letters to answer at more leisure.

T

TO *Stephen Spender*   TS Northwestern

30 January 1934   Faber & Faber Ltd

My dear Spender,

This is just to tell you that I and Morley have read Hyndman's first two chapters, and that they are now in Faber's hands. My own opinion is

---

1 – EP gave his proposed list of contents on 24 Jan.:

    1. Preface

    2. Troubadours

    3. Arnaut Daniel

    4. Eliz. Classicists

    5. Trans/ of Greek

    6. French Poets

    7. H. James and Gourmont.

    8. CAVALCANTI (including G[uido]'s Relations/ re/ effect of Italian poetry on Eng/ Elizabethans.)

    9. a. Harold Monro. – dead

    10. Housmann – practically, or say burried

    c. Binbin – considered as crit/ of Inferno.

    Appendix (vermiform).

EP wrote on 27 Jan.: 'I shd/ rather favour proceding with what we've GOT, and if it falls short of 454 pages (as per YOUR collected essays we cd/ shovel in exactly the required page/ age . . . so'z to comply with yr/ longlonglong ago suggestion that I shd. Not appear to have talked less than Yr/ Eminence.'

2 – 'In short EZ/ in various phases as crik/

    1. diskussing

    2. playing abaht, as in Divagation from J. la F.

    3. Muzik, az in setting Mssrs Villon. Cav. And Soredello.

    4. in the highly distinguished omnium gatherum AND sortem out (the latter process not yet very deemonstrated).'

3 – EP, 27 Jan.: 'YEW aint (so far as bulletins recd./ convey) YET bin axd to write for "Esquire"

'THE Quarterly for Men

'"it combines the best features of Vanity Fair, The New Yorker, and a man's edition, if there were one, of Vogue, with a distinctive masculine quality of its own".'

that the possibilities of the book depend entirely on the matter which is to follow, and that it is impossible to come to an opinion one way or the other upon the material so far available. So we shall be glad to see more as soon as any considerable portion is ready.

Yours ever,
T. S. Eliot

Thank you very much for the poem, which I like & am glad to have. Is not the man's name something like *Prakosch*?[1] He has sent me [a] thing of his own similarly printed.

TO *W. H. Auden*[2]   CC

30 January 1934   [Faber & Faber Ltd]

Dear Auden (I think that we might drop the Mr),

I have your letter of the 25th with enclosure, and the copy of *The Orators* has been sent as you request to Mirsky.[3] I have shown your note and the enclosure to Morley and Faber, and they both agree with me that we see no reason why the *Modern Monthly* should be allowed to reprint entire in a periodical the whole of a verse composition which we have published and are still selling as a book. It is likely that a good many copies of *The Dance of Death* reach America, and publication there would, of course, put an end to the sales. If it was a question of your receiving personally any remuneration for this publication, we should be likely to adopt a different attitude. But I really don't see why a literary property like this should be given away by author and publisher, merely because a Review cannot pay its contributors.

1–SS's poem *Perhaps* was printed in a limited edition by Frederic Prokosch in Nov. 1933.
2–W. H. Auden (1907–73), prolific poet, playwright, librettist, translator, essayist, editor: see Biographical Register.
3–WHA wrote: 'Would you be kind enough to give me your opinion of the enclosed? I have no personal objection, but why are they unwilling to write to Faber's. Is there some Hankey-Pankey somewhere.' The enclosure has not been traced.
   Dmitri. S. Mirsky (1890–1939), historian and literary scholar, who had served as a Russian army officer and was wounded during WW1, was Lecturer in Russian at the School of Slavonic Studies, London, 1921–31. Publications include *Contemporary Russian Literature* (2 vols, 1926) and *A History of Russian Literature from the Earliest Times to the Death of Dostoevsky, 1881* (1927). In 1931 he joined the Communist Party of Great Britain (see 'Why I became a Marxist', *Daily Worker*, 30 June 1931), and in 1932 returned to Russia where he worked as a Soviet literary critic. In 1937 he was arrested in the Stalinist purge, found guilty of 'suspected espionage', and sentenced to eight years of correctional labour: he died in a labour camp in Siberia. See G. S. Smith, *D. S. Mirsky: A Russian–English Life, 1890–1939* (2000).

Edmund Wilson[1] is a friend of mine; I do not know Calverton.[2] I should put a very large question mark after the third paragraph of Calverton's letter; I should be very much surprised if any New York publisher would be willing to entertain the suggestion of publishing the *Dance of Death* as a book, after its appearance in this form. It seems to me that the best thing that you could do would be to suggest to Calverton that if he could find a New York publisher who was interested in publishing the book, either printing it or taking sheets, the proposal for free publication in the *Modern Monthly* could be considered by arrangement with that publisher.

If it appeared in the *Modern Monthly* first, I suspect that the publishers terms would be exactly the same as the *Modern Monthly*'s – that is to say, without royalties to the author and ourselves.[3]

Yours ever,
[T. S. Eliot]

TO *Ezra Pound*

TS Beinecke

31 January 1934   *The Criterion*

Bhagavan Shri Shastri Pandit O damb I cant remember what Rabet is in Sanskrit I used to kno it like my own name as well as, so:

There are still one or two points to be cleared up about ESSAYS. viz

1. I presume you want us to go ahead with French Poets as in copy of *Instig.* here, noting also to cut out Régnier and Griffin which I have done and note that you want to abbreviate Merrill and aren't you wrong to spell it Merril I spel it Merrill and you spell Russell Russel but I havent got my v. Bever here so please verify.[4] I gather that you want to make other alterations in galley I hope not TOO Extensive and to include a Vildrac[5] now where is that Vildrac ??? Anythink else ???

---

1 – For Wilson, see letter to him, 20 July 1934, below.
2 – Victor Francis Calverton (1900–40) – originally George Goetz – Marxist literary critic; editor of *The Modern Quarterly*. See Leonard Wilcox, *V. F. Calverton: Radical in the American Grain* (1992); Haim Genizi, 'V. F. Calverton, A Radical Magazinist for Black Intellectuals, 1920–1940', *The Journal of Negro History* 57: 3 (July 1972), 241–53.
3 – WHA replied from the Downs School, Colwell, nr. Malvern, 5 Feb.: 'Dear Eliot . . . I quite agree with what you say about the *Modern Monthly* . . . I have written as you suggested.'
4 – Vielé-Griffin (b. 1864), Stuart Merril (1868–1915), and De Régnier (b. 1864), on whom EP had written brief entries in 'A Study of French Poets', *Instigations* (New York, 1920).
5 – Charles Vildrac (1882–1971), French poet and playwright; author of *Poèmes de l'Abbaye* (1925), *Prolongements* (1927).

IMPORTANT: Can you reassure us about all copyright on quotes? There Is a Hell of a lot of Quotes. We dont want to find out afterwards that we have Got to pay for having used them. IMPORTANT.

THOUGHT FOR THE DAY. 'I wish I could dispose of them as easily as I write them'. From a Letter from Unknown Poet of Brockley S.E.4.

2. You MUST settle in your mind about how to Gum James & Gourmont together Do you want Henry James AND-OR GOURMONT Just like that followed by I and then II ???

I presume OTHER Gourmont (Divisions) is scrapped ???[1]

3. I have been looking through your Correspondence Box to find exact statement of pages of GUIDO to be printed I say GUIDO because it is easier to write than CAVALCANTI but cant find it any more I have got down to the bottom where there is about a gross of cards all Jokers detritus and/or sediment at the Bottom but I kno it wasnt on one of them So please repeat repeat.

Not sure whether '8' Essays will fill the Pages though there is a Lot of French poetry, so must be ready with Monro -Housman)---Banyon which can be set up from *Criterion* Pages I suppose. A-- Appenxix Appendix????[2] am sending Out now Portfolio containing ¼ ½ .,;"/,£_&'() ¼¼¼¼¼¼¼ ¼¼¼¼¼¼""""""&/',(£'_&("_"" ½½½½½""

that key is not wokinb well I mean ½ ½ ½ %% ½

containing Provincialism the Enemy and Contemporanea don't you want to print Provincialism it seems to read allright[3] your etc. for the mombent

TP

Title for Monro
Houseman Banyan:
'The Modern Mind'

1–EP had collected two pieces on Remy de Gourmont in *Pavannes and Divisions* (New York: Alfred E. Knopf, 1918).

EP responded on 2 Feb.: 'All the Gumming of James and Gourmont is done in the list of essays and on the half title
Henry James and Remy de Gourmont
I.
H. J
II (when we git there)
Remy de G.

Yaaas, omit the blurbs about Remy in Pavannes, there is enuff (probably you think too much..) in Instig.'

2–EP, 2 Feb.: 'ANYTHING I have writ/ that YOU think will sell the boo, or bring in any more L/s/d, can go into the Addenda. I pussnly think my present way of riting is more readable than my earlier discomforts.'

3–EP, 2 Feb.: 'No to hell with Provincialism. At least I can't remember whats in it.'

TO *Marianne Moore*   CC

31 January 1934   [*The Criterion*]

Dear Miss Moore,

Thank you for your letter of the 18th.[1]

As for your not having enough for a book – what I had in mind was your collected/selected poems, 'what you wish to preserve' of all your work up to date – the volume you published some years ago (did it include 'Marriage'?) and what you have written since. Little enough, I know – that is to your credit, and also to be expected of your type of mind: but from a publisher's point of view, I know that there is enough. The point at which one has 'enough' for a book (of verse) is not a quantitative matter alone: it comes at the end of a paragraph, or chapter, however short; it's a question of form. One only has not enough, when one feels that the poems written require the cooperation of certain poems not yet written, in order to be themselves quite. I mean that on the one hand I don't want to badger you, on the other hand I think you have enough.

In the sense of the paragraph above, I have not yet 'enough' either to bring out an expanded 'Collected Poems' or a second volume.[2] 'The Hollow Men' ends a period; and I must wait until the next period has enough weight (not necessarily bulk) to balance the first. I don't think this applies to the matter in hand; I want to be clear as to what your scruples are.

The engagement with MacMillan does not interfere; they would take the American rights and we the British, that is all.

There should be time to finish the poem you are working on.[3] As to whether you were to be a loss to a publisher, that is the publisher's business; we should be taking a long view, and wish to illustrate our House.

---

1 – MM was 'in a dilemma' – she had 'not yet quite enough for a book', and she had promised her next work to the Macmillan Company, New York – and yet, she went on: 'I think it goes without saying that if something by me were to come out, I should like to have your hand in it . . . I am sure it is true that there is not money in poetry for anybody and to say that I dislike the thought of being a loss to a publisher is far more than a mere understatement' (*Selected Letters of Marianne Moore*, ed. Bonnie Costello, Celeste Goodridge, Cristanne Miller [1998], 517).

2 – FVM was to tell Geoffrey Grigson, 19 Oct. 1934: 'The sale of Eliot's collected POEMS is round about 10,000. But I don't regard that as a ceiling – I mean in time we will sell a great deal more.'

3 – MM was writing a piece on Henry James for *Hound & Horn*; after that, she said, 'I should like to see what I can do with a poem I have been working on; verse is the work I like best.'

My colleague, Mr F. V. Morley, will be in New York on business in about ten days. He is a dear creature of unusual intelligence, and he will communicate with you. I shall be very glad if you can see him and talk the matter over.

Yours very sincerely,
[T. S. Eliot]

TO *Ezra Pound*   TS Beinecke

1 February 1934   *The Criterion*

To the Enlightened One, Son of Heaven, initiate into the MIY AOU MIY AOU and other Arcane Mystries & other big medecine:

The DATE LINE looks allright what I mean is that there seem to be passages in it susceptible to interpretation etc. & some quite Luminous that clears up In the Votrex etc. & saves all but the most curious from having to burrow in ancient chronicles of the early Wars

Am having material on Hand cast off for no. of pages It looks has if. There would be enough to fill pages. Do you WANY those pages 1–36 (having now found the passage referred to about Guido I wish you could invent some system for indexing various subject matters in your corresponedents dence I am trying to train up an efficient staff but by the time they have mastered it they wont be fit for anythink else) COMPLETE with poems in Engelsk and Italienisch AND notes in smaller print You suggested cutting but nobody can cut that sort of cocoanut except yourself what do you cut it with a piece of string or oxy-acetaline etc.

AM definitely of opinion that PAVEXANNA stuff should be kept for another sort of charivari Foire de Neuilly etc [1]

MORLEY says he has a QUIA but he may forget it I being sperated from my library etc he leaves for New York tomorrow address c/o Harcourt Brace I think returns end of March so will close with Kind regards yours etc

Wilson seems a sensible chap the book is pretty old now but Still these lads need a cool word they dont get much criticism I can tell you and I cant be impresario and critic at once unfortunately[2]

TP

1–EP, 29 Jan.: 'Re/ Pavannes, I dunno. I leave all that to yr/ superior ecclestical polity . . .'
2–EP, 29 Jan.: 'T. C. Wilson has for some reason (diffidence, I believe) sent ME his review of New Country, instead of sending it direct to YOU. I am sending it along, with my own DATE LINE (alias the preface). You might polish one or two phrases (of WILSON, not of ole Ez . . .).'

Am trying to get Marianna to join our select circle of collected/selecteds but blimey that filley is shy if you have any influence etc [1]

TO R. Webb-Odell[2]

5 February 1934   B11 Eliot House, Cambridge

Dear Mr Webb-Odell,

(1) I enclose a note for the Diocesan Leaflet which I think is about the right length.[3] If you think it says the wrong things or is simply not enough of an appetiser for the people, will you please return it immediately with comments?

(2) The title has been a matter of great difficulty, and now Browne is in Arran and I can't consult him.[4] I have tried various 'fancy' titles, but they

---

1 – EP would write to MM ('Deraly Beloved Marianna of the Moated ETC') on 3 Feb. that 'he had received a "plaintive communique from the Rt/ Rev/ bro/ in Xt/ T.S. thePossum of Eliot /codirekr of Faber and Faber London/ who . . . wants to pub/ your poems for reefeened circles in the decaYdent city of Lunnon on Thames . . . I think you better display maidely charity and LET HIM DO IT . . . Besides yr/ mother wd/ like it. I mean yr/ being pubd in Dickens Home Town/."' (Linda Leavell, *Holding On Upside Down: The Life and Work of Marianne Moore* [2013], 270).

EP told TSE on 8 Feb.: 'I done your chore of askin her to let Fan F/ publish her.'

2 – The Revd Rosslyn Webb-Odell, MA (1879–1942), Rector of St Anne's, Soho; Organising Director of the Forty-five Churches Fund for the Diocese of London; editor of *The Christian Faith: a series of essays . . .* (1922) and *Church Reform* (1924). EMB thought him 'a great, jolly polar-bear of a man . . . He was an able organizer' (*The Making of T. S. Eliot's Plays* [1970], 3).

3 – Webb-Odell wrote, 1 Feb.: 'Could you possibly let me have by Thursday next a short article of 500 words telling about the Pageant from your point of view as Author? I am anxious to issue with the next Diocesan Leaflet an extra page concerning the Pageant . . . [S]omething descriptive of your own aim in the composing of the Play is what I think would "get over" to the people. As the Leaflet has a circulation of over 60,000 this means a considerable publicity.'

TSE's text was printed in the Sadler's Wells publicity leaflet for *A Pageant Play/The Rock/ By T. S. Eliot*.

4 – Webb-Odell wrote, '[I]t is *getting really urgent* that a title should be fixed as soon as possible.'

E. (Elliott) Martin Browne (1900–80), theatre director: see Biographical Register.

EMB had written to TSE, 11 Jan.: 'We need a title terribly badly. Is "London Echoes" any good? Conventional, but true in a way. I've also wondered whether something with the word "vision" in it – "London Visions" – "A London Vision" – would do.

'I would like something more interesting, but have nothing to offer . . .

    Stones of London
    Building London
    London the Greater
perhaps are better?'

usually suffer from obscurity, and I think that a simple straightforward title which gives some clue to the subject matter is what is wanted. It ought to include both 'London' and 'Church' or 'Churches', I take it. Is *The Church Bells of London* too flat, or too clumsy, or anything else. 'Bells' has a merry sound, and perhaps Shaw could introduce a few chimes here and there – that would be a good thing anyway, I think. If you will let me know as soon as you can, I should want to wire to Browne for his opinion before settling the title. A title which had some simple familiar allusion would be more pat, but I cant think of one. I wish I could get a more 'catchy' title.

I had lunch with Mayhew the other day, and learnt from him of the participation of St Cyprian's.[1] He is keenly interested.

Yours very sincerely,
[T. S. Eliot]

[Enclosure]

I do not wish to be described as the Author of this Pageant. I am the writer of the Words, so far as these are original, and compiler of the speeches of certain historical personages out of their own works. I have written the choruses, the song, and some modern dialogue. I do not wish to disclaim responsibility, but to give credit where it is due. And, having no experience of writing for the theatre, I am very grateful to have had the opportunity of this collaboration; which also has made it possible for me to concentrate upon the problem, new to me, of trying to write a kind of verse which should produce the intended effect when declaimed from a stage to an audience unfamiliar with it.

I think that Mr Browne and I shared the desire, even before we had begun to discuss the matter, to escape as far as possible from the conventional conception of an 'historical pageant'. I mean that a pageant which should merely be a brilliant review of the more picturesque or impressive episodes in the history of London church-building, however pleasing to the old or instructive to the young, was never in question. The past is employed only because of its relevance to the present, and to bring the attention to the very urgent and anxious problems with which the Church today is concerned. There is no problem of a community to which the presence or absence of a church is irrelevant: and he who is concerned that a church should be built is committed to a concern with all the problems of the community which the church is intended to serve.

---

1 – Volunteers from St Cyprian's, TSE's former parish church in Clarence Gate, represented the second segment of 'Remembering the Past': 'St Michael Paternoster Royal, A. D. 1440'.

The problem of church-building is integral with the problem of more and better housing in general. The employment of men for building churches suggests the whole problem of unemployment. There are many who will say that 'in these times' the money and the labour might be put to better purpose, or at least to satisfy more pressing needs; and, while repudiating the assumptions on which such objections are made, we must assert that these needs are all one need, and that they can all be satisfied. There is sufficient stone, clay, lime, and other materials in the country for all the building of every kind that is wanted; there is sufficient unemployed labour. The world is ready enough to employ money for the purpose of making more money, or for the purpose of destroying competition: it needs more *non-productive* activity.

In the ordinary sense, the pageant is true enough to the pageant form in having no 'plot'; it endeavours to get its coherence from a significance such as I have tried to suggest above; while the separate scenes, it is hoped, will be enjoyed also for their own sake. A continuity of tone is aimed at through the recurrence of the Chorus and the symbolic figure of The Rock; while the modern and the historical scenes are purposely juxtaposed and blended to enhance the effect of contemporaneity. I have not been so ambitious as to hope that what I contribute might be great poetry, but I have tried to write efficient verse of a kind simple and straightforward for the stage, and I think I have succeeded in writing something that is at least wholly lucid and understandable, and have not spared the use of rhetorical devices of great antiquity.[1]

1 – *The Rock* was announced by F&F, Autumn 1934: 'The Rock is the text written by Mr Eliot for the pageant play recently produced at Sadler's Wells on behalf of the Forty-five Churches Fund of the Diocese of London. While in form it approximates a play, the production includes much pageantry, mimetic action, and ballet. The dialogue is mostly in prose, but the choruses, in considerable variety, constitute a piece of work in verse much longer than any of the author's previously published poems. Mr Eliot's success in this attempt to find modern forms of verse suitable for the stage may be judged from the press notices which follow . . .'

5 February 1934   [Faber & Faber Ltd]

My dear Yeats,

I understand from Richard de la Mare that you are willing to publish your introduction to the Bhagwan Hamsa's narrative separately in periodical form.[2]

I should be very glad to have this for publication in the *Criterion*, if you will consent. In this case, and as the book is to appear fairly early in the autumn, I presume that your introduction had best appear in the July *Criterion*; but I could hold it over until the October number, that is to say a few weeks after publication of the book, if you have any strong reason for doing so.

You know our usual terms, and if you approve publication in the *Criterion*, I will take the matter up with Watt.

May I say how keenly I enjoyed both introduction and text?[3]

Yours very sincerely,

[T. S. Eliot]

1 – William Butler Yeats (1865–1939): Irish poet; Nobel laureate: see Biographical Register.

2 – WBY's introduction to *The Holy Mountain*, by Bhagwan Shri Hamsa (1882–1941), was to appear in periodical form as 'Initiation Upon a Mountain', C. 13 (July 1934), 537–56.

3 – TSE's reader's report on *The Holy Mountain*, 5 Jan. 1934: 'Uncle William is looney as ever. He will spell Balzac with an S and he talks about the aphorisms of Patanjali Im not sure but I suppose he means the sutras of the Sanhkya Bashya Barika upon which Patanjali wrote his justly celebrated commentary Never Mind he goes on in his oldtime way about the phases of the Moon etc. It is a good long introduction and I suppose would help the sale of the book I dont mind it being mostly nonsense but it does seem a pity that he tells some of the Holy Man's best stories over in advance in his own fashion but the Holy Man himself writes much better than Yeats for this sort of thing I mean. That is a good one about his scaling a mountain about 25000 feet and tumbling into a cave on top of a still Holier Man who received him with laughter & affection.

'The narrative is wholly delightful and if not authentic at least is extraordinarily plausible and the appearance of the God to the Holy Man after the latter has been meditating for 3 days on a cake of ice in the middle of a frozen lake bears the Stamp of Truth. We ought to find out how Uncle William came by it and what assurance he can give of its genuineness for what an Irishman's assurance is Worth, and my approval is subject to the terms being such as I also approve. P.S. Incidentally the contrast between Uncle William and the genuine Hindu article is food for the discerning.'

The blurb for *The Holy Mountain* is very probably by TSE: 'There is an almost inaccessible Holy Mountain in Tibet, to which only Hindu adepts who have attained a very high stage of spiritual development make their pilgrimage. In this volume we have a very remarkable document: the first-hand narrative which a great Hindu Saint of our time – who is still living – has written of his own journey. It is an account which should interest not only students of Indian Mysticism, but everyone who is interested in extraordinary revelations of human nature, and everyone who is interested in exciting adventure – in fact, *everyone*. The author's

TO *Cyril Strauss*[1]   CC

5 February 1934   [Faber & Faber Ltd]

Dear Mr Strauss,

Thank you for your renewed invitation. I am booked up for the next
two weekends, and after then I must stay at home and work solidly until
Easter, so that I am afraid that my visit would have to be in the summer
term, if you care to invite me then.

I should have liked an opportunity to talk to you about your book.[2]
Candidly, we found it on the whole a disappointment. It is with no
disrespect to your own share in it that I say that the book seems to me
uneven, but not uneven enough. Some of your contributors are inclined
to indulge in rather turgid journalese, and the book as a whole does not
give the impression of clear thinking amongst the young conservatives.
The Scottish article, among others, is interesting, but is rather submerged
amongst unrelated subjects. It seems to me that your group ought to try
again, with a better scheme of division of labour, a simple statement of
principles on which you are all agreed, and a determination to avoid
rhetoric. And I can't say that the chairmanship of Colonel Buchan
ingratiates my opinion; but this is a personal bias.

I hope that I have not spoken too bluntly.

With all best wishes,

Yours very sincerely,

[T. S. Eliot]

---

plain, matter-of-fact style, his simple and unassuming character, his attention to such details
as engage the ordinary traveller as well as to the object of his quest, enhance the credibility
of the amazing vision on the frozen lake which forms the consummation of his purpose. The
Introduction by Mr Yeats is an essay which none of that great poet's admirers will care to
miss.'

1–Cyril Anthony Strauss (1913–44), New College, Oxford; after graduation, he was to
qualify as a barrister-at-law but was killed in action at Assisi, Italy, on 1 Dec. 1944, aged
thirty-one.

2–TSE's reader's report on 'Jeunesse Oblige', 29 Jan. 1934: 'This is a number of separate
essays on social, artistic and political problems of the time by a number of Oxford
undergraduates (I know one of them) introduced by a slick sort of chairman, Mr John
Buchan. Mr Buchan creates an unfavourable impression in advance. These are Young
Conservatives. One of them speaks of an "optimistic note". It rings in *my* ear more like the
death-knell of Conservatism, and of English Prose. The style is almost uniformly turgid and
pompous. But in the circumstances, I wish very much that GCF would examine one or two.'

GCF wrote at the foot: 'Very pretentious immaturity indeed.'

Strauss (3 Feb.) again asked TSE to visit him at New College, Oxford, and went on:
'I hope you will like the book. If you think it fulfils its purpose, perhaps you would be willing
to write a short letter of introduction by way of foreword.'

Undated [after 7 February 1934]   [*The Criterion*]

Dear Mr Bolshakoff,

I have your letter of the 7th. Mr Christopher Dawson's address is as follows:

> Hartlington Hall,
> Skipton,
> Yorks.

As I think I suggested before, in writing to him, I should mention the names of any members of his own community who have given their adherence.

As for Fascism, it is so much a question of the character of the individual leaders, and varies so much from one nation to another that generalisations are difficult.[2] What I should deprecate would be any pronouncement on the part of your group which would give the slightest encouragement to any so-called Fascist associations already formed in this country. I see nothing here at present of that kind which deserves to be treated with anything but abhorrence. So far as the affirmation goes of universal principles, which any Fascism would have to accept if it wished to be good Fascism, that is quite another matter.

Yours sincerely,
[T. S. Eliot]

---

1 – Serge (Sergius) Bolshakoff (1901–90), Russian-born ecumenist: see Biographical Register.
2 – Bolshakoff was to write on 13 Mar. 1934: 'The greatest dangers to Catholic Church now are: modernism, panchristianism, marxism and racism. Any these movements cannot be assimilated by Church without her destruction but Labour Party, Fascism, Democracy can be assimilated in some countries. Not every Labour party or every Fascism are good but they can be christianized . . . I hope and I believe we shall become the closest collaborators after more intimate mutual acquaintance. Our general ideas are the same ones.' On 3 May Bolshakoff reported to TSE that he hoped to invite Konstantin Rodzaevsky (1907–46), leader of the Russian Fascist Party (in exile in Manchukuo), to attend the meeting which would formally inaugurate the Academy of Christian Sociologists: 'he is the most extraordinary man . . . a key man in the Far East, perhaps, in not very distant future the master of Russia. He is profoundly Christian . . . If he will be invited he will be only man of manifest fascist tendencies in our midst.'

TO *R. Webb-Odell*   TS Bodleian

8 February 1934   Faber & Faber Ltd

Dear Mr Webb-Odell,

Thank you for your letter of the 5th.[1] Browne's *Many Mansions* seems to me quite good.[2] My only objection to *The Rock* is that the Rock himself, if he gives the title to the production, will be identified by most people as St Peter pure and simple, which does directly conjure up to my mind the Petrine Claims – which are hardly appropriate. Do you think this is a considerable objection or not? If not, then perhaps this is the best title.

Another point. I saw a poster today which describes me as 'the author'. This is not correct, and gives me what is not due. I should be glad if posters could in future read; 'Produced by Martin Browne. Words by T. S. Eliot. Music by Martin Shaw.'

or something like that?

Finally, I have a favour to ask. I seem to have mislaid the letter in which you gave me bibliography for Rahere,[3] nor do I remember whether you made any suggestion of whence to draw the material for a sermon by Mellitus[4] (I imagine that there is none recorded, from what I find out of

1 – 'As to Title [for the pageant],' wrote Webb-Odell, 'frankly I hate "Church Bells". It reminds me of some transpontine melodrama of my youth.

'Martin Browne today suggests, "Many Mansions", which doesn't seem bad.

'What is wrong with the Title Lady Keeble gave it, *vide* yesterday's "Observer" [4 Feb.] – "The Rock"?

'Anyhow, I think the prime need is to fix on something as soon as possible. Probably, after it is done, a much better idea will come to someone; but that can't be helped.'

See 'The Theatre of the Future: Miss McCarthy and the Poet-Dramatist', *The Observer*, 4 Feb. 1934, 18. Lillah McCarthy had pronounced in her third lecture on Poetry and the Drama at the Royal Institution, 3 Feb., 'The Church has already opened its doors to poetic drama ... Gordon Bottomley's "The Acts of St Peter" is to be given at St Margaret's, Westminster, and later on T. S. Eliot's "The Rock".'

TSE to 'Class of 1910: Fiftieth Anniversary Report', 1960, on the title: '[*The Rock*] was the name of my pageant, but somebody else had decided on that name before it was written ...'

2 – John 14: 2: 'In my Father's house are many mansions: if it were not so, I would have told you. I go to prepare a place for you.'

3 – Rahere (d. 1144), jester and courtier of King Henry I, made a pilgrimage to Rome and fell gravely ill, whereupon he experienced a vision of St Bartholomew who instructed him to build a church and hospital in the 'suburb' of Smithfield, London. Rahere built St Bartholomew the Great – 'Great St Barts' – which he set up as an Augustinian priory in 1123. See *The Book of the Foundation of St Bartholomew's Church in London* (1923).

4 – Mellitus (d. 624), leader of a group of missionaries sent by Pope Gregory I in support of Augustine at Canterbury; first known Bishop of London, 604–16/18, and third Archbishop of Canterbury.

that saint, but perhaps there are early sermons which would do). Would you be so kind as to tell me what you can?

Yours very sincerely,
[T. S. Eliot]

TO *F. O. Matthiessen*[1]

TS Donald Gallup

8 February 1934   Faber & Faber Ltd

Dear Matty,

I have been slow in answering your letter of the 28th December, which gave me much pleasure.[2] I have often thought of the very pleasant memories of Eliot House, and of our weekend in Kittery and on the Ipswich River. I often wish that I might fly over for a few nights at No. B-11.

I am glad to hear, from more sources than one, that 'Bartholemew Fair' was a great success. I hope you will be able to keep up the tradition, though it means a great deal of work.

There is no startling literary news in London. I have had my nose to the grindstone – first, re-writing lectures – the Virginia lectures will be out in a fortnight – and since then trying to write the words for a pageant to be produced during the first fortnight in June at Sadler's Wells. I find that playable dialogue is a very difficult thing to write: all my speeches are too long.

I have been trying to get a copy of the *Advocate* containing Pound's effusion.[3] They (i.e. Wade) have asked me to contribute, but I have warned them that I am hardly in a position to be as outspoken as he can be.

I wonder what your new quarters are like – the last seemed to suit you so perfectly. And whether they meet with the approval of the Matthiascat, to whom my respects.

Yours ever,
T. S. Eliot

---

1 – F. O. Matthiessen (1902–50), author and academic: see Biographical Register.
2 – Not traced.
3 – EP, 'Ignite! Ignite!', *Harvard Advocate* 120: 3 (Dec. 1933), 3–5.

TO *Hallie Flanagan*[1]   TS NYPL Theater Collection

9 February 1934   Faber & Faber Ltd

Dear Mrs Flanagan,

Thank you for your letter.[2] I trust that you will find this reply waiting for you at Brown Shipley's upon your arrival.[3] I hope that you will let me know when you get here, and will be able to lunch or dine with me.

I do not know the School of the Theatre at Dartington Hall, but I may be able to make enquiries. I gather from your letter, however, that you intend to visit the place yourself.

I cannot tell you when or whether there will be more of *Sweeney* but in any case I hope to start something new of the same kind as soon as I have finished with a dramatic pageant which is to be produced in the early summer.[4]

W. H. Auden's address is: The Downs School, Colwall, Nr. Malvern. If possible, I should like to get him up to town to meet you while you are in London, but I am not sure that it is possible for him to get away from his school during the term.

Yours very sincerely,
T. S. Eliot

1 – Hallie Flanagan (1890–1969), theatre producer and director, playwright, author, taught 1927–35 at Vassar College, Poughkeepsie, New York, where she built up the Vassar Experimental Theatre. She was to be National Director of the Federal Theater Project, 1935–42; and she ran the Theatre Department at Smith College, Northampton, Mass., 1942–52. See Flanagan, *Dynamo* (1943); Joanne Bentley, *Hallie Flanagan: A Life in the American Theatre* (1988).
2 – Flanagan wrote (n.d.) to say she was sailing for London on 8 Feb., and would be visiting the school of theatre and dance mime at Dartington Hall, Devon, and also spending time in London. 'I should like very much to see you about possibility of more of *Sweeney* . . . Also, I am decidedly interested in Mr Auden's *Dance of Death*. Do you think he would trust me with it?'
3 – Flanagan asked TSE to leave a note for her at the branch of the bankers Brown, Shipley and Co., at 123 Pall Mall (which dealt primarily with letters of credit for American travellers).
4 – Sidnell, *Dances of Death*, 100–2, and Appendix A, 263–5, argues that this 'something new' was *The Superior Landlord* – 'the complete scenario for a Sweeney play. It was not written before the published fragments – though this has been assumed. In the scenario, Eliot sketched an entirely new version of the earlier work.'

9 February 1934   Faber & Faber Ltd

Now look Here Rabet dont you go visperin in my Ear and a-twitchin my Sleeve[1] whilst I am a-aimin at BEAR.[2] You Might get into the line of Fire.

An don yo go mumlin an prayin ober dat tombstone w'en dat Posum am a winkin at yo fum de top o'dat sycamore tree.[3]

Podesta I have been in communication with a Mr Cullis of Oxford Podesta Mr Cullis is no doubt verree excellent Port Cullis in a storm But he is somewhat lacking in lucidity of style in business letter. IF has I take it this is a question of releasing Part of the existing stock of *Quia Pauper Amawi* (Friday night being Amavi night) God Bless You Podesta and Prosper the Venture and all powwer to Blackwall for it but Podesta I just wanted to assure ourselves beyond the Shadow of a Peradventure that there was no Question of REPRINTING wich would hobvously spike our PROPERTIUS and nobody would make enough money to call it a Day. So may I have your hassurance on this Point.[4]

Podesta the momentary delay over *Selected Essays* is not my fault I am waiting for Production Manager who is overbusy to make cast off of Material but am pressing forward with Zeal and you may with all confidence leave your interests etc.

Please give approximate date of delivery od CANTOTOES MSS.

Yrs etc

Tp.

1 – *Cf.* Cassius in *Julius Caesar*, I. ii. 179–81: 'As they pass by, pluck Casca by the sleeve, / And he will, after his sour fashion, tell you / What hath proceeded worthy note today.'
2 – 'Bear' is in this case FVM.
3 – See the American song (*c.* 1899): 'Way down south where the sly old possum hides in the sycamore tree.' EP replied, 11 Feb.: 'Wot Baaar you pottin at? I sure Is glad you think being "up a tree" izz isilleratin . . . don't you got git too treed. souns like you losin hole ov you lagqidge.'
4 – EP, 11 Feb.: 'RE/ the Portcullis/ this is NO question of Blackwell reprinting. I told Cullis to tell 'em to go to hell. He in prudence is trying to sell 'em Fontenelle. And the Quia Pauper is to be listed in their cats/ of 1st. edtns/ at 5/ bob. So THAT wont interfere with the 2/6 Propertius.
'IZZAT O.K.'

13 February 1934   [Faber & Faber Ltd]

Dear Pollinger,

I have been given your letter of the 15th January to Frank Morley, with the enclosed post card which you asked to have returned to you.[1] As Morley left for New York nine days ago, I do not know whether he answered your note, and I am therefore answering it myself. The present position of Pound's *Selected Essays* is that the material is in our hands, and as soon as we have been able to make a cast-off, and estimate the size and cost of the volume, we will draw up a contract based thereon.

I had suggested to Pound that we should now publish his book of *Collected Poems* – that is, of course, everything up to the *Cantos*, allowing the 7/6 edition of the *Selected Poems* to go out of print, and retaining the latter only in the 3/6 edition. Pound, however, preferred to postpone this collected edition in order to publish *Propertius* first by itself, and this we have agreed to do. *Propertius* is a short poem about the length of *H. S. Mauberley*, which appeared as part of the volume *Quia Pauper Amavi*, which was published some years ago by the Egoist Press, and is now nearly out of print. *Propertius* by itself would probably make not more than a 2/6 volume. There has been, however, some suggestion of Basil Blackwell reprinting *Quia Pauper Amavi* entire. I have written to Pound to clear up this point, and as soon as I hear from him that this republication has been abandoned, we will prepare a contract for the *Propertius*. The terms were the usual straight 10%.[2]

Furthermore, we are expecting from Pound another ten or more Cantos, to be published by themselves in the autumn. Not yet knowing how many Cantos there will be, nor how long they are, we cannot fix the price of the volume.

Is there anything else in connection with Pound's affairs that is not clear?

Yours sincerely,
[T. S. Eliot]

1 – Not traced.
2 – *Homage to Sextus Propertius* was to be published by F&F in Nov. 1934.

TO *Rupert Doone*[1]   CC

13 February 1934[2]   [Faber & Faber Ltd]

Dear Mr Doone,

I am sorry I was unable to see you the other day, and thank you for
your letter. I should be very glad if you could let me have two seats for the
performance of *The Dance of Death* on Sunday the 25th instant.[3]

I should be very glad if you could notify Mrs Hallie Flanagan, c/o Messrs
Brown Shipley & Co., 123 Pall Mall, London s.w., of the performance,
and ask her if she will be able to be present. Mrs Flanagan is the Directress
of an experimental theatre in America, and is arriving in London within
the next few days. She produced *Sweeney Agonistes* very well indeed, and
has asked me about the possibility of her doing *The Dance of Death*,
so that I think it would be to Auden's interest to let her know about the
performance.

I am not quite clear what you have in mind when you say that you
would like to discuss a play with me, but I should be very glad to see you
by appointment any morning, if you will ring up my Secretary to fix a
time and date.[4] I should be pleased to discuss your dramatic affairs with
you.

Yours sincerely,
[T. S. Eliot]

TO *Herbert Read*[5]   CC

13 February 1934   [Faber & Faber Ltd]

My dear Herbert,

I wonder if you could find time one day before long to look in and help
me by running through a very select batch of verse to give me the benefit
of your opinion. You know that I have almost lost my sensibility as a
result of reading so much youthful verse, and am very distrustful of my

---

1 – Rupert Doone (1903–66), dancer, choreographer, producer: see Biographical Register.
2 – The top copy was with Robert Medley: he sent EVE a copy on 23 Mar. 1983.
3 – Doone wrote on 9 Feb. to say that the Group Theatre was producing WHA's *The Dance
of Death* (with costumes by Robert Medley and masks by Henry Moore) at the Westminster
Theatre on Sun., 25 Feb., and he would be happy to send TSE the number of seats he asked
for.
4 – 'I want to see you to discuss a play . . . It is quite important to me that I should see you.'
5 – Herbert Read (1893–1968), English poet and literary critic: see Biographical Register.

unaided decisions. If it isn't convenient, I could meet you somewhere at your greater convenience, in tea room or public house.

I am sending you a copy of my new book, which appears next week.[1] I can at least say for it that it is very short, and I hope that it may be the last volume of lectures that I shall have to publish.

Yours ever,

[Tom]

TO *Dorothy Richards*   MS Magdalene

15 February 1934   Faber & Faber Ltd

Dear Mrs Richards,

I am trying to do this with a pen in order to express (through physical discomfort) my enjoyment and appreciation of a wholly delightful weekend. I would have written before but on my return immediately was engaged in moving. I have now left boarding house life and am installed in a furnished flat – nicely furnished and practically a flat, having its own door – and the servant can do the bedroom without disturbing me in the sitting room & vice versa, that makes it a flat – and later I shall be equipped to ask people to tea & possibly dinner. It's the house of the local vicar, but I don't have to see any more of him than I want.

A disaster has happened. My secretary, who is under notice for cumulative irritatingness,[2] now announces that she has not the slightest recollection of my having given her one gramophone record to put away. I think she must have thrown it away in the wrappings. It is exasperating & means ordering some more, which means months if at all.

I am coming tomorrow afternoon, & am very sorry I can't dine afterwards. But I hope I may be asked to Cambridge again in the summer.

I have written to Read (re Jennings) to ask him how people get museum jobs.

---

1 – *After Strange Gods.*

2 – GCF wrote in his diary, 3 Jan. 1934: '[Lister the caretaker] said he was tired of being ordered about by Miss G. [Tacon Gilbert] as if he were a dog; & if it went on, or I expected that of him, it wld. be better for him to go. Confirmed my opinion that Miss G. cannot stay – she is not only not really efficient, but she gets unbearably on my nerves, & apparently has put almost everyone in the building up against her. So in the morning I gave her notice – a most disagreeable business.'

Gilbert eventually quit the *Criterion* in the week beginning 6 Mar. 1934 – 'to take up private coaching' – and handed over to Erica Wright.

I am anxious to know what I. A. R. thinks of Bottrall.[1]

Yours sincerely

T. S. Eliot

TO *Ernest Bird, Messrs Bird & Bird*   CC

19 February 1934   [Faber & Faber Ltd]

Dear Bird,

I am not at all surprised or shocked, and I shall settle this account in a few days; I should like to wait until my December royalties come in.[2]

I enclose a letter from Mr James on a matter about which he spoke to me the other day when I was in his office because of income tax business. I said that I should have no objection to paying this bill; but I think it better that the matter should pass through your hands. Will you give him the authority?[3]

For official use, and private information, I have now moved (decidedly for the better) to a small furnished flat at 9, Grenville Place, South Kensington s.w.7. The telephone, which is not mine but my landlord's the local Vicar, is Western 1670.[4]

Yours sincerely,

[T. S. Eliot]

1 – Ronald Bottrall (1906–89), poet, critic, teacher and administrator: see further, letter to him, 25 Oct. 1935, below.

2 – Bird had written on 9 Feb. that he was 'almost ashamed' to have to send TSE a statement of his indebtedness to his firm, to the end of 1933, amounting, with disbursements, to £116. 5. 10. (TSE had at some point sent a cheque on account for £50, so in fact he now owed £66. 5. 10.)

3 – James & James (VHE's solicitors) had sent on a bill amounting to £8. 9. 11 (supplier unknown); and on 22 Feb. Bird received from James a masseuse's bill for £2. 5. 0d. Bird authorized the discharge of both items. 'I have done so for the reason that it goes to the end of last month which is really prior to the revised arrangement coming into force. I have impressed upon him that you cannot be responsible for any more payments of this character . . . I think it is at least debatable whether you are responsible for any fees incurred by your Wife with Messrs James & James, but it may be that you are right in accepting what I may call a moral responsibility up to that date.' (VHE had a number of treatments by a masseuse between 18 Dec. 1933 and 19 Feb. 1934, and TSE paid for all of them. VHE also ran up bills at Selfridge's, but TSE closed his account there by Jan. 1934.)

4 – Gordon, *The Imperfect Life*, 251: 'His rooms were drab, with hideous purple covers in a small, angular sitting-room, and meagre dribbles from the hot tap (he shared a bathroom with the curates).' EVE, '"Owls and Artificers"' (letter), *TLS*, 16 July 1971, 835: '"Burnt Norton" and "East Coker" were written in the Royal Borough, in Grenville Place and Emperor's Gate respectively, and contain local allusions – for example, "a place of disaffection" is Gloucester Road Underground Station. And in "Little Gidding" the line "We trod the pavement . . ." is a reference to the surface of the Cromwell Road.'

TO *Herbert Read*   TS University of Victoria

19 February 1934   Faber & Faber Ltd

Dear Herbert,

Many thanks for museum information. I have sent your memorandum to Richards, asking him to convey to the young man[1] by word of mouth what the latter ought to know, and then destroy the paper. It's a pity to destroy it, however.

I think it quite likely that you *meant* something different[2] – that you were thinking only in an artistic frame and not in a more comprehensive moral one; but I maintain that there is danger in further meaning that the words will *bear*. Any statement of the sort cannot help being a kind of incitement to action, or having some influence upon conduct. I don't think that there is any question of 'precedence' between ethical and aesthetic judgements; the point is rather that in your whole discussion of character and personality no distinction between the two judgements clearly appears. The ordinary reader might easily be led to the conclusion that (as a kind of moral imperative) *personality* is to be sought and *character* avoided. It does not seem to be made clear that although you can, to some extent, form 'character', you cannot form 'personality'. The statement in your letter is much more acceptable to me; though I don't think that you can leave character out of account even with the artist qua artist.

One of the things I want to discuss is Sykes's *Petron*; I don't feel happy about it.[3]

1–At IAR's request, HR had written a spoof paper on 'How to Get a Museum Job' for the benefit of IAR's student Humphrey Jennings.

2–HR had written ('Saturday'), of *After Strange Gods*: 'I'm not surprised to find myself among the heretics, and though I don't like my company, I feel that in the circumstances one must put up with some strange bedfellows. I am quite unrepentant about the intention of my theory; I am only a little uncertain whether I was wise to try and give definition to such worn counters as "character" and "personality". What I contend for is no more than Keats contends for; and you have expressed approval of Keats's theory in the Use [*UPUC*]. And it seems to me that when you say, for example, that "people who write devotional verse are usually writing as they want to feel, rather than as they do feel", you are tacitly assuming *all* I really care to stand by. It is a question of the intervention of the will. I am quite sure that the will cannot intervene in any form of art without disastrous results – not, at least, at the moment of inspiration.'

'But this gives you no idea of how much I have enjoyed the book. It will do a lot of good . . .'

3–Hugh Sykes Davies, *Petron* (fiction, 1935): an extract would appear, under the title 'Banditti (From The Biography of Petron)', in *C.* 13 (July 1934), 577–80.

I was aware, afterwards, that people may read fascism into it.[1] This may give me the trouble of an explicit disclaimer; we must see if the occasion arises. There is a recent letter of mine in the *Church Times* which should give more than a hint, but that only reaches a limited public.[2] Apart from having, I hope, an ordinary share of reason and humanity, and not wanting to be associated with an uprush of the masses, I observe that the fascist and the royalist ideology are incompatible.

Yours ever

T.

TO *Ezra Pound* TS Beinecke

22 February (Hurrah) 1934   Faber & Faber Ltd

Podesta what a funny letter Podesta the rattle of musketry is reported from the Ligurian Coast and it is Said that that an allgemeine Mobilmachung of the Swizz Army has been ordered Much excitement in Macon Georgia and copies of MAN! A Journal of the Anarchist Ideal and Movement are selling like Hot cakes in the purlieus of the Grays Inn Road But Nevertheless Podesta Votaries of the Beauuuutifffulll like you 'n me 'n Goethre must pursue the paths of Purnesses abovve the battle. So: what is Really serious

WHAT is your Real Idea about Cantotoes?[3] I mean, if (as seems Prudent in view of the Existing State of Legislation) you bring out Farrar

---

1 – 'I regret a little pp. 19–20. I think it will lead to misunderstanding. Hail Mosley! will be written over it, and perhaps *your* bedfellows will be not a little strange.' HR was referring to TSE's remarks in *After Strange Gods* about the desirability of a stable society: 'The population should be homogeneous; where two or more cultures exist in the same place they are likely either to be fiercely self-conscious or both to become adulterate. What is still more important is unity of religious background; and reasons of race and religion combine to make any large number of free-thinking Jews undesirable' (19–20).

2 – See TSE, 'The Blackshirts' (letter), *Church Times* 111: 3706 (2 Feb. 1934), 116: written 30 Jan., above.

3 – EP wrote on 9 Feb.: 'Farrar is said to be paying an advance (damn it) but not getting into print till autumn/ . . . I spose I'll have to make you a new typescript . . .' On 11 Feb.: 'Re/ Cantos/ I can deliver 'em in 48 hours/ Virginia reported that a contract with Farrar wuzza bein made, and that they thought they wd/ be unable to being 'em out till autimn, and proposed to do so then.

'I don't propose to keep you wating. My hurry to print was for the American edtn/ and I spose for copyright reasons / the Brit/ edtn/ shd/ not precede.

'If Farrar had any guts he wd/ have the stuff in print by now/ and I cd/ the Eng/ edtn/ one canto more . . . possibly . . .

'I suppose eleven cantos make about 56 pages. if you are thinking of printers costs . . .

'anyhow/ the Essays in Early hautumn/ ought to git their reviewes/ and then have the 31/41 [Cantos], late autumn in time for noEl, no hell!! Wot o the XXXXmas cheeUr!!'

& Max first, WHEN can you get those Boys to Name the Day? Should
Morley now in N.Y. try to Rustle them a Bit? If so, answer promptlY for
it means sending him a Night Letter. Or wd. you rather we kept them till
after Xmas? As for us, we take things as they Come but we could keep
ourselves busy selling Select Essats & Proppertius up till then If you Say
the Word Brother Say the Word Essays are being Cast Off and results with
number of pages, price and contact should reach you before Long so Will
close Please give my regards to your Father yours etc

TP

[Postscript written at head of letter]
DO be Fair Podesta that wasnt Gummery Belgion[1] at All that was a Poet
named Bransford who lives in Upper or Lower Austria He calls himself the
White Stallion His wife wants me to see Justice done to him but Podesta
I am too humane for that your little archy. You never tell me what I want
to Know but I will write to Harriette nonetheless.[2]

TO *J. Roy Daniells*[3]   CC

23 February 1934   [Faber & Faber Ltd]

Dear Sir,

Thank you for your letter of February 17th, and for letting me see
your article on myself and T. E. Hulme.[4] I have made one or two trifling

---

1–Montgomery Belgion.

2–On 9 Feb. EP raged against Harriet Monroe, editor of *Poetry* (Chicago), for turning
down his Canto 37: 'Whereas the dried monkey/turd in Chikago ruined the Propertius by
printing/ a frogment . . . That old crusted capon is now sabotaging Canto 37 on the grounds
that it treats of American history/ an that while you and Yeats may have praised the earlier
cantos you haven't praised or printed cantos 31/34 or 37.

'The old twat is getting on fer 80/ so no use expecting any great rush of cerebral
development where the bases wuz allus lacking . . . Harriet's letter is almost at the level of
Squire and de Selincourt.

'obscenely disgusting in the degree of its stupidity . . .

'And that a snivveling pore miserable pityable; wd-be-mother of morons shd/ still be
holding up the traffic. is etc.'

3–J. Roy Daniells (1902–79), British-born Canadian professor of literature; taught for some
years at the University of Manitoba, and from 1946 at the University of British Columbia.
See Sandra Djwa, *Professing English: A Life of Roy Daniells* (2002).

4–Daniells, who had been living in Catford, London, and had heard a reading by TSE
at St Martin-in-the-Fields – 'you looked much more human and approachable than I had
expected' – asked TSE to comment on an essay he had written including remarks on TSE's
indebtedness to T. E. Hulme: see 'T. S. Eliot and His Relation to T. E. Hulme', *University
of Toronto Quarterly* 2 (1932–3), 380–96. See further Michael Roberts, *T. E. Hulme* (F&F,
1938); Alun R. Jones, *The Life and Opinions of T. E. Hulme* (?1960); Ronald Schuchard,

remarks on the margin, but on the whole I think there is very little to correct, and I enjoyed reading your essay very much.

You might find some development of some of the ideas in my recently published pamphlet *After Strange Gods*.[1]

Yours sincerely,
[T. S. Eliot]

TO *H. Watt*[2]

CC

23 February 1934   [*The Criterion*]

Dear Mr Watt,

In reply to your letter of the 20th, the rates of the *Criterion* are £2 per thousand words. These rates are invariable, and are what Mr Yeats has received from us before; we have never made any exceptions in favour of distinguished authors.

The date of publication would be about the 15th of June. I should be glad if you will let me know that our proposal to publish Mr Yeats's essay[3] is accepted.

Yours sincerely,
[T. S. Eliot]

'Hulme of Original Sin', *Eliot's Dark Angel: Intersections of Life and Art* (1999), 52–69; Robert Ferguson, *The Short Sharp Life of T. E. Hulme* (2012).

1–Published on 22 Feb. 1934. Advertised in Spring 1934: 'In this series of three lectures (the Page-Barbour Lectures at the University of Virginia, 1933) Mr Eliot develops, after fifteen years' interval, the implications of his essay *Tradition and the Individual Talent*. He maintains that the weakness of modern literature, indicative of the weakness of the modern world in general, is a religious weakness; and that all our social problems, including those of religion and criticism, begin and end in the religious problem. He proceeds to consider the meaning and the relation of the terms *tradition* and *orthodoxy*, not in the exact theological sense, but as they can be used in criticism; and discusses the consequence of heterodoxies as displayed in modern literature, adducing instances from the work of several distinguished contemporaries.'

2–H. Watt, A. P. Watt Literary Agency, Hastings House, Strand, London.

3–WBY's introduction to *The Holy Mountain*, published as 'Initiation Upon a Mountain', C. 13 (July 1934), 537–56.

73

TO *I. A. Richards*[1]   TS Magdalene

24 February 1934   Faber & Faber Ltd

Dear Richards,

Thank you for your letter.[2] Your invitation revives the temptation – a letter from Rylands had nearly put me off it. I ought not to come – still, it is three weeks off – yes I will, just for the night – any night you like except Wednesday. I console myself by pretending that I ought to see plays – have just been to Sean O'Casey's, which has real merit mixed in with maudlin sentiment.[3] Thank you very much.

Abercrombie was certainly a shock.[4] I didn't think he could be as bad as that.

Herbert can be very good when he relaxes like that, but that seldom happens in his public utterances.[5] When he gets into philosophical matters it seems to me that there is always something of the amateur about him.

I rather hope that Bottrall will improve on you with time.[6] There seems to me good solid work in it, nothing flashy, and at least greater maturity than in the Oxford Group.

If you find you *have* anything very damaging to say about the *Strange Gods* I had rather hear it from you than anybody.[7] It will get so much abuse of a stupid sort, and that sort of criticism always tends to confirm one in one's prejudices, which is bad. I wish some of my reviewers could be compelled to rewrite their articles in Basic, bazic, Bassic (I think I am

1–I. A. Richards (1893–1979), theorist of literature, education and communication studies: see Biographical Register.

2–IAR wrote (20–3 Feb.) to invite TSE to the undergraduate Marlowe Society production of *Antony and Cleopatra*, dir. George ('Dadie') Rylands (Mon. 12 – Sat. 17 Mar.), and to stay with them for the weekend. See IAR, *Letters*, 74–5. The party went to the play on Tues. 13 Mar.

3–See 'Mr Eliot's Pageant Play', TLS, 7 June 1934: '[W]hat might be called the modest or non-sublime approach to poetic drama has become almost a convention. They take the popular stage forms today (the modern "folk" forms), such as musical comedy or *revue*, and use them as a basis. There was recently Mr O'Casey's *Within the Gates*; and echoes of its sing-song choruses, its pervasive harping on modern down-and-outs find their way into *The Rock* . . .'

4–'Yes Lascelles Abercombie it was – like a mouthful of dry slightly mouldy flour. I did immensely enjoy your charitable grins.' Lascelles Abercrombie (1881–1938), poet and critic.

5–Referring to HR's spoof 'How to Get a Museum Job'.

6–'[Ronald] Bottrall I've read through two or three times at intervals – without anything yet more definite than reminiscent smells of other poets coming into my head.' Bottrall's *Festivals of Fire* (F&F) was published on 22 Feb. 1934.

7–'*After Strange Gods*. Well I don't see really anything I must disagree with – but I'll read it again with a less sympathetic eye. But there are lots of things I should sometime like to say . . .'

being converted, but must read the book before I commit myself, at present my attitude is similar to that towards Social Credit). There will be a very animated review by Pound, at all events.

Yours ever
T. S. E.

TO *Valentine Dobrée*[1] MS Brotherton

24 February 1934 Faber & Faber Ltd

Dear Mrs Dobrée

I postponed writing to thank you for a delightful weekend until I had the photographs to enclose.[2] You will not thank me for them. The photographer is maladroit: but there is just sufficient likeness to the originals (no more) to serve the purpose for which they were taken: a reminder to myself of pleasant memories. I am sorry not to have been able to include Georgina;[3] but *if* I may be invited again, I shall hope to include her.

Yours very sincerely,
T. S. Eliot

TO *Henry Eliot* TS Houghton

24 February 1934 Faber & Faber Ltd

Dear Henry,

Thank you very much for your letter of the 13th.[4] I have been worrying rather about you in this extreme cold weather, which could not have made the operations on your teeth any pleasanter. But if you were having abscesses I hope that you will feel better in the event. I was poisoned by abscesses in 1925, you know, and have a permanent slight cloud in my right eye which is attributed to them. I suppose Chardy went to a nursing

1 – Valentine Dobrée (1894–1974) – née Gladys May Mabel Brooke-Pechell, daughter of Sir Augustus Brooke-Pechell, 7th Baronet – was a noted artist, novelist and short-story writer. She published novels: *Your Cuckoo Sings by Kind* (1927), and *The Emperor's Tigers* (F&F, 1929); a collection of stories, *To Blush Unseen* (1935); and a volume of verse, *This Green Tide* (F&F, 1965). She married Bonamy Dobrée in 1913. See further *Valentine Dobrée 1894–1974* (The University Gallery Leeds, 2000).
2 – At Mendham Priory, Harleston, Norfolk.
3 – The Dobrées' daughter Georgina (1930–2008) was to become a renowned clarinettist.
4 – Not traced.

home; and I hope she will be none the worse for the cold weather either. Six pounds is rather on the small side, isn't it. I hope she will have several children. I sent a wire in reply, addressed it to 'Miss Priscilla Stearns Talcott', which I hope was delivered to somebody. I will write a line to Agnew. Priscilla[1] I suppose is named for great grandmother Priscilla Cushing Stearns, a formidable looking old lady.[2]

By the way, I think that Eliot House Library ought to have up a copy of that miniature of the Rev. Andrew Eliot which Cousin Jenny gave me. If she could provide another, I believe Merriman would be glad to have it framed and stuck up. He was for a time President of Harvard, and he's an ancestor of Mrs Merriman as well as of C. W. Eliot.

I am grateful to you for all your and Theresa's kindness to Mrs Monro. She has been very kind. She may not have told you that she rendered great assistance in helping me to get off to America. But for her I should have had to go without my bag which held razor, pyjamas etc.; she went back and fetched it, I having left it behind in the excitement, and got to the train just in time.

Morley went straight to Baltimore, I think; but you will have seen him by now.

After Strange Gods is out here (I sent you a copy, our books are better than Harcourt's) and has had one (abusive) review on the day of publication (but the *New Statesman* is definitely anti-clerical anyway).[3]

I am now in very pleasant furnished lodgings, two rooms, excellent servants, and meals served in my rooms, so that I am quite to myself. And I visit friends at weekends now and again, but I must not again till after Easter, as I have too much to do writing the words for a pageant. I was glad to leave the boarding house; the landlady had an eccentric (to say the least) uncle living with her who must be a great trial to the poor lady, who tried to keep up genteel appearances without any natural gifts for

1 – TSE's great-niece Priscilla Stearns Talcott, newly born on 19 Feb. 1934.
2 – Priscilla Stearns, *née* Cushing (1779–1856), wife of Thomas Stearns (1778–1826), maternal great-grandfather.
3 – K. John, 'The Grand Inquisitor', NS 7 (24 Feb. 1934), 274. TSE 'does not want the beliefs of a group at all, but the beliefs of *his* group: no other form of orthodoxy need apply. In other words, you must *start* from dogmatic theology . . . The enjoyment school will never understand this complacent advocacy of the rack and the thumbscrew, this horror of all diversity in opinion, taste, feeling, this old-maidish dislike of "nature boon". Is it the mere love of priesthood and dictatorship, or a kind of spiritual agoraphobia, a blind fear of the complexities of life and thought? "Worm-eaten with liberalism" – in Mr Eliot's own words – we cannot judge.'

running a boarding house; he is irascible, and I believe is the reason why the servants were constantly changing.

> With love to Theresa,
> Your affectionate brother,
> Tom

TO *Laurence Pollinger*

27 February 1934   [Faber & Faber Ltd]

Dear Pollinger,

There is a young man from Cambridge named *Alistair Cooke*, at present in America on a Commonwealth Fellowship who is devoting himself to dramatic criticism. He has not yet produced anything, but I have some hopes of him, and I think he is worth getting hold of.

He has sent me a short article on Eugene O'Neill's new plays:[1] it is not suitable in form for the *Criterion*, and he did not suppose it would be, so he has asked me to pass it on to an agent to try to place. Would you, or the appropriate department of Curtis Brown's, undertake this if I sent it to you?

Personally, I don't think this article is suitable for publication in England at all, as it is primarily concerned with two new plays of O'Neill's, which I don't think have been produced here. What I have in mind is not so much this article, but the possibilities of future books from him.

> Yours sincerely,
> [T. S. Eliot]

1 – 'Salvation and Eugene O'Neill'.

TO *Marianne Moore*   TS Rosenbach Museum & Library

27 February 1934   Faber & Faber Ltd

Dear Miss Moore,

Thank you for your letter of the 15th.[1] I shall now wait to hear the result of Morley's talk with you, and I must say that I should be very sorry if *Observations* were not included. What I really had in mind was a complete volume of your work up to date, leaving out only such poems as the author wished absolutely to suppress; and I hope that these may be very few.

Yours very sincerely,
T. S. Eliot

TO *Hallie Flanagan*   TS NYPL Theater Collection

27 February 1934   Faber & Faber Ltd

Dear Mrs Flanagan,

I am glad to hear from you at last, as I had been wondering whether you had ever arrived in England at all.[2] I had hoped that you would have been in London last week, as I had arranged to have tickets kept for you for the production of the Chester Mystery Play and *The Dance of Death* at the Westminster Theatre last Sunday evening. The plays were produced by Tyrone Guthrie and Rupert Doone, and I thought extremely well done. The producers were very sorry that you were not present. There is to be another performance of them next Sunday evening, and if you are free, I do hope that you will go. In that case, will you write to Rupert Doone, 5 Albany Terrace, N.W.1? I am sure that he would like to meet you after the performance, if you could arrange that with him; and I am very sorry that I shall not be free to go myself.

---

1 – 'I am much helped and encouraged by this [TSE's letter of 31 Jan.], if you are not taking too cheerful a view . . . My scruple was that I could not offer work to anyone before offering it to Macmillan; but also, I hesitate to revive *Observations* [her second volume, 1924]; at least for the present. I shall show my newer things to Mr Morley and shall see what I can do to finish what I had spoken of offering you ['The Frigate Pelican'] for the *Criterion*.' C. 13 (July 1934), 557–60.

FVM called on MM and her mother at 260 Cumberland Street, Brooklyn, on 27 Feb., and she was charmed by him. 'His much mind and his kindness of heart,' she reported to TSE the next day, 'would lead one almost into particularizing. People laid hold of such a person . . .'
2 – Flanagan wrote from Dartington Hall, Devon, that she had been having 'a most interesting time', and that she could be reached at Dartmouth House, London, over the next week.

Would you be free to lunch with me on Saturday next the 3rd? If you can, I will suggest a restaurant at which to meet.[1]

Yours sincerely,
T. S. Eliot

P.S. If you are only to be in town this week, and if you can't lunch on Saturday, would you please let me know, so that we can arrange some other meeting?

TO *M. le Marquis de Champvans de Farémont*[2]   CC

27 February 1934   [Faber & Faber Ltd]

Dear Sir,

I have to thank you for your letter of the 6th February, and to express my appreciation of the great honour which you and your Council have done me in making me a Corresponding Honorary Member of the Institut Littéraire et Artistique de France.

Please convey my deep sense of appreciation to your Council.

I am, my dear Sir,
Yours faithfully,
[T. S. Eliot]

TO *Francis Underhill*   CC

1 March 1934   [Faber & Faber Ltd]

Dear Father Underhill,

I now have your letter of the 27th, and I am writing to confirm what I said in conversation, that I will gladly come to address the school on the Speech Day, June 30th.[3]

1–Flanagan had lunch with TSE, and tea the next day. 'We have had the most crazy and amusing times, and we talk entirely in Sweeney-ese. Eliot thinks [her production of] Sweeney the best play he ever saw, and of course this makes me think him very discerning' (cited in Bentley, *Hallie Flanagan*, 149).

2–Le Marquis de Champvans de Farémont, historian; editor of the journal *Diplomatie et Salons*; member of L'Académie Royale Hispano-Américaine des sciences et des arts.

3–Underhill invited TSE to speak and to distribute the prizes at the King's School, Rochester, on Speech Day, Sat. 30 June. 'I am Chairman of the Governors of the School which is a very ancient one, it seems to have been founded by Ethelbert and Augustine at the same time as the Cathedral in 604, and was refounded by King Henry VIII. It is a very good public school . . .'

I shall be glad to have a word about this ceremony when I come down for the night on Monday of Easter week.[1]

Yours very sincerely,
[T. S. Eliot]

TO *Ottoline Morrell*[2]

TS Texas

2 March 1934 — Faber & Faber Ltd

My dear Ottoline,

Thank you for your card. I continue to feel that my presence at large gatherings of a purely social nature is unsuitable, and I have no great stomach for them, though I mind less when wholly amongst complete strangers. I except the theatre, of course: to that I sometimes go.

I should be happy to come in late any other day than on your Thursdays – except that Wednesdays are always inconvenient, as I have a committee that lasts late. On the whole I should prefer to wait until after Easter for making *new* acquaintances! as I am confoundedly busy trying to finish my Pageant. But I should like to come to see you.[3]

1–Underhill (21 Feb.) invited TSE to stay for the Monday night of Holy Week: 26 Mar.
2–Lady Ottoline Morrell (1873–1938), hostess and patron: see Biographical Register.
3–OM's journal, 10 Feb. 1934: 'I saw T. S. Eliot last week – quite nice – & quite sympathetic – but of course really so American – he never knows English people – nor their queer humanity the thing that interested him was whether a Catholic priest had really told Asquith that a man whom Asquith had not pardoned was guilty – He was indignant that any priest could have given away confession. – . . . He & I were lamenting that so few of the young men were aware – spiritually – or had any religion . . . & we both agreed how arid & dull it made them – & then I felt how hard it is of us sitting here at tea, condemn them . & I said but isn't it horrid of us criticising them thus – can they give themselves Faith? He was quite angry at this & said that "it was *necessary* to criticise" – What an *Ecclesiastical* mind he has. – Rule – Order – paramount – none of the good old English Compromise, & human leniency . . . Will such an Ecclesiastical mind as he has – ever – remain happily in the Anglican Church?' (BL Add Ms 88886/04/034)

OM's journal, 17 Mar.: 'T. S. E. came in & we were then talking about Virginia. I said she had "developed" & grown more human. T. S. E. said "Mellowed" Oh no she is too young to mellow. I perhaps have mellowed. – Tom said that he had mellowed. I said Not in your writings Tom! & I winked at Stephen. I fear T may have caught the wink in Transit . . . Tom talked of France – & the French – I asked him if he liked them – & he said he did as he understood their minds & could foresee how they would work. – [. . .] Tom said that [Joyce] was the most Self centred man – that he knew *entirely* self engrossed. I understand that & I expect his blindness helps it. . . . Tom said that Virginia's writing seemed Passé to him – quite out of date . . . T. S. E. never seems to me very clear, or very intelligent or illuminating –

'He said he had lost all power of enjoying anything he read – He read so much stuff very critically that he had got the Habit now of only criticising what he read.'

Affectionately
Tom[1]

TO *Marianne Moore*   CC

2 March 1934   [Faber & Faber Ltd]

Dear Miss Moore,

I may have given you the impression that I was anxious to impose upon you a selection of a kind different from what you wanted to do. I should like to clear this up. It seemed to me very regrettable that your earlier work was unobtainable in England, and what I wanted was a volume containing this and all subsequent work that you wanted to include. If you prefer to put the emphasis on your more recent work, we should be equally pleased to have the book; but at the same time I shall continue to put in a plea for including at least some of your previously published poems.

Yours sincerely,
[T. S. Eliot]

'March 21 . . . Last Mon: I had a very interesting tea party – Stephen Spender – & T. S. Eliot . . . Maurice Bowra & later on Virginia. T. S. E. looked very green & unwholesome – I am sure he suffers from some poisoning . . . he is very *unhygienic*. – We talked at tea about nondescript things . . . But after Virginia came. – I said to Tom that I thought he had treated Hardy badly in his book – & that opened the Sluices of our minds. Spender talked up very boldly about things in the books . . . The Jews . . . etc. & ask[ed] Tom if he realised that these things could be taken by the Nazi – to cite him as sympathising with them. That this book could be taken politically . . . He said that he himself was often accused by the Communists of treating some Social & Political Subjects in a purely intellectual way – & he knew it was True – & that is what he considered Tom was doing – quite apart from the real Importance of the subject.'

'Stephen may say things he doesn't hold to but he is sincere. T. S. E. says things from complicated motives, & is *never sincere* to himself. He has the belief in evil .. which works in people like DHL. – but doesn't evil also work on the members of the Church?'

'I believe his Church views were first started by his feeling against Bertie [Russell] – he said so in a letter to me once that he thought B *was definitely Evil* & that converted him to being a Christian. – . . .

'He is a Churchman rather than a Christian. Newman was a Churchman *&* Christian. Tom is an orthodox Churchman – not a Saint. – He is a man who is timid & needs the backing & *Safety of the Church – He loves order . . .*'

1 – OM would write to JDH on 2 Apr. 1934, presumably not long after a visit from TSE: 'tho I am very fond of him & *think he is a lovely poet* I never liked his criticism & I think he knows that we come from diametrically opposite "Traditions" . . . I cannot bear *Ecclesiastical* Religion – & he I suppose finds it necessary . . . & it gives him certainty & security' (King's OM/JDH/31).

2 March 1934   [*The Criterion*]

Dear Miss Monroe,

I have had some mysterious correspondence from Pound, from which very little emerges in a form apprehensible to my intelligence: but I gather that you have either declined or held in suspense one of his Cantos, on the ground that I had either not seen it or failed in some way to express my approval.

Whatever the facts may be, let me make clear my own position with regard to future Cantos. Pound has never been enthusiastic about releasing Cantos one or two at a time for the *Criterion*, and in consequence I have never pressed the matter. Several years ago he gave me the Malatesta Cantos, since included in the volume of Cantos which Farrar and Rhinehart published in New York and which we published here. He made an exception in offering these, because he considered that they formed a kind of unity within the whole.

I have not, in consequence, seen any of the Cantos which he has written since the first thirty. I believe that one or two have appeared in the *New English Weekly*, which I seldom see. But Pound knows perfectly well that I should be glad to publish any Canto that he cared to have appear in the *Criterion*. My firm expects to publish in book form all subsequent Cantos in such sections as he wishes, and we expect to bring out a volume containing the next ten or twelve in the autumn.

The fact of my not having seen etc. a particular Canto in question is, accordingly, irrelevant to the whole matter.

Yours sincerely,

[T. S. Eliot]

1–Harriet Monroe (1860–1936), founder and co-editor of *Poetry: A Magazine of Verse* (Chicago). See Ann Massa, 'Harriet Monroe and T. S. Eliot: A curious and typical response', *Notes and Queries* 230 [32: 3], Sept. 1985, 380–2; *Dear Editor: A History of* Poetry *in Letters: The First Fifty Years, 1912–1962*, ed. Joseph Parisi and Stephen Young (2002).

3 March 1934   [Faber & Faber Ltd]

Dear Mr Bolshakoff,

Thank you for your letter of the 28th February. I note your new arrangements for the academy.[1] Your intention of limiting the membership to a very restricted number is, I think, sound. But if you do secure the adhesion of any important Roman clergy in this country, I would urge you strongly to try to interest also Mr Christopher Dawson, who is to my mind the most important social philosopher in England. I find Mr Dawson's views nearer to my own, on the whole, than those of anyone else of whom I can think. Fr Victor Demant,[2] whose name has already been mentioned, and who is a friend of Mr Maurice Reckitt,[3] would also be most valuable to you.

I am likely to be able to attend a preliminary discussion soon after Easter; I certainly could not make the time to do anything of that sort during Lent.

I must say, in reply to a previous letter of yours just before you left England, that I am very sceptical of the possibility of Catholic association with any fascist movement that is likely to prosper here. I am indeed doubtful whether the principles of the Church and those of fascism are not wholly opposed.[4]

> With all good wishes,
> Yours sincerely,
> [T. S. Eliot]

---

1 – Bolshakoff's 'Declaration of the International Academy of Christian Sociologists' characterised the organisation as 'a society of Christian social thinkers, workers and statesmen, founded for the study of social problems along the principles laid down by the Encyclicals "Rerum Novarum" and "Quadragesimo Anno" accepted as the best exposition of Christian Sociology by the majority of Sociologists of various denominations. The membership of the Academy is open to every Christian; i.e., to all validly baptised persons professing the Nicean Creed, rejection of which involves forfeiture of membership . . . The purposes of the Academy are the study of social problems along the principles given in its declaration; promoting social and international peace; defence of the Christian religion and morality against persecution or defamation . . . The number of Academicians is restricted to forty and they all are elected for life.'
2 – The Revd Vigo Auguste Demant (1893–1983), theologian: see Biographical Register.
3 – For Reckitt see letter to him, 31 Aug. 1934, below.
4 – Letter not traced; but Bolshakoff told TSE on 29 May 1934: 'I just published in Shanghai my study "The Christianity and The Fascism". My leading ideas there are accepted by the pact of Tokio signed . . . by leaders of Russian Fascists of Far East and in America, who are united now in a single All-russian Fascist Party. General Araki, wellknown philosopher

5 March 1934   Faber & Faber Ltd

Cheer Up Br. Delano[1] Here's another letter from Old Posum well well after all this time whats there to talk About Well I DID write to Arriett as clearly as posbil considerin your obnubbilation of the subject Thanks about Marianne I have wrote again.[2] SELECT ESSAYS or Little Flowers of Br. Rabbit is still being cast off PRUDENTIUS i mean PROperetc. thats settled Nothink to do but Whait for Cantoos Does Orage[3] still consort with Ourspenskys etc.[4] I hope not. I see what hes after all editors has the delusion that controversies etc. cheer things up and increase circulation They rarely if ever.

Futility of controversy.

Where facts are wrong that should be stated. But the what the Hell IS a fact?

All good men should be united upon etc. but how get em to agree as to what IS the vital issues etc.

Alteration of financial system etc. one of few things praps Stavisky is Dead[5] but what Good does that do Rothermere & Mosley is still alive

My ed is wooley from tryin to write verse (I said verse not pottery) that that can be delivered 'recited' by any sort of people that can be got to recite it but what the Hell they alltalk like maple syrup I mean the imitation kind

---

and leader of Japanese people, approved the pact cordially. His declaration to the General Secretary of Allrussian Fascist Party is truly remarkable. By Pact of Tokio the Party recognizes in its first article that the Holy Christian and Orthodox Faith is the source and the basis of the ideology of the party which promises solemnly to work under the guidance and the advice of Russian Episcopacy and not to undertake anything against the Church faith or morality. So after one year of work I obtained the full and unconditional acceptance of my ideas by the most powerful Russian party, which in [. . .] future will rule over Russia. That been for me a great consolation. Certainly the ideology of Russian fascists is very distant from that of Germany & even of Italians.'

1 – Delano was a seventeenth-century French Huguenot ancestor of Franklin Delano Roosevelt (1882–1945), Democrat and 32nd President of the USA, 1933–45.

2 – EP informed TSE on 27 Feb.: 'MARIANNE SEZ if you'll "make it new instead of selected" she'll be DEE/lighted . . . . Marianne now okkpyd writing crit of Bull WMS [William Carlos Williams.] I dunno IF M/ ever got yr/ invitation/ her letter dont read as if she had had it.'

3 – A. R. Orage, of the *New English Weekly*; see letter to him, 16 Mar. 1934, below.

4 – P. D. Ouspensky (1878–1947), Russian esotericist: exponent of the doctrinal 'system' of George Gurdjieff.

5 – Serge Alexandre Stavisky (1886–1934), a Polish Jew, became a French citizen in 1930. He was charged with massive frauds which somehow involved senior members of the French government; and he was almost certainly assassinated, by persons unknown, on 8 Jan. 1934.

Did I say Wilson seems good to me but that other fellow Farrel is it praps the books he was reviewing didnt give him afair chance
My Air is growin a bit and its white pretty when washed.

Yours etc.

Tp

I See I forgot to take a carboon of this valble letter. Anyway, nothing in it about terms.

TO *Idris Davies*[1]   CC

6 March 1934   [*The Criterion*]

Dear Sir,

I have read the enclosed poem with much interest and approval.[2] After careful thought, however, I have come to the conclusion that the *Criterion* is not quite the place for it. I think that the *Adelphi* is the obvious vehicle for publication, and I hope that you will send it to the editor, Sir Richard Rees, telling him at the same time that I liked the poem, and thought it suitable for his review.

Yours faithfully,

[T. S. Eliot]

TO *T. O. Beachcroft*   CC

6 March 1934   [*The Criterion*]

Dear Beachcroft,

I should be very glad if you cared to undertake Basil Willey's book *The Seventeenth Century Background*. I think Willey is worth treating carefully; and I can, alas, give you plenty of time, because I have had such an abundance of reviews that the June issue is now practically filled. I hope you will like to review this book; please drop my Secretary a line for it.[3]

1–Idris Davies (1905–53), Welsh poet: a former coalminer who lost a finger from hacking at the coal face; a veteran of the 1926 General Strike; and a self-taught man who became a schoolteacher and highly respected poet. See his *Gwalia Deserta* ('Wasteland of Wales', 1938); *The Collected Poems of Idris Davies*, ed. Islwyn Jenkins (1972, 1980).
2–Davies submitted a free-verse poem 'Rhymney' – about the colliery township in Monmouthshire where he had started work as a miner on leaving elementary school.
3–Review in C. 13 (July 1934), 692–6.

I should also like to know whether a story you left with me before I went to America has subsequently been published anywhere else. It is the story about the physician observing a case of meningitis through a microscope, looking into a child's eye. I thought it fascinating and particularly gruesome, and have a mind to publish it if you have not published it elsewhere.

Yours ever,
[T. S. Eliot]

TO *Stephen Spender*   TS Northwestern

6 March 1934   *The Criterion*

Dear Stephen,

I enclose two poems which I have had in reserve for some time, as I thought that you ought to have them back. I don't mean to call upon you very often for poems for the *Criterion*, although on the other hand I shall always be delighted to have anything which you would particularly like to have published in the *Criterion*; but in general I like to keep the poetry in the *Criterion* for people who are unknown or only beginning to be known.

Yours ever,
T. S. E.

TO *Dorothy Richards*   TS Magdalene

6 March 1934   Faber & Faber Ltd

Dear Mrs Richards,

Thank you for your letter.[1] Tuesday 13th will suit me very well, and I can eat anything you like (not tripe), as fish is only compulsory on Wednesdays and Fridays. I am very glad to hear that the Coultons will be coming.

I will take the 11.50 on Tuesday morning.

1 – Letter not traced.

I shall be interested to know what you think of *The Dance of Death*. I wondered whether your alteration of the title to *Paid on Both Sides* was a conscious or unconscious criticism.[1]

Yours sincerely,
T. S. Eliot

TO *C. A. Siepmann*[2]   cc

6 March 1934   [Faber & Faber Ltd]

Dear Siepmann,

I wonder whether you could find time in the midst of your official duties to read for us and give a reader's report on the manuscript of a new book by Rudolf Arnheim? A couple of years ago he wrote an excellent book on the Film, the translation of which we published,[3] and he has now produced a similar volume on Broadcasting.[4]

I have only skimmed through the book myself, and there is a certain amount of technicality which is rather beyond me.

We should of course pay the usual reader's fee for your trouble in the matter, but I wish that you might consider it also almost as coming within the scope of your official duties. If you consent to read it, I should like [you] to consider at the same time whether the book is important enough to be valuable from the point of view of the B.B.C., both for the use of people actually engaged in broadcasting work and also for the edification of the general public.

As I say, the book seems to me excellent, but we feel that we must have an expert opinion.

Yours sincerely,
[T. S. Eliot]

---

1 – Richards diary, Tues., 13 Mar. 1934: '*Eliot & Antony & Cleopatra*. Coultons arrived just after one! . . . Eliot, lunch partyish! Afterwards G G C [Coulton] & TSE discussed patriotism & Chr. Dawson. G G C says there is so much intellectual bootlegging in Catholicism . . . The Index itself is too holy for the Laity to read it! In afternoon . . . Iv went for Eliot over his last book, . . . Takes his *Pageant* very seriously (D. feels he is vain: and it shows in his prose) He didn't think much of *The Dance of Death*. Goodish dinner . . . Sat up till 1.0. Talking about it & drinking whiskey heavily. T. S. E. seeming very content.'
2 – Charles Arthur Siepmann (1899–1985), radio producer and educator: see Biographical Register.
3 – Rudolf Arnheim, *Film* (F&F, 1933).
4 – Rudolf Arnheim, *Radio*, trans. Margaret Ludwig and Herbert Read (F&F, 1936).

TO *Denis Devlin*[1]   CC

6 March 1934   [*The Criterion*]

Dear Mr Devlin,

I was glad to get your letter of the 30th January, and to hear from you
after having talked with Brian Coffey.[2] I like some of the enclosed poems,
but I don't think there is anything here which I like quite enough. I am
sorry, and I do hope that you will send me other things from time to time.

Thank you very much indeed for your kind letter. I hope that if you are
ever in London you will let me know.

I now see that you ask me to send back the poems in a fortnight. I am,
as a matter of fact, dealing with them much more promptly than is my
habit, but I do apologise for the delay.

With all best wishes,
Yours sincerely,
[T. S. Eliot]

TO *Evan Charteris*[3]   CC

7 March 1934   [Faber & Faber Ltd]

My dear Sir,

The information has reached me, indirectly, that you have a set of postcards which is being delayed by my failure to produce a biography of
Coleridge. I therefore enclose such a biography, which I hope will suit
your purposes.[4]

---

1 – Denis Devlin (1908–59), Irish poet and career diplomat; close friend of Brian Coffey, with
whom he published *Poems* (1930). *Collected Poems* was edited by J. C. C. Mays (1989).
2 – Devlin, who in his letter praised TSE's work as poet and critic, submitted 'a few poems'.
He added that he was 'trying to persuade Mr Yeats to publish them. I'm afraid he won't,
alack!

'I think you will not like what I write, though you may admit that it is well done. It is
too sensual and lacks control, I know that myself. But perhaps you will find something to
praise.'

For Coffey, see letter to him, 5 June 1934, below.
3 – The Hon. Sir Evan Charteris (1864–1940), biographer, barrister, arts administrator;
Chair of the National Portrait Gallery Trustees from 1928; Chair of the Board of the Tate
Gallery, 1934.
4 – This text was written to accompany the reproduction in black and white of the portrait
of Coleridge by Peter Vandyke (1795) on the verso, and was no. 192 of a series of postcards
issued by the National Portrait Gallery in which living writers summed up those of the past.
It was issued in early May 1934, at 3d. TSE posted a copy to his sister Ada Sheffield on 11
May 1934.

I am,

Yours faithfully,

[T. S. Eliot]

[Enclosure]

SAMUEL TAYLOR COLERIDGE 1772–1834

When five years old had read the *Arabian Nights*. Christ's Hospital and Cambridge. Metaphysician and poet. His life was ill-regulated: weak, slothful, a voracious reader, he contracted an unhappy marriage and much later the habit of taking laudanum. Described his own character in his great *Ode to Dejection* (1802). The greatest English literary critic, he was also the greatest intellectual force of his time. Probably influenced Newman, Maurice,[1] and the Young Tories; and died as the guest of Mr Gillman of Highgate.[2]

T. S. Eliot

(81 words).

TO *Gabriel Hebert* CC

8 March 1934 [Faber & Faber Ltd]

Dear Father Gabriel,

Thank you for your letter of the 6th with the enclosed outline of your book, which I have discussed with Geoffrey Faber.[3] As I have said,

---

Charteris replied on 21 Mar., 'I am so very much obliged to you for your admirable Coleridge – It will be a valuable addition for the Coleridge Lamb exhibition which we are proposing to hold this summer – I only hope we have not bothered you too much about the postcard but we were nervous lest you might have forgotten it.'

1–F. D. Maurice (1805–72), theologian; religious author, controversialist; Christian Scientist.

2–When copying out these lines for EVE in the 1960s, TSE added an apologetic postscript: 'Slothful? but of incessant mental activity, and immense output of writings.'

3–*Liturgy and Society* (F&F, 1935). Hebert wrote: 'I have taken counsel with others, and I am also clear in my own mind, that I want to offer this Book to you rather than to S.P.C.K.: if, that is to say, it turns out to be written in a manner that is suitable for the public whom you reach.' His proposed volume, a theological survey to be entitled *The Liturgy and The Church*, was to cover an immense amount of ground, from 'The Early Church: Christianity as a Mystery-religion', through 'The Middle Ages' and 'The Return of Classical Christianity', to the present opportunity for the Church of England. 'The reunion of Christendom is possible only on the basis of the common faith, not of religious idealism,' he wrote in his outline. In his letter he concluded: 'I feel sure that the idea is sound and is capable of being carried through.'

whether the book ultimately comes to us or to the S.P.C.K. depends on the ultimate form it takes; but I hope very much that the book may be ours.

I find your outline extremely interesting. I have at the moment only one criticism to offer, which I put with all modesty and with a proper sense of my lack of qualification to criticise at all. Your book covers very much more ground that I had expected. I am afraid lest the importance of what you will have to say about the present and the future in connection with the place and conception of the function of Liturgy in Church life may be rather submerged in such a comprehensive historical treatment. I cannot help wondering whether you are assuming too little knowledge, or rather, I think, too little previous thought, on the part of the public, rather than too much.

I take it that with such a book we aim to reach the many people who are sympathetic to the Christian faith, and whose minds are frequently concerned with it; but who have no conviction and who are not active members of the Church. There is, of course, a much larger public again outside of that, which I fear simply refuses to look at any book dealing with such matters at all. But for the public which I believe it is possible to reach, I feel that such a long preface in the way of historical treatment as you seem to have in mind might be somewhat discouraging. For example, I feel with reference to page 2 that the type of reader the book will meet hardly needs to be put through any elaborate discussion of the question whether Christianity is merely one amongst a variety of religions. I think you may almost assume an acceptance of the uniqueness of the Christian faith.

Perhaps it is merely a matter of arrangement. I believe at least that the reader ought to be given a clear grasp of the actuality of the problems you have to discuss, in the beginning, even if you revert to a historical account afterwards, as a necessary preparation. In short, the outline given suggests a book which might appear to most readers an historical account without any special emphasis. But I know from experience that a brief synopsis of a projected book is often capable of giving quite another impression to the reader than what is in the author's mind.

I want you to remain convinced, however, that I am tremendously interested in the subject and in your book on it. I shall hope to hear from you again as soon as you have time to write.

Yours very sincerely,

[T. S. Eliot]

TO *George Barker*[1]   TS Texas

8 March 1934   Faber & Faber Ltd

Dear Mr Barker,

I am finally writing to return you 'Elegy Anticipating Death', because I simply can't see what can be done with it. I like the poem, though not as much as 'Daedalus', the rhythms of which are more interesting. The point is that our Ariel series has been discontinued, and this poem is too short for anything but periodical publication. I obviously couldn't use it very soon in the *Criterion*, because in a quarterly you cannot have the same poets appearing very frequently. So I am afraid that it is a question of saving this for inclusion in a small book: the smallest that we publish are those of the size of Herbert Read's *End of the War*, or *The Dance of Death*, which can be sold for half a crown.

Of course a volume of poems would be a different matter. If you are ever in London I should be glad if you would come and see me.

Yours sincerely,
T. S. Eliot

FROM *Ezra Pound* TO *The Editor,* The New English Weekly[2]

8 March 1934

MR ELIOT'S MARE'S NEST[3]

Mr Eliot's thesis, nowhere so clearly expressed in his text as in the jacket-announcement, is that: 'The weakness of modern literature, indicative of the weakness of the modern world in general, is a religious weakness, and that all our social problems, including those of literature and criticism, begin and end in a religious problem.'[4]

---

1 – George Barker (1913–91), poet and author: see Biographical Register.
2 – *The New English Weekly* (1932–49), ed. A. R. Orage, 1932–4, and Philip Mairet, 1934–48.
3 – This is a review by EP of *ASG*, in *New English Weekly* (*NEW*) 4 (8 Mar. 1934), 500.
4 – The blurb of *After Strange Gods* – probably written by TSE – reads: 'In this series of three lectures (The Page-Barbour Lectures at the University of Virginia, 1933) Mr Eliot develops, after fifteen years' interval, the implications of his essay *Tradition and the Individual Talent*. He maintains that the weakness of modern literature, indicative of the weakness of the modern world in general, is a religious weakness; and that all our social problems including those of literature and criticism, begin and end in the religious problem. He proceeds to consider the meaning and the relation of the terms *tradition* and *orthodoxy*, not in the exact

As there is muddle and confusion even in this statement, one is not surprised that a verbatim reprint of lectures gives no solid ground for argument.

In the first place the main idea is neither true nor expressed with sufficient precision.

The fact is that 'religion' long since resigned. Religion in the person of its greatest organised European institution resigned. The average man now thinks of religion either as a left-over or an irrelevance.

In the 'Ages of Faith,' meaning the Ages of Christian faith, religion in the person of the Church concerned itself with ethics. It concerned itself specifically with economic discrimination.

It concerned itself with a root dissociation of two ideas which the last filthy centuries have, to their damnation, lost.

In Dante's intellectual world certain financial activities are 'against nature'; they are damned with sodomy. The Church was not abrogating her claim to judge between good and evil along one of the most vital and intimate lines of social relation.

Creative investment, productive exchange, sharing the profits of shared risk, were considered good. Destructive parasitism was forbidden. I am not arguing, I am stating historic fact. I am not saying that the detailed regulations of mediaeval business can to advantage be resurrected in the identical forms. I am not making a plea for a return to the past.

I am asserting a known and established fact: when religion was real the church concerned itself with vital phenomena in ECONOMICS.

This is, perhaps, not the place to give the history of Protestant revolt, Leo X's desire for taxes, etc. In any case they fall outside a review of Mr Eliot's brochure, which does not even concern itself with the history or the dogma he mentions (or asserts to be a personal reality to himself).

The weakness he is gunning for [is] NOT a *religious* weakness *in something else*, but an ethical weakness *in* organised Christianity. The sacerdos has been superseded by the (often subsidised) ecclesiastical bureaucrat.

This decline was not unexpected and the Middle Ages are full of propaganda and warning against this particular danger.

---

theological sense, but as they can be used in criticism; and discusses the consequence of heterodoxies as displayed in modern literature, adducing instances from the work of several distinguished contemporaries.'

See also Christina C. Stough, 'The Skirmish of Pound and Eliot in *The New English Weekly*: A Glimpse at Their Later Literary Relationship', *Journal of Modern Literature* 10: 2 (June 1983), 231–46.

The battle was won by greed. The language of religion became imprecise, just as the language of all forms of modern flim flam, including popular and philological lectures, has become imprecise.

Mr Eliot, in a moment of inattention, has interpreted part of his bargain with the Virginia institution literally. He was asked to lecture, and then apparently found he was expected to publish what he had said verbatim, or at least he so construed his contract, and as a result the pages of this book probably say both more or less than he means, and in any case are full of lacunae.

It is highly confusing to find half way through the book that what he means by 'orthodoxy' is merely the extension of literary subject matter to certain ranges of human consciousness that inferior writers now neglect as have inferior writers in other times.[1]

E. P.

TO *Ernest Bird, Messrs Bird & Bird*   CC

8 March 1934   [Faber & Faber Ltd]

My dear Bird,

Referring to your letter of the 9th February, I enclose herewith my cheque for £66. 5. 10d. together with your statement of account. This is the most convenient moment for me to settle it.

There is one small matter which puzzles me. I want to restore (a) to my wife a canvas trunk and a leather jewel case, (b) to her mother a leather trunk and a camera. If I ask Carter Paterson to fetch them it might be the means, through the carters, of disclosing my address, which I prefer not to do. If you think of any device for concealing the traces, I shall be grateful.[2]

1 – TSE's sister Ada commented, 29 Apr. 1934: 'Does not Ezra Pound give rather free rein to his emotions? He seems a bit intemperate in his tone.'
2 – Bird suggested (9 Mar.) that TSE should send 'the effects in question' to his office, and he would then undertake 'to dispatch them in accordance with your instructions. Alternatively, I would send someone in a taxi to pick them up . . . and deliver them at the respective addresses.'

So far I have had no communication from my wife or from any of her family.

Yours sincerely,
[T. S. Eliot]

P.S. I cannot help wondering (you must have been asked) how your firm came to choose its telegraphic address.[1]

TO *Edwin Muir*[2]   CC

9 March 1934   [*The Criterion*]

My dear Muir,

I am writing to thank you for your review of my book, which I read in *The Spectator* last night.[3] It is much the most satisfactory that I have had so far – in fact almost the only one in which the writer has really criticised the book, instead of merely talking from a previously adopted point of view. You probably know as well as I do how seldom it is that a review says anything of the slightest use to the author of the book, and I find your identification of several obscurities and ambiguities very helpful. It is quite true that in several places I have either said too much or too little.

Yours very sincerely,
[T. S. Eliot]

TO *Bonamy Dobrée*[4]   CC

9 March 1934   [*The Criterion*]

My dear Bonamy,

I am quite ready to sign such a letter if there is the slightest possibility of its doing any good.[5] There are one or two points which I should like to raise first, however.

---

1 – Bird & Bird's address for telegrams was 'MORBID', which Bird explained on 9 Mar.: 'For very many years from about 1850 until the early nineties this firm was known as "Bird & Moore" although I have always understood that the said Moore was only a partner in it for a few years. By juggling the two names they eventually got at "Morbid". There is the story as I have always understood it but I cannot vouch for its accuracy.'

2 – Edwin Muir (1887–1959), Scottish poet, novelist, critic, translator: see Biographical Register.

3 – 'Mr Eliot on Evil', *Spectator* 152: 5515 (9 Mar. 1934), 378–9.

4 – Bonamy Dobrée (1891–1974), scholar, editor and critic: see Biographical Register.

5 – BD had sent (5 May) a draft of the letter that was to be published in *The Times*: see below, letter of 4 Apr. 1934. Other proposed signatories included Richard Aldington, GCF,

First, I don't quite see the principle on which the signatories are chosen. Herbert explained to me last night that it was desired to get a group of people who were without obvious political labels, and I quite see that; but isn't the present list a little too exclusively literary, with only one exception? I can't see that I have any suggestions in mind at the moment, and I am against having such a list too long; if I can think of any suggestions, I will make them: possibly a few people like the Archdeacon of Northumberland,[1] or perhaps Sir Wyndham Deedes.[2] I am a little afraid that the detachment of the present list will only signify to the readers a group of literary people who don't know what they are talking about. All this is nothing to do with my private distaste for signing anything in company with Richard Aldington, as I think one ought to swallow that sort of objection.[3]

My other chief point is whether you have, at the back of your mind, any definite proposals of the form which such a public enquiry should take? I seem to remember that there was some sort of enquiry made some years ago which was probably of a rather partial nature. We know pretty well, I think, what would come of an investigation by a committee which had on it, let us say, people like Keynes, or Stamp, or Salter. I am anticipating the sort of public correspondence which this letter might provoke, and want to be sure that the answers to objectors would be forthcoming.[4]

Eric Gill, Storm Jameson, J. B. Priestley, EP, and J. B. Trend. 'I would like comments on the proposed signatories . . . The letter of course will not go forward unless a fair proportion of people sign.'

1 – Leslie Hunter, DD (1890–1983), Archdeacon of Northumberland, 1930–39; later Bishop of Sheffield.

2 – Brigadier General Sir Wyndham Deedes (1883–1956), distinguished for his service in WW1; civil administrator (Chief Secretary to the British High Commissioner of the British Mandate of Palestine); staunch, stoic Christian: he was a social worker in Bethnal Green, London, 1931–45.

3 – In 1931, Richard Aldington had published *Stepping Heavenward,* a merciless lampoon of TSE – portrayed as 'Blessed Jeremy Cibber' – in his relationship with Vivien ('Adele Palaeologue'), which caused a permanent breach in their friendship.

BD responded to this letter, 11 Mar.: 'The principle of selection was one not only of disinterestedness from politics, but also, in my view, to suggest that there was a compact body of opinion among the intelligentsia in favour of having Douglas at least seriously considered . . . As for Aldington, I am quite prepared to drop him: I don't suppose he would carry much weight. I have not written to him yet.'

4 – 'My idea of a public enquiry would be an impartial board before whom everybody who wished to talk would come . . . I would exclude professional economists, who could be summoned, if they did not want to come of their own accord; but they would.'

My third point is a very small one. It seems to me that the first sentence is a little weak and hesitant. Wouldn't it be better to begin with a sentence put in an affirmative rather than an interrogative form?[1]

I had some words last night with Orage about this matter. He knew nothing, of course, of your letter, but gave me some information of the accuracy of which you will probably be able to gauge better than I, as I know Orage very slightly, and have never quite made him out. He told me that a certain Conservative group, either including or supported by Walter Elliot,[2] was about to issue a similar letter, also in the Correspondence Columns of *The Times*. This appears to be a kind of feeler of public sentiment. If he is right, then I think it makes this all the more desirable, possibly more useful, than it seemed to me on first reading.

Yours ever,
[T. S. E.]

TO *Ezra Pound*

TS Beinecke

9 March 1934   Faber & Faber Ltd

Well well I think now you better let me see the original version, bein as how you seems to ave boiled it down so theres nothink left but syrup.

Well only tagable tangable result so Far that I ave suscribed to the *New English Weekly*, that comes partly from havin met Orige at a cocktail party.

McNair Wilson[3] will receive notice, I have read it, good exposition I think.[4]

I shall write just to say which of your 15 points I accept and which few dont seem to mean anything..

There are some youngsters who are not too bad. Desmond Hawkins looks as if he might shape well, and I have a young Primo Carnera[5] in training at Oxford I mean although at Oxford; and the school-children of Rochester (Kent) are champin at the Bit.

1 – 'I agree that the first sentence should be positive rather than interrogatory.'
2 – Dr Walter Elliot Elliot (1888–1958): prominent Scottish Unionist Party politician; Minister of Agriculture from 1932; later Secretary of State for Scotland.
3 – R. McNair Wilson (1882–1963), Scottish physician and historian; writer of detective stories under the pseudonym Anthony Wynne.
4 – EP wrote on 10 Mar.: 'McNair Wilson might add to yr/ Econ/ library if you're fed up wiff me. Or get him into Criterion. (he's on the Times, so he must be respekkabl.' McNair Wilson's *Promise to Pay* (1934) was reviewed by BD in C. 13 (July 1934), 703–4.
5 – Walter Tomlin: see Biographical Register.

Praps us & Walter Elliot may get something done. I dont kno.

T. C. Wilson writes affably, I encourage him to Do his article on the Palgrave-Untermeyer tradition.[1]

You better trot over in June & see my Pageant.[2]

Aaron Tanu Rosen as sent me another copy of is Poems, saying e fears the first copy may have gone a Stray. I have had second immediately acknowledged. Marianne conscentiously refuses to review Williams, sayin she as already done so elsewhere.[3] What Can I do as I cant make Very much out of it myself.

yrs etc.
TP

<Forgot to add, Warm Regards.>
Please return to E/P at convenience/ and when you next write. VIDE VERSO[4]

TO *Christopher Dawson*[5]   cc

12 March 1934   [*The Criterion*]

My dear Dawson,

I have taken the liberty of giving your address to Mr Bolshakoff, who will no doubt write to you extremely fully and somewhat incoherently about his ambitious projects. I feel that I ought to tell you just what I know and what I don't know about this curious Russian. He came in to see me once and I have had a good deal of correspondence with him. One feels instinctively that this is a rather pretentious Russian nonsense, yet,

---

1 – Not done. For Wilson, see letter to him of 12 Mar. 1934, below.

2 – FVM to EP, 2 May: 'I send you a book called What's the Use of Poetry by Brer Tarbaby. What I look forward even more to sending you is his pageant play euphemistically called The Rock of Gibraltar which he has written for 45 bishops to perform somewhere in the brick-laying part of London. This is all very conferdential. Don't say a word till you see the thing yourself.'

   Whereupon EP posted off to TSE (also dated 2 May, presumably in eager error) this note: 'Lines in prospect of Mr ElYiot's Paggy/ant in Saddling Wells . . .

    Milord the BisHOP of Chichester
    Persuaded twenty three bitches ter
    Perform certain rites
    In exiguous tights
    That the devil couln't get witches for.'

3 – MM to TSE, 28 Feb. 1934: 'I was obliged to return the William Carlos Williams, having already reviewed it for *Poetry* . . .'

4 – Sentence typed at head of letter; EP had written an obscure note on the other side.

5 – Christopher Dawson (1889–1970), cultural historian: see Biographical Register.

at the same time, the man seems extremely energetic and has managed to get in touch with, and at least attract the notice of, a surprising number and variety of people. It is the sort of project which one feels one should look into very carefully before refusing to be associated with it. Some of the people I feel rather doubtful of, such as Lord Tavistock, whom however, I don't know personally. I am not greatly impressed either by the adherence of Maurice Reckitt who is a very nice fellow and an extremely zealous worker, but, I think, he is ready to take up with almost anything for a time.

I don't propose to be formally associated with this for myself unless they also secure the support of Victor Demant, who is, I think, not only a much keener intelligence but a more level head than Reckitt.

I do hope that you will be able to contribute to the *Criterion* before long, we do need your support. May I say how much I liked your recent article in *Theology*. There was hardly a word in it which I should not have liked to have written myself.

Yours sincerely,
[T. S. Eliot]

TO *D. G. Bridson*[1]   cc

12 March 1934   [*The Criterion*]

Dear Mr Bridson,

I have your letter of March 8th.[2] Mr Morley had given me the impression that you were intending to come to London to live, and I had been waiting to hear from you when you were established here.

I am afraid that I do not know very much about your reviewing, and I should be very glad if you would send me specimens which will be returned to you. Of course, you will understand that in any case there is not in the *Criterion* very much reviewing from any one reviewer. I do like to take on new people as often as possible but nearly everybody wants to review the same type of book; and I like to keep the proved reviewers as well.

1–D. G. Bridson (1910–80), radio producer, dramatist and poet, worked for thirty-five years (from 1935) as one of the most innovatory writer–producers on BBC radio, for which he produced two authoritative series, *The Negro in America* (1964) and *America since the Bomb* (1966). Later books include *The Filibuster: A Study of the Political Ideas of Wyndham Lewis* (1972) and *Prospero and Ariel: The Rise and Fall of Radio* (1971).
2–Bridson wrote from Manchester (8 Mar.) to request some reviewing.

I like your poem in the *Active Anthology* better than any of the things in that book by people whose work was unknown to me.[1] I like it better than any of those which you have sent me. I hope you will let me see more of your work from time to time.

Yours sincerely,

[T. S. Eliot]

TO *T. C. Wilson*[2] TS Beinecke

12 March 1934   *The Criterion*

My dear Mr Wilson,

I have your letter of the 27th February. I have already sent you two new books about poetry, asking you if you would review them, and if they have not arrived by the time you get this letter, they must have gone astray, and I should be glad to hear from you about it.[3] I shall certainly keep you in mind for other reviews as often as possible.

Such an essay on Palgrave as you suggest might be very valuable, and while I have always been on friendly terms with Untermeyer, I am convinced that the influence of his anthologies must be pernicious. I should be very glad to see this essay, when it is ready, as it ought to be most suitable for the *Criterion*.[4]

Yours very sincerely,

T. S. Eliot

1 – 'Second Hymn for the People of England', 221–3, opens – after citing the opening of 'The Hollow Men' – 'We are the hollow men. We are the fools / Who run the business . . .'
2 – Ann Arbor, Michigan. Wilson, the young editor of *Westminster Magazine*, had already written a review of *New Country, an Anthology of Prose and Poetry by The Authors of New Signatures*, ed. Michael Roberts, which EP encouraged him to send on to TSE: see C. 13 (Apr. 1934), 485–7.
3 – Wilson, review of Charles Williams, *Reason and Beauty in the Poetic Mind*; James Sutherland, *Meaning of Poetry*: C. 13 (July 1934), 673–5.
4 – 'I am working on an essay dealing with Palgrave and his influence, wherein I hope to show the fundamental defects of Palgrave's method of selection and how these defects have been present in the anthologies since Palgrave's time, particularly in those of Mr Louis Untermeyer. I believe further that Palgrave's influence has been limited not only to anthologists, but has left its mark on much present-day criticism of poetry.' In the event, the essay was not written.

12 March 1934   Faber & Faber Ltd

Dear Ezzum thts all right only you forgot to say whether pharaohs used camels or not he seems an intelligent boy[1] and has found out that what old A. J. Penty has been preaching for many years partly in the pages of the *Criterion* but I'll see what I can do Wazzat about music[2] Rabbit I don't mind much what you do so long as you don't go involve yourself with that Mosley that is only a place fit for Bad rabbits coneys and such cavies you always *said* you didn't like Rothermere and you mustnt go back on it now Rabbit sometimes I 'ears a bit o' English news in London but always of course yes always subject to confirmation from Rapalloo I just got my eye trained on zoze conservastiffs just before you spoke I dont know how it was but I xpect something moved in the bushes Rabbit I mean Podesta theri is a certain amount of properganda in my Paggant Rabbit I wouldnt dream of contradictin anybody but there is a certain amount what you put into that note which you arks me to contradict by the fact of puttin it in so I just says no doubt Mr Oound means to say here something that I cordially approve but its only that he cant ex press himself very Well ere anthere the writin is slipshod if he dont look out he will be reincarnate as a Capybara[3] about that corporeal I am dinging to night with someone

1 – This curious question had been raised in a letter to EP from William Bird (1888–1963), American journalist and publisher – 'the wise guy and satirist' who 'wuz head of a press syndicate, and got wise' – dated Paris 5 Mar. 1934, which EP sent on to TSE. EP commented: 'I dunno if his style is up to Criterion level/ but the satire is too fine to get printed otherwhere.'

Enclosed was an essay by Bird entitled 'A Plea for Waste', opening: 'The account books of the Pharaoh's are lost, as are other statistics of the period, but it is reasonable to estimate that the pyramids alone must have cost a very large proportion of the Egyptian national energy.

'The pyramids, as well as the rest of the Egyptian monuments, were constructed by hand labor, with crude tools, and with only such auxiliary power as could be supplied by camels and ~~mules~~ oxen.'

The burden of Bird's argument is summarised on the final page: 'prosperity under the present economic system is proportional (within, possibly, limits that might be mathematically determined) to the "waste" or "extravagant expenditure" of public funds . . .

'This note is intended only to suggest that by substituting scientific and methodical "waste" for the haphazard waste of war, modern States might attain to a permanent prosperity equal to the temporary prosperity of war-time, without the discomforts and horrors of war.'

Bird remarked to EP about his piece: 'I question two words in it. Page 1, line 6, am not certain whether camels were used by the Pharaohs. If not, substitute mules.'

EP replied to this remark by TSE, 15 Mar.: 'Wot th/ do I care if the pharos used camels . . . I think old Bill zSOiseau [*sic*] heard about it before Penty . . .'

2 – EP announced in a card dated 9 Mar.: 'I wants teh be musical in de next Criter/+erium.'

3 – Capybara: large South American rodent.

who has a dictionary a big one[1] As for the use of Poetry what the ell I KNEW *that* was a bd book bad book & no mistake about it all same[2] Orage MIGHT have sent you THAT at the time as there ARE errors in that book and praps should have been pointed out as for these New economic etc. works why the only thing is we are launching 3 three of your works this autumb that the only thing but youi best tell Porringer to consult us first Morley will be back in about a 4tnight I didnt mean I ad anythink Aganist Orage I havent seen any writings of MC A. for years Years si so I I dont no anyth ink Thats not a bad idea McNair Wilson he knows how express himself but to return Podesta I am ready to forgive a great deal to anybody what lived many years in the Shadow of St Mary Abbot[3] thats a experience no man could come out of un Scathed and he never wants to talk about it and Kensington is NOT wholesome Hiler unfortunately went to Hinks[4] he is not so bad he is one of the new school pro-Stokes anti Try T Fry I dont want to do I forget what had to sign some cheques here Now then terms on cantos was I understood to be the same as previous cantos warnt that right? Morley had this in hand not me Oh yes I remember now thats it I dont want to say anything publicly about Rothermere at present lest he get interested and think I have put him into my Paggant thats a fact.

Tp

---

1 – EP asked, 10 Mar.: 'IS there any authority for corpo*real* instead of corpo*ral*. I am using "extra=corporal" soul, re Donne. Nothing in any dictionary I have, that seems to forbid it, and the extra *e* is a bore. Yaas corporeus. In lat. but . . .'

2 – *The Use of Poetry and the Use of Criticism* (which EP was to style 'The Uses of poetry and self abuses of critics'). EP wrote, 15 Mar.: 'Yaas I shall admire to see yr/ Pagent. But in the mean (oh very) time, you better lemme have the BAD book . . . I don't want it merely fer to shoot off me fyce in N.E.W. Nor do I care a kuss about lyrics re/ Blathermere and Rotherskite. My questions aint allus financial.' On 6 May: 'I am reluctantly compelled to grant the justness of yr/ view. Started in to lay wreathes, and have writ too long a review . . . but thaa sss thaaat.'

3 – EP lived in 1909–14 at 10 Church Walk, Kensington, adjacent to the steepling Victorian edifice of St Mary Abbotts Church (where he was on occasion bothered by the bells).

4 – EP, 10 Mar.: ''I wd/ cheerily review Hiler's bk/ on Painting technique/ if you think . . . oh well . . .' Hilaire Hiler, *Notes on the Technique of Painting* (1934), was not reviewed by Hinks.

TO *William Empson*[1]   CC

13 March 1934   [*The Criterion*]

Dear Empson,

I shall be delighted to use your poem in the *Criterion*, though I don't understand it in the least. That is exaggeration. I mean that I do find it difficult.[2]

Yours sincerely,
[T. S. Eliot]

1 – William Empson (1906–84), poet and critic; author of *Seven Types of Ambiguity* (1930), *Some Versions of Pastoral* (1935), *The Structure of Complex Words* (1951), *Milton's God* (1961). TSE would later take pains at F&F to publish *The Gathering Storm* (poems, 1940). See further *Complete Poems*, ed. John Haffenden (2001); Haffenden, *William Empson: Among the Mandarins* (2005); *Selected Letters of William Empson* (2006).

Empson liked to recall certain encounters with TSE: 'My most impressive memory is of walking up Kingsway with him after some lunch . . . when finding myself alone with the great man I felt it opportune to raise a practical question which had been giving me a little anxiety. "Do you really think it necessary, Mr Eliot,' I broke out, "as you said in the preface to the Pound anthology [*Selected Poems*, 1928], for a poet to write verse at least every week?" He was preparing to cross into Russell Square, eyeing the traffic both ways, and we were dodging it as his slow reply proceeded. "I had in mind Pound when I wrote that passage," began the deep sad voice, and there was a considerable pause. "Taking the question in general, I should say, in the case of many poets, that the most important thing for them to do . . . is to write as little as possible." The gravity of that last phrase was so pure as to give it an almost lyrical quality. A reader may be tempted to suppose that this was a snub or at least a joke, but I still do not believe it was; and at the time it seemed to me not only very wise but a very satisfactory answer. He had taken quite a weight off my mind . . . There was a party (I forget everybody else in the room) where Eliot broke into some chatter about a letter being misunderstood. "Ah, letters," he said, rather as if they were some rare kind of bird. "I had to look into the question of letters at one time. I found that the mistake . . . that most people make . . . about letters, is that after writing their letters, carefully, they go out, and look for a pillar box. I found that it is very much better, after giving one's attention to composing the letters, to . . . pop it into the fire." This kind of thing was a little unnerving, because one did not know how tragically it ought to be taken; it was clearly not to be regarded as a flippancy' ('The Style of the Master', in *T. S. Eliot: A Symposium*, ed. Richard March and Tambimuttu [1948]; repr. in Empson, *Argufying: Essays on Literature and Culture*, ed. John Haffenden [1987], 361–2).

2 – Empson wrote (n.d.) of his poem 'Bacchus': 'The first bit was published in *New Verse* (and will be in a volume with some notes by April); this is the second, and I shall do some more of it if I can. The thing seems clear enough with the remark at the top, but perhaps it would be better manners to put remarks like "This is Humpty-Dumpty" or "the beasts in the Revelation" at the bottom. It is a nice little theme, but I am afraid my air of having to be clever all the time to manage such solemn difficulties makes it ridiculous.' See 'Bacchus II', C. 14 (July 1935), 572.

14 March 1934   [*The Criterion*]

Dear Sir,

I have read your essay on Lawrentian principles with considerable interest,[1] although I have found it very difficult reading, and I hope I may say without offence that you may still learn a good deal about expression from Lawrence himself. I don't like the rather slip-shod Americanism which he introduces in the *Faustus of the Unconscious*[2] but that, after all, is a surface decoration which he might easily have spared, and Lawrence's book itself seems to me very lucid indeed.

The other and more material difficulty is the impossibility of doing anything with an essay of this length. We have found the publication of pamphlets unprofitable except when the sale is very high indeed, and we have practically abandoned this form of publishing. I write, therefore, merely to say that I am interested in your work, and should like to be able to follow its developments.

Perhaps you might care to submit an essay from time to time of the proper length for the *Criterion*. Essays for this purpose ought not to be more than five thousand words. It would be interesting if you would develop your ideas about Major Douglas,[3] with whom, so far as I understand his ideas, I do not think I can agree.

Yours very truly,

[T. S. Eliot]

---

1 – The 22-year-old Donald Main (Glasgow) submitted his essay on 22 Feb. 'I hope to have an introduction from the popular pen of Aldous Huxley or, on his dissenting, Mrs D. H. Lawrence, whom I know well and who assents to my conceptions . . . I believe I have something vital to say to the younger thinkers.'

2 – *Psychoanalysis and the Unconscious* (1923).

3 – C. H. Douglas (1879–1952), engineer and economic theorist, propounded the theory of 'social credit' (his catchy notion was that prices for goods might be kept lower than actual costs by supplying more money to consumers, or else subsidies to producers). His works include *Economic Democracy* (1920) and *Credit-Power and Democracy* (1920). The Labour Party discountenanced the theory in the 1920s, but it was promulgated in the 1930s, in the periodicals *New Age* and *New English Weekly*, and in Douglas's own organ *Social Credit*, as a panacea for the Depression. EP proselytised for Douglas's ideas: see Roxana Preda, 'Social Credit in America: A View from Pound's Economic Correspondence, 1933–1940', *Paideuma* 34: 2–3 (Fall and Winter 2005). See too David Bradshaw, 'T. S. Eliot and the Major: Sources of literary anti-Semitism in the 1930s', *TLS*, 5 July 1996, 14–16; and follow-up correspondence, 9 July and 9 Aug. 1996; Meghnad Desai, *The Route of All Evil* (2006).

TO *The Editor,* The New English Weekly

[published 15 March 1934, 528]   [No address given]

MR ELIOT'S VIRGINIAN LECTURES[1]

Sir, —

I have read with keen interest Mr Pound's kindly note upon my Virginian lectures, in your columns; and I find myself in cordial agreement with the major part of what I am able to understand of it. What I do not understand includes statements which, to me, have no meaning.

I agree with paragraphs 5, 6, 7, 8, 12, and 13, though not necessarily with every inference that might be drawn from them. Though I fail to see their relevance to the subject of Mr Pound's note, the truths contained are so important that no opportunity should be missed for repeating them.

I find that paragraph 4 has no meaning for me. That has sometimes been one's experience with statements beginning with the words *the fact is that.* I am also a little surprised to find Mr Pound, who does not, in his literary criticism, show any great deference towards that spectre, the 'average man', citing him as an authority in this context.

Paragraph 11 puzzles me a little. Many of us would admit that there has been and is great ethical weakness within organised Christianity. I do not know whom he means by the '(often subsidised) ecclesiastical bureaucrat'.

As for the second sentence of paragraph 14, your readers may find some of these lacunae, and some of the statements which say either too much or too little, pointed out in an admirable review of this book by Mr Edwin Muir in *The Spectator* of March 9.

If Mr Pound would rewrite paragraph 9 in Basic English, avoiding phrases like 'when religion was real', and 'vital phenomena', it might possibly turn out to be a statement which I could accept.[2] I do not understand paragraph 15, but I believe that it contains something which might be put in a form in which it would have some meaning for me.

T. S. Eliot

1–EP, 'Mr Eliot's Mare's Nest', *NEW* 4: 21 (8 Mar. 1934), 500: see above.
2–EP wrote in his review: 'I am asserting a known and established fact: when religion was real the church concerned itself with vital phenomena in ECONOMICS.'

TO *A. W. G. Randall*[1]   CC

15 March 1934   [Faber & Faber Ltd]

My dear Randall,

                    History of German Literature

I brought your suggestion of the 12th instant before the Editorial
Committee, who expressed a lively interest.[2] While we don't believe that
such a book would be profitable, we agree that it is a book which ought
to be written and which could be of considerable importance. Our first
opinion is that the sale within the first two seasons would be about 500
copies, which only makes it possible for us to offer a 10% royalty; this
is on the assumption that the book would be sold at 12s. 6d., though a
somewhat cheaper book might be possible, and on the other hand if it
were bigger than we estimated it might be possible to charge 15s.

We are quite ready to come to an agreement with you on this basis, if it
is acceptable. It would be an advantage if you could let us have some sort
of an outline of what you propose.

                              Yours ever,
                              [T. S. Eliot]

1 – Alec (later Sir Alec) Randall (1892–1977), diplomat and writer, entered the Foreign
Office in 1920. In the early 1920s he was Second Secretary to the Holy See. He ended
his career as Ambassador to Denmark (where he was awarded the Grand Cross, Order of
Dannebrog), 1947–52. He wrote on German literature for *C.* and *TLS*. Later works include
Vatican Assignment (1956) and *The Pope, the Jews and the Nazis* (1963).
2 – 'It appears to me that, particularly with present events in Germany in mind, the time has
come for the publishing of a history of German literature since 1914, or even 1900.'

TO *W. K. Lowther Clarke*[1]   cc

16 March 1934   [Faber & Faber Ltd]

Dear Mr Lowther Clarke,

Thank you for your note of the 14th, and for sending me a proof of your article in *Theology*.[2] I do not get *Theology* regularly, and always read as much of it as I can but with so many periodicals to look at in the intervals of labour, I very easily overlook things of the first importance.

I have glanced at your proof and the subject seems to me most fascinating, especially as I have always been an admirer of James, and particularly of *The Sense of the Past*.

I am very happy to hear about More's book, and it's a great satisfaction to me to feel that I have played some part in bringing you and More together.[3]

Yours sincerely,
[T. S. Eliot]

TO *Mary Hutchinson*   TS Texas

16 March 1934   Faber & Faber Ltd
                                       [from St. Stephen's Vicarage]

Dear Mary,

I dined with Doone and Medley[4] on Wednesday, and they talked to me about their plans for raising the money they need in order that their group may settle in Suffolk for six months or so. It appears that they have about

---

1–The Revd William Kemp Lowther Clarke, DD (1879–1968): Editorial Secretary of the Society for Promoting Christian Knowledge, 1915–44; Canon Residentiary of Chichester Cathedral, 1945–65; Prebendary of Chichester Cathedral from 1943. Works include *New Testament Problems* (1929) and *Liturgy and Worship* (1932).

2–Lowther Clark sent a proof copy of an essay written for the Apr. number of *Theology*. 'A very good dogmatic theologian said to me: "No one has ever thought along those lines before".'

3–'We propose to publish P. E. More's Anthology [*Anglicanism: The Thought and Practice of the Church of England*, ed. Paul Elmer More and Frank L. Cross (1935)] as a 950 pp. book . . . to sell at 21/-. Not till I read the MS. did I decide on a big edition & a low price. It is astonishingly interesting & I must thank you for bringing me into touch with More 3 years ago.'

4–Robert Medley (1905–94), artist, theatre designer; teacher; from 1932, artistic director of the Group Theatre, designing sets and costumes for productions by his partner, the dancer, choreographer and director Rupert Doone (1903–66), of plays by TSE, WHA, SS and Louis MacNeice. See further Medley, *Drawn from the Life: A Memoir* (1983).

£200 and think that another £300 will see them through. They propose to make a public appeal in the form of a letter to the press. I suggested that they should issue circulars of invitation to the public for a kind of associate membership, at a guinea or so subscription, such membership to carry privileges but no control. Doone thought that they might not have enough to show at the end of six months to satisfy the associates that the money was well spent. What he wants to do is to get a smaller number of benefactors to contribute larger sums, as he would be able to explain in greater detail, and more personally, to a small number, exactly what had and had not been accomplished at the end of that time.

He is writing, I believe, to a few people like Mrs Matthias to ask directly for contributions; and to a few others, like Ottoline, to ask them to use influence with wealthy friends. He will probably be writing to you in the latter capacity, to ask for your advice, and to ask you to write to any suitable wealthy people among your acquaintance.

I am very willing to do all I can to help them. Turning it over in my mind since seeing them, my only doubt is about the morality of encouraging young people to throw over jobs (as a few, I expect, will be doing) for what is possibly only a quixotic enterprise. What do you think about that? Of course they are modelling their procedure upon the Quinze,[1] but one is inclined to feel that anything of the sort is much more uphill in this country than in France. And on the other hand one does not want to discourage them with purely prudential counsels of timidity!

I said I was willing to sign an appeal in the form of a letter to the press, amongst others.

The pageant text so far has been very well received by the people concerned in it. I have to try to complete it in the next two weeks, which means every moment I can spare. I hope to see you again when that pressure is relieved – soon after Easter that should be.

Affectionately,
Tom

1–The *Compagnie des Quinze*: theatre production company organised by Michel Saint-Denis (nephew of Jacques Copeau), along with the playwright André Obey, at the *Théatre du Vieux-Colombier*, Paris, 1929–34; influential on English theatre in the succeeding years.

TO *F. R. Leavis*[1]   TS Texas

16 March 1934   *The Criterion*

Dear Mr Leavis,

Thank you for your letter of the 13th. Your response to Cooke's article is very much what I expected.[2]

I am sorry to hear that the direction of *Scrutiny* has been such a strain upon its Editors, and I hope that both Editor and the review will quickly recover.[3] I still hope to let you have a contribution, but the only thing I am sure of is that I shall have no time to consider any such work until the autumn.

> With all best wishes,
> Yours sincerely,
> T. S. Eliot

TO *A. R. Orage*[4]   TS Mrs Orage?

16 March 1934   Faber & Faber Ltd

My dear Orage,

I should like very much to meet AE, whom I do not know; but alas Wednesday afternoon is the one impossible; I have a committee every Wednesday which usually lasts till about 6.[5] So I must decline.

1–F. R. Leavis (1895–1978), literary critic: see Biographical Register.
2–Leavis had replied to TSE's letter to L. C. Knights of 8 Mar. (see tseliot.com/explore/letters), to explain that since Knights was now at Manchester, he himself was having to 'do most of the *Scrutiny* work'. He agreed with TSE that there seemed no point in printing an article by Cooke on plays that had not been produced in England. 'Anyway, I don't think Cooke is desperately in need of encouragement.'
3–FRL ended his note: 'We look forward to having something from you some time – if we can keep going. At the moment I feel that *Scrutiny* may end by the collapse of the present editor from overwork. An end-of-term feeling, no doubt.'
4–A. R. Orage (1873–1934), owner-editor of the *New Age*, 1907–24; founder of the *New English Weekly*, 1932; disciple of the occultist P. D. Ouspensky and later of the Russian mystic G. I. Gurdjieff; major proponent of C. H. Douglas's economic system of Social Credit. See P. A. Mairet, *A. R. Orage: A Memoir* (1966); Orage, *Selected Essays and Critical Writings*, ed. Denys Saurat and Herbert Read (1935); *Orage as Critic*, ed. Wallace Martin (1975).
5–Orage invited TSE to meet 'AE' before his return to Ireland: 'perhaps next Wednesday for coffee at the Kardomah Café at the top end of Chancery Lane?' Æ: pseud. of George William Russell (1867–1935), Irish poet, painter, nationalist, mystic; friend of WBY and JJ; worked for some years as Assistant Secretary of the Irish Agricultural Organization Society; editor of the *Irish Homestead*, 1905–23; *Irish Statesman*, 1923–30. Works include *Collected Poems* (1913, 1926). Known for his generosity towards younger writers. See Nicholas Allen, *George Russell (Æ) and the New Ireland 1905–30* (2003).

I must say I was disappointed with Ezra's letter. I wish he would stick to the points worth debating, or to pointing out the faults that certainly glare out of my terminology, or to criticising my particular judgements etc. By talking about 'religion' he just encourages the tendency for people to line up according to their previous prejudices or convictions. I tell him he lived too long in Kensington; or maybe Rapallo is another Kensington. His longer version is better, but he will drag in Van Buren![1]

The letter we spoke of the other evening is being prepared; whether the *Times* will print it is another matter. If you have any news about the other letter and the designs of the group I should like to know.

Yours ever,
T. S. Eliot

TO *Derek Phit Clifford*[2] CC

16 March 1934 [*The Criterion*]

Dear Mr Clifford,

I am now returning to you your typescript, together with a few detailed comments, which I have taken the liberty of scribbling in pencil. You will find that the comments are copious and diminish on the latter pages. There seemed to me no need to say the same thing more than once.

I am not going to discourage you in the least. I feel that in this phase you have usually a pretty good notion of where you want to get to but are apt to be very confused about the route. Or to put it less metaphorically you know what your ends are more or less but not what means to use. I do feel that you must get a much greater respect for the individual souls, so to speak, of the various words in the English language. There are a good many words in the language[;] I am not sure that there are not too

---

1 – EP had written to Orage (TS on the back of TSE's letter, which Orage had forwarded to EP):

'Dear A/R/O/

'If the Rt/ Rev/ is too god damn lazy to reread his own book and correct his own OVERSIGHTS . . . plaster his own errors of simple detail/ minutes of small fly size . . . what the HELL!! . . .

'He is not interested in Van B/ because his is IGGURUNT and has lived in British bog so god damn long he has acquired London habit of not wanting to learn or HEAR of anything that hasn't already grown onto his feet.

'Like Mike Agnolo's boots did, because he was averse from changin' 'em.'

2 – Clifford was a sixth form student at the King's School, Rochester: he was introduced by Francis Underhill on 20 Feb.

many. I hope that you have access to, and occasionally browse in a book which is most valuable for anyone who wants to write poetry, I mean the complete Oxford English Dictionary. The numbers of meanings which one word may have, as given in that dictionary, should help to impress on anyone the great care and respect with which words should be used.

Also it is a good thing sometimes to examine microscopically the way in which Shakespeare uses words. You will find again and again that his use of a word will be perfectly proper according to previous usage, but that it will bring it a further meaning not previously used, and that often a word will have also a meaning in a particular context, which while true to the general meaning of the word will exist in that place alone. I think that this sort of consideration helps to throw light on the extraordinary vigour of Shakespeare's language.

Yours sincerely,
[T. S. Eliot]

TO *Aldous Huxley*[1]   CC

17 March 1934   [Faber & Faber Ltd]

Dear Aldous,

Here is a matter upon which (if that is the right preposition) your support is very much wanted. A letter has been written to *The Times* (Dobrée has seen a copy) by a group of Conservatives who are backed by Walter Elliot, to the same effect as the enclosed, but of course at greater length and in greater detail, and in a different style as coming from politicians and not literary blokes. The letter is to be a *ballon d'essai*, and upon the response the possibility of any action depends. A few of us who are profoundly dissatisfied with the way things are going, but who are neither communists nor fascists, want to back that letter up. The enclosed was

---

1–Aldous Huxley (1894–1963), novelist, poet and essayist, whose early novels *Crome Yellow* (1921) and *Antic Hay* (1923) were successful satires of post-war English culture. While teaching at Eton, Aldous told his brother Julian in December 1916 that he 'ought to read' Eliot's 'things', which are 'all the more remarkable when one knows the man, ordinarily just an Europeanized American, overwhelmingly cultured, talking about French literature in the most uninspired fashion imaginable'. For his part, Eliot thought Huxley's early poems fell too much under the spell of Laforgue (and of his own poetry), but Huxley went on to become, not only a popular novelist, but, as the author of *Brave New World* and *The Doors of Perception*, an influential intellectual figure. See Nicholas Murray, *Aldous Huxley: An English Intellectual* (2002); Aldous Huxley, *Selected Letters*, ed. James Sexton (2007).

written by Read, and revised with Dobrée, Miles and myself. I have ticked the names of those who have assented in principle, though the others have not yet seen the revision. I am not so keen myself about having the Dean of Canterbury, but Bonamy wants him. At my suggestion, we are particularly keen on getting you and Dawson (to whom I am writing by the same post) and for obvious reasons I think that you would both carry great weight.[1]

The letter purports to come from people who are not committed to anything, who do not profess to be economists, but predominantly men of letters. The form in which you see it is to be sent if *The Times* does *not* print the other people's letter; if *The Times* does print that letter, we shall prefix a sentence referring to it.

If the Elliot group letter does not appear, we have plenty of time; but if it does, we shall want to get this one in as quickly as possible; and in that event I shall send a reply-paid wire, to which you need only answer 'yes' or 'no'. But I do hope most earnestly that you will consent.[2]

Yours ever

[Tom]

TO *David Cecil*[3]   CC

17 March 1934   [Faber & Faber Ltd]

Dear Cecil,

Here is the letter as revised yesterday afternoon. The final list of signatories is longer than I should have wished, but it appeared that Dobrée had already approached one or two people, and I don't suppose Abercrombie or Sadler can do any harm.

---

1 – The draft letter TSE circulated was the same as that eventually published in *The Times* on 5 April 1934: see below. The proposed signatories were Lascelles Abercrombie, Lord David Cecil, Christopher Dawson, Bonamy Dobrée, TSE, Aldous Huxley, The Very Revd the Dean of Canterbury, Edwin Muir, Hamish Miles, Herbert Read, I. A. Richards, and Sir Michael Sadler.

2 – Huxley responded *c.* 18 Mar.: 'Yes, I will certainly sign – do sign in fact, and return the letter herewith. Douglas may be wrong – tho' I can't detect the error in a good exposition of his theory, such as Marshall Hattersley's *This Age of Plenty* – but anyhow he – and Soddy [Frederick Soddy (1877–1956), Nobel Prize-Winning radiochemist; author of *Wealth, Virtual Wealth and Debt: The Solution of the Economic Paradox* (1926)] – are obviously talking about something very important which ought to be looked into' (*Letters of Aldous Huxley*, 378).

3 – Lord David Cecil (1902–86), historian, critic, biographer; Fellow of Wadham College, Oxford, 1924–30; Fellow of New College, 1939–69; Professor of English, Oxford, 1948–70; author of *Early Victorian Novelists: Essays in Revaluation* (1934) and *Jane Austen* (1936).

I have written to Dawson and Aldous, *both* of whom I am anxious to get.

I hope you won't feel that this commits you to too much! I am myself a horse of no colour, being neither fascist nor communist (disliking both) and not being a Douglasite because I don't understand it, and considering that 'Conservative' does not mean enough at the present time and is almost synonymous with whiggery anyway; and to me the point of this letter is that it should be signed by people in a position like mine.[1]

I am sending you the *Theology* I mentioned, and also an address I gave last summer to the Anglo-Catholic Summer School, copies of which have just turned up.

Yours sincerely,
[T. S. Eliot]

TO *Ezra Pound*

TS Beinecke

19 March 1934   Faber & Faber Ltd

Dear Podesta that's surprrisin about old Buchan and I dont much admire what I seen of is prose style he must ave ad a singular change of eart of Late[2] I alwys thought he was as dead as dead and I dont kno what my Fenian friends in the Ighlans of is navite native country would say thay ave been wantin is scalp for a generation or more but praps that worth lookin into but as he wrote to you in Such a nice guarded way Ill try to get up the form to write him dont kno the bastard.

What About MASONS?[3] Never eard of anyone taking em seriously in this country ave they been up to their monkey tricks here too R. W. Child was a numskull when I knew him or praps his lookin such a numbskull should have made One suspicious

---

1–Cecil responded, 24 Mar.: 'I am very much afraid I do not see my way to signing the letter. I am, as I told you, in sympathy with the spirit which inspires it; but I am really too ignorant of these economic questions to feel myself justified in assisting to put forward any suggestion, however tentative, in public with regard to them. I dislike having to refuse all the more because I felt, during our talk, so sympathetic to the attitude to political questions I gathered you held.'

2–EP, 17 Mar.: 'Mr John Buchan writes me that he agrees with some of Dougs premises / but being a conservatie, I take it he don't want to say which . . .

'However he'd be a catch for the Criterion, yan I suggesss that you AX him to say which. You can say I dun tole you as he write to me pally and perlite.

'I also onnerstan (not from him) that he writes nice hist'ry pieces

'so ef he wunt come into the hopen on ECON// you might with muchool ggglory and yoner print his historical diggin'.'

3–EP asked on 17 Mar.: 'Wot about MASONS?? anybody on that tick? in yr/ country?'

Morley as been dealin with Frankie[1] and should be back this week with the spoils.

I like your little cameo about B.U.F.'s and may make use of it weavin it into my conversation now n them then Relieved to find you now not so black as you was panted shirted I mean But I rather agree with C. H. about working from the ground up rather than from the air down.

No you dont know about all that we just make both ends meet, under the present economic syst.

THOUGHT FOR THE DAY.

Dear singer of the ravaged years that weep
Within the ranks of joys funereal train,
Forgive my love . . .

From TO FRANCESCO PETRARCHA by James Clough. Want to see his portrait? Name should rhyme with TOUGH which he looks.

This is nicer   (TURN OVER

When I was a delicate slip of a maid
    What couldn't eat more than a couple o' chops,
Of a Sattaday night I occasion'ly strayed
    Along the New Cut just to look at the shops.[2]

(T. S. Eliot)

Yrs. for the momint
Tp

TO *W. H. Auden*   CC

20 March 1934   [*The Criterion*]

Dear Auden,

I really don't feel that the enclosed poem is quite up to your best level.[3] I might have accepted it, were it signed by some more obscure name than yours. But I feel that at the present moment it is more judicious for you to go out for quality rather than quantity, even if it means remaining in eclipse for a short time.

Do send me something more whenever you have a mind to.

Yours sincerely,
[T. S. Eliot]

---

1 – President Franklin D. Roosevelt.
2 – See Bert's 'Song', in *The Rock*.
3 – The poem (title unknown) had been submitted by WHA on 5 Feb. 1934. (Ed Mendelson, Auden's literary executor and editor, is not able to identify the poem.)

TO *Christopher Dawson*   cc

20 March 1934   [*The Criterion*]

My dear Dawson,

Thank you for your letter.[1] I am all the more sorry that you cannot see your way to signing this letter, because the doubts you express are so much of the kind that I feel myself. It is partly because of my doubts, and partly because I see so little hope elsewhere, that I have signed the letter; and I know that Read is hardly more convinced than I am. I should like an opportunity to know more. I have expressed my doubts again and again, both privately and occasionally publicly. The usual reply is that we must have Credit Reform in any case. If that is so, or rather if we do get something of the sort, then it seems to me important that people like ourselves should be interested, and should keep our eyes open for such dangers as those you speak of. I have myself grave doubts about the dangers of authoritarianism, although Douglas himself is very strongly anti-fascist. And Credit Reform arouses my suspicion by appearing to promise too much. I cannot believe that financial change without moral change can possibly set things right. And how can one depend upon people for whom values, of the first importance for oneself, simply do not exist?

A reason which seems to me to make it more important to take an interest in such schemes, however, is that many Christians, certainly in my communion, are inclined to throw themselves into the arms of Credit Reform out of a kind of despair: they are very unhappy about the world as it is, and find communism and fascism quite unacceptable. I think a good many of these people are blind in their allegiance.

I think that Credit Reformers (I mean the ones who really understand what they are talking about) merely narrow their outlook as other economists do. I do believe that *some* change in the economic system is necessary, and I believe that some change – not necessarily for the better – will come about. There are a few people – a very few – who are concerned

---

1 – Dawson wrote on 19 Mar.: 'As to the *Times* letter, it was most kind of you to think of including my name & I should have been delighted to sign had it been on almost any other subject (for I always agree thoroughly with the principles you state so clearly in *After Strange Gods*). On this credit question, however, I feel very serious doubts indeed. It seems to me that all these schemes of national credit ignore the real difficulties of our economic situation. I can quite see that it might help the world situation if it were applied internationally or even in some great self-sufficient continental area like USA or USSR. But our peculiar difficulties arise from the fact that we are a specialized industrial commercial state existing for & by the world market. That market has failed us & we cannot change over to a self contained national basis without living on a much more restricted scale.'

about the other profounder changes which must come about as well if any economic change is to be a wholesome one.

I wish that you might think this over again.

I am not satisfied with my book. I am satisfied with what I was trying to say, but I do not think that I have expressed myself well: there is a not altogether happy terminology. And it seems almost impossible to convey one's meaning to those who do not more or less agree with one already. The reviews have been most perplexing. I suppose I ought not [to] be astonished at being accused of fascist tendencies. The most useful review that I have seen was one by Edwin Muir in *The Spectator*. I sometimes feel that I am not the person to meddle with these matters, but ought to stick to verse. I haven't the erudition; and I doubt whether I have the power of abstract thinking.

I met the charming G. G. Coulton[1] at Cambridge last week; he spoke of your work in terms of the highest praise.

Yours ever,
[T. S. Eliot]

P.S. I don't know the Nashdom people. They don't come exactly within my circle. I believe there is at least one good man there (I forget his name) but on the whole they do not appear to be rated very high. So far, the support of Nashdom does S. B. neither good nor harm in my eyes. I am somewhat prejudiced by his chaotic manner of correspondence and by his excessive zeal for organisation.

TO *Hallie Flanagan*   TS NYPL Theater Collection

20 March 1934   Faber & Faber Ltd

Dear Miss Flanagan,

Thank you very much for taking the trouble to write me such a kind note.[2] I think that everyone enjoyed the party very much; and I hasten to assure you that no evidence appeared of the strain you were under. On the

---

1–See letter to him, 2 Dec. 1935, below.
2–Flanagan wrote (n.d.) from Genoa: 'It was a beautiful party [thrown by TSE at the Ritz] and I liked meeting your friends and I think it was very lovely of you to ask me. I hope you could not tell from the outside that I was very crazily and insanely unhappy because I have gotten my life into a complete tangle and my work suddenly seems utterly useless and I feel as if I were made of cotton wool.' To make matters worse, she had arrived in Genoa to spend two weeks, by invitation, with Mr and Mrs Gordon Craig – 'the *maestro*'– only to discover that they were not expecting her: they had never received any letter from her.

contrary. Sometimes one is particularly cool and collected at such times, though hardly aware of what one is doing.

I do hope that your affairs will straighten themselves out, at least to the extent of restoring your belief in your own work. That I know is indispensable, as I often suffer from the absence of it. I know also that words of consolation often sound like a mockery when they come from someone who is ignorant of the real trouble; but please accept them for what they are worth.

I am grieved that you had such a fiasco in Genoa. Had I known you were going to Genoa I should have wanted to arrange for you to meet my friends the Pounds in Rapallo.

I do think on retrospect that the *Dance of Death* was rather a mess.[1] Perhaps Doone spent his time in trying to arrange choreography for people who couldn't dance – when I saw the bathers I thought there was something to be said for the ordinary musical comedy chorus after all – and so the verbal part got rather neglected. Certainly it was impossible to hear what they said.

I look forward to seeing you on your return; meanwhile I hope you will enjoy your travels as much as you can in the circumstances.

Yours very sincerely,
T. S. Eliot

1 – 'By the way, I couldn't say anything to nice Mr Doone about *The Dance of Death* because I thought, aside from a moment or two, it was a very bad performance. It was messy, and people were thinking about themselves and *not* about the play. And such horrible stage movement. It seemed motivated only by a desire of the actors to keep from falling over each other.

'The mystery play made me feel quite ill.

'Quite often I hate all theatres including my own.'

TO *Walter Lowenfels*[1]   CC

20 March 1934   [*The Criterion*]

Dear Mr Lowenfels,

Your news is so pleasant that it almost breaks my heart to be obliged finally to return this manuscript to you.[2] I do think it is good but I don't see what we can possibly do about it. It doesn't fit in to our programme anywhere. I have given a good deal of thought to it and also consultation.

If you would like me to put in a word with any other particular publisher, I should be glad to do so.

I wish to send my most cordial good wishes to Mrs Lowenfels and the twins.

Yours sincerely,
[T. S. Eliot]

1 – Walter Lowenfels (1897–1976): American poet, journalist, author, activist; member of the Communist Party; editor of the *Daily Worker* from the late 1930s until 1953. After working for his father (a butter manufacturer), 1914–26, he lived in Paris, 1926–34, where he came to know expatriates including Ford Madox Ford and Henry Miller, and where he co-founded in 1930 the Carrefour Press. In 1953 he was arrested by the FBI and charged with conspiracy to overthrow the US government: his conviction in 1954 was overturned for lack of evidence. His works include *Episodes & Epistles* (1925) and *Steel, 1937* (1937). See too Hugh Ford, *Published in Paris: American and British Writers, Printers, and Publishers in Paris, 1920–1939* (1975).

2 – Lowenfels wrote, 8 Mar.: 'My wife is in the hospital, just having had twins (girls), and she says she likes my Lawrence poem because it stays propped up on her knees without being held while she nurses the twins in bed, but the Suicide doesn't. Can you imagine a more compelling argument for its publication before it is too late and the twins become a grown-up, non-nursing dancing act?' He had submitted 'The Suicide' (short version) on 30 Sept. 1933, and asked about it again on 28 Oct. 1933.

TO *C. M. Bowra*[1]   CC

20 March 1934   [*The Criterion*]

Dear Mr Bowra,

I have hesitated for some time over your interesting essay on Rilke but have finally decided with regret that it does not quite fit in to the *Criterion* programme for the immediate future.[2]

Yours very truly,
[T. S. Eliot]

TO *Herbert Read*   CC

22 March 1934   [Faber & Faber Ltd]

Dear Herbert,

We shall be greatly obliged if you will let us have a reader's report in the usual way on the MS which I am sending you, entitled 'Hoere Israel'. We know nothing whatever of the writer, who describes himself as a young German Jew who has been living in London for the last four years.[3] I have myself been able to give it only a very cursory reading, and can give no

---

1 – C. M. Bowra (1898–1971), educated at New College, Oxford, was a Fellow and Tutor of Wadham College, Oxford, 1922–38; Warden of Wadham, 1938–70; Oxford Professor of Poetry, 1946–51; Vice-Chancellor, 1951–4. President of the British Academy, 1958–62, he was knighted in 1951; appointed CH in 1971. Works include *Tradition and Design in the Iliad* (1930), *Greek Lyric Poetry* (1936), *The Romantic Imagination* (1950), *Memories, 1898–1939* (1966). See Leslie Mitchell, *Maurice Bowra: A Life* (2009).

To Theodore Spencer, 5 June 1948: 'If you don't know him, I may mention that he is extremely social, a very amusing talker, with a trained palate (it is well known that he has at Wadham the best chef in Oxford) and a keen interest in people and their humours . . . He likes wealth and fashion as well as intelligence and wit.'

Mary Trevelyan recorded TSE calling Bowra, on 23 Dec. 1949: '[a] philologist posing as a dillettante [*sic*] in literature – and an insecure man' ('The Pope of Russell Square', 22).

2 – Bowra had submitted his essay on 14 Feb. 'Rilke has swum into new fame lately because [critics] are sharply divided over his claims, and I think that for a German poet he is very well known in England.' See further Bowra, *The Heritage of Symbolism* (1967).

3 – Joachim Lucius Brandler (1912–98) had written to Faber & Faber, 4 Mar. 1934: 'On April 1st it will be exactly one year that Nazi Germany staged the boycott against the Jews. And the Jews – the first who should have learned their lesson – are the last to have done so. Be it in this country or any other. They still cling to values which are out of date, relive the lives of their forefathers instead to look out for new ways which may be those the whole world is looking for [*sic*].

'I know that books on the subject of Germany and the Jews have been published by the dozens lately. Indeed every retired German Government Official suddenly remembering that he is called a Jew is now their champion. Those who have been hid [hit] hardest and if things

---

account of the argument if there is any. At the same time I was impressed to the point of enthusiasm by the author's sincerity and passion. This happened at the end of a long evening during which I had been reading much duller MSS, and my first impression was so very favourable that I feel that I may be completely mistaken, and that the book is only froth.[1]

Therefore we want to ask you to read it in cold blood, and tell us what you think of it from every point of view.

Yours ever,

[Tom]

---

are going to be repeated elsewhere are going to be hid [hit] hardest again are now allowed to talk – the young men.

'As a very young Jew who has been enjoying the hospitality of this country for the greater part of the last fore [sic] years I have tried – and hope succeeded – to learn the essential parts of the lesson. And whilst by necessity talking to those who are nearest to me I mean of course not only the Jews.

'Just let me add a few words. I am not trying to establish myself as an author. I may lack the brilliance of style of those whose business it is to talk cleverly. I, and with me thousands of young people, have been waiting for the call and all we see and hear is fear, business, wish to forget, quarrels.'

1 – TSE's reader's report on 'Hoere Israel', by Joachim L. Brandler (19 Mar. 1934): 'I cannot say that I have read this book thoroughly, word for word. I have read it rather hurriedly, and have skipped a number of pages. Nevertheless, I was fascinated by it, and only skipped in order to have something to say about it in time for this committee. I cannot make a summary report on it. But that is not altogether my fault. I should find it difficult to sum up and give the committee a fair impression of Isaiah, or Ezekiel, or Jeremiah. This man has no important argument: he is a Hebrew Prophet, though a minor one. He is a sort of Jewish Péguy. The whole thing is a tremendous exhortation to his own race: it appealed, not to my reasoning powers (such as they are) but to my emotions. If, after a slow re-reading over 2 or 3 days with nothing else to think about, this book moved me as much as it did on this hasty perusal, it would be a book to which I should be glad to write a preface (I don't mean that I think a preface by me would help it or would be in any way called for but I put this in for a kind of emphasis in a manner of speaking).

'This man seems to me quite out of the ordinary. It is the sort of book I should like to publish whether it sold 10 copies or not. Thank God for sending the fellow to us and not to Gollancz, but I don't believe Gollancz would like it. This man is not an English Jew, or a German Jew, but a Jew.

'I have even exaggerated my enthusiasm in order to provoke a reaction. I should like the Chairman to spend an hour over it and see if he gets the same queer impression of sincerity that I do. And then perhaps someone like Dr [Herbert] Read should take it and spend some time over it and give an opinion. I was so excited by it that I feel it was praps a kind of intoxication, so long as you don't distort my meaning.'

TO *Ormerod Greenwood*[1]   CC

22 March 1934   [*The Criterion*]

Dear Sir,

In reply to your letter of March 20 with enclosures, I wish to say that I shall be glad to sign the letter for the Group Theatre.[2]

I have one minor suggestion to make. It seems to me always best, when making an appeal to the widest public, not personally acquainted with any of the people concerned, to give the name of a bank to which donations should be sent, marked 'for the account of the Group Theatre' or something like that. There is nothing in it, of course, but I know that even I, when I read in a newspaper an appeal for some cause by people I do not know, get more impression of solidity and seriousness when I see that contributions are to be sent to some bank. There must be many people still who are reassured by seeing a banker's name on a prospectus – or at least, who are suspicious if they don't see it there.

I confess also that on reflection I feel a little worried by the responsibility of appearing to encourage people to throw up jobs (i.e. like Auden) for an indefinite future. I should like to be given some estimate of the amount of personal disaster that would be caused if the scheme eventually led to nothing! I hope very much for its success; but I know enough about being out of work, and of having uncongenial work, to feel anxiety about younger people. Also I should very much like to know more about the practical arrangements for the *séjour* in Suffolk. Who will be in charge? What will be the routine? Have expenses been calculated so that you may be sure, given a certain sum – the £500 – twenty people may be sure of decent living accommodation and convenience and enough to eat? Who will do the cooking? I hope that all this will not appear an impertinence on my part, but I don't want any responsibility for 20 young people living

1 – Michael J. Sidnell, *Dances of Death*, 48: 'Just down from Cambridge, where he had been President of the Mummers, Greenwood [1907–89] was twenty-four years old, a Quaker, a devotee of Edward Gordon Craig and an idealist imbued with a strong sense of mission to the theatre'; executive secretary of the Group Theatre. Greenwood became a BBC radio producer, and taught for eighteen years at the Royal Academy of Dramatic Art.
2 – 'I believe that Mr Rupert Doone has spoken to you of the Group Theatre's scheme for six months training, and that you are willing to sign the appeal for funds which we are issuing to the press.'
  TSE was to be identified on a Group Theatre advertisement as one of five 'ladies and gentlemen' who had 'agreed to vouch for its integrity'; the others were Lilian Baylis, CH (Director of the Old Vic and Sadler's Wells theatres); Michel Saint-Denis (Director of the *Compagnie des Quinze*); Charles Laughton (actor); and E. McKnight Kauffer (designer).

miserably and half fed. Will they all have enough private funds to supply any other personal expenses they may have?

If you get all the other signatories you mention, it will make a very good list. I hope you will.

I ought to have gone into these questions when I last talked with Doone about the venture. But that was the first I knew about it; and such reflexions do not always come at once.

Yours sincerely,
[T. S. Eliot]

TO *Ezra Pound*   TS Beinecke

23 March 1934   Faber & Faber Ltd

Dear EZ -

Your last post card incomprehessible as Usual Podesta what next what ave I to say. Marianne as melted so thank you v. much ver moosh Was dispointed to See nothink by You in last english weekly Well I said to Mr Orgae Orage well Mr Orage I Said that Rapallo I wonder if it aint a lot like Kensington its probably the place they calls South Kensington I said well Podesta I hope there aint so many Mice in Rappalloo as in S. Kensington they gnaws ones Toes Podesta I sent you greetings by Mr Stokes Now look Here its Sad to think ow few english Periodicals there Are where a Man can place anythingk All I can do I can write a Leader in the Supplement on some minor Elizabethan author if I Want to but I dont much any more want to that belongs to my youth I can also if I wanted place some sorts in Life & Letters which is now out of hands of Desmond Mkciarty[1] and run by Hamish Miles who is pretty white why not try him with somethink sometime c/- Jonathan Cape 30 Bedford Square there is also New Verse prints prose too but that pays nothink and has small circulation I have not entrée to any daily or Sunday or to any but the Litry columns of any weekly if the *Criterion* went Out I should ave nowheres to express myself and a good job too you ses Podesta a letter as been prepared this is a secret signed by self, Read, Dobrée, Richards, Huxley, Muir and others a few others includin O Lord Abercrombie Lassells advocating consideration of Credit Reform does thatsprise you or Not but in any case I misdoubt the Times won't print it Now if you can tell me what youre drivin at with this

1–Desmond MacCarthy.

music[1] and how much space well see the trouble about music and art is that avin regular chronicles such as they are and they seem to me pretty good I dont like goin over eads of Radcliffe & Hinks and usually consult em about such contributions first you understand not that there is any reason why opinions contrary to theirs or as often appens to Mine should not happear and no reason why anybody shouldnt wrangle with anybody else its also a question of space but Lets see I cant Think of anythink more at the momint so will close yours etc.

Tp

Podesta I hope you are following the Stavisky case closely that's a good one about how he fixed the playincards at Nice and the racehorse at Longchamps Maurras says evidently there is a CHEMIST in the Gang.

Might raise that 10% after oooo coppies well see.[2]

TO *Marianne Moore*   TS Rosenbach Museum and Library

23 March 1934   [Faber & Faber Ltd]

Dear Miss Moore,

Thank you for your kind letter of the 15th instant, which gives me great pleasure.[3] We are expecting Mr Morley back within the next few days, and I will discuss the matter with him. Meanwhile I hope you will proceed with a collection or selection of your poems, new and old.

What a very kind thought of you to get me a copy of the original edition of *The Waste Land* but what a pity from my point of view that you didn't do me the honour of inscribing it for me.[4] Thank you very much indeed.

1–EP, n.d.: 'My muzik. Wd/ be news that Jinks and Kinks/ havent GOT . . . it wouldnt cut into yr Eng/ muzik. it wd. be European.'

2–EP had asked, 10 Mar.: 'How come I'm only getting 10% on Cantos . . . I fergit . . . oh well . . .' On 15 Mar.: 'Re/ Cantos/ 10% aint a classy royalty fer the higesest lichery monnyment of the age. Wotever the present econ/ shiststem. I notice that is wot I got on XXX . . . Of course the firm still exists in a prewar econ/ system, and the firms' jewty is to buy as sheep as possible, and to sell fer the highest, and fer to collect interest on all funds for six months. I know all about that.'

On 24 Apr. FVM would make this proposal for what EP termed his 'Elected essays': 'will you accept 10% to 1500 copies with a rise to 15% after that on a proposed price of 12/6 for the volume? I would suggest an accrued advance. These are the figgers allowed for in the estimate, and we are counting on selling 1270 copies in order to get our money back.'

3–'I feel very earnestly your interest in thinking you might like to publish work of mine and I should like to be guided by your advice. When Mr Latham [of the Macmillan Company, New York] wrote to me in October, I thought I preferred not to hazard old work with new, but your attitude to the former alters my objection.'

4–'I am sometimes asked if I would like to make a great deal of money by selling my Boni

As a matter of fact, not being a collector of first editions, I have almost none of the earlier editions of my own work. I admit, however, that the first thing I do when I receive a second-hand bookseller's catalogue, is to look for my own name, and usually find '*Daniel Deronda*, two volumes, uncut'.

Yours sincerely,

T. S. Eliot

TO *Bonamy Dobrée* TS Brotherton

23 March 1934 Faber & Faber Ltd

Dear Bumbaby,

Yours of 22nd to hand.[1] I am glad that Richards has come Through.[2] Huxley's acceptance must be in your hand by now, so I think that will do nicely. I'd wait a couple of days in any case for the possibility of Dawson's relenting. I do regret him. I don't think Cecil[3] cuts any ice, except possibly with the public which has never heard any of the rest of us: I only asked him because I happened to be seeing him at the moment; and my retrospective impression now is that he is not an individual at all, only a member of his family.

Faber suggested that when we are ready to try to place the letter I might try to see Barrington Ward first.[4] Not much use to try to see Geoffrey Dawson; you get put off onto a secretary. If *Times* won't, I don't know where else. *Daily Telegraph*? Don't know anyone on *Post* except Grigson.

& Liveright Dial Award copy of THE WASTE LAND – a query that led me to think you ought to have any copies that could be secured. Although I felt it useless to ask, I did ask at 152 13th Street last week if they knew of copies, and our former telephone operator – now a secretary for the Dial Press, thought she knew of one – an uncut soiled copy, which she found for me. I have done what I could to restore it and am sending it to you in care of Faber & Faber.'

1 – BD named those who had agreed to sign, so far – Lascelles Abercrombie, BD, TSE, the Dean of Canterbury, Edwin Muir, Hamish Miles, HR, IAR – 'leaving your group, David Cecil, Christopher Dawson, and Aldous Huxley. Sadler says no. I enclose his letter . . . The other letter is apparently not going to appear. The question will no doubt arise as to what we are to do if they don't print ours. Is it worthwhile sending it to any other paper?'

2 – *Cf.* D. H. Lawrence, *Look! We have come through* (1917).

3 – Lord David Cecil.

4 – Robert Barrington-Ward (1891–1948), barrister and journalist; from 1927, assistant editor of *The Times*, under Geoffrey Dawson; deputy editor, 1934–41; editor, 1941–8. See Donald McLachlan, *In the Chair: Barrington-Ward of 'The Times'* (1971); Iverach McDonald, *The History of 'The Times'*, V: *Struggles in War and Peace, 1939–1966* (1984).

Ez suggests McNair Wilson might like to contribute to *Criterion*. I await your considered opinion of his book.[1] Muggeridge has gone to Cournos for long review in June number.[2] Ez also says he has a letter from Buchan (John) expressing some sympathy with unorthodox financial theory, but I can't believe Buchan would ever wet his feet.

I ears as ow you was at a weddin, all drest up.

I have got to write a brief conversation (for Paggant) over the weekend between WREN, PEPYS and EVELYN (does that constellation too flagrantly violate probability?) so may I submit it to you afterwards to put into good English of the period?

Yours etc.

T.

You didnt enc. Sadler's letter[3] – Never mind.

TO *Aurelia Hodgson*[4]   TS Beinecke

25 March 1934   Faber & Faber Ltd

My dear Aurelia,

I am a Beast (to put the best foot forward, and the best complexion on it) not to have written to you (1) to thank you for your welcome letter to me in America (2) to thank you for your pretty Japanese card (3) to thank you for the Japanese comfits or sweetmeats or savoury biscuits, which were very much enjoyed both by myself and by my brother-in-law[5] who

---

1 – BD review of McNair Wilson, *Promise to Pay* (1934), C. 13 (July 1934), 703–4. BD told TSE, 22 Mar. 1934, of Wilson's book: 'Seems very good'; and on 24 Mar.: 'It is a sound and lucid exposé of the banking system, but runs off a little too much into wanting to be an exposure . . . I think that to ascribe it all to the inherent wickedness of bankers is a mistake. They did the job society asked them to do, and society must take the blame with them. Perhaps I am prejudiced in their favour. My great grandfather was the Governor of the Bank of England.'

2 – John Cournos reviewed Malcolm Muggeridge, *Winter in Moscow*, in C. 13 (July 1934), 670–3.

3 – Michael Sadler (The Master's Lodgings, University College, Oxford) to HR, 18 Mar.: 'I am glad you are sending this letter but, as I have had to sign another very important one (on another subject) which is still unpublished but may appear any day, I feel that I have done enough for the present to prefer to stand aside.'

4 – Aurelia Bolliger (1898–1984): born in Pennsylvania, studied at Heidelberg College, Ohio; taught in Wisconsin before journeying to teach at a mission school in Tokyo, 1922–3, and for the next seven years at the Women's College of Sendai, where she met and fell in love with the English poet Ralph Hodgson: she married him in 1933.

5 – Alfred Dwight ('Shef') Sheffield (1871–1961), husband of TSE's sister Ada, taught English at University School, Cleveland, Ohio, and was an English instructor, later Professor,

was born and brought up in China his father having been a President of A Missionary College in Pekin in consequence of Which he speaks Chinese like a native language as you might say and sits crosslegged quite natural being double jointed. Well as I was Starting to say I was Overjoyed as you might Expect to Ear your news and wish you both the best of Everythink wich is no more than you deserves I did send a cable wich I ope may go towards the remission of my omissions if you take my meaning.

I might mention (as perhaps you may not have heard it otherwise) that I have been living alone since my return and expect to do so for the rest of my natural life. Vivienne is not yet very pleased about it and it has all been very difficult, but I think in the end it will prove to be the best for both. I was most of the summer in the country and should have been glad of the company of R. H.[1]; these English Birds you can identify them from a Book when you see them but their Notes for that you need the company of someone who knows them. Still there was a lovely pair of Bulfinches in the neighbourhood, and plenty of dishwashers, wrens, and tits about the place. I have been working very hard and have published two Bad books of Lectures and have been writing no end of verses not poetry for a Paggeant which is to be produced in June. I wonder what Ralph will think of the following EPITHALAMIUM which is to be in the paggeant:

When I was a lad what had almost no sense,
    A gentle flirtation was all my delight;
And I used to go lookin for ex-pe-ri-ence
    Along the New Cut of a Saturday Night.
It was on a May evenin I'll never forget
    That I found the reward of my diligent search:
And I made a decision I'll never forget,
    Wich led to a weddin at Trinity Church.

When I was a delicate slip of a maid,
    What could eat nothing more than a couple o' chops,
Of a Saturday Night I occas'nally strayed
    Along the New Cut for to look at the shops.
Me avin no other design at the start,
    You may well be surprised at the end of my search:

---

of Group Work, Wellesley College. His works include *Lectures on the Harvard Classics: Confucianism* (1909).

1—Ralph Hodgson (1871–1962), Yorkshire-born poet; husband of Aurelia Hodgson: see letter to him, 31 Oct. 1934.

For a andsome young mason e captured me heart,
And led me all blushin to Trinity Church.

When this is done I have a Nonsense Book which I have been working on by fits and starts.

Do let me have your news some time. I am sure that there are many people looking forward to your return to England.

Ever yours affectionately,
T. S. Eliot

TO *Mary Hutchinson*   TS Texas

27 March 1934   Faber & Faber Ltd

Dear Mary,

Thank you for your letter. I am afraid that it is impossible for me to come in tomorrow or any day this week, so I shall not be able to see you until you return from Naples. Nothing particular to Aldous except affection, as I have been having some correspondence with him.

I have also had some correspondence with someone named Ormerod, no Ormerod Greenwood, who signs as the secretary of the Group Theatre. When I wondered whether the Group should be supported, my point of view was that of conscience – whether one should take the risk of encouraging these children to give up jobs or prospects of jobs for a wild goose chase – having in mind that they did not appear to have anyone of really distinguished ability and inspiration to lead them. My correspondence with Greenwood dealt with such questions as whether they were likely to be underfed, or to suffer from inadequate living conditions, etc.

However, as they will do it anyway, if they can raise the money, the question is how the money is to be raised. The public letter, which I was quite willing to sign, would really only have point if (a) they were applying for a very large sum or (b) if they were asking people of moderate means to subscribe a guinea or so. Doone was averse to the latter until they felt that they had something to show for their efforts, and therefore they seem well advised to postpone the public letter.

As for private wealthy benefactors. I confess that my heart sinks for them at the mention of Guinness. People who have an axe to grind, and want to be authors themselves, are not patrons in the proper sense, but merely scroungers on the poor. I know the type. I have seen Guinness's

Jonah (but don't tell him or *anybody* that I have), and I assure you it illustrates only lack of taste, lack of humour, lack of virility, and lack of the mildest literary gifts. My hopes are gone for these poor young people if they sell themselves to a twirp like that. E just aint got no manhood e aint. It is just as hard to find £300 honestly now as it ever was. Is it impossible to find a generous racketeer of some kind WHO DOESNT WANT TO WRITE. The trouble is one just doesn't mix in low enough circles to find such people. If one only knew a few folk like Capone and Stravisky [*sc.* Stavisky] – there must be heaps of them about.

Well, I suppose there's nothing more to say until we meet again. I do wish you a most happy holiday.

Affectionately,
Tom

I would put up five pounds on them. But I don't know where to find 59 others.

TO *Bonamy Dobrée*   TS Brotherton

27 March 1934   Faber & Faber Ltd

Dear Bonamy,

Very many thanks for your letter[1] – I had to go down to Rochester last night, and have been busy all of today – tomorrow committee most of the day, and Holy Week lots of services – I shant be able to do a hands turn about the matter till after Easter – suppose I should go to see Barrington Ward, but will confer with Herbert first – Morley returns tomorrow) Ezra also worritting the life out of me – Dawson (Chris.) still unready to sign, but always ready for long correspondence) Dawson showing alarming tendency towards fascism – question there rightly put by Ezra 'WHO are these fascists?'[2] – have more hope of fascist practicies [*sic*] to be made use

---

1–BD wrote, 24 Mar.: 'I don't think the list is bad as it stands, but I hope Dawson will relent. Am I to understand that Cecil Definitely Says No? I don't think it matters very much. Dawson's objections come largely, I venture to think, from not quite understanding the question. Douglas could be applied not only locally, but regionally, or to one great industry.'
2–See EP to TSE, 15 Mar. 1934: 'When Y/Brown had the toodle paper, he sez "Ez will you write me a nice piece about Fascism"

'so wiff me uzul takk [usual tact] I writes

'"The question is not so much: what is fascism but WHO are these fascists"

'That is the kind of simple statement that keeps my verbal manifestation OUT of so many papers.'

of by astute quiet people than by cabotins[1] like Mosey[2] – likely to take all the worst features and leave the best. S. Dark saying Church never more alive than today – A. Orage saying it is all ready to walk the plank, domb damn everybody – will answer your letter adequately according to my ability over weekend – meanwhile HERE is my dialogue do not laugh at my simplicity: I am told to have Wren talking to Pepys and Evelyn (First, does this too far violate probability) and saying he is designing St Pauls. His predicting jerrybuilding of future is MY idea and I should like to keep it – please PLEASE try to put this into good period language for me and hash it about as you will, shall be grateful and will acknowledge in preface yrs etc.[3]

T.

1 – Cabotin: 'low-class actor' (*OED*); barn-stormer; histrionic politician.
2 – Sir Oswald Mosley.
3 – BD replied, 28 Mar.: 'I hasten to return your admirable little conversation [in the text of *The Rock*], with one or two suggestions: but as it stands it seems to me excellent – distant in time without being at all "quaint".

'The meeting is not wildly improbable, though I know of no record of the three actually meeting. But no doubt they must often have met at the Royal Society, of which they were all members and Pepys, if not the others, at one time president. The first record, however, of Evelyn meeting Pepys is in 1684, two or three years, I would gather, after the date of your conversation. Still, I only have the Everyman Evelyn. Any way, Pepys knew Wren, Evelyn knew Wren, and Pepys and Evelyn knew each other: and that is enough.

'I have, however, one or two other observations to make. The bulk of Pepys's speech should go to Evelyn, who admired Wren as an architect. What impressed Pepys most about Wren was his instrument for drawing in perspective, and he ordered one to be made for himself. He does not mention Wren as an architect in the diary, but still, that was in early days. Pepys did not really care for the arts, except music. He loved organising the Navy Office, and he had a passion for gadgets. Evelyn was the real virtuoso.

'There is one thing, however, I implore you to delete, and that is the reference to port. Port did not become a usual drink until after the Methuen treaty with Portugal in 1703. They probably drank Burgundy: but in case of error, why not just say wine? Anyway, not port. Most unlikely.

'I must take you to task also about distorting the standard biography of Wren. This runs, if I remember right

> Christopher Wren
> Went to dine with some men.
> He said, if anyone calls,
> Say I'm designing St Pauls.

'It says, you observe, that he went to *dine* with some men, not to *wine* with some men. Still, I have no doubt you will be able to reconcile this with your artistic conscience, especially as the biographer quoted does not give his authority.'

TO *Ormerod Greenwood*   CC

29 March 1934   [*The Criterion*]

Dear Mr Greenwood,

Thank you for your letter of the 23d.[1] I am not sure that I *am* relieved by your decision not to make a public appeal. On the whole, I think you are right. But the attempt to raise £300 privately also bristles with difficulties. You don't want it all from one person if you can help it, unless that person has absolutely no desire to write, paint, compose or act. There are always rich people who want to do one or more of these things, and if you get into the clutches of any such folk God help you. At any rate, if you do have to take such money, be firm and give nothing in return, but show them who's master.

O yes, I know about gambling, and am quite used to living on the edge of one abyss or another. Incidentally, publishing nowadays is not one of the safer occupations.

Your account of ways and means, feeding and work is encouraging. Let me know whenever I can be of any use. I hope to have a talk with Mrs Hutchinson about the financial possibilities when she returns from Italy.

> Yours ever sincerely,
> [T. S. Eliot]

TO *The Editor,* The New English Weekly

[published 29 March 1934, 575–6] [No address given]

                    'The Theology of Economics'

Sir,

To some, at least, of your readers it must be a matter of regret that a paper which is able to express itself so clearly on political and economic matters should have to take refuge (p. 523, lower right hand corner) in cloudy truculence when it concerns itself with ecclesiastical polity. As one who was in sympathy with the Archbishop of York's proposals before

---

1–'I think you may be a little relieved to know that we have decided not to make a big formal public appeal through the press at this time. We feel that the sum we require is so minute (as appeals go), our organisation so unknown . . . that it is wiser not to court the limelight; it would spoil our chances of any public appeal later . . . There is no escaping the fundamental gamble of the whole business. Everyone in the theatre is a gambler . . . We are going to use your valuable suggestion about the bank in making our appeal (which will now be a private appeal).'

they were known to the *New English Weekly*, I should be interested to know what this paper thinks of them; and as you say only that 'there can be no hesitation in the minds of normal people about the side they are to take,' I have what is to me the still more vital interest of wanting to know whether I am, according to the judgment of the *New English Weekly*, a normal person.

It strikes me further that your Theological Editor is inclined to interpret the words *Thy Kingdom come . . . in earth* in a way of his own. I do not know what he means by its '*native* condition of spirituality': at what date was the Kingdom of Heaven born? And when he speaks of 'agony and passion' he is transferring to the incarnation two terms which are properly applicable to the Atonement. What does your Theological Editor or Leader Writer *mean* by the 'Kingdom of Heaven upon Earth'? What does he mean by saying that the ideal mission (I do not know how an ideal mission differs from a mission) of the Church is not of *saving souls alone* but of creating a divine society of Mankind upon Earth? Is not the saving of souls the only way to create a divine society upon Earth? I should like some assurance that by 'the Kingdom of Heaven upon Earth' your Theological Editor does not mean the National Dividend.

I trust that I have not been prejudiced – though in the spirit of one laying his cards upon the table I mention the point – by your writer's using the verbs *to pose* and *to sense*.

T. S. Eliot

TO *Martin Shaw* TS Houghton

Good Friday [30 March] 1934   Faber & Faber Ltd

Dear Shaw,

Here is a new copy of the Girl Guide Song with a different third verse – better I think than the last I sent you. Poor enough, in all conscience. Had I realised at the beginning how perfectly regular such a song had to be (and of course we did not know that it was to be applied to Sunday School treats) I should have chosen a longer and easier metre – this one is not well adapted to the purpose, and it is very difficult to find words with meanings, that will fit exactly. I am afraid I can do no better than this, so go ahead with Novello!

No more songs for you – I have got to the final chorus now.

Sincerely yours,
T. S. Eliot

3 April 1934   Faber & Faber Ltd

My dear Ottoline,

Thank you very much for your letter. I think it would be very pleasant to come on Saturday – if that or Friday is all one to you – and so I will do, to tea, unless I hear to the contrary.[1]

I wanted to send you lilies – but florists' lilies are never quite as one would like lilies to be – there is something both *astiqué*[2] and enervated about them.[3]

> Affectionately,
> Tom

---

1 – TSE went to tea, with Dilys Powell, Elizabeth Bowen and L. A. G. Strong, on 7 Apr.

2 – *astiqué* (Fr.): polished.

3 – OM's journal (BL), Easter Sunday 1934 (1 Apr.): 'I was very humiliated yesterday, when we arrived home . . . to find a large Bunch of White Lilac a present from T. S. Eliot! . . . After all my anger & annoyance & abuse of the poor man, about his book [*After Strange Gods*]!

'– I don't know why he sent it – except that I suppose he finds me in thought after all – sympathetic as a Christian but he gives me the impression always when I see him of disapproving of my religion. He is *Ecclesiastical* more than Religious but still I know he *prays*.'

OM recorded too, when at tea with VW, that 'Leonard Woolf told a long Story of Eliot, who in the war called himself Capt. Eliot & had rooms in Charing X Rd. – he gave a Party – with weeks of elaborate preparation & had the Hutchinsons – R. Fry, & the Woolfs – & he turned greener & greener. The food was all put out on little tables . . . at last he was so green that he had to fly to the WC & be sick – He was so drunk – How the evening ended I don't know . . . but next morning he rang up all his Guests .. & Virginia heard a Despairing Voice imploring her to forgive him – "Virginia, can you ever – Will you ever . . . . It was Terrible – but I was so nervous & excited that I drank a little to steady my Nerves – etc. . . . etc . . . Will you ever forgive me" & this he did to every one –

'TSE is a queer lonely isolated figure – without the Capacity of friendship – he only can be polite & formal.. – Never intime.'

Later in the same diary: 'T.S.E. & I are religious – but he is not a Mystic – he is Ecclesiastical – & he has never been very friendly or consistent with me . . .'

OM noted further: 'On Saturday last [7 Apr. 1934] I had Tom Eliot to tea & Dilys Powell to meet him. It was very interesting because I got T. E. to reveal himself more. He is rather crazy really .. his *complete* removal from the ordinary world .. the intense absence of feeling with the ordinary mortal – He simplifies Life – There is only Black or White, & *very* little White – I talked to him about Lawrence – He was not interested nor would he really believe that Lawrence wasn't a Devil. – I assured him that L was really *very good* & religious & I said how orthodox he was . . . & tried to explain problem[?] of L & F – he said that L liked being outraged by her – .. I could equally have said Did you like being outraged by Vivienne ..? He really is very superficial he hadn't taken the trouble to read L last Poems, . for he is frightened, . he is in TSE eyes definitely _Evil_. [. . .] Tom is an *Ostrich* who hides his head to prevent himself seeing Life, – he has a temperamental Dislike of Life, . & I think his Calvinist forefathers must have *hated* Beauty – for when I was showing him & DP some books of

TO *Stephen Spender*

TS Northwestern

3 April 1934　　　　　　　　　Faber & Faber Ltd

Dear Spender,

You are, I imagine, leaving tomorrow or the next day for Serbia, and I shall not have seen you again after all. So this is simply to convey my warmest good wishes for your southern sojourn; my hope that you will find Dobrovnik (or wherever it is) a happy place in which to work; and that you will return refreshed in body and spirit.[1]

I have been puzzling over the Twelve. Perhaps when you come back I shall be able to tell you whether I like it or not. It is compact, and needs careful reading. Only the end seems to me ignominiously picturepostcardy.

Ever yours,
T. S. E.

In any case, I shall prize it as a personal reminder.

TO *I. A. Richards*

TS Magdalene

3 April 1934　　　　　　　　　Faber & Faber Ltd

My dear Richards,

I am rather at a loss to know what to do about Jennings and his article on Gray.[2] It is extremely ingenious and rather fascinating but it is much too long for a periodical and too short for anything else. I should like to have your candid and confidential opinion of the value of a whole book of this sort of thing, which he looks capable of turning out with the greatest facility. He didn't give me the impression of having a mind anywhere near the class of Empson's, although extraordinarily clever. Of course a book on this subject of Jennings would have no chance of success, but would

---

Greek Statues V & IV Centuries he said they repelled him for he felt they were not far removed from Serpent Worship! I looked at him with mouth Open . . . I don't feel happy or at ease with him – for I feel he isn't frank – or really sincere – Also if he really is sincere in his cruel views then he & I have *nothing* in common. We asked him what "shocked" him most in Life. He wouldn't say. I said Cruelty – and I felt he knew that I knew that he was cruel. – I don't know if he also has a *very* kind side – or if that isn't sincere – I *have* seen the kind side very often, – altho it may be only courtesy that has been trained in him by his bringing up – He is really a very sick man – or else crazy – or a very very odd survival of some Calvinist Ancestor.'

1 – Spender was spending time in Mlini, about five miles outside Dubrovnik.

2 – Humphrey Jennings had undertaken postgraduate research at Pembroke College, Cambridge, on Thomas Gray, under the remote supervision of IAR.

it be a book which one might consider it a duty to the world to publish? I rather doubt it but I should like very much to do something to help Jennings, if it were possible.

The lady who consulted you about sending me some articles, has sent them, and merely says discreetly in her letter that she had spoken to you about it first.

Yours ever,
T. S. E.

TO *The Editor,* The Times   cc

4 April 1934[1]   [Faber & Faber Ltd]

Sir,

In view of the publication of a letter of Sir Geoffrey Clarke and others in your issue of today,[2] we beg to submit without further delay the following statement which we have had in preparation independently.

In consideration of the continued difficulty experienced by all countries, whatever their political system, in adjusting consumption to production, the undersigned believe that it would be of value to have a thorough and public examination of some scheme of National Credit. It would appear that the possibilities of production throughout the world have enormously increased, so as to give every individual a certainty of adequate provision for the necessities of life. There appears to be lacking some machinery for distribution, by means of which the enormous values inherent in the national capacity to produce could be made available to every man and woman. One such scheme has been before the public for some years, and is attracting increasing attention; and though it has been severely criticised,

1–Published as 'The Money System: Industry and Orthodox Finance', *The Times*, 5 Apr. 1934, 6.

2–'Poverty in Plenty: Faults of Monetary System: Call for Parliamentary Inquiry' (letter signed by Sir Geoffrey Clarke and eight others inc. Lord Sempill), *Times* 4 Apr. 1934, 8: '[T]he present monetary system, the proper function of which is to facilitate the production of goods and their distribution to customers as required, has broken down, both in its national and international aspects . . .

'We, the undersigned, in common with a large and rapidly growing body of citizens who are genuinely concerned at existing conditions, have come to the conclusion that gold is not essential as the basis for the issue of national money, and that nations should not be under obligation to make payments internationally with gold. A system must, in our view, be established under which the issue and recall of currency and credit will be regulated on a rational, national, and scientific basis, so that the correct number of money-tokens shall be available to consumers to enable them to enjoy the output of production.'

the scheme shows a surprising vitality. The criticisms, when they are free from prejudice, do not seem to amount to more than academic objections. What we feel to be essential is a thorough and impartial survey of any proposal which offers a solution of the most urgent problems of the day, without committing the nation to a political programme involving other issues on which there can be no general agreement.

Yours faithfully,

[Signed by] Lascelles Abercrombie, Bonamy Dobrée, T. S. Eliot, Aldous Huxley, Hewlett Johnson,[1] Edwin Muir, Hamish Miles, Herbert Read, I. A. Richards.

TO *Alistair Cooke*

CC

4 April 1934   [*The Criterion*]

My dear Cooke,

As I expected I have had no success in placing your article on O'Neill,[2] for the obvious reason that the plays which you criticise are still unknown in this country. I did, however, take up the matter with Curtis Brown Ltd, one of the best known agencies, who, I thought, might be useful for you to know as they have an office in New York as well as offices here and on the Continent. They would be interested in doing business with you, if you should care to let them handle any future books and they might deal also, if you wished, with such periodical writing as could be placed here. They suggest that you should get in touch with their American manager, Mr Raymond Everitt at 10 East 49th Street, New York, mentioning my name.

I don't see myself that there is any particular point in your bothering at the moment, and I am assuming that you will be back in England at the end of the summer. I look forward to hearing from you about your book, when you have anything further to say about it, and shall always be glad of your news. I don't envy you the experience of a winter such as I never met in America myself.

Do let me know when you expect to return.

Yours sincerely,

[T. S. Eliot]

1–Hewlett Johnson, Dean of Canterbury Cathedral since 1931. (BD to TSE, 11 Mar. 1934: 'Hewlett-Johnson was put in to give it a tinge of not being exclusively literary or artistic.')
2–David Higham had written to Erica Wright (TSE's secretary) on 28 Mar., that they could not manage to place Cooke's article 'Salvation and Eugene O'Neill'.

TO *I. A. Richards*   TS Magdalene

4 April 1934   Faber & Faber Ltd

Dear Richards,

I am delighted by your letter of the 22nd and look forward with the keenest interest to reading your Coleridge.[1] What you tell me you find about Coleridge is what I have always wanted to think, and what I have wanted to find out for myself. I think I told you, or if not I have told other people, that I have felt that in my lectures I have underrated him and some day I should like to make amends for this. I shall accordingly be quite ready to accept calmly any strictures that you feel obliged to make on my remarks about him.

The current *Criterion* has already appeared and the June *Criterion* should go to press at the end of this month. I shall be very happy to have a review from you of Gustav Stern, whoever he is, and will put it in if it arrives in time.[2]

I have been on the point of writing to ask whether you and Mrs Richards could come up to town and go to see Charles Laughton's *Macbeth* with me.[3] It will run through April but I imagine that your vacation activities will make such an expedition impossible.

Beechcroft[4] is a very charming young amateur, a contemporary of David Cecil's at Oxford, who is now in some advertising business in London. That is about all I can think of to say about him.

Yours ever,

T. S. E.

When you return, may I send an essay by a Chinese, on English translations of Chinese poetry, for your opinion?

1–IAR wrote on 22 Mar.: 'My *Coleridge* [*Coleridge on Imagination*] – after having been a goods train heavily if richly laden – has suddenly turned into a sort of meteor and gone up into the Heavens. It's now a revelation of the essential mythopoeic faculty and settles provisionally all such things as the status of poetic belief (and some others) . . . When people have seen that he has all this, I think they will make him out to be quite as big as philosopher as he was a poet . . .'

2–'I'd rather like, if I can, to send you a review of Gustav Stern on *Meanings*.' IAR had written on Stern's *Meaning and Change of Meaning* (1931) in *Psyche* 13 (1933), 185–96.

3–Charles Laughton's *Macbeth*, dir. Tyrone Guthrie, with Flora Robson as Lady Macbeth, played in the 1933–4 season at the Old Vic, London.

4–IAR asked: 'Who is T. O. Beachcroft, who writes on Nicholas Ferrar and Herbert in *Criterion* October 1932? He's provided a sort of cannibal feast for me there and I think I should know who it is I've been biting. Really he's near to a limit!' 'Nicholas Ferrar and George Herbert', C. 12 (Oct. 1932), 24–42. (See *Coleridge on Imagination*, ch. 9, for IAR's feasting.)

TO *Louis MacNeice* CC

5 April 1934 [Faber & Faber Ltd]

Dear Mr MacNeice,

I am very glad to get your letter of April 2nd, especially as, having had no reply to my earlier letter, I had wondered what the present situation was.[1] I shall look forward to the new volume when you think it ready to send.

Of course, you will understand that I can't in advance give any positive assurance of publication. It depends upon a number of business factors, as well as upon the merit of the book. I can only say that I am confident that I shall be able to recommend your poems to my firm. Incidentally the fact that they will not be ready, as you say, before the early autumn is an advantage because we have a rather heavy programme of poetry for the autumn season, and there would be much more chance of the firm's accepting your book for the early spring.

With all best wishes,
Yours sincerely,
[T. S. Eliot]

TO *John Maynard Keynes*[2] TS King's

5 April 1934 Faber & Faber Ltd

My dear Keynes,

How charming of you to write to me about my very unsatisfactory lectures.[3] This is approval from an unexpected quarter. I am glad of your

1–MacNeice had been rearranging his poems, and cutting out some (mostly early ones). 'I have lately been writing some longer poems which, for want of a better name, I am calling "Eclogues". Two of these, I think, I could put at the beginning of my book.' He would be able to submit the revised collection in the early autumn. 'I had much rather . . . they were published by you than by any other firm' (*Letters of Louis MacNeice*, ed. Jonathan Allison (2010), 239).

2–J. M. Keynes (1883–1946), influential economist and theorist of money (expert on macroeconomics); pamphleteer; patron of the arts (begetter and financier of the Arts Theatre, Cambridge), government adviser and negotiator; editor of *The Economic Journal*, 1912–45; columnist for the *Nation and Athenaeum* (of which he was chairman from 1923); intimate of the Bloomsbury circle; Trustee of the National Gallery; author of *The Economic Consequences of the Peace* (1919), *A Treatise on Money* (2 vols, 1930), and *The General Theory of Employment, Interest and Money* (1936).

3–Keynes's letter not traced: TSE sent it to his sister Ada, in part because he could not decipher one particular word in the missive. Ada responded, 29 Apr. 1934: 'Looking over Mr

support in my avoidance of the economic problem. That, of course, is what particularly annoys my friends of the Social Credit persuasion but I remain of the opinion that I should not discuss matters about which I am ignorant. Furthermore it would, from my point of view, weaken my case if I attached it to any particular vision of economic paradise.

Although it may seem outside of your interests I venture to hope that you may come to see my church pageant at Sadler's Wells in June. I have taken the liberty of engaging two of my characters, a bricklayer and an agitator, in a discussion concerning yourself.

Yours ever,

T. S. Eliot

I have just decyphered [*sic*] one word as 'nonsense'. I am afraid I can't go the whole way with you!

TO *Virginia Woolf*[1]   TS Berg

[? 5 April 1934]   Faber & Faber Ltd

[No salutation]

I recognise at once the numerical importance of the Venns, but as modern experts on warfare favour a small professional force against a large army of ill-trained conscripts, I think that at this point we ought to introduce the concept of quality. Every Head of a House, or President of Harvard, or Founder of a University or College, to count as 10. What about itinerant preachers and fanatics? that is a doubtful point. I am anxious to include John Brown of Ossawatomie, but am afraid that I should really be giving you the advantage. For the moment, I will post the Revd Dan'l Greenleaf, the Revd Dr Asahel Stearns,[2] the Revd Obadiah Smith, and (among Moderns) the Revd Fred. Eliot (author of *Hammered on the Anvil*, a book of parochial talks to Young Men) in charge of skirmishing parties and raiders. The body of hollow square (heads) behind. It is unfortunate that Julius Caesar Eliot never took orders.

Keynes' letter again, I think you are mistaken in taking a very illegible word as "nonsense". He writes "if you're going to treat that (dogmatic theology) as more than perhaps valuable —— I fancy that I should find it a very cheap escape from the problem." Valuable nonsense does not make sense. I fancy it is some word meaning "example" or "confirmation". It is an awfully nice letter. How was he to talk with? at the Wolff's [*sic*]? Perhaps he told you what that word was.'

1 – Virginia Woolf (1882–1941), novelist, essayist and critic: see Biographical Register.

2 – Asahel Stearns (1774–1839) – descendant of Isaac Stearns, who migrated from England to Salem in 1630 – Massachusetts state senator; Professor of Law at Harvard Law School; author of *The Revised Statutes of the Commonwealth of Massachusetts* (1836).

I have marked down the 18th of the month in red Ink. I wonder should I wear my new Dinner Jacket (Tuxedo) or my new Sports Suit. I have had a touching letter from the Wizard of Finance, & shall be glad to grasp his hand.[1]

T. S. E.

I have just been made a Churchwarden.[2] That ought to count 3 points.

At 8 o'clock.

Monks House might count ½ point.

I forgot to say that *future* clergy are barred.

TO *Gavin Ewart*[3]   CC

5 April 1934   [*The Criterion*]

Dear Mr Ewart,

I have your letter and have made a few suggestions towards the improvement of your translation of my poem into French.[4] I should urge you strongly, however, to submit it to some French writer for criticism as I don't feel confident of my own capacity. While I approve warmly of

1–On 18 Apr. VW noted: 'Tonight Tom & Maynard [Keynes] dine to discuss Tom's book: *After Strange Gods*. Julian [Bell] & E[lizabeth] Bowen come in afterwards. I want to try & make myself write down the discussion tomorrow, as I am keeping off fiction' (*Diary 4*, 208). On 19 Apr. she reported: 'It began at dinner. Tom & Maynard talking about his book. You have brought up again one of the primal questions, & nobody has even tried to consider it. No, said Tom, much like a great toad with jewelled eyes.

'Morality. And JM [Keynes] said that he would be inclined not to demolish Xty if it were proved that without it morality is impossible. "I begin to see that our generation – yours & mine V., owed a great deal to our fathers' religion. And the young, like Julian, who are brought up without it, will never get so much out of life. Theyre trivial: like dogs in their lusts. We have the best of both worlds. We destroyed Xty & yet had its benefits." Well the argument was something like that, I pressed Tom to define belief in God; but he sheered off' (*Diary* 4, 208).

2–He was appointed Vicar's Warden (the highest lay position in the parish) after High Mass on Easter Monday, 2 Apr. The position meant that he was an ex-officio member of St Stephen's Parochial Church Council, from 1934 to 1959.

3–Gavin Ewart (1916–95), poet; reluctant advertising copywriter, 1952–71; Chair of the Poetry Society, 1978–9; author of *Poems and Songs* (1939); *Pleasures of the Flesh* (1966); *The Deceptive Grin of the Gravel Porters* (1968); *Collected Poems, 1933–1980* (1980).

4–Ewart, who was staying until 17 Apr. at the Château de Nanteuil, Huisseau-s-Cosson, Loir-et-Cher, wrote in an undated letter that he had been trying to translate into French 'Triumphal March', which he aspired to publish in a French periodical. He enclosed the MS of his effort.

translations both from and into a foreign language as a valuable exercise for the translator, I would dissuade you from attempting to publish any such translation until you have a more complete mastery of the French language. You will observe that I have corrected the spelling of the French word for sausages.

As a matter of fact there are very few French writers whom I can trust to translate my own writings into French: I have only known one who was completely satisfactory. I could not possibly authorise the enclosed translation.

With all good wishes,
Yours sincerely,
[T. S. Eliot]

TO *Mélodie Stuart-Fergusson*[1]   cc

5 April 1934   [Faber & Faber Ltd]

Dear Mrs Stuart-Fergusson,

I have been thinking about your letter of April 3rd but I am so far at a loss to find any way in which I can help.[2] I assume from what you say that the boy is too much of an invalid to be able to come to see me. I should like to know a little more about him.

In the first place can you tell me approximately what his age is and what is the kind and extent of his general education? Was his knowledge of French, German and Italian acquired by living abroad or solely by study in England? Has he had any technical instruction in typing and shorthand, and has he had any experience in proof reading? It seems just possible that I might from time to time be able to direct proof reading work towards him, if I can produce any evidence or assurance of his ability. You will understand that knowledge of a reader's general education and interests is

---

1–Mélodie Stuart Fergusson, The Three Arts Club, 19A Marylebone Road, N.W.I.

2–'Have you, by any happy chance, a little typing, or indeed any other work which has to do with the making of books, to a really brilliant boy, to help in saving a brave little family from disaster?

'They are gentle people . . . The boy, Anthony Lawrence, is an only child and an invalid; the father is out of work and ineligible for any kind of unemployment pay; the mother has serious heart trouble, and will not last long, I am afraid . . .

'The boy speaks and writes fluent French, German and Italian, and would, I am sure, be perfectly reliable with proofs, an index, or anything of that kind. And his typing is *excellent* in *every* way. I have assured myself on that point before asking others to employ him.'

very useful in deciding what types of book he could most efficiently read
in proof.

Yours sincerely,
[T. S. Eliot]

TO *Germaine Berder*[1]   CC

5 April 1934   [Faber & Faber Ltd]

Dear Miss Berder,

I must apologise for having kept your stories so long.[2] I assure you that
they are only two amongst a great many sufferers, some of much longer
duration; but that is no excuse.

Of the two, I like 'Portsmouth Lights' the better. 'The Joy of Her' seems
like a succession of images and thoughts without form, or with a form
which escapes me. One supposes that the episode of the little dog must
have some allegorical significance, as it has no apparent connexion with
Marie. The story reads rather like a dream to which one has no key.

'Portsmouth Lights' on the other hand has a beginning, a middle and an
end; and the conversation with the farmer in the darkness is real enough.
But here again there seems to be more intended than reaches the reader.
What is the significance of this apparition, if such it was? One would
expect that the mysterious farmer had appeared, at some critical moment,
to give a hint of guidance to the narrator. The conversation – except for a
slight stiffness of phrasing here and there – is good; but the effect which is
built up by this curious talk under odd conditions is just allowed to drop
plop at the end. The man seems much more like a being from another
world *during* the conversation than at the end of the story! And it is not
enough to give the impression of a supernatural visitor; it is necessary to
give the impression that there was some *reason* for his appearance.

Both pieces give me the impression that you have a keen interest in the
occult etc. but this is not put across to the reader. There is, however, a
slightly spooky intensity which might be developed. You need a good deal
more practice! [*sic*] and look at first rate short stories to see at what points
the author concentrates the interest.

---

1 – Germaine Berder was to be author of *Your Hands Can Help to Heal You* (1954).
2 – Mollie Culpin had submitted Berder's stories to TSE on 6 Nov. 1933.

With all good wishes,
and renewed apologies,
Yours very sincerely,
[T. S. Eliot]

TO *H. C. Crofton*[1]   CC

6 April 1934   [Faber & Faber Ltd]

My dear Crofton,

It is good to see your initials again and to get in touch with you once more.[2] This has been a very busy winter for me, and I have thought often of our postponed lunch. I don't expect to be quite so busy in the immediate future, and should be glad if we could now arrange it. Almost any day in the week except Wednesday is possible and I would come to the City if that is more convenient for you than joining me in the West-end.

Is this Freeman the same Freeman who [came] into the bank on demobilisation, and who has only one arm? If so, salute him from me. I have read the poems but I must admit that while they have a somewhat fragile charm I cannot see very much hope of a distinguished future.[3]

Do let me hear from you about lunch.[4]

Yours ever,
[T. S. Eliot]

1–H. C. Crofton (d. 1938), who had been a colleague and friend at Lloyds Bank, was the senior of the four managers of the Colonial and Foreign Department. Crofton's son John told the Archivist of Lloyds Bank, 1 Aug. 1980: 'I have memories of my father inviting T. S. for several week-ends to our home. My mother . . . used to speak of him and of how much they enjoyed his visits. (If I may add that in those days it was a little unusual for the Chief Foreign Manager to invite "a clerk" for week-ends!!!) I do know that the object of the visits from my father's side, was to persuade T. S. to give up the Bank and devote himself to his obvious real calling.'

2–Crofton wrote, 4 June: 'I owe you a very great deal in having been enabled to see "The Rock"; there is only one word for it, which, incidentally, one of the critics used – "stupendous".'

3–Crofton wrote, 28 Mar., 'I enclose some poems written by one of my Staff, which came as a great surprise to me and which, as a layman, strike me as being exceptionally good.'

4–Crofton (9 Apr.) proposed lunch in the City at 12 o'clock on Mon., 16 Apr.

TO *Derek Phit Clifford*   CC

6 April 1934   [*The Criterion*]

Dear Mr Clifford,

Thank you for taking my criticism so nicely. It is all right to be led first by ear, so to speak, and then to make sure of the sense. That seems to me the proper order. As for your aversion to *The Golden Bough* as a source of inspiration for poets, I am inclined to think that that period is over and done with. I think, however, that one should continue to respect the Oxford Dictionary because one is not entitled to use a word in a new way until one is fully aware of all the ways in which it has been used previously.

I think that just as the ear takes precedence over the eye, and reason in poetry so the [words missing on carbon copy] This, however, does not absolve one from the duty of using exactly the right word.

> With all best wishes,
> Yours sincerely,
> [T. S. Eliot]

TO *William Force Stead*[1]   CC

6 April 1934   [Faber & Faber Ltd]

My dear Stead,

Many thanks for your letter from the [RMS] 'Berengaria'.[2] I am very happy, as will be all of your friends, to welcome you back, and merely send this line to conjure you to try to arrange a meeting as soon as you can.

What you say about the situation in America interests me very much, and I long for an opportunity to discuss it with you, and I pray that your affairs may take a more hopeful turn.

> Yours ever affectionately,
> [T. S. Eliot]

1–William Force Stead (1884–1967), poet and critic; Chaplain of Worcester College, Oxford: see Biographical Register L6.
2–Stead was returning to the UK because he had been unable to secure a job at a US university. 'So far as my experience goes, things over there are fundamentally unsound. The Govt. is spending billions in an effort to improve things – the improvements can hardly be measured in millions – So it seems a bad bargain. And the Govt is honeycombed with grafters and chisellers.'

7 April 1934   Faber & Faber Ltd

Dear Shaw,

Here is the result of my fiddling with that damn'd syllable; and small pride have I in the result.[1] This abominable jingle seems to grow more and more ignoble the more I work over it: here I hope is its last derisible phase. Don't tell me once more there is a jot or tittle too few or too many!

I didn't know you wanted the final chorus.[2] But if so here it is. There is more to come, but that will be merely the monologue by S. Peter! I am finding it very difficult to get him in the role of chairman, introducing the speaker of the evening, Winnington Ingram.[3]

Yours sincerely,

T. S. Eliot

I seem now to have written everything that will concern you; but I should be glad if you would let me know if I am right.

1–Shaw reported in an undated note (Bod MS. Don. d. 44, fol. 20ᵛ) that he thought the latest version of the 'Girl Guide's Song' – properly, 'The Builders' Song' – 'first-class'. In the third verse, however, there was 'one awkward musical place. Last line really wants another syllable at beginning. This is pattern

    In this London of ours
    Oh of yours & of mine

'Without that syllable there is a *musical* hiatus. V. 3 is the only penultimate line with a masculine ending.

'Could this be done? Otherwise it won't sing well.

'"Ours" can't be sung like "towers" unfortunately! Shall we print 3 verses & say "go back to 1st verse to end with if you want to"?

'I think 3 enough for singing.'

'The Builders' was printed in *The Rock*, 19 (first stanza, repeated at the end of the play) and 28–9 (third stanza). The second stanza of the musical setting did not appear in *The Rock*.

2–'*I am panting for final chorus. Times hastes away!*'

3–Arthur Foley Winnington-Ingram (1858–1946): Bishop of London, 1901–39.

8 April 1934   *The Criterion*

Dear Mr Otaké

I have your letter of March 23rd and will answer your questions as well as I can, point by point.[2]

(1) a. So far as I know there are no literary sources whatever for Sosostris or Phlebas or Mrs Equitone. To the best of my knowledge both names and persons were pure inventions but as you are a student of Coleridge, you will know how large a part memory plays in invention.

b. Himavant is Sanskrit for the Himalayas in general.

(ii) I had no deliberate intention of dividing the poems according to the divisions of Elizabethan drama. There may, of course, be some analogy but it formed no part of my conscious purpose. What similarity there is between *The Waste Land* and Mr Pound's *Cantos* lies I think in versification, in the use of allusion and in a similar kind of concentration. There is no similarity in form.

(iii) 'The Song of one bird, 'the leap of one fish'. That I imagine comes from a well-known poem of Wordsworth. <'Song of one Bird' Yes. Woodthrush (American)>

---

1 – Taken partly from the carbon copy, and partly from the frontispiece reproduction of the original letter, containing manuscript additions, in *Ishin o motomete*, Masaru Otaké's translation of *After Strange Gods*, 'Tradition and the Individual Talent', and *Thoughts after Lambeth*.

2 – Otaké, a Japanese graduate student in the English Department, Syracuse University, New York – working on a thesis, 'The Waste Land and the Ancient Mariner: a Comparison' – asked:

'I (i) The literary sources of Sosostris and Phlebas, if there are any; are they purely your creation? Do they have some meaning in the sense Mrs Equitone has? I have in mind naturally Sosostris, and the "afflicted" or "the oppressed", as used by Aristophanes and Theocritus. (ii) The location of Himavant.

'II I have noticed the structure of the poem, namely the five divisions and their function, has the same kind of scheme, as seen in the Elizabethan plays. Is this view valid? It is said that there is a very close similarity between the Waste Land and Mr Pound's Cantos, but is it not true that in this sense of totality and form, both differ greatly? . . .

'III "The song of one bird, the leap of one fish . . ." P. 141 The Use of Poetry. Is this passage from your actual experience? I was struck by the fact that all these images appear in the Waste Land.

'IV Are you fond of the Mermaid series?

'(V) Even Mr P. E. More seems to think that Ash-Wednesday is radically different from the Waste Land, whereas I feel that the Waste Land itself is profoundly religious, infinitely sad and lyrical, and yet wistfully hopeful, though it is very far indeed like the fragrant pessimism of the East. In short, the chaos is not of the mind of T. S. Eliot, but the world of "appearance" confronting him.'

(iv) The Mermaid Series are extremely useful because of the form and size but the establishment of the texts leaves something to seek.

(v) I am inclined to agree with this against what you state to be the opinion of my friend Dr More. I am not clear, however, as to what 'the fragrant pessimism of the East' may be.

Yours very truly,

T. S. Eliot

I cannot think of Buddhism, or of any of the Higher Religions, as 'pessimistic'.

TO *J. L. Brandler*   CC

10 April 1934   [Faber & Faber Ltd]

Dear Sir,

I have read your essay HOERE ISRAEL with very great interest and sympathy, as has also another reader who was able to bestow more time upon it than I had at my disposal. While we feel that this is a document which ought to be published and which appears to be quite translatable, we don't believe that our firm is the one which could publish it to the greatest mutual advantage. It is a small book: we publish a considerable number of books every season, and I fear that a book of this sort would be rather submerged in our list, and that we should not be able to give it the attention which it deserves.

The firm which seems to me the most suitable to undertake this book is the Hogarth Press. If the suggestion appeals to you, I shall be happy to send the MS round there with a personal letter to Mr Leonard Woolf, the proprietor, who is a very old friend of mine. Or if you prefer to call and see Mr Woolf, I will give you a note of introduction and also write to him separately. Meanwhile I hold the MS until I receive your instructions.

Yours faithfully,

[T. S. Eliot]

Director

TO *Ford Madox Ford*¹   CC

10 April 1934   [Faber & Faber Ltd]

Dear Ford,

I am nearly always in town, and if you are going to be here for a little time, I should be very glad to drop in and see you.² Would you care to suggest one or two alternative days after this week?

Yours sincerely,
[T. S. Eliot]

TO *Walter Richard Sickert*³   CC

10 April 1934   [Faber & Faber Ltd]

Dear Mr Sickert,

I don't suppose for a moment that you will remember me but, as I appear to be the only one of my Board of Directors who can lay claim to the honour of having met you, I have been delegated to write to you on a matter about which we are unanimously agreed.

I don't know whether you have ever contemplated writing your memoirs but if not, I hope very much that we may persuade you to contemplate such a task. We believe that you ought to write such a book, and that it would be both extremely interesting and successful.

1–Ford Madox Ford (1873–1939), novelist – *The Good Soldier* (1915) – memoirist, critic and editor, joined the Welsh Guards in 1915, and fought on the Somme and at Ypres before being invalided out in 1917. The four novels of *Parade's End* (1924–8) drew on his experiences. See further Max Saunders, *Ford Madox Ford: A Dual Life* (2012)

2–Ford (9 Apr.) invited TSE for 'a cup of tea' at 31 Southampton Street, Fitzroy Square.

3–Walter Richard Sickert (1860–1942), painter, printmaker, controversialist, teacher, writer, was the son of a Danish painter and illustrator who in 1869 moved with his family to London, where they took his wife's nationality. He studied briefly at the Slade School of Art, then in 1882 became an apprentice to the US-born painter James McNeill Whistler. He spent periods in France, where he made friends with Jacques-Emile Blanche and Edgar Degas; he painted in Dieppe, then in Venice; and he developed his reputation in France. From 1905 he lived in north London, working in Camden Town: he founded the London Impressionists and the Camden Town Group; and after WW1 he migrated with his second wife back to Dieppe. From 1925 he called himself 'Richard' Sickert, and until the mid-1930s his distinction as portrait painter, landscapist, and painter of music halls, theatres and conversation pieces, became celebrated. His work as commentator on art, journalist and diarist, is collected in *A free house! or, the artist as craftsman being the writings of Walter Richard Sickert*, ed. Osbert Sitwell (1947). See further Richard Shone, *Walter Sickert* (1988); Matthew Sturgis, *Walter Sickert: A Life* (2011).

Incidentally, I may say that we have had plenty of experience with this type of book: I have no doubt that you have seen Rothenstein's memoirs.[1] Can you be induced to undertake something on the same scale? I am sure that we would not only produce the book in a way which would satisfy you, but that we are in a position to reach the right public at least as successfully as any other London firm.[2]

Yours very truly,
[T. S. Eliot]
Director

TO *The Editor,* The New English Weekly

[published 12 April 1934, 622–3]   [No address given]

Mr T. S. Eliot's Quandaries

Sir, —

Wishing to engross as little of your space as may be, I shall try to comment upon Mr Pound's observations (p. 558) and your own notes (p. 576) briefly in one letter.[3]

---

1 – William Rothenstein, *Men and Memories* (F&F, 1932).

2 – Mrs Sickert (Thérèse Lessore, his third wife) replied (11 Apr.) that her husband asked her to say that 'he has no intention of ever writing his memoirs as he writes them on his canvases. He says he has already told you this but I expect it is another publisher he is thinking of.'

3 – EP wrote, in 'Mr Eliot's Quandaries' (*NEW* 4 [29 Mar. 1934], 558–9): 'In dealing with his Primer of Heresy I start with the initial irritation of finding a book treating what are to me mainly irrelevant and frivolous topics; but which at certain points brushes the edge of a vital problem . . . The danger of Mr Eliot's reprint is amply illustrated by the efflux in the *Observer* which can be taken, I suppose, as gauge of 'average' London intelligence?'

'To deal with Mr Eliot's answer to my review:

'His surprise at my mentioning the "average man" seems to me a purely personal matter, part, that is, of Mr Eliot's autobiography. I have for years respected Mr Eliot because of my belief that he did not and does not read his own Quarterly publication (which is the most authoritative and distinguished in England, and is unmatched in America; but which does descend or has descended to a series of authors too numerous to mention in this place, and analysis of whose natures might lay the *New English Weekly* open to libel action.

'Nevertheless I did, in the pages of Mr Eliot's own august organ, say a few words on society at large, and on the unlikelihood of genius getting a decent break UNTIL the whole economic order were so changed that EVERY MAN would get a break quite good enough for the first-rate artist or writer. (Vide 'Murder by Capital', *Criterion*, July 1933) . . . [M]y mention of the "average man" was not intended as a surprise, even to Mr Eliot. His being surprised is, however, useful, as it sheds light on a peculiar malady of his logic. I mean that the kind of fallacy he commits in his Primer, he commits in his letter . . .

First, I suggest to Mr Pound that the review mentioned in the *Observer* is definitely below the level of 'average London intelligence'. I do not know how to prove this.

Mr Pound does not make clear to me what *is* the peculiar malady of my logic. I should like to know. Naturally, *if* my diagnosis is wrong, my remedy is likely to be an irrelevance.

I had no intention of distracting my readers from the vital problem of economics; and Mr Pound's objection seems to depend upon the assumption that this is the *only* vital problem.[1]

I still do not know whether Mr Pound means, by 'ecclesiastical bureaucrats', the whole of the Anglican and Roman hierarchies, or not. Is the Pope, for instance, a bureaucrat according to Mr Pound's definition?

Mr Pound has now re-written the paragraph which stands as the last but one on p. 599, in such a way that I cannot only understand it but agree with what it asserts. I thought that this was what he meant; but only goodwill could supply the interpretation.

Now, Sir, as to your notes. Our difficulties seem to turn primarily upon the use of words in different senses. As for (1) I apologise for having overlooked your previous comment upon the Archbishop of York's letter.

'But Mr Eliot is . . . in fact treating the sickness of the age. His diagnosis is wrong. His remedy is an irrelevance . . . Mr Eliot's book is pernicious in that it distracts the reader from a vital problem (economic justice); it implies that we need more religion, but does not specify the nature of that religion . . . He claims that "orthodoxy" has lost its grip on mankind, but he fails to SEE why . . .

'To answer some of his other requests by definition:

'A bureaucrat (ecclesiastical or any other god damn'd variety) is a man in a safe or safeish job whose mental attitude is coloured by his wish to retain that job, often to such a degree that the truth becomes of secondary or tertiary importance to him, and the translating of the concept of justice into action seems to him impractical, or infinitely deferable.

'My phrase "When religion was real", is, I admit, vague, and was used for brevity's sake . . . Let me rewrite it thus: During those centuries when organised Christianity, namely, the Roman Catholic Church, was most active in the life of Europe, both in affairs spiritual and in affairs temporal, during those Ages when religious verbal manifestations in Europe reached their most admirable heights, whether in the writing of Scotus Erigena, Albertus de la Magna, Aquinas, Francis of Assissi, Dante himself; and when ecclesiastical architecture triumphed in San Zeno, St Hilaire, the Duomo of Modena and an infinite number of churches, the CHURCH had not abrogated her right to dissociate ECONOMIC right from Economic evil.

'The abrogation of such discrimination is unpardonable . . .'
1 – Stough, 'The Skirmish of Pound and Eliot . . .', 237: 'Herein lies their major split: Pound thinks economics of central importance; Eliot, religion. Other problems, for both, are subsumed by these major areas. Pound believes the Church's major weakness is that it no longer emphasizes that usury is a sin against nature (in fact, that the Church generally ignores usury). For Eliot, a Christian society, based on Christian ethics and morals, will eradicate such a problem as usury. Both men recognize the same problems, but their emphases differ.'

(2) I find that you mean by *native* something like what I mean by *eternal*. I find it hard to dissociate the meaning of the adjective *native* from the process of *birth*. A 'Whitstable native' is surely an oyster which was born at or in the vicinity of Whitstable, even though of American parentage. (3) As for the Atonement, Sir, you might consult, among others, the essay on the subject by Dr Kirk in *Essays Catholic and Critical*. (4) However admirable may be 'a classless but functional society distinguished only by objective merits', it seems to me only a *means* to the Kingdom of Heaven on Earth, not that Kingdom itself. (5) Again, we differ as to the possible meanings of the word *mission*. A mission is an *errand*. The extension of the meaning to cover what is actually accomplished should be made clear in its context. (6) I suspect that by 'saving souls' you mean 'creating a divine society of Man on Earth' (whatever you may mean by divine). In other words, where you put *complementary*, you mean *identical*?

T. S. Eliot

P.S. I have just read a book recommended to me by Max Rychner: *Die Götter des Abendlandes* by Theophil Spoerri (Furche Verlag, Berlin, 1932) which expresses some of the opinions of *After Strange Gods* much better than I have done.

TO *Alistair Cooke*   CC

12 April 1934   [Faber & Faber Ltd]

Dear Mr Cooke,

It is surprising to hear from you all of a sudden from an address like Blackpool, when I had imagined you were still in Massachusetts.[1]

I should like very much to arrange a meeting with you during your flying visit to London. Very unfortunately I have made a luncheon engagement for Saturday, the 1st [*sc.* 21st], which I can hardly break. As Saturday morning is impossible for you, will you let me know how early in the afternoon you must leave for Cambridge. My luncheon is in Chelsea but I could probably get to my office soon after 3 o'clock, if there was any possibility of meeting then. Or, if it were not too inconvenient for you, the Oxford and Cambridge Club would suit me better. It would also be more comfortable. Would it be possible for you to meet me there

---

1–Cooke wrote (1 Apr.) from the family home in Blackpool that he was back from the USA for a few days, and planning to pass through London on 21 Apr. en route to Cambridge: he hoped to be able to meet up with TSE. He would bring with him the manuscript of 'Hollywood Prospect'.

in the afternoon and catch a train for Cambridge after tea? One can get to Liverpool Street very much more quickly now because of the new junction of the Piccadilly and the Central London at Holborn.[1]

Yours ever sincerely,
[T. S. Eliot]

TO *George Barker*

TS Texas

12 April 1934   Faber & Faber Ltd

Dear Mr Barker,

I am now answering your letter of March 27th and am reporting on the poems which you enclosed with it.[2] I am very much impressed by these poems and so also was Mr Herbert Read, to whom I showed them for confirmation of my own opinion.

I feel very strongly, however, on a point of policy. I think that it is really important, both for us and for you at this point, that your first volume of verse with us should be a bigger one, and Mr Read agrees with me. These very small volumes of the form and size of *The End of A War* or the *Dance of Death*, are really only suitable and successful when the author is already pretty well established. We are bringing out several more of that type in the autumn, and, if your poems were done in the same way,

1–Alistair Cooke to EVE, 20 Dec. 1983: 'When the Commonwealth Fund (the sponsors of my two-year American fellowship) sent me over to England in the spring of 1934 to be interviewed by the BBC for their vacant job of film critic (which I became on my return in the autumn) TSE invited me to lunch at the Oxford and Cambridge Club. By that time I was 150% American, and I told him that if I lived permanently in America, the only reason I should want to return to England would be to buy my shoes there, since American shoes were so awful. He said, in his grave, careful way, that the only reason he would ever choose to go back to America would be to buy his shoes there. I noticed on the way out that he was wearing a type of sharp-pointed, yellowish brown shoe that was exclusively American and that most Englishmen, I should guess, would associate with racing touts!

'He was very kind to me in those early days and seemed to think that I would develop into a serious literary and/or dramatic critic. But I came to find a high brow very uncomfortable to live with and soon acquired an ambition, which I have never lost, to try and write and talk sense for a large general audience. Hence my attraction to radio and, later, television. Inevitably, I lost touch with the *Criterion* and most other intellectuals, except (later on) people interested in politics: e.g. Isaiah Berlin.'

EVE to Cooke, 31 Jan. 1984: 'I am charmed by your anecdote, and may include it in the Correspondence with appropriate acknowledgements to you. Rather in the same vein, a fellow clerk [at Lloyds Bank] remembered him in "immaculate black jacket and sponge-bag trousers with spats, and his large tortoiseshell-rimmed glasses which, at that time, were a new thing and not generally worn, even at managerial level!"'

2–Barker had submitted two more recent poems.

I feel sure that they would miss the attention they ought to get. What I hope you will agree to do, is to wait until you have enough material, that satisfies you, to make a volume of about the same size as Stephen Spender's poems, to be sold, say at 5s. In the position of publishing at the present time, I am convinced that this would be the wisest step.

Please think this over and let me know when you think you are likely to have enough material for such a book. I will say again that I like your poetry very much.

Yours sincerely,
T. S. Eliot

PS. Meanwhile I am holding the MS.

TO *Marianne Moore* CC

12 April 1934   [Faber & Faber Ltd]

Dear Miss Moore,

This is primarily to acknowledge the receipt of the poems which you have sent. I am not quite clear whether this represents your own selection, or whether it is the gross amount from which you wish me to select. In the latter case I warn you that I am not likely to want to leave out very much. But in any case, I will send you my list of selection, and tentative order for your approval.

I understand from Morley that there has been some mention between you of a preface by myself, and the publication of a volume somewhat similar to my selected poems of Ezra Pound some years ago, (if you have never seen this I shall be glad to send you a copy.) Of course, I should be proud to contribute such a preface or introduction, if it was wanted but I should not think of doing so unless it was your express wish. Please do not allow politeness to prevent you from saying exactly what your preference is.[1]

Yours very sincerely,
[T. S. Eliot]

1 – The idea that TSE might write an introduction to MM's *Selected Poems* had come from MM herself, in conversation with FVM. However, feeling selflessly concerned that TSE might harm his own reputation by the association, she told him (18 Apr.): 'Mr Latham says something about an introduction by you as if it were a certainty. I had suggested it to Mr Morley; to be based perhaps on your *Dial* article . . .' Later, on 16 May, she made this more direct approach: 'If you would be willing to introduce the book, or preface it with a comment, I should be grateful. That the things would profit by being sponsored is perhaps

TO *Donald Brace*[1]   cc

12 April 1934   [Faber & Faber Ltd]

Dear Brace,

Frank and I have been discussing the possibility of doing something
with your edition of Pareto[2] in this country. We are both handicapped by
the fact that we are entirely ignorant of his work. All that I have ever heard
about him has been from Aldous Huxley, who has been an enthusiast for
Pareto for some years.

We should be very glad if you would send us along some proofs in due
course, so that we may know what it is all about to begin with. I don't
think that we shall be able to read all five volumes, even between us, but
we are serious in the matter, and want to investigate fully.[3]

With all best wishes,
Yours ever,
[T. S. Eliot]

---

a reason against your undertaking them, so I leave it to you; you must safeguard yourself
in any way that seems best, against permitting this venture to be a bugbear. I have not seen
the Pound, and though I have been intending to buy it, surely would not need to see it in
connection with what you might do for me' (*Selected Letters of Marianne Moore*, 322–3).

1 – Donald Brace (1881–1955), publisher; founder in 1919 – with Alfred Harcourt, whom
he befriended at Columbia College, New York: they graduated in 1904 – of the firm of
Harcourt, Brace & Howe. See *The History of Harcourt Brace and Company: 75 Years of
Publishing Excellence* (1994); *American Authors and Books: 1640 to the Present Day* (3rd
edn).

2 – Vilfredo Pareto, *The Mind and Society*, 4 vols (*Trattato di Sociologia Generale*), trans.
Arthur Livingston (1934). Pareto (1848–1923) graduated from the Istituto Politecnico
of Turin and was for twenty years a railway and mining engineer. Enormously erudite in
history, philosophy, social sciences, metaphysics and mathematics, he was appointed in 1893
to the Chair of Political Economy at the University of Lausanne, where he spent the rest
of his career. *The Mind and Society* was his masterpiece: a far-reaching study of thought,
sentiment and conduct in society that was specifically addressed to an intellectual élite.

3 – Brace replied to TSE on 23 Apr. that 'arrangements about English publication were made
years ago – in 1927, in fact. Cape became interested in it independently of us, and then
found that we had acquired the rights. He was over here in 1927, and we fixed up with him
then that he was to publish it in England when the time came.' FVM had in the meantime
also written to Brace (13 Apr. 1934): 'Eliot and Faber and all are tempted by the thought of
Pareto; yet on anything so big it would be enormously helpful to be able to see the material
if it is available. I very stupidly forgot to take a note of your publication plans . . .' FVM
sought to advise Brace further, 4 May: 'About Pareto . . . What I wanted to record was that
when I reported the matter to the others, they were interested; Eliot, Aldous Huxley, etc.,
aren't ignorant of P., and we should be very glad to make an estimate for what we can do if
we can see material.'

TO *Bonamy Dobrée*   TS Brotherton

[?13 April 1934]   Faber & Faber Ltd

God damb it Bonamy I have just been to your lecture[1] if that doesnt show
that Friday the 13th is Unlucky I don't know what does so I barged into
a meeting where I wasnt wanted and they looked oldfashioned at me they
did God damb it I wanted to hear that lecture I wonder what you thought
had happened I spose I thought these lectures were always on a Friday
I put it down so on my pad Well Now this is to express my manifooled
regrets and at not having a talk with you what shall we meet Again so
now will close respecfully.

                                        T. S. E.

TO *Leonard Woolf*   cc

17 April 1934   [Faber & Faber Ltd]

Dear Leonard,
    Many thanks for the cheque. I enclose formal receipt. I should not have
expected it to go on selling to that extent.[2]
    I was on the point of writing to you about a typescript which came our
way almost by accident, and which I want to commend to your attention.
We have had to turn it down because we are already pretty well down to
the deck level with non-commercial books for the next season or two, and
because I think that you (publishing fewer books) would be able, if you
took the book, to do better by it than we could.
    It is called *Hoere Israel* and is in German. The author is a young
German Jew who says he has been four years in England, in business. He
is not a writer by profession. I thought him a very attractive fellow. It's
impossible to give you any analysis of the book – it is not a long one; it is
a passionately prophetic sort of utterance, which quite carried me away
when I read it.
    I would like to have a word about it tomorrow night, to which I look
forward.[3]

                            Yours ever
                            [Tom]

1 – BD's note on letter: 'Lecture to R. S. L. Wed 11th.'
2 – Sales information not traced.
3 – LW to J. L. Brandler, 24 Apr.: 'Mr T. S. Eliot handed me the enclosed MS *Hoere Israel*.
I have read it with the greatest interest and realize its great merits. I am however extremely
sorry not to be able to make an offer for its publication as it does not quite suit our list.'

17 April 1934   *The Criterion*

My dear Spender,

I have two practical reasons for writing to you. The first is to remind you that you have promised to let me have an essay for the next number. To make publication possible I ought to have it very soon, certainly by the first week in May. May I know whether the essay will be ready in time?[1]

The second part is that your poems are in measurable distance of going out of print. I am therefore asking you to consider whether you would like to make any alteration in the text, or to include any new poems or poems previously omitted. You will remember that Auden made several such alterations in his volume, so that we were able to call the reprint a second edition. This is a distinct advantage in publication, though I don't want to urge you to make any changes for that reason alone, and of course, we must keep in mind the small autumn volume of poems which is to come.[2]

I do hope that you are enjoying yourself on the Adriatic, and finding it a good place for work. I shall be glad to hear from you as soon as may be.

Yours ever,

T. S. E.

1–SS, 'W. B. Yeats as a Realist', C. 14 (Oct. 1934), 17–26.
2–FVM to Donald S. Klopfer, Random House, 4 May 1934: 'I have just heard from Spender that in a reprint which is called for of his POEMS we should make an alteration in the text. He wants to delete two poems and to add nine; which will make his text forty instead of thirty-three poems. We are reprinting them over here, and I shall be able to let you have proofs of the new POEMS in a week. I hope they will come in time for you to make the corresponding alteration in your text. Perhaps it is too late for you to be able to hold up pending the material.'
    (In 1934 there were new editions of *The Orators*, and of SS's *Poems*.)
    F&F Catalogue, Autumn 1934: 'Mr Spender's *Poems*, after running through two impressions, now appear in a second, and we believe definitive edition. The author, finding that this volume (by which his reputation was first definitely established) represents a stage of his poetic development through which he has now passed, has removed two of the poems included in the First Edition, but added nine more which belong to the same period. The present volume, therefore, includes "all that the author wishes to preserve" of his work up to the present year.'

TO *W. H. Auden*

17 April 1934   [Faber & Faber Ltd]

Dear Auden,

Many thanks for your letter.[1] First about a possible meeting. I am
engaged on Saturday for lunch and dinner, and I have asked Alistair
Cooke to have tea with me as he is passing through town on that day;
so I very much hope that you will be staying over the weekend. Could
you have either lunch or dinner with me on Sunday at the Oxford and
Cambridge Club at 1.15 or 7.30 respectively? Do let me have a line as
soon as you get this.

Thanks for your gentle comments. As for the possible interpretation
of what you mention in the book I am not unaware of it but I can't
take the danger so seriously as Stephen does. On the whole I don't regret
those remarks because I don't think one should be entirely muzzled by
the fear of being misunderstood or made use of for purposes one does
not approve. Furthermore having said this much I propose to make other
remarks in future to discourage such people from claiming me as a friend.

Yours ever,

[T. S. Eliot]

1–WHA wrote ('26. 4. 34': actually 16 Apr.): 'I can hardly now even apologise for not
writing before to thank you for the Primer [*ASG*] and your letter. They arrived during the
rush hours of producing a school play, and since term ended, I have been so absorbed in one
of my own, that I have neglected all the duties of friendship and politeness . . .

'I read the Primer with very great interest. With your comments on individual works I
found myself almost always in agreement. Some of the general remarks, if you will forgive
me saying so, rather shocked me, because if they are put into practice on a political scale,
they would produce a world in which neither I nor you I think would like to live. But you
must be very bored with hearing the book talked about, and anyway criticisms by the bright
young juniors like myself . . . are rather impertinent.'

Auden was taken aback by TSE's remarks in *ASG* concerning a stable society that have
often been taken to be notorious: 'The population should be homogeneous; where two or
more cultures exist in the same place they are likely either to be fiercely self-conscious or
both to become adulterate. What is still more important is unity of religious background;
and reasons of race and religion combine to make any large number of free-thinking Jews
undesirable' (19–20).

TO *Edwin Muir*

CC

19 April 1934   [Faber & Faber Ltd]

My dear Muir,

Yes, I have seen the name of D. Gascoyne[1] in several places but I don't believe I have ever taken the trouble to read the poems. I must say that I should think it very unlikely that we should be able to publish a volume of his poems. But if he is only 17, I should think that encouragement was a good deal more important than publication. My policy has been to try to avoid presenting more than one new poet a season, and as I have two possibles in view, the chances for the immediate future are not good. Nevertheless, I should very much like to see Gascoyne's volume.

                                        Yours sincerely,
                                        [T. S. Eliot]

TO *E. W. F. Tomlin*[2]   TS Lady Marshall

19 April 1934   Faber & Faber Ltd

Dear Mr Tomlin,

I have read your essay dealing with Rowse's book, and although I must read it again before committing myself to a formal opinion, I must say that from practical points of view it seems to me a great improvement over anything previous. On the first reading it seemed to me that I agreed with everything you said but this is such an uncommon experience that I must read it again before taking my oath on that point.[3]

I wonder how you feel about publication. The essay will no doubt annoy Mr Rowse, who doesn't always find it easy to understand why everybody doesn't think as he does. But I don't know that that matters very much from any point of view, even his own. You are not, I take it, in any way a pupil of his but only attend his lectures. I can imagine any man being rather hurt at having his ideas publicly attacked by anyone who was at the time in the status of being his pupil; and it would hardly be good form on the pupil's part. But I am under the impression that your relations with him consist of no more that attending his lectures, and that

1–For David Gascoyne (1916–2001), see letter to him, 6 Oct. 1934.
2–Walter F. Tomlin (1914–88), writer and administrator: see Biographical Register.
3–'Slaves to the Future' was an essay in which Tomlin 'attempted [as he wrote in an undated letter] to combine a précis of my original answer to Mr Rowse's book [*Politics and the Younger Generation* (1931)] with some extra matter.'

you have very little to do with him personally. Is he likely, for instance, to be one of your examiners in any subject? I really ask this sort of question in consideration of your interests.

I don't know the book of George Sorel which you mention.[1] Indeed, I believe that the only one which I have read is the *Reflexions sur la violence*. I think the best thing that I can do is to get hold of a copy and read it myself first. In general translations of French books do very badly unless they are very popular works, for the reason that the majority of people who are interested are usually able to read them in French; furthermore some of the leading periodicals will already have reviewed the French text. But I should like to read anything that you recommend so warmly, and if I see any chance for a translation I will write to you again about it.

Yours very truly,
T. S. Eliot

TO *Harriet Monroe*   cc

19 April 1934   [Faber & Faber Ltd]

Dear Miss Monroe,

I have read with interest your letter of the 2nd instant.[2] The whole matter had been incomprehensible to me before. I think what you have told me

1 – 'Having recently taken up the study of the works of Georges Sorel, I have been wondering . . . whether a translation of "Les illusions du progress" might be a profitable undertaking. Although Sorel's reputation in England seems to depend solely upon the "Réflexions sur la violence", the thesis of that book seems to have lost most of its relevance – a charge that cannot be made against "Les illusions du progress", which possesses, I think, all that is of permanent value in Sorel's thought, and has the merit of being much less topical than its predecessor.'

2 – Monroe explained the limits of her patience with EP and the *Cantos*: 'In April 1933 *Poetry* led off Volume XLII with *Canto XXXIV*, which was chiefly about early American politics – Adams, Jefferson, Madison, Napoleon, J. Q. Adams, etc. I can't say I was enthusiastic about its quality as poetry, and when, soon after, he sent us *Canto XXXVII*, all about Martin van Buren, and, in my opinion, merely choppy prose, I was in no great haste to print it. In January he wrote raging about the delay because he thought (though we couldn't see it) that some speech of President Roosevelt (he enclosed clipping) had stated ahead of him one of his own pearls of political wisdom. Also, he challenged my right to be less appreciative of his Cantos than you and two other authorities. I replied, somewhat less mildly than usual, that *Canto XXXVII* was listed for March, but that it would be the last one of that kind which we should care to print, that if he was writing politics and not poetry why didn't he send it to the *N. Y. Times*, and that I doubted whether you had ever read the two Cantos *Poetry* printed. (I guessed it right in this detail, it seems.)

'Evidently you like his recent cantos better than I do if you are willing to print any or all of them in the *Criterion*. I violated my artistic conscience in giving space to *Canto XXXVII* . . .'

is quite enough to enable me to see the outlines of the correspondence between Pound and yourself.

I have since read the Canto about Van Buren, or about the politics of that party in *Poetry*, and as I know very little about the period and still less about the party from Pound's point of view, I found that it conveyed almost nothing to me.[1] It didn't seem to me a particularly suitable Canto to appear in isolation, although if you have been printing his Cantos consecutively and complete that is a different matter. At the same time I have so much admiration for the technical merits of the remaining Cantos that I should certainly be inclined to take it on faith, pending the appearance of the rest of the work. As for his letters, I hope that you don't take the violence of his style too seriously; I am completely habituated to it myself.

With all best wishes,
Yours sincerely,
[T. S. Eliot]

TO *John Garrett*[2]   CC

20 April 1934   [Faber & Faber Ltd]

Dear Mr Garrett,

I have your letter of the 12th instant, together with a copy of the magazine of the Croydon Repertory Theatre, of which I had not before heard.[3] I should be very glad to let you have a small contribution at some

---

EP's letters to her had always been 'incredibly violent and abusive,' she said; but his replies to this latest letter from her had been 'unspeakable' – 'missives . . . which might surprise you, however accustomed you may be to his epistolary style'.

1 – Canto XXXVII draws on the memoirs (written in 1860) of the Democrat Martin van Buren (1782–1862), lawyer, who was 8th President of the USA, 1837–41.

2 – John Garrett (1902–66), pioneering schoolmaster: see Biographical Register.

3 – Garrett was at this time Head of English at Whitgift School – he taught E. W. F. Tomlin – and also edited a magazine called *REP* on behalf of the Croydon Repertory Theatre. He wrote, 'Now the churches at the moment seem to be risking a return to the ancient alliance of religion and drama. I have just returned from America, where the movement as you know has gone much further and revealed far more potentialities of danger. Could you possibly do me an article (750–1000 words) on this subject? The prestige of your name as a contributor would be of enormous value to a magazine which is going through a critical stage in its career.'

See TSE, 'Religious Drama and the Church', *REP* i (6 Oct. 1934), 4–5: 'The writer of religious drama must be allowed a considerable liberty and experiment – we have not to paraphrase the mystery plays but to devise new forms . . . The Church has the opportunity, greater now than in the period of industrial expansion, of gathering to itself, of educating

time when I have rather more leisure than at present, that is to say, I shall not have time to do anything of the sort until the autumn.

I am not quite clear what you mean by 'the alliance of religion and drama'. You speak of something which has been going on in America. I wonder whether you were referring to the very much over-done practice over there of preaching sermons about plays – not only very much over-done but sometimes, it seemed to me, choosing plays of more than doubtful suitability. I don't know very much about this practice, I have never listened to any such sermons, and I don't know that there is anything that I can do about it. Or do you mean the revival of religious drama, such as is being particularly active in the Chichester diocese? I know something about this, and could find out more. But if this is what you mean, I don't know enough to be aware of the potentialities of danger of which you speak. Perhaps if we could clear these matters up and settle on a subject, I could let you have something in the latter part of the summer.

Yours sincerely,
[T. S. Eliot]

TO *Stephen Spender*   cc

20 April 1934   [Faber & Faber Ltd]

Dear Spender,

I was glad to get your letter of April 12th enclosing your essay.[1] Meanwhile I had written you a note addressed merely *poste restante*, which I hope you will collect.

I like your essay and think that your notion about Yeats's realism versus his occultism etc. is good and new and deserves to be considered. I am trying to obliterate, however, any reference to myself in the essay because it would obviously be unsuitable for me to publish in the *Criterion* any criticism in which comparison between Yeats and myself, or indeed Pound and myself, was involved. Fortunately the references are mostly asides.

---

and spiritualising, all the potential forces of civilisation. And these forces, gathered in the Church, will consequently radiate out from it. So that we may perhaps come to a time, in which a play as fundamentally Christian and Catholic as *Polyeucte* may be written and may be performed successfully to audiences which will not be consciously attending a "religious play", because they will be imbued with the Christian and Catholic way of feeling, even when they ask only to be entertained.'

1 – 'W. B. Yeats as a Realist', C. 14 (Oct. 1934), 17–26. 'I'm afraid I do not praise Yeats enough: however I am aware of such a feeling of BUT when one praises Yeats: & that was the feeling I wished to explore.'

I am a little unsettled in my mind as to whether it is possible to use this essay in the next number or not. The reason is that I have unfortunately to publish an essay by Yeats himself, and as this essay has a good deal of mystical chatter in it, the immediate collocation with yours might be invidious. His essay is the introduction to an extremely interesting travel diary of a Hindoo Holy Man.[1] When the book comes out I think that you will find some amusement in the contrast between the delightfully matter of fact style of the Holy Man and the occultism effect of Yeats.

In either case, however, I will try to arrange to send you in a few days a cheque on account, leaving the exact sum for this essay to be determined when the printers have counted the words. I have taken the liberty of making one or two very minor suggestions on the margin.

Your account of Dubrovnik makes it so attractive that I should be tempted to come out for a short holiday if it were not that I am tied to London until the middle of June.[2] When do you return? Good luck to your play.[3]

Yours ever,
[T. S. E.]

1–Bhagwan Shri Hamsa, *The Holy Mountain: The Story of a Pilgrimage to Lake Manas and of Initiation on Mount Kailas in Tibet*, trans. Shri Purohit Swami, with Intro. by W. B. Yeats.
2–Spender (12 Apr.) called Mlini 'the most beautiful place I have ever been to . . . There are beautiful pine trees outside our windows . . . A waterfall runs down the mountain side through the village into the sea. Behind are the mountains with rows of cypresses going up them.' (But soon the place was to be crowded out with German and Austrian Nazis, taunting the Englishmen.)
3–'I am doing a play for Faber's in the autumn. I hope it will not be too long. It will probably be (if I do not scrap it) at least twice as long as Auden's. I am more excited about it than anything I have attempted.'

TO *Phoebe Fenwick Gaye*[1]   CC

20 April 1934   [Faber & Faber Ltd]

Dear Miss Gaye,

Thank you for your letter of the 13th instant.[2] I think that I should probably enjoy airing some of my views in your periodical, and I should like to know the date by which you would want them. When you say 'in the month of January next' does that mean four separate contributions with or without some continuity, and in that case what number of words to each instalment?

Yours very truly,
[T. S. Eliot]

TO *Bonamy Dobrée*   TS Brotherton

[1934]   Ty Glyn Aeron, Ciliau Aeron,
                                Cardiganshire

Dear Bumbaby,

Very good[3] but not at 24 Russell Square (I find your attempted witticism[4] flat, pretentious and in doubtful tast e) this is not my typewriter nor even my kind of typewriter,. What I wished to say was Oxford & Cambridge will do? or if you have better ideas preferring Soho or what you could let Frank know and he would tell me I shall see him the day before. Otherwise one 0%clock precisely for sherry.

Yours etc.
T. S. E.

1–Phoebe Fenwick Gaye (1905–2001), novelist; assistant editor of *Time and Tide*.
2–Gaye invited TSE to contribute to a series 'Notes on the Way' – 'notes about the world at large, in which each writer is given an absolutely free hand to comment upon contemporary events . . . Lady Rhondda would very much like to have you also as a contributor in this series, and wonders whether you would consider writing them for the month of January next.' (Margaret Haig Thomas, Viscountess Rhondda [1883–1953], writer and feminist, was editor from 1926 of *Time and Tide* [1920–79].) Among those who had already taken part were Sean O'Casey, Aldous Huxley, Rose Macaulay and Rebecca West. The fee was £8–0–0.
3–Letter not traced.
4–Dobrée wrote at the foot of this letter: 'I think this is when I referred to Faber & Faber as Smith & Smith.'

TO *Aldous Huxley*   CC

20 April 1934   [Faber & Faber Ltd]

Dear Aldous,

We have been toying with the idea of doing something in London with
sheets of the translation of Pareto's *Sociology*, which Harcourt Brace are
bringing out in America. There are various difficulties to be considered,
primarily, of course, the possibility of selling any copies. But my first
point is the following – I don't know Pareto in the original and you do.
Furthermore I should have to know the original very well indeed to be
able to hold any opinion of the merits of the translator. I don't know who
the translator is. If, when the time comes, I send you a few, I hope very
few, sheets of translation would you be able to give me your opinion of
the accuracy of the translation? Have you got the original text by you?
Second, would you be willing to write a few words of commendation
which we could use in advertising the book? Third, I should very much
like to know what you think of the possibility of selling any copies in
London; of course it is a big book, five volumes.[1]

We were very grateful for your support for the letter to *The Times*.
I think that the letter probably helped a little to increase interest in the
matter: I suppose you have seen the correspondence on the subject.
I saw Maynard Keynes last night, who, of course ridiculed Douglas but
admitted that it was probably better than our present system. His portrait
of Norman[2] is quite grotesque.

Yours ever,

[Tom]

1–Huxley replied on 28 Apr. 1934: 'With regard to [Vilfredo] Pareto – yes, I will willingly
look at a few specimen pages. I will also willingly write an introduction . . . [I]f you like
and think fit, I shall enjoy saying something about the old man, because I like and admire
the book . . . But whether the public has the money to buy five volumes is another question'
(*Letters of Aldous Huxley*, 379–80). F&F was considering publication of Pareto's *Sociologia
Generale* (*The Mind and Society* as it was titled in the US, ed. A. Livingston, 1935; also
issued in four vols by Jonathan Cape, 1935).
2–Montagu Norman, Governor of the Bank of England, 1920–44.

20 April 1934   Faber & Faber Ltd

Dear Richards,

Many thanks for your letter of the 17th.[1] I should certainly like to publish Jennings's book but I don't see any immediate prospect. We have to keep a very careful eye on the amount of non-commercial stuff we publish in any one season, and I am convinced that this would fall very short of paying for itself. But I should like to give him some encouragement. I have written therefore to say that I should be delighted to use it in the *Criterion* if he could bring it down to six thousand words.[2]

Your young men do seem to suffer from delusions of size with regarding [*sc.* regard to] the *Criterion*. Here is Madge[3] also whose essay on Coleridge has just turned up, which is quite interesting, entirely psychoanalytical, fortified by many pages of quotations, and is exactly four times the length of the longest article we could publish. I am asking him to come round and talk to me about it. I am a little disappointed in his treatment as I had hoped that he might deal with Coleridge's general philosophical ideas. Nevertheless this is a competent piece of work.

Now that I know what Madge's paper is about I can ask you with more confidence whether there is any bit of your Coleridge book which it would be possible for the *Criterion* to publish before the book appears.

I am very sorry that you are going to be so busy until the end of May.[4] My own pressure is slightly relieved now. You must both try to come up to London during the first week of June. The Lord Chamberlain and the

---

1–In response to TSE's question of 3 Apr.: 'I seem to think very much as you do about [Humphrey] Jennings. I agree he isn't in Empson's class or near it – but then I can't quite think of any young person who is . . . If I were asked, say by the Cambridge University Press, what I thought and I neither knew him nor cared what they thought of me, I would urge publication strongly . . . (Could you serialise some of it in the *Criterion*?)' Jennings was working on a postgraduate thesis on the work of Thomas Gray.

2–TSE's letter to Jennings has not yet been found; but Jennings responded to it on 7 Oct. 1934: 'I cannot say how ashamed I am not to have answered your very kind letter about my work on Gray. At the moment of receiving it I was asked to do some film work which I am still doing & which has left me practically no time in which to cut down the MS I sent you, from 10,000 to 6,000 words, as I had hoped to do.

'With luck however I may manage this in the next few weeks & I will then send you the shortened copy.'

3–Charles Madge (1912–96), poet and sociologist: see letter to him 14 Nov. 1934, below.

4–Having just returned from Coniston, IAR pleaded that he was under huge pressure of work – writing lectures, setting exam papers, etc. – or he would 'have jumped at going to *Macbeth*'.

Bishop of London have both passed my text, rather to my surprise, so I feel more cheerful.[1]

Yours ever,

T. S. Eliot

1–The pageant was licensed for public performance at Sadler's Wells by the Lord Chamberlain's Office, 12 Apr. 1934. The official reader was G. S. Street:

'There are a multitude of scenes in this "pageant play" but they succeed one another without pause. A serious study of it would take a day's hard reading, not that it is obscure – as I find much of the author's other poetry – but because the incidents and characters and the ideas expressed by them are so numerous. It is partly in verse and partly in prose dialogue: in the case of the modern workmen introduced slangy and topical. It goes to and fro in time and I think T. S. Eliot has attempted to cram too much into it. The scene is an open space, we learn from inference on the banks of the Thames. A male and female chorus begin and resume at intervals: it expresses the poet's point of view, I suppose. Then "The Rock" comes on. It is not until the end of the pageant that The Rock is identified with St Peter. He speaks of man's labours. We then have some modern workmen who are building a church. Rahere, who built St Bartholomew, appears to them and his workmen lend a hand. I think that not to weary the Lord Chamberlain I had better from this point merely give a list of the personages who appear: he will readily imagine the ideas and arguments for which they stand. A Modern Agitator. The Jews rebuilding Jerusalem. A crowd incited by the Agitator against the workmen. The Danish invasion. Shock Troops and Black Shirts. A Plutocrat with a long speech to them. The Rock again. Part II The Chorus and The Rock. Bishop Blomfield. Young men setting out in Richard's Crusade, with a Latin service for them and investment with their Crosses. An argument between modern people about art and religion. Very long sermons by a Reformation preacher, ending in a Priest's going to be burnt. The Rock, or St Peter, again. A ballet of Dick Whittington and his Cat(!) Pepys, Evelyn and Wren conversing after dinner and Mr Eliot positively gets in the Chesterton joke about Wren. St Peter again and a benediction by the Bishop – of London?

'The author's religious view and the auspices of the Bishop of London guarantee the reverence of the religious portions of the pageant, nor would anyone object to the lighter passages. I think Mr Eliot goes out of his way to exaggerate the views of "The Blackshirts", if he means the followers of Sir Oswald Mosley and this introduction of political animus seems a great pity. I should be inclined at least to suggest to the author the excision of these passages. See I, 34. There is a conversational bloody (I, 4) but I should not interfere with that. Recommended for Licence.'

The Lord Chamberlain, the Earl of Cromer, commented at the foot: 'This is a curious play to receive the blessing of the Bishop of London, but as it seems to be the case I hardly think any interference necessary.'

EMB had suggested a ballet to TSE on 9 Dec. 1933: 'We have the offer of the services of a first-class child-dancer of 11. What do you think about a ballet of Dick Whittington & his cat, choreography based on contemporary British painting?' See letter to Ida Shaw Page, 7 June.

21 April 1934   Faber & Faber Ltd

My dear Ted,

I have been very dilatory in answering your letter of so long ago – which I found very cheering. I am not a good correspondent. Anyway, I now write officially to announce the publication of 'Marston' in the June *Criterion* – this being his tercentenary, so they tell me. Whether you will get proofs in time for correction I don't know, but I hope so.[2]

I am delighted to hear that you are coming over this summer, and that you will be seeing Nancy and John.[3] The question is, whether and when you will be in London? If you *could* manage to run over here between the 28th May and the middle of June, I should like you to see my pageant play which is to be produced at Sadler's Wells during that period, and no longer. The text is now finished and has been passed by the Lord Chamberlain and by the Bishop of London; we have an excellent cockney comedian for the leading part, and everything promises well. Whether there will be any political demonstrations during the performances I don't know; but that would add to the interest.

Perhaps you can't tear yourself away in time to escape the Final Examinations and the Doctors' Examination, but do try. If you can't get to England, I shall have to run over to Normandy perhaps, later. I have not seen Richards very recently and don't know how his schemes for exchange lecturers progress. The sticking point seems to be that the Cambridge lecturers are naturally appalled at the prospect of having to give so many lectures and do so much irrelevant work as you have to do at Harvard.

The last time I saw Richards was when I stayed with them to see *Antony and Cleopatra* done by the Marlowe Society. All things considered – the play being much too ambitious for undergraduates to undertake anyway – it was well played. I think modern electric light effects can easily be overdone; and the costumes were bad. Cleopatra not only indecent, but what's worse, ridiculous. Her sea-fight costume made her look like a

---

1 – Theodore Spencer (1902–48), writer, poet, critic, taught at Harvard, 1927–49; as Boylston Professor of Rhetoric and Oratory from 1946. Co-editor of *A Garland for John Donne 1631–1931* (1931), to which TSE contributed 'Donne in Our Time'; and author of *Shakespeare and the Nature of Man* (1951).
2 – Spencer, 'John Marston', *C.* 13 (July 1934), 581–99.
3 – Spencer wrote (31 Jan.) that he was planning to visit the UK in the summer. 'Probably we'll go to Austria again & then have 2 weeks or so in England towards the end of the summer.'

comic Britannia; and really, if a lady is to appear with bare legs, it should not be in a scene in which she has to kneel several times in supplication, so that she goes about with dirty knees and the effect of majesty is rather diminished. But that was Rylands's doing, whom God preserve and the Devil pickle in brine. This was the first time the female parts had been done by Newnham and Girton. I think John Hayward will be disappointed if you don't come to London. He seems to get about a bit, with help; but I have never seen him except sitting in his room; and I don't for the life of me know how he gets to the bathroom even; I never see him even stand up. But you know how proud and reserved he is about his physical condition. Otherwise, he seems pretty cheerful; I go in to supper with him and a game of chess every week or two.

Please don't leave this letter unanswered so long as I did yours; because I really want to know your plans as soon as may be.

Affectionately,
Tom

My colleague Frank Morley was a couple of days in Boston, and lunched at Eliot House – with David McCord[1] – expressly in the hope of meeting you; but you weren't there that day.

TO *H. S. Latham*   CC

23 April 1934   [Faber & Faber Ltd]

My dear Latham,

Morley has handed me your letter of April 12th concerning the selected volume of poetry of Miss Marianne Moore.[2]

1–FVM wrote on 20 Apr. 1934 to David McCord (1897–1977) – poet and fundraiser; executive director of Harvard College Fund – that F&F did not 'dare make an offer for THE CROWS [by McCord]. This and two other collections of poems in which Eliot and I are interested have had to be jettisoned because of our commitments and the state of the Trade. You know the problems about as well as I do; Eliot and I are allowed just so much for poetry, and we have already exceeded the allowance for this year.'

2–H. S. Latham, The Macmillan Company, New York, to FVM, 12 May 1934: 'Since you were here I have been considering off and on the suggestion that we publish a selected volume of the poetry of Marianne Moore, the selection to be made by Eliot, and to be prefaced by him. We have decided that if you are ready to go ahead, we are, and I have made a royalty proposal for the American market to Miss Moore, which is acceptable to her. All of this is subject to Eliot's doing the selection and introduction. What is the next step to be taken?' FVM replied to Latham, 17 May, evidently after consulting with TSE:

'I had the feeling that when I was in New York talking about Eliot's collaboration in the book I mentioned that we could hardly expect him to do this for pure love of literature.

It is quite true that I am to make a selection from amongst the work of Miss Moore, which is now in my hands. Also Morley brought back to me the account of the conversation which he had with her, in which it was proposed that I should do an introduction to the poems, as I previously introduced a volume of Ezra Pound's poems selected by myself. As Miss Moore's wishes on this point only reached me verbally, I thought it only courteous to write to her and ask for her confirmation and to ask also whether she had any other wishes with regard to the selection and order. As soon as I hear from her I will set to work and will, of course, let you have a typed copy of my introduction, together with a list of the selections in order, as soon as they are ready, unless you prefer to wait for proofs. We should like to produce the book in the autumn season if possible.

Yours very truly,
[T. S. Eliot]

TO *Lilian M. Case*   TS Beinecke

24 April 1934   [Faber & Faber Ltd]

Dear Madam,

Mr Richard de la Mare has handed me your letter to Mr Walter de la Mare asking if I would present a manuscript for a sale in aid of the Shoreditch Housing Association.[1]

I can provide two kinds of manuscript. The first kind is genuine, is written in pencil on odd scraps of paper and is usually illegible. I send you a specimen of the genuine kind, which is a first draft of a chorus from a

---

I am sure you will agree that as his collaboration will materially help the book, it should be budgeted for; and what I had in mind for the American use of Eliot's introduction was a fee for £25 in addition to the royalty to the author. This is a moderate fee, but Eliot is agreeable to it, and I am sure you won't feel it is out of the way.

'The fee to Eliot would, of course, be inclusive; that's to say, you wouldn't need any other editorial expenses of any kind; and naturally you would not wish to alter his selection if the book is to carry the introduction referring to that selection.'

Latham wrote again to FVM, 1 Aug. 1934: 'I appreciate your being willing to put over the publication of Miss Moore's book until January. Our poetry list is rather long this autumn, and Miss Moore's book will have a better chance next year. If you can send us proofs of the English edition in August, we should have no difficulty in getting our edition ready for January. I would propose tentatively January 22nd, 1935, as a date for publication . . .'

1 – Lilian Case (Crewe House Auction in aid of the Shoreditch Housing Association, Toynbee Hall, London) asked Walter de la Mare on 20 Apr.: 'We are anxious to ask Mr T. S. Eliot if he could spare us a manuscript of one of his poems for sale, and we wonder if you would be so very kind as to ask your son Mr Richard de la Mare to mention it to Mr Eliot for us?'

play.¹ The other kind of manuscript is artificial, and is written legibly and painfully in ink. If you prefer the latter kind, will you please return the enclosure and let me know if you have a preference of which of my poems you would like to have a manuscript. It should not be long, however, as writing with a pen is physically painful for me.²

I am,

Yours very truly,

T. S. Eliot

TO *Janet Adam Smith*³   CC

24 April 1934   [Faber & Faber Ltd]

Dear Miss Adam Smith,

Thank you very much for your kind invitation of the 23rd.⁴ I am afraid, however, that the subject is too big a one for me to tackle in the time.

1 – TSE sent her the first complete draft of the final chorus of *The Rock*, along with the closing speech by 'The Rock, now St Peter': five leaves dated Mar. 1934 – now in Beinecke. Donald Gallup to TSE, 12 Jan. 1948: 'I cabled recently for five pages of the original manuscript of the final chorus from *The Rock* (the firm of Elkin Mathews, Bishops Stortford had this) but the item was reported sold. I hope that someone in England bought it for the Bodleian, where, of course, it belongs.' TSE to Gallup, 12 Feb. 1948: 'I cannot think where the five pages of manuscript of *The Rock* came from. I thought that all of the preparatory script for *The Rock* was included in what I gave to the Bodleian.'

2 – Mrs Case responded, 26 Apr., 'We are most grateful to you for your very kind gift of a manuscript for our sale, & we should much prefer to keep the pencil MS. you sent rather than have an ink one specially written.

'I am enclosing the manuscript because we should be so glad if you would add to your kindness by signing it & also if you would either add a title & any brief explanation or send us a brief note (which could be sold with it) explaining what it is – the title & signature would add a good deal to its value.'

She wrote again on 30 Apr.: 'Thank you very much for your kindness in signing your manuscript & for sending an explanatory note with it.'

3 – Janet Adam Smith (1905–99) read English at Somerville College, Oxford. She was assistant editor of the *Listener*, 1930–5; assistant literary editor, 1949–52, and literary editor, 1952–60, of the *New Statesman*. In 1935 she married the poet and editor Michae Roberts, and TSE was to become godfather to Adam (b. 1940), the third of their four children. Her works include *Mountain Holidays* (1946), *John Buchan: A Biography* (1965), and *John Buchan And His World* (1979), as well as anthologies including *The Faber Book of Children's Verse* (1953). See further Jason Harding, 'The Criterion: Cultural Politics and Periodical Networks in Inter-War Britain* (2002), chap. 8: 'Michael Roberts and Janet Adam Smith'.

4 – Smith invited TSE to contribute an essay on the American moralists, for a series being run in *The Listener* later in the summer: possibly up to 2,500 words? She asked too to be allowed to call on him to discuss various points relating to other articles in the series. (At their meeting, TSE suggested, among other ideas, that Ford Madox Ford might be asked to contribute a piece.)

I am not really a very well read person and it seems to me that I know almost nothing about the American moralists. In fact, I am not quite sure whether you mean contemporaries or whether you have in mind such people as Emerson. I am not a very good person to talk about Emerson, as I dislike him and his works. Of course I do know something about the modern American humanists but I am afraid that in any case, I shall be too busy to prepare anything for you in the time.

I should be very happy, however, to discuss the general subject with you, if I can be of any use. Almost any time would do except Monday mornings and Wednesday afternoon. Perhaps you will ring up and make an appointment with my secretary.[1]

Yours sincerely,
[T. S. Eliot]

TO *Leonard Woolf* TS Berg

26 April 1934 Faber & Faber Ltd

Dear Leonard,

I am sending you round, with the consent and approval of the author, a biography of Geraldine Jewsbury by a Mrs Noble of New York. While I don't pretend that the book is a particularly brilliant biography, I read it through with considerable interest and enjoyment. We hesitated over accepting it, and as our list for next season is such that it is a question of keeping it within limits, we eventually decided against it: this, in spite of the fact, which you should keep in mind, that Mrs Noble is prepared to pay some of the expense of publication. Just how much, I don't know as we didn't get to the point of discussion, but you might find that she was willing to bear the heavier part of the burden.

With the biography comes a separate envelope containing a selection of letters to and from Miss Jewsbury. Some of these are very interesting but they don't seem to me as a whole impressive enough to print as a separate section of the book. I suggested to Mrs Noble that it would be better to select the more interesting of these letters, such as those from Carlyle, and incorporate them in the text in the appropriate places, and to this she agrees.

1–Adam Smith recalled, 'I met Mr Eliot for the first time, when I went to consult him at Fabers' about a proposed supplement [for *The Listener*] on American Literature. He couldn't contribute himself, but gave me excellent advice on possible subjects and writers' ('Tom Possum and the Roberts Family', *T. S. Eliot: Essays from the 'Southern Review'* [1988], 213).

As I imagine that Virginia is the chief living authority on Geraldine Jewsbury, the Hogarth Press seemed to me the most appropriate destination for the manuscript.[1]

Yours ever,

T. S. E.

TO *Algar Thorold*[2]   CC

26 April 1934   [Faber & Faber Ltd]

My dear Thorold,

I should perhaps have acknowledged your letter immediately but should not have been able to reply to it, as I wished to discuss your suggestion with one or two other directors.[3] In the absence of the Chairman I can only reply rather tentatively.

First of all, however, let me express my deep regret at the loss to English periodical literature through your ceasing to edit the *Dublin Review*. I consider it also a loss to myself as the *Dublin* was almost the only established periodical which could use some of the same contributors as the *Criterion*. In writing in this way I admit that I am assuming that the *Dublin* will deteriorate and become, without your direction, almost negligible outside of the R.C. sphere.

1 – See VW, 'Geraldine Jewsbury', *TLS*, 28 Feb. 1929, 149–50; repr. in *The Common Reader: Second Series* (1932); and Susanne Howe, *Geraldine Jewsbury: Her Life and Errors* (1935).
2 – Algar Thorold (1866–1936): editor of the *Dublin Review*. TSE wrote in a memorial note in C. (Oct. 1936, 68) that Thorold 'had been a frequent contributor [to the *Criterion*] since very early in our history: his knowledge especially of modern French philosophy and theology was invaluable. Having written very few books – his *Masters of Disillusion* has been out of print for many years – he was not known to a very wide public, and another generation will not be aware that *The Dublin Review*, under his editorship, was one of the most distinguished periodicals of its time. Being half-French by birth, and at the same time thoroughly English, with the culture of the past and the curiosity of the present, he held a position as a man of letters such that we could say of him, that he was the sort of man whom we could ill afford to lose.'
3 – Thorold wrote on 19 Apr. that he was being made redundant as editor of the *Dublin Review*. He had edited the periodical for eight years. 'Messrs Burns & Oates find themselves unable to meet the expense of carrying on the review as at present, & have obtained the Cardinal's permission to bring it out in their office without an Editor.' His private means being small, he was obliged to try to make money by writing a book: he proposed to undertake a study of French philosophy, 'From Pascal to Bergson' – covering 'intermediate thinkers' including Maine de Biran, Marcel Blondel, Lucien Laberthonnière, and also T. E. Hulme . . . The point of view from wh: I shd write would of course be "R.C." but not, I trust, in any merely narrow, sectarian or conventional sense . . . I think it wd have a better chance if not brought out by an R.C. firm.'

Now about your book, we don't feel that a book covering such a wide field, with a succession of authors, some of whom are hardly known in this country, could possibly appeal to more than a small and select public. The connection between the authors is by no means obvious to those who haven't already made some study of the subject. The attraction of the book would lie wholly in the name of the author, and it would be useful if the subject had some immediate appeal also. What has occurred to us is that you might be able to say a great deal of what you want to say and introduce the authors whom you wish to discuss if you wrote a book primarily about T. E. Hulme. There is, of course, a great deal of interest in Hulme amongst younger people today; many of the things in which you and I believe could be made more acceptable to them if protected by Hulme's authority; and I believe that we are as closely in touch with the public interest in Hulme as any other publisher in London. In fact I might have said that we are obviously the publishers to whom any new book on Hulme should be submitted; and sooner or later someone is sure to write a book about him. I put out this suggestion very tentatively and when I know what your response is, I will discuss the matter again with my Committee.

Yours ever,

[T. S. Eliot]

P.S. I should be glad to have the Newman as soon as possible.[1]

Herbert Read's address is

'The Burlington Magazine'

16a, St. James's Street

s.w.1.

of which he is now the editor. He is no longer 'Professor'.

TO *Ezra Pound*   TS Beinecke

26 April 1934 AD   Faber & Faber Ltd

Podesta leavin aside for the moment this vital question of cruelty to animiles, I think praps I ought to come down to see about that, but why oh why do the wops[2] allow such goins on, these Americans what thinks when they're away from home thay can do as they likes, skylarkin about

---

1–Review of Jean Guitton, *La Philosophie de Newman*: C. 13 (July 1934), 680–1.
2–wop: 'An Italian or other southern European, esp. as an immigrant or foreign visitor . . . Now considered offensive' (*OED*).

Montmarter and drinkin vichy and bitin animiles in zoos where they are penned up and elpless poor little pretties;[1] leavin all this to one Side for the moment I say,

let us return to the question already broached of a COLlected edition of your Juvenilia up to cantoes at 7s. 6d. the SElected bein out of print at that price and sellin very pretty at 3s. 6d. Of course that sale will be slightly Reduced by COMplete edition at higher price but not very appreciably our Sales Manager thinks. And your royalties on the higher price of Course better. This you will remember was deferred as at the Time you was unable to set your mind on anything but the Propertius. But I mean this for some time in 1935, after givin the Propertius a reasonable run to get its money back.

I dont kno if we could run to a Beaooootifull Portrit of Ezzum as well.

Cor blimey this bitin of animiles blest if I dont blieve youll take to flagellation next Rabbet cant you sate your vicious lusts some other more normial way than bitin animiles yours truly

Tp

EG. SIG. Ezzum Lomax Pound, sub judice,
    via marsala 12 int 5.
    RAPPALLOO.
    Italien.

1–EP had reported on 18 Apr.: 'DESPITE the fakk of yr/ TOTEM [the possum] having BIT me during my recent peerambe thru the Rome Graden of living zoological specimens, I hasted ter kommunicate that from that snot Zabel's review of yr/ Use and Misue I think I might give you some favourable publicity on the bk/ . . . Even if yr. "Use and masturb// of Poesy" is as bad as you say, mebbe one cd/ quote something USEFUL from it . . . admitting that the main use of your talkin in, instead of walking thru, the Eu/S/Ah wuz to line yr/ pocket with baloney dullars.' (On 26 Apr. EP gave the title as 'Uses and self-abuses of Poesy' or wotever its masturbly called.')

TO *Geoffrey Grigson*[1]   TS Texas

26 April 1934   *The Criterion*

Dear Mr Grigson,

Thank you for the copy of *New Verse* with the poems by MacNeice and Smith[2] which I will read.

I will send you Edwin Muir's poem and a few other poems which have just come in.[3] There doesn't seem to be very much poetry worth reviewing on hand at the moment. I should be glad if you would hold such books as I send and let them collect (intransitive), separating out those which deserve any mention at all until a review is needed for the September number. If any books appear which you think are suitable for review in a collective review, please let me know.

Yours sincerely,
T. S. Eliot

TO *The Editor,* The New English Weekly

3 May 1934[4]

MODERN HERESIES[5]

Sir, —

There appears to be left one matter upon which Mr Pound and I do not agree: namely, the vital problem of what is and what is not blue china. Let Mr Pound dust his own blue china and let me potter about with mine.

---

1 – Geoffrey Grigson (1905–85), poet, prolific anthologist, literary and art critic, writer on natural history and travel, and of non-fiction for children, worked for the *Yorkshire Post*, as literary editor of the *Morning Post*, and for the BBC. Founder and editor of the influential magazine *New Verse*, his other publications include *The Arts Today* (1935), *New Verse: An Anthology* (1939), and *The Crest on the Silver: An Autobiography* (1950).
2 – A. J. M. Smith (1902–80): Canadian poet and anthologist.
3 – Grigson wrote (25 Apr.), 'If you let me review some more poems for the "Criterion" I should like to have Edwin Muir's "Variations on a Time Theme" among them, but not "Festivals of Fire" which I don't like and have already been perhaps rude about in *New Verse.*'
4 – Published on that date in *NEW*, 71–2.
5 – This letter is in answer to a letter from EP published as 'Mr T S Eliot's Quandaries' (*NEW* 5 [26 Apr. 1934], 48), which read (in part): 'It is not that economics constitute "the ONLY vital problem", but that poverty and the syphilis of the mind called the Finance-Capitalist system kill more men annually than typhoid or tuberculosis. I would not stop to discuss blue china in the midst of a cholera epidemic if I possessed means to combat the epidemic, and, in the present circumstances, I consider certain kinds of aesthetic discussion on a par with such a course.'

Incidentally, the personalities of Mr Chesterton and Dean Inge, and Mr Pound's lack of respect for them, seem to me to be totally irrelevant.

I am not convinced that my own concern for the future of society, in England A.D. 1934, is any less than that of Mr Pound in Italy *anno* 12. On the contrary, as Mr Pound is not interested in the survival of the Christian Faith, his demands upon the future are much more likely to be satisfied than are mine. And this is the point, and indeed the only point for me of embarking upon or pursuing this correspondence. It is only a step from asserting (what appears to be true) that the economic problem must be solved if civilisation is to survive, to asserting (what I dispute) that all other problems may be or ought to be neglected until the solution of the economic problem. And from this point it is only one step more into complete Securalism. The political alternatives which we are offered as alternatives to the present rotten state of affairs both seem to me wholly secular. The reason why I have been able to support the *New English Weekly* is that the doctrines it advocates do not appear to be necessarily and exclusively secular. The kind of fanaticism which Mr Pound applies to economic reforms with which I am, in any case, in sympathy, and which he applies in a different sense to a religious institution of which I am a member, seems to me to degrade the former, and to leave the latter unaffected.

Mr Pound has been kind enough to inform me about the works of Alberto de la Magna, the Collection Migne, and Larousse. I may recommend in return a small pamphlet, *Le bien commun*, published by Desclée de Brouwer et Cie., fr. 2.50. I have also found *Le meilleur régime politique selon S. Thomas* (Marcel Demongeot) and *Fragments de*

—

'For the rest I refer Mr Eliot to Migne's collection of the early Church Fathers, the *Encyclopedia Britannica* or Larousse and/or any passable history of the Church. I certainly do not intend to stigmatise the "whole of the Anglican and Roman hierarchies" ... Obviously an organisation that presents itself publicly in the person of Dean Inge does not inspire *my* respect.

'On the other hand a church containing Father Charles E. Coughlin is not otiose in ALL its parts.

'P.S. – I take it from Mr Eliot's signature of the *Times* letter that he is not wholly blind, and his *Criterion* (current issue) carries a note by Bonamy Dobrée indicating a disposition towards daylight.

'Perhaps the measure of religion's degradation in England in our time may be measured by the fact that Chesterton is the most vocal Catholic, and Inge the noisiest and most persistent verbal manifester of the Anglicans.'

sociologie chrétienne (Tristan d'Athayde) of some interest. I have no doubt that he is already familiar with *Quadragesimo Anno*.[1]

T. S. Eliot

TO *Stephen Spender*

TS Northwestern

3 May 1934   Faber & Faber Ltd

Dear Spender,

Thank you for your letter of the 27th.[2] I have given the new poems, together with the list of contents and your instructions, to de la Mare. I don't think that it will be necessary to raise the price to 6/- but we can be more definite about that when they actually go to press.

We have come to the conclusion that the present stock of your poems will probably be exhausted within a month or so, which will allow sufficient time to announce a new edition in the autumn. We see no reason why that should conflict with the publication of your play for the Christmas market, only if we don't get your manuscript until October, it will allow a very narrow margin for publication, as it is useless to publish any book

---

1 – EP replied to this letter with a further letter of his own, published as 'Mr Eliot's Looseness' (*NEW*, 10 May 1934, 95–6): '[T]here are Christians, at least in the Roman Church, to whom the faith implies ethical discrimination and direction of the will toward righteousness . . .

'I wish I could lead Mr Eliot to a more precise use of language. "Not interested in the survival of the Christian faith." It is most slanderous to accuse me of any such lack of purely scientific generosity as this sentence implies . . . Does he mean to accuse me of disapproval of Christian *faith*, or disapproval of Christian *doctrine*? . . .

'I have not read the recent French literature recommended by the earnest Eliot. I found, as nearly as I remember, four absolutely unwarrantable assumptions in the opening pages of the summary of the Summa. Theologians frequently offer possibilities as if they were facts . . .

'Mr Eliot has been able to live in England, and that may or may not imply that he is less nauseated by drivelling amateurism than I am. If he dreams of a Christian Church manned or priested by adepts, I agree that his "demands" are apparently made on a very *far distant* future . . .

'Again Mr Eliot tries to bludgeon me with terminology. Again he is loose in his applications of words. You can assume the aesthetic attitude, as when Gourmont remarks that certain ideas would be spoiled if you translated them into action, but Mr Eliot uses the term "fanatic" as if any man who believed that his ideas SHOULD be put into ACTION, were by that sole fact a fanatic.'

2 – Spender wrote on 27 Apr. that he wished to make some alterations for a possible new edition of his *Poems*. 'I wish to cut out the poems no VI and XI. When I sent in the MS, I realized that these were weak links, and, of course, Dr Leavis in his review pounced on them to say I was a Georgian, unconsciously influenced by Meredith etc. Really, they are just rather forced . . .'

between the 15th November and the new year. Could you possibly let us have the manuscript of the play by September 15th?[1] Certainly you need not worry about two thousand lines being an excessive length. If we find that the book cannot be published at half a crown, we will publish it at 3s. 6d. It is possible to allow certain variations of size and price between publications of this type. The main thing is to maintain some similarity of form and to bring them out at the right moment.

I am having your essay on Yeats set up in order to ascertain the exact number of words, and will send you the cheque with the proof.

I will write to you again as soon as I can answer your question about the American edition.[2]

Yours ever,
T. S. Eliot

TO *Bonamy Dobrée*   TS Brotherton

4 May 1934   Faber & Faber Ltd

Dear Bomany God damb it I find I Have a meeting of the Council of the Church Literature Association (First meeting since the amalgamation of the E.C.U. and the A.C.C. which no doubt you have followed with intense and palpitating interest[3]) and then to lunch with Roger Hinks.[4] I shall

1–Spender asked, 'will the play be possible for you to do at Christmas? I will finish it by October . . . It is about the German Revolution, and I'm afraid it will be at least 2,000 lines. Is that too long for you?' Spender to RdlM, 19 May 1934: 'Could you mention to Eliot that I shall have the play ready by Sept 15. It will be better than these poems [*Poems*, 1934], I trust.'
2–Spender had asked in a postscript, bluntly: '? What about the American Edition?'
3–The English Church Union fused with the Anglo-Catholic Congress to form The Church Union, and so the old Church Literature Association (CLA) had amalgamated with the Literature Committee of the English Church Union to form the Church Literature Association. TSE was one of twenty-nine members of the Council, and the Revd Charles Harris was Chair of the Book Committee – whose mission was to be 'responsible for the publication of learned books for the exposition, defence and propaganda of Catholic Faith and Practice, and all subsidiary subjects'.
4–See Roger Hinks, 8 May 1934: 'At lunch today Eliot gave me his impressions of America while he was there last summer. He said that among ordinary, unthinking people the one idea was to get back to the conditions of 1926 which was looked back upon as a kind of golden age. A few, somewhat more perspicacious, realized that such an ambition neither could nor should be gratified. Owing to technical improvements there would still be, under the existing system, about two million more unemployed than there were then if the plants worked at the same capacity. The enthusiasm for Roosevelt, and the optimism that his policy was evoking (things have changed somewhat since), were the final throw of the gambler, not the reflection of a new spirit. The gambling spirit of the American masses, fostered enormously in the

look in at Hastings's[1] after lunch with or without Hinks. I have a chorus rehearsal in Eccleston Square at 6, and some other rehearsal at Bound's Green after dinner. Otherwise I am free. Is there any chance of your being over night. Very regretful to miss opportunity to sherry and lunch with you.

I wrote Aldous the next day but too soon to have a reply. I know however that he is at home as I had a letter from him on a different subject crossing mine.

Herbert is back from Paris, where he interviewed Thierry Maulnier.[2]

yrs. despondently

T.

TO *Elizabeth Bowen*[3]   CC

8 May 1934   [Faber & Faber Ltd]

Dear Mrs Cameron,

Thank you so much for your kind invitation of May 7th.[4] I do frequently go away at weekends, and it would give me great pleasure to stay with you at Headington, but, unfortunately, the weekend of May 26th is quite impossible [because] we shall be rehearsing on the Saturday and having the first performance on Monday evening. The run is for a fortnight, during which I ought not to leave town, and after that I am intending to go away for a fortnight's rest. I wish that your invitation had not coincided with this engagement, and I hope that you will be kind enough to ask me again at some other time.

---

boom years, has no outlet in any sport; it is satisfied only by speculation on Wall Street. The materialism of America appalled Eliot: it is far worse than European materialism. Not even adversity has taught Americans the futility of worshipping "Success"' (*The Gymnasium of the Mind: The Journals of Roger Hinks 1933–1963*, ed. John Goldsmith [1984]).

1 – Presumably the studio or home of the sculptor Donald Hastings.

2 – Thierry Maulnier (1909–88): French journalist, essayist, playwright, critic; contributor to *L'Action française*; author of *La crise est dans l'homme* (1932), *Nietzsche* (1933), *Miracle de la Monarchie* (1935), *Mythes socialistes* (1938); he was elected to the Academie française in 1964.

3 – Elizabeth Bowen (1899–1973) – Mrs Alan Cameron – Irish-born novelist; author of *The Last September* (1929), *The House in Paris* (1935), *The Death of the Heart* (1938), *The Heat of the Day* (1949). TSE told A. Desmond Hawkins on 26 Jan. 1937 that he respected Bowen's opinion; and on 3 Feb. 1937: 'She has a very definite place, and a pretty high one, amongst novelists of her kind.'

4 – Bowen invited TSE to Waldencote, Old Headington, Oxford, for the weekend of 26 May. They were just back from Ireland, where the Woolfs had enjoyed visiting them for a day.

I am very glad to hear that you had good weather at Bowen Court, and that the Woolfs enjoyed the experience of Ireland. I thought that they would.

Yours very sincerely,
[T. S. Eliot]

TO *The Editor,* The Times   CC

9 May 1934[1]   [Faber & Faber Ltd]

Sir,

In view of the great number of enquiries we have received consequent upon the letter from ourselves which you were good enough to print in your columns of April 5th, and the impossibility of dealing with them individually, may we further trespass on the hospitality of your pages to say that the scheme we had in mind as notably requiring thorough discussion, is that concerned with Social Credit and associated in particular with the name of Major C. H. Douglas?

Yours etc.

(Signed by) Lascelles Abercrombie, Bonamy Dobrée, T. S. Eliot,
Aldous Huxley, Hewlett Johnson, Hamish Miles,
Edwin Muir, Herbert Read, I. A. Richards.

TO *Christopher Dawson*   CC

10 May 1934   [Faber & Faber Ltd]

My dear Dawson,

I have left your last letter unanswered for a long time, during which I have been occupied with immediate practical matters, principally a sort of play for which I am partly responsible. But your letter has been on my mind, and I should like, however hastily, to try to formulate my points of disagreement.[2]

---

1 – Published in *The Times,* 10 May 1934, 10.

2 – Dawson wrote (n.d.): 'What you say about the appeal of Credit Reform to well intentioned people rather explains my own attitude to it. I feel it is being preached (especially by the clergy) not on its own merits, but because people feel that Credit Reform seems the mildest & most palatable economic remedy on the market.

'I agree that economic changes are necessary, but I do not think they can be safely carried out except by a very strong & far-sighted government. The first necessity is the restoration of political authority, & the restoration of economic order can only follow. This may sound

First of all, you say: 'I feel that there is more danger of violence from the left than from Fascism in this country.' For the immediate future, which I take as the frame of reference, I should prognosticate the exact contrary. You cannot fill the Albert Hall with people interested in communism: if you half filled it, you would have a cordon of police as numerous as the audience. It depends on what you mean by 'violence'. If you mean a dramatic 'revolution' as in Russia, I agree; but if you are willing to include as 'violence' such sporadic affairs as the Matteoti case,[1] or the insurgence of young roughs in Germany, then I should say that I hold the opposite view. Personally, I should expect to get rather more humane treatment from the communists than from the fascists, because the former would include some intelligent and intellectual element, and the latter would not.

As for the 'corporate state, hierarchy and authority' being the essentials of Catholic social doctrine expounded by Leo XIII, very well. But in practice, I believe that the authority claimed by a fascist state would conflict with ecclesiastical authority. The Papacy is strong in Italy, and Mussolini is a wise and astute statesman; but, even in Italy, I cannot believe that a Concordat is the ideal relation of Church and State. The Papacy is not so strong in Germany, or we may say the Catholic German States are not dominant: and we see the result. The Papacy, and what I call Catholicism, are still weaker in England: and we may predict the result. I am quite ready to agree to anything you say about Communism: I may have said it already. But I question whether English Communism would be any more spiritually destructive than English Fascism. Communism, or even a few years of government by the Labour Party, would certainly generate a 'strong force of resistance'; but I cannot see the faintest reason for expecting that that resistance would be, as you say, *spiritual* resistance. We should probably get merely the conflict of one temporal set of interests with another.

---

fascist, but I must confess that so far as principles go, setting aside their practices, I have very little quarrel with Fascism. I am sure that the corporate state is the right basis for both a political & an economic solution. Equally I feel in the principle of hierarchy & authority. After all, these 3 principles are the essentials of Catholic social doctrine as expounded by Leo XIII. The weak points of Fascism are its militant nationalism & the all-important question of personnel. As to the question of violence, I feel that there is more danger of this from the left than from Fascism in this country . . . Of course the danger is that here as in Germany this force will ally itself with a blind intolerant nationalism, but it need not necessarily be so.'
1–Giacomo Matteoti (1885–1924), leader of the United Socialist Party in the Italian Chamber of Deputies, had denounced the violence of the Fascists and was thereupon assassinated by them.

I may be only reiterating your own quotation: 'come out from among them, and be ye separate'.[1]

I am not quite sure what you mean by 'the restoration of political authority'. But it seems to me that any political authority that we are likely to get through fascism, a 'restoration' financed by industrialists, is the last thing to favour the restoration, or the creation, of economic order. It is just as likely to mean the further oppression and exploitation of the lower classes.

I don't think that Credit Reform is preferred by intelligent people merely as the 'mildest' medicine. I think that a small number, at least, realise that it implies a spiritual conversion of a very radical kind. Both fascism and communism, however, rely upon exploiting the comforting sentiment of hatred.

And what you call 'the all important question of personnel' is indeed important. That alone seems to me enough to make it impossible to hold any traffic with fascism in England until the present movement has been stopped and forgotten.

Yours ever.
[T. S. Eliot]

TO *Bonamy Dobrée*

TS Brotherton

10 May 1934   Faber & Faber Ltd

Dear Bonamy,

AS you dont see the *Times*, I enclose our masterpiece in print.

And, for the same reason, I enclose a dreadful, and I believe ominous, specimen of the brilliant wit of Mr Oliver Stanley.[2]

To-day I interviewed Mr Odle, of the XI Hour Emergency,[3] a pleasing young man, whom I engaged to keep in touch with me. But I fear that *New Albion* needs a bit of editing. Nevertheless, Mr Odle should be encouraged. I promised to write something for them.[4]

I regret, again, having had to be absent from the sherry of Hastings and Drinkwater; indeed, I have not yet had time to visit the exPOsition.

1–2 Corinthians 7: 17.
2–Oliver Stanley (1896–1950), British Conservative politician.
3–John Elsden Odle, Eleventh Hour Publishing Company, 16 Queen Anne's Gate, London.
4–Odle had written to TSE, 29 Apr., that he wished to explain 'who we are, and the deeper purpose behind the campaign for unity in Monetary reform'.

Yours etc.

TP

The only really interesting thing about the *Rock* (28th inst.) will be to see how the public responds to the political allusions in it. But I fear a dull and lethargic audience for this sort of affair.[1]

TO *S. C. Carpenter*[2]   CC

11 May 1934   [Faber & Faber Ltd]

Dear Carpenter,

My colleagues have been considering the need for a fairly comprehensive book on the Church of England, and my suggestion of yourself, as a possible author, was received with great approval. What they have in mind is not simply a history of the Church of England, covering the whole period, the sort of book of which your 'Church and People' covers part but a book which, besides historical treatment, should be a kind of handbook explanatory of the Church for the information not only of the faithful but for the intelligent unfaithful, and also people outside the Church with an intelligent interest.

I say 'they' rather than 'we' because I am referring to a public they represent and which I do not. For this reason I am enclosing a copy of an outline drawn up by one of them, rather than attempting to re-state the notion in my own language.

I don't know what your commitments are for the immediate future but we would rather, I think, wait for any definite period, if you are willing to undertake the book eventually instead of approaching anyone else. This letter aims only to enquire whether you are interested in principle in writing such a book. If you are, I should be glad to take up immediately the question of satisfactory terms.

Yours sincerely,

[T. S. Eliot]

1 – 'He need not have feared,' wrote BD. 'The audience (which included my wife and myself) seemed far from lethargic' ('T. S. Eliot: A Personal Reminiscence').
2 – S. C. Carpenter, DD (1877–1959): Master of the Temple, London, 1930–5; Chaplain to the King, 1929–35; Dean of Exeter, 1935–50. His works include *The Anglican Tradition* (1928). He was a member of the Book Committee of the Church Literature Association.

TO *R. Webb-Odell*

CC

11 May 1934   [Faber & Faber Ltd]

Dear Mr Webb-Odell,

Here is a draft of a note for the programme. I am sorry it has taken me so long. Please consider yourself free to knock it about in any way you like, or re-write completely.[1]

1 – 'The Story of the Pageant', signed by TSE and EMB, was printed in the Sadler's Wells Theatre programme – 28 May–9 June 1934 – p. 7:

'*The Rock* is not a pageant in the usual sense. It does not consist of a number of historical scenes or tableaux in order of time. The aim is not merely to remind people that churches have been built in the past, but to employ the historical scenes to reinforce, in appropriate places, the emphasis upon the needs of the present.

'The direct action of the play is concerned with the efforts and difficulties of a group of bricklayers engaged in building a modern church. At the beginning of the play they are seen working upon the foundations; later the half-built church is shown. When the builders have finished, decorators of various kinds complete the work, and the church is shown ready for its dedication. And during the course of construction the builders experience difficulties – from poor soil for the foundations, from the fear of lack of money to continue the work, from an agitator and a tumultuous mob, from critics who complain that the church is too ornate, or that it is too "modern". Besides the immediate troubles experienced by the group of workmen represented by Bert, Alfred and Edwin, the more general difficulties of the Church in the Modern World are symbolized in the action: the difficulties of the Church opposed, ignored, or interfered with by the secular tendencies of the present age.

'A Chorus, as in Greek Tragedy, comments in verse from time to time upon the needs and troubles of the Church to-day, and upon the action. This Chorus opens both parts of the play, and from time to time appeals to "The Rock," who, though he takes little part in the action, symbolizes the permanence and continuity of the Church of God, and its resistance to the forces of evil and dissolution.

'After the opening chorus, and some words of encouragement and consolation by "The Rock," a chant of Builders is heard, followed by a chant of the Unemployed, to which the Builders reply. The light then discovers the modern bricklayers discussing their work and many other things as well. A remark by one of them leads to an "experiment with time," in which the builders find themselves spectators of the conversion of Sabert, King of London, and his Saxon followers, by the Roman missionary Mellitus. After this scene they resume their work, but under great difficulties: the ground is swampy. To them appears Rahere, the builder of St Bartholomew's, and after reassuring them he and his men give them supernatural aid in the work. They are next confronted by social opposition, in the form of an agitator and a mob; and their momentary conflict with the mob calls up to our memory, as so upon the stage as the following scene, the troubles of Nehemiah in rebuilding the Wall of Jerusalem.

'In the second part the building (interspersed with other historical scenes) is completed. A scene of the Reformation reminds us of the dangers of destruction. A group of scenes towards the end recall the dedication of other churches: Westminster Abbey, St Michael Paternoster Royal, and St Paul's. At the end "The Rock" reappears; and the play is completed by the Bishop's benediction of the audience.'

It did not seem to me worthwhile, in the space, to give an exact and complete synopsis of the play, but merely the hang of it. Perhaps you may think it desirable to add a note about the Builders' Song.

I want to buy two *more* seats. I want two stalls for the first night, and if possible near to those which you gave me, in Row C. If not, as far forward as possible. I have only just heard that the two friends in question want particularly to go on the first night, and if possible near my other friends.

Yours sincerely,
[T. S. Eliot]

TO *David Higham*[1] CC

11 May 1934   [Faber & Faber Ltd]

My dear Higham,

Many thanks for your suggestion of the 9th May.[2] For one thing, however, I am rather averse in general to entering into collective volumes published by another firm, and I have one such commitment already. For another thing, there are other activities which I had rather spend my time on. And third, although I used to attend Bergson's lectures in 1910, and at that time studied all of his works very carefully, I am now wholly incompetent to write about such subjects. You want a man who is a practical philosopher. I might possibly consent to write an essay on Bergson, if you could induce Bergson to write an essay about me, but otherwise this just is not in my line. Finally it is quite impossible for me to undertake any work whatever which would have to be finished within the next month.

With many thanks,
Yours sincerely,
[T. S. Eliot]

1 – David Higham (1896–1978), literary agent, worked for Curtis Brown Ltd, 1925–35; then for David Higham Associates; author of *Literary Gent* (memoir, 1978). FVM told Helen Jacobs, 20 May 1935, of Higham: 'He is an ebullient young man with a curly moustache, and an eager but not very accurate tennis player'; and he reported to Joseph Chiari, 7 Feb. 1953 (when Higham was a director of Pearn, Pollinger, & Higham): 'Higham is a very active and pushing agent.'

2 – Higham advised TSE that Cassell was contemplating a volume to be entitled *Great Contemporaries*, consisting of forty 4,000-word essays on 'great living contemporaries': Curtis Brown had 'ventured to suggest' TSE as 'the best possible author for an essay on [Henri] Bergson', with a nominal advance of £20 payable on publication and a small royalty.

TO *Ezra Pound*   TS Beinecke

11 maggio [May] AD 1934   Faber & Faber Ltd

[PICTURE incomplete]
Podesta this is my new invention, Chas chastity girdle for ellefunts, pat.
pend. as offered to the Duce and all the other Heads of Zoos in Europe.[1]

I have given FVM two Beauttiful Budgerigars, you'd better come over
and see em, theyre in a Cage, and we could arrange for your transport
to Lingfield (Surrey) without passing through London. It is done by
parachute.

1–EP responded to 'the Rt. Rev. Wunkus T. Possum', 17 May: 'Your ceinture de Cluny wd/
seem to have been anticipated in all essential features (with rather less fuss) by our known
local inventor the neolithic Heinz . . . As to the aim and purpose of yr/ invention we are
opposed on both moral and theological grounds.
    'ref Encyclical DE VONUPTATE, of Gregory VII
        Cap. 7, Lib. 23.
    'De Coitu bestiarum/ Marcellus. Lib. 4. Cap. 87.
    'De bestialitas, Rev. Sinistrari of Ameno . . . But whether in this case the protection wd/
be effective against Mahouts there seems to be some doubt.'
    On 25 May EP referred again to 'the ceinture de chasteté wherewith the Rev/ Elepunt's
. . . design was garnizshed.'

I am all ready for a Campaign about Education, world wide. At least, I Did tell my pupils (sic) at Harvard that I only flung em my opinions for them to Bite at, that they wouldnt get anything out of my lectures that would help to pass examinations, but I expected them to come just the same.

I have a feelin you are about right on Abuse.[1] If so, I am not going to argue about It. What with the matters on which you are Right, and the matters you just don't understand, there aint so very much to argue about after all. This will be continued shortly.[2]

Tp

Bad E ducation IS at the bottom of all the rottenness today, mostly.

1 – 'Abuse': EP's shorthand for TSE's *The Use of Poetry and the Use of Criticism*.
2 – EP responded on 13 May: 'You jess get right DOWN to it/ and make a li'l list
    1. OF WHAT EZ is right about
    2. wot Ez dont understand; cause I got a few years left barin accident;
'Seereeyussly/ The ABC of Lit. ought to be out any day now/ and you cd do an honest mornings work reviewing it yourself in the Criterion . . .
'AS the means of blasting all the fahrting pseudo=crits.'

TO *Thomas MacGreevy*[1] TS Trinity College Dublin

11 May 1934 Faber & Faber Ltd

Dear Tom,

Thank you for your note[2] and for Beckett's note,[3] both of which are after my own heart. Your book[4] had come in and has gone out again to a reviewer, but, I am afraid, not in time to be mentioned in this next number.

I wish you would occasionally suggest books yourself, which you would like to review. Your short notes are invaluable but when there is any book that you would like to review at length, I wish that you would let me know. And, incidentally, I should like to remind you that you have

---

1–Thomas MacGreevy (1893–1967) – the family name was 'McGreevy', but by the 1930s he assumed the more Irish spelling 'MacGreevy' – poet, literary and art critic, arts administrator – worked for the Irish Land Commission before serving in WW1 as a 2nd lieutenant in the British Royal Field Artillery: he fought at Ypres and the Somme, and was twice wounded. After reading History and Political Science at Trinity College, Dublin, he moved in 1925 to London, where he met TSE and started to write for the *Criterion, TLS* (with an introduction from TSE) and *N&A*. His poem 'Dysert' appeared in *NC* 4 (Jan. 1926) under the pseudonym 'L. St. Senan' (the title was later changed to 'Homage to Jack Yeats'). In 1927 he took up teaching English at the Ecole Normale Supérieur in Paris, where he became friends with Beckett and JJ (to whom he had been introduced in 1924) and with RA. (His essay on JJ's *Finnegans Wake* – 'The Catholic Element in Work in Progress' – appeared in *Our Exagmination round his Factification for Incamination of Work in Progress,* 1929.) In addition, he journeyed through Italy with WBY. Back in London in 1933, he lectured at the National Gallery and wrote for *The Studio.* Ultimately he became Director of the National Gallery of Ireland, 1950–63. He was made Chevalier de la Légion d'Honneur, 1948; Cavaliere Ufficiale al merito della Repubblica Italiana, 1955; Officier de la Légion d'Honneur, 1962. In 1929 he published a translation of Paul Valéry's *Introduction à la méthode de Léonard de Vinci*; and in 1931, two monographs: *T. S. Eliot: A Study* and *Richard Aldington: An Englishman.* Publications on art include *Jack B. Yeats: An Appreciation and an Interpretation* (1945) and *Nicolas Poussin* (1960). See also *The Collected Poems of Thomas MacGreevy: An Annotated Edition,* ed. Susan Schreibman (1991).

2–See MacGreevy's review of Leon Pierre-Quint, *André Gide: Sa vie, son oeuvre*: *C.* 13 (July 1934), 707–9.

3–MacGreevy wrote on 9 May: 'I asked my friend Sam Beckett to make a few notes on the Rilke book as he is familiar with the original. He produced the second text enclosed and as it seems to me more competent than anything I could do myself on the subject I venture to send it to you. The suggestion that I should do so is mine not his.' Samuel Beckett's review of J. B. Leishman's translation of Rilke's *Poems* appeared in *C.* 13 (July 1934), 705–7. See Anthony Cronin, *Samuel Beckett: The Last Modernist* (1996), 202–3: 'The fact that Beckett never reviewed for the *Criterion* again proves nothing either way. He was the opposite of pushy and a little pushiness is usually needed to maintain connections, even with such editors as T. S. Eliot.'

4–McGreevy's *Poems,* published by William Heinemann in May 1934, was not reviewed in *C.*

made several suggestions when we met at the new year, none of which has yet been realised.

I am very busy up to the first part of June but after that I want to get you to have a meal and talk.

Yours sincerely,
T. S. Eliot

TO *Randall Swingler*[1]

11 May 1934   [*The Criterion*]

Dear Mr Swingler,

I must apologise for the delay in reporting on your play 'Crucifixus' (by the way you didn't date your letter so I don't know just how long the delay has been), but I wanted to make time to write to you rather fully about it.[2] The time has not yet shown itself so please accept this letter as a substitute.

In the first place, I am interested in your wanting to write a play and believe that this one is good enough to justify encouraging you to go on and write more. Here under the reasons why I do not consider this play acceptable. I assume as a general principle that a verse play should be written for future performance if it is to be worth writing.

In the first place, the Lord Chamberlain would not and could not permit the performance of a play in which the person of God appears. That is one quite sufficient reason, at present, why it is not worthwhile writing plays in which He or any figure symbolising Him has a part.

---

1 – Randall Swingler (1909–67), poet, playwright, editor; alumnus of Winchester College and of New College, Oxford; joined the Communist Party in 1934 (leaving it in 1956, in advance of the Hungarian rising), and became involved with the Workers' Music Association, the Left Book Club, Group Theatre and Unity Theatre. His editorial career spanned the *Daily Worker*, *Left Review* (of which he was the last editor), *Poetry and the People*, *Our Time*, *Arena*, *Circus*, and *New Reasoner*. In WW2 he was awarded the Military Medal for bravery. Works include *Poems* (1932) and *The Years of Anger* (1946).
2 – 'I was rather diffident of sending it to you because I know you have already had verse plays showered upon you . . . I have endeavoured to make my play as catholic as possible, so that it would be effective for performance in churches or elsewhere. It is perhaps more definitely religious than John Pudney's or *The Dance of Death*, and I have tried to found it on the Greek mode (particularly Aeschylus' *Prometheus*) . . . I do not know if with this in view, I have avoided the commonplace, and the sanctimonious. I realise both as dangers. But I believe it will be more effective in performance than in reading and that it could be produced with a certain simultaneous dignity and gusto.'

Secondly, I think it is a very poor dramatic device to have a person suffering the agony of crucifixion and at the same time delivering long harangues. It is hardly in keeping with what we know of Jesus Christ, and hardly credible that an ordinary human being in such torture should have so much to say for himself. Indeed, I fear that on the stage the effect might even be dismally comic. And in general I think that your characters have too much to say and too little to do. Versification alone cannot take the place of dramatic interest.

I think that you might on the one hand read verse drama, particularly the Greek drama, with a view to finding out how interest and suspense are maintained, and how and where the climax is produced. And on the other hand I think it would help you to talk with people like Robert Medley and Rupert Doone, who are interested in the realities of putting modern verse drama across on the stage. But I do recognise merit in this piece, and I do hope that you will go on with this sort of work. It is extremely difficult for any of us, who have begun life as poets to adapt ourselves to the theatre, and we have to be willing to learn, and to adapt ourselves.

Yours sincerely,
[T. S. Eliot]

TO *Ernest Bird, Messrs Bird & Bird*   CC

11 May 1934   [Faber & Faber Ltd]

My dear Bird,

I had no wish to pester a busy man about matters which might be of no urgency; but I did not know whether one was urgent or not, and I wanted to assure myself that you were neither ill nor away, and that the letters had come under your eye.[1]

As to the Frenchman, I will write to him as you suggest. There is one point in your letter which does not make itself clear to me. You say 'under no circumstances can you be held responsible for the rent'. But you add 'provided that she gives up possession as I am led to hope she will'. I take

---

1 – Bird had failed to respond to two (now lost) letters that TSE posted on 3 and 4 May. TSE had been petitioned by a French writer who wrote to him at Clarence Gate Gardens for the return of a manuscript. Bird suggested that TSE should reply that the MS had been mislaid 'with other papers at your flat in which you are not now living and that you are making enquiries'. It seems too that TSE had been advised by W. L. Janes (see next footnote) that VHE had taken a flat in South Kensington. As to the rent of Clarence Gate Gardens, Bird said: 'Your liability will be at an end at Midsummer – always provided, of course, that she then gives up possession as I am led to hope she will.'

this to mean that so long as she retains possession *without* signing a new lease, I am responsible. And I should think that the fact of Bournstone's making a fresh lease with her, after having dealt with me for so many years, would imply his recognition and acceptance of the situation. He would presumably take up *her* banker's reference. By the way, I do not know whether her bank, the District Bank of Cornhill, are acquainted with the present situation. They have been the bankers of her family for many years.

I shall be grateful for any information you can extract from James. I feel some delicacy about applying to her brother; and I do not wish her to suspect that I am in communication with old Janes or with any friend of hers.[1]

Yours sincerely,

[T. S. Eliot]

1 – William Leonard Janes (1854–1939): ex-policeman who had worked as general factotum for TSE since 1924. 'If I ever write my reminiscences, which I shan't,' TSE reminisced to Mary Trevelyan, 2 Apr. 1951, 'Janes would have a great part in them' ('The Pope of Russell Square'). TSE told Adam Roberts, 12 Dec. 1955: 'I . . . knew a retired police officer, who at one period had to snoop in plain clothes in the General Post Office in Newgate Street – he caught several culprits, he said' (Adam Roberts).

VHE wrote in her diary, 24 Apr. 1934: 'Janes says he is 80 years old, & I say to him I feel 80 years old & the *good* old gentleman *understands* & sympathises with me & indeed he has a most sensitive & sympathetic & *fine* nature. He is a man in a decade, & it is an honour to have known him.' On 7 July 1934: 'I took a taxi to 68, where I found Janes waiting, with high blood pressure, having walked the *whole* way & he wished me to understand that he is close on 80 years old & *my* troubles are no affair of his. However, he got over it later.' (Janes's eightieth birthday actually fell on 11 July.) On 2 Aug. 1934: 'during the last 2 *years* the *only* people who have shown any *heart*, any *good-breeding*, or refinement, to me, are Johanna Culpin and W. L. *Janes*. These 2 persons are the only 2 persons in all the *vast* numbers I know to whom I feel I owe the *least* consideration, & these 2 are both *old* people, who can *expect nothing from me, gain nothing* by my death, & there is *no* way in which I can reward them, *nor do they look for reward. Compare* them, you who in later years *will read these very words* of *mine* & will be able to trace a *true history* of *this epoch*, by my Diaries & papers – compare these 2 *old* people, with *my* mother, *my* brother, *my* aunts – My Husband, IF, IF, I say, these persons are *really what they claim to be.*'

Johanna ('Jan') Culpin (mother of TSE's deceased friend Karl Culpin) kept in touch with TSE in the months following his separation from VHE, and would give him occasional news of VHE's activities and demeanour. On 5 Sept. 1934: 'I think V. is in her flat again. She met me at the station and came here to Gordon Sqr. I have not seen her the last few days, she thinks of going to France.' 30 Sept.: 'For quite a long time, I had no news whatever from V. This afternoon I had gone to Kensington Gdns for a lonely walk and when I returned Miss [illegible name] told me V. had been to fetch her laundry and had hoped to find me at home. She had been at the sea side and then had been unwell at home, the usual thing I suppose. She said she would go to Paris next week for a long long time. She wants to see me. I'll ask her to tea for Thursday – I wonder how you succeeded about your pictures and books. It seems a long time since you came to see me.' 5 Oct. 1934: 'V. had tea with me yesterday

TO *George Barker*   TS Texas

18 May 1934   Faber & Faber Ltd

Dear Mr Barker,

I have thought over the situation again and discussed it with Herbert
Read, and less exhaustively with Edwin Muir. Read certainly is of the
same opinion as myself, and I think that Muir would be if he had read *The
Bacchant*. You may have heard from Read before now.

I am convinced that from your point of view quite as much as ours, *The
Bacchant* should be held over until the *Poems* have prepared the way. As
for the *Poems*, I think I can say definitely that we want to publish them.
While there is nothing in your additions so far that impresses me more
than the first set, I think they are quite good enough to support it; and

---

afternoon of which I'll tell you when we meet. She says now she is not going to Paris.' 15
Dec. 1934: '[Gretel] still goes to V. every day. She told me about your belongings being
fetched.' But TSE tended to distance himself from Jan Culpin as the weeks wore on: perhaps
he could not bear the thought that Jan might also gossip about him with VHE (who would
sometimes stay with Culpin in her lodging house at 20 Roland Gardens, Kensington).

VHE was to write in her diary on 26 June 1934: 'The *19th* (nineteenth) Anniversary of
the wedding day of Thomas Stearns & Vivienne Haigh Eliot. And what an exhibition of
Puritan morality, New England culture & tradition & the value of learning & education
on highly civilised man. What an example to hand down from generation to generation, &
what an *invaluable* gift I have made to the *Bodleian* Library Oxford. I must make a note to
my Will that the papers & M.S.S. & Diaries are *not to be used in any biography* & *not* to be
paraphrased, but published if published at all, *without alterations.*' On 22 July 1934: 'On
July 13th I signed my *last Will* at 1 Great Winchester Street. I am perfectly satisfied with it
& I foresee no reason why I should ever change it –.' However, she appears to have made a
further will on 24 Apr. 1935, superseded by her final will and testament, dated 5 May 1936,
which included these provisions:

'5. I GIVE to the Bodleian Library absolutely and free of duty all my papers manuscripts
diaries journals photographs albums and sketches except securities and books of account on
condition that the said library shall not permit any of the same to be altered erased added to
quoted from or used for the purpose of any work of fiction.

'6. I BEQUEATH free of duty (a) to my husband THOMAS STEARNS ELIOT or in case
he shall die before me then to his said brother HENRY WARE ELIOT such of my family
portraits as he shall within twelve months after my death select (b) to my said brother
MAURICE all my other family portraits and all articles and effects at any time given by
him to me and it is my hope that if my family portraits shall come into the possession of my
brother he will keep them in his own possession and will not sell or dispose of them and (c)
to my said husband or in case he shall die before me then to his said brother Henry Ware
Eliot all other my personal chattels not hereby or by any codicil hereto otherwise specifically
bequeathed and I direct that the expression "personal chattels" shall have the meaning given
thereto in Form 2 of Part I of the Statutory Will Forms 1925.

'7. I DESIRE that my Yorkshire terrier "Polly", my dog "Rip" and my cat "Whiskers" be
offered to my husband but if he shall not wish to take them or either of them or in case he
shall die before me THEN I DIRECT that they or such one of them as my husband shall not
wish to take be painlessly destroyed.'

indeed the collection could bear the addition of a few more. May we now come to terms about the *Poems*? I am prepared to recommend my firm to make some improvement beyond the terms we ordinarily give on first-volume *Poems* – beyond, that is, what is really practical – in consideration of your holding over *The Bacchant*.

I don't know that I need to recapitulate our reasons, which I think I gave in conversation. But the point is not merely that *The Bacchant* could have no success *except* as the work of a man already well-known for his poetry; it is that its premature publication and consequent failure, would militate against the success of the poems. In publication, everything that does not help a man's reputation, hinders it. *The Bacchant* is the prose of a poet, and will only be intelligible and acceptable (the latter adjective is the more suitable) to a public of more than 100, when they have learned to see you through your poetry.

I do like *The Bacchant*, but from every point of view its publication NOW would be a great mistake. What I have in mind to lay before my firm is to offer you a small advance on the *Poems* (something we have never done before, and something I have never had myself) instead of the profit you would NOT make on *The Bacchant*.[1]

I'll look into the possibilities of the Royal Literary Fund; but I don't know whether that is ever given except to down & outs whose work is behind them.

Yours ever sincerely,
T. S. Eliot

---

1 – On 14 Aug. 1934 Barker submitted two typescript copies of *The Bacchant*. 'The newer copy . . . contains a number of corrections and alterations not inserted in the earlier draft. Therefore, if Messrs Simon and Schuster find themselves unable to enter on the publication of the work, I should think it better if Messrs Faber & Faber retained the second copy, which, apart from being altogether clearer and cleaner, represents, actually, the finished book.

'On the subject of revision, I have effected a number of betterments in the text of several of the poems now in your possession . . .

'P.S. I was also hoping to hear whether you liked the two particular poems against which I remember your fixing a small spot.'

TO *Olivia Shakespear*[1]   Lilly Library

18 May 1934   [Faber & Faber Ltd]

Dear Mrs Shakespear,

I am delighted to hear from you again, and should be very happy indeed
to come to tea with you.[2] I am under the impression that I have had some
business acquaintance with Shri Purohit Swami, the one I mean is the
apricot-coloured one.[3] I am tied up with some rehearsals until the end of
next week. Could it be one afternoon after the 28th of May? Any day in
the week except Wednesday is possible for me.

Yours sincerely,
T. S. Eliot

1 – Olivia Shakespear (1864–1938), mother of Dorothy Pound, and second daughter of
Major General Henry Tod Tucker (1808–96), made an unhappy marriage in 1885 with
Henry Hope Shakespear (1849–1923), a solicitor. She published several novels including
Love on a Mortal Lease (1894) and *The Devotees* (1904). Through her cousin, the poet
Lionel Johnson (1867–1902), she arranged a meeting with W. B. Yeats, which resulted in a
brief affair, 1895–6, and a lifetime's friendship. Yeats wrote at least two poems for her, and
she was the 'Diana Vernon' of his *Memoirs* (ed. Denis Donoghue, 1972).
2 – Shakespear wrote from 34 Abingdon Court, Kensington, 15 May: 'My friend Shri
Purohit Swami is anxious to meet you quietly & have a talk. I wonder if you would come
to tea . . . The Swami is a most interesting man, & I expect you would like him on further
acquaintance . . . [P]erhaps you could fix a day next week?'
3 – Shakespear to TSE, 25 Aug. 1934: 'Dear Possum (I can't resist it), It is indeed good of
you to send me the guru's book [*The Holy Mountain* (F&F, 1934)]. I am greatly taken with
his photograph. I had imagined him to be a withered old creature, whereas he looks much
younger than our Apricot Swami. Perhaps, as an initiate, he has attained eternal youth –
which I shouldn't envy him.'

TO *Hugh Sykes Davies*[1]   CC

18 May 1934   [*The Criterion*]

Dear Hugh,

Thank you for the case of Petron, which went immediately to the printers.[2]

I should think that it was rather a waste of time to debate about poetry with a man like John Sparrow who, I daresay, is a good debater but who doesn't understand poetry.[3] I should take the line myself that there was no such thing as modern poetry but possibly a few modern poets, who have perhaps more in common with previous poets than with the mass of their contemporaries. Otherwise you get let in for defending people who you may not care much about. Try him with Marianne Moore, I don't believe he has ever heard of her.

I should have written in any case to thank you for the weekend, which I enjoyed immensely. I only felt some compunction at being probably partly responsible for keeping us up so late.

                              Yours ever,
                              [T. S. Eliot]

1 – Hugh Sykes Davies (1909–84): author and critic. Educated at St John's College, Cambridge – where he edited, with William Empson, the magazine *Experiment,* and where he took the Jebb Studentship and the Le Bas Prize, 1931 – he became University Lecturer and Fellow of St John's, Cambridge. In the 1930s he was a Communist and Surrealist, and co-created the London Surrealist Exhibition, 1936. Works include *Full Fathom Five* (novel, 1956) and the posthumous *Wordsworth and The Worth of Words* (1986). Sykes Davies would praise TSE for his 'diligence, courtesy, and personal concern for the recruiting of young writers, for exploring the temper of their generation, and encouraging them to put as good a face as possible on being themselves'.
2 – Sykes Davies, 'Banditti (*From* The Biography of Petron)', *C.* 13 (July 1934), 577–80.
3 – Sykes Davies wrote from Cambridge (n.d.): 'I have allowed myself to be manoeuvred into a debate with John Sparrow about modern poetry, before a literary Society up here, and am under a positive necessity in consequence of acquiring some passable convictions in the next fortnight – unless Auden or Spender or some of them can write something that I really like before then.'

TO *Basil Bunting*[1]   CC

Dear Mr Bunting,

I have your letter of the 9th instant.[2] I am sending you Williams's *Collected Poems* to review; it is rather late in the day but I sent them first to Miss Marianne Moore, who returned them on the ground that she had already reviewed them in New York. Williams's poems mean very little to me but I want them to have a fair chance.[3]

Yours sincerely,

[T. S. Eliot]

1 – Basil Bunting (1900–85), Northumberland-born poet, lived in Paris in the early 1920s, working for Ford Madox Ford at the *Transatlantic Review*. From 1923 he was mentored by EP, whom he followed to Rapallo; and it was through EP that he became acquainted with JJ, Zukofsky and Yeats. EP published his work in *Active Anthology* (1933); but his enduring fame came about after WW2 with the publication of *Briggflatts* (1966). EP told TSE, 6 May 1934: 'Bunting is slower than coaltar/ but NOT a complete ass . . . [H]e had some regard for precise expression, and absoLOOTly will not drool to order. I can read his criticism, which is a damn site moren can be said fer that of most of his god damn direvveling apes of contemporaries.' TSE to J. R. Ackerley, 17 Aug. 1936, of Bunting: 'He is a good poet and an intelligent man'; and in a reference for the John Simon Guggenheim Memorial Foundation, 30 Dec. 1938: 'Bunting . . . is a very intelligent man and an able poet. I say "able", because I am still doubtful whether he will ever accomplish anything of great importance as an original author. I think he has just the qualities to qualify him as a translator of poetry . . . I back him strongly for the sort of work that he proposes to do [translations from the Persian] – work, also, which is in itself worth doing.' See Bunting, 'Mr T. S. Eliot', *New English Weekly*, 8 Sept. 1932, 499–500; Richard Burton, *A Strong Song Tows Us: The Life of Basil Bunting* (2013); and *The Poems of Basil Bunting*, ed. Don Share (2016).
2 – Bunting asked whether TSE was willing to send books for review to him in Tenerife. 'I'd be more interested in poetry or matter touching poetry, but could deal tolerably well, in my own opinion, with a wide variety of other matters. I have French and Italian pretty well, Latin and Persian less well, only a smattering of German, Spanish, Arabic etc.

'I have the good allround ignorance proper to journalists and did actually get a sort of living out of Fleet Street for a couple of years before they heaved me out.

'Pound has been interested in my rather exiguous product for some years now. I think I can rely on moderate approval from him.'

He asked in particular to review William Carlos Williams's *Poems* (Objectivist Press).

EP had told TSE on 12 Mar.: 'Get Bunting (Basil) . . . to review the Williams. He is slower than you are/ solid, conscientious, and does understand. Best grade critical SENSE . . . B. OUGHT to be used, employed. Start Basil NOW, and he may have a three page article in time for Summer issue.'

3 – In the event, Bunting did not review Williams's *Poems* for C.

18 May 1934   Faber & Faber Ltd

My dear Richards,

I have two matters to mention to you, and one I should have written about at least a week ago. I have been interested in the theatrical efforts of a young man named Rupert Doone and his friends. I enclose their prospectus which he has probably sent you himself. He is anxious to put on a performance, which will include *Sweeney Agonistes* and *Fulgens et Lucres*,[1] somewhere in Cambridge during this term, and as the time is short I promised to write to you to support him, in asking whether you could give him any advice and help in finding a place for the performance. While I can make no promises for the future of the Group Theatre, it seems to me an experiment worthwhile trying out.

The other matter concerns two old friends of mine, the Reverend John Carroll Perkins and Mrs Perkins. Dr Perkins is the retired master of King's Chapel, Boston, and is over here for some months.[2] They intend to come to Cambridge during the end of next week, and want to find good lodgings there until the end of June. I am merely writing to ask if you know of any.

I have received a bill from Harvard for gramophone records, which, I hope, means that some are on the way. I expect that they will be held up by the Customs, so that I may not be able to let you have one for several weeks. I see that the Harvard University Press now advertises them in their catalogue at two dollars each.

Will you be coming up to town during the fortnight of the 28th? If so I should like to get you tickets for my show.

Yours ever,
T. S. Eliot

P.S. Records arrived. One side is the HALLOW Men, sic.[3] I don't want to trust the post for breakages – shall it wait till you come to town?[4]

---

1 – The sole copy of *Fulgens and Lucres* [*Lucrece*] by Henry Medwall, the earliest surviving English secular play, had been sold at auction in 1919 and reproduced in facsimile in 1920.
2 – See TSE to Perkins, 29 May 1934.
3 – The Harvard record label gives 'Hallow' for 'Hollow' (*The Hollow Men*).
4 – Richards diary, Sun. 3 June 1934: 'Brought down T. S. Eliot record of *The Hollow Men* & *Gerontion* – strange deep voice like a high Priest & too amplified.' Entry by Dorothy Richards: 30 June 1934: 'Ivor sent a tremendous note to Eliot on "The Rock" & his speaking of verse.'

TO *Susan Hinkley*[1]   TS Houghton

22 May 1934   Faber & Faber Ltd

Dear Aunt Susie,

Thank you for sending me the interesting family documents. I am glad
that the matter has been satisfactorily settled. I was particularly interested
in the information about Uncle Will, and his colleagues. It is odd to think
that I never knew till now that Uncle Will was a Presbyterian! that is most
interesting.[2]

I also want to tell you that Grandfather's doorplate reached me safely
and is now safely put up on the door of my room here, where it looks very
well.[3] It can of course be removed upon our quitting these premises or in
the event of my demise. Thank you very much indeed for it.

I am in the middle of a very busy week: the last week of rehearsal of my
show, and the time when (with amateur performers) it seems a complete
chaos!

Affectionately your nephew,
Tom

TO *E. R. Curtius*[4]   TS University of Bonn

22 May 1934   *The Criterion*

Dear Curtius,

Welcome to London![5] But I wish first that you might be staying longer;
and second, that I had known of your coming, because I was in town
throughout the weekend, and should have been delighted to see you. And
alas! this week finds me immersed in the final rehearsals of a kind of Play

1 – Susan Heywood Hinkley, née Stearns (1860–1948): TSE's maternal aunt.
2 – William Augustus Stearns (1805–76), minister and teacher; President of Amherst College,
Mass., 1854–76.
3 – The plate, which TSE kept mounted on his office door for many years, reads 'T. Stearns'.
4 – Ernst Robert Curtius (1886–1956): renowned German scholar of philology and Romance
literature; author of *Die Französische Kultur* (1931; *The Civilization of France*, trans. Olive
Wyon, 1932), and *Europäische Literatur und Lateinisches Mittelalter* (1948; trans. by
Willard R. Trask as *European Literature and the Latin Middle Ages*, 1953).
5 – Curtius and his wife stayed at the 'shabby-genteel' Thackeray Hotel, Great Russell St,
22–5 May. He had written on 18 May: 'Ich hoffe sehr, Sie endlich kennen lernen zu können.
Bitte sprechen Sie nicht von meiner Ankunft. Es gibt Leute, die ich nicht sehen möchte, z.
B. E. Alport': ('I very much hope to be able to meet you at last. Please do not talk about my
arrival. There are people I do *not* wish to see, e.g. E[rich] Alport.') TSE and he had lunch
on the Friday.

which I have written, which is to start on Monday. That means that all my evenings are taken up. But could you and Frau Curtius lunch with me on Friday, the first day I have free for lunch? If so I will call for you at about one o'clock. If not, could you come to tea with me here on Thursday? I do wish that you could stay over into next week!

I ought to explain that I live apart from my wife, and therefore have no home of my own in which to entertain.

I am writing this to leave at your hôtel, in case you are out when I pass by.

Yours very cordially,
T. S. Eliot

TO *John Garrett*   CC

25 May 1934   [Faber & Faber Ltd]

Dear Mr Garrett,

Thank you for your second letter.[1] I have no doubt from what I have seen of religious activities in America that what you say about their so-called religious drama is quite justified. Unfortunately I have not the first hand knowledge, which would make it possible for me to write about it.

Furthermore, I am afraid you are under the impression that I know a good deal more about contemporary activity in England than I do. If you want an informative article about what has been, and is being done, then I think Martin Browne is the man to give it to you; and I think that such an article might be well worthwhile. What I could likely do for you would be merely a note on my own opinions, as to the lines which such drama ought to follow in the future. I mean that the John Masefield or the Gordon Bottomely [*sic*] sort of thing is, in my opinion, not what is needed at the present time, and that something much more vigorous and

---

1 – Garrett asked TSE (n.d.) to contribute to *REP* (the magazine of Croydon Repertory Theatre): 'When I was in America I was horrified at the nature of play masquerading there as religious drama. Particularly with the Nonconformists one found that anything that paid could be called uplifting. The "danger" that I spoke of was one that I felt might perhaps come to injure what seems to me to be one of the most interesting movements in the religious life of this country.

'But that is neither here nor there and if you would be so good as to write us an article on what is being done in Chichester and elsewhere we should be very grateful. If, further to that, you could add your own impressions of the value of this instruction of the laity in the basic truths of the Faith through the medium of drama the article would have an even added value.'

contemporary is needed: but the possible audiences, I am afraid, require a good deal of education.

Yours very sincerely,
[T. S. Eliot]

TO *Rupert Doone*

TS Berg

25 May 1934   *The Criterion*

Dear Mr Doone,

I also had a letter from Richards explaining the difficulty of doing anything so late in the term. I am afraid that you will get a similar answer from Rylands, whom I only know very slightly, and to whom I did not myself write.[1]

I am, myself, very doubtful of the suitability of doing *Sweeney* in the open air.[2] It would certainly be impossible in the daylight, and I don't know whether you could possibly get lighting effects at night, which would suggest the proper surroundings. I should think it unlikely.

I am glad to know that Granville-Barker is taking some interest.[3]

The pageant at the moment, except for a few bright performers, seems to me to be in a limp and chaotic state. I don't know whether it is a peculiarity of amateurs belonging to parochial congregations, or whether it is found in all very amateur collections, but most of the players seem to me dismally lacking in vitality.

Yours ever,
T. S. Eliot

1–Doone wrote on 22 May to say that IAR had sent a discouraging letter, though IAR had recommended Doone to contact George Rylands (1902–99), Fellow of King's College.

2–It was possible that the Group Theatre might be allowed to perform in Wadham College (Oxford) gardens, but Doone considered the place unsuitable for a performance of *Sweeney Agonistes*.

3–Doone had received a letter of encouragement, and a cheque, from Harley Granville-Barker – 'just when we were feeling a little depressed'. Harley Granville-Barker (1877–1946), English actor, director, playwright and critic.

TO *Eric Gill*[1]   CC

25 May 1934   [*The Criterion*]

Dear Mr Gill,

I have your letter of the 11th instant and must begin with an apology.[2] I had intended to do what was only proper – to send you a copy of the April *Criterion* immediately it appeared and offer you the opportunity of replying in the next number. Owing to having many other things on my mind at the moment, I completely over-looked this courtesy. I shall be delighted to publish your reply but, owing primarily to this piece of negligence on my part, the June number has now been completely made up, and I can't find the room for it.

I hope, however, that you will send it as soon as complete, and that you will allow me to give it prominence in the September number, in which I shall have room for as much space as you require up to 5,000 words.

With renewed apologies,
Yours sincerely,
[T. S. Eliot]

TO *Henry Eliot*   TS Houghton

26 May 1934   Faber & Faber Ltd

My dear Henry,

This will be only a short letter of thanks, as I am in the midst of rehearsals. I have sent you a copy of the text, which is very much cut in acting. I will write again after Monday night.

The doorplate arrived safely, and I thought the best thing to do with it was to have it put up on the door of my room at Faber's, which I did.[3] It looks very well there.

1–Eric Gill (1882–1940), artist, type designer, sculptor, draughtsman, wood-engraver, essayist, social critic; convert to Catholicism, 1913; member of the third order of St Dominic, the lay order of the Dominicans, 1919–24; neo-Thomist; socialist; practitioner of the ideal craft community; devotee of a 'holy tradition of workmanship'. Publications include *Art-Nonsense* (1929); *Art and a Changing Civilisation* (1934); *Work and Leisure* (1935); *Autobiography* (1940).
2–'I have received a copy of Criterion (April) with Mr Penty's article. I do think it's a lot of nonsense but I have written a long reply to it (about 3000 words). I hope you will agree to publish it . . . You will, I hope, get the typescript by June 3 or 4.' See Arthur J. Penty, 'Beauty Does Not Look After Herself', C. 13 (Apr. 1934), 353–70 – a hostile essay on Gill's *Beauty Looks after Herself* (1933) – and Gill's long letter in retaliation: C. 14 (Oct. 1934), 114–20.
3–Henry's note at foot of letter: 'Thomas Stearns plate from Lexington house'.

Sometime at your leisure I wish you would look up the names of all clerical ancestors, collaterals, and connexions by marriage that we have. The point being that I have a bet of half-a-crown with Virginia Woolf as to which is descended from more parsons. She has been rather boastful on the point.[1] What's the relationship to Richard Sterne, Archbp. of York? I shall count Laurence Sterne, as a collateral.[2]

Thanks for the stamps (for Donald Morley).

Affectionately,
Tom

FROM *Vivien Eliot* TO *Mary Hutchinson*   PC MS Texas

Monday 28 May 1934[3]

Mary dear, today is my birthday. At present I have no address but should love to go to a Film with you & will come on the chance of yr. being able to go – at 2 p.m. on Monday next. *Dont answer*. If you are out you can leave a message. V.H.E.

1 – VW to SS, 10 July 1934: 'The rock [*The Rock*] disappointed me. I couldn't go and see it, having caught the influenza in Ireland; and in reading, without seeing, perhaps one got the horror of that cheap farce and Cockney dialogue and dogmatism too full in the face. Roger Fry, though, went and came out in a rage. But I thought even the choruses tainted; and rather like an old ship swaying in the same track as the Waste Land – a repetition, I mean. But I cant be sure that I wasn't unfairly influenced by my anti-religious bias. He seems to me to be petrifying into a priest – poor old Tom' (*The Sickle Side of the Moon: The Letters of Virginia Woolf*, V: *1932–1935*, ed. Nigel Nicolson [1979], 315).

2 – Reporting on this letter in a letter (28 Jan. 1975) to 'Jo', EVE commented: 'result unknown'.

3 – VHE noted in her diary (Bod Eng. misc. e. 877), 28 May 1934: 'T. S. Eliot's Pageant, at Sadler's Wells Theatre, starts tonight. He *did* it for my birthday, *I knew*. I had got the cheap seats, & I left Polly with Janes, & went to fetch Margaret Smith who was going with me. I had no supper or food. In the Interval we went to the theatre refreshment room & had coffee & Sandwiches. We were faint & sick. In the stalls we saw St John Hutchinson smoking a big cigar. We waited till the very end & saw everyone leave, & we saw the Fabers in evening dress – at the entrance – we walked all round & hung about, but *no* sign of T. S. Eliot at all & I am not at all sure he wrote it. I still believe all this is a *HOAX*. I am waiting to get to Paris, *& then to America*.'

TO *Charles du Bos*[1]

29 May 1934   [*The Criterion*]

My dear Du Bos,

Again I find myself in delay in answering your letter, and for the same reasons. I now have two letters from you of considerable length, and shall treasure them in the hope of their eventual appearance in your *correspondence complete* (1 vol.?).

First I have not at the moment access to my books but I remember that your essay on [the] Leonardo da Vinci of Valéry gave me much pleasure. It has always been against my principles to publish in the *Criterion* any work which has appeared elsewhere. I may have made one or two exceptions – and in the circumstances, and as there seems no prospect otherwise of adding you to our roll of contributors, and if Miss Mayne will collaborate in the translation, *I shall be delighted to have it*. I think that I could use it in the September number, if I could be assured at an early date of its arrival in good time.[2]

I am dreadfully afraid that in the pressure of other business, which has been exceptional this spring, I may have neglected to write to Professor

---

On 4 June: 'Today – a year on – I have *no idea where* my husband Tom *is*, or whether he is alive or dead.'

On 7 June she went again to see the pageant, standing in the very hot gallery: 'No sign of Tom. I waited until everyone was out and hung about a long time . . .'

On Sat., 9 June: 'Last performance of The Rock at Sadlers Wells Theatre. It is a *beautiful* peice [*sic*] of work & appeals to me utterly. It is moving & terrible & childish & just what it should be except for a very horrible Ballet pushed in & an unpleasant scene in the middle – speech by a sort of Winston Churchill, in a grey bomber hat. The Chorus is the great triumph I think, it is masked & groups of voices speak together, in twos and threes. It is a very *extremely emotional* peice of work, & it is has been terrible for me to endure it, in the heat & the horror. Tom, *if he wrote it*, is certainly a very wicked man, to so play (& prey) on the *emotions* to such an extent. It is *wrong*. It *is* Immoral in the highest sense of that word. I say it is an *Immoral* Pageant. And without doubt I am right. No no. The Pageant is *very* beautiful, & quite perfect. It is the man who wrote it, *if that is T. S. E.*, whose soul must be saved.'

GCF noted in his diary, 28 May: 'To Sadler's Wells for 1st night of *The Rock*. A gt. success – the choruses marvellous, & their diction *superb*. Hot, & long, & rather tiring.'

1 – Charles du Bos (1882–1939), critic of French and English literature – his mother was English, and he studied at Oxford – wrote one review for C. in 1935. He published *Réflexions sur Mérimée* (1920), and became famous for his posthumously published journals (6 vols, 1946–55).

2 – Charles du Bos, 'On "Introduction à la méthode de Léonard de Vinci" by Paul Valéry', trans. Ethel Colburn Mayne, C. 14 (Jan. 1935), 218–38. Mayne (1865–1941), Irish novelist, biographer, translator and literary critic, had translated du Bos's *Byron et le besoin de la fatalité* (1932) as *Byron and the Need of Fatality* (1932).

Abercrombie. I don't know him but I am sure that he knows my name, and I should certainly have written to him. I can only apologise humbly for this piece of neglect. I hope very much that Miss Starkie was successful in her application.[1]

You say truly that you have written me, on this occasion, a business letter, and I am afraid that in return I have given you a very poor impression of my own business abilities. I can only again plead the unusual number and pressure of preoccupations during the last three months.

Always sincerely your friend,
[T. S. Eliot]

P.S. I had long expected that Fernandez[2] would find himself turning in that direction.

TO *J. C. Perkins*[3]   TS Donald Gallup/Beinecke

29 May 1934   Faber & Faber Ltd

Dear Dr Perkins,

I am glad to know that you received the tickets safely.[4] One way of getting to the theatre is the 38 Bus, which you can get at Victoria, and which will stop at the theatre door. I am worried because, although we have cut the text ruthlessly, the performance last night did not end till nearly 11.30! It will have to be cut still more, though I do not know what we can cut. I advise you, during the interval, to rest yourselves by going

---

1–Enid Starkie (1897–1970), Irish literary critic; Fellow of Somerville College, Oxford; ultimately Reader; author of *Baudelaire* (1933), *Arthur Rimbaud in Abyssinia* (1937), *From Gautier to Eliot: The Influence of France on English Literature, 1851–1939* (1962), *Flaubert: The Making of the Master* (1967). Appointed CBE, 1967. See Joanna Richardson, *Enid Starkie: A Biography* (1973).

2–Ramon Fernandez (1894–1944), philosopher, essayist, novelist, was Mexican by birth but educated in France, where he contributed to *NRF*, 1923–43. Works include *Messages* (1926) – with 'Le classicisme de T. S. Eliot' – and *De la personnalité* (1928). In the 1930s, he was a fierce anti-fascist, but during WW2 he became a collaborationist.

3–The Revd Dr John Carroll Perkins (1862–1950): Minister of King's Chapel, First Unitarian Church of Boston – the oldest church (1717) in the USA. TSE, in his letter of condolence to Edith Perkins (31 Dec. 1950), felt he could say only 'what you know already, and what must have been said already by many friends: what a good and beautiful person Uncle John [Perkins] was, and how much loved he was. Like everyone else who knew him, I shall continue to cherish every memory of his very Christian soul, of essential integrity and innocence ... His own patience and humility made one rather ashamed, and his readiness to see people at their best.'

Emily Hale was their niece, and had grown up in their care.

4–No letter traced.

out into the foyer, instead of listening to the Bishop and the Choir. And unless you both feel up to a long evening, I should really advise leaving altogether after the end of Part I. The performance (and the patchwork thing itself) is very uneven, but the chorus stood up to their job splendidly.[1]

I was under the impression that you were going back to Cambridge, but I see that you are going next to Chichester. Bosham used to be very charming, and little places like Appledram and Birdham. There *might* be houses to let at Itchenor or Wittering, out on Chichester Harbour. All the country about there is very lovely.

Sincerely yours,
T. S. Eliot

TO *Martin Shaw*
TS Houghton

30 May 1934 — Faber & Faber Ltd

My dear Shaw,

As I have not seen you since Saturday – when I was too much worried with my own part of the show to attend – I must write to tell you how very much I like your music throughout. One thing that impresses me, and that has been most valuable for the success of the play, is your versatility and adaptability. I have myself been irked by having to write bits and snippets, seeing how I should have liked to develop them dramatically if I had had the scope; and I imagine that you have had to curb yourself, and subdue your inspiration, still more than I. It is the music that justifies, for instance, the ballet and the scene (which would otherwise become very boring) of the Craftsmen.

I am quite unqualified to criticise or praise, technically; I only write as a collaborator to express my satisfaction.

I hope that this effort will not be the end either of our acquaintance as human beings or of our collaboration as workmen; and I hope also that Mrs Carpenter (sic) [*sic*] if she will forgive me, will also be with us in some future venture.

Yours sincerely
T. S. Eliot

---

1 – The Perkinses went to *The Rock* on 30 May. Dr Perkins wrote to TSE, 31 May: 'Our interest was held closely all the evening through. And it seemed to me that the large audience followed the various changes with a keen sympathy and their responses where evidenced by slight or marked movements appeared right and intelligent.'

TO *Marianne Moore*   TS Rosenbach Museum & Library

30 May 1934   Faber & Faber Ltd

Dear Miss Moore,

This is to acknowledge the receipt of your letter of the 16th May and the enclosed notes.[1] I hope to get to work on your book in about a fortnight's time. I propose to deal with the poems first and then write my introduction.

I am sending you a copy of our edition of Ezra Pound's poems.

Yours very sincerely,

[T. S. Eliot]

Supplementary note and *N.Y. Sun* arrived today. Very many thanks.

TO *T. W. Earp*[2]   CC

30 May 1934   [Faber & Faber Ltd]

Dear Earp,

Thank you for your letter of the 28th [*sc.* 29th].[3] This is merely to say that your assumption is quite correct, and that if it is impossible to get the one kind of book, we should still then be very much interested in the second. I shall hope to hear from you again in a few days, and wish you success.

Yours sincerely,

[T. S. Eliot]

1–See *The Selected Letters of Marianne Moore*, ed. Bonnie Costello, Celeste Goodridge, Cristanne Miller (1998), 322–3. 'If you would be willing to introduce the book, or preface it with comment, I should be grateful. That the things would profit by being sponsored is perhaps a reason against your undertaking them, so I leave it to you; you must safeguard yourself in any way that seems best, against permitting this venture to be a bugbear.'

2–T. W. Earp (1892–1958): noted art critic and translator.

3–Earp was going to sup with Walter Sickert. 'I will try my best for a personal, autobiographical book in some form or other. But I assume, after our conversation, that Faber and Faber would take a collection of papers, entirely or as much as possible, on questions of art, of contemporary interest . . . It would be lively . . .'

30 May 1934   Faber & Faber Ltd

Dear Aunt Susie,

This is just a short note, on one not very pleasant matter. I have received through Henry a list of yours of the silver which Aunt Marian left me. My memory is not very good: but I am under the impression that this silver was *not* a wedding present, but a *bequest* to me which I received after Aunt Marian's death.

I should be glad if you would kindly confirm this, by return, as Vivienne has to leave the flat at June quarter day, and I am giving my solicitors a list of the property there which belongs to me.

Incidentally, are the two spoons with crests ancestral, or were they purchases of Aunt Marian's?

This is not a letter. My time is too taken up with my pageant, until ten days hence!

> Affectionately your nephew,
> Tom

TO *Polly Tandy*[1]   CC

30 May 1934   [Faber & Faber Ltd]

Dear Mrs Tandy,
    Thank you for your note.[2] I am looking forward with great pleasure to
seeing you at the weekend. I think the arrangement is that I shall pick up
your husband at the Museum for lunch, and that we shall journey down
together.

                                    Yours sincerely,
                                    [T. S. Eliot]

TO *Mélodie Stuart-Fergusson*   CC

1 June 1934   [Faber & Faber Ltd]

Dear Mrs Stuart-Fergusson,
    Referring to your letter of the 8th April concerning Anthony Lawrence,[3]
I am now writing to ask if you would be so kind as to let us have his

---

1–Lyndall Gordon, *Imperfect Life*, 255: 'Polly [Tandy] . . . was a practical, religious, warm-
hearted countrywoman who mothered Eliot . . .' Geoffrey Tandy (1900–69) was Assistant
Keeper in the Department of Botany at the Natural History Museum, London, 1926–47,
and did broadcast readings for the BBC (including the first reading of TSE's *Practical Cats*
on Christmas Day, 1937). During WW2 he served as a commander in the Royal Navy,
working at Bletchley Park. He and his wife Doris ('Polly') were to become intimate friends
of TSE. Tandy was to write to Martin Ware (who had invited him to talk about TSE to a
small literary society), 20 Nov. 1935: 'I believe that anything I may be able to do to help
anybody to a better understanding of Eliot's work will be a good work. Against that I
have to set the fact that he is a pretty close personal friend (whatever that locution may
mean) and my judgement may be vitiated in consequence. The text of "this side idolatry"
may be used against me. However, having asked the man himself if he have any serious
objection, I say yes and hope that you will not regret having asked me.' See further Judith
Chernaik, 'T. S. Eliot as "Tom Possum": The "good grey Poet" and the Tandy family', *TLS*,
1 Nov. 1991, 13–14; Miles Geoffrey Thomas Tandy, *A Life in Translation: Biography and
the Life of Geoffrey Tandy* (thesis for MA in Arts Education and Cultural Studies, Institute
of Education, University of Warwick, Sept. 1995).
2–Polly Tandy wrote from Hogarth Cottage, Hampton-on-Thames, 26 May 1934: 'Dear
Mr Eliot I do hope that you will find it possible to pay us your promised visit next weekend.
We are much looking forward to seeing you. Yours sincerely Doris M. Tandy.'
3–Stuart-Fergusson wrote from the Three Arts Club, 19A Marylebone Road, London:
'I think I can tell you everything you would like to know. First of all, alas, he can only
undertake work which can be done in his own room . . . Anthony is nearly 21, and has
been extremely well educated. He is in fact one of the most thoughtful, well-informed boys
I know. Also he took Honours at Cambridge in English, and also in French and Italian
afterwards. His mother is Italian, and they were much in Italy in his earlier days, and they
always talk Italian or French in their home even now. French he also acquired in France, and
among many French friends over here; and his German has mostly been learnt here.

---

address so that we might communicate with him if any work turns up. Would you please give this address direct to Mr Richard de la Mare at this office as the work, if it appeared, would issue from his department.

Yours sincerely,

[T. S. Eliot]

TO *Margaret C. Branford*   CC

1 June 1934   [Faber & Faber Ltd]

Dear Mrs Branford,

I have given a good deal of thought to Mr Branford's poems, and frankly I do not know what to do.[1] I have also discussed the matter with one or two friends. But I cannot but feel that it is impossible to do much to forward the recognition of another man's poetry unless one is in sympathy with the form, as well as the content and message. I have a different, and partly un-English, tradition behind me, and my habits in metric and vocabulary are different. I do not pretend to understand, still less to judge, any of my contemporaries: I can only really understand what I try to do myself.

For reasons which we both appreciated in conversation, I do not suggest Squire; but there must be other poets and critics, of more serious weight, who could sympathise better with Mr Branford's aims, and methods. Have you thought of writing to Edmund Blunden (at Merton College, Oxford)? His tastes are very different from mine; and he is one whom

---

'He *has* had technical instruction in typing, and his work is admirable . . . And also he is of a wholly studious turn of mind, and with no real interests outside books and music, both of which are a passion . . . [E]ven a trifling job would be a godsend to this boy, and I am sure you would be pleased with the result.'

1 – TSE had talked with Mrs Branford in the second week of Apr. Frederick Victor Branford (1892–1941), poet, was educated at Edinburgh University and Leiden University. While serving during WW1 as a captain in the Royal Naval Air Service, he was shot down off the Belgian coast during the Battle of the Somme: having been severely wounded in that action, he remained disabled for the rest of his life. His publications include *Titans and Gods* (1922) and *The White Stallion* (1925). He had written to TSE (7 Apr.), from their home in Hove: 'My Foreword to the *White Stallion* caused, wherever it was read, scarifying misunderstandings. D. H. Lawrence, for example, who read it (and no further) concluded that the verse was a metrical version of the Upanishads.' He believed that 'the social influence of Art . . . operates through the release of energies of a bio-electric character, of which little is known in the west. Through an illness which brought into relief processes normally silent I became conscious of these energies, and learned something about them.' He ended up: 'But I hope you will be able to consider my work purely as verse . . . Everything else has been thrust upon me.'

I respect both as a writer and as a man. His support would be as valuable, amongst serious people, as you could get.

I should always be glad to discuss matters with you further.

Yours very sincerely,
[T. S. Eliot]

I enclose the leaves from the *London Mercury* which you wished returned. Would you like me to write to Blunden, and send him the two volumes you left with me?

TO *The Editor,* The Spectator[1]

1 June 1934   *The Criterion*

'The Rock'

Sir,

Mr Verschoyle's amiable review of *The Rock* in your issue of to-day leaves me wondering what he thinks that the production was intended to be.[2] The 'play' makes no pretense of being a 'contribution to English dramatic literature': it is a *revue*. My only seriously dramatic aim was to show that there is a possible *rôle* for the Chorus: an aim which would

---

1–Text from the *Spectator* 152 (8 June 1934), 887.

2–Derek Verschoyle, 'The Theatre', *Spectator*, 1 June 1934, 851: 'The production of Mr Eliot's pageant play is organized by the Diocese of London, in aid of the Forty-Five Churches Fund, the president of which is the Lord Bishop of London. Apart, therefore, from its place as a contribution to English dramatic literature, *The Rock* is to be considered as an official *apologia* for the campaign of church-building which the fund was started to finance. In both respects it is an extremely interesting work, and in both it is at least partially a failure ... The main theme of the whole production is, in Mr Eliot's words, the conflict between the Church and the World.

'It is a defect of the play, considered as an apologia, that the case for neither of these opposed causes is conclusively stated. Mr Eliot's defence of the Church is based rather on invocations than on definition, and he seems reluctant to commit himself to logical justification. For the most part the Church's cause is assumed and not stated, and at times Mr Eliot's unwillingness to substantiate his beliefs makes him appear to be doing little more than strike an attitude. His picture of the society in which the Church must work is simplified and thereby distorted. He satirizes Fascists and Communists, plutocrats and social parasites, but admirable as much of his satire is it is not conclusive. The elements in society which he satirizes do not represent the only, nor even the main, reasons for indifference to the Church today. Acceptance of Fascism or Communism is for many of their followers the result, not the cause, of dissatisfaction with the Church. The causes in many instances lie elsewhere; in, for example, despair of the Church's attitude towards such questions as Housing and Population. Mr Eliot does not touch upon the latter problem, and only deals fragmentarily with the former. And he neglects altogether opposition to the Church which has other than a materialistic basis.'

have failed completely without the aid of a perfectly trained group of speakers like Miss Fogerty's.[1] And to consider *The Rock* as an 'official apologia' for church-building is to lay a weight upon it which this rock was never intended to bear. It is not an apologia for the campaign, but an advertisement. If I had meant to write an apologia – I do not know whether any other people besides Mr Verschoyle think that one is needed – I should have written a prose pamphlet.

I also wonder what Mr Verschoyle wanted, when he speaks of my 'reluctance to commit myself to logical justification' and my 'unwillingness to substantiate my beliefs'. He does not make matters clearer by referring to 'despair of the Church's attitude towards such questions as Housing and Population' – a despair which we are to believe has helped to convert people to Communism or Fascism. Let me recommend for reading, to Communists, Fascists, and Mr Verschoyle, the Archbishop of Canterbury's speech at the Guildhall on March 12th, on the subject of Housing. And as for Population, would Mr Verschoyle have wished me to tax my poetic resources by making my Chorus declaim about Birth-Control?

In conclusion, may I repeat what every author knows: that criticism is only valuable to an author when it is particularised.[2]

I am, Sir,
Yours faithfully,
T. S. Eliot

---

1 – Elsie Fogerty, LRAM, Principal of the Central School of Speech Training and Dramatic Art. EMB: 'The most important part in Eliot's script [*The Rock*] was given to a mixed Chorus: with this he boldly sought to capture the attention of a popular audience for poetry, by combining prophetic grandeur of utterance with a sharp ironic humour at the expense of contemporary follies. To me it seemed essential that Miss Fogerty should provide and train this Chorus: and the success which the production made was very largely due to the understanding with which she divided and interpreted the lines, and the assurance, finish and conviction with which her students spoke them. From the success of *The Rock* arose the invitation to its author to write for Canterbury the next year' (*Fogie: the life of Elsie Fogerty, CBE*, ed. Marion Cole [1967], 155).

2 – Verschoyle replied to TSE's letter at once, on the same page of the *Spectator*, 8 June 1934: 'Mr Eliot's letter leaves me in rather the same state of wonderment as my review apparently left him. He declares that *The Rock* "makes no pretence of being 'a contribution to English dramatic literature': it is a *revue*." What Mr Eliot's reasons are for holding that a *revue* cannot be considered as a contribution to dramatic literature, I do not know: my belief that in any case *The Rock* could be so considered was based upon what I took to be the view of Mr Eliot himself. At a meeting of the "Friends of New London" at Londonderry House on May 7th he remarked of it: "It is a play, not pageantry, which is only illustrative and incidental."'

TO *Ezra Pound*   TS Beinecke

1 June 1934 AD   *The Criterion*

Podesta whats this about me refusing to shake hands with a man named
Mr McA. or whatever whoever it is[1] Rabet are you circulatin Liebels
like That about me When did I ever refuse to shake hands with anybody
because he was drunk May be you mean Squire but if so it wasnt because
he was drunk bit Because he was Squire Rabet this is a monstrous thing
for anybody to say about Me you know perfectly weel I could Drink you
under the table before breakfast given my choice of beverages any rate if
it was Gin or Whisky I could makes Rings round you Dambit there are
some SOME subjects I know about and this is one of them So no more for
the Present more serious subjects in the worldly sense but no more serious
to me will be discussed when I have recuperated from this Revue of mine
Godam it meanwhile I expect a written apology yrs etc.

                              Tp

TO *Ezra Pound*   TS Beinecke

1 June 1934   *The Criterion*

Sir,
    My attention has been drawn to the fact that you have either invented
or set in circulation a rumour to the effect that I refused to speak to some
individual not clearly specified, on the ground that he was drunk before
lunch. It should be unnecessary to point out that for a person occupying
an official and public position like mine, such a scandal is likely to have
serious consequences. I must therefore call upon you to make public an
adequate recantantation and apology without delay; otherwise I shall be
compelled regretfully to place the matter in the hands of my legal advisers.
                              I am, Sir,
                              Yours etc.
                              T. S. Eliot [signed]
                              Vicar's Warden.

1–EP had asked on 30 May, 'What's this about yr/ refusing to shake hands with Mr McA.
[McAlmon] because he was drinking at high noon?'

1 June 1934   Faber & Faber Ltd

Dear Mr Barker,

I am now in a position to make a definite suggestion for the publication of your poems, which we wish to undertake.

I think I have already made quite clear that we are convinced that it is necessary for the sake of your future reputation to bring out a fairly substantial volume of verse before publishing any prose work like *The Bacchant*, however excellent. I not only believe that there is a greater possible market for the poems than for *The Bacchant* but I should further hope that *The Bacchant* would get its sale chiefly through the reputation which we hope you will make as a poet. I have, therefore, persuaded my Board to offer an advance of £25 on a 10% royalty for the poems on condition that we have an option on *The Bacchant*. We not only don't want to publish *The Bacchant* ourselves before the poems have established your reputation, but we feel that it would be equally unfortunate, both for ourselves and for you, if anyone else was to publish it: and naturally when we undertake the work of a new poet, we wish to feel that he has sufficient confidence in us to wish us to publish his later work. An advance on a book of poems by an author who has not hitherto received general publicity is not, of course, economically justifiable but we are making the offer because we believe in the future of your work and are ready to back it.[1]

If you are in accord with the foregoing I will then urge my Board to agree to payment of this advance upon delivery of MS. and signing of contract. The point being that we have several volumes of poetry already on our list for the autumn, and we believe that we could do best for your

---

1–Barker had remarked on 23 May: 'money worries us wretchedly all the while. Do you think that Faber would, if convinced of the necessity, allow me some within the next six weeks or so? My wife has a hospital bill to meet by then . . . The point is simply that we have no money.'

Robert Fraser, *Chameleon Poet*, 66–7: 'On Saturday, 2 June a daughter was born . . . [T]he baby would have been conceived in September and the marriage had not been solemnised until November. Though born within wedlock, the baby would have been regarded by Jessica's parents as illegitimate. At least, this is what Jessica seems to have feared. She wanted the baby to be adopted, an unsatisfactory solution so far as George was concerned, and psychologically disastrous for her. Without a doubt, both of them were motivated by fear of disapproval from the Woodwards and by the general stigma still attaching in the mid-1930s to any suggestion of illegitimacy. Through a local priest . . . they arranged for Clare to be baptised. She was then confidentially adopted through a Catholic Adoption Society. She grew up a judge's daughter, not learning the secret of her birth until 1986.'

book by launching it very early in the new year; meanwhile using our efforts to attract attention to the forthcoming publication.[1]

Could you by the way let me see a few specimens of reviewing that you have done as I should also like to get you to review from time to time in the *Criterion?*

Yours sincerely,
T. S. Eliot

TO *E. W. F. Tomlin* TS Lady Marshall

2 June 1934 Faber & Faber Ltd

My dear Tomlin,

I must apologise humbly for my delay in dealing with what I know is an urgent matter; I can only plead that I have been extremely busy. It was several days before I could read carefully the paper which you had taken the trouble to copy out; and more than several days before I could make up my mind about it. I hoped that I might be able to pass the little article after only a few minor changes; but now I must face the fact that, with the exception of one or two points worth making, I want to scrap the whole thing.

I remember now that the article was written for a special purpose.[2] I had no desire to associate myself with that group of 'humanists' at all: it was only out of courtesy and regard for my old master Irving Babbitt that I took part. I considered it only as a volume in honour of Babbitt; and I took the only possible line that I could at the moment, in his support. To reprint now what is in any case a rather feeble piece of writing, would give it a stamp of my own endorsement which I don't want it to have.

I do not see furthermore that the essay has any close relevance to the subject of your symposium. If I had not been so busy during these recent weeks, or if your book was to appear in the autumn instead of immediately,

---

1 – 'Bacchant' was to be included in the volume *Janus* (F&F, 1935). *Poems* (6s) was announced for Spring 1934: 'Those who look for new poets will remember a few poems, in the *Criterion*, the *Listener*, *New Verse*, and one or two other periodicals, which could not be classified as paraphrases or imitations of any of the living poets now generally admired. Some of these poems have been over the signature of George Barker. There are many people who have wanted to see more of George Barker's work, so that they might make up their minds about him. This volume gives them the opportunity of committing themselves to an opinion of a poet younger than those whom they have recently been discussing.'

2 – TSE's essay 'Religion without Humanism', in *Humanism and America* (1930), ed. Norman Foerster.

I would gladly try to write something new for you. But I am busy all the coming week, and am then taking a holiday of a fortnight, during which I must get done two other pieces of work. So I can only wish you the best of success with your other contributors, and hope to see a brilliant book.

Yours ever sincerely,
T. S. Eliot

I am very sorry indeed about this, especially after the trouble you have been put to.

TO *Donald Brace* CC

2 June 1934   [Faber & Faber Ltd]

Dear Brace,

I am sending you four copies of my latest production, a kind of play called *The Rock*, which was written for performance on a specific occasion here in London.

One copy is with my compliments to yourself. As for the others, I am going to ask of you the kindness of doing the possible in the way of securing American copyright.

I don't know whether the text is likely to have any interest for American readers, and if so, whether you would care to take some sheets. The interest aimed at was local: the play had to deal with London, and London alone, and the cockney dialogues may be boring for other people. The only point about it worth making is that the choruses do represent a new verse experiment on my part; and taken together, make a sequence of verses about twice the length of *The Waste Land*.[1]

When are you coming over for another outing on the moors?

Yours ever,
[T. S. Eliot]

P.S. The English publication date was Thursday, May 31st.

---

1 – Coincidentally, on 20 Aug. 1934 Harper & Brothers wrote to FVM: 'Gene writes me that he was talking the other day with Dr Bernard Iddings Bell of St Stephen's College, New York. Dr Bell told him that the sequence of poetic choruses in *The Rock* might be segregated into a charming volume, especially if they could be supplemented with other short works. Do you think there is anything in this idea, or is Mr Eliot tied up for all his work elsewhere?'

5 June 1934   Faber & Faber Ltd

Sahib Goddamb you Heres a question that demands an answer its about the Title of your Essay-Book now about that book I mean about that Title what we want is a Title. I don't think that NINE ESSAYS is a good title no not a good title and I do think SEVEN ESSAYS is still worse a Title yes still worse. It's not snappy but rather liverish so to speak what we want is a GOOD title. Possibly some title that would suggest that this is just one side of your critical work would be a good title? Unity of this Lot. Other volumes of this many-faceted spiritualist and conjuror to follow. What we want is a good totle. Title I mean title. Now you try usin your Brains for once and start to try to think Up a good tutle title. And be quick about it see. Snap right into it. Put the pround House of Faber on the intellectual Map. And I dont mean any title I mean a GOOD tatle is what we Want. I can't put it plainer than that so will Close.

TP

P.S. What about a Mother's Day Canto. Theres a good idea. You come to me to teach you Sales Sense.

P.T.O.

SAPODESTA I would myself pay 10/6 one half guinea for a Elephunt, a nice Elephunt, just his ead Ezzum havin bit off the rest, but must have tusks TUSHES and trunk or proboscis turned upwards with a kind of frisky flourish That would make me a nice seal to seal my letters with.

TO *Brian Coffey*[1]   CC

5 June 1934   [*The Criterion*]

Dear Mr Coffey,

I have been considering your question about the poems you sent me in odd moments from time to time.[2]

It is difficult to say whether these poems ought to be printed by themselves or not, but, on the whole, I think they are quite good enough to justify it. But whether you make a book of them depends on whether they represent something which is, for you, complete – that is to say, if you feel that the phase in your own history, which they represent, is one out of which you have passed; and if you feel that your work will represent a different stage of maturity, then I should say that you had nothing to lose by their publication. If, on the other hand, you are not certain that they belong altogether to the past, then you may regret publication because you will later wish to alter, delete or amplify. I shall be interested to know how you feel about it and any news about yourself.

> With all best wishes,
> Yours sincerely,
> [T. S. Eliot]

---

1 – Brian Coffey (1905–95), poet, critic and educator, attended Clongowes Wood School and University College, Dublin, where he read medicine and then mathematics, physics and chemistry; from 1930 he studied in Paris, where he befriended Samuel Beckett and Thomas MacGreevy; and in 1933 he enrolled at the Institut Catholique where he studied philosophy under Jacques Maritain. During WW2 he worked as a teacher in England, and he then emigrated to the USA where he was Assistant Professor of Philosophy at St Louis University, Missouri, 1947–52. From 1954 to 1972 he taught sixth-form mathematics in London (he taught among others the young Haffenden). His collections of poetry include *Poems* (co-written with Denis Devlin, 1930); *Three Poems* (1933); *Third Person* (1938); a much-anthologised long poem called 'Missouri Sequence' (*University Review*, 1962); *Selected Poems* (1971); and translations from Paul Éluard, Stéphane Mallarmé and others. See further *Brian Coffey Special Issue, Irish University Review* 5: 1 (Spring 1975); Donal Moriarty, *The Art of Brian Coffey* (2000).

TSE to Edith Sitwell, 28 Aug. 1945: 'Brian Coffey always seemed to me a nice, sensible young man . . . He is really a philosopher but the Irish haven't very much use for philosophers who are not in Holy Orders and he has been teaching in a Roman Catholic school near Sheffield.'

2 – Coffey submitted a group of poems on 19 Apr. 1934. 'I had spoken of them to you at Christmas. Now I think of having them printed here, so as to be rid of them. First, however, I should like to know your opinion of them, and of the utility of publishing them. Myself, I am out of sympathy with them. But friends urge me to have them printed.'

5 June 1934   [Faber & Faber Ltd]

Dear Bird,

Thank you for your letter of the 2nd.[1] I hope that my wife is more than 'contemplating' leaving at Midsummer. I have a letter from Janes (in fact I will enclose it) which suggests that perhaps she has returned to the room which she took, and according to his report left after a week, in South Kensington. Fortunately I am going to the country, until about the 25th, on Monday next. (Address: c/o F. V. Morley, Pike's Farm, Lingfield, Surrey, as last summer).

I am quite willing to renew the offer of £50 on prompt vacation, so long as the proposal is made to appear as a concession or gesture of kindness, and does not give the impression that I am in a panic lest she stay. I wish that she might be pressed again (as in her own interest) to sign the Agreement, but it would seem rather undignified to make the £50 contingent on that. In any case, the £50 must be payable *after* complete evacuation, and also after all my property has been accounted for. I have already sent you a list of silver; I could draw up a pretty clear list of pictures and odd objects of sentimental value (such as a brass tea-kettle of my mother's) whenever required.

It is quite reasonable that I should have satisfaction before paying over the £50, because she would not have any considerable *cash* expenses. The offer might possibly, at least, elicit some indication of her intentions. Anyway, I authorise you to give the undertaking to James if and in such form as you think fit.

Yours sincerely,
[T. S. Eliot]

1 – Alfred E. James told Bird 'that although he has not been able to get into direct touch with your wife he understands from her mother that she is contemplating leaving the flat at Midsummer. He went on to remind me that in the draft deed of separation – which was, of course, never completed – it was provided that she should receive a sum of £50 towards the expenses of removal and enquired whether that sum would be forthcoming – so to speak as an inducement to her to go. In a sentence he suggested that if you remain of the same mind it might be well to offer to pay her this amount provided she is out by the stipulated date and you receive your personal effects.'

TO *Polly Tandy*

TS BL

6 June 1934   Faber & Faber Ltd

Dear Mrs Tandy,

I don't know whether the ancient practice has been generally abandoned or not, but I like to write and thank my hosts for a pleasant visit. It was very refreshing, and I was extremely tired – I do not want you to think that I ordinarily sleep for two hours between lunch and tea. I only hope that I may be asked again; I have certain gifts as a guest which I like to exhibit: making beds, sweeping, bathing dishes, and cooking corned beef hash.

I trust that Richard's cough was *not* a symptom of measles.[1]

Yours very sincerely,
T. S. Eliot

TO *T. W. Earp*

CC

6 June 1934   [Faber & Faber Ltd]

Dear Mr Earp,

Many thanks for your very full letter of May 7th and also congratulations upon your partial success.[2] The prospect seems to me very satisfactory but I will bring up your letter before our committee, which meets this week on Thursday, and let you know more definitely after that.

Morley and I will be very glad to lunch with you but the only day on which I am free for lunch is next Monday at 1.30. I am engaged every day until then, and after that I am going away for a fortnight, so I hope that day is possible.

Yours very sincerely,
[T. S. Eliot]

1–Richard, only son of Geoffrey and Polly Tandy.
2–Earp wrote on 7 May to say that Sickert was against writing reminiscences as such ('his life has not been especially eventful'), but that he was perhaps interested in publishing a collection of his various writings – 'Luckily Miss Sylvia Gosse had made a typed copy of these' – and Sickert added 'that he has for some time meditated and is anxious to write a book on painting, or what he calls the psychology of paintings . . .' He had authorised Earp to 'treat' on the matter; and Earp hoped TSE might be able to discuss it with him over lunch at the Etoile that week.

TO *F. Scott Fitzgerald*   TS Princeton

6 June 1934   Faber & Faber Ltd

Dear Fitzgerald,

Thank you for your letter of May 21st.[1] I don't remember what the line was which Scribner's have used on the jacket, and I haven't yet seen a copy of either the American or English edition, but I am sure that it is nothing to worry about. I know how easily these things happen.[2]

I look forward with great interest to reading the book. When are we likely to see you over here? I was under the impression that you had some notion of returning to the Riviera.[3]

> With all best wishes,
> Yours ever sincerely,
> T. S. Eliot

1 – 'I want to thank you for your generous remark about my work which you permitted Scribner's to use and also to apologize and regret most terribly that they used a line from a personal letter of yours on the jacket. They promised me that they wanted to see some such material only to show to their salesmen, and I was shocked when I saw what they had done. If Chatto & Windus would be inclined to use the American edition blurbs I think you could head it off by phoning them to cut out the one about Henry James. I know how I would feel if anyone used as publicity what I had written in a personal letter.

'With my very best wishes always and a great desire to see you again.'

2 – Charles Scribner's made use of this blurb by TSE on the dust jacket of *Tender is the Night: A Romance* (1934): 'I have been waiting impatiently for another book by Mr Scott Fitzgerald; with more eagerness and curiosity than I should feel towards the work of any of his contemporaries, except that of Mr Ernest Hemingway.'

3 – Fitzgerald responded from 1307 Park Avenue, Baltimore, 19 June: 'Sent you a book from the first batch. Terribly sorry it didn't arrive and am sending substitute.' He inscribed the copy:

T. S. Eliot

from

F. Scott Fitzgerald

with all admiration

all respect

all——

all everything from one who believes that Dr Johnson's sneer at

'reciprocal courtesy between authors' must have been

tossed off in a bitter moment.

TO *Katherine Oliver*   TS National Library of Scotland

6 June 1934   Faber & Faber Ltd

Dear Mrs Oliver,

It was with very real grief that I read in *The Times* of your husband's death.[1] I had always known of his frail health and fortitude, and realised that he might never return to London; and I imagined this winter that he was failing. But somehow I had hoped that I might see him again, on some visit to Scotland; and it is difficult to reconcile myself to the impossibility.

I owed him a very great debt of gratitude, for his kindness to me and to the *Criterion*; and though it would be excessive to boast of his friendship, I remain proud of having had his acquaintance. *The Times* eulogy was if anything too moderate.

His is one of the deaths which, with an increasing realisation of lack of sympathy on my part with the world of today, make me feel that I am growing old.

Please forgive me for typing. I suffer from a writer's cramp which renders me dependent upon this machine.

Yours very sincerely,
T. S. Eliot

TO *Ezra Pound*   TS Beinecke

6 Cuspidor an I. [6 June 1934]   Faber & Faber Ltd

Dear Rabbet Sir There again there you are thats how wars start[2] I see our old friend Urp in the Etoile on daye at lunch and I see with him a face

---

1 – F. S. Oliver (1864–1934), businessman, author and polemicist, was educated at Edinburgh and Trinity College, Cambridge, before joining forces in 1892 with Ernest Debenham in the firm of Debenham and Freebody (drapers, wholesalers, manufacturers), which they caused to flourish and expand (buying up Marshall & Snelgrove and Harvey Nichols). Oliver, who had become a wealthy man, retired as managing director in 1920. A radical Tory, he engaged himself in many public causes. Works include *Alexander Hamilton* (1906), *Ordeal by Battle* (1915), and *The Endless Adventure* (3 vols, 1930–5). Oliver died on 3 June. See 'Mr F. S. Oliver: The Business Man as Historian', *Times*, 5 June 1934, 19.

2 – EP had written on Sunday, 3 June: 'America's leadin' prosateur writes me Bro/ Possum done but him daid in a restaurant. He low you is mouldy in deh liver, and got religion up to the navel . . .

'Bob he low you must ha' knowd it quz him because he was eatin with Tommy Yearp and Yearp done jess TOLE you he (the proeseater) wuzza lunchin.

'Of course if you have refused to shake with Squire that wd. get you a lot of kudos with the nex generation and wipe oft a lot of high hattin'.

what looked kind of familiar the sort of Face you might See along the King's Road or Charlotte Street any day and I stares at it and thinks to my self That's. a face I seen before. So I stared hard but then I pulls my self. Up. Didn't want to be impolite. But that Face never grinned at me nor anythink so I thought it didnt know Me. Kindly convey to America's leading prosecutor the suggestion that I hadnt seen it for so Long that I didnt recognise it. I wasnt drunk. He wasnt drunk. Urp wasnt drunk. Eddie wasnt drunk. Nobody wasnt drunk. Theres no Story in this at all.

Podesta can your central european Craftsman design a good OPossum because if you can see to it that he makes a good OP ossum I will gladly convey another half guinea for another Seal Two seals is a good Idea so will close.[1] I dont know about fittin Brer Whale into that little tub out in front of your piazza but I think it would do him good to come down during a Hot spell and Sweat some of the fat off round his umbilical we must press the matter[2] so will Close yours etc

                          T P

Earp did NOT tell me whom he was lunchin with. He just come up and speak to me about a point we ad been discussin a few days afore.

I cant find anythink in the Sermon on the Mt. about cutting people because they is drunk.

'Tenny rate the prose eater lows you "doesn't approve of" him and putts it down to yr/ anglo/Xtianity. but mebbe it was only yer English manner wot had become incomprensible to the orfsprung of the open spaces.'

1 – EP responded, 8 June: 'About the stone cutter/ how much damn zoo/ do you want. You is done gittin ONE elefunt aza triboot to yr/ glory. offert by the admierer. EF you sendz along the photo/ of a real ZOO possum (cause there jess aint no specimen in Rapallo) I rekon it can/ be did.

'also if you want yr/ bdy. Heraldric tooter/ send on yr/ belted earldom/ and I'll see what the blighter can rize to.'

2 – EP had asked, 30 May: 'When are you and FV/ comin out here to breathe a li'l AIR.'

TO *S. L. Bethell*[1]

CC

6 June 1934   [*The Criterion*]

Dear Sir,

I have had your article for some time, and I now think that I may be able to make use of it.[2] You are dealing with a very interesting subject and one that ought to be approached. It is the first attempt that I have seen to examine the really important implications of Dr Richards' theory of value.

I cannot at the moment tell you when I shall be able to use it as I have a good deal of material previously accepted but I shall hope to be able to do so before the end of the year.

Yours faithfully,
[T. S. Eliot]

TO *Ida Shaw Page*

TS Valerie Eliot

7 June 1934   Faber & Faber Ltd

Dear Mrs Shaw Page,

Thank you very much for your kind and appreciative note. Let me reassure you about Patricia's delivery of the verses.[3] I thought she recited

---

1–S. L. Bethell was to be author of *Shakespeare and the Popular Dramatic Tradition* (1944) and *The Cultural Revolution of the Seventeeth Century* (1951).

TSE wrote on 25 Nov. 1947 to the President of Bowdoin College, Brunswick, Maine (which was considering inviting Bethell as a Visiting Lecturer): 'He was as I remember one of the ablest of the students in the English tripos at Cambridge of his time, and he was a frequent reviewer and contributor to the *Criterion* under my editorship.

'I regard Mr Bethell as a very able man indeed, and I should say that he will certainly in time accede to a good chair of English at some one of the provincial universities. I am sure that he will make his mark as he is not only extremely able but energetic and ambitious . . . He is a practising Christian and a Christian in the further sense that his religious attitude is apparent in his literary interpretations and valuations. He is not merely a good scholar in English literature but a scholar with a sound theological background.'

2–Bethell wrote on 14 Mar. 1934: 'I endeavour to show the relevance of beliefs about the world-order to theory of value, basing my constructive suggestions upon an examination of Dr Richards' theory of value.' 'Suggestions towards a Theory of Value', C. 14 (Jan. 1935), 239–50.

3–Patricia Shaw-Page recited the following verses of 'Cat's Prologue' to a ballet interlude, produced by the British choreographer Antony Tudor, in *The Rock*:

> Be not astonished at this point to see
> Creep on the stage a little cat like me.
> This pageant is a kind of pantomime
> Where anything may come at any time;

them very nicely indeed; and I did try to write verses that would not sound inappropriate when delivered by a child of eleven.

I believe that the whole ballet is extremely popular with the audience; and I am sure that it deserves its popularity.

Yours sincerely,
T. S. Eliot

TO *R. Webb-Odell* CC

8 June 1934   [Faber & Faber Ltd]

My dear Webb Odell,

Many thanks for the cheque and for the letter which accompanies it.[1] I feel that I have at least the equivalent of that sum, in the pleasure of doing the work, the collaboration, and finally in such testimonial rewards as your letter.

I go away on Monday for a fortnight's holiday, and I hope you can do likewise. I look forward to a future reunion of the principal workers.

—

> And what's a pantomime without a Cat?
> And I'm no ordinary puss at that.
> For I was to a worthy master loyal
> Who built St Michael Paternoster Royal:
> I am the Cat who was Dick Whittington's,
> And now we'll show you how our story runs.
>   (Houghton [EMB Papers]: see *Poems*, ed. Ricks and McCue, II, 165.)

Cf. 'Gus: The Theatre Cat', 31–2: 'In the Pantomime season I never fell flat, / And I once understudied Dick Whittington's Cat.'

(For Antony Tudor, see Susan Jones, *Literature, Modernism, and Dance* [Oxford, 2013].)

Sadler's Wells programme note: 'Dick, miserable as a scullion, is loved by his master's daughter. He ventures his Cat on a ship going to the Barbary coast; the Cat rids the Court of vermin and the king buys it for much gold. Meanwhile, Dick has run away; but Bow Bells bring him back to find fortune and his bride.'

R. Webb-Odell assured TSE, in a letter of 3 June 1934, that Patricia was '*the* "hit".'

Years later, on 18 Sept. 1961, Patricia Shaw-Taylor, finding that she could no longer remember the entire speech she had been given to recite, asked TSE if he could remind her of the words. 'The original scripts of my little bit which I possessed was destroyed in the bombing when my mother and I were squashed under a bomb! However, the photographs of us children . . . survived.' TSE replied via his secretary (15 Dec. 1961) that he too had no copy of the text.

1–Letter not traced.

I am sending you a copy of *The Rock* with my compliments.[1] By the way, I want to know the name of young Ted, who is given on the programme as 'Emck'.[2] That can't be right: you can't even pronounce it.

Yours very cordially,

[T. S. Eliot]

TO *A. Desmond Hawkins*[3]

TS BL

8 June 1934   Faber & Faber Ltd

Dear Mr Hawkins,

I am very glad to be able to enclose the cheque for your essay on the Drama which is to appear in September.[4]

I shall be extremely interested to learn how your affairs proceed, if you care at any time to impart the information. I hope that you will not think it an impertinent intrusion to say that I hope a divorce will follow quickly. In such cases it seems to me, where there are no religious prohibitions to prevent, the only satisfactory conclusion. One strong reason is that I believe that any union in which having children is wholly out of the question – I mean has to be prevented deliberately from the start – is a great strain; and has less hope of being permanent. (Furthermore, your legal position with your first wife ought not to be left unsettled). I have known of cases in which the woman changed her name by deed poll to the surname of the man she lived with, for the benefit of the children: that is one way, but not quite the most satisfactory. Find out what a divorce costs: I had the impression that there was some 'poor man's divorce' relief facility.

Forgive my offering suggestions. It may seem odd to you that I should write in this way; but I should find it quite impossible to take any part in the world unless I held to some extent two standards: one for churchmen and one for others.

With all good wishes,

Yours sincerely,

T. S. Eliot

---

1 – TSE inscribed a copy of *The Rock* to Webb-Odell 'with grateful thanks, T. S. Eliot, 9.vi.34' ('Modernisms' catalogue, Blackwell's Rare Books 2015, item 44).
2 – The role of 'Edwin', in the opening section of *The Rock*, was played by John Emck.
3 – A. Desmond Hawkins (1908–99), novelist, critic, broadcaster: see Biographical Register.
4 – Hawkins, 'The Poet in the Theatre', C. 14 (Oct. 1934), 29–39.

P.S. I have of course typed this myself, and am leaving it gummed up with my secretary. Sealed – but no seal to stamp it.

TO *The Editor,* The New Statesman and Nation   cc

9 June 1934[1]   [Faber & Faber Ltd]

Sir,

Mr Francis Birrell's notice of *The Rock* in your issue of today is, I dare say, quite excessively laudatory; but I am naturally disposed to accept without protest any praise that is not robbed from others.[2] But when he says that 'all the way through, both in prose and verse passages and in what the film writers would call the continuation', I show myself 'a greater master of theatrical technique than all our professional dramatists put together', he is unknowingly assigning to me a good deal of the work which was done by the producer, Mr E. Martin Browne.[3]

Yours faithfully,

[T. S. Eliot]

TO *I. A. Richards*   TS Magdalene

10 June 1934   Faber & Faber Ltd

Dear Richards,

I am taking the liberty of giving a card of introduction to you to my old friend Frederic Manning, who will be staying at the Jolly Brewers, Milton, for a time. He is the author of *Her Privates We,* and of an earlier book *Scenes and Portraits,* which is worth reading. Fred is a distinctly post-war type (in his early fifties, I suppose) and was a friend of Whibley, but is extremely intelligent in his way.

1–Published on that date in *NS&N*, 880.
2–Francis Birrell, 'Mr Eliot's Revue', *NS&N* 7 (2 June 1934), 847.
3–EMB to TSE, 15 July 1934: 'Looking at "The Rock" from this distance, I realize more & more clearly how much I owe to you. Your magnificent statement of Christian truth in exciting poetry made the play, despite all the limitations & faults of its scenario & performance, a thing of memorable distinction. Yet you were ever tolerant of the conditions with which production burdened you; & I have been touched to see you troubling to write to newspapers to give me credit for a part in the creation of the play. I cannot adequately express my appreciation of all this, nor the joy which your writing in the play still continues to give me, nor the personal pleasure which it has given me to work with you.'

Do let me know if you pass through London in July. I expect to be in London, though my movements depend somewhat upon a sister (not one you ever met, I think) and a niece who will be here.[1]

Yours ever,
T. S. Eliot

TO *C. Marshall Hattersley* CC

13 June 1934 [Faber & Faber Ltd]

Dear Sir,

I feel much honoured by your invitation to address the West Riding Credit [*sic*] Association, and I have been greatly tempted to accept, although the moment will not be entirely convenient.[2]

On sober reflexion, however, I think that I should not. The cause of monetary reform, whether or not one accepts Douglas's scheme, or any other, in its entirety, is something for which it is now a public duty for every man to use his influence; and if I believed that I could forward it by addressing the Social Credit Association, I would put aside any other engagement. But I do not believe that this cause will benefit by speeches from those who would only appear to be incompetent zealots. At present, the best that I can do is to let it be known publicly that I believe in the necessity for reform or revolution on Social Credit lines. For the past two years I have been incessantly occupied with immediate tasks, and only now am beginning to enjoy a little leisure for study. I hope that I may qualify myself to be more vocal; and should be gratified if the invitation might be renewed a year hence.

Yours very truly,
[T. S. Eliot]

1 – Sister Marian; niece Theodora 'Dodo' Eliot Smith (1904–92), daughter of Charlotte (Mrs George Lawrence Smith).
2 – C. Marshall Hattersley, a solicitor from Mexborough, wrote on behalf of the West Riding Social Credit Association on 8 June to invite TSE to address their Summer School at Skegness for a fortnight from 4th Aug. He suggested a talk of about an hour, plus half an hour for questions. 'The subject should, of course, have some bearing on the monetary question, but need not be a technical exposition, nor need it be essentially from the Social Credit point of view.'

TO *George Bell*[1]   TS Lambeth Palace Library

13 June 1934   Faber & Faber Ltd

My dear Lord Bishop,

Thank you very much for your kind letter. It has been a gratification to me to find that my work in the pageant is approved by several

---

1-Rt Revd George Bell, DD (1883–1958): Dean of Canterbury, 1924–9; Bishop of Chichester, 1929–58; President of the Religious Drama Society of Great Britain from its foundation in 1929; chairman of the Universal Christian Council for Life and Work, 1934–6; President of the World Council of Churches from 1954 – he has been called both a true 'world churchman' and 'the father of modern religious drama'. Though shy, modest and soft-spoken, with a high voice, he was a man of uncompromising conscience, courage and energetic commitment, especially to the work of international ecumenism and the place of the Church in public life. 'Not for me', he said, 'a fugitive and cloistered Church, which refuses to face the problems and crises of the modern world.' In 1944 his denunciation in the House of Lords of the Allied policy of bombing cities and civilian homes in Germany caused much resentment: his stance was believed to have dashed his chances of succeeding William Temple as Archbishop of Canterbury later that year. His works include *Randall Davidson, Archbishop of Canterbury* (2 vols, 1935), *Christianity and World Order* (1940), *The Church and Humanity* (wartime speeches, 1946). While at Canterbury he invited John Masefield to write for the Festival: *The Coming of Christ* (nativity play, 1928), with music by Gustav Holst and settings by Charles Ricketts, was the first play to be performed in the Cathedral for 400 years. Other plays commissioned for the Festival have included Laurence Binyon, *The Young King* (1934), Charles Williams, *Thomas Cranmer of Canterbury* (1936), Dorothy L. Sayers, *The Zeal of Thy House* (1937), Laurie Lee, *Peasant's Priest* (1947), and Christopher Fry, *Thor, with Angels* (1948). See further Ronald C. D. Jasper, *George Bell: Bishop of Chichester* (1967); Kenneth Pickering, *Drama in the Cathedral: A Twentieth Century Encounter of Church and Stage* (1986, 2001); Andrew Chandler, *George Bell, Bishop of Chichester: Church, State, and Resistance in the Age of Dictatorship* (2016).

See TSE, 'Bishop Bell', *The Times*, 14 Oct. 1958: 'I hope it is not too late for a reader who has been abroad and has just returned to England, to add a personal postscript to your obituary notice of Bishop Bell, and to Sir Charles Tennyson's tribute to his services to the arts.

'On a summer afternoon in 1934, walking in the garden of his Palace, Dr Bell proposed to me that I should write a play for the next Canterbury Festival. I accepted the invitation and wrote *Murder in the Cathedral*. To Dr Bell's initiative (and subsequently, Mr Ashley Dukes's enterprise in bringing the play to London) I owe my admission to the theatre.

'I am only one among other artists and poets who have benefited from the patronage of Bishop Bell, and who have reason to remember him with gratitude and affection.'

On 30 Dec. 1958 TSE recorded a contribution for the programme 'The Way of Life' (broadcast on the Home Service, 18 Jan. 1959): 'In my memories of Bishop Bell, four meetings stand out. The first memory is of a weekend, which must have been in 1930 or 1931 [actually Dec. 1930, when TSE had recited *Ash Wednesday* to a party which was at once impressed and bewildered], when I was a guest at the Palace in Chichester. Mr Martin Browne had been appointed by the Bishop [in 1930] his Adviser on Religious Drama for the diocese, and Mr and Mrs Browne dined with us: out of that meeting came the invitation in 1933 to write the Church Pageant which became "The Rock". I remember also that Dr Bell travelled up to London with me on the following Monday; not having consorted much

discriminating critics who like my previous work, as well as by a number of persons who had never heard of me before.[1]

It has also gratified me, and I think is not without interest, that my first opportunity to do anything like the sort of work that I want to do, has come through the Church. And the working on the play, apart from the many moments when I felt that I had bitten off more than I could

------

with bishops in those days, I found it strange to be journeying with a bishop in a third-class railway carriage. On that journey, the Bishop spoke to me about Dr J. H. Oldham and his work for the Church and the World: and so that weekend brought about my acquaintance with two men, Mr Browne and Dr Oldham, with whom I was later to be closely associated in quite different activities. The second of those four meetings which are clearest in my memory was also to have important consequences for me: it was on a summer afternoon in 1934 walking in the garden of the Palace that Bishop Bell proposed that I should write a play for the Canterbury Festival, the Festival which he had originated when Dean of Canterbury and in which he retained a warm interest. The result was "Murder in the Cathedral". A third meeting was in Stockholm in 1942: the Bishop arrived on the day on which I was to leave. We all know now, what I did not know then, why Dr Bell had come to Sweden: it was no fault of his that the conversations he had there led to nothing. [While lecturing in Sweden for the Ministry of Information, Bell had been made privy to a German plot to assassinate Hitler: when he conveyed this information to the Foreign Office no credence was given to his report – but it turned out two years later that the names he had vouchsafed to the British authorities turned out to be those of officers executed by Hitler after the attempt on his life.] And the fourth meeting was at a conference which he had assembled in Chichester, I think also during the War, to discuss the place of the Arts in the life of the Church: among others present, I remember Mr Henry Moore, Sir Edward Maude, and Miss Dorothy Sayers.

'These four meetings, chosen by my memory from among others, illustrate the varied interests and activities of the Bishop, outside of the regular duties of a diocesan which he carried out so faithfully: his interest in the service which Art could perform for the Church, and no less in the inspiration and employment which the Church could give the artist; his interest in the Oecumenical Movement, of which there is ample documentary evidence; his interest in foreign affairs and his sense of the international responsibility of the Church and of churchmen. He and another of my friends, Duncan-Jones the late Dean of Chichester, were men of very different type, but in two respects in which they were both outstanding, they had much in common. The Dean made the Cathedral the musical centre of the diocese; the Bishop, by his patronage and encouragement of drama and of the plastic arts, made his diocese an exemplar for all England. And both Bishop and Dean, during the 1930s, were tirelessly outspoken in their protests against the religious and racial persecution taking place in Germany.

'My first impulse, in speaking of the impression which George Bell has left upon me, is to say that he was a "loveable man". On reflection, I find that in applying this adjective, I am making it a compendium of all the qualities for which I loved and admired him. These include a dauntless integrity: no ambition could ever have deflected him from whatever course he felt to be right, no fear of the consequences to himself could ever have prevented him from speaking the truth as he saw it. With this went modesty and simplicity of manner, the outward signs, I believe, of inward humility. A friendly man, and a man of genuine piety – in short, a good man and an honest man.'

In 2015 Bell was formally and privily anathematised by the Anglican Church – more than fifty years after his death – as a paedophile, following a single anonymous accusation.

1 – Bell's letter not traced.

chew, brought much happiness. The collaboration, on all sides, was most harmonious; our ideas developed and expanded in the process of construction; and the sense of working together with sympathetic and understanding people was exhilarating, even exciting. Incidentally, I am grateful to you for having first brought me into contact with Martin Browne.

I should never have got the opportunity through the ordinary stage. I have at times been tempted to feel, except that it seems presumptuous about anything in which oneself is involved, that the guidance of Providence was present.

I am sorry to hear of the postponement of the conference, which I hope is only a postponement.

I have taken the liberty of giving a letter to you to some old friends who will be in Chichester. Dr Perkins is a specimen of the almost extinct Right Wing American Unitarian minister, and has read a good deal of Anglican theology. They would like to find a furnished house in Sussex for themselves and their niece (through whom I know them) but I fear they have left it rather late.

With best wishes for yourself and Mrs Bell, I am,

Yours very gratefully,
T. S. Eliot

TO *Edmund Blunden*[1]   TS Texas

13 June 1934   Faber & Faber Ltd

Dear Blunden,

I have taken the liberty of sending you two books of verse by F. V. Branford. I have not met the author, but his wife has called upon me and discussed his affairs. The enclosed copy of a letter from her will give you the situation as it was given to me.

1–Edmund Blunden (1896–1974), who won the Military Cross for valour in Flanders in 1916, was Professor of English at the Imperial University, Tokyo, 1924–7; and in 1930–1 literary editor of *N*. He was Fellow and Tutor in English 1931–44 at Merton College, Oxford (where his students included the poet Keith Douglas and the Canadian critic Northrop Frye); and for a year after WW2 he was assistant editor of the *TLS*. In 1947 he returned to Japan with the UK Liaison Mission; and he was Professor of English, Hong Kong, from 1953 until retirement. He was made CBE in 1964, and in 1956 received the Queen's Gold Medal for Poetry. In 1966 he was elected Oxford Professor of Poetry (the other candidate was Robert Lowell), but stood down before the completion of his tenure. See Barry Webb, *Edmund Blunden: A Biography* (1990).

It seems to be a pathetic case. I had never heard of Branford before; but he seems to have suffered by having been first encouraged and then ignored by Squire and suchlike. Candidly I can't do anything for him because I can't conscientiously recommend or publish his verse. But I am very diffident about my judgement of contemporary writers. The work is obviously rather old-fashioned, and may be quite second-rate; but different people can understand and tolerate different kinds of old-fashionedness and second-rateness; and it occurred to me to hope that you might find more in this than I do. There may be a very deep content, but the Shelley–Francis Thompson echoes put me off.[1] She sent me a cutting about Einstein (which I am afraid I have lost) and it seems that some statement by Einstein is supposed to confirm some intuition of Branford's.[2]

Anyway I apologise for troubling a busy man, but if you can do anything to help or encourage these poor people I shall be grateful. They are not financially in want; fortunately he has a small private income; but his wife craves a little recognition so that he may be encouraged to go on writing, as it is the only thing he can do.[3]

Yours sincerely,
T. S. Eliot

1 – HR had written to TSE on 16 Apr., in response to his request apropos Victor Branford's two books of poetry: 'Twenty years ago I might have been enthusiastic about them, but now they seem pale intellectual flames. There is something to respect there – a mind, a mysticism – but the form does not survive. It dates so desperately – Shelley, Francis Thompson, etc.'

2 – Margaret Branford (15 Jan.): 'In "The White Stallion" – the title poem – he has taken the horse as the symbol of destiny. In this connection I enclose a cutting of a lecture delivered by Einstein two years ago (ten years after the poem was written). This conception of the material universe is obviously identical with that of the great horse ridden by the god who sayeth "Naught", the "first and last Fate" – going "No-where" from "No-whence".'

On 6 Feb.: 'Since the early days of the "Adelphi" my husband knows nothing of modern literature as for years he could not even read a newspaper. He concocted a literary landscape from what little information I could give him.'

3 – Blunden responded on 27 June that while he felt deep sympathy for Branford, he could be of little help in encouraging his poetry. 'So though as you suggest I am probably soused in various inferior poetry, and am moderately patient under the miscellanies urged upon me, I fear there's nothing practical I can attempt to improve Branford's situation as a poet.'

TO *A. L. Rowse*[1]   TS Exeter

13 June 1934   Faber & Faber Ltd

My dear Rowse,

I was very much touched and pleased by your letter, which conveys your characteristic kindness.[2] And I am grateful for commendations from anyone of discrimination who has liked my previous verse, because I was deliberately trying to strike out a new line, which I felt might alienate some of my earlier supporters. Except for the abortive *Sweeney Agonistes* it is my first complete attempt on a major scale, and I often felt, while working on the pageant, that I had bitten off more than I could chew. I hope at least that it will put an end to the nonsense about 'intellectualism' and 'obscurity'. I am anything but an intellectual; more nearly a pure *émotif*. And nobody with anything to say *wants* to be obscure. But one isn't naturally simple or lucid; it takes work and experience to get there. One has to shed a great deal, or work out a lot of poison; and perhaps simplicity only comes through a gradual mastery of one's own emotions. But perhaps when I say 'simplicity' here I mean objectivity. Am I being in the least lucid now, I wonder?

I am at present in the country; I shall be in London for one night at the end of the month, and shall be paying a visit in Stepney for the first week in July. After that, if you are about, I shall try to get you to lunch.

With grateful thanks,
Yours ever,
T. S. Eliot

TO *The Editor*, The New English Weekly

[published 14 June 1934, 215]   [No address given]

'The Use of Poetry'[3]

Sir,

Now, Mr Orage, Sir, it seems to me the time has come to engross a little more of your space to do some sweeping up after Ezra. One can't be

---

1 – A. L. Rowse (1903–97), historian; Fellow of All Souls, Oxford: see Biographical Register.
2 – Letter not traced.
3 – This letter was written in response to EP's review of *The Use of Poetry and the Use of Criticism* – 'What Price the Muses Now', *NEW* 5 (24 May 1934), 130–3 – which opened disobligingly by asserting that it was at least a better book than the other one that TSE

everywhere at once; and a good deal of litter has accumulated: I will only deal with what concerns me.

Mr Pound has done your readers a disservice in suggesting that a book of mine, which is an unsatisfactory attempt to say something worth saying, is more negligible than another book of mine, which is an unsatisfactory attempt to say a variety of things most of which were not worth saying. There was, however, one notion running through my book on *The Use of Poetry*, something about the development of critical consciousness, which seemed to me interesting; but Mr Pound has not mentioned it, and I do not propose to discuss it. What Mr Pound really has to say is this: that my lecture on the Countess of Pembroke (pawky humour) was good enough to include in a new edition of Selected Essays, and that the rest might well be scrapped. I wholeheartedly agree. But I cannot help being exacerbated [*sic*] by a critic who takes a great space to condemn an inferior book for the wrong reasons, and who cannot stick to the point, because he refuses to see it.

Mr Pound might have been usefully occupied in saying that I overrated the criticism of Dryden; and that through ignorance, inattention, and haste, I both underrated and misunderstood the criticism of Coleridge. He might have told you, in so many words, that my lecture on Arnold was prejudiced, ill thought out, and wholly superfluous. He might have said that my lecture on 'The Modern Mind' was undigested. He might have said that I had spent eight hours in coming to no conclusion. But he

published in 1934, *After Strange Gods: A Primer of Modern Heresy*: 'it becomes apparent . . . that this volume was meditated, and its introduction considered. By comparison the Heresy book would seem to have been chucked together on Mr Eliot's receiving an invitation to say something he hadn't said already at Harvard.' Of this more recent volume, EP favoured the Introduction and the second essay ('Pawky humour in the title. Essay full of meat, acute observation, Mr Eliot's own view with highly respectable knowledge of the matter'), but he dismissed the remainder as dealing 'with inferior and in some cases vile matter'. EP proceeded to declare that the worst case – the 'gravest charge against his rank as critic' – was the final essay, 'The Modern Mind', in which the author had 'found none of the more vigorous intellectuals of the past century worth even passing mention': 'His high-water mark is an allusion to Levy-Bruhl . . . Fabre, Fraser, Frobenius, Fenellosa would appear to mean nothing to him . . . [Eliot] composes his list from obtuse and unqualified writers of tertiary or *n*th intensity, and from dabblers in minor theories.' EP thus glanced at Jacques Maritain and I. A. Richards, though without naming them: 'The nastiest blasphemy is quoted from the typical French religious faddist, and a racketeer on the borders of aesthetics.' He feared that the essay might be an index of TSE's 'gross insensitivity to the history of the past 150 years', and that he might therefore be disqualified 'from any perception of poetry in relation to life or to any thought outside the interlocking cenacles of just such racketeer-aesthetes and theorists.' It was perhaps time, he reckoned, to tell 'the dean of English essayists: What you need is a bit of good solid reading matter.'

has done none of these things. Instead, he wastes time flinging tomatoes at Mr Richards and Mr Maritain, whose works I do not suppose he has read; for as he says himself, one cannot read everything. Still, one need not call them 'racketeer-aesthetes and theorists'.

Mr Pound suggests that 'Fabre, Fraser, Frobenius, Fenollosa' mean nothing to me. I at least know how to spell Frazer, but beyond that, Fabre and Frazer mean to me two very valuable collectors of facts. Fabre was, so far as I am qualified to judge, a great observer; Frazer a great collator; but neither of them was, so far as I know, and in the sense in which I was using the word *mind*, a great exemplar of the modern *mind*. To Fenellosa I am grateful for having provided the material and occasion for Mr Pound's *Cathay*. And Frobenius, to judge by what I have read of his work (*Schicksalskunde*) is to me an example of the modern 'mind' in its most unpleasant form.

I should like to know what Mr Pound means by *nasty blasphemy*. I should be still more interested to know what he means by the phrase: 'the fall of the church, in its failure to deal with evil when that evil menaces the comfort of its subsidised professors and professional racketeers'.

It is interesting to learn that the church fails to deal with evil menacing the *comfort* of its professors, but the compliment expressed hardly seems to have been intended.

Now, Mr Orage, Sir, I am going to set round the chimbly and have a chaw terbacker with Miss Meadows and the gals; and then I am going away for a 4tnight where that ole Rabbot can't reach me with his letters nor even with his post cards.

I am, dear Sir, Your outraged,
POSSUM[1]

---

1 – See further EP, 'Ecclesiastical History, or the Work Always Falls on Papa', *NEW* 5 (5 July 1934), 272–3; repr. in *Selected Prose 1909–1965*, ed. William Cookson (1973), 61–3. A week later again, however, perhaps feeling he had gone too far to damn the recent work of his friend and publisher, EP allowed in a further appraisal, 'Mr Eliot's Solid Merit' (*NEW* 5 [12 July 1934], 297–9): 'If Mr Eliot weren't head and shoulders above the rank of organised pifflers, and if he didn't amply deserve his position as recognised head of English Literary criticism I would not be wasting time, typing-ribbon and postage, to discuss his limitations at all.'

TO *Guy Vernon Smith*[1]   CC

15 June 1934   [Faber & Faber Ltd]

My dear Bishop,

How kind of you to repeat your offer! I am at present in the country, so cannot find out immediately the prices of books; but the book which occurs to me (which I had been intending to get) is Volume I (the only one yet appeared) of Allison Peers' translation of St John of the Cross. Mrs Stuart Moore[2] tells me that it is much better than the previous Lewis translation. If that is within the price (and I expect it is) I should prize it with your inscription, and should go on to get myself the other two volumes as they appear. I believe it is published by Burns & Oates.[3]

There is another matter I must speak to you about, because I don't know to whom else to speak. A Mrs [Roberta] Carter took on the publicity of *The Rock* after the collapse of Mr Neville, and only a few days before it opened. I only met her once; and as I was not in any way concerned with the publicity (except to grumble at it, but that was before she came upon the scene) I have no notion of what she did, or of what proportion of the work was done by her and what by the Revd Vincent Howson,[4]

1–Guy Vernon Smith (1880–1957), Bishop of Willesden, 1929–40: Vice-Chairman of the Forty-Five Churches Fund, Diocese of London.
2–Evelyn Underhill.
3–The Bishop presented TSE with a copy of *The Complete Works of Saint John of the Cross, Doctor of the Church* I, trans. E. Allison Peers from the edn of P. Silverio de Santa Teresa, CD: 'To T. S. Eliot, A Helper of the Diocese and A True Friend of New London in Middlesex with gratitude from G. Vernon Willesden, Sadler's Wells, June 1934' (Valerie Eliot Bequest, Magdalene College, Cambridge).
4–The Revd Vincent Howson (d. 1957), St James' Vicarage, Ratcliff, London. Founder and producer of the East End Amateurs, he had been a member of Sir Frank Benson's Shakespearian Company.
  TSE wrote in his prefatory note to *The Rock*: 'The Rev. Vincent Howson has so completely rewritten, amplified and condensed the dialogue between himself ("Bert") and his mates, that he deserves the title of joint author.' Elsewhere he called him a 'Cockney comedian'.
  JDH, 'London Letter', *New York Sun*, 19 May 1934: 'The truth is that the actor, playing the part of Ethelbert, the foreman builder, revised and, in places, altered Eliot's original text, but the credit is nevertheless Eliot's.'
  EMB: 'Already on 7 December [1933] he [TSE] sent me the draft for the workmen's first scene. This group gave him the most trouble, because its leading actor, an old Bensonian turned East End vicar, insisted on re-writing Eliot's cockney into a cockney of his own. The latter appears in the published text . . . A sample of Eliot's original script for these scenes is printed in my book, and the whole may be studied in the Bodleian Library. The comparison shows Eliot as the better workman. But the experienced actor was indispensable to us. This was one of many frustrations which Eliot accepted for the sake of seeing for himself how a stage production comes to life' (E. Martin Browne with Henzie Browne, *Two in One* [1981], 80–2).

who I know collaborated with her to some extent, voluntarily. Her letter, which is marked 'Private', so I suppose I ought not to enclose it, seems to me slightly hysterical. She tells me that she drew £15 (out of the £25 earmarked for Mr Neville) and 'most of my expenses. I say most', she continues, 'because I am, as a matter of fact very much down over the whole business' . . . 'there is practically nothing to show for my work, financially at all.' The statements that she got 'most' of her expenses, and that she has 'practically nothing to show for her work, financially', are perhaps not completely consistent. Anyway she seems to be hard up. She wrote to me to ask if she might have a 'tiny percentage' on the takings of the sale of the text in the theatre (she says it was she who took steps to see that it was properly exhibited). I have told her that I have no voice in this matter, as the whole of the profits of the sale in the theatre go to the Forty-Five Churches Fund.

There seems to be no point in my speaking to Webb Odell about this matter, because she confesses that she did not get on very well with him. Yet I always feel that something should be done about a person with a grievance; that if it is genuine, it should be put right, and if imaginary, she should be told off. So I leave it in your hands, with apologies for having to trouble you.

I do hope that the 'Friends of New London' will make progress. They need a good deal more advertisement than I can give them!

I am, my dear Bishop,
Yours very sincerely,
[T. S. Eliot]

TO *Ernest Bird, Messrs Bird & Bird*   CC

16 June 1934   [Pikes Farm, Lingfield, Surrey]

My dear Bird,

I must apologise for not answering your letter sooner. Last week was a very busy week, and I left London on Monday; and have spent all the time I could spare from sleeping and idling in tidying up some business arrears. My address is as before: c/o F. V. Morley, Pikes Farm, Lingfield, Surrey, until the 28th. I return to London on that day, go to Rochester to

---

EVE later disclosed that the idea of 'Gus: The Theatre Cat' 'benefited from an old Bensonian actor, the Reverend Vincent Howson, who took part in a pageant play . . . to which TSE contributed. Howson would repeat, "Watch me – I act with my back."' ('The long march of the Practical Cats', *The Sunday Telegraph*, 12 May 1991, xiii.)

distribute prizes on the 29th, and from the 30th shall be in London till further notice.

I am annoyed to find that in the confusion I have left your last letter, about the insurance, in town. So I must answer, I fear, at random.

I should say that the possessions were probably over-insured. I know nothing about the furniture at Cadogan Gardens, which obviously is furniture lent by my wife to her brother, or about furniture elsewhere than at Clarence Gate. I believe that the list I gave you includes all my objects of importance: I think I mentioned a brass tea kettle of my mother's, and all the pictures not obviously of members of my family. But I enclose a list, previously mentioned, which my surviving aunt has sent me, of the objects which she sent me. (I do not recall any Tristram Shandy, and the portrait of Priscilla I had framed). These were *not* wedding presents.

Would it be possible to take out an ad interim insurance on the whole lot of stuff at present insured, and split it up after the division of property? If at any moment before the 28th you should think it desirable for me to come up to town to see you, you have only to let me know by letter or telephone.[1]

Yours sincerely,
[T. S. Eliot]

TO *Walter de la Mare*[2]

TS de la Mare Estate

16 June 1934   Faber & Faber Ltd

My dear de la Mare,

I am writing to ask you to let me know if there is anything more that you can do, or that you can suggest that I could do, to help a boy to whom you have already been very kind, George Barker.

1–Ernest Bird replied, 18 June: 'I am sorry to say that I am still without any further news from James or of your Wife's intentions. There is now but little time to elapse before the 24th inst., and I am becoming the more apprehensive . . . Having reminded James over and over again of the critical date I have written him a line today enquiring what arrangements have been made (a) for your Wife to vacate the flat on the 24th inst. and (b) as to the delivery of your effects . . .

'Do not worry about the insurance for the present. We have fifteen days from the 24th inst. in which to pay the present premium and between now and then we shall I hope have arrived at some conclusion.'

2–Walter de la Mare (1873–1956), poet, novelist and short-story writer, worked for the Statistics Department of the Anglo-American Oil Company, 1890–1908, before being freed to become a freelance writer by a £200 royal bounty negotiated by Henry Newbolt. He

We have accepted a volume of poems from him – or a number of poems from which a volume is to be selected – and have given him a small advance – quite contrary to custom and wisdom in publishing young poets! But his wife has just had a baby, under rather terrifying conditions, though he says they are now doing well; his grant from the Royal Literary Fund has come to an end, and I have been racking my brains to think what work could be found for him. He is very young, and unfortunately not well enough educated to be of much use as a reviewer, reader, or any of the odd literary jobs which one is able to dispense. I believe him to have unusual imaginative and emotional gifts, and a deeper feeling for rhythm than most of the younger poets; and once we can get him established, if we can, things may not be so difficult. But the next year or two present a serious problem. Would it be possible, for instance, to obtain a renewal of the Literary Fund grant?

Yours very sincerely,
T. S. Eliot

TO *Ezra Pound*

TS Beinecke

18 June 1934   Faber & Faber Limited

Now then, podesta, we must get to Work again. But first of All, Podesta, I want to know something about your Climate, podesta, this English climate is ceasing to suit me as it Did the trouble is we don't get enough RAIN and I cant stand all this sunshine day in and day Out Now so dry and Hot it is if your climate has plenty of rain every few days and fairly cloudy I might like to make a change but then again I hear your regime is fairly strict about Garb I have taken up nudism and I find that a loincloth and a sarong is just about all I can stand about me I have a lot in common with Gandhi yes Gandhi not Gandi Grandi Gantry[1]

As soon as the weather cooks if it ever does I will rustle round and see if I can get a photo of a Opossum I know a man in the Natural History Museum[2]

---

wrote many popular works: poetry including *The Listeners* (1912) and *Peacock Pie* (1913); novels including *Memoirs of a Midget* (1921); anthologies including *Come Hither* (1923). He was appointed CH, 1948; OM, 1953. See TSE's poem 'To Walter de la Mare'; Theresa Whistler, *Imagination of the Heart: The Life of Walter de la Mare* (1993).

1–EP had asked, in an undated letter: 'How does the bloody Mahatma spell hiz nyme/ Gandhi or Ghandi. Mebbe I better have page proofs/ after all.'

2–EP, 15 July: 'The recent event in the zoo/ you have kepp from me. 2 gnu possums/ but not fotoed in way that wd/ aid iggurunt skulpter to incisify.'

The serious matter is that Brer Bar and self dont feel altogether happy about your new title MAKE IT NOO we may have missed subtle literary allusion but if we do I reckon genl public will also[1] Podesta these essays is you heavy stuff and we want to get the heavy readers there is enough virus however in the essays to affect their metabolism if you dont frighten them off with a title like that we want to suggest (a) that this is not just 'Selected Essays' miscellaneous like mine but a particular corpus berrin on the history & appreciation of literature from special angle, so that second volume will not give impression of being second best pickings but something DIfferent do you take my meaning. Essays in . . . Essays on . . . You have to consider the future; Collected Works In XVIII volumes tome premier de proses Please please consider Yours etc.

TP

Can you give any lowdown on a bird named Mitrinovic (?) who looks like a devil doctor I dont like folks with no back to their head has mixed up with these New Britain New Albion 11th Hour emergency crowd and I dont know how far one should get involved with them.[2]

P.S.

HERE I see you have written typed something on the back of your letter. Yes but MAKE IT MEW may have authority I dont dispute that but ut doesnt give an Inkling of whats inside Yes of the 2 I prefer 7 notes on the tradition even it if give you the Sick fit to make you pewk govner but why say notes 7 epistles to the corinthians etc.[3]

1–EP had protested on 8 June (with a sideglance at William Empson's *Seven Types of Ambiguity*): 'Of course if you expect me to descend to the British level I cd/ call it
'Seven notes on the tradition.
'But it give me the nausea I shd/ prefer
'"Make It New".'
2–EP, 21 June: 'Know nowt of Mitrinovitch save name/ and incline strongly to agree with you that heads shd/ have back as well as front.
3–EP replied on 21 June that Make It New 'izza good title . . . MAKE IT NEW: seven critical essays/ on why literature shouldn'y stop where it is . . . Cardinal essays might dew for yew . . . DAMN the tradition bizniz/ I dont care a fhart about its being tradition.'
On 22 June: 'But IF you mean to do right, you can call it Collected Essays, vol. I. with sub title "Make it New". I think that wd/ be good publishing.'

TO *J. C. Perkins*   TS Donald Gallup/Beinecke

18 June 1934   Faber & Faber Ltd

Dear Dr Perkins,

It is very kind of you to write to me; and I am more than flattered that you should have cared to go to see *The Rock* again.[1] I was there myself on the last night, and thought that the performance had considerably improved since you saw it before. I have been on the whole highly gratified by its reception, and by its having seemed to appeal to more than one type of auditor. And particularly by the fact that the more important members of the cast – who were mostly the younger ones – including the chorus – have expressed much enjoyment in doing the work. Both Browne and I were anxious to avoid raising or suggesting any controversial issues within the Church: sometimes with amusing results. One lady is said to have objected to the Reformation Scene because it was 'so very High Church', while a friend of hers was delighted because she said it proved that the Anglican Church was still 'essentially Protestant'.

I am grateful to you for letting me know about your plans, and rejoice that you have found a satisfactory habitation. Chipping Campden is only a name to me, but I know its reputation; the Cotswolds I only know from the motor route between Oxford and Hereford. I hope indeed that I may be allowed to see you there, and could save household trouble by staying the weekend at some local inn.

I am all the more glad if your having settled will induce Emily[2] to take an earlier boat – resting in the Cotswolds will be better for her than running about New England in the hot weather, from visit to visit.[3]

1 – Perkins wrote from London, 17 June: 'I went on the last night, the Saturday – alone, for Mrs Perkins had gone to Chipping Campden. It seemed to me that many details were carried out rather better than when we saw it first . . . I should not suppose that your grandfather Eliot had a very different spiritual purpose from yours or would have read "The Rock" with anything but approval. I felt that all your statements of vital religious truth were universal and I had something of the emotion of a disciple.

'At Chipping Campden Mrs Perkins found a house near the north end of that fascinating street, not far from the church, which appealed greatly to her, especially as there was a beautiful and intelligently planned garden. I went down yesterday to see it with the result that I am writing Miss Sunderland-Taylor [the owner who passed her summers in Yugoslavia] that we will take it for three months, beginning July 15. We have cabled Emily Hale to that effect. The house is called Stamford House and we shall hope to see you there one day.'

2 – Emily Hale (1891–1969): drama teacher; intimate friend of TSE: see Biographical Register.

3 – Gordon, *Imperfect Life*, 258: 'On 15 July, Emily Hale sailed from Boston . . . Eliot went [to visit them at Chipping Campden] at once . . .' For details of TSE's doings with Hale and the Perkinses, see Gardner, *The Composition of 'Four Quartets'*, 35; Gordon, *Imperfect Life*, 257ff.

As you are not going there till the 15th, I hope I may see you again in London, unless you are to be in Chichester or elsewhere. I have just heard from the Bishop that his conference is postponed, so I shall not be going to Chichester after all.[1] I shall spend the first four or five days of July with 'Bert' in Stepney, but after that will be in town, except for any visits I may make with Marian.

With many thanks,

Yours very sincerely,

T. S. Eliot

Lyndall Gordon, 'Eliot and Women', in *T. S. Eliot: The Modernist in History*, ed. Ronald Bush (1991), 17: 'in September 1934 she and Eliot went together to view the rose-garden of the Gloucestershire country house, Burnt Norton, a visit that, in a sense, set off Eliot's poetry for the next eight years during which he wrote his masterpiece, *Four Quartets*.' TSE to John D. Stephenson, 13 July 1945: 'Burnt Norton is a manor house in Gloucestershire. I know nothing of the history of the house or of its owners. I merely happened to walk through the grounds one summer day at a time when the house had evidently been unoccupied for at least several years.' Raymond Preston asked on 31 July 1945 whether in *BN* TSE had in mind 'the house of that name near Aston Subedge, Gloucestershire, and the death by fire of Sir William Keyt, the eighteenth century owner of the original Norton?' TSE responded, 9 Aug. 1945: 'Burnt Norton is certainly the house near Aston Subedge which you mention. I believe it belongs to a family of the name of Ryder but I know nothing of the history of the house and what you tell me about Sir William Kyte is news to me. I daresay that I found some obscure attraction in the name, but otherwise I am afraid this house was only a point of departure for my poem. Indeed I suspect that anyone visiting the house with my poem in mind might find the house and gardens disappointingly commonplace.' TSE advised Hermann Peschmann, 12 Sept. 1945: 'You are quite correct in identifying the manor house Burnt Norton, and no doubt when you saw the house you were disappointed. The poetry – if any – is in the poem and not in the house. It is a perfectly third-rate manor house built on the site of an older one which had been destroyed by fire. I merely happened upon it one day when it was unoccupied; I think there was someone living in the lodge but I wandered through the grounds quite freely and it provided the suggestion for a deserted house.' Stephen Cross, while working on the BBC TV programme 'The Mysterious Mr Eliot', related to EVE, 24 Mar. 1970: 'I found there were three pools, all "drained" and all "dry concrete". There is the long, rectangular pool which I know is generally accepted as the one in the poem; a semi-circular pool adjacent to it; and, a little distance up the hill and hidden among trees, a third, round pool. For some reason I feel strongly that this last pool is the one your husband referred to, and it certainly fits exactly with the line "Along the empty alley, into the box circle", which the rectangular pool does not. The round pool is in fact set in a circle of box trees.' EVE responded to Cross, 10 Apr. 1970: 'I have always understood that the rectangular pool was the one my husband described, although I never heard him say so.'

1 – The Chichester Conference had just been postponed. For various reasons, the organisers had failed to secure a Roman Catholic participant: Fr Robeyns of Louvain had to refuse the invitation, and 'the economic situation in Germany has put the finances of Maria Laach in a serious state'. The formal bulletin, issued by the Bishop's Palace on 11 June, stated: 'To our great regret, the Roman Catholic members of the Liturgical Conference at Chichester, to which we had been looking forward so much, find themselves unexpectedly unable to be present this year. We feel that without their presence the Conference would lose a large part of its value.'

TO *Walter de la Mare*   TS de la Mare Estate

20 June 1934   Faber & Faber Ltd

My dear de la Mare,

Many thanks for your letter of the 18th about Barker.[1] I know nothing whatever of Barker's, or of his wife's, family; but I imagine that there is no money anywhere. I feel that it is not at the moment a question of providing for his future indefinitely, but much more pressing than that: of getting them through say the next year. I would gladly be one to contribute say 5s. a week guaranteed for a year, and if four or more would do the same it should contribute materially to relieve the situation. I suspect from his appearance that they have been living very poorly indeed, so that £50 or more a year would help considerably. I believe that such a fund should be applied as impersonally as possible – better that he should not know who the contributors were. It could be arranged so that the payment might be made weekly or monthly through a bank. I am trying to think of people who would be willing to contribute, not as a 'charity', but whole-heartedly. If we could find *two* others on the same terms, for a year, it would be worth starting. Can you think of anyone to ask?[2]

Yours ever,
T. S. Eliot

TO *Alida Monro*   TS University of Victoria

20 June 1934   Faber & Faber Ltd

Dear Alida,

I am very glad to hear from you. It is now my turn to be away – I am taking a country rest, and sha'n't be settled in town again until the 5th

1–De la Mare suggested that a small group of persons might make a weekly allowance to Barker 'It probably couldn't free him from anxiety, but it would take the worst edge off, and I would very gladly be one of the contributors. As regards the R.L.F., George Barker's age is a difficulty, and there is a regulation as to the interval between the first application and a second.'

2–De la Mare responded to this letter on 21 June, to say that he 'would very gladly contribute the sum you have mentioned. I agree with you as to the method of sending it on.' On 2 July he forwarded to TSE a letter of 29 June from H. J. C. Marshall, Royal Literary Fund, indicating that TSE's letter 'contained some useful sentences' and that he had suggested a grant.

Arthur Pottersman, 'After 28 years his true confession is made public', *The Sun*, 24 Apr. 1965: 'In the 1930s he survived only because the late T. S. Eliot got five friends – Barker has never known their names – to provide him with £4 a week. "Eliot to me was saintly," he says.'

July – my sister Marian (whom you have not met) and one of my nieces arrive on the 8th. I will ring you up on my return, and ask to come to tea with the poodle.

Some of the acting was indeed pretty bad, but considering that the people were mostly suburban church parishioners I think we came through it pretty well. The Rock would have been good if he had had a voice; Rahere an epitome of all theatrical faults. If they hadnt cut that scene he would have looked still more the fool than he did. I really found the chorus far above my modest expectations, and my respect for Elsie is increased. I managed to tone down their sweetness a bit myself. The girls were better than the men; the leader, Janet Lewis, has a really good speaking voice. The first candidate for the Rock, one Clifford Turner, was unspeakably syrupy. I didnt get to *Aurung-Zebe* [*sic*], and have had not further truck with Lady Keeble; but I have been moved to a violent attack upon the English Association in the *Criterion* for their new anthology 'The Modern Muse'.[1] Have you examined it?

I had a letter from Henry yesterday, but his designs of coming over have not yet become definite enough for him to mention them to me.

Yours ever,
Tom

I see that Ottoline is back.

The matter at the moment on my mind is the question whether Vivienne is really going to move out of Clarence Gate on the June Quarter Day. If she doesn't, it may become unpleasant, as I shall be responsible to the landlord for her vacating.

---

1 – 'A Commentary', C. 13 (July 1934), 624–8. 'It is the mixture of good and bad that makes the book dangerous. There is a sense in which the word "catholicity" means something pernicious, and in this sense the book is fully catholic. The editors do not show bad taste: they show no taste at all . . . It should have taken as one of its aims, instead of the brainless balderdash of its preface, the aim of educating the public taste . . . It has preferred, in a spirit of addled Imperialism and Anglo-American amity of the most futile kind, to offer a marketable ware to English-speaking people in "the four quarters of the globe"; and to talk about it in the language used by politicians without policy, whose only programme is to stay in power.'

TO *Theodore Spencer*   TS Harvard Archives

20 June 1934   Faber & Faber Ltd

Dear Ted,

Many thanks for your letter of June 10th. It was cheering to think of
you and the Pickmans reading my play aloud. The performances went off
well – houses quite well filled – bishops pleased as some money was made.
The music was good, and the chorus (pupils trained by Elsie Fogerty at
the Central School of Dramatic Art) did their job admirably. And we had
a fellow come down from Stepney with a piano-accordeon to provide the
accompaniment for the bricklayer's song.

Let me know your address when you get one. I thought Cannes an ugly
place, but I did not see it under the best conditions.[1] However, to sit on
a beach with no clothes is my notion of a holiday, and you will have heat
and sun. But I have heard better of Hyeres, though you would probably
be picked up there by Edith Wharton.[2] Give me as much notice as you can
before you are coming to England. I don't expect to go abroad this year,
but I might be in Scotland or Wales.

                                    Affectionately,
                                    Tom

TO *Henry Eliot*   TS Houghton

20 June 1934   Faber & Faber Ltd

My dear Henry,

Thank you for your letter of the 8th.[3] Also for list.[4] I think there are
a few omissions – there were two Rev. Andrew Eliots in succession, one
during the Revolution – and wasnt Uncle Oliver Stearns, Dean of the
Divinity School, a parson? The relationship to the Sternes ought to be
established somewhere, as they used the same arms, but perhaps our

---

1 – The Spencers were to spend part of the summer in Cannes.
2 – Edith Wharton went south in the winter to her villa in the commune of Hyères, south-
east France, 1919–37.
3 – Not traced.
4 – The list, in answer to TSE's enquiry (26 May) about clerical ancestors, included Revd
Daniel Greenleaf (1679–1743), Revd Andrew Eliot (1683–1749 (Minister of New North
Church, Boston), Revd William Smith, Revd William Greenleaf Eliot, Jr., St Louis, Missouri
(1811–87); and over a dozen parsons, direct and collateral, among the descendants of
William Greenleaf.

Stearns's had no right to it.[1] Aunt Susie has produced (unasked) a Revd John Rogers, admired by Hooker. The relationship with Sir John Eliot (who was a scoundrel)[2] is shown in a *Genealogy of the Eliot Family* by Walter Graeme Eliot of New York; father had two copies which should have gone to you. There is another in the British Museum. The family came from Cotlands in Devon and that branch settled at Port Eliot in Cornwall – the Earl of St Germans (formerly a cashier in Lloyds Bank) is a lunatic – his brother just got a K.C.V.O. however – another brother is the 'bad case' described in the police court notice I sent you. Our people, you remember, went to [East] Coker, near Yeovil in Somerset.[3]

I sent you a copy of *The Rock* which you must have by now. The whole business I enjoyed immensely, having a very able producer and agreeable people to work with. The bishops are very pleased, as the run was well attended and they made several hundred pounds, having expected only to make expenses. About 2000 copies were sold in the theatre, the small profit on those going to the Fund.

I am in the middle of a couple of weeks holiday in Surrey, in the same lodgings next door to the Morleys in which I spent last summer. I shall be back in London by the 1st of July ready to receive Marian and Dodo[4] when they arrive. I dont know what they will want to do; but I should think Marian ought not to bustle about much; and I think it would be good if I could find some quiet country or seaside lodgings for two or three weeks with them, later: and Dodo could whisk about alone if she wants to. At present I myself only want to lie in a deck chair, on the lawn, in as few clothes as possible – shorts and no stockings; but I have several odd jobs to do, and have to think up a speech to make to the boys of the

1 – HWE responded to this query, in an undated letter: 'I don't think I have ever seen the genealogy of Isaac Stearns, or Sterne (16– ? – 1671) traced back, and don't know whether Laurence Sterne or Richard are connections or not . . . It would be interesting to know.'
2 – HWE responded (7 July) to this remark: 'As for poor old Sir John Eliot, I should judge him sufficiently punished by his imprisonment and consequent death (of t.b., wasn't it?) at the hand of Charles I. What a vessel of wrath you must be to conserve all this anger against your scoundrels and your damned!'
3 – An Eliot family was living in East Coker in 1563. The Revd George Mullard, vicar of East Coker, who looked into this connection after TSE's death, found from church records that by the end of the sixteenth century there were four Elliott (*sic*) families headed by William, Stephen, Jehrome and Henry. Of these there are records of the burials of Stephen (1600) and William (1642). 'Church Records of T. S. Eliot's Ancestors', *Western Gazette* (Yeovil), 15 Jan. 1965.
4 – Theodora 'Dodo' Eliot Smith (b. 1904) – TSE's niece, daughter of Charlotte (Mrs George Lawrence Smith) – was visiting from Baltimore.

King's School, Rochester, next week, when I distribute their prizes.¹ I am at the moment trying to write an introduction to the *Collected Poems* of Marianne Moore. You and Theresa ought to know her, by the way; she is an eccentric and extremely intelligent person, very shy, lives with an elderly and difficult mother in Brooklyn (260 Cumberland Street) you might ask her to tea one day. One of the most observant people I have ever met.

I am glad if you can get into the country from time to time during the summer. I hope you will get a prolonged holiday later. I wish we could repeat the week at Randolph every year!²

Love to Theresa,

Affectionately,

Tom

I was interested to get the cutting about Liverpool. I have followed the case with great interest and satisfaction. It was Lord Hugh Cecil who started the rumpus, and conducted his part of it in a masterly way. It is a good step in the direction of stricter discipline.³

TO *Paul Elmer More*⁴   TS Princeton

20 June 1934   Faber & Faber Ltd

My dear More,

Many thanks for your letter of June 1st, which was very welcome.⁵ Your words about *After Strange Gods* are especially gratifying, first

---

1 – Commemoration Day, 30 June.

2 – TSE had passed a week with members of his family at Randolph, New Hampshire, in 1933.

3 – Lord Hugh Cecil had presented to the Archbishop of York a petition calling for action against the Bishop and Dean of Liverpool for having permitted persons holding heretical opinions (Dr L. P. Jacks of Oxford and the Revd Lawrence Redfern, a Liverpool Unitarian) to preach in the Cathedral. 'I trust to procure an authoritative declaration that those who reject the deity of Christ shall not preach in our cathedrals.' His petition was refused by the Archbishop.

4 – Paul Elmer More (1864–1937), critic, scholar and writer; author of *Shelburne Essays*: see Biographical Register.

5 – More wrote of the essays of *After Strange Gods*: 'Your conception of tradition and orthodoxy, and of the relation between the two, strikes me as subtle and profound, and the application of these canons to Lawrence and Hardy and Thackeray and George Eliot (not to mention Babbitt) seems to me an admirable example of the proper use of general concepts, or principles, in the judgement of particulars. And you have come out into the open nobly, as you have not done before, perhaps were not prepared to do before. You have opened a big field for criticism. Possibly one of the things you will undertake to show how and why

---

because (without flattery, only because you are one of the few people who would have both the knowledge of literature and theology, and the point of view from which I accept judgement on these lectures) your good opinion of this book means as much to me as anybody's; and second, because I felt compunctions at having defended a good cause less skilfully and carefully than it deserves. Both of my sets of lectures in America had to be prepared under difficulties and at short notice; as this was for reasons which I would not want to make public account of, I desire and deserve no mitigation of severity therefore. But the subject of *The Use of Poetry* was undertaken merely because it seemed the one on which I could write with the minimum of new reading and thinking; the field of *After Strange Gods* was one to which my real interest had turned. I therefore feel more regret at the inadequacy of the latter than of the former.

I am painfully aware that I need a much more extensive and profound knowledge of theology, for the sort of prose work that I should like to do – for pure literary criticism has ceased to interest me. I do not know whether I shall ever have the time to acquire it. And I am not a systematic thinker, if indeed I am a thinker at all. I depend upon intuitions and perceptions; and although I may have some skill in the barren game of controversy, have little capacity for sustained, exact, and closely knit argument and reasoning.[1]

---

the orthodox tradition (in which certainly you were not brought up) is the right soil for great and true and permanent art . . . And that brings me to James Joyce. To reverse matters, I cannot see him as the moralist he still appears to you, or feel as you do that he is "penetrated with Christian feeling". Unless his use of the stream of consciousness should be regarded – as certainly he does not regard it – as a sense of original sin. I just cannot escape the notion that in your attitude to Joyce you have not quite caught up with yourself – if you know what I mean by that – and that you ought logically now to place him with Lawrence and Hardy, though for somewhat different reasons. But these are minor points in comparison with my admiration of your book as a whole, and with my whole-hearted acceptance of your main thesis.'

1 – More to Lester Littlefield, 1 Mar. 1935: 'It has always seemed to me that Eliot started out with the initial romantic error of believing in pure art, art for art's sake. That has led him into some perfectly incomprehensible bits of criticism – notably his dicta about Shakespeare and Dante (they are in his *Selected Essays*, I forget now just where). But I have thought too that he was gradually working himself out of that nonsense. His last volume of criticism, *After Strange Gods*, shows indeed that he has at last pretty well found himself.' Years later, when Littlefield posted More's letter to TSE (15 Dec. 1962), TSE would comment on 19 Mar. 1963: 'I cannot say that I agree with him even now and I am surprised he speaks so well of *After Strange Gods* which I consider an intemperate attack on the people with whom I disagree' (Princeton).

TSE to JMM, 21 Nov. 1956: 'As for Lawrence, you may or may not know that I insisted long ago that a book of lectures called *After Strange Gods* should be allowed to go out of print. Not only about Lawrence perhaps but in general there was a violent and intemperate

Apart from one intelligent review by Edwin Muir in *The Spectator*,[1] reviewers either praised or damned the book according to their predispositions, without apparently studying the text with any care. The *Times* review was typical of the *Times*, as well as symptomatic of the chasm between 'literary' reviewers and 'theological' reviewers in the Anglo-Saxon world.[2] The editor, Bruce Richmond, has always been a good friend of mine, and a kind one. But he has a *Times* mind, the Oxford specifically All Souls' mind: such minds have one very strong principle and conviction, which is the absence of principle and conviction erected into a principle and conviction itself. And that indeed is the way the country is being governed. Is not the upper middle class today almost utterly destitute of principle and conviction? Is there anything that they would, as single individuals and not as a mob, die for?

----

tone about these lectures which may have had something to do with my state of mind during that year [1932–3], but which tended to disqualify the lectures as literary criticism. I should say that my feelings about D. H. Lawrence have with years very much mellowed, and that I am more inclined to recognise his admirable qualities than his shortcomings. The latter have not vanished from my sight, and I would say that the trait of Lawrence which always offended me most still does offend me, and that is a strain of cruelty, which I find not only in such a book as *Lady Chatterley's Lover* but in *Sons and Lovers*. I am less blinded by this to the insights and independence of mind, however, and Lawrence's opinion of Bloomsbury seems to me thoroughly justified' (Northwestern). On 20 June 1963 he reiterated, apropos a draft typescript of Northrop Frye's *T. S. Eliot*: 'It should be mentioned somewhere that I became dissatisfied with *After Strange Gods*, which I came to consider rather intemperate, especially in speaking of Thomas Hardy, and no longer keep [it] in print in this country.'

To Roy Morrell, 15 May 1964: 'The book in which I criticized Thomas Hardy severely is one which I have subsequently regretted, and I regret in particular what I said about Hardy. Since publishing that book, which by the way I no longer keep in print, I have come to the conclusion that I do not find it worthwhile to write about any author, especially one who is no longer alive, merely to express antipathy, nor do I feel that dislike of Hardy's novels which I then felt. I particularly admire *The Mayor of Casterbridge* and parts of *Far from the Madding Crowd*. There are scenes in both which remain permanently in my memory, such as that when the mayor of Casterbridge looks over the bridge and sees his own effigy floating in the water.

'I entirely agree that some of Hardy's poems are very moving indeed. My only complaint against them is that there are too many of them, and the effect would be more impressive if he had pruned down his collection to the best. There is, however, at least one story in the volume *A Group of Noble Dames* which seems to me quite horrific (horrible).'

1 – Edwin Muir, 'Mr Eliot on Evil', *Spectator* 152: 5515 (9 Mar. 1934), 378–79.
2 – TSE's sister Ada wrote on 20 May 1934: 'The review of After Strange Gods in The Times Literary Supplement strikes me as another instance of a reviewer reading inattentively. Several others have impressed me that way also. They read with preconceived notions in their heads. Most people are slow to take in careful distinctions, in my experience, especially when they catch sight of some word, like "orthodox" or "tradition", which they associate with what is outworn and discarded.' A. Clutton-Brock wrote in the *TLS* (anon.), 19 Apr. 1934: 'We may not have any very imposing tradition, but surely we have enough "inherited wisdom of the race," wisdom acquired by learning from mistakes, to be rather shy of attributing to the devil opinions with which we do not agree.'

It is quite possible that I overestimate Joyce, in that context, or use him as a stick to beat the others with. I should not (and cannot remember that I did) consider him as a 'moralist'; and to say that his work is penetrated with Christian feeling is not to say that the man is established in Christian principle and conviction. I mean something for which he cannot, morally, be given any particular credit; an accident, if you like, of birth and education from which he draws the advantage. I say nothing as to his *intentions*. And if I condemned him, it would not be *with* Lawrence and Hardy, but in quite another *giro*.

You must by this time have received the copy of *The Rock* which I sent you. It represents, so far at least as the verse choruses go, a venture on a wider sea than before; and I shall be curious to know whether you find as deep a fissure between 'actuality of form' and 'actuality of content' as you do in its predecessors.

I am grieved to hear of your overworked winter and your accident, and hope that the summer will restore you to perfect health.[1] I look forward eagerly to the appearance both of the lectures and of *Anglicanism*. But I am sorry that you no longer have the compulsion of the latter to bring you to England. When shall we see you here again? I hope to visit America next year.

Ever yours cordially,
T. S. Eliot

TO *Marianne Moore*   TS Rosenbach Museum and Library

20 June 1934   Faber & Faber Ltd

Dear Miss Moore,

Having now somewhat recovered from my pageantry and from arrears of other matters which have now been partially cleared away, and being for the moment in the country where I can expand a little, I have set myself first the question of selection and order.

First selection. What we contemplate is a kind of companion volume to the *Selected Poems of Ezra Pound*. That book has 184 pages. Your total

---

1–More had laboured through the winter, though troubled by 'a complex of horrid diseases', to finish the lectures for *The Sceptical Approach to Religion* (1934), as well as his introduction to *Anglicanism: The Thought and Practice of the Church of England* (1935). 'I had given myself time enough for preparation, but unfortunately had a fall which just missed smashing my face to jelly and laid me up, so that I had to compose the address at the last moment under great strain.'

manuscript, even with the notes, will hardly run to that length; so I see no reason whatever for omitting any of the lot that you have typed out for me. I therefore propose to retain them all.

I take it that the order which you give them, which is the same as in *Observations* (a title, by the way, to which you have better claim than I) is the order of composition. The fact that your omissions are chiefly of the first numbers of that book lends colour to my assumption. If the chronological order were retained I think dates ought to be given. But I am inclined to a re-shuffle, which is more or less arbitrary in that it could be varied considerably without damage; and I enclose a tentative list for your approval.

I want to start with the new poems hitherto uncollected, and shove some of the slighter pieces towards the end. At your simplest, you baffle those who love 'simple' poetry; and so one might as well put on difficult stuff at once, and only bid for the readers who are willing and accustomed to take a little trouble over poetry. I think this will pay better; and will excite the booksellers more.[1]

I want to call the book 'Selected Poems' just like Ezra's. One point is to assume that *everybody knows your work*. Some people, especially in cathedral towns and the like, are very backward in this country. A fancy title might make them think that you were a hitherto unknown author, just being launched; and that gives ignorant reviewers a chance to be patronising.

The price to be, I think, 7s. 6d.

Now for the very difficult task of providing a fitting prefatory eulogium.[2]

---

1 – According to Molesworth, *Marianne Moore* (1990), TSE's 'influence was greatly felt in the selection and arrangement of Moore's *Selected Poems*. Not only did he prevail upon her to reprint all of the earlier *Observations*, but it was he who arranged the book so that the poems published after 1924 should open the volume . . . Eliot's suggested order, with "The Steeple-Jack" as the first poem, remained unchanged by Moore throughout her lifetime.' Leavell, *Holding On Upside Down*, 288: 'By obscuring her early development, the arrangement of the poems had the desired effect of making her seem difficult. And since she reproduced Eliot's arrangement in her *Collected Poems* (1951) and *Complete Poems* (1967), she would appear to decades of readers as a kind of Athena born fully grown from the mind of the Modern.' See too *A-Quiver with Significance: Marianne Moore 1932–1936*, ed. Heather Cass White (2008).

2 – MM responded on 2 July: 'Eulogium even used humorously makes me shrink to nothing.'

Moore's *Selected Poems* (F&F, 7s. 6d) was announced for Spring 1935: 'In that poetic renaissance with which the names of Eliot and Pound are associated, there is at least one other name the place of which is assured. The work of Miss Marianne Moore is already known to those who provide the opinions that are later accepted by all; she herself has been indifferent to wider appreciation. Her poetry is unlike that of either of the other poets just mentioned, as it is unlike that of anyone else. The present volume contains all of her work,

Yours sincerely,
T. S. Eliot

P.S. 'The Fish' is a good one to put well forward. That, I predict, will figure in anthologies of the English Association. Do not misinterpret this remark, I like the Fish very much, but I think it will frighten anthologists less than some.

P.P.S. I have always heard the tree referred to in this country as 'Monkey Puzzle' not puzzler. And

in line 4 of 'Silence' should not we read 'or' for 'nor'?

It will be a looovely book.

In line 2 of 'The Rock' please read 'Dog' instead of 'dog'.

[Enclosure with letter to Marianne Moore of 20 June 1934]

ORDER.
Part of a Novel, Part of a Poem, Part of a Play
The Jerboa
Camellia Sabina
No Swan So Fine
The Plumet Basilisk
The Frigate Pelican
The Buffalo
The Fish
In This Age of Hard Trying
To Statecraft Embalmed
Poetry
Pedantic Literalist
Critics and Connoisseurs
The Monkeys
Roses Only
Black Earth
In the Days of Prismatic Colour
Peter
Picking and Choosing
England
When I Buy Pictures
A Grave

---

up to the present year, that she cares to preserve, and since the publication of a very small book of *Poems* by the Egoist Press in 1921, is the first collection of her verse to appear in this country.'

Those Various Scalpels
The Labours of Hercules
New York
People's Surroundings
Snakes, Mongooses
Bowls
Novices
Marriage
An Octopus
Sea Unicorns
The Monkey Puzzle
Injudicious Gardening
Is Your Town Nineveh?
To Military Progress
An Egyptian Pulled Glass Bottle
To a Steam Roller
To a Snail
'The Bricks Are Fallen Down'
'Nothing Will Cure'
To the Peacock of France
The Past is the Present
'He Wrote the History Book'
Like a Bulrush
Sojourn in the Whale
Reinforcements
Silence.

TO *A. Desmond Hawkins* TS BL

20 June 1934   Faber & Faber Ltd

Dear Hawkins,

   I am glad that you got the cheque, though six pounds does not go very far in such circumstances. I hope that you have [not] been been cast off without a job; and that you will write again when the temperature is more normal.

   I mentioned the 'poor man's relief' thinking that your wife might have recourse to it, if she were willing and ready to divorce you. But of course it would be unwise for you to negotiate directly with her; and it would be best to take the advice of an experienced lawyer first.

When I spoke of 'two standards' I am not admitting any permanent compromise, or recognising the World as a 'positive order' beside the Church. I merely mean that one cannot expect to impose (in the present state of affairs) the same moral judgements upon *individuals* that one does upon a society as a whole, or expect those individuals to live according to a morality which is founded upon dogmas which they do not accept. The Church is, from one aspect, as Eric Gill says, 'in the catacombs'; and it is more important to make converts than to try, at the moment, to impose a theocracy upon a rebellious and triumphant pagan world.

In such a society as I would see, of course, marriages would be made with a full sense of their sacramental finality. The present situation is neither one thing nor the other. Today, I know, it is difficult for the ordinary young person to realise that anything is *final*, once for all; they can hardly be expected to be willing to reap the harvest unless they were told what they were planting. We cannot abolish divorce unless we abolish the registry office: the two go together.

You are bound to be rather confused at present, that will clear up later. I shall be in London again, off and on, throughout the summer; you have only to ring up (any time after the beginning of July) and find out whether I am there; and we could lunch quietly somewhere.

Yours sincerely,
T. S. Eliot

TO *Maurice Haigh-Wood*[1]   cc

23 June 1934   [Faber & Faber Ltd]

Dear Maurice,

I quite see the difficulty, and if James approves, what you suggest seems to me the best way out of the present difficulty. It is most unfortunate that the Irish income should fail just when you are beset by other difficulties.

I hear, by the way, from Bird, who hears from James, who has spoken to the landlord, that V. has taken on the same flat in her own name. But as no one knows where she is at present, no one can communicate with her about it. I wish she would take the advice of responsible people before taking such steps.

---

1 – TSE's brother-in-law: see Biographical Register.

Let me know as soon as you have heard from James.

Yours ever,

[Tom]

TO *Ernest Bird, Messrs Bird & Bird*   cc

23 June 1934   [Faber & Faber Ltd]

Dear Bird,

I should be willing to contribute a reasonable sum to my wife towards redecorating the drawing room of the flat after my pictures, books and bookcases are removed. You remember that she made this request last year, but it was refused because I was leaving articles there until the expiry of the lease, and was offering a sum to cover cost of moving.

My books are, or were, all those in the open bookcases; her books, a small number, were all contained in the glassed top of a bureau. If there were any of her books by chance among mine, I could identify them and return them. There were various files, odd papers, photograph albums of mine in a desk and in a deal wardrobe. I cannot itemise the pictures better than as follows:

A number of photographs etc., framed or passe-partout, of members of my family, or of portraits of earlier members of my family. Two drawings, framed, made by my father when a boy: Brutus & the Ghost, and a carthorse. A framed drawing of myself as a small boy, made by my deceased sister, and a framed worsted cat made by myself as a child. An engraving of the portrait of my friend Charles Whibley. A drawing in green ink of an elephant, by the sculptuor Gaudier, which doesn't really belong to me but to a friend.

I cannot remember any others that I want. Drawings etc. by various artists (Wyndham Lewis, Raoul Dufy, Kauffer etc.) she may keep. I only want those of sentimental value to me, and the one mentioned which is only lent.

There were some odd garments, no longer of any value to me.

Sincerely yours,

[T. S. Eliot]

TO *Horace Gregory*[1]   TS Syracuse University Library

25 June 1934   Faber & Faber Ltd

Dear Mr Gregory,

I was glad to hear your very pleasant news.[2] I am at present in the country for a short holiday, and shall not be settled in town again until the 5th of July. I will write again on my return and hope to see you and Mrs Gregory. I hope however that you will get a bit of time in the country or at the seaside as well.

I shall probably be at this address during most of the day from the 2nd of July, but the first four days of that week shall not be available at night. But if you should be in the neighbourhood drop in and ask for me.[3]

1–Horace Gregory (1898–1982), poet and critic, majored in English at the University of Wisconsin before moving to New York. His poetry includes *Chelsea Rooming House* (1930), *Poems, 1930–40* (1941), *Medusa in Gramercy Park* (1961). He won a Guggenheim Fellowship in 1951, and the Bollingen Prize in 1965. His Russian-born wife, Marya Zaturenska, won a Pulitzer Prize for her second volume of verse, *Cold Morning Sky* (1937).

2–Gregory wrote that, thanks to TSE, he had secured a job teaching poetry at Sarah Lawrence College, New York, for 1934–5; also he and his wife and children were to visit Bryher (pseud. of Winifred Ellerman [1894–1983], English heiress and novelist, who paid for their passage) in London for two months in the summer, when they hoped to see TSE. Gregory was ultimately to teach classical literature in translation and modern poetry at Sarah Lawrence College, 1934–60.

3–Gregory and his wife were to call on TSE at his office in the afternoon of 3 July. On another day TSE took them to lunch in Soho, in company with Herbert Read – 'the best time we've had in London,' as Gregory wrote (n.d.).

He would recall, in his memoirs: 'T. S. Eliot invited Marya and me to lunch; we met in his office at Faber and Faber in tree-shaded Russell Square. There, with a wave of his hand, he introduced us to Herbert Read. Read, though gray-haired, looked youthful and quick, and his boyish grin, though permanent, and perhaps professional, was ingratiating, apparently ready for anything that proved itself amusing. For the moment, he seemed entirely at Eliot's service, and was swept along with us on a brisk walk to Soho.

'Eliot, too, seemed younger than when I had first met him in New York – more sensitive, more volatile, more alert. We stepped into a French restaurant, where we were swiftly seated, and I saw a wine list placed in Eliot's hands. For several seconds, he considered it gravely, consulted the waiter – then his face cleared, the trial and ritual over. With less caution, he gave orders for lunch to the scarcely visible waiter at his side.

'The wine performed its miracles. Almost at once, the table, chairs, and floor were slightly elevated. Wherever I turned my head, things took on a rosy hue; everything looked preternaturally clear and bright. Eliot was saying how vehemently he detested the charms of *Elia*, the essays of Charles Lamb – he abhorred their everlasting *whimsy*. Whimsy was the curse of Lamb. (Years later, when I saw *The Cocktail Party* in New York, I realized that the side of Eliot that was uppermost in that Soho restaurant resembled Sir Henry Harcourt-Reilly, the victorious, lighthearted psychiatrist of the play.) He later asserted that the most heinous crime a writer could commit was dullness – all the other vices resulted in lesser offenses – and this prompted me to bring up the verses of T. Sturge Moore – which set Eliot off into an imitation of Moore and Robert Bridges, the two of them seated in a restaurant,

I was very much interested in your review of one of my lecture books.[1] What you say about my not being an intellectual is something that I discovered about eight years ago; but whenever I have made the statement I have met with incredulity: my motive for saying it being taken to be either irony, false modesty, or love of paradox. Another myth I cannot destroy is that of my vast learning. And it is as well for my future reputation that these things should be discovered as soon as possible. Other remarks of yours I did not quite understand. E.g. I do not want to pose as a 'persecuted' man, and I can't see why you should think that I am. I think that I have met with as much kindness and appreciation as anybody can expect to receive.

Yours sincerely,
T. S. Eliot

---

tapping out each other's metrics on the edge of the table. "Sheep in sheep's clothing," he called them.

'He seemed moved and pleased when Marya spoke her admiration of "Ash Wednesday", for at that moment the poem had yet to receive the praise that it deserved. And then as if in fear of hubris, he reassumed the manner of a cheerful host, catching us off guard with talk of baseball, quoting batting averages or standing of the clubs, with particular reference to the St Louis team. Read looked blank' (*The House on Jefferson Street: A Cycle of Memories* [1971], 223–4).

1–'The Man of Feeling' (on *ASG*), *New Republic* 79 (16 May 1934), 23–4.

TO *John Hayward*[1] TS King's

25 June [1934] Faber & Faber Ltd

No John you have got it all Wrong. you dont think that Mr Austin Read would turn me out like that now do you Now hear is a diagram correctly drawn if La Marjolaine is interested to know

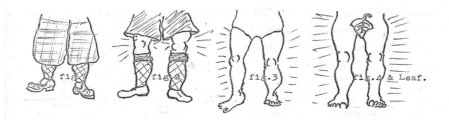

the truth.

EXPLANATION
Fig. 1 . . . . Cold
Fig. 2 . . . . Cool
Fig. 3 . . . . Hot
Fig. 4 . . . . Torrid

Yours etc.
T. S. E.

P.S. The radial lines indicate that peculiar emanation or rather effulgence which usually accompanied with the odour of Violets is accustomed to envelop the Limbs and torso of very Holy persons.

1–John Davy Hayward (1905–65), editor and critic: see Biographical Register.

28 June 1934   [Faber & Faber Ltd]

Dear Miss Moore,

I have now received your letter with the 'Nine Nectarines' which shall be included.

I ought to have explained that your book will not look like the edition of Pound's poems which I sent you.[1] Pound's poems were originally published in a more expensive looking form at 7s. 6d., and what I sent you is a subsequent cheaper edition in the Faber Library. I think that you will find the production of your poems more to your liking, although I hope that they also will go into this library at some future date.

I note that Macmillan's agreement with me for the introduction calls upon me to provide the MS. of the poems as well. It seems to me, however, more satisfactory for everybody, as well as giving me less work, that you should yourself see the American text through the press. Have you a duplicate copy of the poems as sent to me, which you can let Mr Latham have? I feel that in any case the author should have the opportunity of correcting her own proofs.

May I ask whether you have sent me all of the notes that you want used? I can't find any notes on 'Part of a Novel' or 'The Buffalo'.

I shall be grateful if you would let me know without delay whether my arrangement of the poems is satisfactory. If not please let me know exactly how you wish to have them; and your wishes shall be obeyed. The book is all ready to be set up here, pending your approval or correction of the order.

I am not very happy about my introduction but I don't believe that I should be satisfied even if it were much better. One feels something of the fatuity and superfluity of the chairman in after dinner speech-making: I am so conscious of an introduction being an impertinence, only justified by temporary considerations, that I am not happy writing one.[2]

1–MM wrote (16 June) of EP's *Selected Poems* that she was 'much interested in your carefully unequivocal analysis and in the choice of poems . . . I like a book to open flat as this does, the clear type, and the unsnobbish price. I question the color and certain details perhaps' (*Selected Letters*, 324–5).
2–MM (14 July): 'I allowed you – I asked you – to write an introduction; yet now I am troubled by the thought of having trammelled you with it.'

I have only just got back from the country and will write to you again when I have had time to read the Ross poems.[1]

Yours sincerely,
[T. S. Eliot]

TO *George Barker*   TS Texas

29 June 1934   Faber & Faber Ltd

Dear Mr Barker,

I have your letter of the 28th and, after consultation with the Chairman and with Mr Morley, I have pleasure in sending you herewith a cheque for £15, being the balance of the advance agreed upon for your poems.[2]

I hope that your appeal to the Royal Bounty will be successful, and shall be very glad to give you any support within my power.[3] If nothing comes of this we will explore in some other direction.

Yours very sincerely,
T. S. Eliot

TO *Donald Brace*   cc

6 July 1934   [Faber & Faber Ltd]

Dear Brace,

Many thanks for your letter of June 27th.[4] All that I need to say about the matter, I think, is that I am quite pleased by your decision to publish the book yourselves, and to confirm our reply cable accepting your terms.

I am glad that you found *The Rock* readable. In spite of what you say, however, I think it is desirable to emphasise the fact that it is a patchwork affair, done strictly to order, and that the design was not my own; the

1–MM had sent poems by Mr Ross (husband of Mary Lowry Ross), a *Dial* contributor whose work interested her: he was a chemist for the Canadian government, and he also wrote music.
2–Having signed the contract for his poems, Barker asked if the second instalment of £15 advance against royalties might be made available to him forthwith: 'we are endeavouring to live without income or a capital'.
3–'I have been advised to appeal to the Royal Bounty, introducing yourself and Mr de la Mare as aware of my or our circumstances. I trust I have not infringed?'
4–Brace thanked TSE for *The Rock*. 'I remember your speaking during our trip on the moors of your promise to do this play, but I had no idea it was to be so considerable a work as this . . .

publication was an after-thought; even the choruses were written to a strict time sheet. The text that is, was written for delivery on a particular occasion and not as a book.

I do hope that you will change your mind and pay us a visit in the autumn.

Yours ever,
[T. S. Eliot]

TO *George Barker* TS Texas

10 July 1934 Faber & Faber Ltd

Dear Mr Barker,

In reply to your letter of July 2nd,[1] I think that a volume of about the length of Stephen Spender's poems is what we ought to aim at but I don't want you to cudgel your brain for poetry merely in order to have enough. I don't wonder that you have found writing difficult of late and I think that the best thing you can do is not to worry about it. The moment that your anxieties are somewhat relieved I am sure that you will find that you have plenty to say.

Yours sincerely,
T. S. Eliot

'And as a matter of fact, the subject is not merely of local interest. I enjoyed the book very much. I think your regular readers will want it and that perhaps it may appeal in some circles beyond that . . . I should like to produce the book here rather than take sheets . . . I think it would be best for us to publish it at one dollar, or at any rate not less than that, and to bind it in cloth.' He offered a royalty of 10 per cent.

1 – 'I am experiencing extreme difficulty in writing lately, and have composed no verse at all. About how many poems more are required for the volume?'

TO *Sherard Vines*[1]   CC

10 July 1934   [Faber & Faber Ltd]

Dear Vines,

I know I promised to give you a title shortly after I saw you; and every time I have thought about it, which has been very frequently, I have finally given up and postponed it till the next day. But one must make the plunge some time. I have got a lecture (which I would rewrite to give again) on 'The Bible as Literature' – a fairly mild sort of thing objecting to what one might call the Quiller-Couch literary 'approach' to the Bible. This would be specially pleasing to Non-Conformists; nothing in it about the Church. Or there is a subject chosen for Leeds (not yet written) on 'Literature in the Modern World' (or something like that), which would touch on some of the points raised in *After Strange Gods*. Would that suit better, and would you mind the duplication? And the third possibility would be to write a third lecture, and the fourth to split the last mentioned into two and give part to you and part to Leeds.[2]

When are you to be in London again?

Yours ever,
[T. S. Eliot]

TO *Mary Hutchinson*   TS Texas

10 July 1934   Faber & Faber Ltd

Dear Mary,

I see that there is a Sadlers' Committee tomorrow – Wednesday is never possible for me, unless my proper committee on that day is very brief, so I shall probably not be able to come. I should probably not have gone to the last one if I had realised that it was a *general* meeting – you never know whom you may meet[3] – I was sorry to miss you on the way out, but

---

1 – Sherard Vines (1890–1974), poet and academic, taught at Keio University, Tokyo, 1923–8, and was then G. F. Grant Professor of English at University College, Hull, 1929–52. Works include *The Pyramid* (1926) and *Tofuku: or Japan in Trousers* (travel, 1931).

2 – Vines responded on 16 July, 'we [at Hull] should like the lecture you are giving at Leeds . . .'

3 – TSE might well have bumped into VHE at one such Sadler's Wells meeting: she wrote in her diary on 28 June 1934: 'I ought to go to a meeting of Saddlers [*sic*] Wells Theatre at 6 p.m. at Lord Howard de Walden's in *Belgrave Square*. My only reason for hesitating is the only

Lilian[1] insisted on introducing me to her Mr Cass.[2] At the moment I am rather annoyed with Lilian for another reason.

I have been away most of the time until recently – in Surrey, Rochester, and Stepney. Met Sir Frank Benson at the enclosed.[3] We were given 7 boxes of kippers in Billingsgate.

I am now waiting to hear from my sister, who is, I suppose, in Chester. I hope I may see you again before you leave for Dell Quay, unless you are very busy.

Affectionately,
T. S. E.

TO *W. H. Auden*   cc

10 July 1934   [Faber & Faber Ltd]

Dear Auden,

I find that *The Orators* has just gone out of print. We shall, of course, reprint it without delay but before we do, I am writing to ask whether you wish to make any alterations or additions which would constitute a second edition: also if there are any errors in the text which ought to be corrected.

Do let me know whether you are going to be in London at all during the holidays and what you are doing. It seems a very long time since you

---

reason I *now* have for hesitating to attend *any* function, & that is the *determination* I have formed NOT to meet my husband *any where* but *in his* (& my) *own home*. *Alternatively*, at the Sanat: de la Malmaison in the presence of *witnesses* of *my own choosing*. When I say in *his own home*, I mean of course 68 Clarence Gate Gardens which I have taken on a further lease of 5 years. Never having seen him in his own home since *September 17th 1932* I have *formed* the *determination* for my own protection & it is very necessary.' On 16 Apr. 1934 she had attended a party at Sadler's Wells, where she 'sat close to the door keeping my eyes fixed for Tom'. On that occasion she did meet up again with VW and LW, and with Mary and Jeremy Hutchinson.

1–Lilian Baylis (1874–1937), redoubtable and legendary English theatrical producer: manager from 1912 of the Old Vic Theatre, and from 1931 of the Sadler's Wells Theatre.
2–Henry Cass ran the Old Vic Shakespeare Company, 1934–6.
3–An announcement of a Garden Fete at St James', Ratcliff, E.14, on Thursday 5 July.

have produced any major work, and I am wondering when we may expect something from you.[1]

Yours ever,
[T. S. Eliot]

TO *Michael Roberts*[2]

11 July 1934 [probably not sent]   [*The Criterion*]

Dear Mr Roberts,

Thank you for your letter of the 3rd and for enclosing your essay.[3] It is extremely interesting and the book ought to be a good one. I am just wondering whether this essay is a particularly suitable one to print by itself. I should like to keep it for a bit, and meanwhile you might let me know if you think any of the other parts of the volume would be more complete in themselves for periodical use. Which of the two books is likely to be finished first?

I didn't see either you or Madge or Miss Adam Smith on the evening you speak of, and I didn't hear any comments except from one of the parishioners, who remarked that it was interesting but very difficult.[4] I am interested in the comments of the programme seller and am certainly

1–WHA replied from Cumberland, 5 Aug. 1934:
'Here is the copy of the *Orators* with corrections.
'I also enclose a poem for the *Criterion* if you like it.
'I have written to Miss Powell.
'Just getting my old crock of a car ready to take me to the Carpathians; so I am rather doubtful if I shall ever see you again but hope to in September.'
The enclosed poem ('Poem') opens: '"Sweet is it," say the doomed, "to be alive though wretched".' Written in Mar. 1934, it was to be printed for the first time in W. H. Auden, 'Five Early Poems', ed. Ed Mendelson, *TLS*, 16 Jan. 1976, 53.
2–Michael Roberts (1902–48), critic, editor, teacher, poet: see Biographical Register.
3–Roberts had two books in hand: (i) *The English Critic* – 'a handbook giving a summary of critical doctrines in historical order . . .' ; (ii) *The Single Mind* – 'ten essays on science, metaphysics & theology, again in historical order . . .'
He enclosed a first draft of the first essay.
4–Roberts wrote: 'I went up to the last performance of The Rock, and sat with a Presbyterian (Janet Adam Smith) on my right, and a Communist (Charles Madge) symbolically on my left. I don't think we made any irritating comments, though it was not until you were going out that I noticed you had been sitting in the seat in front of me.
'At the interval, I talked to a programme-seller. She complained that [they] had been over-worked during the show, that they had no pay for overtime, that the audience gave no tips. "Now, sir, isn't it the understood thing, that if you buy a cup of tea, you give a girl a penny? Of course, these aren't our regular patrons . . . Or they spend 6/9 or 7/6, and still you don't get a penny. Well, I used to be a regular church-goer, but I reckon I'm not going after this . . ."

not prepared to defend the audience. But I think it is a fairly general experience that once you are committed to any cause the hardest cross you have to bear is the character of the people you are associated with. On the whole, and with exceptions both ways, most of the people I like best are not connected with the Church. I found that some of my Communist friends in New York have much the same feeling toward their party, but that doesn't really affect the matter. At any rate I don't think I made any attempt to conciliate the sort of people you have in mind.

I hope you will get the job you want.[1] Let me know if you are in London any time during the summer.

Yours sincerely,
[T. S. Eliot]

TO *Bonamy Dobrée*

TS Brotherton

11 July 1934   Faber & Faber Ltd

Dear Bonamy,

I apologise for not writing before – I apologise for everything – I hope I have not held you up over this weekend – I was waiting until I could let you know definitively about the story[2] – I think it is very good – but it IS long, which means that I must be sure how long the rest of the contents will be. Now, I dont feel I can leave London on the 14th – my sister & niece have just arrived[3] – I should have liked nothing better than a visit to Mendham. However, I hope you will ask me when you are settled again. I believe you are addressing the W. Riding Summer School.[4] Mr Hattersley of Mexborough asked me to speak, but I said

---

'Now I know the girl was wrong: you can't judge church by the people in it [. . .] but hadn't she got at the root of the trouble? Isn't she more likely to find kindness & understanding among people who have been driven out of the church?'

1 – Roberts had been summarily dismissed by Mercers' School on 1 Feb. (the governors had been upset by reports of lessons looking into religious and scientific belief). He now had an offer of 'an attractive job' from the Royal Grammar School, Newcastle, where he had taught from 1925 to 1931.

2 – A story by Valentine Dobrée: not published in C., included in her *To Blush Unseen* (1935).

3 – VHE noted in her diary, Sun. 15 July: 'Sun, 15 July. I have been told that on this day Theodora Eliot Smith & Margaret Dawes [*sic*] Eliot (who I did not know *were* in *England* nor had any intention of coming) went to tea at 3 Compayne Gardens. Mother told me this & said they were staying at The *Constance Hotel*. *If this* is *true* – IF – & I am going to The Warrior House Hotel, St Leonards [where her father had died] this week – *it is, indeed, Point Counter Point.*'

4 – BD was due to lecture on 15 July, on 'Resistances to Social Theories', at the West Riding Summer School, Skegness.

I would not spoil a good cause with an ignorant speaker, and perhaps when I knew more I might speak; now he invites me to be a pupil as I cannot be a teacher. But I have forgotten when it is. Will you be there? I hear you were lately in town. Herbert is smart and smiling in silk underwear; I am hot and wilting in no underwear.[1] I am in a fit of depression. I have to think of three subjects to lecture on next winter, and there is nothing at all that I want to talk about or know enough to talk about. I don't think my poetry is any good; not *The Rock*, anyway, it isnt; nothing but a brilliant future behind me.[2] What is one to do?

> I was lunching one day in the Princess Louise[3]
> When I passed some remark to a man in white spats
> Who was eating a plate of fried gammon and peas;
> So we soon fell to talking of thisses and thats –
> Such as Pollicle Dogs and Jellicle Cats.[4]
>
>   * * *
>
> I have teeth, which are False and quite Beautiful,
> And a Wigg with an Elegant Queue;

1–BD responded, 12 July: 'Don't you wear underwear? I too find it much more economical not to. But then Herbert is so very dressy. But silk is a delusion; it is hotter than cellular aertex . . .'

2–BD, 12 July: 'And perdie, what is all this about your poetry? The choruses in *The Rock* are certainly as good, and perhaps better, than anything you've done. Of course the play was no play because it was a pageant, and you can't do anything with a pageant, especially if people will insist on putting in wearisome art and crafty tabloids. As a matter of fact I want to talk to you about your choruses when I see you: the method and the form seem to me to hold infinite possibilities. Are you really bothering about your brilliant future behind you? Is it possible ever to live up to one's past?'

3–Compare lines 1–5 of 'Pollicle Dogs and Jellicle Cats':
> I was lunching one day at The Princess Louise,
> When I passed some remark to a man in white spats
> Who had ordered a plate of fried gammon and peas,
> So we soon fell to talking of thisses and that –
> Such as Pollicle Dogs and Jellicle Cats. [*Poems* I, 294]

4–C. S. Kreiter (16 June 1959) asked if he might use the words 'jellicle cats' in a children's book he was writing: 'I recall that you use these words in a poem, and since I am unable to find the word "jellicle" (which I assume is a diminutive for "angelical") I thought perhaps your copyright might cover the use of the two words in combination, or "jellicle" alone.' TSE's secretary replied, 25 June 1959: 'Mr Eliot has asked me to write and say that he does not wish to copyright the word "jellicle" and is quite content that it should be used without acknowledgement, so long as its use conforms to the definition of Jellicle Cats given in his poem about them. And jellicle, by the way, is not a diminutive of "angelical" but is a diminutive of "Jellylorum" which was the name of a cat of that description which Mr Eliot once owned.'

And in closing I send my most dutiful
Respects to your lady and you.

Apologetically,
T. S. E.

TO *Christopher Dawson* CC

11 July 1934   [*The Criterion*]

Dear Dawson,

Thank you for your review of Niebuhr which is being set up. From what I looked at of the book I am much inclined to agree with you.[1] I found myself irritated that the author should be so intelligent without being more so, but the atmosphere of America is very unfavourable to theological precision, which seems to be preserved there only by the Jesuits.

I am very much interested in your article on 'Religion and the Totalitarian State' and I don't think it at all unsuitable for the *Criterion*.[2] I don't mean that I altogether agree with you by any means. I agree that something of the sort is likely to happen, especially if the talk of Walter Elliot means anything. But I don't feel sure that there mayn't be some better solution, if people would look for it. Furthermore I should like to be clearer on the relation of economics and politics. While there seems no reason for the Church to oppose any political organisation as such, it is called upon to express itself in the economic world, for instance in such matters as usury. But I shall be very glad to print your article either in September or December.

I should be interested to know whether you had got any further with Bolshakoff, and whether you have come to any conclusion about the utility or futility of his project.

Yours ever
[T. S. Eliot]

1 – Review of Reinhold Niebuhr, *Reflections on the End of an Era*: C. 14 (Oct. 1934), 131–3. Dawson wrote to TSE (27 June) that he was rather disappointed in Niebuhr's book: 'He is full of catchwords like "religious insights" & worse.'
2 – 'Religion and the Totalitarian State', C. 14 (Oct. 1934), 1–16. Dawson remarked of his piece, 'which I contributed to an Anglican Conference on Church & State': 'I am afraid that it is much too ecclesiastical for the *Criterion*, but I thought that you might like to have a look at it, in spite of that.'

TO *Laurence Whistler*[1]   CC

13 July 1934   [Faber & Faber Ltd]

Dear Mr Whistler,

Mr Ian Parsons, who is one of the partners in Chatto & Windus, would be very glad to see you with reference to a possible future opening in that firm.[2] He suggests that you should write to him and let him know of a day when you will be in town, for the purpose of fixing an appointment.

I will let you know of anything else as it turns up.

Yours sincerely,

[T. S. Eliot]

TO *Ezra Pound*   TS Beinecke

13 July 1934   Faber & Faber Ltd

Dear Sir that a fine elephent I am rt. proud to have that eleplent and I thank you for the bootom of my heart I asked your good lady wasnt I to pay anything I thought I was undertaking to help support in that small way a Victim of nationalism or something as well as Artist but she said No that was somehow included in his paying off pecuniary favours done to him by you[3] Well if I cant get a picture of a Oppossum I cant think of anything else to order for the moment does he do Tasteful Jewelry I Wonder one can always find uses for that curiously carved semi-pretious stones and the like but even so how to Get it to me I asks, rings for small Fingers etc. Ald also Podesta I have to thank you for a charming Obbituary thats real andsome of you and if it does not make me look more lifelike will at Least preserve a delightful Fragrance round my Tomb But I having just wrote you up in our Catalogue as our best living Critic praps the young folks will begin to smell skunks where they aint there.[4]

I have a good Piece what Lord Rothermere said in a speech about his Mother in Case you missed it I think it should come in some canot canto.

1–Laurence Whistler (1912–2000), poet (recipient of the King's Gold Medal for Poetry, 1935) and artist specialising in glass engraving – he later undertook commissions for TSE and GCF.

2–Whistler had approached TSE on 6 July at the suggestion of Humphrey Sumner of Balliol College, Oxford; TSE saw him the very next day, 7 July.

Ian Parsons (1906–80) worked for Chatto & Windus after graduating from Cambridge, becoming a director in 1953.

3–A Rapallo stonemason had cut in stone the head of an elephant to serve as a seal for TSE.

4–TSE hailed EP, in his blurb for *Make It New*, as 'the most vitalizing critic of literature in our time'.

The W'ale is in bed with Wimbledon Throat. Hes been carryin on too much with Helen Jacobs.[1]

yours
TP

TO *Alida Monro*   TS University of Victoria

13 July 1934   Faber & Faber Ltd

Dear Alida,

I have had a few words with our Sales Manager on the subject of selling up stock.

He says that the first thing to do, when one has made up one's mind, is to write to all the publishers and ask them whether they care to take their stock back. Most of them won't; but he says that we would.

Apparently once you have given the publishers this opportunity, however, you are at liberty to do anything with the books that you want to. He recommends strongly Wilson at Bumpus as a man to approach with a view to buying the whole stock; Wilson would give a fairer price than anyone, and next in order Simpkin Marshall, and last Foyle's. Or, if you like, he could recommend somebody who could negotiate for the sale of the books in lots to different people, according to their character. I imagine, however, that your stock is pretty homogeneous. Such a man would work on a commission. He says he is too busy to undertake such a job himself; but I could ask him to look in some time and have a talk with you about it.

I feel pretty sure that we ourselves would be interested in buying the children's anthology you mention. Or you might get tenders for it from several houses. You might be able, with that anthology, to sell the dozen or so books as a lot.

Do you know Miss Lyn Irvine?[2] I don't. Young, zealous, Scotch – I believe the daughter of a moderator. She runs an odd little mimeographed

---

1–EP replied, 18 July: 'I am sorry the Whale is throated/ and that yr/ arrival is so prorogued.'
Helen Jacobs (1908–97), outstanding US tennis player: winner of ten Grand Slams.
2–Lyn Irvine (1901–73): journalist and author. Daughter of a Presbyterian minister, she studied at Aberdeen and Cambridge. Following the success of her first publication, *Ten Letter Writers* (Hogarth Press, 1931), she set up a little magazine called *The Monologue* (26 issues p.a.), with contributors including Elizabeth Bowen, Graham Greene, J. M. Keynes and LW. See William Newman, *Married to a Mathematician: Lyn Newman's Life in Letters* (2002).

magazine. Someone suggested to me that she was the sort of person who might like to take over a bookshop.

Possibly, at the same time you started to try to sell the stock, you should take steps to enforce the payments of the debts; or sell the debts to some collector as a block. I dont know about these things; we should have to find out more.

I think this is all I have gleaned so far.

Yours ever,
T. S. E.

TO *Mary Hutchinson* TS Texas

16 July [1934]   Faber & Faber Ltd

Dear Mary,

Thank you for your letter.[1] I telephoned to Deal to say that I am engaged for both Wednesday and Thursday evenings, and hope that you will have a free evening next week. Especially as I suppose you will be leaving for Chichester the week after. I am wrestling with problems of American relatives and acquaintances. As for relatives, it is difficult to know what to do with the combination of a sister considerably older than myself and a niece considerably younger, both very nice but with no pronounced tastes. I want to take them for a week or so into the country and can't think, at short notice, of any appropriate place. As for American acquaintances, they are numerous and miscellaneous, and do not by any means all fit together – and nothing is worse than to try to fit incongruous Americans together when they are abroad.

I hope you know more about Mr Cass than I do – he did not inspire me with confidence. He comes, I believe, from the Croydon theatre. And a play called *Elizabeth's England* (or *England's Elizabeth* I forget which) rouses me to no enthusiasm either. I know Miss Byrne, who is an Elizabethan pundit.[2] She smokes the same cigarettes that I do; but I was once annoyed by her about something else.

Ever
Tom

1 – Not traced.
2 – Muriel St Clare Byrne (1895–1983), scholar and lecturer; author of *Elizabethan Life in Town and Country* (1925) and an edition of the letters of Henry VIII; but most famous in later years for the fifty-year labour that produced *The Lisle Letters* (1981) – a selected edition of the private and public correspondence of Arthur Plantagenet, Lord Lisle: Lord Deputy of Calais, 1533–40 – which TSE had encouraged at the first.

TO *Brian Coffey*   CC

16 July 1934   [*The Criterion*]

Dear Mr Coffey,

I was glad to get your letter from Dublin and to hear that the past academic year has been so very successful.

I am always doubtful about studies of the work of living authors.[1] At any rate to judge from my own experience, they make the author himself feel quite dead and efficiently buried. However I do think that criticism of modern poetry from a scholastic point of view, done by someone like yourself, who knows both modern poetry and scholasticism, might be extremely useful at the present time, and I shall await further news of your undertaking with great interest.

With all best wishes and hoping to see you if you pass through London in the autumn.

Yours very sincerely,
[T. S. Eliot]

She published too *Common or Garden Child: A Not-unfaithful Record* (1942), with this blurb by TSE: 'This is an unusual account of a usual child – or at least, as the title denotes, that is what the author considers herself to have been. It is not an autobiography, nor is it an evocation of a period, but an attempt, renewed at intervals over the space of twenty years, to remember – and to revive the experience of life of a small person early in this century. Whether this was, after all, a "common or garden" child the reader must judge for himself: another possibility is that every child is an exception from this category, but that only a writer of uncommon sensibility, memory and skill in expression can elicit the uniqueness of any childhood.'

1 – Coffey wrote (n.d.): 'During last year I saw several editors about a projected study of your work and influence. But, as they did not become very definite – I had no manuscript to show them – I have now decided to write the study, and then to try these editors again.'

17 July 1934   [Faber & Faber Ltd]

Dear Auden,

I was glad to get your letter of the 13th after having had no news of you for such a long time.[1] If you haven't succeeded in getting hold of a copy of *The Orators*, will you let me know and I will find one myself.

I now find also that the poems will be out of print before very long, and I should like to know whether there are any corrections to be made in any of them before we start re-printing.[2] What I am in favour of is to reprint the poems and keep the book in stock in its present form and publishing your new lot with the play. I am sure it would be better policy to wait till the play is ready rather than to publish the new lot of poems by themselves. I believe that the public is now expecting more dramatic work from you and if the poems appear without the play people might be disappointed; and there is always the danger of reviewers muttering merely more of the same stuff. I believe that the play would be a great advantage to the next book, although it seems a long time to wait.

I noticed that the *Times Literary Supplement* critic believed that I had learnt something to my advantage in writing *The Rock* by studying *The*

1 – 'There are several corrections to be made in the *Orators*. As soon as I can get hold of a copy, I will send you them.

'As to another book, I have been working for some time on a long play, which I hope to get finished by about next Easter. The trouble is that during the term time it is almost impossible to get anything connected done. One is too tired even when one has the time. Having read "The Rock" has done me no good either, as I have to spend some time resisting the temptation to imitate . . .

'It seems a long time since I saw you. I should be passing through town at the beginning of September, so I hope we shall meet then.

'I enclose a copy of our school magazine in case the boys' work should interest you . . .

'P.S. There are enough poems, I think, for a book by themselves, but I think it would be better to wait till I have finished the play. What do you think?'

2 – FVM to WHA, 9 Aug. 1934: 'We want to put in hand a reprint of the POEMS as well as the reprint of THE ORATORS. I gather that the corrections for THE ORATORS have been received and that that reprint has been arranged; but in Eliot's absence I cannot find any record about the corrections of the POEMS. He wrote to ask you whether you had any, and it may be that you let him know; but there is, unfortunately, no trace of the answer.

'Could you let me know? I am sorry to bother you again, but the stock is low and the reprint is becoming urgent.'

WHA to FVM, 12 Aug. 1934: 'There are no corrections to be made in *The Poems*.' He added, 'Will you tell Eliot when you see him that the play I wrote to him about is just finished, and that I will send him a copy as soon as the typeing [*sic*] is done.'

Dance of Death. One is never fully aware of these things oneself but I am glad if I have profited from your work.[1]

Your *Badger* (by the way what is the symbolism of that name, not the usual I hope?) is quite interesting, and the boys have nice faces.[2] I like Mr Yates' oil painting but I have not yet had time to read much of the prose or poetry. It reminds me, however, to send you a book which appears to be very much in your line. If you have time do let me have a review of it whenever you like, if you find it worth it. It is a collection of children's plays performed at Dora Russell's school.[3]

I look forward to seeing you in September. I am pretty certain to be here during the first week and probably away the second week.

Yours ever,

[T. S. Eliot]

1 – 'Mr Eliot's Pageant Play', *TLS*, 7 June 1934: 'Mr Auden is another experimenter; he is marked by strangeness and an arrogant threatening of a doomed society, as he sees it. Him, too, Mr Eliot recalls on occasion:–

Though you forget the way to the Temple
There is one who remembers the way to your door.

His gift of parody may unconsciously lead him to this. But conscious parody appears elsewhere, as in the Communists' verses – typographically parodied also.

'The scene where this occurs, set in 1934, is most characteristic of the Eliot known through his poems ... The chorus, despondent, wonder if the young offer hope of better things. Bands of Redshirts and Blackshirts are questioned. Their replies are, with exaggeration, unsatisfactory. The chorus says: "There seems no hope from those who march in step." A Plutocrat enters, criticizes the Church and, instead, offers to the crowd a golden calf, for which they fight. As a comment on our modern situation, it cannot be said that in this the pessimism of *The Waste Land* has been abandoned.'

Michael Sidnell, in *Dances of Death: The Group Theatre of London in the Thirties* (1984), argues that WHA's play was an influence on *The Rock*: 'Eliot's ophidian Plutocrat ... is a close equivalent of Auden's Theatre Manager ... The Redshirts and Blackshirts portrayed by Eliot ... strongly resemble Auden's Chorus in its Communist and Fascist phases. As in *The Dance of Death*, Eliot uses choric formations, facile rhymes and broad caricature for his satiric effects.'

2 – *The Badger* was the school magazine of the Downs School, where WHA taught, 1932–5.

3 – Dora Russell and Bertrand Russell set up in 1927 a 'free' school (akin to A. S. Neill's progressive school Summerhill) at Carn Voel near Land's End. In 1932 she separated from Russell, but the school carried on for a long time. See Rosemary Dinnage, '"Human beings are what's needed"' (a profile of Dora Russell), *Times Educational Supplement*, 28 Mar. 1980, 21–2: 'In *The Right to be Happy* [1927] I wrote: "Animals we are and animals we remain, and the path to our happiness lies through our animal nature." T. S. Eliot said if I could think that, I wasn't fit to bring up children!'

TO *Hallie Flanagan*

18 July 1934   [Faber & Faber Ltd]

Dear Mrs Flanagan,

Thank you for your letter and for sending me the 'Delian Apollo' and the essay, both of which I have found very interesting.[1] I expect to be in London when you arrive and shall count upon you to let me know, so that we may have an opportunity of meeting and discussing these things.

With all best wishes,
Yours sincerely,
[T. S. Eliot]

TO *Ezra Pound* TS Beinecke

19 July 1934   *The Criterion*

Ezzling my blessling the prooves of a book which you will he intrested to Ear we have decided to call by the novel tittle of *Make It New*[2] are proceeding prettily BUT my Eye having fallen on the text of a sonnet by Mallarmé I saw a verb *brûle* it said and Coo! I says I'll be hooooooooooo I

1–Flanagan wrote from Athens, 8 May 1934, to say she had been spending much time on Delos (birthplace of Apollo). She enclosed some translations that she called 'Chorus for the Delian Apollo'. 'Then, too, I've been studying ancient theatres in Sicily and North Africa and Greece – and wondering about the chorus – I also enclose an article on the chorus because it explains how the Chorus to the Delian Apollo ought to be done – now by a full chorus, now by individual or group dancers.' She wrote again on 28 June: she would be back in London from 29 July – 'perhaps we can talk a little about the Chorus to the Delian Apollo'.

2–*Make It New: Essays by Ezra Pound* was to be published in Sept. 1934, with this blurb by TSE (with FVM's help): 'This is the first volume of Mr Pound's critical essays to be published in England. From two volumes of collected papers, both unobtainable in this country, and from his edition of the Poems of Guido Cavalcanti, published in Florence, Mr Pound has chosen seven long essays which form a whole, and has written an introduction for this new volume.

'This series of essays, each dealing with one of the significant points in the development of European literature, and ranging from the Troubadours to Henry James, represents only one aspect of Mr Pound's prose writing. The essays serve, however, to confirm the growing awareness that his criticism is neither haphazard nor capricious, but is a coherent defence of essential literary values. They will also, to many readers, reveal Mr Pound as the most vitalizing critic in our time.'

FVM to EP, 28 June: 'You orta see the beeyewty blurb pawsum & I compressed in a moment of unsleep . . .'

Contents: Date Line; 1. Troubadours: Their Sorts and Conditions – *about 1912*; II. Arnaut Daniel – *1920*; III. Notes on Elizabethan Classicists – *before 1918*; IV. Translators of Greek – *before 1918*; V. French Poets – *February 1918*; VI. Henry James and Remy de Gourmont – *August 1918 and February 1919*; A Stray Document; VII. Cavalcanti – *1910/1931*.

mean h . . . . if I dont think that oughtnt to be *brûlé* so I turns up the *NRF* definitif Poésies and blasted if I wasnt right Well then I looked into the Matter. and I found 6 other small errors in that and the next Podesta I presume these minute errata exist only in the additional matter prepared by you in Italy which has no doubt Caused some blunting of your sensibility towards French tongue, and that the Liverwright edition from which we set up was correct because being cut off from my books in any case I cant verify the whole lot of these poems theres was two small errattums in Gourmont I believe Athènes is right also Pourrions. I have No doubt the Wop stuff[1] is all applepie I am elpless there

ABC[2] is being reviewed by Bridson I dont kno if he is right man or not[3]

Here you are a Ware that canotetoes cantose would have been acceptable in the Mortuary[4] A Quarterly Review at any time but you never offered any on the contrary you said etc of course that was some time ago but why should not a intelligent man change his Mind Im askin you not sure about room in September but send it along one at a time one at a time or perhaps two in any case at this Rate the choirs where late the etc will he bare and Ruined[5] before the book comes along so send some along send them along Before the fall of the Leaf Shall I go to Social Credit Congress at bracing Skegness or not that is a Question now Why dont you Podesta concentrate your views on What the World Needs into 900 words and send it to New Britain they wont pay but they will probably print it tell um with my urging you send etc.[6] They do print a lot of bull shit which is a Pity well no more for the Present so will close

TP

1 – TSE is picking up EP's term from the previous letter.

2 – *The ABC of Reading*.

3 – Bridson review of *ABC of Reading*: C. 14 (Oct. 1934), 123–5.

4 – One of EP's wisecracks was to refer to the *Criterion* as the *Crematorium* and *Moratorium*.

5 – 'Bare ruined choirs, where late the sweet birds sang' (Shakespeare, *Sonnet* 73, l. 4).

6 – TSE, 'In Sincerity and Earnestness: New Britain As I See It', *New Britain: A Weekly Organ of National Renaissance* 3: 62 (25 July 1934), 274: 'It is probable that the politicians, bankers, economists, &c. of tomorrow will be the same sort of people as those who pursue these vocations today . . . I do not suggest that all vocations will remain the same in New Britain . . .

'The Churches cannot, of course, pick out any one political form and maintain that it is essential for the Christian Life; but they can and should denounce any political form which is either hostile to or subversive of the Christian Life. Nothing accordingly need be said about the necessary Christian attitude towards Communism, except to repeat the obvious warning against accepting any other form simply because it is anti-Communistic. As for Fascism, we have been told by its English exponent [Oswald Mosley] that it "synthesizes" the Nietzschean and the Christian doctrines. The Christian ought to know what to think about a doctrine which "synthesizes" Christianity with something else. And the Christian

TO *Algar Thorold*

19 July 1934 [Faber & Faber Ltd]

My dear Thorold,

I have thought a good deal about your letters of the 15th and 17th and have discussed the situation at length with the Chairman and Mr Morley.[1]

While we see very readily the difficulties that you have discovered, we are very doubtful of the prospect of a Hulme book if the other matter (about which, beyond doubt, you know more than anyone, certainly any layman, in England) cannot be treated too. A book exclusively about Hulme ought, I believe, to treat of all departments of his activity. In some of his fields of thought you say you are ill equipped, and are certainly not specially interested. That is the trouble with a full length book on Hulme; I can't think of anyone who is qualified to cover all of Hulme's interests. I am, like you, most interested in his theological side; Herbert Read could

---

cannot possibly agree that any simply political reorganization can be "the greatest cause and the greatest impulse in the world".

'There is another ground for rejecting Communism and Fascism, which is simply that they do not appear to have any solution, or even any awareness, of our real and urgent economic problems . . .

'While the Churches cannot advocate any particular political system, or any particular economic machinery, they can and should oppose openly all systems that make Christian virtue more difficult of practice. The present system is worse than that: it elevates Christian sin into worldly virtue . . .

'We must remember that voluntary poverty is a high Christian state; but that involuntary misery or wage-slavery is an anti-Christian state . . .

'We need both intelligence and passion. Otherwise we are helpless against unintelligent passion. Both Fascism and Communism exhibit a diversion, to material ends, of passion which should only be devoted to religious ends.'

See further Richard Rees, 'Mr Eliot and "The Adelphi"', *New Britain* 3: 63 (1 Aug. 1934), 328; K. S. Shelvankar, 'Mr Eliot and Current Problems', *New Britain* 3: 64 (8 Aug. 1934), 362.

1 – FVM had assured Thorold that a contract for a book on T. E. Hulme was on the way, with a modest advance of £25. All the same, wrote Thorold on 15 July, 'various considerations have occurred to me in connection with the book as modified by your first letter to me on the subject.

'It was very evident in that letter that my original idea of a study of French philosophy – "from Pascal to Bergson" – seemed to you too exotic to give much hope of success . . . What I would now suggest is that I should do the "Hulme" for you – not of course forgetting his mental genealogy & affinities – and the French philosophers as such for someone else.'

On 17 July: 'I should also say that there are points on wh: I am out of sympathy. His "Action Française" side & all the "Athée catholique" business . . . There is also the fact that on his aesthetic criticism and philosophy, I feel myself very deficient. All this makes me rather doubtful. I feel myself exclusively interested in the religious philosophy side of him; but can it be so definitely distinguished? I am distinctly doubtful whether I am the man you want for the sort of book you propose.'

handle the aesthetics, but is weaker on general philosophy, and unfitted to tackle theology. (I am not sure that a real synthesis is possible, or that all of H.'s views are compatible).

Now, as the sum at stake is so pitiably small anyway, I do feel, frankly, that the best thing for you is probably to go ahead with the book you want to write, and which you have at your fingertips, leaving the 'Hulme' in abeyance. It does seem as if the Hulme work would entail far more labour than the book was worth financially to you. And if you do not succeed in getting the book on French Philosophers commissioned, I need hardly say that we should be very happy to consider it when it is done. (It is probably not wholly reasonable, but publishers will often accept books when they see them, that they would be too cautious to commission!)

My fellow-directors agree that, as things stand now, that is probably your best course.

Yours ever,
[T. S. Eliot]

TO *Leonard P. Moore*[1]   cc

20 July 1934   [Faber & Faber Ltd]

Dear Mr Moore,

I am returning herewith the typescript of Mary Butts' short stories, which came with your letter of June 28th.[2] I have always been interested in Miss Butts' work and also consider that it ought to be much more widely known than it appears to be at present. We are too doubtful, however, of the success of a volume of short stories at the present stage to be able to consider this projected work just now. What we should be interested in would be a full length novel of contemporary life of the kind

---

1–Leonard P. Moore (d. 1959), Christy & Moore, Literary, Film and Dramatic Agents, 222 Strand, London.

2–In the hope that F&F would add Mary Butts to their published list, Moore posted some 'specimens of some short stories she proposes to include in a volume which she is desirous of publishing'.

Mary Butts (1890–1937), writer, was married to the poet and publisher John Rodker (1894–1955) from 1918 to 1926; to the artist Gabriel Aitken/Atkin (1897–1937) from 1930 to 1934. Works include *Speed the Plough and Other Stories* (1923) and *Ashe of Rings* (1925). She remarked on 25 Dec. 1927: 'T. S. Eliot, with his ear on some stops of english speech which have not been used before, the only writer of my quality, dislikes me & my work, I think' (*Journals of Mary Butts*, ed. Nathalie Blondel [2002], 275). See further Nathalie Blondel, *Mary Butts: Scenes from the Life* (1998); *A Sacred Quest: The Life and Writings of Mary Butts,* ed. C. Wagstaff (1995).

that Miss Butts handles with such remarkable skill, leaving the matter of the short stories to be taken up at a later phase. We believe that this would be to the interest of Miss Butts as much as to that of her publishers.

Alternatively it has been suggested that Miss Butts might do a very interesting study of the life of one of the peculiar, more or less abnormal, propagators of religious or other cults, such as Oliphant. One or two obvious examples of contemporaries come to one's mind but it would have to be, of course, some figure from a slightly earlier period in order to avoid the obvious complications.

We should be glad to hear what you and Miss Butts think of these suggestions.

> Yours sincerely,
> [T. S. Eliot]

TO *Hugh Walpole*[1]   CC

20 July 1934   [Faber & Faber Ltd]

My dear Walpole,

I have heard that you are at present out of England but I hope, nevertheless, that this letter will reach you in time to perform its task.

In the last two autumn seasons we have experimented with the publication of a number of small and pleasant looking books for the Christmas market. The original intention was to supply a substitute for the failing inspiration of our 'Ariel' poets, and we have found that these small volumes at 2/6 each have sold quite as well for that purpose, as the shilling poems. I don't know whether you have seen any of these 2/6 volumes. They include a piece of Joyce's new work, poems by Sassoon, Herbert Read, and Auden, and a fragment of my own.

We should like to pursue the venture in a more comprehensive way, and we are wondering whether you have anything unpublished or in mind, which you want to write, of something like a suitable length. It might be of any form, either a long 'short' story or a self-contained part of an unpublished novel, or an essay.

1 – Novelist, man of letters, bibliophile, and generous patron, Sir Hugh Walpole (1884–1941) became first chairman of the selection committee of the Book Society and of the Society of Bookmen. His novels include *Mr Perrin and Mr Traill* (1911), *The Cathedral* (1922), and the Herries saga (1930–3). OM noted in her journal, 26 Mar. 1934, apropos a tea party with VW – 'old Hugh Walpole was a good butt to tease & laugh at. He knows Eliot & dines with him sometimes. I asked him if he was a "follower of Eliot"[:] he said E. was ashamed of him!'

None of the things we have published so far was written specially for the purpose, and we are appealing primarily in the hope of your having something on hand, though, of course, we should feel still more flattered if you were moved to some new piece of work.

We, of course, don't ask for any other rights than the right to publish in this particular form, nor do we require the right to sell the book in America, though, naturally, we should be glad to have it.

I am sending you, in order to give you some notion of the form, a copy of Joyce's *Shem and Shaun*, which is probably the one most worth possessing.[1] But we don't want to confine ourselves to the kind of public which is interested in Joyce, and I hope you can help us to make this list of books more catholic.

Yours ever sincerely,
[T. S. Eliot]

TO *Edmund Wilson*[2]

TS Beinecke

20 July 1934   *The Criterion*

Dear Wilson,

I was very glad to hear from you, as I had lost your address: that is to say, I have it on a letter of yours buried in a mass of manuscript and correspondence which I brought back with me, and which I have never had the time or courage to sort out.[3]

---

1 – *Two Tales of Shem and Shaun: Fragments from 'Work in Progress'* (1932).
2 – Edmund Wilson (1895–1972), literary critic, cultural commentator and memoirist, worked in the 1920s as managing editor of *Vanity Fair*; later as associate editor of *The New Republic* and as a prolific book reviewer. Works include *Axel's Castle: A Study in the Imaginative Literature of 1870–1930* (1931) – which has a chapter on TSE – *The Triple Thinkers: Ten Essays on Literature* (1938), *The Wound and the Bow: Seven Studies in Literature* (1941); and the posthumous *Letters on Literature and Politics 1912–1972* (ed. Elena Wilson, 1977). TSE to Geoffrey Curtis, 20 Oct. 1943: 'Edmund Wilson is a very good critic except that, like most of his generation in America, he has mixed his literary criticism with too much political ideology of a Trotskyite variety and perhaps he is also too psychological, but I have a great respect for him as a writer and like him as a man.' See too Wilson, 'T. S. Eliot and the Church of England', *The New Republic*, 24 Apr. 1929, 283–4; 'T. S. Eliot', *The New Republic*, 13 Nov. 1929, 341–9.
3 – Wilson wrote on 26 June 1934: 'Thank you very much for sending me *The Rock*. I like parts of the choruses, and if the rest of it doesn't seem to you up to your standard, I blame it on the fact that the scenario was imposed on you. – Your point of view and mine are so far apart that there is no use arguing about them, but it does seem to me that you ought to explain how the building of forty-five churches is going to provide "work for us all".'

I wish that you might turn up here at some time, and give me the opportunity of returning your very generous hospitality. But in any case, I wish to say that I should like you to regard the *Criterion* as a possible vehicle for an essay now and then.

Yours ever sincerely,
T. S. Eliot

TO *Ottoline Morrell*

TS Texas

20 July 1934   Faber & Faber Ltd

My dear Ottoline,

I am so sorry that I could not come yesterday afternoon. I hope to see the Bussys in the autumn.

I will come on Thursday, then, to meet Miss Williamson.

I think my sister and niece greatly appreciated your asking them and enjoyed having tea with you, though they are not very vocal. And I very much appreciated it too. My sister has suffered from youth from the conviction that she was the most ill-favoured and least intelligent of the family, and is rather tied up in consequence.[1]

Affectionately,
Tom

1 – TSE guided Marian and Theodora to tea with OM on 17 July; the other guests were Juliet Huxley, Simon Bussy and his wife Dorothy (Strachey), Stephen Potter and T. Sturge Moore.

OM's journal (BL), 19 July: 'Yesterday I had T. S. Eliot to tea and his sister & niece. He looked ill & grey & unwholesome rather. The sister is such a complete Old Maid as hardly exists in England now – a specimen. She must have been very pretty once – a quite [?queer] charming face. – Niece tiresome – silly & conceited – & Ignorant.

'He was as I thought he would be rather reserved & formal . . . in their presence . . .

'I had the impression that Tom was happier than he had been & was more relaxed & certainly less strained.

'It is very good of him to look after the Relations. They are very Trying – as you can imagine from this photograph.'

TO *Paul Elmer More*   TS Princeton

20 July 1934   *The Criterion*

My dear More,

Your letter of the 4th July was a welcome surprise, as I had not expected to hear from you again so soon; and your generous praise gives me encouragement at a time when it is needed.[1]

I was very much struck by Cowley's book, but not in a favourable sense.[2] It was interesting by the obvious sincerity of his feelings about the *Waste Land*, though I wonder whether he was aware of what was 'wrong' about it quite so quickly as he intimates. On one point I think the poem was, at the time, and to some extent still, misjudged. I was not aware, and am not aware now, of having drawn a contrast between a contemporary world of slums, hysterics and riverside promiscuity etc. with any visibly more romantically lovely earlier world. I mean there is no nostalgia for the trappings of the past, so far as I can see, and no illusion about the world ever having been a pleasanter place to live in than it is now. There is no *time sense* there, in that literal way; the glories and the sordors are both aspects of futility.

But what interested me about Cowley's book was his prodigious effort to make an episode in the life of a few young people, not many of them of any important talent (Hemingway probably the best, and what a sad best!) into something of continental importance for America. (Incidentally, they left Montparnasse a pretty messy place instead of the rather quiet and industrious artists' quarter that it was in 1910, anyway). He makes a significant figure out of that poor neurotic, Harry Crosby. I have no desire to cast stones at that young man as a war-shocked waster with talents which he wasted, and financial and social advantages which he abused. Why should such a figure be elevated to the symbol of a generation's malaise? Cowley is so very very parochial, his vision so narrow, his values so distorted. I suppose he considers himself a very hard one, but surely there is something very *soft* at the very inside, and some shrinking from reality? Am I wrong?

1–'Since I wrote last I have been rereading *The Rock*, and closer acquaintance with the work strengthens my delight in it as an outspoken expression of your true self.'
2–Malcolm Cowley, *Exile's Return* (1934). Cowley (1898–1989), fellow traveller; literary editor of the *New Republic*; friend of Hart Crane. See further *The Long Voyage: Selected Letters of Malcolm Cowley, 1915–1987*, ed. Hans Bak (2014).

I dare say we shall be more agreed about Joyce than you expect.[1] I am probably prepared to admit that he is a great writer gone wrong, so long as it is admitted that he is a great writer, and his errors are of a very different seriousness from those of the majority of talented drifters and provincials of our time.

When I come, I shall certainly try to include a visit to you in Princeton – rather longer, I hope, and without the distraction of a public performance.[2]

Yours affectionately,
T. S. Eliot

TO *I. A. Richards*

TS Magdalene

20 July 1934   *The Criterion*

Dear Richards,

Many thanks for your letter.[3] I hope that by the time you return I shall have an uncracked record to offer you. There is perhaps something to be said against, as well as for, an author reading his own works. For the reader of rather slow perceptions, there seems often to be great help in it; but for the alert and sensitive appreciator of poetry it may merely provide an interposition of the author between reader and poem. In any case, I don't maintain that the author's reading is the only 'right' one – which certainly brings one to the threshold of the very obscure problem you touch on in your letter. I should expect that there would be fewer ways of reading bad poetry than good: bad poetry being either vague (and so not an utterance at all) or literal, and so not poetry.

This problem interests me in a practical form in dramatic poetry. I mean that owing to the necessities of the form, of presenting definite

1 – 'You may be interested, or alarmed, or disgusted, or just amused, to know that I have undertaken to write an essay on Joyce . . . What you say about the Christian sense of moral values in *The Dead* as compared with Katherine Mansfield and D.H.L. appeals to me as acute and thoroughly right. Joyce I hope to show is a genius and a moralist gone to the bad through false theories of art and of life. I trust this does not shock you too much.'

2 – More had written: 'I do hope you will fashion your plans so as to include a real visit to me here in Princeton. If I may say it without self-flattery and without offence against the reticencies of polite speech, I feel myself at the bottom of my heart, whatever superficial differences there may be, more in unison and sympathy with you than with any one else I meet.'

3 – IAR wrote, 29 June: 'I should long ago have told you how I have liked *The Hallow Men* [*sic*] and *Gerontion* as they are recorded . . . Now I've heard you reading them so often, I don't know how I should read them or how near it would be to the way I used to read them before' (*Selected Letters*, 81–2).

human beings in human actions, the play has to have a fairly consistent *skin* of literalness, and the excitement comes with the tension between this literal action and the implications of poetry. I get more excitement, for instance, out of the 'poetry' in say Racine or Shakespeare, than in a writer of the type of Mallarmé, whose form requires the minimum (perhaps less than the minimum) of literalness. It's all something to do with that 'other world' of action going on, of which I once spoke in connexion with Chapman and Dostoevski. These two are interesting specimens because the dédoublement[1] is so apparent; but I am not sure that it is not present in all great poetry.

Something might be elicited even from a study of what is called 'children's poetry'. Bad children's poetry is poetry written for children; the eminence of Lear and Carroll is due I believe to the fact that they wrote primarily to please themselves, not the children.

I think that the verse in *The Rock* does at times get too near to what I have called literalness, to be really important – perhaps very often. And one had to stick to very crude symbols.[2]

I sent a book of Coleridge's *Treatise* on Method to you in Cambridge.[3] If you don't want to do anything with it, there is no one else whom I want to give it to, that's all. A centenary volume appeared (with Blunden of course) mostly bilge, I think.

Spencer is now in Austria – I wonder if he has not tried to get in touch with you to join them there, somewhere in the Salzkammergut, I fancy. In any case he should be in England by the time you return.

> With best wishes to both,
> Yours ever,
> T. S. E.

1 – Writing in his 'Commentary' about the functions of irony, TSE noted its 'use (as by Jules Laforgue) to express a *dédoublement* of the personality against which the subject struggles' (C. Apr. 1933, 469). (See further Lee Oser, *T. S. Eliot and American Poetry* [1998], 33.) VHE was to note in her diary (31 July 1935): 'I see now the significance of the French word *dédoublé*. It was used a *great* deal when I was at the Sanat. de la Malmaison. So, as Edith Lawrence always said, I seem mad, but *am right* – I presume that back in 1926 they were faking up a double for T. S. Eliot.' *Dédoublement* – now known as multiple personality – was first discussed in 1875 by Eugène Azam: see further Ian Hacking, *Rewriting the Soul: Multiple personality and the science of memory* (1995), 159–70.

2 – IAR reflected on *The Rock*, which he had seen twice – once with TSE: 'Hearing it a second time – without your presence as a kind of orthochromatic screen – the prose-scenes and the verse seemed to me fall apart, to become not merely as different planes but actually discrepant, the prose profaning, where it touched the same matter, what was worthily handled in the verse' (*Selected Letters*, 82).

3 – IAR's review *S. T. Coleridge's Treatise on Methods*, by Alice D. Snyder: C. 14 (Jan. 1935), 308–11.

TO *Mary Hutchinson*   TS Texas

22 July 1934   Faber & Faber Ltd

Dear Mary,

I had a message to the effect that dinner was tomorrow night (Monday) at 8. I presume black tie, unless I hear to the contrary.

Can you think of any people whom I could approach to contribute 5s. a week for a year for a young Poet? I have two subscribers, but I want eight, to get him about £100 for that period. They would have to take my word for him, and I won't guarantee anybody to be a poet – but he is as good a gamble as any I have met. Within that time, he should either have some little reputation, or have failed of it – then he must get an ordinary job. He isn't eligible for any of the ordinary hacking, or schoolmastering, or the usual things, because he has had very little education. He has just had a Baby, and is very hard up, but can apparently live on very little. I am writing about this, because I don't want to discuss him publicly: he should not know who the contributors are, and it would be better if as few people as possible except the contributors knew anything about it. (This has no connexion with the Rupert Doone lot!)

I look forward to seeing you tomorrow.

                                     Yours
                                     Tom

TO *Ezra Pound*   TS Beinecke

23 jugglio [July] 1934   Faber & Faber Ltd

Podesta it is refreshin strike me Dead if it aint to meet a man to admit his limbitations so touchinly modestly etc as you well I never I always said now didnt I theres some subjects on which the Buck Rabbit is touchinly ignorant such as French literature, drama, philosophy and theology *exceptin* Lope de Vega etc. Japanese drama, Javanese hip dancing, some French literature in the middle ages and some scholastic or pre-scholastic works to me be found in Migne of which He as a Spattering. As for your general thinkin ability Podesta the less said about that the Better specially as thats my weak Point to and we mustnt let down the Union Podesta I have been rereading Marianne's Poem about the Gerboa and it come to me like that maybe Hes not a Rabit at all but a Gerboa a Little Animil wich I understan does illustrate the Quantum Theory by bein at two Places at once even if he dont understand it Podesta it was Never I what sent you

Frankie's book[1] & I was always Sceptical about Him especially after his letting the Banks reopen besides Podesta I thought that was just a usefull exercise you was lettin off besides it is not intelligible to Engelsk readers no I dont mean Quite what you think although I admit my old friend Bronson Cuttin[2] seems more alert than most of our peers what I mean is nobody has ever heard of Hull or Woodin or Wigin Who is Beevers[3] Besides you dont seem to have answered my last letter yet of perhaps not at all of my letter Our little friend thinks he might like a seal of a whale thats his business not mine only if and when the next whale turns up on your lido you might tell your Boy to make a few rough sketches in case I shall be visiting the zoo before long and will verify the enclosed but sir rabbit I didnt know as I was Plurial, so will close for themoement yours sir

TP

TO *Rupert Doone*   TS Berg

25 July 1934   Faber & Faber Ltd

Dear Mr Doone,[4]

I am glad to hear from you further about your plans, and sympathise with you on the point of theatrical construction.[5] I don't see how I can

---

1−FVM, who met President Franklin D Roosevelt in the USA, wrote to EP on 24 Apr.: 'I send a copy of On Our Way which the big boss has just autographed for you. What transpires from the text is primary that he is a decent feller.' On Our Way (1934) outlined Roosevelt's economic programme including the New Deal. EP thought it was a review copy and promptly submitted a review to C., chasing it on 15 July: 'Wot I wanter kno IZ/ wotter bout my note on Frankie . . .' (Yet FVM had explained to EP, 2 May: 'I don't believe you have been studying the mathematics studiously else you would scarcely be writing 300 page reviews of Frankie without consulting the Big Boy [TSE] whether he wants anyfin so up to date as Frankie in the *Criterion*.')

2−Bronson Cutting (1888−1935), who was TSE's contemporary at Harvard, served as a US Senator for the Republican Party. See further *Ezra Pound and Senator Bronson Cutting: A Political Correspondence, 1930−1935*, ed. E. P. Walkiewicz and Hugh Witemeyer (1995).

3−EP, 15 July: 'Do you know the plural BeeverS? now on "Time and Tide".'

4−This letter was previously published in Browne, *Making*, 39.

5−The Group Theatre had received an expression of interest from Dartington Hall in Devon, but the trustees there had decided to put off a decision until 1935. In the meantime, Dartington Hall was proceeding to reconstruct its stage, though without consulting the producers who might wish to use it. 'The producer is never consulted over theatres. That is why so often they are reconstructed, I imagine.' Doone went on: 'One thing that would make me happier, would be if we could count on a new play from you?? If ever we are to have a season we shall need a background of more than 2 plays . . . Wyston [*sic*] has promised his play for October. He has only gussed [*sic*], I imagine, at the date, it might easily [*sic*] be later.'

definitely promise a play at any particular time. With the amount of time I have to give, there might be a full year's work in writing one play, and one can never anticipate what distractions and interruptions might not appear during that time. In any case it is extremely unlikely that I could even think of finishing it until next summer.

If I write the play I have in mind, it would require a chorus, and my recent experience warns me that choruses need long and arduous training.[1]

I hope that your summer programme will be very successful.

Yours very sincerely,

T. S. Eliot

TO *W. H. Auden* CC

25 July 1934　　　　　　　　[Faber & Faber Ltd]

Dear Auden,

I have just had a letter from Doone telling me that he expects a play from you in October. I haven't told him that you mentioned next Easter to me because that is none of my business, and also you may have been referring to something else. But are there really two plays or is the October one now postponed to Easter? I am asking just in case there should be something in the autumn which might be published in the same way as *The Dance of Death*, but I hardly think that you can have meant that.[2]

Yours ever,

[T. S. Eliot]

1 – Doone responded on 26 July: 'It is curious that you should be contemplating a play with a chorous [*sic*], because we are concentrating this next year on the vocal side of the Group Theatre . . . Of course in "The Dance of Death", we tackled the most difficult of all forms of chorous [*sic*] work, that of singing words. (Auden, as you know had no experience of writting [*sic*] words for a singing chorous [*sic*]). I believe the secret of that is to have only key words that can be deciphered instantly by the listener . . .

'What I would like to announce was that you are writting [*sic*] a play which we hope to produce. It would help us very much.'

2 – WHA replied on a PC, postmarked 27 July 1934: 'No. There is only one play.'

TO *Hermann Broch*[1]   CC

25 July 1934   [Faber & Faber Ltd]

Dear Herr Broch,

I have been awaiting a letter from you as our friend Edwin Muir had told me that you might be writing to me.[2] I have read most of your essays with great interest and sympathy, and admire their quality. I might as well say at once, however, that the market for such a volume of essays, even when they are by a well-known English author, is very poor, and they could only be published at a definite loss. My private opinion is that such a volume could most successfully be published by the same firm as published your other works in this country. There is, on the whole, an advantage, both for author and publisher, in having one firm produce the whole of one's work.

I am very sorry because the quality of the essays fully justifies their publication here. I should, however, be glad to publish something more of yours in the *Criterion*. I should be glad to know if you had anything in mind which seemed to you suitable, or perhaps Edwin Muir could advise.[3]

With many regrets and most cordial good wishes,

Yours very sincerely,

[T. S. Eliot]

1–Hermann Broch (1886–1957): Austrian writer. TSE was to write to Alvin Johnson, The New School for Social Research, New York, 30 Mar. 1951: 'I should like to feel that I could support the candidature of Hermann Broch, because I do believe that he is an author who has to be most seriously considered for a Nobel Prize, but this belief is not one which I could defend from adequate knowledge of Mr Broch's writings. I have read a good deal of his *Death of Virgil*, but only in the English translation, and I hope that you will understand that it is not lack of goodwill on my part, but merely conscientiousness, that makes me feel that to know only a part of one work by a man, and that only in a translation, is an insufficient qualification for a sponsor, and I also feel a responsibility towards the Swedish Academy, all the greater because of their generosity to me.'

2–Edwin Muir wrote to GCF, 15 June 1934: 'I am sending herewith a volume of essays in German by Hermann Broch, the author of *The Sleepwalkers*. You may remember that selections from that book appeared in the *Criterion* . . . I have a feeling that this book would interest Mr Eliot; it is of wide literary and philosophical interest, and contains among other things a very fine essay on Joyce. Herr Broch would very much like Mr Eliot to see it . . .'

3–No further essay by Broch appeared in C.

TO *Donald Hastings*[1] cc

25 July 1934   [Faber & Faber Ltd]

Dear Hastings,

Many thanks for sending me the photograph.[2] I am glad to know that copies are obtainable.

I do hope that your show was a real success, at least by the modest ambitions which I suppose are imposed by the conditions of today. I wish very much that somebody would buy my head. Candidly I don't know anyone to whom to give it. I mean I don't know anyone who would want a bust of me if I gave it to them, and, apart from not being able to afford it, the last thing which I should ever want to keep in my own surroundings would be a bust or portrait of myself. This means no disrespect to yours, which you know I like, but having to look at oneself in the mirror every day takes the edge off the pleasure of contemplating one's own effigy.[3]

With all good wishes for the future.

Yours very sincerely,
[T. S. Eliot]

TO *Mary Hutchinson* TS Texas

27 July 1934   Faber & Faber Ltd

My dear Mary,

This is most kind of you. I had not meant to solicit you personally, because the same small number of people are always being asked to

1 – Donald Pierre Hastings (1900–38), English sculptor; son of the sculptor William Grenville Hastings (1868–1902); noted for ecclesiastical, architectural and portrait commissions.

2 – Hastings wrote on 18 July, 'I am clearing up after my show and selling off, if you would like to buy your head for £15 as it stands or in Bronze at £25 I should be prepared to sell at that price (half the advertised price at show), or it can be bronze plated, it would then be £20.

'I am very much indebted to you for having sat to me and your kindness in coming to my show and thank you very much indeed.'

3 – TSE's sister Ada wrote on 4 Mar. 1934: 'The photos of your bust have arrived. They are very good. The more I look at them the better I like them. At first I had to grow accustomed to the appearance of whiteness. It made the face seem unalive. But now the expression stands out. In bronze (Mr Morley says the bust is to be bronze) it will be a fine head, I should think. The expression does the family credit! Only a good background produces a face like that.'

VHE wrote in her diary on Fri. 18 May that she went by taxi with a friend to the New Burlington Galleries. 'I took with me 2 photographs (signed) of Tom. We went to look at a Bust (*Head*) which is labeled T. S. Eliot. We did not say anything. I refused to answer any questions. The sculptor – *Hastings* – was extremely polite & kind & considerate in *every* way. He asked us to sign his book. So we did' (Bodleian).

contribute to the same kind of cause; and it would be pleasant if one could interest a few people who had never been interested in that sort of thing before. However, I shall not refuse. If I could get one more 5s. subscriber that would be enough to start with – I believe £1 a week would mean a good deal to them; though I should like to get four more to make £2, but I dont suppose I can. With four, I should write to Barker and say that I had been asked by donors who wished to be anonymous, to take charge of the sums, and ask him if he knew some local bank through which it could be paid. If not, I would deposit the money (people could pay in such sizes as they found convenient, I think I would pay my whole amount at once) in a special account with my bank, and ask them to pay him a cheque once every four weeks.[1]

Yes, that is the sort of thing. I am going with them to Canterbury on Tuesday, and after bank holiday to Gloucestershire I think, for another week. And I am away this weekend and next, on my own. Wednesday I must go to see John Hayward, and Thursday I take them to the ballet. So I do not appear to have any time for a fortnight or more. But I will let you know as soon as I get back – there will surely be time to meet before you go away.

I enjoyed the other evening very much. I had never heard Leonard seriously tackled on his political theories before. I thought Jack had the better of it; I was surprised to find how antiquated some of Leonard's views appeared.[2]

I hope you will get rested – again grateful thanks.

Affectionately,

Tom

1 – VW noted, at a Hutchinson dinner on 23 July: 'Tom read Mr Barker's poems, chanting, intoning. Barker has some strange gift he thinks & dimly through a tangle of words ideas emerge. He thinks there is some melody some rhythm some emotion lacking in the Audens, & Spenders. Wants 5/- a week for this young man, who has wife & child' (*Diary* 4, 231).

2 – VW noted, of the Hutchinsons' party: 'Talk gets upon whether we frighten or are frightened. Tom said I made him feel I saw through all his foibles; which perhaps I do . . . Tom remained on the verge; yellow, bony; but I regretted having denounced the Rock – so much melancholy in his face . . . So to politics & then, what with Jack [Hutchinson]'s cross examination, & Tom's intentness, & . . . Leonard's specialised convictions, the argument blazed: how the Labour party wd come in: what it would do. But how can you make any such ridiculous claim Jack boomed. What is it going to do about unemployment, about agriculture? All these questions were put from the point of view of here & now, capable business men; L. ideal by comparison . . . They heckled L. between them . . .' (*Diary* 4, 230–1).

27 July 1934   [Faber & Faber Ltd]

Dear Maurice,

I am writing to you to ask if you can try to induce Vivienne to be reasonable in the matter of my property at Clarence Gate Gardens. I have there a considerable library, which is really necessary for my work; also some miscellaneous papers, some pictures of personal value (family matters), a little family silver and a few other such objects. I did not want to remove these things until the lease expired, as I assumed that she would be moving. Now she has taken on the same flat. My solicitors have asked, through James, that she should arrange for me to have these things taken away. James has told Bird that he can get no reply to his letters, and that one of his clerks who called found no one at home, and practically suggests that the only resource is for me to take legal action to recover my property.[1]

Now, I am naturally loath to do this, but if Vivienne persists in ignoring these appeals, the only thing I can do (as I am advised) is to apply for a writ. I must have these things which belong to me – some of them, as the books, I need; and others are family property – the absence of none of them would inconvenience her, as all of the furniture proper and fittings is excluded – as for furniture I only want the bookcases which belong to me, and which are useless without the books.

I felt that, before I applied for a writ for my property, I ought to let you know what the situation is; and ask you to use any influence you have, to induce Vivienne to consent to parting with property which is mine and which she does not need. I have talked this over with Bird, and have told him that I would write to you; and have told him that if I did not hear from you within a few days, or if I heard from you that you could make no impression upon Vivienne to accede immediately, I would authorise him to take the legal steps.[2]

1 – James had written to Ernest Bird (as Bird advised TSE in a letter of 20 July): 'As regards Mr Eliot's effects, we have written several times very urgently to Mrs Eliot but she takes no notice of our letters so we are afraid that legal proceedings will be necessary to enable your client to get possession of his property.' Bird added for TSE's benefit: 'I have told [James] that he may pay on your behalf the gas, electric light and telephone bills to the end of last month but that as from then your liability is at an end – in other words, that he is restricted to the £5 per week.'
2 – MH-W responded on 31 July that VHE had been away at Hastings. 'I think I am in pretty good odour at present & that she will listen to me if to anyone. I am writing today & will endeavour to see her the moment she returns to town, so I suggest that you wait a

I hope things are going well, and that your Lingfield excursion is successful.

Yours ever,

[Tom]

TO *Edith Perkins*[1]   MS Donald Gallup

30 July 1934   Faber & Faber Ltd

Dear Mrs Perkins,

As gratitude seems most genuinely expressed by pen – when one is incompetent to express it by word of mouth – I am taking what is certainly a painful action for my hand, and probably equally painful for your eye. I have already, not expressed, but at least 'formulated' my appreciation of your asking me so soon. I should like to formulate, if not express, my appreciation of a delightful weekend in a lovely household. From an experienced weekender. As the advertisements say, 'it is different'. I shall not try to trace the ramifications of gratefulness in detail; but my perceptions are at least superior to my power of expression, and I think exceed the need of it.[2]

Again with gratitude to you all,

Very sincerely

T. S. Eliot

That blanket story is just a yarn of Haysum's. The blanket was sat upon by the Indian Student and an elderly clerk in holy orders, and on the unblanketed side sat an elderly spinster (as I gathered from her luggage label, and she was going to Edinburgh to visit Mrs Penner) who had recently broken her ancle [*sic*] and complained to the cleric that it Retarded her Speed. So I sat indignantly on the same side with her.

---

week or so before taking any action & I will use all my efforts to get her to arrange about the books &c.'

1 – Wife of Revd J. C. Perkins; aunt of Emile Hale.

2 – TSE's sister Ada wrote to him, 28 Oct. 1934, in response to his gossip about the Perkinses: 'How could the Perkins family consume two roasts in two days? Our Sunday roast lasts every week until Thursday, or even to Friday sometimes. We had beef this noon, and probably shall buy no more meat till Friday's fish, and may have beef hash on Saturday!'

TO *Ezra Pound*   TS Beinecke

30 July 1934   Faber & Faber Ltd

Yassur Podesta I gass your bour right,[1] I kno I am Erritatin podesta I
cant elp it its something in my natur that just Erritates people exceptin
those what is Pure in eart and they are not Erritated only mildly amused
but what I have to say is to Ell with Francklin what about a canto for
December sein that there is no plausibility of the book before that given
date we might have a canto canto canto three cheers fot the Headmaster
three cheers for the governors three cheers for the Dean hip hip canto
cantoo cantooo yrs etc.

                              TP

P.S. Got any more southpaw laurel wreathes for me???

TO *Vernon Bartlett*   CC

1 August 1934   [Faber & Faber Ltd]

Dear Mr Bartlett,

I have read with a good deal of interest the story by Philip Jordan, which
you sent me.[2] I confess that I had never heard of him before; but that
means nothing. I was very much interested in this story, which is far above
the usual run of stories submitted to the *Criterion*. I don't, however, think
that this story quite succeeds. There is a sudden, and I think, disturbing
change of angle late in the story, from the point of view of the author, so
to speak, to the point of view of an eye-witness, and the two parts simply
don't fit. I think it would be a much more successful story if the author
didn't attempt to introduce himself as an eye-witness at the end. I suggest,
however, that this might be a good story to send to *Life and Letters*.

1–EP wrote (n.d.): 'Yerr a niritatin little kuss/ why don't you say what about that rev/ of
Frankie/ [Franklin D. Roosevelt's book]
    'I supposed the bk/ was a review copy/ and there is such a process as cutting when the
cake is too large . . . If you had said 900 words for Frankie/ you wd/ prob have got 900.'
2–Vernon Bartlett, director of John Quill Ltd (Literary, Lecture and Dramatic Agents),
submitted Jordan's 'A Love Story' on 6 July, and explained: 'He has written two novels
under his own name and several "shockers" under the name of Victor France, or, I think,
Philip Spain.'

At all events the story has interested me to the extent of making me want to see more of this author's work.[1]

Yours very truly,
[T. S. Eliot]

TO *Christopher Dawson*   CC

1 August 1934   [Faber & Faber Ltd]

My dear Dawson,

Thank you for your letter of July 28th.[2] I am thrown into some consternation by your saying that you would not have had anything to do with this Academy, if you had not thought that I was taking part. I hope that nothing that I have said in writing to you has given you the impression that I was definitely pledged to become a member. On the other hand it is quite likely that Bolshakoff has sought to give you that impression. I have tried throughout to make it clear to him that I was entirely friendly to the ideals of the organisation, that I was in accord with the statements on the Creeds and the three Encyclicals as a basis for defining the Christianity of the members; but that I was a very busy man, and that I did not wish to be identified with any society until I was convinced, not only of its utility, but of my own usefulness in it. I don't want if I can help it to give a lot of time to mare's nests, which one is constantly being invited to make one's bed in.

On the other hand I can assure you that I have no present intention of dropping the matter entirely or of retreat. I shall be very glad to attend the first meeting possible. So far the meetings have taken place mostly at Nashdom and at times inconvenient for me. Furthermore Bolshakoff wrote as if my attendance at this coming meeting would imply my becoming a member of his Academy. You may be assured that I will attend the next meeting I possibly can but without giving any guarantees in advance. I should certainly like an opportunity to confer with some of the other

1–FVM reported to TSE, in an undated note written on Bartlett's letter: 'I think he is worthy. The end seems to me to fail. This might do for *Life & Letters*, which wdn't be a bad title for its present construction. The first part, until the break, is good.'

2–'I do hope you will stick to the Academy in spite of its weaknesses. I should never have had anything to do with it if I had known that you were not taking part. But as things are it is difficult for me to resign, as B. has given all the undertakings for which I asked, & my only reason for standing out would be his own irresponsibility & that is not a reason that I can offer publicly.'

members. I presume that you know Sir William Milner, who is, I believe, a neighbour of yours.[1]

I should be very glad to publish your paper on the Catholic Philosophy of History in due course but I don't think I want to give up the paper which you sent me.[2] The fact that I don't see quite eye to eye with you on some of the matters there discussed is not a sufficient reason for not publishing an article, which certainly raises some of the most important questions of the day for people like ourselves.

Yours ever,
[T. S. Eliot]

TO *Messrs James & James*   CC

1 August 1934   [Faber & Faber Ltd]

Dear Sirs,

I thank you for your letter of July 30th with statement of sums owing by me to the Inland Revenue. There are one or two points on which I should be glad of enlightenment.

First, I should like to know where there figure the sums already paid on account, through yourselves.

Second, I should be glad to know what steps I can take to recover the Irish Income Tax. Do I take it that I have to pay the British Government before I can recover from the Irish?

Third, I note that while you have me down for £250 Director's fees etc. in 33/34, you put them at £500 for 32/33. This is incorrect: they were £250 in each year.

Yours faithfully,
[T. S. Eliot]

1–Dawson affirmed on 6 Aug.: 'Yes Milner is a neighbour of mine, an Anglo Catholic architect, very well off. I don't know his political opinions but I think he is a social crediter.'
2–'As to that article, I am wondering if you would care to have instead the paper I am reading at Oxford on the Catholic philosophy of history. It is a more serious piece of work than the other & perhaps more suitable . . .'

TO *W. H. Auden*   CC

2 August 1934   [Faber & Faber Ltd]

Dear Auden,

A friend of mine, a Mrs Payne, who writes under her maiden name of Dilys Powell, has written a book of essays on contemporary poetry, and has applied to the various authors concerned as well as to the publishers. I have gladly given her permission to quote from my poems. I saw her the other day and she said that she had received permission from all of the authors to be quoted except from yourself. I haven't seen the book but Mrs Payne seems to me a very intelligent woman, and I hope you can see your way to giving her the necessary permission, which is, I understand, only for a few lines consecutively. She told me that she had written to you but had had no reply. As she is in a state of uncertainty and her book is in suspense, I should be grateful if you would drop her a line in any case to say whether or no. The only other poets I know of as being concerned are Siegfried Sassoon and Stephen Spender, and I understand that they have both given permission.

Her address is 55, Connaught Street, w.2.

Yours ever,
[T. S. Eliot]

TO *W. B. Yeats*   CC

2 August 1934   [Faber & Faber Ltd]

My dear Yeats,

Our friend, Swami Shri Purohit, has tackled me lately in the matter of forwarding his designs for the publication of his translations from the Upanishads and other canonical literature.[1] I understand from him that you are acquainted with his translation of the Sankhya Bhysya Karika and the comments of Patanjali, and that you like them. I have myself only examined a translation of the Kena Upanishad, which seems to me excellent but I have not had an opportunity of comparing it with the only good translation I know, which is in German.[2]

1–Shri Purohit Swami – (1882–1941) Hindu philosopher, translator and teacher – and WBY translated *The Ten Principal Upanishads*.
2–Paul Deussen, *Sechzig Upanishads des Veda* (1897).

The Swami is anxious to enlist your support as well as mine but says he is diffident of approaching you as you have taken so much trouble on his behalf in the past. I think that what he wants is something in the way of prefatory notice and comment which might facilitate a friendly reception by editors.

The only periodical that occurs to my mind as a possible vehicle for such translations is the *Hibbert Journal*. I told him I was quite willing to write to the editor of the periodical on his behalf, although I don't know him personally. Indeed, at the moment I can't remember who the editor of the *Hibbert Journal* now is. In any case do you think you can do anything for him or can you make any suggestions to me?

Yours always sincerely,
[T. S. Eliot]

TO *Frank Morley*[1]

MS Faber Archive

13 August [1934]   Lechlade (i.e. in the lounge of the
Fleece, Cirencester)

Now Mr Morley Sir you mustn't expect anything in the way of a letter. Me being separated from my typewriter. Sir the New Inn has not belied you and is quite comfortable but I dont know about which elems elms from hornbeams But one is a bit homesick a weeny bit so far from the Commercial Road E. There are many boy Scouts. Now as to Marianne it will be a relief to you to know as Nothing can be done nothing the MS is at Grenville Place but All will be in order by Monday early Me returning on Friday & aving the week end.[2] *Hold* Pareto and Rundfunk for me my Hand is tired so will now close.[3] yrs rsp fly

T. S. Eliot

1–Frank Vigor Morley (1899–1980), publishing colleague and close friend of TSE: see Biographical Register.
2–FVM had asked, 9 Aug.: 'The Macmillan Co. of New York is wery anxious to have proofs of Miss Moore, her book, by the end of this month, or so soon after as plausible . . . I thought that you and Dick were counselling about it; but Dick persuades me he ain't yet heard nothing.

'In that case where is the Tar Baby and how can I get it to Dick pronto?'
3–FVM (9 Aug.): 'Dr Rudolf Arnheim's DER RUNDFUNK [*Radio*, to be published by F&F in 1936]; the first 84 German pages have arrived: I suppose they ought to be looked over before making a contract: when would, or could you look them over?? . . . One-and-a-half volumes of Pareto have turned up, but I don't propose to make your life hidjus with them till you get back.'

Pickwick X word makes some progress but always at the xpense of Pickwick.

I dont quite get ARCANE??

secrets?[1]

TO *Christopher Dawson*

CC

20 August 1934   [Faber & Faber Ltd]

My dear Dawson,

Many thanks for your letter of August 6th.[2] I have heard nothing from Bolshakoff for some time, but I assume from him not mentioning the matter that the projected conference at the beginning of this month did not take place. I still hold myself ready, without committing myself any further, to attend any conference within my power, preferably, of course, in London.

I agree with you that the scheme itself is a good one, and that it would be a pity if it came to nothing. One point that still puzzles me is that although nothing has been said about the financial aspect, it appears naturally that Bolshakoff would want a stipend. How, I wonder, are the expenses to be defrayed?

---

1 – The game was to take a crossword puzzle printed in a newspaper and to devise a fresh set of questions to fit the available number of clues and spaces. In the case of this particular exercise, FVM's new clue for 28 Across (nine letters) was 'What you must do to see Ralph Hodgson (2, 2, 5)', to which the answer was 'GOTOJAPAN'; or, for 2 Down: 'What Tom wears when swimming (6, 3)', where the answer is 'RUBBERCAP'. In the case questioned here by TSE, FVM had stretched his ingenuity so as to frame the question 'You know a secrets (6)', to fit a 6-letter space: the answer was of course 'ARCANA'. FVM responded to this letter on 14 Aug.: 'Dear Mistah Eliot, / I is ashamed for you; reelly ashamed. How you expect to hole yo haid up among classical people and not know the plural of "Arcanum" is "arcana". These yere arcana is sposed to be part of your pereperations, but now I guess you is all a pious fraud. I could blaret yo reputation wiv this, but I wont, not till after you have come through with Marianne.'

2 – 'I quite understand your position with regard to Bolshakoff's Academy. I feel myself that he is not the sort of person to make a good organizer for such a society. On the other hand I do think that the scheme is a good one: that such a society would have to be composed primarily of laymen & that if the leader or organizer were an Orthodox, it would probably be better than having either an Anglican or a Roman Catholic.'

294   TSE at forty-five

I am sorry that I could not come to the Summer School as the controversy between Hecker and Berdiev sounded very lively.[1] I hope you will send me your own paper.[2]

Yours ever,

[T. S. Eliot]

TO *F. O. Matthiessen*   TS Donald Gallup/Beinecke

20 August 1934   Faber & Faber Ltd

Dear Matty,

Many thanks for your letter of August 8th.[3] There has [*sic*] been considerable, and sometimes heated, discussions about your manuscript. In the first place, I haven't been allowed to see it, but both of the directors who had read it, speak of it with the highest praise. In the second place, I raised very strong objections to our publishing a book about myself, however good. This is not pure modesty, but the belief that it would be better all round, and much better publicity for me, if some other firm undertook it. Your first version is now, I understand, in the hands of the Oxford University Press, and I have heard from a friend of mine whom they asked to report on it, that he has recommended them to publish it. If they do not want it, I dare say we shall in spite of my personal protests. I look forward to seeing the revised version.

1 – 'I have just been at Oxford at the A. C. summer school . . .

'The Communist element was very sticky at this meeting, & if only Hecker [*sic*] had been a little less drastic in his elimination of God, I think he would have had the majority with him . . . I was rather struck by the evident appeal of Communism to the religious minded & the fact that there was no *moral* objection to revolutionary violence as there is, for instance, to war between nations.'

2 – Dawson wrote again on 31 Aug.: 'I forgot to say in my last letter that I had decided to let the A. C. summer school people have my paper, as they were very insistent. Of course I would much rather have published it in the *Criterion*, but I thought it would be rather redundant on top of that article you have already got, as they both deal broadly with the same subjects.'

He added too, 'I have finally let myself in for Bolshakoff's Academy, but I very much doubt if anything will come of it.'

3 – 'Having sent you what I thought was an almost complete manuscript [of *The Achievement of T. S. Eliot*], I am now somewhat embarrassed to have to report that ever since I arrived here [his vacation home at Kittery, Maine] a month ago I have been adding steadily, with the result that the whole is half as long again as the original draft. But I certainly won't inflict you with this, other than to say that I think its organization is much clearer and sharper – it is now divided into six chapters; and that my principal addition is a fairly long analysis of "Ash Wednesday" . . .'

I am glad to hear that you liked Charlottesville. I was enchanted with the place. I intend to propose myself for a visit to Kittery next summer.

With best wishes for the Mathias cat and yourself.

Yours ever sincerely,

T. S. Eliot

TO *W. B. Yeats* CC

20 August 1934   [Faber & Faber Ltd]

Dear Yeats,

Many thanks for your letter which I found on my return from the country.[1] I will write to the editor of the *Hibbert Journal,* and do anything else I can for the Swami.

I am very sorry that you did not let me know before about your poems. The *Criterion,* you must know, is always delighted to have anything you care to give it but, of course, verse especially. My October number, which actually is supposed to appear in the middle of September, has already gone to press, and I am afraid it is quite impossible to put anything else into it, but if you have anything which you could let me print in the December number, I should be delighted.

As for American periodicals, I do not know any that pay liberally nowadays, but I can recommend the *Virginia Quarterly,* published at the University of Virginia, Charlottesville. They do pay something, and if your main intention is to preserve copyright, I think it would be as good a vehicle as I can think of. You probably know the *Hound & Horn* in New York, which is a kind of successor to *The Dial.*[2] I think that might

---

1 – WBY wrote from Dublin (n.d.): 'Dear Eliot, All I could do for the Swami's book is write a couple of pages taking up some one point. I gave three months to my essay in The Holy Mountain but now I am writing against time to keep my sister's press going. His work wants one or other of two things, or both of them, to introduce it. One of those things is a scholarly introduction by a learned orientalist. [Francis] Younghusband would probably be ready to write such an introduction. The other thing (supplement or substitute) is a few words by some man of letters (not me; my bolt is shot). [. . .] It would be a mistake to send him forth again as my god-child . . .

'I have a good deal of verse. I have a short dance play just produced here with success. I have not sent it to you because you are a quarterly & I imagine my sister will publish it about Xmas. Your October number is probably full, and because I am shy about it. You have to insist upon certain characters in the verse you publish & I am of an older school. But can you tell me of any Review or magazine in U.S.A. where one can send verse.'

2 – *The Hound & Horn,* founded at Harvard and later published in New York, ran from 1927 to 1934. Editors included Varian Fry, Lincoln Kirstein, Bernard Bandler II, and R. B. Blackmur.

do equally well, though it is an irritatingly feeble production, and am sure would be delighted to publish anything of yours.

Yours ever sincerely,
[T. S. Eliot]

TO *Geoffrey Faber* CC

20 August 1934   [Faber & Faber Ltd]

Dear Geoffrey,

I am sending you, by registered post, the manuscript of *The Unfinished Universe*. I like the book very much in its present form and am prepared to recommend its publication on the lowest possible terms; say 10 per cent up to so many thousand, with no advance. The man came in and saw me this morning, and I was rather impressed by his appearance of sincerity. Says he intends to quit being a Methodist minister and become converted, but wants to publish the book first. It is a relief to find that he is in no particular hurry about publication. Says he intends to submit the book to Martin D'Arcy for his approval for publication, which step I strongly endorsed.

I found the book quite easy to read once I got started. What I should specially like you to consider is the first section dealing with the history of Greece, as I imagine you remember more Greek history than I have ever had the opportunity to forget. My first reading left me with the impression that, although what he had to say about Greek civilisation was extremely arresting, he hammered and repeated his point more often than was necessary, and one or two of the long quotations from Frazer or Gilbert Murray seemed to me unnecessary.[1]

1–GCF replied, 28 Aug., 'Right – I'll read some, at any rate, of the Unfinished Universe [by T. S. Gregory]. I also liked the man, & was predisposed in favour of the book.'

GCF wrote to Gregory on 6 Sept.: 'I am glad to be able to write making you an offer for the publication of "The Unfinished Universe". As you know, Mr Eliot read this and was much interested by it. I have not, unfortunately, been able to read the whole of the revised text myself; but I have read considerable portions of it, and I fully share Mr Eliot's view of the book.

'We should propose to publish it next spring, probably at 7/6, and to give you the following rates of royalties:- 10% to 2500, 12½% to 5000, and 15% thereafter, and to pay you at the time of publication a sum in advance and on account of future royalties equal to the amount earned by the number of copies subscribed.'

The Unfinished Universe (Mar. 1935) came with this blurb (presumably by TSE): 'This book is the record of a passionate and sincere pursuit of spiritual conviction, of the journey of one human mind. But the author, who was until recently a nonconformist minister in

I hope you have recovered from the effects of highland weather, and also that the swimming pool is no longer quite so empty as you depicted. I have just come back from a week in Gloucestershire with my sister where we didn't do so badly.

Yours ever,

[Tom]

PS. I am enclosing a letter from a lady named Ursula Roberts for your consideration in case the question of adding to the staff comes up. I am not sure whether I know Ursula Roberts or not, but if I do, she is either the wife of Ellis Roberts,[1] or of his brother, the Revd W. C. Roberts. In the former case she is an American bore. In the latter case she is a tartar. I am telling her that I have pleasure in referring the matter to you and (aside) am washing my hands of it. As the lady writes from Wales, that is an additional reason for your dealing with her.[2]

TO *Phyllis Woodliffe*[3]   CC

22 August 1934   [*The Criterion*]

Dear Miss Woodliffe,

It was very nice to hear from you and to be assured that you suffered no lasting ill effects from the fortnight's orgy – I have a photograph of you grasping the bottle of gin – and I am glad to know that you have had a holiday in Cornwall.

Now, *my* personal acquaintance with the stage, and what is much more important, with managers etc. is *very* limited; I was once mistaken for Leon M. Lion,[4] that's about all. I really am about the most helpless person to ask – though I still hope that my acquaintance (and influence) may become more extensive. I do know one troupe of ambitious young

Wales, has also elaborated a kind of Christian philosophy of history. He examines Greek civilization from a point of view which to many will be new and disturbing; he considers the Middle Ages and the Renaissance and Reformation, and finally the modern illusion; and he is led to conclusions from which the reader himself will find it difficult to escape. This is a book for the theologian, for the historian, and for every reader, however ignorant of theological science, who is interested in the Christian answer. An argument of absorbing interest, leads to a conclusion which the reader may or may not be prepared to accept.'

1 – Richard Ellis Roberts (1879–1953), author, editor; literary editor of the *New Statesman & Nation*, 1932–4; *Life and Letters Today*, 1934.

2 – 'I've written a nice NO to Mrs Roberts.'

3 – Phyllis Woodliffe (Wanstead Park, Essex), who had played 'Mrs Bert' in *The Rock*, asked TSE (n.d.) if he could recommend a good dramatic company which she might join.

4 – Leon M. Lion (1879–1947): English stage and film actor.

people, but their dramatic prospects at present do not seem likely to lead to anything more certain than starvation. Of course if I *do* ever get a play written, and what is more difficult, get it accepted, something might be possible, but at the most optimistic that would be not less than a year hence. I wonder if Browne could be of any use to you? But if chance should put anything in my way I would let you know.

With all good wishes,
Yours very sincerely,
[T. S. Eliot]

FROM *Frank Morley* TO *Bennett A. Cerf*[1]   CC

23 August 1934   [Faber & Faber Ltd]

Dear Bennett

I am typing this with my own fair hands, so you may conceivably expect some irregularities; but all that I say is from the horse's mouth & all above board.

We want Saroyan.[2] It isn't going to be easy sledding to put him over in this country. I don't see how we could better the terms which I cabled you last night: Viz:

   10% to 2500
   12½% from 2500 to 5000
   15% after

No advance; or say, if you prefer, accrued advance. Option on the next two books by Saroyan, on specified terms. The above applies to British Empire book rights, and though you will have covered Canada, we should like not to be shot if our agents should forward a few orders from there & we supply em. If we can place any second serial rights, we ought to go shares, don't you think?

1–Publisher, of Random House.
2–FVM to GCF, 16 Aug. 1934: 'I have, by the way, discovered a genius called William Saroyan; an Armenian living in California. I am struck all-of-a-heap with him. Dick [de la Mare] is rather bothered about him, and the Goblin [C. S. Stewart] can't see it at all. What makes it worse is that it is short stories.'

William Saroyan (1908–81), from Fresno, CA, was author of *The Daring Young Man on the Flying Trapeze* (1934). Novelist, playwright, screenwriter, essayist, Saroyan became a prolific author: later successes included *Inhale and Exhale* (1936); *The Time of Your Life* (play, 1939), which won the Pulitzer Prize (though Saroyan declined the honour) and the New York Drama Critics' Circle Award, and was adapted for a 1948 movie starring James Cagney.

Now as to the present book, DARING YOUNG MAN, the above offer ought to be conditional on some slight rearrangement. The prefuss don't go in this market, and T. S. Eliot suggests a little shuffling of the contents, in an attached memorandum. I am hoping there is nothing in these suggestions which would heartburn you or Mr Saroyan. They are suggested as helping to make this a wedge-book into the English market.

Win or lose, I am exclusively excited about the daring young Saroyan; want to handle him; hope you'll let.

Hurrah. Cheers. Yours
[F. V. Morley]

[Memorandum from TSE]   23 August 1934.

1. Omit Preface.

2. I suggest for the order

   1 Seventy Thousand Assyrians
   2 Snake
   3 Love, Death, Sacrifice and so forth
   4 1, 2, 3, 4, 5, 6, 7, 8
   5 The Earth, Day, Night, Self
   6 The Man with the French Post Cards
   7 And Man
   8 Seventeen
   9 Laughter
   10 War
   11 Harry
   12 A Curved Line
   13 Big Valley Vineyard
   14 A Cold Day
   15 The Big Tree Coming
   16 Dear Greta Garbo
   17 The Daring Young Man on the Flying Trapeze
   18 Among the Lost
   19 Three Stories
      ~~Love~~
   20 Aspirin is a Member of the NRA
   21 Sleep in Unheavenly Peace
   22 Fight your own War
   23 Common Prayer

There might of course be a number of arrangements just as good. But I want to start with Assyrians because that is straight stuff and something that ought to get everyone by the neck at once, and Snake is different enough to make anybody suspect that this man has a lot of picturecards in his fist. Then follow some more good 'short stories'. Then the juveniles, and I want to bury The Daring Young Man and Among the Lost in the middle of the book because they seem to me immature. Then some shorter and miscellaneous bits, following closely the American order – the social criticism should be felt more strongly towards the end, I think; and I should like to end with Myself upon the Earth because the portrait of the father seems to me a superb finale.

I should rather like to omit Love as following too conventional a pattern – there ought to be some bits at the end but the trap or the alarum clock or whatever you call it just doesn't go off. But I hesitate because it is not a long book anyway. If included I think it would be improved by being called 'Number 8' instead of 'Love'.

T. S. E.

TO *Clara Leiser*[1]   CC

24 August 1934   [Faber & Faber Ltd]

Dear Miss Leiser,

Your letter of the 13th has been forwarded to me here.

Unfortunately I do not know William Ellery Leonard[2], either personally or through his work. I have heard his poetry very highly praised, but I have never read any of it.

You see, I have to read so much contemporary verse, especially of course that of younger men, that in consequence I never read modern poetry if I can help it. I agree that contemporary opinions always form

1–Clara Leiser (New York) was engaged in 'a really serious undertaking' – a biographical and critical study of William Ellery Leonard – and she wished to 'have an estimate' of his work from his contemporaries. 'As you are one of the major American poets, I should like to know how familiar you are with William Ellery Leonard's work and, rather specifically, what you think of it.'

2–William Ellery Leonard (1876–1944), poet, playwright, translator and scholar; studied at Boston University and Harvard, and in Germany; taught English for many years at the University of Wisconsin; translated Aesop and Lucretius, and the Old English *Beowulf*.

an interesting document, whether the valuations are right or wrong. But I never know what I think about my contemporaries anyway; and reading their work is only disturbing, more so if it is good.

With many regrets,
Yours sincerely,
[T. S. Eliot]

TO *Ezra Pound*

St Bartholomews Day Hurrah.   Faber & Faber Ltd
anno XLVI [24 August 1934]

Dear Epsum yes Sir but yours too late about alterin that bootiful titel page[1] sir its too late we cant go bugrin about with that lovely bathroom idiogramme Hot & Cold becides what the hel aint essays good enough anybody what has enough mathematical ability to read your hoakum can probably count up to seven. Well I left your cantoes at home so they cant go off now to Hon. Farrer till Monday your command having arrived this morning Podesta do you know anythink about SALAZAR the dictator of Portugale they claim he is some kind of punkins[2] There is not much news here Orage bein on oliday but your wife has gone and sent me a pretty post card with a wreath of pansies on it whats that mean I want to Kno possums and pansies dont naturly lie together[3] Br. bear is off to the island of Egg with his phillibegs so everythink is at 6s and 7s poor old possum Barnum wasnt far wrong when he Said theres a poet born every minute[4] Listen to this: as these poems were conceived by the union of emotion and intellect, the reader will do well to bring both these faculties to bear upon them as they are read Thats what he says no I ask you what kind of coition is that. I have been Marking time for most of the last page because there is somethink else I Kno at the back of my Mind I had to say but there it is I cant remember Well I am now out of debt for the first time since 1927 and thats an awfully dismal feeling to have rabbit being out of debt makes one feel poor as dirt. Wishing you so will close

TP

1 – *Make It New* (F&F, 1934).
2 – EP answered, 26 Aug.: 'No, boss, I aint got no dope on th Portagoose Salazar . . .'
3 – EP replied, 26 Aug.: 'I try not to interfere with my wife's private life; but if she send you dem pan's eyes, I spekk you done som efink FURST.'
4 – The saying 'There's a sucker born every minute' is often attributed, without foundation, to the nineteenth-century showman P. T. Barnum.

TO *The Editor,* Social Credit   CC

27 August 1934[1]   [*The Criterion*]

Sir,—

Economics is a subject I have never been been able to understand, but
I suspect that one reason why I cannot understand it is that orthodox
economics rests upon moral assumptions which I could not possibly
accept, if they were laid bare. The moral foundations of Communism
and Fascism seem to me equally unacceptable, and their economic and
monetary theories, if any, do not seem to me to differ very interestingly
from the old theories. Furthermore, while I do not pretend that I
understand Major Douglas's theory yet, I cannot see that his opponents
are in a strong position, so long as they continue to support a system
which simply does not work.

                                Yours sincerely,
                                T. S. Eliot

TO *J. W. Scott*[2]   CC

27 August 1934   [Faber & Faber Ltd]

Dear Sir,

As Mr F. V. Morley, with whom you have been in correspondence, is on
holiday, I am replying to your letter of the 24th instant.

Mr Morley and myself are both warmly in favour of accepting your
proposal,[3] but the matter has not yet had the consideration of the other
members of the Board. I will bring the suggestion forward at our meeting
on Wednesday, and write to you before the end of the week.

---

1 – Published in *Social Credit: The Official Organ of the Douglas Social Credit Secretariat*,
7 Sept. 1934, 45. B. J. Boothroyd, editor of *Social Credit*, wrote on 6 Sept. 1934 to thank
TSE for his letter – 'part of which I had published in this week's issue'.
2 – J. W. Scott, Hon. Secretary, The National Homecraft Association Ltd., was a Professor at
the University College of South Wales and Monmouthshire, Cardiff.
3 – Scott proposed in a letter to FVM (24 Aug.) to write a short book (40,000–60,000
words) entitled 'Self-subsistence for the Unemployed: an economic study of the Homecraft
system'. He had written an article called 'Paradox of Progress', and a letter to *The Times*,
13 Aug. 1934. *Self-Subsistence for the Unemployed: Studies in a New Technique* (F&F) was
published in Jan. 1935.

May I tell you how very much I was interested by your article in *The Times*. I have long hoped that something might be done along these lines; and this experiment seems to open out great possibilities.

Yours faithfully,
[T. S. Eliot]
Director

TO *Ormerod Greenwood*   CC

28 August 1934   [Faber & Faber Ltd]

Dear Mr Greenwood,

I apologise for the delay in answering your letter, but I have been, owing to holidays and illnesses, without a secretary for some days and am rather in disorder.

I dislike speaking in public and do it badly, which is one reason why I take a long time in preparation. I am about as booked up as I can afford to be until the end of November. If you want me to do this I suppose I ought to; but could it be some time in December?[1]

I thought Auden did not expect to get his play done until next year.[2]

With best wishes,
Yours sincerely,
[T. S. Eliot]

TO *Ezra Pound*   TS Beinecke

28 August no 29 August 1934   Faber & Faber Ltd

Well ol Ezum Heres how it Is The Yale University Press has got to Hear about Seven Essays they dont know the right title That is to say Viginia Rice who is a sister of a woman whose husband is a professor at the University in Buffalo where I stayed once and they had some very nice sweet Port with the Soup she is the assistant to Gov. Cross whom I never heard much about but dont get her name wrong its Virginia Rice not Victoria Cross she writes to say what do we quote for sheets or for printing 1000 copies photographically Now it struck me there are two parts to this problem viz

---

1 – Greenwood (16 Aug.) invited TSE to give a talk for the Group Theatre in a series called 'The Theatre and the World Today'; he wished TSE to speak on 'The Theatre and Faith'.
2 – Greenwood announced in a postscript to his letter that WHA had finished a new play. (This would have been *The Chase*, which turned into *The Dog Beneath the Skin*.)

(1) What would the publishers of *Instigations* & *Payannes* have to say to this? Pollinger refuses to commit himself and says Thats none of his business and he wont soil his fingers with it so you see nobody knows but ol Ezum if he and its his business to give written undertaking etc. if the copyright is hizn and nothing to do with Knopf Liveright etc.

(2) The Yale University Press OUGHT to print and not take sheets if you said alright sheets we would get the best terms possible but not much in it for anybody. If they print from photographs besides getting better print than they have cases of over there anyway would be better. We should just get a fee and you would get a royalty. Anyway

This is all more your affair than ours but you say the word what you Want and we will negotiate Perhaps you would like to add Virginia Rice 175 West 72nd Street New York City to your correspondence List so will Close

Tp

TO *Donald Brace*

cc

29 August 1934   [Faber & Faber Ltd]

My dear Brace,

The Congregational Publishing Society, of 14, Beacon Street, Boston, have written me a letter about which I enclose a copy.[1] I am very happy to have the opportunity of pushing this little matter on to you. It seems to me quite impossible to change the title, and I am certainly not prepared to change it for publication in England. The title was not chosen by me in the first place, but by the people who commissioned me to do the job. It would cause no end of confusion if the published words were dissociated from the play as produced in June. But would you care to take the matter up with the Congregationalists?

1–Sidney A. Weston, General Manager of the Congregational Publishing Company, told TSE on 14 Aug.: 'Miss Mary P. Hamlin, the author of "The Rock" a play which we published for her in 1925, reports to us that you have recently published a play by this same title in England.

'Inasmuch as Miss Hamlin's play is used in England and has been produced several times there, we feel that the title of your play will be misleading to the English public and that it will have an unfavourable effect not only on our sales of "The Rock" but on your sales of the play.

'We are sure that upon being informed of this fact, you will realise the situation and will want to change the title of your play before any difficulty arises.'

Many thanks for the author's copies, especially as I am glad to have some in a less perishable form than our own edition.

I am not sure whether I wrote to you to say that I do hope you will be taking Herbert Read's *Poems*. The new volume does strike me as a very substantial piece of work which will stand up after some greater contemporary reputations have completely collapsed.[1]

Yours ever,
[T. S. Eliot]

TO *John Pudney*[2]

TS Texas

29 August 1934   Faber & Faber Ltd

Dear Mr Pudney,

Thank you for your letter of the 28th. I am glad to have a copy of 'Joseph', though, as the book is coming out in September, you say, it is too late for me to do very much about it.[3]

There are some young fellows in the B.B.C. who are interested in what they call radio drama; they have got one from D. G. Bridson which they haven't produced yet.[4] They want to get hold of poets and teach them what they need to know about the technique. It might be worthwhile seeing them while the fit is still on them; one is named Val Gielgud,[5] but the one I had most conversation with is named Gilliam[6] – I don't know

---

1 – Brace had written to FVM a week earlier (21 Aug.): 'With regard to the poems of Herbert Read, I am not disposed to disagree with you in your estimate of the value and enduring quality of the work . . . Read can scarcely be said to have become established as a poet here, and everything considered, I am afraid it would take a very long time to sell an edition.'

2 – John Pudney (1909–77), poet and journalist, was at Gresham's School, Holt, Norfolk, with W. H. Auden and Benjamin Britten. In his early career he worked intermittently for the *Listener*, the BBC, and the *News Chronicle*; later he gained success with a plethora of short stories, TV and radio plays, children's books, and ten adult novels. His works include *Collected Poems* (1957). See further Pudney, *Home and Away* (1960) and *Thank Goodness for Cake* (1978); Frederick Alderson, 'John and "Johnny": John Pudney 1909–1977', *London Magazine*, 21: 9/10 (Dec. 1981/Jan. 1982), 79–87.

3 – The play 'Joseph' was printed in Pudney, *Open the Sky: Poems* (1934).

4 – *Prometheus*, which Bridson offered to TSE for C. on 5 Oct. 1934. Bridson told TSE, 10 Oct. 1934: 'I'm sorry I didn't make myself clear, but thought you knew that "Prometheus" would not be broadcast in any case.'

5 – Val Gielgud (1900–81), actor, director, producer; author of detective fiction; elder brother of the actor John Gielgud. He was for many years Head of Productions at the BBC, where he had complete responsibility for radio drama.

6 – Laurence Gilliam (1907–64), inspirational radio producer, led the development of BBC radio features. See *BBC Features*, ed. Gilliam (1950), D. G. Bridson, *Prospero and Ariel: The Rise and Fall of Radio* (1971); Asa Briggs, *The History of Broadcasting in the United*

his first name or initial – I mentioned you. There may not be anything in it – the B.B.C. usually gets shifted about before anybody has time to do anything; but you could ring up Gilliam and tell him I told you to try to see him.

I know, having to think about politics etc. does get in one's way badly. The only way to get anything done nowadays is to take a period of time and refuse to think about anything extraneous till it is over. Or else to get oneself into a position such that the thing has to be written or you will get into difficulties with other people.

Yours sincerely,

T. S. Eliot

TO *Hugh Walpole*   CC

29 August 1934   [Faber & Faber Ltd]

My dear Walpole,

I cabled to you on receipt of your welcome letter[1] to say that it would be quite possible for us to print a contribution from you in time to catch the Christmas market if you despatched the manuscript by the end of September, and if you are willing to leave the proof reading in our care, which I think you may safely do. This, of course, is cutting it pretty fine, but we are very anxious to have something by you, and hope that your official duties in Culver City will not interfere. I should, of course, be grateful if you would let me hear from you as soon as you can definitely promise the manuscript by that date.[2]

It seems very odd that *David Copperfield* should be produced in California whilst *Treasure Island*, as I hear, is being produced in England. There ought to be a brisk export trade between the two countries in fogs and palm trees. I hope you are not finding the matter too impracticable.

———

Kingdom (4 vols, 1961–79); Douglas Cleverdon, 'Radio Features and Drama at the BBC', *TLS*, 26 Feb. 1970, 229.

1 – Walpole replied from the Metro-Goldwyn-Mayer Studios, California, to TSE's letter of 24 July, that he felt 'pleased and flattered' to be invited to contribute something to the Ariel series, but that at the moment he was busy with work on the film of *David Copperfield*. He asked if it would be possible for him to try to write something for TSE by the end of September. (The MGM film of *David Copperfield*, adapted by Walpole, directed by George Cukor, and starring W. C. Fields, was shot entirely on sets constructed in California, and released in 1935.)

2 – Two days later, on 31 Aug., Walpole posted off a chapter from his forthcoming novel *The Inquisitor* (1935). 'It seemed to me detachable as a picture of a number of human beings enclosed for an hour by the Cathedral.' It did not appear in *C*.

I have heard rumours that your producers have been importing voices from Boston. I look forward to the film with the greatest curiosity.

With all best wishes,

Yours ever,

[T. S. Eliot]

TO *Michael Roberts*

TS Janet Adam Smith

29 August 1934   Faber & Faber Ltd

Dear Mr Roberts,

I must apologise for my delay in answering your letter of the 11th [*sc.* 3rd] July. I did indeed write an answer, but was dissatisfied with it; and have kept on postponing trying again. My summer has been rather broken up, as my summers are apt to be – brief occasional holidays, American visitors etc.

I am interested in your essay. The book ought to be a good one, and I want to hear more about it as it progresses. I am wondering whether the chapter you sent is likely to be the best for publishing in the *Criterion*. Have you advanced to a point at which you can say whether it, or some other part, is the most satisfactory to stand alone? I am just putting this question in your ear; if you say this is the best, I will use this one. But I don't quite see from this where the book is aiming to end up.[1]

I didn't see either you or Miss Adam Smith or Madge on the evening you spoke of – I might have been cowed by such a battery of critics. I heard a parishioner in front say, in the intermission, that it was 'interesting, but *very* difficult'. I am interested in the behaviour of the audience towards the lemonade sellers. I thought the audience pretty awful at that; and I am quite sure that most of it got an entirely different impression from what I intended to convey. But I have had to see a good deal more of such people than sitting among them in a theatre, I assure you. I suppose that they are no worse than the corresponding element in the Communist Party; they only happen to irritate me more because I see more of them. I think that if you identify yourself with any cause you have to put up with yahoos of some sort. My sort is pretty tough, I know. But of course I shouldn't judge the Communist Party by the sort of people who belong to it.

1 – Roberts responded (22 Sept.) that he hoped to complete the book – 'essays on philosophy of science, insufficiency of "survivalism" & pragmatic necessity of something more than pragmatism' – within a few months. 'I think that when I have tidied it up, the essay I sent you in July will point more clearly to the direction which the book is to take.' No essay appeared in *C*.

Do let me hear from you. I shall be away from the 8th to the 17th September, otherwise probably here; and should like very much to see you. I hope you have found the job you want.

Yours ever sincerely,
T. S. Eliot

TO *Maurice Reckitt*[1]   CC

31 August 1934   [Faber & Faber Ltd]

My dear Mr Reckitt,

Thank you for your note of the 27th. I am interested in your memorandum,[2] which is certainly well sponsored (by the way I wonder if the Arthur Mayhew who signs is my friend Arthur Mayhew of St Cyprian's, Lancaster Gate?). I should be very glad to attend the meeting in October, and depend upon you to let me have due notice when the time comes.

The only suggestion that occurs to me at the moment is to wonder who is to do the selection of the books. Obviously in any sort of bookshop the management must be prepared to order for a customer any book that he wants but, as for the books to be stocked, will not the Archbishop of Westminster wish to exercise control over the selection of Roman Catholic literature? I don't suppose that for us any such supervision is possible, though I confess in passing, that I am much more anxious to

---

1 – Maurice Reckitt (1888–1980): editor of *Christendom: A Quarterly Journal of Christian Sociology*, 1931–50; primary organiser of the Oxford Summer School of Sociology. He was a dogmatically outspoken contributor to Christian policy conferences; and at his bidding, numerous thinkers and strategists – including TSE, Dorothy L. Sayers and Philip Mairet – were to participate in the discussion groups he promoted. 'The Christendom group stood for autochthonous thought and activity and was once denounced as "the rudest group in the Church of England"' (*ODNB*). Other works include *Faith and Society* (1932), *Maurice to Temple* (1947), and *Prospect for Christendom* (ed., 1945), to which TSE contributed. See Reckitt, *As It Happened: An Autobiography* (1941); V. A. Demant, *Maurice B. Reckitt: A Record of Vocation and Versatility* (1978); J. S. Peart-Binns, *Maurice B. Reckitt: A Life* (1988).

See too Reckitt, 'Eliot's entire corpus' (letter), *The Spectator*, 12 May 1967: 'I was one of a small dining club which Eliot often attended in the 'thirties when he was never "aloof" but always "the gay, witty companion". I recall on one evening, when he had ordered that rather noxious concoction a poire Belle Hélène, one of us remarking that he could not imagine how a poet could choose such a thing. "That only proves that you are not a poet," replied Eliot, "but I am a poet and I can imagine it quite easily." To such a knockdown argument there could be no reply.'

2 – Not traced.

keep away from books of a wobbly Catholic kind than from the out and out modernists, who are not so insidious. I don't want to make difficulties. This is just an attempt to anticipate a possible point that someone else may raise later.

With all best wishes,
Yours sincerely,
[T. S. Eliot]

TO *Stephen Spender*

CC

4 September 1934   [Faber & Faber Ltd]

Dear Spender,

I was glad to get your letter of September 1st enclosing a letter from a Miss or Mrs Codman, whom I don't know.[1] Before going into that matter, however, there is one question that I should like to ask you. You will remember that we were expecting from you at the beginning of this month your play to publish for the Christmas market. As you say nothing about the play, do I understand that your poem on Vienna is instead of the play and for publication at the same time in the same way? This is the first point to get settled.[2]

On the assumption that the poem is instead of the play I will bring up your questions about the *New Republic* and Mrs Codman at our meeting

---

1–Mrs Codman had approached Spender with a view to printing in the USA a limited edition of *Vienna*. Spender added: 'There are some replies to you in my poem. I hope they may amuse you.' Also: 'I have written two essays on you [TSE] in my [Henry] James book.'

2–'I have finished all but 30 lines of a poem called *Vienna*, which is about 700 lines long, & which I will send as soon as it is completed . . . I think it is the best thing I have done.'

'A Play' (untitled) by Spender had been advertised in the F&F Autumn catalogue 1934 – along with 'A New Work' by T. S. Eliot (p. 32). Spender to FVM, 11 Aug. 1934: 'I have written the most part of a long poem for the slim book in September. It is much the best thing I have done, the only mature poem really. It is called Vienna 1934, and is about the socialist rising and things connected with it.' Spender wrote again to FVM, 27 Aug. 1934, 'I have done ¾ of a poem [*sic*] of 600–700 lines called VIENNA, which I shall send to Eliot early in September. I like it.' FVM to Bennett Cerf, Random House, 28 Sept. 1934: 'Stephen Spender has just completed a poem of 600 or 700 lines called VIENNA. I don't know whether it is narrative verse or a play; and there seems to be no way of finding out because it is at the printers. Never mind, as soon as there is a proof to send you, you shall have one. Auden is also busily engaged, and I think his is a full-length play.' The proofs of *Vienna* were sent in mid-Oct. to Cerf, who responded to FVM, 7 Nov.: 'I wrote to your Mr Stewart yesterday telling him how enthusiastic we are about Spender's VIENNA. I heartily believe that Spender will be a very big name before a great deal more time has elapsed.'

tomorrow. But it would have been a help if Mrs Codman's letter had given some indication of the form and number of copies that she had in view.

I shall be in London when you get back and look forward eagerly to seeing you.

Yours ever,
[T. S. Eliot]

TO *Geoffrey Curtis*[1]

5 September 1934   Faber & Faber Ltd

My dear Curtis,

I was happy to get your letter after this long while, and as often happens in such cases, had been thinking about you for a day or two before it came, and wondering how you were faring. I have been pretty preoccupied since before last Christmas, first of course with the *Rock*, which took all of my spare time until after Easter, and most of it until the production was over. After that I took a half-holiday (if you take a holiday anywhere under two hours from town it is only a half-holiday). The summer, with American visitors, and weekends visiting friends, is always a broken period for me; and this year I was confined for the better part of two months by the happy duty of entertaining a sister and a niece from America. And tomorrow I go away to Wales for a week, after which, I think, the summer is over.

I am glad you have had a holiday in such a sanctified, as well as naturally beautiful part of Britain as that which holds the memories of S. Columba.[2] I am more a believer than most, I think, in the influence which the spirits of others exert through places, both for good and evil, and I know that it is good to be where holiness has been.

I am interested, but not really enlightened, by your comments on *The Rock*.[3] It is possible that my very superficial acquaintance with Barthian

---

1–The Revd Geoffrey Curtis (1902–81): Vice-Principal, Dorchester Missionary College, Burcote, Abingdon, Oxfordshire.

2–Curtis wrote (8 Aug.) from a ferry off the Isle of Mull: he had been to Iona. 'I think it will carry you S. Columba's blessing for my eyes can still distinguish Iona Abbey in the distance.'

3–'*The Rock* brought me joy, delight and misgiving. Joy because of your having accomplished so valuable and arduous a task for God's church. Delight because of the mastery of your verse which increases rather than decreases misgiving because I find hints that the Renaissance's shortcut to humanism, its not wholly evangelical catholicism (a religion of Revelation rather than of Redemption) has not yet wholly unmasked for you its siren falsity – that to speak theologically you belong to the pre-Barthian era.'

theology[1] is from the wrong end. That is, I got the impression that it was a movement back to Luther; that as a counter-reformation of Liberal Protestantism it was all to the good; but that it had little to offer to the less Protestant minded, and indeed held dangers in stressing the chasm between the spiritual and the temporal order. In fact, the Bishop of Stepney asked me if I had been influenced by Barth because he thought that I was emphasising the division of 'Church' and 'World' to such an extent! So I should like to know more of what you mean by the 'shortcut to humanism' of the Renaissance, and in what passages you detect in *The Rock* dubious matter.

I think that by some oversight Knight's book *The Christian Renaissance* was not reviewed in the *Criterion*.[2] At the moment I cannot lay my hand on a copy. Knight strikes me as a man of remarkable insights, which, when translated into theses, he is apt to ride too hard. I should not think of him as altogether sound, and I am not surprised to learn that he has some association with 'Groups'.

Don't you think that the metaphysical and the sensitive or parabolic approach, representing types of mind, have both to be maintained? I should not like to see the 'language of metaphysic' wholly abandoned in favour of that 'myth, analogy and parable' in theology, because I think the practical result would be a relaxation of precision in language and a luxuriance of modernism. Anyway, I should not like to dispense with the Johannine element. By the way, did you ever read Hoskyns & Davey's book?[3] I should think you would find my friend More's attitude sympathetic – did you ever read his *Greek Tradition* and in particular vol. IV – from the second century to the Council of Chalcedon.

I do want to visit you for a weekend if you will still have me – would some time in November or December be convenient? And I like the country as much in the winter as in the summer.

Affectionately in Christo,
T. S. Eliot

1–Karl Barth (1886–1968), Swiss Protestant theologian; author of *Epistle to the Romans* (1919; 2nd edn, 1922; translated into English from the 6th edn by Sir Edwyn C. Hoskyns, 1933).
2–Curtis asked what TSE thought of *The Christian Renaissance*, by G. Wilson Knight: 'It is the book I have longed to write for so long, only I venture to think damaged by lack of acquaintance with the Biblical part of his subject-matter.'
3–Sir Edwyn Hoskyns and Noel Davey, *The Riddle of the New Testament* (F&F, 1931).

TO *Leonard P. Moore*

7 September 1934   [Faber & Faber Ltd]

Dear Mr Moore,

I must apologise for the delay in answering your letter of August 15th,[1] which has been due partly to absences and partly to illness amongst the staff. I am afraid that I am not able to make any definite suggestions which will appeal to Miss Butts; but what Mr Morley and myself had in mind was a study of a figure like Laurence Oliphant.[2] As I don't know Miss Butts's address or her present name I am sending to you a book which I shall be glad if you will forward to her: *Group Movements of the Past* by Mrs Strachey, which contains some information about Laurence Oliphant and similar personages.

I don't know, however, how Miss Butts's difficulty with regard to books is to be overcome. I presume she is a member of the London Library. I only hope that she may be able to find some subject which will interest her enough to persuade her to come up to London at a later stage to consult such books as are [un]obtainable elsewhere.

Yours sincerely,
[T. S. Eliot]

TO *Serge Bolshakoff*

7 September 1934   [Faber & Faber Ltd]

Dear Mr Bolshakoff,

I have been considering your letter of the 21st August with the reference list enclosed.[3] The more I consider the matter the more I feel that it is impossible for me to be associated so closely as to become a Foundation Member of the Academy. It is not worthwhile from your point of view

---

1 – 'She is not able to write a novel at present, but she is very interested in your suggestion that she might do a study of the life of one of the peculiar, more or less abnormal, propagators of religious and other cults. Her difficulty is the necessary research. As you may know, she lives down in Cornwall and cannot get there the books she would want.'

2 – Laurence Oliphant (1829–88): British author, traveller, diplomat, and Christian mystic. He was a cousin of the Scottish novelist and historical writer Margaret Oliphant.

3 – Since Bolshakoff had failed to get enough interested parties to attend the 'inauguration meeting' of his proposed academy, he was now seeking 'to know how many of my friends will really support the idea of [the] Academy by more than an expression of general sympathy only'.

Christopher Dawson had agreed to become Librarian of the Academy.

to have in this nucleus members purely for the value, whatever that may be, of their names; for obviously there is a great deal of work to be done and no one should be involved to that extent who is not in a position to assure his giving a good deal of time, especially during the first year or two of existence.

I should be glad to be an Associate and to be permitted to attend meetings and, on occasion, participate in discussions. You may be assured that I accept the principles laid down in question 1, and especially approve the dependence upon 'rerum novarum' and 'Quadragesimo Anno'. I shall be grateful if you will keep me in touch with the progress of the Academy, and let me know of any future meeting which I might be able to attend.

With all best wishes,
Yours sincerely,
[T. S. Eliot]

TO *Laurence Gilliam*[1]

CC

7 September 1934   [*The Criterion*]

Dear Mr Gilliam,

Thank you for your letter of the 4th instant and for letting me see the script of Bridson's 'Prometheus' which, as I am going out of town for a week, I have read and return herewith. It seems to me on the right lines and a thing which I should very much like to hear produced. I have the impression that Bridson's balance of interest is right and that his interest is really in the dramatic and not simply in spoken verse. I do hope that you will be able to produce this as soon as possible, and shall be grateful if you will let me know as far in advance as possible the date and time.[2]

Thank you very much for taking up the wireless question with your engineers.[3] As I say, I shall be away next week but shall be back permanently on the 17th. An essential part of the problem is to find a good set at a price which I shall feel justified in paying.

With many thanks,
Yours sincerely,
[T. S. Eliot]

1 – Laurence Gilliam (1907–64), legendary radio producer: pioneer of BBC Features.
2 – *Prometheus* had been broadcast by the BBC on 27 Aug. 1934.
3 – Gilliam wrote, 'I have got the Engineers on to the problem of your wireless set and a Mr Endicott will get in touch with you about it.'

TO *Hermann Broch*   CC

7 September 1934   [*The Criterion*]

My dear Herr Broch,

I must apologise for my long delay in answering your kind letter of the
1st August.[1] I had wished that the suggestion of a subject for the *Criterion*
might come from your side. Any subject dealing with the arts, especially
in their more philosophical and social implications, or an essay concerned
with the general problems of our time would certainly be of interest.
The essay you mention would not be too long and the title sounds quite
suitable. I hope that you will let me have this and if you care to send a few
more also, I should be delighted to read them.

I am having a copy of *Anna Livia Plurabelle* and *Haveth Childers
Everywhere* sent to you.[2] Unhappily the series of pamphlets in which
these appeared has had to fall more or less into abeyance as we find that
at the present time it is only a rather exceptional publication in this way
of which we can sell enough copies to justify the undertaking.

                              With best wishes,
                              Yours sincerely,
                              [T. S. Eliot]

1 – 'Naturally I regret that you cannot consider publishing the essays at the moment, though
I completely understand your reasons. But I am pleased that you would like to publish
contributions by me in the *Criterion* . . . Can I therefore ask you to tell me which topics
would come under consideration in the *Criterion* and how long the contribution may be.
I have just finished an essay for the Schönberg festschrift (Arnold Schönberg is turning 60)
entitled "Thoughts on the Problem of Irrational Knowledge in Music", which, if it is not
too long – it consists of approximately 12 typed pages – you may wish to consider. Please
let me know about it.'
2 – 'Edwin Muir told me that you once considered printing my Joyce lecture in that small
series in which Joyce's "Anna Livia" has also appeared. Is this something you are still
considering? In any case, I would like to ask you a favour: can I ask for a copy of this "Anna
Livia" to be sent to me?'

TO *Carl Wildman*[1]

7 September 1934   [Faber & Faber Ltd]

Dear Sir,

We have considered in Committee the suggestion contained in your letter of the 4th instant.[2] I am afraid that we are very doubtful of the prospects of a translation of any play by Cocteau at the present time. Our experience with translations of French works which are likely to appeal only to the more fastidious public is that those who wish to read them at all will always prefer to read them in French; so that the only effect of an English translation is to provide a slight stimulus to the sale of the French original. I can see that persons interested in the developments of the modern theatre would want to have the English translation because of the actual production of the play in this country. I should, indeed, want to get it myself but I am afraid that the number of people so minded is very small.

We do, however, see greater possibilities in your second suggestion of your own study of the modern French theatre, especially if you are likely to have some interesting illustrations. I hope, therefore, that when this book is ready you will let me see it, particularly as I take a warm interest in the subject myself.

Yours faithfully,
[T. S. Eliot]
Director.

---

1 – Carl Wildman (1912–90), translator.
2 – Wildman invited TSE to consider a version of Jean Cocteau's *La Voix Humaine – Woman Speaking –* that he had been preparing for Flora Robson. 'My English version of Cocteau's *Orphée* was published last year by the Oxford University Press, and kindly reviewed by Herbert Read in the *Criterion* and Stephen Spender in the *New Statesman*.

'I am at the moment considering making an English version of Cocteau's latest classical play (a tragedy in four acts concerning Jocasta and Oedipus), *La Machine Infernale*, produced with great success in Paris last season – would this interest you?'

In addition, Wildman was preparing a study, *Modern French Theatre* – 'roughly from Diaghilev to Jouvet . . . showing not only the tendencies in production, scene and theatre designs, but also in the creation of the written work intended for the stage – this part includes principally Claudel, [Henri-René] Lenormand, Gide, Romains, Giraudox, Cocteau and Obey.'

7 September 1934   Faber & Faber Ltd

Dear Spender,

I have now discussed with the Committee the questions raised in your letter of September 1st. Assuming that your poem of 700 lines is a substitute for the play we do want to publish it among the Christmas books, in a form rather similar to that of *The Dance of Death* and presumably at about the same price. Accordingly we should certainly not wish *The New Republic* to print the poem, as I am sure that it would have an adverse effect upon the sales.[1]

Thirdly, we shall be obliged to let Random House make an offer for it and this makes it impossible to accept Mrs Codman's proposal. I don't believe, however, that there would be any more money in Mrs Codman's publication than in that by Random House. At the present time the market for very expensive books is pretty dead in America and I think that at a practical price Random House would be at least as satisfactory. Besides, we do know about them and we know nothing whatever about Mrs Codman.

I should like very much to know also what has happened to the play. Have you scrapped it altogether or will it be finished at some later time?[2]

Yours ever,

T. S. Eliot

P.S. I return Mrs Codman's letter herewith.

1 – SS notified TSE (1 Sept.) that the *New Republic* wished to print extracts from *Vienna*. 'If I send it to them, I would like to make them publish the whole thing. It has so much news about Viennese politics in it that they might do so.' He hoped that F&F would not object.
2 – On 17 Sept., SS requested Erica Wright to 'tell Mr Eliot that the poem I sent is only by way of an experiment for the play. I have done about 1/3 of the play, and I think it should be ready by January, but I can't quite say as I have been working on & off on it for about 2 years now . . .'

TO *F. O. Matthiessen*   TS Donald Gallup/Beinecke

17 September 1934   Faber & Faber Ltd

Dear Matty,

Thanks for your letter of September 2nd.[1] I hear that the Oxford Press
have already made an offer for your book.[2] I don't know what terms they
suggest but I hope that they will be acceptable. I look forward with much
interest to reading the book in its final form; and if meanwhile you have
any questions to ask me, I will do my best to answer them.

I saw Ted Spencer twice during his very brief stay in London, and heard
either from him, or some other source which I cannot remember, that
you were having a year's leave but the rumour was that you were to be
in England so I am much disappointed to hear that you are travelling in
the opposite direction. I am glad of your free year if it makes possible
the writing of a book which, from what little you say, sounds extremely
promising.

Hoping to see you a year or so hence,

Yours ever,
T. S. Eliot

1 – 'I can most certainly understand your having objections to Faber and Fabers publishing
a book with the subject of mine . . .

'Naturally I was very pleased to hear the good opinion of my work held by the directors
of your firm; and will be fully content whoever decides to publish it. The now revised and
more-or-less final version left my hands about ten days ago . . .

'I forget whether I have told you that I am luxuriating in the present [*sic*] prospect of a
leave of absence this year from Harvard. I shall spend some of my time reading towards an
ultimate book of critical definition of the general artistic movement represented by Emerson,
Hawthorne, Thoreau, Whitman, and Melville.' The book that Matthiessen had in view was
to become *American Renaissance* (1941).

2 – *The Achievement of T. S. Eliot* (OUP, 1935). FVM wrote to Ferris Greenslet, Houghton
Mifflin Co., 30 July 1934: 'I should have written before to thank you for Matthiessen's essay
on Eliot. It is a very good essay, and certainly ought to be published without loss. At the
same time, it would be better for some other English firm to do it, and I hope you will not
mind our mentioning it to the Oxford Press. If nobody else here will publish it, I think we
should be glad to; the only reason we hesitate is the unusual reason of sparing a director's
blushes. A French publisher would have no hesitation in publishing a eulogy of one of his
own firm, but somehow there is a certain amount of embarrassment about that here.'

TO *Gerald Graham*[1]

17 September 1934   Faber & Faber Ltd

My dear Graham,

I was delighted to get your letter of the 5th this morning. This is indeed good news.[2] It is always the cause of pleasure to hear of anyone's fortunes turning so completely and I rejoice particularly that such good fortune should be yours. I remember the period of your great anxiety most vividly; and I trust that your original work, as well as the 9 a.m. lectures, is flourishing exceedingly. I hope to hear more from you about the book as it approaches completion.

Please give my most cordial regards and felicitation to your wife, and believe me,

Sincerely your friend,
T. S. Eliot

TO *A. L. Rowse*

TS Exeter

18 September 1934   Faber & Faber Ltd

My dear Rowse,

I have read your essay once with much interest and sympathy; and pending a second reading here are my first comments.[3]

I am in agreement with you on some important points, at least. My valuation of Aldous Huxley's views in general is hardly likely to be higher

---

1–Gerald S. Graham (1903–88), a graduate of Trinity College, Cambridge, was instructor in History at Harvard, 1930–6. After a period as Assistant Professor of History at Queen's University, Kingston, Ontario, he was a Guggenheim Fellow, 1940–1; and during WW2 he served in the Canadian Army. He was Rhodes Professor of Imperial History at King's College, London, 1949–70; Life-Fellow and Vice-President of the Royal Commonwealth Society; general editor of the Oxford *West African History* series. A world authority on naval power and the British Empire, his works include *Sea Power and British North America, 1783–1820: A Study in British Colonial Policy* (1941). Graham told EVE, 28 July 1984: 'T. S. E. was a most compassionate man. That is why he "picked me up" in Eliot House in 1932. We were brought close to each other because (unbeknownst to me at the time) we shared a common misery.'

2–Graham (Cambridge, Mass.) announced the birth of a son on 31 Aug.; his wife Emily was 'terribly happy, and the event will make a different person of her . . . The dark days seem far away now, but I shall never forget your wonderful kindness to us both, at a time when you were so occupied yourself.'

3–Rowse submitted on 13 Sept. a long article, 'War and Psychology' – 'a complete exposure of the threadbareness of this stuff that Aldous Huxley goes on writing about the psychological origins of war . . .'

than yours. He seems to me to offer sedatives for suburbans; he does not hold any of the positions which are tenable for the present day; and his scepticism is thoroughly jejune.[1] As for his theory of war, I agree that it is not only wrong, but dangerous. I agree with what you say about the economic foundations of war, and also (if I understand you) about the redherring effect which may follow the present interest in armament scandals. The latter is all to the good in so far as it makes people realise what a sordid swindle war is; but of course the armament firms are only behaving as one should expect capitalism *to* behave, and it is absurd just to make them the scapegoats. What isn't an armament firm? In the present state of things, a firm which supplies cotton-machinery to a foreign country which has been an important customer for cotton goods, is just as 'treasonable' as a firm which supplies 'munitions of war'.

And also, having put the 'passions' of war in their proper place (and one ought to add that sentimental fancies and wrong thinking count for more with most people than passions, though there is a proportion of thugs everywhere) I agree in disapproving of referring matters eventually to the necessity of a 'change of Heart', 'spiritual awakening' etc. I have no patience with muddling things by putting spiritual and moral issues where they don't belong, which only means shelving these issues as well as others. And I don't believe that an orthodox Christian viewpoint can support it: we are not taught to expect mass transformations of human nature by outbursts of sentiment.

A few points of detail:

P.   1. 'common sense voice' not very persuasive so early; leave it to be discovered.

   5. reference to Angell might be more effective if he had not already been mentioned?

(it is a good point to make, that nations *do* profit by war; it is true, and implies that the social reorganisation needed is far more drastic. The Angellism view that war is silly is pleasant for superior minds, but only induces a superior laziness).

P.   13. 'Thank God'; feebly overemphatic?

'descendants': I was under the impression that the feudal barons had pretty well killed each other off in the Wars of the Roses; and

1 – *Cf.* TSE's Reader's Report on Roger Lloyd, 'Aldous Huxley and the Christian Religion' (1931): 'The way to deal with Huxley is exactly to sneer at him, and for this purpose there is, I think, a chance for a good pamphlet by some real ruffian – not a gentleman, and preferably not even an Etonian, but, let us say, one who has plumbed life to the very dregs of Carlton House Terrace . . . [I]n short, I can think of no one except Wyndham Lewis or myself.'

that the present representatives you mention are more likely to be descended, at most, from Tudor parvenus, if not from industrialists and financiers. I defer [to] your knowledge of history, however.

14. 'Junkers & industrialists': are they fundamentally the same or not, in their motives and interests?

17. Whose poem!

18. Query *different than*?

23. Rhetorical question to Mr Huxley seems a rather stale form.

27. Are you not sure that Blum is such a worthy person? Is he or is he not an F . . . ?

37. Monks. Hy VII great statesman. Naturally, can't agree with you at all about the monkeries. Are dukeries a great improvement? Mem: full morning on Aug. 22nd.

The last part I had to read rather hurriedly. My own feeling that Huxley most suitable for FREEZING than BURNING, but it may be a personal preference for the former style. If I don't disagree TOO violently with the latter part on re-reading I am favourably inclined.[1]

Yours ever
T. S. E.

Lunch any day next week possible for you?

TO *K. de B. Codrington* CC

18 September 1934   [Faber & Faber Ltd]

My dear Codrington,

I must apologise for not writing yesterday, but my first day back was a pretty full one, and I had unfortunately an evening engagement. Here is the position as it appears after a careful consultation.[2]

If the possibility of the boy's being baptised depended upon finding godparents, then it seems as if I ought to accept. But godparents, I am told, are not an absolute necessity. The plan suggested is that the case should be put to the local vicar, who ought to be willing to baptise without this

---

1 – ALR's essay did not appear in C.

2 – Codrington ('Thurs.'): 'I am in difficulties over the Christian up-bringing of my offspring, especially of my newly born son . . . I cannot boast myself a Christian but would do nothing to put obstacles in the way of anybody else being one . . . My difficulty is that I cannot take on the responsibilities implied in baptism myself, unless I can find someone who is willing to advise in these matters with faith, when the time comes . . . Would you be Christopher's god-father?'

formality. What I would do, with your approval, would be to get some higher dignitary to write to the vicar first, and ask the latter to get in touch with you. You would have to let me know what your parish is.

The point which has elicited is this: that by merely being in the background, as a person whom your son could talk to when he arrived at an age at which it is appropriate to be interested in such matters, I shouldn't really be carrying out my undertaking, which is to see that the child is brought up from the earliest suitable moment in religious instruction, habitual prayer etc. later the meaning of prayer etc. etc. As for being available later, I could (and of course would be glad to) be of just as much use without being a godparent – assuming that by the time he did not have any other preference as to whom to talk to – he might more likely approach some schoolmaster whom he knew and liked.

Of course I believe that it is highly desirable from any point of view that a child should be baptised, however it is to be brought up. Also, I shall be happy to be at your service in any way possible: but it does not seem as if my having the status of godparent would render me any more acceptable to the boy later as an adviser, unless he had been brought up in that belief beforehand – and even then, he might think a godfather too compromised by his position to be a person worth consulting! But do let me hear from you again quickly about the matter.[1]

Yours ever,

[T. S. Eliot]

TO *Maurice Haigh-Wood*   CC

19 September 1934   [Faber & Faber Ltd]

My dear Maurice,[2]

I must give you the following news, although it is not very pleasant.

I saw Janes a couple of weeks ago, and he handed me a sealed envelope (Janes, not James) which Vivienne had given him some weeks before, with

---

1–Codrington wrote again by return: 'The position is a difficult one – and of some importance. With astonishing lack of imagination I had not realised that you had been troubled with this sort of thing before . . . Things, however, led me, also, to take advice, and having done so, a solution was at hand . . . [T]he obvious relation *asked* to be allowed to act. I accepted and the child was christened at even-song – very beautifully . . . I of course had no right to depart from tradition or to implicate you, because I see things in a certain way . . . I was very moved at the service, which was beautifully done. My father's obvious satisfaction was sufficient in itself.'

2–MH-W had turned thirty-nine on 29 Aug.

instructions to deliver into my hand if he saw me, but not in any other way. Bird was away, and I was just going off to Wales, so I sent it to Bird's office to hold, saying that I would open it when I saw him.[1]

I opened the envelope in his presence this morning, and it proved to contain only the letter which you wrote her about my property (after our correspondence on the matter) and a note to Vivienne from her mother. Both letters were torn in two, and there was no message from Vivienne.

In the circumstances I trust you will understand my reading your letter to V., which was, if I may say so, a very good one. You have done all you could, and I appreciate what you have done.

The note from your mother had no bearing on anything. It was written to the flat and stated that your mother had written to V. at Hastings, that her letter had been returned, and begged V. to let her know where she was.

I hope you have had a satisfactory summer at Lingfield, and that Ahmée and the boy are well.

Ever yours,
[Tom]

P.S. I see that I have omitted the conclusion of the matter, which is that I have instructed Bird to proceed with the writ.

1–Compare VHE's diary, 22 Sept. 1934: 'W. L. Janes came to 68 Clarence Gate Gardens & told me that he had *seen* Tom, in the street, yesterday & that he had stopped him & had *handed* to him the sealed envelope which I had given to Janes to *keep* until my death (*or his*).'

According to VHE's record, the statement she handed to Janes read: 'There is no reason why Mr T S Eliot should not come to 68 Clarence Gate Gardens NW1 at any time and no reason why he should not live at Clarence Gate Gardens NW1 and there is *nothing* to prevent his doing so, as 68 Clarence Gate Gardens is his home. Anyone making any statement to the contrary is lying.'

In a separate ledger (Ms. Eng. lett. c. 382, fol. 1), VHE recorded: 'William L. Janes *says he met Tom* in *Leicester Square* (*or* the Army & Navy Club) & gave him certain letters which I had given Janes to keep until my death.

'There may be more to this. Janes said that Tom said "*I'm fine*" in reply to his enquiry about his health. The last words that Tom wld. use.'

On 11 Oct. 1934, after Janes had been to call on TSE at Faber & Faber (on VHE's orders), she noted in her diary: 'He reported to me that he had *seen* him, for a very hurried few minutes & that he seemed well. I cannot help feeling that Tom *likes* to have people call to enquire for him, & to *show* their anxiety, even although he acts in this queer way, & by his *apparent* [illegible word] *indifference* & callous cruelty *makes us* act in a queer & abnormal way. But I feel sure & *more* sure, that *if all is* as it is said to be, the poor fellow was, & has been for 2 years, a [illegible] under some delusion which makes him *not* understand that we here are his friends & *true champions* & loyal *to the death*, & that we *still* wait for him with *open* arms.'

19 September 1934   Faber & Faber Ltd

Dear Enid,

I waited to write until I had the photographs developed – which brings it rather late, but I think you should just receive this before you start for London. I was not sure which pictures were properly yours and which mine – so I send you all the negatives, with apologies for not sending all the positives – but although I had several copies taken, I found that I wanted them all for myself – there are two excellent ones of Ann which I think would bear enlarging, and one nice one of Tom; Dick does not fare so well. I am grateful to you for giving me such enormous shoulders, but note that my legs appear very spindly.

I enjoyed the holiday immensely[2] – for it was the only week I have had this summer which really deserved the name of holiday – just as much as last year – my enjoyment was only slightly marred by your & Geoffrey's conscience over teaparties and shoots – because I don't like to have the time of a visit specially planned for me, but prefer to fall in and fit in with whatever is happening in a household. And I slept particularly well, and felt singularly remote from anxieties of every kind – which helps me to face with equanimity the possibility of an action in the King's Bench division of the High Court, or whatever it is. Another year I shall bring a machine gun and give John and Lewis Lloyd Thomas something to carry home.

Ann seems to have made an impression upon Miss Wright. I trust that the journey back will be comfortable, and that you will not run out of petrol. I trust that Eleanor Farjeon will provide the Christmas play, which will give my imagination until Easter, – over this weekend I must try to elaborate a little essay upon Swamis for the Book Committee.

Yours ever gratefully
T. S. E.

1–Enid Faber (1901–95), née Richards, daughter of Sir Henry Erle Richards, Chichele Professor of International Law and Diplomacy and a Fellow of All Souls, Oxford, married Geoffrey Faber on 30 Dec. 1920. The couple had two sons and a daughter.

2–GCF's diary records these small details of TSE's holiday week in Wales:

'Sat, 8 Sept. Down to T. G. with Tom Eliot.

'Mon, 10 Sept. I brought Tom & children out to lunch.

'Weds, 12 Sept. Sunbathed with Tom, & bathed in pool. Afternoon shot rabbits . . . 33 in all. Tom watched persistently, & I hope not with boredom.

'Thurs, 13 Sept. E. took Tom & children to sea.

'Fri, 14 Sept. took Tom & E & children to Cei Bach in morning.

'Sat, 15 Sept. Took Tom into Lampeter, & got the washing.'

TO *Alastair W. R. Miller*[1]   TS Professor Andrew M. Miller

25 September 1934   Faber & Faber Ltd

Dear Mr Miller,

I have taken some little time over looking at your poetry, but I assure you, rather less than the usual.

I like some of the poems in 'The Man of Gingerbread' very much, because they are accomplished work in a light kind, instead of being ambitious failures. They do what they set out to do; and you have here and there made a skilful use of a Hopkins trick without attempting to do anything so pretentious with it as what he could do. There is a tone, well held, of your own.

The newer poems aim at something much more substantial. It is impossible to say whether the fragment of a play[2] is good, because it depends entirely on whether the play is good. I am afraid, however, from this small piece, that I do not feel either that something is happening or that something is waiting to happen or not happening. The result is to give the dialogue an effect of obscurity and artificiality. I do not think it is necessary that stage dialogue should be extremely simple language, and in that rather disagree with Cocteau's remark about making designs in rope rather than lace.[3] What I do think is necessary is to have a plot that gets somewhere and never wastes a minute. If the audience have a general notion of what is going on, and of the relation between the characters at any given moment, then you can make your poetry as elaborate or difficult as possible without bothering them; because they will not try to take in every word, but only the general direction of the speech. There are plenty of speeches in Shakespeare which are so complicated that you can spend no end of time trying to decipher them; but they do not give trouble, because the audience has a clear enough notion of what a character is feeling, and why, and that something is going to happen in consequence. The audience doesn't hear very many of the words anyway. And a chorus can't say very much for the audience to hear: if they speak all together

---

1–Alastair W. R. Miller (1912–74), author and schoolmaster, educated at Christ Church, Oxford, was to teach for many years (English, Latin, History) at a prep school in Santa Barbara, California. Works include two volumes of poetry, *The Man of Gingerbread* (1933) and *Stages of Pursuit* (1935), and a children's book, *The Quest of the Cat-Nip Mouse* (F&F, 1967).

2–Miller's play was called 'The Life of Alexis'.

3–Jean Cocteau, preface to *Les Mariés de la Tour Eiffel* (1922): 'Poetry in the theatre is a delicate lace, impossible to see at any distance. Poetry of the theatre should be a coarse lace, a lace of ropes, a ship at sea.'

nothing much will come through except refrains and reiterated single words. What I don't get is the feeling of action. And I am doubtful about the songs, which are interruptions, rather than essential moments in the drama, as in Shakespeare, and in themselves are a brew of Beddoes and Auden. I should also say, forget Elizabethans and try a dose of Aeschylus and Sophocles. But first of all, have you a good Plot? I mean something that Edgar Wallace would not have been ashamed of? And I should say at a venture, cut out the rough stuff, I don't think it's your cup of tea, leave it for Auden, and just be serious in the ordinary way.

The second poem with the queer name seems to me to belong to a transition stage between the volume and the play. It is really early Tennyson ('The Sea Fairies' etc) and I think should be condensed into something more lyrical and with less break between movement and movement. The last poem 'Testament' seems to me the most successful thus far.[1] You have a considerable and not uninteresting sense of rhythm, but could do with a greater sense of the importance of the individual word (Mallarmé and Shakespeare, not Swinburne). I fear that in writing a play you may be distracted from your true moods by obvious models.

Do let me see more in six months time, or the play when finished.

Yours sincerely,
T. S. Eliot

I'll get my secretary to send the poems back to you separately.

FROM *Vivien Eliot*   PC[2] Valerie Eliot

[?26 September 1934][3]   [No address given]

Thomas Stearns Eliot Esq. A. M. Litt. D, Columbia of the family of St Germains in the county of Cornwall wishing him many happy returns of *his birthday* from his wife –

---

1 – 'Testament' was to appear in *Stages of Pursuit*.
2 – The postcard shows a portrait of Sir Thomas Bodley (1545–1613), founder of the Bodleian Library.
3 – VHE was to write in her diary on 6 Oct. 1934: 'This is a *return* of a type of nervous collapse which I have experienced very many times. It always had a phase of severe pains in the head, a heavy dazed sleep all day & night, & may continue so for weeks, or months – .' On 1 Nov. 1934: 'The *only thing* I yearn for & *bleed* for is the day when Tom *calmly turns the keys* in this *front door*, walks *leisurely* in, finds the *room* door key, & then has a good look all round, smiles with quiet satisfaction, draws a *long breath*, & goes *quietly* to his *dear* books & to his bed. And if he *can then* say, God bless my little Welsh wife Vivienne. Surely he *will* say that' (Bodleian).

Vivienne Haigh Eliot.[1]

The Constance Hotel[2] 23 Lancaster Gate London w.2.
  and
Dartmouth House, 37 Charles Street Mayfair London w.1.

TO *F. R. Leavis*   CC

26 September 1934   [Faber & Faber Ltd]

Dear Dr Leavis,

It is extremely kind of you to lend me *The Experimental College*, which I shall read carefully and return in due course.[3] If it seems to me a book which might be possible for publication in this country, I should like to keep it a little longer to show to one or two other directors. I am afraid, however, that this will probably not be possible. People are really too lazy to make the necessary transposition in their minds between American conditions and ours; they require the evidence to be as near at hand as possible.

I may be publishing in the *Criterion* an article on American education by Canon Iddings Bell, who is almost the only clergyman in America, Roman Catholics excepted, whose mind didn't seem to me to be completely stuffed with wool.[4] I wonder if you have heard anything about his educational

1–VHE had noted on 17 Sept. 1934: 'At Smith's Bookstall / Will Thomas Stearns Eliot Director of Faber & Faber 24 Russell Square return immediately to his home & his wife at 68 Clarence Gardens which he left on September 17 1932 if he is free to do so.' (Bod MS Eng. let. C. 382). Among her papers (MS Eng. let. c. 624) is a receipt from Messrs W. H. Smith, St Leonards Railway station, dated 15 Sept. for placing an advertisement in the *Times* on 17 Sept. However, no such advertisement appeared in the *Times*.
  On 26 Sept. she recorded: 'This day was Tom's 46th birthday. I was too stunned by pain during the early part of the day to remember . . . By about 4 o'clock my head quite cleared and I saw at last just what I needed to do. So I took 2 extra keys of this flat which I had always kept in the cash box, and found a label. On the label I wrote "September 26 1936 [*sc.* 1934] keys of 68 Clarence Gate Gardens for T S Eliot wishing him many happy returns." When this was done I felt very calm and peaceful. I just lay down and waited for Janes to come. I ordered him to take the labelled keys at once with Polly to 24 Russell Sq and demand to see Tom, and hand him the keys. But if he could not see Tom, to ask for Lister, the caretaker, to leave the keys at Faber and Fabers in any case. He obeyed. I started out after him and met him outside 2 Gordon Sq, where he reported to me, handed me Polly, and left me . . . I had walked all the way back to this flat as I have arranged it all now is my birthday present to Tom.'
2–VHE took 'refuge' at the Constance Hotel on several occasions over the next two years.
3–FRL offered on 22 Sept. to lend TSE his copy of *The Experimental College* (1928), by the academic and philosopher Alexander Meiklejohn: he was keen to see it published in the UK.
4–Dr Bernard Iddings Bell, Canon of Providence, Rhode Island, attended a performance of *The Rock*, and lunched with TSE at the Oxford & Cambridge Club on 4 June 1934.

experiment at St Stephen's College New York, which was finally stamped out by Nicholas Murray Butler.[1] If I print the article, however, I shall feel it necessary to say something in the Commentary about its having some pertinence for English readers.

I take the liberty of congratulating you on the work you are doing in *Scrutiny* in stirring up examination of educational realities and probabilities. In the long run this seems to me as important and as neglected a problem as any we have.

Yours sincerely,
[T. S. Eliot]

TO *Daniel Cory*   CC

28 September 1934   [*The Criterion*]

Dear Sir,

I must apologise for the delay in returning to you your essay 'The Realism of Common Sense'.[2] My final opinion is that the work of Santayana is as yet too little known in this country for such an essay to have its full effect. What I should like, if you would care to consider writing it for the *Criterion*, would be an essay on Santayana's philosophy with particular reference to its latest developments, which might serve as an introduction and arouse greater interest to his writings in this country. I hope you will consider this suggestion favourably.

Harper & Brothers, London and New York, reported to FVM, 20 Aug. 1934, the suggestion from Iddings Bell 'that the sequence of poetic choruses in THE ROCK might be segregated into a charming volume, especially if they could be supplemented with other short works. Do you think there is anything in this line, or is Mr Eliot tied up for all his work elsewhere?'

1–Nicholas Murray Butler (1862–1947), philosopher and diplomat; President of Columbia University, 1902–45; winner of Nobel Peace Prize.

2–Daniel Cory (London) – 'I am a disciple and the literary executor of Mr George Santayana' – submitted the introductory chapter of his book *A Primer of Epistemology for the Laity*.

He added: 'Mr Santayana is a devoted reader of your magazine, and if it is possible that you would like an article by him, I think I can arrange it in the future.'

See further *The Letters of George Santayana*, ed. Daniel Cory (1955); Santayana, *The Idler and His Works, and Other Essays*, ed. Cory (1957); *Santayana: The Later Years, A Portrait with Letters* (1963); *The Birth of Reason and Other Essays by George Santayana*, ed. Cory (1995).

TSE to William B. Goodman, Harcourt, Brace & World, Inc., 12 Oct. 1961: 'While Santayana's title *Three Philosophical Poets* did make a deep impression on me, I never regarded myself as to any degree a disciple of Santayana himself. As a matter of fact, I thought the man rather a poseur, who chose to look down upon New Englanders as provincial protestants. Most of his early books, *The Life of Reason*, seem to me very dull, and he was certainly much at his best on the borderline between philosophy and literary criticism.'

It need hardly be said that I should be delighted to have a contribution from Mr Santayana, and should indeed have been glad to have had one at any time in the past. When you are next writing to him, I should be grateful if you would let him know that a contribution from him would always be more than welcome.

Yours faithfully,
[T. S. Eliot]

TO *Mary Hutchinson*

TS Texas

3 October 1934   Faber & Faber Ltd

My dear Mary,

Thank you so much for your letter. I had been wondering whether you are back; but I had heard that Barbara's baby had arrived (I send her, if you remember to convey them, my felicitations) and I seem to have heard also that Jack had not been very well; so I did not want to bother you.[1]

Very many thanks for your cheque for £3:10:0d. I want, before I start sending the money, and before I say anything to Barker about it, to secure one more subscription. This is only three, and I want to be able to send at the rate of £1 a week before I start. So I propose to hold your cheque for the moment; and when I have one more subscriber, I will call in the rest of the quarter's subscriptions. I think we might stop there for the present; and if I find his needs becoming greater for any justifiable or inevitable reason, I shall be glad if you will help me in getting more. He is more likely, I should say, to need subsidising for another year, than more money at once; and in that event it would be good to have four more subscribers to step in instead of the actual ones.

Oh yes, it was Maria Huxley who told me about Barbara.

I should like to see you whenever you find it convenient. Or would you come to the theatre? I have been told on pretty reliable authority that one ought to see *The Moon in the Yellow River*.[2] I am very well I think, and hope you are. I paid visits to Gloucestershire and Wales, but have not been out of England, as I had a sister and a niece with me for nearly two months. I am in a bit of a legal mess too, about my books etc. at Clarence Gate.

Ever affectionately,
Tom

1–Sarah, daughter of Victor Rothschild and his wife Barbara Hutchinson: born on 13 Sept.
2–Denis Johnston, *The Moon in the Yellow River* (1931).

TO *Audrey Duff*   CC

4 October 1934   [Faber & Faber Ltd]

Dear Miss Duff,

Monday afternoon the 26th November would suit me the best, as I am
not free on the following Thursday.[1] Or the following first Monday in
December would do.

Your letter of today suggests to me that I had better read other people's
poetry instead of my own. What do you think? When you speak of
'choosing my material' you perhaps do not realise that it is very hard
for me to read for 50 minutes or so without reading my complete works.
I have written very little, you see; and some of my best pieces sometimes
shock people unless they are very humble folk or people who like poetry.
But I like reading poetry, especially when it is better than my own; and
I could make up a nice selection with Shakespeare and border ballads
etc. So little of mine appeals to the 'low brow' unless the low-brow is
REALLY simple & pure in heart. I should like your advice.

                                Yours sincerely,
                                [T. S. Eliot]

TO *F. S. Flint*[2]   CC

4 October 1934   [*The Criterion*]

Dear Frank,

I have been worritting about your communications and have taken
the liberty of discussing with Morley and also Dobrée, and finally the

1 – Duff had asked TSE (4 Oct.) to name a date for his appearance at the Fulham Skilled
Apprenticeship Committee: 'will you be so kind as to remember that it will be a mixed
audience; & include what will be acceptable to the "low brow".' TSE gave a reading on 26
Nov.
2 – Frank Stuart ('F.S.') Flint (1885–1960), poet, translator, civil servant, grew up in poverty
– 'gutter-born and gutter-bred' – and left school at thirteen. But he set out to educate himself
in European languages and literature (he had a deep appreciation of the French Symbolists
and of Rimbaud), and in history and philosophy. In 1908 he started writing for the *New
Age*, then for the *Egoist* and *Poetry* (ed. Harriet Monroe). Gaining in authority (especially
on French literature: his influential piece on 'Contemporary French Poetry' appeared in
Poetry Review in 1912) – he became associated with T. E. Hulme, EP, RA and H.D. Between
1909 and 1920 he put out three volumes of poetry, though his essays and translations were
the more appreciated: he was a contributor to C. from the 1920s – a member of TSE's inner
circle – while working full-time in the statistics division of the Ministry of Labour (Chief
of the Overseas Section). See *The Fourth Imagist: Selected Poems of F. S. Flint*, ed. Michael
Copp (2007).

best thing I can do is I think to publish communication no. 1 in the Correspondence section. I'd like to give your views an airing certainly, but the point is that if printed as articles or reviews they might give [the] impression of being the official *Criterion* views. There is no general rule possible about that: each case on its own merits. For instance, I could *not* publish a pro-fascist article because people might think the *Criterion* was going fascist; but I *could* publish a pro-communist article because nobody would imagine that the *Criterion* was becoming communist; I can publish things by people I am known to be in substantial agreement with or by people with whom I am known to be in emphatic disagreement; but here we are on a vague ground. I hope you see my difficulty. I think it would be a good thing to publish this as correspondence and if possible get a controversy going; but I want to keep the body of the paper out of the technical economics if I can. You shall have a proof to knock about in good time.[1]

yours ever aff,
[Tom]

TO *Louis MacNeice*   CC

5 October 1934   [Faber & Faber Ltd]

Dear Mr MacNeice,

I am sorry that we have taken such a long time over your poems, and I hope that the delay has not been annoying.[2]

We should like to publish your volume if possible during next season, and I am authorised therefore to make you an offer of the usual 10% royalty. We envisage a volume of a somewhat similar format to that of Spender's poems, published at 5/-. As soon as I hear from you I will have a contract drawn up.

I like the new poems very much, and the book seems to me to show a vast improvement over last year's. It seems to me that the new poems are quite the best that you have done, and if you go on in this way, you may have a

---

1–Flint argued in a long letter, replete with algebraic formulations, against the 'logic' of Major C. H. Douglas's economic nostrums, in 'Correspondence', C. 14 (Jan. 1935), 292–7. He concluded: 'The scientific solution of the problem of issuance and cancellation appears to be socialism (or economic communism).'

A letter by EP, headed '1934 in the Autumn', followed Flint's communication (pp. 297–304), expatiating at equal length in favour of Douglasite theory.

2–Submitted on 29 Aug. 1934.

few more to add or to substitute for a few of the earlier poems before the book goes to press. In any case I congratulate you on this collection.[1]

Yours sincerely,
[T. S. Eliot]

TO *Marianne Moore*   TS Rosenbach Museum and Library

5 October 1934   Faber & Faber Ltd

Dear Miss Moore,

We are sending you two copies of your proofs. I have corrected one copy of the Introduction in accordance with the corrected copy here. Please forgive me for sending the other copy uncorrected from lack of time. In any case please see that my corrections on this galley proof are used by Macmillans.

I have not had time to run through the proofs of the poems, but that hardly matters as we shall presumably be receiving from you a note of any errors or changes to be made.

I feel more than ever diffident and miserable about this puny Introduction. It seems to me to fall very far short of doing you justice, at best, and I hope that if there is anything in it you definitely dislike, you will not fail to say so. I dare say that it will seem to you a travesty.

With very humble apologies,
Yours sincerely,
T. S. Eliot

TO *Alexander Langridge Ford*   CC

5 October 1934   [Faber & Faber Ltd]

Dear Mr Ford,

You have no need to apologise. That is what I am here for, and if it was any relief to you, so much the better. I should not expect anybody to

---

1 – On 9 Oct. 1934 MacNeice accepted the offer from F&F.

TSE's blurb for MacNeice's *Poems* (F&F, 1935): 'After a distinguished reputation while an undergraduate at Oxford, contemporary with Mr Auden, Mr Louis MacNeice has allowed his verse to appear only rarely in periodicals and anthologies. His classical scholarship has informed a genius representative of the spirit of his Northern Ireland. The most original Irish poet of his generation, dour without sentimentality, intensely serious without political enthusiasm, his work is intelligible but unpopular, and has the pride and the modesty of things that endure.'

accept my 'philosophy' at 19; neither did I; at 19 one is still a conservative, and thinks in 19th century terms.[1] What you need at the moment I should say is more sleep. With eight or nine hours sleep every night and regular meals you will do more credit to Roberts.[2] The kettle has been boiling too hard to look into it; I should be glad to examine the product when it has been off the fire for a little time.

It is equally undesirable to think oneself a poet and to think that one is not a poet. That is something that we never find out.[3]

Yours sincerely,
[T. S. Eliot]

TO *Algar Thorold*   CC

6 October 1934   [*The Criterion*]

Dear Thorold,

I apologise for our packers having mishandled your name but I have no personal responsibility in the matter as the book was obviously meant for the *Dublin*, and was not sent by me.[4] You need not bother to return the book as it is our own mistake, and I have ordered another copy to be sent direct to the *Dublin*.

By all means do *The Holy Mountain*[5] and *Salvation* separately. I will apply to Alcan for a copy of the Bergson book and, if it comes in time for you to review it for December, I suggest that you should let me have a long review of Bergson[6] and rather short notices of the other two.

1–Ford wrote on 25 Oct. to apologise 'most profusely for wasting your time last week': he appeared from his letter to accept he had been 'MAD'. Last night he slept – 'the first time in 7 days except about 5 hours.' He had shown TSE some verses that were evidently 'DOGGEREL'. He noted too, 'I admired Pound; & you were the 1st POET I read, but @ XIX [i.e. 19 years of age] I cannot accept your philosophy – I wish I could – (forgive my ravings of last week).'
2–Ford had been taught by Michael Roberts, who 'at school told me that I would go far'.
3–On 18 Oct. Ford's mother (A. J. Ford) wrote to Erica Wright, 'I regret to inform you that his recent fit of mental excitement has culminated in a nervous breakdown from which he is not likely to recover for at least another six months.'
4–Thorold had been sent – addressed to 'A. Thorogold' – a book entitled *After Hitler's Fall*, by Hubertus Loewenstein.
5–Bhagwan Shri Hamsa, *The Holy Mountain: The Story of a Pilgrimage to Lake Manas and of Initiation on Mount Kailas in Tibet*, trans. Shri Purohit Swami, with an Introduction by W. B. Yeats, was reviewed by Thorold in *C*. 14 (Jan. 1935), 334–5.
6–Thorold's review of Henri Bergson, *La Pensée et la Mouvant: Essais et Conférences*: *C*. 14 (July 1935), 690–4.

I unfortunately have a previous engagement to take the chair at a meeting on the evening of your dinner[1] but I told Dru that I hope that the meeting will be over early and that your dinner will be prolonged late so that I can look in after dinner to add my tribute and salutation to that of the others.

Yours ever,
[T. S. Eliot]

TO *Sally Cobden-Sanderson*[2]   TS Hornbake Library

6 October 1934   [No address given]
St Bruno & St Faith

Dear Sally,

I cannot on this occasion Write to report my voyage & successful making my moorings Because as you so kindly gave me my passage you know that already But. any [*sic*] excuse is better than None so I take the opportunity of sending You a photograph to replace the one you were Exposing this [*sic*] is a Good one it is called the Angelus & shows me at my Best would you like an enlargement this will do until I have a Cabbinet portrait taken by Elliott & Fry As I say any excuse is better than none and this is to express my pleasure & delight in a happy evening with you and yr Consort & hoping that there may be many more here and there Some day I hope I may live to deserve a Portrait Study of Mr & Mrs Cobden-Sanderson so will close yours respectfully I hope I did not talk too much I sometimes do,

> I have teeth, which are False & Quite Beautiful,
> And a Wigg with an Elegant Queue;
> And in Closing I send my Most Dutifull
> Respects to your Consort & You.

T. S. Eliot

1 – 'I hope you are coming to my dinner on Oct. 16.'
2 – Sally Cobden-Sanderson (d. 1972) was working for Hutchinson's Agency ('for Domestic Help Male and Female'), Carlton Chambers, Regent Street – a firm which also catered for travel arrangements. She and her husband Richard Cobden-Sanderson (1884–1964), printer and publisher, were friends of TSE.

TS Hornbake Library

[postmarked 7 October 1934]

> O Postman! take a little skiff
> And ply your oar to HAMMERSMITH;
> And let your nearest Port of Call
> Be No. 15, UPPER MALL.
> Demand, before your task is done,
> The name of COBDEN-SANDERSON.
> The house is plainly built of bricks;
> The district, clearly, is
>> W.6.

TO *D. G. Bridson*   CC

6 October 1934   [Faber & Faber Ltd]

Dear Mr Bridson,

I must apologise for the delay in answering your letter of the 26th September.[1] I have asked my secretary to see that a copy of Bottrall's poems is sent to you. I think, myself, that a few of the shorter poems are more interesting than the title poem.

I understand that the *New English Weekly* have had a review copy of *Make It New*, and the Propertius is not yet ready.[2]

Yours sincerely,
[T. S. Eliot]

P.S. I don't think that a book by Calverton is likely to be worth notice in the *Criterion*. The man can't write English, he doesn't know anything, and I don't believe he has any standing in America among Communists or any other people. I am trying to get Wyndham Lewis' book for you, and I am sending the Story of Troilus[3] but shan't have room for a review of more than one printed page.

1–Bridson had been asked by *Poetry* (Chicago) to review Bottrall's collection. He asked TSE: 'Are you interested in a notice of V. F. Calverton's *Passing of the Gods*, a copy of which has reached me from him?'
2–EP's *Homage to Sextus Propertius* was to be published on 8 Nov.
3–Ed. R. K. Gordon.

TO *David Gascoyne*[1]   CC

6 October 1934   [Faber & Faber Ltd]

Dear Mr Gascoyne,

I must apologise for the delay in dealing with your poems, which were
given to me by Edwin Muir. While they seem to me to have considerable
merit and perhaps excessive fluency, I feel that your stuff ought to simmer
for a good bit longer before it boils down into a proper book. I should
be glad if you would let me see a few from time to time with a view to
publication in the *Criterion*, and I should be delighted to see you if you
cared to make an appointment by telephone with my secretary.

Yours sincerely,
[T. S. Eliot]

TO *Sally Cobden-Sanderson*   PC[2] Hornbake Library

[postmarked 8 October 1934]

Perhaps you will have been appal-
led by rhyme of upper mall and call.
For everybody knows that Sal-
ly lives at 15, UPPER MALL;
Long may the Thames serenely run
By house of COBDEN-SANDERSON.
Until death leaves me cold & stiff: I'll praise
the town of HAMMERSMITH (W.6.)

1–David Gascoyne (1916–2001), poet, playwright, translator and novelist, had published,
by the age of twenty, two volumes of poetry, *Roman Balcony and Other Poems* (1932)
and *Man's Life is This Meat* (1936), and a novel, *Opening Day* (1935), as well as *A Short
History of Surrealism* (1935). Other works include *Collected Poems* (1970) and *Paris
Journal 1937–39* (1978). See further Robert Fraser, *Night Thoughts: The Surreal Life of the
Poet David Gascoyne* (2012).
2–Postcard depicts the Central East Window of Winchelsea Church.

TO *Charles Williams*[1]   TS Marion E. Wade Collection

7 October 1934   [Faber & Faber Ltd]

[No greeting][2]

I seem ungrateful to have delayed writing to you for so long; but I am both grateful and have had pleasure and excitement.[3] It was good of you to send the books the next day, so that I was able to take *Place of the Lion* away with me for my weekend, with the peculiar appropriateness of its being Michaelmas.

The book gave me the same kind of unusual thrill as did *War in Heaven*.[4] I won't say 'more', because the other has for me, as you know, a special interest of subject matter – I have never before met anyone who was interested in the subject matter in quite the same way as myself. What you have attempted in *The Place of the Lion* seems to me more difficult, and therefore perhaps not so easily successful. On the other hand, in the character of Damaris and her scholarly interests there is a very important lesson for everybody. I suppose that what the ordinary reader gets out of

---

1 – Charles Williams (1886–1945), novelist, poet, playwright, religious and theological writer; historical biographer; critic; member of the Inklings; went to work for Oxford University Press in 1908 and remained there, in positions of increasing editorial seniority, for the rest of his career. His oeuvre embraces novels – 'spiritual shockers', he styled them – including *War in Heaven* (1930), *The Greater Trumps* (1932), *Descent into Hell* (F&F, 1937), and *All Hallows' Eve* (F&F, 1945); and non-fiction and theological writings including *The Descent of the Dove: A Short History of the Holy Spirit in the Church* (1939) – which TSE considered 'one of the most interesting and readable books on any theological subject that I have ever read'. – and *The Figure of Beatrice* (F&F, 1943) – 'at once a good introduction to Dante and to the thought of Charles Williams'. See further Grevel Lindop, *Charles Williams: The Third Inkling* (2015).

2 – Text taken from a TS copy of the letter.

3 – TSE and Williams spent the evening together on 28 Sept.; the next day, Williams sent TSE a copy of *The Place of the Lion* (fantasy novel, 1931) – 'it will give me pleasure if you'll have it'.

4 – TSE later wrote of *War in Heaven*: '[Williams's] novels . . . are not all equally good . . . Fortunately, the first is also one of the best . . . It is the story of what happened when the Holy Grail, the famous cup in which Joseph of Arimathea is reputed to have taken some of the blood of Our Lord when on the Cross, turns up in modern England; and of the struggle for its possession, in which supernatural powers, both good and evil, join. The nearest comparison I can make to these stories is Chesterton's *The Man who was Thursday*. I admire that story very much: but I think it is Chesterton who suffers by the comparison. Williams has not Chesterton's gift for humour and paradox. But, on the other hand, he is not writing his story in order to point a moral; he has no obvious design to instruct and convert the reader. It is rather that he wants to write an exciting mystery story, and knows how to do it: and he writes about good and evil, about the inevitable progress of every human being to heaven or hell, simply because these are the most exciting things to write about that there are' ('The Significance of Charles Williams', *Listener*, 36 [19 Dec. 1946], 894).

your stories is just what he gets from a thousand other well built 'thrillers', but for me they mean something quite different and special, and I hope you will be inspired to write more. In fact, you must take it as altogether a compliment when I say that I have found these two books so exciting that I am incapacitated from making any purely literary judgement of them; though the visualisation of the immaterial, and such scenes as the rippling of the ground in *The Place of the Lion*, seem to me marvellously successful.

It is surprising how few people seem to have any awareness of other than material realities, or of Good and Evil as having anything to do with the nature of things – as anything more than codes of conduct. I suppose it is because there is something so terrifying, like a blast from the North Pole, in spiritual reality that just natural cowardice and laziness makes us all try to evade it as much of the time as we can.

[incomplete]

TO *Ezra Pound*   PC TS Beinecke

[8 October 1934]   Faber & Faber Ltd

Shall be writing BUT this is to try to stop you from spelling Quincy Quincey[1] where did you get that Quincey from Old John was no Opium Eater[2] though they do say Mrs John was a Great Trial to him you aint got that bit of gossip in yet but you can take it from me Come on we mustnt let you show your ignrance of American Literature. TP.

TO *Maurice Haigh-Wood*   CC

9 November 1934   [Faber & Faber Ltd]

My dear Maurice,

I wrote to you on September 19th to tell you that I had instructed Bird & Bird to proceed to secure a writ for the possession of my property.

This was done in due course, and the Court issued instructions that Vivienne should deliver up the property.[3] In accordance with the usual

---

1 – Canto 34, published in *Poetry* (Apr. 1934), makes arbitrary (Humphrey Carpenter's word) use of the diary of John Quincy Adams.

2 – *Confessions of an English Opium-Eater* (1821), by Thomas de Quincey (1785–1859).

3 – Bird & Bird notified VHE, 9 Oct. 1934: 'We have been instructed by your husband to commence proceedings against you for the delivery up of certain books, silver and other

articles belonging to him at the flat, 68 Clarence Gate Gardens, N.W.1., now occupied by you.

'Our representative has called at your flat on two occasions for the purpose of serving the Summons upon you, and although he was informed by the person who answered the door that you were not at home, we have reason to believe that you were in the flat at the time.

'The Summons was originally fixed for hearing on the 12th inst., but as we have been unable to serve it upon you personally up to the present, we have obtained an adjournment of the hearing until the 26th inst., at 10.30 a.m., when it will be heard by the Judge in chambers at the Royal Courts of Justice, Strand.

'We now write to inform you that our representative will call at your address, 68 Clarence Gate Gardens, on Friday next, the 12th inst., at 9 a.m., for the purpose of serving you with the Summons. If this appointment is inconvenient to you perhaps you will kindly let us know at what other time and place he can see you.'

Bird & Bird advised TSE on 15th Oct. that VHE had been served with the Summons on Sat., 13 Oct. 'Several abortive attempts to that end were made last week by two or three members of my staff against whom the door was shut in their respective faces. Ultimately a process server was employed to wait outside the flat indefinitely and she was eventually caught. I gather that she acknowledged her identity but refused to receive the papers which were, however, thrust into her hands.'

TSE's suit was heard before Mr Justice Goddard, Judge in Chambers, in the High Court of Justice, King's Bench Division, on 26 Oct. 1934:

'In the matter of the Married Women's Property Act 1883 and

'In the matter of certain questions between Thomas Stearns Eliot and Vivienne Haigh Eliot his Wife as to certain property.

'Upon hearing Counsel for the Applicant Thomas Stearns Eliot and upon reading the Affidavit of Arthur Parlett of service of the Originating Summons upon the Respondent filed this day and the Affidavit of the Applicant filed this day and the exhibits therein referred to.

'It is hereby declared that the Property set forth in the Schedule hereto is the property of the Applicant.

'And it is ordered that the Respondent do deliver the said property to the Applicant or to any person authorised by him to receive it on 24 hours notice.

'And it is ordered that the following questions herein namely as to which items of furniture and effects (other than those set forth in the said Schedule hereto) at present at 68 Clarence Gate Gardens in the County of London are the property of the Applicant and which are the property of the Respondent, be referred to the Master for enquiry and report.

'And it is ordered that the Applicant and his Solicitors be at liberty to enter upon the flat at 68 Clarence Gate Gardens aforesaid on giving 24 hours notice to the Respondent to inspect the furniture and effects and to make inventories thereof.

'And it is ordered that notice may be given by leaving written notice at the flat.

THE SCHEDULE

BOOKS AND BOOKCASES
  1. Two open bookcases formerly fitted to the wall in the drawing room
     immediately prior to September 18th 1932.
  2. Two standing bookcases.
All the books the contents of the two book cases mentioned in item 1 above and all the books in one of the bookcases mentioned in item 2 above immediately prior to September 18th 1932.
  4. 1 Bound set of Addison's "Spectator"
  5. 1 Hymn book previously the property of Priscilla Cushing Stearns.

procedure, she received a notification that Bird & Bird would appear at the flat on Monday morning last to take over the goods listed in my application. This they did, having a van from Maple's in waiting. They were unable to obtain entry, although it was quite evident both to them and to Maple's men that the flat was occupied, as voices, and other noises, were heard.

———

SILVERWARE PLATE ETC.
    6. 10 Silver knives.
    7. Bottle corks with silver tops
    8. Silver cheese scoop
    9. 11 Silver dessert forks.
  10. 1 Silver sugar spoon.
  11. 1 Silver butter knife.
  12. 2 Silver table spoons
  13. 1 Small green trunk studded with brass nails
  14. Brass stamp box.
  15. 1 Silver pie knife.
  16. 1 Silver soup ladle.
Items 4–16 hereof inclusive were formerly the property of Miss Marian Cushing Stearns
  17. 1 Brass tea kettle
  18. 1 Small table bell in brass ("The Four Evangelists")
PERSONAL JEWELLERY AND EFFECTS
  19. Seal ring formerly the property of the applicant's great grandfather.
  20. Files and loose papers.
PICTURES ETC.
  21. Photographs of members of applicant's family
  22. Two drawings of applicant's father ("Brutus and the Ghosts" "a Cart horse")
  23. Drawing of applicant as a boy by his deceased sister.
  24. Framed worsted cat.
  25. Engraving of Charles Whibley
  26. Drawing of Elephant by Gaudier
    (The property of a friend temporarily loaned to Mr Eliot).'

Ernest Bird told TSE the same day, 'For reasons which I will not here set forth but can be reported verbally to you some little difficulty was occasioned in obtaining it. The result may I think be regarded as satisfactory but the question of enforcing it will no doubt be a source of difficulty. The original of this Order has to be served personally upon Mrs Eliot . . .'

(Bird sent TSE a bill of his 'indebtedness' to Bird & Bird, for the period up to the commencement of these proceedings, for £38. 14. 9 – 'for which please only let me have a cheque at your convenience'. His bill from the firm of Bird & Bird for the year ending 31 Dec. 1933 had run to £116. 5. 10d.: the bill was issued on 9 Feb. 1934, and he paid in full on 8 Mar. 'I would that all clients were as prompt,' wrote Ernest Bird on 9 Mar., 'and I might add as appreciative of what one tries to do.')

Messrs Bird & Bird duly served formal notice to VHE on 30 Oct. that she had to deliver up – at 11.30 a.m. on 5 Nov. – the property of TSE specified in the schedule to the Order (MS Eng. lett. b. 20).

VHE recorded in her diary, Tues. 11 Dec. 1934: 'I woke in confusion to a loud banging on the door. I was of course in only a nightdress & dressing-gown. I stumbled to the door thinking it was Mrs Read *& opened* it. A man put his *foot* in & *pushed me* violently, *forced*

If the law takes its course, the Court will next summon Vivienne to appear before it; and if she ignores the order, she will be in a very serious position indeed. I understand that the officers of the law will be entitled to break in by force and remain in possession; and persistent recalcitrance will inevitably render her liable to be removed to prison for contempt of court.

———

the door open, & 5 or 6 men pushed their way in. I screamed for Louie [Purdon], & she came very quickly. I told her to telephone for Janes at once & she looked up the number & did it very very quickly. In the meantime Mrs Read had come. She behaved both stupidly & *badly*. She took Polly out & *left* me here with the men. However, Louie & *Gibbons* were on guard outside all day. Janes came rushing, I think he took a taxi. I stayed locked in my room *all* day, with no food. When Gretel came she came in to me & sat with me for 3 hours.'

On 12 Dec.: 'Of course I was completely ill & in a very bad state of nervous collapse. The flat was wrecked. All Tom's books had been taken, & a great many of my books also. All the *Criterions*, both bound & unbound had also been taken. The shelves had been wrenched off the walls leaving scars & marks which I shall have to repair. The *Clock*, which Mother had given me had been swung about so violently & passed from hand to hand that it never went again. I felt indignant enough to write at once to Geoffrey Faber to tell him what had been done, & to say I would order one copy of every Criterion which had ever been published, as I care 'excessively' about the Criterion. He replied to this at once & said he would make it his business to see that all Criterions & all my books were returned to me. Janes *seemed* quite dazed, but of course he *may* have known about it in advance.'

(Michael Hastings, who interviewed MH-W in his eightieth year, recorded Maurice's observation: 'Tom got Fabers to enter 68 [Clarence Gate Gardens], but Vivie held on to all the things in 177' [Seymour-Jones, *Painted Shadow*, 528]. Maurice's putative recollection relies on the notion that Vivien had arranged to rent an additional flat in the same mansion block.)

In fact, TSE learned that VHE had deposited some of his possessions in two separate banks. Then W. L. Janes found out that the articles claimed 'and not already recovered', as Bird put it on 17 Dec., 'are to be found in the packages deposited with the two banks. Unfortunately, as I rather anticipated, although in both cases the managers are disposed to be helpful and seem, from their own knowledge of Mrs Eliot, to appreciate something of the difficulties in which we find ourselves, they have intimated – after consulting their legal advisers – that in the circumstances they cannot permit us to inspect the contents of the cases – of the nature of which they are not themselves aware – without some definite directions from the Court.'

VHE would write to her solicitor A. Moxon Broad, 3 Jan. 1935: 'Dear Sir, I shd. be very much obliged if you could see me in yr. office for 5 mnts, before going to the Bank. I want to be quite clear in my mind what we are to do. At the same time I want to make a very urgent appeal to you to let me deliver my husband's parcels, *un*-opened, direct to 24 Russell Square. I know that Mr Faber would be agreeable & in fact glad if this were done. I am indeed sorry to trouble you so much. I am writing at the same [time] to the Manager of the District Bank to say I am to meet you there at 2.15. I am writing at the same time to my husband's *sister* with whom I correspond to explain all. How I wish we could at the last minute save the whole situation. I shall remove all my own things from the Bank at the same time as I feel that individual Trustees would have more respect for the rights of the individual.'

(VHE told her solicitor, in an undated note (Jan. 1935): 'I have found the peice [*sic*] of silver described as a pie knife, it is what I call a *fish slice* . . . There is no *soup ladle*, & I dont remember having one for years. Soup is always served in plates. You know I still & always shall believe there has been foul play.')

I want to put the seriousness of the situation as clearly and forcibly to you as possible, because it is inconceivable that she should continue to behave as she is doing, if she realised herself how serious the matter is, and is likely to be for her. I wish to implore you, by every means in your power, and in cooperation with your mother if you think best, to induce Vivienne to agree to the inevitable, in her own interest. You must see how lamentable it would be if things came to this extremity, and also how totally unnecessary it is. There is no time to waste; but I have confidence that you will use every means to make her see what the consequences of her attitude must be, and to make her agree to the removal of my property.[1]

Yours ever,
[Tom]

I am sending another copy of this letter to your business address.

1–TSE's sister Ada had written to him on 20 Sept. 1934: 'First let me say how delighted I am to hear that the business with V. is getting settled at last. You will feel a great relief from strain, I am sure, when that is all over. She certainly is odd. It always seems to be the people who are not certifiable who do most harm to others.'

TO *Dylan Thomas*[1]   CC

9 October 1934   [Faber & Faber Ltd]

Dear Mr Thomas,

I have read your three stories[2] and am very much interested. The first one is definitely much too horrible to be possible to print in a periodical and could only be published in a collection of your own work. I am keeping the second one, *The Visitors*,[3] and return the other two but I should like to see more of what you write, either prose or verse, whenever you care to send it.[4]

Yours sincerely,
[T. S. Eliot]

---

1 – Dylan Thomas (1914–53), Welsh poet, short-story writer, dramatist, broadcaster. TSE to Hugh Gordon Porteus, 17 Dec. 1957: 'I did not know Dylan Thomas very well and never took to him particularly, although I have been impressed by the warmth of affection for him of people whose opinions I respect including Vernon Watkins . . . whom I like very much, but I was rather too senior perhaps to see the side of him that must have been so very lovable. Anyway your account seemed to me as fair and unbiased as anything I have read' (Beinecke). When Thomas applied for assistance from the Royal Literary Fund, TSE wrote in an undated letter to H. J. C. Marshall: 'Mr Thomas has, from time to time, contributed both prose and verse to *The Criterion*, which I edit; and I am publishing another poem of his in the next issue. I consider him one of a very small number of notable poets of his generation whose names will survive the test of time; he has the additional distinction of being the most brilliant (in my opinion) of younger Welsh writers. I wish to support wholeheartedly his application; and I do not know of any way at the present moment in which a grant from the Royal Literary Fund could be more suitably bestowed.' When A. Desmond Hawkins advised TSE on 20 Apr. 1940 that Thomas was going to register as a Conscientious Objector, and asked if TSE would 'sign a round-robin testifying to his talent as a poet, and/or the probable genuineness of his convictions', TSE replied, 6 May 1940: 'I should certainly sign a letter testifying to his gifts and accomplishments as a poet and a prose writer, and could also say that I had not the slightest reason to doubt the genuineness of his convictions, but as I have never talked to him on the subject . . . I don't see how I could say more than that.' EVE to Miss Barker (secretary at F&F), 16 Feb. 1964: 'Please write to Mr Bill Read of 69 Revere Street, Boston 14, Mass. and say that TSE thanks him for his letter of January 8th, which amused him, and say that he has no recollection of Dylan ever paying him back, but then he never expected him to. He regarded any money he gave to Dylan as a gift.' TSE to Paul Horgan, 1 May 1964: 'My wife, before she married, saw something of Dylan in connection with her work and found him a very likeable rapscallion, as I did too . . .'
2 – Not identified.
3 – Dylan Thomas, 'The Visitor', C. 14 (Jan. 1935), 251–9.
4 – On 5 Feb. 1937, the agent Spencer Curtis Brown was to write to FVM, enclosing 'THE BURNING BABY and other stories': 'Here are the Dylan Thomas short stories about which Richard Church spoke to you. I shall look forward to hearing from you as soon as you have come to a decision on them.' The word 'NO' is written by unknown hand on the letter.

TO *Hugh Ross Williamson*[1]   CC

9 October 1934   [Faber & Faber Ltd]

Dear Mr Williamson,

I must apologise for the long time I have taken over writing to you about the poem by R. F. Waller.[2] It puzzled me so much that I was obliged to take another opinion. I won't say, even now, that I understand it but I do think that it shows very considerable ability, and is, at least, a remarkable *tour de force* for a boy of 20. What disconcerts me is that he writes in such a middle-aged way. I suppose that is the result of his invalidism but I wish that he could have a more youthful outlook. I suppose from what you say that it is impossible for him to get about; otherwise I should ask you to send him to see me. But I do think that it is just worthwhile giving him

---

1 – Hugh Ross Williamson (1901–78), author, historian, dramatist, journalist, broadcaster, worked on the *Yorkshire Post* (leader writer, drama critic) before editing *The Bookman*, 1930–4. Geoffrey Grigson recalled that Williamson 'worked hard to drag that tame old-fashioned literary journal from allegiance to the Squirearchy to support of Eliotry and Audenism [and] to conduct what we thought was the necessary game of harassing the Sitwells as pretenders to modernism' (*Times*, 21 Jan. 1978). Robert Waller wrote of him, in *Pilgrimage of Eros* (1992): 'He was exuberant, witty and a bit of a dandy.' In 1943 he was ordained in the Church of England and was for twelve years an Anglo-Catholic curate before converting to Roman Catholicism in 1955. A prolific author, he wrote over thirty-five books, including *The Poetry of T. S. Eliot* (1932), biographies and histories. See too *The Walled Garden* (autobiography, 1956).

2 – Robert Waller (1913–2005), poet, writer, radio producer; see further, letter to him, 19 Mar 1935, below.

Williamson (*Strand Magazine*) asked TSE on 12 July to read a 'badly-titled poem': 'Waller is 20: he has been most of his life an invalid, secured in an odd suburban house. He came to me originally when he was 17, with some derivative romantic poems: rather bad. He has developed (making allowance for environment and illness) rapidly, I think, and this particular poem seems to me worthy of a better eye than mine . . . I feel so definitely that he is worthy of encouragement.' TSE wrote on 20 Feb. 1946 to Theodora Bosanquet, editor of *Time and Tide*, 'to ask if you could find any reviewing work for a young friend of mine named Robert Waller who has recently been demobilised after six years in the Army and having taken part in the Normandy invasion and the Occupation of Germany. I knew him for several years before the war and he has always struck me as a distinctly remarkable young man of incessant intellectual activity who thinks for himself. He is to a large extent self-educated, coming from some obscure part of South London and with a somewhat sordid family background, but he was for a year or two at London University.'

Waller to EVE, 22 Dec. 1981: 'thanks to your husband sending an essay of mine on *Hamlet* to (Sir) Desmond McCarthy, I became his private secretary in 1936/37. After that I shuttled between London and Paris; spent six years as a private in the army and after being demobbed was a producer in the BBC: at first on literary, religious and artistic programmes, then, dramatically, on agriculture and rural life! I was submerged in a passionate interest in ecology . . . [TSE] was, as you can imagine, immensely kind and helpful to me in a great crisis in my life . . .'

some encouragement and sympathy, and I should like to see subsequent work by him.[1]

> Yours very sincerely,
> [T. S. Eliot]

TO *James Laughlin IV*[2]

TS Houghton

10 October 1934   Faber & Faber Ltd

Dear Mr Laughlin,

I have your letter of the 3rd.[3] It seems to me that the best thing to advise you to do is to send a copy of the typescript over to me as soon as it is ready. If it appears to be unsuitable for Faber & Faber, I shall at least be in a better position to advise you where to send it.

I hope for original as well as critical work from you in due course. I am delighted that you like Pound's book.[4]

> Yours sincerely,
> T. S. Eliot[5]

---

1 – An abbreviated version of this letter was relayed by Williamson to Waller: see Waller's *Pilgrimage of Eros*, 95; letter in BL Add MS 71231. TSE talked with Waller in mid-Nov. 1934.

Williamson replied, 19 Oct.: 'Actually he is almost well now: his heart still troubles him at times, but he is living a fairly natural existence. So I am presuming on your kindness to tell him to write to you and ask if he may see you. That . . . would encourage him more than anything.'

2 – James Laughlin IV (1914–97), scion of a wealthy steel family; poet; major publisher of modernist and experimental writers; launched New Directions Publishing Company in 1936 while in his Junior year at Harvard (bringing out the first of the annual anthologies *New Directions in Prose and Poetry*, 1936–91). His authors included EP, William Carlos Williams, Elizabeth Bishop, Henry Miller, MM, Wallace Stevens, E. E. Cummings, Lawrence Ferlinghetti, Thomas Merton, Kenneth Rexroth and Delmore Schwartz. See further Ian S. MacNiven, *"Literchoor is my beat": A Life of James Laughlin, publisher of New Directions* (2014).

3 – Laughlin was finishing a 'little book on dear old Gertrude Stein', and wondered whether TSE could suggest a British publisher for the work, if not F&F itself. 'It is ragged and sometimes strong writing, which wavers between Pound dynamics and Eliotine [*sic*] suavity . . .'

4 – Laughlin praised the F&F production of EP's *Make It New*. 'It is a beautiful book, and you have done a great service in making that stuff available.'

5 – In reply (11 Oct.), Laughlin warned TSE that his work on Stein was 'thin cloth indeed . . . [I]t is hardly the kind of thing I could show you with an open heart. The book is not my criticism of Miss Stein, but an impartial elucidation of her intentions and aesthetic opinions.' On 9 Nov., while staying with EP in Rapallo, he wrote that he had decided not to submit his work on Stein.

TO *Bernard Iddings Bell*[1]

10 October 1934   [*The Criterion*]

Dear Canon Bell,

Thank you for sending me your article 'The Decay of Intelligence in America', which I ought to have acknowledged before. While it is superficially of only local application, I think it is of significance here also, and if I can, I want to use it in a number in which I shall have room to point out its application in a few editorial remarks.[2]

Looking forward to seeing you again next summer.

I am,
Yours sincerely,
[T. S. Eliot]

TO *Ezra Pound*

11 Oct[ober] 1934 A.D.   Faber & Faber Ltd

Dear Ez ez first place I suppose you have recd copies of *MIN*[3] by now I am thinking About whom to give it To review have you any personal ideas or preferences?? Second what the ell is the Use of sending p.c. about

1 – Bernard Iddings Bell (1886–1958), Episcopal clergyman and influential High Church conservative, served from 1919 to 1933 as Warden of St Stephen's College (now Bard College), New York, where he taught too at Columbia University. He was Canon of the Cathedral of Saints Peter and Paul, Chicago, and William Vaughn Moody Lecturer at the University of Chicago. His works include *Beyond Agnosticism* (1929), *In the City of Confusion* (1938), and *God is Not Dead* (1945). See further Cicero Bruce, 'Bernard Iddings Bell, Rebel Rouser', *Modern Age* 41 (1999), 252–61. Russell Kirk called him 'an Isaiah preaching to the Remnant'.

2 – 'The Decay of Intelligence in America', C. 14 (Jan. 1935), 193–203. TSE's 'Commentary', 264: 'We print in this number some observations on the condition of Education in America by Canon B. Iddings Bell of Rhode Island. As some readers may hold the mistaken belief that education in America has no lessons or warnings for education in England, a word of comment may not be amiss. So far as I have had the opportunity to observe, the problems of education in England and in America are likely to become more, rather than less similar. The problems of the provincial universities appear very similar, and the importance of the provincial universities relative to that of the older foundations is in both countries increasing. It is therefore pertinent to know what an American educator, whose attitude is similar to that which *The Criterion* might be expected to take up, thinks of American Education to-day. Canon Bell was for some years the head of a college which he ran in a way opposed to the general tendencies of the time; a college which, I imagine, has altered its character since he left it.'

3 – *Make It New*.

Mockel[1] when nobody knows where or if Mockel is. Careeers napoleonlic have been blasted by lack of attention to details. Well. Now I like that new piece of yours & wish to publish it[2] But there is one peculiar kind of difficulty affecting mode of presentation which is. Here's Flint been going over a theory of his own which he thinks demolishes Douglas and nearly everything else anyway he thinks he has found what the world needs and it is preying on his mind brain.[3] Well I dont know it is all tricked out with algebra and cymbals Morley says the mathematics is allright for the matter of that but that the theory would be just as true or false without em and a damb sight lucider But now heres It I have staved off Frank in this way for I dont want to be responsible for him going to the loonybin with this theory I says tactful Well I dont mind printing things I disagree with no one can say I am narrow in the mind in that respect even though I Have a paleo-devonian cephalic index But I do worry about printing what I dont Understand So I will print this as a letter though a heell of a long one Now the point is that if I print yours simulataneously or soon after as artikel that will ruffle his sensibilities and make him unhappy because then he will feel that I have been deal dealing doubly by him, which no doubt there is a good case to be made out So . yours being desirable to print rapidly I propose to print as correspondence[4] which brings me to the next Point it would make still possible to print Canto in Same number I Think, I shall pro-propose to print No. 36 I think it is because I am afeared that that about Jeff and John Quincy might frighten off the

1 – Albert Mockel (1866–1945), Belgian symbolist poet.

2 – EP responded, 13 Oct.: 'As to yourn of the 11th, I suppose it refers to my note on Mussolini's Milan speech?? Tho it wd/ be clearer if you had referred to it specificly by its title.'

3 – F. S. Flint wrote to TSE on 5 Aug. 1934: 'Here is the "Essay in Arithmetic" in its extended form. There are three things to be said about it:

'(1) If it is new and true, it is very important.

'(2) If it is true and not new, what are the economists bleating and braying about? – they ought to be shouting it.

'(3) If it is not true, it is unimportant.

'Frank Morley may be right in saying that the text states all that the arithmetic states, but he must know that a verbal text is unconvincing without the proof.

'If you print this in the "Criterion", I should like an offprint of a hundred copies . . .'

4 – EP answered, 13 Oct.: 'As you have never showed any leniency to my sensibilities I don't see why you shd/ bother about Frankie's, or BOTHER ME about Frankie's.

'I can't believe his algebra or his econ/ are likely to be much use, but am allus willin' to learn . . . I suppose if you print me as a letter it saves Faber the expense and enables the firm to feed some god damn shit who ought not to be . . . Frank/ sends you something incomprehensible, therefore you print it as a letter.'

See 'Correspondence' (by F. S. Flint and EP), C. 14 (Jan. 1935), 292–304.

publikum which is not yet being acquainted with niceties of American history;[1] and will send rest to Orage asking him to return BUT Is this the Copy WE ARE SUPPOSED TO SET UP FROM??? Had already sent Miss James out for review[2] no more for moment so

Tp

TO *The Editor,* The Church Times

12 October 1934[3]   22 Russell Square, W.C.1

'Our Mr Eliot'

Sir,

In your last week's issue, under the rubric The Editor's Table, I read that I recently shocked the *New Statesman* 'by writing the most important and moving of my poetry to provide money for building churches in London's new suburbs'![4]

1–EP, 'Canto XXXVI' ('A lady asks me / I speak in season . . .'), C. 14 (Jan. 1935), 204–7.
2–EP (8 Oct.) urged TSE to run a 'GOOD article' on *The Diary of Alice James* (1934).
3–Published in the *Church Times* 112 (372) on that date.
4–'The Editor's Table': 'Our Mr Eliot', *The Church Times* 112: no. 3741 (5 Oct. 1934), 355: a review-essay on TSE's *Elizabethan Essays*. 'Scepticism can count nowadays among its adherents (if it is possible to adhere to a negation) many distinguished writers. The Roman Church has its Christopher Dawson, its Alfred Noyes, its Chesterton, its Belloc – four of a noble cohort. But Catholics of the English obedience have little distinction in the world of literature and art . . . [N]one the less, they may properly preen themselves that Mr T. S. Eliot, a poet of genius and a critic, individual, courageous, and sometimes bewildering, is among their fellows.

'T. S. Eliot judges and writes from a definitely Catholic point of view, recently shocking the New Statesman by writing the most important and moving of his poetry to provide money for building churches in London's new suburbs! We say that some of his judgments are bewildering. We do not, for example, profess to understand his high estimate of James Joyce . . .

'Here we are not concerned to discuss Mr Eliot's aesthetic judgments . . . We are concerned first with the problem suggested in the essay, *Shakespeare and the Stoicism of Seneca*, as to how far the personal realities of a great writer may be deduced from his writing, and then since, as Mr Eliot says, "the great poet, in writing himself, writes his time," to consider the character of the later years of the Renaissance, in which Shakespeare was the supremely great figure . . .

'If . . . "the great poet, in writing himself, writes his time," it is also true that in writing his time the poet writes himself, that he expresses the dreams and the fears, the peculiar and fundamental character of his age. Mr Eliot continually asserts that the end of the sixteenth century was a period of "anarchism, dissolution, and chaos". This is only partially true. The century began with dreams and ended in something like despair . . . Christendom was divided; the *respublica Christiana* was destroyed, the faith was largely lost.

'The tragedy for England was that it was untouched by the counter-Reformation.'

If my memory is accurate, this statement is incorrect. It was not the *New Statesman*, but Mr Francis Birrell writing in the *New Statesman*;[1] and, as I remember, Mr Birrell merely expressed incredulity as to whether the building of forty-five new churches would in itself abate the materialism at which I expressed indignation. This was silly of Mr Birrell, inasmuch as a little reflection would have brought him to the conclusion that I never expected that it would. His remark, in fact, was merely a rhetorical Liberal flourish. It is because I support your activity in calling attention to the overt anti-clericalism of the *New Statesman* that I feel obliged to make this correction.

If you were referring to some other statement in that paper than Mr Birrell's notice of *The Rock* I offer my apologies for writing this letter.

When I said that 'the poet, in writing himself, writes his time', I was, I believe, explicitly, quoting Remy de Gourmont.

T. S. Eliot

[We had Mr Birrell's letter in mind. – ED.]

TO *A. L. Rowse* TS Exeter

12 October 1934 Faber & Faber Ltd

My dear Rowse,

I have got your revised version and brought it home to read tonight – but I find myself too tired this evening to apply myself to anything but patience.[2] So I will just answer the

PRIVATE & CONFIDENTIAL

part of the letter.[3] The notion of sharing a house, or dividing some largish set of rooms, had occurred to me at the time <we were discussing living arrangements>. The trouble is that at the moment I dont see my way to

---

1–Francis Birrell, 'Mr Eliot's Revue', *NS&N* 7 (2 June 1934), 847.
2–ALR had submitted his revised version of 'War and Psychology' – his smack at Huxley. 'I considered over and over again how I could cut down the last section: but it seemed such an integral part of the argument . . . directed to answering the crucial difficulty "Won't there be just as much nationalist rivalry in a world of nationalist states, as under capitalism?" . . . that I have left it in.'
3–ALR proposed in his (undated) letter, 'If both you & I have some difficulty in finding a suitable place in which to live in comfort, but inexpensively, in town, why don't we share, either a little house, or a half a house? . . . [T]here's a good top-half of a house – 6 rooms – in Mecklenburgh Square now: it's such a quiet & lovely square.

'Two celibates like you & me ought to be able to get on without too much noise, with a servant to look after us; and I'm away from town a great deal.'

any change. If I get my books, I shall need more room; for the present the chief out about my present place is the noise and vibration of the railway; though, as my sleep began to give way about 1927, that is certainly a consideration. But I don't know when or whether I shall get my books; the chief point is not that but hanging on that. I am now engaged in litigation, which at present is private and I hope will remain so, with my wife, for the possession of my books and a number of objects of sentimental value which remain in her flat. I don't know how expensive this is going to be; and of course one feels very unsettled while such a business is going on. I am expecting a pretty large bill from one firm of lawyers for settling my arrears of Income Tax – the taxes are paid, I sweated in America to do that, hence the poor quality of the lectures; and I shall get another from my regular lawyers for this miserable business. And when I settle I shall have to buy furniture, I haven't a stick of my own except three bookcases or so – and bedding and what not. I don't mind other people's furniture except for its ugliness; but when one settles it is of course more practical in the long run to buy one's own. So I can't see myself thinking seriously about settling for another season or so.

By the way, equally confidentially, would you care to express any opinion of the legal abilities of Quintin Hogg? It seems that my solicitors have got him as counsel in this case – God knows why one needs counsel at this point. The head of the firm is a friend of his father. I have no reason to doubt the choice, but one wonders.[1]

Ever yours,
T. S. Eliot

1–ALR replied (n.d.): 'I don't think you need fear about Quintin: he's a damned good lawyer, very conscientious and hard-working, which means that he won't scamp your work for you . . .'

Quintin Hogg (1907–2001), lawyer and politician, was called to the bar by Lincoln's Inn in 1932, after taking firsts in Classical Moderations and in Greats at Oxford (where he was also President of the Oxford Union Debating Society). He was elected to a prize fellowship at All Souls in 1931. A gifted lawyer with a volatile personality, he was to take silk in 1953, becoming head of his chambers in 1955. His career as Conservative MP saw him hold office as First Lord of the Admirality, Minister of Education, Lord President of the Council, Minister for Science, and finally Lord Chancellor in the administrations of both Ted Heath (who granted him a life peerage as Baron Hailsham of St Marylebone) and Margaret Thatcher. His publications include *A Sparrow's Flight: The Memoirs of Lord Hailsham of St Marylebone* (1990).

16 October 1934   [Faber & Faber Ltd]

Dear Father D'Arcy,

Mr Eliot has asked me to write and ask you if you know whether there is any Roman Catholic organisation in this country for the relief of Roman Catholic emigrants from Germany. He has been asked to help in the case of a boy of about 20 who is described as a tailor's assistant, and who is very likely coming to this country. It appears that the boy is likely to be deprived of his livelihood owing to his religious allegiance, and that if he goes abroad, his father desires at least that he should keep up his religious duties. The boy does not yet speak English.

Mr Eliot would be grateful for any information you could give him. He also wishes me to say that he is very sorry to have seen nothing of you this summer, and hopes that you will let him know when you return to London at the end of the term.

Yours very truly
[Erica Wright]
Secretary.

TO *John Garrett*   CC

16 October 1934   [*The Criterion*]

Dear Mr Garrett,

Thank you for sending me the number of *Rep*, which I think as a whole does you much credit.[2] I should very much like to see the magazine regularly.

I should be very glad to add you to the reviewers for the *Criterion* when the opportunity presents. I am not quite clear what type of book you are

---

1 – Martin D'Arcy (1888–1976), Jesuit priest and theologian: see Biographical Register.
2 – Garrett sent (12 Oct.) the issue of *REP*, Sept. 1934, 'containing your authoritative article'.
   TSE, 'Religious Drama and the Church': 'I doubt whether there is anything to be done with the contemporary theatre-going public: you have got to assemble new audiences . . . Only a cause can give the bond, the common assumptions between author and audience, which the serious dramatist needs . . . There are only two causes now of sufficient seriousness, and they are mutually exclusive: the Church and Communism.'

specially interested in reviewing, and should be glad if you would let me know.

Yours sincerely,
[T. S. Eliot]

TO *James Hanley*[1]　　　　　　　　　　　　　　　　CC

16 October 1934　　　　　　　　　*[The Criterion]*

Dear Sir,

I have read the story 'Stoker Hoglitt' [*sc.* 'Stoker Haslett'] which you sent in and I like it. I should like to publish it in the *Criterion* but I am afraid it is about twice too long to be possible. However, I should like to keep it for a short time to consider and show to one or two other people. Meanwhile I should like to know if you could let me see any shorter stories or sketches; and if you are ever in London, I should be glad if you would let me know so that we might arrange to meet.[2]

Yours very truly,
[T. S. Eliot]

TO *Michael Roberts*　　　　　　　　　　　　　　　　CC

17 October 1934　　　　　　　　　*[The Criterion]*

Dear Mr Roberts,

Thank you for your letter of the 12th.[3] Your pupil's antics have not caused me much personal inconvenience, although I believe he has taken up a certain amount of my secretary's time. I have not yet seen him and I can't see that there is any particular point in my doing so just yet. I am

---

1–James Hanley (1897–1985): prolific British writer of novels, short stories, and plays (for radio, TV, theatre); author of *Drift* (1930), *Boy* (1931; repr. 2007 with an essay by Chris Gostick, 'Extra Material on James Hanley's *Boy*'), *No Directions* (1943), *A Kingdom* (1978).

2–Hanley (16 Oct.) expected to be in London in late Nov. He asked, 'I hope you will be kind enough to excuse my asking you if you would be good enough to read in proof the 1st volume of my tetralogy – *The Furys*, which is being issued in January (a saga of a working class family). I would look on this as a favour, as I have no contacts with the literary world.'

Hanley's story 'A Changed Man' was to appear in *C.* 14 (Apr. 1935), 374–8.

3–'I believe that you have been troubled by the antics of a former pupil of mine [Alexander Langridge Ford] . . . The poor lad has been through a rather difficult time, and fired with sudden literary ambitions has made himself ridiculous and pathetic. I think he will be all right now, and

always ready to be sympathetic to anyone who has a superficial appearance of lunacy, and I hope that he will turn out for the best. Certainly I don't want to be a correspondent with him on the same basis as you are; but I think he is probably worth the trouble you and Miss Adam Smith are taking over him.

> With very many thanks,
> Yours sincerely,
> [T. S. Eliot]

TO *Stephen Spender*   TS Northwestern

17 October 1934   Faber & Faber Ltd

Dear Spender,

What the Devil do you Mean by writing to Miss Wright in that way.[1] If you havent any clothes that the police will allow on the street, come in a barrel or I will lend you an old suit which would not be too bad a fit only I must have it back. As the Revd Chas. Smyth[2] is coming dressed as a Scoutmaster,[3] I dont see that you have anything to complain of unless you have some Grievance against me, in which case you should speak Out like a Man. In any case, feelings will be Hurt if you do not come so will close.

> T. S. E.[4]

I am getting Miss Adam Smith to keep an eye on him till I come down. He is, or will be, a very able person, but there is no reason why he should badger you at the moment. Some idiot has been psychoanalysing him, but I think we can put that right. He writes me seven pages a day.'

1 – Spender wrote on 16 Oct.: 'Mr Stephen Spender regrets that he cannot accept the kind invitation to the Criterion party [on 31 Oct.], as he has no morning dress.'

2 – Charles Smyth (1903–87), ecclesiastical historian and preacher: see letter to him 12 Nov. 1935, below.

3 – Smyth had asked (n.d.): 'Could you tolerate me in Scout uniform, or would that shock the company too much? If I have to come home & change, it will make me frightfully late.' In another letter (n.d.): 'may I take it that Scout Uniform will pass as "Morning Dress"?' Smyth reaffirmed in another undated letter, 'I look very nice in Scout uniform – not at all "hearty".'

4 – Spender responded (n.d.): 'I'm so sorry. I thought Morning Dress was clothes with swallow tails, or rather like your elephant in the seal. However, I took [William] Plomer aside today and had a Frank Chat with him and he told me that they are just clothes one wears in the morning.'

TO *George Bell*   Lambeth Palace Library

18 October 1934   Faber & Faber Ltd

My dear Lord Bishop,

I believe that in writing to you in June I mentioned some friends of mine from America to whom I had given an introduction. They did not visit Chichester at the time, but I understand that they are coming for a week or so within a few days, so I am giving a fresh introduction, and I hope very much that you will be able to see them. They are the Revd John Carroll Perkins D.D. retired minister of Kings Chapel (Unitarian) in Boston, and Mrs Perkins, and their niece Miss Emily Hale.

Incidentally, I am expecting to spend the weekend of the 21st at the Dolphin with them; and I hope you will not be too busy for me to come to see you in their company, if you have any free time on the Sunday.[1]

With all best wishes to Mrs Bell and yourself,

I am, My Lord,
Yours very sincerely,
T. S. Eliot

Gabriel Hebert has just finished a book, which ought to be very good.

TO *F. O. Matthiessen*   cc

18 October 1934   [Faber & Faber Ltd]

Dear Matty,

I have your letter of September 30th, and am returning the enclosure.[2] I marvel at your industry and cleverness in digging out such information. I have made a few corrections and notes on the typescript. The only thing I am still uncertain about is that I had been under the impression that my grandfather had 14 children, and it is something of a disappointment to me to be told that he had only 9. I will look this matter up; but I think the quickest thing for you to do would be, assuming that you want to mention this interesting fact, to write to my brother (H. W. Eliot, 315, East 68th Street, New York City), who knows all about such things.

1–Dr and Mrs Perkins, Emily Hale, and TSE all signed the Visitors Book at the Deanery of Chichester on 30 Nov. 1934: Helen Gardner, *The Composition of 'Four Quartets'* (1978), 35.
2–'The offer of the Oxford Press is of course highly satisfactory, and . . . gladly accepted.'

I am glad that you have got the book off your hands and can now turn to something more important. I see that you ask another question.[1] The quotation from the Dante is indeed from Charles Maurras, and is to be found in a little essay called, I think, *Dante et Béatrice* or some such title. I can't lay my hand on it at the moment but it is a good essay. Also I didn't know T. E. Hulme personally although I had heard much about him. I never read anything he wrote until *Speculations* came out.[2] Herbert Read didn't know him personally either: only people living in London before the War knew him.

I had a very pleasant evening and a very pleasant lunch with Ted but, unfortunately, his and my engagements were from town which made it impossible for me to see as much of him as I should have wished.

Yours ever in haste,
[T. S. Eliot]

P.S. It is quite correct that the 1917 pamphlet on Ezra Pound was written by me.[3]

TO *Hope Mirrlees*[4]   TS Hornbake Library

22 October 1934   Faber & Faber Ltd

Dear Hope,

I was so sorry to find your letter this morning – my secretary tells me she let you know that I was away – first in Leeds to lecture, and then for the week-end. I have a snuffling cold, caught in the Leeds train, so perhaps it is just as well. I hope we may meet soon – I will write and make a suggestion. I hope the biography is progressing.

Yours ever sincerely,
T. S. Eliot

1 – Matthiessen wanted to know the source of TSE's epigraph to his *Dante*.
2 – EVE told Lyndall Gordon, 16 May 1975: 'He never met Hulme, and did not remember (in 1954) reading any of his essays in the *New Age*. After the poems he moved to *Speculations*.'
3 – *Ezra Pound: His Metric and Poetry*.
4 – Hope Mirrlees (1887–1978), British poet, novelist, translator and biographer, became a close friend of TSE; author of important works including *Paris: A Poem* (1918), *Lud in the Mist* (novel, 1926) and *A Fly in Amber: Being an Extravagant Biography of the Romantic Antiquary Sir Robert Bruce Cotton* (1962). See too *Collected Poems of Hope Mirrlees*, ed. Sandeep Parmar (2011).

(On 18 Mar. 1934, VHE went to tea with Hope Mirrlees – 'one of the few among Eliot's friends to take trouble with Vivienne' (Gordon, *Imperfect Life* 281) – '& had a most diverting conversation – I found her as usual a very brilliant companion & a most peculiar personality'.)

TO *John Hayward*   MS King's

24 October [1934]   Faber & Faber Ltd

Dear John

How very kind of you. *The New Yorker* to nourish my mind and the
Turtle Soup my body. I had never tasted it before.

Back & head be full of aches

Or Weasand?[1]   Chest be full of croup,

But Belly see thou have store enough
Of jolly good turtle Soup.

Its lovely. I may be up on Friday, if so, to go to Chichester Sat – Mon[2]
– I have a very old friend from America who will be in London from next
week & would like me to bring her to tea with you, if you consent.[3] Also
will settle Faber & Richmond.

I caught this cold lecturing in Leeds but went to Morleys for weekend,
& played GO, or as the Chinese say KI, 1000 times more difficult than
chess. Invented by Emperor Shosun in 2225 B.C., to improve the mind
of his son. I took to my bed on Monday. And will ring you up on next
Monday.

Very grateful thanks –
Affectionately
Tom

TO *T. S. Gregory*[4]   CC

26 October 1934   [Faber & Faber Ltd]

Dear Mr Gregory,

I believe you have had the typescript of *The Unfinished Universe* for
some little time now. Please don't think that I am trying to hustle you in

1–Weasand: gullet.
2–Emily Hale's birthday fell on 27 Oct.: TSE planned to spend the weekend with her and
Dr and Mrs Perkins in Chichester.
3–Smart, *Tarantula's Web*: 'Emily Hale's name was duly inscribed in the visitors' book
[at JDH's flat in Bina Gardens, S. Kensington] for 9 November . . . At first Hayward felt
pleased to be treated as one of Eliot's intimates when he was introduced to her. But soon,
like Virginia Woolf and Ottoline Morrell, he took against "that awful American Woman"
and her "sergeant major manner". He particularly disliked the way she seemed to boss Eliot
about. She was a "grim, prim, school-ma'amish female who takes a dreadful proprietary
interest in poor Tom", he wrote to Ottoline Morrell' (100–1).
4–T. S. Gregory (d. 1975), convert from Methodism to Catholicism. Author of *The
Unfinished Universe* (F&F, Mar. 1935). The blurb was almost certainly by TSE: 'This is a book

any way by writing to ask its present position. It is only that we like to lay our plans as far as possible in advance, and we are anxious to know when the script will be ready for the printers.

I trust that by this time you have been able to get Father D'Arcy's opinion.

With all good wishes,
Yours sincerely,
[T. S. Eliot]

TO *Ottoline Morrell*   MS Texas

29 October 1934   Faber & Faber Ltd

My dear Ottoline,

I have just realised that I am taking some people to *Richard II* on Friday evening; which means being at the restaurant, dressed, at 6.45; so that I shall have to leave you *very* early. I am sorry; I actually made the theatre engagement before you asked me; and it did not occur to me that there was any conflict. So I will come at 4.30, hoping to find you in.

My friend, about whom I wrote to you, will be glad to come with me on the 8th. No doubt there will be a number of other people; but I hope you will be able to talk to her a little, as I have been anxious that you should meet. She is quite an exceptional person, though it may not be immediately obvious.[1]

---

which is not easily classified. On the one hand it is the record of a passionate and sincere pursuit of spiritual conviction, of the journey of one human mind. But the author, a nonconformist minister in Wales, has also elaborated a kind of Christian philosophy of history. He examines Greek civilization from a point of view which to many will be new and disturbing; he considers the Middle Ages and the Renaissance and Reformation, and finally the modern illusion; and he is led to conclusions from which the reader himself will find it difficult to escape. This is a book for the theologian, for the historian, and for every reader, however ignorant of theological science, who is still interested in the Christian answer, and who will find himself following an argument of absorbing interest, to a conclusion which he may or may not be prepared to accept.'

Gregory wrote in his Preface: 'I wrote this book as a Methodist minister, and began work upon it without any suspicion that I should ever become anything else. There are questions – so it seemed to me – which must assail any sincere Christian in these days, some of faith and others of practice; and it was in attempting to find a Christian answer to them that I was led into the Catholic faith.'

1–TSE and Emily Hale went to tea with OM on 7 Nov.; the other guest was Baroness Budberg. Maria (Moura) Budberg (1892–1974), daughter of a Ukrainian nobleman and diplomat, is believed to have been a double agent for OGPU and the British Intelligence Service – becoming known as the 'Mata Hari' of Russia. Married in 1911 to Count Djon

I had lunch with Yeats today. Not only my admiration, but my *liking*, for him, grows with time: he is one of those few of whom one can say without exaggeration, that it is a 'privilege' to know them.[1]

My cold, I think, is cured.

Affectionately,
Tom

TO *John Hayward*   TS King's

30 October 1934   Faber & Faber Ltd

Dear John,

I cannot as yet lay claim to bearing comparison with a fiddle, a trivet, or a fighting-cock – I am not yet quite up to the mark: but you are to understand from this that I am on deck and in fighting trim. Branle-bas.[2] But jesting apart, as they say, or Plus de Baddinadge, I had lunch with Richmond today, and found him Primed for your Nuts & Wine; you have only to say the word, and I will find out what nights Faber has at his disposal. And I should like to know when I might bring my friend to tea. Tuesday is impossible, and Wednesday. And I warn you that I have to drink poteen with Pat Mullin and possibly Mrs Kiernan on Monday, so I shall probably be sick all the week, but no matter. Perhaps you will ring me up for a chat.

Your obedient
T.

---

von Benckendorff (who was killed in 1918), she had a perilous love affair with the British diplomat Robert Bruce Lockhart, was secretary and common-law wife to Maxim Gorky, 1922–33; and from 1920, and again from 1933 until his death, mistress of H. G. Wells (she declined to marry him). She was also married, briefly, to Baron Nikolai von Budberg-Bönningshausen. She was in addition a writer, and worked on the scripts for films including *The Sea Gull*, dir. by Sidney Lumet (1968), and *Three Sisters*, dir. Laurence Olivier (1970). See Nina Berberova, *Moura: The Dangerous Life of the Baroness Budberg* (2005); Deborah McDonald and Jeremy Dronfield, *A Very Dangerous Woman: The Lives, Loves and Lies of Russia's Most Seductive Spy* (2015).

1–OM noted in her journal, 3 Nov. 1934: 'I was expecting T. S. Eliot & Gerald Heard to Tea – & rather Dreading it . . . However after a little they got going & began about Yeats whom Tom had recently seen . . . – Eliot had liked him very much' (BL).

TSE to Donald Hall, 16 Apr. 1959: 'Yeats was always very gracious when one met him and had the art of treating younger writers as if they were his equals and contemporaries.'

2–Branle-bas: the taking down and stowing of hammocks in the morning.

TO *Laurence Irving*[1]   CC

30 October 1934   [Faber & Faber Ltd]

Dear Mr Irving,

The Bishop told me something about your designs, and kindly promised to put us in touch. I told him that I would keep as much of the day free as possible on both Thursday and Friday in the hope of hearing from you. Since then, unfortunately, I have learnt that the young people who are producing my *Sweeney Agonistes* in 10 days' time, are to have a rehearsal at 2.30 on Friday, at which they want my presence; and I have arranged to ask a few friends to lunch and to go on with me to the rehearsal. So now the only times I have are Thursday and Friday mornings. I am very sorry that I can't lunch with you but I could see you either here or at the Garrick, or wherever you like at any time in the morning. Alternatively, I should be delighted if you could dine with me on Thursday evening.

Yours very sincerely,

[T. S. Eliot]

1–Laurence Irving (1897–1988): theatre designer and author; grandson of the legendary actor-manager Sir Henry Irving. He served with distinction as a pilot during WWI (Croix de Guerre, 1916) before spending time in Hollywood as art director to Douglas Fairbanks Sr. From 1931 he worked in London, designing for theatre and film and elsewhere. His writings include *Henry Irving: The Actor and His World* (1951); he was a director of the Times Publishing Company, 1946–62; and he campaigned for the establishment of the British Theatre Museum.

John Miller, '"His shadow still stretches down the years"', *The Listener*, 12 Feb. 1981, 200: 'The Dean of Canterbury, George Bell, persuaded John Masefield to write and produce *The Coming of Christ* in the Cathedral in 1928, and talked Laurence Irving into his one and only acting performance, as King Gaspar the Wealthy. Laurence also designed a permanent setting for the Festival, which became an annual event, commissioning new religious plays from leading poets. He explains how, after the success of Tennyson's *Becket* (in which Henry Irving had given his last performance) and Laurence Binyon's *The Young King*, George Bell was keen to commission T. S. Eliot:

'"I was empowered to offer the poet a commission of £150 to write the play, with performance guaranteed, which really meant more to them [*sic*] than anything else. We spent the morning in the Cathedral and I showed him the stage and everything. I said: 'Does this suggest any idea to you for a play?' 'Oh, yes, I think I'd like to write about Thomas à Becket.' Of course I was utterly dismayed. I thought 'worn-out Thomas à Becket', but then I realised that he'd make something entirely new, as he did."'

FROM *Bird & Bird* TO *Vivien Eliot*   TS Bodleian

30 October 1934   3 Gray's Inn Square, W.C.1

Dear Madam,

In accordance with the Order made by Mr Justice Goddard on Friday last, the 26th instant, and served upon you yesterday, we write to give you formal notice that we shall call at No. 68, Clarence Gate Gardens, on Monday next, the 5th proximo, at 11.30 a.m. and that by the said Order you are then required to deliver to us as the duly authorised agents of your husband the property specified in the Schedule to the said Order.

We further give you notice that at the same time we propose to make the inventory of the other furniture and effects by the said Order.

> We are, dear Madam,
> Yours faithfully,
> [Signed] Bird & Bird

FROM *Erica Wright* TO *Jan Culpin*[1]   CC

30 October 1934   [Faber & Faber Ltd]

Dear Mrs Culpin,

Mr Eliot has asked me to let you know that his enquiries have not brought to light the existence of any organisation in this country for helping Roman Catholic refugees from Germany. But Mr Eliot has been advised that the best thing to do immediately is to get in touch with the priest in charge at the church of St Boniface, 47, Adler Street (Bishopgate 4933). If the boy has any Jewish blood, Mr Eliot has also heard that the Guild of Israel, C.S.I., Our Lady of Sion, Chepstow Villas, W.11, would probably help.

> Yours very truly.
> [Erica Wright]

1–Mary Johanna ('Jan') Culpin (b. 1897) was the sister of TSE's deceased Oxford friend Karl (Charles) Culpin (1893–1917), who had graduated with a first in Modern History, 1915, and died of wounds in France on 15 May 1917. Their father was Henry Culpin (1861–1912), first curator of the Doncaster Museum and Art Gallery; their mother was Johanna Culpin, née Staengel, who was born in Germany in 1862.

TO *Harry Levin*[1]   TS Houghton

31 October 1934   Faber & Faber Ltd

Dear Mr Levin,

You may by this time have received the October *Criterion* with your
Cleveland in it, which was probably sent to your St Paul address.[2] The
cheques have not yet been sent out, so yours will now go to Eliot House.
I congratulate you and the Committee. It is good to know that the Fellows
now include at least one humanist amongst the scientists and poison gas
researchers.[3]

I shall await your article on the Academy with interest.[4]

I have not yet been allowed to see Matthiessen's book, which several
people here tell me is very good. Anyway, the Oxford University Press are
to publish it, so I can wait. Thank you for your remarks about *The Rock*.[5]

                          Yours sincerely,
                          T. S. Eliot

1 – Harry Levin (1912–94) graduated *summa cum laude* from Harvard in 1934. An authority
on Renaissance literature, and nineteenth- and twentieth-century American, English and
French literature, he rose to become Irving Babbitt Professor of Comparative Literature;
author of *James Joyce: A Critical Introduction* (1941). Levin was to recall: 'I had written a
senior essay for Theodore Spencer, who showed it to TSE. Though it had taken issue with
his views on Metaphysical Poetry, he responded by expressing a willingness to publish it in
his distinguished journal . . . Discussing my first article with him over a cup of tea in his
rooms on the River Charles, I encountered that helpful benignity which so habitually graced
his relations with younger and minor writers' ('Old Possum at Possum House', *T. S. Eliot:
Essays from the 'Southern Review'*, ed. James Olney [1988], 154). At a symposium at the
University of Kent, Canterbury, 8 May 1983, Levin remarked too that TSE's 'stateliness' at
Harvard had been 'mitigated by shyness' (Ackroyd, *T. S. Eliot*, 195). See too Levin, 'T. S.
Eliot: A Reminiscence', *The Harvard Advocate* 100: 3–4 (Fall 1966), 34–5.
2 – Levin, 'John Cleveland and the Conceit', C. 14 (Oct. 1934), 40–53.
3 – Levin reported on 4 Oct. that the Society of Fellows was supporting his 'leisure' at Eliot
House, Harvard, 'for a while'.
4 – 'I have been puttering . . . with some material on the elaborate and unsuccessful attempts
to develop an English academy in the early seventeenth century.'
5 – 'We have just been going through the final stages of Matthiessen's book with him and are
curious to know how it will strike you. May I say that I was particularly impressed by some
of the choruses in *The Rock*?'

TO *Arthur Waley*[1]   CC

31 October 1934   [*The Criterion*]

My dear Waley,
    Would you be willing to review Ezra Pound's volume of essays, *Make It New*[2] for the next *Criterion*? You may not, at first thought, consider it is particularly in your line but Ezra is very worked up because of some reviewer, who criticised his knowledge of Chinese;[2] and I am sure he would like to have the book reviewed by someone whose authority would be unquestionable. Of course Ezra may or may not be right, and I doubt whether either he or his reviewer knows very much about the Chinese language. But I, myself, should be very much interested to have a review from somebody who knows what Ezra is talking about when he is discussing 'ideograms'. If you are willing to do this for me, I will try to find the review in question.[3]

                                     Yours sincerely,
                                     [T. S. Eliot]

TO *Marianne Moore*   TS Rosenbach Museum and Library

31 October 1934   Faber & Faber Ltd

Dear Miss Moore,
    I trust that your first impression, if it is what it appears to be, will survive.[4] If you have any objections, you clothe them in a luminous and

---

1 – Arthur Waley (1889–1966), esteemed orientalist and translator from the Chinese, worked at the British Museum, 1913–29.
2 – D. G. Bridson observed in C. 14 (Oct. 1934), 125: 'The fact that Mr Pound is both hasty and inaccurate is rather hard to deny . . . If he were not congenitally disposed to regard it favourably, surely he would have realised that the Chinese ideogram for "the East", which he carefully and diagrammatically explains as "sun tangled in the tree's branches, as at sunrise" might equally suggest "the West" or the sun tangled in the tree's branches, as at sunset – more especially so, since China's coastline happens to face East.'
3 – Waley replied on 3 Nov.: 'I am afraid I should only make matters worse, as far as Ezra's feelings are concerned. He does not of course pretend in private that he knows Chinese. But he likes to give the world at large that impression, to tell them that his credo is a belief in the "Ta Hio", and so on.' He had 'always admired' EP and would gladly tell TSE over lunch 'whether I think that the part about ideograms is true'. BD reviewed *Make It New* in C, Apr. 1935.
4 – Moore (23 Oct.) felt utterly gratified by the 'comments' that TSE was 'granting' her book. 'To be elucidated is a spur both as regards rectitude and abandon and I begin to find myself on a better level by being even in the Barrie Dear Brutus sense, understood. I might tell you with regard to my froward rhymes that my mother acknowledges being

pleasing mist which makes them invisible – I will try to get the attribution 'Poetry' 'Egoist' corrected.[1] As for mothers,

Whenever I am disposed to be vainglorious, I should remind myself of a remark my mother once made to Sally Bruce Kinsolving of Baltimore.[2] 'Mrs Kinsolving, I like your poetry, because I can understand it and I dont understand my son's.'

There is something in that.

I hope you will like the book from every point of view when you see it.

Yours very sincerely
T. S. Eliot

TO *Shri Purohit Swami*[3]   CC

31 October 1934   [Faber & Faber Ltd]

Dear Swami,

In reply to your letter of the 18th, I hope that you will hear favourably from Dr Jacks.[4]

I spoke to Mr Yeats on Monday, who would be willing to write a prefatory note to your translation of the *Mandookya Upanishad*. I am afraid it is doubtful whether I could include this in the *Criterion* before

---

converted from what for years has been an aggrieved sense of the family gone astray. When a friend recently noted my "using no rhymes," she said, "Don't enlighten him." Even now she thinks she ought to read the Introduction at least once a week' (*Selected Letters*, 329). (In J. M. Barrie's play *Dear Brutus* (1922) a man named Purdie complains that his wife fails to understand his finer points.)

1 – 'I wonder if you know that it was by the Egoist I was first published, not Poetry; it is only loyalty however that leads me to mention this' (*Selected Letters*, 329–30).

2 – Sally Bruce Kinsolving, née Sally Archer Bruce (1876–1962); author of *Depths and Shallows* (1921), *David and Bathsheba and Other Poems* (1922), and *Grey Heather* (1930).

3 – Shri Purohit Swami (1882–1946), who was born into a wealthy and religious family in India, studied philosophy and law at university but elected to spend his entire adult life in spiritual devotion. At the direction of his mentor he married and had three children, but otherwise lived in celibacy. Author of poems, songs, a play, a novel, and an autobiography, he lived from 1930 in England, where he undertook translations of the *Bhagavad Gita*, Patanjali's *Aphorisms of Yoga*, and (with W. B. Yeats) *The Ten Principal Upanishads*.

4 – TSE's secretary had advised Shri Purohit Swami, 17 Oct.: 'Dr Jacks says that [the *Hibbert Review*] is always overwhelmed with matter but that he would be able to consider publishing one Upanishad if the total length is not over 5000 words. Mr Eliot suggests that you should send one to Dr Jacks, and Mr Eliot will be writing to you about other matters in a few days.'

Purohit submitted his translation of 'Katha-Upanishad' (5,000 words) to Dr Jacks. He wrote too that W. B. Yeats had told him of his regret that the 'Mandookya-Upanishad' had not been included in *The Holy Mountain*: Yeats had even referred to it in his essay for C. Yeats indeed thought it would be good to publish it in C. – 'with a very small note by him'.

the March number, and I don't believe that Mr Yeats would have time to do his preface for the December number in any case, but if the later date is agreeable to you, I should be very glad to hear.

Now about the three books.[1] First of all, I don't believe that much could be done with your *Stories of Indian Mysticism* for the British public. They are, of course, of varying merit and some are extremely interesting but I feel that they could only appeal to a public, which is already educated in Indian thought and imagery. I don't find that English readers are very much interested in miracles. I am sorry to say that very few of my friends are sincere believers, even in the Christian miracles; and I must confess

---

1–TSE wrote on 26 Sept. 1934 a reader's report, 'Murder of my Swami (Feast of S. Cyprian & S. Justina)', with this slightly misremembered epigraph from Byron's 'The Bride of Abydos': 'O wild as the accent of lovers' farewell /Are the deeds that they do and the tales that they tell':

I.

Especially the Cock & Bull tales that they tell. The tales are full of miracles, and the number of miracles that anybody can believe is limited, for instance that one about the buffalo reciting the Vedas. As the author says, 'it is very easy to tame a tiger, though not so easy to ride him in public, but to ride a wall was beyond imagination'. There is a story about a saint being cured of colic by his disciple appealing to a tigress to give her milk, which to me is incredible. When these people are not performing miracles they are bursting into song, and the worst of it is that the songs are given in full. The only sensible thing he says is that the English are materialistic.

II.

Swami's translation of the Bhagavad Gita. There is no doubt of the importance of this poem, and I must say, without having had the opportunity to compare this translation either with the original or with other translations, that it seems a good translation, though not so good as the original. BUT I don't see how we could sell a translation of the Bhagavad Gita or Holy Song unless it had an apparatus and scholarly introduction etc. which is not what the Swami wants. He wants to appeal to possible disciples, being a missionary: wouldn't he do better to try the occultist and theosophical presses?

III.

Swami's translation of seven Upanishads. I have seen one of them – I think it was the Kena Upanishad, and without having had the opportunity to compare it with Muller or Deussen or the original it struck me as a good translation. Seven Upanishads, with prefatory note by T. S. Eliot, is the idea. I don't like the idea, but it is less unpractical than I or II. The idea of [a] prefatory note by T. S. Eliot is that W. B. Yeats has struck and says he can't do more, which in itself is all to the good.

Epilogue.

What I really need is names of other publishers to steer the Swami onto. I am willing even to write an introduction to one book if somebody else will publish it, if I get a fee from Faber & Faber for not publishing it as well as a fee from the other publisher for publishing it. The point is that My Swami should NOT murder Faber & Faber. I am paid to PREVENT as many books from being accepted as possible.

that even to myself some of those recounted in your stories are frankly incredible. I simply don't know what to do about this or whom to suggest as possible publishers. I think, however, that the most likely publishers for all or any of the MSS., which you have sent me, are George Allen & Unwin.

Of the two sets of translations, I am most interested in the *Upanishads*, and feel that this book has a better chance of success than the *Bhagavad-Geeta*. Here again to the ordinary occidental reader who has no first hand experience of Indian thought, and no real perception of the seriousness of the subject, the *Bhagavad-Geeta* is likely to seem at first sight repetitious and prolix. I believe that it might seem so to me, if I had not many years ago read it in the original. The *Upanishads* on the other hand are short and varied, and should interest many more people. I would definitely urge you to attempt to get this volume published first. It should be a valuable and interesting volume, and I think that it ought to interest Messrs Allen & Unwin.

I am returning to you the *Stories of Indian Mysticism* and *The Bhagavad-Geeta*, and returning for the moment the copies of *Six Upanishads*, one of which is the *Mandookya*.

With all best wishes,
Yours very sincerely,
[T. S. Eliot]¹

TO *Ralph Hodgson*²   TS Beinecke

31 October 1934   Faber & Faber Ltd

Now then Mr Hodgson Sir I aint done with you yet though it did take me indeed some time to recover from your letter of Aug. 31st but now I

1–TSE's secretary wrote to Shri Purohit Swami, 7 Nov.: 'I am enclosing five of the Upanishads as arranged yesterday. The sixth, the Mandookya Upanishad, Mr Eliot is keeping in the hope that he may be able to publish it later in *The Criterion*.'
2–Ralph Hodgson (1871–1962), Yorkshire-born poet – author of *The Last Blackbird* (1907); winner of the 1914 Edmond de Polignac Prize of the Royal Society of Literature – taught English at Sendai University, Japan, 1924–38. He was awarded the Order of the Rising Sun, 1938; Annual Award of the Institute of Arts and Letters, 1946; Queen's Gold Medal, 1954.
    TSE and Hodgson were introduced by OM on 11 Dec. 1931. See Stanford S. Apseloff, 'T. S. Eliot and Ralph Hodgson Esqre', *Journal of Modern Literature* 10: 2 (June 1983), 342–6; Vinni Marie D'Ambrosio, 'Meeting Eliot and Hodgson in Five-finger Exercises',

have recovered my Wind and here it Is.[1] I can only suppose this sort of attitude comes from your associating so long with poor little Orientals what you can bully with your Fist but Sir you cant treat big men 6000 miles or more away like that. Well what if Morley IS Looney? What has that to do with it? I said set a lunatic to catch a lunatic and besides you dont treat him fair. Its like Ambolocles and the Lion when the Lion came up and licked his paw at him supposin that Ambolocles had hauled off & hit the Lion on the side of the Jaw he never would have become a great hero and have had plays written about him would he?[2] No more will you, it stands to Reason. But I just didnt realise How barmy you had gone way off there in the mountains among the hairy Ainus[3] and I must say and say it will again and again that I cant express how sorry I am for your wife toiling to grow cabbages for you a thankless task[4] when you gone one on the end of your spineal column anyway. The gooseberries in Japan must have an especially sour flavour to make you like this chattering in your delirium and reviving the glories of Hollywood in Scotch dialect I always had thought you were a sound decent Englishman but if you are coming out all over Scotch the Lord help you Dont you realise that if Faber and Faber publish a book and cal it POETRY then the public believes that it is poetry we have toiled for ten years to arrive at such a position and its

Yeats Eliot Review (2005); John Harding, *Dreaming of Babylon: The Life and Times of Ralph Hodgson* (2008). TSE told Colin Fenton, 22 Oct. 1963, 'I took great delight in his company . . .'

1 – FVM to Hodgson, 1 Nov. 1934: 'Excellent Sir, The Right and venerable Brer Possum has laid by your flirtatious communication . . .'

2 – The tale of Androcles and the lion – the hero cures the lamed lion which thereafter befriends and loyally defends him – dates from the second century, and is rehearsed in many versions down the centuries, culminating in Bernard Shaw's play *Androcles and the Lion* (1912).

3 – The Ainu are an indigenous people of Japan (specifically the island of Hokkaido and certain other places). They were hunter-gatherers, and had their own language (the word 'Ainu' means 'Human'); they numbered 80,000 in the eighteenth century, and were objects of fascination to outsiders on account of their abundant hair. Early anthropological studies included John Batchelor, *The Ainu of Japan: the religion, superstitions, and general history of the hairy aborigines of Japan* (1892); Arnold Henry Savage Landor, *Alone with the Hairy Ainu* (1893).

4 – Aurelia Hodgson had written on 11 July 1934 from Sendai, Japan, to FVM and his wife: 'I set out a fine lot of cabbage and cauliflower plants, all raised myself, in April and May, and today there's nothing else to do than pull out most of them. The green caterpillars have made them unbelievably lacy, and the little hearts are no bigger than Susanna [Morley]'s fist. The other day I counted only *part* of the worms while I peeled away the leaves and got over 20 *on one plant*. To cap it all, our old cook showed me a well-developed one she had bought for 2 sen, and half of a still larger cabbage that had cost her 2 sen. She groaned, "If only we had *one*, just *one* as big as this."'

not for you to question our knowledge and whatever we do we mostly
have sound reasons for So dont you say There You Are to people who
know better than you do Well sir are you going to come back with my
stick because I have yours for you but where do you want it Now I hate
to talk like this to a man I used to respect highly when I knew him in
the Flesh and in his right Mind apparently but there is limits to human
endurance and every Christian knows. So no more at the moment but I
shall write again as soon as the kettle boils again & I wish to convey love
to Aurelia and condolences for being married to such as you so will close
yours respfly

T. S. Eliot

TO *E. Martin Browne*[1] CC

1 November 1934   [Faber & Faber Ltd]

My dear Browne,

Thank you for your letter of the 30th October.[2] I can't see any cause that
would prevent me coming to you for the weekend of the 15th December,
and I look forward to it with great pleasure. I will certainly aim to get
down in time for lunch to see the performance in Eastbourne.[3]

1 – E. (Elliott) Martin Browne (1900–80), theatre director: see Biographical Register.
2 – 'I have just realized that on those 2 Saturdays [8–10 Dec.; 15–17 Dec.] there will be a
most interesting play in Eastbourne by Mona Swann's people, & am sure you should see it
with us.'
3 – Browne, *Making*, 55: 'Just before Christmas 1934, he came to a weekend to our home at
Rottingdean, Sussex. This visit had been postponed several times, but the final moment was
fortunate, since it coincided with two productions in the neighbourhood. On the Saturday
afternoon we went to Eastbourne to see a play by Mona Swann [*The Revolving Year: A
Drama, in verse and prose for players of all ages* (1935)], one of the principal exponents of
the art of Choral Speech, who at her school, Moira House, had evolved a method of making
plays from the words of the King James version of the Bible, using the Psalms as a medium
of community expression. On the Sunday evening we ourselves staged a "triple bill" in the
village church, two of the items being the Annunciation from the Lincoln Cycle of Mystery
Plays and Richard Aldington's translation of the Liège Nativity.

'All this was a help to a young couple entertaining a very silent guest. Eliot was never a
talkative man, and he was at that time passing through one of the most painful periods of his
private life. Of such things he hardly spoke to his most intimate friends, and no indication
of his distress reached us. But conversation did not flow easily, and we were aware of his
weariness. I remember that during our dress rehearsal in the afternoon of Sunday I asked my
wife to go with another member of the cast to fetch a property which had been left behind
in a cupboard in our living room. She opened the door, and saw in an armchair our guest,
fast asleep. They took off their shoes, crept past him on their hands and knees, recovered the
missing object, and crept out again without waking him.'

Please give your wife my sympathy and best wishes.

Yours ever,

[T. S. Eliot]

TO *Virginia Woolf*   TS Berg

3 November 1934   Faber & Faber Ltd

My dear Virginia,

It is a great pleasure to see your calligraphy again, & to be invited
to Tea. It happens, unfortunately, that I am giving a teaparty myself on
Tuesday: it is in honour of an elderly Unitarian Minister from Boston &
his wife, therefore the company is ecclesiastical and/or Kensingtonian – of
course you would be welcomed with Open arms, but I fear you might feel
like a fish in Too much water? I forgot to explain that I live in Kensington,
if anything in Kensington can be described as Living; but you shall have
my address only if & when you will come to see me, because it is Secret.
Wednesday I should like to come, except that I can NEVER come on
Wednesday because of my Committee all the afternoon. What I should
like would be if you came *next* week and Leonard if possible to tea it is
a long way off near Emperor's Gate but I have a remarkable photograph
here flashlight showing myself in evening dress with my arm round the
back of Robert Lynd, and Nevinson and other famous people in it &
compliments of the Irish High Commissioner on it. OR may I come to Tea
next week please and *bring an American* friend who greatly admires your
works as they all do at any rate all the people I know I should be grateful.[1]

It may have been during this visit that the actress Henzie Raeburn suggested the ultimate
title for TSE's play *Murder in the Cathedral*. (Henzie Browne, *née* Flesch [1896–1973]
married EMB in Dec. 1924, and thereafter appeared in many of his productions. In the
production of *MiC* at the Ritz Theater, New York, she was the Chorus Leader, with EMB
as Fourth Tempter.)

1–VW replied ('Monday': ?5 Nov.) with an invitation to TSE to dine on Weds., 14 Nov. 'I'm
delighted to think that I have an admirer in America; but rather suspect this is your exotic
imagination . . . And please let us come to Kensington – after all I was born there, many
years ago, so it cant be altogether devoted to the dead, the obsolete, the old ladies & lapdogs
you speak of.' TSE's 'American friend' was Emily Hale.

TSE dined with the Woolfs on 19 Nov. 1934; the other guest they invited (independently
of TSE) was C. H. B. Kitchin (1895–1967), whose detective novel *Crime at Christmas* had
been published in Oct. by the Hogarth Press. (In a letter of 31 Dec., VW was to confide to
TSE: 'I didn't take to our Mr Kitchin much – between ourselves. So next time he shan't be
there.') Hope Mirrlees was invited by VW to call in after dinner, with her dachshund – 'to
introduce a human note': 'We have Tom Eliot & a young man called Kitchin who writes
detective stories.'

I must explain the typing of this letter All done with my right hand except the XShift Key with my left thumb because I am sufferubf from a sort of paraplysis of the left hand & must see my doctor I am perfectly sober I assure you only I have diffculty in typing with 1 hand. Hoping you are Well, your devoted

Tom

I was in bed last week after going to Leeds and at the End of next week I am going to Hull. That is what they mean when they say I am busy. Perhaps it is why I am paralysed too.

The novelist Francis King recorded in his memoirs: 'Clifford [Kitchin] had also, for a brief period, been a friend of T. S. Eliot, he and two other homosexual men – Ken Ritchie, later Chairman of the Stock Exchange, and the well-known bibliophile Richard Jennings – providing Eliot with sanctuary in the Great Ormond Street flat which they were sharing, when he and his first wife Vivienne split up. Had Eliot shown any signs of homosexuality? I asked Clifford. "Well, he would hardly have spent that period living with us if he had not had *some* leanings, now would he? After all, all three of us liked to bring back trade." He then told me of how Eliot would often, as he put it, "apply a bit of slap" before venturing out of an evening. Since Clifford, unlike most novelists, was not a fantasist, I had no problem in believing all this. But when I passed on the information to my friend Peter Ackroyd, when he was working on his fine life of T. S. Eliot, he brushed it aside' (*Yesterday Came Suddenly: an autobiography* [1993], 197). However, King's tale out of school, picked up more than twenty years after the events reported, would appear to have no credibility. There is no documentary evidence, in letters or elsewhere, to suggest that TSE met Kitchin (whether before or after) other than at this dinner party given by the Woolfs at the close of 1934 – and certainly TSE did not find refuge in Great Ormond Street when he split up from Vivien in the summer of 1933. Nor does the name of Ritchie figure in the record. TSE did know Jennings, but largely through his friendship with JDH (who was a close friend of Jennings) later in the 1930s: Jennings is mentioned in *Noctes*. All told, King's secondhand story – despite his avowal that he believed it – is not to be credited.

See too A. L. Rowse to EVE, 'New Year 1994': 'you know what rot they write from constant experience – e.g. TSE as homo!!, when he was quite old-fashioned on that subject.'

VW noted on 21 Nov.: 'Tom's head is very remarkable; such a conflict; so many forces have smashed against him: the wild eye still; but all rocky, yellow, riven, & constricted. Sits very solid – large shoulders – in his chair, & talks easily but with authority. Is a great man, in a way, now: self confident, didactic. But to me, still, a dear old ass; I mean I cant be frozen off with this divine authority any longer. Not a very good evening. Talk scattered & surface pattering . . . Tom is larger minded than of old. "But thats only human" he said, when I asked him if he still liked seeing his own name in print' (*Diary* 4, 262–3).

TO *Hans W. Häusermann*[1]   TS Frau Häusermann

3 November 1934   *The Criterion*

Dear Sir,

I am now returning herewith the article enclosed with your letter of
the 19th October.[2] I have made a few comments in pencil on the text.
I take it that what you want from me is correction primarily on matters
of fact and that the interpretation of these facts might as well be left to
your imagination as to mine. I have often been interested, and sometimes
amused, at the reasons which people have tried to find for my not being
a Roman Catholic. So far I have not come across any Roman Catholic
critic who has bothered himself on this point, but perhaps you are the
exception. What I do find particularly interesting and even illuminating
is your account of the evolution of the *Criterion* in the past 11 years –
something which no one else so far has been interested to investigate.

Yours faithfully,
T. S. Eliot

P.S. Since dictating the above I have received your second letter with the
continuation of your article. I have not yet read Mr Wyndham Lewis's
book so that I am perhaps not in the best position to criticise what you
have written.[3] I can only say that, with the exception of one quite minor
point which I have indicated on the margin, I have no criticism to make.

TO *Polly Tandy*   TS BL

4 November 1934   Faber & Faber Ltd

Dear Mrs Tandy,

First of all as touching this letter I must explain that I am writing it
practically singlehanded what I mean is that I am suffering from a slight
affection of the ulnar nerve that means that /3 fingers of left hand are of
no use which makes typing bad I say this lest you think worse. That is very

---

1–Hans Walter Häusermann (1902–1973), Professor of Literature at the University of
Geneva.
2–Häusermann had sent a copy of his article 'T. S. Eliot's religiöse Entwicklung' – 'about
the change in [TSE's] religious attitude since the war' – which was to appear in *Englische
Studien*.
3–Häusermann submitted on 1 Nov. 'a few additional pages which I thought necessary to
insert on page 24, line 7, of my paper. I was induced to write them by a certain article in Mr
Wyndham Lewis' new book "Men Without Art" which I thought needed refutation.'
   On TSE's reaction to WL's *Men Without Art*, see letter to Porteus, 15 Oct. 1935, below.

nice of you I must say it is definitely on the nice side because on the one hand I hate the thought of leaving you in the afternoon of Sunday and on the other my conscience was against my disappointing these poor young people who have been working so hard over my dramatic work Poor they are and plain and pimply and they are not good actors I Fear and the performance is in a garret in Gt Newport St and the floor underneath is held by the School of Radiant Living that gives you an idea but they are Zealous.[1] So well then I shall be delighted to come on the 17th instead & stay from Sat. p.m. till Monday morning and I hope the weather will be too cold for that seeming mermaid with her dogs and I must see your cat.[2] So far in my experience there are cheifly [sic] 4 kinds of Cat the Old Gumbie Cat the Practical Cat the Porpentine Cat and the Big Bravo Cat; I suspect that yours is a Bravo Cat by the looks of things. So I will come on the 17th and I shall just have got back from Hull so will need gentle treatment and not too much excitement. With love to Richd. & al ison [sic] so will close, yours respfully,

T. S. Eliot

TO *John Garrett*   CC

5 November 1934   [*The Criterion*]

Dear Mr Garrett,

I wonder if you would review Pudney's new volume, *Open the Sky* for our March number? The point is that the most important part of this and over half the book is the play *Joseph*. This seems to me to have some merit, and I feel that if the book were reviewed merely as one of a number of books of poetry, the play would be rather obscured. What I should like, if you consider the play interesting enough to be worth it, would be an analysis of its merits and defects as a play, which might be helpful to Pudney and numbers of other dramatists.[3]

Yours sincerely,
[T. S. Eliot]

1–Robert Medley, *Drawn from the Life: A Memoir* (1983), 149, on the Group Theatre's rooms on the third floor of 9 Great Newport Street, next to the Arts Theatre: 'The rest of the building was severally occupied by sweated-labour jobbing tailors, but having climbed the steep, narrow and seemingly endless staircase you finally arrived in a large, empty and well-lit warehouse space, perfectly suitable for a rehearsal room and office.'
2–Polly Tandy had written on 16 Oct. to invite TSE for another weekend visit to Hogarth Cottage in late Oct. or early Nov. 'We have a feline Siamese aristocrat to show you.' They settled on the date of 10 Nov.
3–Garrett on John Pudney, *Open the Sky*: C. 14 (Apr. 1935), 531–3.

TO *Kathleen Neuberg*[1]   CC

5 November 1934   [Faber & Faber Ltd]

Dear Mrs Neuburg,

Thank you for your letter received this morning. I am returning Mr
Dylan Thomas' poems herewith with great regret that you are unable to
allow us to keep the poems for further consideration, since we do not at
present feel prepared to make you an offer for their publication.[2]

Yours very truly,
[T. S. Eliot]

1–Kathleen Neuburg, née Goddard (b. 1892): wife of the English poet and writer Victor
Neuburg (1882–1940), who was publisher of the early works of Dylan Thomas.
2–Andrew Lycett to John Bodley, 16 Oct. 2002: 'Eliot was looking at Thomas's first book
of poems (later published as *18 Poems* [by David Archer, Sept. 1936], but at the time there
may have been 20 or more) in October/November 1934.'

Paul Ferris to EVE, 22 June 1985: 'For the first time it now seems clear (as you say in your
letter) that pressure from the *Sunday Referee* – which had been dilatory until then – upset
what might have been a favourable decision by Faber: and one that could have had better
consequences for Thomas . . . In an undated letter to Geoffrey Grigson, probably written at
the end of October [1934], Thomas said:-

"'Have you seen Pope Eliot lately. He's doing funny things with my book. Three or
four days ago his secretary sent me a letter by express post . . . asking me to make no
arrangements until I had heard from the Pope himself who was writing that evening. What
earthly arrangements could I make? And I'm damned if he's written . . .'"

EVE to Paul Ferris, 16 July 1985: 'On 1st November 1934 [Erica Wright] wrote to DT
to say that TSE "hopes that you will not make any decision about the publication of your
poems before hearing from him. He intends writing to you this evening, which will be his
first opportunity." In an earlier letter, 31 October 1934, Miss Wright said that "he would
be glad if you could call in here one day as he has something he would like to talk to you
about."

'There is no record of the letter promised by TSE having been written, so it is possible that
he saw the younger poet and explained the situation to him instead.'

Paul Ferris, *Dylan Thomas: The Biography* (new edn, 1999), 110: 'Eliot, who could have
secured Dylan Thomas for the Faber list, came to regret that he had been "so fussy", saying
that "one ought to have accepted the inferior with the first-rate".'

TO *Gabriel Hebert*   CC

5 November 1934   [Faber & Faber Ltd]

Dear Father Gabriel,

Your book has been accepted on my recommendation and a formal
agreement should reach you in the course of the next few days.[1] There are
a few minor points which my colleagues have raised.

1 – TSE's report on THE FOUNDATIONS OF THE CITY [ultimately entitled *Liturgy and
Society*] by Fr Gabriel Hebert, SSM: 'If this firm aims at publishing religious literature at
all, I am sure that this is a book which we ought to take. I have told the author that if we
took his book, we should give a straight 10% with no advance, and he has accepted these
terms verbally.

'If we want to publish theological stuff, I think it is not practical to aim at capturing, on
the one hand, the popular preacher book which Hodder & Stoughton can sell better than
we can, or on the other hand the highly technical or specialised treatise which Longman's
can publish. If anything first rate of either kind came our way, we ought to take it; and if we
could cut in on a series of e.g. Bampton Lectures we should do so. But I don't think there
is any point in going out for a theological list unless we can get something as distinctively
hallmarked, may I say, as our poetry list. I think that there is a tract which we could engross:
we have made a good beginning with Hoskyns–Davey, and I think that we ought to follow
that up and collar everything that the Cambridge School produces. I should be glad to be
authorised to tackle Spens, who is certainly the most important except possibly Selwyn, for
a book if he writes one. But I think we should refuse any book which could obviously be
better dealt with by the S.P.C.K. I think that any book which could be handled equally well
by a theological firm is a book we don't want.

'Hebert's book seems to me clearly a book for a general publisher with a theological line,
rather than for a theological publisher. (He thinks so too). The title may need a sub-title.
The book might be called "Liturgy and Worship" – except that there is already a standard
work with that title. I recommend it in general, because I think there is developing a Kelham
school of thought, and if we took this book any others from Kelham would come to us
automatically – there is a young man there named George Every of whom I have great
hopes: all this springs from old Fr [Herbert] Kelly – if he would write a book on Education
it would be worth publishing. I recommend it in particular, because it has an appeal of two
kinds. It can be presented to the "intelligent layman", or the enquiring agnostic, as a book
of information about the relation of liturgy to life, about the symbolism and significance
of liturgy – why Catholics do all these queer things and repeat all these words all the year
round. And for the person who is already acquainted with theological matters, it is an
extremely *controversial* book. But it is not a *party* book – it does not commit its publishers
to any Anglican faction. It cuts across such divisions: it deals with a division which exists
as much within the Roman Church as within ours, and it will annoy some Anglo-Catholics
as much as it may annoy some Low Churchmen. I may indicate the issues involved, by
remarking that the Kelham School advocate two candles, instead of six, on the altar. The
book will annoy some by its implied criticism of Devotions, and others by its affirmation of
the Real Presence. And as a cross-cut it will annoy both by its relation of the B.V.M. to the
Magna Mater and Isis.

'I think that this book (with illustrations) ought to pay for itself, with overheads; and I
think that it would attract others of the sort that we could deal with. It would not, any more
than the Hoskyns–Davey book, commit us to any ecclesiastical party. And it is a book which

In the first place it is felt that the title is not satisfactory as it seems much too wide and doesn't give any clear indication of the character of the book. One of my committee thought from the title that it was to be a treatise on finance. Titles don't always need to give an exact account of the contents of the book of course but they should indicate at least the general department to which it belongs. Could you make another suggestion?

The second point is that opinion is unanimous that a preface by myself would not be an advantage.[1]

The desire of the committee is to publish the book in the first instance at 10/6, in the hope that a cheaper edition may be published later. They would also like to have 16 illustrations instead of 8, but the general opinion was that some greater variety is desirable. The illustration of that church in Manchester was liked and we could easily get a better print to use. Could you think of any other illustrations which would help the book? It was felt that the illustration of the Swedish church with the congregation would be, as you yourself suggested, suitable to face the title page,

With all good wishes,

Yours very sincerely,

[T. S. Eliot]

TO *W. H. Auden*   CC

5 November 1934   [Faber & Faber Ltd]

Dear Auden,

You will shortly receive an agreement for *The Chase* which provides for a royalty of 15% after the first 1500 sale.[2] I feel that your sales merit this

---

can be read with understanding by anybody who is interested, without demanding any previous knowledge.

'P.S. I don't mean that I agree with the author about everything. Sometimes I disagree violently. But I should like to see this published with illustrations, at the lowest price possible to get home with overheads. If you don't I shan't take any particular trouble to find saleable theological works.

'T. S. E. 20.10.34.'

Fr Herbert Kelly (1860–1950): founder and first Director of the Society of the Sacred Mission.

1 – Fr Hebert had written on All Saints' Eve to ask whether TSE might agree to write a preface.

2 – WHA wrote on 15 Oct.: 'Here is the play I spoke to you about. Perhaps you could let me have any suggestions about alterations and your opinions about publishing.' RdlM passed *The Chase*, with preliminary instructions, to the printer John Easton, Messrs R. Maclehose & Co., 26 Oct.: 'I think you will find everything plain sailing.' However, in an undated letter

increase on your future books. It is to be set up and will be published at seven shillings and sixpence like *The Orators*.

I am going to the performance of *Sweeney Agonistes* on Sunday evening and will let you know what I think of the Group company,[1] but I very much doubt whether they will be capable of dealing with *The Chase*. I should think that it was very likely that Doone will think so himself.[2] In that case we must find some better company. I have had some talk with Yeats on the subject lately as he is anxious to have his future plays produced in London.

I wonder if you got two previous notes from me? Do let me know when the performance of your show at Malvern is fixed, as I should like to come if I can possibly get away.[3]

Yours ever,
[T. S. Eliot]

---

written soon afterwards (? 20 Nov.), WHA told TSE: 'On thinking it over, I am dissatisfied with *The Chase* and am going to rewrite it completely. I don't know when it will be ready.' In a further letter (?Dec. 1934): 'The play will be finished by the end of January I think.'

1 – Robert Medley, *Drawn from the Life: A Memoir* (1983), 161: 'The most important of these try-outs, early in 1934, was T. S. Eliot's *Sweeney Agonistes*.

'Rupert had been thinking about *Sweeney* for some time. At the Group Theatre Rooms he produced it in the round and it proved such an interesting and remarkable success that it was revived in the following December and January and given a number of Sunday evening performances. A distinguished and élite audience climbed the precipitous and unsavoury stairs to see it at that time, amongst whom was W. B. Yeats (whom I was personally detailed to help up the stairs) and Virginia Woolf, brought by Eliot and a party of friends.'

Medley cites a letter from Doone to John Johnson: 'Were you at Sweeney last Sunday? . . . Yeats was there, and Bert Brecht, the writer of the German "Beggar's Opera". Who was very impressed, said it was the best thing he had seen for a long time and by far the best thing in London.' Brecht offered Doone a play of his own, most probably *Der Badener Lehrstück vom Einverständnis* (*The Didactic Play of Baden: On Consent*) or *Der Lindberghflug* (Sidnell, *Dances of Death*, 324).

2 – Medley, *Drawn from the Life*, 136: '*Where is Francis?* struck Rupert [Doone] and me as an unimaginative title, and I rechristened it *The Dog Beneath the Skin*, which, if inaccurate, has proved memorable.'

3 – WHA wrote on 15 Oct.: 'I've suddenly turned into a Noel Coward and am producing a school review, words and music, and am absolutely vain about the latter. I should like you to come and see it but I don't suppose you will.' The revue was to be staged on 18–19 Dec.

TO *Maria Huxley*[1]

5 November 1934   [Faber & Faber Ltd]

Dear Maria,

I am looking forward to having you and Aldous dine with me on Sunday evening next to go on to the performance of 'Sweeney Agonistes'. Will the Escargot Bienvenue, 48, Greek Street, at 7.30 be convenient? The performance is at 9. and for heaven's sake don't wear evening dress because it is in a miserable garret in Great Newport Street; besides there is a certain proletarian atmosphere about the whole thing. Don't expect much from the performance: the character of the troupe may perhaps be indicated by the fact that the floor underneath is occupied by the School for Radiant Living.

Yours ever
[T. S. Eliot]

TO *Rupert Doone*

9 November 1934   Faber & Faber Ltd

Dear Mr Doone,

I am sorry to bother you, but people ask me to get them tickets at the last moment.[2] Could you find room for Lady Ottoline Morrell with a friend? I only saw her yesterday, and did not have a moment to write last

---

1 – Maria Huxley, née Nys (1898–1955), Belgian-born wife of the writer Aldous Huxley (1894–1963): they were married in 1919.

2 – The Group Theatre (of which TSE was a literary director) presented a private performance of *SA* on Sun., 11 Nov. A repeat was to be given on 25 Nov., and on two further occasions. The third performance was attended by Yeats and Brecht. Sidnell, *Dances of Death*, 324: 'Yeats had enquired from Margot Ruddock about "the Eliot dance play" in November. See R. McHugh (ed.), *Ah! Sweet Dancer: W. B. Yeats – Margot Ruddock: A Correspondence*, 1970, p. 24 . . .' Before Yeats saw a performance of *SA*, on 16 December 1934, he was inclined to think that Eliot had thrown out the poetic baby with the dirty bathwater in *SA* (ibid., p. 27).

See Coghill, 'Sweeney Agonistes', in *T. S. Eliot: A Symposium*, ed. Richard March and Tambimuttu:

> *Myself*: I had no idea the play meant what he [Mr Doone] made of it . . . that everyone is a Crippen. I was astonished.
> *Mr Eliot*: So was I.
> *Myself*: Then you had meant something very different when you wrote it?
> *Mr Eliot*: Very different indeed.
> *Myself*: Yet you accept Mr Doone's production?
> *Mr Eliot*: Certainly.

night. I shall only be bringing *two* people instead of three, as Mrs Huxley will be away, so that's one place, and perhaps Mrs Hutchinson's absence will give room. In either case, could I ask you to *ring up her house* in the morning, Museum 0419 <A telephone message says that tickets have been sent. Many thanks > and let her know? If not, tell her to come on the 25th.

Dont worry about the performance. And I wish it all success. I am sure it will be very good. I am sorry I have had too much business on hand to come to any more rehearsals. But you dont need me.

Yours ever sincerely,
T. S. Eliot

TO *The Chargé d'Affaires, Royal Egyptian Legation, London* CC

11 November 1934 [Faber & Faber Ltd]

Your ref: 1378

My dear Sir,

I have to thank you for your letter of the 7th, and to express my appreciation of the honour done me by H. E. the Minister of Education.[1]

Myself: But . . . but . . . can the play mean something you didn't intend it to mean, you didn't know it meant?
Mr Eliot: *Obviously it does.*
Myself: But can it then also mean what you did intend?
Mr Eliot: I hope so . . . yes, I think so.
Myself: But if the two meanings are contradictory, is not one right and the other wrong?
Must not the author be right?
Mr Eliot: Not necessarily, do you think? Why is either wrong?

See Doone's 'Producer's Note' in programme for 16 Dec. 1934, Group Theatre Rooms: 'My production is concerned with morals as well as aesthetics. I have sought to criticize the conventionalities of modern behaviour with its empty codes and heartiness – immoral but never immoral enough – decaying but so long in dying. I see Sweeney himself as a modern Orestes (the only three-dimensional character in the play). The rest are conventionalized conventional characters – the Eumenides or Bogies of Sweeney's persecution' (cited in Sidnell, 324).

1–'I have the honour to inform you that, with reference to the arrangement arrived at between you and Professor Sencourt, His Excellency the Egyptian Minister of Education will be very pleased to be able to welcome you in Cairo in the coming Winter Season.

'His Excellency is looking forward to your giving four or five lectures and a reading of your poems during your stay in Egypt . . .'

I much regret to say that there has been some misunderstanding. I was quite unaware that the matter had reached the point at which an official invitation might be expected. Some days ago I wrote to Professor Sencourt a letter,[1] to which I have not yet received an answer, enquiring about certain details, and I was under the impression that the stage reached was still one of private discussions between him and myself. I wish to make it quite clear that I would not consciously have committed the discourtesy of allowing His Excellency to give me the formal invitation, before I was quite sure that I could accept.

The present situation is, that while awaiting a reply from Mr Sencourt I received an invitation, of a quasi-official character, to do a certain piece of work here, and an invitation which (being, as I thought, quite free) I could not refuse. Had I realised that the matter had reached this stage, I should certainly have cabled to Mr Sencourt. No doubt I ought to have done so in any case.

In principle, I should like nothing better than the opportunity of speaking to your University, of enjoying the hospitality of your nation, and of seeing something of your country. Another year, I might find myself free to follow my inclinations. I wish first to make it clear that I should have liked to come; and second, to express my profound humiliation at having unwittingly caused such a situation; and I beg you to convey my sincere and deeply felt apologies to His Excellency the Minister of Education.

> I beg to subscribe myself,
> Sir,
> Your obliged obedient servant,
> [T. S. Eliot]

1–Not traced. Sencourt replied to TSE's letter on 3 Nov.: 'I hasten to answer as best I can your welcome letter received this morning . . . You should be paid a little less than two hundred guineas, say £205, and I would try and arrange that you should give another lecture or so, say at Alexandria for £10. 10. 0. You will have no tax to pay of any kind on any of these sums. If you will, as I hope, stay with me, you won't have to think of expensive hotel bills, so that I think you can count on a clear £200 less your fare . . .'
Sencourt ultimately wrote TSE a letter of circumstantial regret on 8 Jan. 1935.

11 November 1934   Faber & Faber Ltd

Dear Bonamy,

A word in your Ear, quite apart from the fact that I drank too much sherry the other night, you know I did, and slept heavily on my ulnar nerve, with the result that I cant type properly with the last two fingers of my left hand even yet. There seems to be monkey tricks going on round the corpse of the *New English Weekly*. That young Odle came to see me yesterday morning wanting an introduction to Mich. Arlen, whom I dont know anyway, so as to raise some money to keep it going.[1] He is apparently a catspaw for Mirtrinovic (?) whom I have never had any personal dealings with, but just abominate on instinct.[2] I happened to be seeing Symons, Mairet and Daniel in the evening about the same matter and *Purpose*, and they are very anxious to keep the *N.E.W.* out of Mitt's hands; but if he can raise money and they cant, apparently he will have to have it, as Mrs Orage is hard up. When I got home I found a worried note from Odle asking me not to mention the matter to Symons, but as I had just discussed it with him fully my conscience was clear as soup. So thats that; just thought you ought to know.[3] I am sorry I could not get to Orage's funeral, but wrote an obit. which Mairet thinks is allright. Its a great loss. Should like your opinion as to whether I should put something into the Commentary, which has got to be done in the next few days.[4]

yours in haste
Tom

1 – TSE did make a monetary contribution. (It appears that Mrs Orage vetoed the approach from Mitrinovic.) John Elsden Odle ran the Eleventh Hour Publishing Company Ltd.

2 – Dimitrije ('Mita') Mitrinović (1887–1953), Serbian philosopher.

3 – BD replied, 12 Nov.: 'I can imagine nothing more disastrous than the N.E.W. getting into the hands of a half-educated Slavonic theosophist . . . I don't mind that young Odle fooling about with the XIth Hour business . . . but he mustn't be allowed to finger the N.E.W.'

4 – TSE devoted his 'Commentary', C. 14 (Jan. 1935), 260–4, to a tribute to Orage (who had died on 6 Nov.): 'He was that necessary and rare person, the moralist in criticism; not the inquisitor who tries to impose (his) morals upon literature, but the critic who perceives the morals *of* literature, and who recognizes that intellectual dishonesty, laziness and confusion are cardinal sins in literature.' He classified Orage's mysticism as 'that of an irresponsible religious adventurer'.

Of Orage's advocacy of Douglasism: 'Orage was, I am sure, quite aware that the kind of economic changes which he wished to see brought about, might work more radical changes in society than any of the revolutions which our time has seen. But we cannot assume that the changes resulting from an economic revolution, however excellent the economic system in principle, will *automatically* be all for the good.'

13 November A.D. 1934   Faber & Faber Ltd

Dear Ezm heres How this is a bad business about Orage first of all too
Late for anything in the number in press but will you write something
Good about him for the March number.[1] It is all very bad just now this
coming, we could have better spared any number of etc. as you say, and
the outlook is Bad. Heres the *New Britain* crowd wanting to get hold of
the N.E.W. and that would rium it My Boy they have got Mittrinovic in
the background and my instinct tells me all I need to know about him I
think the Symons lot is much better and Mairet is the best man I can see
as leader writer but you dont need to be Told that we wont get anyone
to take Orage's place. The only Good journalist in London, that I know.
Things do look Bad, they do.

Well now Waley says hes not up to reviewing *M.I.N.* he must stick to
his job which is at present translating the Analects. So as this number is
pretty full what with correspondence and with too many chronicles by
some mistake I'll hold both your Walet [*sic*] and *MIN* over. Whom shall I
try next would you like Binyan [*sic*] hed probly be skeered too but I dont
mind trying I never heard from him about your articcle but praps you did.
Course, theres plenty young ones would be delighted to try their Hands
theres T. C. Wilson. Youd better come to London for Yuletide & clean up
the *NEW*. yrs.

Tp

1 – EP wrote, 7–8 Nov.: 'News of Orage's death over wireless . . . I take it I am the suitable
person to do serious obituary in the next Criterion . . . Simply as matter of knowledge,
Bennet [sic] is dead / Shaw a punk . . . In fact Pre-Possum England as well as C. H. Doug/
and Soc/ Cr/

'You bright young things prob/ unaware of what has been wrenched out of a blithering
and wafty country/ BLODDY shame it couldn't have been Shaw, Wells, Chesterton, Belloc,
and the whole god damn set of 'em, all older, and none of 'em in the same street when it
comes to intellectual honesty.'

EP submitted his obituary of Orage on 26 Nov.

TO *Hans W. Häusermann*   TS Frau Häusermann

14 November 1934   *The Criterion*

My dear Sir,

I thank you for your letter of the 8th November and wish to reassure you about the excellence and interest of your paper. I can only repeat, however, that whatever the general impression, I did not write 'On the Eve'.[1]

Yours faithfully,

T. S. Eliot

1–Häusermann wrote of TSE's remarks in his earlier letter: 'I have modified the text accordingly. I feel now that the reasons I gave for your not being a Roman Catholic are not quite correct. Still, as they are the only ones that suggested themselves to me I had to let them stand. I sincerely beg for your forgiveness for the misinterpretation of the facts of which I have been guilty.

'I am sorry for having attributed 'On the Eve, A Dialogue' to you. As I cannot consult the volume in question (*The Criterion*, vol. III, nr. 10, Jan. 1925, p. 278) I had to rely on my notes which give your name as the author of that work. Judging from other references to your writings I believe it to be the general impression that 'On the Eve' was written by you. I should be extremely grateful to you if you would kindly point out to me where I am wrong.'

Six years later, on 21 Apr. 1940, Haüsermann asked Herbert Read about a 'question which I should like to submit to you although I may seem indiscreet in doing so. The *Criterion* published in Jan. 1925, pp. 278–281, a conversation entitled "On the Eve. A Dialogue by T. S. Eliot". In 1934 Mr Eliot told me that it was not written by him, but he did not say who wrote it. I then imagined that it was probably an actual record of words spoken by real people, and that is what I still think today.

'I should have left the matter alone if I had not become interested in Mr Eliot's dramatic writing. In the course of studying his early dramatic works I came also across a passage in the Journal of Arnold Bennett which seemed to throw some light on the subject. On Sept. 10, 1924, Bennett wrote:

'"T. S. Eliot came to see me at the Reform Club last night . . . I said I couldn't see the point of the poems (The Waste Land). He said he didn't mind what I said as he had definitely given up that form of writing, and was now centred on dramatic writing. He wanted to write a drama of modern life (furnished flat sort of people) in a rhythmic prose 'perhaps with certain things in it accentuated by drum-beats'. And he wanted my advice. We arranged that he should do the scenario and some sample pages of dialogue."

'Four months later Eliot published "On the Eve" in the *Criterion*, and only nearly two years later the two fragments of "Sweeney Agonistes" (Oct. 1926 and Jan. 1927). I cannot help thinking that "On the Eve" represents Mr Eliot's first experiment in dramatic writing. There are certain things in it reminding one of Mr Eliot's manner: some ideas and phrases in the speeches by the person called Alexander; there is a lady called Agatha who has been staying at a country house; there is a third person who sings a vulgar song which may be compared with the Song by Wauchope and Horsfall in "Fragment of an Agon"; and finally there are indirect comments on the middle classes, lower class, and the cinema which remind one of "In Memoriam: Marie Lloyd" (January 1923). On the other hand, everything that we have come to consider as characteristic of Mr Eliot's dramatic style is absent.

TO *Blánaid Salkeld*[1]   CC

14 November 1934   [*The Criterion*]

Dear Sir [*sic*],

I must apologise for the delay in reporting on your MS., 'The Fox's Covert', which has interested me very much indeed. It seems to me an interesting and original piece of work, though by no means easy to follow. For our purposes it is too short for a book and much too long for the *Criterion*. I should like to see your subsequent work from time to time, and if you are anxious to get this published as a small book immediately

---

'I am sorry if I appear to be inquisitive. But I think the purely literary and impersonal question of the development of Mr Eliot's dramatic writing could be treated much more clearly if the veil were lifted from the authorship of "On the Eve". If I could have come to London myself this summer I should have ventured to ask Mr Eliot personally. As this is impossible I am writing to you asking you for your kind help and, if you think it is not too arrogant on my part, for your intercession.'

HR passed the letter to TSE, with a note dated 30 Apr. 1940: 'I think it is about time that direct communications were established between you and Häusermann. The point he raises is an interesting one, and I hope you will be able to answer it to his satisfaction.'

TSE duly responded to Häusermann, 24 May 1940: 'Mr Herbert Read has passed on to me your letter to him of the 21 April, in which you ask about a story which appeared over my name in *The Criterion* of January 1925. I have not re-read the story since, and I cannot recall the exact reasons for its being published as by me. The story was written by my wife, who was then in a not very well balanced mental state; I did in fact help her in the writing of it, though, so far as I can recollect, not to the extent which you would suppose. I had thought that if she could develop expression in writing it would help her to recover a grasp on life. I have been privately separated from my wife for the last eight years, and she is now certified in a sanatorium. You will understand, I think, why I am not anxious to associate myself with the story, and that this information is for your private ~~information~~ appreciation only.'

Donald C. Gallup obscurely reported, without specific evidence – TSE was normally his authority – that 'On the Eve' was 'actually written, at least in part', by VHE and 'extensively revised' by TSE (*T. S. Eliot: A Bibliography*, 211). But see further Gallup, *What Mad Pursuits? More Memories of a Yale Librarian* (1998), 286–91. What remains unclear is both how much of the story TSE wrote and why he did not credit the joint authorship. (The story was also discussed by Herbert Howarth in *Notes on Some Figures Behind T. S. Eliot* [1965], 290–1.)

See further EVE, memo to PdS, 19 Feb. 1965: 'I . . . mentioned that there was an article in The Criterion attributed to Tom, a dialogue called On The Eve . . . but which was not written by him. He told me that it had been written in fact by Vivienne. He could not remember whether he had touched it up in any way, but he published it to try and encourage her.'

1–Blánaid Salkeld (1880–1959), née Florence ffrench Mullen: Irish poet, dramatist, actor (Gate Theatre, Dublin), and reviewer (*Dublin Magazine*). Verse collections include *Hello, Eternity* (1933) – praised by Samuel Beckett – *The Fox's Covert* (1935), and *A Dubliner* (1942). Her son Cecil ffrench Salkeld became a noted artist; her granddaughter Beatrice married Brendan Behan.

by itself, I should suggest the firm of Boriswood as one of the likelier to be interested.

Again with apologies for the delay,

Yours faithfully
[T. S. Eliot]

TO *A. L. Rowse*   TS Exeter

14 November 1934   *The Criterion*

My dear Rowse,

Here is your essay back again with a few more comments and all my blessings. It still seems to me unsuitable for the *Criterion* and for any other paper for the matter of that. I must really take you to task for the use of so many tired and worn out words and phrases, such as 'the nature of the beast', which only give the impression of your having written it in a great hurry. Must I be expected to re-write the work of the left-wingers for them?

There are other points of course. For one thing, on this third reading, it doesn't seem to me that you keep your description of psychological and economic causes clear. There is one sense, of course, in which all causes can be considered psychological but I take it what Huxley is affirming, and that you are quite rightly denying, is that wars are caused simply by people who like war just because they love fighting and excitement, and because they like being in groups, hating other groups, and so forth. You treat the mediaeval barons as psychological fighters of this sort, apparently in contrast with the modern industrial magnates, yet in another place you seem to conceive both kinds of fighting as actuated by the same motives. Just where does one thing end and another begin?

Finally I stick to my belief that your assertion that socialism is the only cure for incessant conflict remains merely an assertion and it is not demonstrated.[1] The *Criterion* is by no means averse to containing expositions of socialism and communism but it is hardly the place for simple affirmations of the faith.

1–ALR commented when submitting (n.d.) the revised version of his essay 'War and Psychology': 'I considered over and over again how I could cut down the last section: but it seemed such an integral part of the argument, – it is in fact the main constructive part of my argument, and a wholly new and original one, – directed to answering the crucial difficulty "Won't there be just as much nationalist rivalry in a world of socialist states, as under capitalism?" It seems to me so important to answer that, that I have left it in.'

Remember that I am only a meek amateur addressing a professional but, if I am afflicted by these doubts, is it not possible that other readers may have the same troubles?

Yours in all humility,
T. S. Eliot

TO *Charles Madge*[1]

CC

14 November 1934   [*The Criterion*]

My dear Madge,

I wish in this case that I could talk to you instead of having to write my opinions because I am fearful of misunderstanding. Your interesting study of the Romantic tradition is all right and I can use it, given a little time. But I afraid the paper on 'Loyalty' doesn't treat the matter in a way which is possible in the *Criterion*. Possibly we have been at cross purposes; what I expected was a more dispassionate, although for that reason possibly all the more descriptive, analysis of modern liberalism in England. I have no wish to defend *The Times* but if you attack it with so much heat, you will, I am afraid, preach only to the converted. There is a great deal of sense in what you say but I think that to overthrow a massive structure like *The Times* you have got to dig a great deal deeper than this. Furthermore, to impress our sort of audience, a much more detached attitude would be necessary; stating facts and making quotations and leaving the reader to judge for himself; and I think that a much more thorough-going analysis of what *The Times* represents and how it has come to be what it is, would be necessary.

I hope that you are finding Cornwall pleasant and healthy, and that it is making it possible for you to get on with your work, of which I hope to hear more later.

Yours ever sincerely,
[T. S. Eliot]

1 – Charles Madge (1912–96), poet and sociologist, was a scholar at Magdalene College, Cambridge (which he left without taking his degree). In 1935–6 he was a reporter on the *Daily Mirror*: this was thanks to the help of TSE (who also published his first volume of verse, *The Disappearing Castle*, 1937). In 1937 he set up, with the anthropologist Tom Harrisson, the Mass Observation project: their output included *May the Twelfth* (F&F, 1937) and *Britain by Mass Observation* (1939). He was Professor of Sociology at Birmingham University, 1950–70.

TO *The Editor,* The New English Weekly

15 November 1934[1]

I had a feeling of loss when Orage gave up the *New Age* and went to America; I had a feeling of relief when he returned and started the *New English Weekly*; I had a feeling of very deep loss when I read of his death the other day. It was not a personal loss, for my meetings with him, over a period of some eighteen years, had been infrequent and in public places. It is something quite as disturbing as a private loss: it is a public loss.

Many people will remember Orage as the tireless and wholly disinterested evangelist of monetary reform; many will remember him as the best leader-writer in London – on Wednesday mornings I always read through the first part of the *New English Weekly* before attending to any other work. A smaller number will remember him, as R. H. C. of the *New Age*, as the best literary critic of that time in London. Some will remember him as the benevolent editor who encouraged merit and (what is still rarer) tolerated genius. He was something more than the sum of these. He was a man who could [be] both perfectly right and wholly wrong; but when he was wrong one respected him all the more, as a man who was seeking the essential things and therefore was unafraid of making a fool of himself – a very rare quality indeed. What was great about him was not his intelligence, fine as that was, but his honesty and his selflessness. Most of us have not the self-knowledge to realise how parasitic we are upon the few men of fixed principle and selfless devotion, how the pattern of our world depends, not so much upon what they teach us, but just upon their being *there*. But when a man like Orage dies, we ought to admit that his no longer being *there* throws us, for the time, into disarray; so that a more thorough reorganisation is necessary than we should have believed possible.

[T. S. Eliot]

TO *Bonamy Dobrée*   TS Brotherton

15 November 1934   Faber & Faber Ltd

Dear Bonamy,

I hear (In Confidence) that the *N.E.W.* has been saved from the New Britain group and is to be continued in some form under Philippe Mairet.

1–Published in *NEW* (100) on that date.

I did not thank you for your review of *Eliz. Essays*, which I appreciate.[1]
I now agree with you about the superiority of the *Dutch Courtesan* over
the *Malcontent* – I dont know why I ever thought otherwise.

In haste
T.

TO *William Force Stead*   TS Beinecke

22 November [1934]   Faber & Faber Ltd

My dear Stead,

Very harebrainedly I forgot to answer the point of your last letter.
Please forgive me. OF COURSE I shall be delighted to back you up in
any way possible, & for whatever my name may be worth – Just let me
know when, in what form, and to whom to address the letter. Or shall I
just write an open letter containing an appreciation and send it to you?
Command me.[2]

Yours in haste,
T. S. E.

Fr Reginald Tribe, the Director of Kelham, has just been reading your
Mt Carmel and liked it immensely.

TO *Elsie Fogerty*[3]   cc

22 November 1934   [Faber & Faber Ltd]

Dear Miss Fogerty,

I have just returned from a visit to Kelham and find your letter.[4] I am
so sorry that I cannot accept your kind invitation to the English Verse

1–BD, 'Views and Reviews: the Elizabethans', *NEW* 4 (8 Nov. 1934), 91–2.
2–Stead responded, on 22 (presumably 23) Nov.: 'All you need say is that you have known
me for a number of years, that I am a very nice person and a horrid old-fashioned poet, that
my morals are not openly notorious but my religion is, that I talk fluently and almost always
off the point – off the point, aye, but on the pint . . .'
3–Elsie Fogerty, CBE, LRAM (1865–1945) – teacher of elocution and drama training;
founder in 1906 of the Central School of Speech and Drama (Laurence Olivier and Peggy
Ashcroft were favourite pupils) – was to train the chorus for the Canterbury premiere in
1935 of *MiC*. See further *Fogie: The life of Elsie Fogerty, C.B.E.*, compiled and ed. Marion
Cole (1967), 164–8.
4–Fogerty wrote on 20 Nov. to invite TSE to the Luncheon of the English Verse Speaking
Association on Sat., 24 Nov., at the Trocadero Restaurant.

Speaking Association, but I have to go to Canterbury on Friday night and shall not have returned.

It is a coincidence. I am going down to see Laurence Irving, as there is a suggestion of my doing a play for the Canterbury Festival in June. I had been on the point of writing to you about it. I should want to do a verse play with a chorus. Probably a smaller chorus of half a dozen speakers, which would have more to do with the action than in *The Rock*, as this would be more of a play. The subject of St Thomas of Canterbury has dramatic possibilities unexplored by Tennyson. Both Irving and myself, especially myself, are very anxious to persuade you to take an interest in this, and consider whether it would be possible for you to supply (and train) a small chorus? Much would depend upon that, as I should probably write the play differently – and better! – if I had hope of such support on a smaller scale, as you gave to *The Rock*. I shall be grateful if you will think this over and let me know if it is in any way possible. I believe the Festival is about Whitsun, and that the run is for a week.

Yours very sincerely,
[T. S. Eliot]

TO *Mary Hutchinson* TS Texas

22 November 1934   Faber & Faber Ltd

My dear Mary,

There has been no opportunity to mention this on the infrequent occasions on which I have seen you, but I do want to raise the matter now, because young Barker my poet has a Grant which will run out at Christmas, after which his situation will be serious. I have been holding your cheque in my pocket all this time, waiting to get a fourth person. Now can you think of any serious person whom you would, or I could, approach for 5s. a week for a year in quarterly payments? I say serious, because once the thing is started, if anyone fails to pay up, I shall have to make up the deficit out of my own pocket, and I shall be rather pinched myself after Christmas, what with Income Tax still to pay on what I earned in America, and heavy legal expenses. I am not sure whether Ted Kauffer[1] is not too flighty – you know the affair was to be kept private, and I found he had told John Hayward all about it without any secrecy – John will not tell anybody but Ted may have told all sorts of people. I dislike to

---

1 – Edward McKnight Kauffer (1890–1954), American artist and illustrator; friend of TSE.

approach benevolent folk who would dislike his poetry, because I think it is wrong to ask people to give money just out of charity to what they do not understand, when there are so many other deserving causes which they can understand. I should be grateful for any suggestions.

I hope you will be in town and can go to the Group Theatre on Sunday next for the second performance. The first was very much better than I expected, and I think really very good, although it was definitely a conception quite alien to my own.[1]

I have been à 4 chemins for the last ten days or more – going to Hull, Hampton, Newark, and tomorrow to Canterbury. Come December I hope to settle down a bit and get some work done. Would you care to see St Joan, if we could agree upon an evening?

Affectionately,

Tom

TO *Ottoline Morrell*   TS Texas

27 November 1934   Faber & Faber Ltd

My dear Ottoline,

Emily would like to come on Thursday very much if she can get done in time[2] – she is leaving for Italy the next day and has shopping and packing to do. If she comes, I will; but I have to catch a 5.50 train from Victoria for a long, and much needed weekend – so if she doesn't come I should prefer on my own account to come next week instead, when I shall not have to hurry away.[3]

1–Compare Bob Scott (President of O.U.D.S.), 'Living for the Theatre', *The Isis*, 19 Jan. 1966, 13: 'I remember a performance of "Sweeney Agonistes" in a room about this size and Mr Eliot sitting there looking at it absolutely stunned. He was so surprised by the way it was done. But afterwards he said to me, "That was obviously what it meant".' The programme notes for the production stated: 'The American accents are meant to be impressionistic and not authentic.' According to TSE's friend Jack Isaacs, in *An Assessment of Twentieth Century Literature* (1951), the production highlighted the farcical aspects of SA and neglected its tragic quality.

2–OM wrote (15 Nov.): 'I should be delighted if you would come on the 29th. Also Miss Hale.

'I was very much impressed & moved by your Play. I thought it was very fine & so interesting to realize how much it was enlarged & filled out by the acting . . .

'I wish you had been here today. There were several interesting people. I have set my heart on you knowing Charles Morgan for I feel you & he would have much in common.'

3–OM would note in her journal, flatly: 'Miss Hale and TSE to tea.'

I much enjoyed having sherry with Julian and her husband, on Saturday afternoon.[1]

I wonder if you can make any suggestion in the following difficulty. I have a young poet, a volume of whose verse we are bringing out next, who is married and very poor. I won't guarantee his genius, or that of anybody under thirty, but I think he is a good gamble. He is not well educated, so there is not very much employment to be found for him. Much more sensibility than intellect, and not very tough. I want to provide him with at least £1 a week for a year – that would make a great difference as his standard of living is low, though they have a baby. I have got two, and I think three, people to promise 5s. a week to be paid to me quarterly to pay over to him without his knowing who the donors are; but I want at least one, and preferably three more. I don't like asking people who are simply generous but don't care about poetry, or people who would see nothing in *his* poetry. But I want *reliable* people, because once the thing is started, if any benefactor defaults, I shall have to make up the deficit myself. Can you suggest anybody whom I might ask? He has had small grants from the Royal Literary Fund twice (got for him by Walter de la Mare) and that is coming to an end at Christmas and cannot be renewed. I should be grateful.

Ever affectionately,
Tom

P.S. His name is George Barker; but I don't want this to get about beyond the people who are likely to contribute.

I hope Bristol benefited you.

TO *Laurence Irving*

CC

29 November 1934   [Faber & Faber Ltd]

Dear Mr Irving,

I have heard from Elsie Fogerty, who is quite enthusiastic and anxious to provide all the assistance she can as soon as I can tell her more about the play. I have not yet had a reply from Martin Browne, and can only suppose that there is delay in forwarding from Rottingdean, which is the only address I have from him.

Now about the shilling edition, which is still a stumbling block to my firm. The first question is: is such an edition absolutely necessary?

1 – Julian's Morrell's husband was Victor Goodman (1899–1967), later to become Clerk of the Parliaments.

If so, the first point is that we cannot afford to undertake a shilling edition of 750 copies at our own expense, because we should have to sell many thousands at that price to make any profit, and 750 at a shilling means a definite loss. On the other hand, the more copies are sold at a shilling the fewer copies of the full version at 7s. 6d. would be sold. They would of course much prefer that there was no cheap edition at all; but if there has to be, the only possible way is for us to print it specially for the Canterbury authorities, and take a commission as well as the cost to us, to cover overhead expenses and the loss of a number of sales of the more expensive edition. Of course we don't assume for a moment that all of the people who buy the shilling edition in Canterbury would otherwise have bought the 7s. 6d. edition; but some certainly will content themselves with the cheaper who would otherwise have bought the other. We think that we could afford, all things considered, to produce the limited shilling edition for you for about £50 or £60.

I must recall what I said to you before, that my firm had commissioned me to write a play already, and that I cannot ask them to sacrifice probable sales merely because the play happens to be produced. The putative gain in publicity by performance at Canterbury would be more than offset by the loss of sales through a cheap edition.

I do not really see what the Festival has to gain by producing a cheap edition at all. Presumably the Festival, or at least the dramatic entertainment, aims to make money rather than lose it, and it is quite certain that the cheap edition will lose money. But if the shilling edition is considered essential, then what I have indicated above seems to us the only way in which it can be financed.

Yours very sincerely,
[T. S. Eliot]

TO *Ezra Pound*

TS Beinecke

29 November 1934   Faber & Faber Ltd

Yes as I said above 29 November 1934 Well Podesta the royal Nuptuals bein more or less Complete[1] I can again return to business Podesta you're about right There only a POSSUMA can Pet a Possum and they're skeercer than hen's teeth no ratels, raccoons or itchneumonia need apply mark that

---

1–On 29 Nov., Prince George, Duke of Kent, fourth son of King George V, was married to Princess Marina of Greece and Denmark, at Westminster Abbey.

well now thats a interesting narticle about this & that my only comblaint bein that there isnt so much about orage[1] and that mostly hindtail on fore but what of that what of it I guess or callate that a big man like Brer Rabbitt can spit whar he please and Again only objection to lil note on Parker & Tyler Too is that it leaves the reader much in the dark as to what Mr P. T. has been up to[2] Yes we did assume that proofs of Cantoon had been corrected by the old man and that if they were accurately reproduced all would be acceptable Podesta it strikes me that a visit from you might be helpful here in London sometime when the weather permits you dont know we have bathing in the Serps[3] now and what with Orage bein absent there is room for an active mind with me on the job acting as a kind of useful Fly-trap to interview all the boob and suckling poets and prevent them from getting any further you have a freer hand to collect the more intelligent I dont know if we could induce Wyndham to sit still in the back seat of the open barouche between us bowin graciously to the multitood horsely cheering or not but he might get in to the flash-light at Victoria station besides you could talk more and type less. However however its no use coaxin so will close yours

Tp

---

1 – EP had submitted an essay entitled 'In the Wounds (Memoriam A. R. Orage)' – published belatedly in C. 14 (Apr. 1935), 391–407 – dedicated to filling out 'the ideas to which [Orage] devoted the last fifteen years of his life . . . [I]t is with Douglasism that Orage was concerned. "Social Credit" and "New Democracy" give weekly and fortnightly counsel to the converted and nearly-converted . . . I doubt if Orage had any political talents whatsoever. He was a moralist, and thence an economist . . .'

Given TSE's response, EP added this endnote: 'If I have inadvertently left any obscurities in this article, I apologize. I also refer the reader who finds the statement lacking in detail, to a brief shilling pamphlet by Major Douglas *The New and Old Economics* (Scotts Free Press . . .).'

2 – EP had sent in a short review of *Modern Things*, ed. Parker Tyler (New York, 1934): 'When a young and quite impractical critic can include as much acute criticism as the Introduction to this brief anthology contains, I am ready to give thanks for his existence . . .' EP wrote in a covering note: 'The kid is not a blockhead but *very* ignorant.' His note on Tyler was not used.

3 – A swimming area on the southern bank of the Serpentine, the recreational lake in Hyde Park, London, had been opened in 1930.

TO *Walter de la Mare*   TS de la Mare Estate

29 November 1934   Faber & Faber Ltd

My dear de la Mare,

I am now taking up once more the problem of George Barker. His Grant, that you got him, is coming to an end at the end of the year, and he is beginning to be worried about the future.[1]

This seems to me the appropriate moment for carrying out the scheme we discussed, which was, if you remember, that you and I and two other persons should provide 5s. a week for a year, each. I have now got the two other persons. One of them prefers to pay quarterly, the other has sent me the £13 in one sum. What I propose is to ask you as well, if you are still disposed to contribute, to let me have a cheque, and I will give my bankers instructions to pay Barker £13 a quarter, commencing at Christmas. My bankers can then confirm, at any time if the question is raised, that the money has reached its destination. I shall try to make some arrangement so that any money in hand should still go to Barker in the event of my death meanwhile; but I think the best arrangement would be for you to pay me on quarter-days so that the money should go out as soon as it comes in.

I may secure one or two more subscriptions, but I do not want more than that. I feel that it will be better to keep a few possible benefactors in reserve, so that if necessary a similar arrangement could be made another year. That I think is more important than that he should receive a larger sum the first year. The number of people to whom I can apply is limited.

Yours very sincerely,
T. S. Eliot

1 – Barker had written to TSE, 14 Nov.: 'I am hesitant of mentioning a matter which is now worrying me profoundly – I mean money. The Royal Grant expires at Christmas, leaving us as we were before, without any. I should be infinitely grateful to you, if, hearing of any work in England or abroad, you would notify or suggest me, – please forgive this if it transgresses.'

4 December 1934   [Faber & Faber Ltd]

Dear Sir,

I enclose herewith five cheques for the credit of my Current Account as
follows:

Per			
	The Hon. Bryan Guinness	...	£14
	Victor Rothschild Esq.	...	£13
	Walter de la Mare Esq.	...	£3:5:0
	Mrs St John Hutchinson	...	£3:5:0
	Siegfried Sassoon Esqre.	...	£5:0:0

Against these when collected will you kindly draw a cheque for £22:5:0
(twenty-two pounds 5s) to George Barker Esqre. and send it to him at

> Gaulter,
> Kimmeridge
> Corfe Castle, Dorset.

His receipt should be obtained.

The point is that the first four of the persons listed, *and* myself, have
undertaken to pay £3:5 quarterly each, *anonymously*, to Mr Barker who
is in need. Mr Guinness and Mr Rothschild preferred to let me have the
whole sum at once; Mr De la Mare and Mrs Hutchinson will pay me
quarterly, and you will debit my £3:5:0 quarterly, of course. The five
pounds from Mr Sassoon, and an extra pound from Mr Guinness, are
gifts and not regular payments. Hence the sum of £22:5 is made up by
five times £3:5:0 plus six pounds. For the following three quarters you
will pay Mr Barker only £13:5:0. The names of the donors are not to be
revealed to him.

I trust that this is clear. The only question I have to ask is whether you
could earmark the balance of what Mr Rothschild and Mr Guinness have
paid, so that in the event of my death during the year, it might be paid to
Mr Barker without being involved in my estate.

Apologising for the trouble I am giving you,

I am,
Yours faithfully,
[T. S. Eliot]

TO *George Barker*   TS Texas

4 December 1934   Faber & Faber Ltd

Dear Barker,

Four persons who wish to remain anonymous, and who are interested
in your work and in helping to a small extent through your present
difficulties, have asked me to act as treasurer. The money collected, or
promised, will amount to twenty-five shillings a week for a year. This is
not very much, but it should ease the situation a little. I am to receive, and
to pay out the money quarterly. So you will shortly be receiving a cheque
for £16: 5:0 and three quarterly payments of the same amount, unless we
get a little more.

In addition, we have gifts totalling £6, so that the *first* cheque will actually
be for £22: 5:0. Your receipt to the bank will be all the acknowledgement
needed.[1]

                              Yours sincerely,
                              T. S. Eliot

TO *Mary Hutchinson*   TS Texas

4 December 1934   Faber & Faber Ltd

My dear Mary,

I meant to write to you last night – but was too tired to write any letters
– and tried to telephone today but you were out. Very many thanks for
your kindness – Victor Rothschild sent me £13;[2] and I have another from
an unexpected quarter – so now I can give Barker twentyfive shillings a
week for a year – and we have another six pounds for a gift to him. I didnt
see the poem[3] – somebody asked if it meant that his baby was dead –
I dont know that either – I hope not. I should love to go to *St Joan* with
you, but Friday is a bad day[4] – I have an old man coming to sherry with
me – he is very eccentric, and his daughter killed herself, I am told, not
long ago – I have to try to cheer him up, and I dont know when I shall be

---

1 – Barker acknowledged on 5 Dec.: 'I have received your letters and am at a loss to express
adequately the extent of my gratitude & thanks.'
2 – Mary Hutchinson had written, 2 Dec.: 'I had asked Victor [Rothschild] if he would like
to subscribe some time ago and I was waiting to hear definitely before writing to you.'
3 – 'I thought Barker's poem in the *Listener* ['The Multiple Figure', 14 Nov. 1934, 827] the
week before last very remarkable and I was glad to think I could help a little towards his
leisure.'
4 – 'Could we go to St Joan together next Friday?'

able to escape exhausted. I couldnt get away till 7 anyway, and shouldnt be able to dress. Have you any evening NEXT week for it? I am free on Monday Wednesday and Thursday. Please let me know if you can and I will get the tickets. If Birrell is in a nursing home in London and would like to see me let me know – I should like to see him, I always liked him.[1]

Affectionately,

Tom

TO *Ottoline Morrell*   TS Texas

4 December 1934   Faber & Faber Ltd

My dear Ottoline,

I had yesterday your letter enclosing a cheque for £5 from Siegfried Sassoon, and I have also a letter with a cheque for £14 from Bryan Guinness. I am extremely grateful to you for your help in the matter.[2]

I look forward to seeing you on Monday the 10th.

Yours ever affectionately,

Tom

I don't know whether I *like* Gerard Heard or not – but I felt that we could probably *understand* each other's languages, whether we talked them or not![3]

1 – 'Poor Francis Birrell has gone again into a nursing home in rather a desperate state. [H]e suddenly became very much worse and they fear a recurrence of his illness. I saw him on Thursday when he was better and he spoke of you and would like to have seen you.' Francis Birrell (1889–1935), critic, joint owner with David Garnett of a Bloomsbury bookshop, wrote for *NS&N*; and he was author of two biographies: his life of Gladstone was published in 1933.

2 – OM wrote on 28 Nov.: 'Now about your young friend [George Barker]. I am writing to Siegfried Sassoon who *likes* to help young poets, but of course he may have too many on hand. Then I am also writing to Bryan Guinness.' She added, 'I believe Virginia [Woolf] of course would help your young man gladly. They are I fancy well off & have no children & I believe are very generous in such cases. It would be best if *you* ask Virginia, I think.'

3 – OM had asked on 8 Nov., ' I wonder if you liked Gerald Heard.' She wrote again on 1 Dec.: 'Siegfried S. sends £5 toward the fund & cannot give more at present.

'I think it's best to accept it but we could hardly count him as a permanent subscriber can we? . . . He has given £100 towards W. Owen's MS for the British Mus. which seems to me a waste of money, unless the owner was very poor.'

TO *Walter de la Mare*   TS de la Mare Estate

4 December 1934   Faber & Faber Ltd

My dear de la Mare,

Many thanks for your letter of the 20th enclosing a cheque for £3:5s. I am very much obliged to you. I have now enough to provide Barker with 25s. a week for a year, as well as two odd gifts amounting to £6, which he shall have with one instalment before Christmas.

I did not see Barker's poem in the *Listener*, and have had no news from him about the child.[1] I know that it was born in the most difficult circumstances, but had not heard about its having died. If this is true, it must be most recent, but I hope very much that it is not so.

We are bringing out his volume of poems in the spring. He tells me that he has produced another prose piece, which I am to see after Christmas. The trouble with his prose pieces is that they are such a completely unpractical length for publication. The new one is again, I believe, about twenty thousand words. I have told him that the only chance for stuff of this kind is that it may float on the reputation to be made by his poems. I think that you would agree with me about this. An imaginative work of twenty thousand words by an unknown author is an almost impossible undertaking.

                          Yours ever,
                          T. S. Eliot

TO *William Force Stead*   CC

4 December 1934   [Faber & Faber Ltd]

Dear William,

Here we are. It is a bit high-flown, but I thought one ought to employ a rather orotund style to hold the attention of the Oriental. If there is anything to alter or to add or to subtract I am at your service, and will write any number of drafts to get it right. May your fortunes prosper.

                          Ever yours,
                          [T. S. E.]

1–De la Mare wrote on 30 Nov.: 'Did you see Barker's poem in *The Listener* not long ago? Does this mean that the child that was born is dead? I hope indeed that this is not so.' Barker's poem 'Elegy', in *The Listener* 12 (26 Sept. 1934), 530, carried the epigraph '*Luctus in morte infantis*'.

4th December 1934

I have known Mr William Force Stead for over eleven years and count him as a valued friend. He is, first, a poet of established position and an individual inspiration. What is not so well known, except to a small number of the more fastidious readers, is that he is also a prose writer of great distinction: his book *Mt Carmel* is recognised as a classic of prose style in its kind. And while the bulk of his published writing on English literature is small, those who know his conversation can testify that he is a man of wide reading and a fine critical sense.

Mr Stead is, moreover, a man of the world in the best sense, who has lived in several countries and is saturated in European culture. By both natural social gifts and cultivation, accordingly, he has a remarkable ability of sympathy with all sorts and conditions and races of men.

I would say finally that I know from several sources, that Mr Stead was most successful as a teacher of young men at Oxford; that he gained both the affection and the respect of his students; and that he exercised upon them a most beneficial influence. He has the scholarship necessary to teach English literature accurately, and the personal qualities necessary to make the subject interesting to his pupils; and I could not recommend anyone for the purpose with more confidence.[1]

TO *Cyril E. Hudson*[2]   CC

4 December 1934   [Faber & Faber Ltd]

Dear Father Hudson,

I enclose herewith the manuscript of the lecture which I promised you for the *Teaching Church Review*, and which I have abbreviated as best I could. You are welcome to abbreviate it further for your purposes if necessary, but I should like to see the proof. I should also be glad if you would make the acknowledgement with it, that this is the shortened form of an address delivered at the University of Leeds, and at the University College, Hull.[3]

1 – Stead had prompted TSE on 3 Dec. – TSE had asked for this – 'you can say that we have been friends for about ten years – that is praise in itself – that I had a long experience of university life – that Oxford thought highly enough of me to elect me to a Fellowship – that my prose book Mt Carmel has been widely read and praised and that my poems have their admirers also, and that you believe – I hope you believe – that I can make the subject of English Literature interesting to my students – Could you bring in some of these points?'
2 – The Revd Cyril E. Hudson (1888–1960), Canon of St Albans; Hon. Sec. of the Teaching Church Group for Adult Religious Education; editor of the *Teaching Church Review*.
3 – 'Literature and the Modern World', *The Teaching Church Review* 5: 1 (Feb. 1935), 11–15.

With reference to the second paragraph of your letter, I dare say that what you suggest is advisable.[1] I should think that this point might well be raised at the next Committee Meeting. I have not amassed the necessary acquaintance amongst Non-conformists to make any suggestions. I think, however, that if the Committee is much enlarged, it may be desirable to nominate a small Executive Committee within it, in order to get any business done. What I have been doubtful about, however, is not whether the complexion of the Committee itself is too Catholic, but whether the list of names proposed as signatories of the letter to *The Times* is not too preponderantly Roman and Anglican. Here again, however, I have no suggestion to make.

Yours sincerely,

[T. S. Eliot]

TO *Mary Trevelyan*[2]

CC

4 December 1934   [Faber & Faber Ltd]

Dear Miss Trevelyan,

I must apologise for my delay in answering your letters of the 20th and 30th of November, which has been due to pressure of work.

I should be very glad in principle to accept your invitation to lecture at the Student Movement House, but I find that all my spare time from now until the middle of June will be taken up by one piece of work, and I am now obliged to decline any further invitations to speak during the first part of 1935.

With many regrets, and apologies for the delay.

Yours sincerely,

[T. S. Eliot]

1–Hudson wrote on 29 Nov.: 'I have been rather wishing that the Committee could be strengthened from quarters less conspicuously Catholic than at present: don't you think this would be advisable, if we are going to appeal for funds to the Christian public generally?'

2–Mary Trevelyan (1897–1983), Warden of Student Movement House, worked to support the needs of overseas students in London (her institution was initally based at 32 Russell Square, close to the offices of F&F). An international student club founded in 1917 as a memorial to students of all countries who fell in the Great War, it catered for the more than sixty colleges in London. Later founder and first governor of International Students House, London. In a letter of Nov. 1939 TSE would refer to her as 'the hearty Warden'. She was appointed CBE in 1968. She left a memoir of her friendship with TSE – 'The Pope of Russell Square' – whom she long desired to marry. See obituary in *The Times*, 12 Jan. 1983. See also Humphrey Carpenter, 'Poor Tom: Mary Trevelyan's View of T. S. Eliot', *English* 38: 160 (1989), 37–52.

TO *Ernest Bird, Messrs Bird & Bird*   CC

4 December 1934   [Faber & Faber Ltd]

My dear Bird,

Thank you for your letter of the 3d.[1] The procedure as you now state it seems to me more satisfactory than the other. I had not been happy about the necessity of breaking open the doors; and if the Sheriff, once he has obtained entry, is in a position to remove what belongs to me, so much the better. I shall foresee difficulties in recovering *all* the property; but I endorse the proposals set forth in your letter. I only regret that the Sheriff does not wear a uniform.

Yours very sincerely,
[T. S. Eliot]

TO *W. B. Yeats*   CC

6 December 1934   [Faber & Faber Ltd]

My dear Yeats,

I am sorry that I was much too pressed and short-handed to give you my immediate impressions of the performance of Rupert Doone's troupe, but no doubt you have heard from Miss Cullis.

I must say that, although the presentation was in important respects entirely alien to my intentions, I was very much pleased with the skill and intelligence of the production. Whether they are up to anything more ambitious than *Sweeney* I am not sure. I should think, unless you now have other plans maturing, that it might be worthwhile letting them do a similar private performance of one of your smaller plays, and see how

---

1 – 'Following our last interview on the 19th ult., and as then arranged I write to say that we have obtained a writ enabling the Sheriff to enter your Wife's flat for the purpose of obtaining your effects. It now appears that, contrary to the opinion previously expressed to you, the Sheriff to whom the writ will be delivered is not entitled to break down the door but must seize an opportunity of entering peaceably [*sic*]. In these circumstances I think that it will be wiser not to address any previous letter to Mrs Eliot as to do so will put her on her guard. My proposal is that when the Sheriff is in possession he shall get into touch with Higginson who will then go himself with a view of collecting what belongs to you.' (G. F. Higginson, a new partner at Bird & Bird – a graduate of Winchester College and of Balliol College, Oxford – had previously arranged to call at VHE's flat, accompanied by a 'suitable van' supplied by Maples, on 5 Nov. – 'for the purpose of taking over the articles belonging to you and making the Inventory directed by the Order of the Court' – but that visit had evidently availed nothing.)

you like it. I think, however, that it ought to be at a time when you could be in London to direct them.

Yours very sincerely,
[T. S. Eliot]

TO *Edith Sitwell*[1]   CC

6 December 1934   [Faber & Faber Ltd]

My dear Edith,

I was very much gratified and honoured by receiving from you the inscribed copy of *Aspects of Modern Poetry*. I have not yet had time to read it thoroughly, but I look forward to reading it with a keen and possibly somewhat malicious enjoyment.

I admit that it is pleasant to see a book which does not treat all of us merely as precursors of the next generation, doomed to perish in the wilderness. I am also glad to see Ezra Pound receiving really critical and appreciative attention.

I hope I may see you again when you are next in England.

With many thanks,
Ever yours,
[Tom]

1–Edith Sitwell (1887–1964): poet, biographer, novelist; editor of *Wheels* 1916–21. Her collection *The Mother and Other Poems* (1915) was followed by *Clown's Houses* (1918) and *The Wooden Pegasus* (1920). In 1923, her performance at the Aeolian Hall in London of her cycle of poems, *Façade* (1922), with music by William Walton, placed her briefly at the centre of modernistic experimentation. Other writings include *Collected Poems* (1930) and *Taken Care Of* (memoirs, 1965). She was appointed DBE in 1954. See John Pearson, *Façades: Edith, Osbert and Sacheverell Sitwell* (1978); *Selected Letters of Edith Sitwell*, ed. Richard Greene (1997); Greene, *Edith Sitwell: Avant-Garde Poet, English Genius* (2011). TSE to Mary Trevelyan, 16 Oct. 1949: 'Edith and Osbert [Sitwell] are 70% humbug – but kind – and cruel' ('The Pope of Russell Square').

TO *W. H. Auden*

6 December 1934   [Faber & Faber Ltd]

My dear Auden,

I haven't been able to think of anyone fitted to vet your cockney dialect.[1] The trouble is, from my experience, that one wants somebody who not only understands that language thoroughly, but who understands your own purposes, and can adapt the former to the latter. A pedantic literalist is no good, and it is much better to take the risk. Anyway, your dialect is at least as good as mine, and you don't have to tackle the problem of making people express completely inappropriate sentiments.

I think you must have heard from Stephen and others about Doone's performance of *Sweeney*.[2] It seems to have been a success, as he has repeated it once, and will repeat it again. The conception was entirely different from my own, but that does not matter. I was really very pleasantly surprised by Doone's skill in presentation in these circumstances, and the general level of intelligence. I think that they put their backs into it. I am still uncertain whether the company are up to a play which will make such heavy claims upon them as yours, but I am a good deal more hopeful than I was.

I wish that I could get down to Malvern for your stream-lined revue, but it looks as if I should have too much to do from now on.[3] I shall be very sorry to miss it.

Yours ever,
[T. S. Eliot]

---

1 – WHA wrote in an undated letter, in reply to letters from TSE that cannot now be traced: 'I quite agree with your criticisms. I want to rewrite the end, so will you hold up the printing. The cockney wants revising. If you could put me in touch with someone really competent, I should be most grateful.'

2 – VW recorded on 12 Nov.: '& so to hear Sweeney Agonistes at the Group Theatre; an upper attic or studio: I sat by Tom: an audience, containing Ottoline & Hope [Mirrlees] & Raymond [Mortimer]. The acting made more sense than the reading but I doubt that Tom has enough of a body & brain to bring off a whole play: certainly he conveys an emotion, an atmosphere, which is more than most: something peculiar to himself; sordid, emotional, intense – a kind of Crippen, in a mask: modernity & poetry locked together' (*Diary* 4, 260–1).

Dr H. H. Crippen was hanged in 1910 for poisoning his wife.

3 – WHA's revue at Downs School was to be staged on 18–19 Dec.

TO *Cyril Ray*   CC

7 December 1934   [Faber & Faber Ltd]

Dear Sir,

I must apologise to you for the delay in answering your letter of
November 28th, which by an oversight was not brought to my attention
until yesterday.¹ Your suggestion is one that needs some rather careful
consideration. I will write to you again when I have had an opportunity
of discussing it with my directors.

Believe me,
Yours truly,
[T. S. Eliot]

1 – Cyril Ray (1908–91), journalist and author; war and foreign correspondent; wine writer,
wrote from Liverpool, 28 Nov. 1934:

Dear Sirs, / As the publishers of [Rudolf] Arnheim's *Film* and of *For Filmgoers Only*,
I wondered if you would be interested in the following suggestion.

A number of publishers have produced books on the cinema but no one publisher has as
yet identified himself with that subject as, say, Gollancz with popular economics. I suggest
that a publisher could 'cash in' on a very definite public interest with a 'library' or series of
short monographs on film topics. Small books at about 3s. 6d., each written by an authority,
on various aspects or personalities of the cinema would, I think, be assured of a steady
sale. There could, for example, be a book on Chaplin, one on René Clair, on The Russian
Cinema, on Cartoon and Silhouette Films, on Montage etc.

There are many obvious authors: C. A. Lejeune, R. S. Lambert, Rotha, John Grierson,
Olive Baldwin and others. I think that the British Film Institute would probably lend its
support very gladly.

I am not suggesting myself as a possible contributor – although I have contributed to
various periodicals on film subjects I have neither the time nor the ability to write a book on
the cinema – but I offer the suggestion to you for what it is worth. I should very much like
to see such a series as I suggest and I am sure that the series could be made a profitable one.
/ Yours truly, / Cyril Ray

7 December 1934   [Faber & Faber Ltd]

Dear Miss Forwood,

I thank you for your letter of the 2nd. It is a pleasure to know that the Pivot Club would like me to speak to them, and I should very much like to be able to do so. I assume what you want is something similar to my reading the other day, but I think for the Pivot Club it might be somewhat more advanced.

As a matter of fact, I have been declining all invitations to speak from now until the middle of the year, because I shall be much too busy, but as I am so indebted to the Central School, I should like to make this one exception, if I can. As you say it is impossible to make engagements more than three weeks ahead, would you care to write to me somewhere about the end of January, when I shall hope to be in a position to take the time?

                    With many thanks,
                    Yours sincerely,
                    [T. S. Eliot]

1 – Hon. Sec. of the Pivot Club (President, Elsie Fogerty) – the Social Club of the Central School – Muriel Forwood invited TSE to give them a lecture and a reading from his work during the next term. 'I passed on your charming remarks about the "Rock" choir to the proper quarter, and they were much appreciated.' Robert Sencourt explains that next door to Eliot's lodgings in Courtfield Road 'lived a prominent Anglo-Catholic, Miss Muriel Forwood' (*T. S. Eliot*, 121). 'Miss Forwood . . . would drive him about in her car. Once she was taking him to a poetry reading. "I hate reading my poetry aloud like this," he told her. "It's like undressing in public." "You needn't worry," she reassured him. "You never take off too much"' (ibid., 130).

TO *Laurence Irving*   CC

7 December 1934   [Faber & Faber Ltd]

My dear Irving,

I postponed writing to you until Miss Babington's letter had arrived and been discussed with my Board.[1] Geoffrey Faber is now taking up the matter with Miss Babington, and I hope that they will be able to arrive at an agreement satisfactory to all parties.[2]

1–Irving had written on 29 Nov. 1934: 'I have shown your letter to Miss Babington, and she, as Festival Manager, is writing to you about the shilling edition and the general financial aspect.

'I think you know how keen the Bishop of Chichester and I are that you should write a play for the Canterbury Festival . . . If at the moment, the position in which are you placed makes it temporarily impossible for you to write a Canterbury play, I am sure that we would rather postpone it for a year than that you should feel hurried or dissatisfied with the conditions under which it would be written.'

2–Margaret A Babington was from 1928 Hon. Steward and Treasurer, Friends of Canterbury Cathedral; Hon. Festival Manager for the Festival of Music and Drama, 15–22 June 1935. Irving was to remember her as 'tall, trim and purposeful', a person of 'fervour and boundless energy [and] cheerful assurance . . . ebullient and warm-hearted . . .' And above all else: 'Within a year she had enrolled 1,430 Friends' (*The Canterbury Adventure: An Account of the Inception and Growth of the Friends of Canterbury Cathedral 1928–1959* [1960]: Canterbury Papers no. 10). See also letter to her, 29 Jan. 1935.

Babington wrote to TSE, 1 Dec. 1934: 'Mr Irving has shown me your letter to him, and has suggested that I write to you about our experience here in connection with the shilling edition of "Becket" and the "Young King" and [John Masefield's] "The Coming of Christ".

'Such an edition has proved to be absolutely necessary. The acoustics of the Chapter House demand it, the audience like to read the play before they see it, and moreover the Festival is intended primarily for lovers of the Cathedral, the great majority of whom could not afford to pay 7/6 for a book. And certainly our Cathedral Players, with scarcely an exception wage earners, could not afford an expensive copy of the play; they number about 30.

'In the case of "The Coming of Christ" Heinemann were glad to print and publish the shilling edition; in the case of "Becket" and "The Young King" a shilling edition was printed and published locally with profit to the printer. For "Becket" a 2d royalty was paid to Macmillan. These editions were both published by the Friends of Canterbury Cathedral, so that I can be quite sure of the facts. We had the royalty of 2d on "The Young King", which will tell you that there is certainly no loss on the edition, for our printer himself first mentioned the question of the royalty at this year's Festival.

'I am wondering whether the Canterbury Play could be a thing apart, and not connected in any way with a book that would be sold for 7/6, otherwise you would I suppose either have to diminish the play for us or else expand it for the book, as our plays run only for an hour and a half. With the rather complicated mechanics of the Chapter House, I imagine that a play specially written would have to be very concise. If you could do this the Festival Committee would pay you £50 in advance royalties; the percentage could be agreed on. The takings during the last three years have been round about £400, and such a play as you would write would be bound to be revived at frequent intervals.

Meanwhile, I have heard from Miss Fogerty, who would be delighted to co-operate; but of course nothing definite can be decided until I can tell her exactly what I shall need.

'I hope that my letter does not seem importunate, but I think you know how much we should like to have a play from you. I have seen the Dean and have told him of your visit when staying in the neighbourhood. He was most interested and very greatly pleased to hear of the possibility of a play from your pen. At the same time neither Mr Irving nor I should like to think of your doing anything that would place you in difficulties; and if these seem to be insuperable we must, in the very near future, turn our minds to something else.'

GCF replied to Babington on 7 Dec. 1934: 'Mr Eliot has given me your letter to him of December 1st, and has asked me to reply to it. I am writing with his knowledge and approval.

'The circumstances are these: Mr Eliot had already agreed to write a full-length play, for us to publish at 7/6, before he received the invitation of the Friends of Canterbury Cathedral. He is anxious to accept the invitation, if he can do so without upsetting the terms of his agreement with us. The play which he is writing for us will be considerably longer than the plays acted at Canterbury, but I understand from him that it would be perfectly possible to prepare from the full-length play an abbreviated version for performance at Canterbury.

'We should be willing to give the Friends of Canterbury Cathedral a license to print not more than 750 copies of the abbreviated version and to sell these, in Canterbury only, at one shilling, provided that any copies remaining at the end of the Festival are withdrawn from sale. We should require a fee of thirty guineas for this license, but there would be no other fees or royalties to be paid either to Mr Eliot or to ourselves.

'The question of reissue of the acting edition, in the event of later revivals, would have to be left over until it arose.

'It is possible that our 7/6 edition will be published at a date near to that of the Festival. The sale of the acting edition is bound to have an unfavourable effect on the sale of our own edition; so that we are obliged to make the stipulations set out above.'

Babington responded on 14 Dec. 1934: 'I note that you ask a fee of thirty guineas as license for the publication of 750 copies of an abbreviated version of such a play to be sold at one shilling, on the understanding that any copies remaining unsold at the end of the Festival are withdrawn from sale.

'Meanwhile I write to ask if Mr Eliot can give us any date for the completion of the play to be published by you? After it is written, the acting edition would have to be prepared (as in the case of Mr Laurence Binyon's play, "The Young King") by our producer, Miss Eileen Thorndike. All this, as you would realise, takes time.

'We were proposing to get together a band of voluntary workers to make some of the costumes. They ought to start by the end of January and rehearsals ought to begin not later than the first or second week in April.

'If Mr Eliot could give you information on these points to pass on to me by the end of the month I should be very grateful. But as Mr Eliot had definitely agreed to write a play for you before we discussed the subject with him last month, you are no doubt already in a position to reply.'

Babington wrote again to TSE, 19 Dec. 1934: 'I have written an official reply in answer to the letter I received from Mr Geoffrey Faber written on behalf of the Firm. Meanwhile I write to you to say how greatly we hope that the play from your pen may be possible without your being too greatly hurried.

'I shall be in London from Christmas Eve until Thursday, December 27th, so that if by any chance you would like me to ring you up on the latter date to ask any questions I hope that you will not hesitate to let me know.'

I enclose the first and relevant page of a letter from Martin Browne. You will see that he is definitely interested, but he asks questions which you, probably, are in a better position to answer than I am. May I suggest that you should now write to him direct. As I told you, I am spending the weekend of the 15th with him, at Rottingdean. I have just had a note from him at that address, and presume that he should be addressed there, instead of at York.[1]

Yours sincerely,
[T. S. Eliot]

TO *Cosmo Gordon Lang*[2]   CC

8 December 1934   [Faber & Faber Ltd]

My Lord Archbishop,

As Secretary of the Book Committee of the Church Literature Association, I have been requested, by the unanimous wish of the Executive, to ask Your Grace to do us the great honour of taking the Chair at the Annual Meeting of the Association on Thursday, January 31st.[3]

I and my Executive are quite sensible that it would be improper to ask such a favour of a personage like Your Grace, if any reasonably satisfactory substitute could be found. I must allow myself to say that if Your Grace declines, we shall most regretfully be compelled to make much more modest arrangements.

This is to be the first Annual Meeting of the newly formed Church Literature Association, which, as Your Grace is aware, is formed out of the old Catholic Literature Association and the Literature Committee of the English Church Union of which Dr Charles Harris is the Chairman. As it is vital at the present time that the New Church Union should really be a Union, so it is of great importance that this new affiliated organisation should present itself, on its first public appearance, as an organisation for combining and raising to the highest degree of effectiveness the intellectual forces of the Church in print. The new Association starts with a determination to maintain unity within against the forces of Secularism

1 – In Nov. 1934 EMB had taken up the post of producer at the York Repertory Theatre.
2 – William Cosmo Gordon Lang (1864–1945), known as Cosmo Gordon Lang, served as Archbishop of York (1908–28) and Archbishop of Canterbury (1928–42).
3 – This letter was written at the behest of Charles Harris (letter to TSE, 6 Dec.). 'You might inform His Grace that the Book Committee has preserved its complete identity with the old English Church Union Literature Committee, whose work it continues . . .'

without: the subject of the meeting, therefore, will be: 'The Christian in the Modern World'. Nothing could so truly affirm this determination as the presence of Your Grace in the Chair.

The meeting will not occupy more than an hour and a quarter. Dr N. P. Williams is being asked to speak for the Book Committee, and Mr Maurice Reckitt for the Tract Committee, and the Principal of Pusey House, the Revd A. F. Hood, is asked to make some general remarks on behalf of the Association as a whole. The place is the Hoare Memorial Hall, The Church House. The time is 5.30 or a later hour if Your Grace prefers.

Hoping that Your Grace will consider this request favourably,

> I remain,
> Your Grace's obedient servant,
> [T. S. Eliot]
> Secretary of the Book Committee.

P.S. I enclose for Your Grace's perusal a copy of a letter which I have just received this morning from Dr Charles Harris. Your Grace will observe that Dr Harris mentions January 31st, or a later date at Your Grace's convenience.

TO *George Barker*   CC

8 December 1934   [Faber & Faber Ltd]

Dear Barker,

As your Poems are now wanted for the printers, I have a few last points to raise.

You have three poems all named *Narcissus*. For purposes of identification I think they should each have a name or be numbered Narcissus I, II and III.[1]

I cannot trace a poem 'Luctus in morte infantis'. Can you send another copy?[2]

I can see no reason why all the poems you have added should not be included; it will depend somewhat on how the paging works out. But I should like to include 'Northumberland bound down' which you wished to omit, because I think it is a good one and because it has a concreteness and intelligibility which will be useful.

1–Barker responded on 11 Dec.: 'Regarding the three Narcissus poems, I have numbered these I II & III in the contents list, as you suggested.'
2–Barker explained (11 Dec.) that 'Luctus in morte infantis' was the title he had added to the poem opening 'Count them as they cluster'. The poem was ultimately called 'Elegy'.

The revised 'Colocinth' is called, I observe, 'The Bloom of Creed'.

Is there any close plan about the order you have given? If not, I doubt whether 'No feeble dream' is the best one to start with. Better have a strong poem like 'Daedalus' or a strong group with some relation.

I understand you reject the following: Count them as they cluster. O in summer he came. I am not wronged. Fragment of a Dramatic Poem. The Erinny. The detonator's phalanxes. The Prisons and the Towers. These cerulean sandals. Great anthropoid.

Your last title-page reads:

No feeble dream
Narcissus
Fistral Bay
Venerable all hills
The Constellation
I am suspicious
I am the land, surrounding sea
The land is you
Narcissus
The Leaping Laughers
The Crystal
Daedalus
I too will end
Lax though the longing wear
Narcissus
His perennial
Elegy Anticipating Death
The Chimaera
The honeycombs of virtue
He comes among
The Seal Boy
Love apart
The webs of action
This destination not to be read
The Cornucopia
The Amazons
This figure, multiple
I, mute immutable, cry
The Tenements of Death

Have you any preference for
The order of the following:

Paradisiacal bird
I am that face
Northumberland, bound down
Though at intervals

The poppy trembling
Luctus in morte *MISSING*
The Wraith-Friend

I should like to settle these points as quickly as may be.[1]

                    Yours sincerely,
                    T. S. Eliot

TO *Stephen Spender*   TS Northwestern

10 December 1934   Faber & Faber Ltd

My dear Spender,

I sympathise with your present feeling of discouragement about *Vienna*, but of course that feeling is in relation to your own standards and ideals rather than to those of the reader.[2] I was inclined to feel myself that the poem could have been strengthened if it had been kept a little longer, and revised by the author at a somewhat greater distance in time from the occasion which provoked it. That is apt to be the case with any piece of work which has been definitely promised for a particular date – not, in general, the best thing to do with poetry, but for that we are as much to blame as you, and the poem has some very fine things in it. I don't think

1–Barker explained on 11 Dec. that 'Luctus in morte infantis' was a title for the poem opening 'Count them as they cluster': 'If I included this poem in my suggested rejections I did so by error, as I am actually fonder of it than of others.' He appended a fresh order for the volume, leading off as Eliot suggested with 'a strong poem'.

2–SS wrote on 8 Dec.: 'I have decided that Vienna is a complete failure. I ought to have realized this some time ago. But now, supposing it should sell out the whole of one edition, will you prevent it going into another impression?' He went on: 'With regard to future plans, I think that when you have subtracted the £10 advance on my royalties, I will of course be in your debt for £15 on the novel.'

John Sutherland comments: '*Vienna* was published by Faber, in a rush, in November 1934 . . . There was little seasonal good-will for Spender's latest effort. Few commentators, in 1934 or later, have had a good word to say about *Vienna*. None the less, the long poem (Stephen's first) represented a major advance – or could have done . . . But the blow to Stephen's confidence was palpable. *Trial of a Judge*, his next ambitious project in verse (and another "political" production) went into limbo. It would not appear until 1938. Nor would he produce another collection of verse until *The Still Centre*, five years later' (*Stephen Spender: The Authorized Biography* [2004], 170, 174). The rushed production may go some way to explain why *Vienna* was produced with no blurb. However, SS had written to RdlM, 27 Oct. 1934: 'I like the Vienna book very much. It is beautifully printed, and I like the wrapper: I even rather like the red cover now. It certainly seems very nice now that the book is bound. The paper is very good too. I greatly appreciate your taking so much trouble.'

in the least that it will damage your reputation, but on the contrary will increase the curiosity about your next work.

I am not quite clear as to how we stand with you financially, but I am enquiring about the matter, and will write again. Don't worry about your work.

Ever yours,
T. S. E.

Yes, you are right. *Vienna* has now earned over £11 so you are on the credit side. The £15 is set against the novel.

TO *Marguerite Caetani*[1]   CC

11 December 1934   [Faber & Faber Ltd]

Dear Marguerite,

I have [been] meaning to write to you daily for some time past, but have been extremely busy, mostly with uninteresting routine and odd jobs – lecturing and speaking and taking the chair and on committees – which do not give much satisfaction, and am tired. First of all, I wanted to thank you for your kindness to Miss McPherrin. She wrote me a long and enthusiastic letter about meeting you; and what is still better evidence, wrote in the same strain to Emily.[2] You may be sure that the visit [was] of great pleasure and profit to her, and I am deeply grateful.[3]

The second matter is less pleasant. I have a letter, just on a month ago now, from Mr Whittaker of Jones and Evans. I do think, knowing something of booksellers' business as a publisher, that he really has shown distinguished patience. It really is rather awkward for me, having made the introduction, especially as I am not in a position to settle the account for you: I have Income Tax claims of £400 to meet on the first of January, and solicitors' bills and counsel's fees to meet in connexion with my domestic affairs, which are still in the hands of the Law. I simply can't ask Whittaker to hold his hand any longer, and he will certainly take

---

1 – Marguerite Caetani, née Chapin (1880–1963) – Princesse di Bassiano – literary patron and editor; cousin of TSE: see Biographical Register.
2 – Jeanette McPherrin wrote her letter of enthusiastic gratitude to TSE on 13 Nov. 1934.
3 – Caetani replied, 19 Dec.: 'I was so happy to meet your sweet friend – I liked her *very* much and I wish I could have seen more of her. I hope I find her in Rome when I reach there the 30th of this month. Please send me her address and that of Miss Hale.'

McPherrin (1911–92), a modern linguist who was to become a professor at Wellesley College, was a close friend of Emily Hale: see further TSE's letter to McPherrin, 13 Dec. 1934.

legal proceedings – he will be forced to in order to justify himself to his shareholders, whoever they are. I know that booksellers are having a hard time at present, as the depression in their business comes back upon us. So do please try to come to some arrangement, and an arrangement which you will be able to carry out, because it is better not to make promises unless one can be sure of performance. I am sending a copy of this letter to Paris, as I can only ask Whittaker to wait a reasonable time for a reply.[1]

My friend Miss Hale, who is the friend of Miss McPherrin, and who is one of my nearest friends, whom I mentioned to you before, is now in Florence, and will be in Rome for the winter. I do very much want you to meet her, and will write again a little later.

Affectionately,

[Tom]

TO *George Blake*[2]   CC

12 December 1934   [Faber & Faber Ltd]

My dear George,

I feel rather lucky in being able to answer your letter of the 12th of October without having had meanwhile the impatient reminder which I

1–Caetani assured TSE (19 Dec.) that she had sent a cheque to Whittaker – 'and I hope never to miss in the future sending them a sum every month. I have been so terribly hard up lately.'

2–George Blake (1893–1961), novelist, journalist, publisher – author of *The Shipbuilders* (1935) – co-founded the Porpoise Press in hopes of refashioning a national publishing industry in Scotland. The Press was taken over by F&F in 1930. GCF wrote to H. M. Cohen, 14 Oct. 1930: 'We recently acquired the stock and good will of a small private business in Edinburgh called The Porpoise Press. The Porpoise Press exists for the purpose of publishing pamphlets, books and poems of Scottish national interest. It has hitherto been run in a very haphazard way by a single individual, and has just about paid its way. There are, however, considerable possibilities in it; and we are now working it up, with the assistance of two Scotchmen, named Blake and Thomson. Blake is one of our directors. Thomson is not. The arrangement with them is that they each take 25% of any net profits there may be arising from the Porpoise Press; and the management of the Press is entrusted to a sort of joint Committee consisting of Blake, Thomson and three of our own people. The whole of the business organisation is provided by us, and we put up all the money and collect all the income.' (See further Alistair McCleery, *The Porpoise Press 1922–39* [1988].) Blake was editor for four years of *John O'London's Weekly*, and for two years of *Strand Magazine*. On 20 June 1930 GCF wrote to offer him a Principal Directorship at F&F, starting on 1 Jan. 1931; but in the event he worked for F&F from 1 Aug. 1930. On 10 Oct. 1930 FVM told Henry S. Canby (editor of the *Saturday Review of Literature*) that 'my very good friend' was 'the recently appointed Fiction Editor to Faber and Faber . . . The fact that we have been able to snaffle him for Faber and Faber, shows the happy reputation which we have been

deserve for my delay.¹ I have now looked over MacEwan's poetry with some care. I should say definitely that the youth has something in him, but that this is definitely not a book to print. He seems to me to have considerable emotional force, and, I should think, some intellectual strength too, but before he can make any impression, he has simply got to develop more individual idiom. He just hasn't yet got the feeling for words which is necessary, and time after time uses the conventional phrase or word which convey nothing either to the eye or ear. In fact, I am by no means sure that poetry is his medium at all. I cannot believe that if he were writing prose he would allow himself to use such conventional phrasing. As I don't know his age or anything about him, I can't say much more. All I am sure is that he is a lad worth encouraging, though I am doubtful if poetry is what he should be encouraged to work at.

I am sorry that we missed making the Scottish visit an annual occasion, but I do hope that it will be possible next year. I have been too tied up with local affairs to get away for any length of time this autumn or winter, and my hands will be pretty full from now until next summer. I hope I may see you before then.

Yours ever,
[T. S. Eliot]

---

establishing . . . There is a very interesting Scottish nationalistic movement; and it is really producing some brilliant writers.' FVM, in a letter to John Livingston Lowes, 12 Dec. 1930, wrote of the Porpoise Press as 'our new and lively subsidiary'. Blake was to take leave of F&F in 1932. On 22 Dec. 1951 TSE wrote to Harry Levin, of 'my old friend': 'George Blake's great-grandfather emigrated from Somerset to Scotland, and the Blakes have married Scotch [sic] wives ever since; and George Blake is about as Lowland-Scots as anyone can be.'
1 – Blake wrote, from *The Evening News* (Glasgow): 'Many a time have I stood between you and the young bards of Scotia – more often than you will ever know – but certain pressures, some from Neil Gunn, – force me to ask you to bestow a glance on the poesy herewith. It is certainly not entirely the work of a slouch, but I am quite incapable of saying whether the youth should be encouraged, and so must throw myself on your indulgence.

'I had hoped we might contrive a Scottish tour by car this month, but I am finding it damnably difficult to clear my feet these days . . .'

TO *Charles Harris*[1]   CC

12 December 1934   [Faber & Faber Ltd]

Dear Harris,

I will meet you and Lowther Clarke at 1.30 on the 20th as you suggest.

I am afraid that, not knowing the people, I am not really competent either to make suggestions of new names or criticisms of those you send. It does strike me, however, that if there is anyone available who would be in other ways suitable, it is desirable to have one or two ladies on the Committee, in order to balance the other Committee, which seems to be efficiently equipped in that way.

I wrote to the Archbishop on Saturday, but have so far had no reply.

Yours ever,
[T. S. Eliot]

TO *Messrs James & James*   CC

13 December 1934   [Faber & Faber Ltd]

Dear Sirs,

I have your letter of the 11th instant; and having examined the statement of account, regretfully return it pending settlement of the matter of responsibility.[2] Apart from the fact that some of Mrs Eliot's items appear trivial and totally unnecessary, there are many items which appear to be her liability and not mine. Furthermore, I am under the impression that Mr Ernest Bird informed you that we would be responsible for all the expenses of the Separation Arrangement *if it was signed by Mrs Eliot*, but that I could not be responsible for *any* of her legal expenses thereafter – or after the failure to obtain satisfaction on this point.

I should be glad to hear further from you in this matter.

Yours faithfully,
[T. S. Eliot]

1–The Revd Charles Harris, DD (1865–1936): Prebendary of Hereford Cathedral from 1925; Vicar of South Leigh, Witney, Oxfordshire, 1929–34; Chairman of the Book Committee of the (English) Church Union from 1923; Assistant Editor of *Literature and Worship*, 1932. His works include *Creeds or No Creeds?* (1922); *First Steps in the Philosophy of Religion* (1927).
2–James & James commented on their bill – £106. 13. 4d, for the period Aug. 1933 to Dec. 1934 – 'we may say we are prepared to accept £100 in settlement'.

TO *Jeanette McPherrin*[1] TS Ella Strong Denison Library

13 December 1934 Faber & Faber Ltd

Dear Miss McPherrin,

I have been meaning for exactly a month (I mean for just under a month) to write to thank you for your charming letter (of November 13th): this is rather too late to be an acknowledgement and too early for

1 – Jeanette McPherrin (1911–92) studied at Scripps College and Claremont College, California, at Harvard University, and at the École Normale Supérieure de Sèvres. She taught French at Reed School, Portland, Oregon, and at Kent School, Denver, Colorado (her home town), and went on to become Director of Admission at Scripps, 1939–43. Following war service in the Women's Reserve of the U.S. Navy, she worked for the rest of her career at Wellesley College, Wellesley, Massachusetts: as Dean of the Class of Freshmen, 1946–56; Dean of Freshmen and Sophomores from 1956; and she was a Lecturer in French from 1948 until retirement in 1975.

McPherrin to EVE (?1974/75): 'I was a graduate student at Scripps College during the years that Emily Hale was a member of the faculty. I won a scholarship in 1934 to pay for a year of study at the Ecole Normale Supérieure de Sèvres in the suburbs of Paris. The depression was in full swing and I was able to accept the award only because the father of a wealthy undergraduate offered me a round-trip ticket (San Francisco to San Francisco via the Panama Canal) in exchange for chaperoning his daughter during a month of travel in England. This was a windfall, if not quite a God-send since it left me with two and a half months of living to finance on my own before the opening of the universities in France. Emily Hale persuaded her relatives, the Perkins, to rent me a room at their house in Chipping Campden [from 27 Aug. 1934]. I stayed only a few weeks because Mrs Perkins invited me to move out when she had the opportunity to entertain some visiting Brahmin from Boston. I was glad to exchange my quarters for less pretentious ones in the home of the local bus driver and his wife. Because Emily had qualms of conscience about my eviction, I was still invited to meals quite frequently at Stamford House, included in excursions, and asked to help entertain weekend guests who were walkers, your husband among them. A common feeling for Dr and Mrs Perkins helped me to forget my intellectual inadequacies as I set out to explore the village with my celebrated walking companion.

'Your husband was very kind to me during subsequent holidays which I spent with Emily in London and during my year in France when he provided letters to a number of interesting people. Since I was a very unsophisticated and rather gauche little Westerner, the doors which he opened for me, both through his introductions to people and through the advice he gave about my studies, were truly doors into an enchanted country . . .

'As you will have surmised, I knew Emily Hale well, or perhaps "intimately" would be a better word. I was too inexperienced and unworldly a young woman to understand the sources and the depth of her self-preoccupation as I came in middle age to recognize the clues I'd picked up along my youthful path. If you will permit me the liberty of a personal remark in what was intended to be a business letter – I've been so happy to know that Tom had a real marriage of mutual love and shared dedication to spiritual and moral truths as well as to intellectual ones.'

Of Emily Hale she wrote further, 19 Apr. 1976: 'She was a very fine person and it was her most earnest desire to be a good woman. The circumstances of her life had created habits of introspection that led to an increasing preoccupation with her inner world. (As you probably know, her mother became hopelessly insane when Emily was a girl in her teens and was confined in a mental hospital in a Boston suburb until Emily was past sixty). Her dramatic

Christmas.[1] You made it clear that your letter required no answer; but as I get many letters from people who *do* require answers (though I am afraid they do not always get them) I perversely prefer to answer one which does not. I am glad you enjoyed the Princess and I hope that you have not been bankrupted by following my friend's or any other person's financial advice. Sevres (I have no accents on this machine) sounded in anticipation very dreary, as French suburbs can be; but I hope it will be an experience you will look back upon with pleasure, even if you do not feel any at the time – like so many experiences.

I do hope that you will be able to get to Rome (either by speculating in francs or honest saving) for Christmas, as much for Emily's sake as for your own. What with dentistry and other medical attentions, and the

---

gifts made it possible for her to project scenes from the inner drama into the stage of her outward life. The result was a series of beautifully portrayed scenes that charmed and held the imagination of the observer. Mr [T. S.] Matthews has described the impression that she created on an audience of young people most effectively, though he was misinformed about the circumstances of her life and didn't understand the sources of outwardly demonstrated attitudes. As a young woman I, like the young women Mr Matthews has described, was quite captivated by her. When I found her again after the War and the problems in my own family had taught me to read human nature with a more careful eye, I realized that what had seemed glamorous to me was really an unconscious compensation for the sufferings and disappointments of her family life. I do not believe that she would have been able to put aside her preoccupation and give herself fully to a life shared with another human being after the death of her father with whom she had shared so much. I do not mean to suggest that she was a hypocrite, a conscious self-dramatist. I'm sure she never dreamed that she was playing a series of beautiful roles in her associations with other people. The Perkins aggravated her problems. They were people with whom *nobody* could have had a real human relationship, and she kept feeling that she should be loving them!'

Of TSE, she said: 'I am grateful above all for the fact that he took me seriously as an intellectual being. He gave me a confidence in my capacity to arrive at valid conclusions through a reasoned consideration of available evidence which has affected both my career and my personal life. His deeply sensitive kindness was unique.'

EVE replied to McPherrin, 28 Apr. 1976: 'I appreciate your scrupulousness with regard to Emily Hale and the Perkins and can assure you that what you say has been confirmed by my husband and other people.'

Writing to Judy Sahak, Librarian of Scripps College, 6 July 1980, McPherrin remarked that her own letters contained 'no revelations about the relationship between Mr Eliot and Miss Hale . . . which modern readers would find unbelievably "proper" in the Victorian sense'.

McPherrin to EVE, 3 Oct. 1984: 'My clearest memories of him include a mental picture of him sitting in a big armchair reading to us from the manuscript of his first poems about cats.'

1 – McPherrin thanked TSE for having introduced her to Marguerite Caetani, with whom she had spent a day. 'Madame Bassiano is a delightful person in such an amazing variety of ways . . .

'I have had vivid and enthusiastic accounts [from Emily Hale] of London festivities and, however stupid I may sound, I can't help saying that I have blessed you for them, because I think it is exactly what she needs beside the happiness it has given her.'

scrubbiness of London hotel bed and board, she did not seem to me any too robust when she left; and I suspect strongly, though I shouldn't dare say so, that the Perkins's must be rather a drain upon her vitality – I know that they are on mine, though I have never been with them any longer together than that weekend. Anybody one can't argue with is fatiguing; especially elderly people who don't seem to have been knocked about or have had to fight for their lives when younger.[1] So I think if you can get to Rome it will buck her up a bit. I hope that she will be able to have some time again in London in the summer; and I hope that you will join her here before you return. London is really very nice in May and June, you know, and even in July – and you will, I hope, have had your walking tour (or some other form of locomotion) though I wish you were going to Perigord, where there is so much more beautiful country and such entrancing small places few people know, than to Touraine. Not that the wine is not very good all down the Loire, and the river itself lovely; and the chateaux would be beautiful if they hadn't served as models for so many New York millionaires' houses in the past. Anyway, with all best wishes for Christmas, whether you get to Rome or have to keep the *réveillon*[2] in Sevres.

Yours very sincerely,
T. S. Eliot

TO *Gabriel Hebert* CC

13 December 1934 [Faber & Faber Ltd]

My dear Father Gabriel,

Thank you for your letter of the 12th.[3] I shall have to keep you waiting till next Wednesday in order to bring the united brains of my Board onto

---

1–TSE's sister Ada Sheffield wrote to him on 9 Dec. 1934: 'I'm afraid I'm less patient of bores than you . . . As for Mrs Perkins, I know her kind. We have a cousin not unlike her.'

2–*réveillon*: midnight supper.

3–'That title! I am not sure whether your Board see that for a theological work one may be almost driven to a symbolical title that seeks to give the right idea by suggesting some imagery. On the other hand, they are doubtless right in desiring that the relatively few theological books on your list should bear clear labels, and thus rejecting titles which would be entirely satisfactory for an S.P.C.K. book. What do you say to

    Liturgy and Society

    Or Common Faith and Social Life

    A Common Faith and Social Life

I will tell you what I think of these when I have thought over them more.'

    The book became *Liturgy and Society: The Function of the Church in the Modern World*.

the subject of your title, so will say nothing more about that subject till then. On the same occasion I will bring up the question of the date of publication and of payment for the right to reproduce illustrations.

I have made diligent enquiry, but the agreement which you posted from Kelham on November the 20th does not appear to have reached us.[1] I am, therefore, enclosing a carbon copy, which I will ask you kindly to sign and initial, whereupon the counterpart will be forwarded to you.

I am very much interested by what you say about your own development, and about Paul More.[2] I am sure that he would be very much pleased to have a copy of your book from you, although, as a matter of fact, I was thinking of sending it to him myself for review. I don't know whether you would consider him a suitable reviewer or not; neither do I know how familiar he is with the works of Maurice. I remember, a year or so ago, Brother George brought up the question of Maurice while speaking of More, and I mentioned it subsequently in a letter to More, but I don't think that I have ever heard More mention his name. I shall be interested to see up to what point sympathy with More will go.

I hope you will drop me a line when you get to London, and will come and lunch with me one day.

Yours very sincerely,
[T. S. Eliot]

1–Fr Hebert had in fact given the signed agreement to TSE by hand on about 21 Nov.
2–'I have been reading with great delight Paul Elmer More on "The Sceptical Approach to Religion". I have been thinking how in my Oxford days, when I woke up to religion for the first time, & soon after went off into Modernism, I used to attend Schiller's lectures and announce myself as a Pragmatist. *I never took the absolutist philosophers seriously.* I blundered into Pragmatism & Modernism, because here at least human truth was distinguished from Divine. Thereafter I began to disgorge Modernism, but still never took the theologians quite seriously, till I came across Father Kelly's teaching . . . Here was the same distinction between human truth & divine, between opinions and faith; only now it was put in a way that threw floods of light on Christianity and the Bible. Thus I find P.E.M. on Scepticism very illuminating. I am going to write to him and tell him this . . . and perhaps I shall criticise his Platonic view of the nature of Evil, and ask him if he has read F. D. Maurice, and suggest that the doctrines of the Trinity and of Original Sin are the only sound forms for a sceptic's faith.' F. D. Maurice (1805–72), theologian, was founder of Christian Socialism

TO *Gavin Ewart*   cc

13 December 1934   [Faber & Faber Ltd]

Dear Mr Ewart,

I have read the poems which you sent us on November the 24th. I find them interesting but unripe, which means that I should like to see some more of your work from time to time. One reason for thinking that you may not yet be quite ready for a book is that a number of poems at the beginning remind me too closely of the cadences and feeling of Pound's *Mauberley*, and that some of those toward the end, such as your *Ode on a Distant Prospect of Eton College*, seem to me too close to the Auden school. You seem to me to have a definite gift for a satirical kind, but of course satire is one of the poetic kinds which needs the most mellowing in the wood before it is bottled.

I hope that you will send me more of your work from time to time,

Yours sincerely,
[T. S. Eliot]

TO *Charles Harris*   cc

14 December 1934   [Faber & Faber Ltd]

My dear Harris,

I enclose the reply from the Archbishop's Chaplain, by which I am grievously disappointed, though not surprised. Now I beg you to reflect once more, and take council with Rosenthal, before asking me to take the chair. Unfortunately, the time is very short, but I do feel that some conspicuous public man, like the Lord Chief Justice, would be much more suitable, and would command a wider interest. I feel that my own influence and standing is not nearly so great in the outside world as some people in the Church seem to think. I mean, especially, Rosenthal. It is true that I am very busy, and that I have no strong stomach for public appearances of this sort in any case, but of course as a last resort I will do it, if you can't get anyone better.

As Rosenthal is only in town apparently one or two days in the week, and as one cannot be sure which days those will be, I suggest that it would save time if you would communicate with him direct at Birmingham rather than through me.

I shall look forward to seeing you next Thursday at 1.30, and hope that the excursion to London will not prove very tiring for you.

Yours ever,
[T. S. Eliot]

TO *William Force Stead* CC

14 December 1934   [Faber & Faber Ltd]

My dear Stead,

Thank you for the review.[1] I am taking advantage of your permission, and cutting out the first page and a little over. It is not that I think it bad, but that I think the best review technique is to get right to work on the book, as I think readers of reviews are a little impatient of preliminary generalisations. One can generalise as much as one likes afterwards, but I think that such remarks ought to come in unobtrusively later, as if they were suggested by the matter of the book, after you have told the reader what the matter of the book is.

I have heard nothing from Cairo either.[2] I don't think Robert is a very good correspondent, and I always rather dread his letters anyway, because there is usually at least one important-looking word which is completely illegible. His handwriting seems to get more slovenly all the time. I don't think you have any reason to worry yet. It is probably simply the usual dilatoriness of the Oriental.

Yours ever,
[T. S. Eliot]

TO *E. W. F. Tomlin* TS Lady Marshall

14 December 1934   Faber & Faber Ltd

Dear Tomlin,

I shall certainly be glad to stand as one of your referees in your application for a scholarship, and will do my best when the authorities

---

1–Review of Theodore Haecker, *Virgil: Father of the West* – on Virgil's place in the growth of Catholic Christianity – sent on 13 Dec.: 'You can cut it down to prescribed limit by omitting the first page & half the second.' See C. 14 (July 1935), 680–1.

2–'No news from Cairo. Has somebody bagged my job? I thought that great plotter Professor Sencourt could always contrive & carry through a good plot.'

apply to me for my opinion.[1] I rather hope, however, that this scholarship is to be tenanted after you come down from Oxford, rather than as a break in your work there, but I may be mistaken in this opinion, and would gladly know more of your designs. Anyway, I hope you get it. If you go to Harvard I should like to give you some introductions there.[2]

I look forward to receiving another essay from you, and shall write to you to suggest a date for lunch soon after Christmas.

Yours sincerely,
T. S. Eliot

FROM *Frank Morley* TO *Patience Ross*   CC

14 December 1934   [Faber & Faber Ltd]

Dear Miss Ross,

Many thanks for sending us HARMONIUM by Wallace Stevens.[3] We have a long standing interest in the author, but it isn't possible to make an offer for this book. From our point of view it is almost a disadvantage that the poems exist in book form. Most of such resources as we can devote to poetry are reserved for poets who would not get into book form unless we started them. Sounds rather complicated, but I think you will see what I mean.

Yours sincerely,
[F. V. Morley]

TO *Ezra Pound*   TS Beinecke

19 December 1934   Faber & Faber Ltd

To our venerable father, Ezra, by the grace of God Supreme Coney, at his Palace at Rappaloo, greetings.

1–Tomlin reported (13 Dec.) that he was thinking of applying for a Henry Scholarship – 'which involves research-study in the U.S.A. (Harvard or Yale) for one year' – and accordingly asked if TSE could supply a reference for him: the deadline for submission was 1 Jan. 1935.

2–Tomlin confirmed on 20 Dec. that indeed he would not be able to undertake research until after he had taken his degree – a fellowship would be tenable only from the next autumn.

3–Patience Ross (A. M. Heath & Co.) wrote to TSE, 4 Dec. 1934: 'We are sending you HARMONIUM, poems by Wallace Stevens, published in America by Knopf . . . I hope you will find them suitable for your list.' A handwritten note on Ross's letter reads: 'R. FVM write.'

As touching your injunctions and tender admonitions towards immediate action in the direction of Leavis and other of the lower infusoria,[1] in so far as this is a sign of your great benevolence towards, and paternal care over ourself, we accept them in a spirit of humble gratefulness.[2] So far as the inception of such action is concerned, we are minded that Joseph was found in the house of Pharoah, Lot in Sodom, Daniel in Babylon, Obadiah in the palace of Ahab and Jezebel, and they kept silence because they could do no good by speaking. I had some hope, furthermore, that the whole lot of amateurs and pedants might exterminate each other without any outside assistance. And whereas, at the present moment, there is a scuffle going on in the pages of the *New Statesman* between Edith and somebody who says she got her quotations from Leavis, in which the Sitwell forces are embattled, and whats more Wyndham has, they say, plunged in,[3] but

1 – *Infusoria*: 'A class of Protozoa, comprising ciliated, tentaculate, and flagellate animalcula, essentially unicellular, free-swimming, or sedentary; so called because found in infusions of decaying animal or vegetable matter' (*OED*).

2 – EP wrote on 16 Dec.: 'Laughlin has imported, and dumped upon this clear and serene coast several protuberances of anglo/yittish and other diseased pituitrin secretions/ notable a mess by Leavis

'I know it is difficult to get you to give serious attention to ANY damn thing whatsoever/ 'BUT

some attempt to deliver decent writing from this sort of parasitic scab SHOULD be undertaken. Your own voice wd/ be the most useful/ a Criterion editorial wd/ be better suited to the purpose / tho if you are too damn lazy to think it would I will submit a memorial of POINTS to be stuck thy the god damn cheese rind . . .

'The Leavis louse attempt to beslime his letters . . . by flattery of real authors/ e/g/ spewing his Whitechappel spittle upon the Sitwell, in effort to aggrandize his putrid self, and trying to make the pore bdy/ stewddent think that our Olympianity wd/ notice his sizzle.'

3 – Edith Sitwell wrote to TSE, 14 Dec.: 'I am very delighted to know that you are pleased with such of the book [*Aspects of Modern Poetry*] as you have read; and I hope very much that you have by now had time to read it all, so that you will know how disgraceful is the attack made upon me in the *New Statesman*. The reviewer accuses me of copying from a review of Mr Grigson's, (which I have *not* read), a passage from Mr Yeats' "Packet for Ezra Pound", – a book which was given me by Mr Yeats when it first appeared. Naturally, when writing about Mr Pound, I turned to your Preface to the Selected Poems, and to Mr Yeats' book for information.

'Now, a lower grade mental defective from Liverpool, a Mr Pickering, who has apparently only just learned to read, and that very incompletely, – he has never read any books excepting Dr Leavis's "New Bearings" and my "Aspects of Modern Poetry", – is accusing me of plagiarizing from Dr Leavis, because, amongst other things, we both say that the Waste Land appeared first in the Criterion, and that the title was taken from Miss Westons "From Ritual to Romance". A brief study of your notes might have established the latter fact! In addition, this unfortunate believes that "inert resignation" (Dr Leavis' phrase) and "giving up of the will" (mine) mean the same thing!! He does not know, either, that talk about the use of ordinary speech rhythms, and the breakdown of rhythm in life, is a commonplace in modern criticism.

I dont like to slime my hands on the *N.S.* any oftener than need be (That boy just never wont sit still. Allus afidgetin). I agree that to be praised by Edith brings one out in a cold sweat BUT

something might be said about general principle of unauthorised people writing books ABOUT modern poetry. WE dont publish em because they dont pay. If you was one this spot you would realise that Leavis dont swing so much lead as he may look to from afar; but hes worse than Edith because he keeps poundin away on his little maggazine. And dambitall, you just cant keep things straight very long in this place; just when you got it swepngarnished in bust the amateurs again and begin redecoratin with the neo-georgian trimmins, only chromium plated this time and karl-marxed still I have got two boys in view who never been to Oxford.

I have now got your proof corrected and Quincy spelt right but I wont tamper with the Greek you are more versed in the Homeric dialect than I am So will close wishin you the compliments etc.

Tp

'Mr Grigson has entered the fray also, and accuses me of copying Herbert Read, because we both say that Sprung Rhythm is not an innovation, and that it is the rhythm of Piers Ploughman and of Skelton . . .

'The Editor, too, has not printed a letter written by a certain critic defending me, although he allows all this nonsense to be talked.

'The book is full of the most appalling misprints, due to hasty proof-reading, and my only comfort in the midst of these tribulations is that Milton and Hopkins are dead, and so cannot know the fate they have met with. Nor can they complain.

'Mr Wyndham Lewis has taken refuge with the dear old ladies of "Time and Tide", and in that congenial and suitable atmosphere of lavender and old lace, is simply *howling* with rage. – I gave him a good bang over the head, too, on the subject of "Men without Art" in the Sunday Times.'

See further Sitwell's letter to the *TLS*, 3 Jan. 1935, in *Edith Sitwell: Selected Letters*, ed. John Lehmann and Derek Parker (1970), 48–9.

TO *Oliver Morley*

TS Susanna Smithson

27 December 1934   *The Criterion*

DEAR OLIVER:

THANK YOU VERY MUCH FOR THE BEAUTIFUL NAPKIN RING I SHALL
GET A NAPKIN FOR IT BUT I DONT EXPECT TO FIND A NAPKIN BEAUTIFUL
ENOUGH FOR THAT RING. I LIKE IT VERY MUCH AND HEAR THAT YOU
MADE IT AND DESIGNED IT. THANK YOU AGAIN. I HOPE TO SEE YOU AT
THE END OF THIS WEEK AND HOPE I SHALL FIND YOU WELL.[1]

YOURS AFFECTIONATELY,
UNCLE TOM [signed]

TO *Joseph Gordon Macleod*[2]   CC

27 December 1934   [Faber & Faber Ltd]

Dear Mr Macleod,

I have done the best I could to give you a quick decision about your
play, but it was necessary to get another opinion as well as my own, and
its arrival so soon before Christmas made it impossible to reply sooner.[3]
I have read it with a great deal of interest, and think that it must have
been very interesting on the stage, but it does seem to me definitely an
acting play rather than a reading play, and I am afraid, therefore, that it

---

1 – Brigid O'Donovan, 'The Love Song of T. S. Eliot's Secretary', *Confrontation* (Long Island
University), no. 11 (Fall/Winter 1975), 7: 'TSE got on so well with the families of his friends
it was a tragedy he could have no family life of his own. The Morley children used to
come often to the office. The six-year-old son would spend an hour or so typing elaborate
multiplication tables, which he would make up correctly and type accurately.'

2 – Joseph Macleod (1903–84), poet, playwright, actor, director, historian and BBC
newsreader, was educated at Balliol College, Oxford (where he was friends with Graham
Greene), and in 1929 joined the experimental Cambridge Festival Theatre, of which he
became director, 1933–5 (his productions included Chekhov's *The Seagull* and Ezra Pound's
Noh plays, and five of his own plays). In 1938 he joined the BBC as announcer, retiring
to Florence in 1955: it was during the BBC period that the poetry he produced under the
nom de plume 'Adam Drinan' became sought-after in Britain and the USA: he was admired
by writers including Basil Bunting and Edwin Muir. His first book of poems, *The Ecliptic*
(1930), was published by TSE at F&F. His plays included *A Woman Turned to Stone* (1934)
and *Overture to Cambridge* (1936). See *Selected Poems: Cyclic Serial Zeniths from the Flux*,
ed. Andrew Duncan (2009); George Bruce, 'Fine poet recollected', *The Scotsman*, 26 Mar.
1984; James Fountain, 'To a group of nurses: The newsreading and documentary poems of
Joseph Macleod', *TLS*, 12 Feb. 2010, 14–15.

3 – Macleod submitted his plays to TSE on 19 Dec., requesting a quick decision. FVM,
who also read them, wrote on Macleod's letter: 'it is outside scope it can go back with
melancholy'.

is outside of our field. I should think that it would be best to try to get this play published in Cambridge if possible. I am afraid that the majority of readers of plays, who are not very many, would imagine that the play was much more local in its significance than it really is, and therefore one might as well start from the place where it is most assured of attention.

I should very much like to see the next thing you do, especially if there is more verse in it, and if it is intended for a wider audience.

Yours very sincerely,
[T. S. Eliot]

TO *Philip Mairet*[1]   CC

27 December 1934   [*The Criterion*]

Dear Mr Mairet,

As I have heard nothing from Symons, I am now answering your letter of the 22nd.[2] I should be very glad to see you at your convenience next

---

1–Philip (Philippe) A. Mairet (1886–1975) – who had a Swiss father and English mother – was educated at Hornsey School of Art and worked under the architect C. R. Ashby, 1906–9, before becoming a designer and artificer in stained and painted glass windows for churches. After war service in the British Red Cross and the French Red Cross in France, and having served a term of imprisonment as a conscientious objector in three different prisons, he was a member of the Shakespeare Company at the Old Vic Theatre, London. He then became a journalist, 1926–31, and worked at the formation of the Alfred Adler Society (International Society for Individual Psychology) in London: he published *The ABC of Adlerian Psychology* (1926); and in 1932 joined the staff of the *New English Weekly* under its founder A. R. Orage. On Orage's death, Mairet became editor, 1934–49. TSE contributed to *NEW*, and was also an active member of the editorial board. Mairet convened the group of high-level psychiatrists who wrote the symposium *Christianity and Psychiatry*, and he edited and contributed to the publication under the auspices of the Christian Frontier Council to the Student Movement Press. He was the dedicatee of *Notes towards the Definition of Culture*. See further Mairet's contribution to *T. S. Eliot: A Symposium for His Seventieth Birthday*, ed. Neville Braybrooke (1958); Mairet, *A. R. Orage: A Memoir* (1936); Mairet, *Autobiographical and Other Papers*, ed. C. H. Sisson (1981); *Poems*, 182–3.

2–'Since that very interesting talk I had with you in company with [W. T.] Symons [editor of *Purpose*; associate of Orage], the decision to continue the New English Weekly has been taken.

'I should be very glad to have a chat with you some time on points which arise from this. For instance, I wonder whether you might sometimes like to use the paper to write in yourself: and if you would occasionally advise with us as to editorial policy. Maurice Reckitt, who is playing a leading part in the reconstruction of the paper, thought you might find it, in some respects at least, a congenial medium . . .

'There is a hope, I believe, that we shall meet on January 1st when, Symons said, he would ask you to dine with Reckitt and others of us at Chandos. If so, there is no need to answer this letter.'

week to discuss these matters. In particular, there is a point in connection with Ezra Pound on which I must obtain your views. Will you suggest a time of meeting by letter or telephone?

Yours sincerely,
[T. S. Eliot]

TO *Humphry House*[1]   CC

27 December 1934   [*The Criterion*]

Dear Mr House,

It has just occurred to me that possibly there might be some bit of the Hopkins which could be published in the *Criterion* before the book comes out. Of course, I have no idea how soon you expect to have all your material ready for publication, but I am sure that an advance fragment in the *Criterion* would arouse a good deal of interest. Not that there is not already an unusual amount of expectation about the book.[2]

Yours very sincerely,
[T. S. Eliot]

1–Humphry House (1908–55), literary scholar and lecturer, taught for two years at University College, Exeter, then for several years in India. After WW2 he taught at Peterhouse, Cambridge, and as University Lecturer in English Literature at Oxford. His publications include *The Note-Books of Gerard Manley Hopkins* (ed., 1937) and *The Dickens World* (1941).

2–House replied on 29 Dec.: 'I am preparing two separate books:

'(i) The texts of Diary, Sermons, some letters & fragments: in fact all from the papers which I think can stand independent use: this much with a formal introduction about the fate of the papers etc is now very nearly ready for press . . .

'(ii) A critical book of my own incorporating further material from the papers, & from the forthcoming Bridges letters: this will be ready I hope by the early summer.

'I expect what you would like for the *Criterion* would be extracts from (i). The Copright belongs to Gerard Hopkins of the O.U.P., whom I shall be seeing next month. The matter is really in his hands as representing both the family & the publishers, but is further complicated by the fact that the actual MSS are (?) the property of the Jesuits . . . I will put the suggestion to Hopkins.'

TO *A. J. Mathews*   CC

27 December 1934   [Faber & Faber Ltd]

Dear Sir,

I have your letter of the 10th December,[1] but I am afraid that I regard
the 'prose poem' as a minor form of a past era, and of less importance
for English literature than for French. As [for] the only one which I have
committed myself, I regard it as a kind of note for a poem, but not as a
poem. My feeling about most of Mr D. H. Lawrence's poetry is that it
does not get very much further than that.

I am not surprised that you find my essay 'Verse and Prose' unsatisfactory.
I have not seen it for many years, but I doubt whether it is worth your
attention.

                            Yours faithfully,
                            [T. S. Eliot]

TO *Ernest Bird, Messrs Bird & Bird*   CC

27 December 1934   [Faber & Faber Ltd]

Dear Bird,

I am very sorry to ask you to involve yourself, even indirectly, in any
difficulty over James & James's bill; and indeed I should prefer to pay it
and have done with it; but the sum is so large that I must, in my present
circumstances, reduce it if I can.

I enclose the account and the second letter. Of course I do not dispute
their charges for the weekly payment or for my income tax affairs; I don't
know why they mention them. But I am writing to explain that in view of

---

1–Mathews (Instructor, Department of English, University of Oregon) was studying the
development of the *poème en prose*, hoping to discover what the poets have thought of the
'prose poem': 'whether they have written it as a relief from more rigorous techniques, or as
a liberation from too limited forms; whether they have considered it a rough draft of verse
material or a finished thing of its own kind; a poem or a prose. (I do not mean to establish
any antithesis here.)

'Now I have come quite accidentally . . . upon a copy of *The Chapbook* for April 1921
with your essay "Verse and Prose". From it I have tried, perhaps without reason and
certainly without much success, to derive what must be your attitude toward such of your
own poems as "Hysteria" . . . Do you call "Hysteria" a prose poem? Understanding the
term *prose poem* to mean "poetic content in a prose form" (Mr Richard Aldington's phrase),
would you call it a prose poem? Do you recognize the "poem in prose" as an art form
in English? If my request is pertinent and not presumptuous will you say what your late
judgments upon "Hysteria" are?'

the fact that they now pay the money not direct but to Mrs Eliot's bank, I shall instruct Lloyds Bank to make the payment to the District Bank direct, which will cost me 3s. 6d. a week. And I have said that I am giving attention to their suggestion.

It is of course annoying that so many of Mrs Eliot's items are either futile or frivolous. But the point is whether I can hold that after a point they were acting for her and not for me.

Yours sincerely,
[T. S. Eliot]

TO *Geoffrey Faber*

TS Faber

28 December 1934   Faber & Faber Ltd

Dear Geoffrey,

Wyliau Dedwydd![1] Aeth blwyddyn! Fo eich ran and many of them, for 1935.

You were quite correct in telling Vivienne that she should get her own books back. It is annoying that she did not either keep them separate or tell the men at the time. I hear now that she has got some solicitors (quite good people, whom I used to know) to deal for her; so that I shall probably get everything back except my ring.[2]

I imagine that Christmas in Wales always involves you in social obligations such as you mention, which must be very tiring. I managed to

---

1 – *Wyliau Dedwydd!*: Happy holidays! TSE's Welsh is otherwise wonky.

2 – EVE wrote to Ian Carruthers, 17 Oct. 1972: 'My husband was never a collector, and tended to borrow his books from the London Library and such places rather than possess them. Twice his library was dispersed, once on the breakup of his first marriage, and again during the war.'

Robert Crawford to EVE, 16 June 1983: 'I have discovered recently in the Bodleian Library a list of some six hundred and fifty books in T. S. Eliot's library around nineteen thirty. The lists are typed with handwritten additions and comments by T. S. Eliot and Vivienne Eliot. I enclose a photostat of my transcription, prefaced by a brief description of the documents. I have shown the transcription to my supervisor, Professor Richard Ellmann, who suggested that I write to you about the possibility of publishing it, as lists of the libraries of Joyce and other major modern writers have been published and are valuable aids to scholarship.'

EVE to Crawford, 28 June 1983: 'With regard to the book list, I am afraid I cannot let you publish it, partly because it is incomplete. I have reason to believe it was drawn up at the time of the Eliot separation in 1932 [*sc.* 1933–4], and my husband was recovering his property through solicitors. Most of the books are now in my possession, but some of his most precious ones, such as his Virgil, Dante and heavily annotated copy of *Appearance and Reality* which I have, are not on it. I shall probably include a detailed account of his library in one of the volumes of letters mentioning his markings and comments, which are so important.'

get through without having to eat any turkey till boxing day – it is a bird which I do not admire so warmly as in my childhood. Did the children get their play from Eleanor Farjeon, I wonder, as I failed to produce one for them. Another year, I hope, when I have had more practice.

I am glad to hear that Jowett has become active.[1] But I should imagine that with any biography like that one's reading must in the end be limited arbitrarily at some point by the impossibility of giving a lifetime to it. I share your doubts as to whether you can read Hegel now. I know I couldnt. Even when I did read what I did read of him it all seemed too wildly improbable to keep my attention. Yet nowadays some of the young intellectuals like Charles Madge read Hegel, because he was a predecessor of Marx. That alone is enough to damn Marx for me; the dialectic seems to me a mythology with no foundation.

If you think I felt any severe scruples about Loisy,[2] you just havent plumbed the deps of my cynisme [sic]. I dont say I mightnt mind the Bp of Birmingham or Dr Major or Professor Raven or the like, but Loisy is dead. At least, I think so. I may have been prejudiced by the fact that in 1910 I used to go every week and hear Loisy mumble about burnt offerings among the Early Persians, and he wasnt regarded as a very live issue in Paris then. I may be wrong, but I should have thought that the interest which the French Modernism of that epoch could arouse would be nil. Thats all I was conscious of.

I know my great etc. gnd. father used to hang witches (I dont mean with his own hand), but you dont know what Captain Eben Lake of Jonesport said to Captain Joe Tibbetts of East Machias; he, said, barring Old Ike Carver of Mosquito Cove, he said . . . . but I mustn't boast.

The only point about theological literature is, what is mutually exclusive. I mean, what is going to drive other authors away, and who pay best. I dont see why Loisy should, but I havent read the book.

At any rate, he hanged 'em, he didnt burn 'em. And if it come to that, there hasnt been a Papist in *my* family since the Reformation. I am, by temperament but not in doctrine, an old-style hellfire calvinist. But as Captain Eben Lake said about me . . . but I mustnt mention that.

Why should I strain at a Lousy and swallow a Sitwell?[3] I mean, the other way about, why should I swallow a Sitwell and then etc Barring Old Ike Carver of Mosquito Cove, and he had 70 years reputation behind him.

1 – GCF's labours would eventually produce *Jowett: a portrait with background* (F&F, 1957). Benjamin Jowett (1817–93), theologian, Master of Balliol College, Oxford.
2 – Alfred Loisy (1857–1940), French theologian.
3 – Matthew 23: 24: 'You blind guides, who strain at a gnat and swallow a camel!'

T. S. Eliot with his sister Marian and niece Dorothea in the gardens
at the Morrells' house in Gower Street, photographed by
Lady Ottoline Morrell, 1934.

Three views of a plaster portrait bust of Eliot by Donald Hastings for
his *Exhibition of Sculptured Celebrities* at New Burlington Galleries,
London, 1934.

T. S. Eliot, photographed by
Man Ray, 1935.

Vivien Eliot in a suit by Philippe
et Gaston, which she wore for
presentation to the Prince of Wales
at Londonderry House,
October 1934.

E. Martin Browne (*right*) with friends
(including George Bernard Shaw, *left*), c. 1934.

The Revd Vincent Howson as 'Bert' in *The Rock*, performed at Sadler's Wells, May–June 1934.

Ashley Dukes, producer and proprietor of the Mercury Theatre, Notting Hill Gate, *c.* 1935.

Rupert Doone, dancer, choreographer and founder of the Group Theatre, mid-1930s.

Elsie Fogerty of the Central School of Speech and Drama, at Lawnside, during the Malvern Festival, 3 August 1934.

TSE reading a newspaper, *c.* 1935.

Lady Ottoline Morrell, photographed probably by Philip Morrell, 1935.

George Bell, Bishop of Chichester, 1935.

TSE with Emily Hale and two friends, probably at Chipping Campden, *c.* 1935. The figure on the far left is thought to be the Revd J. C. Perkins (1862–1950).

TSE having a cigarette break, on the moor.

TSE with Frank Morley and Donald Brace (*left to right*) on their
motoring trip to Scotland in 1935.

Marianne Moore, *c.* 1935.

George Barker, photographed
by Lady Ottoline Morrell,
August 1936.

Louis MacNeice with his son
Daniel outside their home at
Highfield Cottage, Selly Park,
Birmingham, 4 June 1935.

Programme for *The Rock,*
first performed at Sadler's Wells,
May–June 1934.

Michael Roberts, reading *Petite anthologie poétique du surréalisme*
(1934) at Val d'Isère, France, 1935.

Frank Morley, Geoffrey Faber and TSE (*left to right*), at the Fabers'
house in Wales, 1935.

Two photographs of the first production of *Murder in the Cathedral*,
performed at Canterbury Chapter House, June 1935.
From an album presented to TSE by the Friends of Canterbury
Cathedral, inscribed and dated 22 June 1935.

Three Sitwells make a swallow.

However, I should like to read the book one day. I might be converted. Old Jacks is a friend of Cousin Annie[1] but I wouldnt take the word of a Unitarian for the saleability of a book; because they're always out-of-date and touch.

And after all, the bigger a firm gets the dirtier tricks it can afford to play. Look at the Civil Service.

Why we may get into the pornographic racket yet. I have got you a nice cigar, a rubber one. Yours for better breaks, and Love to Enid and the children.

Tom

P.S. Lousy? The Greeks had a word for it.

TO *Ezra Pound* TS Beinecke

Holy Innocents' Day   *The Criterion*
[28 December] 1934 AD

Podesta I am thinking about your generous offer re *N.E.W.* and am seein Mairet sometime next week I Expect. and will write again about the matter.[2] Youre right about their ought to do something that Orage Didnt do or did BADLY rather than try to make exact facsimile. If anythink ever comes of it might be as well (as I told you before) to come over (quite a small aeroplane would do) and meet some of the personalities involved specially the younger ones or ones you thought worth worth lookin over.[3] I dont know has you ever clapped eyes on Bridson, but If not I aint goin to tell you what he looks like you must have a few surprises. I think Dylan Thomas has some punch behind the fist and bein a welshman he is pretty tough. I will try to impress upon Mairet that literaryart section ought to be a lot more constructive CONStructive. But Podesta whats this rumour about me bain COARSE you know better than that Podesta mirthful I am

---

1 – L. P. Jacks (editor of the *Hibbert Journal*) was a friend of TSE's cousin Mrs Horace Lamb, and had known her since 1887 when she was Annie Rotch.

2 – EP, 20 Dec.: 'what is your real opinion of the AMOUNT of me, the N/E/W public or ANY bleeding brit/ pubk/ wd. stand in 1935?? Wd/ a greater explositivity in the licherary pages of N/E/W/ be any use/?? . . . Would fer exampl Faber take a half page for book advertisng IF I took a FIRM grip on the literary section of N.E.W/ and run her full tilt, a la Egoist, or little Review . . . If you have ANY ideas re/ what I ought to advise the N/E/W/ to DO, send 'em along . . . Or shd/ I regard myself as one of Orage's excentricities / pardonable because Orage permitted it.'

3 – EP had anticipated this suggestion on 1 Dec.: 'who wd/ PAY for my trip to London?'

tuneful I am drunken I am and when I get with those Harvard professors hilarious I sometimes may be but no never Coarse thats just your joke or somebody gettin a rise out of You:[1] That said Columbo was a Joke/ But *I call it crude & coarse/ Such conversation I have heard / From the lips of Maltese whores* etc. etc. so heres yours for better breaks,

Tp

About that lady well I dont know praps I might allow you credit for that does she insist on Montrachet or Châteauneuf du Pape or would a seidel of Pilsner and some Limburger and Frankfurters do. You could pay me back samewise but you would have to go to Rome to do it and she likes a moderately not dry Pouilly will do.

AGREED about title of *Cantos* yours right on that point too.[2] God ddamb it I WOULD like to come to Italy in spite of the climate & the Food but I am HARD UP, with solicitors bills to pay and not money to pay em but I have got your GAUDIER ELEPHANY back will you come and fetch it dont like to trust it to the Poast.

1−EP had heard stories about the 'emerstus dtr, the Harvard lecturer': 'I hear the pink profs left yer tea parties when you told about Lil. cause yr/ COARSE language was not that of the Hawvud facultee . . .'
2−FVM reported to EP, 20 Dec.: 'Proofs XI CANTOS just received . . .' Accordingly EP barked at TSE on 20 Dec.: 'Cantos CANT simply be called XI/, got to be XXXI/XLI otherwise it looks like same old start I/XI all muddled again.'

TO *Barbara Barclay Carter*[1]   CC

28 December 1934   [Faber & Faber Ltd]

Dear Miss Carter,

I must apologise for the delay in reading and considering Don Sturzo's play and in answering your kind letter of November the 8th.[2] I must apologise particularly for not having answered your letter at once because I see that you kindly suggested my coming to tea to meet Don Sturzo. I should have been very glad to do so, but November and December have been particularly busy months for me, and I am still having to forgo all the engagements that I can avoid, but I hope that you may repeat the invitation when I have more leisure.

The cycle of plays is extremely interesting. I do not see how it could be played except as the libretto of an opera. That, however, is irrelevant. I also think that the translation is very good, although I am not sufficiently at home in Italian for my judgement to be of the highest value. I must, however, say candidly that the market for this kind of thing is almost non-existent. We do publish as much poetry as we can afford to publish, but the majority of books, even of English verse, hardly pay for themselves, even over a period of several years, and the chances of translation from a foreign language are still less. I have some personal knowledge of the matter because I myself translated what I consider a very fine French poem and the book only sold a few hundred copies.

I don't want to be too discouraging. The important point is that my own firm has taken on as much unsaleable literature as it can possibly handle for the next year or so, but there may be some other firm which is in a position to add distinction to its list. I hope, therefore, that you will try elsewhere.

1 – Barbara Barclay Carter (1900–51), Catholic convert and writer who devoted her career to translation and the Italian democratic movement under Don Luigi Sturzo. (At an unknown date, TSE dined in London with Carter and Luigi Sturzo.)

2 – Carter had submitted on 8 Nov. Don Sturzo's 'Ciclo della Creazione' – 'the original Italian, which the author would be very glad if you would accept, "for keeps", and my translation of the first two parts.' The first parts of the cycle were entitled *Angels* and *Adam*. She added: 'Yesterday Don Sturzo signed a contract with Herr Jessner (the late Director of the Berlin State Theatre, and controlling all the State Theatres of Germany) conceding to him the right of representation for 1935 and five succeeding years.' Jessner hoped to be able to produce the play.

Luigi Sturzo (d. 1959, aet. 87), Secretary General of the Partito Popolare – the most influential Catholic opponent of Mussolini – had gone into exile, moving first to London in 1924. EP was to call Don Sturzo a 'clerical ballyhoo artist' (letter to the Editor, *NEW*, 28 Mar. 1935).

I am very pleased indeed to have a copy of the book signed by Don Sturzo, and I should be very much obliged if you would kindly thank him most gratefully for me.

With best wishes for the New Year,

Yours sincerely,
[T. S. Eliot]

TO *Henry Miller*[1]

CC

28 December 1934   [*The Criterion*]

Dear Mr Miller,

I should be very glad if you would submit a part of your book on Lawrence to the *Criterion*.[2] From what you say, however, it sounds as if the section you have in mind might be much too long to be possible. The longest length of essay we can publish is 7,000 words, and I much prefer articles of not more than 5,000 words, as the longer ones take some fitting in and often have to be delayed. Furthermore, it is impractical in a review which appears every three months to serialise; but do send me something, as I should be most interested to see it.

I should certainly like to see your *Tropic of Cancer*, about which Mr Pound has told me, if it is possible to get a copy to me.

Yours sincerely,
[T. S. Eliot]

1–Henry Miller (1901–80): expatriate American author (supported for many years by his lover, the diarist Anaïs Nin) of autobiographical novels including *Tropic of Cancer* (1934), *Black Spring* (1936), *Tropic of Capricorn* (1939), and the *Rosy Crucifixion* trilogy (1949–59). Put out by the Obelisk Press, Paris, his works were for many years banned in the UK and the USA.

2–Miller asked (n.d.) whether TSE would like to consider publishing in C. a fifty-page section – 'Universe of Death' – from his forthcoming work on DHL – 'concerned primarily with Proust and Joyce, with the world they sprang from and the world they represent. A background of death for the emergent Lawrence.' To date he had drafted about 200 pp. of the whole book, which he intended to 'compress considerably' when he came to revise it. He wondered too whether EP had mentioned his *Tropic of Cancer*, which he would be happy to post to TSE. 'It may be inconvenient, however, for you to receive it, as it is not supposed to be imported into England.'

432   TSE at forty-six

1935

Thomas Stearns Eliot[1]

BORN: St Louis, Mo., Sept 26, 1888. PARENTS: Henry Ware Eliot, Charlotte Chauncy Stearns.
PREPARED AT: Smith Academy, St Louis, Mo.; Milton Academy, Mass.
YEARS IN COLLEGE: 1906–1910. DEGREES: A.B., 1910; A.M., 1910; Hon. Litt. D. (Columbia University), 1933.
OCCUPATION: Company Director.
MARRIED: Vivienne Haigh Haigh-Wood, London, England, June 26, 1915.
HARVARD BROTHER: Henry Ware Eliot, Jr. '02.
ADDRESS (business): 24, Russell Square, London w.c.1., England.

After graduation I spent a year in Paris, attending lectures mostly on philosophy, and then three years in the Harvard Graduate School working for a Ph.D. in philosophy, and also studying Sanskrit and Pali. I was given a Sheldon Fellowship for a year, which I spent at Oxford working at Aristotle under Harold Joachim. At the end of the year I married, and took a job as a master at High Wycombe Grammar School at £140 p.a. with dinner. I never returned to take my final examinations for the Ph.D. but perhaps the dissertation on 'Meinong's Gegendstandstheorie considered in relation to Bradley's Theory of Knowledge' is still preserved in some archive of Emerson Hall. It was accepted, I suppose, because it was unreadable.

After one term at High Wycombe I got a better job at the Highgate School, which brought me £160 p.a. with dinner and tea. I stayed at that for four terms, then chucked it because I did not like teaching. I had a couple of months out of work, and then got a job in the Colonial and Foreign Department of Lloyds Bank at £120 a year and no food. To supplement this I assisted in editing *The Egoist*, which was pleasant, and gave Workers Educational Lectures in the evening, and reviewed books for several periodicals: this meant often enough a fourteen or fifteen hour day.

1–*Harvard College Class of 1910: Twenty-fifth Anniversary Report* (1935), 219–21.

433

I entered the bank under the false pretence of being a linguist; nevertheless I was earning £600 p.a. with income tax paid at the time when I left to join the board of Faber & Gwyer, a newly constituted firm which is now Faber & Faber. I was on inward bills, foreign coins and notes, and documentary credits until I was sent to Head Office to take charge of Pre-War Enemy Debts for the bank and its customers. This was a really interesting job, requiring a bookkeeping system which nobody could understand but myself, and a good deal of legal work.

When that petered out, I was put in joint charge of the Foreign Information Bureau, and when the other man left for a better job I was the sole head. We had to look through twenty or so foreign papers a day and turn out a daily sheet of 'Extracts from the Foreign Press', which a couple of typists printed on a machine in the office. Sometimes they used too much ink, sometimes not enough. I also wrote a monthly commentary on Foreign Exchange Movements for the Bank Monthly, and had general charge over the ordinary Confidential Reports. I liked the bank and most of the people in it; but I was luckier than most in getting interesting work.

In 1922, as an evening employment, I undertook the *Criterion*. Lady Rothermere wanted to start a literary review, so I ran it for her; but I couldn't take any money for that, as a bank official is not allowed to hold any other regular job. I gradually gave up reviewing, but in 1919 I wrote very regularly for the *Athenaeum* under Middleton Murry; and continued to write leaders for the *Times Literary Supplement*.

Since 1925, when I joined the board of Faber & Gwyer Ltd, my public life has been less eventful. I was Clark Lecturer at Trinity College, Cambridge, in 1926; but the rules of that enlightened college did not require that these lectures be printed. In 1932 I returned to Harvard for a year as Norton Professor.

My ordinary day's work is that of a publisher and an editor.

(When I joined Faber & Gwyer the *Criterion* was rearranged as a limited company under the ownership of the firm and Lady Rothermere; later Lady Rothermere retired and the review now belongs solely to Faber & Faber.) I spend a great deal of time talking to authors whose work I do not want to print. And I have to read a great many manuscripts, most of which are uninteresting. I find that the number of things one is called upon to do, in middle age, increases much more rapidly than one's income – such as taking the chair at meetings, speaking on behalf of good causes, and giving lectures to institutions which can't afford to pay for them.

I have been serving on the Council of the Shakespeare Association, on the Executive Committee of the Sadler's Wells Society,[1] and as Secretary of the Book Committee of the Church Union. My hobbies are theology, Social Credit, and occasionally, when I can find time, writing a little poetry. I have had two quasi-dramatic productions, one at Vassar College and one at Sadler's Wells; and I wish I could write a really good play. I forgot to say that I am obliged to spend a great deal of time answering letters from Ezra Pound, but my firm pays for the stamps.[2]

I like eating and drinking, with a preference for Burgundy and Hock; and I prefer sherry (light dry) to cocktails. I play a bad game of chess, and like such games as poker, rummy and slippery Ann for low stakes. I like certain very simple and humane kinds of practical joke. Which reminds me that I am also, at the moment of writing, a Churchwarden. I never bet, because I never win.

I have travelled a little in foreign parts, such as California, Scotland and Wales; but I become more and more sedentary, although I have only put on seven pounds in twenty-five years, and find it an effort now even to get as far as Paris. I cannot afford yachting, but I should like to breed bull terriers. I am afraid of high places and cows.[3] I like detective stories but especially the adventures of Arsene Lupin. I tend to fall asleep in club armchairs, but I believe my brain works as well as ever, whatever that is, after I have had my tea.

P.S. I believe I am an Honorary Vice-president of the Distributist League of Glasgow, but I am not sure.[4]

---

1 – Other members of the Executive Committee of the Sadler's Wells Society included Lilian Baylis, Bryan Guinness, Mary Hutchinson, J. M. Keynes. Capt. Malcolm Bullock was Chair.
2 – FVM would write to EP on 27 Mar. 1935: 'The ingenius reverend elefunt has been writhing for stage purposes, and seems to fatten on it. I am a little worrited by the growth of his corpulation. Efter keeping his shapely figger for I don't know how many years, it upsets me (as mkfr of underwear) to see him swelling. Better be guarded in any rufferences you make to his girth, for he is perty sensitive – and damn it there's a lot more waist-line to be sensitive than there ever was when you saw him' (Beinecke).
3 – See 'The Country Walk', in *Poems*, ed. Christopher Ricks and Jim McCue (2015), I, 296.
4 – J. Griffin, Hon. Secretary, invited TSE on 9 July 1930 to become Hon. Vice-President of the Glasgow University branch of the Distributist Club (of which G. K. Chesterton was President). TSE accepted the honour in a letter to A. J. Montague (Glasgow President) on 29 Oct. 1930. (On 25 Nov. 1936 TSE was to consent to become honorary Vice-President of the Chesterton Club.)
Building on encyclicals by Pope Leo XIII (*Rerum Novarum*, 1891) and Pope Pius XI (*Quadragesimo Anno*, 1931), G. K. Chesterton and Hilaire Belloc advocated the economic philosophy of Distributism: a decentralisation of the means of production based on an organic and artisan view of economic order and culture. Distributism seeks to put productive property directly into the hands of families and local communities (as against control by the

PUBLICATIONS: The following is all I can bother with: Verse: *Poems: 1909–1925*; *Ash Wednesday*; *Sweeney Agonistes*; *Journey of the Magi*; *A Song for Simeon*; *Animula*; *Marina*; *Triumphal March*; *Difficulties of a Statesman*; *The Rock*; "Pollicle Dogs and Jellicle Cats" (unfinished at this time). *Anabasis* (translated from the French of St J. Perse). Prose: *Selected Essays*, *The Use of Poetry*, Harvard University Press, *After Strange Gods*, *Elizabethan Essays* (mostly contained in *Selected Essays*). All published here by Faber & Faber. Such as are published in America are by Harcourt Brace, except where indicated. Various things of mine have been translated into French, German, Spanish, Italian, Modern Greek, Dutch, Swedish and Esthonian; and a selected volume has been published in English with introduction and notes in Japanese.

MEMBER OF: Oxford & Cambridge Club, London, England.

TO *Maurice Reckitt*   CC

1 January 1935   [Faber & Faber Ltd]

My dear Reckitt,

I have just sent the copies of a new draft to Fr Hudson. I hope that it is superior to the first; but unfortunately, I may not have got down all of the suggestions agreed upon, and it will probably need further revision.

Meanwhile, however, I have thought more about the project, and the more I have thought the more doubtful I am (a) of the suitability of launching it with a letter to *The Times*, and (b) of its feasibility at all.[1]

State, big business or a few wealthy individuals). Notable texts include Chesterton's *What's Wrong with the World* (1910). In a review of two other works – *The Outline of Sanity* by G. K. Chesterton, and *The Servile State* (1912; 3rd edition 1927) by Hilaire Belloc; and *The Conditions of Industrial Peace* (1927) by J. A. Hobson – TSE noted: 'One has much sympathy with the Belloc–Chesterton gospel of Distributive Property. It is a fertile idea; and in the form of exposition which they have chosen there is material for one excellent essay. But in full books we expect more than that: we expect some indication of a "way", answers to some of the objections that occur to us, and an admission that the problem is simplified for expository purposes . . . There could be no greater contrast than that between Mr Belloc and Mr J. A. Hobson [who] is a serious economist of the old school . . . [H]e knows his subject matter in detail . . . On the nature of Capitalism, he is at one point far more illuminating than Belloc. He observes, in effect, that the "evils" of capitalism are not primarily due to the concentration of ownership, and are therefore not mitigated by the multiplication of owners. On the contrary, the multiplication of small security-holders places more power in the hands of the few directors who have the knowledge; diffusion of ownership diffuses their responsibility. The "Capitalist" is this director or manager' (*MC* 6 [July 1927], 72–3).

1 – At a meeting to discuss the prospects of a 'Pro Fide' bookshop, held in London on 9 Apr. 1935, it was decided that a number of prominent persons would be asked to sign a letter to

As for the letter to *The Times*, I do not think we can *count* upon getting any considerable benefaction that way. The letter will be an advertisement, but I believe that the money will be obtained by direct approach to individuals and societies; and until we are sure of perhaps the major part of the financial subsidy needed, it may be injudicious to advertise something which may never come into existence.

As for the scheme, I see several difficulties. I do not imagine that the kind of bookshop (of which there are two or three at least) that we have in mind as the opposition, has the same kind of official sanction. I do not know that there is any either supported or officially approved by the Communist Party. I suspect that such shops as there are, and in so far as they prosper, owe their success to their being run by able and convinced individuals. If, that is, we could find a private individual with the necessary zeal, ability and personality to want to run a Christian bookshop, we should certainly try to obtain support for him; but to start the bookshop by cooperation of sects, and then look for a manager, will, I fear, condemn the undertaking to be merely one more religious bookshop. An individual with the right nose for books can be free, and can afford to make mistakes; a manager under the supervision of a committee will be more likely to play safe. We cannot ignore the fact that the combination of forces of denominations is, after all, a weakness; that it may have all the weaknesses of a coalition, rather than the strength of an alliance. And the strength of alliances is usually a temporary strength; it is brought about by an emergency; the emergency does not even have to end, it merely has to endure long enough, for a great strain to be placed upon the bond of union. And such a combination of forces against *one* (supposed) force, gives the effect of a last-ditch defence of frightened people.

I think that in my mind all the time, and I suspect in yours, the attraction of the scheme has been largely the possibility of the propagation of Christian economics – but a Christian economics along certain general lines. There are many Christians, I have no doubt, who look for economic reform in the same direction as ourselves; but we must not overlook the fact that [to] many Christians, as well as many 'Christians', our own brands of economic and social reform are just as repugnant as any other. In short, we have to deal not only with internecine conflict among Christians on doctrine, but with internecine conflict in economics and sociology: and

---

The Times: the Archbishop of York, the Dean of St Paul's, Mr J. H. Oldham, Father Martin D'Arcy, G. K. Chesterton, the Revd J. S. Whale (Principal of Cheshunt College, Cambridge), the Revd S. M. Berry (Secretary of the Congregational Union), and Sir Henry Lunn.

what is more, the confusion will be great because the division on dogma will not coincide with the division on economics.

I have been tending to concentrate my own attention, not on associating Christianity, so much, with social and credit reform, as on associating social and credit reform with Christianity. I do feel that it is a more instant problem to leaven the Reformers with Christianity, than to leaven Christians with Reform.

Practically, I believe that the thing is to find the bookseller first; to let him have a free hand – under the right influence. I very much doubt the success of a 'stand' made by 'the churches'.

I must stop at some point –

Yours ever sincerely,
[T. S. Eliot]

TO *Dorothy Bussy*[1]   CC

2 January 1935   [Faber & Faber Ltd]

Dear Madame Bussy,

I must apologise for the delay in reporting to you about *Veronicana*.[2] The translation seems to me admirable, although I have not read the original, and the book itself is extremely interesting. I am very glad to have read it, and I quite agree with you that it was worth translating, and that it was worth publishing, but it is obvious at once that the book is one which would have an extremely small sale apart from the people who either have read it in French, or who would, as so often happens, merely be impelled, by hearing of a translation, to get hold of the original. I don't believe there are more than a couple of hundred people in the whole of England who would want to buy it and would understand it if they did.

I don't want to be discouraging. Every decent publishing firm produces every season a few books which have no better prospects than this. It would add distinction to any list. The trouble is that my firm has already invested in more good unsaleable books than it can afford to do for the next year. I should very much like you to try someone else because I

---

1 – Dorothy Strachey (1865–1960), eldest of the Stracheys, novelist and translator, was married to the French artist Simon Bussy and lived between England and France, where she was friendly with Matisse and for many years lovingly obsessed with André Gide. See further *Selected Letters of André Gide and Dorothy Bussy*, ed. Richard Tedeschi (1983).
2 – *Veronicana* by the writer Marcel Jouhaudeau (1888–1979).

should like to see the book published. Therefore I am not returning you the manuscript until I hear from you again, as you may have some other firm in mind.

With best wishes for the New Year to Monsieur Bussy and Janey[1] and yourself, and looking forward to seeing you again in the summer,

I am,
Yours very sincerely,
[T. S. Eliot]

TO *Ezra Pound*

3 January 1935 A.D.[2]   Faber & Faber Ltd

Respectit Boguscat,

Yuss, I thought it was Miss Rudge.[3] You dont say how long she is stopping and therefore I dont know how immediate the emergency, but I will write to her at beginning of next week. So.[4]

Bridson does NOT look like Brooke, nor quite Clive Brooke either, he looks like Anthony Eden, only his dress is louder and he has a ginger mustashe.[5]

Not knowing HOW you compile matter for Wilson anthology cant say why you dont know Dylan. But I thought your Wilson anthology was to be purely American exclusive of Cardiff and the Rhondda valley.[6]

I understand about the Elephant.[7]

---

1 – Jane Simone Bussy (1906–60).

2 – Misdated 1934.

3 – Olga Rudge (1895–1996), American-born violinist and musicologist (brought up in London and Paris); long-term mistress of EP. See TSE's letter to Rudge, 10 Jan. 1935, below.

4 – EP had written (n.d.): 'The lady as you probably surrmize is Miss O. Rudge temporarily chez/ Mrs Richards, Gorse Cottage, Hook Heath Woking, surrey. Violinist for bread, a reader at the call of her personal tastes etc. NOT a heavy eater/ and wd/ do wiff a bottle of bass. at any rate a trusty means of communication of whatever nuances of the London licherary sityvashun that you are too lazy to translit by letter . . . If you do lunch the gal/ tell her I said you shd/ meet Don Arturo/ . . . and she adores perlite conversation/ very little left in these days//'

5 – EP: 'Bridson has attempted to prepare me for his northern aspect. Dont tell me he looks like Rupe Brook !! or the late Charlie 2nd, or even Sacheverel.'

6 – EP: 'I take it Dylan'z no poET, or shd/ have seen mss/ for the Wilson anth?'

7 – 'I enc/ a foty/cart by th missus/ re/ taking the elepant to 34 Abingdon Court, when and if you go there. no hurry.'

About COARSENESS I dont want to boast,[1] so I wont tell you what Capn Eben Lake of Jonesport said to Capn Joe Tibbetts of East Machias about me.

Barring, of course (he added) old Ike Carver of Mosquito Cove.[2] And HE was the man who fucked the whole of Marshall's Island in one night, at the age of 70, so what do you expect. Its only fair to except a man like that.

I am inclined to agree with you about Flint.[3] Superstitious he is; that algebra dont get you nowheres.

Richards is not NOT a oupain, but again a Welshman.[4] Type that was in Wales befoe the Celts arrived. By the way the Rassenkunde number of L'Italiano has some good photographs in it. Richards good idea on basic in *N.E.W.*

I think they may ask us to join editorial committee of *N.E.W.* Better than bein responsible for a department. My idea rather some young feller whom we could deal with but who could be allowed to make just enough mistakes to preserve appearance of independence. Desmond Hawkins posbly. Mairet quite in accord en principe on your point of strengthening previous weak Parts of *N.E.W.* I discouraged any notion of any kind of union with *G.K.'s* because I think there ~~would~~wont be much left to that when G.K. dies, and one doesnt want to be saddled with his leavings and officeboys.

I said that *N.E.W.* ought to get a certain number of Poems from the right people to sprinkle in, as it has previously mostly given appearance of

---

1 – 'I suppose what Haavud felt wuz that you spoke english and call a rooster a cock (whereas the english for phallus is penis, with biological reason).'

2 – TSE to Leon M. Little, 11 Aug. 1956: 'I wish I could see North Haven again, but how? I should also like to put in to Jonesport (another generation of Dyers and Carvers no doubt – I shall never forget Pete leading the Grand March at the Jonesport Summer Ball with Mrs Willie Carver, you never saw anything more respectable) . . .'

3 – '[F. S.] Flint is a worse ninny than I thought. 4 pages, prolix statement of A plus b/, commonplace Douglasism and then a statement that Flint having said water is wet, refutes the Doug/ite theory as to the wetness of water. Fortunately too unreadable to do much harm/ save to apes, who dont understand Doug/ and MAY suppose all that algebra shows that F. does.'

4 – 'What about this BASIC ENGLISH, anyhow/

'Couldn't yr/ boy friend Isaac Arooon Agahsh Richards [IAR] do something on it in N.E.W. that would be topical, without interjuicin caststrated cx/ onto crit/ of licherchoor.'

EP would write to TSE, 10 May 1934: 'You have never told me I. A. Richard's [*sic*] was anything but something to write about in Brit/ critical reviews? Has the abstracting bleater any perceptions? or not? or merely the better prof/ in contrast to schlimey Leavis etc??'

dustbin for people who cant get verse paid for and for objects of Orage's benevolence.

Well well.

TP

TO *R. Ellis Roberts*[1]   CC

4 January 1935   [Faber & Faber Ltd]

My dear Roberts,

I must apologise for the delay in answering your letter of December the 18th, but I trust that you know as well as I that business of importance occurring during the second fortnight of December cannot always be dealt with quickly. I had to present the matter before our Book Committee before I could say anything definite to you.

I believe that there is some possibility for a children's magazine, but the rest of the Committee confirm my view that it is not for us to undertake. In order to make such a paper worthwhile I know that a great deal of time and money must be spent to build up a circulation. I should expect it to be run at a considerable loss for the first three or four years. Furthermore, it would involve a considerable addition to our staff, and this at present is out of the question for reasons of space alone. Nor do we feel inclined to divert a sufficient amount of our capital into what is at best a very promising gamble.

It seems to me that some syndicate controlling a variety of papers might be more likely to entertain the suggestion than a publishing house of our type.

Nevertheless I thank you for suggesting the project to us. With all best wishes,

Yours sincerely,

[T. S. Eliot]

1–Richard Ellis Roberts (1879–1953), author, critic; literary editor of the *New Statesman & Nation*, 1932–4; *Life and Letters Today*, 1934; biographer of Stella Benson (1939).

4 January 1935   [Faber & Faber Ltd]

Dear Father Gabriel,

I can now answer your questions.[1] The title *Liturgy and Society* was accepted by my Committee who, however, think as I do that the sub-title should be simply 'The Function of the Church in the Modern World'. 'Essay' has become rather a debased word and does not do justice to the book.

I am assured that we can, without altering the date of publication, provide one or several proof copies of the book in good time for the Bishop of Chichester and his friends.

As for the Alinari[2] illustrations, when you have got these and if you and we find them suitable for the book, we will take up the matter of payment direct. I am told that Alinari's price could be made a matter of negotiation.

Don't worry about the index, but wait until you have got all the illustrations and until you have had page proof.

De la Mare liked Donald Maxwell's drawing and thought that it would be very suitable as a frontispiece, but he was not able to say at the moment whether the copy you gave me would do for reproduction, or whether we had better get another copy or use the one in Skeffington's book.[3]

Finally, do you think that the Bishop of Chichester would be willing to contribute a sentence or two on behalf of the book which we could use in advertising it? We should not expect him, of course, to make any definite promise until he had had an opportunity to read the book, but as I suggested above, we should let him have a proof copy in ample time. Unless you have any objection to this suggestion I will write to the Bishop myself when the time comes.

Yours very sincerely,
[T. S. Eliot]

1–Fr Hebert wrote on 31 Dec. 1934: 'As for the title: "Liturgy and Life" is rather a hackneyed tag . . . Does not "Liturgy and Society: An Essay on the Church and the Church Service in relation to the modern problems of belief and of social life" or "An Essay on the function of the Church in the modern world" meet the case adequately?'
2–Fratelli Alinari, Florence: fine art publishers, founded in 1885.
3–Donald Maxwell's drawing of the interior of St Paul's Cathedral was reproduced in *Famous London Churches*, by C. B. Mortlock (Skeffington & Son, 1934).

TO *Charles Harris*

CC

January 1935   [Faber & Faber Ltd]

My dear Harris,

I have received the enclosed letter from Lowther Clarke, who has asked me to return it to you.[1] In his covering letter to me he also mentions the Revd Dr Box in Cambridge. As I have no knowledge of the men mentioned either by Lowther Clarke or by Milner White[2] I have no suggestions to make.

Although it is not my particular business I am seriously concerned about the projected volume of sociological studies; and please keep in mind that I know so little of Lockhart that nothing I say is to be considered as casting any reflection upon his abilities. It is the design of the enterprise itself which I should wish to see more clearly. If the book were to be merely a collection of essays by well-known churchmen who are also zealous in social and economic activities, I should not feel that it was worth doing. It would undoubtedly express [a] very different point of view, and might be merely a nest of inconsistencies, and there may be people who appear to be qualified to contribute merely from the fact that they are known to have this dual interest. I am thinking specifically of Ivor Thomas, who is active in social and political work, but whose calibre seems to be small and who might tend to identify himself too closely with the Labour Party.[3]

It seems to me that what is wanted is a clear statement of the division between the permanent requirements of the Church and the application of one or another social programme none of which is in itself specifically Christian. Such a volume might have very great value, but it would be a work for trained philosophical minds rather than for social workers, however devoted. Some attention might also be given to the social and economic theories of the Scholastics, which are often referred to in economic controversy, but very seldom with anything like authority. And finally, it occurs to me that it might be an advantage if none of the contributions was signed, although the names of all the contributors might be given on the title page. Such an arrangement would make each contributor more responsible for the other contributions and would therefore tend toward unity. If the book says more than what we feel the Church as such can commit itself to I think it would miss its point. These

1 – Not traced.
2 – The Revd E. Milner White, King's College, Cambridge.
3 – Ivor Thomas (1905–93): journalist and author; devout Anglican; later a Labour MP.

443

are only somewhat random preliminary misgivings, and you may find it easy to settle them all.

I have one other matter on which I want to consult you. It has been suggested to my firm, not through me, that a useful volume for parents and teachers would be a kind of companion to the Prayer Book, explaining the Book for children of between, say, the ages of 10 and 15. I cannot, in the first place, offer this idea to the Book Committee because it is not my own and therefore belongs to my firm. Secondly I don't think that it is a suitable undertaking for the Book Committee. It was intended for all church people without any particularly catholic cast, and it obviously covers a very different ground from your projected children's Missal. First, do you think such a book is possible and desirable, and if so have you any suggestions of a suitable person to write it? It should be a book which could be useful for instruction in all Anglican schools, including such as only teach the usual brand of Public School Christianity, but if the book is done I should like to see that it is in the right hands.

I have not yet received the typewritten notes of the last meeting. I understand that when I get them I am to make such alterations and excisions as I think desirable, and send them on to you for your approval. Then, I take it, they go back to the secretariat to be formally entered in a minute book, and read at the next meeting.

With all best wishes for the New Year,

Yours ever,

[T. S. Eliot]

TO *The Manager, Lloyds Bank* CC

6 January 1935 [Faber & Faber Ltd]

Dear Sir,

I should be obliged if you would kindly *cancel* the power of attorney which has been exercised over my account since September 1932, by Messrs James & James of 23, Ely Place, E.C.1.

At the same time would you kindly take note to pay to the District Bank, 75 Cornhill, E.C.3. the sum of £5 (five pounds) *every Friday* beginning next Friday, to the account with them of Mrs T. S. Eliot, 68 Clarence Gate Gardens, N.W.1.

Messrs James & James have heretofore been drawing on my account with you for this weekly allowance, and I prefer to have it paid direct. I am sorry to put you to this trouble, but for certain reasons it is desirable that Mrs Eliot should have the allowance in weekly instalments, rather than at longer intervals.

Yours faithfully,
[T. S. Eliot]

TO *Ottoline Morrell*   TS Texas

Twelfth Night [6 January] 1935   Faber & Faber Ltd

My dear Ottoline,

Your letter arrived the day you left – I rang up Millie, who suggested that I should write to Gower Street and she would forward it.[1] I am *delighted* that you like Barker's poems – and very happy to get your cheque – and it is so much pleasanter to accept money for a poet from people who like what he writes.

The subsidy has helped to make him much more cheerful and hopeful about next year. When his poems come out, I will send a copy to each of the benefactors, and keep one against your return. Bryan Guinness seems a nice lad, and rather pathetic.

I do hope that India will give you all it can – somehow I can't hope that anyone or you particularly should *enjoy* it – but that it will prove an experience you will be glad to have had.

Yours ever affectionately,
Tom

It seems likely that Yeats's theatre season will come off, in May.[2] My Canterbury play is for the middle of June.

---

1 – OM wrote on 28 Dec. 1934: 'I have read George Barker's Poems & also his Prose Volume & I was very much moved & impressed by it. For it has great intensity & beauty. I have been given some money by my brother for my journey & I should go forth happier if I sent you this small sum to add a miserable 2/6 a week to the fund . . .'

2 – WBY told his wife on 3 Jan. 1935: 'Last Wednesday we had the first meeting of our dramatic committee. Edmund Dulac, Rupert Doone (ballet master and producer), T. S. Eliot [*sic*], myself, Margot Collis's secretary. Ashton was absent dancing somewhere. Next morning I 'phoned to Dulac: "I won't have Rupert Doone spreading mustard and molasses over my brown bread. I shall produce all my own plays." Result, a visit from Dulac to Ashley Dukes, who owns the theatre we are to play in and who supplies the finances, and to Ashton. General agreement that I don't know enough about London actors to cast my plays – somebody else has to be found. We are now in pursuit of that somebody else, and there is to be a committee meeting on Tuesday. It has been decided that the actual performance of the plays will be from April 29th to May 19th, or longer if we have a success, and the rehearsals will last about a month' (W. B. Yeats and George Yeats, *The Letters*, ed. Ann Saddlemyer [2011], 387–8).

Twelfth Night (Or What you Will)   Faber & Faber Ltd
[6 January] 1935

My dear Virginia,[1]

If you write to me without anything to say, that I take as all the greater compliment.[2] If I now write to you in the same vacancy, I hope that the feeling of being complimented may be, however faintly, reciprocated. Add the fact that I have so many other things I ought to be doing that I cannot remember them clearly. P. G. Wodehouse says something about being so deep in Gore that one might as well wade through as try to step out, I think he was quoting MacBeth.[3] I wish you would tell me what to say to the Shakespeare Association on Jan. 27th about Shakespeare and the Modern Stage: it seemed to me a catchy sort of title when I was asked what I would talk about, but I cant think of anything to say. I have also got to make a Speech on the 30th as Secretary of the Standing Committee of the Book Committee of the Joint Council of the Book & Tract Committees of the Church Literature Association, and meanwhile am contributing Notes by the Way for January to *Time & Tide*[4] – I expect you have done that long ago. It is easy to make promises: but when I have finally to sit down and write something for something, I realise that I have nothing to say about anything. Does any other scribbler feel like that? I wonder – I mean the MSS. submitted to Faber & Faber multiply, increase in geometrical ratio, as they say. One crowded hour of Glorious life Is worth a cycle in Cathay[5] I know, but what about hours crowded with manuscripts? I had rather be a mandarin and con the sacred texts of Tao. Waley tells me that the early Chinese texts are so few that he can work on them anywhere, even in the Hotel Russell. And if I was a mandarin I shouldnt be involved

1–VW noted, 11 Jan. 1935: 'A very long, rather formal, I mean affected letter from Tom this morning, which I must put away, as it will be so valuable. Did he think that when he was writing it?' (*Diary* 4, 273).
2–VW wrote on 31 Dec.: 'I have been meaning to write to you – not that I have anything to say: mere affection ... When we come back, on the 14th, then I hope you will make a resolution to drop in at 52 for a cup of tea sometimes. Please do. I get less & less able to invite people. And dinners are a bore ... And I saw Francis Birrell, who had been pleased, poor man, by seeing you. Forgive this scrawl; & love from us both.'
3–'I am in blood / Stepp'd in so far that, should I wade no more, / Returning were as tedious as go o'er' (*Macbeth*, III. iv).
4–TSE, 'Notes on the Way', *Time and Tide* 16: 1 (5 Jan. 1935), 6–7; 'Notes on the Way', 16: 2 (12 Jan. 1935), 33–4; 'Notes on the Way', 16: 3 (19 Jan. 1935), 88–90.
5–Sir Walter Scott, 'Answer': 'One crowded hour of glorious life / Is worth an age without a name.' Tennyson, 'Locksley Hall': 'Better fifty years of Europe than a cycle of Cathay.'

in a Yeats-Auden-Eliot season at the Mercurey [*sic*] Theatre at Notting Hill, which means another committee with Yeats in the chair, and Auden taking an aeroplane for Copenhagen;[1] and I shouldnt be writing a Play for the Canterbury Festival and I shouldnt be rung up by Miss Babington[2] and I shouldnt have to help edit the works of A. R. Orage and I might be able to keep Bees in Sussex like Sherlock Holmes & Mrs Woolf.

I wish that I might have Seen the Old Year Out with you at Rodmell. As a matter of fact, I wasnt asked to. If I had been, I should have brought a bottle of Champagne, and sung one of my songs, viz.:

> I dont want any Wurzburger –
>   I'd sooner drink gasoline.
> I dont care to tarnish
> My throat with such varnish:
>   It's allright to oil up a sewing-machine.
> I don't care for Budweiser,
>   And Anhauser [Anheuser]-Busch[3] I decline:
>   The platform I stand on
>   Is Moet & Chandon –
> The bubbles that blow off the troubles for mine![4]

There is another song for the occasion called 'The Miner's Dream of Home'; but I dont remember the words, but the Miner was in Australia, in a red shirt and a widebrimmed hat, and

>   the bells
>   were ringing
>   the Old Year OUT
> and the
>   New
>   Year
>   IN.

The bells were in England, of course, and he heard them in imagination, you could tell that from his eye.

1 – In Dec. 1934 WHA had asked to borrow money from F&F to be able to fly to Copenhagen to work on his play with Isherwood. 'I don't want to have to sell my car to do it.'
2 – See footnote to TSE's letter to Lawrence Irving, 7 Dec. 1934.
3 – A brewing company in St Louis, Missouri.
4 – According to Ricks and McCue (*Poems* II, 177), this was a popular song by the Hungarian-born Jewish American songwriter Jean Schwartz (1878–1956).

I should have liked to see Francis Birrell again – I had arranged to go with John Hayward – but by that time it was too late.[1]

I agree with you about dinners. If I might drop in to tea once a fortnight I should be happier. I await (champing at the Bit) your return on the 14th.

> With love to both, I am,
> yours
> T. S. E.

I have another good song, it goes:

> I met you first at Spring St.
>> And then upon my word
> I thought id known you all my life
> When we reached 23d.
> I won your heart at Haarlem,
>> At the Bronx you murmured Yes:
> We lost no time
> On that ride sublime
>> On the Subway
>>> Express.[2]

And several more.

9 January 1935

I wrote the foregoing several days ago. You see, I am more terrified of writing to Mrs Woolf than to anybody, because her standard of letter-writing is so high – one feels that a letter to Mrs Woolf should compare favourably to, let us say, a letter from Gibbon to Madame du Deffand. But I, alas, am not so important as Gibbon; and you, alas, are more important that Madame du Deffand. I hesitated to post my Twelfth Night Letter because I thought of you saying, on reading it: 'He was drunk when he wrote that.' But he wasnt: I cant even live up to your standards of inebriety. The proof is that I didnt try to tell you what Captain Eben Lake of Jonesport said to Captain Joe Tibbetts of East Machias, he said, Barring Old Ike Carver of Mosquito Cove, he said . . . nor did I tell you

1–Francis Birrell died on 2 Jan. 1935, aged forty-five.
2–*The Subway Express* (1907), words, James O'Dea; music, Jerome Kern. From the musical *Fascinating Flora*.

what the Parrot in the Public in Islington said after seeing the barman rob the till . . .[1]

The point is, that I agree with you about dinners, and that I shall be pleased to come to tea every day except Wednesdays, shall I bring some Patum Papericum or Gentleman's Relish: and if you will ask me if only once, I will retail to you in confidence the news of the last meeting with W. B. Yeats in the chair and Miss Margot Collis as secretary – the only actress living, Yeats declares, who has the Tragic Face.[2] I MUST go to bed.[3]

Yrs humbly
T. S. E.

TO *Laurence Binyon*[4]   CC

7 January 1935   [*The Criterion*]

Dear Mr Binyon,

I have heard rumours, which I hope are true, that you are continuing your translation of the *Divine Comedy*. If, as I hope, this is true, I should

---

1 – See 'Billy M'Caw: The Remarkable Parrot' (*The Queen's Book of the Red Cross*, 1939). TSE wrote to his friend Jack Isaacs, 29 Dec. 1948: 'I am pleased that you liked the Parrot . . . I daresay it was composed about the same time as *The Rock*, or a year or so later . . . [T]he episodes in the Life of Billy M'Caw are entirely my own invention. His figure was inspired by a very gifted parrot which used to belong to the licensee of a bar in Islington. The adventures of the real parrot were just as incredible as those of mine!' The public house in question, the Prince Albert, Angel, Islington, London, is now the Charles Lamb.

2 – Margot Collis (1907–51), actress and poet, took part in W. B. Yeats's *The Player Queen*.

3 – TSE next went to tea with VW on 4 Feb. 1935, as she recorded: 'An admirable way of seeing him. And how he suffers! Yes: I felt my accursed gift of sympathy rising. He seemed to have got so little joy or satisfaction out of being Tom. We – L[eonard] rather – argued, about the T & T correspondence. [In Jan. TSE had contributed the 'Notes on the Way' column to *Time and Tide*; and his criticism of A. A. Milne's anti-war tract *Peace with Honour* had provoked correspondence.] Highly philosophical: on war; suddenly T. spoke with a genuine cry of feeling. About immortality: what it meant to him – I think it was that: anyhow he revealed his passion, as he seldom does. A religious soul: an unhappy man, a lonely very sensitive man, all wrapt up in fibres of self torture, doubt, conceit, desire for warmth & intimacy. And I'm very fond of him – like him in some of my reserves & subterfuges' (*Diary* 4, 277). VW noted in addition: 'After abusing booksellers yesterday for some time, I said to Tom, do you ever buy a new book? Never he said. And I said, I sometimes buy poetry, thats all' (ibid.).

4 – Laurence Binyon, CH (1869–1943), Keeper of Prints and Drawings in the British Museum, 1932–3; noted translator of Dante. In 1933 he succeeded TSE as Charles Eliot Norton Professor of Poetry at Harvard. See further John Hatcher, *Laurence Binyon: Poet, Scholar of East and West* (1995). No further extract from the Binyon translation was forthcoming in C.

be delighted and honoured if you would let me have a canto of the *Purgatorio* for publication in the *Criterion*.

> I am,
> Yours very truly,
> [T. S. Eliot]

TO *Dulcie Bowie* CC

7 January 1935   [Faber & Faber Ltd]

Dear Miss Bowie,

I thank you for your letter of the 2nd instant inviting me to be a member of the Board of Judges for your Verse Speaking Competition at Oxford in July. The question of fees is not an important consideration in connection with such an event, and your remuneration is quite adequate.[1] I do not feel, however, that I am qualified to be a judge of such competitions, and it is a task from which I should beg to be excused. This involves no reflection on the English Verse Speaking Association, but is the reply that I should make to any invitation of the kind from any quarter.

Incidentally, I cannot help questioning the suitability of *Kubla Khan* and Francis Thompson's *Corymbus* for choral speaking.[2] This, however, has nothing to do with my decision.

> With many regrets,
> Yours sincerely,
> [T. S. Eliot]

1–The Association offered no fee, but an 'expenses grant' of two guineas for each of the three days of the event.

2–'A Corymbus for Autumn' (*The Works of Francis Thompson: Poems*, vol. I, 1913, 141–6) opens tongue-twistingly (and carries on in the same vein):

> Hearken my chant, 'tis
> > As a Bacchante's,
> A grape-spurt, a vine-splash, a tossed
> > tress, flown vaunt 'tis!
> > Suffer my sing,
> Gipsy of Seasons, ere thou go winging!
> > Ere Winter throws
> > His slaking snows
> In thy feasting-flagon's impurpurate glows!

FROM *Vivien Eliot* TO *Elizabeth Wentworth*[1]   MS Bodleian

7 January 1935   [No address given]

Dear Miss Wentworth

I have just read your last letter over again & I realise I did not reply to it at all. I am *terribly* sorry that you say you find *Marion* is not at all well. I do not wish to worry her with letters but I should be so grateful if you will tell her I am sorry to hear of her bad health, & beg her to take care of herself. I think she does too much *work* in her apartment. She never was strong. I think it is *very hard* on her & I should be very ill indeed if my brother started such a course of behaviour I really dont know what I *should* feel, especially being in another country & so far away. If it is any comfort to her to know it, do tell her I keep this *HOME* still for Tom, & keep it as nicely as I *can* in the circumstances, but I have been *very sick indeed* for the last 5 weeks & am in a very low state of health myself. Much *worse* in health, please tell her, than my Mother is, whom she saw in June last. – Tell her I leave the Door open *every evening*, & at *certain hours*, always, for Tom, & that I *wrote* & *told* him *it is so*. So that he has *no excuse* to lead a life without the very necessary <u>*protection*</u> of a wife. It is indeed a tragedy, & tell her the personnel of these Mansions are always loyal & *never* give up the hope of seeing him walk in. That is all I can tell her but it *is true*.

The cold weather here is quite dreadful. It has gone on so *long*. I am sorry you found your apartment in such a terrible state. It was nothing for you to be ashamed of, however, considering *all* the time you had been away. Did you remember about the *E.S.U.*? You *ought* to *come back* here for the Silver Jubilee. I shd. be so glad to have you stay here. It will be a most extraordinary year, here in England. A great historic event.

> With my love to you & Marion –
> Sincerely,
> V. H. Eliot

1 – A distant relative of the Eliot family.

8 January 1935   *The Criterion*

My dear Rowse,

Many thanks for your letter of the 5th.[1] I should be very glad to have such an article from Hudson, and cannot foresee any likely reason for rejecting it, though I am not clear as to what his point of view may be. I don't know that that matters very much so long as he represents it adequately. Do tell him to go ahead.

The present *Criterion* is, I agree, rather scrappy.[2] One of the difficulties was the long letters from F. S. Flint and Ezra Pound which they both wrote for publication as articles, and which I declined to use except in an epistolary form. It was really Flint's that caused the trouble. I do not, as you know, object to publishing articles which I cannot understand, and I remain unconvinced that Flint's mathematics express anything that cannot be expressed in words.

I read your Supplement leader with some care,[3] and although I saw nothing wrong with it I felt as if you were writing in a state of depression rather than in enthusiasm. I attributed this, of course, to the terrifying influence that the *Times* has on all of us whenever we write for it, and I thought you could probably have done better with the subject elsewhere. Those were two books which I should certainly have asked you to review for the *Criterion* if you had not been committed to the *Times*.

By the way, can you tell me the best book to read on the reign of Henry II? I should be grateful if you could tell me or find out for me.[4]

Yours ever affectionately,

[T. S. Eliot]

---

1 – Rowse lauded G. F. Hudson of All Souls – 'an extremely interesting man' – who wished to write for the *Criterion* an essay on Toynbee's *History of Civilisation*. 'Hudson is, you may remember, a remarkable fellow: he has a very wide range of historical knowledge, has written a book on "Relations between Europe and China", another on "The Huns", and I dare say knows as much about the history of civilisations as ever Toynbee does . . .'

2 – ALR remarked that the latest issue of *C.* was 'a bit patchy': 'It needs a substantial long article to begin with, like my "Débâcle of European Liberalism"! – of course I couldn't say what I intended to say on the subject in the "Times Lit. Supp."'

3 – 'Did you see my T.L.S. leader when it came out? It had one or two of its quips & sallies removed, & arranged v. respectable.' [ALR], 'New Light on Swift' – on *The Letters of Jonathan Swift to Charles Ford*, ed. David Nichol Smith; *Swift: Gulliver's Travels and Selected Writings in Prose and Verse*, ed. John Hayward – *TLS*, 10 Jan. 1935, 13–14. (The issue was available in advance of publication date.)

4 – Rowse replied on 14 Jan. 1935: 'As it happens, there is no one good book on the reign of Henry II: you will have to read several shorter things. The best is to read the three or four

FROM *The Manager, Allen & Hanbury's*
TO *Vivien Eliot* TS Bodleian

8 January 1935 7 Vere Street, Cavendish Square,
London

Dear Madam,

The undersigned has noticed that you are using a large amount of the Faivres' Cachets,[1] and he feels it is his duty to mention that taken in excessive quantities these might prove harmful. In the doses recommended they are quite useful, but all preparations of this type are intended only for occasional use.

> Yours faithfully,
> Allen & Hanbury's, Ltd.[2]

TO *Paul Elmer More* TS Princeton

9 January 1935 Faber & Faber Ltd

My dear More,

Father Martin D'Arcy, whom you know, is to give a series of sermons in New York during Lent, and he would like very much to visit a few other parts of the country and places of learning. He is not of course keen on emolument, but wherever he went he would have to have his expenses paid at least. I am writing in the hope that Princeton may be able to invite him to speak. Do you think this is possible, and would it be possible for your brother to get him an engagement in Cincinnati? I hope that St Louis

---

essays on the Reign in Bishop Stubbs' "*Historical Introductions*" (ed. by A. Hassall); and in his "*Lectures on Medieval and Modern History*". These are very good.

'The articles in the Dictionary of National Biography on Henry II and Becket are short but excellent.

'The most useful text-book covering the whole period is H. W. C. Davis: "England under the Normans and Angevins" – I should read the Angevin section. (A fuller work is Kate Norgate, "England under the Angevin Kings".)

'Then on Becket, there is Dean Stanley's old-fashioned but useful – "Historical Memorials of Canterbury" (Everyman Library) . . .

'I think the above should cover the ground – oh, also the chapter on Henry II in the *Cambridge Medieval History* – and you won't find in all it amounts to a great deal.'

1 – Cachets du Docteur Faivre, a medication containing quinine and caffeine, were prescribed for pain, headache and toothache.

2 – Allen & Hanbury's (chemists of 7 Vere Street, off Oxford Street, London) to VHE, 22 Aug. 1935: 'From Saturday onwards we shall prepare and deliver to you each morning 2 Adalin Tablets, 2 Phenacetin Cachets, and 1 Draught No. 18.157.' VHE noted: 'This denotes great reduction to sleep draughts since staying at the Constance [Hotel].'

University may invite him out there. I should be grateful for anything you can do. I don't think he wants to tie himself up with any lecture association, but would prefer to arrange privately.[1]

I have just started *The Sceptical Approach to Religion*[2] with keen interest and enjoyment, but have to lay it aside until at least the end of this month. I shall write to you again when I have read it. It has aroused warm interest at Kelham, and I believe my friend Father Gabriel Hebert has written to you. We shall be publishing a book of his in the middle of the year which I think will interest you.

With all good wishes for the coming year, and in the hope of seeing you here,

> I am,
> Yours ever,
> T. S. Eliot

P.S. Lowther Clarke says that he has got the two Archbishops to write commendatory words to be used in advertising *Anglicanism*, and he has asked me to do a note also, calling attention to the literary value of this hitherto buried treasure.[3] This I am very glad to do.

Your friend Mr Went has just been in to see me – but your letter of introduction has never arrived!

1–Elmer More replied on 22 Jan. that he had no formal connection with the university, but would do what he could. 'That able but somewhat sly S. J. was never any favourite of mine, since the day (if you won't mind my saying it) when I first met him in London in your house. And apart from personal considerations, I don't like what he stands for. He belongs to the band of R. C. scholars who are making a concerted drive, almost a conspiracy I might say, to foist the scholastic philosophy and the cruder side of the Middle Ages upon us; and they are succeeding to a remarkable degree.'

2–New Shelburne Essays, vol. II (1934).

3–Lowther Clarke, Editorial Secretary, SPCK and the Sheldon Press, on 27 Dec. 1934: 'What we should especially value would be something, such as you could say with authority, about the value of the book as an Anthology of stately English prose.' *Anglicanism*, ed. Paul Elmer More and Frank Leslie Cross (SPCK, 1935), is an anthology about 'the thought and practice of the Church of England, illustrated from the religious literature of the seventeenth century'; it consists of two short essays by More and Felix Arnott, followed by some 800 pages of extracts.

See too TSE's remarks in his 'Views and Reviews' column – in praise of *Anglicanism* – *NEW* 7: 10 (20 June 1935), 190–1, on the subject of prose style.

TO *Frederick May Eliot*[1]   CC

9 January 1935   [Faber & Faber Ltd]

My dear Frederick,

My friend the Revd M. C. D'Arcy S.J. is coming to America for the first time to give a series of Lenten Sermons in New York, and while he is in America he would like to give a few lectures elsewhere in order to make some acquaintance with the country. I expect the Jesuits at S. Louis University will ask him out there, and I am wondering if St Paul or Minneapolis would be interested? I am sure that your friend Father Moynihan will know about D'Arcy, who enjoys a distinction which extends far outside of his own communion; indeed, he is recognised as one of the ablest philosophers in England at the present time. I am just writing to you at a venture, but if anything came of it I should be extremely grateful. I think also that you would find D'Arcy a man whom you would very much like to meet.

With all best wishes for the New Year to Elizabeth and the children and yourself.

                              Yours ever affectionately,
                              [Tom]

TO *William Temple*[2]   CC

9 January 1935   [Faber & Faber Ltd]

My Lord Archbishop,

In your Grace's communication to *The Church Times* of January 4th, occurs the following sentence:

1–The Revd Frederick May Eliot (1889–1958), educated at Harvard Divinity School (graduating *summa cum laude* in 1911), was Minister of Unity Church, St Paul, Minnesota, 1917–37; President of the American Unitarian Association, 1937–58. He married in 1915 Elizabeth Berkeley Lee. Works include *Fundamentals of Unitarian Faith* (1927) and *Toward Belief in God* (1929). See too *Frederick May Eliot: An Anthology*, ed. Alfred P Stiernotte (1959); John Kielty, 'Frederick May Eliot', *The Inquirer*, 26 Mar. 1960, 489: 'It is rare that in one man are found the qualities of a good executive officer ably directing the day-to-day business of a religious body; the qualities of a mystic with a deep philosophic mind; and those pastoral qualities that reveal a deep concern for men, women and children as persons of infinite worth. Rare indeed that one man should possess all-round qualities to such a high degree . . .'
2–William Temple (1881–1944) – son of Frederick Temple (1821–1902), Archbishop of Canterbury – taught Classics at Oxford University; ordained in 1908, he served as Headmaster of Repton School, 1910–14, and was Bishop of Manchester and then (from

'If, when a communicant leaves the church, he has in his heart no more of self-giving love than when he entered, he has not received the Real Presence.'

I have hesitated to trouble Your Grace with a letter on the subject, but if I wrote to *The Church Times* it would come to the same thing, and I am seriously interested to know what Your Grace would wish us to infer from this pronouncement. The following questions suggest themselves:

(1) If the communicant has not received the Real Presence, can he be said to have taken the Host unworthily, since it is not the Host that he has taken, but only, I suppose, the elements as if unconsecrated? If what he has received was not the Real Presence, can he in any sense be said to have eaten and drunk damnation?

(2) If an unbaptised person, or Unitarian, leaves the church, after making a communion, with more of self-giving love in his heart than when he entered, has he received the Real Presence? If so, is he in a better spiritual state than if, as an unbaptised person, he had refrained from making his communion?

Your Grace continues: 'The first thing which that self-giving love must long to do is to win others to seek it at its own source.' Does Your Grace mean that the first result, in the order of time, of receiving the Real Presence in the Sacrament of the Altar, will be a missionary zeal? Or that the first thing, in the order of value, which the person who has received the Real Presence will long to do, is to convert others?

I could enlarge upon these points, but I wish to keep this letter as brief as possible, and I think the foregoing is enough to suggest the possible implications in my mind.

Apologising for encroaching upon your Grace's time,

I am,

Your Grace's obedient servant,

[T. S. Eliot]

1929) Archbishop of York. He became Archbishop of Canterbury in 1942. His writings include *Christus Veritas* (1924), *Nature, Man and God* (1934), *Christianity and Social Order* (1942). In the 1920s he won authority as a leader of the movement for international ecumenism – 'this world-wide Christian fellowship', as he invoked it.

TO *Henry Eliot*   TS Houghton

9 January 1935   Faber & Faber Ltd

My dear Henry,

I have left my Christmas letter to you till the last, because it was the most important. I received, some days before Christmas, a parcel which I could not understand, but refrained from opening. It was explained to me by Morley. The dressing gown which I had in use was a cheap affair of coloured towelling, some years old and very dishevelled: what I have now is much the most elegant that I have ever had, and must have cost you a pretty sum. It is so elegant that I take it off before cleaning my teeth, so as not to spill toothpaste on it. It is a really useful and needed present; and I am especially touched by the thought and ingenuity you put into getting a present of this kind to me in this way. It was chosen by Mrs Morley (Christina). I presented a watch to Donald, a xylophone to Oliver, a crib with sheets, blankets and eiderdown to my goddaughter, and a Mickey Mouse cinema to the family. I went down there and saw the New Year in with them – with a proper haggis and pre-war whisky (Christina being Scotch) as well as roast duck and champagne.

Also, your and Theresa's Christmas cards gave me pleasure.

I did very little for Christmas this year, beyond Christmas cards. I appreciate your sending the 'toy bears' for Tom. As the Faber family are still in Wales for the holidays, I thought that they would cheer him up better if kept as a surprise upon his return to school, in about ten days, so he hasn't had them yet, as I am keeping the box here.[1]

1–In response to a thank-you letter from young Tom, HWE wrote directly to the boy on 10 Feb. 1935 (enclosing four photographs by himself of some captive bears): 'My dear Thomas: It was very nice of you to write me a nice letter thanking me for the two bears. You write beautifully and you do not mis-spell (is that word spelt right?) any words. I was glad to know that Jim and Jam, the twin bears, arrived safely. I gave them jam next week, just before they went on board ship, so that they would not be hungry. I am sorry that I couldn't send any gammel-ost [a standing joke: gammel-ost is a Norwegian cheese] for them, but I don't know what it is. But Mr Frank Morley knows all about it, he knows more about gammel-ost than any living man, and if you ask him I am sure he will get you some. He gets it from Norway and eats it between meals. Now you must be careful not to give the bears more than a tiny crumb of gammel-ost, for if they get too fond of it they will grow up to be as big as Mr Frank Morley, and while that is all right for Mr Morley and nobody minds, it would not be so nice to have two bears that size. When you go in to see Mr Morley about this, give him my best regards, also the same to your godfather who is my brother Tom. I hope that explains who I am and that you are convinced that I did not make myself up and am only imaginary. Maybe I am imaginary but I don't think so as I have just been to the dentist and that is very convincing.

I have not written for so long that I do not know what to try to say. I had an arduous October November December, with several odd lectures to give, meetings to address etc., and I have a hard three months ahead of me, as I have a play to write in the next three months, which means abstaining from all weekends, from as many evening engagements as possible. Correspondence with, and interviews with solicitors have not lightened the burden. I have from time to time given Ada brief reports – Vivienne by a policy of inaction made matters as difficult as possible, and at one point I was afraid that the only thing to do would be to have her sent to gaol for contempt of court – at any rate she has given me the maximum of trouble and legal expense in getting my property, but I think I have now got most of it – certainly all that I shall trouble to get. Apparently, I can dismiss from mind the fear of her molesting me. With what I provide, she now should still have an income of nearly £600 a year[1] – a good deal more than Margaret or Marion has to live on, I think; but my chief fear is that she will get into financial difficulties. At present, I couldn't very well help her out except at sacrifice of capital – I am still paying heavy taxes on my income while in America – and she has involved me in enormous legal expenses. So, if it came to helping her out financially, I could only do it by insisting on somebody having control over her actions in future. The other possibility is that she may become irrationally miserly, and starve herself. Her father had a tendency to think that he would die in the poorhouse, but he was able to leave £30,000. I think Vivienne and Maurice have each about £350 a year, and their mother £600 a year or more, which will be divided between the two when she dies.

This leads me to a point mentioned in a letter of yours some time ago, which I have not answered. You spoke of the family having to share, probably, expense of paying taxes on Mill Creek property. I want to bear my share of this: I am only afraid of your trying to pay the whole sum yourself in order to save your sisters; so I shall be glad if you will write to

---

'Here is a birthday card that was sent to me and as I don't care for birthdays you can have mine. You can have all the rest of mine, but you can't have my Christmasses.'

See TSE's verses 'The Jim Jum Bears', evidently inspired by his brother's happy gift – although, curiously, one TS is typed on paper headed 'B-11 Eliot House, Cambridge', which suggests either that he first thought them up during his year at Harvard, 1932–3, or that he was using up old paper – in *Poems*, ed. Ricks and McCue, I, 302–3, 1206–8.

1–On 1 Feb. 1935 VHE declared for tax purposes for the years 1927/1933 that she was beneficially entitled to an income of £569. 3. 4d. This was derived from a one-third share of rents of properties at nos. 1, 3, 4 & 5 Haigh Terrace, 16 Tivoli Road, 1–10 Eglington Park, and Eglington House, all in Dun Laoghaire, outside Dublin (Bod MS Eng lett. b. 22).

me again explaining the situation up to date. I imagine that you are more pinched than I am, even now. My income would be good enough, in a more rationally organised society. The trouble is that one may acquire a position, which involves living on a certain scale, more rapidly than one acquires income. I have to entertain a lot of young writers to lunch, etc. occasionally help them out with a five pound note, and that sort of thing; as well as sometimes reciprocating the hospitality of people richer than myself. Also, the sort of reputation that I have gained, involves being asked to do all sorts of worthy things which don't bring in any money – give addresses, take the chair, serve on committees etc. One can't do everything one is asked to, but one must do some of it. I am sometimes asked to give a lecture, or a poetry reading, on behalf of some excellent charity. And so on. I am not grumbling about this, but it is pleasant to yarn on about it.

I certainly cannot afford to take a holiday in America till 1936. That lets me out of the Class of 1910 Reunion, however.

I am quite contented with my lodgings in South Kensington; the food is not very good – it is surprisingly difficult to tell whether the meat is beef, veal or mutton – but I lunch heartily at my club – and I am very well – my resistance to cold is much greater this winter than last. Everything but the food is good, and unless the Underground Railway decides to demolish this house, I may stay indefinitely – of course, as it is a Clergy House, I have to be Churchwarden, but I rather like that. I intend to move in the books that I have recovered, which are in storage.

I am very busy with my regular work, with the Church Literature Association, with the Orage Memorial and the *New English Weekly,* and with writing a play to be performed at Canterbury in June, and with cooperating with W. B. Yeats and W. H. Auden in a season of poetic drama at the Mercury Theatre in May (this is not yet public news).

I feel that you have got discouraged about writing to me, because I have been such a poor correspondent. When I envisaged a celibate life,[1]

---

1 – TSE had taken a vow of celibacy in Mar. 1928, after bringing VHE back to London from the Sanatorium de la Malmaison in Paris (see Ronald Schuchard, "'If I think, again, of this place": Eliot, Herbert and the Way to "Little Gidding"', in *Words in Time: New Essays on Eliot's "Four Quartets"*, ed. Edward Lobb [1993], 56). TSE wrote on 17 June 1938 to Henry Swabey, who said he was feeling a certain resistance to the life upon which he had embarked at theological college in Chichester: 'I should, I confess, feel more unqualified sympathy with your revolt against social deadness, if it wasn't coupled so oddly with a protest against celibacy. For one thing, you are not compelled to remain unmarried, in the Church of England; and I ought not to need to remark that the "homosexual type" hardly makes the best celibate: though I dare say that if one is homosexual (that is, of a feeble or

I thought that I should have an infinity of leisure for writing letters; but I have found that the more time you have the more duties come to fill it, and things which were impossible become obligations. But please do write to me at length, once, about yourself and about anything and everything, and see whether I reply adequately.

With much love to both of you, and Priscilla,[1]

Affectionately your brother,

Tom

TO *Michael Roberts*   CC

9 January 1935   [Faber & Faber Ltd]

My dear Roberts,

I should be glad to know whether I have sent you all the poetry books that you feel able to cope with in one review. It goes without saying, of course, that the great majority of the books I have sent you are destined only for the waste-paper basket, but there are others which certainly need attention. I am asking because Dylan Thomas's small book, eighteen poems, has just come in. He interests me very much, and I should be sorry to see him receive enforced inadequate notice merely owing to the fact that you have too much on hand to deal with properly. Please don't think that I want you to say any more about the book than you feel inclined to, only I should like to feel that you were able to give it whatever space you felt it deserved.[2]

Yours sincerely,

[T. S. Eliot]

---

incomplete sexuality) it is very easy to imagine that one has a vocation for celibacy. But to deny that celibacy is the highest ideal (however few people may be fitted to practise it) seems to me to be in a very bad spiritual muddle. I am really wondering whether you are called to be a priest at all.' E. W. F. Tomlin noted of one lunch (undated) with TSE: 'Referring to living the celibate life, he said, quite simply but placing both hands flat on the table, as he often did when stressing a capital point, "It *can* be done, as I know." This was the only time I heard him refer directly to his sexual life. I was convinced he was sincere. In *Thoughts after Lambeth* he had referred to sex as "the most imperative of our instincts". The inference therefore was that he had found this, understandably, no easy task' ('T. S. Eliot: An Expostulation by way of a memoir', *Agenda*, 23: 1–2 (Spring–Summer 1985), 146).

1–Priscilla Stearns Talcott (b. 19 Feb. 1934).

2–Roberts reviewed six volumes – including Dylan Thomas, *18 Poems*; Stephen Spender, *Vienna*; Ezra Pound, *Homage to Sextus Propertius* – in C. 14 (Apr. 1935), 496–9.

FROM *Vivien Eliot* TO *District Bank*   Bodleian

9 January 1935   [No address given]

Dear Sir, I have been ill in bed since last Friday when I saw you, & have only got up today. Otherwise I shd have *brought* you this note. I must ask you not to give up those articles of silver until I have brought you the most recent photograph of my husband. I should have asked you this but I did not like to in front of Mr Broad. But I am never able to concentrate my mind & am therefore extremely handicapped in dealing with anything so serious as this. For my part I cannot see that a signature is a sufficient identification. If it were anyone could claim anything from a *weak minded* or feeble person by declaring it is theirs & by their signing their name. It sounds to me childish. What I have a right to ask you is that you shd arrange for me to be present & hidden in some way so that I can see if it is my husband. For my part, if this is not arranged I shall never be convinced however many signatures you show me that these articles of silver & that very important Dead Box were actually claimed by my husband. At the same time why was this not arranged while his *sister* was in London (*in June*)? This is the whole of my defence. I swore that I would keep his things in my protection until I gave them up *into his own hands*. It was only by Brute Force that his things were snatched from me & I have no proof that my husband ever returned from America, but it is easy, as time passes, to see what a *help* it is to say that he is living & in England, & to *scare* me by every kind of bogey from *seeing* him. I call it a scandalous affair.

You brought up the point that he & I once had a joint Account. Are you aware, dear Sir, that *from* July 1933 for at least *a year* I was writing letters (or I was appealing, the whole time) to Messrs James & James, appealing for a *joint* Account with my husband, for I *knew* I was incapable of managing my own financial affairs – Mr Moxon Broad holds 17 or 18 or 19 of these letters (copies of these letters) – I *enclose* herewith a photograph which was taken just before my husband left for America.

                    I am
                    Yrs. faithfully
                    V. H. Eliot.[1]

1–VHE wrote in her diary, 18 Feb. 1935: 'As my books & all the Criterions, bound & unbound, which were stolen from my flat have never been returned, I shall now order, through Foyle's, all the Criterions in print . . . As for my books, I must still rely on Mr Faber getting them back for me.

'This was not done.'

(The photo enclosed is a snapshot of Tom, me, & Lillia Symes, outside the Gate of 3 Compayne Gdns. taken by Aurelia Bollinger [*sic*].)

TO *Geoffrey Faber*   TS Faber

10 January 1935   Faber & Faber Ltd

Dear Geoffrey,

I have just had a letter from Charles Harris, that is, Prebendary Harris of Hereford, who is Chairman of the Book Committee of the Church Literature Association of which I am Secretary. Amongst other subjects he raises the question of our publishing from time to time any books produced under the auspices of the C.L.A. for which a wider public is desired than that accessible through the S.P.C.K.

Hitherto all the books which the C.L.A. (which is really a department of the Church Union) has sponsored have been published by the S.P.C.K. The arrangement has usually, and, so far as I know, always been that the C.L.A. and the S.P.C.K. go half and half in sharing the costs and in taking the profits.

I don't know whether Harris has at the moment any particular books in mind, though he speaks of being still uncertain to what publisher to take the book on Convocation. (You will probably remember that this was a book in which he expected to get some collaboration with Lord Hugh Cecil, and which has been mentioned at Book Committees.)[1] Obviously each book would have to be considered on its own merits. I don't know whether you would consider an arrangement similar to that with the S.P.C.K. good enough, but there is nothing immutable about this arrangement. The chief point in my mind is whether we should care for the appearance of being so closely associated with any one church organisation as that. It might not matter once every two years or so, but I should doubt its advisability in general.

I don't know whether that would be a vital matter to the Church Union, and I think that probably there would be books which the C.L.A. would like to back, but without having their name connected with. I should like to know what you think of the notion in general. The only other publisher

---

On 27 Mar. 1935, with regard to the Criterions: 'They were marked copies, & contain all the writings of Irene Fassett & myself [& TSE] . . . all under the names of Fanny Marlow, Feiron Morris, Felise Morrison, & T. S. Eliot.'

1 – Harris, 'Convocation: its past, present and future' (unpublished).

on my Committee is J. G. Lockhart,[1] which means that if we did not take such books they would go to Bles or to the Centenary Press. I have a feeling that Harris and Lowther Clarke, who are the only people who really count on the Committee, would much rather work with us than with Bles, as being a firm of much greater prestige.

Also, I want to tell you that Harris thinks that your scheme for a Child's Companion to the Prayer Book is a very good one, and agrees that it is a project for a general publisher, certainly not for any particular church organisation. I think that he might be able to suggest a few names of people who could do such a book without giving it any pronounced bias one way or another.[2]

Yours ever,
T. S. E.

TO *Alastair W. R. Miller*   TS Professor Andrew M. Miller

10 January 1935   Faber & Faber Ltd

Dear Mr Miller,

I got your letter yesterday, but did not answer it at once because I wanted to think the matter over carefully.[3] It is always a temptation to accept this kind of suggestion when one has liked the author's poems that one has seen, but I feel that this is the kind of thing that I ought not to do, however happy I should be to do it in particular instances. It is not the first time that I have been asked, and I have always refused. My objection to assisting books in this way is less firm on any subject but poetry, but you see if I did so once I should find it impossible to refuse

---

1 – J. G. Lockhart was a Director of the Centenary Press, London. TSE contributed 'Religion and Literature' to *Faith that Illuminates*, ed. V. A. Demant (Centenary Press, 1935), 29–54.

2 – GCF replied, 13 Jan.: 'this is just to say that I don't see anything agin the idea, provided that it didn't lead to the appearance of a too close connection with the C.L.A. I don't think this would be so, if the books published through us were only a percentage of their books.'

GCF told Captain B. Liddell Hart, 14 Oct. 1935: 'As a publisher, I must necessarily publish a great many books expressing views which I do not hold myself. For example, I do not agree with Professor Macmurray's "Philosophy of Communism", nor with T. S. Eliot's religious standpoint, and so forth.'

3 – Miller asked (n.d.): 'I showed Mr Basil Blackwell yr. letter, in which you dealt kindly with "The Man of Gingerbread" – to cheer him at having published it. Now he is bringing out another book of poems: and has mentioned that he would like (as obviously I would greatly) to use a few words from that letter – quoted as being "in a letter" – on the wrapper, along with excerpts from reviews by Mr Blunden, the Times Lit. Sup. – and perhaps others . . . May it be done?'

similar invitations, and I should end by putting myself in a position where my word carried no weight at all. Similarly, I never *review* books of verse, and feel that the only important way in which I can express my opinions of younger writers than myself is in my capacity as editor and publisher. I have, of course, written introductions to volumes of selections from the work of Ezra Pound and Marianne Moore, but these people are my own contemporaries who had been working for many years, and who had not received the recognition in this country that they should have had.

I am deeply sorry to disappoint you, but I am afraid that an acceptance would land me in an impossible position.

I am keeping your French translations by me for publication when they fit in conveniently. With many regrets and best wishes for the success of your book,

Yours sincerely,
T. S. Eliot

TO *Olga Rudge*[1]   TS Beinecke

10 January 1935   Faber & Faber Ltd

Dear Miss Rudge,

Ezra has informed me that you are at present in England, but does not say for how long. I hope that you are here long enough to have lunch with me one day. Would next Tuesday the 15th be possible? If so, I suggest the Escargot Bienvenu, 48 Greek Street, unless some other part of town would be more convenient. If not Tuesday do please let me know when you are free.

Yours sincerely,
T. S. Eliot

1–Olga Rudge (1895–1996), American-born violinist and musicologist (brought up in London and Paris); long-term mistress of EP. In 1936 she began to champion the work of Vivaldi, having unearthed in Turin twenty-five volumes of his music (309 concertos for violin and orchestra): she formed a Vivaldi Society in Venice and published a comprehensive catalogue (1939). See obituaries in *Times*, 21 Mar. 1996; *Guardian*, 20 Mar. 1996; and Anne Conover, *Olga Rudge and Ezra Pound: 'What Thou Lovest Well . . .'* (2001).

TO *A. S. Duncan-Jones*[1]   CC

10 January 1935   [Faber & Faber Ltd]

My dear Duncan-Jones,

I have just had a letter from Martin Shaw to which I do not know how to reply, and I should like to explain the situation to you.

Some time ago Shaw came to me in a high state of excitement with his notion for a grand pageant on the subject of Peace. At that time I was already negotiating with the Canterbury people for a play for their festival, and told him that in any case I could not touch such a project until the Canterbury business was over. At the same time I tried to hint to him:-

1. That the making of pageants was not my business, and that all I had done last year was to write words for a scenario.

2. That my only interest as a workman in last year's pageant had been in experimenting with choruses.

3. That I was much more anxious to try play writing than to be involved in any more pageants.

4. That I was extremely sceptical over the possibility of a pageant about Peace making the slightest difference to the future of Europe.

Dear Shaw is such an ardent enthusiast for Peace that I did not want to put these points brutally, and he probably carried off the impression that the only difficulty was my desire to get the Canterbury job over first.

I simply can't see a Church pageant about Peace making any impression or having any strength in it. One's hands would be tied by the official character of the show, and half of the things that I should want to say myself would have to be left out. The only possibility that I can envisage for handling the subject at all is in the form of Aristophanic farce, which certainly could not be produced under official auspices and which would probably be too libellous to be produced at all. But what use is there in dealing with the subject unless one can deal frankly and freely with the whole swindle?

If, however, somebody else produced a scenario with which I could feel in sympathy, I might be able to do a few choruses or something of

1 – The Revd Arthur Stuart Duncan-Jones (1879–1955) was Dean of Chichester Cathedral, 1929–55. TSE informed the General Meeting of the London Library, July 1955: '"D-J" had several claims to eminence, and a variety of interests which complemented each other. He shared with his Bishop a love of the arts and a sense of public responsibility which extended far beyond the bounds of their City and Diocese. Duncan-Jones was, as a Dean should be, a lover of music, an art in which he possessed both knowledge and taste, and the Cathedral of Chichester became known as a centre of music both liturgical and extra-liturgical. He was

465

that sort, but I should hardly want to tackle even that seriously until the autumn. What shall I write to Shaw?

Yours ever sincerely,
[T. S. Eliot]

TO *The Editor,* The Times Literary Supplement[1]

10 January 1935   24 Russell Square, London W.C.1

Sir, –

In the interesting review of Ernest Dowson's Poems in your last issue,[2] your reviewer suggests that I caught the phrase 'Falls the shadow' from

---

a distinguished theologian. He knew well Germany and the German language, and he had a discriminating taste in German wines. Like his Bishop, he early wrote and spoke with condemnation of the Nazi persecution of Jews and their campaign against the churches. He was an accomplished speaker both in private discussion and in debate, and a formidable disputant in Assembly. I may, of course, be somewhat influenced by the fact that I was in general sympathy both with his theological views and with his political and social views, and that I often found myself supporting, or supported by, his opinion. What I most admired, however, was his fearlessness and independence. He is a loss to the Church and to the Nation and, I will remind you again, a loss to the London Library.' To the Revd Dr S. C. Carpenter, TSE wrote on 27 Sept. 1955: 'My affection for Duncan-Jones was quite out of proportion to the intimacy of our acquaintance, for indeed I cannot say that I knew him well. I used to see him regularly at our All Souls Club, of which he was one of the mainstays. He was unsurpassed for clarity, fluency and vigour in discussion, during which he gradually became pinker in the face. But so far as I remember, he had the gift of being downright and blunt without ever being quarrelsome or giving legitimate ground for offence. Indeed, the only man of my acquaintance whom I ever remember as quarrelling with Duncan-Jones, was a man who was known to be brusque and ill-mannered. Apart from meetings of All Souls Club and two or three visits to Chichester – I am happy in the memory of having given an address to the Friends of Chichester Cathedral which earned his warm commendation – I was also with him on a rather short-lived and ill-fated Committee, of which the less said the better. Of this Committee, as of other occasions, I may say that Duncan-Jones and I saw eye to eye. I shall always be painfully aware of the absence of his support on occasions when I know we should share the same views' (quoted in part in S. C. Carpenter, *Duncan-Jones of Chichester* [1956] , 75).

1 – Published as 'Dowson's Poems' (letter), *TLS*, 10 Jan. 1935, 21.

2 – Anon (Geoffrey Tillotson), 'Ernest Dowson' – on *The Poetical Works of Ernest Christopher Dowson*, ed. Desmond Flower – *TLS*, 3 Jan. 1935, 6: 'The loosening of rhythm connects Dowson with Mr Eliot, some of whose many roots may be found gripping Dowson's best poem "Non sum qualis eram bonae, sub regno Cynerae". It seems less than fantastic to note, among more elusive communications, that the repeated "Falls the shadow" of the "Hollow Men" seems to derive partly from this poem:-

> Last night, ah, yesternight, betwixt her lips and mine
> There fell thy shadow, Cynara! thy breath was shed . . .
> But when the feast is finished and the lamps expire,
> Then falls thy shadow, Cynara! the night is thine . . .

Dowson's 'Cynara'. This derivation had not occurred to my mind, but I believe it to be correct, because the lines he quotes have always run in my head, and because I regard Dowson as a poet whose technical innovations have been underestimated. But I do not think that I got the title 'The Hollow Men' from Dowson. There is a romance of William Morris called 'The Hollow Land'. There is also a poem of Mr Kipling called 'The Broken Men'. I combined the two.[1]

I am, Sir, your obedient servant,
T. S. Eliot

TO *Geoffrey Faber*   TS Valerie Eliot

14 January 1935   Faber & Faber Ltd

Dear Geoffrey,

If you havent mentioned that photograph of me to anybody, please dont; if you have, please tell them not to. I dont want it to get any farther.[2] What happened was that the B.B.C. have been clamouring for a long time for a portrait, saying that their fans have been writing in and asking to see a portrait of Uncle Tom; and I have always refused, but it came to this, that I should probably lose the job if I held out, so I said I would pose if they would undertake that the portrait should be unrecognisable. Confound it, if they had only let me wear the black beard, and elastic sided boots I wanted to wear, nobody would have been any the wiser and the children would have been satisfied, but they had some silly scruple about lending themselves to that kind of deception. And as you have spotted me it is possible that others will; on the other hand most people dont think of me as 'Uncle Tom' and not expecting to find me in the *Radio Times* like that they may overlook it, which is why I ask you not to mention it.

And a favourite phrase of Dowson's is "the hollow land". It comes three times, and twice with the symbolic deepening of initial capital letters.'

(This review was collected in Tillotson's *Essays in Criticism and Research* [1942].)

1–See too TSE, 'The Unfading Genius of Rudyard Kipling', *The Kipling Journal* 26 (1959), 9–12: 'I could never have thought of this title [*The Hollow Men*] but for Kipling's poem *The Broken Men*. One of the broken men has turned up recently in my work, and may be seen at this time on the stage of the Cambridge Theatre.' TSE was referring to Lord Claverton in *The Elder Statesman*.

On the title *The Hollow Men*, see further *Poems*, ed. Ricks and McCue, I, 715.

2–GCF had sent a cutting from the *Radio Times*, issue dated 4 Jan. 1935, with an illustration on p. 56 of a man in a cap – not TSE – crouching by a penguin. The caption reads: 'Uncle Tom and a Penguin Friend: Uncle Tom will tell the Children about the "New Year in the Zoo" this afternoon at 5.15.' GCF wrote by hand on the cutting: 'You didn't tell us about this? We are *so* disappointed to have missed it.'

There is another matter to take up with you when you return: I told T. S. Gregory[1] that he would find it impossible to retain his position as a Methodist minister after his book was out; but he must have [been] talking or writing elsewhere, because he now writes to say that the Methodists have already kicked him out, and how can he earn a living? I dont know the answer; but we shall have to think of something to tell him to go and do. Married, and has what he calls a Bairn. If he joins the R.C.s they have a society or something for helping converted parsons.

Wishing you a swift & easy journey. Portrait of myself as I wanted to appear on next page.

T.

Correct Uncle Tom outfit –

As I meant it to be

TO *Messrs James & James*   cc

14 January 1935   [Faber & Faber Ltd]

Dear Sirs,

I have considered your letter of January 7th and have again consulted Mr Ernest Bird, who tells me that he considers that the amount I have already offered, £52:10:0d., is in the circumstances entirely reasonable.[2]

1–See TSE's letter to Gregory, 15 Jan. below.
2–James & James reported (7 Jan.) that they had gone carefully through the bill of charges with a view to 'eliminating such charges as we think may not be fairly charged against you . . . We suggest therefore that a sum of £75 (a reduction of £30) would fairly meet the position . . .'

If you can come to accord with me on this sum I will arrange to send you a cheque forthwith. You will understand, I trust, that I am not simply standing on a point of principle; but that in my present circumstances I am very hard pressed indeed.[1]

Yours faithfully,
[T. S. Eliot]

TO *Ernest Bird, Messrs Bird & Bird*

cc

14 January 1935   [Faber & Faber Ltd]

My dear Bird,

Thank you very much for your letter of the 10th instant.[2] I have today written to James & James, offering £52:10:0d. at once, and hope that they will accept.

At the same time, however, I should feel happier if I began to pay you something on account. Your firm is presumably out of pocket, to the extent of counsel's fees, Court charges, etc. I should like to have some idea of what I owe you on the whole operation, so that I may budget for it in instalments.

I shall try to make a memorandum for you of the changes for a new will, which I should like to simplify, to make it easier to execute. What I want to know first of all is whether, if I left nothing to my wife – in view of the fact that she will get the income of my two trust estates, and five thousand dollars life insurance, and will be rather better off than during my lifetime, to say nothing of her mother's – whether, if I leave her nothing, she could successfully contest the will.[3]

The shares in Faber & Faber do not yet pay a dividend, and I want to bequeath mine back into the firm (or to their children) to spare them the inconvenience of having my wife as a shareholder. I think I should want

1 – James & James replied on 17 Jan. that they were prepared to accept the sum of £52. 10. 0d 'in settlement of our bill subject to reserving our rights against Mrs Eliot, regarding the balance'.

2 – Bird & Bird reiterated that in their opinion TSE should inform Messrs James & James that his offer of £52. 10. 0 had been made 'after full consideration and that you do not see your way to increase it . . . I do not know whether you have already told them that the bill has been submitted to me but you are quite at liberty to do so and inform them that all things considered I think the suggestion is in the circumstances entirely reasonable. Such assuredly is the fact but if it became a question of defending a lawsuit I might be compelled to modify my opinion.'

3 – Bird replied on 23 Jan.: 'Let me say without hesitation that if you leave nothing to your wife – as in the circumstances I do not think you should – she most certainly could not successfully contest the Will or even attempt to do so.'

my executors to dispose of my library as they thought best, giving them perhaps a short list of friends whom I should like to be remembered. Certain inherited objects, such as silver, could all go to my brother to distribute among members of the family.

Yours sincerely,
[T. S. Eliot]

TO *Charles Davies*[1]   TS The National Library of Wales

15 January 1935   [Faber & Faber Ltd]

Dear Mr Davies,

I hardly know what to say about your play except that I don't believe any publisher could sell it. That is no slight upon its merit, but simply means that you have put your ideas into what happens to be an unreadable form. I do not think that a play which is only written to be read is ever really readable unless it is a sort of lyrical poem like *Atalanta in Calydon*. You have a lot of material here, but I think you ought to take it to pieces and try to write a play (if that is to be your form) which can be staged or alternatively broadcast. Whether you get it produced is a secondary matter. My point is that it ought to be written with a *view* to production. Then, of course, you would not be able to assign your characters such extremely long speeches, which no living actor would be able to remember. What makes this difficult to read is a cardinal error of form.

I should like to see the next thing you do.

Yours sincerely,
T. S. Eliot

TO *Francis Younghusband*[2]   CC

15 January 1935   [Faber & Faber Ltd]

Dear Sir Francis Younghusband,

Thank you for your letter of the 10th of January inviting me to become a member of the National Council of your World Fellowship.

1 – Charles Davies, of Bangor, Wales.
2 – Sir Francis Younghusband (1863–1942) – army officer, explorer; writer on spirituality – undertook explorations into Central Asia including Manchuria, 1886–7, Chinese Turkestan, and Tibet, 1903–4, all the while reporting to the British governments his intelligence regarding the strategic threat posed to the British Raj by the military infiltrations of Russia. In 1890 he was made the youngest member of the Royal Geographical Society, receiving too

While I sympathise with any society which aims at the realisation of peace and brotherhood I am already associated with as many committees, societies, etc. as I can take active part in, and I never care to give my name to any society in which I am not taking an active part.

With all good wishes and many regrets,

I am,

Yours very truly,

[T. S. Eliot]

TO *George Barker*

TS Texas

15 January 1935   Faber & Faber Ltd

My dear Barker,

I can now tell you that my firm have decided that they would like to publish *Documents of [a] Death* and *The Bacchant* together in one volume presumably in the autumn, and on the same terms as your poems, i.e. 10 per cent. royalty.[1] We find that the two together make a larger book than I had anticipated as the estimate is actually for 288 pages. I think this is very satisfactory, and if you will let me know that you approve I will have a contract prepared for you directly.

Hoping that everything is going well with your wife and yourself,

Yours very sincerely,

T. S. Eliot

TO *Lady Keeble*

CC

15 January 1935   [*The Criterion*]

Dear Lady Keeble,

Thank you very much for your letter of the 11th and for your kind invitation to become a Vice-President of the Oxford Branch of the English

---

the Patron's Gold Medal (he served as President of the Society in 1919). In 1908 he was promoted to lieutenant-colonel. In later years he espoused an eccentric religiosity – he has been dubbed a 'premature hippy' – incorporating quasi-pantheistic elements, and set up the World Congress of Faith. See further Patrick French, *Younghusband: The Last Great Imperial Adventurer* (1997).

1 – *Janus* (1935) carried this great blurb by TSE: 'Here are two narratives of Love and Death. They are told in the form of a prose which Mr Barker has invented, unprecedented. They will give pleasure to readers who are civilized enough to be primitive and honest enough to recognize their own feelings.'

Verse Speaking Association, but I wrote last July to the Secretary declining an invitation to be a Vice-President of the Association itself.[1] My reason is that I have made a rule not to accept such positions which carry no obligation, and I am already connected with as many societies which do include obligations as I have time to cope with. I don't want to appear ungracious, but I do feel that the general principle of societies carrying the names of many people with no obligations, responsibilities or control is an unsatisfactory one. I know that it is very generally followed, but I cannot feel happy about it for myself. With many regrets,

Yours very sincerely,

[T. S. Eliot]

TO *William Temple*   cc

15 January 1935   [Faber & Faber Ltd]

My Lord Archbishop,

I am especially sensible of Your Grace's kindness in replying so quickly and so explicitly to my enquiry, in view of the fact that my theological knowledge is so incomplete and inexact as to give me no right to appeal direct to so high an authority.[2]

1–Lady Keeble (Lillah McCarthy) had been asked to form an Oxford branch of the Association; Gilbert Murray was to be President 'and nearly all the Heads of the Oxford Colleges have consented to be Vice-Presidents also Laurence Binyon & other poets . . . The office carries with it no obligation . . .'
2–Temple replied on 10 Jan. to TSE's letter of 9 Jan.: 'It is, I think, agreed on all hands that the Res Sacramenti, as distinct from the Sacramentum, is, as you put it, "received into the soul by faith, not into the stomach by the mouth". There is a difference of emphasis among theologians with regard to the pre-requisites of effective reception . . . Unbelief may be of indefinitely varied grades, from total disbelief to failure of completeness of self-surrender; and the extent of its hindrance varies accordingly . . . It is impossible to set up a sharp dilemma – *either* a man receives worthily and obtains grace *or* he receives unworthily and obtains judgment – and then apply this to particular instances.

'No doubt I exposed myself to the implied difficulties which you mention by the deliberately crude form of my own statement. To make what I said secure from such criticism I should have said that a man who leaves the Church with no access of love "has not received the Real Presence *in its fullness*." But then some would have said – "After all, no one does all that"; and I wanted to press home the point that the Real Presence is the Presence of the Incarnate Love Divine, so that to receive it is to receive Love.

'This leads to your question whether by "the first thing" (which self-giving love must long to do) is first in time or in value: certainly, in value – but therefore in time also so far as the self-giving love is itself complete.

'There may be a devout reception which actually wins grace to the extent of the gratitude, and an intention to serve God better. But the tremendous language of Catholic devotion

I appreciate Your Grace's distinction of degrees of unbelief and of reception. Some of my difficulties are disposed of; if I say not all, it is not for the purpose of soliciting further correspondence but only to be honest about them. I do not recall, and probably have never read, the context in which Gore[1] makes the distinction between the reception of the *Res Sacramenti* through faith, and the *Sacramentum* through the mouth: I should have thought that at the moment of reception, the relation of the stomach to the soul was, so to speak, identical with the relation of the Host to the Body of Christ. But my chief difficulty is this: I should have the thought that the 'degrees of worthiness' etc. were degrees which applied only to members of the Church. Your Grace observes that the unbaptised person, receiving the sacrament, neither expects nor receives the Real Presence. But I am not clear what he does receive; nor where there is any sin in his communicating; nor, if so, on whose part: his, or that of a priest who knowingly gives him the Sacrament. Obviously, it will only be a very few, among the faithful, who in taking the Sacrament realise its full significance – these few either through theological knowledge and aptitude or through special gifts of grace – and perhaps not on every occasion. There would be an obvious danger in allowing people to believe that they should not take the Sacrament except when they *believe themselves* to be in a state of unusual grace.

I must apologise for allowing myself to pursue the subject at such length; and I have no intention of trespassing further by provoking a reply.

With very grateful thanks,

I remain,

Your Grace's obedient servant,

[T. S. Eliot]

---

shews that what is offered in the Sacrament is something far more than this. It is real union with Christ – which must shew itself in the doing of the works of Christ.

'I have omitted your question about a Unitarian or unbaptized person. To answer this would involve a distinction between various senses of the words "Real Presence". If this means only true or genuine Presence, then I say that wherever Christian love is found there Christ is "really" present. If what is meant is "Presence as a *Res*" – i.e. the objective spiritual presence of the human nature of Christ offered in sacrifice – then I should suppose that such a worshipper neither expected nor received that; but I don't think it is possible to dogmatise negatively. What is to be noticed is that the Real Presence in the latter – strict – sense carries with it the former – more vague – sense, while this does not necessarily carry with it the other. And I have but very imperfectly received the *Res* if I have not received such love as will make me eager to win others to the experience of it.'

1 – Bishop Charles Gore (1853–1932), leading Anglican theologian; Bishop of Worcester, then Birmingham, and eventually Oxford; founder of the priestly Community of the Resurrection: see further Alan Wilkinson, *The Community of the Resurrection: A Centenary History* (1992).

I notice that Dom Vonier says: 'It would be a disastrous day for the Christian cause if, in the minds of the faithful, the Eucharistic mystery were shorn of that all-important social character, if their frequent eating of the heavenly Bread meant to them nothing but individual spiritual satisfaction, without furthering the great cause of Christ's spiritual Body, the society of the elect.' I should suppose that the participation of unbaptised persons in communion would be tolerating a kind of 'individual spiritual satisfaction' of a kind, and therefore shearing the Eucharistic mystery of its all-important social character.

TO *T. S. Gregory* CC

15 January 1935 [Faber & Faber Ltd]

Dear Mr Gregory,

I am very sorry that what I expected has happened so very much sooner than I expected it.[1] I am seriously concerned about what is to happen. Mr Faber returns tomorrow after his Christmas holiday, and I will take the first opportunity of discussing your position with him and will write to you at once, and hope to be able to make suggestions.

> With much sympathy,
> Yours sincerely,
> [T. S. Eliot]

TO *Stephen Spender* TS Northwestern

16 January 1935 Faber & Faber Ltd

Dear Stephen,[2]

I enclose a formal note giving your credit balance, as I thought you might like to have a separate statement which you could show your

---

1–Gregory wrote on 12 Jan.: 'At an interview which I had with you some time ago, you said that having written such a book as mine (*The Unfinished Universe*) I could not remain a Methodist. The Methodist authorities are now asking for my resignation and by the end of next month I shall be out of work. I am writing to ask you whether you could give me some advice as to how to begin life as a journalist, whether you know of any editors who might have some use for me . . . I do not know what kind of thing is saleable or where to try to sell it.'

2–Spender asked from Vienna, 12 Jan.: 'Perhaps, as no one ever calls me by my surname, you might adopt the "Stephen" now!'

bank.[1] Is the existence of this balance sufficient for your purposes for the moment? If you want cash let me know. I won't swear that this is exactly what is owing to you, because I have the impression that there is a small advance upon *Vienna* to be deducted. I can't find out at the moment because Stewart, who deals with such matters, is away ill, and in any case there is no need to present such details to the bank. Let me know about your cash position, and we will do all we can to help out.

I am glad you like the new *Criterion*.[2] The Valéry essay is not quite what I wanted, but the unpublished essay on Stefan George which Du Bos sent me was much too long, and also rather dull to anyone not already acquainted with George's poetry. Besides, I think Du Bos has passed his prime. His first series of *Approximations* was decidedly the best.

I will send you a book to review as soon as I can, though I may not have room in the March number. It does fill up very rapidly. I hope you have got over your feeling of depression about *Vienna*. It is a much better poem than you thought. I only felt, as I may or may not have told you, that you were a little too close to the subject matter, and that the separation of yourself from the object by a longer interval of time might have been a good thing. On the other hand, that delay would have somewhat impaired the point of immediacy as social criticism which you wished to give, so I think the best thing is to consider that poem as a successful exercise in a special kind, and get on with something else. I think that your Cape book is looked forward to with a good deal of interest, and I also look forward to the novel.

I wish that your play might have been ready sooner, not that I want in the least to press you to finish it before you are ready.[3] I expect you have heard from Wystan or someone about the projected season at the Mercury Theatre of three or four weeks, to do plays by Yeats, Auden and myself. I hope that it will come off, because I want Doone to be having something to do on a larger scale than the Group Theatre performances,

---

1 – Spender asked to be sent any money that was due to him for his book *Vienna* – 'or . . . send me a brief statement of what credit I have with Fabers. My bank has been making a fuss again.' He was in credit with both *Poems* (£19. 10. 9d) and *Vienna* (£6. 14. 11d), a total of £26. 5. 8d.

2 – Spender thought the new issue of *C.* 'the best': 'I think Canto 36 is one of the most beautiful of the Cantos; the essay on Valery, your commentary and also the discussion about Social Credit are very interesting.'

3 – 'I am working hard here, doing a sketch of this play. I shall probably put it aside when it is finished, and do the novel first, as it would be nice to publish two fairly long prose books before I do any other verse book.'

now that the latter have proved so successful. *The Chase*, in its revised form, is expected at the end of the month.[1]

Vienna (I mean the metropolis this time) sounds extremely depressing to me,[2] but I hope that there is still social warmth under the surface, at least among your own friends.

Yours ever affectionately,
T. S. E.

TO *Ezra Pound*   TS Valerie Eliot

17 January AD [1935]   Faber & Faber Ltd

ROAR Podesta ROAR, like any efficient druid, shanachie or scop:
And if you hear anyone else talking, tell him from me that I wish
                                                          him to stop.
ROAR Podesta ROAR, the only original Anglo-American wop.

Let us celebrate the Podesta's merits: they say his prick has
steel springs in it like a tape-measure,
So that it can be adjusted to fit any size or shape of cunt,
thus giving the maximum of pleasure,
Thus solving completely various problems of work and of leisure.[3]

Podesta I will try to deal with serious problems as they arise but I keep thinkin of the time Uncle Jud Calkins fell off the forty foot ladder and I cant help larfin. At the moment I have troubles of my OWN: fust place I am bein Abused by the rabble in Time and Tide (2½ pages of letters) for suggestin that if people left off gettin up prayer meetins and rallies on behalf of Peace and tried to think out the economic causes of modern war, something might be accomplished.[4] Podesta, they call me a militarist, an imbecile and a vulgar person. God dambit you think that I jest set in my rockincheer and chaw terbakker but I tell you that rockincheer has a steel back to it like Al Capone's and I have to wear steel combinations too. 2nd

1–WHA wrote in an undated letter ('~~Tuesday~~'): 'I understand that a copy of *Where is Francis?* the new version of *The Chase* has been sent to you. I hope it has arrived safely, and that you think it will do.'
2–'Vienna is covered with a thick layer of snow, which is extraordinarily impressive. It seems more dead and quiet than ever – under a white shroud.'
3–See *Poems*, ed. Ricks and McCue, II, 256.
4–Letters to the Editor, *Time and Tide* 16: 3 (19 Jan. 1935), 94–6: from A. A. Milne, Rebecca West, TSE himself (answering West's of 12 Jan.), John Brophy, N. A. Smith, George van Raalte.

place there is a dinner of the Orage Society comin off; it is bad enough havin to pay 12s. 6d. to join and go to the dinner, but worse to have to speak at it, you dont have to do that, just squat in your billets eatin macaroni or skippin down to the beach in your triangle.

Brother, the trouble with Miss Rudge is not only that she dont eat much but that she dont drink ANYTHING. Now one can understand that in Alida Monro, but I hope Miss Rudge hasnt got some secret sorrow; dont she drink with anybody or just wont she drink with me? Nevertheless, I hope she was not too bored.[1]

TP

to *The Editor,* Time and Tide[2] cc

18 January 1935   [Faber & Faber Ltd]

Sir,

In his letter in your issue of January 19th, Mr A. A. Milne[3] says that he supposed that when he had finished thinking about war, everybody would know exactly what he thought. Not knowing that Mr Milne had begun thinking about war, I did not know that he had finished. Long before I had finished reading his book, I knew what he *felt* about war; and with his feelings I have a warm sympathy. If everyone felt about war as Mr Milne does, I am convinced that we should never have war; if everyone thought as he does, I do not know what would happen.[4]

I cannot see that there is anything absurd in the question, 'Why do you consider it important that people should not lose their lives?' though I

---

1 – EP replied, 19 Jan.: 'I aint never seen her drunk at midday/ . . . but a glarrs of simple wine in the country, many a time at her table, etc. . . . . The only secret sorrow that I knows on wuz that she feared you might be bein bored but too perlite to show it/

'now with me the company is NEVER in doubt . . .

'Somthing or other/ you didn't get the gals confidence . . .'

2 – The text is taken from the issue of 26 Jan. 1935, 191, under the heading 'Mr Milne and War'. (The issue of 19 Jan. was released in advance of the official date of publication.)

3 – A. A. Milne (1882–1956), author and playwright; best known for *Winnie-the-Pooh* (1925) and *The House at Pooh Corner* (1928). A pacifist, he published in 1934 a work on *Peace with Honour*, but his stance was modified for *War with Honour* (1940).

4 – TSE, in 'Notes on the Way', *Time and Tide*, 12 Jan. 1935, challenged Milne's book *Peace with Honour* 'as an instance of . . . a frequent type of confused and insufficient thinking about war . . . I do not see how you can condemn War in the abstract unless you assert (a) that there is no higher value than Peace; (b) that there is nothing worth fighting for; and (c) that a war in which one side is right and the other wrong is inconceivable. I am prepared to admit that any number of particular wars have been unjustifiable by either side but not to admit the foregoing assumptions . . .'

dare say the 'militarist' who asked the question was an absurd person. But Mr Milne's answer, especially now that he has underlined one phrase,

—

'I think, furthermore that writers like Mr Milne suffer from two prejudices. One is that the great thing is to go on living. "If," he says, "the intelligent man of war wishes to know why death is taken so seriously by so many people, I will tell him." After this portentous preparation, Mr Milne . . . continues: "The reason is this: Death is final . . . Death is the worst thing that can happen, because it is the last thing that can happen." Well, I felicitate Mr Milne; he is haunted neither by the thought of Achilles among the shades, nor by the terrors of death that beset the Christian. "Death is final." If I thought that death was final, it would seem to me a far less serious matter than it does . . . And life would seem to me much less important than it does . . .

'The second prejudice is that Peace is a valuable state in itself: not simply because Peace gives the possibility of the amelioration of the material and spiritual state of man, but because Peace is beautiful . . . War is in itself a bad thing, we all agree. But what, as things are, is Peace?'

Milne, letter to the editor, *T&T* 16: 3 (19 Jan. 1935), 94: 'Mr Eliot says that I suffer from two prejudices. "One is that the great thing is to go on living." In order to convict me of this prejudice he quotes me as saying "Death is final." He does not mention that, when I said this, I was answering a militarist's absurd question: "Why do you consider it so important that people should not lose their lives?" He does not mention that, in case anybody was so stupid as to misunderstand me, I said six lines later: "Whatever you do to a man, if you leave him his life, you leave him, not only life, but, if he prefers it, death. If you take away his life, you leave him, *in this world*, nothing." He does not mention that the whole chapter was an argument on the theme that if the men who made war died in war, they would be less callous about the lives of others. No, he just seizes on the phrase "Death is final"; reflects comfortably on "the terrors of death that beset the Christian" (himself), but not, apparently, the agnostic (Mr Milne); tells us that, if death were final, he would be much less afraid of it than he is; assures us that it is his Christianity which makes life seem to him so very important; and in some extraordinary way supposes that all this is convicting me of attaching too much importance to life . . . When I am meeting the common military argument that anyhow a soldiers' war is more humane and gentlemanly than an economic war, I don't defend the economic system, and say that we all live happily under Peace; I point out that in the last war a million women and children died of starvation . . . I should not have considered it possible that anybody could read my book and suppose that I regarded Peace as beautiful in itself, or the social system as perfection . . . For [Eliot's] rule of life seems to be that nothing is worth doing unless you can convince yourself that there is nothing better worth doing, and as you can never do this, you had better do nothing . . .

'I should have supposed that you could (a) condemn adultery without asserting that there is no higher value than not living in adultery; (b) believe that there are things worth fighting for, and worth dying for, but *not* worth bombing babies for; and (c) condemn duelling in the abstract without asserting that a duel in which one side is right and the other wrong is inconceivable. Mr Eliot, however, will not admit any of these assumptions. And thinking like this in his third column; stating that for these reasons he cannot condemn war in the abstract; he arrives in his fourth column at the remarkable conclusion: "War is in itself a bad thing, we all agree." A bad thing, but he cannot condemn it – nor help us to make an end of it.

'So we must go on by ourselves, hoping not to distract Mr Eliot's attention "from the matters which are more urgent". It was an awareness of these matters which made me assume in my book that I felt more passionately about war than the Pope or the Archbishop of Canterbury. Mr Eliot, standing, I suppose, somewhere between these two prelates, rebukes me for my assumption.'

does seem to me absurd. 'If you take away his life, you leave him, *in this world*, nothing.' In other words, if you kill a man, you kill him. But M. de la Palisse, apparently, is not dead yet.[1]

Mr Milne presently makes an assertion, or to be more exact, a supposition, which I find a little more difficult. He says he should have supposed that you could condemn adultery without asserting that there is no higher value than not living in adultery. I should say that unless you can affirm some higher value than 'non-adultery', you have no business to condemn adultery, which in itself differs from war in being, as a rule, pleasant for both parties engaged. It is quite a different thing to assert that non-adultery is a positive value, and to assert that chastity is a positive value. You might, for the sake of argument, assert the value of non-adultery from the point of view of eugenics; you only assert the value of chastity from the point of view of religion. To complete the analogy, we might say that Mr Milne is in favour of non-war, and I am in favour of peace.

As for the belief that there are things worth fighting for, and worth dying for, but not worth bombing babies for, I should suppose that the *intent* to bomb babies was one which no practical militarist had ever cherished. I have no militarist friends, but I should suppose that most militarists would declare that intentional bombing of babies was a waste of bombs, inasmuch as they would all count upon a war being over before the babies reached fighting age. I would distinguish between intentional bombing of babies, and the bombing of some babies while aiming to hit a railway station. But if Mr Milne, and Miss West, think that I am defending unlimited warfare, they are mistaken. I only say that I dislike as much the idea of people being killed in the firing line, as behind the firing line; I object as much to the killing of men as of women and children.

The 'common military argument' that a 'soldiers' war is more humane and gentlemanly than an economic war' is of course nonsense; but not apparently to me in quite the same sense as to Mr Milne. For my point was exactly that a soldiers' war is the outcome of an economic war; I suggested that we ought to enquire more closely into the economic causes of war and try to stop *them*; but Mr Milne still ignores this point.

I am obliged to Mr Milne, at any rate, for his civility. I do not find anything in Miss West's letter that calls for comment, but there are two

---

1 – The joke derives from the epitaph of the nobleman and officer Jacques de la Palisse, or Palice (1470–1525) – '*Ci gît le Seigneur de La Palice: s'il n'était pas mort, il ferait encore envie*' ('Here lies the Seigneur de la Palice: if he weren't dead, he would still be envied') – which wags misread as '*il serait encore en vie*' ('he would still be alive'). A *palissade* is thus a statement of the obvious, a comic truism or tautology.

points in Mr Brophy's letter which need mention. Mr Brophy says that I insinuate that 'Mr Milne and those who agree with him advocate peace chiefly out of a desire for their own personal comfort and security'.[1] I meant nothing of the kind. I did suggest that peace might be more pleasant for Mr Milne (and for myself for that matter) than for some other less fortunate members of society. I was not suggesting that Mr Milne hated war because it interfered with his personal comfort and security. If the tone of his book is any indication, I am sure that Mr Milne would cheerfully lay down his own life to avert war, if that were possible. Mr Brophy then asks whether I cannot realise that 'to go on living is . . . a necessary condition of all human activity'. I do realise this. For Mr Milne had already told us that when you have killed a man, he is dead.

I am, Sir,
Your obedient servant,
T. S. Eliot

TO *Walter de la Mare* TS de la Mare Estate

18 January 1935   Faber & Faber Ltd

My dear de la Mare

I only know that Barker was in town at Christmas time.[2] He came in to see me, apparently in very good spirits, but he had just bought a new suit, bright red, with which he was extremely pleased. He had got it very cheap because the man said no one else would buy it. Furthermore, I dare say that the pleasure of having received the first instalment had not yet worn off. The first instalment included gifts amounting to £6, and since then I have secured another adherent, making the total weekly sum up to 27s. 6d.

It is very difficult to know what to do beyond this to help him. He can write a good review when the subject happens to be just the right one. I saw a rather brilliant review which he wrote on Middleton Murry's

1–John Brophy, 'T. S. Eliot's Notes on the Way' (letter to the editor), *Time and Tide* 16: 3 (19 Jan. 1935), 95–6.
2–WdlM reported on 15 Jan. that Astbury, secretary of the C. O. S., had asked him in a recent letter about Barker. 'He says: "I am still terribly worried about him. He does not seem to be able to get hold of any work. I administered a grant of £50 from the Royal Bounty. This finished at the end of January, and I am in a position to carry him on at a slightly reduced rate until March when his book is published. Do you think that when it is published, he will be on his feet?" He then suggests that living so far from London may be a hindrance to his getting reviewing and so on . . . [Astbury] doesn't seem to have heard yet about out little scheme, but this of course makes some difference in the situation.'

Blake,[1] but the trouble is that he is so very uneducated and, to judge from his own account, very much dislikes reading. I sent him to Verschoyle of the *Spectator*, but I don't think he has got any work there. He has had a little in the past from the *Listener*. I hope the situation may be changed before the end of this year. We have now undertaken to do a prose book in the autumn whether the poems succeed or not.

Personally, I was rather shocked to hear about the baby. It appears that they have disposed of the baby to be formally adopted by other people. I have no doubt that the baby is in good hands, but at the same time it is a little shocking to me that young people should not wish to make a little harder fight before surrendering their first child. Please regard this paragraph as in complete confidence.

With best wishes to Mrs de la Mare and yourself,

Yours ever,

T. S. Eliot

TO *John Garrett* CC

18 January 1935 [Faber & Faber Ltd]

Dear Mr Garrett,

I may not have made quite clear to you what it is that I want. I should like to have a longish review of Yeats, treating him primarily as a dramatist, and writing somewhat from the point of view of a producer. We have had several reviews and at least one article about Yeats all discussing him as a poet, but so far I have had no critical treatment of him as a dramatist. I cannot help hoping that your attitude will be on the whole favourable, because of the possibility of one or two of Yeats's plays being produced in London in the summer.[2] I should have liked an article, but Stephen Spender's article on Yeats is so recent that I think it is too soon to have another.[3] Then, if you will deal with Pudney, also from the dramatic point of view, to the length of 500 to 800 words, I shall be grateful for that also.[4]

Yours sincerely,

[T. S. Eliot]

---

1 – See Barker on JMM's *William Blake* in *The Twentieth Century* no. 32 (Nov. 1933), 115–16.
2 – Garrett on Yeats: C. 14 (Apr. 1935), 488–91.
3 – Spender, 'W. B. Yeats as a Realist', C. 14 (Oct. 1934), 17–26.
4 – Garrett on Pudney: C. 14 (Apr. 1935), 531–3.

TO *The Editor,* Time and Tide[1]

19 January 1935   24 Russell Square, London W.C.1

Sir,

There is one point in Miss Rebecca West's[2] letter in your issue of January 12th, which seems to me to call for an answer. I feel that Miss West fails to represent accurately the attitude of Father Herbert Thurston; so that the uninformed reader might imagine that Fr Thurston's interest in 'supernormal manifestations' was of exactly the same kind as that of Messrs Huxley or Mr Gerald Heard.[3] One does not even need to *read* Fr Thurston's books to be made aware of the difference. On the jacket of one that I have at hand are the words: 'The Church has forbidden spiritualistic practices to her children, and that her prohibition is just and wise can be seen from evidence'. And if the reader gets only as far as the Author's Preface, he will read that the three contentions of the book are as follows:

'The first is that genuine and inexplicable phenomena, – even of the physical order, do occur in the presence of certain exceptionally constituted persons called "mediums"; secondly, that for the mass of mankind, and notably for Catholics, spiritualistic practices, quite apart from the Church's prohibition, are dangerous and altogether undesirable; and, thirdly, that people have learned nothing from their attempted intercourse with the spirits of the departed – an almost inevitable result when the

1–Published *Time & Tide* 16: 3 (19 January 1935), 95.
2–Rebecca West (1892–1983) – Cicily Isabel Fairfield ('Rebecca West' was a *nom de plume*) – author and journalist, wrote for newspapers including *The Freewoman, The Star, Daily News,* and *New Statesman;* later for the *New Yorker.* Her novels include *The Return of the Soldier* (1918); her non-fiction includes *The Meaning of Treason* (1949). Made a dame in 1959, she was also a Chevalier of the Legion of Honour and a Companion of Literature.
3–West ('Mr T. S. Eliot's Notes on the Way', *Time and Tide* 16: 2 [12 Jan. 1935], 43–4) questioned TSE's 'pretensions as a thinker', especially his claim that the Church provided 'the last asylum of the true sceptic'. TSE's essay included the remark: 'And Mr Aldous Huxley, who passes for a sceptic amongst the general public, and whose intelligence and learning I greatly admire, is interested in spiritualism and ghosts. The real sceptic knows that even if one return from the dead, that will not settle the doubts of those who are not convinced by Moses and the prophets.' West countered that TSE's words obviously imply 'that Mr Huxley does not desire the name of a sceptic because he is interested in spiritualism and ghosts; but if a sceptic may not do that, how can he find an asylum in the Church, which (as the Penny Catechism will tell you) holds firmly to the belief in spirits? Even if Mr Eliot is speaking of the Anglican Church, he speaks in error, for it has never renounced this belief . . . Mr Eliot had better consult such Roman Catholic investigators of psychical research as Father Thurston, S.J., who within the Church and in the service of the Church has for many years studied supernormal manifestations.'
See Herbert Thurston, *The Church and Spiritualism* (1933).

fact is borne in mind that the identity of the supposed communicator can never be established with certainty.'

I am, etc.,

T. S. Eliot

TO *Hope Emily Allen*[1] CC

21 January 1935   [Faber & Faber Ltd]

Dear Miss Allen,

I am writing to tell you that my Board have unanimously expressed a very keen interest in your modernised version of Margery Kempe, and look forward very much to having the offer of it.[2] I gathered that all that you wanted at the present moment was to know whether we were interested or not, in as much as you are not yet in a position to make any positive proposal. Of our interest I can definitely assure you.

With all best wishes, and looking forward to hearing more definitely from you at a later date.

I am,

Yours sincerely,

[T. S. Eliot]

TO *Theodore Spencer* TS Harvard

22 January 1935   Faber & Faber Ltd

My dear Ted,

I must apologise for the delay in reporting on your manuscript, but as you know, it is a long book and it had to be read by another director as

1–Hope Emily Allen (1883–1960), Canadian scholar of medievalism, specialist in the works of Richard Rolle, and discoverer of the Book of Margery Kempe.

2–Prompted by Hope Mirrlees, Allen had written on 6 Jan. about her research work on the medieval mystic Margery Kempe, whose writings (dictated in 1436 and 1438, some of it from a copy of *c.* 1432) had lately come to light in the library of Lieutenant-Colonel W. Butler-Bowdon, DSO. The 'Book of Margery Kempe of Lynn' – Kempe was the daughter of a prominent citizen of Lynn, and had been married for many years to John Kempe, 'a worshipful burgess', bearing fourteen children, before taking a vow of chastity – combines lofty spiritual devotions with an account of her travels throughout Europe and to the Holy Land, emotional and weeping. This newly discovered text was to place her as one of the foremost mystics of the age, alongside contemporaries including St Bridget of Sweden, St Catherine of Siena, and St Joan of Arc. See Hope Emily Allen, 'A Medieval Work: Margery Kempe of Lynn' (letter), *TLS*, 27 Dec. 1934; *The Book of Margery Kempe*, trans. Anthony Bale (2015).

well as myself, and everybody has a great deal to do.[1] I enjoyed reading it, but I feel, as does the other director, that it remains a book for the scholar rather than for the general reader, and we are both definitely of opinion that it is a university press book. Therefore I am holding it for your instructions, which I presume will be to send it on to Roberts of the Cambridge Press.[2]

And may I send you a book to review for the *Criterion, Themes and Conventions of Elizabethan Tragedy* by Miss M. C. Bradbrook, which is also published by the Cambridge University Press? I won't send it until I hear from you, but I hope you will let me know in time to have the review for the June number.[3] This is also an excuse for getting a letter out of you. Have you made any plans about next summer, and has anything come of the Cambridge exchange project?

Yours ever affectionately,
Tom

With best wishes to Nancy.

TO *Messrs James & James*   cc

22 January 1935   [Faber & Faber Ltd]

Dear Sirs,

I enclose herewith Assessment for '34–'35 Tax received from H. M. Inspector this morning, and should be obliged if you could give it the favour of your immediate attention. I have not your figures before me, but I query the sum of £1,975 Lecture Fees, as I seem to have remitted only something over £1,500. It will be a considerable strain upon me to pay this year's tax in any case, and I am anxious to keep it down to what I actually owe. I cannot give you the figures for Rebate on Life Insurance; but I have these at home and not at my office.

Yours faithfully,
[T. S. Eliot]

1–Spencer had submitted 'Death and the Elizabethans' with a covering letter of 17 Oct. 1934.
2–S. C. Roberts, Cambridge University Press.
3–Not reviewed by Spencer.

TO *Harold Rosenberg*[1]

CC

23 January 1935   *[The Criterion]*

Dear Sir,

I must apologise for the inordinate delay which I have taken over your manuscript.[2] I am afraid that for a time it was mislaid, and when it was found I wished to consult the opinion of someone[3] who was more of an authority on the work of Thomas Mann than I am.

Though the essay is indeed very interesting, I doubt whether many of the readers of the *Criterion* are interested in such a highly specialised study, and I therefore return it with many regrets.

Yours very truly,
[T. S. Eliot]

TO *David T. Pottinger*[4]

CC

23 January 1935   [Faber & Faber Ltd]

Dear Mr Pottinger,

I thank you for your full explanation of the 9th instant, and am sorry to hear that the edition of my lectures has sold so badly.[5] In the circumstances, naturally, I shall be glad to waive any claim upon royalties for the present. If the book ever did sell in any considerable quantity perhaps the situation might be revised, but I see no reason to believe that it ever will.

1–Harold Rosenberg (1906–78): American writer, educator, philosopher; best known for his art criticism (later in life he would become the influential art critic of the *New Yorker*).
2–Rosenberg (New York) had submitted an essay called 'Thomas Mann and the Analogical Method' in June 1933; he asked after it on 9 Oct. 1933.
3–A. W. Randall.
4–The Secretary, Harvard University Press.
5–Pottinger wrote from Harvard University Press, in response to TSE's letter of 27 Dec. 1934 – (see www.tseliot.com) : 'At the present time there is a deficit of about $140.00 on our American edition. We have sold eleven hundred and seventy (1170) copies, have twenty-one (21) out on consignment, have distributed sixty-nine (69) review and other complimentary copies, and have two hundred and forty-seven (247) on hand. The sale of the present stock will bring us out just about even.' Did TSE desire him to take up with the Corporation the question of royalties? 'In the meantime, I might say that we have not given royalty on the American sales of any of the Norton lectures.' The record of *Gerontion* and *The Hollow Men* sold 67 copies in the year ending 30 Apr. 1935.

485

The six gramophone records have not yet arrived, but I am very much obliged to you for sending them, and for having them packed with special care.[1]

> With many thanks,
> Yours sincerely,
> [T. S. Eliot]

TO *George Barker*   TS Texas

24 January 1935   Faber & Faber Ltd

My dear Barker,

We are of the opinion that your prose book containing the *Documents of a Death* and the *Bacchant* ought to have a title which should be neither of these, but which might have some application to both. You are pretty good at titles, and I think in this case it would be difficult for anyone but the author to invent one. Will you think it over and let me have any suggestions?

> Yours sincerely,
> T. S. Eliot

TO *Walter de la Mare*   TS de la Mare Estate

24 January 1935   Faber & Faber Ltd

My dear de la Mare,

In reply to your letter of the 23rd[2] I must say that it was a complete surprise to me to learn that George Barker is getting assistance from another source. However, the overlapping is not very great. I made the first quarterly payment to him early in December, so that he will not get anything further from us until early in March. If Astbury had only promised to continue his support until March I should think that it would

---

1 – Pottinger expressed regret that the records had been found to be broken on arrival. 'We are therefore sending you six other records to replace the first shipment. I shall see that these are wrapped with especial care, and I trust they will reach you in sound condition.'

2 – De la Mare enclosed a letter just received. 'It was impossible to answer Astbury [Bernard Astbury of the Royal Literary Fund] without referring to the fact that G. B. is receiving a small allowance from a few friends – though I did not, of course, go into particulars. Did you know that the C. O. S. was sending him 30/- a week? Do you think it would be a good plan for Astbury to have a word with G. B. and to see what comes of it? It is a slightly difficult situation.'

be simplest for him to go on for the remaining weeks, if he would, without saying anything about it. After all, the sum which I am sending only represents what I could raise, and £2 a week would be nearer the sum that I should like to provide. If Astbury feels that he must stop the gratuity at once, than I see nothing to be done except for him to explain that you have told him about the other scheme. I return his letter to you herewith.

Yours ever,
T. S. Eliot

TO *Charles Williams* CC

24 January 1935 [Faber & Faber Ltd]

My dear Williams,

In reply to your letter of the 22nd instant:-[1]

1. It is true that I referred Mr Yano to you under the rights of that essay. I'd like to ask him for three guineas, but I don't believe he will pay it. This book is to be one of a series of English texts, and I think the terms he gave me are very low. I only agreed to it because it did not appear that sales of the volume were likely to interfere with my other sales. You might get a guinea out of him, but if you consider that too troublesome a sum to spend postage upon, just turn the matter over to me.

2. As for 'Shakespeare and the Stoicism of Seneca', my impression is that the rights belong to me. I think that I consulted G. B. Harrison about it as a matter of courtesy when I included it in my *Selected Essays*, so that as I consider that you have now applied to me for the right to use it, I reply that I have no objection, and would like to know what you are prepared to pay me.[2]

3. I have not yet written to thank you for your kindness in sending me *The Greater Trumps*. You know that I enjoy everything that you do in this kind, and only clamour for more. It is a thing that nobody else, so far as I know, can do at all, so I hope you will not mind when I say I don't think it is quite up to either *War in Heaven* or *The Place of the Lion*. I feel that instead of, as in the other books, seducing the reader almost without

---

1 – Williams reported that Professor K. Yano wished to reprint TSE's Introduction to Johnson's *London*, from *English Critical Essays: Twentieth Century*; but all rights in the essay rested with TSE. Also, OUP was projecting a volume on Twentieth Century Shakespeare Criticism in the World's Classics series, and wanted to include 'Shakespeare and the Stoicism of Seneca'.

2 – TSE was paid four guineas.

his knowing it from the natural into the supernatural world, you have here bumped him straight into the supernatural too violently, so that I was not either very credulous or deeply impressed by the dancing figures, although the idea behind them is a very good one. Perhaps also I find the characters, with the exception of the aunt, unsympathetic. Also (although quite irrelevant) the fact of my having been born south of the Mason and Dixon line makes me somewhat colour-conscious, so that I dislike the notion of the young lady marrying a gipsy. Besides, what have gipsies got to do with Egypt, and why should they attach so much importance to Isis and Osiris? I always thought that the generally accepted theory about gipsies was that they were a race of aboriginal Indian origin, cognate to the Tamil or Telugu tribes along the Coromandel coast. Perhaps I am wrong here.[1]

4. I have been very busy indeed this month, but, as I have told Belgion, I want to fix a date in February for a return dinner. Is any evening of the week better than any other for you?

Yours sincerely,
[T. S. Eliot]

TO *I. A. Richards*

TS Magdalene

24 January 1935   Faber & Faber Ltd

My dear Richards,

First of all, I want to know if you have seen an article on Value by one S. L. Bethell in the last *Criterion*. If so, would you be interested in replying to it? You can have all the space you want if you will let me know. If you haven't seen the *Criterion* I will send you a copy.[2]

---

1 – Williams responded on 30 Jan.: 'You are of course entirely right in most of what you say about *The Greater Trumps* and perhaps all. My own feeling was that about two-thirds of the way through the book came back instead of going in; it was a case of the super-natural that took the wrong turning. And in general I realise that there were too many loose ends. I shall try and do better when I really get down to *Descent into Hell*.'

Williams wrote to Mary Butts on 21 Feb. 1935: 'It may amuse you to know that Eliot has been reading the novels during the last year or so and wrote the other week after I had sent him *The Greater Trumps* to say that he did not like that as much as the others – like you, and you are both quite right – but that he simply ate them up and asked for more. I have always liked Eliot but for a moment I felt he was much more bright and good than I had supposed' (quoted in Nathalie Blondel, *Mary Butts: Scenes from the Life* [1998], 371).

2 – S. L. Bethell, 'Suggestions towards a Theory of Value', C. 14 (Jan. 1935), 239–50.

IAR replied (30 Jan.): 'I did read Bethell. Just why his arguments seem to me irrelevant to my suggestions & not about what I was concerned about would be a very tedious thing,

Second, are you in a position to tell us anything more about the procedure for the King's Medal?[1] Walter de la Mare seems to know nothing at all, and we have had a very unsatisfactory reply from Masefield's secretary saying that any books sent will receive attention. So far as it's either incumbent upon or free to a publisher to do anything in the matter, we naturally want to do what we can to see that our own poets satisfy the requirements.[2]

Third, Ezra Pound has suddenly waked up to Basic English, and seems to be developing an enthusiasm for it. I believe he is writing something on the subject for the *New English Weekly*, and is anxious to know whether you would be willing to write in reply, correcting any mistakes and developing the matter further.[3] I also should like to urge you to do something in the way of a short article or notes for the *New English Weekly* whenever you can. It is being edited chiefly by Philip Mairet, who, I think, is quite the best man available for the job, and I have promised to help in an advisory way, and by trying to get good contributors.[4] We are anxious to strengthen the non-political and non-economic side of the paper, which has always been very weak. I do hope you can help. I assure you that we only want the right people if we can get them.

I am very busy at present on the 'Archbishop Murder Case'.

Yours ever,

T. S. E.

I think, to try to show. And that is all I c'd do. So, with my thanks, *no*; I won't reply.'

1 – IAR was serving on the committee chaired by the Poet Laureate John Masefield to award the King's Gold Medal for Poetry: first offered for the year 1933, to be awarded in 1934.

2 – IAR (30 Jan.): 'I think I know *all* about the procedure for the King's Medal and that there isn't any. No submitting or anything. I don't think you need be uneasy. The only risk any publisher (or poet) runs is that the book won't come into the field of attention of any of the judges at a moment when the judge is awake & taking notice! But you need hardly fear that . . .'

3 – EP, 'Debabelization and Ogden', *NEW* 6: 20 (28 Feb. 1935), 410–11.

4 – Mairet was to recall TSE at the editorial committees of *NEW*: 'He gave his complete attention to what was submitted to him; and you knew it, though his comments were usually brief, even laconic. His words were not subject to the usual discount for politeness or the desire to be encouraging' (*Philbeach Quarterly*, summer 1965; cited in Ackroyd, *T. S. Eliot*, 221).

26 January 1935   [Faber & Faber Ltd]

Sir,

I have to thank you yet a third time for giving Miss Rebecca West the hospitality of your columns. But this time I am not so thankful to Miss West, since she has finally said something[2] to which I must reply. She scores this success by making an allegation: to the effect that I have accused her of dishonesty.[3] She says that my phrases 'seek to suggest' that she has not read the works of Father Thurston. I never dreamt of such a thing: I only sought to suggest that perhaps Miss West had read them without quite understanding them.

I am inclined to believe that my suspicions have some foundation. Miss West says that I remark in dispraise of Mr Huxley's interest in psychical phenomena that it would be of no importance whether psychical phenomena were established or not, and she says that Fr Thurston is evidently not of the same opinion. Well; the effect of Fr Thurston's writings on my mind is to persuade me that psychical phenomena are *not* important; and I should have thought that that was what he intended. But I do not know Fr Thurston, and Miss West has interviewed him.[4] I have it from a mutual friend[5] that Fr Thurston has never attended a *séance*; perhaps Fr Thurston did not have time to tell Miss West that. One's imagination runs riot (to use the kind of phrase that flows from Miss West's pen under inspiration and circumstances of unusual difficulty) in wondering what *was* said at that interview. Did Miss West, I wonder, tell Fr Thurston that he was a 'most charming and contented ornament of the Church'?[6] and was Fr Thurston charmed by and contented with Miss West? We may never know.

1–Published in abbreviated form in *Time & Tide*, 2 Feb. 1935, 155.
2–As published: 'has said something'.
3–Sentence not in published version.
4–West, 'Mr T. S. Eliot's Notes on the Way' (letter), *Time and Tide* 16: 4 (26 Jan. 1935), 123–4. West claimed that she had met Fr Thurston with a view to discussing the contents of his books – though she does not proceed to cite any evidence at all from such personal encounters with Fr Thurston. She goes on immediately: 'What is significant is that there is not the smallest suspicious fact in my argument which would have given Mr Eliot grounds for his assumption. It is a purely gratuitous attempt to bolster up the Eliot legend of the Great White Literary Spirit who, all-wise and happy in having read not only all the books that have been written but that are going to be written, broods in solitary grieved majesty over a literary world, the only other inhabitants of which are barely literate, imbecile, and wholly unacquainted with literature . . .'
5–Presumably Hope Mirrlees, from whom TSE borrowed the book.
6–The remainder of this paragraph, from 'and was', not used in published version.

As for my own honesty, which Miss West impugns,[1] I leave that for others to judge. In her first epistle, Miss West suggested that, after saying that 'it is better to suspend decision than to surrender oneself to a belief merely for the sake of believing something', I ought to dissociate myself from the doctrine of Charles Maurras and all the Action Française group, who 'blatantly recommend that France should practise Catholicism whether she believed it or not, for the sake of the unifying power of religion'.[2] Miss West did not pause to point out that to surrender oneself to a belief for the sake of believing something, is not the same thing as practising a religion without believing it; nor did she mention[3] the possibility that I supported Maurras and the Action Française group for some other reason than what she calls their 'blatant recommendation'. But perhaps I am asking too much of human honesty, especially in the warmth of controversy. If Miss West would come up and see me some time,[4] I should enjoy talking these matters over quietly.

I should like to dissociate myself from the 'Eliot legend' which Miss West (still writing, I suppose, under circumstances of unusual difficulty) accuses me of 'gratuitously' trying to 'bolster up'. As for the 'powerful flood of suggestion that has been turned on us in England during the last twenty years', I admire Miss West as a sort of Mount Ararat, the first to rear her majestic head from the subsiding waters. But perhaps Miss West was never submerged at all: in which case I admire her still more, and am happy to regard her as[5] 'that most charming and contented ornament' of the Ark, Mrs Noah.

I am, Sir,
Your obliged obedient servant,
[T. S. Eliot]

P.S. I again call your attention to the misprint *voleuntade* for *volontate*, repeated in Miss West's quotation, which I mentioned in the footnote,

---

1 – As published: 'which Miss West does not seem to think highly of'.
2 – West had concluded her letter published on 12 Jan.: 'The only encouragement I find in Mr Eliot's article is the sentence: "It is better to suspend decision than to surrender oneself to a belief merely for the sake of believing something." That is a point of view many of us have been urging on Mr Eliot for some time, and we must all be glad to see that he is adopting it. But had he not better dissociate himself from the doctrine of Mr Charles Maurras and all the Action Française group, who blatantly recommend that France should practise Catholicism whether she believed it or not, for the sake of the unifying power of a religion? He has certainly spoken kindly enough of them in the past.'
3 – As published: 'entertain'.
4 – A popular misrendering of a saucy line spoken by Mae West, as 'Diamon Lil', in the movie *She Done Him Wrong* (1933): 'Why don't you come up some time, and see me.'
5 – As published: 'admire her still more as'.

which you did not print, to my last letter.[1] If you print Miss West's postscripts, won't you please print mine too?[2]

TO *Ernest Bird, Messrs Bird & Bird*   CC

26 January 1935   [Faber & Faber Ltd]

My dear Bird,

Thank you for your letter of the 23d.[3] The shock is not very great; I had anticipated that it would be over £150; so I hope that the shock of learning that I cannot pay immediately will not be very great either. I have had to pay out over £1600 to Somerset House since my return from America, and I have another £180 to account for to them in June. James & James, I am glad to say, have finally accepted £52: 10s. in final settlement from me, without prejudice to their claim against Mrs Eliot: so that I have ended my business with them for a total of £127: 10s. It will take a little time for the well to fill up to its normal level; and I cannot do much until the latter part of the year; but I shall try to make a token payment quite soon.

1–*Paradiso* III, 85: '*e la sua volontate è nostra pace*' ('in his will is our peace'). See 'Shakespeare and the Stoicism of Seneca' (1927): 'When Dante says *la sua voluntade e nostra pace* it is great poetry, and there is a great philosophy behind it. ' 'I like this passage because it seems to me to express, better than any other lines of Dante or of any other poet, one of the greatest ideas of the Christian religion' ('My Favourite Passage from Dante', 1928). '[T]he statement of Dante seems to me *literally true*. And I confess that it has more beauty for me now, when my own experience has deepened its meaning, than it did when I first read it' (*Dante*, 1929). To Laurence Binyon, 28 Apr. 1941: 'I am flattered that you should want my opinion about Sua Voluntade. I should think it was one of the most difficult things to translate in the whole Commedia: partly because it is one of the few lines that everybody knows, and therefore no translation of it can come with such a bang as to satisfy the reader. By itself, I do prefer just "in his will is our peace" which is what 99 readers out of 100 will expect and want: but how you are to fill out the line I don't know, unless you can append an extension, or begin the following line.'
2–Final sentence not used in published version.
3–'I have purposely deferred replying to your letter of the 14th inst. Until I was able to comply with your kind request and send you – as I now do – a statement of your indebtedness to my firm in respect of their fees and disbursements amounting, in all, to £177. 16. 6 – including, of course, the previously rendered bill. To be frank, the amount is as alarming to me as no doubt it will be to you. At the same time, I think that I may fairly say that you have been treated with consideration. No one knows better than you do the work and complications that have been involved in the state of affairs with which we were compelled so unfortunately to deal. I can only assure you without reservation that my firm are not pressing creditors and that you may discharge the account by instalments or otherwise at your leisure.'

I will send you notes for a new Will shortly; and I sincerely hope that I shall not have to require any other legal aid from you until my account is cleared.

With many thanks for your indefatigable exertions,

Yours very sincerely,

[T. S. Eliot]

TO *T. S. Gregory* CC

28 January 1935   [Faber & Faber Ltd]

Dear Mr Gregory,

I have been thinking over your affairs since I wrote to you last. I feel strongly that journalism is an occupation to be considered only as an avocation to add to one's income, but not as a profession to be pursued. I will gladly give you letters of introduction to any editors whom I know, with a view to reviewing books. Apart from this kind of journalism I know hardly anyone connected with the daily press. The life of a reviewer is a hard one, and further than that, it is not possible by reviewing to make the whole of the necessary minimum to live upon, and the lower types of journalism, I imagine, are occupied by men of far less culture and education, who have begun early in life.

My natural suggestion would be work as a schoolmaster; possibly also Extension Lecturing. Have you thought of either of these careers?

You probably know that the Roman Catholic Church has an organisation for assisting converts who have previously been clergymen of other denominations, and whose conversion therefore deprives them of their livelihood. I do not know, of course, how soon you will be in a position to make any claims upon this society, but I should think they could judge each case on its own merits.

Meanwhile, however, if you want reviewing work, I wish you would let me have both a list of your qualifications and of the kinds of book which you feel best fitted to review, and also a short biographical note, giving such facts about your education and activity as are pertinent for editors to know, or would recommend you to their attention.

With all sympathy,

Yours sincerely,

[T. S. Eliot]

TO *James Hanley*

28 January 1935   [*The Criterion*]

Dear Mr Hanley,

Many thanks for your story.[1] It is a good story and all right as to length. My only regret is that I would rather have a story of a type which you seem to me to do better than anything else, rather than something which is merely good in a type of fiction which many people write. Nevertheless, I want to keep this and use it, unless you write anything in the meantime which you would prefer me to use, as being more typical of your work.

Yours sincerely,
[T. S. Eliot]

TO *Joseph Gordon Macleod*

28 January 1935   [Faber & Faber Ltd]

Dear Mr Macleod,

Thank you for your letter of the 26th.[2] There was no irony intended. I quite agree with you that poetic drama must be created in the theatre, and I am sure that your methods are right. I do not expect very much of either Auden or myself in the way of dramatic merit, as we have both had so little dramatic experience. My point was, however, just that your play did seem to me an acting rather than a reading play. The plays we are publishing will probably read a good deal better than they will act, but I am looking at the matter from the point of view of the publisher, not that of the dramatic writer, and my attitude toward your play, and that of the

---

1–Hanley had met TSE on Thurs. 3 Jan. 1935, and submitted on 9 Jan. a 'short MS': 'A Changed Man', C. 14 (Apr. 1935), 374–8.
2–'I suppose the irony was unintentional – or was it a hint? A week or two after receiving your rejection of my plays on the ground that they were acting plays, arrived your spring list, advertising plays by yourself and Auden.

'As a poet of repute I cannot claim equality with you nor priority with him. But as a playwright I do register the most emphatic and earnestly-worded protest. *Sub specie aeternitatis.*

'If poetic drama is to be what I believe it must be, it must be done by theatre means, not by literary ones. There are plenty of poets about, and more than a few would-be dramatic ones. But there are very few dramatists and no poetic ones, except myself.

'Auden is trying to do what I am trying to do, but crudely, ignorantly, and remotely. Studying the arty movements of studios does not make a dramatist. Theatre sense must be in the blood from long practice: as with all the great dramatists of history, European, British, or Japanese.'

other director who read it, was dictated by the doubt of its commercial success as a published book. It involved no comparison whatever between your dramatic abilities and those of Auden or myself.

Yours sincerely,

[T. S. Eliot]

TO *E. Martin Browne*   CC

28 January 1935   [*The Criterion*]

My dear Browne,

Thinking the matter over afterward, I think I may have given you the impression that I was personally keener on letting Ashley Dukes[1] and Doone do that job than I really am. My feeling is that in the long run it might be more to my personal advantage, to say nothing of any other consideration, to have the first production one which I know I can rely upon, and which will have the further advantage of Miss Fogerty. This, I think, really outweighs the temporary advantage of having it in London, where more people will see it. My only real motive is that I was touched by Doone's appeal, as he made it appear a vital matter for his company.[2]

I am taking the liberty of sending you herewith a small Church play, to ask the favour of your opinion. I have not read it, and do not know who the author is. It comes to me through a friend of the author, who says that the author is a vicar somewhere, who has produced it with success in his own parish, and would like to get it taken up elsewhere. I should be grateful for your candid opinion on its value and prospects, and for any suggestions as to what could be done with it.

Yours ever,

[T. S. Eliot]

1–Ashley Dukes (1885–1959), theatre manager, playwright, critic, translator, adaptor, author: see further, letter to him, 1 Oct. 1935.
2–EMB replied, 31 Jan.: 'I was afraid, the very grudging admission I made of the possibility of using Miss Haffenden has been seized upon eagerly; & I don't think we can hope to get them off this track unless Doone does the play with Miss Pearce and hires us the costumes.'

29 January 1935   [Faber & Faber Ltd]

Dear Miss Babington,

I have lately been approached by Mr Ashley Dukes and Mr Rupert Doone in connexion with a projected season of three weeks in May at the Mercury Theatre, Notting Hill, of verse plays by W. B. Yeats, W. H. Auden and myself. I have no old piece that they could use except a fragmentary play which only takes twenty-five minutes. They are therefore very anxious to have permission to perform for four nights the play of which the Canterbury play will be a reduced version.

I should not feel any strong enthusiasm for this on personal grounds, but they have put it in a way that makes it difficult to refuse. I have been a supporter of Rupert Doone's Group from the beginning, a group of earnest young people anxious to dedicate themselves to poetic drama. They have lately attracted a good deal of favourable notice to themselves by doing my *Sweeney Agonistes* fragments, and Doone feels, rightly I think, that they must either go forward at once to something more ambitious, or fail. The season with Dukes is a great opportunity for him; and he is convinced, rightly or wrongly, that a few nights of a new full length piece by me would just make the difference between success and failure. He may not feel the same about it when he sees the text; however, he has made a most touching appeal to me to let them have it for a run of four nights. He feels that the whole future of his company depends upon it. I should like to give him all the help I can. They are convinced that this could not have an adverse effect upon the success of the play in Canterbury; especially as their theatre is very small, holding only 150 audience, and rather out of the way; and also as the two versions of the play will have different names.²

---

1 – Margaret A Babington, Hon. Steward and Treasurer, Friends of Canterbury Cathedral: Hon. Festival Manager for the Festival of Music and Drama, 15–22 June 1935. Browne, *Making* 58: 'This remarkable woman had been chosen by George Bell as steward and treasurer of the Friends when he founded them. She was the daughter of a retired clergyman living in the Precincts, and had had a long experience of upholding her eccentric widower-father in the care of a large country-town parish. She was tall, trim and dignified, with a tremendous dynamic energy, but also with a keen sense of humour and the voice of a young girl. Throwing herself with unsparing dedication into the service of the cathedral, she had gathered 1430 Friends within a year, and 4000 by the time of *Murder in the Cathedral*.'
2 – The Mercury Theatre accommodated only 130 people; the proscenium was 18 feet wide by 8 feet high, and the stage was just 11 feet 6 inches in depth. (The theatre features in the movie *The Red Shoes* (1948), by Michael Powell and Emeric Pressburger.)

I should like to know, however, how Canterbury feels about it. One possible advantage would be that it might settle the question of costumes; I would see that they got proper costumes, which they would be willing to let Canterbury use (I should see to that too) for the Festival. I should doubt whether the rather sombre costumes (for the most part) that I should want would be of much use for any other play.

Yours sincerely,
[T. S. Eliot]

TO *George Yeats*[1]   CC

1 February 1935   [Faber & Faber Ltd]

My dear Mrs Yeats,

I am very sorry to hear that your husband has been ill; indeed, I had heard it from another source before you wrote, and I hope that it is not serious.[2] Yes, I do know what he means by 'that Upanishad'. As a matter of fact, however, I had much rather publish the Upanishad in June than in March, as I find I have already too much for the earlier issue, and it will be very inconvenient even to add a short Upanishad. Besides, I should like Mr Yeats's preface to be as long as he [is] willing to make it. Do you think that he would be ready to concur, and find the later date more convenient? If not, I really ought to have the preface at once. I think on the whole I should prefer it if he were willing to write a little more, and let me have it by the end of April.[3]

Please give him my best wishes for a speedy recovery.

Yours sincerely,
[T. S. Eliot]

1–Bertha Georgie ('George') Yeats, née Hyde Lees (1892–1968), married W. B. Yeats in 1917. See W. B. Yeats and George Yeats, *The Letters*, ed. Ann Saddlemyer (2011).

2–Mrs Yeats wrote on 29 Jan. to say that her husband, who was ill, wanted to know the latest date by which he could send his essay on 'that Upanishad'. 'He says that you will know what he means by "that Upanishad".'

3–Mrs Yeats responded on 8 Feb. to say that WBY would submit his preface to 'that Upanishad' by the end of Apr. Yeats, 'Mandookya Upanishad', C. 14 (July 1935), 547–56.

TO *E. Martin Browne*   CC

Dear Browne,

This is very mysterious. Miss Babington's letter arrived just when I was expecting a reply from her to my letter sounding her feelings about the other production. I assumed that for some reason she was writing about it to you instead of to me, and I am still waiting for a reply from her to my letter.

The letter you enclose is very depressing, and comes at a time when I am already a little depressed at the idea of being involved in the other venture, so that I feel as if I was between the two grind stones, or mill stones, or whatever they are. I don't feel that the introduction of the Colonel's lady is a happy augury either. However, we can't do anything more about the costumes until I hear from her myself. It may be that her interest in Miss Haffenden will make the other proposal have a still less, rather than a greater appeal to her.[1]

Many thanks for your instructions about the *Man and Everyman* which I will pass on.[2]

As to that proposal about *The Rock*, emanating from West Virginia, Shaw suggests the simplest thing would be for us to put our interests in the hands of Miss Fassett.[3]

That seems to me a good idea, which might save us a lot of trouble. I don't know what Miss Fassett's present name is, but I believe she is at the same address.

                              Yours ever,
                              [T. S. Eliot]

P.S. I have forgotten one thing. I am sending you the first 396 lines of the Archbishop, and hope to send you more in a few days' time. This should

1–Margaret Babington wrote to EMB, 29 Jan. 1935: 'I was very glad . . . to find that you and Mr Eliot more or less favour the idea of Miss [Lettice] Haffenden for the costumes. It will be an enormous help to me personally . . . I believe that when Mr Eliot came here I did mention to him that we had one very good actress here, who played the leading lady with Laurence Irving's father. She is the wife of Colonel Findlay, and a charming person. I wondered whether she could be the eleventh lady with ten of Miss Fogerty's pupils.' She asked too to be told the title of the play once chosen. Rachel Field wrote to F&F (n.d.: early 1964): 'Lettice Haffenden and I were members of St Stephen's Gloucester Rd. when he was Churchwarden there and she was in the original cast of Murder in the Cathedral when we were students at the Central School.'
2–EMB found *The Man and Everyman* 'an admirable scenario for a church pageant-production of the strictly devotional kind', and recommended sending it to the Religious Drama Society.
3–Dorothea Fassett, Managing Director of the London Play Company.

be about half of Act I. You must remember that it will be longer than you will want, as I have to make a pretty full length play to fulfil my contract with my firm. The full length should be between sixteen and eighteen hundred lines, and as I don't suppose it could be acted at the rate of 20 lines a minute, it must be cut down. That I shall leave to you, but the cutting down will be the least of our troubles. I feel that so far it not only tends to be stationary, but that I am apt to overlook the importance of the visual effect of scenes.

TO *A. L. Rowse*   TS Faber

1 February 1935   Faber & Faber Ltd

Dear Rowse,

Thank you for sending Hudson's essay, which I have read. My chief criticism is that from the point of my interest there is rather too much Spengler and not enough Toynbee. I am, of course, in sympathy with the point of view. By the way, the essay seems to end rather abruptly with a quotation about the breakdown of irrigation in Ceylon. I suppose, however, that there is no page missing? I shall use the essay as soon as I can, but the next issue is already complete.

By the way, I should like to call your attention to the current number of a paper called *Time and Tide*, in connexion with your essay, over which we had some discussion. I had merely been trying to point out to sentimental pacifists like Mr A. A. Milne that the most important practical step to take against war was to investigate its economic causes, and attempt to control them. It is amazing that this kind of people seemed to regard such an attitude as a form of militarism.[1]

Yours ever,
T. S. E.

1 – See too *The Idea of a Christian Society* (1939), 73–4, 98: 'I cannot but believe that the man who maintains that war is in all circumstances wrong, is in some way repudiating an obligation towards society . . . Even if each particular war proves in turn to have been unjustified, yet the idea of a Christian society seems incompatible with the idea of absolute pacifism; for pacifism can only continue to flourish so long as the majority of persons forming a society are not pacifists . . . The notion of communal responsibility, of the responsibility of every individual for the sins of the society to which he belongs, is one that needs to be more firmly apprehended; and if I share the guilt of my society in time of "peace", I do not see how I can absolve myself from it in time of war, by abstaining from the common action . . .'
'And I believe that modern war is chiefly caused by some immorality of competition which

TO *Maria Huxley*   CC

2 February 1935   [Faber & Faber Ltd]

My dear Maria,

I am not social [?anti-social] in the least, and I will not put up with such insinuations and taunts.[1] Wednesday I always have a committee beginning at one, and on Tuesday of next week I have another committee, which is lunching in order to economise [on] time. I am very sorry not to see you before you depart, but do please let me know when you return from Dartington. I have so far no engagements.

Yours ever,
[T. S. E.]

TO *George Every*[2]   TS George Every

2 February 1935   Faber & Faber Ltd

Dear Brother George,

Thank you for your letter of the 30th. Your review has gone straight to the printer, and I look forward to reading it in proof. From what you say about your attitude in your letter, I should think it ought to be right. I hoped for a review which would praise More's great work without ignoring the occasional slips and errors. Besides, More is the sort of man who is never too old to learn.[3]

------

is always with us in times of "peace"; and that until this evil is cured, no leagues or disarmaments or collective security or conferences or conventions or treaties will suffice to prevent it.'
1–Maria Huxley wrote from E2, Albany, Piccadilly, London, on a postcard postmarked 31 Jan.: 'Sorry you *arent* social – Monday is no good for Aldous as he has an early afternoon engagement – I shall write again when we return from Dartington . . .'
2–George Every (1909–2003), historian and poet. Educated at the University College, Exeter (where he was tutored by Christopher Dawson), he joined in 1929 the Anglican theological college, House of the Sacred Mission, at Kelham, where he lived until 1973. His works include *Christian Discrimination* (1940) and *The Byzantine Patriarchate* (1947); and articles and reviews in periodicals including *Eastern Churches Review* (of which for a time he was editor). Converting in 1973 to Roman Catholicism, he lived at St Mary's College, Oscott (seminary of the Archdiocese of Birmingham). His friends included Charles Williams, C. S. Lewis, Norman Nicholson and Kathleen Raine. See George Every, S.S.M., 'T. S. Eliot 1888–1965', *I.C.F. [Industrial Christian Fellowship] Quarterly*, Apr. 1965, 8–11; 'Recollections of Charles Williams and Eliot', *Mythprint: The Monthly Bulletin of the Mythopoeic Society* (Whittier, California), 2: 4 (Apr. 1975), 2–3. TSE considered Every 'a charming and saintly young man'.
3–Every wrote of his review of Paul Elmer More: 'I like the book enormously, and it is very difficult to balance appreciation and criticism in a review of this kind. But I do not think it

I have been thinking over your discussion with Reckitt, and have been feeling rather inclined to take a hand in it myself.[1] On further consideration I may not feel that there is any place for my intervention. My first impression is that I am somewhere between you and Reckitt, or at least that I should want to add certain qualifications and safeguards against either point of view. In any case, I shouldn't be able to take the matter up seriously until April or May, so that my entry might possibly be too late.

I am interested in what you say about the S.C.M. series. Will you ask Fenn[2] if he could send me the issues as they appear, or is it something to which I ought to subscribe? I take in so many things already, most of which I don't have time to read, that I am not anxious to subscribe to more. I am very sorry for your news about Geoffrey Parks. On the other hand I should like to know how far Norman Hester's operation has been successful.[3]

I hear from all sides that the Hopkins letters are extremely good. The more actual knowledge we have about Hopkins the better, as without that

---

would be right to evade the issue and ignore the unorthodoxies, however convinced one may be that they are not central to his thought.' Review of *The Sceptical Approach to Religion: New Shelburne Essays* II: *C.* 14 (Apr. 1935), 494–6.

1 – 'I heard from Maurice Reckitt the other day that David Peck, Fr Demant's curate, is answering me in the March *Christendom* . . . I have written a very short letter of protest against being made into an empiricist for ever and a day . . .

'We must see what David Peck's article is like. Being younger than the Committee people, and not without intelligence and sensitiveness, he may be very much more reasonable than Reckitt when writing on the raw. (Not that M. B. R. isn't reasonable enough in private!) But if he is worth replying to I wish you would do it rather than Charles Smyth.'

2 – The Revd J. Eric Fenn (1899–1995): presbyterian minister, ecumenist and broadcaster; editor of *The Student Movement* (published by the Student Christian Movement of Great Britain and Ireland, which Fenn joined as assistant general secretary in 1926). From 1936 he worked with the ecumenist J. H. 'Joe' Oldham, helping to organise the important Oxford conference on 'Church, Community, and State', and participating in the meetings of Oldham's 'Moot', 1938–47. From 1939 he was assistant director of religious broadcasting for the BBC; literary editor for the British and Foreign Bible Society, 1947–56. See further K. M. Wolfe, *The Churches and the British Broadcasting Corporation, 1922–1956: The Politics of Broadcast Religion* (1984); *The Moot Papers: Faith, Freedom and Society, 1938–1947*, ed. K. Clements (2010).

3 – 'The S.C.M. series. You'll be interested possibly to hear more of that. I did the introduction myself eventually – terribly cramped for space; but I liked it, and afterwards at least one S.C.M. secretary liked it. The Lawrence article is put off until March, which is rather trying . . . I come back in June to do Joyce and sum up. Unhappily Geoffrey Parks has been "invalided" out of the series. There is nothing at present seriously wrong but his health is giving a good deal of cause for anxiety again . . . Norman Hester is back and catching up well.'

he is likely to remain a mere peg for biassed [*sic*] theories. The publication of the Journals in the autumn will be a help also.

I hope that you will shake off your cold quickly, but I don't think of Kelham as the easiest place to get well in. I shall defer discussion of your poetry until you can send me the other poem which your cold has postponed.

Yours very sincerely,
T. S. Eliot

TO *Stephen Spender*   TS Northwestern

2 February 1935   Faber & Faber Ltd

My dear Stephen,

Not being able to answer your letter of the 18th at once, I waited until about the date that you said you expected to be back.[1] Please let me know of your return, and come and lunch again as soon as you can. I should like to hear more of what you are doing. I quite agree with your diagnosis of the failure of Yeats to find a successful medium, the result of which is that he remains a lyric poet in the theatre.[2] I am afraid that his difficulty is the same that we shall all find, and it is really impossible to know whether one has found a suitable kind of verse until one has heard actors deliver it. One's own reading of it is no clue.

Yours ever,
Tom

1 – SS wrote from Vienna: 'I have done some of the play, and I am doing some short stories. I have also sketched the opening of a novel. I shall not work intensely at the novel until I have finished the play. My idea is to write a book called *The Liberal Cage*, a title which excites & amuses me. It is founded on *The Temple*. I want to do a very full study of the completely free life made possible by the liberal idea of free individuality – that is free for a few people. That's what *The Temple* really was getting at, though it wasn't formulated.'

2 – 'I read all of Yeats's plays a few weeks ago. I think his history as a playwright is simply the history of his failure with blank verse, and his failure to find any other medium. Perhaps Auden may find the medium, but much as I like *The Chase* [by Auden], it doesn't offer any solution of the problems that bother me in my own style.'

TO *The Editor,* Time and Tide

[published 9 February 1935, 191]   [Faber & Faber Ltd]

Sir,

As Mr Milne continues to involve himself, like a cat in fly-paper, in comparisons or analogies which he cannot control; as he is impervious to irony; and as he consistently misses the point, I shall content myself with re-stating briefly what I meant the main point to be.[1]

I did not criticise Mr Milne's book from pure love of destruction, but from a belief that essays like his are harmful in so far as they distract people's minds from more practical effort to minimise the chances of war. I pointed out that, instead of inveighing against War in general, we should do better to study the causes of the particular kind of war which we should be likely to have in contemporary circumstances. I believe the causes of modem wars to be largely, even preponderantly, economic; and I suggested that we ought to try to modify the world economy, beginning with our own, in order to do away, for instance, with the 'struggle for markets'. The ultimate cause for War may indeed reside in human passions; but these passions operate through a long series of interests. I think that the passion for fighting and the motive of hatred are quite secondary among the causes of modem war. If Mr Milne, like Lady Rhondda, is quite satisfied by Mr Huxley's intelligent but superficial reflexions on the conflicts of Central America, there is no more to be said.[2]

1 – For Milne's letter of 19 Jan., see notes to TSE to *Time and Tide*, 18 Jan., above.

Milne's next letter appeared on 2 Feb. 1935, 154: 'It is all very difficult. The question is asked (absurd to me, intelligent to Mr Eliot): "Why do you think it so important that people should not lose their lives?" I make the only possible answer: "Because death is final" – i.e. the end of human activity . . .

'And I should not have thought it necessary to explain to anybody but Mr Eliot that my book was an enquiry into the way to end war, not the way to improve Peace; nor should I expect anybody but Mr Eliot to announce this fact with an air of discovery a week after I had specially called his attention to it. For Mr Eliot said in his article that I suffered from the mistaken prejudice that Peace was a valuable state in itself; I replied in my letter: "I have made it perfectly clear throughout the book that by 'Peace' I simply mean 'Not-war'; and now he announces as climax to a paragraph of triumphant reasoning: 'Mr Milne is in favour of non-war, and I am in favour of peace.' And where in the world does he think he has arrived – except at the "mistaken prejudice", of which, simultaneously, he acquits me and accuses himself, that Peace is valuable.'

2 – Lady Rhonnda, editor of *Time and Tide*, wrote on 2 Feb. 1935, 150: 'I am not going to pretend that I am on Mr Eliot's side in respect of the hornets' nest he has brought about his ears by his article on Mr Milne's *Peace with Honour*. Mr Eliot has not convinced me. I still believe that the elimination of war and the fear of war is the task laid upon our generation.'

She goes on: 'Aldous Huxley . . . in an analysis of the pleasure of national hatred, which is the best thing of its kind I have yet read (he and Heaven alone know why he has entitled it

Mr Milne says, in rejoinder to Miss Mary Butts: 'there is not one single page in my book which indicates whether I do or do not believe in individual immortality'.[1] This is a very significant omission; and I am glad that Mr Milne has called attention to it. The fact that Mr Milne does not realise its significance only makes it more significant.

I am grateful to Mr Edwards for correcting me: I could not remember how *Palice* was spelt. I was indeed referring to the *vérité de la Palice* rather than to the gallant officer, of whose death I had heard. I must call Mr Edwards' attention, however, to the difference between a *truism* and a *tautology*.

> I am, Sir,
> Your obedient servant,
> [T. S. Eliot]

"Guatemala City" and embedded it in the middle of travel notes in *Beyond the Mexique Bay*), follows Norman Angell in so far as he points out once more that war never pays . . . and seems to suggest that since, as every honest thinker must admit, economic interests are all against war, it must follow that all that any nation ever gets out of war is gratification of the pleasure of national vanity and hatred.' She hails Huxley's chapter on Guatemala City as 'so extraordinarily fresh, vivid and illuminating'.

TSE would write to *Time & Tide*, 26 July 1958: 'I hope and believe that the death of Viscountess Rhondda will not bring to an end so valuable a periodical as *Time and Tide*, but her death does seem to mark the end of an epoch . . . I have been a reader of *Time and Tide* for more years than I can remember; I had been impressed by the integrity and independence of its Proprietor and Editor long before I had met Viscountess Rhondda herself.

'Many who knew her will have spoken of her kindness, of her hospitality . . . of the wide scope of her interests, and of her passionate sense of public responsibility.'

1 – Mary Butts, in a letter to *Time and Tide*, 26 Jan. 1935, 124, argued against Milne and in favour of TSE: 'Surely the only valid arguments, for and against pacifism, depend entirely on the question of individual immortality. What significance worth two pins has human life without it? . . . [M]an must not sacrifice too much for mere safety or mere comfort. (While, since we are all going to die, there are worse deaths – and here death is Mr Milne's point – than death in battle.)

'But, as Mr Eliot hints, the question of a change in world-behaviour as implied by pacifism cannot wholly be argued without its religious implications.'

Milne wrote in his letter to *T&T*, 2 Feb.: 'As for Miss Mary Butts, I hardly know what to say to her. There is not one single page in my book which indicates whether I do or do not believe in individual immortality. I gather from Miss Butts that if, privately, I do believe in it, then the arguments in the book are valid; if not, not. It seems odd. Does she apply her test equally to arguments about flogging, capital punishment, the provision of lifeboats on liners, and the inspection of collieries? I suppose so. As I began by saying, it is all very difficult.'

See Milne's final letter reiterating his position on 16 Feb. 1935, 237–8.

5 February 1935   [Faber & Faber Ltd]

Dear Sirs,

I am writing to inform you that the books, pictures, and two other objects were delivered to my private address this morning, satisfactorily.

For regularity's sake I will point out what I know to be missing. I have a number of my small pictures, but not all: I remember photographs, or photographs of portraits, of my grandfather, the Revd William Greenleaf Eliot, my sister Marian Eliot, my greatgrandmother Priscilla Cushing, as well as Sir T. Eliot and Sir J. Eliot (the last don't matter). What is more serious is the absence of a considerable section of my books. I had a considerable library of French books, paper-bound; literature, theology, politics and history; including a very pretty collection of books dealing with the Condemnation of the Action Française in 1926 which I believe to be unique in England, and in particular one book borrowed from a French friend which I wanted to return to him as it is irreplaceable having been suppressed at the instance of the Vatican. These books in French I kept all together: not one of them has come, only a few French books in outsizes which had been scattered among my other books.

Incidentally, I have a few of my wife's books among the lot, which will have to be returned to her. In the present confusion, I cannot tell whether I have all my English and other books; but I should not think many could be missing. I shall take the first opportunity of opening the cupboard at the warehouse; but from what the man said about its light weight I do not believe for a moment that it could contain the missing French books, which should number a couple of hundred or so. I thought that I ought to let you know about this defect, in case you think it advisable to notify Broad that I am not satisfied. The pictures can probably be replaced; the books cannot.[1]

Yours sincerely,

[T. S. Eliot]

1 – Higginson (Bird & Bird) responded, 11 Feb.: 'I saw Mr Broad on Friday last and further discussed with him the position with regard to your missing books and other articles of property. As I anticipated, I found him very ready to do all that he can to assist . . . Unfortunately however he is in the difficult position of being unable to obtain instructions from Mrs Eliot though he promised to renew his efforts to get in touch with her . . . [S]hould these be unsuccessful I certainly should not allow the matter to rest there but would suggest that we proceed with our Order and inspect the contents of the parcel at Martins Bank. I trust however that such extreme measures will not be necessary.'

FROM *Vivien Eliot*   MS Valerie Eliot

6 February 1935   68, Clarence Gate Gardens,
                                       Regents Park, N.W.1.

This front door is *always left open for T. S. Eliot from 10.30* until *11 p.m.* –
No words needed. Love from *Polly, & V. H. Eliot.* ------------
Here is your <u>*home*</u>, & here is your *Protection* which you NEED.
I *know*.

TO *Edith Perkins*   TS Donald Gallup

8 February 1935   Faber & Faber Ltd

Dear Mrs Perkins,

I was very much pleased to get your kind letter, and to know that you
were enjoying sunshine and good weather. I have never been in Rome in
the winter, but remember it in May with nightingales, and the gardens
very pleasant to stroll in. I know too, that Rome seems inexhaustible in
the way of things to see and study – so much so that I think after a time
one would need to go away to some place where there was nothing to
see or study, in order to rest. When I was there, in 1926, it was noisy;
I hear that now noise has been abolished; but I do not know whether what
seems like quiet to a Roman is what seems so to us.

Here the weather has been normal: that is to say we have had enough
rain, and a few cold days but not too many, and pale sunlight in the
morning; the chief pleasure of this time of year is the evident 'drawing
out' of the days.

I look forward to your return with the spring, and am happy to think
of you returning to Campden.

With all my best wishes to Dr Perkins and Emily, as well as yourself,

                                       Yours very sincerely,
                                       T. S. Eliot

'Mr Broad has, I understand, not heard anything from Mrs Eliot since he went with her to
the Bank and she has not forwarded to him the one or two articles of silver which she then
informed him were still at the Flat. Incidentally he told me that he was much troubled by the
position of her affairs in general which he regarded as unsatisfactory and I think that if the
immediate problems can be disposed of he will do all he can to endeavour to get her to adopt
a rational view of the whole situation and to place matters on a more satisfactory basis.'

TO *Ezra Pound*

TS Beinecke

8 February 1935   Faber & Faber Ltd

Now look here, Podesta, to begin with I am just recoverin from a acute coryza & my secretary <is ill> and I aint got time to deal with much until next Week but theres one or two points first I thought I explained to you about Old Uncle Jud Calkins fallin off that forty foot latter, after the 4th of July celebrations of the Ancient & Honble Artillery Company of Jonesport it was. Peekin in a window he was; and as he was gettin on for 82 the fall did shake him up some Didnt we laugh though I shant forget it. I was thinkin of raisin a complaint about that Beachopper[1] Roberts who the hell is he but the immediate point is this that me and also Faber who ought to know some more Greek than I do bein a 1st in Greats have been tryin to emend your greek qootations Podesta why dont you ever read your proofs and verify your references and Podesta why dont you adopt some SYSTEM of transliteration if you got to transliterate at all But he as well as I is handichapped by not knowing the sources and perhaps less familiarity I might say indeed on your part Gross familiarity Podesta with the Yomeric Ymns dont know where ALL the dambed things come from, can you give exact refs. those two big quotes especial they are certainly Meaty when it comes to errors of one Kind or another[2] Do you want the proof back or what damb your eyes liver lights etc. so will close.[3]

TP

---

1 – Beach hopper: a crustacean, a marine arthropod which burrows under piles of seaweed on the beach: it even jumps from place to place, though not a relative of the flea.

2 – EP replied on 10 Feb.: 'Gordamm that greek/ I putt the line numbers on fht margint, thinking anybody that cd/ reed it at all cd/ tell wot buk it cum frum, namely the Circe or Kirke book K. of the O/dishy. and I putt the numbers of the lines from which the small quotes are taken, on some set of proofs . . .

'I dont quote in full, I leave out woidz that dont comport with wot I'ma driving at.'

'Wall I'm sorry to be orl thes trubbl to th bruvvren/ but still I hev me trubbles/ an I'm sorry about the coryza, wot iz it? me wife sez it sounds like a plant/ I think shd/ wuz thinkin or cryzia mutica, if I aint fergot to speell it.'

3 – EP, 10 Feb.: 'NO, I dont want to see any MORE proofs/ the bdy/ thing orter bin out befo/ noo yearz . . . only for Xtzache don't send me any MORE proofs.'

TO *Theodore Spencer*

12 February 1935   Faber & Faber Ltd

Dear Ted,

I have your letter of the 31st, and am sending your manuscript to the C.U.P. directly.[1] I am also having Miss Bradbrook's book sent on to you. I don't know how long the Cambridge Press are likely to take. I have asked them to write to you direct. I should think you might hear in a couple of months.

I am very glad to hear your news, especially the good news that you will be in England for a short time during the summer.[2] I expect to be here, partly because I can't afford to go abroad at present, and partly for other reasons. In any case I shall not be going to Boston until 1936, so there is no danger of missing you in that way. I wish, however, that the Cambridge idyll might have been realised.

Your news of Eliot House theatricals is also very pleasing.[3] The Giant Rat of Sumatra seems to me an excellent subject. I presume, by the way, that this giant rat is identical with the animal known as the Bandicoot,[4] whose habits you might investigate before starting your scenario. I am at present, in fact it is taking up all my spare time and more, on a murder play, which is probably to be produced in London in May, along with plays by Yeats and Auden, and at Canterbury in the middle of June. I am glad to say that I have been able to make some use of the Musgrave Ritual, but am finding some of the writing very difficult to manage.

With love to Nancy,
Yours ever affectionately,
Tom

1–Spencer assented to TSE's judgement that his book on death and the Elizabethans was 'a University press affair': 'If you feel that you can honestly do it, I suppose a word or 2 of recommendation from you would be of great help in influencing Roberts in its favor.'
2–'Probably we'll go to Austria again & then have 2 weeks or so in England towards the end of the summer. What are your plans?'
3–Spencer related that he and Harry Levin had put on a production of *1 Henry IV* at Eliot House; he had also co-written a musical farce that had been performed at the Tavern Club. 'We are now planning a similar thing – with music – about Sherlock Holmes – I think the story of the Giant Rat of Sumatra – "a story for which the world is not yet prepared".'
4–Bandicoot: 'A large Indian rat (*Mus malabaricus* or *giganteus*), as big as a cat, and very destructive' (*OED*).

TO *E. Martin Browne*   CC

12 February 1935   [*The Criterion*]

My dear Browne,

I ought to have written to you before, but I was away ill several days last week, and my correspondence is rather congested. In the first place, I have completely re-written my dull dialogue after the first choral part, and have shown it to Doone, who likes it much better than the first version.[1] It is much more formalised, with no attempt at realism, and more in the mode of *Everyman* or a Morality play. I hope, however, that it is free from quaintness. As soon as I have completed this scene I will send it on to you. As I intend it at present, the four actors who interview the Archbishop in Part I can double for the four murderers in Part II. In fact, I should rather like to emphasise this by having their facial make-up remain the same, and changing only their costumes. Also, Doone and other people think it would be very much pleasanter to have the murder take place actually on the stage. What do you think about this?

Now about the costumes, about which I have spoken to Doone. I find that he would be perfectly willing to arrange to let Canterbury use his costumes, but his costumes would be made by Robert Medley, of whose work he has a very high opinion. I know nothing about Robert Medley's work. Do you? Do you imagine that his costumes would be satisfactory for the purpose, or at any rate more likely to be satisfactory than anything Miss Haffenden can do?

> Yours ever,
> [Tom]

---

1 – Medley, *Drawn from the Life*, 154–5: 'Following the success of *Sweeney Agonistes* Eliot had sent Rupert a first version of the play, which to Rupert's surprise was written entirely in prose. Rupert went to see Eliot and told him that by abandoning verse he was denying his essential genius; at this meeting they discussed scenes from the projected play in some detail. Rupert had hoped that the Group Theatre might mount the first production of what was clearly destined to be an important work.' In the prefatory note to the first edition of *MiC*, TSE was to thank Rupert Doone, along with E. Martin Browne, for 'help in [the] construction' of the play.

12 February 1935   [*The Criterion*]

My dear Henry,

I have had an enquiry from a young man in Manchester,[1] who has been working for the B.B.C. there, as to the possibilities of his getting a job with some American broadcasting company. He seems to be an ambitious lad, and apparently does not feel that the possibilities for him here are as interesting as they might be. It occurred to me that you might be willing to enquire of young Strauss how one gets into broadcasting work, and whether there would be any possibility of an Englishman breaking in.

I can recommend this fellow, although I know little about him personally. He does work for the *Criterion*, and I believe has a good deal of practical experience of programme work in broadcasting. He is especially interested in radio plays, and besides what he mentions in the enclosed letter, which you may show to anybody whom it might interest, has written an unproduced broadcast play, which I am printing in the *Criterion*.[2]

I should imagine that the competition for any jobs would be too keen to make it likely that an Englishman would have any chance, but I promised him that I would try to make enquiries. I should be extremely grateful for anything you could do, but I doubt whether you can do anything, and I don't want you to take excessive trouble over it.

> Yours ever,
> [Tom]

TO *Margaret Babington*   CC

12 February 1935   [Faber & Faber Ltd]

Dear Miss Babington,

Please forgive my delay in answering your letter of the 1st, but I was away ill for part of the time, and my secretary was also ill, so that my correspondence is in arrears. I am very glad that you do not feel that the performance at Notting Hill will interfere in any way with Canterbury, because, as I told you, Mr Rupert Doone sets such store by it.[3]

1–D. G. Bridson.
2–'Prometheus', C. 14 (Apr. 1935), 408–30.
3–'Of course you must give permission for the longer Play to be performed at the Mercury Theatre, Notting Hill, on four nights in May. Indeed Canterbury would be churlish to say

As for the sombre costumes, as the play alters I feel that I have exaggerated their sombreness.[1] The only really sombre costume necessary is that of the Archbishop himself. I particularly don't want him to appear in gorgeous robes, but in his usual garb during the latter part of his career, a simple monastic costume. I should think, however, that the contrast of black and white could make him visible enough. There will also be three priests or minor canons, and I don't see how they can be put into very highly coloured clothing either, but perhaps it is proper that minor canons should be heard and not seen. Some of the other characters, there are not very many altogether, could be as gorgeous as one pleased. I think, in fact, that the Mercury people are likely to want a good deal of colour. In any case, they will not be using Miss Pierce [*sc.* Pearce]. I have had a talk with Rupert Doone about this. He depends for his costumes on Mr Robert Medley, of whose work he thinks very highly. He would be quite ready to make some arrangement to let you have his costumes for Canterbury if you wished. I have not seen any of Robert Medley's costume work myself. Possibly Martin Browne or Lawrence Irving will know enough to form an opinion. I am writing to Browne on this point also.

Yours sincerely,

[T. S. Eliot]

TO *The Secretary, Cambridge University Press* cc

12 February 1935   [Faber & Faber Ltd]

Dear Sir,

I am sending you at the request of Dr Theodore Spencer, the manuscript of his dissertation entitled *Death and the Elizabethans*. The manuscript is based on his thesis for the degree of Ph.D. at Harvard. He sent it to me because I am a friend of his, and I send it to you because Dr Spencer is an M.A. of Trinity College, and because I felt that it was eminently a University press type of book.

---

anything else. I am interested to know that the two plays, the short and the long versions, will have different names.'

1 – Babington wrote on 1 Feb.: 'I am rather afraid that the possible advantage you suggest may not be possible. The sombre costumes of which you speak will literally not be seen in the Chapter House, save at the (perhaps) three evening performances of the Play . . . And, in a place that is not too good for sound, it would be disastrous if the actors were not seen, for that always makes hearing more difficult, does it not. Moreover the audience would assuredly depart showering curses and maledictions on the head of the unfortunate Festival Manager . . .'

The book strikes me as an excellent and scholarly treatise, and I found it very interesting to read. You will no doubt understand when you examine it that it is hardly a book on which a general publisher could afford to take risks. I hope that the Cambridge University Press will be able to consider it seriously. I should be obliged if you would make known your decision direct to Dr Theodore Spencer, whose address is 43 West Cedar Street, Boston, Massachusetts.[1]

Yours faithfully,
[T. S. Eliot]

TO *John V. Simcox*[2]   CC

12 February 1935   [Faber & Faber Ltd]

Dear Sir,

I have your interesting letter of February the 8th, which I cannot answer as fully as I should like, because it is some time since I have read the works of Maurras and his colleagues, and because at the moment I have not access to my collection of these books.[3] I can, however, say quite positively that I don't accept Miss West's description of the Maurrasian doctrine. It is true that in my letter I left the point unsettled, because I was there concerned only with trying to expose Miss West's confusion of thought and her illicit insinuations. She obviously has never studied the Action Française, and is speaking from pure prejudice. At the same time, her statement is near enough to be a travesty of the opinion of Maurras, so that satisfactory refutation would take considerable space. The adjective 'blatant' is of course a specimen of loose journalistic vocabulary, and is as

---

1–Spencer, *Death and Elizabethan Tragedy: A study of convention and opinion in the Elizabethan drama* (Harvard University Press, 1936).

2–The Revd John V. Simcox, a Roman Catholic priest: St Edmund's College, Ware, Herts.

3 – 'May I ask you to clear up a point arising out of your reply to Miss West in *Time and Tide* of February 2nd? . . . Do you accept Miss West's description of Charles Maurras and the Action Française group? You refer to the description in your reply to her without definitely rejecting it. For my own part, I cannot remember any passage in the writings of Maurras in which he "blatantly recommends that France should practise Catholicism whether she believed it or not, for the sake of the unifying power of religion." To begin with, Maurras is not given to being blatant . . . Secondly, so far as I know, Maurras has never maintained more than that it is to the political interest of France to treat Catholicism with respect and honour rather than with hostility. He is of opinion that France is still largely Catholic, and that, apart from this, Catholicism is in the blood of the country . . . Do you think that he goes further than this . . . ?'

inapplicable to the clean, precise style of Maurras as any adjective could be. I think that your interpretation is a sound one.

Yours faithfully,
[T. S. Eliot]

TO *Ezra Pound*

TS Beinecke

12 February AD [1935]   Faber & Faber Ltd

The first trouble with you Podesta is that you aint Practical. Here you Go place a document in my Hands suggest that I take it up with my lawyers.[1] And you dont say what paper the so-called libel appeared in. I call that Hasty. Secondly you dont seem to realise that I already owe my lawyers £177 and am in no Position to litigate. I dont say that you Dont know any Greek because I am not quite qualified to say That, but I do say you are not Practical.[2] Old Ike Carver of Mosquito Cove was Practical. How do I know what wop rag you read, and may be you sold them that photo yourself and wrote the rubric.[3] But if so Podesta again you aint Practical if aiming malice because I maintain that what is contained in that letterpress is NOT libellous but on the contrary a statement of fact in Which I Glory. I Know quite well that ladies Prize my skin and how do you suppose that I keep 'em off? By the puzzo[4] Podesta by the puzzo of which I am as proud as of that Skin: Not once, nor 2ce, in our rough island story,[5] the Possum's Stink has saved the land of Hope & Glory.[6] Man Ray has taken some good photos of OPossum.[7] BUT I Stink when I PLEASE, and when

1 – EP had sent a magazine cutting with a photo of himself with what he considered a libellous caption (unidentified).

2 – EP responded, 16 Feb.: 'Waal naow, Possum my Wunkas, Dew yew XXXpekk me to be pracTical AWL th time? Aint it enuff thet I write a nice practical XI Cantos to inskrukk the reader in hist/ and econ/ even if I do leave out a greek hack/cent, which most of the readers wd/ learn to copulate WITHOUT, almost as soon/ unless impeded . . .'

3 – EP, 16 Feb.: 'No I didn send 'em that pixchoor/ I was painfully shocked thet le'er press. '"Protest meetin's were held in many parts of the Kingdon" (Social Credit. Nov. 2. Number I. (Feb. 15, 1935 anno dumbeni).'

4 – *Puzzo* (It.): foul smell.

5 – Tennyson, 'Ode on the Death of the Duke of Wellington', 201–2: 'Not once or twice in our rough island-story, / The path of duty was the way to glory'.

6 – *Land of Hope and Glory* (1902): music by Edward Elgar, lyrics by A. C. Benson.

7 – Man Ray (1890–1976): pioneering photographer and artist; born Emmanuel Rodnitsky, the son of a Russian-Jewish tailor who settled in Philadelphia. He grew up in New York, where as a teenager he adopted his redolent pseudonym, and fell under the influence of Alfred Stieglitz's Gallery 291; and he became one of the leaders of Dadaism and Surrealism. For most of his adult life he lived in Paris, where he built his reputation as an experimental

I Please I smell of Violets. I am gettin to Grips with Mairet about that Beachopper. Yours etc.

TP

TO *M. C. D'Arcy*   CC

12 February 1935   [Faber & Faber Ltd]

My dear D'Arcy,

Thank you for your note.[1] It is a relief to hear that Gregory is likely to have some work, as I have not yet got anything for him myself.

I have not yet had much consequence to my enquiries in America. You may be hearing from Paul More, who has promised to do what he can. I hear from Daniel Sargent that the prospects at Harvard are nil. Apparently he has tried several times to make them invite Maritain to lecture there, and has failed. Perhaps the prejudice against orthodoxy is still strong at Harvard. Meanwhile, in case I hear anything further, may I have an address of yours in New York, to which I could refer anybody, and if I don't see you again, I send herewith my best wishes and prayers for the success of your visit.

By the way, I imagine that your feet are much smaller than mine, but in America in the winter it is almost essential to have a pair of high over-

---

photographer; he also made notable contributions to film. With the onset of WW2 he went back to America, though in 1951 he was to return to France. Man Ray met TSE on two occasions, on 21 Jan. and 23 Jan. 1935, at his office in Russell Square (the photos were probably taken there). Man Ray wrote to TSE on 2 Feb. 1935: 'Thank you for your letter of the 29th. [TSE's letter has not been traced.] I am pleased you like the pictures I did of you, and shall be glad to make up some prints for you personally at one guinea each. They will be somewhat smaller, but have better quality. I think your publisher should pay three guineas for the rights of publication. I hope this is satisfactory.

'I left the same day the prints were delivered to you, and am sorry not to have spoken with you. But I hope to have the occasion on my next visit.'

Ray to FVM on 18 Feb., 'I have not yet heard from Mr Eliot, but any request from him will receive immediate attention.'

VHE was to write to GCF, 21 Nov. 1935: 'I do hope you will send me the name of the photographer who took this latest photograph of Tom, as you promised you would, on Monday afternoon, at the Book Exhibition. Please send it on a post card. Yours, V. H. Eliot.' GCF replied, 21 Nov.: 'About the photograph. It was done by Man Ray, 31 bis, rue Campagne-Premiere, Paris. It is the only copy we have, and I am afraid we can't part with it, since we need it for "publicity"; but there is no reason why you shouldn't write to his London agent (Messrs Lund Humphries Ltd., 12, Bedford Square, W.C.1.) yourself, and ask him to send you one. I don't know what his charge is, since he hasn't sent in his bill to us; and I am told that it is very difficult to get him to answer any enquiries!'

1 – D'Arcy wrote on 5 Feb. that Gregory was 'in very fair prospect of getting some work'.

shoes which they call goloshes, which are necessary in the snow. They buckle securely round the leg, and therefore cannot very well fall off, even if much too big. If you could use mine I should be delighted, and it would save the possible expense of $2.50 when you get there.

Yours ever,
[T. S. Eliot]

TO *Henry Eliot Scott*[1]   CC

13 February 1935   [Faber & Faber Ltd]

Dear Harry,

I was much interested by your enquiry of the 19th, particularly as I had supposed that there was hardly any interest in America in any of the forms of fascism. It is not very easy to express briefly any general opinion on fascism, because it varies so much from country to country. At any rate, the Italian and German versions differ considerably, and it seems to be of the nature of fascism to develop its theories after it has become established. At any rate, that was the case in Italy, where it apparently endeavoured to find a basis of political philosophy in the work of Pareto and of Sorel. In Germany, on the other hand, it seems to have started with a few definite ideas of an agrarian and guild socialist type, which have disappeared into the background as the National Socialist Party has got more and more closely associated with big capital.

With regard to Sir Oswald Mosley, it is much easier to come to a conclusion.[2] On the other hand, it is not perhaps wise to put down on paper

1–TSE's fourth cousin, Henry Eliot Scott (1909–89) – son of Grace Cranch Eliot (daughter of TSE's uncle, Revd Thomas Lamb Eliot, Portland, Oregon) – writing from Middlesex School, Concord, Mass., said he had become 'converted' to the principles of the fascists he met during the period he spent in Munich following the Nazi Revolution. He had 'liked tremendously' the Mosleyites he encountered.

Scott to EVE, 4 Oct. 1970: 'After I had graduated from Harvard, I studied for two years as an Exchange Student at the University of Munich, Germany, during which time Hitler came to power. After my return to America in 1934, shaken and yet awed by what I had seen, I wrote to T. S. Eliot to ask if he had any opinion of Oswald Mosley, and he replied that he would rather not say what he knew, but that I could take it to be unfavourable. Since then, I have had no other communication or meeting with T. S. Eliot; I sent him an announcement of my marriage in 1947, and he was one among several others who did not reply. I did not mind.'

2–Sir Oswald Mosley, 6th Bt. (1896–1980) founded in 1932 the British Union of Fascists.

VHE had been a member of the British Union of Fascists for five months. On 5 Sept. 1934 she wrote in her diary: 'After paying [W. L.] Janes & having a short chat I walked back to 12 *Lower Grosvenor Place* which is the Women's *Fascist* Headquarters, which I

what I have heard of him privately and through mutual acquaintances, but you may take it to be unfavourable. Politically, the man is at present pretty well discredited. His political philosophy is clap-trap. He has no economic or financial theory at all, and he appears to have tried to make pleasing promises to various elements, without considering that some of the promises were mutually incompatible. His party was supported for a time by Lord Rothermere in the *Daily Mail*, but I am told that the reason why the *Daily Mail* dropped it is that advertising, in which Jewish interests were involved, fell off.

As for the question of the Jews in Germany, I can't speak of them with any authority, but certainly anti-Semitism is not, and cannot be, a serious political issue in England, nor does it seem to be a very practical way of inflaming popular passion. Mosley's movement has been on the decline since a disgraceful meeting at a big public hall last year, at which interrupters seem to have been treated with considerable barbarity. I do not say that there might not be a recrudescence of the movement if conditions changed, but I should think it unlikely that any movement of the sort would flourish, either under the name of fascism, or under the leadership of Mosley.

I take it from your address that you are now a master at Middlesex. Are you there permanently?

Yours ever,

[Tom]

---

have been trying to get to for so long. This was my *dying* effort. It was after 2 & I was done for & still with *every*thing to do. However I *joined* up, & am now a Fascist, & I was glad & *relieved. Old* days, *like the War*, happy, *organised* & *public service*, than which there is *nothing better.*' On 25 Mar. 1935 she would attend a BUF rally at the Albert Hall: 'I have never seen such a meeting in my life. It was *COLOSSAL. VAST*. Epoch-making. Sir Oswald Mosley's *organisation* must be the best in this country. It is perfectly marvellous. And all the Fascists are bright, healthy, good & kind people & very *very* clever. I got home by 11 with no difficulty & no harm came to me except a very natural fatigue' (Bod. MS Eng. let. 382). 'On March 22nd, 1936. I saw Sir Oswald Mosley for the first time [at the Albert Hall]' (Bod. Eng. let. C. 383, fol. 45v). On 18 June she went to the Fascist headquarters to buy her uniform: 'I was disappointed to be told that Fascists may not wear uniforms in foreign countries.' (She had in mind a trip to France.) On 15 Aug. she wrote in her diary: 'I here & now, if I die tonight, advise Sir Oswald Mosley to hitch T. S. Eliot on to *his* wagon & that quickly. *That is the man Mosley needs today.*'

See too Stephen Dorril, *Blackshirt: Sir Oswald Mosley and British Fascism* (2006), 287: 'T. S. Eliot's wife, Vivienne Haigh-Wood, did join the BUF . . . [T. S.] Eliot distanced himself from the "infection" which emanated from Ezra Pound. In the *Church Times* on 2 February 1934 he invited Catholics who sympathized with Fascism to question its orthodoxy that absolute monarchy "can never return" and that the State was an absolute. On 12 March Eliot warned Pound against Mosley. Not long after, he drafted *The Rock*, satirizing totalitarianism with a scene of Blackshirts chanting anti-Semitic abuse.'

TO *Alistair Cooke*

14 February 1935   [Faber & Faber Ltd]

Dear Cooke,

I have been meaning to write to you for some days. My Committee took to heart your advice, as transmitted by me, about the series of film books, and I think that the project has been abandoned. They were, however, very much interested by the suggestion of the kind of book which you outlined to me, based upon your wireless talks. When you are ready to discuss the matter further, please let me know. This does seem to be a book for which a place should be found.

Yours sincerely,
[T. S. Eliot]

TO *John V. Simcox*

14 February 1935   [Faber & Faber Ltd]

Dear Father Simcox,

Thank you for your letter of the 13th.[1] I also regretted very deeply the condemnation of the Action Française, which I studied very carefully at the time, and about which I accumulated a number of books, upon which I cannot at present lay my hand. Amongst others, there is, or was, an excellent book about Maurras, written by a Jesuit father in France some years before the condemnation, which is now unobtainable.[2]

I had some conversation with Leo Ward at the time, as well as controversy, and formed the impression that he had taken up the matter

---

1 – 'I think that Maurras himself would fully agree with your refusal to associate yourself quite unreservedly with the A.F. After all, even before his condemnation, he had often warned Catholics against a too unlimited adhesion to his school. Personally, I must own up to a feeling of regret over his condemnation. I can, of course, see that there was plenty of justification for it. But, in my own case, Maurras had only helped me to see much in Catholicism that I have never seen before. He had (through his books) been such a good friend to me . . .

'My own impression is that many of his Catholic opponents either could not or would not understand him. Certainly that was so with Father Leo Ward in England. I once asked him whether he really believed in his own case against Maurras as set out in his pamphlet on the A.F.; but he simply refused to discuss it. He told me that you had replied to his pamphlet and that he was still so sore from your handling of him that he wished never to hear of the A.F. again. Unfortunately, I never saw your reply to him.'

2 – Lucien Laberthonnière, *Positivisme et catholicisme: à propos de "l'Action française"* (1911).

with more zeal than knowledge.[1] The book which appeared in England a little later, by Denis Gwynn on the subject, showed a much more intimate acquaintance, although its point of view was one which I could not really accept.[2] My controversy with Ward is to be found in the March and June issues of 1928 of the *Criterion*. The June issue is out of print, but I am sending you a copy of the other.[3]

Yours very truly,
[T. S. Eliot]

TO *The Editor,* The New English Weekly

[published 14 February 1935, 382–3]   [Faber & Faber Ltd]

'Douglas in the Church Assembly'

Sir,

While I feel, as I suppose do other readers of the *New English Weekly*, gratified that some members of the Commission appointed to report to the Church Assembly on the subject of Unemployment, were able to incorporate into the Recommendations such excellent and far-reaching suggestions; and while I am gratified also that the Assembly has 'accepted' (whatever that means) the Report, I cannot feel any happier after reading the report of the discussions of the Report in the Assembly.[4] So far as the

---

1–Leo Ward, *The Condemnation of the 'Action Française'* (1928). See TSE's article 'The *Action Française*, M. Maurras and Mr Ward, *MC* 7 (Mar. 1928), 195–203; reply by L. Ward, 7, 364; by TSE, 7, 372; and rejoinder by Ward, 7, 376. See also correspondence in *L4*.
2–Denis Gwynn, *The 'Action Française' Condemnation* (1928).
3–Simcox replied on 25 Feb., thanking TSE for 'so kindly sending me your reply in the *Criterion* to Father Leo Ward. I can now understand Father Ward's refusal to discuss the subject of the A.F. when I asked him about it. Your reply must have convinced him that he was quite incompetent to deal with the matter. There is, so far as I can see, no reply possible from his side to your criticisms of his competence . . . My own impression is that he simply "got up" his case against Maurras . . . However, I imagine that even Leon Daudet himself would agree that your *Criterion* article inflicted chastisement adequate to the offence committed. Poor Father Ward!'
4–See 'Notes', *NEW* 6: 17 (7 Feb. 1935), 347–8: 'Eight bishops, with twenty other distinguished Churchmen and laymen, drew up a remarkable document for discussion by the Church Assembly this week. This Commission was appointed to enquire into Unemployment, and its report begins with a refreshing novelty in present-day political statements – a clearly-drawn distinction of principle. Whilst "work", these Commissioners explain, has both natural and spiritual sanction, "employment", which is only one form of work – the sale of one's time and energy for purchasing power – is commonly dictated by economic need alone. In short, these enquirers refused to study Unemployment as necessarily a social evil, and on the contrary upheld as a principle of religion that Unemployment may be "a privilege and a benefit to society". The present confusion of Employment with moral

Church Assembly, or its vocal members, may be taken to speak for 'The Church', it would appear that the Church has not made up its mind how far, or in what way, it ought to be concerned with social and economic problems. And until the Church does make up its mind, I do not see that we have much reason either to rejoice that Credit Reform proposals should be debated, or to deplore that they have met with such vague approval.

What is evident to a reader of the proceedings, is that each speaker spoke according to the warmth of his heart, and in the light of his individual reason. Those who, as individual subjects, believed that Reform was necessary, advocated it; those who individually believed that it was all nonsense, concluded that the Church ought not to meddle with economics at all: and many persons, both in and out of the Church Assembly, are probably deterred by the fear of letting the Church back the wrong horse. The more enlightened, such as the Bishop of London and the Bishop of Southwark, made it clear enough that they did not wish the Church to commit itself to any particular theory of reform, but that they would like to see the Church commit itself to the assertion that the present situation is intolerable and unreasonable, and that it devolved upon the temporal authorities to recognise the present situation for what it is and do something about it. That is a perfectly sensible position to take up; indeed it is, in my opinion, about as far as the Church (again, in so far as the Church Assembly can be said to represent the Church) can go. But the debate seems to have resolved itself into a conflict of individual opinions as to the merit of the 'Douglas Plan'. It was perfectly clear that no one who took part had thought out for himself what are the relations of Church and State: so how could they be qualified to discuss the Report? The one attempt, and a lamentable failure it seems to have been, to say what is and is not the Church's business, came from the Bishop of Jarrow, who remarked neatly that 'it was not the business of the Church to make society fit for men, but to make men fit for society'. To employ the Bishop's own turn of speech, we may suggest that if we are respectful enough to believe that this statement has meaning, then it is heretical; and that if we are respectful enough not to question its orthodoxy, we must admit that it is meaningless.

I suggest that we should be more likely to get somewhere if the representatives of the Church in the Church Assembly, instead of merely

---

duty, they averred, is destructive of the Christian conception of vocation, and "the necessity of finding work in order to be employed (to earn a living) reverses the true order of values".'

expounding their own economic beliefs or prejudices – and the opinion expressed against the Douglas Theory was merely a prejudice expressed in favour of the present system, not a demarcation of the limits to which the Church should go in favouring any temporal system – should give their time to considering the fundamental moral laws founded on Christian theology, and content themselves with proclaiming positively any violations of these laws which they observe (as Churchmen) in the present order. If the voice of the Church spoke with authority on that point, the result would be disturbing enough: more disturbing, and more hopeful, than anything that has been accomplished by the present Church Assembly.[1]

T. S. Eliot

TO *Laurence Irving*   CC

14 February 1935   [Faber & Faber Ltd]

My dear Irving,

I am sorry to hear that you are laid up, and hope that it is not serious.[2] Today week would do me quite well – the afternoon better than the morning. But if the afternoon is impossible I will arrange to be in between 12 and 1. Preferably, will you not lunch with me? That would also mean a saving of time.

Thank you for reassuring me about Miss Haffenden.[3] I really had very little to go upon, and I was chiefly prejudiced in favour of the known over the unknown. However, the situation is now changed. Rupert Doone is going to put the play on in London, and his costumes are to be designed by his friend Robert Medley. He would be quite willing to let Canterbury use his costumes for their performance, and Miss Babington would be glad to have them. I should prefer, however, to leave this unsettled until I know whether you and Browne have any acquaintance with Medley's work, and if so, what you think of it. I know very little about it myself,

---

1–See reply by Maurice B. Reckitt, 'The Church Assembly', *NEW*, 21 Feb. 1935, 403.
2–Irving had written to excuse himself on 13 Jan.
3–Irving wrote, 28 Jan.: 'I saw Browne for a few minutes at Canterbury and Miss Haffenden has been down here since her interview with you both on Saturday. I heard, after we had more or less approached her with a view to inviting her to Canterbury, that you would have preferred Stella Mary Pearce. I know them both and they are both excellent practical costumiers and very good designers. I think Miss Haffenden has a good deal more practical experience and she has worked with me on one or two big productions. I really thought she would be the most suitable person . . .'

and one wants to be sure that his designs would be suitable. I shall write
to Browne on this point.

Do lunch with me on Thursday if you can.

Yours sincerely,
[T. S. Eliot]

FROM *Vivien Eliot*   MS Valerie Eliot

14 February 1935   68, Clarence Gate Gardens,
                                     Regents Park, London, N.W.1.

Tom. The front door of this flat is opened every night at *10.30* until *11*
for T. S. Eliot. Your room is ready. You close the door, & there you are,
Safe. You *need not speak a word.* You MUST come home now. Before
anyone else *dies.* — You do not want another death – *do you? Polly* is still
waiting for you. Her anxious, haggard eyes are always questioning me.
When I say – Master – she runs to the door always. *Your* family would be
much happier if they knew you were safely *here.* I *know* they are *anxious,*
unhappy, & *not well.* Put your own feelings *aside. Pocket* your rotten
false pride. Make the few remaining years of those who care about you
less of a Hell than you are doing. You *Must not* make Hell for people –
Now, I *expect* you *every night.* This is your Home, & here you will be
Safe. As *all matters are now settled* you must come home & give us all a
little cup of happiness. Think of *Marion,* Theodora, *Chardy* – Henry —
Come Tom. You are doing wrong.

Your wife
Vivienne Haigh Eliot

Snap your *fingers* at your *enemies.* You can do that better *here,* under my
care. —

A fig for your enemies.

TO *T. S. Gregory*   CC

15 February 1935   [*The Criterion*]

Dear Mr Gregory,

Thank you for your letter of the 29th of January, giving me the
information needed.[1] I have also heard very satisfactorily from Professor

---

1 – 'I rather fancy schoolmastering is ruled out. That is to say that the main reason why
my resignation was instantly required was that a girls' school attended a church in which

Barker.[1] I have written to Mr Richmond, the editor of the *Times Literary Supplement*, about you, but I hear that he has been away, and is returning next week. Meanwhile, I will see what can be done elsewhere, but if you should be up in London it might be a good thing if you could come and have a talk.

If you are sufficiently acquainted with Kierkegaard's work to wish to write an article about him, I should be delighted to have it. You don't need to write any differently for the *Criterion* than for your own book. The only thing to remember is that the *Criterion* is a general literary review, and that the majority of its readers are not people with Catholic assumptions. About five thousand words would be right.

As to what you ask about the 'new world and its fashions', I am not quite clear what you mean, but you don't need to worry about fashions in writing for a paper like the *Criterion*.

Yours sincerely,

[T. S. Eliot]

I preach once a fortnight. I should think that in an overcrowded profession it would be all but impossible for a Roman Catholic to get a job without possessing qualifications far beyond mine. Catholic schools – except for a few like Ampleforth and Downside – are not commanded even by Catholics, and depend for their staff largely on professed religious, or on schoolmasters who have taken their professional training and diploma in the ordinary way.

'In time, I believe, there will be work under one or other of the propagandist societies. The interval is difficult. But, if I could get £2 a week for reviewing I have saved enough to survive for some time.

'There are two other things I should like to ask. A friend of mine, Mr Alick Dru, is very interested in the Danish philosopher Sören Kierkegaard and has kindly invited me to help him with a book. He suggests that if I sent you an article on Kierkegaard, you might include it in the *Criterion*. If so, would you tell me how long to make it. And would you spare time to tell me something of this new world, what fashions there are in it, so that I need not spend time in producing a perfectly decent article on some subject no-one else is interested in.'

1 – Ernest Barker (1874–1960), Professor of Political Science, Cambridge, wrote on 3 Feb.: 'When I was a Fellow of New College, Oxford, we elected [Gregory] a History Scholar of the College from a good field . . . some 20 years ago. He worked with me . . . and I still remember the distinction and the individuality of his work. He became a methodist minister; I left Oxford; and I have only met him again during the last two years. I am a member of the Burge Trust (which exists to promote international fellowship thro' the Churches, in memory of Bishop [Hubert] Burge), and I induced my colleagues to co-opt him on our Trust, as a representative of the free Churches. He has been a good and useful member.

'He is a scholar, with a touch of fine mysticism, and with a fine unworldliness. I think he is a little lost in ordinary mundane things: he moves in a bright world of ideas (Platonic ideas); and he is at home in the history of thought. I commend him to you as a rare man . . .'

15 February 1935   Faber & Faber Ltd

Dear Richards,

I am sorry, I thought I *had* answered your invitation.[1] I should have loved to come, but I simply dare not break the thread of my typing until I have killed the Archbishop – I haven't been out of London since November and I can't go out of London until some time in April – I shall [have] still more than half to go, uphill too. It won't be a very good play either, as it looks at present – of course I depend very heavily on choruses – no it isn't Laud it's Becket, whose dramatic possibilities are greater, to be treated quite unhistorically (after reading up the history) in a kind of Everyman way, in doggerel. I should like to know your opinion about the title – there is some divergence of view – I thought of calling it 'The Archbishop Murder Case' because it is very SERIOUS, but some folk I know will object violently. How does it strike you.[2] I have to pound away at this every morning now. It is to be produced at Ashley Duke's Mercury Theatre in May, in a season with Auden and Yeats (Auden's new play seems very good) and more primly at Canterbury in June. I am awfully sorry I can't get away – I enjoyed that other Pepys dinner very much, especially the session with Ogden afterwards,[3] and your kitchen is excellent and also the cellar. I haven't even had time to read Coleridge[4] yet – it looks to me, in the 'actual writing' as they say, the best thing you have done yet. Please give my regards to Mrs Richards.

Yours ever,

T. S. E.

1–IAR (14 Feb.) invited TSE to the Pepys Feast, 23 Feb.
2–IAR replied, 22 Feb.: 'I don't *at all* dislike *The ArchBishop Murder Case* – as title' (*Selected Letters*, 88).
3–C. K. Ogden (1889–1957), psychologist, linguist, polymath, was educated at Magdalene College, Cambridge, where in 1912 he founded *Cambridge Magazine* and co-founded (1911) the Heretics. He went on to devise 'Basic English' – 'an auxiliary international language' based on a vocabulary of just 850 English words – 'BASIC' being an acronym for British American Scientific International Commercial; and in 1927 he established in London the Orthological (Basic English) Institute. Works include *The Foundations of Aesthetics* (with IAR and James Wood, 1921), *The Meaning of Meaning* (with IAR, 1923), *Basic English* (1930); and with F. P. Ramsey he translated the *Logisch-Philosophische Abhandlung* of Ludwig Wittgenstein (*Tractatus Logico-Philosophicus*, 1922). He was editor of the psychological journal *Psyche*, and he edited the series 'The International Library of Psychology, Philosophy and Scientific Method'. See W. Terrence Gordon, *C. K. Ogden: a bio-bibliographical study* (1990); *C. K. Ogden: A Collective Memoir*, ed. P. Sargant Florence and J. R. L. Anderson (1977).
4–*Coleridge on Imagination*.

TO *W. H. Auden*   CC

15 February 1935   [Faber & Faber Ltd]

Dear Auden,

At the risk of being a nuisance I am going to bring up again a point which we discussed before you went to Copenhagen.[1] I do so now, however, not simply for myself, but as the mouth-piece of the Committee, and can do so rather more forcibly having your final text in my hands.

While we appreciate your anxiety to give full credit to Isherwood[2] for his help, we feel that you could do this more accurately and in as great detail as you wish in the form of a preface than by having his name on the title page. Indeed, it seems to us that to acknowledge your debt in the form of joint authorship is really misleading, and not true to the facts. I imagine that what Isherwood has done is to help reorganise and simplify the plot, and to outline the various scenes which you have worked up. (I do think, on one hasty reading, dramatically the play is very much improved, and more practical, and Doone seems to be highly satisfied.) But the actual writing seems to be altogether yours. Certainly all of it is either definitely Auden, or might as well be Auden as anyone else. Surely joint authorship signifies that the actual writing has been shared?

I have in mind, of course, all the reasons against joint authorship that I mentioned to you before, but examination of the text seems to us to reinforce these reasons very strongly. Do think this matter over again very carefully. I think, even, that Isherwood would get more justice in the end if you indicated your debt in a prefatory note, than he does by having his name on the title page. As it is, no careful reader is likely to believe that he had very much to do with it.[3]

Yours ever,

[T. S. Eliot]

1–TSE and WHA had lunched together in London on Fri., 4 Jan. 1935.

2–On 29 Jan. 1935 Isherwood submitted the MS of 'Where is Francis?'; it arrived on 31 Jan., and the secretary passed it to TSE. Isherwood had clearly referred to it, in a letter to TSE dated 29 Jan., as 'Auden's & my play'. See further the account by B. C. Bloomfield and Edward Mendelson in *W. H. Auden: A Bibliography 1924–1969* (2nd edn, 1972), 15–16.

Christopher Isherwood (1904–86), novelist, dramatist, translator, diarist and writer on religion, published his first novel, *All the Conspirators*, in 1928, and was to collaborate further with WHA on *The Ascent of F6*, *On the Frontier*, and *Journey to a War*. His autobiographical novel *Lions and Shadows* (1938) contains a vivid portrait of the young Auden under the guise of 'Hugh Weston'.

3–WHA replied from Downs School ('Monday', n.d.): 'I have really thought over what you said, but I still feel only a joint title acknowledgement is possible.

TO *H. D. Aldington*[1]   CC

15 February 1935   [Faber & Faber Ltd]

Dear Mrs Aldington,

I shall not be free to come in on Sunday, but I think I could come rather late on Monday, about 5 o'clock or so, and I should like to do so.[2]

Yours sincerely,

[T. S. Eliot]

TO *Margaret Babington*   CC

15 February 1935   [Faber & Faber Ltd]

Dear Miss Babington,

Thank you for your letter of the 13th.[3] Perhaps before deciding to accept the use of the costumes designed by Robert Medley, it would be

---

'As you saw, Isherwood outlined the plan of most of the scenes, but more than that, the whole of the Channel crossing & Financier scenes, (except the songs) the whole of the Customs scene, the asylum scene bar the leaders speech and the song at the beginning, bits of the hotel scenes, and all the last scene except for the sermon are his, so I'm sure you will agree with me, that I couldn't very well do anything else. Nobody reads prefaces and acknowledgments are meant for the careless reader, not the careful.'

1– Hilda Doolittle (1886–1961), American poet, novelist and memoirist – always known by her *nom de plume* 'H.D.' – lived in London from 1911, where she made friends in the literary world, worked as assistant editor of *The Egoist*, 1916–17, and gained a reputation as an Imagist poet (promoted in good part by her old friend EP, to whom she had been briefly engaged in 1907–8). Her debut volume of verse was *Sea Garden* (1916). In 1913 she married the poet Richard Aldington; and although the marriage foundered by the end of WW1, they remained friends and were divorced only in 1938. For thirty years, the bisexual H.D. lived with the heiress, philanthropist and novelist Bryher (Annie Winifred Ellerman), and she brought out noted works including *The Walls Do Not Fall* (1944), *Trilogy* (1946), and *Tribute to Freud* (1956). Posthumous works include *End to Torment: A Memoir of Ezra Pound* (1979). See Barbara Guest, *Herself Defined: The Poet H.D. and Her World* (1985); Rachel Blau DuPlessis, *H.D. The Career of that Struggle* (1986).

2– H.D. wrote ('Wednesday'): 'I shall be in on Sunday; possibly Ernest Freud will be here, with his wife. They are not psycho-analytical. He is a gifted architect, forced to leave Berlin. Or I shall be alone on Monday, or with a Mr Rodeck whom I would like you to meet. He retired from his profession, also architecture, to become a priest – at least, he is waiting for his full orders; in the meantime, he is somewhat baffled by difficulties in getting his final foot-hold.'

3– 'Everything now seems so very satisfactory and as the costumes, apart from that of the Archbishop, are not to be really sombre, I shall with the utmost gratitude accept the loan of them as designed by Mr Robert Medley, for our performances in June . . . Are you going to have completely new costumes for the knights or did you think of using those designed for Becket?'

as well if we consulted Laurence Irving and Martin Browne. I have just written to Irving, and shall write to Browne. I don't think that Doone would want to use the Canterbury costumes, because I imagine he wants the costuming of the play to be all of a piece, but I think it is possible that the costumes you have might be more suitable for Canterbury than his. After all, I feel that this is the producer's business much more than the author's, and I don't want to interfere in what is not my business.

I have been devoting a good deal of thought to the title, and am still wavering, but I am aware of the desirability of settling the name as quickly as possible.[1]

Yours sincerely,
[T. S. Eliot]

TO *Frederic Prokosch*[2]

TS Texas

20 February 1935   Faber & Faber Ltd

Dear Mr Prokosch,

Very many thanks for your kind gift, and for printing my two poems in such a charming way. I am sure that no one could raise any objection

---

1–Babington wrote on 13 Feb., 'The only thing I am wanting badly now is the title of the play, for I cannot announce any more that there is to be "a specially written play by Mr T. S. Eliot . . ."' To TSE's secretary, Babington wrote further on 20 Mar.: 'Would you very kindly ask Mr Eliot whether it is not yet possible for me to know the title of the Play he is writing for the Canterbury Festival? The preliminary Programme is actually waiting to be set up until I know this, for I have every other detail of the Festival Week save this.' FVM to Babington, 26 Mar. 1935: 'I consulted Mr Eliot about the title, and he tells me that he wrote to you last night explaining that the proper title is FEAR IN THE WAY, and that no other title should have been released.' TSE's secretary to EMB, 27 Mar. 1935: 'Mr Eliot has asked me to send you the enclosed typescript of Fear in the Way. Part I has been revised and this copy now takes the place of the one which you have. Mr Eliot would therefore be obliged if you would return the latter to him . . .'

2–Frederic Prokosch (1906–89), American novelist and poet – son of Edouard Prokosch, Sterling Professor of Linguistics at Yale – was educated in Austria, Germany and France; graduated from Haverford College, Pennsylvania, and taught English at Yale for two years. His first novel, *The Asiatics*, published to considerable acclaim in 1935, was to be translated into seventeen languages: André Gide hailed it as an 'authentic masterpiece', and Thomas Mann as 'this astonishing, picaresque romance'. Later novels included *The Seven Who Fled* (1937) and *The Missolonghi Manuscript* (1968). Accomplished as a printer of small private editions, he also translated poems by Hölderlin and Louise Labé. He was squash-rackets champion of France, 1933–9; of Sweden, 1944. See Robert Greenfield, *Dreamer's Journey: The Life and Writings of Frederic Prokosch* (2010).

On 1 Jan. 1950 TSE would support Prokosch for a Fulbright Award: 'I have known Mr Frederic Prokosch slightly, for a number of years. That is to say, I have seen him from

to your printing poems in this way which are not for sale, and I am very pleased by the gifts.[1] It occurs to me that a short poem produced in this way would make a very nice Christmas card, and if you cared to produce something in this way for next Christmas for me, I would write a poem for the purpose. Of course, an arrangement of that sort would naturally involve my paying for your expense and time.

Yours very sincerely,
T. S. Eliot

P.S. I like your poem, and shall be glad to publish it at some time in the *Criterion*.[2]

---

time to time on his passage through London. I do not know him well enough to speak directly of his personality, but I have always regarded him as a very good poet and prose writer. The fact that his novels are now published in this country by my Firm, is sufficient evidence of our esteem of his work, and recognition of his qualities as a writer. His reputation however, is so extensive and well established, that a commendation of his imaginative work seems almost superfluous. I should imagine that he was a good linguist. I regard him as a man of quite exceptional ability, and I should think that the grant awarded to him for the purposes indicated, would be amply justified.' He advised the Bollingen Foundation, 28 June 1955: 'I know Mr Prokosch as a talented poet and writer of prose romances. I have no direct knowledge of the extent of his knowledge of foreign languages, or of his ability as a translator. But Mr Prokosch has always appeared in his prose writings as a man of very cosmopolitan experience, and I have no doubt that any translation he made would be an interesting piece of English verse.'

1 – Prokosch printed twenty copies of *Words for Music* (1934) as a Butterfly Book: comprising 'New Hampshire' and 'Virginia'. 'Here is a present for you,' he wrote in an undated covering letter. 'I had hoped to get them off by Christmas . . . As you surely know, they are meant purely to give pleasure. I hope they do. I enjoyed printing & designing & binding them very much.' TSE sent a copy to Hope Mirrlees on 24 Dec. 1935, 'With Christmas wishes, 1935, from Tom Eliot'; another to George Every, SSM, in Feb. 1935. See further *Poems*, ed. Ricks and McCue, II, 463–4.

2 – 'Going Southward' (submitted on 11 Feb.). Prokosch added: 'in two or three weeks I shall send a long novel called *The Asiatics* to Faber'.

TO *John Masefield*[1]   CC

20 February 1935   [Faber & Faber Ltd]

Dear Sir,

I have to thank you for your letter of February the 15th, and am sending you, under separate cover, two volumes of verse by Stephen Spender, which appeared in the year 1934.[2]

Yours faithfully,
[T. S. Eliot]

TO *I. A. Richards*   CC

20 February 1935   [Faber & Faber Ltd]

My dear Richards,

I am sorry to have to bother you again about the King's Medal, but we have just had a letter from John Masefield from which I learn that the poetry under consideration is limited to volumes published in 1934. Is that quite right? I had been under the impression that 1933 was the first year to be considered. The annoyance is that 1934 puts Auden out of the running, because he did not publish any book in that year. Spender, I suppose, is still eligible, as both the second edition of his poem[s], including a number of new ones, and *Vienna* appeared in that

---

1–John Masefield (1878–1967) won lasting popular acclaim with *Salt-Water Ballads* (1902), followed by other books including *The Everlasting Mercy* (1911). Appointed Poet Laureate in 1930, he also served as President of the Society of Authors in 1937. TSE to John Willett (*TLS*), 19 May 1961: 'If I could find the time at present I should be indeed happy to write something about Masefield because I think he is a poet of more historical importance than is usually put to his credit by writers of my generation and younger. But I should have to give some time to re-reading what I have read and reading for the first time a great deal that I have not read of Masefield's work, and I see no possibility whatever of fitting it in at any time this year. I am very sorry because this is a service which I should have been very happy to do him.' Masefield reciprocated TSE's liking, and wrote on 9 Jan. 1940 that he felt 'very deeply moved and delighted' by *The Family Reunion*. 'Nothing finer has been done in my time,' he told TSE.
2–Masefield invited Faber & Faber to submit books of poetry published in 1934 that might be considered by a committee – Laurence Binyon, Walter de la Mare, Gilbert Murray, and I. A. Richards – for the Royal Medals for poetry. 'The Medals, when awarded, will be given to the first or second book of a writer or to the work of a writer under thirty-five years of age.'

year. I should be very grateful if you could let me know exactly what does come under consideration for the first medal and what does not.[1]

Yours ever,

[T. S. E.]

TO *Derek Verschoyle*[2]   CC

20 February 1935   [Faber & Faber Ltd]

Dear Verschoyle,

Here is the information about the reviewer of whom I spoke. His name is T. S. Gregory, and he lives at 6 Hadlow Road, Sidcup, Kent. Age, 37. Was a scholar at New College, where he got a second in Modern History. As I mentioned on the telephone, he has been a Methodist minister until this year, and having now broken with that denomination, he is badly in need of work. Professor Ernest Barker, who was his tutor, has written to me about him praising him very highly. We are publishing his book, *The Unfinished Universe*. He is specially strong in philosophy and theology, in political theory, and in history generally. He is also very well read in English literature, and is specially strong on Swift and Defoe. He seems to me a very good man, and I should be very glad if you could try him.

Yours ever,

[T. S. Eliot]

TO *Jeffrey Mark*   CC

21 February 1935   [Faber & Faber Ltd]

Dear Mr Mark,

Forgive my delay in dealing with your manuscript *Analysis of Usury*. I found it extremely interesting, and so far as I am competent to judge, a valuable piece of work. I am afraid, however, that my firm cannot see its way to publishing the book. We have always found the market for books on economics, even of a more conventional sort than yours, to be very poor. We make a point of publishing certain kinds of poetry and literature which [do not] command a large sale, so that I do not feel justified in

1–IAR, 22 Feb.: 'You are right! The first year for which a medal was offered was 1933 (to be awarded in 1934). We are a bit late but that 1933 year is not yet settled. After that, will come 1934!' (*Selected Letters*, 88).

2–Derek Verschoyle (1911–73): literary editor of the *Spectator*, 1932–40.

urging my firm to publish economic works at a loss also. I think that Stanley Nott might be interested in this, as he is not necessarily committed to narrowly orthodox Douglas Credit. It seems to me just possible that Kegan Paul or Allen and Unwin might be interested. If I can help in any way I shall be very glad, and I am sorry to have to return the manuscript to you.

Yours sincerely,
[T. S. Eliot]

TO *E. Martin Browne* cc

21 February 1935   [*The Criterion*]

Dear Browne,

Thank you for your letter of the 14th.[1] I hope to let you have Act I complete by the beginning of next week. Miss Fogerty can go ahead

---

1 – 'I look forward to your new style, which I'm sure will be better than what you sent me – I have a strong feeling that the departure from historical "realism" should be as complete as possible. This will of course be assisted by [Robert] Medley's work, which Miss Babington seems delighted to accept – she has just written me a charming letter about it. I don't know it, but feel sure it will at least be stimulating. Oh, yes, it suddenly occurs to me that I've seen Doone's "Dance of Death" ballet, & those were his costumes. They were rather violent – not as distinguished or witty as Stella [Newton]'s – but alive and effective. Yes, we should do well enough. Could you please represent to Doone that it would help us if Medley could become acquainted with, and to some extent remember, our *background* in designing? It is, after all, very definite in character, and though of course I expect & *want contrast* between background & costumes for our purpose, the two should be *complementary*, especially in colour-scheme, if the contrast is to be at all effective . . .

'I'm having a copy of the first chorus made to keep Miss Fogerty quiet. Is that all right? P.S. Miss Babington urgently wants the "title" for the play. I strongly suggest that if Doone's doing it as "The Archbishop Murder Case", we should also use that. But we must decide something soon.'

Elsie Fogerty was to recall: 'The way in which we obtained Eliot's consent to doing the choruses was very interesting. Martin Browne, who was producing, came to me one day and said: "Eliot has written a wonderful play, and he wants to have choric speaking in it. He has heard – so-and-so – and doesn't think he could bear it, after *The Rock*. Will you get your students to learn a chorus he has written, and let him come and hear it?"

'"No," I answered. "Let me have the chorus, and I will have copies made directly. Then, next time you come to the Hall, ask Mr Eliot to come in with you: I won't speak to him or go near him: just let him sit at the back of the Theatre. I'll take through a chorus I think we can do, and then I'll set to work and teach a bit of his chorus to the choir, for the first time: if he likes us, and the way we approach it, we'll go on; and if he doesn't, I shall think no more about it." . . .

'The great peculiarity of Eliot's choric work was the way individual threads of character ran through the whole of the choruses. So, after doing one well-known Greek example, the

with that chorus. There is one other longish chorus for her girls at the end of Act I. About the title, I am still very unsettled. I am sure that the Archbishop's Murder Case wouldn't do. It would offend a good many people, who would think it too flippant. On the other hand, you will gather why I thought of such a title tentatively. I want to avoid any suggestion of conventional religious drama.

I am sorry for your private information about York, but look forward to hearing more about it when we meet.[1]

Yours ever,
[T. S. Eliot]

TO *Henry Eliot*   TS Houghton

21 February 1935   Faber & Faber Ltd

My dear Henry,

I was very glad to get your letter of the 11th. The Ariel Poems are all available except *Marina* (which contrary to rumour went out of print long before Prince George's engagement) so if you will let me know how many you want of which I will have them sent. Be assured that my lawyer has considered the prospect of Vivienne's increase of income when her mother dies. What I pay her now is only voluntary anyway, as she has not agreed to any deed of separation, and on the death of her mother is to be revised. The notion of her having a considerably larger income than Marion or Margaret does not appeal to me. Of course she will get the Trust Income after my death, by the provisions made at the time; but I am making a new will by which she will get nothing else.

---

students took their new copies and sat down and we set to work. Of course, in ten minutes I had forgotten that Eliot was there, and the students never knew. The problem was to find the exact number of speakers needed for each phrase in the chorus, and very soon we realised that we were doing not strictly choral work – but orchestral work; each speaker had to be like an instrument, in harmony with the other voices during the ensemble passages, but repeating a recurring phrase in an individual tone – just as a flute or horn would do in an orchestra: one such phrase I remember is the "Living – and partly living" of the first chorus: we tried four voices before finding the one that could give – quite naturally – the strange discouraged hopelessness of that line.

'I did not wait to hear the verdict after that first attempt. But a few days after, Martin arrived triumphant: "Eliot has written three more choruses!"' (*Fogie*, ed. Marion Cole, 164–5).

1–'I'm not at all happy here [at York, where EMB was producer of the York Repertory Theatre since Nov. 1934], as the management has got into the hands of a person quite alien to me, & I may not be here long. This is confidential. In any case, I shall come down & see you in a fortnight's time.'

The English law is that in a separation the wife is entitled to one third of the *joint* incomes of husband and wife.

I am horrified about the kidnapping threat. It may of course be the work of a deranged or irresponsible person; and I should not have thought that the Danes were so superlatively wealthy as to attract the attention of practical kidnappers. In the present circumstances, after the Hauptmann trial,[1] it would be natural that anyone with a grudge, such as a dismissed servant, might send such a letter merely to excite alarm, but it is a cruel thing to do.

D'Arcy should be in New York now, his address is: Father M. C. D'Arcy, S.J., America House, 329 W. 108th Street. He is a good friend of mine. I can't get him any jobs; I wrote to someone at Harvard. St Louis University, being Jesuit, will very likely ask him. I wrote to Frederick too, but have no reply. He is not anxious to make money; being a member of an order that makes no difference to him personally; but he would have to have his expenses paid, and he would like to see something of America. Anything you could do would be appreciated. I think he would be as interested to meet Unitarian clergy as any other.

The quotation in the enclosed cutting was of course NOT by me, it may have been and most likely was by Gertrude Stein, but there is no connexion between the two firms: I have NOTHING to say on her behalf.[2]

I have only about five weeks to finish my play about the murder of St Thomas à Becket, which is to be produced in London in May (with plays by Yeats and Auden) and at Canterbury in June; so I have to avoid all possible engagements in order to work.

With love to both,
your affectionate brother,
Tom

1–Richard Hauptmann (1899–1936), a German-born carpenter, was convicted in New Jersey of the abduction and murder of the twenty-month-old son of the flying hero Charles Linbergh and his wife – the so-called 'Crime of the Century'. At this date, he had just been sentenced to death.
2–Not identified.

TO *Michael Roberts*   TS Berg

21 February 1935   Faber & Faber Ltd

My dear Roberts,

I have read your poems with a good deal of liking, and rather mixed feelings as well. It seems to me that this book needs a few longer and stronger poems to start off with, if it is to make its way. There is a certain monotony about the descriptive form of a good many, and there is rather too much of the cultured traveller, Matthew Arnold at the Grande Chartreuse. I don't feel that the collection is yet quite ripe enough for picking. At the same time, I am quite willing to believe that there are other publishers who would disagree with me.

Miss Adam Smith has very kindly invited me to dinner on the 9th or 10th of March, and I look forward to seeing you then.[1] I have a proposal which I should like to discuss with you when we meet. My firm has conceived the idea that there is room for another anthology of modern verse, and we wonder whether you would consider editing a collection for us. I should very much like to know whether you are interested in principle, and we can discuss the details when we meet.[2]

Yours ever.
T. S. Eliot

TO *Herbert Read*   CC

22 February 1935   [Faber & Faber Ltd]

Dear Herbert,

I should be grateful if you would look through the enclosed poem by a lad at Oxford named Frank Prince,[3] who is a friend of Stephen Spender. I can't make up my mind about it, and should like to have your opinion. It will do the next time I see you.

Yours ever,
[Tom]

1–Adam Smith wrote on 19 Feb. to invite TSE to join them for dinner at 5 Ladbroke Square, W.11. (Michael Roberts had notified TSE on 24 Jan. that he and Janet Adam Smith had become engaged to be married. TSE had sent his congratulations in a letter that has not been traced.)
2–First mention of *The Faber Book of Modern Verse* (1936).
3–Frank Templeton Prince (1912–2003), poet, critic and editor. See further TSE to Prince, 10 Sept. 1935, below.

TO *Bruce Richmond*[1]

22 February 1935   [Faber & Faber Ltd]

Dear Richmond,

I agree with you that the content of the enclosed letter is mere pepper-pot criticism.[2] I did not myself think very highly of the edition. The notes were inadequate, and were sometimes, like G. B. Harrison's, rather prudish. I thought it was a laudable enterprise on the part of the publishers, who deserved encouragement. I don't think that any of the points that your correspondent makes justify the truculence of his tone. I have ticked a few points which seem to me more worthwhile mentioning than others.

It was stupid of me not to have given you Mr T. S. Gregory's address, which is 6 Hadlow Road, Sidcup, Kent.[3] His book has not yet been published. It is to be called *The Unfinished Universe*.

Yours ever,
[T. S. E.]

TO *Stephen Spender*   TS Northwestern

22 February 1935   Faber & Faber Ltd

Dear Spender,

I understand that Random House are considering publishing *Vienna*, but I doubt if they will publish it just yet, as for them it comes rather close on the heels of your poems.[4] I should certainly advise you to let them

1–Bruce Lyttelton Richmond (1871–1964), editor of the *Times Literary Supplement*: see Biographical Register.
2–BLR had forwarded on 21 Feb. a letter (writer unknown) of complaint about TSE's review 'John Marston' (*TLS*, 26 July 1934, 517-18), on *The Plays of John Marston*, vol. I, ed. H. Harvey Wood; and *The Malcontent*, ed. G. B. Harrison. 'I cannot form any opinion of my own, as you have got the book; and, even if I had it, I should come to you for advice! It seems to me that it is all very small beer, and that, even if the points are sound, to publish it in full would be gibbeting the book unfairly. If on the other hand you think that five or six of the points are really worth making, it might be worth while to return the letter to the writer and offer to print a letter containing those points . . .'
3–TSE wrote about Gregory on 8 Feb. (letter now lost). BLR replied, 21 Feb.: 'I will certainly try to find something for Mr Gregory . . . I hope his book has not been sent out in my absence . . .'
4–Spender asked (21 Feb.) if *Vienna* was due out in the USA. 'If I had known, I would like to have re-written it, but now I really don't care very much, as I am writing so much else that I feel less dissatisfied when I look back on it . . . The first English reaction is one of annoyance: Why write about Austrians, when we have our own slums? Of course, there is something in that.

publish it, if they do, with the same text as in the English edition, and get on with what you are doing, instead of worrying about *Vienna*. I am glad that you have got over your first impression about the poem. Possibly Michael Roberts will have cheered you up a bit. I don't think that the English public is yet prepared for occasional verse. I have noticed myself in the last year or so that criticism of what I write is apt to be very much biassed by whether the critic agrees with my views or not. Unfortunately the people who do agree are often just as incompetent to criticise because of their agreement, as are the people who are biassed by their dislike of one's views.

I haven't the slightest idea who Prokosch is, but he seems a very amiable person. I printed one of his own poems last year, and he has just sent me another, which I also like. I look forward to seeing you on Friday.

Yours ever,
Tom

TO *A. J. Penty*[1]   CC

22 February 1935   [Faber & Faber Ltd]

My dear Penty,

I must apologise for the very long delay over your manuscript. I am really shocked to see what a long time I have had it. It has been read by others, and I held it from day to day because I was anxious to read it through myself, for my own interest, whether I agreed with the opinions it expressed at all. I have thoroughly enjoyed reading it, but I must say that I agree with my colleagues that it is a book which would be very difficult to sell. I think the trouble with it is that if falls between two types of literature. It is too biographical to be successful as a book on social and economic theory, and it contains too much economic theory to be successful as a biography. We feel that for this reason it would fail to have more than a very small sale. I am afraid, also, that the young people who are interested in economic theories of today are not interested in what was going on in the early part of the century.

'I see that 970 copies of this poem have now sold. Well my own feeling is that when this edition has gone (which will be fairly soon), it might be better to print no more: to let it fade out. But I only suggest this to you: it is just a matter of my inclination. If you feel that the work can stand the strain of a 2nd printing, I shall trust your judgement.'

1 – Arthur J. Penty (1875–1937), architect: see Biographical Register.

I wish we could publish it, as most of your views are so sympathetic; but I am afraid that we cannot afford to do so.

> With many regrets,
> Yours very sincerely,
> [T. S. Eliot]

TO *The Editor,* Time and Tide

[published 23 February 1935, 272]   24 Russell Square, w.c.1

Sir, –

Mr Milne has begun to formulate the differences between him and myself.[1] He believes that it is 'simpler' to stop war than to stop conflicts between nations; I believe that there is more hope of preventing the causes of conflict than of stopping war so long as the conflicts continue. That is one point; and Mr Milne and I hold contradictory views. Second, Mr Milne and I dislike war for different reasons: I adopt an explicitly Christian view, and Mr Milne is explicitly non-committal. Third, Mr Milne believes that analogies from conflicts between individuals prove something about conflicts between nations; and I do not.

> I am, etc.,
> T. S. Eliot

TO *Philip Mairet*   CC

25 February 1935   [Faber & Faber Ltd]

Dear Mairet,

I have read Mr Playfair's Survey of the Pornographic Press with some interest, and amusement. It seems to me good enough to print, as I can't see that it interferes with a profounder treatment of the matter by some

---

1 – Milne's final letter summed up his position: *Time and Tide* 16: 7 (16 Feb. 1935), 237–8:

'(1) I believe that wars are sometimes due to economic causes, sometimes not.

'(2) I believe that, whatever the causes which bring nations into conflict, the form in which the conflict works itself out need not, and should not, be war.

'(3) I believe that it is simpler to break the sequence from "conflict" to "war" than to break the sequence from "cause" to "conflict" or to eliminate all possible causes of conflict; just as (if I may be allowed a comparison in which I shall try not to involve myself too deeply) our ancestors found it simpler to break the sequence from "quarrel" to "duel" than to break the sequence from "cause" to "quarrel", or to eliminate all possible causes of quarrel.'

one else later. My only question is whether the publishers of any English paper mentioned, or indeed of any of the American papers mentioned which are circulated here, would have any grounds for libel action on account of being mentioned as pornographic or indecent.

Of course, this little essay is a very slight affair, and if you had anybody in mind to do something better in the near future, I should say scrap this.

Yours ever,

[T. S. Eliot]

TO *Ezra Pound*

ts Beinecke

25 Feb[ruary] 1935 AD   Faber & Faber Ltd

Once again, Podesta, I have to inform you that you are Not Practical. Here I have had the Accountant on the Mat, and been through the Books; and if we render a perfectly accurate account to Curtis Brown and Curtis Brown garbages it, what about it? You write to your Agents about that: you take your little Polligner and have your supper there/ He wondered much what he had found/ That was so small and hard and round/[1] It was 1d. royalties after Curtis Brown had taken their slice off the mellon. And what more Podesta I must ask you not to write in your usual Lewse and Blasphemious fasion when you are dealing with accounting matters; its jam for the secretaries in the usual way, thats all right, but our Accountant has a sensitive nature and is easily shocked by prophaning lunatics I object Podesta[2] I object God damb it if I can get up early enough in the morning I have got to go to Fred Manning's funeral Goddamb it God rest his soul[3] so will close

TP.

---

1 – A version of this couplet appeared as light verses published as 'Der Tag' ('The Day') in *The Spike or Victoria University College Review*, Sept. 1925; it is not known how TSE came upon it.

2 – EP had written, 17 Feb.: 'My Dear Possum / FER XTZ acke get a book keeper, and start yr/ firm using DECENT and clean accounting forms.

'Who say   13   18   9

$$\frac{11 \qquad 6 \qquad 3}{37 \qquad 5}$$

'M.I.N. [*Make It New*] 436 @ 10%   £37.5

'Is this De La Mares dept/ or have you got someone practical . . . The doggymints are being returned to Plngr/ [Pollinger, his literary agent].

'Thirty [*sc.* thirteen] and elevent equal thirty seven

'Possum's bloody book=keeper wont ever get to heaven.'

3 – Frederic Manning died in Hampstead, London, on 22 Feb. 1935 and was buried at Kensal Green Cemetery on 26 Feb.

I always suspected you were an ingoramus in matters of Practical Finance. There's a snaphaunce[1] for you.

TO *E. Martin Browne*   CC

25 February 1935[2]   [Faber & Faber Ltd]

My dear Browne,

Thank you for your letter of the 25th.[3] In the circumstances, it seems to me quite unnecessary that you should trouble to come up to town before March 16th. I am sending you herewith the revised version of Act I. You will observe that I have so far done nothing to the first ten pages of script, so what you have to do is to destroy pages 11 ff. of what I have sent you, and insert these. There are, of course, I am quite aware, some rough places in the versification to be polished, and what I need, of course, at present, is criticism from a dramatic point of view. Frankly, there is not really time to re-cast the act, but I should be able to make any modifications that might help to render it a little more actable. Act I is round about 700 lines, and Act II will probably be the same. I shall ask you to do the cutting when the time comes, but I have indicated a passage out of the very long final speech on page 34 which could easily be omitted without damage.

There will, of course, be more action in Part II, and it will be on a natural plane altogether.

Thank you for your own suggestion; but first, what do you think of my new title? My idea was to give it a title which would suggest a detective story, without being open to the criticism of attempting cheap wit. My title seems to me to sound enough like such titles as *Murder on the Links* or *The Corpse in the Car* and that sort of thing, and as it will appear on the title page to be a quotation from Ecclesiastes, nobody ought to be offended. I shall wait anxiously to hear from you.

Yours ever,

[T. S. Eliot]

P.S. I also am particularly anxious that the four tempters in Act I should double with the four murderers in Act II. Different costumes, but the same faces.

---

1 – snaphance/snaphaunce: 'An armed robber or marauder; a freebooter or highwayman; a desperate fellow or thief' (OED 1).

2 – Misdated, according to EMB, who thought it is more likely to be 28 Feb.

3 – Browne had written on 25 Feb., 'Would "Doom on the Archbishop" (from 1st chorus) strike the happy mean between religious and frivolous? It has a firm sound!'

TO *Rayner Heppenstall*[1]   TS Texas

27 February 1935   *The Criterion*

Dear Mr Heppenstall,

I have your letter of the 22nd, and will send you Barker's poems when they are ready. As for the Ballet article in June, I am afraid that will be impossible for reasons of space.[2] The March number is overflowing into June, and obviously I could not let you write such an article unless I could be sure of publishing it in that issue, so I think we shall have to wait until October. If I see any way of getting tickets I will do so, but I have had previous experience some years ago in trying to get ballet and theatre tickets for the *Criterion*, and it is practically impossible to get tickets for a review appearing so infrequently as every three months.

The other volumes you mention will certainly be sent to the *New English Weekly.*[3]

If I have read your postscript correctly, I must take lively exception to it.[4] The word 'unscrupulous' seems to me an imputation of malicious motive, and I could see nothing in Spender's review which exceeded the legitimate bounds of criticism.[5] I speak, of course, without having read your book. I am sorry that I have not read it, but I simply have not had the time.

Yours sincerely,
T. S. Eliot

1– Rayner Heppenstall (1911–81): novelist, poet, radio producer; author of *Middleton Murry: A Study in Excellent Normality* (1934); *Apology for Dancing* (1936); *The Blaze of Noon* (novel, 1939); *Four Absentees: Dylan Thomas, George Orwell, Eric Gill, J. Middleton Murry* (1960).

2– 'Yes, an article summing up the season, in October, would be excellent. I think Ballet at least as important as the other matters, and feel, etc., etc.; and I would like to divide the season up into two, if there is any chance at all that you could put in a shortish article in June . . . Also, is there the chance that extra (press) tickets for performances could be had through *The Criterion?*'

3– 'Also, shall copies of Auden, Marianne Moore, and the new Cantos be coming to the *NEW?*'

4– 'Spender's review of MURRY was the most *unscrupulous* of many: I was surprised.' SS on Rayner Heppenstall, *Middleton Murry: A Study in Excellent Normality*: C. 14 (Jan. 1935), 311–13: 'Mr Heppenstall does not seem in the least anxious to "convert" people to his prophet; for I assume that conversion is the only conceivable attitude to the man who is not only the perfect norm, the super-synthesizer, but also the multiplicator of Jesus, Shakespeare, Blake and Marx . . . It is a pity that Mr Heppenstall is not more explicit both in his hatred and in his admiration. For he gives the impression of being a genuine hater . . . Undoubtedly, Mr Heppenstall will write much better books: here he has done himself a disservice, and Mr Murry far less than justice.'

5– In his next letter (n.d.), Heppenstall apologised for the postscript: 'it is a matter between Spender & myself . . . I apologise . . . for having stupidly made the remark in a letter *to you*.'

FROM *Vivien Eliot*   MS Valerie Eliot[1]

27 February 1935   68 Clarence Gate Gardens,
                                  Regents Park, N.W.I.

Tom, I have been ill since last week, & a prisoner. *Like yourself.* But you must know, unless your correspondence, *even*, is interrupted, that I work day & night on your behalf & that every thought I have is for you & all my strength is used that way but often I am not able to move for weeks at a time & have no strength left. I take notes of *all things* so that it *will be* known, in time, if you receive my letters & IF YOU ARE FREE. Yr. wife, V. Haigh Eliot.
    9 p.m. Front door *open* —

TO *The Editor,* The New English Weekly

[published 28 February 1935, 422] [Faber & Faber Ltd]

                 The Church Assembly and Social Credit
Sir,
    I hope and believe that the difference between myself and Mr Maurice Reckitt is more verbal than real.[2] I assumed, even if I did not make explicit, the difference between the Report of the Commission and the debate on the Report in the Assembly. I was not finding fault with the

---

1–Also transcribed in VHE's diary.
2–Reckitt, 'The Church Assembly', *NEW*, 21 Feb. 1935, 403 – with reference to TSE's letter about the Church Assembly's debate on the Report of its Social and Industrial Committee – 'I am entirely in agreement with him when he says that "it would appear that the Church has not made up its mind how far, or in what way, it ought to be concerned with social and economic problems." Membership of the Commission in question gives me some qualifications for warmly endorsing this assertion. I agree again with Mr Eliot that "we should be more likely to get somewhere if the representatives of the Church in the Church Assembly (and not only there) . . . should give their time to considering the fundamental moral laws founded on Christian theology." Christian social values will only begin to achieve authenticity when they are plainly rooted in moral theology . . . But the Report did, at least to some extent, do what Mr Eliot desiderates – it did "proclaim positively violations of moral laws" which its authors "observed, as Churchmen, in the present order" . . .
    'Where I seem to differ, however, from Mr Eliot is in regard to his suggestion that this is as far as Churchmen can legitimately go in this matter. I do not indeed think that they are justified in associating religion categorically with any particular secular theory, for reasons which this journal is perhaps scarcely the place to elucidate. But I do think that those who have taken the pains to found themselves upon an authentic foundation in theology and Christian tradition ought not to be inhibited from drawing any constructive deductions from their premises.'

Report, but with the debate. When I wrote, my feelings were inflamed by the words of Lord Hugh Cecil, Mr Assheton, Sir Francis Fremantle, and the Bishop of Jarrow.

I should like to draw a distinction between the use of the terms 'the Church' and 'Churchmen'. I indicated a point beyond which I thought that 'the Church' should not go; but I should think poorly of Churchmen, as human beings, if they were unwilling to go farther: I might even say that it seems to me to be the duty of Churchmen to go farther than the Church should go. When Mr Reckitt says that he does not think that Churchmen are justified 'in associating religion categorically with any particular secular theory', I am in agreement, except that instead of the term 'religion', which I do not much like, I should prefer 'the Faith'. But I should add that I feel that Churchmen, as individuals, might well advocate whatever secular theory seems to them most nearly compatible with their Churchmanship. By all means let Churchmen 'draw constructive deductions from their premises': Mr Reckitt does that, and so, I hope, do I. In so doing, we commit no one but ourselves. It is not the business of the Church to commit itself to any particular secular solution; but it is very much the business of individual Churchmen, as they take their membership of the Church seriously, to be ready to commit their individual opinions.

T. S. Eliot

FROM *E. Martin Browne*   TS Valerie Eliot

2 March 1935   87 Clifton Green, York

My dear Eliot,

I am sorry to have delayed answer to your letter and the complete Act I, but have been earnestly considering them – in fact this is the third letter I have started to you.

I frankly confess myself worried about the Act from a dramatic point of view. It now consists of a series of entrances and no exits, involving the gradual construction on the stage of a group in the manner of Orcagna or Duccio;[1] and that is absolutely all that can happen. There is no possibility of movement unless one artificially inserted it, which would only spoil the

---

1–Andrea di Cione di Arcangelo (c. 1308–68), known as Orcagna: Florentine painter, sculptor and architect. Duccio di Buoninsegna: 13th–14th-century Sienese artist (d. 1319) best known for the *Maestà*, a double-sided altarpiece (1308–11) commissioned for Siena Cathedral.

whole. Added to this, an audience will find those Tempters very hard to understand. They talk in abstract and difficult language, and it would be hard even for a very experienced verse-speaking actor to make a difference between any of the first three which an audience could get firmly hold of. They all talk in the same tempo, and in rhythms not so different as to offer much relief; and they again are not so different from the Priests in style. This matters mainly because there is no clash between the parties; the Chorus seem to take the arrival of the Tempters without protest, so do the Priests, and what they say later is meek in the extreme. Thomas necessarily goes on saying just 'No' all the time, so he doesn't help much either.

This is extremely destructive criticism, but I think it better to say now what I feel, especially because the Act is full of good poetry and fine thought, and my criticism is solely from the stage point of view. As a producer, I frankly confess to feeling that Roger and Robert, though less distinguished, were better drama than the Tempters are now. So the question is – what can be done to make the Tempters dramatic?

Here are some ideas:

(1) They should be violently different, in tempo, rhythm and looks. The first should be THE WORLD, gay, speaking trippingly and liltingly, dressed in fantastic profusion of colour and line. The second THE POWER, hard, grand, ermined, speaking heavy regular lines. The third INTRIGUE, slinky, speaking perhaps prose or a very fluid long line, dressed in narrow kaleidoscopic stripes; attacked by the first two. The last THE GLORY, in white monastic garb but with a black face, speaking either blank verse or a freer five-accented line; rouses the expressed horror of all the other three, but playing in a spiritual key which should for a time captivate Thomas – his discovery of the true nature of this temptation should be the most dramatic moment of Act I.

(2) Before, during and between scenes we need the reactions of Chorus and Priests; and Thomas' reactions should be much more marked.

(3) The Tempters must *explain their stories*. At present it would need a 30-page essay to make any of the audience understand what they have to do with Thomas. In each case a concrete fact or incident shd. be told as illustrating what Thomas is offered, and told in detail, not just referred to.

(4) The end of the scene must have movement. Could not Thomas' final dealing with the Tempters lead to his desertion, first by them, then by the Chorus and then by the Priests, till he is alone on the stage? Then, to link Act I to Act II, a sort of Gethsemane, quite short but preparing

for the martyrdom. Some of the material now in your final speech should come in here, for at the end of the Act you *don't* want a long exposition.

One other problem of the producer needs attention. The first entrance of the Chorus is what we call 'cold' – i.e. it happens for no reason and without anything happening, nor can they speak while they walk in without spoiling your poetry. In a play of this kind we can't do what we did in the Rock – there are no 'scenes' and no curtains; so they ought either to have something to bring them on or else to be there from the beginning. This may not apply so much in London, but at Canterbury it will be really essential. Music might be used, but I can't quite see how.

All this seems complex and you certainly won't agree with all of it. Would it be a great help if I came up and saw you and we went over it together? I could manage to get up for a single day I think; the best would probably be Saturday, but I would try to fit in with you; or I could easily come any day next week after Monday (11th).

Please believe at the end of it all that I do think the writing excellent and have faith in the play's ability to become successful for acting. And forgive my presumptions.

Yours ever,
Martin Browne

TO *E. Martin Browne*   CC

Shrove Tuesday [5 March] 1935   [*The Criterion*]

My dear Martin Browne,

I trust you did not expect me to reply by Return of Post: because your letter needed a deal of mulling over; and if I had replied in the spirit of the moment I should have told you to go to hell entirely, and take Canterbury with you, and begin thinking about somebody else's play for the bloody festival etc. Even as it is, I am not sure that the last suggestion is not pertinent.

However, I am now in a more Lenten mood. I have discussed the matter with a friend (male) whose opinion I value, and this afternoon with Rupert Doone; and I can begin to separate the wheat from the chaff.

I don't deny that the play as you outline it would be a good play; it might be a better play than mine; but it wouldnt be MY play. OF COURSE the play is entrances and no exits (I mean Act I) and is building up a group, a group of various points of view all alien to Thomas's; and their all sticking on to the end is meant to emphasise his isolation more brutally than if he were left alone; I meant to emphasise his loneliness, but you can only do that by showing a man in a crowd of people who from different points of view dont understand what he is after. OF COURSE there is no clash between the parties: you have their clash with Thomas, and as they are all against him it would only weaken the effect to have them against each other as well; they dont take any notice of each other, in fact that [they] are all together against HIM.

WON'T have tempters given individual abstract names: wont have pseudo-morality play pre-raphaelite simplicity. Let the audience adjust planes of reality for themselves. The last shall Not be a Blackbird of 1935. Point is that at each temptation Thomas is a lap ahead: what is offered is a memory of temptation: everything offered is what Thomas has ALREADY thought about. He does not NEED to say much, because the four voices are himself. By the time 3 comes on Thomas is already past 3, when 4 comes on Thomas has already dealt with 4. GETHSEMANE NO: wont have mere Saint going through analogous struggles to our Lord; there is only one God, but human beings become saints in human ways.

Now then, turn over:

POINTS ACCEPTED:

Tempters do talk (or begin to talk) too much alike. I think something concrete and particular should be introduced at the beginning of each of their speeches. Let them begin, each, looking particular and become symbolic gradually. Beginning of each of their speeches (at any rate the first three) to be re-written, with more marked rhythmic difference.

POINTS IN DOUBT:

Whether the Chorus should join in, as individuals, in comment on the action. Don't agree about first activity of chorus, which may be cold, but like the embraces of the Devil, a heat which freezes.

BUT

If Chorus don't comment individually, some other common human measure is needed against which to gauge the super-normality of the planes of reality of the scene.

In Act I a normal human element is needed as a measure; in Act II the problem is reversed; it is all scuffle. In Act I the audience needs to be reminded of ordinary human attitudes; in Act II it has to be reminded of the general in the particular.

Useful to keep Chaucer in mind: relation of St Thomas to the Wife of Bath etc. But Wife of Bath no more 'human' than Nun.

I think that you underrate audience. If not, nobody ever did anything worth doing in writing down to an audience.

Yours ever,
[T. S. Eliot]¹

TO *Stephen Spender*

8 March 1935   Faber & Faber Ltd

My dear Stephen,

I am afraid that my Committee did not look upon the projected translation of Hoelderlin with at all a favourable eye.[2] In the first place, I think I mentioned to you my own experience with *Anabase*. Although Hoelderlin is of course a much greater poet than Perse, and is recognised

---

1–Browne replied (n.d.: ? 7 Mar. 1935): 'Many thanks for your excellent letter, and first for refraining from consigning me to hell. My stupidity deserved it, I know, but the results of your forgiveness may be good all round. You have made clear to me how definitely you desire a certain presentation of your problem; & as long as we are sure what effect we want, I entirely agree that the audience must accept it – and, if I can get it properly done, I'm sure enough of them will do so.

'I think your decision to define the Tempters more will really help the audience. My pre-raphaelite way of putting it wasn't meant to be taken literally, but was the most vivid means at my disposal of suggesting the particularity I felt was needed. The names were, I confess, an excess of provocative zeal!

'I still hope you will help me solve my producer's problem of the end of the Act. Understanding that no one is to leave Thomas, and why, I have to ask, on an open stage in daylight, how is the end of the Act to be marked?

'I am grateful for the expression that "Thomas is a lap ahead" of the Tempters – that illuminates the scenes for me.

'I must say I rather hope you will use the Chorus for individual comment, rather than introduce others; it seems to me that they *do* clearly stand for ordinary humanity, by their first speech, & to introduce another "common human measure" might tend to confusion? Incidentally, you would get the individual comments better spoken.'

2–Spender proposed an edition in translation of poems by [Friedrich] Hölderlin, to be undertaken in collaboration with Edwin Muir. His submission to F&F has not been traced. See further SS, 'The Influence of Hoelderlin on English Poetry', *The Listener*, 15 Aug. 1946, 217: 'In Eliot's *The Waste Land* the three elements which are obsessive in Hoelderlin are present. One of these is paganism, widened in *The Waste Land* beyond the Greek to an interest in primitive cultures; the second is the almost oppressive sense of the past, that is to say the sense of the past not as the past but as inescapable and omnipresent; the third element in common with Hoelderlin is the idea of Christ as the resurrection of a whole civilisation in which the past is projected into the future and the rituals of more primitive civilisation reborn within Christianity. I do not suggest that Eliot was directly influenced by Hoelderlin in *The Waste Land*, though this is undoubtedly the poem in which he is most influenced by German thought, and, as I have said, after the last war German literature had rediscovered Hoelderlin.'

as a classic, yet I think that for sales purposes he is so little known in this country that his name gives no advantage over a poet completely unknown. The book would sell, therefore, merely as a minor work of your own. As such, and for the sake of keeping all your work together, we might be glad to publish it, but candidly we would not consider paying Edwin Muir £35 to collaborate with you where actually the collaboration of Edwin Muir would be a disadvantage to the sales. I am speaking without compliment, but quite practically, and, you will understand, in entire confidence, when I say that having Muir's name attached to the book would be a real draw-back to its sales. Your name alone would excite a good deal of curiosity even about a poet whose name is almost unknown in England, but the addition of the name of a man who, however excellent a writer, is too well known as an ordinary translator, would damage it very much.

The Committee would still like you to entertain the notion of a semi-autobiographical book, or what you call a novel, as your next considerable piece of work. If you find you can't do that, I think that the volume of stories is the next thing to come. I am inclined to agree with you that in the long run it would be a better policy to delay the next volume of poems for a few seasons. Let me know what you think about all this.

Yours affectionately,
Tom

TO *W. H. Auden*   CC

8 March 1935   [Faber & Faber Ltd]

Dear Auden,

It is true that I sent you the two poems which were printed by the friendly Prokosch.[1] Don't send me in return any that he has done for you, because I should certainly mislay them at once. These nice little poems make very good Christmas cards, but they are pleasanter to give than to receive, so you can throw mine away as soon as you are ready. I did *not*, however, send you the Pound *Cantos*. I should not have dreamt of sending you the Pound *Cantos*. I find on enquiry that they were sent to you by the

---

1–WHA wrote on 5 Mar.: 'I ought to have written before to thank you for the poems in which I fancy I see the hand of our mutual admirer Mr Prokosch. He's sent me some of mine which I'd send you only I don't like them.' WHA, *Two Poems* (1934) – from *New Verse*, Oct. 1933.

firm as a present and testimonial of esteem, but if you dislike them as much as all that it is perhaps as well that you have returned them.[1]

We do not think the enclosed photograph suitable for enlargement and reproduction.[2] What you have got to do on your next visit to London is to make an appointment with Elliott and Fry to have a portrait made for us, without expense to yourself.

We had a meeting last night at the Mercury Theatre, and decided on the following dates: the 21st of May, Yeats; the 28th, myself; the 4th of June, yourself. We propose, therefore, to publish your play on Thursday the 6th of June. The date for mine is as yet unsettled. It is a pity that Yeats is ill, as he would have been useful at this meeting, but you will probably hear all about that from Doone.

I hear from Doone that considerable alterations are taking place in your play, that he is cutting out all the stage directions, and making you alter some scenes. I am finding producers a considerable nuisance myself, but I have the advantage of having two producers instead of one, which gives me a certain advantage in sometimes getting my own way. But the point is, how radically is your play going to be altered in proof, and I am wondering whether it was not premature of us to send your typescript to the printer. I wish you could give me some idea of the extent of the changes to be expected. Incidentally, I do think that *The Dog Beneath the Skin* is a much better title than *Where is Francis?*, and I hope that it will be published in that name.[3]

Yours ever

[T. S. Eliot]

1–WHA, 5 Mar.: 'I'm sending the Pound *Cantos* back. I dislike his work so much that I do not feel competent to review it. Please forgive me.'

2–WHA, 5 Mar.: 'Fabers have sometimes worried me for a photograph. If you think the enclosed suitably severe will you pass it on to the proper quarters.'

3–As it happened, 'copy' and lay-out for the preliminary pages of *Where Is Francis?* was sent to the printers Robert MacLehose & Co. by RdlM on 11 Mar. 1935.

TO *Randall Swingler*   CC

8 March 1935   [Faber & Faber Ltd]

Dear Mr Swingler,

I am finally returning to you your collection of short pieces called *Star in the Firmament*.[1] I am afraid that the unity or continuity of the pieces is not sufficiently obvious to establish itself in the mind of the ordinary reader, even the reader who is willing to take trouble, and I find that the subject matter is often not clearly objectified enough to prevent the attention from wandering. My general impression is, in short, that it would be a pity to publish this collection at the present time, and that you would do best to try to write something, either prose or verse, of such a positive kind as to give yourself a clearer and more definable position in the public mind. I think that this had better wait until you have done something with a clearer single purpose, and I shall be glad to see your future work.

                              Yours sincerely,
                              [T. S. Eliot]

TO *T. S. Gregory*   CC

8 March 1935   [Faber & Faber Ltd]

Dear Mr Gregory,

I have put forward to my Committee your design of a book about the five men of the 18th century, and the general impression is that this is not likely to be a popular subject or the book which the prospective readers of *The Unfinished Universe* are likely to want next from you.[2] I am afraid we must leave the search for a subject to you, but I should think you might try to find some subject issuing out of *The Unfinished Universe* which could show some continuity with that. It might well, I should think, be a book of a more definitely theological turn, although I dare say that at the moment you do not feel ready yet for anything that could be classified as

---

1–Swingler had submitted his collection of short prose works on 21 Jan. 1935: 'I realize that work of this kind has practically no commercial value at all . . . On the other hand, the pieces have a kind of unity of theme . . .'

2–Gregory ventured on 29 Jan.: 'Perhaps the English 18th century is what I know best, have read every published word of Jonathan Swift and almost of Defoe. I had designed offering to Fabers a book on the 18th century written about its five giants, Swift, Fielding, Wesley, Johnson and Burke, and called Five Rebels . . . I was advised that it was a threadbare topic and that you would not consider it.'

theology. However, if you have turned over other subjects in your mind we might well have another meeting and discuss them.

> With best wishes,
> Yours sincerely,
> [T. S. Eliot]

TO *Roland de Margerie*[1]   CC

8 March 1935   [Faber & Faber Ltd]

My dear Sir,

Our mutual friend Mr John Hayward has told me that you would be so kind as to read and let us have your opinion of the typescript of a biography of Louise de Lavallière,[2] which I am sending you. This book is offered to us for publication, and unless your opinion is sweepingly and completely condemnatory, we should be glad to have as much detailed criticism as you cared to give.

I may save you a little of your trouble by remarking myself that the style of the author is extremely flowery, and at places obviously crosses the line which divides the decorative from the absurd. It would obviously require a good deal of re-writing, but the subject is such a good one that we are anxious to know whether the writer's knowledge, accuracy and historical judgment can be trusted. The author informs us that there is only one other book on the subject in English, which is translated.

> With many thanks,
> Yours very truly,
> [T. S. Eliot]

1–Roland de Margerie (1899–1990), Secretary of the French Embassy, London. De Margerie and his wife Henriette ('Jenny') were to become close friends of JDH.
2–Louise de la Vallière (1644–1710), a mistress of Louis XIV. Margaret Trouncer, *A Courtesan of Paradise: Louise, duchesse de La Vallière, or Sister Louise of the Order of Mount Carmel* (F&F, 1936).

TO *Hugh Sykes Davies*   cc

11 March 1935   [Faber & Faber Ltd]

Dear Hugh,

I am returning to you *Petron*, which I have enjoyed immensely, and
which others here have read and enjoyed also. I am returning it simply
because we don't see how we could possibly sell it. The audience which has
anything like the background required for appreciating such a narrative
must be almost negligibly minute. I think, however, one of the smaller
firms such as Boriswood, which seems to publish books because it likes
them rather than with any commercial necessity, might be very favourably
inclined.[1]

I hope you will be up in London during the vacation, and will have
some time to spare. The Lotinga piece, after all, was only a short act in a
general variety programme.[2]

Yours ever,
[T. S. Eliot]

TO *Rayner Heppenstall*   TS Texas

11 March 1935   *The Criterion*

Dear Mr Heppenstall,

I have now read your article on the Frankness of the West, which I
found interesting and full of suggestive points. Your remark about ritual
preceding belief or mythology came home to me because it is quite
consistent with the results of a study which I made myself many years ago
about various savage tribes, and the investigation of which was suggested
to me by the work of Lévy-Bruhl.[3] In that I argued that in the study of
primitive tribes, any actual belief or explanation of practice is apt to be
a rationalisation of ritual, the origins of which they have forgotten. But I
was inclined to believe that the ritual, in the form in which it was found,
might also be based on an earlier belief which itself might be a still more
primitive rationalisation. That is to say, one can take ritual and belief as
affecting each other. I should hesitate to affirm any absolute priority. Your

1–Hugh Sykes Davies, *Petron* (fiction, 1935).
2–Ernie Lotinga (1876–1951), legendary music hall performer.
3–TSE, 'The Interpretation of Primitive Ritual' (1913–14), in *The Complete Prose of T. S.
Eliot: The Critical Edition, I: Apprentice Years, 1901–1918*, ed. Jewel Spears Brooker and
Ronald Schuchard (2014), 106–19.

decisions about the differences between East and West are interesting, but belong to a class to which German philosophers are addicted and of which I am naturally suspicious. I am thinking at the moment of Spengler and Frobenius.

However, the article is provocative, and I should like to use it. I could not use it in June because that number will be very full, and if I have space for anything on dancing I shall be obliged to give it to something by Adrian Stokes. In October I want your review of the year's ballet, but I could use this, I think, within a year's time.[1]

Yours sincerely,
T. S. Eliot

TO *A. Desmond Hawkins*

TS A. Desmond Hawkins

11 March 1935   *The Criterion*

Dear Hawkins,

This is in reply to your letter of the 26th.[2] I am sorry to say that Barker's poems had already been promised when you wrote, and I have asked John Garrett to review Auden's play when it is ready, because I was especially anxious that it should be treated primarily from the dramatic rather than from the poetic angle. There remain Pound's Cantos and Marianne Moore, Read also having been given out. To my mind Marianne Moore is the most important item on the programme. The fact that I have written a preface for the book does not add to its significance, but it does indicate how highly I think of it. But either one likes Marianne Moore immensely or sees nothing in it except ingenuity. If you are one of the latter, I am afraid you had better do something else, but I am holding the Marianne Moore and the *Cantos* until I hear from you.[3]

Yours sincerely,
T. S. Eliot

1–Heppenstall, 'The Year in Ballet', C. 15 (Oct. 1935), 57–64.
2–'I am particularly keen to review Auden's new play [*The Dog Beneath the Skin*] & Barker's poems . . . [Herbert] Read & Marianne Moore can flavour the pot if you wish.'
3–Hawkins on *The Collected Poems of Marianne Moore*: C. 14 (July 1935), 697–700.

TO *Michael Roberts*   TS Berg

11 March 1935   Faber & Faber Ltd

My dear Roberts,

I had been meaning to ask you the other evening, but never remembered at the right opportunity, whether you would care to do a review of Day Lewis separately for the June Number. There is a volume of collected poems, and simultaneously a new poem, and after Grigson's treatment of him I should like him to have a decent break. Not that he is not getting enough notice, though Desmond MacCarthy's review was pretty feeble. On the other hand, all the more so, because I don't make much out of it myself. It seems to me pleasantly pastoral, but perhaps our conversation is a sufficient commentary on that remark.[1]

I await your outline with much interest. Meanwhile, I should like to say how very much I enjoyed dining with you and Miss Adam Smith.

Yours sincerely,
T. S. Eliot

Your letter just arrived. Will answer on Thursday. Many thanks.

TO *F. O. Matthiessen*   CC

12 March 1935   [Faber & Faber Ltd]

Dear Matty,

Many thanks for your letter of the 23rd and for your news.[2] You seem to have been having a delightful time, and I can see that your native country, speaking in a large and general sense, has a strong pull on your emotions. I thought myself that the New Mexican desert was one of the most beautiful things that I had ever seen.

This is only to tell you not to expect me over this year. In the first place, I haven't enough money, having spent all the profits of my year in America on paying arrears of British income tax. The second reason is that I am having a play produced in June in London, and subsequently in Canterbury, and I want to be on the spot – that is to say, if I get it finished

1–Roberts on C. Day Lewis, *Collected Poems, 1929–1933*, and *A Time to Dance and Other Poems*: *C.* 14 (July 1935), 700–3.

2–'My friend Russell Cheney and myself motored out here in December . . . and I am very glad to be in contact once more with this Western country. The beauty of its mountain sun is like no other that I know, and we have been particularly fortunate in the number of Indian ceremonial dances. Certainly if D. H. Lawrence wrote anything of lasting value, it was his accounts of such dances in "Mornings in Mexico".'

in time, and if it proves to be playable. I hope it will, because it has kept me steadily in London since the end of October, and I am beginning to feel the need for a break.

Please give my regards to Russell Cheney.[1] I am glad to hear about young Joe Barber, whom I liked very much.[2] I also hear that there is some possibility of seeing Ted[3] again this summer, on his way to or from somewhere else.

Yours ever,

[T. S. Eliot]

TO *Paul Elmer More*   CC

12 March 1935   [Faber & Faber Ltd]

My dear More,

I think you were probably right about Cornford's book, but I am having it sent to you in any case, with my compliments, and if you care to write a very short note for the *Criterion* it will be welcome.[4] But I have another book which is much more important, and which I should rather you would review than anyone else. It is Temple's *Gifford Lectures*. I hope you will let me send you that because it is not an easy book to find the right reviewer for. From what I know of Temple's work it would be extremely subtle, tending to Oxford Greats hair-splitting, slightly tainted with idealism, and full of good things, and not a few dubious modernisms. It is not suitable for an R.C. to review, and your approach to it is just what I should like to have.

Yours very sincerely,

[T. S. Eliot]

1–Russell Cheney (1881–1945), American painter; Matthiessen's partner. See further F. O. Matthiessen, *Russell Cheney, 1881–1945: A Record of His Work* (1947); *Rat & the Devil: Journal Letters of F. O. Matthiessen and Russell Cheney*, ed. Louis Hyde (1978).
2–'You will be glad to hear that young Cesar Lombardi Barber [known to his friends as "Joe"], who reported on Katharine Mansfield in your course [at Harvard], has won a fellowship to be at Cambridge (England) next year.' C. L. Barber (1913–80) was to become a distinguished Shakespearian scholar: author of *Shakespeare's Festive Comedy: A Study of Dramatic Form and its Relation to Social Custom* (1959).
3–Theodore Spencer.
4–Brigid O'Donovan wrote on 14 Feb. 1935 to offer *Plato's Theory of Knowledge*, by F. M. Cornford, to More: 'The book consists of a translation of the *Theaetetus* and the *Sophist*, with an introduction and a running commentary.' More responded, 23 Feb.: 'I should suppose it doubtful whether it would furnish material suitable for notice in the *Criterion*. From your description of it I should take it to be the sort of scholarly work to be reviewed only in the more technical journals.'

TO *Robert Speaight*¹   CC

13 March 1935   [Faber & Faber Ltd]

Dear Mr Speaight,
    Thank you so much for your invitation.² I should like very much to
see you and to meet your wife, and I should also like to meet Charles
Morgan,³ but unfortunately I shall be too busy on Friday to be able to
join you. But if you are in London do please give me another opportunity.
                                    Yours sincerely,
                                    [T. S. Eliot]

TO *William Empson*   CC

13 March 1935   [*The Criterion*]

Dear Empson,
    I shall be delighted to use your poem in the *Criterion*, though I don't
understand it in the least.⁴ That is exaggeration. I mean that I do find it
difficult.

                                    Yours sincerely,
                                    [T. S. Eliot]

1–Robert Speaight (1904–77), actor, producer and author. A graduate of Oxford University,
he developed as an actor through taking parts at the Liverpool Repertory Company, and
at the Old Vic and Haymarket Theatre in London, before creating the part of Becket in
TSE's *MiC* at Canterbury Cathedral in 1935 and later at the Mercury Theatre, London.
Indeed, over a period of many years he played the role more than a thousand times in
numerous revivals all over the world – travel was a passion – and he presently became
a Roman Catholic convert. In addition to his work as an actor, he wrote many books,
articles and lectures: monographs on figures including George Eliot, Ronald Knox, Hilaire
Belloc, William Rothenstein, Eric Gill, Teilhard de Chardin, Georges Bernanos, and François
Mauriac, as well as studies of Shakespeare.
2–Speaight invited TSE (12 Mar.) to lunch at the Queens Restaurant, Sloane Square, in
company with Mrs Speaight and Charles Morgan, and 'a very interesting Bavarian girl'.
3–Charles Morgan (1894–1958), English playwright, novelist and essayist; author of
novels including *My Name is Legion* (1925) and *The Fountain* (1932). He was chair of
International PEN, 1953–6. In the late 1940s he employed Valerie Fletcher (EVE) as his
private secretary.
4–WE wrote (n.d.): 'The first bit was published in *New Verse* (and will be in a volume with
some notes by April); this is the second, and I shall do some more of it if I can. The thing
seems clear enough with the remark at the top, but perhaps it would be better manners to
put remarks like "This is Humpty-Dumpty" or "the beasts in the Revelation" at the bottom.
It is a nice little theme, but I am afraid my air of having to be clever all the time to manage
such solemn difficulties makes it ridiculous.' 'Bacchus II', *C.* 14 (July 1935), 572.

TO *F. R. Leavis*   TS Valerie Eliot

13 March 1935   *The Criterion*

Dear Dr Leavis,

I have been very dilatory in writing to Bottrall, and as a matter of fact
I mislaid the poem for some little time.[1] ~~As a matter of fact~~ I don't think I
particularly want to use it, and so I hope you will. I have been hoping for
new things from Bottrall, but I confess that this does not seem to me as
much of an advance as I should have liked to see.

I still have your Meiklejohn book, and hope to return it to you before
long.

Yours sincerely,
T. S. Eliot

TO *Michael Roberts*   TS Berg

14 March 1935   Faber & Faber Ltd

My dear Roberts,

Your outline for an anthology has been accepted unanimously by the
Committee.[2] The only comment that I am asked to put forward is that

---

1–FRL wrote on 11 Mar.: 'When [Ronald] Bottrall sent me his poem, "Preamble to a Great
Adventure", some months ago, I replied that we should like to print it. He in his turn replied
that he had submitted it for the *Criterion*. He now writes suggesting that I should ask you if
you want it, & I do so. If not, we should like to have it for our next number.

'Please forgive this démarche: the remoteness of Singapore makes things difficult, & I
should like to do what I can for Bottrall.'
2–Roberts wrote (11 Mar.): 'As editor, it would please me to have a royalty interest in
the book rather than receive a lump sum. In any case, it seems that the book will require
considerable thought, and I hope that Mr Faber will not extend to compilers of anthologies
his argument that authors enjoy writing and therefore do not really need to be paid anything
more than a token.'

He enclosed his outline for the proposed 'Anthology of Post-Georgian Poetry' – which
was to become *The Faber Book of Modern Verse* (1936) – 'I suggest that this should be a
book of about 320 pages, including an introduction of 16 or 20 pages indicating the various
currents: the "European" influence in Pound and Eliot, the development of the insular
tradition in Graves and Auden, the return to an outward-looking poetry of affairs in Spender
and Day Lewis, and finally the appearance of a new group of romantic poets, influenced by
the French surrealists rather than the earlier writers. If I were to edit the book I should try
to produce a collection which would not only appeal to the habitual buyer of new poetry
as a kind of epitome of his own tastes, but would also serve for some years to illustrate
the development of English poetry from its "Georgian" position. I should include only
poems which I appreciate and which I think I understand: I should not attempt to represent,
however, some of the tendencies in American poetry which have produced poems which
seem good to me but which have not had, and are not likely to have, any influence over here.

we should be glad if Yeats could be included, even if you decided not to include Hopkins. I hear, however, that Yeats is inclined to ask rather high fees for anthology rights. As for the other names about which you are uncertain, we should leave that entirely to you.[1]

What we wish to offer you is an advance of £30 on delivery, plus a 10 per cent royalty after the sales of the book have made up to us this advance and the fees of the contributors. We should, like you, count upon the book's continuing to sell for some years, and I therefore agree with you that you had better have a royalty than a larger advance. This also suits us, because of the expense at the outset. We can allow you £150 to cover contributions. What you will be asking for from each contributor is British Empire rights, but we should be obliged if you would please find out from them who hold the American rights of the respective poems, the point being that if we sold the book to an American publisher for distribution in the United States, that publisher would have to negotiate for the American rights with the authors or their representatives. I should be glad to know if this is satisfactory.

'About 28 poets would be included, notably:– Pound, Eliot, Monro, Graves, Marianne Moore, the Sitwells, Owen, Read, Rosenberg, Ransom, MacDiarmid, Hulme, Empson, Spender, Auden, Madge, MacNeice, Day Lewis, Barker, Thomas, Gascoyne.

'I am doubtful about Wallace Stevens, Aiken, Aldington, Bottrall and Laura Riding, and in a different way, about Yeats and Hopkins, who certainly belong to the literary history of the period. No doubt there are others whom I have overlooked at the moment, and if I were to undertake the work I should be glad to have an indication of the publisher's preferences in this matter.

'The book would require some time to prepare, but as I have my own work to consider, I would prefer, if I agreed to do this book, to work hard at it during the summer, and to get the material into the publisher's hands by the end of October, rather than let the work drag on over a longer period. Of course, difficulties in negotiations with authors and their publishers might delay the book.'

See further Janet Adam Smith, 'Mr Eliot's Proposal: The Making of *The Faber Book of Modern Verse*', *TLS*, 14 June 1976, 726–8.

1–TSE to Ronald Bottrall, 3 July 1951: 'I am distressed by your letter of June 29th. I am personally very sorry that you are not represented in *The Faber Book of Modern Verse*, and I can assure you that Faber's have no responsibility for your absence, except in so far as they are responsible for choosing the editors of the book. We gave a completely free hand to Michael Roberts, in the first place, and have done the same with Anne Ridler. If publishers invite anyone to compile an anthology, they may lay down the framework in advance, but I think it would be improper to interfere beyond that point, and dictate inclusions or omissions. It is within the bounds of possibility that I may have suggested new inclusions, but I have certainly never for a moment suggested that either editor should omit anybody. I do not believe for a moment that either Michael Roberts or Anne Ridler would be impelled to anything that could possibly be called a "boycott", and while I regret their decisions in this particular matter, I must defend both of them warmly against any imputation of prejudice.'

I am glad that you will review Day Lewis.[1] Detecting as I do a slight note of irony in your defence of him, I look forward to further enlightenment.

Yours ever,

T. S. Eliot

TO *A. Desmond Hawkins*   TS A. Desmond Hawkins

18 March 1935   Faber & Faber Ltd

Dear Hawkins,

Thank you for your letter of the 14th.[2] As for Pound, I don't by any means admit what you say, but it is still possible that most of such criticism of a writer might be true, and that yet there was something more, and more important, which it missed. I feel certain of one thing, and that is that Pound and Marianne Moore ought to be reviewed separately. I also feel that they are not poets whom anyone should review unless he is fundamentally an admirer of their work. I don't mean that it is necessary to admire these particular Cantos, but I do feel that unless one has a general admiration for Pound's work one has not got the right angle from which to criticise these poems, even in the most damaging way. But there is plenty of time before the June number, so I am sending you a copy of the Cantos, and a proof copy of the Marianne Moore book. Would you please stew over them for ten days or so, and then let me know how you feel about reviewing one or the other. Do not return, or rather, please keep these copies in any case.

1 – Roberts wrote (13 Mar.), in reply to TSE's request (11 Mar.), that he would be pleased to review Day Lewis. 'Obviously he lacks the subtlety, the high differentiation, of some of the Elizabethans and the metaphysicals and the Symbolistes, but he seems to me to show more than a capacity for modernised lyricism or "Communist Kipling" although it is no doubt the apparent bluntness of his perceptions which is leading him into popularity. I'll try to define the virtue which I find in his "pastoral" poems . . .' Roberts on C. Day Lewis, *Collected Poems, 1929–1933*, and *A Time to Dance and Other Poems*: C. 14 (July 1935), 700–3.

2 – Hawkins answered TSE's letter of 11 Mar.: 'I have sucked in an amount of Pound from the surrounding atmosphere . . . but I have not swallowed him. He is still foreign . . . I have always suspected his reverence for the quack annexe to everything, the distant & esoteric, the obscure and minor thing. It is the planned pedantry of a tremendously inferior man. I think he is a gutter-boy, gamin, fingers to the nose, dosing his anxiety with sudden whimsies . . .

'I have seen little of Marianne Moore. I think of her as the one item in Active Anthology which stood up to the introduction. She had some good work there, but I am without any informed impression of her.

'I associate her with William Carlos Williams among the American poets who should be known here but are not. (I hope one day to edit an edition of Williams.) I have, as you see, no initial prejudice!

'I should very much like to review the two. I want an occasion for digesting them.'

I shall be interested if you can do something with *Purpose*.[1] I have known Symons,[2] the Editor, for a long time, and he is an extremely nice fellow. I hope you will get something out of it. That is the main thing.

With all good wishes,

Yours ever,

T. S. Eliot

TO *Edouard Roditi*[3]

TS UCLA

18 March 1935   Faber & Faber Ltd

Dear Mr Roditi,

I have owed you a letter for a very long time, and I am answering one when I should be answering several. I am glad that matters have improved a bit.[4] I should suppose that there was more to be done in the way of translating English into French than from French into English. It is extremely rare that anything in the way of French fiction can be produced in an English translation with any profit. The sort of people who are able to appreciate French novels are usually able to read them in French. In fact, I believe it has sometimes happened that the chief effect of the publication of a French novel in English has been to stimulate the demand for the original French edition. There is, of course, more to be done with volumes of memoirs, especially anything of a slightly sensational character, which would appeal to a much larger public than that which can read them in French.

Candidly, I did not think that your translations of Hopkins in *Mésures* were very successful.[5] This is no reflection upon your abilities, because Hopkins' poetry seems to me about as untranslatable as it could be. It is not only the rhythms and verbal effects that are impossible to reproduce,

---

1–Hawkins was to be literary editor of *Purpose: A Quarterly Magazine*.

2–W. T. Symons was editor of *Purpose* and a director of C. W. Daniel, London publishers.

3–Edouard Roditi (1910–92), poet, critic, biographer, translator: see Biographical Register L6.

4–Roditi wrote (n.d.): 'Things are gradually easier for me now, though far from brilliant yet. I have "moved up" in the novels I translate from detective-stories to John Masefield . . . and have enough work to keep me busy & alive for a couple of months.'

5–Roditi asked in the same letter, 'It would interest me to know what you think of my Hopkins translations that Paulhan included in the first number of "*Mésures*". I . . . am now working on Kavafis with a Greek friend who, by the way, has translated some of your poems – rather well – into Greek . . . Kavafis interests me . . .' (*Mésures*: a French literary magazine founded and edited by Jean Paulhan and Henry Church.)

but there is something, to my mind, extremely insular about the spirit which informs the poetry. I admire what I have seen of Kavafis translated into English, and he seems to me an eminently translatable poet.[1] Have you ever thought of trying to translate any of Hölderlin into French? There again I believe you have a more translatable poet than some more recent Germans. What I have seen of George or Rilke in English look extremely dull in this language. I shall be interested to hear whether the project for publishing your early poems is to be realised.[2]

I sympathise with your political difficulties.[3] I don't think Spender would ever become a fascist. His traditions are of another kind, and there is too much of the best of liberalism in them. As for Auden and Day Lewis, I don't think it matters very much whether they call themselves communists or fascists. This is with all due respect to their abilities as poets.[4]

Yours ever sincerely,
T. S. Eliot

TO *T. O. Beachcroft*   CC

18 March 1935   [*The Criterion*]

Dear Beachcroft,

I enjoyed your story, and want to keep it on the understanding that you are at full liberty to place it elsewhere. I mean that I prefer to stick to *The Man Who Spoke to Lenin* for the June number for two reasons.[5] One reason is that I have just printed a fairly bloody prize fight story, although not nearly so ghastly as yours, in fact rather on the comic side.[6]

1 – Konstantinos Petrou Kavafis – C. P. Cavafy (1863–1933) – acclaimed Greek poet who worked without self-advertisement as a journalist and civil servant; translated *TWL* into Greek.

2 – 'A friend of mine has suggested printing my love-poems separately in a limited edition . . . I shall probably decide next week. I am rewriting nearly all my earlier poems so as to reduce the vocabulary to a bare minimum of "significant" words.'

3 – 'Paris is depressing – we seem to be heading towards some collectivism or other. All my family turned fascist last year; unfortunately, I am incapable of such enthusiasms and ceased to see them – hence my worries. Still, I am incapable of following Spender and becoming an ardent communist . . . And I feel quite sure that Auden & Day Lewis – perhaps not Spender – may conceivably turn fascist pretty soon.'

4 – See further 'Shortly before his death C. Day Lewis talked to Hallam Tennyson', *The Listener*, 27 July 1972, 108–10.

5 – Published as 'May-Day Celebrations', C. 14 (July 1935), 573–85.

6 – W. H. Boggust, 'Dave Hadley's Last Fight', C. 14 (Jan. 1935), 208–17.

But I think the *Criterion* would be criticised on the ground of monotony and of excessive specialisation if it published two ring stories so close together. Secondly, the Lenin story seems to me the better story. To me there is something just a little artificial about *Pretty Face*.[1] I don't feel that the peculiarity of the hero's temperament is sufficiently accounted for, and Rachel seems to me rather a superfluity. She would, of course, be expected in the kind of story that would be printed by the kind of magazine which on other grounds probably wouldn't print this story at all, but I speak with diffidence, as I don't feel that I am a very good judge.[2]

Yours ever,
[T. S. Eliot]

TO *Roger Roughton*[3]　　　　　　　　　　　　　CC

18 March 1935　　　　　　　　　　[Faber & Faber Ltd]

Dear Roughton,

Our attempts at supper do seem to have been most unfortunate, and I feel all the more regret at not having been able to come before, added to the unfortunate reason and the misfortune of its coming for you at this time.[4] I hope that your jaundice will not keep you long in confinement, and that we may renew the occasion before you do leave for America.[5]

Yours sincerely,
[T. S. Eliot]

1 – 'I'll spoil your pretty face' was 'written in a type of jargon,' said Beachcroft.
2 – Beachcroft responded on 7 Apr.: 'there's not really much merit in the "Pretty Face" story . . . I entirely agree with your criticisms of it. It was very kind of you to say you enjoyed it. I should be very unwilling to be placed in a position of wondering whether you had spoken the truth.'
3 – Roger Roughton (1916–41): English poet and critic; editor of *Contemporary Poetry and Prose*, 1936–7; friend of David Gascoyne, Dylan Thomas and John Davenport; and sometime member of the Communist Party. FVM to C. K. Broadhurst, 8 May 1933, apropos Roughton's 'interesting' poems: 'On this evidence I should say he had a good deal in him; which means he is on the road which calls inevitably for patience and endurance; for as you know as well as I, or better, it is a painful and well-nigh impossible task to publish poems. We cannot do anything with these at the moment, though I am telling Mr Roughton that we will do whatever we can to help him when T. S. Eliot is back with us – he is, as you know, in America just now.' See further Bernard Gutteridge, '"You can't abdicate and eat it": A note on Roger Roughton', *London Magazine* 23: 11 (Feb. 1984), 76–9.
4 – Roughton wrote on 4 Mar. that he was confined to bed for a fortnight with jaundice; he had had to cancel his sailing the following week. He was sorry to have to cancel supper with TSE.
5 – Roughton went to the USA in mid-summer 1935, in company with John Davenport.

19 March 1935   Faber & Faber Ltd

My dear Barker,

I have received your poem, which looks exciting, but I have not yet had time to give it the attention which it needs. I will write again before long. I should, of course, feel honoured by the dedication.[1]

As for your excursion to Capri, I quite understood the conditions under which it was made.[2] But in any case, let me say that once funds have been collected to cover a certain period it does not seem to me to be either my business, or that of the contributors, what you do, or what other assistance you receive. The money was definitely promised for a year, and that is as far as our interest goes. At the end of the year we shall have to go into the situation again to see what is to be done next.

I doubt myself whether we shall be doing any half-crown Christmas books this year, but the matter has not yet come up. It is a little too soon to decide what is the best policy to pursue with regard to this new poem.

Yours ever,

T. S. Eliot

1 – Barker wrote on 13 Mar.: 'I send this poem [unidentified] with more optimism and with more excitement than usual – partly because I feel it to be indubitably better than any of my previous verse, and partly because I feel that you may also think so. I am the more anxious that this work should not displease you firstly because it constitutes my first effort at the long poem proper, and secondly because, if you find that you conspicuously like it, I want to ask your permission to dedicate it to you.' He hoped F&F might be able to make use of it in one of their half-crown volumes.

2 – Having recently gone on an excursion to Capri (in company with a male friend), Barker hastened to explain: 'I feel that it would be wretched and unfair of me not to assure the persons who have supplied us with money that all the expense of the affair was covered by the friend with whom I went. I hope you are not hurt by the saying by me of this . . . Please forgive me and disregard it if it ought not have have been said.' Fraser (*The Chameleon Poet*, 75) explains more exactly: 'It was the first time that Barker had been outside England and his real motive for leaving was, as his notebook confirms, the possibility of sexual adventure.'

TO *Michael Roberts*   TS Berg

19 March 1935   Faber & Faber Ltd

My dear Roberts,

I was glad to have your letter of the 16th.[1] If you will give me a list of
the Faber books that you want I will see about getting them to you. There
is also Louis MacNeice, whose poems we are bringing out in the autumn.
I can probably let you have a proof copy of them early in the summer.[2]

Yours ever,
T. S. Eliot

TO *Robert Waller*[3]   TS BL

19 March 1935   Faber & Faber Ltd

Dear Mr Waller,

I am now returning the various poems and writings which you left with
me.[4] I am glad to have had the opportunity of reviewing your work, and
am sorry I have kept it so long. *Fumes and Flames* is certainly not only the
most ambitious but the most successful thing you have done so far, but I

---

1 – Roberts accepted the terms given in TSE's letter of 14 Mar. He determined: 'If Yeats is to
go in, then Hopkins should be represented also.' He asked for a set of Faber books that were
likely to be represented: he wanted to cut them up, and so avoid introducing typing errors.
2 – MacNeice, *Poems* (1935).
3 – Robert Waller (1913–2005), poet, writer, radio producer; 'ecological humanist' who
helped to found the magazine *The Ecologist*. His writings include *Prophet of the New Age:
The Life & Thought of Sir George Stapledon, F.R.S.* (F&F, 1962).
4 – 'I found Eliot himself puzzling. He was very kind to me and found time to comment on
the verses and essays I sent him. He even took me out to lunch.

'But from the first I found him a difficult person to talk to. His personal defences, so it
seemed to me, were invulnerable and he seldom lowered his guard so as to talk on a personal
level about his own experience or one's own. It was like meeting a bank director rather than
a poet, even though we talked about poetry, religion and culture rather than money. In his
presence I felt wild and uncouth, irresponsible, something of a thoughtless chatterbox: the
worst sort of Shelley. He would listen gravely with knit brows and a puzzled expression; he
always seemed to have a puzzled expression, even when he wasn't talking to me. I did not
know the anguished background to his own life at that time . . . His dark suits and breast
pocket handkerchief and cuff links, his horror of the mob, the yah-hoos as he called them,
all made me feel that temperamentally we were not on the same wavelength. Later on his
essays on *Milton* and *Hamlet* and *Blake* seemed to give me evidence for this. Yet in his essays
we catch glimpses of how sensitive and intense his responses to people could be, as when he
is talking of Dante's *Vita Nuova*. I was too young, too shy, too nervous, no doubt, to know
how to talk to him. I recognise now that underneath the waistcoat and the formality was a
romantic struggling to get out' (Waller, *Pilgrimage of Eros* [1992], 101–2).

don't quite see what is to be done with it at the moment. It is a very hard and abstract piece of writing to start the ball rolling with, and it doesn't seem as if you had enough other stuff suitable to make up a book. For the moment I am keeping one poem called 'Girl in Exeter Cathedral', which I like, especially the first half, which is more apprehensible, and might, I think, bear printing by itself.

When you have some more poems that you would like to show me, do come in and have another talk.

Yours sincerely,
T. S. Eliot

TO *E. W. F. Tomlin*

20 March 1935   [Faber & Faber Ltd]

My dear Tomlin,

I have taken another chew at 'Interpretation by Economics', and while I think I like it, it seems to me, as it did at first, not quite in a form suitable for general consumption. As it stands, I feel it is more fitted to appear in *Mind* or some other philosophical journal than in a general periodical. At the same time, it is handling a problem which I want to see handled, and I think that so far as I can understand it, you have the right end of the stick, but the ordinary reader would not, I think, be quite clear either where you start from or where you are going. One would like to have stated somewhere, perfectly simply:

a. What the problem is.
b. What your own conclusion about it is.
c. What are the alternative theories which you reject.

There is a great deal which is rather in the abstract form of Greats philosophising, so that one is somewhat distracted from the point by the brilliance of the gymnastics. I am returning it to you for the moment so that you may collate my comments with your text, and let me know whether you think I am entirely missing the point.

Yours sincerely,
[T. S. Eliot]

20 March 1935   Faber & Faber Ltd

My dear Doone,[1]

I am so very sorry to get your letter of the 18th, and to know that after you have taken so much time and trouble over this business, you feel obliged to retire.[2] Obviously it is impossible for any one man to produce five plays in the time at your disposal. I am afraid that the whole thing has been badly muddled. Whether the issue would have been more successful had Yeats been able to be in London I do not know. And also, unless there was someone behind such a scheme with the time and the influence to get adequate support it could come to nothing. This end of it was obviously not your business and I don't consider that it was mine.

I am sorriest on account of Auden, and I hope that you will be able to make arrangements with the Westminster Theatre to give him a show in the autumn. As for myself, I want to assure you that I have found your criticisms very valuable, and but for this abortive undertaking I should not have had the benefit of them.

I should like to have a talk with you about this and the future as soon as convenient. Wednesday afternoon is never possible for me. How about Thursday?

Yours ever,
T. S. E.[3]

1 – Much of this letter was previously published in Browne, *Making*, 39–40.
2 – 'Tyrone Guthrie is unable to take any part in the proposed season. His next production has been advanced 2 weeks. This means that it will be impossible to find a producer of known goodness to give his services free as I should have to.

'Three weeks rehearsals with as many as five plays to do would be impossible for me, even should the committee (I should say Yeats) perhaps would desire it. So I am afraid I have had to inform Ashley Dukes and others that I personally must retire from the scheme . . .

'This means that I have given you enormous amount of trouble, for which I do apologise.'
3 – Doone wrote by hand at the foot of this letter: 'About Ashley Dukes starting a Poetic Drama Theatre at the Mercury Theatre.

'Yeats & Eliot did not get on well.'

See too Medley, *Drawn from the Life*, 153: 'Dukes had approached Rupert to join discussions with T. S. Eliot, W. B. Yeats, and Tyrone Guthrie about the possibilities of creating "a home for poetic drama" at the Mercury [Theatre]. It would be initiated by a season of plays possibly including *Sweeney Agonistes*, *The Dance of Death* and something by Yeats. However much respect Eliot and Yeats had for each other, there were disagreements. Eliot told Rupert after one meeting that he felt like "kicking Yeats downstairs".'

TO *The Editor,* The New English Weekly

[published 21 March 1935, 482]   [Faber & Faber Ltd]

'The Church and Society'

Sir,

In replying to Fr Demant's letter in your issue of March 7th, I have had still more difficulty than in replying to Mr Reckitt, to decide what the points of difference are.[1]

I did not speak of the obligation of the Church to 'pass beyond' saying that the state of things is bad, to saying *why* it is bad, because I assumed that the Church should know why it is bad before saying that it *is* bad. But *Why* may mean several different answers: here, I suppose, we mean the reason why the state of things controverts Christian faith and practice. The answer to the *Why* is not quite the same for the Christian and the non-Christian.

'The Church fails socially because she fails theologically,' says Fr Demant. With that I wholly agree. If I and another Churchman advocate the same economic changes, but disagree in our theology, then our agreement is as ordinary citizens and not as Churchmen. I do not want to say with any Churchman: 'let us sink our theological differences, and unite on a social policy' *as Churchmen.*

What I find difficult to understand is Fr Demant's distinction between 'the nature of the re-ordering of society which will remove the evil' – with which he thinks the Church should occupy itself – and prescribing 'the political or economical means for that re-ordering'. I should be glad if he would make clear the difference between the *nature of the re-ordering* and the *political or economic means for that re-ordering.* Until he does that, until we agree as to what are ends and what are means, I shall not know whether we disagree or not.

I should think that it was quite within the scope of the Church's business to give us a definition of *work* and *leisure*; and certainly to have an opinion between collectivism and distributism, the latter in view of the confusion between *ownership, control,* and *title to interest.* One might also wish that the Church might be more positive even in its negative pronouncements. It sometimes seems as if the Church was opposed to Communism, only because Communism is opposed to the Church. I have at hand a book containing statements by Sir Oswald Mosley, which anyone with the merest smattering of theology can recognise to be not

---

1 – V. A. Demant, 'How far can the Church go?', *NEW* 6: 21 (7 Mar. 1935), 442–3.

only puerile but anathema. So far as I know, the Church has given no direction to the Faithful in response to these statements.

But I should like to qualify Fr Demant's statement that 'Sir Francis Fremantle . . . is representative of the Church in her official congresses' by suggesting that the Church is not really represented by her official congresses – or at least by the Church Assembly. Fr Demant knows as well as I do how the Church Assembly is recruited.

T. S. Eliot

to *George Bell* cc

21 March 1935   [*The Criterion*]

My dear Lord Bishop,

Thank you for your note of the 20th, which followed upon one from Oldham.[1] I feel honoured by your invitation to join the Advisory Council and should be very glad to serve on it, unless the duties involved are greater than I can adequately perform. I should be extremely grateful if you could let me know before next Tuesday what is expected of members of this Council, and how often it is likely to be meeting. I don't want to undertake anything which I cannot adequately carry out, but on the other hand I should be very much interested in this work.

I am, my Lord Bishop,
Yours very sincerely,
[T. S. Eliot]

1–'[J. H.] Oldham has told me of your keen interest in the problems before the World Conference 1937 on Church Community & State. Will you join the Advisory Council?' The first meeting was due to take place on the Tuesday following. For Oldham, see letter to him, 26 Dec. 1935, below.

21 March 1935   Faber & Faber Ltd

Dear Stephen,

Thank you for your letter of the 19th.[1] I should be glad to use one article about Hölderlin in the *Criterion*; you and Muir might plan out several articles, not too overlapping. One for either the *Mercury* or *Life & Letters*, and one for the *Spectator*. Or it might be better if articles appeared in the *Mercury* and *Life & Letters*, and a few poems, with the text opposite, in the *Criterion*; because other reviews will print articles, but only the *Criterion* will print translations of poems with the original texts. Payment as for original poems, when the author has been dead long enough not to claim anything.

As you like the Pound cantos,[2] I thought for a moment of asking you to review them for me; but then I thought, people already will have been thinking that *Vienna* was influenced by the Cantos, and you say you hadn't read them; and if a laudatory review of cantos appears by S. S. they will be all the more likely to think that. Besides, poets shouldn't waste their time reviewing poetry, however good.

I have ordered a copy of Barker to be sent to you.[3] Are you going abroad again? If so, let me know in good time, as I should not like that to happen without seeing you again first.

                     Affectionately,
                     Tom

1–'I think I understand what you mean about the translation [of Hölderlin's poems], and I suppose it's just my perversity which convinces me that we could sell 1,000 copies. How did Carlyle ever get Goethe known in England? Besides translating him, he wrote various essays about him, published lectures etc. If Muir and I manage to publish one or two articles in the London Mercury etc, on H's poetry, we shall probably get quite a few people interested.'

2–'I never thanked you for sending me Pound's Cantos XXXI–XLI. I have now read all the cantos about six times, and I get to like them more and more. What strikes me almost most about him is that he is a poet who can write about light and the sun.'

3–'If you could let me also have [George] Barker's poems, I think I can push a review of them into the *Yorkshire Post*. Otherwise, they may not send them out . . . I think I could put in a good word for Barker.'

TO *Geoffrey Grigson*   TS Texas

22 March 1935   *The Criterion*

Dear Mr Grigson,

I congratulate you on having become a father and hope that you will convey my felicitations and best wishes to Mrs Grigson.[1]

I am afraid that it is going to be impossible for me to do a note on Hopkins for you within reasonable time. It is not as if I had the subject at the tip of my tongue and knew exactly what I wanted to say about it. I should have to spend two days rereading Hopkins and making up my mind about him before I could get down to even the shortest note. In fact, the length of the note would be the least of my difficulties. I look forward very much to the number. Humphry House ought to be very good.

With best wishes,
Yours sincerely,
T. S. Eliot

TO *Stephen Spender*   TS Northwestern

22 March 1935   Faber & Faber Ltd

Dear Stephen,

Thank you for your note. As you are going away so soon, could you lunch with me at the Oxford & Cambridge at 1.30 on Monday? That would be a good day for me, as I have to go to the Home Office at 3.30 to see about a German boy they want to deport; so we should not be hurried. If not Monday Tuesday? but I hope Monday is convenient.

Affectionately,
Tom

1–Grigson wrote on 19 Mar.: 'I would have answered before and thanked you, but for the complications of possessing a child, which has just been born.

'If you can manage the note on Hopkins can I have it as soon as possible, preferably before the end of March? It should be a good number: the article on Hopkins and Scotus is good and so is one by Humphry House on Hopkins as a priest.'

TO *Virginia Woolf*

22 March 1935　　　　　　　[*The Criterion*]

My dear Virginia,

I am sorry about April the 4th, but an engagement such as you have is not one that can lightly be broken.[1] On April the 11th I am sorry to say I have just arranged a committee meeting. If other days of the week are possible what about Friday the 5th? It is apparently the Mohammedan New Year and a day upon which dividends are due. Or indeed, this very next Tuesday, the 26th? but I have forgotten whether either Tuesday or Friday is a bad day for you or for Leonard.[2]

　　　　　　　　　　　　Affectionately,

　　　　　　　　　　　　[Tom]

1–TSE had evidently invited the Woolfs to tea at his Kensington lodgings on 4 Apr. VW wrote *c.* 20/21 Mar.: 'Monday April 4th is of course the day chosen for my niece's school concert which (though it is a painful occasion, in Essex) I have promised to attend. If the following Thursday April 11th would do, may we come then? If so, we should be happy & would follow the map gladly. But its a long way off.' TSE had taken tea with her, in company with Stephen Spender, on 16 Mar., as VW recorded: 'Tom's writing a play about T a Becket to be acted in Cy Cathedral. Asks us to tea – very easy & honest & kind to Stephen, Said he wrote the last verses of W[aste]. L[and], in a trance – unconsciously. Said he could not like poetry that had no meaning for the ear. Read lacking in sensuality. Poor Stephen so hurt by reviews of Vienna that he told Tom to withdraw it. Tom advises him to abstain from poetry for a time' (*Diary* 4, 288).

2–In the event, VW went to tea at 9 Grenville Place on Sat., 30 Mar. – the one other guest was Alida Monro – as she described it the next day: 'A small angular room, with the district railway on one side, Cornwall Gardens on the other. A great spread; rolls in frills on paper. A dark green blotting paper wall paper, & books rather meagre, stood on top of each other; bookcases with shelves missing. Not a lovely room. A coloured print from an Italian picture. Nothing nice to look at. Purple covers. Respectable china. "A present" said Tom; he was perched on a hard chair. I poured out tea. There was Mrs Munro, a handsome swarthy Russian looking woman in a black astrachan cap. And it was heavy going. All about cars; the jubilee [the Silver Jubilee of George V and Queen Mary]; publishing; a German boy; a little literary gossip; feet conscientiously planting themselves in the thick sand; & I not liking to go too soon, & so sitting till we were all glad when Mrs M. got up, & Tom was glad, & showed us his bedroom – a section, getting the railway under it. "I forgot to ask you to drink sherry" he said, pointing to sherry & glasses on the bedroom window sill. A pallid very cold experience. He stood on the steps – it is the Kensington rectory & he shared a bath with curates. The hot water runs very slowly. Sometimes he takes the bath prepared for the curates. A large faced pale faced man – our great poet. And no fire burning in any of us. I discover a certain asperity in him towards the woman[?] – a priestly attitude. Here he gets warmed up a little. But the decorous ugliness, the maid in cap & apron, the embroidered cloth, the ornamental kettle on the mantelpiece all somehow depressed me. And as I say it was a bitter cold day & we have seen too many literary gents. How heavenly to sleep over the fire! Tom's was a gas fire' (*Diary* 4, 294).

TO *F. W. Chambers*[1]   CC

25 March 1935   [Faber & Faber Ltd]

My dear Mr Chambers,

I thank you for your letter of March the 20th. I of course know about the work of the Converts' Aid Society[2] and regard it as a most useful institution deserving every support. I feel, however, as a member of the Church of England myself, that I am unable to take any active part in supporting it.

Yours very sincerely,
[T. S. Eliot]

TO *E. McKnight Kauffer*[3]   TS Pierpoint Morgan

26 March 1935   Faber & Faber Ltd

My dear Ted,

Thank you for your note of March the 24th.[4] I am sorry to say that the copies of the limited edition of the poems you like have all been distributed. It isn't really an edition, for that matter. They were printed by a poet in America who must have come across the verses in the *Virginia Quarterly*. When he sees a poem he likes he prints off a few copies in this way and sends them to the author.

I think the Man Ray photographs a brilliant piece of work and certainly better likenesses than any I have ever had taken. Like all photographs their reception among my friends has been mixed.

I should very much like to see you soon but am pretty busy for the next ten days. What about Tuesday the 9th for lunch?

Yours ever,
T. S. Eliot

---

1 – F. W. Chambers, KSG, Secretary, The Converts' Aid Society – founded by Pope Leo XIII to assist 'convert clergymen from the Church of England and other protestant bodies, who, by reason of their conversion, are often rendered quite destitute'.
2 – President: His Eminence Cardinal Bourne, Archbishop of Westminster.
3 – Edward McKnight Kauffer (1890–1954), American artist and illustrator; friend of TSE.
4 – Kauffer hoped to obtain a copy of 'your *private limited edition* of two very beautiful poems' that he had seen at Mary Hutchinson's. Did TSE like the Man Ray photos? Also: 'If you have a luncheon time free in the next fortnight could you let me have the pleasure of seeing you?

Thursday. 28 March 1935   Faber & Faber Ltd

Dear Geoffrey,

I was discussing my play this evening with Martin Browne (who produced the *Rock* and who is to produce the play at Canterbury): he doesn't like 'Fear in the Way' as a title (no more do I)[1] and he especially

---

1 – Browne had written (n.d.): '*Title*. I've tried "Fear in the Way" on various people, & as I expected they don't expect a thriller but a "highly symbolic play" – they all use the word "symbolic". It has only the *rhythm* of a detective-story title, it lacks the other characteristic – concreteness. A detective-story title always contains "*the Car*" or "*the Links*" or "*the Barn*". What about "Murder in the Cathedral", if you want one of those? But personally I believe that "Doom on the Archbishop" is a better *kind* of title; it fits the play, with those Tempters etc., because the play has almost none of the kind of contemporary allusions that came into "The Rock" – though it is modern, it is much more universal – like a Greek Tragedy of a Christian story.'

Evidently TSE, in a now lost letter, asked Margaret Babington for her opinion, for she wrote to him on 22 Mar.: 'I think that "FEAR IN THE WAY" would be better than simply "IN THE WAY" as title for the play and will understand that you would be willing for this to be stated.' However, she went on: 'Strangely enough, Gouldens, the bookshop here, have . . . told me that they have just received the printed list from Messrs Faber and Faber stating that a play "THE ARCHBISHOP'S MURDER CASE" is to be published and "tried out in the Mercury Theatre and afterwards played at Canterbury" – all this in print with the title. I am rather wondering what is the meaning of it.'

TSE evidently wrote to her again on 25 Mar. (letter now lost), because she replied on 26 Mar.: 'The question of the title is now quite clear and I will take it as "FEAR IN THE WAY".'

'The bookseller was so insistent that their title must be the right one and that made me feel a little nervous, but I agree with you that it might have given the impression you rather feared.'

Babington wrote also to GCF, 25 Mar. 1935: 'I am in a state of some confusion as regards the title of the Play by Mr Eliot that is to be produced at the Festival in June.

'Mr Eliot wrote that the title he suggests is "Fear in the Way", whereas our bookseller tells me that he has received printed intimation that a Play entitled "The Archbishop's Murder case" is to be tried out at the Mercury Theatre, and then played at Canterbury. It is impossible for me to get my preliminary Programme (giving all details of the Festival) printed until this matter is cleared up; for you will agree that it would be most unfortunate were two titles to be mentioned for the Canterbury Play, it would create the utmost confusion in the minds of intending visitors who would assuredly think that two different plays were to be performed during the Week. The Programme is already late, as it has been waiting for the title of the Play. May I therefore ask that you will very kindly inform me immediately what title shall be printed on the Programmes that should be ready by the end of the week.'

FVM replied on GCF's behalf, 26 Mar.: 'I consulted Mr Eliot about the title, and he tells me that the proper title is FEAR IN THE WAY, and that no other title should have been released. We all entirely agree that it would be unfortunate to create confusion, but I very much hope that the bookseller you mention will help to clear up any confusion there may have been.'

GCF wrote again to Babington on 28 Mar.: 'Since Mr Eliot wrote to you on the 25th, and Mr Morley on the 26th, we have had a further discussion about the title of Mr Eliot's play.

doesn't like the idea of its being produced and published under different titles – perhaps better for the sales if one and the same title. But he doesnt like 'Archbishop Murder Case' because, when you read the text, you see there isnt any 'case' about it, and he suggests MURDER IN THE CATHEDRAL as a possible title for *both*. He thinks he could persuade Babs (Miss Babington, your correspondent) to agree to that, and it seems good enough to me. It didnt when he first suggested it, several weeks ago, but I have rejected so many titles since then that I think much better of it. Would you turn this over in your mind before 3 p.m.?

Yours etc.

[Signed only with the drawing below]

<hr />

'We all feel that "Fear in the Way" is not a very good title for the *book* of the play, and that Mr Eliot's earlier suggestion "The Archbishop Murder Case" is an excellent title. I understand, however, that it would not be considered suitable for the Canterbury performance, or for your acting edition.

'As the full text of the play is to be published by us at the end of May, before the Canterbury performances, we should naturally prefer to use the more effective title. Would the difficulties, expressed in your letter of the 25th, be met if we announced our publication under the title "The Archbishop Murder Case", with a note to the effect that the acting version, prepared for the Canterbury Festival in June, is to be called "Fear in the Way"?'

On 29 Mar., presumably prompted by GCF, TSE sent Babington a (now lost) telegram, to which she responded with relief on 29 Mar.: 'I am very glad to have your telegram this evening, just in time before the Preliminary Programme is printed. MURDER IN THE CATHEDRAL seems to me excellent, and I have immediately communicated this title to the Canterbury Book shop as the only title to be used for the Play.'

FROM *Vivien Eliot* TO *Geoffrey Faber*   MS Bodleian[1]

28 March 1935   [No address given]

Dear Geoffrey

I should be so grateful if you will have my books & my *'Criterions'*
returned to me. I had hoped to have them by now. It is *not* a question
of their monetary value but a question of the names & *signatures* which
are inscribed on the front pages & of the personal notes & markings
which they all contain. I think it is a *serious* matter that these books with
names in them should be floating about. I have been advised to notify
Bookshops that if they are brought for disposal they shall be *stopped* &
sent to me. As to the *Criterions* I do not need to repeat that they cannot be
replaced, & their loss is a serious matter to many people *besides* myself.
Do, please, do *all* you possibly can to get these back for me without fail.
I hate troubling you but I *must* –

Yrs. ----

I sent a signed copy of 'Marina' to the Duke & Duchess of Kent.[2]

TO *Michael Roberts*   TS Berg

1 April 1935   Faber & Faber Ltd

Dear Roberts,

I am somewhat annoyed by Pound's attitude, but I hope that I can
smooth that out.[3] Possibly he felt that he should have been approached
by us first. I am writing to him about the matter.

---

1 – VHE's diary 1935, fol. 88.
2 – On 28 Nov. 1934, VHE had posted off a copy of *Marina* to Prince George (fourth son
of King George V) and Princess Marina as a wedding present, and noted in her diary that
day: '*Realising* that Princess Marina's Father was assassinated not 3 weeks ago I felt that she
might find *comfort* in the words of this really beautiful poem of my husband's. . . . I wrote
in it For Prince George Duke of Kent & Princess Marina Duchess of Kent Nov 29th 1934
from *V.H.E & T.S.E*. With sincere wishes for their happiness.' . . . It looked very well and
I posted it myself. The copy of Marina which I sent away was among the few books by
him and photos of him which I stole from 3 Compayne Gardens. It was not signed and the
publishers no on the back is 29.'
3 – Roberts reported (28 Mar.): 'Pound is being difficult (I have not heard from Yeats yet).
I first of all offered the standard rate for the anthology (Hopkins, Spender, Day Lewis,
Owen, Read, Aiken, with minor reservations, are all available at that rate). Pound roared.
I then made another offer. Pound says, very sensibly,
    1. How does he know the anth. is critical?
    2. He has two friends in Fabers, but they have not appealed to him.
    3. All publishers should be made to pay.
    4. Never heard of me.

There was one point in our agreement which was left obscure, and which makes it desirable that we should redraft it. There is one clause which leaves the American rights for the anthology unsettled. We naturally want to control the world rights of the volume, and our notion of what is fair is that we should pass on to you 25 per cent of whatever we receive from the American edition.

When I asked you to try to find out in each case who held the Author's copyrights in America that was for the purpose of giving the information to any American firm which should be interested.

I am very sorry for giving you extra trouble on account of this oversight, but I should be grateful if you would let me have your copy of the agreement back, and I will have that item reworded.

Yours ever,
T. S. Eliot

TO *R. J. G. Johnson*[1] TS Texas

1 April 1935 Faber & Faber Ltd

Dear Mr Johnson,

I have read your pamphlet *A New Theatre* with much interest and enjoyment, and I feel that it was well worth while doing.[2] I have no suggestions to make except on one point which concerns myself. You must remember that *Sweeney Agonistes* really *is* a fragment from my point of view, and that my intention was a full length play on an Aristophanic model. The present fragments would have looked very different in a complete text from what they appear to be in isolation; and they are consequently, even after ten years' interval, still a different thing in my mind from what they can be in the mind of any producer. In order

---

5. If Fabers want to add 5% on his royalties in return for putting him in anth., that is a business affair.'

Roberts had offered £21 to EP for over a dozen poems, including five sections from *Hugh Selwyn Mauberley* and two complete Cantos. 'Can any pressure be put on him?'

1–R. J. G. Johnson had spent a year with the firm of Jonathan Cape and was now on the managerial staff of the Times Book Club.

2–Johnson had met TSE after his address to the Group Theatre in ?Jan. 1935, and submitted with his letter an essay on modern verse drama: 'it has been carefully revised several times following the suggestions and help I have had from Rupert Doone . . . and Wystan Auden who pleased me very much by saying that he thought it would do admirably.' (He added in a postscript, 'Auden tells me that the long quotation I have given from his new play is "now obsolete" and he sent me in proof the new version but as both are substantially the same and as you must have seen the new version I have not enclosed it.')

to be produced at all, in fact, with any effect, the fragments have to be interpreted differently from my original meaning. It should therefore be made clear that the character of Sweeney as you describe it is Doone's Sweeney and not mine. To say this is not in any way to criticise Doone's production, but I think it is worth making the point that a fragment like this is a very different matter for the producer than a complete play.

Now for the practical side of it. I confess that I don't see what could be done with a pamphlet of this kind. We no longer publish pamphlets because the overhead cost, that is to say the amount of labour that has to go into the production and marketing, is prohibitive except for a pamphlet which is going to sell many thousands. And I doubt if such a pamphlet could possibly have enough effect on the sales of my work and Auden's to justify it as an advertisement. Possibly one of the newer and smaller firms such as Boriswood might be interested.

With many thanks, and much appreciation,

Yours very sincerely,

T. S. Eliot

TO *Ruth Harrison*[1]   cc

1 April 1935   [Faber & Faber Ltd]

Dear Miss Harrison,

Thank you very much for sending me a copy of your *Approach to French Poetry* which I have enjoyed reading very much. I am only sorry that you could not have found room to say something about Molière as a poet, and I should have liked to know why you think him a writer of good spirits. I should have thought that in at least one aspect he was an extremely sombre writer who could give points to Wycherley, if not perhaps to Swift. And I wish that at the end you could have included something on Laforgue and especially on Corbière, who seems to me much the greatest French poet after Baudelaire. But apart from things like

1–Following six years at the École Supérieure, Vevey, Switzerland, Ruth Harrison won a scholarship to Westfield College, London, where she gained a first-class degree in French (with English subsidiary); she then took a six-month secretarial training course at Mrs Hoster's College. After a year of working in temporary posts at Girton College, Cambridge, she spent five years as Secretary to the Headmistress, Roedean School, Brighton.

this, which are perhaps inevitable in a book of restricted length, I liked it very much indeed.

Yours sincerely,
[T. S. Eliot]

TO *Roland de Margerie*   CC

1 April 1935   [Faber & Faber Ltd]

Dear Mr de Margerie,

Thank you very much for your kind letter of the 30th.[1] As you show so much delicacy about the use of my language, which you speak a great deal better than I speak yours, I cannot do less than reply in the same fashion and refrain from massacring a language towards which I feel such a deep affection.

I am sure, also, that you are far better qualified to acquaint me with the unknown treasures of French literature than I am to perform the same service for you in English.

Thank you very much for your prompt response to my appeal for a report. Your remarks about the lady's style are very just. The problem is whether she is capable of writing with greater restraint. I quite agree about the inappropriateness of her ardent language to a period of Jansenist theology. Your report will be extremely helpful, and is indeed a model.

I am taking the liberty of enclosing our usual cheque for your report.

With most cordial good wishes,
Yours very sincerely,
[T. S. Eliot]

1–'*Il me semble que l'on peut en tirer parti, à condition de l'émonder comme un arbre trop touffu. Mais le sujet est beau; il n'a guère été traité jusqu'ici: le public préfère prèfère les pécheresses qui ne repentent point, et réserve ses faveurs à Madame de Montespan. Et puis Madame de Montespan avait de l'esprit, alors que Louise de la Vallière n'avait que du cœur.*' He added in a handwritten postscript: '*Dirai-je que l'ouvrage de Miss Trouncer parait un peu "high Church" à mon goût de catholique janséniste?*' ('It seems to me that one could make good use of it, provided that one prunes it like a tree with too many leaves. But the subject is nice; it has hardly been treated up until now: the public prefers [female] sinners who do not repent, and is favourably disposed towards Madame de Montespan. Moreover, Madame de Montespan had some wit, while Louise de la Vallière only had a heart . . . Shall I say that the work of Miss Trouncer appears a little bit "high Church" to my Catholic Jansenist taste?' (Roland de Margerie's report on Trouncer is in the Faber Archive.)

TO *J. H. Cyriax*[1]   CC

2 April 1935   [Faber & Faber Ltd]

Dear Dr Cyriax,

Mr James Courage's novel, of which you are in charge during the author's absence in New Zealand, has been carefully read by several directors.[2] We do not feel that it is a book which is likely to have enough sale to justify our publishing it.

In saying this, however, I also wish to say, on my behalf and on behalf of the other members of the Board, that we have always been and are still interested in Mr Courage's work. The present volume, however, does not seem to me to mark any very great advance on Mr Courage's earlier autobiographical account of childhood in New Zealand, which first attracted our interest. It shows the same sensibility, the same precision and delicacy in recording both the external scenes and the feelings of childhood. The first part of the book is undoubtedly the more successful. Mr Courage is an unusual recorder of the experiences of childhood. It is the second and short part of this book which seems to us a failure. The grown man is not nearly so real to us as the boy, and does not hold our interest sufficiently to give the whole volume dramatic effect. The first part, therefore, instead of leading up to and re-inforcing the second, remains by itself as an independent piece of slight though thoroughly delightful writing. In the second part the characters and feelings are too vague to have the seriousness which such a long prologue requires of them.

I write at this length in the hope that you will convey to Mr Courage our continued sympathetic interest in his future work.

Yours very truly,
[T. S. Eliot]

1–The physiotherapist Dr James H. Cyriax (1904–85) practised with his wife Dr Anna Cyriax and his father Dr Edgar Cyriax at 41 Welbeck Street, Marylebone, London.
2–James F. Courage (1903–63), New Zealand-born novelist, was educated at Christ's College, Christchurch, and St John's College, Oxford. Works include *Our House* (1933), *The Fifth Child* (1948), and *Desire Without Content* (1950).

TO *Susan Hinkley*   TS Houghton

2 April 1935   Faber & Faber Ltd

My dear Aunt Susie,

I was very glad to get your letter, which I am disconcerted to find was posted nearly a month ago. It would be very pleasant if you could come over this summer, as there are several reasons to prevent my coming to America until next year. I hardly like to speak of my play, although it is, in a sense, finished. It is now in the painful stage of being altered in accordance with producer's suggestions. It is, however, definitely to be produced in Canterbury for a week beginning June 15th. It is still possible that there will be a production in London; but I hope not, because the man who was to have produced it has dropped out; and even if they get another producer I doubt whether they can do it properly in the time: verse, and antiphonal chorus work, takes a great deal of rehearsing. I should have withdrawn it, but for not wanting to disappoint Yeats, who is anxious to proceed with the season if possible. But the Canterbury production will be the one to see, if you should come; Martin Browne is directing, and Elsie Fogerty is training a chorus, as before.

I will not report your thoughts of a voyage to anyone; but I hope you will come. What good plays there will be I don't know; but the Russian Ballet will be here in any case.

With love to Eleanor – if you *don't* come, I hope she will write one day; but if you do, she needn't.

                                  Affectionately your nephew,
                                  Tom

TO *Henry Eliot*   TS Houghton

3 April 1935   Faber & Faber Ltd

My dear Henry,

I can now thank you for your letters of the 7th and the 21st.[1] I am sorry my ribbon is so faint. As you have sent a draft for two pounds, it is easier for you if it is cashed, so I have turned it over to the accountant with instructions to credit you with anything left over after the booklets and subscriptions are paid. Another time, you could order what you want and wait for an invoice from us, so as to pay no more than the exact amount due. Thank you also for your kindness to D'Arcy, which I am sure he

1–Not traced.

enjoyed. And again for your good offices on behalf of Bridson, for whom I think you have done enough, as he is only a professional acquaintance.

I am distressed to hear about the Harveys, whom I remember by name as having been friends of yours in Chicago; you once sent me a photograph of them. The great difficulty about getting translating work here is that preference is naturally given to English people – not for patriotic reasons, but because *a priori* an American is expected occasionally to use some word or idiom not current in England (e.g. 'meet with' instead of 'meet'), and publishers do not want the bother of going through a translation to alter these little things. And of course the majority of people who want translating work are necessitous and many deserving: if they weren't hard up they wouldn't want to do such drudging and ill-paid work. If you could get hold of something that Dorothy Dudley has translated, for me to see, it would help. There is a kind of Society of Translators, which Morley was instrumental in founding, which you can join after submitting specimens for approval; publishers often apply to them for translators. But really there is more work translating French books in New York than in London; because people here who would read French books (especially novels) mostly read them in French. That does not mean that there is any larger French-reading public here, only that the people who don't read French are not interested in French literature. I will consult Morley.

The play is nearly finished. I wish that you could come over and see it at Canterbury, because I doubt whether it would have enough interest in America for anyone ever to want to produce it. The subject of Church and State is important in England and Europe, but not in New York. It is finally called *Murder in the Cathedral*. I have no illusions about its dramatic importance, but I think some of the verse, which is largely choral, is good ranting stuff; and Miss Fogerty's pupils, who were so very successful in *The Rock*, may be depended upon to make a good job of the delivery.[1] And I have the same producer, Martin Browne. There was a scheme afoot

---

1 – Robert Speaight, *The Property Basket* (1970), 173: 'Fogerty knew everything about speech, but her ideas about acting were derived from *matinée classiques* at the Comédie Française. Like some good wines, they did not travel. She was a formidable woman who gave the impression – and perhaps it was no more than an impression – of monumental insincerity . . .

'The chorus for *Murder in the Cathedral* spoke their intricately varied verse with exquisite precision and feeling; but Eliot's Women of Canterbury are types of the medieval poor and these dulcet-tongue damsels from South Kensington suggested neither poverty nor the Middle Ages. The difficulty is nearly insuperable, and Eliot used to say that the best chorus he had seen was at the National University in Dublin, where the Irish brogue conveyed an unforced impression of the "folk".'

for a joint season of Yeats, Auden and myself in London; but I believe and hope that it has fallen through.[1] I don't think that this play is even suitable for an ordinary London audience, though it is not 'religious drama' in the usual sense. I undertook it in order to get more practice: you don't get any practice out of writing plays which are not produced; and if I can learn in this way, I might get an opportunity to do something eventually for the regular stage, not the little theatres and juvenile companies.

I have just made a new will, quite simple. Inasmuch as V. should have eventually an ample income – more than either of our sisters she has already – and will have the benefit of two trust estates of mine, and in view of everything, I am leaving her nothing. After Theodora and Chardy and my god-children are remembered, you are residuary legatee. This will do for the present, as there is so little to leave.

I am rather stale after having been in London all the winter without going away for even a weekend, working at this play taking up all my spare time. I hope to get to the North of Scotland for a week at the end of April. If I can afford it by then, I want to take a month abroad next winter. In the summer, I pay a few visits, a week or two and numerous weekends, and then there are always American relatives and friends to look after, so that the summer is not good either for work or for long holidays. And I want to come over at some time in 1936. I could not afford to come this spring, and I have to be in Canterbury off and on during June, which gives me a good excuse for escaping the 1910 reunion at Harvard – I am not fitted for that sort of thing, and I hate having to try to be pally with men I hardly knew, and many of whom time does not seem to have improved.

With love to Theresa,
Ever affectionately,
Tom

---

1 – W. B. Yeats would write to his wife, 15 Apr.: 'Early last week theatre project went Smash – T. S. Elliots new play cannot be done before Canterbury performance, & Ashley Dukes wanted it first. General despair! On Thursday I got Dukes to dine at Savile and started project again. He was struck by a letter from [Bladon] Peake [theatre director] about Elliot's play & has asked him to come to London at his expense. If their talk is satisfactory, simultanious [sic] London & Canterbury performances of Elliot. Peake general producer & Ashley Dukes in general charge. I much prefer this arrangement. Ashley Dukes suggestion is to give two weeks of my plays to celebrate my 70th birthday – then comes Elliot. Then after an interval will come other poets mainly new school Auden etc. It may mean much of my work in London. Elliots play is about murder of Becket, half play half relegous [sic] service as spoken poetry exceedingly impressive. I had proposed cutting it but Peake says no & is perhaps right. I only understand the play on a Greek or Ibsen model, a single action. It will require magnificent speaking, its oratory is swift & powerful' (W. B. Yeats & George Yeats, *The Letters*, 394).

TO *Camillo Pellizzi*[1]   CC

3 April 1935   [Faber & Faber Ltd]

My dear Sir,

   I thank you for your kind letter of the 31st ultimo, and highly appreciate
the honour which you and the other authorities of University College pay
me.[2] I regret all the more that I cannot see my way to accepting the dignity
of a Barlow Lectureship.

   In the first place I am, as I have declared, merely an amateur, and am
wholly unqualified to lecture on Dante from a Chair in which Moore
and Gardiner have sat. I am very gratified that you should have liked
my small essay, but if this essay has any merit that is all the more reason
for remaining silent in future, as I am convinced that this essay contains
everything on Dante that I am qualified to say. To say anything more
on the subject I should have to prepare myself by many months of hard
work, but even if I were prepared the composition of a series of twelve
lectures would require all my spare time for a year, and with the other
tasks and interests which I have at present I simply cannot afford the time.
So I really feel no hesitation, although deep regret, in declining your very
kind invitation.

                              I am, dear Sir,
                              Yours very truly,
                              [T. S. Eliot]

TO *N. M. Iovetz-Tereshchenko*[3]   CC

4 April 1935   Faber & Faber Ltd]

Dear Dr Iovetz-Tereshchenko,

   I am sorry to be obliged to inform you that my Board, although finding
your book a very interesting and valuable piece of work, have come to
the conclusion that it is not a type of book with which we are really

---

1–Camillo Pellizzi (1896–1979), sociologist and political scientist; Professor of Italian
Studies, University of London.
2–Pellizzi invited TSE to give the Barlow Lectures on Dante – 'an old and small endowment'
– for the next academic year, for a payment of £28 p.a. 'The Lecturer in expected to give
twelve lectures, on any subject connected with Dante but preferably on some of aspect of
his work.'
3–Nicholas Mikhailovich Iovetz-Tereshchenko (1895–1954), B.Litt. (Oxon), PhD
(London): Tutor in Psychology and Philosophy under the University of London Tutorial
Classes Committee and the Workers' Educational Association.

qualified to deal.[1] If published by us we do not feel that the book could be made for itself. As I think I said in conversation, it is a kind of book which is ordinarily done by Kegan Paul, or possibly Allen and Unwin. My next suggestion would be the Hogarth Press, who publish a considerable number of serious and scientific psychological works, and I should be glad to write a line to Mr Leonard Woolf, the proprietor, about you, if you would like to try there. Alternatively, I think there is a fair possibility that one of the American university presses, such as, particularly, the

---

See Robert Crawford, 'T. S. Eliot, A. D. Lindsay and N. M. Tereshchenko', *Balliol College Annual Record* 1983: 'In 1920 Nicholas Mikhailovich Iovetz-Tereshchenko left Russia for Yugoslavia where he became for six years a secondary schoolmaster in schools for Russian refugees. In 1926 he came to Oxford, and two years later graduated B. Litt. in Russian Literature from St Catherine's Society. By 1929 he was lecturing in Oxford in Slavonic subjects. His first and only book, *Friendship-Love in Adolescence*, published in 1936 by Allen and Unwin, was the outcome of Iovetz-Tereshchenko's doctoral dissertation in psychology written at London University where he was by that time a tutor in psychology and philosophy under the auspices of the University of London Tutorial Classes Committee, the Workers Educational Association, and the University of Oxford Extension Lectures Committee. One of those thanked in the book's preface for reading the original typescript is T. S. Eliot.

'That Eliot was interested in such a book should not be surprising. As a graduate student of philosophy at Harvard he had taken a laboratory course in experimental psychology, and had been interested in the work of Janet and Ribot. In *Dante*, published in 1929 . . . Eliot discusses in the context of Dante and Beatrice what was to be the subject of the Russian's book:

> In the first place, the type of sexual experience which Dante describes as occurring to him at the age of nine years is by no means impossible or unique. My only doubt (in which I find myself confirmed by a distinguished psychologist) is whether it could have taken place so late in life as the age of nine years. The psychologist agreed with me that it is more likely to occur at about five or six years of age.
> (*Selected Essays*, 3rd enlarged edn [1951], 273)

'Eliot and Iovetz-Tereshchenko had other interests in common in addition to that dealt with in this passage. Both men were Christians . . . And both, of course, were interested in literature. In 1941 Iovetz-Tereshchenko was lecturing in Oxford on "Some Psychological Theories concerning the Aesthetic Experience, Love, and the Religious Experience."'

1 – The blurb-writer (unidentified) for *Friendship-Love in Adolescence* (1936) was to characterise the work in these terms: 'This is a book written to describe scientifically the friendships and loves of adolescence and to establish the special character of romantic experience at that age. It deals in particular with the mental development of an individual boy and his attachments to other adolescents, both boys and girls; the account covers the boy's life, in its different aspects, from the age of 13 years 4 months to the age of 16 years 1½ months. The research of which the results are embodied in the book was based upon the author's large collection of original documents – such as diaries, letters, and stories – written by adolescents and for years kept secret by them. On the evidence of these documents the author claims, in opposition to much modern dogma, that love is not a sexual phenomenon, and he has had the courage to clarify his argument by giving an exact definition of the sexual.'

University of Chicago Press, might be interested, and might have funds at its disposal for the publication of scientific books.

I will keep your 2 books here awaiting your instructions. We will send them to you or you may call for them as you prefer; or we could, if you wish, send them round to the Hogarth Press.

I am extremely sorry that we cannot see our way to publishing your book.

Yours very sincerely,
[T. S. Eliot]

TO *Alistair Cooke*   CC

4 April 1935   [Faber & Faber Ltd]

Dear Mr Cooke,

I am sorry for the delay in reporting on your typescript, but like everything else it has had to have several readings, and I gave it to others before going over it myself.[1] Candidly, we do not feel that the material in this form, successful as I am sure it must have been on the microphone, makes a book. It is too scrappy and discontinuous, and as I think you mentioned yourself, a great deal of the light humour needs to be removed. I really feel that this material should go back into the melting-pot so that a real book may eventually be made.

With many regrets,
Yours ever,
[T. S. Eliot]

---

1 – Cooke left at Faber on 6 Mar. what he called 'a bunch of manuscripts for his proposed film book – a book for the multitude. I thought glibly of a title and at the time "TALKING OF GARBO" seemed a good one. Its public could I think, and should, be implied in the title that is fairly genial and inviting and popular . . . But I wanted to avoid the line of either A PRIMER OF CINEMA; or TALKS ON THE ART OF THE CINEMA.

'I've indicated roughly where the deletions should be. I'd need to go over each script carefully and take out some of the immediate confidences and whimsy . . .

'The preface is now written for the book, and – I think – necesssary to make clear the often deliberate over-simplification of a process and the general confidential tone of the talks.'

4 April 1935   Faber & Faber Ltd

This time you really did think I was dead Podkesta and once more have
I to some extent fooled you Well you are being snooty over and above
that anthology Personally I disapprove of anthologies but they wanted
an anthology Well I said if you must have one Mike Roberts is the man.
This is a critical critical anthology[1] whatever WHatever that means it
means illustrations of influences types and directions from the Creation
in or about 1908 to the present day It is a contemporary anthology in
the sense in this sense that you and I & Yeats are there to show what
good or harm we have done if either which I am inclined to doubt when
I read what is turned out now a days. Furthermore it is to illustrating
the development of English ENGLISH poetry such as it is for there is a
point at which English and American divaricates[2] So far as I can make
out American poetry consists of YOUR imitators from Macleith leish to
Zukovsky etc. Robt. Fitzgerald and what not and Ame I mean English
poetry consists of the neo-pastoral and pylon-pastoral and practical joker
schools. We leave the reader to judge for himself at what point gangrene
sets in and draw his own moral more or less This will be a case book
perhaps painful reading but critical critical AND Roberts will no doubt
include a few whom I wouldnt or you wouldnt or you & I wouldnt be
he wont be allowed to leave OUT anybody really vital. At any rate I
have talked it over with him and shall keep an eye on it; and Roberts
has only been given a certain sum of money to play with so please be
kind to him If any more complaints please refer to me dogone I might
have written perhaps to warn you Roberts was comin but I been working
most of the time for some time because I need the money and I have to
write something else before Xmas because I shall need more money Dont
pick on the little man but if any more complaints make them subject of
a epistle to Russell Square note the spelling[3] Well now about this Gesell[4]

1–EP replied on 6 Apr.: 'Again re/ anthol/ [*Faber Book of Modern Verse*] I do NOT see
why I shd/ sell outright in perpetuity the rights: to a large hunk of my stuff, which is what it
amounts to./ practically a selected of E/P/ enough to make one of them little volumettes of
T.S.E. that you pub/ . . .'
2–Divaricate: 'To stretch or spread apart; to branch off or diverge from each other or from
any middle line' (*OED* 1.a. Intrans.)
3–EP invariably spelled 'Russell' as 'Russel'.
4–EP had written to TSE in mid-Jan. 1935 recommending *The Natural Economic Order*
by Silvio Gesell (1862–1930): 'This here Nacherl Econ/ order by Brother Gesell izza g/reat
bukk . . . In July/ how much Gesell can you stand/ very clear and incisive dissection of Marx

if this is serious I think October the circulation of the *Criterion* has a
certain periodicity about it which could be illustrated graphically if I took
the paper out of the typewriter and didnt mind getting ink on my fingers
that is to say its best sales are Autumn and Spring, January worse and
July worst of all it has always been so October is a good number to say
anything if you think it is important people are fresher then and at the
same time sad and readier to for thought[1] Also have large amount of junk
to work off As for Frankie[2] the less said the better I think something went
wrong inside him some years ago and is now coming out all over As for
the *Criterion* well well it would be nice to have an adequate number of
ideal contributors the term ideal comprehending being approved of by
both you and myself, but they dont seem to be there and Anyhow how
can one see eye to eye with a crosseyed man without regret as for your
Henry Miller and his novel thats all very well but whats the use when
one cant get the novel he said he would try to get one to me and I might
have got it if I had had time and money to go to Paris for it but I havent
I dare say it is all you imptimate it is but your little nOtise seemed to
written be for people who had read it or could read it what good would
that do anybody[3] Very difficult to get anything good in the way of Fiction

---

and Proudhon/ an artcl/ ought to quote say 12 pages of Gesell, and have from six to 8 of
comment.

'It is a basic book. If anybody can cut the guts out ova subject bettern old Ez/ let 'em go
to it. Othersiwe the ang/sax mental life demands that Gesell be known/ both azza RITER
and azza kneeconymist.

'Spotting Marx' false dilemma/ is of great use and the buggarin bitches hat MAKE the
brit/ press such a middan, jess don't do nothing else but . . . all proletarian hokum starts in
that . . .

'Might be able to get it into less/ but wdnt want to feel cramped proposed title / "The
Critical Mind of Gesell", with attention to his perception of Marx and of Proudhon".'

See EP, 'Leaving out Economics', *NEW* 6: 16 (31 Jan. 1935), 331–3; 'The Individual in his
Milieu', *C.* 15 (Oct. 1935), 30–45: 'You can not make good economics out of bad ethics.'
1–EP responded, 6 Apr.: 'Gesell for October. O. Kay, cheef.'

GCF wrote on 1 Apr. 1935 an article for the Jubilee Number symposium of *John
O'London's Weekly*; his piece included these words: '*The Criterion* (Mr T. S. Eliot's quarterly
review) is a first-class instance of a publication which is inadequately patronized. One would
have supposed that there were enough intelligent people in London – letting the provinces
alone – to support a high-brow literary review. There are not. *The Criterion* does not pay,
and never has paid; and for several years it has cost my firm several hundred pounds a year.
Yet its influence has been considerable, its value to the community is analogous to that of
a research laboratory. The importance of experiment, in fields other than literature, is to
some extent appreciated by the public at large; but few people realize that literature itself
advances by experiment.'
2–F. S. Flint.

3–EP's four-page notice of *Tropic of Cancer* (Paris: Obelisk Press) includes these remarks:
'The bawdy will welcome this bawdy book with guffaws of appreciation, but the harrassed

very few authors Saroyan is a clever boy whatever you say[1] Hanley is overrated I mean he isnt so good as I thought he was going to be theres those two girls Kay Boyle[2] and Mary Butts sometimes does something

———

and over serious critic (over serious as measured by the reviewing trade) will be glad of deliverance from a difficult situation. For 20 years it has been necessary to praise Joyce and Wyndham Lewis (author of "The Apes of God") not in an attempt to measure them, but in a desperate fight to impose their superiority, as against the ruck of third rate stuff tolerated through the era dominated by Wells, Shaw and the late cash-register Arnold Bennett. In this D. H. Lawrence held an intermediate position, that of an almost solitary writer in the second category, between Joyce, Lewis, a few prose writers of high quality but not of very great dynamism, and the definitely THIRD rate authors welcomed by the trade, inventors of nothing, adapters and diluters of everything according to the demands of laziness, popular hand-over and the grossness of standards . . .

'As against Joyce's kinks and Lewis' ill-humour we have at last a book of low life "incurably healthy". Bawdy the book is, and is so proclaimed by its publishers who were probably blind to other dimensions, but if an obscene book is obscene because of any vileness in the author's mind, this book is certainly not obscene. It is a picaresque novel, or life little above that depicted by Smollett . . .

'For a hundred and fifty pages the reader, not having started to think very hard, might suppose the book is amoral, its ethical discrimination seems about that of a healthy pup nosing succulent "poubelles", but that estimate can't really hold. Miller has, and has very strongly, a hierarchy of values. In the present chaos this question of hierarchy has become almost as important as that of having values at all . . .

'Miller's sense of good and evil is probably sounder than that of either Joyce or Lewis . . . The lack of Dantean top floors is, I admit, apparent in certain chapters, but the gamut of values goes up at least to the finest burst of praise and appreciation of Matisse, a better evaluation of Matisse' particular gift, than I have found anywhere else. Throughout the whole book there is an undercurrent of comfort in Miller's eminent fairness. He paints, in honest colours, life of the café international strata as seen by a man with no money, whose chief preoccupation is FOOD, with a capital F and all the other letters in majuscule. [Signed] Ezra Pound.'

Cf. TSE, 'Ezra Pound II', *The New English Weekly*, 7 Nov. 1946, 88: 'If I am doubtful about some of the Cantos, it is not that I find any poetic decline in them. I am doubtful on somewhat the same ground as that on which I once complained to him about an article on the monetary theory of Gesell, which he had written at my suggestion for the *Criterion*. I said (as nearly as I can remember): "I asked you to write an article which would explain this subject to people who had never heard of it; yet you write as if your readers knew about it already, but had failed to understand it." In the Cantos there is an increasing defect of communication . . .'

1–EP had written on 3 Feb.: 'JeezKrize wot a lott ov buks Faber do pub/ish . . . Do peepul reed all them buks? . . . If you casionally reviewed Faber buks in the Criter/ium one might know whozzis zawl erbaout.

'Mr Hmnwy/ pears to hav dealt with Saroyan. Of course IF there is anything on the list a human being can read/ I can boost it . . . in N.E.W. but do give us the inside.'

2–Kay Boyle (1902–92): American author, editor, teacher and political activist, whose early novels, including *Plagued by the Nightingale* (1931), *Year Before Last* (1932) and *My Next Bride* (1934), were published by F&F. From 1923 to 1941 she lived primarily in France, marrying in 1932 Laurence Vail (ex-husband of Peggy Guggenheim) and enjoying friendships with artists and writers including Harry and Caresse Crosby (who published in 1929 her first fictions, entitled *Short Stories*, at their Black Sun Press), and Eugene and Maria

good but not always and they dont send anything in will report soon on Firadausdi[1] but o well I dont like poetry much I mean what people write with now and then a canto from you or a canto from Binyan a canto here and a canto there and a occasional Beast from Marianne's menagerie a pangolin this time but I have to give the lads their chance I dont suppose Barker will appeal to you but there is something in that nevertheless I am more doubtful about Thomas (Dylan). I cant remember just what I told Porteous to say about Propert. but he didnt say it because he had already said something else so I had to eat that vile Chinese food for nothing and they bring it in half cold and half warm I forward your card in an envelope to Dobrée[2] but you DO consider Landor a good critic when you agree with him I dont agree with you about Milton myself but then I dont like Milton much on the Whole I mean hes not the kind of man I like so its not important but if you are not careful you will be caught saying that Racine is a bad poet I dont think Cocteau much of a poet myself but I Wish I had a 3/8 1/8 a fraction of his theatrical ability and thats where his poetticle gifts comes out best too Well now about Knott[3] I told him some time ago that I would dash out a pamphlet some time if I got an idea and had time but I havent that flooncy needed for a good pamphletteering so now for the moment will close Professor Knickerbocker[4] is amiable

———
Jolas; she also contributed to *transition*. See further Robert McAlmon and Kay Boyle, *Being Geniuses Together, 1920–1930* (1968); Jean Mellen, *Kay Boyle: Author of Herself* (1994); *Kay Boyle: A Twentieth-century Life in Letters*, ed. Sandra Spanier (2015).

1–Anu l-Qasim Ferdowsi Tsu (940–1020) – Ferdowsi/Firdusi – Persian poet; author of an epic entitled *Shahnameh* ('Book of Kings').

2–BD revealed later, in a letter to TSE (17 May), that EP 'was peeved with me about my *Criterion* review [of *Make It New*]. So I wrote him an extremely rude letter, withal good-humoured, which is what he likes, & he has since written in better vein.' BD on EP, *Make It New*: C. 14 (Apr. 1935), 523–6: 'Whatever one may think of some of Mr Pound's conclusions, and criticism of criticism becomes wearisome, these collected essays are for the reader a valuable exercise in intelligent criticism . . . [T]he only serious quarrel I have with him is on the score of Milton. Admitted that much of what he did was horrid, much also is of the best: he was not always contorted into repellent latinisms. To argue the case would take more room than is here possible to grant me, but I would take the liberty of asking him to do something . . . and that is, to read Landor. Landor was an admirer of Milton, but no infatuate; and I would like to think that if Mr Pound were again to read the two conversations between Landor and Southey dealing with Milton, he might a little, just a little, revise his opinion. Perhaps by so doing he might forfeit something in the esteem of Dr Leavis, but that is a risk he may be prepared to take.'

3–Stanley Nott [*sic*] had invited TSE to write about Social Credit.

4–William S. Knickerbocker (1892–1972): Professor of English, Episcopal University of the South, 1926–43; editor of *The Sewanee Review*, 1926–42. His writings include *Creative Oxford* (1925). He was visiting Britain under the auspices of the Carnegie Endowment for International Peace, based at Manchester and Aberdeen Universities.

but not very interesting do you know anything about the Southern Review in Louisiana and tell me what you know about Huey Long[1]

TP

TO *Homer L. Pound*[2]   TS Beinecke

4 April 1935   Faber & Faber Ltd

My dear Mr Pound,

I have just got round to thanking you for your kind letter of October 8th[3] – when I have done that I shall try to tackle some of my longer-dated liabilities. And I cannot write very intelligently at the moment, because I have just written to Ezra and that takes it out of me rather: I'm not so young as I used to be. I was also glad to get the snapshot, which has decorated my mantelpiece ever since.

I still hope to get to Rapallo eventually, and make your acquaintance; it is nearly ten years since I was there. As Ezra can't afford (or doesnt want) to come to London, and as I can't afford to leave it, we shan't meet presumably until I have paid my debts. Perhaps I can just manage it before the 10 years is up.

I hope you like the production of the cantos as well as *Make It New*. I feel a certain personal pride in the Cantos too, because it was my giving Ezra a set of the Complete Works of Thomas Jefferson that started him off studying American history.

With cordial wishes to Mrs Pound and yourself,

Yours very sincerely,

T. S. Eliot

---

1 – EP replied, 6 Apr.: 'Wot I know about Huey, is that he is on the wagon, and has been eddikated, and got sense NOT to show it to the wrong peepul, and he has now cut in with Cutting . . .' Huey Long (1893–10 Sept. 1935, when murdered): radical Democrat; fortieth Governor of Louisiana, 1928–32; Senator, 1932–5.

2 – Homer Loomis Pound (1858–1942), father of EP, who had worked at the U.S. Mint in Philadelphia, had retired with his wife Isabel to Rapallo in 1929.

3 – Not traced.

TO *E. Martin Browne*   cc

4 April 1935   [Faber & Faber Ltd]

Dear Browne,

Thank you for your note of the 3rd which is very encouraging.[1] I shall
be engaged on Tuesday afternoon from 4 o'clock until I come to the City
for you. I could manage from 2 to 4, or an earlier hour if you could be
in London and have lunch with me. Otherwise I am free on Wednesday
morning, and can spend that time with you.

Yours ever,

[T. S. Eliot]

TO *George Bell*   Lambeth Palace Library

5 April 1935   Faber & Faber Ltd

My dear Lord Bishop,

I am taking the liberty of sending you a proof copy of Gabriel Hebert's
Liturgy and Society, which we are publishing in June, in the hope that
you will find it enough to your liking to be able to write a few words of
appreciation which we could quote on the jacket to help the sales of the
book. I have seen this book through from its inception to its printing,
and it strikes me as a valuable and important contribution. I need hardly
say that the few words over your name would be of the greatest value in
arousing interest in it. It is all the more necessary to do everything we can
in the way of stimulating interest as it is a book which ought to appeal
to a very much wider public than the persons in whose way it would
ordinarily come.

I should be extremely grateful if you could do this, and if you cannot
I should be obliged if you would let me have a word from your secretary
to that effect.

I am, my Lord Bishop,
Sincerely yours,
T. S. Eliot

1 – 'The reading was very successful, & I can see that, with thorough drilling, I may get the
men's parts, except Becket & possibly Fourth Tempter, cast to our reasonable satisfaction.
The play reads magnificently, & I had great joy in doing it.

'I have been, and am, working on cuts (which I regret for the most part very much) for
the 1½ hour Canterbury version. Could we spend a little time on this? As I am suggesting a

TO *Elsie Fogerty*   CC

5 April 1935   [Faber & Faber Ltd]

Dear Miss Fogerty,

I had been intending to write to you ever since I discussed matters
with Martin Browne on Sunday; but it slipped my mind on the only free
evening I had. Now he has sent me your letter to him of the 2nd. I had
meant to write to you sooner, and you ought to have heard from me
before you heard from Miss Collis.[1]

This affair started with Yeats, who had been offered the Mercury
Theatre by Dukes, and who wanted to use it for a season of three weeks
of plays by himself, Auden and me. The original idea was to produce
Sweeney as that was all I had to offer. Then they got hold of Doone, who
would have produced Auden. Doone was enthusiastic for a time, and I
yielded finally to his persuasion that if I would let him have the play which
is now *Murder in the Cathedral* it would be a great help to the Group
Theatre – his organisation. I consulted Miss Babington at Canterbury
first, of course. Later, Doone withdrew – for perfectly sound reasons,
I think – leaving me however in a somewhat awkward position. I felt that
Yeats had set his heart on this season, and I hesitated to retire; especially
because he has been very ill, and apparently still is.

But I don't know anything about Miss Collis and do not know anyone
who does: she is a protégée of Yeats, but even he has never seen her *act*.
I have not definitely said that I would authorise a production, but only on
condition that she found a producer and company who would satisfy me.
I mentioned that Browne and you were doing it at Canterbury, and that
is why you heard from me [her]. It is obscure how much of this is Yeats's

---

number of things which do seem to me to "crudify" your thought, though I can't see how
to avoid doing so in the time-limit; and I don't want to adopt such cuts without your
concurrence.'

1–Elsie Fogerty had written to EMB, 2 Apr.: 'I had a curious letter to-day from a Miss
Margot Collis. She tells me that she is producing "T. S. Eliot's new play 'Fear In The Way'
which has been written for the Canterbury Festival". She further informed Miss Sargent
that Eliot had given her permission to do the play and that it was the one he was going to
do at Canterbury. Surely this cannot be, as it would be a great pity to have any anticipatory
performance. She wants me to do the choric work for it, and will be very pleased if I will
produce the whole play!!! in Ashley Duke's little Notting Hill Theatre.' Browne wrote at
the foot: 'I think you'll like to see this. I've advised her to give NO encouragement.' Margot
Collis: stage name of Margot Ruddock (1907–51), Irish actress, poet and singer, who had a
relationship with WBY beginning in 1934: she is the subject of his poem 'A Crazed Girl', and
he published some of her work in the *Oxford Book of Modern Verse*; their correspondence
in *Ah, Sweet Dancer* (1970).

desire and how much her own. But I am not at all keen about it, and I had hoped that she would fail quietly, *faute d'appui*. And I had meant to ask you not to encourage her unless you really took kindly to the idea.

I had thought that I would let the matter rest for a bit and then say that I was convinced that there was not time to do a good job. I shall at least mention it when I go to Canterbury on Wednesday.[1]

Yours sincerely,

[T. S. Eliot]

FROM *Vivien Eliot*   TS Valerie Eliot

5 April 1935   68 Clarence Gate Gardens,
                                        Regents Park, N.W.1.

Private

Dear Sir,

T. S. Eliot Esq.
Editor of the Criterion Quarterly Review
24, Russell Square, W.C.1

As a member of the Committee in aid of Queen Charlotte's Hospital re-building fund (Queen Charlotte's National Mother-saving Campaign) I am writing to ask if you will *advertise your Quarterly Review* in the Programme of the Third Gala Celebrity Concert at Queen's Hall on Monday, May 20th at 8.30. 1935.

You will find all particulars of the Programme and rates of advertisement etc on enclosed sheet.

It would be a great kindness if you will advertise in this Programme, and if you could persuade any of your friends to do so. You will see by the enclosed sheet that it will be a very important advertisement.

1–Fogerty replied to TSE's letter on 6 Apr.: 'I saw Miss Collis. She seemed a nice thing, but I gather her idea is to play with amateurs, some of whom I know and who are just – – – [*sic*] good!

'I think far the best thing would be to do the two Yeats plays, or possibly three, and nothing else. I told Miss Collis that if it was your wish and you considered the time possible I would do the Canterbury play, but that I could only undertake it at your explicit instructions, as in these cases I never hold myself responsible to anyone but my author. I thought that was the best thing to do, as, like you, I do not want to antagonise Yeats. If they would bring into it Lillah McCarthy [Lady Keeble] who is now in London, is a great actress and could play the Player Queen, she would bring it through [*sic*]. I will try and get her to write to Yeats about it.' (Fogerty produced Lillah McCarthy, Lady Keeble, as Boadicea, in *Boadicea* by Laurence Binyon, at the Playhouse, Oxford, on 30 July 1935.) See further Ronald Schuchard, *The Last Minstrels: Yeats and the Revival of the Bardic Arts* (2008), 365.

This letter will be followed by a personal call early next week.

I am, dear Sir,
Yours, & etc.
Vivienne Haigh Eliot

TO *Jeanette McPherrin*

TS Denison Library

8 April 1935   Faber & Faber Ltd

Dear Miss McPherrin,

Would you care to meet my friend Jacques Maritain and his wife, who live at Meudon? I don't know Madame Maritain, who was Jewish, but I am told that she is very charming; and as for Maritain himself, he is one of the most charming and even saintly men that I know. I did not mention this before, as I thought he was lecturing in Toronto; but I have just received a book from him so I suppose that he is back in Meudon. Of course it isn't worthwhile unless you know who he is and have a mild interest in his writings; but they are nice people, and are not far from you, and are usually at home on Sunday afternoons. If you would care to meet them let me know, and I will write to him about you. In any case, I don't suppose you will want to bother till after the Easter holidays. I am so glad that you and Emily will be having a holiday in Guernsey, if not in Anjou; it is time she had one. I hope to see her on Thursday for a moment between Guernsey and Campden.

Yours sincerely,
T. S. Eliot

TO *Henry Eliot*

CC

12 April 1935   [Faber & Faber Ltd]

Dear Henry,

I am giving a note of introduction to a very young poet named Roger Roughton. I think he is only about 18. He believes that he is going to buy a Ford car in New York and tour about for some months in North and South America. I think at his age he might be much better employed in other ways, but he has not asked my advice on this point. For heaven's sake don't bother about asking people to meet him or make a fuss of him, but if you could ask him to tea and get him to talk about his plans and give him fatherly advice, that is all I want to ask. He is a rather attractive little thing, however.

Yours affectionately,
[Tom]

TO *Sydney Schiff*[1]
CC

12 April 1935   [*The Criterion*]

My dear Sydney,

Your letter of the 8th gave me much pleasure.[2] Please believe that I have always remembered you and Violet with affection and respect, and that you have been in my mind more often than you are likely to think likely. But I believe that when one has not seen old friends for a long time, and when one's life has changed radically meanwhile, it is best not to force things, knowing that if there is any reason for renewing contact, the occasion will surely come.

I shall be very glad to do what I can for your young friend Paul Lucas, and will look out for his manuscript. If he would address it to me personally that would save time. I will also read it, though of course it will have to be read by others as well; and if we cannot publish it, I shall be glad to advise him as to where to try.

I make bold to enclose a circular. If you and Violet could find your way from Abinger to Canterbury one of those days, I should value your

---

1–Sydney Schiff (1868–1944), British novelist and translator, patron of the arts and friend of WL, JMM, Proust, Osbert Sitwell, published fiction under the name Stephen Hudson. Works include *Richard, Myrtle and I* (1926); and he translated Proust's *Time Regained* (1931). In 1911 he married Violet Beddington (1874–1962), sister of the novelist Ada Leverson (Oscar Wilde's 'Sphinx'). See AH, *Exhumations: correspondence inédite avec Sydney Schiff, 1925–1937*, ed. Robert Clémentine (1976); Richard Davenport-Hines, *A Night at the Majestic: Proust and the Great Modernist Dinner Party of 1922* (2006); Stephen Klaidman, *Sydney and Violet: Their life with T. S. Eliot, Proust, Joyce, and the excruciatingly irascible Wyndham Lewis* (2013).

2–Schiff wrote from Abinger Manor, Abinger Common, near Dorking – a 'secluded and peaceful spot' (though they had not given up their flat at Porchester Terrace in London) – 'Your existence has become mythical . . . I have never ceased thinking of you and with the warm affection you inspired in me which sixteen years have not diminished.' His immediate reason for writing was to ask whether TSE might do something for a young man named Paul Lucas who had written a PhD thesis on Keats entitled 'A Study in Poetic Experience', which Schiff (who had not read it) understood to be 'a serious contibution to the literature on the subject'. (The initial recommendation came from Schiff's friend Rowland Alston, Curator of the Watts Gallery near Guildford – 'a man whose judgement I think well of'.) Lucas himself (Godalming) submitted a copy of his thesis to TSE on 14 Apr. – 'I hope you will excuse this trespass on your time.'

criticism; and I can assure you at least that the choral work by Miss Fogerty will be above reproach.

Affectionately,
[Tom]

TO *Jeanette McPherrin*   TS Denison Library

12 April 1935   [Faber & Faber Ltd]

Dear Miss McPherrin,

Thank you for your letter of the 11th, though if today is only the 12th, I don't see how yours could have been written on the 11th. But perhaps I am merely being old-fashioned.

As I understand from Emily, whom I saw yesterday – in fact I went to Thomas Cook's with her – that you are meeting in Guernsey on Tuesday, no Wednesday next, for a fortnight, I shall delay writing to the Maritains for about that length of time. Yes, I think you qualify as knowing quite enough about him to start with: especially as I think the man himself more remarkable than any of his writings.

It is difficult enough to cope with Emily's sense of duty at any time, and much more difficult when her income is so limited as it will be next year. One can only try cautiously to affect her (a) behaviour (b) attitude towards her relatives, to whom she seems to me exasperatingly respectful. But as I was once put in my place for commenting not too favourably about the behaviour-towards-her of a relative of hers not nearly so closely related as these, I am very careful; and you can perhaps do more in this way than I can. In a way, I think it is as much her fault as theirs that they have such a repressive effect on her and make her so depressingly humble. I mean if she adopts such a humble attitude, they, being what they are, can't be expected *not* to accept it from her.

English mosquitoes are as inferior to French as French are to American; on the other hand there are smaller creatures, called midges, gnats etc. in England, which are very active. But nothing is equal to the Italian flea.

While you are in Guernsey I hope to visit your (so to speak) birthplace again, Inverness; the air of which, as has been remarked, nimbly & sweetly recommends itself unto our gentle senses.[1]

Sincerely yours,
T. S. Eliot

1 – *Macbeth* I. vi. 1–3.

TO *Geoffrey Tandy*

12 April 1935   [Faber & Faber Ltd]

Mr Tandy Sir. I have investigated the matter of Faber's comments on your original prospectus and specimen chapter. Apparently the comments were either transmitted by word of Mouth or else by sole of exchange of which no copy was preserved. Anyway, we are not worrying about that now, the opinion being that such comments are out of date and incidental to the scheme. Go ahead on the lines of our discussion and of the chapter on eels which you showed me, barring my criticisms which are matters of detail and can be settled when the whole thing is complete. Your scheme Sir seems to me a good one. So go ahead. And move fast and rapid.

Mr Tandy Sir I have been told off to ask you two questions. One is what do you know about Sir Chalmers Mitchell retired director of Zoo: is he a man who could write an interesting book of reminiscences or not? Has he anything to reminisce, think you, except the birth of Jubilee, the presentation of two striped pangolins by the Government of Rhodesia, the escape of two minkets I mean monkeys into Park Street, and such small beer? Is he a card, or not? Confidential?[1]

Second, do you think that your friends who climbed four mountains in E. Africa in Search of giant lobelias, pygmy castorbean plants (Ricinus) and other monsters had (1) any amusing experiences worth telling the public. and have (2) any ability to put them across? Especially your Lowland friend Taylor. Confidential.[2]

Third, what do you know about one Italian named Gatti, who claims to have discovered the henna-haired Gorilla or animated giant carrot in the Congo, the pschee-bird (which you remember flies backwards to keep the sand out of its eyes), the tightskinned armadillo, and other unknown beasts such as anthropophagi in the Congo: is he a fake or not. Confidential.[3]

1–Tandy replied (15 Apr.): 'Sir Peter Chalmers Mitchell is by way of being a card and, I shd think, might produce some distinctly entertaining reminiscences if properly prompted. He's the man as told reporters . . . that the Zoological Society was a learned society only in the sense that the Bar was a learned profession.' Sir Peter Mitchell (1864–1945), zoologist; Secretary of the Zoological Society of London, 1903–35; creator of the open-air zoo at Whipsnade, Bedfordshire.
2–'My colleague Taylor is tied hand and foot in the matter of publication. I think he does not wish to write about the expedition anyway.' George Taylor (1904–93), botanist, was joint leader in 1934 of an expedition to the mountainous regions of East Africa. He ended his career as Director of the Royal Botanic Gardens at Kew, 1956–71; and was knighted in 1962.
3–Commander Attilio Gatti (1896–1969), gorilla hunter, published *The King of the Gorillas* (1932). Tandy wrote: 'I think your friend Gatti has a distaff side relationship

All part of the filthy business of making books. You cant touch pitch without etc.[1] and a rolling stone etc.

Confidential.

Enclosed leaflet.

Enjoyed weekend enormously.[2] I know I ought to write to your Lady also, but have been in Canterbury, and am going tomorrow I mean Monday to Rochester where I shall take advice on the point we discussed and will write again So will close.

[T. S. E.]

TO *Michael Roberts*   TS Berg

15 April 1935   Faber & Faber Ltd

Dear Roberts,

I hope that this address on your postcard is permanent enough for you to receive this letter.[3] After writing to Pound I talked the matter over with Morley, and we agreed that your selection is rather too comprehensive. That is to say, it is not to our interests or his that so much of his work should appear in the anthology as to give anyone the impression that they were getting all the Pound they needed to read. I should suggest using only one or two sections of Mauberley, and possibly no Cantos at all, and perhaps you could afford to dispense with one of the shorter ones also. 'The Exile's Letter', 'Near Périgord', and 'Provincia Deserta' seem to me excellent choices and should be kept in, and I think that both Mauberley and Propertius should certainly be represented. Furthermore, we are in favour of keeping the fee to Pound as high as possible. His notion of five guineas a poem is of course absurd, and I think that the method of paying so much a page is more satisfactory. I shall be glad to hear from you, at least to let me know at the moment that you have received this.[4]

Yours ever,

T. S. Eliot

---

with Munchausen. His father, it is suspected, was either Dr Cook or his faithful Eskimo companion Etukisuk.'

1 – 'He that toucheth pitch shall be defiled therewith' (*Eccles.* 13: 1).

2 – TSE had spent the weekend of the Oxford and Cambridge Boat Race with the Tandys at Hogarth Cottage, Hampton-on-Thames.

3 – Roberts wrote from Switzerland (9 Apr.): 'I find that I only have room for 24 pages of Pound in any case & for these I have offered him £18.'

4 – Roberts responded *pro tem* (24 Apr.): 'I had already decided that Pound's representation must be decreased, simply for lack of space.'

TO *James Le B. Boyle*   cc

17 April 1935   Faber & Faber Ltd]

Dear Boyle,

Thank you for your long and informative letter of April the 4th, which I must answer briefly.[1] I return herewith the Shakespeare pamphlet which I have inscribed. Second, I don't feel that my conscience calls upon me to provide a lead for Copey's garland.[2] I did take one course with him, from which I think I learnt nothing. At any rate I have always regretted that I did not employ the time otherwise. I wish him well, but I never got on with him, and have literally nothing to say about him. Third, you were much better employed drinking sherry with Desmond Macarthy than in hearing him lecture.[3] His social gifts are admirable, his critical gifts less dependable.

I remember quite well the unhappy event mentioned in the sixth paragraph of your letter.[4]

Laurence Binyon has been doing some very good work in translating Dante. I would call this to your attention.[5]

1 – James Le B. Boyle, Secretary of the *Harvard Advocate*, wrote: 'You must indeed weary of innumerable importunate widows and it must seem to you that you seldom hear from the *Advocate* save when a request or petition is the cause, still it is to be hoped you do not regret a complaisant good humour that encourages these visits by toleration . . . All of this preamble, as you may suspect, prefaces an earnest desire that since I procured this copy of Shakespeare and the Stoicism of Seneca with some difficulty (an auction, mind you) you will sign it.'

2 – 'You will notice that the office illustriously filled in 1910 is now held by a miserably unworthy wretch. We actually, complacently, expect to make up a C. T. Copeland issue (rather like the Santayana Memorial) for June . . . How do you feel about it? Speak and spare not . . .' C. T. Copeland (1860–1952) was Professor of English at Harvard: see J. Donald Adams, *Copey of Harvard: A Biography of Charles Townsend Copeland* (1960).

3 – 'Theodore Spencer's English 26 deals manfully with C. Day Lewis, Auden and Spender, Pound etc . . . Yet Desmond McCarthy [*sic*] was curiously disquieting in his comments on that group – Spencer bit his lip, he liked it very little. We asked McCarthy over here and he drank a whole mug of sherry at one toss and stepped below to the Dunster House Bookshop to buy me no end of H. G. Wells which he decided should be a part of my education – it had been a gap.'

4 – 'Do you remember the afternoon Foster Damon read your palm with his tickling ivory wand etc.? That was one of the grimmest events. Parlour tricks are fun enough save when they demand one's participation, on the receiving end. That looking very like an imposition to me.'

5 – 'If you by remote chance have a small bit poem [*sic*] you'd like to see the *Advocate* have (o remotest chance!) do send it. Isn't Laurence Binyon a grand sort of man?'

With all best wishes to the Michael Mullins Marching and Chowder Club,

from
The Honourable Member,
[T. S. Eliot]

TO *P. Mansell Jones*[1]   cc

18 April 1935   [Faber & Faber Ltd]

Dear Mr Jones,

I have your translation of Giraudoux's *Racine* which I agree is a very interesting study. I do not feel, however, that it is quite what is wanted for English readers. That is to say it implies an appreciation of Racine which only readers who know French intimately would have. I think that until Racine is better understood in this country his interests here can best be forwarded by English writers who understand the usual prejudices against him.

Yours sincerely,
[T. S. Eliot]

TO *Henry Miller*   TS Jay Martin

18 April 1935   Faber & Faber Ltd

Dear Mr Miller,

I must apologise for the delay in reporting to you on the specimen pages of your Lawrence book.[2] I have laid the matter before my Committee, who are of the opinion that the market for a critical work on Lawrence,

---

1–P. Mansell Jones (1889–1968), educated at University College, Cardiff, and Balliol College, Oxford, was teaching at the University College of South Wales and Monmouthshire, Cardiff; he was later Professor of Modern French Literature, University of Manchester, 1951–6. His works include *Tradition and Barbarism* (F&F, 1930), *French Introspectives* (1937) and the *Oxford Book of French Verse* (ed., 1957).

2–Miller had submitted on 21 Jan. a section from his book – 'the conclusion of a long introduction'. Jack Kahane (Paris), who published *Tropic of Cancer*, had an option on his next two books, but Miller doubted whether he would publish the DHL book – which he ached to be encouraged to complete. Stuart Gilbert had been 'very favorably impressed' by it. Miller told TSE too: 'In order to have my say I must find a man, a lone individual, who has faith in me. The publishers are not interested in me as an individual: they are interested only in exploiting me. It's hard to keep one's integrity.' Miller wrote again in Apr., asking after TSE's judgement; also whether TSE had accepted EP's review of *Tropic*. He

however excellent, would be too small to justify their undertaking it. I am very sorry myself, because I found the material interesting. Perhaps at some later time you could pick out some section of it which might be suitable for publication by itself in the *Criterion*; not more than 5,000 words.

I have not published Pound's notice of *Tropic of Cancer* because what he wrote seemed to me too obscure to be of the slightest use.[1] When a book is unobtainable in this country that seems to me to require a rather special sort of review. I only wish that I myself might have access to the book. What is *Black Spring*? Is there any chance of a copy of this, either in print or in manuscript, getting through to us?

Yours sincerely,
T. S. Eliot

TO *Michael F. Cullis* CC

24 April 1935 [Faber & Faber Ltd]

Dear Mr Cullis,

I entirely approve of practise in versification acquired in the process of translation, and especially translation from Latin and Greek.[2] I hope, therefore, that you will continue in this occupation with enthusiasm. I don't feel satisfied that these two specimens, however, have any other purpose than as exercises. I feel that they are modelled too closely on Ezra Pound, and not so much even on the Propertius as on the Cantos. At any rate, that is how they are bound to strike the ordinary reader. There is nothing wrong about that. You have chosen an excellent model; but I think that in using the model you have also acquired some of the idiosyncrasies such as can only be employed with impunity by the inventor. I think that you need more time in order to filter Pound's style and then

---

concluded: 'It looks as though I have found a publisher here [New York] for the "Black Spring". Miracles happen now and then.'

1 – TSE's secretary to Hank van Gelre (Nijmegen, Netherlands), n.d.: 'Mr Eliot is very sorry that the only work of Mr Miller's which he has read was his first book *Tropic of Cancer* and it is so long since he read it that he cannot now express any opinion without rereading it with some care. He remembers with relish Mr Ezra Pound's epigrammatic description of the book.'

2 – Cullis, a student at Brasenose College, Oxford, submitted on 5 Mar. what he called 'these two frankly retrogressive bits of work / a couple of (mis)translations of Theocritus . . . I hardly like to suggest it, as you must be very busy; but if, when rejecting them, you cd. spare a moment to tell me *why* they're bad, I shd. be most sincerely grateful.'

mix it thoroughly with something more peculiarly your own. I shall be
interested to follow your progress.

With all best wishes,
Yours sincerely,
[T. S. Eliot]

TO *Stephen Spender*   TS Northwestern

25 April 1935   Faber & Faber Ltd

Dear Stephen,

I was very glad to get your letter of the 18th; indeed, if I had known
your address, I should have written before.[1] Your surroundings sound
delightful, and I hope you will find this a good place for work. And no
doubt the season is much more advanced than here. I am going to Scotland
tonight in a cold raw rainstorm.

So far I have had time only to skim through your book very hurriedly,
before sending it off to a reviewer – I am not sure whether he is the right
reviewer or not.[2] You may be sure, to begin with, that there is nothing
in it to offend *me*, whether I agree with everything or not. I shall have
much more to say when I have had time to re-read it carefully. My first
impression is that it is full of good things, and *apercus*, but that you have
chosen a very treacherous form for the book. I mean that by adopting a
thesis for the series of essays, you are, as anyone is, putting yourself more
or less into blinkers. I know I did this in *After Strange Gods*. Furthermore,
for this type of criticism, one needs to know one's authors from cover
to cover and inside out – where again, I failed. I think that your case
about James appears stronger than it really is, from your emphasising
particular books and stories and ignoring others. But everything that can
bring James to his own is to the good; and the possibility of different
interpretations is testimony of his greatness. You are right about his not
being so very 'American'; fundamentally, I feel that I am very much more
American than he was, or at any rate 'New England'; for 'American' does
not mean quite the same thing in different generations. (Two minor slips:
there is no such thing as an 'English citizen' and no such thing as the

---

1 – Spender was staying in a village on the edge of the Wiener Wald, near Vienna.
2 – Spender hoped that TSE had received a copy of his book *The Destructive Element*.
'I notice that a huge quantity of it seems to be devoted to you . . . I hope you will let me
know if you think any of it is impertinent. Because of course I don't write in order to
apologize in private for what I say in public . . .'

'Anglo-Catholic Church'. And is the 'war' (which was the Boer war at that) the key to 'The Shadow in the Rose Garden'? I stick to my opinion about that story).

That is about all that comes out of my head at the moment, not having the book by me. But there will be more later.

One practical point. Faber has been a little worried by this book because someone asked him whether it meant that you had left us. He quite understands the position himself, but he does not like such rumours to get about. Of course authors often do commissioned books on special subjects – or in some series – for another than their regular publisher; but I think he would like some informal assurance – a word through me would do – that you would give us the first offer of books you do – prose or verse – because you *want* to do them. And I hope you won't have to do many of the other kind. I take it we may count upon the book of stories in the autumn?

Ever affectionately,
Tom

P.S. I think there are a few spots where the actual writing might be improved.

There is more in your letter to answer – I'll write again soon.

TO *John Masefield*   CC

25 April 1935   [Faber & Faber Ltd]

Dear Mr Masefield,

Thank you for your letter of the 24th.[1] It had been on my mind of late that something ought to be done about Yeats's 70th birthday, and I am delighted and relieved to know that you have taken the matter in hand. I shall of course be very happy to join your Committee of friends, and

1 – 'Mr W. B. Yeats will be seventy years of age on the 13th of June.

'I am writing to ask you if you will be so very kind as to join a small Committee of friends of the Poet: Binyon, Sturge-Moore, Rothenstein, Murray, Augustus John, Dr Vaughan Williams; in order to organize a birthday gift to him from the artists and writers of this country. We felt that, if the money were forthcoming, we might be able to procure him a drawing by William Blake.

'Committee members will have practically no duties beyond signing an appeal sent privately to possible subscribers. It will be a very great pleasure to myself and the other Committee members if we may have you among us.'

if there is anything further for me to do in the matter, I await your instructions.

Yours very sincerely,
[T. S. Eliot]

TO *Geoffrey Tandy* TS BL

25 April 1935 Faber & Faber Ltd

Dear Mr Tandy Sir, this has required considerable excogitation. My director was at first of opinion as I described the matter that the child was reasonably likely to be brought up as a Christian any way and that perhaps I should reserve myself (having already made two shots and being really entitled to not more than 4 in all) for some wretched infant where it would make just the difference, just tip the beam between heaven & hell if you take my meaning. Well, I says, what between infants whose parents is going to bring em up right anyway and infants whose parents is going to bring em up wrong anyway, there arent many infants left and how can I tell where I am going just to tip that beam and where not. Always a risk of Umiliation. But there it is, now it come to me that perhaps this infant was after all just in that class and no offense meant I'm sure so I ope none will be taken after all I am more or less with the dark and I never had a word with your parson about you so if you and your Lady so wish it on mature reflexion I am content to assume responsibility if we could have a gentleman's agreement about not letting me down but on the other Hand. If you have thought better of it well no bones broken as they say so will close bein at your disposial [*sic*] for better or worse I fear dont like leaving any fast fortun [*sic*] behind to remember me By but jamais triste Archie jamais triste.[1] yours[2]

T. S. E.

1–Don Marquis, *Archy and Mehitabel* (1931; repr. F&F, 1934), 196: 'jamais triste archy jamais triste'.
2–TSE had been asked to be godparent to the Tandys' second child, Anthea. 'I dont suppose you knows,' replied Tandy (26 Apr.), 'how near you was to being asked to take office when that Richard was christened . . . It aint no use for me to pretend to be a faithful and obedient son of the Church because I aint nor dont see my way to it yet awhile . . . But I dont mind telling you as we be pretty middling glad you didnt find it necessary to turn down the job. Thankee Dr Thankee.'

TO *Martin Turnell*[1]   CC

25 April 1935   [Faber & Faber Ltd]

Dear Mr Turnell,

I must apologise for having kept so long your essays on Corbière and Laforgue. They both impressed me very well indeed, and so far as I know are by far the most searching criticisms of these authors in English. I hope that they may both be published in some form or another. I should like to use the Corbière in the *Criterion* if it could be abbreviated by about ten pages. It is at present 36 pages, which is inconveniently long. Do you think it would be possible to shorten it to the desired extent without mutilation?[2]

                        Yours sincerely,
                        [T. S. Eliot]

TO *Rayner Heppenstall*   TS Texas

29 April 1935   *The Criterion*

Dear Mr Heppenstall,

I am sorry to have taken such a time over writing to you about your review of Barker.[3] On the whole it seems to me perfectly fair in substance, and you make some excellent points. I am only afraid, however, that in its present form the review may be more likely to distress the feelings of a sensitive author than to help him to purify his style and to clarify his thinking.

I don't think that the review needs any drastic changes, but I am sure that it would be more satisfactory if it could be submitted to a little rearrangement. I don't want to ask you to say anything more in praise of the book than you have done, or to diminish your strictures, but in its present form the article begins and ends on a severe tone, and the complimentary remarks are buried in the middle. I think that it would be gracious if you could rearrange it so that the praise you bestow could be given at the beginning and be followed by the censure as qualification. Even when one says exactly the same things it often makes a good deal of difference in what order one says them.

1–Martin Turnell (1908–79), critic, scholar and translator of French literature; author of *The Novel in France* (1950) and *The Art of French Fiction* (1959).
2–G. M. Turnell, 'Introduction to the Study of Tristan Corbière, *C*. 15 (Apr. 1936), 393–417.
3–Submitted on 7 Apr.

I of course do not want Faber and Faber books to have any preferential treatment in the *Criterion* over other books, but in a case like this when it is a book for which I am personally responsible, and which I am known to be supporting, it would appear a little odd to publish a review which is superficially, at least, rather derogatory. It would therefore be of assistance if you could make some rearrangement of it on the lines suggested, and let me have it back by Tuesday the 7th.[1]

In your letter you mention three other books which you would like to review, but I am sorry to say that I cannot read the names of any of them. Could you let me have these names again?

Yours sincerely,
T. S. Eliot

TO *Sydney Schiff*   CC

30 April 1935   [Faber & Faber Ltd]

My dear Sydney,

Your letter contains nothing but bad news.[2] I am very sorry indeed to hear about the young man. I had been going to write and ask him to come and have a talk with me whether we accepted his book or not. I have not yet had an opportunity of discussing it with my Committee, or of getting a second reading, but my own opinion is that this is a University press book rather than a general publisher's. By all means let me see his other book.

I had not seen Lady Rothermere for about eight years, and indeed we did not part on the best of terms, but I am extremely sorry to hear of her illness.[3] It is all the sadder to think of it for a person who valued good health so highly and who had hitherto enjoyed so much vigour.

With love to Violet,
Yours ever affectionately,
[Tom]

1 – Heppenstall on George Barker, *Poems*: C. 14 (July 1935), 677–80.
2 – Schiff wrote on 29 Apr. with the news that the young Paul Lucas, whose thesis on Keats was in TSE's hands, had shot himself: he had suffered from 'despondency' and was 'introspective'. He mentioned too that Lucas had written another book entitled 'On the Margin of Youth'.
3 – The other piece of news retailed by Schiff was that Lady Rothermere, TSE's old patron and founding owner of C., was 'desperately ill with cancer in a clinic in Switzerland'.

TO *Frederic Prokosch*   CC

30 April 1935   [Faber & Faber Ltd]

Dear Mr Prokosch,

Thank you for your letter of the 17th and for sending your poems, which have just arrived and which I shall read with interest.[1] It is too late to substitute any of them for the one I have taken for the *Criterion*, but I will pay special attention to the ones you mention.

We shall certainly consider these poems seriously for publication, but I must warn you in advance that under present conditions it is very difficult to sell English poetry in England and American poetry in America. *A fortiori*, therefore, it is still more difficult to sell American poetry in England or English poetry in America. And if we consider your poems it will be in the hope of coming to some arrangement with an American publisher. As for your prose book, I should say that the sooner we were able to read it the better, and therefore if you have a fair typescript which you can send us, I should be glad to have that.[2]

Yours very truly,
[T. S. Eliot]

TO *Alastair W. R. Miller*   TS Professor Andrew M. Miller

30 April 1935   *The Criterion*

Dear Mr Miller,

I don't think this is quite the poem that we want.[3] It strikes me as rather broken up between several reminiscent styles, conspicuous among which is William Blake, rather than *A Shropshire Lad*. You are trying to do something more ambitious than your earlier poems, and it is therefore less accomplished and is not crystallised. Let us try again.

What has happened to Alexis?

Yours sincerely,
T. S. Eliot

---

1 – Prokosch submitted a collection of 40 poems, and hoped that TSE would be able to select some 30 of them for a F&F volume to be called 'Poems' or 'Voyages'. He preferred a number of these poems (he specified five in particular) to the poem 'Going Southward' that TSE had accepted – C. 14 (July 1935), 608–9 – and would be happy for TSE to choose a substitute.
2 – Harper's was publishing in Sept. his novel *The Asiatics*: he hoped F&F might want it too.
3 – 'Towards a Blessing' was not published.

2 May 1935   [Faber & Faber Ltd]

Dear Alida,[1]

I have now had an opportunity of talking with Mr Crawley, our sales manager,[2] about the Poetry Bookshop books, and also with the Committee. The next step should be for you to have a talk with Crawley about the several items. I am merely writing before hand to give you a general idea of the position at which we have arrived.

In the first place, we are in general agreement about the price of *For Your Delight*.[3] I am not sure whether we ought to make an agreement with you about this or whether exchange of correspondence and payment will be sufficient, but in any case we should like to see your agreement with the Editor. We think that with the present edition it would be desirable to have the book brought up to date by including a few more writers of children's verse, such as Milne, who are nowadays expected to appear in any children's anthology. I should think that as the Editor would continue to draw royalty she would consider it to her interest to do the work of revision from time to time without any extra payment. As for the present stock, we could, I think, arrange for our own regular binders to store it for us. Then I suppose that you would notify the L.C.C. authorities and any other considerable customer of this book of the transfer.

---

1 – Following Harold Monro's death in 1932, his widow struggled with the management of the Poetry Bookshop at 38 Great Russell Street, London, and had to announce the closing of its doors on 22 June 1935. Alida Monro wrote on 3 Apr.: 'When we were talking of the Bookshop closing down last year you were good enough to say you thought your firm would take over an Anthology for Children *For Your Delight*. I am sending you a specimen copy . . . The sale is steady & would go up again if re-travelled & if put back into its 3 colour jacket.'

On 17 Apr. (TSE was off to Inverness): 'Here are the books I promised you yesterday . . . *Otherworld* is also for your library . . . The Michael Field book I specially want you to read [is] *A Messiah*. Harold & I gave readings of it many times & I feel it ought to be produced somewhere.

'We will discuss the *Delight* terms with your sales manager when he comes back. They seemed satisfactory to me unless you wd prefer to buy the stock at cost & pay me a royalty on sales? I think probably you will prefer the lump sum.'

2 – W. J. Crawley became Sales Manager on 1 Jan. 1934 (he had formerly worked as Methuen's London traveller). TSE to I. M. Parsons, 29 Nov. 1962, about a draft of Howarth's *Notes on Some Figures behind T. S. Eliot*: 'Owing to Frank Morley who knew him, we were joined by W. J. Crawley, who was most efficient as Sales Manager before he became Director.' TSE to WHA, 22 Oct. 1942: 'our Sales Manager, Mr Crawley . . . a very sapient person'. Monteith on Crawley: 'almost incredibly hard-working, often maddeningly obstinate, nearly always loveable . . .'

3 – *For Your Delight: Anthology for Children*, ed. E. L. Fowler (1924), had sold 25,834 copies to date.

About the *Georgian Anthology*. The chief difficulty which occurs to us is the likelihood that if we bring out the Anthology afresh in one volume the contributors will swarm down upon us demanding fees. We liked your suggestion of an omnibus edition, but I am afraid that such an edition would be especially vulnerable in this way. Some of the poets, W. H. Davis for instance, might justifiably complain at having so considerable a number of their poems in any one anthology. A selection out of the five volumes to be made by Eddie Marsh[1] with a new introduction is perhaps more feasible, although open in a less degree to the same danger. The possibility is that we might, if you wished, take over what present stock you have and market it for you on a sort of commission basis.

I am very doubtful about being able to do anything with *Other World*,[2] and the Committee takes no interest in *Michael Field*, at any rate in the poems.[3] The question of the plays must remain open for a little until I have had the time to read and report upon them. My views about the plays might also be influenced by getting an opinion from Martin Browne about their producability.

The second book after *For Your Delight* in which we are particularly interested is the *Collected Poems* of Charlotte Mew.[4] We very much like the idea of producing these in one volume together with the introductory memoir which you would write.

I am afraid we can do nothing with *The Little Green Duck*,[5] but I have given it to Mr Crawley to try on his children.

As we only discussed these books, with the exception of *For Your Delight*, in conversation, I probably don't carry in my head everything

---

1 – TSE was to write to the Hon. Harold Nicolson, 13 Oct. 1952: 'My dear Harold . . . I have no objection whatever to being implicated in the celebration of Eddie Marsh's eightieth birthday, but I should think that Eddie Marsh himself might be happier without me. I am under the impression that he has always regarded me as the great corrupter of English poetry, and that he almost bursts into tears when my name is mentioned. I only know that he always seems to look the other way when I am in sight. That, of course, may be due to myopia or mental concentration, but his expression on such occasions, which is like that of a man who has just bitten into an unripe persimmon, has suggested that he was not unaware of a noxious atmosphere in the street, so I think that out of modesty, I ought to decline.'
2 – F. S. Flint, *Otherworld* (Poetry Bookshop, 1920).
3 – 'Michael Field' was the *nom de plume* of two writers, Katharine Bradley (1846–1914) and her niece Edith Cooper (1862–1913), who were lovers and who together wrote 8 volumes of poetry and 27 verse-plays, plus 24 volumes of diaries they called *Works and Days*.
4 – Charlotte Mew (1869–1928), troubled and reclusive English poet (her family was afflicted with mental illness); author of *The Farmer's Bride* (Poetry Bookshop, 1916); befriended by Alida Monro, who arranged the posthumous collection *The Rambling Sailor* (1929).
5 – Jack Roberts, *The wonderful adventures of Ludo: the little green duck* (1924).

that you said about them, and we should like to have figures of sales and stock for these in which we may be interested.

I should be glad if you would at your convenience ring up Mr Crawley and make an appointment to see him, either here or at the Poetry Bookshop. I would be present too if you like, though I don't suppose I should be needed.

Yours ever,
[Tom]

TO *Margaret Trouncer*[1] CC

2 May 1935   [Faber & Faber Ltd]

Dear Mrs Trouncer,

I am very sorry we have had to take so long in coming to a decision about your book, but I assure you that this is by no means unusual, especially in the case of a book of rather specialised character. We should be very glad to publish your book on the following terms and the following conditions.

Our terms would be a royalty of 10 per cent up to a sale of 1,500 copies and of 15 per cent thereafter for the British and American rights. We should also be glad to give what is called an accrued advance, that is to say upon publication a sum representing the royalties on copies which have been paid by booksellers by that date. We should contemplate publishing it early next spring.

This offer is subject to your willingness to revise the manuscript in a number of places. We feel, as did our French reader, that the style is here and there considerably over-written, and that in places a less purple and more matter-of-fact tone would be suitable. If you agree we propose to have the manuscript gone through by a competent reader in our office, who will make suggestions as to the kind of alteration and the places where it is needed.

Second, we feel that the book would benefit by having more illustrations than the frontispiece portrait which you have provided. Could you provide or at least select seven other illustrations which would be suitable to the subject matter?

Third, we should like to leave the *title* and possibly the *chapter titles* unsettled for the present. Possibly the title you have given the book,

---

1 – Margaret Trouncer (1903–82), writer and novelist: works include *A Courtesan of Paradise: The Romantic Story of Louise de la Vallière, Mistress of Louis XIV* (F&F, 1936).

A Courtezan of Paradise, will prove to be the most satisfactory, but there is not entire agreement on this point.

Finally, the book as it stands is a very long one, and we think that it might benefit and be more widely read if it were *shortened*. Our reader would also be expected to make suggestions to this end. We think also that the apparatus of notes and references might be omitted, as it might appear formidable to the ordinary reader and give the suggestion that the book is only intended for a scholarly audience. Our French reader is satisfied that your scholarship can hardly be called in question, and the greater number of readers do not want to be reminded of this in any case. I am enclosing a copy of part of our French reader's report which might interest you, whether it lead you to make any alteration or not.

I should be very glad to hear at your earliest convenience whether these terms and conditions commend themselves to you.

Yours sincerely,
[T. S. Eliot]

TO *John Hayward*   MS King's

2 May 1935   Oxford & Cambridge Club,
                                    Pall Mall, s.w.1.

My dear John

I found your charming letter on my return from Scotland.[1] If I did not reply at once, it is because I have been torn with indecision. I should gain in practical ways by making the change, as well as by having the satisfaction of your proximity. I don't think that the annual expense would be much more, and I should get a great deal more for my money. Against this there are three considerations. First, I should have to buy furniture. I haven't a stick of my own except bookcases, and I haven't enough of them. And

---

1–JDH wrote from 22 Bina Gardens, London s.w.5, on 26 Apr.: 'I don't know if you really intended to consider seriously taking the flat on the first floor of this distinguished house. I do realize your difficulty in leaving Grenville Place. From a purely selfish point of view I should like you to come here; not because there is any need for you to come any nearer than you are at present in order to play chess &c; but because you would be an ideal tenant. The domestic arrangements here now seem to be so comfortably settled, the cooking improving daily, grace abounding, that it would be a disaster if some unsuitable person spoiled it all. The landlord tells me that he is willing to redecorate the flat, at his expense, to the incoming tenant's choice; and further will instal a h. & c. basin in the bedroom, the bathroom (private) being up a flight of stairs. The rent at present is £120 p.a. but I believe you could knock this down to £115, so anxious is the landlord to find a tenant.'

I shan't be able to buy furniture for another year. It will of course be cheaper in the end, as well as pleasanter: but I must pay my solicitor's bill first, and that will take a long time. Second, I know that I am about as satisfactory a tenant as they are likely to get, where I am, and I don't like to let the Vicar down. He has been very good to me, and he needs the money. My third reason is perhaps more 'psychological' as the saying is. I mean that I have not yet got over the feeling of being *hunted*: in my sleep I am pursued like Orestes, though I feel with less reason than that hero. Where I am I feel relatively *safe*. My status there is highly respectable, they know who I am, they know my circumstances, and if I was ever tracked down and molested I should be in a strong position. Anywhere else, I should be merely an ordinary tenant; I should be more accessible & vulnerable; and if I was tracked down & a disturbance followed I might simply be invited to leave.

I don't know how much ground there is for this feeling, but it is something plus fort que moi, of the character of nightmare, and I have to give way to it.

In another year none of these reasons may survive. I hope they won't. But at the moment they are all powerful, so there it is and I am sorry about it. Quite selfishly, I mean. I may be missing a unique opportunity.

I go down to Lingfield on Friday night till Tuesday. I am free at any time after that, and I shall stay in town over the following weekend. So please suggest an evening.

Scottish tour very successful. I have some photographs.[1]

Ever affectionately

Tom

1–JDH replied to this letter, 4 May: 'My dear Tom: / I couldn't tell you this morning on the telephone how very much I appreciated your letter. Although we've never spoken about those heavy and bewildering cares, I think there is a kind of tacit understanding between us. Any way, I'm sure you know that there is nothing within my power I would not do to mitigate them . . . This is terribly clumsily put, but you're used to me and must make allowances! I hope things will become progressively easier. / Your ever affectionate: / John'

TO *Frederick May Eliot*   CC

3 May 1935   [Faber & Faber Ltd]

Dear Frederick,

Many thanks for your letter of April the 24th.[1] It is a great satisfaction
to me to have been the means of getting Martin D'Arcy his engagements
in St Paul, and I am extremely grateful to you for your good offices. I am
only sorry that he is not in St Paul long enough to see something of you
more privately. I should be very glad if you would remember me most
kindly to Father Moynihan. My brief conversation with him I remember
with very great pleasure.

I am glad to hear that you are well. The children's diseases are, I suppose,
inevitable to their time of life and to the time of year, and it is satisfactory
to have got them over with.[2]

With love to Elizabeth.

                              Yours affectionately,
                              [Tom]

TO *Rayner Heppenstall*   TS Texas

3 May 1935   *The Criterion*

Dear Mr Heppenstall,

I find your revised review of Barker's poems quite satisfactory and have
sent it to the printers.

The name of Norman Cameron[3] is unknown to me, but I will look out
for the book when it comes. *Balletomania* has been out for a considerable
time, and you must remember that what we are now considering is the
review list for the September number. I don't intend to have my play

1 – Frederick Eliot wrote from St Paul, Minn.: 'Father D'Arcy is spending two days in St Paul
– yesterday and today – and I want to send you a word of sincere thanks for letting me be
a link in the chain that brought him here . . . Unfortunately, the very short period of Father
D'Arcy's visit will not let Elizabeth and me have a chance to entertain him at our house . . .
but he is being royally looked after by the Catholics.
    'Yesterday I had the very great pleasure of being present at a small luncheon in his honor
. . . It was a most delightful and charming occasion, and Father D'Arcy was the sort of
"guest of honor" one would go a thousand miles to see and listen to. Then, last evening,
Elizabeth and I went to his lecture on "Catholic Oxford", which was another very pleasant
and stimulating experience. Altogether, his visit here is being a great success . . .'
2 – 'All goes well with us here. The two boys are flourishing, after a prolonged siege of
"children's diseases", which were not at all serious but slightly tiring for the parents.'
3 – Norman Cameron (1905–53), Scottish poet, translator, advertising copywriter.

reviewed at all, and Auden's play and Spender's critical book were both bespoken some time ago.[1] That is one of the difficulties, that there is always a number of people who want to review the same books.

You might ask Heinemann, if you will, to send us a copy of your book of poems when it appears.[2] Otherwise it may or may not be sent. Unless you are already engaged elsewhere I should be glad if you cared to let us see your book on Ballet when it is ready. We publish Adrian Stokes' books, you know, and are rather interested in that subject, although of course we have not so far published any of the more highly technical Ballet books, such as Beaumont produces.

I am afraid I have not the slightest idea how or where to go about getting a job as Ballet critic.[3] If I can find out I will, but I have almost no personal acquaintances in the daily press.

Yours sincerely,
T. S. Eliot

TO *E. Martin Browne*   CC

3 May 1935   [Faber & Faber Ltd]

Dear Martin Browne,

I am writing at once in reply to your letter of the 2nd to say that so far as I know there is no need for a meeting immediately.[4] I think that you are in a position to know better when we ought to meet next than I am. It is merely that I should like to see you to talk things over and learn how the play is going as soon as you are in London again long enough to be able to arrange the meeting conveniently. I have made a few rather important alterations in the proof which you sent me.[5] By an unfortunate oversight

1 – Heppenstall asked, 30 Apr.: 'Did someone do "Balletomania"? I didn't notice. And I'd be very glad to do either your own or Auden's new play. Or Spender's "Destructive Element".'
2 – 'My own poems are appearing, from Heinemann's, sometime, I believe, in June. And I'm supposed to be starting a book on Ballet.'
3 – 'Have you any power to help me to a permanent paid job as Ballet Critic? If so, may I solicit your good wishes?'
4 – EMB wrote on 2 May to excuse himself from meeting TSE on 7 May: 'It seems vital that I should get down in time to see Miss Babington that day, as she is away on Wednesday when the first rehearsal takes place.'
5 – EMB had written on Easter Thursday (23 Apr.): 'I expect by now you've had the proof [of the Canterbury Acting Edition of *Murder in the Cathedral*] you asked for . . . Many thanks for the speeches which will fit excellently. I don't think the *whole* plainsong passage could come after the speech, as it wd. be *very* long: but I do agree that the theme shd be declared by the speaker first, & then the music woven in. But I'll keep them as separate as I can. I'm

I failed to post it back, and it only went off yesterday. I thought that the best person to send it to was Miss Babington. As an instance of the sort of alterations required I found that I had to alter the opening of the sermon to make it do for Christmas morning instead of Christmas Eve. There is nothing in the alterations to put your actors out, but I should be very sorry if the text were printed without them.[1]

Many thanks for returning the book to the London Library. I shall await your further news, and will come down to Canterbury only if and when you want me. I hope that you have succeeded in getting a suitable house or lodgings, and please let me know your address as soon as you have one.

With kind regards to your wife,
Yours ever,
[T. S. Eliot]

TO *N. M. Iovetz-Tereshchenko* CC

3 May 1935   [Faber & Faber Ltd]

Dear Dr Iovetz-Tereshchenko,

I have discussed our conversation of yesterday afternoon with my colleague, to whom I have referred before. He still thinks that one or two other avenues should be explored before definitely accepting the terms which have been offered to you.[2] He suggests first the Cambridge University Press. For this purpose you should write to Mr S. C. Roberts, The University Press, Cambridge, mentioning in your letter that I and Mr F. V. Morley have read your book with very great interest and have made this suggestion to you. Say also that Mr Morley and myself would [be] very glad to answer any enquiries which Mr Roberts might care to make.

The second suggestion is to send the typescript to Dr J. R. Rees, who is the head of the Institute of Medical Psychology in London. If Dr Rees were interested in the book, as I think he might well be, he could be very influential in securing help for its publication. We recommend, however,

---

very anxious to keep the second page, as it explains the point of the whole scene. Forgive haste. I have been making a copy of the new matter with stage directions . . .'

1–Brigid O'Donovan posted proofs to Babington, who replied on 10 May: 'I must apologise for not having acknowledged the receipt of the proof . . . The delay, of course, was unfortunate as the whole thing was already set up, but the part containing the alterations has been re-set and I hope to be able to send Mr Eliot a copy of the completed acting edition at the beginning of next week.'

2–Iovetz-Tereshchenko was considering an offer to publish the book on a subsidy basis.

that you should write to Mr Roberts first. In the circumstances I shall not be writing to Mr Spalding until I have heard from you again.

Yours sincerely,
[T. S. Eliot]

TO *Jessie Gunn*[1]   CC

7 May 1935   [Faber & Faber Ltd]

Dear Mrs Gunn,

I am taking the liberty of sending you copies of the photographs which I took on our Scottish tour. I am only sorry not to have one of yourself, and sorry that there is only one of your husband, and that one taken on a rather dark day. Sending them, however, gives me the opportunity of expressing my appreciation of you and your husband's hospitality. Incidentally, your salmon and your mutton, and of course the whiskey, have given me standards which will make me permanently dissatisfied with any of those viands as provided in the South.[2] But it is much more the spirit of hospitality that remains a valued memory. I hope that this pilgrimage may continue an annual event.

Yours sincerely,
[T. S. Eliot]

TO *Jeanette McPherrin*   TS Denison Library

9 May 1935   Faber & Faber Ltd

Dear Miss McPherrin,

Many thanks for your letter – I was relieved, as I felt some responsibility for recommending the Dieppe route – but a messmate who chews in her sleep was the last inconvenience that I should have thought of – but it

---

1–Jessie (Daisy) Gunn (1887/8–1963) was wife of the Scottish novelist Neil M. Gunn (1891–1973), whose works were published by the Porpoise Press (see TSE to George Blake, 9 Aug. 1932) and subsequently by F&F. The Gunns lived in a bungalow they had built at Inverness, where TSE, FVM and the American publisher Donald Brace had briefly visited them in 1933.

2–TSE would write to George Bruce, BBC Features, 31 Oct. 1961 (Gunn would turn 70 on 8 Nov. 1961): 'Neil Gunn taught me how to educate my palate to the best whisky. In consequence I am a very temperate drinker, for whisky is the only spirit to which I am addicted, and after Neil's whisky in pre-war days the whisky one gets in London nowadays seems very indifferent stuff.'

might have happened anyway anywhere – your description of the lady suggests that she was French – but I hope you are none the worse for it now. It is always pleasant to be thanked, even when one has not done anything particular, and when what one has done has been a pure enjoyment – I am so sorry you could not have staid for another night, and I hope that the chatelaine of Sèvres was not too vinegary when you returned (but French women can express vinegar with more acid content than any others, I think) but what does it matter really? I enclose a note to forward to Maritain – I have just written to him separately, because I never think that a letter of introduction carries conviction otherwise – and I hope you will see them and like them. When you come in July try to give me as much notice as you can – so that I may be able to arrange to have rooms for you and Emily here again, if you can stand it. I shall start trying to do what I can to influence her arrangements for the winter – one has to be very careful with anyone so sensitive and proud (but also, alas, much too humble – I have tried to suggest that there is a wrong way of being humble as well as a right way).[1] Thank you again for your letter: so will close, yours respectfully,

T. S. Eliot

TO *Stephen Spender*   TS Northwestern

9 May 1935   Faber & Faber Ltd

My dear Stephen,

Thank you very much for your good letter of April 30th. First of all, to get them over, business matters.[2]

1–TSE saw Emily Hale on 1 May 1935 (diary with EVE).

See TSE, 'Shakespeare and the Stoicism of Seneca' (1927): 'Humility is the most difficult of all virtues to achieve; nothing dies harder than the desire to think well of oneself.'

2–SS responded to TSE's letter of 25 Apr.: 'When you were in America I had lunch one day with Faber & Morley, and I told them I wd. like to do a book on James. They were not at all interested, and I have dropped the idea, but one evening I mentioned to someone (I forget who) that I had had this book in mind, and the next day Cape rang me up. I asked full leave from Faber before accepting Cape's offer, although I have no binding contract with him.

'I shall do the book of short stories this summer. I plan a book of five or six short stories taking up about 35,000 words, and then a story of 35,000 words, which will be founded on *The Temple*. I shall avoid all possible libels in that, and it will, in fact be completely different from *The Temple*, the MS of which I shall not even refer to when I write it. Is that acceptable to you?

'Secondly, I am doing the Hölderlin.

'Thirdly & fourthly, all the work I am doing now – the short stories on the one hand, and the poems which I am now doing – are sketches for two books which I shall start (I hope)

About the Cape arrangement. I had not known, or if told had forgotten, about your conversation with Faber and Morley while I was away. I should like to think that if I had been on hand things might have turned out differently: I think I should have been excited by the prospect of your writing a book about James – and if I had had anything to say about it, it would have been a book about James, and not including less important people like Lawrence and myself. But it is just as likely that my opinion would have made no difference, as very often happens. Anyway, I don't want you to misunderstand the present point. That was a mistake, but Faber and Morley agree that you consulted them about dealing with Cape, and we have no grounds for complaint against either Cape or yourself. All we want is to feel that you will let us have the first option on any future books – and we want to do the stories, and the plays, as well as your next poems when they are ready – if we can offer terms that will satisfy you as just.

I agree with you that it would be well to publish the group of poems between the novel and the trilogy. But poems can't be written to a date; and if the volume of fifty should not be quite ripe at the right time, I should keep it and publish the other things as they come.

I have felt that if I had been here I should have advised Auden not to let us publish the *Dance of Death* when we did – he didn't mean it to be published then, and only yielded to our solicitations; and I think it was a mistake: but it doesn't matter now, because *The Dog Beneath the Skin* is so good.

I quite agree with you about the kind of criticism that is now most worth while.[1] I think that *After Strange Gods* belongs to a more interesting kind

---

this time next year. The one is a group of Three Plays, called, I think, A European Trilogy, the second is a novel called, I think, The Liberal Cage. I have a few sketches of parts of these, but I still have a great deal of preparation to do. You will realize that *The Destructive Element*, is also an approach to the point of view, from which I hope finally to be able to do the trilogy. I shall offer both of these to Faber.

'Fifthly, I shall have at the end of this year about 20 or 30 new poems, but I don't want to publish another book until I have 50. It would be a good thing, I think, to publish the poems, between the novel and the Trilogy. I shall send them too to Faber.'

1 – 'I quite agree really with everything you say [in TSE's letter of 25 Apr.] about my book. I'm sorry about the small errors.

'The only answer about the question of the thesis, is that I wanted to write a book explaining why, in spite of the qualities which his admirers find to admire, and the prudishness which his detractors attack, I like [Henry] James. The key is in Pound's few remarks in *Make It New* on the qualities in James which his detractors find "cold" – though I had not read *Make It New* when I wrote this book. The answer to my question took me much further into the question of what James's art is actually *about*. Now my thesis is simply that James & other writers, have written books about the moral life of the last two generations of our

of criticism than my earlier work; I only regret that it is not better of its kind. The danger in this kind of criticism is in reading for the purpose of proving one's point. I was not guiltless of that. In this kind of criticism, it is necessary to know one's authors from cover to cover – and I didn't. I am not quite sure that you did either. I ought to have read the whole of Hardy, and the whole of Lawrence, and everything else, without any design whatever, and to have known it ever so well, before generalising about it. And you ought to have read every scrap of James before trying to fit him in to any social theory. I mean that you don't really criticise an author to whom you have never surrendered yourself. Even just the bewildering minute[1] counts: you have to give yourself up, and then

---

civilization. I do not see why this shd. put me in blinkers. But, if it does, I shall, of course remain in blinkers for the rest of my life. Yet, I prefer to be in blinkers [than] to be in the blinkerless, rapidly staring state of Clive Bell on the one hand, or Dr Leavis and his Taste gang on the other, or a mere blinkerless donkey, like Grigson.

'I prefer too your own later criticism in *After Strange Gods*, to the earlier, perhaps more pleasurable, and purer criticism. Because at certain stages criticism has got to stop tabulating, drawing up rules & recording even the most sensitive reactions, and relate art to the life of moral values.

'Of course, this sounds very vague. But the vagueness establishes precisely the problem; to restate the part that literature & music play in religious & political & moral life, in terms which are lucid. Otherwise art on the one hand becomes simply a question of technique & a mysterious snobbery of Taste; on the other hand it establishes a claim that it IS the things which it is about. That it IS religion or morality.

'Anyhow pure criticism finally becomes narrow and even logically misses certain kinds of art. For instance until recently all the Tasteful critics said that Schubert was sentimental – and as for Verdi. The fact that Verdi was one of the men of greatest genius of the last century was so obvious that all highbrow criticism missed it.

'Naturally, I am opposed to this Cambridge & Bloomsbury criticism, because it will always be able to dismiss my work as "glamorous" and obvious. Everything these critics say is perfectly true as to rules that they have laid down. But these rules have nothing to do with what is immediate in art: and the people who make them have no realization of what art is about, or even more important, of *how* it is related to its subject. If any of these critics were contemporaries of Beethoven they wd. either dismiss the Eroica Symphony by saying it was about the ideas of the French Revolution, and Fidelio by saying that it was about freedom; or they would accept these works, by saying that really they have no connection with Beethoven's own ideas. Now, my conviction is that both these critical positions are false, and even hypocritical.'

1–From Tourneur's *The Revenger's Tragedy*, as quoted by TSE in 'Tradition and the Individual Talent' II (1919): 'Are lordships sold to maintain ladyships / For the poor benefit of a bewildering minute?' See too TSE's 'Cyril Tourneur' (1930), and Frank Kermode's introduction to *The Selected Prose of T. S. Eliot* (1975). EVE wrote to Mary Lascelles on 11 Aug. 1974, with reference to this passage: 'Now you will know that "the bewildering minute" comes from "The Revenger's Tragedy" by Tourneur, but will other readers of Tom's correspondence? I have drawn attention in a footnote to what he has written about the play, and the importance of this line in his work. Please tell me truthfully: do you think I am being pedantic?' See too John Worthen, *T. S. Eliot: A Short Biography* (2009), 292 n. 61.

recover yourself, and the third movement is having something to say, before you have wholly forgotten both surrender and recovery. Of course the self recovered is never the same as the self before it was given. That is why my essays on Jonson, and Tourneur, and Bradley are good, and my essay on Machiavelli is rubbish. Now with your book I don't feel that you had at any time given yourself completely to James. If you had, you would not have been quite so selective, I feel; you would not have ignored (relatively) *The Altar of the Dead,* and (completely) a story which to me is of the greatest significance, *The Friends of the Friends.* I think that a thorough study of the latter would perhaps make otiose and irrelevant your questions about James's virility. Which are due partly to a failure to understand the period, and partly to a failure to understand James. (Not that I can pretend to any advantages for understanding James, for, as I said, James wasn't an American. I mean that although he had an acute sense of contemporary America, he had no American Sense of the Past. His America is always his present; he is indifferent to the American tradition: for an American like myself – and I think this applies to Virginia as well as to Massachusetts – *our* America came to an end in 1829, when Andrew Jackson was elected president. In this respect he has nothing in common with our Hawthorne. But James had unconsciously *acquired,* though not inherited, something of the American tradition. He was not a descendant of the witch-hangers.)

And as for 'vulgarity' – that is a dangerous epithet, for the word means so many things, that it is apt to recoil. Flaubert vulgar? You have got to define your peculiar use of 'vulgar' very precisely first; and you can't sweep away so big a man as Flaubert with a word. Still less Stendhal. Balzac of course was 'vulgar', like Dickens; but that's a cruder use of the word than yours.

Of course, it is better to be as you are than to be as Clive Bell or Leavis – but why mention such triflers – or descend with such a thump to the bottomless sound of Grigson? You are diminishing your effort by referring to such puny standards.

'To relate art to the life of moral values'! Certainly, there you have Corneille and Racine with you, except that they were not aware of any unrelation to be made relation. I haven't myself any awareness of Art, on the one hand, and (my) moral values on the other, with a problem set: how to relate them. My own 'art' (such as it is) has always been at the disposal of my moral values. *Ash Wednesday,* for instance, is an exposition of my view of the relation of *eros* and *agape* based on my own experience. I think and hope that I have overcome any desire to write

Great Poetry, or to compete with anybody. One has got at the same time to unite oneself with humanity, and to isolate oneself completely; and to be equally indifferent to the 'audience' and to oneself as one's own audience. So that humility and freedom are the same thing.[1]

Affectionately,
Tom

TO *Philip Mairet*

CC

9 May 1935   [*The Criterion*]

Dear Mr Mairet,

Thank you for your letter of the 7th.[2] I am glad to hear that your meetings hereafter are on Thursdays, as I appear in general to have fewer engagements on that afternoon than on Fridays. At such short notice I am not sure whether I can look in today, and therefore am writing to you in any case.

I am returning Mr Angold's poem.[3] It seems to me quite good enough for a weekly, but not up to the standard which a quarterly ought to try to maintain. There is a lot of undigested Hopkins in it, and that is an influence which seems to me to lead up a blind alley. The poem is able, however, and shows promise.

I should like to express my appreciation of your article in the current issue. I think it is over favourable, but there is only one point I want to make. I am sure that there is nothing that could rightly be called 'animus' in any of Spender's remarks.[4] I mean that the word animus is apt

1 – See too SS's account of this exchange, in 'Remembering Eliot', in *T. S. Eliot: The Man and His Work*, ed. Allen Tate, 255–6.

2 – 'I feel to blame for not having pressed you to come to Committees here . . . Will you please note that we are meeting now on *Thursdays*, not Fridays: and if you should be able to join us this Thursday, about 4.30, or any time between that and 5, we shall be very glad to see you.'

3 – Mairet had written on 7 May: 'I enclose a short poem by J. P. Angold, wondering, at his own suggestion, whether you might think it worthy of the *Criterion*. If you don't, we'll print it.' (John Penrose Angold [1909–43], poet, translator, critic – his work was admired by EP – died while serving in the RAF. See *Collected Poems by J. P. Angold* [1952].)

4 – SS – in two chapters ('T. S. Eliot in His Poetry'; 'T. S. Eliot in His Criticism') of *The Destructive Element* (1935) – criticised TSE's critical beliefs. Mairet – in 'Belief and Criticism', *NEW* 7 (9 May 1935), 71–2 – took issue with Spender: 'The writer Mr Spender idolises is Henry James, the most tentative stylist that ever wrote; and the one writer whom he assails with something like animus, despite genuine admiration, is T. S. Eliot. What he dislikes in Mr Eliot is the definite traditional faith he has adopted, and seeks to apply, even to literary judgment.'

to suggest to people a touch of personal malice. Spender is a very good friend of mine, and he is, I think, one of the last people to nourish such sentiments. I don't mean that you are wholly unjustified in drawing such a conclusion from his book, but that he has given you a false impression.

The *New English Weekly* seems to me to be looking up. I have been trying to think, now that I have finished a major piece of work, which has taken my spare time through the winter, of some subject on which I could write for you from time to time more or less connectedly.

Yours ever sincerely,
[T. S. Eliot]

TO *Ian Parsons*   TS Reading

10 May 1935   Faber & Faber Ltd

My dear Parsons,

I am afraid that I cannot confirm my provisional acceptance of yesterday.[1] I have talked the matter over with my Chairman and one other of my colleagues, and I find them strongly of the opinion that I ought to be very chary of prefaces. This is not simply a desire to retain my services of this kind for Faber books, because the same question arose at the same time in connection with a book we are publishing ourselves.

I am sorry about this, but I really agree with them. What I would gladly do is to allow the use of some remark I have made about Rosenberg in the past on the jacket of the book, if you wished it. Or I would be glad to write a new little blurb for the purpose.

Yours every sincerely,
T. S. Eliot

'Mr Spender, however, makes no serious effort to understand what Mr Eliot means by his "traditional" standards in literature. He only tries to discredit it, by making out that Mr Eliot's use of it is vague, wrong or unintelligible.'

1 – No corresponding letter traced. Parsons had invited TSE to write a preface to his edition of Isaac Rosenberg's poetry.

11 May 1935   Faber & Faber Ltd

Dear R.H.,

Well you are a rum un and no mistake.[1] Well I am sorry for your disabilities but there you are I sometimes feel very poorly with phlebitis

---

1 – Hodgson wrote from Sendai, 9 Apr.: 'My dear Eliot – My old bodily disability came back last Autumn, which by compelling me to keep an unnatural position when I write [drawing by RH of himself in a reclining position, with feet raised high] allows but little ink to flow down my pen [drawing of two hands holding pens at different angles] and makes the act irksome to such a degree that I can't get on unless I'm feeling unusually free from the trouble. (This position [drawing of figure sitting up and writing at a desk] – I haven't written a letter in it for 30 years – sends me to my medicine chest & hot water for days – ½ an hour of it) . . . Last night I went to bed full of heavy thoughts about our over-rated human race, presently dozed off to the other world, dreamt interestingly – dogs etc (one a B.T. most grotesque, wall eye, one of them grinning face & a canine tooth broken off midway but as *big* as a *lion's* – kindly-pleasant etc) and woke up refreshed for early tea . . . While taking tea I turned over the pages of a kennel paper that came yesterday – naturally after such dreams, & my eye caught the enclosed cutting. ['*Even in their palmist days Manchester Terriers were never a breed in which large kennels prevailed to any extent, as they have always been to a great extent in the hands of fanciers who kept a dog and a couple or so of bitches, and the total of the inmates of whose kennels, including young stock, rarely exceeded half a dozen specimens. I should say that in the late eighties Mr T. Ellis, of Cheetham Hill, possessed the biggest kennel of the breed that ever existed, numbering possibly 40 all told. His noted Ch. Pearl was practically invincible, and he sold her to Col. C. S. Dean, who also got together a big kennel, usually containing fully 30 inmates.*'] You see I remember Pearl and her K. mate B. Turk. (A type now lost – the last I saw of this blood belonged, oddly rather, to "Q", the writer (bought fr. Col Dean) 12 or 14 years ago). So I fell into thinking about Pearl, her qualities, particularly her foreface which was remarkable – far more than that – her outline, legs & feet, her wonderfully sprung rib – and *there!* down went my paper, my thoughts & everything about Manchesters to verse & to you & your last letter. Awful guilt came over me. I said 'today I'll write him' & here I am, above angle but pen running sweetly – fairly.

   'Now about that verse business. Did you ever come across a tale – Aug. Birrell's I think – of an old gay buck, rake of the Regency who in about the '40's sauntering up Bow St met an old lag forgotten face posting south; he asked after salutation 'Why such haste, where are you going?' His friend said (Hansards under arm) 'Fearfully busy, House you know good bye' – and his astonished 'Really! does that still go on?' Well, that's rather how I feel over verse of my day (& most others), I feel that it is definitely *over* & done with. I don't like the feeling . . . I know perfectly well that if F. & F. publish a book of verse, anybody's, people will pay attention. But it wont do. What you & M[acmillan] propose is the friendliest thing imaginable & I'll keep the memory of it like everything else really worth keeping. More than that (*no*, not more) if I have anything new that may seem worth publishing in some way to Macmillans, who have first call, I think, by my agreement, are agreeable I shall be only too happy to offer it to you & M. This tomorrow; in the future if any, sometime. The association would be particularly pleasing to me. That is, of course, we'd love to see you again, but I'm not certain when we shall get to England, not this year. You must have plenty of opportunities for hearing nightingales in Surrey, I should expect them to be pretty close round Pike's Farm. They'll be over in a couple of weeks – by the time you get this letter, easily . . . Love to everybody at Pike's Farm. I do hope you hear a good nightingale to pair

myself but what should I expect I say to My self gettin on in years as I am. Still I envy you bein able to dream of bull Terriars I only wish I ever dreamt of anything so lovely as that I don't know whats to be done about the Manchester breed unless you come back to England pretty quick and reform things the world is I agree in a bad Way but something might be done beginning with Terriers and you are the only man who can do it. I had wanted you back here pretty urgently this summer to help me get a Dog for a Lady[1] but now the Lady finds that she probably wont be able to keep a Dog next winter so it isnt so Urgent. The Lady without a Dog. Well to return to poetry it is my Ambition to be the best dressed man over 70 in Pall Mall and I shall beat you at it Well now how long are you going to stand on one leg sucking your thumb havent you realised yet as I have painfully that once you have written and published writings you cant suppress them and that if you dont let your Poems be republished properly now somebody is going to come along and do it after you are dead for 50 years or so in a way you wont like as much. I am not talking about your future work knowing what a lazy devil you are there is more hope of that if we deal with the present first and no use worrying about the future till you get back to Ridgeways and we can fill you up with gooseberry tarts. As for the past now so far as Macmillan is concerned you leave that to us to see what can be done Well now to give you a breath of air for a moment

The Nightingales HAVE been something extra this year I heard them all round Pikes Farm this last weekend that ever was singing all night and all day I never heard so many and on the whole a very fair average of quality though you know my convictions a good mockingbird can beat the nightingale all holler if you discount the fact of the latter having the advantage of the stage all to himself and people feeling sentimental at that time of night and there are even other birds here that I prize as highly blackbirds etc. and I think the hermit thrush superior on his own habitat but there is a very good chorus of birds this year and I have never seen the bluebells more flourishing. Chaffinches & greenfinches very common. But

All you have to do is to think that as your poems are in existence anyway it cant do any harm to have them all in one volume and you can at least let us see what we can do about It with macMillan. I am sorry you are not coming back this summer I have been counting on it for three years Will

---

with your hermit-thrush & that the budgerigars are flourishing & coming along. Yours ever R. H.'

1 – A reference to Anton Chekhov's story 'Lady with a Lapdog' (1899).

you come next year if I come and meet you half way say at Omaha and help with the Akitas Please give my love to Aurelia so will close

T. S. E.

TO *Susan Hinkley*

11 May 1935   Faber & Faber Ltd

Dear Aunt Susie,

I was glad to get your letter.[1] The name of Constance Cummings is vaguely familiar, but perhaps I have merely seen her portrait on a cigarette-card. Anyway, why the devil does she only accept plays that her husband likes? That is a degree of conjugal fidelity that I cannot approve. I wait in breathless suspense. But if the play is not accepted, then I hope there will be the minor compensation of seeing you and Eleanor in London in June. Please let me know what is to happen without delay, because otherwise I may have difficulty in getting you seats for Canterbury. This is not boastfulness; it is only that I know that the Canterbury Festival has a regular clientele which always goes – and the room only holds 500 uncomfortably – and the run is only for a week. I think most of them will be very indignant about what I am giving them, and will dislike its political innuendoes. Don't you think that vanity is one of the great obstacles to a sense of humour? and if so, is that not one of the reasons why actors are so often pompous and stupid?

Emily has been up to town, and seen the King & Queen, and we took a taxi-ride to see the flood-lighting. I encourage her to come up as often as she can afford to. Between ourselves, I find the Perkins's, with all their amiability, very trying. To say nothing of the newly arrived aunt, but then she has just had a holiday in Guernsey with her young friend Jean McPherrin. California was a very great blow to her and it will take her some time to get over the disappointment.

Affectionately,

Tom

1–Susie Hinkley reported on 14 Apr. that her daughter Eleanor's play *Aphra Behn* was causing 'a good deal of excitement' in New York: the American-born British actress Constance Cummings (1910–2005) was especially interested in the role. 'But her husband [Benn Levy] is now in London, and therefore she is waiting to hear from him, whether he likes it. He is a playwright himself, and she said as a rule, he only cared for his own plays. This is, of course, true, and disheartening. However he may like it for her. If so, she would do it in London in the autumn. This would mean, of course, that we would cross then, and not in June . . . The girl, herself, is really charming.'

TO *H. N. Spalding*[1]

15 May 1935   [Faber & Faber Ltd]

Dear Sir,

Although I am unknown to you, I take the liberty of writing to you about the book of Dr Jovetz-Tereshchenko.[2] I do not pretend to any expert knowledge of psychology, but write merely as a publisher and as a Churchman.

Dr Tereshchenko came to me, some weeks, indeed several months ago, with an introduction from a mutual acquaintance. I read his book with great interest and approval, as did also one of my colleagues. We felt sure that it ought to be published. But my firm has so far done so little in the field of psychology, that we considered that we were not the people who could best sell the book; and in any case, it seemed obvious that the book would have only a small public to begin with, and could hardly be published at all without a subsidy.

What I feel about the value of the book is this. I have taken an interest in the psychology of Freud from the point of view of a Christian, and I see that this book directly challenges – I am not qualified to say that it overthrows – Freud's fundamental assumptions; and all the more impressively, in that it is not apparently concerned with Freud at all. So far as I remember, the name of Freud is not mentioned. Dr Tereshchenko's main thesis is one, I think, of the greatest importance in the difference between traditional Christianity and the new psychology; and his book ought to be of great support to Christian apologists.

Incidentally, of course, I was touched by the author's personal plight; and I feel that the publication of the book might be of the greatest help to his future. It would certainly help one who seems to me, on very slight acquaintance, to be a worthy man, to overcome the discouragement under which he might already have succumbed.

1–Henry Norman Spalding (1877–1953), barrister and philanthropist. With his wife Nellie he founded at Oxford a Chair in Eastern Religions and Ethics and other research and lecturing posts. They also supported the Workers' Educational Association and wildlife projects. He was one of the founders of the Association of British Orientalists, and of the Museum of Art at Oxford. He was Vice-President of the World Congress of Faiths; and his published works include *Civilisation of East and West* (1939) and select volumes of poetry.
2–Tereshchenko had prompted TSE on 6 May: 'I . . . would be indeed grateful to you if you would write to Mr Spalding, not withholding from him, of course, the position as regards Cambridge. I cannot help wondering also whether I could ask you to write a few words to Mr Roberts directly; it would make all the difference to his approach to the book.'

It is impossible for the book to be published without a subsidy. Messrs Allen & Unwin, who are as well qualified for selling such a book as any in London, have made an offer, requiring a subsidy, and have undertaken to publish the book within four months of the signing of the agreement.[1]

Knowing nothing of your circumstances, and being a stranger to you, I am not in a position to ask you to help financially. What I can do is to write, as I am doing, to assure you of my own belief in the value of the work. From what Dr Tereshchenko has said to me, I understand that he is very sensible of your great kindness to him in the past.

I am, my dear Sir,
Yours very truly,
[T. S. Eliot]

TO *David Gascoyne*   CC

15 May 1935   [*The Criterion*]

Dear Mr Gascoyne,

I am sorry to have kept so long the poems which you sent me on the 19th of March.[2] They seem to me quite good, and showing development, but I feel that you will do still better before long, and I should like to wait for the next stage before printing anything in the *Criterion*.

Do come and see me again at some time when you are in this part of town.

Yours sincerely,
[T. S. Eliot]

---

1 – In the event, Allen & Unwin brought out *Friendship-Love in Adolescence* early in 1936.
2 – Gascoyne had submitted two poems (titles unknown). HR to TSE, 13 May: 'I think he is improving, but I have seen better poems of his than these. I should wait for something better.'

TO *Emilio Coia*[1]   CC

15 May 1935   [Faber & Faber Ltd]

Dear Mr Coia,

Thank you so much for leaving the caricature for me to see.[2] So far as the victim himself can judge it seems to me excellent, and besides being a good caricature and a good drawing is really far less unflattering than other drawings which have been made. The only bit I don't understand is the red aura projected from the face, which I find a little distracting. Is it meant to symbolise anything, such as an emotion of rage?[3]

If you care to leave it here a few days I will see if Herbert Read can come in and have a look at it. I shan't have time to take it out to Hampstead for him to see[4] before he leaves for Sussex, and in any case I should not like the responsibility of carrying it about the streets in showery weather.

Yours very sincerely,
[T. S. Eliot]

TO *Louis MacNeice*   CC

15 May 1935   [Faber & Faber Ltd]

Dear Mr MacNeice,

Thank you for your letter of the 14th.[5] I had thought that you might be wanting to add a few poems to your volume. Indeed, I had hoped so, because I like so much the more recent ones already in the volume. So I will have the manuscript sent back to you, and will let you know by what date we shall need to have it for the printers.

Yours sincerely,
[T. S. Eliot]

1–Emilio Coia (1911–97), Scottish caricaturist (son of an Italian immigrant), worked for many years in advertising, and after the war for *The Scotsman*.
2–Coia, who lived in Hampstead, left the caricature on Mon. 13 May 1935.
3–A caricature of TSE by Coia is reproduced in *The Scotsman*, 1 Sept. 1958, 4 – but perhaps not the same one as referred to here.
4–HR was living at 3 The Mall, Parkhill Road, London N.W.3.
5–'I have been thinking that, if you are going to do my book of poems some time in the autumn, perhaps I should rearrange it during the summer. I have several new poems I should like to add and I will cut out several from the present collection. Also minor changes. I think perhaps I ought to have back the typescript which you have, as I have not, in all cases, got exact copies?'

TO *Jessica Dismorr*[1]   TS Cornell

15 May 1935   *The Criterion*

Dear Jessie,

I found your note on Wyndham Lewis interesting,[2] and I should like to publish something in the *Criterion* about Lewis, but I feel that this is in itself too slight for the purpose, and really is more suitable for a periodical which could publish a number of illustrations of Lewis's work to support what you say.

I shall be writing to you later about your poetry.

Yours always cordially,
T. S. Eliot

TO *I. A. Richards*   TS Magdalene

16 May 1935   Faber & Faber Ltd

Dear Richards,

'Murder in the Cathedral' now off my hands (title gives less offense than 'Achbp. [*sic*] Murder Case') (I will send you a copy as soon as available – I don't know whether it is good or bad, I never was so in the dark about anything I have written). I should like to see you when convenient – come to Cambridge for a night when we can arrange it.

I am glad to see that the Climbing book is having such a hearty reception.[3] It must be very good.

1–Jessica Dismorr (1885–1939), English artist and illustrator of independent means, associated with Vorticism; intimate friend of WL, whom she met in 1913: she was a signatory to the Vorticist manifesto published in *Blast*, 1914. In the 1930s she did portraits of poets including Dylan Thomas and William Empson. See Catherine Elizabeth Heathcock, *Jessica Dismorr (1885–1939): Artist, Writer, Vorticist* (PhD thesis, Birmingham University, Sept. 1999).

2–Dismorr submitted on 13 Apr. an article called 'The Painting Periods of Wyndham Lewis'. 'It was originally written for the quarterly "Art", which has been abandoned. Lewis liked it ("Great stuff!") which made me think I should give it a chance with another editor.' HR to TSE (13 May), of Dismorr's submission: '"Great stuff" said Lewis – because it is mostly quotation from his own works. It won't do for the *Criterion* – suggest the new art magazine *AXIS*.'

3–Dorothy Pilley (Richards), *Climbing Days* (1935).

Any news of you would be welcome. Whazzz matter with Leavis? He seems to be bilious.[1]

Yours ever,
T. S. E.

TO *Alida Monro*   cc

17 May 1935   [Faber & Faber Ltd]

My dear Alida,

The matter of *For Your Delight* is now quite settled as far as we are concerned, with the exception of getting in touch with the editor and being assured that when the time comes, that is to say when the present stock is exhausted, she will be willing, without extra fee, to bring the book up to date in the way I suggested in a previous letter. Would it not be best, as we do not know her, if you wrote to her yourself and explained the situation?

Mr Crawley would still like to have a short talk with you about the matter of sales arrangements, and about re-arrangements for the transfer to stock, and he would be glad if you would telephone and give him an appointment.

The question of Charlotte Mew needs further consideration. Could you tell me first how many copies of the two present volumes you have in stock, and could you lend us a copy of each volume, and let us know about how long your memoir would be? We want, you see, to have an approximate notion of the size of the contemplated volume, so that we may make an estimate of the cost of production before making an offer. Would it be possible to give me an idea of the length of the other pieces which you considered including? And I should also be grateful for any figures of past sales.

1–IAR answered (n.d.): 'What *is*, indeed, the matter w. Leavis? I've not been informed, except through that article. I suppose it was just my turn (as his last friend here in the faculty!) You mind what you do, it will be your turn before long!'

F. R. Leavis had issued (in his own words) a 'completely adverse' review of IAR's *Coleridge on Imagination*: 'Dr Richards, Bentham and Coleridge', *Scrutiny* 3: 4 (Mar. 1935), 382–402. He summed up his indictment: 'Dr Richards does seem to me to be heading completely away from any useful path . . . It is a great pity, when one thinks of what, had he limited himself by any given discipline, he might have accomplished' (402). TSE, on the other hand, FRL applauded: 'If anyone may be said to have been for our time what Coleridge was for his, then it is Mr Eliot. Mr Eliot, like Coleridge, combined a creative gift with rare critical intelligence' (383).

You have not rung up and suggested a day for lunch. I hope that you can find a day either next week or the following.[1]

Yours ever,
[Tom]

TO *Reginald Tribe*[2]   CC

17 May 1935   [Faber & Faber Ltd]

Dear Father Reginald,

I am honoured by your invitation, and I shall be pleased to speak at the Kelham Reunion on October the 23rd.[3] I should be grateful if you give me some notion in advance as to what you would like me to talk about. I take it that somewhere between 15 and 20 minutes would be right. Probably nearer 15 than 20.

When I last saw Father Gabriel I made a tentative engagement with him for my coming to Kelham for the weekend of June the 30th. I shall look forward to seeing you then.[4]

Yours very sincerely,
[T. S. Eliot]

---

1 – Alida Monro wrote on the same day (her letter crossed with TSE's): 'We have barely 20 copies of FOR YOUR DELIGHT in the shop now and I wonder whether it would be possible for us to come to terms by the time these copies are gone . . . ? . . . Also I have been going into the figures and I think [Mr Crawley] was misleading us when he said (I think you said he said) that your offer of £30 represented about two years profits! . . .

'With regard to the Charlotte Mew I will get into touch with some friends of hers and see what their ideas are. I should prefer a royalty on the book I think.'

2 – The Revd Reginald Tribe, SSM, Director, House of the Sacred Mission.

3 – Tribe wrote on 16 May to ask TSE to be the lay speaker at their annual Kelham Reunion to be held at Church House, London, on Wed., 23 Oct.

4 – Helen Gardner relates (*The Composition of 'Four Quartets'* [1978], 38), with regard to experiences that informed *Burnt Norton*: '[George] Every tells me that on a hot day in the summer of 1935 when Eliot was staying at Kelham he saw a kingfisher on a stream running into the Trent by Averham Church over the fields from Kelham and that there is a yew in the churchyard there and masses of clematis in the rectory garden next to the churchyard by the same stream. He was not himself with Eliot but two students who were told him how excited Eliot was at seeing the bird. Mr Every remembers a conversation about *Burnt Norton* in the year after when Eliot spoke of this summer scene. I had always a little wondered at the sudden irruption of a kingfisher into *Burnt Norton* [IV], for the garden is so remote from the water . . .'

17 May 1935   Faber & Faber Ltd

My dear Roberts,

I am now replying to your letter of the 3rd instant.[1] We feel that your first suggestion for dealing with the situation is preferable to the second. We are anxious in Pound's interest, and our own as his publishers, that he should not be *too* fully represented in the book, and it seems to me that 19 pages is quite enough. Exactly how many pages do you figure that the book will come out at, and what other contributors do you want to have represented at this length? I like the selection that you have made. That is to say, you have chosen poems all of which are favourites of mine. As for their being the most suitable ones to play their part in the total design of the book, no one can know that in the present stage except yourself.

Did I tell you that if the somewhat larger payments to Pound exhaust the resources, I should prefer to help by forgoing part or all of my own fees rather than have you raid your editorial fee? We might leave that matter open until you have tackled what may be the most difficult problem of all, that of Yeats.[2]

The agreement is being redrafted and should reach you in a few days.

Yours ever,
T. S. Eliot

1 – 'I suggest two ways of dealing with the Pound situation:
First:
    Offering £20 for:
        Near Perigord
        Exile's Letter
        E.P. Pour l'election . . . .. I II III IV V
        Propertius XII
        Canto XIII (or XVI if Pound prefers)
This makes nineteen pages, and I should be compelled to cut the book down by twenty-one pages, for if I exceed the £150, then . . . the loss falls on myself . . .
Or *Second*:
    Offering him the standard rate (10/- a page) accepted by everyone else (Yeats and yourself are the only important contributors whom I have not approached) *plus* some private douceur offered by Fabers independently of my contract, for a selection of twentyfour pages . . . This would obviously give the better book . . . I urge that Fabers could afford to do this, for they are getting a very saleable book for their money.'
2 – Roberts responded, 21 May: 'Your offer is very generous indeed: may I suggest that if I am compelled to exceed the £150, we share the loss?' W. B. Yeats's agent A. P. Watt had asked two guineas each for 'Self and Soul', 'Easter 1916', 'Red Hanrahan's Song', 'An Irish Airman', 'The Second Coming', 'The Tower', 'Byzantium', and 'For Anne Gregory' – which Roberts said he found 'quite reasonable'. He added that he was glad TSE liked his selection from EP.

17 May 1935   [Faber & Faber Ltd]

Dear Earp,

Many thanks for the information about Jarry and Villiers.[1]

I have reported our conversation to my Committee with the following result. We should very much like to do the volume of Sickert's essays, especially with a new introduction by Sickert and a self portrait.[2] We should not anticipate a very large sale, however, and we cannot see our way to increasing the advance to £100. In order, however, to make £75 seem more palatable we should like to couple it with an offer of £250 advance on publication for Sickert's memoirs. What we have in mind in making that offer is one volume to be sold at about 18s., and the advance

---

1 – Not traced.

2 – TSE's reader's report, 14 May 1935: 'I went through very rapidly a considerable mass of material, dating over the last 35 [years] or more. I should think there was quite enough worth preserving to make a book of 75,000 or 80,000 words, if that is the length you want. Discussing the matter with Earp, we agreed that he should first go right through it chronologically, selecting everything possible, and then again to make a book of the right length and proportions. He suggests that the arrangement should not be simply chronological, as that might give the impression that the book was without interest for the present generation; but that he should arrange the material in three or four large divisions of subject matter, putting the general essays on art theory and practice first, and classifying those referring to particular periods and artists later. There is a good deal on Whistler etc. some of which is quite interesting. There are also odd reviews of exhibitions, letters etc. bringing the survey up to within the last five years or so.

'The suggestion is that Sickert should provide a new introduction, and Earp thinks he might be induced to do a new self-portrait for the frontispiece.

'While I believe the book is well worth doing for itself, and that it would probably get a good press, as Sickert has had something of a comeback in the last few years, I should hardly anticipate a very large sale, and it is a question how large an advance such a book would carry. Earp is very anxious that we should raise the offer to £100, and would be willing to forgo remuneration himself. I think that all we need offer Earp would be expenses – he would probably have to have all the articles typed out, as they are in several albums.

'What Earp really wants for himself is that we should publish the 60,000 word book on Stendhal which he wishes to get to work on quite soon, after he has cleared up the Sickert MSS. and had his summer holiday. He wishes to put aside his other projects and do Stendhal first. I encouraged him in this, and I think there is a place for a good book on Stendhal in English. There is none at present; a great deal of correspondence and other inedited matter of Stendhal has lately been published. Somebody is sure to write a book sooner or later, and I think Earp would do a good one. I did not discuss terms.

'I pointed out to Earp that we should be much more interested in Sickert's essays if we could feel that the Memoirs would follow, as the latter would be much more likely to pay for themselves. He says Sickert is in very good form at present; but as Sickert is 75, the possibility of getting memoirs is very speculative. I suggest that we might consider sticking to the £75 for the essays but coupling with it a definite temptation for the memoirs.'

mentioned would be on a royalty of 15 per cent. But I don't want to put this in such a way as to frighten Sickert. I mean that he would not be bound in any way to write his memoirs. It would merely be that if he did write them they would come to us on these terms.

Of course, if the memoirs took the form, which we once discussed, of your talking to him and working out a book on his conversations, we should naturally make a different arrangement, in order to be fair to both you and Sickert, but the figures I have mentioned would give us a basis for an amicable adjustment.

We should not really expect to make any money to speak of from the essays, but we should like to publish this book because they are worth doing, and because of the possibility of memoirs to follow.

Your general suggestions about arrangement of material were agreed to. I hope that you will find the series of articles which you mentioned as probably having been printed in the *Southport Guardian*.

Finally, about your book on Stendhal. We should like to do this and are prepared to commission it. Here again we should not anticipate a very large immediate sale, as Stendhal is a writer much more mentioned than read. But we should be glad to offer for a 60,000 word book an advance of £50, on a 15 per cent royalty, for a book to be published in the first place at 12s. 6d.

You know best how Sickert should be approached, so I will wait to hear from you.

Yours ever,
[T. S. Eliot]

TO *Henry Miller*   TS Jay Martin

17 May 1935   Faber & Faber Ltd

Dear Mr Miller,

Thank you for your letter.[1] I hope that your book will get through to me, as I am most anxious to see it. The section of your Lawrence

1–Miller had asked Jack Kahane to send TSE a copy of *Tropic of Cancer*; and wrote of *Black Spring*: 'It is an autobiographical novel – novel in the sense of Unamuno's words: "the novel of the novel, the creation of creation. Or God of God, *Deus de Deo*." It is quite unlike the *Tropic of Cancer*, but I am afraid equally unacceptable. It's an attempt to describe that reality of which I wrote at some length in connection with Lawrence. It is irritating to the American mind because there is no reality here [in New York, where he was staying until going back to Paris in May], only realism. The intellectuals have gone over to the collectivity and the mass is what it always was and always will be, I guess – interested only in

book was so long that I thought it better that you should make from it yourself an extract of the right length. I should doubt from what you say whether *Black Spring* was a book which could be published in London, especially in view of certain recent misfortunes which have befallen other publishers here. Our laws concerning obscene libel in England are still more exasperating than those in America.

I am very glad you like Saroyan's book,[1] and I am glad to say that, for a volume of short stories by an unknown author, we have done better with it than we expected. I have not read anything by Wolfe, and to judge by his productivity, by the time I do get around to it I shall feel that it is not worth while beginning, because I shall never be able to catch up. That is why I never read Proust. If you should happen to be going to London at any time I hope you will let me know.

Yours sincerely,
T. S. Eliot

<I should like to see *Black Spring* nevertheless.>

TO *George Malcolm Thomson*[2]   CC

17 May 1935   [Faber & Faber Ltd]

My dear Thomson,

I have read your pamphlet with interest and appreciation, and as you know, with sympathy.[3] So I hope you won't mind my saying frankly why I think that it would misfire.

"consumption" literature. The individual is rapidly being stamped out, and I insist on remaining an individual, and consequently not of the age. Add to this that the book contains a number of frankly obscene passages and a kind of spiritual mockery, a burlesque which is not at all to the Anglo-Saxon taste. Voila tout!'

Miller went on in his letter to compliment TSE for his *Dante*, which had impressed him 'very very much'. 'If in this age there should arise an artist of towering genius then I do believe he will resemble Dante.' He ended by mentioning the only two recent American books which he believed had showed 'quality' – those by Thomas Wolfe and William Saroyan: 'And strange to add, though Saroyan's book is thinner and lesser it is his book which contains the most promise. It also contains something absolutely rare in this country – mention of *God and the earth*.'

1 – *The Daring Young Man on the Flying Trapeze* (1935).

2 – George Malcolm Thomson (1899–1996) worked for the *Evening Standard* and *Daily Express*, and served during WW2 as Principal Private Secretary to the 1st Lord Beaverbrook. Works include *A Short History of Scotland* (1930) and *The Lambeth Conference* (1930). He was awarded the OBE in 1990. See further George McKechnie, *The Best-Hated Man: Intellectuals and the Condition of Scotland between the Wars* (2013).

3 – *Scotland: That Distressed Area* (Porpoise Press, 1935).

I think, in the first place, most people who take an interest in Scottish affairs at all are prepared to believe that Scotland has been losing both in population and in industrial activity at an already alarming rate of acceleration. This is what your pamphlet sets out to show, and does show. But it seems to me that this is just what everybody believes already, even if they have not studied the figures to prove it, and that therefore you leave off just where I should have liked to see you begin. You want to show not only that Scotland is getting poorer, and not only that it is not getting a fair deal from Whitehall, but how these things come about. Some people will try to have arguments to show that the decline of Scotland is due to other causes than those you allege, and these people, I feel, ought to be refuted in advance. Also, people are sure to suspect that there is more to be learned from a comparison with Southern Ireland before and after Home Rule than with the smaller states which you bring into the analysis. Finally, one inevitably asks what has been done about it. How far, also, is the condition of Scotland merely a symptom of the centralisation of money power and the abuses of an anachronistic financial system.

In short, I feel that not only should the arguments of your opponents, whatever they are, be dealt with, but there is probably a much stronger case to be made on your own side than you have here made. The chief fault seems to me a fault which is particularly vital in a pamphlet that one is very uncertain to what audience you are addressing yourself.

Let us meet some time and discuss these matters.

Yours ever,
[T. S. Eliot]

TO *Denys W. Harding*[1]   CC

17 May 1935   [Faber & Faber Ltd]

Dear Mr Harding,

Many thanks for obtaining for me a copy of Rosenberg's poems,[2] but I feel that I am receiving them under false pretences, and must therefore

1–Denys W. Harding (1906–93), academic psychologist and literary critic; associate of F. R. Leavis; Lecturer in Social Psychology, London School of Economics, 1933–8; Senior Lecturer in Psychology, Liverpool University, 1938–45; Professor of Psychology, Bedford College, London, 1945–68; author of *Experience into Words* (1963), which includes three notable essays on TSE.

2–Sent by Harding on 16 May.

Jack Isaacs reported in a letter ('Eliot's Friends', *The Observer*, 18 June 1967) that TSE first heard of Isaac Rosenberg from Sydney Schiff – 'and Eliot praised [Rosenberg] and

return them to you. I wrote to Parsons a day or two after our meeting to say that I had discussed the matter with my colleagues, and found them unfavourable to my writing any preface. This, as I tried to explain to Parsons, was not a desire on their part to restrict my preface writing to books that we are publishing, because what really brought the matter up was a question of a book of our own to which the author wanted me to contribute a preface. They were equally unfavourable to the one as to the other. I am sorry if I excited false hopes, but I think I made clear at the time that my acceptance was only provisional.[1]

With many regrets,
Yours sincerely,
[T. S. Eliot]

TO *S. Elisséeff*[2]   CC

17 May 1935   [Faber & Faber Ltd]

Dear Sir,

I have your letter of May the 3rd.[3] While I should be happy to be able to contribute to do honour to the memory of James Haughton Woods,[4] a teacher whom I regarded with both respect and affection, I do not see that there is any subject upon which I could write which would be suitable for

---

spread his fame long before the bandwagon rumbled. He once said to me that no English anthology that did not include Rosenberg was worth anything.' Isaacs added, in the same published letter: 'I knew T. S. Eliot for 42 years and I saw no signs of anti-semitism. Very much the contrary, only kindness and understanding. The finest evidence can be found in his rich and warm obituary notice in *The Times*, in July, 1962, of Mrs Violet Schiff.'

1 – Harding replied with regrets, 18 May. 'If you have not already sent the poems back – and if they are any use to you – please keep them. I know Rosenberg's sister would prefer that you should.'

2 – S. Elisséeff, editor of *Harvard Journal of Asiatic Studies*, Harvard-Yenching Institute.

3 – Elisséeff invited TSE to contribute an article to a volume of studies in honour of the late James Haughton Woods, Professor of Philosophy at Harvard. These studies would form the first volume of the *Harvard Journal of Asiatic Studies*.

4 – James Haughton Woods (1864–1935), Professor of Philosophy at Harvard, 1913–34, and chairman of the department, 1914–16. He introduced courses in Indian philosophy, and his *Yoga System of Patanjali* (1914) was the first American scholarly study of Indian philosophy. TSE studied Greek Philosophy with him in 1911–12, and 'Philosophical Sanskrit' in 1912–13. After TSE submitted his thesis, Woods told him he wanted to create a 'berth' for him in the Philosophy Department at Harvard. TSE recorded later that 'a year in the mazes of Patanjali's metaphysics under the guidance of James Woods left me in a state of enlightened mystification' (*ASG*, 40). TSE's notes on Woods's lectures in 1911–12 are in the Eliot Collection, Houghton.

your memorial volume. I abandoned my oriental studies many years ago, and for me to write on such a subject now would only be an impertinence.

With many regrets,
Yours sincerely,
[T. S. Eliot]

TO *Polly Tandy*   TS BL

21 May 1935   Faber & Faber Ltd

Mrs Pollytandy Ma'am I have your letter of the 19th instant[1] and am duely Thankful I am. expecting to catch the Green bus from the Windsor Castle on Saturday the 1st June and this Time I shall come with a Knappsack instead of a Gladstone bag. and I hope I shall not forget to bring my Razor with me too. As for those Cats with short names they may wag their tails at Mr Kipking But I bet half a Crown he will outlive the pair of them and

> Jellicle cats & dogs all must
> Like cocktail mixers, come to dust[2]

So will close, Yours thankfully

Thomas S. Eliot[3]

Hopeing the Family is whell.

1 – TSE was to spend the weekend with the Tandys at Hogarth Cottage, Hampton-on-Thames.
2 – Cf. 'Lines to a Yorkshire Terrier', in 'Five-Finger Exercises', 11–12: 'Jellicle cats & dogs all must / Like undertakers, come to dust.'
3 – Unusually, TSE signed himself thus.

21 May 1935   [Faber & Faber Ltd]

Dear Mrs Mirrlees,

Thank you for your kind letter.[2] I don't really believe that from the point of view of lighting it will make any difference whether you go to an afternoon or an evening performance. As the evening performances are over at 9 o'clock and as they come during the longest days of the year, and as, if I am not mistaken, the window of the Chapter House through which all the light comes is the west window I should think that there might be even more daylight at the evening performances than in the early afternoon.

I look forward to seeing you next Tuesday.[3] Will you let me know whether we are lunching at your house or whether we shall lunch at a restaurant further east. If the latter appeals to you I hope that you and Hope will be my guests.

                         Yours very sincerely,
                         [T. S. Eliot]

1–Emily Lina Moncrieff (1862–1948) – 'Mappie' (otherwise 'Mappy') – daughter of a family of Edinburgh lawyers, was Hope Mirrlees's mother. Through much of WW2, TSE was to retreat from the blitz by spending long weekends at Shamley Wood, Shamley Green, nr Guildford, home of Mappy and Hope, of whom he was deeply fond. 'Mrs Mirrlees is a remarkable woman,' TSE told Sencourt (*T. S. Eliot*, 140). TSE told Philip Mairet, 21 Feb. 1941: 'my hostess here [at Shamley Wood] . . . is a very intelligent, though not intellectual, Scotch lady – but distinctly high in brains as well as character . . .' Soon after Mappie's death, Margaret Behrens wrote to TSE, 30 May 1948: 'Yes! Mappie's going will make a big blank in all our lives. I can't realize that she wont be there when I get back. Her welcome was one of the things that made coming home seem really cosy. Like you, I know no one who has made a deeper impression on me. She was such an extraordinary compound of fantasy, Scotchness, cleverness and, above all kindness and generosity. I never knew anyone with so warm a heart. All her "lame dogs" will be lost without her, though Hope will do her best to carry on in memory of Mappie, I know.'
2–Mrs Mirrlees wrote (19 May) that they had decided to go to the performance of *Murder* on 18 June – 'but then we wondered whether the setting might not be more impressive at night'.
3–Mrs Mirrlees had invited him to lunch on 28 May.

TO *S. I. Hsiung*[1]

22 May 1935   [Faber & Faber Ltd]

Dear Mr Hsiung,

I very much appreciate your kindness in sending me inscribed copies of your books.[2] I had heard well of Mencius, and I have been meaning for a long time to go to see *Lady Precious Stream*, of which I have heard high praise from Major Dobrée and from others.

I shall read *The Western Chambers* [*sic*] with great interest, but I am afraid it is impossible for me to write a preface. I only write prefaces in very exceptional circumstances, and I have lately declined two invitations, one of which was for a book which we are ourselves publishing. It would therefore be a breach of etiquette for me to make an exception now. I am sure that the play will have the success that it merits without any introduction by myself.[3]

With grateful thanks and cordial regards,

Yours sincerely,

[T. S. Eliot]

---

1 – S. I. Hsiung (Hsiung Shih-I, or Xiong Shiyi) (1902–91), writer and playwright, taught at universities in China before emigrating in 1932 to London, where he studied at University College and translated Chinese plays into English. *Lady Precious Stream* (1934) was his first huge success in the UK, and was later produced on Broadway and in many other countries; followed by *The Dream of the Western Chamber* (1935). See Zhou Yupei, 'Shih-I Hsiung', in *Asian American Playwrights: A Bio-bibliographical Critical Sourcebook*, ed. Miles Liu (2002); Diana Yeh, *The Happy Hsiungs: Performing China and the Struggle for Modernity* (2014).

2 – Hsiung wrote on 20 May: 'May I venture to present you with two little works of mine? You will find that facing the title page of "Mencius Was a Bad Boy", there is a little announcement for my next work, "The Western Chambers", a lyric drama. Methuen's is going to publish it early next month. Both Abercrombie and Dobrée have read it and thought it worthy of publication. I would deem it a great honour if you would kindly write a brief Preface for me.'

3 – FVM to Donald Brace, 18 June 1935, of the problem posed by the new play *The Western Chambers*: '*Lady Precious Stream* was published as a translation with illustrations by Methuen in book form in 1934 at 8/6, and is now in its second impression. *The Western Chambers*, also a translation with illustrations, is to be published this summer. The Play of *Lady Precious Stream* has caught on here; It's possible that you saw it while you were over; it's possible that it may catch on in New York; it's possible that it may be a total loss there. It's possible that, even if the play catches on in New York, the book of the play might be a flop.'

TO *C. A. Siepmann* CC

22 May 1935 [Faber & Faber Ltd]

My dear Siepmann,

I can tell you, I think, all that you need to know about George Barker.[1] He is a young poet in whose work I have been interested for several years past, and a volume of whose poems we have just published. Gambling on poets is a still less likely way of making money than gambling on horses. Nevertheless I have great hopes of this one. He has written a new poem, better even than any in our volume, and Janet Adam Smith suggested that he might be given an opportunity of delivering it over the wireless. I should be very glad indeed if this could be arranged. I have the best copy of the poem here and could let you have it. If you think that the suggestion can be entertained I am at your disposal for any support that may be needed.

Could you lunch with me in about a fortnight? My possible lunch days are filled up until then, but I am certainly free for lunch on Friday the 7th, and should be delighted if you would join me.

Yours sincerely,
[T. S. Eliot]

TO *Elsie Fogerty* CC

22 May 1935 [Faber & Faber Ltd]

Dear Miss Fogerty,

I did not acknowledge your letter at once because I was waiting to find out whether I could rearrange another engagement so as to be able to come on Monday next. I now expect to be able to come in for about an hour, and look forward to hearing your chorus with great interest.[2]

I was sure that the chorus you mention would be the one to present the greatest difficulties.[3] The choruses after that seem to me comparatively

---

1 – Siepmann (20 May) had received a letter from George Barker on the subject of a new poem he had written. Barker referred Siepmann to TSE for further information.

2 – Fogerty was to write on 15 Oct. 1943: "It was so good to see you & hear you the other day, above all to realise the development of your whole outward personality since the day, do you remember it, when you were to be allowed to slip in unobserved into that little Theatre & sit in a corner, while I, equally nervous, taught the first sketch of a "Becket" Chorus to Students on that stage.'

3 – Fogerty had written on 21 May from the Central School of Speech Training and Dramatic Art about the difficulties she was experiencing with the choruses: 'No 1 we only now need

easy. Possibly some of the difficulties are such as I could amend myself by a little rewriting. If so, I am at your disposal. I should like to come again, if I may, on a Thursday morning.

Yours sincerely,
[T. S. Eliot]

TO *H. M. Spalding* CC

22 May 1935   [Faber & Faber Ltd]

Dear Mr Spalding,

Thank you for your letter of the 18th.[1] I do not of course profess to any specialised knowledge of psychology. The studies of the subject that I made in the days when I expected to become a professional philosopher antedate the period of psycho-analysis. I don't myself believe that Tereshchenko's work is epoch-making, but I had thought it interesting and valuable. What militates against its popular interest is the fact that the diary is not only that of a Russian boy, but apparently of a very Russian boy. It will be difficult for the ordinary reader to make the transposition between Eastern and Western mentality. I know that this was the reason

---

to get Mr Browne's direction on movement. I have arranged four little stools so that some of them can sit, to help out the lines like "stretched out his hand to the fire".

'No 2 I am not too ill pleased with. It will not need much action as it is in the nature of a prolonged appeal.

'No 3 I have not yet done.

'No 4, ignorant women, is quite fair.

'The great one on page 27, "I have smelt them" is terrifying me at the moment and I find the section on page 28 from "I have lain" down to "Rings of light" a little too long. I think it is the last paragraph "Corruption in the dish" which seems to wander just a little bit from the straight line, but I expect that will be quite right when I have done it.

'We have worked the two chants, but not done them against the chant.'

1 – 'I too have a very high regard for Dr Tereshchenko as a man, and several of my friends who are well qualified to judge have an equally high regard for his abilities . . . The exact value of his twin books seem, unluckily, more open to question. From what he said while they were in course of preparation I was in great hopes that they would prove an effective counterblast to Freud – a consummation which, to me as to you, is devoutly to be wished. I feel doubtful however to what extent it is attained.'

He remarked further that his brother, K. J. Spalding, Senior Research Fellow in Philosophy at Brasenose College, Oxford, had read the books at an earlier stage: 'while thinking Tereshchenko mistaken in claiming the work as epoch-making, he thought it interesting and valuable . . . Tereshchenko writes that Allen & Unwin are prepared to publish it for a subsidy of £140. My wife and I should probably be prepared to make some contribution towards this. Do you know of other friends of Tereshchenko who would be prepared to do the like . . .'

given by one firm for not accepting the book at their own risk, as they otherwise thought very highly of it.

I don't, unfortunately, know any friends of Dr Tereshchenko, and I don't even know who his friends are. The only suggestion that I could make would be that he should try to interest one or two of the authorities at the Institute of Medical Psychology, such as Dr J. R. Rees. Possibly in this way some support might be obtained from London University. But Dr Tereshchenko is naturally rather impatient after such long delays, and would like to be able to settle with Allen and Unwin. I should like to see the book published, not only for its intrinsic value, but in order to save Dr Tereshchenko from utter discouragement.

Yours very truly,
[T. S. Eliot]

TO *Denys W. Harding*

CC

22 May 1935   [Faber & Faber Ltd]

Dear Mr Harding,

Many thanks for your letter of the 18th. I shall be very glad to keep the Rosenberg volume, although I believe Parsons is sending a proof or advance copy of the new book so that I may write a few words of commendation.[1]

Yours sincerely,
[T. S. Eliot]

---

1 – 'A Commentary', C. (July 1935), 611: 'I believe that the future vitality of English literature will depend very much upon the vitality of its parts, and their influence upon each other.

'This point deserves a little elaboration. It is not a matter of indifference that poetry written by an Irishman, a Welshman, a Scot, an American or a Jew should be undistinguishable from that written by an Englishman: it is undesirable. The poetry of Isaac Rosenberg . . . does not only owe its distinction to its being Hebraic: but *because* it is Hebraic it is a contribution to English literature. For a Jewish poet to be able to write like a Jew, in western Europe and in a western European language, is almost a miracle . . . What is essential is impossible fully to define, but it is most effectually expressed through rhythm. It is something which can best be expressed, and most successfully maintained, through poetry. And poetry of this kind may have a fertilizing effect upon *English*: and fertilization, either from its own relations or from foreign languages, is what it perpetually needs.'

TO *W. H. Auden*   CC

23 May 1935   [Faber & Faber Ltd]

Dear Auden,

I have investigated the question of any announcement of the play having been made without Isherwood's name on it.[1] An announcement of a play by you alone was made in an advance catalogue before we knew of your collaboration.[2] In the final spring catalogue, which I enclose, you will see that it is given correctly. So far as the Trade is concerned I am assured that they have been correctly informed. The only thing I can find is that on a Press notice, the text of which I wrote myself, Isherwood's name was omitted, but this notice was only sent out last night, and I am having correction slips circulated today. I trust, therefore, that no incorrect statement has been made, but if you hear of any, please let me know where they are to be found.[3]

Yours ever,
[T. S. Eliot]

TO *George Scott Moncrieff*[4]   CC

23 May 1935   [Faber & Faber Ltd]

My dear Scott Moncrieff,

Did I thank you for your letter of April the 14th? I like your review and the book sounds a good one.[5] I was in Scotland for a few days after I got your letter, in the company of George Blake[6] and Neil Gunn, and

1–Auden wrote on 22 May: 'I'm told (I haven't seen it) that in Faber's list *The Dog Beneath The Skin* is announced under my name only. I wonder if you could see that this is corrected.' He asked too, 'When is *Fear in the Way* coming on?'

2–F&F's catalogue announced '*The Chase*: A Play by W. H. Auden' (p. 36).

3–WHA replied on 27 May: 'Thanks so much for your letter. I'm sorry I made a muddle about the catalogue but it was on hearsay only.'

4–George Scott Moncrieff (1910–74) – 'Scomo' – journalist, author, playwight and novelist. Educated in Edinburgh and at Aldenham School, England, he won praise for his first novel *Café Bar* (1932) – 'low-life vignettes of London'. Other works included *Scottish Country* (1935), *Lowlands of Scotland* (1938), *Edinburgh* (1946), *Death's Bright Shadow* (1948). See Morley Jamieson, *George Scott Moncrieff and a Few Friends: A Brief Memoir* (privately printed, 1987).

5–Scott Moncrieff on Colin Walkinshaw, *The Scots Tragedy*: *C.* 14 (July 1935), 647–9

6–Blake lived at The Glenan, Helensburgh, Dumbartonshire. TSE was to write to Ellie Blake, 1 Nov. 1961: 'I have often thought of the happy visits to the Highlands, when George motored Frank Morley and myself up from Glasgow to Inverness. Those visits were very memorable and very happy, and were my first introduction to the wonderful Highland

had several days motoring through extraordinarily fine Highland scenery in the best of weather. I was sorry that we were never anywhere near your part of the country, but our time was very restricted. I do hope that you and your wife will be able to come up to London at some time in this year. I look forward to the anthology.

Yours ever,
[T. S. Eliot]

TO *George Malcolm Thomson* CC

28 May 1935   [Faber & Faber Ltd]

My dear Thomson,

Thank you for your letter, which does make your point of view more reasonable, although not quite.[1] I am not quite clear why you don't want to come out as a nationalist. I can only think of two valid reasons: one, that you have not made up your mind; and the other, that it would be impolitic in view of your political situation. And I still think that Southern Ireland ought to be discussed, even if only to demonstrate that it is irrelevant. But could we not lunch one day and talk it over? What part of town suits you best, or is the matter indifferent? My lunch times are all taken up until the week after next, but I could arrange a day in the first half of the week beginning on June the 9th.

Yours ever,
[T. S. Eliot]

---

scenery. But I remember with equal clarity and pleasure my visit to both of you, when you were living in Dollar. It was a shock to read of George's death, he was a younger man than I and I thought of him as one who would outlive me. It is a real wrench, I assure you, and although I did not know you and George intimately I regarded you both with warm affection and, believe me, I still do and wish you to know that I have often thought of you, ever since George has gone, and wish that I could have expressed my feelings about him face to face.'

1–Thomson wrote on 18 May to thank TSE for writing 'sympathetically' about his 'pamphlet' (a term he did not like). As to TSE's specific points: 'I set out as a fact-finding agent. Anything that is not pure fact in the pamphlet is either "comic relief" or tendentious in the direction of nationalism. This latter element I have tried to weed out . . . In particular, I do not think that I would command so much respect if I emerged as a candid propagandist of Scottish nationalism, although it is my present view that nothing less than drastic political change will serve . . . I do not at all agree that the condition of S. Ireland affords us any comparisons of value. S. Ireland is 95 per cent agriculture. Scotland is one of the most highly industrialized countries in the world. And so I have sought to compare her with Sweden, Denmark . . . and the others.'

TO *António Ferro*[1]   CC

28 May 1935   [Faber & Faber Ltd]

My dear Sir,

Salazar

I feel it my duty to express to you certain opinions about the translation of *Salazar* which has been submitted to us – opinions by no means solely my own. Perhaps I should explain first why I have not transmitted these opinions sooner.

I myself read *Salazar* only in the French translation. When the English translation was given us, I did not have time to study it myself; and it was sent, for the corrections which Mr O'Dwyer Greene warned us might be desirable, to a trusted reader who has done a good deal of work for my firm. Our reader does not know Portuguese, but availed himself of the French translation. He took a good deal of time and trouble over his revision – for which he must be remunerated – and only returned the typescript shortly before we heard from Mr Greene that you were expected in England. In returning the typescript, our reader accompanied it with a letter criticising it so severely that I examined it carefully myself. The translation is conscientious, but – quite apart from a number of minor errors which our reader has corrected – it is not in idiomatic English. I find myself in entire agreement with our reader in the opinion that the translation is not such as to do credit either to the author or to the publisher, nor is it such as to promote the cause for which the book is intended.

So far as we are concerned, it rests with yourself and your Government to decide whether we shall publish the translation as it stands, or whether the book shall be thoroughly revised. In my own opinion, the value of a really good translation would be well worth the delay in publication. Our reader has done all that he could, but a satisfactory revision could be the work only of someone equally at home in the Portuguese and the English language, and the master of a good English style.[2]

1–António Ferro (1895–1956), Portuguese writer, journalist, politician – author of *Viagem à Volta das Ditaduras* ('Journey round the Dictatorships', 1927) and *Salazar: o Homem e a Obra* ('Salazar: The Man and his Work', 1927; eventually published in translation as *Salazar: Portugal and Her Leader* [F&F, 1939]) – was a firm supporter of the authoritarian regime of António de Oliveira Salazar (1889–1970), Prime Minister of Portugal, 1932–68. Ferro served as Director of the Secretariado de Propaganda Nacional.
2–See António Ferro, *Salazar: Portugal and her Leader* , trans. H. de Barros Gomes and John Gibbons (F&F, 1939).

We therefore await your official instructions in the matter.

> I am, dear Sir,
> Yours very truly,
> [T. S. Eliot]
> Director

TO *Geo. Paul Butler*[1]   CC

28 May 1935   [Faber & Faber Ltd]

Dear Mr Butler,

Thank you for your kind letter of April the 5th.[2] I am sorry to disappoint you, but the work to which you refer, and which has to do, strictly speaking, not with royalty but with royalism, has never been written, and I am afraid I am unlikely to contemplate now undertaking such a work for many years to come.[3] The longer any piece of work is postponed the more one becomes aware of one's ignorance and the amount of study that would be necessary. And at my time of life it is hardly possible to contemplate giving so many years to a task of this kind. It is still possible, but it is hardly likely. The Divine Right of Kings is a branch of the subject which is somewhat outside the field I had intended to cover, which excluded historical and philosophical origins, and was restricted to political actualities. I very much regret that I am unable to help you in your interesting work.

> Yours faithfully,
> [T. S. Eliot]

TO *Geoffrey Tandy*   TS BL

Thurs. [postmark 30 May 1935]   Faber & Faber Ltd

Sir Tandy Sir I apollogise for not haven given you a coup de telephone but what With the dentist four people wanting money an Oxford poet a

---

1 – Geo. Paul Butler, Los Angeles Junior College.
2 – Butler wrote, 5 Apr.: 'In conversation with some of my friends at Columbia University recently we discussed the publication of your new work on royalty. Because of the great amount of research which you have undoubtedly given to this field, I wonder if you would be kind enough to write me concerning your views on the *Divine Right of Kings*.'
3 – TSE noted in *FLA* (1928), x: 'The uncommon reader who is interested by these scattered papers may possibly be interested by the small volumes which I have in preparation: *The School of Donne*; *The Outline of Royalism*; and *The Principles of Modern Heresy*.'

lunch engagement and emerods and alopecia and one thing and another. Sir I am sorry I cannot join you on the Friday Bus but I have got to say goodbye that evening to an old Lady who I am glad to say is going back to Germany for a few months So. will you in that case be in S. Kensington on Saturday morning? I hope so. I could join you at the Windsor Castle or could call for you at your Museum by easy stages because I have a sore heel and a bad wisdom tooth at any time in the morning you Like. I should be grateful for a blow on the telephone tomorrow 'Friday' morning, as I shall have to be Out all the p.m. at a meeting of the Working Committee of the Book Committee of the Church Literature Association, which is hot work I tell you. If not I mean if you are not here on Sat. will You please give me specific instruction as to how to reach Hogarth Cottage by my self. Yours etc.

T. S. E.

TO *Antonio S. de Mendonça*[1] CC

30 May 1935   [Faber & Faber Ltd]

Dear Mr de Mendonça,

The question of a new translation of *Salazar* has been discussed by my Committee. The figures have been reviewed, and we find that we should be able to contribute £10 towards a new translation on the understanding that we had the opportunity of approving the translator. Of Mr Duff's abilities in this way we have no doubt, but we feel that an excellent translation could probably be secured from the Translators' Bureau for a much more modest figure, and we should be glad to make enquiries at your request. Whether you wish us to do so will perhaps depend on the outcome of another conversation with Mr Duff.[2]

We are in agreement with you and Senhor Ferro that no time should be lost, and that the translator chosen should be able to devote his energies to preparing the best possible piece of work in the shortest possible time.

1–Manager of Casa de Portugal (Portuguese Information Bureau), London.
2–Charles Duff (1894–1966) – Cathal Ó Dubh – Irish-born writer (plays, travel essays, satires) and translator, served in the British Merchant Navy in WW1 and subsequently served for several years in the Foreign Service. A gifted linguist, fluent in seven languages, he taught linguistics and languages, and translated writers including Francisco de Quevedo, Émile Zola, B. Traven, Maxim Gorky, and Arnold Zweig; and was author of *James Joyce and the Plain Reader* (1932).

I am,

Yours sincerely,

[T. S. Eliot]

P.S. The existing translation of Salazar with the corrections made on it in green ink by our reader seems to me an important document in the case, which Senhor Ferro ought to have by him in Lisbon. It was stupid of me not to suggest that he should take it with him. I should be obliged if you would tell him that. I hold it here pending his instruction

TO *Jeanette McPherrin* TS Denison Library

30 May 1935   Faber & Faber Ltd

Dear Miss McPherrin,

Thank you so much for your letter – I am delighted to think that you enjoyed your afternoon with the Maritains, and in just the way that I hoped you would.

If you should hear from a M. or Mme. Charles Du Bos I hope you would be able to go to one of their Thursdays, I think it is. Du Bos is a queer old Bird – someone must have told him long ago that he looked like Walter Pater, because he has made himself look as much like that person as possible, and has been writing a book about him for years, as well as the various books – *Approximations*, *Journal*, *Byron*, and *Entretiens avec Gide* etc. His mother was Scottish – a point of sympathy – and he likes talking, or rather haranguing, in English of the idiom of about 75 years ago. He is one of the intellectual leaders of the Catholic *monde*.

My offer to shelter you and Emily is subject to rescission only if there should not be *two* bedrooms available – I dont know whether you could manage with the couch, though it is fairly long. But as (this is highly confidential) our two curates are leaving in June, to everyone's satisfaction, and the vicar intends to replace them with one stout curate-of-all-work, it seems to me likely that there will be room for two. If you take a Norwegian boat, you should insist on being served with Gammel Ost (i.e. Old Cheese). It is made of reindeer milk, and then kept for two years by the peasants under their beds, and it is wonderful.

Your suggestion of what I should suggest is, I am afraid, something that I have said Again & Again. But one cant tell the truth too often, once one starts. Mrs H.[1] is rather terrible. When we sat down to lunch she looked

1 – Mrs Philip Hale: see letter to Susan Hinkley, 7 June 1935, below.

at me piercingly and remarked that I looked like her deceased husband; and before I got over that, she added that very likely he was in the room with us now. She is addicted to spiritualism. I am afraid that E. will be worn out between the *marteau* and the *enclume* – between being fatigued by Mrs P. and being fatigued trying to save Mrs P. from Mrs H., though I think Mrs P. is much better able to stand it than E. For myself, I should find Mr H. much the easier to deal with. Mrs H. is a rather pathetic fool, and she is not a powerful personality. Besides, E. is able to regard her with a good deal of detachment, whereas she seems haunted by the feeling that she ought to be a great deal happier with Mrs P. than she actually is. Mrs P. is a type of stupid woman that I have come across before, and I know that the only way to save oneself from them in the long run is to run away. She is terrifically powerful; her husband is only a pawn in her hands. This type has a gentle relentlessness that no one can stand up to. But I mustnt think about such people too long at a time, or I shall rave.

Sincerely,

T. S. Eliot

A great deal of fuss is being made now over Lawrence of Arabia;[1] but if you could get hold of the *Vie de Charles de Foucauld*, by René Bazin, you would learn something about a much greater man in the same genre.[2]

1–T. E. Lawrence (b. 1888) had died on 19 May, six days after a motorcycle accident.

2–Alec Guinness wrote to TSE on 2 Apr. 1941 that he had just heard the broadcast talk 'The Church Looks Ahead': 'I found it so stimulating and exciting and I would like to thank you most sincerely. I would like to read the biography of the French priest.' René Bazin's *Charles de Foucauld* (1921) was translated by Peter Keelan and published by Burns, Oates & Washbourne at 6s. (*La vie de Charles de Foucauld explorateur en Maroc, eremite du Sahara*).

Charles de Foucauld (1858–1916), explorer, monk and priest; a wealthy aristocrat who served in the early part of his life as an army officer in Algeria. In 1882 he resigned from the army and joined a perilous exploration of the Sahara, travelling in disguise through Algeria and Morocco; he also journeyed into south Algeria and Tunisia, and he would later visit the Holy Land. He subsequently took Holy Orders and elected to lead a life of penury and hardship: having been ordained a priest in 1901, he proceeded to live for the next fifteen years as a hermit missionary in the central Sahara near Morocco, ultimately in a Touareg village at Tamanghasset in southern Algeria. He was shot and killed by passing Muslim insurgents of the Senussi order.

In a reader's report ('Good Friday 1934') on *Shifting Sands* by N. N. E. Bray, TSE noted: 'The author criticizes Lawrence severely, even bitterly; in fact his allegations are extremely damaging. To me they ring rather true: but I have long conjectured that a man who behaves in the eccentric fashion of Lawrence–Shaw must be a person of almost maniacal egotism and vanity: what else can account for such conspicuous research for obscurity?' To Geoffrey Curtis, 14 Feb. 1936: 'I don't *think* that religious vehemence puts me off: indeed, it is just the lack of it that worries me (during my convalescence) in reading Prestige's biography of your founder. For me, Gore (and of course Halifax) was not queer enough. The only

TO *Eugene F. Saxton*[1]   CC

3 June 1935   [Faber & Faber Ltd]

Dear Mr Saxton,

I have a letter from Mr Frederic Prokosch telling me that you have by this time sent me proofs of his novel.[2] I hope that this is so, as I have been interested in Mr Prokosch's poetry for some time, and have a very good opinion of it, and am consequently very much interested by the prospect of our having his novel for consideration. When we have had the opportunity to examine it I presume that we ought at once to acquaint Mr Hamilton with our attitude.

Yours sincerely,
[T. S. Eliot]

TO *Sydney Cockerell*[3]   CC

3 June 1935   [Faber & Faber Ltd]

My dear Sir,

I have to thank you for the courtesy and kindness of your letter of the 26th May. It is all the more interesting to have the quotation that

---

contemporary queer enough for my taste was Charles de Foucauld. Compare Lawrence of Arabia: the only kind of queerness England produces is what fits in to the programme of the *Evening Standard* and a tablet in St. Paul's. We need a *really ascetic* (and from an English point of view, quite *useless*) order.' To Curtis, 2 Apr. 1936: 'A man like Foucauld, however different he is from any of the Frenchmen one has known, represents somehow a continued potency in the race; he truly operates for the salvation of the world, but of his own race primarily, in practice. If I say that England needs English saints, this is not to be taken as an addiction to the race heresy of our time!' (Mirfield)

Jonathan Sale, when producing *The Family Reunion* at Clare College, Cambridge, asked TSE on 20 Aug. 1963: 'While reading the book on your plays by D. E. Jones, I discovered that during rehearsals for the first production, Michael Redgrave asked what Harry does when he leaves Wishwood; and I understand that you wrote an addition [25 lines] to the effect that he gets a job in the East End.' TSE replied on 23 Aug. 1963: 'I am sorry that I have no recollection of any additional words being written for Michael Redgrave, nor do I recall settling on the East End of London as the terminus of the protagonist's pilgrimage. It was certainly indefinite in my mind, and what I had in mind was something more like the career of Charles de Foucauld.'

1 – Eugene F. Saxton, Harper & Brothers, New York.

2 – Prokosch told TSE on 15 May that proofs of *The Asiatics* were almost ready, and that he had asked Harper's 'to send off a set of them to you as soon as possible. They should reach you soon after this letter.' Saxton suggested to Prokosch on the same day that he post the proofs to TSE.

3 – Sydney Carlyle Cockerell (1867–1962), director from 1908 of the Fitzwilliam Museum Cambridge; bibliophile; knighted 1934.

you give me, as I never met the late T. E. Lawrence and never had any communication with him whatsoever.[1] I am looking forward to the future publication of his letters.

With many thanks,
I am,
Yours sincerely,
[T. S. Eliot]

TO *H. C. Crofton*   cc

3 June 1935   [Faber & Faber Ltd]

My dear Crofton,

It seems a very long time since I have seen or had any communication with you or with Aylward. I have been extremely busy through the winter, and shall be until the end of this month, and then I venture to hope that we may lunch together again. Once a year seems to be about all we ever manage. Incidentally, I wonder if you would feel sufficiently interested, especially as you are a man of Kent by adoption, to get over to Canterbury to see the fruit of my winter's labour, which is to be performed in the Chapter House from the 15th to the 22nd of June, under the title of *Murder in the Cathedral*.

My second paragraph is rather a desperate venture. I do not need to be told how difficult it is nowadays for any lad to get a job in the City, but one of the young men who come to show me their verse appears to be a particularly pitiful case, and I feel I ought to make every exploration that occurs to me. He is a boy of 22 who has been writing very interesting verse, though I have not thought any of it ripe enough for publication. He comes of ordinary South London suburban folk, and from what I have seen of him, and what he has told me of his family, I should say that [he] is very much superior to his parents, and in fact has considerable refinement. He

---

1–Cockerell sent TSE this extract from a letter he had received from T. E. Lawrence (1888–1935), dated 29 Dec. 1925: 'at Cranwell this year I have been very fortunate. The rest of "B" flight went on leave, so that I have the hut to myself. Sixteen beds at choice. Sometimes I feel like the last survivor of a sinking doss-house. Still it is very pleasant to have a solitary bedroom & quiet, & lack of talk. I even lent away the gramophone, so that there should be no disturbance, & passed my spare time reading T. S. Eliot's *Collected Poems* (he is the most important poet alive) . . . It's odd, you know, to be reading these poems, so full of the future, so far ahead of our time; and then to turn back to my book [*The Seven Pillars of Wisdom*], whose prose stinks of coffins and ancestors & armorial hatchments.' See *Letters of T. E. Lawrence*, ed. David Garnett (1938), 488, no. 278.

suffered from a nervous illness which seemed to be due to his father being an unpleasant person and making life at home hideous. At any rate he has been in much better health during the last three years which he has spent at London University, apparently in omnivorous reading of philosophy and literature. Even so he only comes up to London for the day, and is only allowed half-a-crown a week pocket money, but is in much better health during term than during his vacations. He is very anxious to get a most modest sort of job of any kind which would enable him to live, however poorly, in London.

One of his motives for wanting to get a job that will allow him to live away from home is that his father regards him as a nuisance; and another is that he says his father's behaviour towards his mother is such that he fears that his mother may become a nervous wreck, or even insane. He believes that if he were self-supporting he might have more influence at home, as well as being able to save his own health.

I have only the boy's account of the domestic affairs, but in any case the boy himself is well worth saving. I have put the matter of his health quite frankly to you, although I know that it might be considered a drawback, but I sincerely believe that a position, however humble, of independence would keep him quite fit for a City job. Can you give me any shred of help or advice?[1]

Ever yours,
[T. S. Eliot]

TO *Frederic Prokosch*   TS Texas

4 June 1935   Faber & Faber Ltd

Dear Mr Prokosch,

Thank you for your letter of May the 21st, with the enclosure from Mr Saxton.[2] I should think, so far as I can tell, that your book was as likely to be for us as for anyone, but there is no reason why Hamilton should

---

1 – Crofton kindly forwarded TSE's letter to Dick Shepherd, St Martins-in-the-Fields (who responded to Crofton on 7 June that regrettably he could not help).

2 – Prokosch forwarded a letter of 17 May from Eugene F. Saxton (Harper & Brothers), to the effect that while he understood that Prokosch had a special interest in F&F, he would still like to call the book to the attention of Hamish Hamilton. 'I think he may very well be [interested], and I presume that you are free to consider and choose among the offers you receive.

'As to the poems, I feel it would be wise to deal with these after the novel is out.'

Prokosch told TSE, 'I personally am frantically eager to have Faber and no one else . . .'

not be seeing it as well. I presume that we shall get the proofs in a few days' time, and we shall attend to them promptly. I agree with Saxton that the matter of the novel ought to be settled before dealing with the poems.

With best wishes,
Yours sincerely,
T. S. Eliot

TO *W. H. Auden*   CC

4 June 1935   [Faber & Faber Ltd]

Dear Auden,

I am just writing to add that of course we had no doubt that you wanted Doone to have the copies of *The Dog Beneath the Skin*, but of course you understand that it would never do to send out copies of books to the debit of the author's account without having his explicit permission direct.

I hope you are satisfied with the appearance of the book. I feel confident of its success, which it fully deserves. Some of the scenes are magnificent.

Yours ever,
[T. S. Eliot]

TO *Hugh Mason Wade*   CC

4 June 1935   [Faber & Faber Ltd]

Dear Wade,

I have your letter of the 23rd.[1] I am very sorry to hear about your missing both the scholarships, but there is so much machinery in these affairs, and so many considerations involved that I have no doubt they are very much a matter of luck. I am sorry, however, if you have left Harvard without bothering to take a degree, and hope that it will not prove a disadvantage later. Harcourt, Brace and Company is, I think, as good a publishing firm as you could find. At any rate I know them better than any others. I have only met Harcourt once, but I have seen a good deal of Brace at one time or another, and like him very much indeed.

1-'Belated thanks for the trouble I put you to in connection with my application for the Rhodes and Henry Scholarships. In the first case I was eliminated quite early by a Yale committee (I applied from Connecticut) and in the second I finished fourth in the competition, three being chosen from Harvard. Being somewhat disgruntled, I have since left Harvard and the academic world and am now doing editorial work.'

I am interested in the article you are writing about Pound and Stein.[1] As you suggest yourself, it is very difficult for me to express opinions about contemporaries, and also about junior poets. Through a good many years of a man's career, and for more years with some than with others, the main thing is to get people to read his works, and not attempt serious criticism until they have done so. But if I can be of help to you, I shall be glad. As you do not say what you want of me in this connection, I will wait to hear from you again.

I am also interested in the essays that you are writing on Catholicism.[2] It is not quite clear whether you are writing them all yourself, but I hope so, and as you mention *Axel's Castle* I suppose that you are. Sheed and Ward are obviously the right people for it in New York, and in that case no doubt they would publish it in London also. The only man I know was the editor of the London office, T. F. Burns, who has now left the firm and is editing the Catholic department of Longmans in London. Burns is extremely able.

Yours very sincerely,
[T. S. Eliot]

TO *Christopher Dawson* CC

4 June 1935 [Faber & Faber Ltd]

My dear Dawson,

I have just had a long letter from Bolshakoff about the progress of his academy. The point is that he now broaches for the first time the financial question.[3] I have no doubt he has written in the same way to you, and

1 – 'I am writing you for help in connection with an article wch would deal with Ezra Pound and Gertrude Stein as influences on other writers, rather than as writers themselves. I feel rather strongly that ultimately their influence will be recognized as infinitely greater than their work . . . You could give me a great deal of help as far as Pound and the English group are concerned . . . I have some scruples about asking you for this help, both on the grounds that it might be personally distasteful to you and that you have already, through your letters and your time when you were in Cambridge, been of infinite and quite unrepayable assistance to me.'

2 – 'You might be interested to know that I am engaged on a series of essays, now appearing in the American Jesuit magazines, on the influence of Catholicism on English and American writers since the War. I believe there is a book, of the *Axel's Castle* sort, in it . . .'

3 – Bolshakoff raised the question of finances in more than one letter. On 30 May he reported that the Abbot of Nashdom was offering gratis full board for Bolshakoff, as well as free correspondence, secretarial and office fees. 'The other members are expected to provide the stipend of the Permanent Secretary, his travelling expenses, and the reserve fund for the library, conferences, publications and so on . . . [I]t is better to rely upon ourselves only. Each

am rather anxious to take counsel with you in the matter. At no time has the question been raised with me before, although of course it has been in my own mind. In view of a previous misunderstanding I want to say that I have never engaged myself to make any subscription, and indeed the question was never raised. In view of my means and various other commitments I should be unable to contribute more than a nominal sum. Possibly a few of the eminent people whose names continually recur in Bolshakoff's letters will be able quite easily to provide the necessary sum, a large part of which, presumably, will be necessary for his own support.

Another point about which I have been uneasy concerns Bolshakoff's apparent flirtations with real or so called fascist organisations, particularly in the Far East.[1] I do not know whether these organisations are practical or fantastic, and I do not know anything one way or another about the character of this General Araki in Japan. But if there were any risk of this Academy being politically compromised in Fascist organisations I should certainly withdraw at once, and so, I am pretty sure, would Maurice Reckitt. If you are not too busy I should be grateful for a word from you before I reply to Bolshakoff.

Yours ever,
[T. S. Eliot]

TO *Philip Radcliffe*[2]   CC

4 June 1935   [Faber & Faber Ltd]

Dear Mr Radcliffe,

Very many thanks for your kind efforts on behalf of the friend of Maritain. If neither you nor Dent know anything about him then I shall despair of finding anyone in London who does. Do you think that Constant Lambert would be likely to know, and if so do you think his opinion would be worth having?

Now I am going to trouble you again, but there is no great hurry about this. I am enclosing an offprint of an article by Herr Hermann Broch,

---

member is invited to contribute according to his means who are very different between us.'

1–Bolshakoff reported obscurely on 30 May: 'Our Academy attracts very wide sympathies in Far East Japanese Government and General Araki himself comprizing . . . comments with great sympathy Tavistock's Social Credit proposals . . . I convinced Russian Fascists in Far East to accept our ideology as stated in Declaration and give up the racialist kind. The deep religious sentiments of these people please me much.'

2–Philip Radcliffe (1905–86), Fellow of King's College, Cambridge, from 1931; University Lecturer from 1948.

an Austrian writer of some profundity, to whom I was introduced by Edwin Muir, who has a great admiration for his work. I find this article rather too deep for me, but perhaps it may be intelligible to some one more familiar with German theorists about music. Would you be so kind as to run through it at your leisure and let me know if you think that a translation would be suitable for the *Criterion*?[1]

I hope that I am not imposing too heavily upon you.

Yours sincerely,

[T. S. Eliot]

TO *Charles Williams*   CC

5 June 1935   [*The Criterion*]

My dear Williams,

By all means send the stuff along when it is ready, but I am afraid I shall not be able really to give any attention to it until after the end of this month.[2] If that is not too late I shall be glad to look it over promptly at the beginning of July, and then I hope that we can arrange to lunch. I had not meant to part so abruptly the other evening. I thought that I would be coming out in your company, and merely turned back as Hayward wanted to say a few words to me, and then you had gone.

Sincerely yours,

[T. S. Eliot]

TO *Susan Hinkley*   TS Sturtevant/Houghton

7 June 1935   Faber & Faber Ltd

Dear Aunt Susie,

This is a very busy time for me, but I must write to thank you for your last letter, and to say that I hope that the cable has been confirmed. This is very exciting. I had never heard of Constance Cummings, because I am

---

1 – Radcliffe replied on 6 June: 'Judging from a passing glance, I should say that it would be extremely hard to translate into readable English.'

2 – Williams wrote on 4 June, with respect to *The New Book of English Verse* which he was editing: 'I hope, if all goes well, to have a fair amount of this stuff ready for your oversight by, say, the end of Whitsun week. Will it be convenient to you if I send it to you then . . . But I don't think that actually it will take you a great while to utter celestial remarks about it.'

not in the theatrical world; but all the world has heard of C. B. Cochran.[1] I don't know him; and I had never associated him with plays at all, only with monster revues. I don't know anything against him – I will try to find out what I can – but I should think it was advisable, if making an agreement with him, to make sure that he would produce the play more or less as the author intended, and not introduce a bathing beauty chorus or a couple of comedians in unexpected places. However, he is very shrewd; anything he picks is likely to go; and his name alone carries great weight. I am eager for further particulars; and I rejoice in your coming in the autumn. Incidentally, it is possible that *Murder in the Cathedral*, if it has at all a good press at Canterbury, will be revived (as the term is) in London in the autumn.

I have somewhat revised my opinion of Miss Ware. Not absolutely but relatively. My present impression is that she does Emily no harm, and occasionally may be sensibly helpful. At present Emily is at Campden – a beauty-spot of England, or an eyesore, according as you look at it – with Dr and Mrs Perkins and Mrs Philip Hale.[2] The last is very trying, of course, and she will wear Emily out. But in a deeper way, I don't feel that even Mrs Philip Hale is as bad for one as Mrs Perkins. At any rate, Emily doesn't feel it her duty to admire Mrs Hale, and is able to say just what she thinks about her; but she forces herself to feel towards Mrs Perkins what I don't believe she really feels. Mrs Perkins strikes me as one of those gentle, stupid, kind, tyrannous, prejudiced, oppressive and tremendously powerful personalities who blight everyone about them. I may be wrong. I may be completely wrong. But she makes my back hair bristle; and confound it one can't help trusting that bristle. Dr Perkins is a very lovable, lazy-minded, muddleheaded man who is completely dominated by his wife, and who is really happier in Emily's company than he is with Mrs Perkins, but he doesn't know it.[3]

1–C. B. Cochran (1872–1951): distinguished English theatrical manager and impresario; producer of revues, musicals and plays; collaborator with Noël Coward.
2–Irene Hale, née Baumgras (1854–1934) – Emily's aunt – widow of Philip Hale (1854–1934), journalist, celebrated as the prolific and influential music critic of the *Boston Herald*, 1903–33, who also wrote a multitude of programme notes for the Boston Symphony Orchestra, 1901–34: see Jon Ceander Mitchell, *Trans-Atlantic Passages: Philip Hale on the Boston Symphony Orchestra, 1889–1933* (2014). Irene Hale, who was herself an accomplished pianist, had studied at the Cincinnati Conservatory of Music, where she gained the Springer Gold Medal 1881, and continued with her studies in Europe under Raif and Moritz Mosckowski: she later wrote music under the name Victor Rene.
3–Perkins would write to TSE on 17 June 1935: 'Now we are looking forward to Canterbury. I read a very interesting review of "Death in the Cathedral", in the "Church Times". Apparently the play is just as good by any other name. Judging from the review

I have changed my mind about California. It is an awful place, certainly. But compared to Milwaukee and to her family environment in Boston, and among a few comparatively intelligent, liberated and educated people at Claremont, Emily was much better off there; and I should feel happier if she was going back. Her young friend Jean MacPherrin [*sic*] is really a very intelligent and sensitive girl, and the best possible companion for her.

All this is to explain why Miss Ware seems to me relatively a suitable person. Private and confidential.* More information about the Cochran engagement eagerly awaited.

Affectionately
Tom

* Except to Ada.

TO *Bonamy Dobrée* TS Brotherton

7 June 1935 Faber & Faber Ltd

Bumbaby If you are going to talk in a patois of that sort I hope you realise you won't get any Hon.Litt.D.'s, which if you talk more natural will come as thick as punkins. No Sir, if you can't talk PURE American dont talk at all.[1] But praps you were talking a kind of Talk in Progress or trying to be as indecipherable in your speech as in your calligraphy. If so, no need to mention the matter again. Now then. The most possible date appears to be the 18th. You don't appear to be inclined to perceive that you have chosen Canterbury Week to see the Ballet Well Well perhaps you didnt mean it and perhaps you Did anyway by now you will have

---

in this morning's "Times" the actors are judged as doing well even if the rhymes, which I liked very much, did not please one reviewer . . . P.S. Thank you too for sending the copy of "Murder in the Cathedral."' On 3 July: 'The "Murder in the Cathedral" still remains the chief topic of our conversation at Stamford House. And when Mr & Mrs Martin Brown[e] came to tea with us last Friday you can imagine with what delight we recalled the splendid performances at Canterbury in the light of their many comments and their intimate part in it all. Personally I am most impressed by your work as very elevated literature, to which the drama seems to me to be a most worthy contribution. For this I have great enthusiasm. I have less ability to understand the dramatic art of the work, but the philosophy, morality and religion in your thought gives the play for me a supreme value.'

1–Letter not traced: possibly it was a cover letter sent with BD's short notice of H. W. Horwill, *A Dictionary of Modern American Usage*, C. 15 (Oct. 1935), 173. 'This companion to Fowler's book . . . throws many sidelights on another civilization by means of the extracts it gives. To the reader of American books it will reveal such mysteries as those of stopping over, or stopping off, though it is to be regretted that stopping in is not explained. One is given to understand that stopping in for someone means calling for them, not staying at home for them.'

received a complimentary copy inscribed.[1] Anyway, on the 17th what do you think I have to go to a reunion of the 25th anniversary of my Harvard Class that is of the European representatives, peering into depraved faces trying to recognise faces which one didnt know even at the time this day I received the class volume of autobiographies there is in it two photos of every member one taken in 1910 and one recently and I must say Mine was the only One that seemed to me to have improved, yes, I must have been a wretched sap in those days & so I was. The others at best show only deterioration. This is a sad but encouraging thought. Well as I was saying the 18th is the night for the Ballet so tell me what part of the house you frequent I usually take those backer dress circle seats at 7. 6d. or thereabouts anyway I dont mind cheaper but say what price seats you like and I will get the four seats and say what sort of clo'es you will wear I prefer black tie as I have some of those vulgar but comfortable soft shirts or we could go higher in altitude but on this occasion I prefer not if possible. What about your Barcelona for dinner or where? I have told my secretary to get programmes Hurrah yours etc.

Tom

FROM *Vivien Eliot* TO *W. L. Janes*   MS Valerie Eliot

7 June 1935   68 Clarence Gate Gardens,
                                         Regents Park, N.W.1

Dear Janes,[2]
    I am very sorry but I have to go, abroad, immediately, so it is no use for you to come here any more until I come back. I am leaving Polly with my cousin. I am forced to go by my enemies (perhaps *you* know *who* they are). You can speak up for me as you know I never interfere with anybody – and never *speak* unless I am forced to ——
    Please go to 24 Russell Square, and *ask Mr T. S. Eliot* for your 10/s a week. You *must* do this. He will not let you starve. My love to Mrs Janes. I hope this *shock* will not *kill her* ——

1 – BD replied, 8 June: 'I thought Canterbury was Whit-week – but never mind. But thank you very much indeed for the inscribed copy . . .'
2 – This letter came with a covering note from Janes (101 Lumley Buildings, Pimlico), 12 June: 'Dear Mr Eliot I see in the Evening Standard your Buch by Becket [*sic*] also the play. I have not seen Mrs Eliot since last Sunday week but received this letter on Saturday I cant make it out so send it on to you hoping you are well I expect you are Bussee [*sic*]. Yours / W. L. Janes.'

Yours always the same
V. H. Eliot
(Mrs T. S. Eliot)

I have tried my best to let this flat, furnished *or* unfurnished. It is in every Agent's books, and I have walked for miles & miles, but no-one has *an offer for it.*

TO *Edwin Muir*   CC

11 June 1935   [Faber & Faber Ltd]

Dear Muir,

I should be very glad and willing to write a testimonial for you in connection with Edinburgh University.[1] I think I know quite enough about your work to speak very warmly of it. I imagine, for a purpose like this, that it is advisable to stress the value of a man's critical writing rather than that of his poetry. Indeed, I think it may be best to speak much less enthusiastically about the latter, as I always feel that merit as a poet may be looked on rather suspiciously by those who have it in their power to distribute academic posts. Let me know when you want the letter, and to whom, if anyone, I should address it.

Yours sincerely,
[T. S. Eliot]

[Testimonial for Edinburgh University]   [National Library of Scotland]

24 June 1935

I have known Mr Edwin Muir for many years, and was interested in his critical writing before I knew him. I regard him as one of the small number of more considerable poets of today, and as one of a still smaller number of literary critics. His criticism is both sensitive and philosophical, independent and dispassionate, and characterised by a high integrity. If he

1–Muir wrote on 8 June: 'I am standing as a candidate for the English Chair at Edinburgh University, which Professor Grierson has decided to give up. It is a Regius Professorship, that is an appointment in the hands of the Secretary of State for Scotland . . .

'I was very uncertain about standing for this post at first, the reason being that I have no academic qualifications at all and no experience of university life. I approached John Buchan and asked him his opinion, and he replied urgently advising me to stand. Professor Grierson also seems to think that my lack of academic status does not seriously matter . . . John Buchan has offered to write a testimonial for me, and this is to ask whether you too would feel yourself justified in doing so.'

conveys to his students even a part of what he has conveyed to general readers in his criticism, he will be an exceptional teacher. I am all the more assured in recommending him, because of my respect for his personal character.

[T. S. Eliot]

TO *Gerald Heard*[1]

CC

11 June 1935   [Faber & Faber Ltd]

Dear Mr Heard,

Thank you for your letter of the 8th.[2] By all means let us see the book of your American friend, or if you prefer it, ask him to get in touch with us. It sounds most interesting, and your recommendation is enough to assure our taking it very seriously.

Yours sincerely,
[T. S. Eliot]

TO *W. H. Auden*

CC

13 June 1935   [Faber & Faber Ltd]

Dear Auden

I am enclosing a letter to me from Hallie Flanagan, together with a letter to you which she sent in my care.[3] I think I have spoken or written to you before about Mrs Flanagan's theatre. I was very pleased with their production of *Sweeney Agonistes*, although it was completely

1–Gerald Heard (1889–1971): historian, science writer, educator and philosopher.
2–'A friend of mine just over from the United States has completed what I think may prove to be an important book wh: he is calling "Conflict in the Religious Mind". He would like to publish it here . . . I think he not only brings together a great deal of original material but his approach is new & constructive. I would much like your firm to look at it. The author's name is William Sheldon. He was brought up in William James company & has developed his thought.'
    William Herbert Sheldon, Jr. (1898–1977), American psychologist and researcher. His book *Psychology and the Promethean Will* was to appear from Harper & Brothers in 1936.
3–Flanagan wrote to TSE, 3 June 1935: 'At one time you were good enough to say that you would suggest to Mr Auden that he might entrust one of his plays to me.
    'Will you, with the enclosed note to him, send a line on behalf of the Experimental Theatre?
    'We wish to do a production of *The Dance of Death* in the Summer Session . . .'
    Flanagan's letter to WHA has not been traced.

660   TSE at forty-six

different from Doone's. I think that Mrs Flanagan, or Mrs Davis as she now is, would do a good job and you could trust her. Also I think she is considerably in sympathy with your ideas. At the same time I am puzzled by the discrepancy between her letter to you and the enclosed prospectus. If you have already given your permission for *The Dance of Death* to be performed, I don't see why she should be asking for it again; and if you have not given it, then it seems cheek of her to announce it in print. And why the change of title? It isn't nearly so good a title as *The Dance of Death* in my opinion.

It may amuse you to hear that an American cousin of mine has just had a play accepted by C. B. Cochran for the autumn season. I don't suppose that we shall ever reach such exalted rank. Is there any chance of seeing you at the end of term?

Yours ever,
[T. S. Eliot]

TO *Hope Emily Allen*   CC

13 June 1935   [Faber & Faber Ltd]

Dear Miss Allen,

I had been thinking of writing to you in any case to enquire how your labours are progressing, and whether you were anywhere near being able to fix a date for the completion of your modern English version of Margery Kempe. This letter, however, is precipitated by a letter from Colonel Butler-Bowdon[1] which complicates the situation. Colonel Butler-Bowdon starts by reminding me that you spoke to me about his manuscript, and also that Professor Sanford Much [*sc.* Meech] of the University of Michigan sent him a few months ago a copy of his typescript transcription of the text. From this transcription Colonel Butler-Bowdon has been occupied in preparing a modern English version himself and he writes to me to ask whether my firm would be interested in publishing his 'modern edition.'

Naturally I do not like to proceed with Colonel Butler-Bowdon after my conversation and correspondence with you without communicating with you first. Could you let me know immediately how the matter stands? Has Professor Much any knowledge of the Colonel's intentions? You know Colonel Butler-Bowdon and I do not. In any case I should imagine that such a translation into modern English required at least the

---

1–See letter to him, 1 Dec. 1935, below.

collaboration of a scholar in the middle English period, and I have no
reason for supposing that the Colonel has any qualifications. I shall try
to temporise with him until I have heard from you in reply to this letter.
You may think it desirable to cable if what you have to say can be put in
so brief a form. I think, however, that the matter will not become really
urgent for three or four weeks, as Colonel Butler-Bowdon will have first
to have the whole of the long manuscript typed out.

Awaiting, therefore, your immediate reply,[1]

I am, yours sincerely,
[T. S. Eliot]

TO *Henry Miller*

TS Jay Martin

13 June 1935   Faber & Faber Ltd

Dear Mr Miller,

I have now read both *The Tropic of Cancer* and the sections of your
Lawrence book enclosed with your letter of May 22nd, and I hope you
will not mind my saying that my appreciation of the former has rather
eclipsed my interest in the latter. *Tropic of Cancer* seems to me a very
remarkable book. I don't like the title, and the cover design seems to me
deplorable,[2] but the book itself seems to me a rather magnificent piece of
work. There is writing in it as good as any I have seen for a long time.

1 – Allen replied on 24 June that Colonel Butler-Bowdon was indeed so enthused by the
'unexpected clearness' of the translation supplied by Allen's collaborator Sanford Brown
Meech that he had himself been moved to try to modernise it still further with the aim of
affording what he called 'modern fluency'. Allen thus observed: 'I feel that only a publisher
can bring him to reality as to the necessity of rendering Margery's meaning – in whatever
medium is chosen (I am sure he is right that modern idiom is what is most feasible), but I
have just sent him a scrap from a letter of Miss Mirrlees, in which she says very well that
she thinks when Margery is altered the language chosen should be "timeless" – I used that
to illustrate my objection to his changing, in one of the specimens we exchanged, "vexed
[with evil spirits]" to "pestered".' Butler-Bowdon seemed, she added, to be 'suspicious of the
pedantry of scholars', but she feared that any publisher who undertook to publish Kempe in
a 'really Bowdonised form might later have to throw it into a remainder'.

The Early English Text Society edition (Oxford University Press) of *The Book of Margery
Kempe*, with a prefatory note by Emily Hope Allen, was to appear in 1940. Butler-Bowdon's
sole surviving copy of Kempe's *Book* is now in the British Library: MS Add. 61823. Butler-
Bowdon's edition of *The Book of Margery Kempe* was to be published by Jonathan Cape,
1936.

2 – The cover was designed, on a commission of 50 francs, by the fourteen-year-old Maurice
Kahane (1919–90) – who later took his mother's maiden name Girodias to conceal his
Jewish identity from the Nazis – son of Jack Kahane of the Obelisk Press. (Maurice Girodias
went on to found the Olympia Press in 1953.) The design depicts a giant crab bestriding

Several friends to whom I have shown it, including Mr Herbert Read, share my admiration.[1]

Now I do think that this sort of work is where you belong, rather than in literary criticism. Without drawing any general comparisons, your own book is a great deal better both in depth of insight and of course in the actual writing than *Lady Chatterley's Lover*. I candidly think that you are wasting your time writing critical books about contemporaries, and the only excuse for it is if you can make any money in that way. I am looking forward with very great interest to the copy of *Black Spring*. If it doesn't come within a few weeks I shall assume that something has gone wrong and will drop you a line to this Paris address.

Yours very sincerely,
T. S. Eliot

---

the earth and holding in its claws a prostrate, seemingly lifeless, human figure dripping with what appears to be blood.

1–Herbert Read to TSE, 12 June: 'Frank [Morley] perhaps communicated to you my reactions to Miller. The impression he made on me does not wear off. But I don't see what you can do about him. It would be interesting to get a report on his personality.' FVM to Donald Brace, 7 June: 'The best thing I have read lately is a quite unpublishable book called TROPIC OF CANCER by an American named Henry Miller. . . . TROPIC OF CANCER, I repeat, is unprintable under Anglo Saxon laws, but I think the boy writes like a ball of fire.'

On 17 Apr. 1950 George G. Olshausen, Attorney at Law, San Francisco, CA – acting on behalf of the American Civil Liberties Union – approached TSE at Miller's suggestion to ask if he would be willing to testify, as an expert, 'to the quality of the "Tropics" books as literature'. A case was pending in the United States District Court in San Francisco, arising from the ban which the Customs Department had theretofore imposed on the importation of *Tropic of Cancer* and *Tropic of Capricorn*. TSE responded on 24 May 1950: 'I have read Mr Henry Miller's *Tropic of Cancer*, but I have never seen his *Tropic of Capricorn*. As for the former, I read it with a good deal of respect and admiration, and I certainly regard Mr Henry Miller as a serious writer. At the same time, I certainly found some passages of the book very nauseating, and I do not see how it would be possible to refute the allegation that the book was obscene. I am even doubtful whether it is a book which ought to have more than a limited circulation.' TSE told Kristian Smidt, 23 Dec. 1958: 'I don't think I have read anything by Henry Miller except the *Tropic of Cancer*. That was a good many years ago and looking back to the time of its publication and my memories of the book I still think it was a quite remarkable book. But I was unable to interest myself in Mr Henry Miller's later work and didn't even know of the existence of *The Rosy Crucifixion* [trilogy, 1949–59]. Anybody who quotes me in general praise of Miller's work is, therefore, misleading the public. I cannot think of any other statement that I have made, except the one you quote ["a really remarkable book"]. I am certainly not prepared to defend Mr Miller against the charge of obscenity, although I should think that, from what I remember of the *Tropic of Cancer*, his work in general would be obscene but not pornographic.'

TSE's secretary wrote to John Calder (John Calder Publishers), on 23 Jan. 1963: 'It is a long time ago since Mr Eliot read this book, but his impression was at that time that he thought it was most unsuitable for publication over here.'

TO *Stanley Nott*[1]   CC

13 June 1935   [Faber & Faber Ltd]

Dear Mr Nott,

Thank you very much for sending me the advance copy of *Plato*, which I did not have time to do more than look at when you showed me the typescript.[2] If I like it I may be able to say something about it in the *New English Weekly*.

I have kept in mind your suggestion of my doing a pamphlet for you, and I still hope to do this.[3] I should, in fact, much prefer writing a pamphlet [to] introducing a collection of pamphlets by other people. I do not feel that I am quite the right man for the second purpose.

Ezra Pound has been writing to me by fits and starts for some time past about his series.[4] I haven't yet, I am afraid, dug up Eeldrop and Appleplex, which I don't remember with sufficient enthusiasm to feel very anxious to reprint.[5] I will, however, look at them, but even if I still like them, the problem remains of finding anything else suitable to include with them.[6]

Thank you very much for sending me your pamphlets as they appear. I find the series very interesting.

Yours sincerely,
[T. S. Eliot]

1 – Of Stanley Nott (Publishers).
2 – Vladimir Solovyev, *Plato*, trans. Richard Gill (Stanley Nott, 1935).
3 – Nott reminded TSE that he had invited him to write a pamphlet on the New Economics. 'We are contemplating publishing ten of these pamphlets in a bound volume under the title of "Social Credit Pamphleteer" . . . An introduction by yourself would be a fitting crown to the work.'
4 – 'Ezra Pound is editing a series of booklets for us which he is going to call Ideogramic series. No. 1 is "Ta Hio", No. 2 "Fenolossa's Chinese Written Character" . . . The third he would like to have from you . . . He has written to me saying he would like to use "Eel Drop and Apple Plex" [*sic*] which appeared in the *Little Review* years ago. Would you agree to this? and if so would you add something else since Eel Drop and Apple Plex would make only twelve pages.'
5 – TSE, 'Eeldrop and Appleplex, I', *Little Review* 4: 1 (May 1917), 7–11; 'Eeldrop and Appleplex, II', *Little Review* 4: 5 (Sept. 1917), 16–19.
6 – TSE's secretary to Jackson Bryer, 29 May 1964: 'Mr Eliot thinks that he may at that time have had some idea of continuing the dialogue and does not know why it remained a single fragment. On re-reading it some years later it seemed to him an inferior piece of work and he never cared to reprint it.'

TO *Bernard Iddings Bell*

17 June 1935   [Faber & Faber Ltd]

Dear Canon Iddings Bell,

In case I forget to mention the matter when I see you at lunch tomorrow I am writing to tell you that you will be hearing from my friend Dr J. H. Oldham, who is anxious to meet you. I hope that you will be able to see him while you are here, because I think he is most certainly one of the men here whom you ought to know. His main work has been in connection with the International Missionary Council, and he is an authority on certain native problems in Africa about which he from time to time advises the Colonial Office, but his activities range very much more widely than that. He is the prime mover of a great many undertakings in the religious world, and is usually a member of Bishops' Advisory Councils and Conferences, and that sort of thing, and has done most important liaison work between important people in the religious world in different countries. He is also in very close touch with German theologians and ecclesiastics, and is very well informed about the situation in Germany, in regard to which he has advised the Archbishops and the Bishops of Durham and Chichester from time to time. I very much want you to have a talk with him.[1]

Looking forward to seeing you tomorrow,

I am, yours very sincerely,
[T. S. Eliot]

TO *Lucy Raleigh*[2]

18 June 1935   [Faber & Faber Ltd]

Dear Lady Raleigh,

I shall be coming down by the same train on Friday morning, but, as I said might happen, I shall have my niece with me, so that I shall merely leave my bag and return to your house late in the afternoon. I find, also, that some friends have the intention of fetching me after the last performance on Saturday evening, and carrying me away into the country for the weekend.

1 – Oldham met Iddings Bell for a talk on 25 June.
2 – Lady Raleigh (whose daughter was married to TSE's friend, the late Charles Whibley) wrote in late May to say that she would be away in London for some days from 7 June, but that TSE was welcome to make use of her flat in The Precincts, Canterbury.

It is very good of you to have me, and I look forward to seeing you again.[1]

Yours sincerely,
[T. S. Eliot]

TO *Gerald Heard*

18 June 1935   [Faber & Faber Ltd]

Dear Mr Heard,

I have been wanting for some time to ask you to come to lunch with me, and the appearance of *Science in the Making* on my table this morning seems to provide a kind of excuse. I should be very glad if you could lunch with me at the Oxford and Cambridge Club on either Tuesday 2nd or Thursday 4th of July at 1.15.[2]

Yours sincerely,
[T. S. Eliot]

---

1 – Virginia Woolf noted on 20 June: 'Tom last night: supple & sub[t]le, simple & charming. Stayed till 12.15. I never felt so much at my ease. He is a dear old fellow: one of "us": odd: I felt I liked him as I liked Lytton [Strachey] & Roger [Fry] – with intimacy in spite of God. First we talked of his play. He stayed with Lady Raleigh, & she gave him cocoa & Oliver biscuits but never said a word about the play. There was a canon there. And they looked out of the window & saw 3 girls in very short shorts, naked legs & large bottoms go into the Cathedral. "The Dean encourages them" said Lady R, grimly. "I am in favour of St Paul if one must be irrational" said Tom. [1 *Corinthians* 11, 13: "Judge in yourself: is it comely that a woman pray unto God uncovered?"] Now tell me about the marmozets view of Germany." We made a good dinner. And he said he liked Stephen – "What a charming person in many ways" no, I think he didnt even qualify his remark, so kind has he become. "Auden is a very nice rattled brained boy. Some of his plays extremely good, but its superficial: stock figures, sort of Punch figures . . ." Publishers gossip. A story about a party [held by John Hayward at his flat in Bina Gardens, Kensington] to entertain the Reads, Ludo [Mrs Herbert Read] & her sister & German friend. Tom bought fireworks; sugar that dissolved & let out small fish; & chocolates that he thought were full of sawdust. "Theyre very greedy," he said; "And by a mistake the chocolates were full of soap. They set on me . . . And it was not a success. So much so that I forgot the fireworks, until they were going. I then let them off on the doorstep. And poor Herbert had to pay for a cab from Bina Gardens to Hampstead." This was very amusing, & not as stiff as usual. L. made cigarettes. Tom drank whisky. I mused & was at my ease. Tom wants to give me all his works, but thought I didnt read them – would always have given me all his works' (*Diary* 4, 324).

2 – They had lunch on 2 July.

TO *Dorothy Richards*   TS Magdalene

18 June 1935   Faber & Faber Ltd

Dear Mrs Richards,

One usually thanks an author for a book either before having read it, or, if one has faith, after one has read it.[1] In this case, it is not quite the latter. I have kept the book on my desk and have picked it up and read a few pages at a time, and have not yet finished. But I must say that I find it fascinating and well-written, and the technical details make me quite giddy. The book confirms my intention of remaining in the valleys for the rest of my life.

I hope that you have recovered from your illness and I look forward to seeing you on the 9th.

Thank you very much, but I wish you had been able to sign it.

Yours sincerely,

T. S. Eliot

TO *R. Ellis Roberts*   CC

18 June 1935   [Faber & Faber Ltd]

My dear Ellis Roberts,

I must apologise for not having written to you several days ago, but I hope you will understand that spending part of my time in Canterbury is very distracting and crowds a good many other things into the other days, during what is usually a busy time. First of all, I must thank you for your very generous article about *Murder in the Cathedral* in the *Church Times*. It makes me hope all the more that you will have been able to see the play, because I think that Martin Browne has done a very brilliant piece of work with it, and made the very most of its possibilities.[2]

Next, about the P.E.N. Club.[3] I feel not only surprised but greatly honoured to be nominated for such a post, but I have at the same time

---

1 – Richards had sent TSE a copy of her book *Climbing Days* (1935).

2 – R. Ellis Roberts, 'T. S. Eliot's Drama of Faith', *Church Times*, 14 June 1935, 729.: 'Mr Eliot's St Thomas is not the hagiographer's; his pride, his ambition are not glossed over, for Becket was not a natural saint, as was that other king's servant, Thomas More.'

3 – Roberts invited TSE to accept nomination as next President of London P.E.N., in succession to H. G. Wells who was resigning. 'When Goldsworthy died, my candidate for the presidency was Chesterton – as I did not want H. G. for various reasons I need not go into. H. G. has been president for two years, has not given satisfaction, & is tired of it.' This nomination represented a unanimous invitation by the appointment committee. 'Your

no hesitation in saying that it is quite out of the question for me to undertake such a responsibility as being president. I have very little spare time, and all that I can give is claimed already by various Church and similar activities, and I simply could not give the time to perform the task properly. I should be just as unsatisfactory as H. G. Wells, although I hope not for the same reasons. I must repeat, however, that I am pleased and honoured by having my name suggested.

What has given me much more reason for thought and trouble is your All Souls Club.[1] The reason for hesitation which I gave you is the only one that exists, and in principle it would give me the greatest pleasure to be associated with such a society. My conscience, however, is not comfortable about it. What I should like best would be to think that the question might be revived after the beginning of the New Year, when I shall be able to review the financial position and see my way a little more clearly. But I am aware that the membership is limited, and that you want to fill the vacancy in the near future. Nevertheless, I do not feel that I ought to commit myself until I am surer of my position.

With grateful thanks, and many regrets,

Yours ever sincerely,
[T. S. Eliot]

TO *W. H. Auden*   CC

18 June 1935   [Faber & Faber Ltd]

Dear Auden,

Thank you for your letter of Tuesday. Your allusion to the wireless is completely obscure to me, as I don't keep in touch with that organisation, and I can't understand in what context the four knights could have been mentioned. In any case I think there is a good deal to be said for the Music Hall turn.[2]

---

reputation as a man of letters, & your integrity as an author are bigger than that of any other candidate named, except Virginia Woolf, who certainly wouldn't accept the position . . . The only rule for membership – except that it is confined to authors – is that no religious, racial or political barriers should be made . . . So at present there is no Russian P.E.N . . . and the German P.E.N. when it expelled most of its members for disaffection to the Nazi regime, was removed.'

1 – 'The next dinner is tomorrow, & I know the members will be anxious to know if you have decided to join.' TSE had not attended a dinner of the All Souls Club even by Feb. 1936.

2 – Auden had written: 'That idiot on the wireless last night said that the four knights [in *MiC*] talked like the Western Brothers.

I am rather puzzled by your allusion to Curtis Brown.[1] Having looked up our agreement with you I don't see what Curtis Brown can do for you except take 10 per cent off the royalties. Do you mean that you want us to pay the royalties to Curtis Brown instead of to you? That doesn't make any difference to us. It only means, as I say, that your profits will be slightly diminished.

Yours ever,
[T. S. Eliot]

TO *I. A. Richards*   CC

18 June 1935   [Faber & Faber Ltd]

Dear Richards,

Many thanks for your letter.[2] I have just discovered that Saturday night is supposed to be reserved for the Friends of the Cathedral, so I am writing to Miss Babington to put in a plea in case it is necessary. I have got to dine beforehand with the Dean (described by the rest of Canterbury as a Boshevic [*sic*]), and the Morleys say that they are motoring over from Surrey that evening to fetch me for the weekend, but we must have a few minutes at least after the show, and I will look for you at once.[3]

Yours ever,
[T. S. E.]

'Lets write a turn together and appear in it at the Holborn Empire – I suggest a dialogue between a French Impersonator and a Goose.'

(The Western Brothers were a popular English music hall and radio act, flourishing from the 1930s to the 1950s.)

1 – 'I forgot to tell you that I've made an arrangement with Curtis Brown about Dogskin because of the problems of double authorship. I hope Faber's don't mind.'

2 – IAR wrote in an undated letter: 'Saturday we will be at Canterbury [for the performance of *MiC*]. I have wired as you suggested in your name to Miss Babington.

'I meant to convey succinctly in my telegram that I thought the play merely as a reader's poem extremely good. The First Part in especial. I've read it several times & don't think it will do anything but grow on me.

'The 2 new *Words for music* went off for me like fireworks the moment I looked at them.'

3 – FVM wrote to Donald Brace, 18 June 1935 (his letter may have been begun on 18 June and finished at a later date): 'The production on Saturday at Canterbury of Eliot's play, MURDER IN THE CATHEDRAL was a great success, and I am enclosing notices from *The Times* and *Telegraph*, and also some reviews of the book. You might like to have a couple of copies of our edition, so I am sending them off by this mail too. The publication of the book was on the 13th, done in a ferocious rush to keep as close as possible to the production of the play.' The *Times*' review of *MiC* appeared on 17 June 1935: 'The play is an exposition,

TO *Mario Praz*   copy of TS

19 June 1935   Faber & Faber Ltd

My dear Praz,

Morley has handed me your letter of the 15th.[1] I never republished my Clark Lectures at Cambridge, and I have no intention of doing so. I may have changed my mind on many points, and I am certainly conscious of having written outside of my actual knowledge. I used some of the material in a series of three lectures given in Baltimore, but I have not republished these, and have no intention of doing so. The point is that to rewrite the Clark Lectures in any form which would be now acceptable to me would be an immense labour and I am now more interested in doing other things and writing about other subjects. The Clark Lectures are of course several years later in date than the three essays contained in *Homage to John Dryden,* but I am willing to let the earlier essays stand.

I am sorry to have lost touch with you for so long. I suppose that you are very busy, but whenever you should have a mind to review something for the *Criterion* I hope you will let me know.

With best wishes,
Yours ever,
T. S. Eliot

---

in Becket, of the nature of saintliness, and contains an urgent suggestion that the problems by which he was beset are present to-day . . . For the greater part of the play Mr Eliot has succeeded in combining lucidity and precision with an uncommon vigour that fully justifies his departure from the customary forms of dramatic verse. The Chorus is never a group of women dully chanting. Taught by Miss Fogerty how to use Mr Eliot's rhythms, it has at once dramatic and intellectual impact . . . Mr Eliot's writing and Mr Martin Browne's production are continuously keen and clear . . . and . . . its merits most movingly appear in the prose sermon and in those passages of verse that are direct in their attack and are not twisted to irony or humour' (repr. in *Specimens of English Dramatic Criticism XVII–XX Centuries,* ed. A. C. Ward [1945], 326–8).

GCF diary: 'Fri, 21 June. Just got to C[anterbury] in time for the beginning of Tom's play (Murder in the Cathedral). It was a very impressive thing indeed – tho' I did not like the chorus personnel or delivery (nothing like so good as in The Rock, & the non-use of masks was a mistake). Robert Speaight's performance as the Archbishop was masterly. No question of TSE's dramatic sense. It's an A1 play – even if one has to accept a premiss of which one is unconvinced or even to which one is hostile. It moved me greatly.

'Tea with Lady Raleigh in the Precincts, & then to Pike's Farm [the Morleys' home in Surrey], where we feasted with the Morleys.'

1–Praz asked FVM: 'Are Eliot's lectures on the metaphysical poets (the Clarke [*sic*] lectures) published in his *Selected Essays?* I have to mention his contribution in an article on *Secentismo* for the *Enciclopedia Italiana* and, although I have read those lectures in ms., I do not know whether they have been published, at least in part.'

TO *Stella Mary Newton*[1]   CC

20 June 1935   [Faber & Faber Ltd]

Dear Mrs Newton,

Thank you so much for your kind letter of the 17th.[2] I am delighted to know that you enjoyed the play. I was sorry to see that one of the papers, I think it was the *Telegraph*, seemed inclined to give me the credit for the conception of the Tempters' costumes which was so entirely your own. May I say also that I had been particularly anxious that the costumes should be designed by you, and that I feel fully justified by the results?[3]

I am sending you a copy of the complete text.

Yours sincerely,
[T. S. Eliot]

TO *Feliks Topolski*[4]   CC

20 June 1935   [Faber & Faber Ltd]

Dear Mr Topolski,

I must apologise for not having written to you before, but I have had a very busy week, and have had to be away much of the time. Our production manager was much attracted by your drawings, and thought that he would like to keep you in mind for illustrations or cover designs when a suitable book presented itself. As there is nothing at the moment he would be glad if you could let him have a few specimen

---

1 – Stella Mary Newton (1901–2001), fashion designer and dress historian – she designed the costumes and sets for both *The Rock* and *MiC* – was married to the art critic Eric Newton.
2 – 'I feel I must write and tell you how enormously I enjoyed your play on Saturday . . .

'I had not been able to pay much attention to the only rehearsal at which I was present, and I found the first performance thrilling beyond all my expectations, although I realised when I read it that it would play magnificently.'
3 – See Stella Mary Newton, 'The First Three Plays by T. S. Eliot: Designs for Settings and Costumes', *Costume* 24 (1990), 97–110.
4 – Feliks Topolski (1907–89), expressionist painter, draughtsman, portraitist. Born and educated in Warsaw, he migrated to Britain in 1935 and took British citizenship in 1947. He painted portraits and caricatures of many contemporary writers and politicans including TSE, William Empson, H. G. Wells, Graham Greene, Evelyn Waugh and Harold Macmillan; and is perhaps best known today for *Chronicles* (1953–79) – a series of 3,000 depictions of notable figures and aspects of world history. See further Topolski, *Fourteen Letters* (F&F, 1988).

drawings which he could keep as a reminder of the style and quality of your work.[1]

> Yours sincerely,
> T. S. Eliot
> [signed by Brigid O'Donovan]

TO *Frederic Prokosch*   CC

Telegram, 25 June 1935   [Faber & Faber Ltd]

SAXTON THINKS YOU SHOULD DECIDE STOP FEEL SURE YOU BETTER OFF
HERE STOP LET ME KNOW QUICKLY[2]

ELIOT

FROM *Vivien Eliot*   PC MS Valerie Eliot[3]

28 June 1935

Dear Tom – Come to this hotel & fetch me away on *July 13th* (or before).
VOTRE FEMME – YOUR WIFE Vivienne Haigh Eliot

TO *Stephen Spender*   TS Northwestern

1 July 1935   Faber & Faber Ltd

My dear Stephen,

I am ashamed to be answering your letter, late at night, with only a half hour or so to spare, and long after I received it. In addition, I have had an earlier letter of yours which requires a careful answer, but which I shall not attempt to answer tonight. What I want chiefly to say tonight is, that your letter (is it June 12th) gave me more pleasure, and pride and satisfaction in the *Murder in the Cathedral* than any expression of

---

1–Topolski submitted on 27 June 'a few of my specimen drawings but I should like to remark that they do not represent my most finished work as I am preparing an exhibition and must therefore keep my best drawings for that purpose.' On 3 July Brigid O'Donovan acknowledged receipt of the specimen drawings – 'which have been filed for reference'.

2–Prokosch cabled TSE on 22 June: 'RECEIVED IDENTICAL OFFER FROM CHATTO WEEK AGO AM REQUESTING SAXTON TO CONFER WITH YOU REGARDING CHOICE.' Prokosch again, 30 June: 'FEEL COMMITTED TO CHATTO LETTER FOLLOWS EXPLAINING DESPERATELY SORRY ABOUT WHOLE AFFAIR SHALL TRY TO RETAIN OPTION PLEASE TAKE POEMS'.

3–Postcard of Hotel Cecil, 30 Rue St-Didier, Paris.

opinion private or public that I have received. In getting a letter like this, I feel that it does not matter whether the subject deserves it, but that one would be equally happy in having written something inferior, if it called forth such comments. It does not seem to matter whether the text deserves praise, so long as it can evoke such immediate comments from a person like yourself.[1]

As for 'calmness', I often refer to a phrase of Goethe's which you no doubt know. Someone complimented him on his serenity. Yes, he said, but it is a serenity which has to be composed afresh every morning.

Verdi, that is for me *Otello* one of the greatest of operas.[2] Farewell the tranquil mind. Farewell content . . . [3]

Please remember that my comments on *The Destructive Element* were based on a first reading – and do not take them too seriously – only I still regret that you could not devote one whole book to James and leave all the other people out. I have not yet had the time to read your friend's story, but will write about it later: at the moment I have an enormous mass of correspondence to clear away. I'm glad about the swimming:[4] that was the only proficiency I had at school, but for twentyfive years [I] am out of practice. What is odd is one's pleasure in overcoming one's feelings of inferiority as a schoolboy. Let the stories come as they will, and never feel that it's TIME to produce something new.

Ever affectionately,
Tom

1–SS wrote, 12 June: 'Thank you so much for sending me your play which must have crossed my letter. I am extremely proud to have it, with your inscription in it. It seems to me that this play is the most beautiful work you have done: I read it yesterday and again today and can think of little else. It is impossible to express the feeling of gratitude I have when I say it is beautiful.'

He enclosed a short story by someone (unidentified) he had met in Spain: 'it is so well written & put together', albeit 'a little "exquisite"'.

When VW described to Julian Bell, 1 Dec. 1935, the violently adverse reactions that she and LW had experienced at a performance of *MiC*, she added: 'Then we met Stephen Spender, who also was green at the gills with dislike [of the production]' (*The Sickle Side of the Moon: The Letters of Virginia Woolf, V: 1932–1935*, ed. Nigel Nicolson [1979], 448).

2–TSE is picking up on Spender's reference to Verdi in his letter of 30 Apr.

3–*Othello* III. iii, 358.

4–'Lately I've learnt to swim very well, which gives me great satisfaction. It's funny how one can miss even the pleasures of mild physical prowess at school & then enjoy them later.'

TO *Will Spens*[1]   CC

2 July 1935   [Faber & Faber Ltd]

Dear Spens,
    Thank you for your letter of the 29th June, and for the very prompt and
agreeable fee of ten guineas. Whenever the dissertation recurs to my mind
I feel more convinced that it does not show evidence of the ability which
you would desire in electing a man to a fellowship.[2]

                                        Yours sincerely,
                                        [T. S. Eliot]

TO *Crane Brinton*[3]   CC

2 July 1935   [Faber & Faber Ltd]

Dear Sir,
    I have your letter of June 17th, and wish to express my great pleasure in
the honour bestowed upon me by the Alpha Chapter of Phi Beta Kappa.[4] I
am deeply sensible of the distinction conferred, and will ask you to convey
my deep appreciation to the members of this Chapter.

                                        Yours very truly,
                                        [T. S. Eliot]

1 – Will Spens, The Master, Corpus Christi College, Cambridge.
2 – *The Janus of Poets: Being an essay on the Dramatic Value of Shakspere's Poetry both good
and bad*, by Richard David (Scholar of Corpus Christi College, Cambridge) – an extended
version of the winning entry in the Harkness Essay Prize 1934 – was to be published by
Cambridge University Press, 1935.
    Spens responded, 29 June: 'This confirms the impression of some of our Fellows, who,
without being members of the English School, are likely to be able to form a competent
opinion, e.g. Pickthorn and our new Tutor, Lee. Their view was much less flattering than
that taken by a member of the English School here, who has reported on the dissertation.
    'I am by no means clear what the College is likely to do in the matter.'
3 – Clarence Crane Brinton (1898–1968), distinguished historian of France and historian of
ideas, taught at Harvard from 1923, becoming full professor in 1942 and McLean Professor
of Ancient and Modern History, 1946–68; elected President of the American Historical
Association in 1963. Works include *The Jacobins: An Essay in the New History* (1930).
4 – Brinton informed TSE that he had been 'chosen an honorary member of the Phi Beta
Kappa, Alpha of Massachusetts . . . If you wish to obtain the Phi Beta Kappa key, please
write directly to the United Chapters of Phi Beta Kappa, 145 West 55th Street, New York
City.' G. Peabody Gardner, Jr., Chairman of the Executive Committee of the Harvard Class
of 1910 (TSE's friend Leon M. Little was Secretary), wrote on 27 June to congratulate TSE
on his election.

TO *John Garrett*

3 July 1935   [Faber & Faber Ltd]

Dear Mr Garrett,

Very many thanks for your kind letter of the 23rd.[1] What you tell me about the effect upon your schoolboys is most gratifying.

I have not seen the Out of Bounds book, which has not been sent to me.[2] I will try to get a copy and will look at it. I hope very much that your appointment as a Head Master, on which I congratulate you, will not keep you too busy to write for the *Criterion*.[3]

Yours sincerely,

[T. S. Eliot]

TO *R. Ellis Roberts*

3 July 1935   [Faber & Faber Ltd]

Dear Roberts,

I have two letters of yours to answer.[4] First, thank you for your good offices in connection with the Little Theatre. Several tentative suggestions have been made from one or two quarters about possible production in London, but nothing as yet very appreciable, and I am not in a hurry to commit myself anywhere without consulting Browne. I will keep Miss Price in mind, and will probably communicate with her later.

Very many thanks to the members of All Souls for their insistence.[5] I should certainly be glad to review the matter in the autumn, as you suggest.

1 – Garrett had taken twelve six-formers from Whitgift School, Croydon, to a performance of *MiC*. 'What I thought would interest you was to know how absorbed these boys were. Afterwards they were quiet and thoughtful in a manner utterly foreign to them, and on the way home and next day, they made continuous reference to this and that in the play which revealed their appreciation of something that was new to them.'

2 – Garrett hoped to review *Out of Bounds: the education of Giles Romilly and Esmond Romilly*.

3 – Garrett had been appointed Headmaster of a new school, Raynes Park, Surrey, from the next term. 'It will be a great adventure but I hope you will allow me still to write for the *Criterion*.'

4 – Roberts wrote on 27 June with the information that Nancy Price, of the Little Theatre, John Street, Adelphi, London, had expressed keen interest in staging a London production of *MiC*.

5 – Roberts wrote ('Corpus Christi') that at the last dinner the members 'expressed their strongest hopes that you would join . . . I shall certainly urge on the club that we wait for you – perhaps you could decide by the October dinner?' (There were 14 members; 10 dinners a year.)

As for the production at Canterbury, I can see that it had many faults.[1] I was not altogether satisfied with all of the costumes, and one in particular provoked its wearer to some rather exaggerated clowning. The chorus also needed more training in rhythmic speaking. But I maintain that Browne is a good producer, and knowing the difficulties under which he was working I am very well satisfied. Furthermore, he was ill in bed for ten days at a most critical moment, and had hardly recovered his voice on the first night, so that he was unable to drill the company as he would have done.

With many thanks,
Yours sincerely,
[T. S. Eliot]

TO *Polly Tandy*   TS BL

3 July 1935   Faber & Faber Ltd

Dear Polly,

Thank you for your letter of the 25th ultimo.[2] The 13th of July is correct, and I am sorry to say it is not a question of my having or not having a mind, because I have to take my turn mounting guard at this office on the morning of Saturday the 13th, and it is quite out of the question to try to change over with somebody else, because I have got to do the same the next Saturday as well, although I am going away for that weekend also, and the real reason is that three weekends, hand-running, were taken for me by somebody, all because of my complications with Canterbury. You

---

1 – Roberts had been to see *MiC*: 'Greatly impressed tho' I was, I cannot agree with you that Martin Brown [*sic*] is really a good producer. Judging only from the results of his work, I should guess he was too modest in his instructions. Speaight, on the whole excellent, failed once or twice . . . He missed, for instance, the lightness of his line about leaving his rooms as he finds them; he was at times monotonous, & all his "Unbar the doors" "Open the doors" were shouted. I feel sure the last, effectual one should be very low and insistent – episcopal not human, the voice of a man already on the other side of the other Door. Then, the murder. This I'd have liked unseen – or rather, over the shoulders & bowed heads of the chorus, huddled round, just the swing of the swords visible – but no Becket.'

2 – Polly Tandy confirmed that TSE was expected for the weekend of 13 July, and from Fri. 12th if possible. 'And I hope you don't write to say that you're taking old ladies out to tea, *or going to Court* to see the "rugs and jugs and candlelights", or making "mumbrian melodies" . . .

'We are all flourishing. The cats have been named Christabel (a pushy insistent female Pankhurst like) Dorabella [*sic*], Una and Thumbeline. The males are Nimrod and Tom Thumb.'

will understand, therefore, that I shall be free to leave Russell Square at about 12.30 on the morning of Saturday 13th, and if Geoffrey is engaged at the Museum on that morning I shall be more than pleased to meet him at 1 o'clock or so, at the entrance of the Windsor Castle Drive, or wherever else he has a mind to if he has a mind to anything. Your news is noted, and I look forward to attempting to photograph the remarkable cats, although I don't understand why one of them should be named Dolabella. Nevertheless I have always maintained that a cat's name should have at least 3 syllables, except in exceptional circumstances.

Yours ever,
TP

TO *Bonamy Dobrée* CC

3 July 1935   [Faber & Faber Ltd]

My dear Bonamy,

Thank you for your letter of the 1st.[1] I only hope that you will not find the overshoes too small for you. The spelling, by the way, is g o l o s h e s, but there is an alternative, g o l o s h e s [*sic*].

But why, my dear Bonamy, should you call upon my devotion, though it is capable of almost anything, to write about an author whose works I have never opened for a good 20 years? What do I know about Bishop Berkeley?[2] Do you think that I am capable of handling anybody in the espicopal line? There are bishops and bishops, and this one is not my pigeon. He is much more in Herbert's way. Can't you find somebody in the whole period of 137 years whom I know more about, or am at least capable of learning more about, than this Bishop of Cloyne? And preferably not, I agree, a merely literary character. Last year, for instance, I read the two-volume biography of Bishop Blomfield, and I don't believe anyone else has read that book since it was published, except a few members of his own family.[3] Unfortunately, Blomfield didn't die in 1837, and I suppose you want somebody who was dead by then. Have you got

1 – 'Firstly, many thanks for the galoshes . . .'
2 – BD (1 July): 'Secondly, au secours! I am editing for Messrs Cassells a series of essays 3500 to 4000 words long, on British Worthies from 1700–1837 . . . Will you, out of your great goodness, jot me down an essay on the good Bishop Berkeley? I shall be bitterly disappointed if you don't, because B. must be in the series, and if you won't do him, who can? I have thought also you might like to, rather than be invited to treat a merely literary bloke.'
3 – Bishop Blomfield features as a speaking role in *The Rock*.

your worthies all listed, or is it worth while my trying to think up a new one whom you have never heard of? And what a job for a retired Artillery man.

With most cordial sympathy.
Ever,
[T. S. E.]

TO *The Librarian, London Library*   TS London Library[1]

3 July 1935   Faber & Faber Ltd

My dear Sir,

Your assistant has so long addressed me as 'T. Steoms Eliot' that I hesitate to introduce any change. But this designation does give me pain, as my middle name is STEARNS (or STERNE); and I should be grateful if she would in future address me simply, as I subscribe myself, as

Your obedient servant,
T. S. Eliot[2]

TO *Marguerite Caetani*   CC

3 July 1935   [Faber & Faber Ltd]

My dear Marguerite,

Your letter arrived while I was away[3] – I spent several days at the Morleys' partially recovering from Canterbury – I have not been so completely exhausted for two years and I am beginning to go bald again – and then I had two very crowded days in London before going away again; and did not get back from Newark until Monday and had to spend the rest of that day at Wimbledon. I shall not be out of town again until

1–First published in Rupert Walters, 'T. S. Eliot', *The London Library Magazine*, issue 1 (Aut. 2008), 15.
2–C. Hagberg Wright, Secretary & Librarian of the London Library, responded on 4 July: 'I beg to acknowledge the receipt of your letter of the 3rd instant, and in accordance with your wish, I have had the necessary alterations made in the records of the London Library.
'I am sorry about this clerical error.'
3–Caetani, who was staying in the Burlington Hotel, Cork Street, had been trying to reach TSE. She wrote again on 23 June: 'You must have been having a wonderful week at Canterbury. I wish I could have seen your play.' In addition, she asked him for Emily Hale's address.

the 13th, so please let me know when I may come and see you. Is Lelia[1] with you? I had to meet Jenny de Margerie[2] yesterday at a cocktail party, and I don't think I ought to see her again for another six months, and I should prefer not to see Lady Colefax.[3] I don't mind most other people, but it would be still more agreeable to see you by yourself or selves.

Affectionately,

[Tom]

TO *A. L. Rowse*   TS Exeter

4 July 1935   Faber & Faber Ltd

Dear Rowse,

Many thanks for your letter of June 20th, which I found extremely interesting.[4] I am trying to get Thomas Lodge for you, but O'Conor was reviewed several issues ago. It is by no means an important book, and I only had it reviewed at all – it was a short notice – out of a kindly feeling toward the author.

I am looking forward to Sir Richard Grenville, which I expect to be a compendium of your political views in application to the Tudor period.[5] I wish that you were now occasionally in London, as my experience is that one finds the points of agreement with another person so much more readily in conversation than in correspondence. Geoffrey took me down to the All Souls Encaenia lunch last week. I imagine that had no attractions for you, but it is worthwhile to see almost anything once, and I was very glad to meet Isaiah Berlin,[6] whom I liked, although I had of course no chance for any connected conversation with him.

1–Caetani's only daughter Lelia was to be married in 1951: TSE did not attend, for he was in Switzerland at the time.

2–Henriette 'Jenny' Jacquin de Margerie (1896–1991) – née Fabre-Luce – wife of Roland de Margerie.

3–JDH described Lady Colefax (*New York Sun*, 25 Aug. 1934) as 'perhaps the best, certainly the cleverest, hostess in London at the present time. As an impresario she is unequaled, but there is far too much circulation and hubbub at her parties to entitle her to be called a salonière.' See Siân Evans, *Queen Bees: Six Brilliant and Extraordinary Hostesses Between the Wars* (2016).

4–ALR asked to review E. A. Tenney's *Thomas Lodge* and Norreys Jephson O'Conor's *Godes Peace and the Queenes*. 'Both rather good, I believe, but the latter for a short notice merely.'

5–ALR reported that the book he had been 'working at all the time' was 'nearing its end now': *Sir Richard Grenville of the Revenge: An Elizabethan Hero* (1937).

6–Isaiah Berlin (1909–97), philosopher and historian of ideas, was born in Riga, Latvia, and brought to England with his family in 1920. Educated at St Paul's School, London, and

As for your essay[1] I maintain my belief, as I hope a dispassionate editor, that you were trying to cover too much ground in one article. If you were writing a book I am sure this essay would fall into two chapters, and the reader at least wants a breathing space after being brought to agreement about the trouble, before being swept on to acceptance of the cure. I feel that it would be a great thing, though requiring much patience, if people could be brought to accept such a diagnosis of modern war as you have given, and I think that it is a pity to force the medicine down their throats at the same time as telling them what is the matter with them. They are anxious enough to avoid accepting the diagnosis; it is easy enough to find faults with any regime prescribed; and they avoid the necessity of looking the facts in the face by concentrating their attention on all the weaknesses of the particular nostrum offered. I hope that this opinion has some value, particularly from the fact that I don't myself find your constructive argument wholly convincing.

I admit that Hoffman Nickerson's article is not so good as it seemed to be when I accepted it.[2] As for the pacific tendencies of fascist regimes, that remains to be tested, but I should have thought myself that fascism, like other forms of demagogy and democracy, might be exposed to the ~~same~~ temptation of staging a war abroad in order to distract the public mind from internal discontents.

You appear to like my play about the man whom you call Thomas à Becket as well as I could possibly have hoped that you would, considering your expressed disapproval of saints, and I am by no means surprised that you found in my sermon an argument in justification of war and a parallel to Reichsbischof Müller.[3] In this, if I may say so my dear Rowse, you seem

at Corpus Christi College, Oxford, he gained a first in Greats and a second first in Philosophy, Politics and Economics; thereafter he won a prize fellowship at All Souls, 1932. He taught philosophy at New College until 1950. In 1957 he was appointed Chichele Professor of Social and Political Theory at Oxford; and in the same year he was elected to the British Academy, which he served in the capacity of Vice-President, 1959–61; President, 1974–8. He was appointed CBE in 1946; knighted in 1957; and in 1971 he was appointed to the Order of Merit. From 1966 to 1975 he was founding President of Wolfson College, Oxford. His many works include *Karl Marx* (1939) and *The Hedgehog and the Fox* (1953).

1 – 'I read through your comments on my Essay on the subject the other day, a second or third time, and was much struck by the fact that in every case where it is a matter of wording or phrasing, you were right. The Essay was written not so much in a hurry as in a passion, and one is apt then to be rhetorical.'

2 – ALR thought Nickerson's article – 'War, Democracy and Peace', *C.* 14 (Apr. 1935), 351–63 – 'rubbish'.

3 – Rowse, 20 June 1935: 'I have got and read your Thomas à Becket, and qua play like it very much; it has some lovely poetry in it which I enjoyed. But I don't like some of the arguments (or rather sentiments) expressed in it; on Peace again, for example: "My Peace I

to me to be running true to form. I observe that my friends who have leanings towards the Left are inclined to suspect me of being a fascist, and if I knew any fascists, which I don't, I should expect them to accuse me of flirting with communism. It is, I think, almost essential to the position of any heretic to suspect anyone who does not share his particular heresy, of being committed to the opposite complementary heresy.

As for my influence in this country or anywhere else, I am afraid that it is exaggerated by your kindly imagination.[1] I of course repudiate the term 'defeatism', unless the meaning you give that term comprehends everybody who attempts to take a Christian point of view towards the affairs of this world. That is to say, a point of view which stands everyday values on their heads. I am trying not to quibble about the world, or take issue with you in any small point-scoring way. I hope and believe that I am in sympathy with the right social and political aims of the Left, but there is a good deal of room for disagreement as to which are the right ones. Incidentally, I should like very much to meet Tawney,[2] and I hope that some day a meeting can be arranged under your patronage. But I think that at the present time it is better that some people like myself should refuse to commit themselves to any political party. The Right is just as alien to me as the Left. I confess that I am not very much impressed by the distinguished names you cite. I have always thought of Lansbury

---

leave with you, my peace I give unto you." "Did he mean peace as we think of it?" you ask; "the kingdom of England at peace with its neighbours, the barons at peace with the King" etc. I don't know how we are to know for certain what Christ meant: but it has always seemed to me as likely as not that he meant by that saying, just what we all mean by it: peace between nations and peoples, and peace within. Certainly that is what it has been taken to mean by innumerable generations of Christian people and I do not see that they are wrong.

'Your argument is not so very different from – in fact liable to lead to – the sort of sermon by Reichsbischof Müller on Xmas Day 1933 on the text "Peace on earth, good will to men", saying that "when Jesus Christ said 'Peace', he did not mean 'No more war'"; he did not mean the peace of the graveyard etc. It is easy to see what this leads to, is designed to lead to.' (Ludwig Müller [1883–1945] – a pastor – was imposed by the Nazi régime as 'Reich's Bishop' of the Deutsche Evangelische Kirche on 28 June 1933.)

1 – ALR went on to make 'a serious and very important point as regards your own development and your influence in this country. Need your arrival at a position of Christian belief involve this kind of defeatism as regards "progressive" ends? . . . It seems to me that a far stronger position intellectually, and a better one morally, is that of a person who has the Christian faith and also is in sympathy with the right social and political ends of the Left, Socialists, Communists and even Liberals. (That is why I have always wanted you to meet Tawney: he has that powerful combination and is as firm as a rock . . .)'

2 – R. H. Tawney (1880–1962) – economic historian, social critic, ethical socialist, Christian socialist; President of the Workers' Educational Association, 1928–44 – was Professor of Economic History at the London School of Economics, 1931–49. Works include *The Acquisitive Society* (1920) and *Religion and the Rise of Capitalism* (1926).

as a lovable and admirable character whose heart was stronger than his head. In any case the mere fact that these people are Anglo-Catholic proves nothing in itself. I have met plenty of ritualists who call themselves Catholics, whose theology was almost non-existent.

I should agree that theoretically there is a great deal in common between Catholicism and communism. On the other hand, Christianity and fascism are certainly opposed, though in some fascist states a precarious modus vivendi may be possible. Obviously an Italian fascism cannot afford to antagonise the Vatican overtly and completely. If the Vatican accepts the political position that is not, in my opinion, descending to a compromise or accepting a pollution.

But I have written long enough for the moment, and I hope we may meet and talk before very long. I have now got to your footnote and see that you suggest also Strachey's *Capitalist Crisis*. I think I will order that for you instead of Thomas Lodge.[1]

Yours ever,
T. S. E.

TO *Sydney Schiff*   TS British Library

4 July 1935   Faber & Faber Ltd

My dear Sydney,

Many thanks for your letter of the 29th.[2] I am glad to know that you obtained a good seat, because the Chapter House is a very unsatisfactory place for a theatrical performance. My own experience was that if you were far enough forward to hear well you were too near to the performers to see the whole scene, so that very few parts of the room were anywhere near satisfactory. I agree with you about some of the costumes, and

---

1 – Rowse on John Strachey, *The Nature of Capitalist Crisis*: C. 15 (Oct. 1935), 107–9.
2 – Schiff, who was hard of hearing, wrote: 'I went to the performance of "Murder in the Cathedral" on the 19th. Thanks to the courtesy of the lady secretary [Margaret Babington] my mention of your name secured me an excellent seat and I heard well almost everything.

'The performance seemed to me almost excellent as a whole . . . The drama is impressive, at moments majestic, especially Part II up to the Knights' speeches which struck me as incongruous & ineffective – not because of the introduction of up to date jargon and allusions but because of the satirical flippancy of tone. In this respect it seems to me to compare unfavourably with "The Waste Land" in which with consummate restraint and power you contrive to put nobility and tragic pathos into the utterance of those women in the pub and a splendour of imagery into such passages as occur and recur in that marvelous "Fire Sermon". I see no point whatever in dressing a knight like a golfer and another in a top-hat. These things seem to my ignorant mind to drag the whole splendid work down.'

consequently about the style of acting which went with the costumes, and I could make some serious criticisms of the chorus. But on the whole I was very well satisfied. As for the knights's [*sic*] speeches, that is the point on which there are conflicting opinions, and I must protest against the suggestion of flippancy of intention. Also I saw none in the execution. The satirical element is quite secondary, and the four speeches as I saw them are intensely pathetic. That, at all events, was my intention, if not my effect. But of course I can see that to most people the political aspect would be much more apparent than the theological aspect.

> With love to Violet,
> Yours ever affectionately,
> Tom

TO *C. A. Siepmann*   CC

10 July 1935   [Faber & Faber Ltd]

My dear Siepmann,

I am writing to you about a matter which must be highly confidential and which I should much have preferred to discuss with you in conversation. But I learn that you are away on holiday until the 22nd and by that time I shall be away myself for a fortnight or three weeks. However Geoffrey Faber will be here until the 26th and would be very glad to talk the matter over with you, if you are so minded.

I enclose a confidential report of a committee of the National Book Council concerning the foundation of a new scheme to be called the National Book League. The committee believe that this Book League might become a very important and influential organisation in the hands of the right man, who will be the organising secretary. Both Faber and Harold Raymond of Chatto and Windus[1] thought of you as the most suitable man who could be found; and, in view of my last conversation with you, I am writing for them merely to ask whether the project interests you. There would be no point in going further at the moment because nothing has been done yet towards securing the necessary support which would make it possible to pay an adequate salary. But I shall be very glad if you will read over the report and consider whether in principle such

1–Harold Raymond (1887–1975): a partner in Chatto & Windus, 1919–53; chairman of Chatto & Windus, 1953–4; celebrated for inventing the Book Tokens scheme which was adopted by the British Book Trade in 1932.

a post would interest you or not. If you feel definitely that it is not the sort of work that you would care to undertake, I should like to know soon; otherwise there is no great hurry. Naturally there is with any new foundation no guarantee of performance but, as I said, if it developed in the way in which its supporters are sanguine enough to believe that it will, it should prove permanent and satisfactory.

Will you in any case drop me a line to let me know that you have received this letter, and consider the possibility of talking to Faber about it on your return. I trust that it will be no unwelcome interruption of your holiday.[1]

Yours sincerely,
[T. S. Eliot]

FROM *Vivien Eliot*   MS Valerie Eliot

11 July 1935   68 Clarence Gate Gardens,
                                    Regents Park, N.W.1
                                    Paddington 8630[2]

Dearest Tom,

I have just bought your 3 books & am reading them. I think *all are wonderful*. I *should* have *been* at *Canterbury* but I *was frightened away from England by threatening letters*. I left England *June 22nd* – returning unexpectedly. I *wrote* to you *from Paris*. Am *returning to France* as soon as I am able. I have posted to you today by *registered post* a *very important printed announcement & invitation to Paris* for the occasion of *Jean de Menasce* being *received into the Church*. It is an important matter.[3] I wrapped the letters in tissue paper & sealed it & put all in covering envelope. I showed this to Miss Swan at 24 Russell Square today (July 10th) when I was in the waiting room at 24 Russell Square at 5 p.m.[4] I am

1 – Siepmann replied from Cornwall (n.d.) that he would be interested in principle.
2 – A new telephone number: TSE would have had only the old one: Ambassador 1518.
3 – The following day (12 July), VHE wrote in her diary: 'The question is whether he will go to Paris to be present at Jean de Menasce's ceremony, or not. It is worth anything to get him back, and I have shown that all through. I shall go to Paris . . . My belief is that he wants to get back to me, and is in *chains*. And that Jean de Menasce has offered him a way of escape, escape *to me*.'
4 – Ethel Swan, a Faber & Gwyer 'pioneer', joined the firm on 12 Oct. 1925, as telephonist and receptionist, retiring in 1972 after 47 years. Peter du Sautoy reported in 1971: 'These duties she still performs with admirable skill and charm . . . She has an amazing memory for voices and it is certain that if James Joyce were to return to earth to telephone a complaint

told you do not often go to your Office Now? Less & less. *Why is this?*[1]
Are the other Directors *rude to you?* Or <u>are</u> *you ill?* WHY do you not *act*

(he called us "Feebler and Fumbler") she would say "Good morning, Mr Joyce" before he could introduce himself, as if he had previously been telephoning only yesterday. Many a visiting author or publisher from overseas has felt more kindly towards Faber & Faber as a result of Miss Swan's friendly recognition' ('Farewell, Russell Square', *The Bookseller* no. 3410 [1 May 1971], 2040).

A profile of 'Swannie' in retirement noted that she had built up an 'extraordinary range of warm and wide personal friendships which later made her a unique character in the publishing trade': 'She remembers some of the many people she met: T. E. Lawrence, whose eyes were curiously vivid, gave his name as Shaw, and would not in any circumstances admit to being Lawrence of Arabia; Ezra Pound, W. H. Auden, a very friendly person who came in when he was a fresh complexioned young man of about 20; Stravinsky, Britten, Epstein and indeed a great roll call of poets and musicians, actors, artists and soldiers who came to Faber & Faber . . .

'Miss Swan had a great affection and respect for Walter de la Mare, but her favourite was T. S. Eliot, whom she admired both as poet and playwright and also as a Faber colleague . . . He was a devoted sender of postcards to "Swannie": over the years there are cards from Montreal, Morocco, Switzerland, Canada, Barbados (where he flourished and was very dark brown) St Louis (where the best waffles were to be had) and many other places. The later postcards are cheerful collaborations between Eliot and his second wife, Valerie' ('At the Faber Switchboard', *The Bookseller*, 2 June 1971, 2662).

In a copy of the first edn of *CP*: 'Inscribed for Ethel Swan by her old friend T. S. Eliot' (TSE library).

1 – VHE had been applying to F&F for some months in an effort to find out more about TSE, if possible to see him. On Fri., 8 Mar. 1935 (as she recorded in her diary), she nerved herself to go to 24 Russell Square, accompanied by the young Franzel, Jan Culpin's son, who had just got out of Germany: 'To think I have allowed myself to be *frightened* & *intimidated* into a state of mind in which I have *never dared* to go *openly* & *honestly* to Faber & Faber's & demand to see *Tom*! *What* a *history* for the English nation to read & marvel at in years to come when these records of mine are *released*. Obviously, having Franz. to go with me, the simple, good boy that he is, made it perfectly easy & *natural*. <u>After all this time!</u> Oh the *cowardly* ----- funks, the English middle classes. It makes me laugh. Only by *thinking*, lately, a *great deal about all* my *intimate* past with *Ottoline Morrell* has brought me to the realisation of how utterly *Alien* to <u>her</u> mind & her feelings all this *mad* behaviour wld. seem. So I saw *dear* Miss Swan, & Tom's secretary, Miss O'Donovan, a very nice, *tired* girl. *We did not see Tom.* They said he was not there & that he is very *erratic*. *Tom* never *was erratic.* He was the most regular of men, liking his meals at home, his Church, his club very seldom, & a most sweet & homely man. It is *not* right of Tom to refuse to come home & it is *cruel*, anti-social, anti-religious, *anti*-economic, *un*tidy, stupid, un-moral, & in NO way excusable . . . Miss Swan said she would come to tea with me.'

On 9 Mar. Brigid O'Donovan assured her that 'all letters & communications do reach Tom, & that all pass through her hands'.

On Weds., 13 Mar. VE called again at F&F, at four o'clock in the afternoon: 'I saw Miss Swan who first said he *was* there. So I waited in the waiting room, & made up how I should be very quiet & gentle with him. Then Miss Swan be-thought her that she had *not* seen him come back after lunch. She offered to get the Secretary down again, & so she did. This time the Secretary, Miss O'Donovan, looked rather *sick*. I said, so Mr Eliot is not always here for the Board Meetings? Then I said of course you know I shall have to *keep* on coming here – & she said "Of-course it is for you to decide" & I said loudly "it is *too absurd*, I have been *with dignity*, & come back here to *me*, your wife, where you can have *space*, & rooms to work in & rooms to sleep in. A <u>clean bed</u> is <u>something</u>, & a quiet room to work in & a *respectable life*. Is it *Isabel Lockyer* who is rude to you & who drives you away from your Office? There is ONLY ONE WAY FOR YOU. You must come back here, & quickly. *I told Miss Swan* & tell *you* that *whenever* you come to *this* door, *day or night*, & *knock with yr. fist*, & *shout out Vivienne, it is Tom*, I shall open, & you will find *all ready*. Or you can *knock* on the *window pane* with yr. *stick*. I enclose cheque for 11/s for books.

Your respectful wife
Vivienne H. Eliot

Vamp vamp vamp —— its enough to drive you *insane* ——

---

frightened away *too long. I am his wife*["] – so then I left. . . . Miss *Swan* was *very nice* & sensitive & assured me that Tom *seemed* well, & so I gave *her* my telephone number – [.]'

(On 14 Mar. she reflected in her diary: 'I wish I could see Bertie again (Earl Russell). I have not seen him for *10* or *11* or *12 years*. . . . I mean only that Bertrand Russell seemed to understand me, as Ottoline Morrell does. They are both mad *fearless aristocrats*.')

On Weds., 28 Mar. 1934: 'Then I telephoned Faber & Faber, and asked for Tom, at 3.30. Mr De la Mare's secretary answered, & said there was a Committee & she cld. not ask him to come. I telephoned again at 5, & was told he had just gone. I telephoned again at 6, spoke to Miss Swan. They were all very nice to me. So I shall *go on*.'

On 31 May, however, she sought to consult GCF: '*Of-course* Faber has got an *Irish* secretary, & a great big *bullying looking woman*. I shd think he would find it difficult to get a *decent* secretary *at all*, in these circumstances. She said she had her *orders*, & I *should* have replied that I have my *RIGHTS*. I am <u>SO</u> feeble, wilted & easily *fooled* by these people. When I said to her that Tom cld come home at *any* moment she said rudely "I *know* he can".'

On Weds. 10 July she went again to F&F, where Miss Swan told her 'that Tom does *not* go there often now, & that has *deeply upset* me'. The following day, VHE recorded in her diary: 'My *belief* is that he wants to get back to me, & *is in chains*.'

See further Brigid O'Donovan's memoir 'The Love Song of T. S. Eliot's Secretary', *Confrontation* (literary journal of Long Island University), no. 11 (Fall/Winter 1975); and Anne Ridler's letter to the *TLS*, 13 Apr. 1984, including this comment: 'while Eliot himself found Vivienne's pursuit of him humiliating and agonizing, he never felt indifference to her pain'.

TO *Stella Bowen*[1]

cc

11 July 1935   [Faber & Faber Ltd]

Dear Miss Bowen,

    I should, of course, be very glad to see any article by Ford Madox Ford with a view to publication in the *Criterion*.[2]

                         Yours sincerely,
                         [T. S. Eliot]

TO *Michael Roberts*

ts Berg

11 July 1935   Faber & Faber Ltd

Dear Roberts,

    I must apologise for not having answered sooner your letter of June 16th, and I now have your letter of July 8th.[3] We have been somewhat

---

1–Esther 'Stella' Bowen (1893–1947), Australian artist and writer, trained in London at the Westminster School of Art, and in 1918 fell in love with the novelist Ford Madox Ford, who was her senior by twenty years (she separated from him in 1927). Her memoir *Drawn from Life* (1940) narrates her experiences among writers and artists in London and Paris.
2–Bowen offered (24 June) to submit an article on 'Techniques' ('about 5500 words') that Ford had sent from New York with the suggestion that it might be of interest to TSE.
3–Roberts wrote on 16 June that work on the anthology was well advanced: already he had permission to include a wide selection by poets including Yeats (12 pp.), Hopkins (20 pp.), Herbert Read (20 pp.), Spender (16 pp), and Auden (20 pp). He had received no further word from EP, and was awaiting replies from various others including Edith Sitwell, John Crowe Ransom and Allen Tate. He found it difficult to make a twenty-page selection from TSE, and suggested:
    Whispers of Immortality
    Sweeney among the Nightingales
    Portrait of a Lady or Prufrock
    ? Waste Land III ?
    Journey of the Magi
    Marina
    ? Fragment of an Agon ?
    ? Animula ?
    Triumphal March
'Of course,' he added, 'I would be very willing to include more than the twenty pages if you could agree – e.g. drop Portrait & Prufrock & Fragment & include more Waste Land.'
    On 8 July he ventured further: 'The more I think about your poems, the more I become convinced that the only selection which would be as fair to you as I have been to Hopkins, Yeats, Pound, Read, Graves & Laura Riding:
    Sweeney among the Nightingales
    The Waste Land (complete, but without notes)
    Journey of the Magi
    Ash Wednesday I
    Animula

worried by the length of the selection from three of your poets, Read, Spender and myself. Hopkins and Auden are admittedly men who need a good deal of space to get their full effect, and I don't think that 20 pages is at all too long for either of them. But Read and Spender and myself are not voluminous poets, and we <i.e. F. & F.> feel anxious to avoid the risk of people feeling that they have got all they need of us <i.e. R. S. & E.> from your anthology. I should suggest 12 pages, the same length as for Yeats, for each of us.

As for your second selection from myself, I have always in the past refused to allow *The Waste Land* to be used either in part or whole in anthologies. To take a part mutilates it, and to take the whole means taking what I regret to say is the only one of my poems which most people feel it necessary to read. You may demur to this last statement, but I am sure there is some truth in it. And, furthermore, if I gave *The Waste Land* for your anthology, I should find it difficult to refuse others in future. I should be glad of course if you thought fit to include 'Fragment of an Agon' and most people would expect 'Gerontion' to turn up, although I have no feelings about that myself. I suppose there is no passage in *Murder in the Cathedral* which you think suitable? But don't think that I want to interfere in any way with your actual selection. All that I am certain of is that I think Read, Spender and myself should be cut down to 12 pages, and that *The Waste Land* should be omitted. You may find that you want to include a few more poets or a little more from the work of some of the other poets.

I hope that you have good climbing in Savoy.

Yours ever,
T. S. Eliot

'You may object that this gives you a little more space than I have given to the others, but it seems to be necessary, and no one but yourself would suggest that it was otherwise.

'I am printing 22 pages of Yeats & 22 of Hopkins.'

TO *George Bell*

photocopy Valerie Eliot[1]

11 July 1935   Faber & Faber Ltd

My dear Lord Bishop,

Very many thanks for your gratifying letter of the 10th and for your kindness in commenting on the play at such length.[2] I had rather suspected that the first impression made upon you was not wholly favourable, and I am therefore all the more pleased to have your considered version. I do indeed intend to pursue my dramatic attempts further.

Again with many thanks, I am, my Lord Bishop,

Yours very sincerely,

T. S. Eliot

TO *Charles Williams*   cc

12 July 1935   [Faber & Faber Ltd]

My dear Williams,

I am very sorry to find that I am too full up next week to be able to take any lunch engagement now.[3] One reason for my being so crowded is that I am going away on the 20th for about three weeks on visits. Would it be too late when I come back?

1 – Though the original is lost, the letter survives as a photocopy made by EVE, and a ts copy by Donald Adamson.

2 – 'I meant before now to have written about "Murder in the Cathedral", following up my brief note immediately after I had seen the play, but various things got in the way. I do want however to repeat what very great pleasure I found in seeing and hearing the play . . . I had heard before – indeed before reading the play – that the last scene might strike me as rather strange, and I was prepared to sit tight and wonder, but I liked the last scene too, very much. The Sermon was splendid, and the whole diction, helped no doubt by the way in which Speaight and the others actually spoke, was so straightforward and so effective. The Sermon was really most remarkable. But, as I say, I liked the whole play. I thought "The Rock" was very fine, but "Murder in the Cathedral" is finer still, and I do think you have found a real métier, and I can only wish that you may continue on it for many years to come, and will give us successive plays on great subjects in the religious spirit, or on great religious themes.'

On 4 June TSE had sent Bell a copy of *MiC*, inscribed: 'To George Bell, Bishop of Chichester † , who must assume some responsibility for this outrage: 4-vi-35. T. S. Eliot' (quoted by Mrs Henrietta Bell in 'Mr T. S. Eliot', *The Times*, 7 Jan. 1965). Bell had then written to TSE on 14 June – 'I have delayed writing to thank you, in the hope of having a couple of hours free to read it' – but commitments had overtaken him, so he would have to see the production first. On 17 June he wrote again to say 'how wonderfully your play moved me'.

3 – Williams (11 July) invited TSE to lunch at Amen House (Oxford University Press), Warwick Square, London E.C.4 – if TSE could give him a choice of one or two days.

Now I have looked over the stuff you sent me and thought about it.[1] Incidentally, if at any moment you need it back you have only to ring up my secretary. I am afraid that I am no longer quite clear as to what were my terms of reference. Without having had time to go through the works of each poet, which I think you hardly expected me to do, and make sure that I agree with you on all the selections, your batch seems to me a very interesting one indeed. A few suggestions occur to me. I am not sure whether it is sufficient for your purpose that nothing you include should be in the *Oxford Book of Verse*, or whether the poems should as well strike the ordinary reader very freshly. In this case it seems to me that there is practically nothing one can quote from Donne's songs and sonnets that is not very well known indeed, and for anything less known you would have to go to his religious verse. Second I have a feeling that you could find a passage or two in Marston's 'Sophonisba' worthy to stand by what you have already taken. Third, Minor Metaphysicals. I should like to see something by Aurelian Townsend, especially his lovely Dialogue of The Reaper',[2] and it seems to me that there are several of the poets in Saintsbury's three volumes of Carolines, who ought to be represented. But as I have already said, I should like to have my memory refreshed as to the terms of reference.

I also want to mention that John Hayward told me the other day that he had seen an announcement of your book which mentioned myself among others, or with one or two others, as an assistant editor. You will understand that I don't wish my name to appear. Partly because any service I have the time and the knowledge to render you will be too slight to deserve mention, and partly because I don't generally care to be associated with books published by other firms than my own. If any publisher used my name in this way without my consent, I should have to take steps to interfere.[3]

1 – Williams wrote on 27 June: 'I am sending you with this the package of stuff for Gollancz's *New Book of English Verse*. I have enclosed a list of the people done and a briefer list of people that I haven't properly done yet. But it would be of considerable help if you could bring yourself to comment on the present collection.'

2 – Aurelian Townshend, 'A Dialogue Betwixt Time and a Pilgrime' (1653).

3 – The Gollancz catalogue ('first Autumn list' issued in July) included this detail: 'Edited by Charles Williams. Associate Editors: T. S. Eliot, Ernest de Selincourt, E. M. Tillyard, Lord David Cecil'. Victor Gollancz himself protested to CW, 15 July: 'I should always hate anyone to think that we had used his name incorrectly: I should particularly hate it in the case of a member of another Publishing House . . .'

Williams responded to TSE's letter with contrition, 13 July: 'it is most frightfully awkward about your name. In the letters that I wrote to Tillyard, de Selincourt, and David Cecil I see I said:

Will you be in London from the middle of August? If so, will you lunch with me at the earliest opportunity?

Yours ever,

[T. S. Eliot]

TO *G. R. Elliott*[1]   CC

12 July 1935   [Faber & Faber Ltd]

Dear Mr Elliott,

I am glad to hear that you are coming to England and that there will be some prospect of meeting you at last.[2] I had better let you know at once that I expect to be away from the 20th of this month until about the 8th of August, so if we cannot meet before then I hope that you will be returning to London later.

I am distinctly puzzled by your essay and should be glad of some elucidation in talk.[3] My feeling about the *Criterion* is that while I am ready to accept interesting essays from a definitely and clearly non-Christian point of view, e.g. of a Communist kind, I ought to be careful about using material which is, so to speak, on the fringes of Christianity. I must confess that I don't know from your essay whether you are a Christian or not, but I am more than doubtful whether this essay is compatible with orthodoxy. I am always suspicious of references to the sacrament of the altar and the objects which it includes as symbols. In so far as the latter is a symbol that seems to me a secondary aspect of it, and I see no interest

---

"It would, I hope, not involve very strenuous work, but I hope that you would have no objection to your name appearing with those of the other assessors, coadjutors, or whatever is the correct term. You will not of course be regarded as having any final responsibility."

'I realize that I didn't write to you, but I was under every kind of impression that I had included this use of your name when I asked you if you would be good enough to help, and I had proceeded happily on this understanding . . . But whatever, under God, is the fact, the world is now more hellish than ever . . . I perfectly understand your position, and you will, I know, be good enough to believe in my own sincerity.'

1–G. R. Elliott was co-editor of *English Poetry of the Nineteenth Century: A Connected Representation of Poetic Art and Thought from 1798 to 1914* (1931).

2–Elliott wrote on 8 July (en route for Germany) that he would be visiting London for two weeks on his excursion and hoped to be able to see TSE.

3–Elliott submitted a piece entitled 'The Altar Among Emblems', which he was also sending to the *American Review*. Not in C.

See too Elliott, 'T. S. Eliot and Irving Babbitt', *American Review* 7 (Sept. 1936), 442–54.

myself in the latter apart from the sacrament of the altar. I hope that we may be able to discuss these matters.

Yours sincerely,
[T. S. Eliot]

TO *Frederic Prokosch*

12 July 1935   [Faber & Faber Ltd]

Dear Mr Prokosch,

Thank you for your letter and for the cable to yourself from Messrs Chatto & Windus, which I return herewith.[1] I congratulate you upon having secured satisfactory terms from such an excellent firm as Chattos, and a firm which is so satisfactory in its relations with its authors. As you say that you yourself don't understand the situation quite, I may be pardoned for failing to understand it myself. In your previous correspondence with me there was no reference to the book having been submitted to Chatto & Windus, and as you entered on discussion with me at such an early stage, I had half expected that we should be receiving a typescript, instead of the galleys which, I believe, Mr Saxton brought with him and which he immediately delivered to us. This question no doubt can be cleared up.

You will remember that you were advised that it would be better to try to launch the prose book successfully before attempting to publish the poems. In the circumstances I feel that Chatto & Windus are the people to whom it would be natural to offer the poems. I will send them on to Chattos if I hear from you to that effect.[2]

Yours sincerely,
[T. S. Eliot]

1–Prokosch wrote that he was sorry that *The Asiatics* had not been placed with F&F. 'How the whole thing happened is too intricate to explain . . . and I myself don't understand the situation quite . . . Concerning my preferences personally there was never a moment's doubt.' It was Saxton and Caufield who had decided in favour of Chatto & Windus. Nevertheless, Prokosch reported that he had retained the option on his next novel – 'so that you will have a chance on that; and . . . you may have the poems of course if you shd wish them, as I desperately hope you do'.

2–Prokosch's next letter, 2 Aug.: 'I implore you to believe that the whole matter regarding *The Asiatics* got out of hand through no fault of mine, and that at no point whatever did I really expect or desire any publisher other than Faber until, at Saxton's suggestion, the deal with Chatto had to be closed.'

TO *John Hampden*[1]

12 July 1935   [Faber & Faber Ltd]

Dear Sir,

I have your letter of July 8th together with the copy of the Nelson Classics edition of Tennyson's early poems.[2] I am interested in your suggestion, and my terms for an introduction of between 2,500 and 3,000 words would be twenty guineas.

Yours very truly,

[T. S. Eliot]

FROM *Vivien Eliot*

MS Bodleian

[14 July 1935]   [68 Clarence Gate Gardens]

MY dear Tom, I wrote to you yesterday and the day before to warn you that Isabel Lockyer is one of your enemies, and I registered both letters, one of which contained a cheque. I also begged you, once more, for the thousandth time, to face up to your enemies and blackmailers by coming here openly where there is nothing but security and safety, for you. It almost makes one doubt your sanity, the way you are hiding yourself up as if you have committed a crime, and the shame and slight on your family, the name of Eliot, is more than one could believe an Eliot could do. Have you lost all shame? and have you forgotten Christianity and

---

See too FVM to Saxton, 29 Aug. 1935: 'I thought I ought to send you the enclosed letter from Prokosch to Eliot; there is something unpleasant about the way it squirms, and I don't like the way he tries to pass the buck. There isn't much profit in post-mortems, and I send the letter to you, not that I am in the least inclined to trust his version, but because you may be glad to keep a weather eye lifted towards – what shall we say – the story-teller. The remark at the top of page 2 is not accurate as to Eliot's letter of 12th July; as you will see by the copy of Eliot's letter enclosed, to which the last letter of Prokosch's was the answer.

'As we school girls used to say, burn this. I mean, I don't see that it is desirable, or necessary, to do anything about it; but as an unpleasant curiosity I thought you would be interested to see it.'

1 – John Hampden (1898–1974), author and publishers' editor; taught English Literature at Queen's College, London, 1929–32; General Editor, Thomas Nelson & Sons, 1932–7. He worked for the British Council, 1942–6; edited *British Book News*, 1942–6; and was a member of the Council and Executive, The National Book League, 1942–6.

2 – Hampden invited TSE to write an introduction of between 2,500 and 3,000 words to a reissue in the Nelson Classics of Tennyson's early poems, omitting the four Idylls of the King.

See TSE, 'Introduction' in *Poems of Tennyson* (Thomas Nelson & Sons, 1936); repr., as 'In Memoriam', in TSE's *Essays Ancient and Modern* (1936).

become a Heathen. Or are you STILL terrorrised [*sic*] and blackmailed to keep out of the way, if so, you know it is a Criminal Offence, blackmail is, and no-one need put up with it for one hour if they have the courage of a dog. I hear from your Office (or is it no longer your Office at 24, Russell Square?) I hear that you now very seldom go there at all. Why is this? Do you mean to tell me that the other Directors there behave in such a way that you feel you cannot even use your Office regularly? If so I say I will make it hot for anyone who is not kind to you, and as you know I have always said that *if a hair of your head is harmed I will* make the whole world pay. I see the others at 24, Russell Square, and they are all very nice and civil people and always kind to me, as they always were. So I can only believe that either you have let yourself go to pieces and will not work at your Office, *or*, that you are being ill-treated and driven away. You should avail yourself of the protection of a wife while you still have one . . .

[incomplete]

Another transcript of this letter in VHE's diary includes these variant readings:

Are you confined? Are you PAID to keep away from me?? *HOW MUCH??* I hope you get a living out of it. On the other hand for all I know you may be living in splendour, squandering money, and leading a bad life.

FROM *Reginald Miller*[1] TO *Vivien Eliot*   TS Bodleian

15 July 1935   110 Harley Street, London W.1

Dear Mrs Eliot,

I turned up at the flat this evening as arranged at about 6 o'clock, but you were nowhere to be found.

I met the solicitor's clerk bringing back some boxes and things which he said they did not claim, and I heard that they had all that they were demanding, and that the men were leaving. Consequently after waiting for some time I came away.

1–Dr Reginald Miller (1879–1948), 110 Harley Street, London, w.1: Consulting Physician to St Mary's Hospital and to the Paddington Green Children's Hospital, London; a general physician with a particular interest in children, he was a recognised expert in the problems of mental deficiency in children and in rheumatic diseases and heart diseases in childhood (on which he wrote several articles). He was the first editor, with Dr Hugh Thursfield, of the *Archives on Disease in Childhood*. Brought up in Hampstead, it is probable that he was an early friend of the Haigh-Wood family. In 1937 he was senior physician, St Mary's Hospital.

I cannot find you in the telephone directory or I would ring you up tonight. But I think I will call on you tomorrow morning, between 9.30 and 10 to see if you are all right and able to proceed to France. I shall call unless you ring up to stop me (Maida Vale, 4192).

I hope that this unpleasant episode will not upset you too much. To get right away again would, I feel sure, be a help.

Yours sincerely,
Reginald Miller.

FROM *Vivien Eliot* TO *Reginald Miller*   TS Bodleian

16 July 1935   [69 Clarence Gate Mansions]

Dear Doctor Miller,

Just a line to thank you very much indeed for your kindness in coming so promptly when I called, and for attending me here all yesterday morning, and for your calling and writing since. All of which I very much appreciate. I have seen our old family Solicitor to-day, and told him all. He was very kind, and will try now to claim back such things which were mine, and also to get compensation for damage to my health and home. It hurt me so terrible [*sic*] that they took away all those photographs of the Eliot family which I have had round me all the last twenty years, and of which many were sent to me and are in point of fact mine.[1]

It seems to me an act of maniacal cruelty, but I do not think our old family solicitor attributes it all to my *husband*, by any means at all. He speaks well of my husband, and says he is still a Trustee and that he is very thankful that he is a Trustee.

---

1 – The second entry by bailiffs took place on 15 July: according to VHE in her diary, two large men forced their way into her flat and seized TSE's files and photographs. VHE called Dr Miller for assistance (he rushed over), and locked the men into her flat – but they managed to escape.

VHE had consulted Dr Miller on 8 May 1935: '[I] had a very fairly satisfactory conversation so far as health is concerned. He said he had never seen Tom again, & that so far as *he* is concerned we might *all* have been *de*-funct. He seemed pleased to see me again . . .' (Diary)

Soon afterwards, she penned this letter: 'Dear Dr Miller Further to our conversation of May 8th my husband only has to return here, *to live*, & everything is open to him & everything is his. All is in perfect order. I have made this clear to all concerned hundreds & thousands of times. – If he had any *friends*, or any sincere people of *honour* around him, they would of-course long ago have urged upon him the necessity of returning here *openly*, no matter how distasteful to his feelings, for the sake of the honour & good name of a very great many people.'

Yes I shall try to get off tomorrow, but I feel very shaken, and the heat is awful. I will send you a card when I get there if I may, and will you please send me your address when you leave town for your holiday.[1]

Yours sincerely,
[V. Haigh Eliot]

TO *Mary Trevelyan*

CC

18 July 1935   [Faber & Faber Ltd]

Dear Madam,

I should be glad to come and speak to your students in October.[2] Sunday evening is never very convenient for me but it would be a little more convenient if the meeting could start at 8.30 instead of 8.15. Would you like me to give a reading of some of my poems with some general remarks on poetry interspersed? In my experience this is on the whole more lovely than a pure reading or a pure lecture.

Yours sincerely,
[T. S. Eliot]

1–See too MH-W to VHE, 18 July 1935: 'I am completely mystified about the men who you told me were seizing papers at your flat. If they came with *no* authority & against your wish you should have called the police & had them thrown out. In these circumstances, Dr Miller who was there, would surely have told you to do so. But as that evidently could not have been the case, they must have had some [verso pasted to page].'

James & James to VHE, 22 Aug. 1935: 'In reply to your letter asking for the return of the articles belonging to you which were wrongfully taken away by the Sherriff's officers we are now informed by Messrs Bird & Bird that those things which were found not to belong to Mr T. S. Eliot have been returned to your flat. We trust the matter may now be considered as closed.'

2–Trevelyan (who had first written to TSE in Nov. 1934) invited him to give a reading or to speak on poetry at Student Movement House, on a Sunday evening in the autumn – specifically she suggested perhaps 13 Oct. at 8.15 p.m. 'Many of the students here are your very fervent admirers, and it would give us all very great pleasure if we might have you as our guest.' She noted in her unpublished memoir 'The Pope of Russell Square', of this event: 'He read *The Waste Land* and *The Hollow Men*, I remember, with his head on one side, a harsh voice, and a face of acute agony.'

19 July 1935   [Faber & Faber Ltd]

Dear Mr MacNeice,

Thank you for the poems with which I am very much pleased.[1] They
have gone to the printer. I should like, however, to take one liberty and
omit all the dates that you have appended. It never seems to me desirable
to date poems at this stage. It might be desirable later with a large collected
edition, although even in that case I think it is better to date poems in
blocks according to what the author recognises to be the important
periods in his development, rather than individually. One should certainly
keep a record of dates but I think at this stage at least they detract rather
than add.

                          With all best wishes,
                          Yours sincerely,
                          [T. S. Eliot]

TO *Michael Roberts*   TS Berg

19 July 1935   Faber & Faber Ltd

My dear Roberts,

Your letter of the 13th has been thoroughly discussed by my committee.[2]
They are a weak-kneed lot of men and your ferocity has had the desired

1 – MacNeice submitted his revised collection on 15 July. 'I have cut out several and put in
eight new ones . . . thirtytwo in all.'
2 – Roberts spoke firmly, and with prescient good sense: 'I enclose the table of contents which
I had proposed for the anthology. In one or two cases, notably that of Lawrence, I am still
negotiating with the holders of the copyright, but you will see that I have already persuaded
many of them to allow me to represent them by a collection which really does give a just idea
of their work, and at the same time illustrates the development of poetic technique in general.
I could not possibly do the same with your work in *less* than 20 pages, and I repeat that a
selection which omits the *Waste Land* [sic] is a misrepresentation. It is quite probable, as you
say, that readers not very keenly interested in the poetry, might argue, after having read my
selection from your poems, that they had read all that was essential. But the same applies
to my selections from a good many non-Faber poets, too, and I presume that I am being
employed by Fabers to cajole poets and publishers into allowing me to make such selections.
Fabers can't expect to skim the cream off other people's list and sacrifice nothing themselves.
   'But this is a short view: if the anthology as I see it is accepted, it is bound to have a notable
effect on public taste. It will be the standard book of this kind for 10 or 12 years, and should
add to the number of people who will buy your *Poems 1925–1937*. Again "Most people"
you say, "would expect *Gerontion* to turn up." But I have tried to avoid overlapping existing
anthologies, and found, indeed, that if I made an honest selection it was easy to do so.

effect; so you are to have the whole of *The Waste Land* without the notes, and my objection of the quantity of Read, Spender and myself is overruled; so go ahead.

The only omission that I regret myself is of Vachel Lindsay. I know it is bad writing with a rather feeble mind behind it. Nevertheless, he did, it seems to me, play a certain part in popularising modern poetry unintentionally. Possibly a few things like 'The Congo' helped to reconcile many people to the work of better writers. This is, however, only a personal opinion.[1]

Yours ever,

T. S. Eliot

Herbert Read occupies, in fact, 19 pages: it is absolutely essential to represent his long poems and *The Analysis of Love* and *Beata l'Alma* is the best way of showing two techniques. Stephen Spender has 17 pages, only 7 of which are in the Faber book, which will soon be out of date anyway. *The Uncreative Chaos* (4 pages), hasn't been printed at all. Yeats, I find, has 19 pages; Auden 15.

'You say that if "The Waste Land" is included, you will find it difficult to refuse other anthologists: I am already introducing a note to say that Laura Riding and Robert Graves have made a concession in this case, not because their feelings about anthologies have changed, but because they believe the book is exceptional. Your name should be added to the list.

'I have tried hard to find a good poem by Aldington, but I can't. The trouble with the Imagists was that they hardly ever wrote a pure Imagist poem: they would keep on dragging in their own sad selves and doing a little public weep. H.D. is a bit better than most, though her poems are trivial. Wallace Stevens is better still. Monro ultimately wrote three good poems, without a dirty thumb mark.

'The Americans, Hart Crane, Allen Tate, John Crowe Ransom, have still a lot to teach the little boys, Barker, Thomas, Gascoyne, who came running on behind the poetical procession. Charles Madge *must* be represented by an amount of the same order as that of anyone under 40, or the book will look silly in 5 years time. There is no question of "promise" in this case. The stuff earns its place on its own merits, which is hardly true of Barker, Gascoyne, Thomas, who go in partly for the sake of the publishers' "up to the minute" blurb.

'The book is over-crowded already. If anyone were to be added, it should be Vachel Lindsay, Edgell Rickword and William Plomer. But no more money can be afforded. Forgive me for arguing so fiercely for the book as I see it. I honestly believe that it happens, at the moment, that a genuine selection of this kind is the one which will pay the publisher best. And in any case, I'd hate to be driven back to second-bests.'

On 25 Sept.: 'I propose to include *Sweeney among the Nightingales, The Waste Land, The Journey of the Magi, Ash-Wednesday I* and *Difficulties of a Statesman.* If one must be ruled out, let it be *Sweeney. Animula* could replace *Ash-Wednesday I* if you prefer it, and *Triumphal March* could take the place of *Difficulties* – unless you cared to offer a third section of the poem, which would be better still.'

1 – Roberts replied on 24 July: 'I am very pleased about the committee's decision and I hope that the anthology will have none of the adverse effects that you fear: it might, for the moment, but I don't think it will in the long run.

'Vachel Lindsay has been in and out of my list several times. I'm rather against the "Congo" which appears everywhere, but there is *General William Booth enters Heaven* &

19 July 1935   Faber & Faber Ltd

My dear Stephen,

I have presented your problem to the committee, and return David Higham's letter herewith.[1] The decision is this, that we are quite ready to publish your story at the same price and on the same terms as the Cresset Press, and bring it out in the coming autumn. It would be still better if you had another story to make the volume bigger, because we think that with two stories we could sell the volume at 5s. instead of 3s. 6d., for the benefit of both author and publisher. Anyway there is the £50 for you.

I should like to know how long it would have to be after that before you could expect to have another full length book. We should of course like to have something to publish in the spring, if you were ready.

Yours affectionately,

Tom

---

some others. *The Virginians are coming again* is interesting Auden-sentiment in a different rhetoric, too. But space is the difficulty: I didn't post my letter to H.D. in the end, and her poems look very thin. Allen Tate's *Oath* might go out, too, but I don't really want to drop anything. The book was to be "about" 300 pages & 20 pages of introduction. How much latitude will the committee allow me? The money question need not worry them; I'm so convinced that the extra pages will make a big difference to the book that I'm prepared to sacrifice all my advance for the moment in the hope of recovering it when advance royalties have been earned.

'Can you tell me when Fabers hope to send the MS to the printers? I have had it sent to you now so that you may make any criticism in good time. I expect that, since the material will be ready, Fabers will wish the book to appear before Christmas. That ought to be quite possible if it goes to press at the beginning of October.

'I am glad that you detected that my "ferocity" was hypocritical editor-to-publisher. But the wish was completely sincere.'

Roberts did ultimately include 'General William Booth enters into Heaven' in the anthology.

1–SS passed on a letter to TSE from the agent David Higham (Curtis Brown) with the news that Dennis Cohen at the Cresset Press was minded to bring out in the autumn a short book of short stories by Spender. 'The total length required is only 25,000 words and I think we could probably get £50 advance. Publication could hardly interfere with any other publisher's plans for you.' Spender asked TSE (11 July) whether such an arrangement would be acceptable to F&F. 'This offer is rather tempting, partly because I am at the moment writing a story which is exactly the length required. On the other hand, since an excision of 25,000 words would blast my volume of stories with Faber, I am inclined to turn the offer down.'

TO *George Bell*   Lambeth Palace Library

20 July 1935   Faber & Faber Ltd

My dear Lord Bishop,

By good chance your letter found me this morning at my office, just before leaving for the country. I am going down into Sussex for the weekend, and thence to Gloucestershire and Wales, and shall not be in town again until the 10th August. So I shall be unable to accept your kind invitation to lunch on July 29th.

But as for a Pageant Play, that is something which I know I cannot do.[1] I can write words for such plays, when the visual design, the scenario and the construction are in the hands of someone like Martin Browne; and this is all that I did for *The Rock*. For a Pageant Play I am convinced that the prime necessity is a producer of imagination, rather than a poet or even a dramatist. I am partly incompetent simply, and partly incompetent because I am not much interested in that off-shoot of drama. Then again, I find that I have to be very parsimonious of my time. Only by unscrupulously restricting my engagements during the winter months – both business and social – am I able to get one piece of original work done; and if I undertook such a job as this, even under Browne's supervision, I should be postponing for a year anything of my own. And I am no longer young enough to be able to postpone things, especially as a great deal of my life has been wasted in the past. I write rather fully, and put the case rather strongly, because I should not like you to feel that I am ungrateful: for I am aware that without your initiative and support I should not have had the most valuable opportunities of writing *The Rock* and *Murder in the Cathedral*. But I feel that what I should try now would be 'religious drama' somewhat in the sense of, let me say without appearance of being over-ambitious, *Polyeucte*.[2]

1–Bishop Bell wrote on 19 July that he had been talking to Francis Neilson, an ex-MP now resident in the USA, who hailed from Liverpool: 'He is very rich and is deeply interested both in Drama and the Church. He has been a great benefactor to Liverpool Cathedral, and gave a large sum of money to the Cathedral the other day. He is very anxious to help the Cathedral to have a Pageant Play about the history of Cathedral building, starting with the earliest Church building and going down to the present day. Remembering our talk about Canterbury Cathedral and the Pageant of Cathedral building there (though it has not come off) I could not help feeling that you were the very man . . . Mr Neilson knows what he is talking about, and has a very strong sense of the Church.'

2–See TSE, 'The possibility of a religious drama', *REP* (Croydon Repertory Theatre), Sept. 1934: 'The Church has the opportunity, greater now than in the period of industrial expansion, of gathering to itself, of educating and spiritualising, all the potential forces of civilisation. And these forces, gathered in to the Church, will consequently radiate out from

If I have not said enough to make my case convincing, I should like to have the opportunity of writing again.

I am, my dear Lord Bishop,
Yours very sincerely,
T. S. Eliot

TO *Rupert Doone* CC

22 July 1935   [Faber & Faber Ltd]

Dear Mr Doone,

I am sorry that you could not come in on Friday afternoon. I was expecting you at 2.30.[1] I am just going away for three weeks, and this is merely to say that I shall be very glad indeed to have you include *Sweeney Agonistes* in your October programme.[2] As for *Murder in the Cathedral*, that is an uncertain matter and I can't give you any decision about it. If it can be arranged, I want Martin Browne to have another chance of producing it and of course in a full size theatre, because I think that he

---

it. So that we may perhaps come to a time, in which a play as fundamentally Christian and Catholic as [Pierre Corneille's] *Polyeucte* may be written and may be performed successfully to audiences which will not be consciously attending a "religious play", because they will be imbued with the Christian and Catholic way of feeling, even when they ask only to be entertained.'

1–Doone wrote on 18 July: 'My reason for wanting to see you was, that Mr Anmer Hall has invited the Group Theatre to collaborate over a six month period at the Westminster Theatre. My proposal to you is, would you allow us to put on "Sweeney" in the first bill? which probably will begin in October next. There is also talk of trying out on Sunday evening "Murder in the Cathedral" later on but we have not definitely fixed upon this proposal.'

2–*SA* was licensed for public performance in the UK by the Lord Chamberlain's Office on 25 July 1935. The reader's report (BL) concludes: 'This "fragments [*sic*] of an Aristophanic melodrama" consist of "fragment of a prologue" and "fragment of an agon". In the former two girls tells their fortunes by cards and one of them, Doris, draws a coffin. They are joined by Sam Wauchope and three American friends who talk about London. In the second fragment besides these five there are Sweeney, Swarts and Snow, the last two merely playing nigger instruments. Sweeney talks in free verse about carrying Doris off to a cannibal island and eating her. Later he tells, also in verse, about a man who "did in" a girl in a bath and was not found out but apparently went mad. Then they all sing a chorus about dreaming they are going to be hanged. Serious poets are seldom happy when they relax – Swinburne's limericks are a notable exception – and I don't think this nonsense amusing. There is no harm in it. The word "copulation" is used on pp. 24 and 25. I don't think it is a necessarily banned word and think it would be rather absurd to cut it out of an eminent poet's verses, even comic ones: it is not indecent. Recommended for License, G. S. Street.' (Street [1867–1936]: journalist and novelist; author of *The Autobiography of a Boy* (1894), a satire on Oscar Wilde and Lord Alfred Douglas.)

could have made a very much better thing of it if he hadn't been so very handicapped. I am afraid that it will be some time before I can come to any decision about an alternative.[1]

Yours in haste,
[T. S. Eliot]

TO *Sidney Dark*[2]   CC

22 July 1935   [Faber & Faber Ltd]

Dear Mr Dark,

While I am certainly flattered by the invitation to write a Collect for the meeting on November 5th, I am terrified at the idea of venturing into what I have always considered an ecclesiastical preserve.[3] I am sure that Cranmer would have turned at the stake if he had any premonition of Collects being composed by people like myself. Don't you think that we still have at least one ecclesiastic who could do better than I could?

Sincerely yours,
[T. S. Eliot]

1 – Doone had written on 25 June: 'Robert Medley and I went to Canterbury to see your play at The Chapter House. We enjoyed it very much. The verse was very clearly spoken, but I felt not understood. None of its colors [*sic*] was used. I thought the Women of Canterbury themselves were too young and elegant. I thought Martin Browne was excelent [*sic*] as the fourth tempter. Robert Speight [*sic*] gave a very good and competent performance as the Archbishop. Particularly he was good in "the sermon", I thought. The costumes were disapointing [*sic*] except for the pale puce and yellow of Martin Browne's costume. The actual clearness [with] which the verse was spoken was really excelent [*sic*]. I thought the speed of "I have smelt them, the death bringers" was too slowly and deliberately spoken . . . We sat a row behind you, the other side of the gangway.'

2 – Sidney Dark (1872–1947), writer and journalist; editor of the Anglo-Catholic *Church Times*, 1924–41. His publications include *Archbishop Davidson and the English Church* (1929), *The Lambeth Conferences: Their History and Their Significance* (1930), *The Folly of Anti-Semitism* (1939), and *Not Such a Bad Life* (memoirs, 1941).

3 – A meeting was to be held on 5 Nov. at the Royal Albert Hall, London, concerning the subject of 'Christian Action in Social Problems', under the patronage of the Archbishop of Canterbury, the Bishop of London, and the Archbishop of York, with a view to expressing a non-party protest against the 'unreason, injustice and ruthlessness of prevailing social conditions'. Sidney Dark, Vice-Chairman of the Organising Committee, contacted TSE on 11 July: 'We are most anxious to have a special Collect for the meeting, which shall suggest the Christian attitude towards social problems, and which shall be phrased in a manner worthy of the occasion. It is the earnest desire of the committee that you may be persuaded to write it for us. Will you?'

TO *Geoffrey Curtis*   TS Houghton

St James's Day [25 July] 1935   Stamford House, Chipping
                                       Campden, Glos.[1]

My dear Curtis,

God bless you for your patience and Christian charity, towards one who
has appeared so negligent. I have thought continually of writing to you,
and have been hoping for a year and more to suggest myself for a weekend
at Shifnal.[2] My return from America involved a very drastic change in my
private life, which has been the cause of considerable strain and taken a
good deal of attention; and for each of the last two winters I have been
engaged on what is for me a considerable piece of work – considerable
not so much in its achievement as in the necessity for continuous effort to
keep enough free time for such work. Then the rest of the year is taken up
with routine and with the things which have had to be left undone in the
winter; and my holidays have been limited, as at present, to two weeks'
visits each summer.

First of all, I shall be in London by the 10th, probably for the rest of
the month, though I hope to get a fortnight or so of needed holiday alone
somewhere in September. I shall want to see you, and not simply for an
interview at Russell Square; the best would be if you would dine with me
one night at my club, which is almost empty in the evening and where we
could talk in peace and at leisure. Either the 12th, 13th or 14th would do:
so please let me know.

I have to absent myself from my hosts to do an hour or two of business
correspondence every morning, so I have not the time to write at any
length even now. But I should like to say that I have always wondered
whether you did not have the (rare) vocation to be a religious, a member
of a community; and also that I believe the development of communities
to be one of the most important tasks of the Church today. So I cannot
fail to rejoice at your present direction. I look forward to hearing more
about your book when we meet. I should also like to have a word with
you about Smyth's position!

1–Address supplemented by the comment, '(until July 31st, after that at Ty Glyn Aeron,
Ciliau Aeron, near Lampeter, Cardiganshire, S. Wales until August 8th)'.
2–Curtis lived at Blymhill Grange, Shifnal, Shropshire, where he was curate of St Mary,
Blymhill, in the Diocese of Lichfield.

And later, I shall hope to visit Mirfield when you are there.[1] I have never been there. I frequently visit Kelham, and have many friends there.

Ever yours in Christo,
T. S. Eliot

TO *Geoffrey Faber*   TS Valerie Eliot

26 July 1935   at Stamford House, Chipping
                                          Campden, Glos.

Dear Geoffrey,

Look that man having played fast & loose with his arrangements and timetables[2] I shall regretfully be compelled to come by train to Aberystwyth Well there is this about it that it is safer and more comfortable and I shall get a glimpse of Wolverhampton which I have never visited I was going to write and say that if I was killed on the journey I bequeath you all parcels that arrive in my name and you might smoke my cigarettes but that seems less necessary now but there is this inconvenience about it how to get from Aberystwyth to Kilkenny or Cillau now I dont want to put you out if the gardenboy or stablelad should be coming to Aberystwyth with a cart or lorry to attend a lecture or for any other purpose he could pick me up at the station at Aberystwyth at 5.05 on Wednesday but if not perhaps I can find a vehicle in Aberystwyth not a taxi which would take me for a price perhaps you know a garage in Aberystwyth and could telephone or have it telephoned to meet me with a car I may not have any money when I arrive because you see this has thrown me all out but I have a chequebook and I presume your credit is good in Aberaeron and no doubt my cheque with your backing would pass anywhere in Cardiganshire dear Geoffrey I am very sorry but you see how it is or not now I should like to suggest two things (1) that Frank should be made to play Golf all the morning (2) that in the afternoons he should shoot rabbits with a bow and arrow and build canoes out of hollow logs and exhibit all those frontier accomplishments

---

1 – House of the Resurrection, Mirfield, Yorkshire: a monastic community within the Church of England, it was founded in 1892 at Oxford by Bishop Gore, and aims to reproduce the life of the early Christians as recorded in the Acts of the Apostles.

2 – FVM to TSE, 23 July 1935: 'for different reasons it unitedly conspires with Enid, Geoffrey and Christina that Monday, 29th, is a more possible day to pick you up than Tuesday, 30th. I do hope that Emily won't be too distressed with us if we come for you at tea-time on Monday instead of Tuesday. We have to leave home on the Monday morning and should, I think, make Campden comfortably by tea-time, and go on as far as Tewkesbury or Ledbury that evening. Geoffrey will then expect us at Ty Glyn on Tuesday. Forgive the change, which is due to a combination of circumstances, and permit us to collect you on the Monday.'

he boasts about and (3) dress for dinner every night. Can I get away from Aberystwyth once there that is the question but I will risk it with many regrets you see how it is with Love to Enid & the family yours in haste

T. S. E.

P.S. I am going completely bald.

FROM *Vivien Eliot* TO *A. E. James*[1]   MS Bodleian

26 July 1935   Constance Hotel, 23 Lancaster
                                Gate, London w.2[2]

Dear Mr James,

Further to our conversation and to my last letter, for which I received an acknowledgement from your firm, on July 19th, you will *not* be surprised to see, by above address, that I have been too much shocked and shaken to remain in my flat. When I saw you on July 16th I had not realised the full extent of the damage done to me. *Alone* in that flat as I am, I now realise the extreme danger of my position. For the last few nights I had my bed out in the corridor, and you need not be told that life in such conditions is intolerable. Apart from recent events, 68 Clarence Gate Gardens is impossible as a 'private' residence. I pay £215 rent, I cannot live there, I cannot keep my little dog there, I cannot induce any self respecting servant to work there, for any wages. A year ago the place was swarming with the filthiest vermin, a kind of cockroach, and I was obliged to apply to the Sanitary Inspector at Marylebone Town Hall. He sent the Insect Pest and Rodent Destruction Society, and I had to leave the flat while the work of destroying the vermin was carried out. I had to pay three guineas and I was told the vermin would doubtless recur, owing to the maniacal over heating of the hot water pipes. The water is kept at

---

1 – VHE characterised James, in her diary (7 June 1934), as 'the most objectionable poseur I have ever come across in any country in all the years of my life. I hope he will meet his dues.'
2 – While staying at the Constance Hotel, VHE took a day trip to Oxford on Sun., 28 July. She walked to Magdalen College 'where the Prince of Wales was, & where Lord Alfred Douglas was, & where Scofield Thayer was, who had the same rooms as Lord Alfred Douglas . . . I took Polly to drink from the river just at the back, where Lucy & I used to punt with Tom & others, & we all had lunch together in Lord Alfred Douglas's rooms. After that I found *my Merton*, the best of all, the oldest College in Oxford, close by Oriel, & the most absolutely quiet & beautiful beyond words. I looked up at the very window of the room poor little loyal Tom had, & where I saw him sitting, *quietly* reading his books in 1915 apparently undismayed by all that lay before him. In his quiet soul no evil, & if he realized that he was later to be *Crucified*, (which are the very words McKnight Kauffer *used*, to me, in October 1932, at the *Ivy Club*, with me & Marion Dorn, as Ted Kauffer *said* T. S. E. would be crucified for the sake of a few worthless cads, & *gutter rubbish*.'

boiling point night and day. It is scalding, and it breaks glass and china and even strips the plating off silver plate.

I have written to the Manager of the buildings many times, and have received the most insulting replies. The steam from the bath and sink destroys all paint, furniture and material. The stench and smell of the whole place is most offensive. It is pitch dark. Owing to the danger of burglars it is impossible to have the windows open at night. The hotter the weather, the more the hot water is insanely kept at boiling point, and the furnaces are stoked night and day. It is no concern of mine that the Landlord employs a maniacal bully to collect his rents and empty his flats. But I refuse to be the dupe of such blackguardism, and to pay a fantastic rent and be obliged to live at a hotel.

Further to this, the tenant underneath my flat is an offensive person. She is in every sense objectionable, rough, noisy, keeps a fierce dog, openly spies on other tenants, and ever since my husband and I were at 177 of those Mansions (you will remember) she has most insolently followed us about, pursued us, and made herself grossly objectionable. Further to that, some weeks ago, she knocked at my door, pushed in, and knocked me down in the corridor. So that I could summons her for assault. Two witnesses were Lift Attendants. To conclude, I object to the Manager of the buildings. I object to his behaviour. To the extent that I will not live there. Although I could supply you with further details I think I have told you enough for you to guess the situation. I write to you to be so kind as to get me released from the lease of the flat. You know that it is on nearly every Agent's books and not one has even got an offer for it. You may say that I have been offered several small houses, with gardens, in the best parts of London – Kensington and Mayfair, for half the rent that I pay for the most disgusting flat in London. As to fittings and fixtures, these were also paid for by myself in 1930 in with the lease, which I bought, for the sum of £340. The Directors of the District Bank will supply you with the exact date, from my pass Book. So all fixtures are mine, and I should expect to be paid a fair sum for them, say £100, or else I should take them away with me. I mean simply the fixtures which were bought with the flat. Of course, I now leave it to you to act for me, and as I wish to settle quickly on a small house which is being held for me,[1] will you please get 68 Clarence Gate Gardens off my hands before the September Quarter Day.

1 – The 'small house' which VHE rented for some months was 8 Edge Street, w.8, towards the Notting Hill end of Kensington Church Street.

I had looked forward to going to Ireland this month, with your kind letter of introduction. But my health is too completely shattered to contemplate any journey at all.

Further to the matter of things wrongfully seized from my flat by means of forced entry, I still await the return of the Files of papers, particularly those marked – Haigh-Wood. I am convinced that these papers are not taken away for my husband's private use, but that they are in the hands of those who will not scruple to use the private information they contain. I must ask you to enquire exactly where those Files now are. They were sealed, and carefully stored by me. I considered it a sacred Trust. Will you inform me if my husband has them in safe custody or if they are still at 5, Gray's Inn Square for anybody's inspection. And the parcels of family portraits of the Eliot family which were particularly left in my care, and framed by me. Are these actually in a private residence owned by my husband, or are they being used to fake up a likeness in order to bolster up a fictitious situation?

I shall remain at the Constance Hotel for some time, but must ask you not to give the address to anyone at all. So I will now leave the matter in your hands and trust that you will act for me in the best way you can.

Hoping you and Mrs James are keeping well in this terrible heat.

I am,
Yours faithfully,
[V. Haigh Eliot]

TO *Geoffrey Curtis*   MS Houghton

Lammas [1 August 1935]   Ty Glyn Aeron, Ciliau Aeron,
                                  Cardiganshire

My dear Curtis

This is a note to say first, that I shall look forward to your dining with me on Monday the 12th at 7.30 at the United University Club, Suffolk Street, my own club being closed. (In asking for me, say 'Oxford & Cambridge Club'.)

Second, your letter requires a *long* reply, which I must give later. But I must say at once: remember that More, for whom I have a warm affection, is a heretic & also not a member of our communion.[1] His services have

---

1–Curtis wrote, 27 July: 'I . . . want to ask you about your American friend [Paul Elmer More], whose Christological thought has been helpful to me. It is an awful thing that he

been great, but the time is coming when some one must analyse his work & make clear what is & what is not acceptable. He is of course more Anglican in some ways than a good Anglican could be. It is some of the things that he puts aside, and some of these you have in mind, that I most want to see emphasised. I might add that an Anglican of my type is one who is *permanently* on the verge of the Roman journey.

Affectionately,
T. S. Eliot

TO *Edith Perkins* MS Donald Gallup

1 August 1935   Ty Glyn Aeron, Ciliau Aeron,
Cardiganshire

Dear Mrs Perkins

I arrived at Aberystwyth at 5.30 – after three changes, and the last stage in a compartment with the Evans's and the Williams's and Mrs Jones and a number of small & dirty Welsh children. The last stage of a railway journey into Wales usually emphasises in this way the foreignness of the country, which is confirmed by this letterhead.

It all goes to make Campden seem a great way off and a long time ago, and to give me a strong feeling of nostalgia. That was a very happy and unforgettable week, with stimulus and rest, diversion and quiet, society and domesticity, combined for me by my hosts according to some recipe with far more skill & thoughtfulness than I could put into a salad. I survive in the hope that I may be given another glimpse of the same household in the same place.

With wistful memories,
Yours very sincerely
T. S. Eliot

---

should have written that polemic against Christian mysticism (chapters of his big work lately republished) if he said in them what reviewers and others say that he said. I've never had the hardihood to read this. But it hurts me even to think of its significance.'

FROM *Vivien Eliot* TO *'Anne'*[1]   CC Bodleian

7 August 1935   [No address given]

Dear Anne,

I was glad to hear that you are well and that you like your new home. I shall look forward to seeing you on your return from Cornwall.

Thinking over our last conversation, I cannot think that any 'loyalty' which you say you feel to my Mother justifies you in saying or doing anything derogatory to my husband or to his family. As always, I put him first, and I do not continue my acquaintance with anyone, however great a friend, who acts treacherously towards him. You know him, having met him at my Mother's house. I disagree with your conclusion to your last conversation. I see much more in this than you can.

Yours sincerely,
[V. H. E.]

TO *Enid Faber*   TS Lady Faber

11 August 1935   Faber & Faber Ltd

Dear Enid,

I have been sunbathing on my bedroom floor this afternoon, which was pleasant, but only a shadow of the sunshine of Wales.[2] We had a pleasant journey back, in mitigation of having to leave at all, and Bath is delightful but we saw the worst picture show I have ever seen (note that 'Abdul the Damned'[3] is to be avoided – the only alternative in Bath was the Triumph of Sherlock Holmes,[4] which would have been too painful). I enjoyed Bath much more, I believe, for not having read Edith's book.[5]

I am writing, however, to tell you that I have had the most pleasant week's visit within memory. Several days of it are individually unforgettable, but what is more important is the recollection of (for me) stupendous physical

---

1 – A friend of the Haigh-Wood family, not otherwise identified.
2 – GCF diary, 27 July 1935: 'We had the Morleys and T. S. E. for most of the first fortnight – a v. successful visit, if it hadn't been for Frank spraining his ankle right at the start.'
3 – *Abdul the Damned* (1935), a British movie directed by Karl Grune, and starring Fritz Kortner and Sultan Abdul Hamid II, is a melodrama about the struggle for power in the Ottoman Empire in the years leading up to the First World War.
4 – *The Triumph of Sherlock Holmes* (1935): directed by Leslie S. Hiscott, and starring Arthur Wontner as Sherlock Holmes, based on Arthur Conan Doyle's novel *The Valley of Fear* (1914).
5 – Edith Sitwell, *Bath* (F&F, 1932).

activity in tranquillity – I mean tranquillity then as well as in recollection;[1] and of the graceful hospitality which made every fresh moment welcome and every past moment regretted. Something or other very disagreeable would have happened to Faust if he had been able at any moment to make a remark which is too hackneyed to repeat: I could have made that remark daily. I hope that I did no great damage to the tennis court. I left my bathing cloth behind, together with the sandals that Geoffrey gave me; but you are not to return them, as that was only my quiet way of suggesting that I hope to wear them again in the same place, and I would not degrade them by wearing them elsewhere. I will repeat, that I have never had a week's visit of more unadulterated pleasure, and will close,

> Yours very gratefully,
> [signed] Tom major

I will send photographs when ready.

FROM *Vivien Eliot*   CC Bodleian

[?11 August 1935]

Tom,

   Meet me in the waiting-room at 66 Wimpole Street on Monday morning Aug. 12 at 11.30 and I will take you home and take care of you. If you can't get there send me a post card c/o Dr Moore and tell me *where* to come and I will come *anywhere*.[2]

> Your wife
> Signed.

---

1 – See William Wordsworth's Preface to *Lyrical Ballads* (1800): 'I have said that poetry is the spontaneous overflow of powerful feelings: it takes its origin from emotion recollected in tranquillity.'

2 – As VHE noted in her diary, it was [her dentist] who disclosed to VHE at this time (12 Aug.) that TSE was living 'somewhere in Kensington'. 'If so I am relieved. The one great horror I had for him was that he should be in the country for I know that that could not be good for him. [The dentist] saw him as recently as July 5, when he says he gave him gas and pulled a tooth out.'

TO *Hamilton Marr*

TS BBC

13 August 1935   Faber & Faber Ltd

My dear Sir,

I have your letter of July 31st, which has awaited my return from a visit to the country, and have no objection in principle to a broadcast of *Murder in the Cathedral*.[1] I think, however, that the fee should be £50, and it would be necessary for the abbreviated version to be submitted for my approval, and I should want to be quite sure that the performers, especially the chorus, were perfectly competent. You could not do better than engage the services of Mr Martin Browne for the production, and if possible, the same performers which he had in the chorus.

Yours very truly,

T. S. Eliot

TO *Enid Hobson*[2]

cc

13 August 1935   [Faber & Faber Ltd]

Dear Mrs Hobson,

I read the poems by your young friend, which you sent with your letter of July 17th.[3] They seem to me to be what one would expect from a precocious child of fifteen. It is, however, unfortunately quite impossible to predict what a child of fifteen will be writing in ten years' time. This may be an early phase of poetic development, it may be a dead end, or she may become a successful novelist. Anything is possible. The poems have no serious intrinsic merit, but are able enough to make the girl's further development seem interesting. I am glad that there are still young people who at that age are writing in regular meters. I think that she should be

---

1–Hamilton Marr, Programme Services Executive, BBC Broadcasting House, London, offered a fee of £20 for the right to broadcast in the autumn a radio version of *MiC*. He asked permission for the BBC to prepare a version which would run for not longer than one hour. See Val Gielgud, 'Radio Play: In the Age of Television', *Theatre Arts Monthly* 21: 2 (Feb. 1937), 108–12.

2–Enid Hobson, Secretary, Women's Auxiliary, The Church Union.

3 – 'The enclosed poems have been written by a young friend of mine aged fifteen years. Her mother is most anxious to have expert opinion on their merit and to know what to do with them.

'One or two of the poems have been awarded prizes in newspaper competitions but the child wants to secure, if possible, more serious consideration of her work.

'Will you be so very kind as to give your invaluable opinion and advice on the work?'

encouraged to practise in difficult set forms such as the sonnet and the sestina, to read good poetry, but very little contemporary poetry, and to keep away from competitions and prizes.

Yours very truly,
[T. S. Eliot]

TO *Ezra Pound*

TS Beinecke

13 Augusto 1935 AD   Faber & Faber Ltd

Now then podesta I hope this finds you well and cheerful and full of benevolence. Now then the purpose of this letter is at least twofold. First and least important in fact of only negative importance I have finally found those two bits of juvenilia which you were alluding to off & on about 6 montsh [*sic*] ago published in the Lil Review[1] and I am grateful to you for bringing them to my attention I read them with keen relish and appreciation it is very pleasant to think that I could write so charmingly and wittily at the age but they will only be republished podesta literally over my Dead body and that charming compound libel on Katherine Mansfield and Brigid Patmore is out of date podesta out of date the old age is out & time to begin a new these chops from a joker's workshop I mean chips need not be repeated and never shall be. I dont quite see what I can do for your series worthy of it Herbert's pamph on essential communism is pretty thin soup as you would say[2] I have wri- hate writing anyway but I shall have to give a few lectures & addresses in the autumn which will have to consist of words the right words in the right order and I might think of something to say on one or two occasions perhaps would you like a fruity little tract on Sunday Observance one of the few things to be said for your country is that the barber shops are open on Sunday.

Now then. A book for the podesta, of the podesta, from the podesta & by the podesta[3] shall not vanish from the face of said Ruggles of Red Gap.[4] A prose book. Those excellent pieces from the *Criterion* ought to

---

1 – TSE, 'Eeldrop and Appleplex, I', *Little Review* 4: 1 (May 1917), 7–11; 'Eeldrop and Appleplex, II', *Little Review* 4: 5 (Sept. 1917), 18–19.

2 – Herbert Read, *Essential Communism* (1935), a Social Credit pamphlet reprinted in HR's *Poetry and Anarchism* (F&F, 1938).

3 – Abraham Lincoln, in his Gettysburg Address (1863), extolled 'government of the people, by the people, for the people'.

4 – *Ruggles of Red Gap* (1935): film comedy, adapted from the 1915 novel by Harry Leon Wilson, directed by Leo McCarey and starring Charles Laughton as Ruggles, an English manservant – a gentleman's gentleman – who is gambled away by his master and finds

be made available to a larger public, and you must have more literary stuff inside your head if you would stop thinking for a moment and stop figgiting about so, I mean more like Binyan Houseman [*sic*] and Monro I mean more or less contemporaneous or recently deceased subjects like the foregoing and in combination bearing on the Art of Poetry in ways less recondite from the general public which in this country sometimes attains a maximum of 2000 souls less recondite I say than troubidours [*sic*] and excluding Gesell. I sketched the matter roughly to your wife when I saw her. Also it seems to Me that the Chinese written character ought to be more accessible, Porteus has had my copy for a long time now. Anyway, anyway, you must have something in your head besides flannel money. Please give my respects to your Venble. Pa whose acquaintance I still hope to make perhaps your family would come and picnic one day with me on the other side of the French frontier so will close for the moment as the other things I have to say have slipped my mind yours etc.

TP

TO *Susan Hinkley*   TS Houghton

15 August 1935   Faber & Faber Ltd

Dear Aunt Susie,

This is only a line to say that I am eagerly awaiting news of when you arrive in London, and when the rehearsals begin. I dont know whether Emily will return in October or in November, but I hope that you will arrive soon enough for us all to meet together. It is unlikely that my Murder will be produced in London in the autumn; but there will probably be a broadcast version of it, and the Group Theatre is to produce *Sweeney Agonistes* and *The Dog Beneath the Skin*.

There are two of my photographs that I have not recovered; I have sent the sheriff's officers in twice and do not intend to send them again; they are Charles Chauncy and Priscilla Cushing. If there is any way of getting new photographs of either of these portraits I should be grateful to be told the way.

Affectionately your nephew,
Tom

---

himself in service to an American *nouveau riche* millionaire couple. With unerring tact and self-discipline, Ruggles earns respect and ultimately his independence.

TO *Messrs Wichern-Verlag*[1]   CC

16 August 1935   [Faber & Faber Ltd]

Dear Sirs,

I must apologise for the delay in consideration of the book by Dr
Walter Künneth, *Antwort auf den Mythus*, which you kindly sent us.[2] The
delay has been due to my absence from London. While I find it extremely
interesting, and have read it with much sympathy, we are of the opinion
that it is not a book for which there is likely to be very much demand in
this country. Those of the general public who are interested in reading
about such matters would of course be very sympathetic to the point of
view. It is rather that there would be no interest here in such ideas as those
of Dr Rosenberg, although there is, of course, an interest in their effects.
But the ideological basis is hardly a reality for the British public. We are
therefore returning the book with many thanks and regrets.

                              Yours very truly,
                              [T. S. Eliot]

TO *Marianne Moore*   CC

16 August 1935   [Faber & Faber Ltd]

Dear Miss Moore,

I am horrified to find that I have left so long unanswered your letter of
May 31st with the four poems enclosed.[3] I think that what happened was
that I put it aside after two readings to let my mind come to a conclusion
about the order. On re-reading again I can see no reason why there should
be any other order than that in which you gave them to me, viz: 'The
Pangolin', 'Birdwitted', 'Pigeons', and 'Half Deity', especially because if
the four are to be printed together *The Pangolin* is an admirable title.
I should like to use 'The Pangolin', and may I ask whether you have any
objection to the *New English Weekly* publishing a shorter poem such

---

1–Publishers, Berlin-Spandau.
2–Walter Künneth (1901–97), German Protestant theologian, was during the Nazi era a
member of the Confessing Church. In the spring of 1935 Künneth circulated – in response
to Alfred Rosenberg's *Mythus des 20 Jahrhunderts* (the standard work on Nazi race theory)
– a 200-page text entitled *Antwort auf den Mythus* ('A Reply to the Myth: the Difference
between the Nordic Myth and the Biblical Christ'), which sold 36,000 copies in three
months. In response to the publication, the Nazis shut down the Apologetischen Centrale
at the evangelical Johannesstift Berlin-Spandau where Künneth was a lecturer, and banned
Künneth's works.
3–MM had asked for advice on the order of the four poems she had enclosed.

as 'Birdwitted'? The out about it is that the *N.E.W.* can't offer to pay anyone, but it is a periodical in which I am interested, and which I am anxious to help, and an occasional poem from an established poet helps to give it prestige in the eyes of the young.

Yours sincerely,

[T. S. Eliot]

TO *John Theobald*[1]   cc

16 August 1935   [Faber & Faber Ltd]

Dear Mr Theobald,

I have read with care the poems enclosed with your letter of August 7th, and I think that 'The Earthquake' represents a considerable advance on the previous work of yours that I have seen. I think, however, that it must be regarded as a piece of experimentation which will be useful to you. It is very ambitious, and I think that the structure has proved to be a prison rather than a scaffold. The fact is that it is not really intelligible without your notes, and even after reading the notes I did not get a comprehensive grasp of the poem on second reading. What I mean by a scaffold is something like the structure of *Ulysses*, very helpful for the author in designing his work, and placing details, but not really essential for the reader. There is all the difference in the world, too, between notes which may be helpful to the reader, and notes which are indispensable to him. If the notes are indispensable then the poem is not quite written. I think that an original design is usually modified during the course of any successful execution. You have, I believe, a great deal of work still to do in the way of simplification. I continue to be interested in what you may do next.

Yours sincerely,

[T. S. Eliot]

TO *Geoffrey Grigson*   TS Texas

16 August 1935   [Faber & Faber Ltd]

Dear Grigson,

If you are really keen about MacNeice's poems I shall be glad to let you have them to review alone. If you do not like them there would of course be no point in reviewing them in this way. I find the volume very satisfying

---

1 – A teacher in Hove, Sussex.

myself, and shall be interested to know your opinion. I will send you a copy as soon as it appears, which will not be soon enough for reviewing in the next issue. It will have to be reviewed in December.[1]

Yours sincerely,
T. S. Eliot

TO *Henry Miller*   TS Jay Martin

16 August 1935   Faber & Faber Ltd

Dear Mr Miller,

I have your letter of August 1st.[2] I have referred to my letter to you of the 13th June, and I don't see anything in it very useful for your purposes. My comparison with D. H. Lawrence is irrelevant, and I warn you against it, because it is just the sort of thing that a publisher might think a useful advertisement. It would not be a useful advertisement to any intelligent reader, because there is no point in comparing the two books, and as a matter of fact, even according to Lawrence's standards *Lady Chatterley's Lover* is a badly written book. If your publisher would like to say 'a very remarkable book, with passages of writing in it as good as any I have seen for a long time' I should think that would do.[3]

1 – TSE's blurb for *Poems* by Louis MacNeice (1935): 'After a distinguished reputation while an undergraduate at Oxford, contemporary with Mr Auden, Mr Louis MacNeice has allowed his verse to appear only rarely in periodicals and anthologies. His classical scholarship has informed a genius representative of the spirit of his Northern Ireland. The most original Irish poet of his generation, dour without sentimentality, intensely serious without political enthusiasm, his work is intelligible but unpopular, and has the pride and modesty of things that endure.'

Grigson on *Poems*: C. 15 (Jan. 1936), 320–3: 'Of my contemporaries who write verse, those I get most satisfaction from are Mr Louis MacNeice and Mr Auden . . . Mr Auden is the Elizabethan Fool-cum-artist, inside and outside life, Mr MacNeice the clear-sighted but less X-ray-eyed Elegant, the experienced Aristocrat who sees life mainly from the outside, with an extensive but less intensive feeling. Mr Auden uses the incantatory symbol, Mr MacNeice the incantation of mood or attitude . . . I must salute Mr MacNeice with the humility and enthusiasm which excellent and peculiar, and if you like, very limited talent deserves . . . [T]his talent has been steadily and severely tended and improved by Mr MacNeice; it has reached its chief excellence so far in the latest of his poems. That is an excitement.'

2 – Miller's publisher Jack Kahane had asked whether it might be possible to quote on the dust-jacket of *Tropic of Cancer* a line or two from TSE's letter to Miller dated 13 June. 'I am naturally eager,' he said, 'to get what attention I can for the book, more particularly because it is a fight to prevent it from falling into the category of pornographic works and thus being buried.'

3 – George Orwell was to write to Henry Miller, 26–7 Aug. 1936: 'I see from the blurb on Black Spring that you got a pretty good write-up from Eliot & Co, also that I am mentioned among them. That is a step up for me – the first time I have been on anybody else's blurb. So no doubt I shall be Sir Eric Blair yet' (Orwell, *A Life in Letters*, ed. Peter Davison [2010], 65).

If I did not give you Herbert Read's address you can always reach him at the *Burlington Magazine*, 16a St. James' Street, S.W.I., of which he is editor. If you are coming to England do let me know. I am sure Read would like to meet you.[1]

Yours sincerely,
T. S. Eliot

TO *Hermann Broch*   CC

16 August 1935   [Faber & Faber Ltd]

My dear Herr Broch,

Thank you very much for your kind letter of the 27th July.[2] I am highly pleased that you should wish to translate any of my poems into German, and you are welcome to publish them in *Patmos*. For regularity's sake I should be glad if you would indicate to me what poems you would like to translate and publish before I give formal permission. I should not care to have too many appear at once lest it should interfere with any prospect of an eventual volume of translations of my verse into German. The only poem which I should not care to have translated is *The Waste Land*, which as you no doubt know has been admirably translated by my friend Curtius, and it might seem a slight upon his [illegible] if I authorised anyone else to make a further translation.

With many thanks and most sincerely good wishes,

I am,
Yours sincerely,
[T. S. Eliot]

1 – Miller was keen to be in touch with HR, and to meet him when he visited the UK.
2 – Broch's letter reads in translation: 'Please forgive me for not thanking you sooner for sending me your poems and those of Mr Spender. But there is a reason for this: not only was I ill for a long time, but I also wanted to attempt to translate into German some of these very fine poems that have moved me, and move me, exceedingly. May I now submit to you a sample of this modest attempt? However, it has to be said in my defence that it is hardly possible to translate the originality of your poems if one really wants to grasp the sense as well as the mood, the rhythm, the metre and the rhyme; one must always renounce one of these aspects and come to a compromise, especially since the German version moves forward much more awkwardly than the English.

'But I would be extremely pleased if this effort met partly with your approval. Would you then have any objections to publishing these translations? For example in the newly founded Viennese literary journal *Patmos*, which promises to have a very high standard and urgently seeks important foreign authors. I think it would be important to bring you closer to a German audience, and I hope that you agree.'

TO *Hamilton Marr*   TS BBC Caversham

16 August 1935   Faber & Faber Ltd

Dear Sir,

Thank you for your letter of the 14th August. I still consider the sum of
30 guineas inadequate, but as I am informed that this is not an unusually
low sum for the B.B.C. to pay for such a licence, I am prepared to accept
it if we can come to an agreement on the other questions.

I note that the Corporation is willing to submit the abbreviated version
for my approval. I think myself that it would be more satisfactory simply
to take the first half of the play, with a few excisions that I should wish
to make, because the first half is quite complete in itself, and indeed more
of a unity than the play as a whole. I should not, however, make this a
condition.

What I am more anxious to know is how you would propose to cast the
play. I think that before going any further in the matter it would be as well
if I could meet and have a talk with whoever was to produce it.

                                        Yours faithfully,
                                        T. S. Eliot

TO *Polly Tandy*   TS BL

19 August 1935   Faber & Faber Ltd,[1]

Dear Pollytandy m'm the 2.45 on a Sattaday will suit me capitally so I
should arrive at Newhaven round 4 BEFORE *TEA* and shall expect to
be Met because I cant identify the house by gorse and blackberry bushes
can I?[2] Did you write that the Seats of his trousers had to be CLEANED
or DARNED before going to Church? I have always found it possible to
kneel in prayer without exposing the Seats of my trousers (2) but perhaps
he was serving at the Altar if so I hope the soles of his Feet was cleaned/
darned too. About bathing I like taking my clothes off too so if there is
bathing I want to have something to do with it I will bring a costume you
leave the landlady to me because I have just received a testimonial (1) it
says I have a magnetic personality so will close your respectful
                                        Possum

1–On the F&F letterhead, alongside the identification of the directors 'T. S. Eliot (U.S.A.
origin)', TSE added in TS: 'and dont forget it.'
2–TSE was to visit the Tandys for a weekend at their holiday home in Newhaven.

(1) from a lady who says I remind her of her deceased husband who was a saint.[1]
<(2) would you like him to borrow my Morning Coat>

Shall bring my tropical costume, and tropical point of view.

[5 photographs enclosed with pictures of Wisbech]

FROM *Vivien Eliot* TO *James & James*   MS Bodleian

20 August 1935   The English Speaking Union,
                              Dartmouth House, 37 Charles
                              Street, Mayfair, London

Dear Sirs,

I have received your letter and do feel that I must reply that your reason for refusing to claim anything for the wilful damage done to my personal chattels when my flat was broken into is weak.[2] You say had I followed your advice the situation would not have arisen. I only wish to remind you that had I followed your advice and succumbed to your pressure in 1933, I should have signed an offensive and damaging paper. I will remind you that at the advice of Messrs Lewis & Lewis, I brought the paper in question back to your office with my friend Mrs de Saxe, straight from Messrs Lewis & Lewis and handed it to Mr Leigh Hunt. As my signature was never obtained for that paper, all subsequent correspondence since that date referring to my husband, T. S. Eliot, becomes waste paper, and has no value. Therefore, the breaking into my flat becomes logically an act of ruthless and insensate violence.

Mr A. E. James states that he sees my husband at 5, Gray's Inn Square, but never alone. If my husband is free, and in his right mind, why should he go to the vast expense of employing hired men to force an entry into my flat to get hold of some old papers when he has had *access* to the flat the whole time? For I must again repeat that the fact that I never did sign any paper referring to him rules out of the sphere of reasoned behaviour all that has passed since October 1933.

1 – Mrs Irene Hale.
2 – VHE's solicitors James & James wrote on 19 Aug.: 'We do not feel we can put forward any further claim on your behalf in connection with the occurrences which took place on 11th December last, because had our advice been taken the necessity for breaking into your flat would not have arisen.'

There are other aspects of the situation on which if I were to enlighten you, I think would alter your point of view.

I am,

Yours faithfully,

Signed.

[The word 'Signed' is written in VHE's hand.]

TO *Geoffrey Faber*   CC

20 August 1935   [Faber & Faber Ltd]

Dear Geoffrey,

I am sending you a book compiled by Miss Perham, which incidently [*sic*] contains one contribution prepared by Miss Audrey Richards.[1] It was agreed by the Committee that you ought to see this book and let us know what you think about it. Stewart and I have both read parts of it. I don't know what Stewart thinks, but I am rather doubtful of its saleability. Some of the Africans, however, have much more interesting stories to tell than others. Those which interest me most were accounts by Africans who had received a more or less European education, concerning their present-day relations with South Africans and English. The more primitive speakers, and elders telling of life before the white man came, I did not find so interesting. Perhaps the interesting parts of their lives were what they could not put into language.

Yours ever,

[Tom]

TO *Dorothy Pound*   TS Lilly Library

20 August 1935   Faber & Faber Ltd

Dearest Dorothy,

Many thanks for your letter of the 19th.[2] I do feel somewhat more refreshed than when I saw you last, and hope that this finds you the same.

---

1 – *Ten Africans*, ed. Margery Perham (F&F, 1936). Audrey Richards was GCF's sister-in-law (sister of Enid Faber): see Adam Kuper, 'Audrey Richards 1899–1984', in *Cambridge Women: Twelve Portraits*, ed. Edward Shils and Carmen Blacker (1996), 221–44.
2 – 'Dearest Possum / . . . I had a letter from Ezra a while ago . . . re new Vol. . . . [T]here are, from N.E.W., articles on E. E. Cummings, J. Cocteau, Toward Orthology . . . I don't see why the next vol. need be all reprints? There is other stuff lying around in Rapallo, I know, which

I have exchanged one letter with Ezra meanwhile on the subject of the new volume, but have not had an opportunity to get from any of my colleagues their opinion about the desirable size of the new book. I should think the *N.E.W.* articles you mention were possibilities, but I haven't got them by me as unfortunately I never keep files, not having the space. It has just struck me that the introduction to the *Active Anthology* might be a possibility, and I am going to re-read that again. I remember liking it very much at the time. I agree that there is no reason why the next volume should be all reprints. That is to say there is no reason from our point of view. In fact I think it would be an advantage to have a few inédits. Perhaps if Ezra won't, you will poke about amongst his manuscripts when you get back and make suggestions. I did rather try to encourage him to produce some new stuff for the book, but I got the impression from his letter that he didn't want to write anything fresh for it. Without having them at hand, I agree with you in principle that the *Dial* letters are likely to be out of date.

No rumour of confiscation of *Jefferson and Mussolini*[1] has reached me. What are the misinterpretations about Italy that you speak of?[2] Let's get that straight.[3]

> Yours devoted[4]
> Possum

TO *Michael Roberts*

TS Berg

20 August 1935   Faber & Faber Ltd

My dear Roberts,

I have found your anthology extremely interesting. As for the length, it seemed to us best to get a cast-off made to see how many pages there would be to the book when set up in a form which de la Mare could approve. So I have given it to him for that purpose, and will write to

---

would be a bit more up-to-date, or lively – or do "they" the d----- public, only want ten-year-old (or more) stuff? The review of "Private Worlds" was good (N.E.W.) & only edging on Economics. E suggests some old Dial letters etc: This seems to me too far away behind . . .'

1 – EP, *Jefferson and/or Mussolini* (1935).

2 – 'I hear of two reviews of Jefferson/Mussolini in Italy ------ has it been confiscated here I wonder! The misinterpretations re Italy in the press here are disgusting.'

3 – Dorothy Pound followed up with this letter: 'I know Ezra doesn't want to write anything new for the next vol: There must be inédits in typescript in Rapallo: I'll have a hunt when I return . . . Yes: Act. Anth. preface was good.'

4 – TSE struck through the 's' of 'Yours' and added 'devoted' by hand.

you again later. I should very much like to know at least for my private satisfaction just how heavy an inroad you have had to make on your own advance beyond the sum allocated for contributors, in order to include so much matter. You will remember my offer to diminish my own fees in order to help toward making a satisfactory anthology.[1]

I find your introduction very interesting indeed, and it represents, as it should, a newer point of view than my own. There is only one point of fact which I should like to call to your attention. You mention me and Pound as the representatives of a group of writers influenced by certain French poets. This seems to me misleading. I arrived at an acquaintance with the poets mentioned independently and before I had come to London. During this earlier period Pound was in contact with a group of people, such as F. S. Flint, who were very much interested in the French poets of the time. But the poets in whom they were interested were rather a different lot from those you mention. They were the later Symbolistes for whom Remy de Gourmont might be described as having been the press agent – poets such as Samain, Kahn, Francis James, Rodenbach, the earlier Verhaeren and others. They were also attentive to the work of more immediate contemporaries such as Vildrac, Romains, Duhamel. But beyond this there is a still further difficulty. I don't feel that Pound has ever been seriously influenced by any French poetry. In fact I don't think that it is even very sympathetic to him. The only name in the whole of French poetry which has really meant much to him is that of Villon, and otherwise what is predominant in his work is the influence of Provencal and early Italian poets.

I don't see that this is worth discussing in detail within your limits, but I think that it might be worthwhile altering your sentence so as to avoid the suggestion that Pound and I developed under exactly the same influences. It is true that about 1917 at his suggestion we both worked under Théophile Gautier, and at a later date still, I think in the summer of 1919, I remember his buying a copy of *Les Amours Jaunes*. But he was not, like myself, moved in the beginning by Baudelaire, Laforgue, or Rimbaud.

Yours ever,
T. S. Eliot

1–Roberts responded, 31 Aug.: 'I think the book as it stands runs to about £174 for contributors – £24 over the £150 allowed, but I'm not sure.'

TO *Perry Blacker*   CC

20 August 1935   [Faber & Faber Ltd]

Dear Mr Blacker,

I have your letter of the 17th. You are quite right in believing that it is impossible to make a living by poetry. I am not sure that it would be a good thing even if one could. That is to say one ought to have other occupations to demand a good deal of one's time. As for converting an enthusiasm for poetry into a means for earning a living, the best thing to do in my experience is to try to find a means of earning a living which is as remote from poetry or literature as possible. For example, journalism is a bad occupation for anybody who wants to write poetry, and if you think of publishing then you might think of some other form of manufacture or commerce which does not pretend to have anything to do with literature. I don't know of course what kinds of employment have been offered you which you have found unsuitable, but I should not be guided by the question of suitability by any supposed relation of the job to writing poetry. The best job is the one which has definite hours, which uses whatever part of your mind has least to do with poetry, and which you can put out of your mind altogether when you leave in the evening.

                              Yours sincerely,
                              [T. S. Eliot]

TO *Christopher Dawson*   CC

20 August 1935   [*The Criterion*]

My dear Dawson,

Would you be willing to look through an article by our friend Penty and tell me whether you think that it is sound enough to publish. It is on the subject of Roman Law, the revival of which, he maintains, caused the collapse of mediaeval civilisation.[1] He also insists that English law is very much more influenced by Roman law than is commonly believed. I don't know anything about the subject myself, but I am naturally suspicious of

---

1–Penty submitted 'Did the Revival of Roman Law break-up Medieval Civilization?' on 18 June.

comprehensive and completely explanatory examinations, and should be grateful if you would have a look at the article.

> With all best wishes,
> Yours sincerely,
> [T. S. Eliot]

TO *F. A. Iremonger*[1]   TS BBC Caversham

22 August 1935   Faber & Faber Ltd

My dear Sir,

I have been in correspondence with Mr Hamilton Marr about a possible production of *Murder in the Cathedral*, and it is suggested that I should discuss the matter with you.[2] I should be very glad if you could have lunch with me on Tuesday next at the Oxford and Cambridge Club at 1.15.

> Yours very truly,
> T. S. Eliot

TO *Hugh Gordon Porteus*[3]   CC

23 August 1935   [*The Criterion*]

Dear Porteus,

I was out of London when you wrote to suggest my coming to supper, but if it is convenient I could come one evening next week, or probably the week after. I should like to very much, when you find that it suits you.

I am sorry to say that the review of Adrian Stokes' book arrived too late to be of any use. I mean to say I am sorry and glad. I am sorry because

---

1–The Revd F. A. Iremonger (1878–1952), eminent Anglican priest; Director of Religion, BBC, 1933–9.

2–Laurence Gilliam proposed a broadcast of *MiC*, in a memo to the Drama Director, 12 July 1935. 'It has the merit of a clear cut dramatic situation, some extremely good verse by Eliot . . . In my opinion the writing of the choruses is the best thing about this play and, although these were effective at Canterbury, they could be still more effective if produced in a rather different way.' Iremonger added: 'I am strongly in favour of doing this.' It was broadcast on Sun., 5 Jan. 1936.

3–Hugh Gordon Porteus (1906–93), literary and art critic; literary editor of *The Twentieth Century* (magazine of the Promethean Society), 1931–3; advertising copywriter; author of *Wyndham Lewis: A Discursive Exposition* (1932) and *Background to Chinese Art* (1935). See obituary in *The Times*, 20 Feb. 1993; 'Forgotten man of the Thirties', *TLS*, 26 Mar. 1993, 13–14.

it struck me as an excellent review, and it is a pity that your wife[1] should have had this trouble in vain. On the other hand it will serve as a specimen of her work, for the review seemed to me a good one because one felt that whatever there might be to be said for the book her objections were well founded, and not capricious or prejudiced. On the other hand the review made me feel that the book was not worth reviewing in the *Criterion*. I always of course feel hesitant about reviewing Faber and Faber books in the *Criterion* for obvious reasons, and as a rule I only include books which I have myself had some interest in from the beginning and more or less sponsored. And when a book is neither good enough to praise nor important enough to damn I think it is better left alone. But I should like your wife to try again with plenty of time, and should be glad if she would at some time suggest another book that she would like to review.[2]

Do you want me to lend you a copy of the *Ta Hao*? I find that I have one.

Yours ever,
[T. S. Eliot]

TO *Jeanette McPherrin*   TS Denison Library

23 August 1935   Faber & Faber Ltd

Dear Miss McPherrin,

Or may I say Jeanie, as I always think of you thereby, and a very good name too and as suitable for Inverness as McPherrin itself – thank you for your charming letter from the Canal Zone.[3] It is the first letter I have ever had from the Canal Zone, I may never have another, and I hope that my next association with the Canal Zone will be your return to Paris by that route if you come that way. The idea of Bath Olivers was Emily's, as well as that of the rations in general, and I hope she has had due credit, but *I* thought of the plums. I must acknowledge the efficiency of Fortnum & Mason who took the matter very seriously and said that if the package was to reach you it must go by Air. How can I thank you for your Card? It touches the sublime. After drinking it in for two days I decided that I ought not to hoard such beauty, and have passed it on for the moment to a

1 – Mrs Porteus was Zenka Bartek.
2 – Porteus responded on 26 Aug.: 'It didn't matter a bit about my wife's review [of Adrian Stokes, *Russian Ballet*]: I think that your remarks on her work, which of course I took the liberty of showing to her, gave her more pleasure than she would have derived, even, from a *Criterion* acceptance.'
3 – Not traced.

crippled friend who is also an amateur of this kind of art. I am afraid that I shall search London in vain to find anything so elevated. I am however enclosing a masterpiece of another kind, but I have had to snip off the top with nail scissors, so it is rather ragged. *I* think it is charming, but I know Emily does not; so I hasten to send it before she tells me not to.

I do hope that this year will be both pleasant and profitable, and that you will get something more worthy in a year's time. It is miserable to think that Emily will probably be spending next year half way between us, subduing herself to relatives instead of expanding. I wish that we were all dining at Foyot's or the Restaurant Perigourdin, or sitting on a bench in the Luxembourg Gardens.

Yours very sincerely,
T. S. Eliot

TO *Pierre de Menasce*[1]

TS Archives Dominicaines, Paris

23 August 1935   Faber & Faber Ltd

My dear Menasce,

I did not receive the card of your first celebration in Paris until after the event, as it had to be forwarded, and I could hardly have come in any case.[2] But I want to let you know, even now, how much happiness the thought of it gave me, and the thought of your own exaltation. I hope that some day I may visit you and talk with you again, whether you are still in Le Saulchoir or whether you are working in France. I think of you often.

Yours in Christo,
and affectionately,
T. S. Eliot

1–Jean de Menasce (1902–73), theologian and orientalist (his writings include studies in Judaism, Zionism and Hasidism), was born in Alexandria into an aristocratic Jewish Egyptian family and educated in Alexandria, at Balliol College, Oxford (where he was contemporary with Graham Greene and took his BA in 1924), and at the Sorbonne (Licence es-Lettres). In Paris, he was associated with the magazines *Commerce* and *L'Esprit,* and he translated several of TSE's poems for French publication: his translation of *TWL* was marked '*revuée et approuvée par l'auteur*'. He became a Catholic convert in 1926, was ordained in 1935 a Dominican priest – Father Pierre de Menasce – and went on to be Professor of the History of Religion at the University of Fribourg, 1938–48; Professor and Director of Studies, specialising in Ancient Iranian religions, at the École Pratique des Hautes Études, Paris. TSE came to consider him 'the only really first-rate French translator I have ever had' (letter to Kathleen Raine, 17 May 1944).

2–VHE, in her diary for Tues., 9 July 1935, copied out a letter in French from Father Pierre Jean de Menasce saying that he had been received as a Dominican: fol. 119.

TO *Margery Fry*[1]   CC

26 August 1935   [Faber & Faber Ltd]

Dear Miss Fry,

Thank you for your letter of the 23rd.[2] I have received the manuscript, which I understand has been acknowledged to you, and look forward to reading it with great interest, all the more so because I had several talks with Roger on the matter long ago, and have heard him discuss the meaning of one or two of the sonnets.

I will try to let you have our decision as soon as possible.

Yours sincerely,
[T. S. Eliot]

TO *Mary Brook*[3]   CC

29 August 1935   [Faber & Faber Ltd]

Dear Mrs Brook,

Thank you for your letter of August 27th.[4] I hesitate to make suggestions in isolation without having the benefit of the criticism of the Committee, and always have the feeling that anything I particularly want to see produced will probably be a financial failure. I don't expect my suggestions to be taken seriously unless somebody else happens to suggest the same thing, but I should like to see *Troilus* done satisfactorily by the Old Vic, and if they were thinking of going outside of Shakespeare for an Elizabethan play, as Mrs Hutchinson has so often advocated, I believe that *Volpone* is the best acting play of the whole period. I expect that *Edward II* is still under prohibition.

1–Margery Fry (1874–1958) – sister of Roger Fry – pioneer penal reformer (she was instrumental in the establishment of the Howard League for Penal Reform and its first secretary), liberal campaigner, and head of college (Somerville College, Oxford, 1926–31).
2–Roger Fry's translation of Mallarmé. 'Charles Mauron tells me that you had spoken to him about the possibility of this book being published by Faber and Faber . . . It should be clearly understood that Charles Mauron keeps the right to bring out later a French edition of his notes and introduction, and I have told him that I should be glad for him to translate Roger's fragment of an introduction as well if he goes on with the plan.' She submitted the MS by a separate posting the same day.
3–Secretary, Sadler's Wells Society.
4–'[Lilian Baylis] says she would be very grateful for suggestions for plays etc, after Christmas . . . Mr Carr told me that he would very much like to do a play of yours, if it were possible.'

As for Mr Carr's suggestion, I don't think we need take such a vague expression seriously. If he wanted to do a play of mine he could always write to me about it. Besides, he ought to know that I have only written one, and I certainly shan't have another ready this year.

I am not frightfully keen about *Boris*.[1] Nevertheless I do feel that extra orchestral rehearsals for the operas is one very good way in which the Committee can apply the Society's money.

Yours sincerely,
[T. S. Eliot]

TO *A. J. Penty* CC

29 August 1935   [*The Criterion*]

My dear Penty,

After much thought and deliberation I have finally come to the conclusion that I do not find your article on the Revival of Roman Law quite satisfactory for the *Criterion*. I am not of course qualified to criticise it by any knowledge of the subject, and I feel that my dissatisfaction and lack of conviction is largely due to a belief that it is too big a subject to be treated in the scope of a single essay. You are making a very important point which is pretty revolutionary in regard to accepted opinions on the Middle Ages, and I feel that it is impossible to be convincing within the space which the *Criterion* can allow. I feel, for instance, the lack of a definition of Mediaeval civilisation when I am told that it began to break up during the 11th and 12th centuries. The uninstructed reader is immediately bothered by the thought that the greatest successes of the Middle Ages in the way of architecture, I mean the late Romanesque, occurred toward the end of the break up, and that its greatest philosophy was produced even after that. To repeat, I don't see how this subject can be treated within the scope of the article.

I hope that you have other suggestions, and I should be glad to hear that you are enjoying good health.

Yours ever,
[T. S. Eliot]

---

1 – *Boris Godunov* (1869/72), opera by M. Mussorgsky (1839–81).

29 August 1935   Faber & Faber Ltd

Dear Mrs Thorp,

Excellent: Tuesday will suit me better than any other night, so I hope it will suit Emily as well; and I had rather see the Shaw play than anything else now playing.² The Cambridge Theatre suggests the Ivy Restaurant, which is close by, for dinner; and if that night suits everyone I will reserve a table there, for seven o'clock. It will be a great convenience to me not to have to dress. If you should hear from Emily tomorrow (Friday) I should be very grateful if you could give me a *coup de téléphone*, so that I shall have plenty of time to make my arrangements. All my other nights next week are free, if she prefers another: but I hope she will let us know soon.

Yours sincerely,
T. S. Eliot

TO *Charles Williams*   CC

29 August 1935   [*The Criterion*]

My dear Williams,

Thank you for your letter of the 26th.³ I don't see how any exception could be taken to your acknowledgements in the form drafted, occurring in the body of a preface, and I am glad to be able to express my appreciation of your considerate behaviour throughout these proceedings.

---

1 – Margaret Thorp, née Ferrand (1891–1970), educated at Smith College (AB, AM) and Yale (PhD, 1934), was a noted author and biographer: works include *Charles Kingsley, 1819–1875* (1937), *America at the Movies* (1939), *Female Persuasion: Six Strong-Minded Women* (1949), *Neilson of Smith* (1956), *Sara Orne Jewett* (1966). She and Willard Thorp were married in 1930.

2 – Bernard Shaw's *Man and Superman*, at the Cambridge Theatre, London.

3 – CW sent a draft of his acknowledgements for 'this tiresome book' (*New Book of English Verse*). 'Tell me . . . if you would like anything altered.' The acknowledgements took a discursive turn beginning: 'My thanks are due particularly, among many friends, to Mr R. C. Goffin, who had persuaded me, long before this book was contemplated, of the justice of his view of Chaucer, and here assisted the choice of extracts; to Mr T. S. Eliot, for his comments on the Elizabethans and Jacobeans – not merely in this relation; to Mr John Hayward, who not only discussed certain poets, but permitted me to use (with the concurrence of the Nonesuch Press) his text of Swift; to Miss Anne Bradby who habitually presented me with more loveliness from the Museum Manuscripts of the 14th and 15th centuries than could possibly be included . . .'

With all best wishes for the anthology.

Yours,

[T. S. Eliot]

TO *The Editor*, The Church Times

30 August 1935[1]   24 Russell Square, W.C.1

This England!

Sir,

Canon Iddings Bell, in his article in your last issue, made several mistakes of approach.[2] He made two generalisations not really necessary to his main point, and therefore distracting. There is as little use in saying

---

1–Text taken from *The Church Times* 114: 3,788 (30 Aug. 1935), 206. Not in Gallup.
2–Canon Bernard Iddings Bell, D.D., 'Is Anglo-Catholicism Conquering?', *Church Times*, 114: 3,787 (23 Aug. 1935), 192. 'It seems to me that the promotion of the Catholic religion in England is possibly more difficult than in any other part of the modern Western world, and this for five reasons . . .

'First of all, by a tradition of several generations, religion in England is closely tied up in the popular mind with social respectability . . .

'Secondly, the English are still a complacent people, perhaps the only complacent people left in a world of violent upheaval in respect of statecraft, economics and morality . . .

'A third difficulty lies in the usual English unwillingness to consider human affairs logically. It has long been of their genius to be pragmatists, vitalists; and it still is. They are suspicious of reason . . .

'Fourthly, there is the Establishment, an arrangement of Church and State now to be found in the Anglican Communion nowhere but in England itself . . . The English Catholic is asked to be loyal, not merely to the Church, but also to this Establishment, a very difficult thing to do; and in particular to be obedient to State-selected bishops, whom . . . he does not wholly trust.

'Fifth, and finally, the general apathy of the English common people is to be considered. The working-people, it is true, still manifest a good deal of the racy, humorous tang that once made England England, though even among them the hopeless quiescence engendered by dole-mindedness has had its effect . . . [T]o any outside observer the deterioration since the war is sure to seem startling and ominous . . . The deadly industrialism of a century has devitalized them . . .

'The English Church, whatever its historical and organic nature, is not yet in practice Catholic, not by a very great deal. It is not even Protestant in any aggressive sense . . . [I]t is essentially respectabilian, and half-asleep . . .

'[T]he Church Union has two sorts of work, equally important, to perform. First, it must be alert publicly to defend Catholic faith and practice . . .

'Second, it must teach . . . the whole of Catholicism to the whole of the English-speaking peoples: doctrine, sociology, morals and religion, convinced that only the whole Catholic faith, uncompromised, can contend successfully with the secularism that is now destroying civilization; convinced, too, that Papalism is a hindrance to Catholicism, not to be endured . . .'

that the English are complacent as there is in the equally common remark that the French have bad manners. If you live long enough in France, you cease to consider French manners bad; and if you live long enough in England, the assertion that the English are complacent ceases to have any meaning. Different nations have different manners and different complacencies. Second, the assertion that the English people is becoming "devitalised" is open to question and to interpretation. Visitors to France now get a similar impression of that country; and it is open to question whether the devitalisation of England and France is not preferable to the galvanisation of Germany.

I think, however, that Canon Iddings Bell had a serious point to make, which deserved serious consideration; and I regret that your leading article chose for comment what was unimportant in his essay – and adopted, if I may say so, a manner which was almost calculated to substantiate his charge of complacency.[1] Canon Bell expressed his doubts as to whether Catholicism was gaining ground in this country; he is a regular visitor who makes a special study of religious conditions here; and I submit that his apprehensions deserve better than to be ignored. To me, at least, his warning seems salutary and by no means over-stated. You suggest that he does not understand the English. Very likely, but that does not disqualify him when he criticises the condition of the Church in England. *Ne nous félicitons pas*. I could not say more without claiming several columns.

T. S. Eliot

1–'We can't be as bad as all that' (editorial), *Church Times*, 23 Aug. 1935, 189: 'Dr Iddings Bell loves England, but England has, to an extent, fooled him.' Of Iddings Bell's charge of complacency: 'History justifies the English in expecting to muddle through. Experience justifies a measure of confidence . . . The Englishman always sees the joke . . . But complacency is certainly not his mood today . . . England is puzzled, not complacent. But, though puzzled, she keeps her head. She will not run after the strange gods of the Fascist and the Communist.

'Again we entirely disagree with Dr Bell that there has been a serious deterioration in the national character since the war . . . Crowd-minded, apathetic! Oh dear no! . . . Modern society does not encourage the development of individuality. But the odd thing is how often the Englishman remains the captain of his soul. The English are essentially individualist. Dr Iddings Bell admits this, and yet he says that the English are mass-minded. They cannot possibly be both.

'It is because of what the English are and not because of what they are not that they so badly need the guidance and the consolation of the Christian religion. And we entirely agree with Dr Bell that an immense responsibility rests with Anglo-Catholics never to rest or sheath their swords until the life of this England be sweetened and quickened by the faith once delivered to the saints.'

FROM *Vivien Eliot* TO *Maurice Haigh-Wood*   cc Bodleian

3 September 1935   The English Speaking Union,
                                   Dartmouth House,
                                   37 Charles Street, Mayfair, w.1.

Dear Maurice,

I wrote to you from the Constance Hotel, on September 1st, and I do not know if you have got my letter. I wrote as follows –

'Following our conversation in Hyde Park yesterday, I must ask you, if you please, to give me the full opportunity of being present the next time you see Tom. *Not* necessarily with his knowledge, but certainly near enough and in sufficient light, to be able to identify him.

Anything but absolutely straight forward conduct in this respect, will as you plainly see, have disastrous consequences. So deal openly with me.

Give me proper notice of your appointment, and full opportunity to identify . . .

If you meet my husband without my knowledge, and without affording me the opportunity to be present, it looks very much like conspiracy, and might be questioned.

Your affectionate sister,
[Vivienne]

TO *William Empson*   cc

2 September 1935   [*The Criterion*]

Dear Empson,

I should be delighted to come and meet Sansom, but dinner on Friday is impossible as I shall be going to the country.[1] I could manage dinner on Monday or Tuesday the 9th or 10th, or lunch on Tuesday, if any of these times suited you and him.[2]

1–Empson wrote (n.d.): 'I should be very pleased if you could come to some meal to meet [Sir George] Sansom, a man I like and admire, Commercial Counsellor in Tokyo. He gets to London tomorrow and stays for a week or two . . . Could you dine on Friday or suggest a day?'

2–WE wrote again (n.d.) to suggest Schmidt's on Charlotte Street on the Monday: he proposed that the party should proceed to call on John Hayward afterwards. TSE's secretary confirmed on 4 Sept. that TSE would be glad to meet him at Schmidt's on the Monday.

Empson was to recall: 'There was some dinner including a charming diplomat's wife [Katharine Sansom], who remarked to Eliot that she too was very fond of reading. She didn't get much time, but she was always reading in bed, biographies and things. "With

Yours sincerely,

[T. S. Eliot]

TO *Richard O'Sullivan*[1]   CC

2 September 1935   [Faber & Faber Ltd]

Dear O'Sullivan,

Thank you very much for letting me know about Father Garrigou Lagrange's lecture.[2] I have already heard of it, and am intending to go with Montgomery Belgion. I should like very much to come into your rooms afterwards and meet Father Garrigou Lagrange if I might bring Belgion with me. But I shall not do so without your consent. Belgion of course speaks French fluently.

The only book of his that I know is *Le Sens Commun*, but in any case his reputation would be enough to bring me.

I should like to ask a favour of you. My old friend A. J. Penty sent me an essay on the break up of Medieval civilisation as a result of the spread of Roman Law. I am not competent to criticise such an article myself, and I have taken one opinion which is not very favourable, but Penty is very anxious to get the article published, and he has referred me to you as an authority on Roman Law. Would you be willing to read it if I sent it to you, and give me a candid and confidential opinion?

Yours sincerely,

[T. S. Eliot]

---

pen in hand?" inquired Mr Eliot, in a voice that contrived to form a question without leaving its lowest note of gloom. There was a rather fluttered disclaimer, and he went on: "It is the chief penalty of becoming a professional literary man that one can no longer read anything with pleasure." This went down very well, but it struck me that the Johnsonian manner requires more gusto as a contrast to the pessimism; perhaps after all, looking back, a mistaken complaint, because if untruth is required to justify this sort of quip it was surely quite untrue that he no longer read anything with pleasure' ('The Style of the Master', repr. in Empson, *Argufying*, 362).

1 – Richard O'Sullivan, KC, KSG (1888–1963), barrister, wrote on the Christian origin of the Common Law of England; and he was founder of the Sir Thomas More Society.

2 – Réginald Garrigou-Lagrange, OP (1877–1964), Dominican priest; leading Catholic Thomist theologian; author of *Le sens commun: La Philosophie de l'être et les Formules Dogmatiques* (3rd edn, 1922), and *Les Trois Conversions et les Trois Voies* (1933): both in TSE library. He spoke under the auspices of the Aquinas Society at the Temple, London, on 'Le Premier Regard de l'Intelligence et la Contemplation'.

3 September 1935   Faber & Faber Ltd

My dear Roberts,

I have your letter of the 31st, and I hope that you can find time to come and see me while you are in London. I shall be going away for the weekend on Friday afternoon, so I hope you will ring up and fix a meeting when you arrive.

The anthology is not being actually set up yet. We are merely having made what is called a cast-off to determine approximately the number of printed pages that the present material will cover. There will be opportunity to make any alterations that you want. It will be quite impossible, however, to produce a book of this size, which will need to be done with care, for the autumn season, and we count upon bringing it out as early as possible in the New Year.

The hint of criticism which you think you detect was certainly not intended.[1] I was simply interested by the differences and thought it right that they should be expressed.

With kindest regards to Mrs Roberts,

Yours sincerely,
T. S. Eliot

1–Roberts wrote on 31 Aug.: 'There is a hint of criticism in your remark [letter of 20 Aug.] that my draft introduction represents a newer point of view than your own: I'm never convinced that a thing is right (even for the moment) because it's new. I'd like you to speak out one day when we meet . . . The error of fact which you mention – relation, or absence of relation, of Pound & Symbolists, is simply hasty writing on my part: I'll correct it with your letter before me.'

3 September 1935   Faber & Faber Ltd

Dear Mr Grigson,

I can see no harm in having a number about poets and the theatre.[1] The great weakness is that so far there has been a great deal of talk about poets and the theatre and very little to show in the way of actual ~~performance~~ writing. I think that such a number ought to be late enough to include a critical examination of Rupert Doone's Group Theatre, both of the aims which Doone has and of the actual accomplishment in his autumn production. It would be a good thing for the Group Theatre to receive friendly but unsparing criticism. I think that such movements are apt to suffer from not getting enough of encouragement and intelligent criticism well mixed. I shall be pretty busy up to December, but I would gladly try to write a short note for you on some general point.[2]

Yours sincerely,

T. S. Eliot

1 – Grigson asked on 1 Sept., 'Do you think it would be a good thing to have a number of *New Verse* about poets and the theatre? And if such a number were planned, and not published before December, could you possibly write something for it, since much of the present activity has come from you?' (Grigson wrote again on the subject on 7 Nov. – 'Can you write, describing the theatre and the kind of plays we can, or should have or something on the principles of a verse drama? . . . Louis MacNeice is writing on Yeats, Humphrey Jennings on yourself and Auden, Rupert Doone on Group Theatre aims.' – but TSE's response has not been traced.)

2 – TSE, 'Audiences, Producers, Plays, Poets', *New Verse*, Dec. 1935:

'It becomes much more difficult to find anything worth saying about dramatic verse, once you begin trying to write it. And theoretically, we should leave theory about contemporary drama until we have produced some contemporary drama to theorise about.

'We admit that we cannot expect to produce a new dramatic literature until we have the audiences and also the producers capable of helping the poets to write for the theatre. On the other hand the producers are checked until they have enough dramatic repertory with which to feed and train the audiences. I believe that the deficiency of plays is more serious at present than the lack of producers or of possible members of audiences. We need not assume that the possible audiences represent one class rather than another, or one political tendency rather than another. So far as the dramatic artist is concerned "the people" is everybody except the present occupants of the stalls at the more expensive theatres.

'In a period in which dramatic verse is the normal theatrical form we may suppose that a poet has better opportunities of learning to be a good playwright than he has today. But at any time it is probably more possible for a poet to learn how to write a tolerable play, than for a playwright to learn how to write tolerable verse. Yet the poet who starts to write plays, today, should not expect to turn himself into a *very* good playwright. He must learn to work hard at an unfamiliar task for which he probably has no native gift, and to learn when (as well as when not) to be guided by those who know the theatre better than he does. As he is attempting to do something new on the stage, he will inevitably theorise a little about what he

4 September 1935   [*The Criterion*]

Dear Porteus,

   I put your outline up to the Committee this afternoon,[1] and am empowered to make the following offer: for a manuscript of 15,000 words on your outline, to be delivered with the necessary (what you think necessary) line-block illustrations by September 25th next, an advance of £10 on publication on a royalty of 10%. The pamphlet would be published, like two of our preceding Criterion Miscellany Art Exhibition pamphlets, at two shillings – we think the people who want it will pay two shillings as easily as one.

   Can you manage this? I hope so. I enjoyed dining with you very much, and I hope you will both dine with me on or before the date of publication.

                                        Yours
                                        [T. S. Eliot]

---

is doing: but I think he will be wise to aim at the minimum, rather than the maximum amount of theory, and for the most part keep his theories to himself. That does not exclude him from communicating to his colleagues any practical lessons he learns in the course of his experiments.

   'The audience does not come to see what he does, in order to rally round a theory, but to be interested and excited. The indispensable merit of a verse play is that it shall be interesting, that it shall hold the audience all the time. And it will not do that, if the audience is expected to do too much of the work. This is a very good exercise for poets, who seem to forget often that poetry, even to be readable, should be interesting.

   'Second, the interest should be one interest throughout, not merely a succession of interests, or of momentary surprises. The play should have form: it needs more form than an ordinary conversation piece; it must have "dramatic form" and also the *musical pattern* which can be obtained only by verse; and the two forms must be one.

   'Third: no models, only suggestions. Continual effort of self-criticism to find out what one can do and what one can't, to build one's form on one's strength. This is expecting of the dramatic poet only the self-knowledge of the successful boxer or tennis-player. To violate every precedent, and break every rule except those mentioned above, if that will help to exploit one's strength and render harmless one's weakness.'

1 – A sketch for *Background to Chinese Art* (1935).

TO *A. A. le M. Simpson*   cc

4 September 1935   [Faber & Faber Ltd]

Dear Mr Simpson,

I have read your volume of poems in its second state pretty carefully, and think that it is an advance over the first selection.[1] I still don't feel that you have got a volume which we could publish, although I am far from saying that you could not get a good house to publish them. While the general effect is often very impressive, I find that the majority do not seem to bear very close analysis. In general, I do not feel that you have yet a sure hand in getting things down to the plain statement. There seems to me to be a very frequent, although slight, inflation – in other words, an infusion of the poetical. It is of course by no means necessary that the reader should be made to feel that the author knows exactly why every particular word is there.

I find two pieces at least which I might like to publish in the *Criterion*, but even about these I have occasional queries. One is a sonnet beginning 'Not more variable the plumed wave'. I don't understand why the substantive 'seas' is qualified by the adjective 'utter'. I should like to be certain why you use 'truckling' instead of 'trickling', and unless 'beyond Euphrates' is an allusion to a particular tigress, it seems to me mere decoration. The other poem is 'Small Warehouse Deserted'. I should like to query the adjectives 'swart' and 'nude'. Otherwise I like the poem. Would you care to consider these points and let me hear from you again? Meanwhile I return you the whole volume.

Yours sincerely,

[T. S. Eliot]

---

1 – Simpson (Newcastle on Tyne) reminded TSE on 13 July that he had first submitted some poems 'a year or two ago'; he had since rewritten the long poem on Nehemiah, and added more.

TO *Merrill Moore*[1]   CC

4 September 1935   [Faber & Faber Ltd]

Dear Dr Moore,

I have kept for a long time Dudley Fitts's poems which you sent me.[2] I like to keep poems for some months and look at them from time to time to try to get new impressions. I still feel unsatisfied with these. They have a good deal of wit and elegance, but on the whole seem to me rather brittle. I hope you will forgive me for the delay.

With all best wishes to yourself and Mrs Moore.

I am,
Yours sincerely,
[T. S. Eliot]

TO *Montgomery Butchart*[3]   CC

4 September 1935   [*The Criterion*]

Dear Mr Butchart,

I have your letter of the 3rd, and am sending you *Jefferson and/or Mussolini*, although I am still wondering how the book can be reviewed

---

1–Merrill Moore (1903–57), poet, psychiatrist and polymath, was educated at Vanderbilt University where he joined the circle of writers called 'Fugitives' (including Allen Tate, Robert Penn Warren and John Crowe Ransom) and contributed sonnets and other short poems to the *Fugitive*, 1922–5; he also edited *Fugitives: An Anthology of Verse* (1927). He studied medicine and psychiatry at Vanderbilt Medical School, and in 1929 moved to Boston where he specialised in neuropathology and psychiatry in various hospitals; and from 1935 he set up in private practice – one of his later patients was Robert Lowell, about whom he was to correspond with TSE. Author of innumerable sonnets (he would write sonnets every day of his life), his publications include *The Noise that Times Makes* (1929), *M: A Thousand Autobiographical Sonnets* (1938); and contributions to scientific journals: he was an authority on alcoholism and suicide. See further Henry W. Wells, *Poet and Psychiatrist: Merrill Moore* (1955). FVM told the publisher Donald Brace, 15 Feb. 1935: 'Eliot has a great respect for Merrill Moore, and I have been gaining one by reading the new sonnets, *Six Sides to a Man* [1935]. But we have got a heavy deck load of poetry ahead of us, and we do shiver at the thought of adding to it. We haven't got such a big hull that we can carry too much canvas; some of it just has to be reefed. Will he understand that it is no disrespect if we feel we cannot make an offer for this book?'
2–Moore submitted 'Fitts' first manuscript of poems' on 3 May.
3–Co-editor of the quarterly *Townsman*. Philip Mairet, in a letter to Maurice Reckitt, 18 Oct. 1936 (Sussex), referred to Butchart as a 'fascist': cited in Jason Harding, *The 'Criterion': Cultural Politics and Periodical Networks in Inter-War Britain* (Oxford, 2002), 193 n. 72.

at all.[1] But I should like to have a review of it if possible, and I should be very grateful if you could see what you can do with it up to 1,000 words.[2]

As for *Money in Industry*, I like to maintain a close contact with the *N.E.W.*, and I think that to some extent the two papers are read by the same people. I am therefore all the more doubtful of the expediency of having the same writers review the same books in both. Otherwise I should have been delighted to let you have it. Would you care to do a short note on the new biography of Basil Zaharoff?[3] It is rather a romantic and journalistic affair, but I think it could bear mentioning.

Yours sincerely,
[T. S. Eliot]

TO *Polly Tandy*   TS BL

4 September 1935   Faber & Faber Ltd

Dear Polly,

Thank you very much for your letter of 3d. instant. No One is more sorry about the September weekend than I am, or as much so, but there it is, as you say, some of my friends are like that but not all, and one occasion after all is to celebrate my Birth Day, which is sooner than you expect, St Cyprian's Day by the Anglican Kalander (why do they spell it with a K it reminds me of the Arabian Nights) but not by the Roman, you will remember he was stoned to death and I used to go to St Cyprian's Church and now I am St Stephen's and that is just 3 months later Dec. 26th and he was stoned to death too and that is a bad horoscope indeed, so if you expect to finish a pull Over by my birth Day I dont see how its to be done and I cant give you my chest measure yes I have found a tape measure and if I breathe in deep as I did it is just 40 inches but that seems nothing in my younger days when I worked by the Sandow system[4] and kept a chart in front of me showing the measurements of Jack Johnson and I hoped that I might expand to 46 O Youth Youth well then I would have been ashamed to be so Puny as I am now Still a Pull over would be

1 – 'The task is not an easy one, but I can, I hope, do something toward drawing attention to the book's chief function, which as I understand it is not so much to praise Mussolini as to stress the fact that political action must be conceived as dynamic rather than static – etc.'
2 – Butchart on EP, *Jefferson and/or Mussolini*: C. 15 (Jan. 1936), 323–6.
3 – Basil Zaharoff (1849–1936): Greek-born arms dealer and industrialist. No review of Robert Neumann, *Zaharoff the Armaments King* (1935), appeared in C.
4 – Eugen Sandow (1867–1925), known as 'the father of modern bodybuilding'.

very acceptable when I step on to the Links with your husband giving Him a Handicap of 12 or 3⅛ a hole I never used that ⅛ before that is why it looks so fresh. But now, what about a weekday? next week I have promised to go down with Morley on Wednesday night today night week and stay over the weekend to rest that is to say I must write an essay on Tennyson whilst there Heaven help me so that brings us to the following week and very likely that is too late to be useful but of course otherwise I am your servant. Now to close will you please give your Husband the enclosed Token it may be of some use to him what some barsted parsed off on me unknowing I am like that never suspecting Evil of no one He'll know how to give it a nick in it some wheres to give it to the English in his next 4-ale bar tourniament [*sic*], also I dont seem to get round to having that photographic enlargement made of Him but you wait and you please ask him to give me a Ring one morning either Western 1670 or Museum 9543 is sure to fetch me so will close with many Thoughts affectionately your indefatigable

Lavender Possum

TO *D. G. Bridson*   cc

5 September 1935   [Faber & Faber Ltd]

Dear Mr Bridson,

Thank you for your letter of 4th September.[1] I will advise the advertising manager that you are no longer reviewing poetry for *Time and Tide*, but you need not send back anything you received. I should have liked you to look at Barker's book, and formed your opinion of it. Incidentally, as you speak of having made use of Bottrall and Day Lewis, do you think you could do anything for Barker?[2] His poems have not attracted a great deal of attention yet, and I should like to get them before the public.

1–Bridson was working as BBC Feature Programme Writer to the North, and no longer reviewing on a regular basis for *Time & Tide*: he was therefore passing the review copy of George Barker's *Janus* directly to *Time & Tide*.

2–'If you feel that I could be of service to Faber's, as a programme material spotter, and feel that the expense would be justified from your point of view, I should be very glad to receive review or proof copies . . . of your poetry publications.

'I have already been able to make use of various good folk, such as Bottrall and Day Lewis, in feature programmes, and suppose that the attendant publicity may possibly have affected their sales, – one way or another!'

I was lunching today with Gielgud,[1] and there seems to be a fair prospect of their doing *Murder in the Cathedral* in the autumn.[2] I have agreed on condition that they get Speaight to take the leading role, and procure a chorus from Fogerty's, and both these conditions appear to be feasible. We also want to get Martin Browne into it if possible.

Yours ever,

[T. S. Eliot]

FROM *Vivien Eliot* TO *Maurice Haigh-Wood*   cc Bodleian

5 September 1935   The English Speaking Union,
                                    Dartmouth House,
                                    37 Charles Street, Mayfair w.1

Dear Maurice,

Further to my letter to you of 3rd inst, I must add, that, during our conversation in Hyde Park, you intimated that the Church has got such an ascendancy over Tom's mind, that it 'will change his point of view'. I see what you mean, but, you cannot accuse the Church of having a sane man of genius, and of middle age, in its power, to such an extent, that his 'point of view' is changed, whether he likes it or not.

England is still a free country, and the Church has no power over the individual, legally.

You will have noted what I say in my previous letter, about your meeting my husband without my knowledge, and without giving me the full opportunity to be present.

Your affectionate sister,

[Vivienne]

1 – TSE lunched at the Langham Hotel with BBC producer Val Gielgud and the Revd F. A. Iremonger, head of religious broadcasting.
2 – 'I understand from Gilliam that there is a probability of "Murder in the Cathedral" being broadcast shortly, and look forward to hearing it, especially if Speaight again takes the lead.'

7 September 1935   The English Speaking Union

My dear Maurice,

I now have your letter of 2nd inst.[1] Since I wrote to you on the 1st, to which yours is an answer, I have written to you twice again, on the 3rd., and on the 5th. You will have had both these letters by now.

In reply to yours I can only say that your letter is evasive and insincere. It is impossible that you do not see the extreme seriousness of the point I have now written to you *four times*.

If you do *not* see Tom, it is very strange, and after 22 years of close friendship and intimate relationship, it is *not right*.

If you do see Tom, and do so without affording me the opportunity to be present, it *looks*, as I said before, like conspiracy.

You say in your letter, that in the event of your seeing him, you would be bound to ask his consent before making any arrangement which would enable me to be present with the object of identifying him. You say that you are sure that I shall agree with you on this point.

In reply, I say that in the circumstances, I do *not* agree that you would have to *warn* Tom beforehand that I should be near enough to see him, and that this statement, coming from you, is strange, and not in my opinion straight dealing. Should Tom wish to see me, I can imagine *no* circumstances in which I should wish to be *warned beforehand* that he was going to be present.

I am bound to say now, that I consider that, ever since July 1933, you have treated me with almost insane cruelty and casualness. I have not said this openly before because I felt your behaviour on this point to be *too* insane to permit of argument. But at this point, I now must say that that is my considered opinion.

I will repeat that I think you ought to see Tom, and to make every effort to ameliorate the situation, and to treat him as the good and affectionate brother-in-law which he always was to you.

It is NOT *sane* to behave as though he no longer exists. But I cannot argue, as I say. Do not juggle with sanity. It is shocking that you say you have not seen Tom for ages and ages.

1–MH-W had replied, 2 Sept.: 'I have no idea whether I shall be seeing Tom at any time – I haven't seen him for ages & ages. But if the occasion should ever arise for making an appointment I would be *bound* to ask his consent to any such arrangement as you suggest. If you reflect, I am sure you will agree that is so. But in any case, as it is very unlikely that I shall be seeing him, the question doesn't arise.'

To me, it sounds like the behaviour of barbarians, and as though all Civilisation is killed.

I hope you will not mind having *both* the photographs of my [*sic*] which I showed you, because I had really intended to have both framed for you in any case.

I hope I shall see Raggy walking bravely out in his red shoes.[1]

Your affect sister,

[Vivienne]

TO *George Dickson*   cc

10 September 1936   [*The Criterion*]

Dear Sir,

I have your letter of the 27th August, and have read with some interest your enclosed poems.[2] I do not feel that they are suitable for the *Criterion*, and in any case you say that you are not offering them for publication. I cannot make up my mind about their merit, but they are certainly peculiar, and different from anything I have seen lately. I shall be interested to hear what happens to 'The Donkeyman'.

Yours very truly,

[T. S. Eliot]

TO *Blánaid Salkeld*   cc

10 September 1935   [Faber & Faber Ltd]

Dear Miss Salkeld,

I think it is time that I returned your translations from Pushkin.[3] I must say that I do not like them as well as your original verse, but I have

---

1 – VHE wrote in her diary, 20 Feb. 1935, that her nephew, MH-W's son 'Raggy', 'looks very delicate & frail, & has a sallow & un-healthy colour . . . his mind & brain are too active & the child is a genius . . . he is so clever and so witty and so sharp that he will always be a popular visitor.'

2 – George Dickson was until the age of twenty-four a fitter in a Clyde shipyard, and had published a long poem entitled *Peter Rae* (1925), plus other items. For the last ten years he had been working at his writing, and had just submitted to Allen & Unwin a new long work, *The Donkeyman*. He asked TSE simply for 'a valuation of what I'm doing. Conceit, I expect . . . I have a funny fancy about poets and others trying to pimp on the muse. I apologise for troubling you.'

3 – Salkeld submitted her translations from Pushkin and Blok on 7 July 1935.

never seen any translations from Pushkin or any other Russian poet which convinced me that the original was really poetry. I shall always be glad to see more of your own work.

Yours very truly,
[T. S. Eliot]

TO *W. B. Yeats* CC

10 September 1935   [Faber & Faber Ltd]

Dear Yeats,

Thank you for your letter of September 3rd.[1] I hope that you have now received back the first draft of your preface. I am unable as yet to give you any information about the decision of my Committee, but I hope that I may be able to let you know definitely by the end of this week. Meanwhile, Lady Gerald rang me up just before she went away, and she understands that the book could not be produced for the autumn season in any case, and is in no hurry.[2]

I was very much interested and encouraged by the two letters which you sent, and which I return herewith.

Very many thanks for your remarks about Martin Browne's lecture. I wish indeed that it were possible to have a performance in Dublin. It would give me a good pretext for a visit.[3]

1–Yeats wrote that Lady Gerald Wellesley was anxious to read his preface to her work: would TSE please hang on to the second, typed copy and return the first for him to send on to her? Yeats reported too that he had attended a lecture on TSE's work by EMB, with readings by Robert Speaight, at the Abbey Theatre, Dublin. 'The passages were most moving.' He would try to find out from the Board of the Abbey Theatre whether it might be possible to arrange for a production of *MiC*.

2–Lady Gerald Wellesley wrote ('Thursday'), in response to a now lost letter from TSE: 'I have looked up my agreement & find that the copyright of my Poems is mine. So there is no obstacle in that direction so far as Yeats' Selection is concerned ... Would it be asking too much if I asked for a copy of Yeats' Preface when convenient to you. I haven't even seen it yet! Yes, he does go the pace.' For Wellesley, see letter to her, 16 Oct. 1935, below.

3–Schuchard relates (*The Last Minstrels*, 365–66): 'Yeats recognized immediately and generously the dramatic force and poetic power of Eliot's *Murder in the Cathedral* ... Yeats went to hear Eliot's director E. Martin Browne lecture on – and the actor Robert Speaight read verse and choruses from – the play on the Abbey stage in September. After attending a performance of Ashley Dukes' revived production at the Mercury in November, he wrote to his wife, "It is to my great surprise a powerful religious play," admitting that it would be a success at the Abbey. But what struck his interest most was the Chorus of Eliot's Women of Canterbury ... "It needs however a chorus of women of five or six they have eight at the Mercury," he explained to George ... In his excitement about Eliot's chorus, he shared his observations with Martin Browne:

I take it that you will not be leaving for the South for another two months or so. Meanwhile I hope that your health remains stable.

Yours ever,

[T. S. Eliot]

TO *Edith Perkins*　　　　　　　　TS Donald Gallup/Beinecke

10 September 1935　　　　　　　　Faber & Faber Ltd

Dear Mrs Perkins,

I begin to feel that you will become as tired of my notes as you might be expected to be of my company; but I fortify myself in the assurance that it is my grateful duty, as well as my pleasure, to write to express my appreciation, whether the letter be welcomed or not. Though the combinations of words may not be inexhaustible (I had to look that word up to see whether it was spelt with an i or an a) I wish to record the fact, on each occasion, that I have added another two days to my store of happy memories: which is not a mere addition of quantity to a general store, because these minute additions (minute in quantity in relation to a lifetime) have a qualitative difference from the parallel occasions that call forth a letter of thanks, a difference of quality due in small part to the place and chiefly to the persons and combination of persons and to the thoughtful planning and hospitable care so unobtrusive as to become apparent only upon analysis. I do not know whether I make myself clear, but I trust that the feeling, if not the sense, is quite evident. Next time, to which I look forward with such keen, I may say in the circumstances poignant pleasure, I shall hope to bring a small piece of good cheese, to return – it would be infelicitous to say a mite – a grain of pleasure in receiving so much. I wish all success to your lecture for the Church Hall, and I hope it will be fully appreciated; though I confess that I seldom feel that the beneficiaries realise all the toil and sacrifice of time that a lecture

---

My only criticism is that the chorus of women speaking in unison was too large by three . . . Florence Farr got great beauty by alternating voices which had a different quality of tone, but that would probably have interfered with your simple massed effects.'

Schuchard quotes further, from the same letter to Browne (*c.* 12 Nov. 1935), Yeats's riddling-obscure judgement: '*Murder in the Cathedral* is a powerful play, because the actor, the monkish habit, certain repeated words, symbolize what we know not what the author knows.'

represents to a conscientious lecturer. Meanwhile if I *could* be of any use in London with respect to house-agents I should be very happy.

Yours very sincerely,
T. S. Eliot

TO *F. T. Prince*[1]   TS Frank Prince

10 September 1935   Faber & Faber Ltd

Dear Mr Prince,

I have your letter of the 9th. I shall look forward to your revision of *Tshaka*, and as I now know a little more about Tshaka than I did when you first introduced me to that warrior, I may be able to judge it more intelligently.[2] Meanwhile it is possible that I may use one of your other poems as soon as I have space for it. 'The Epistle to a Patron' proved too long for me to use in the number which I have just made up.[3]

I am very interested in your notion of completing the 'Ivory Tower'.[4] It is an ambitious attempt, but the exercise may prove very useful to you. If you are thinking of making any commercial use of it I wonder whether you have considered the matter of copyright? I have never known of such a case before, but I should imagine that you would have to offer the book to Macmillan, as Henry James's publishers. Or if any other publishers were interested then they would have to get a licence from Macmillan's to use the part that Henry James wrote.

---

1 – Frank Templeton Prince (1912–2003), poet, critic and editor, graduated first-class in English from Balliol College, Oxford, in 1934. TSE published his first book, *Poems*, in 1938. Following WW2 he taught at Southampton University, becoming Professor in 1957. Other works include well-received collections of poetry including *Soldiers Bathing* (1954), *Collected Poems, 1935–1992* (1993); and *The Italian Element in Milton's Verse* (1954).

2 – Prince had written about his long poem on 20 Feb. 1935: 'It seems to me that in *intention* my work stands in the relation of, say, Milton's to the poetic school of which Mr Auden may be the Fletcher, Mr Pound and yourself the Shakespeare. To press the analogy at any point, and especially where my *results* are concerned, would be to render it quite absurd . . .'

3 – Prince submitted his 'new version' of 'Tshaka' on 2 Nov. 1935 – 'completed . . . to the absolute best of my present ability' – along with revised versions of two other poems. See 'Epistle to a Patron', *C*. 15 (Jan. 1936), 261–4.

4 – 'The summer has been occupied also by my plans for another piece of work. I have decided to complete, with the help of his notes, James' "The Ivory Tower", a third of which was written when war broke out in 1914. The plot is very well suited to my purpose, which is to use the theme as a sort of *persona*, implying a certain view of James' intentions and methods. I shall follow his style, which was even then fluid, [no] more than may be essential to the story and these superimposed meanings.'

I hope that you will very much enjoy your stay at Princeton. If you care to do so I should be glad if you introduced yourself in my name both to Dr Paul Elmer More and Professor Willard Thorp. There is also, or was, a very nice Chaplain named Crocker.[1] The Graduate School is a very attractive place as American universities go.

With all best wishes,
Yours sincerely,
T. S. Eliot

TO *Charles Williams*   cc

10 September 1935   [Faber & Faber Ltd]

My dear Williams,

Thank you very much for your letter of the 5th September.[2] What you say seems to be an adequate recommendation, and I should like to try Miss Fraser. But it was stupid of me not to say that if you could recommend her would you be so kind as to give me her address. The lady who brought her name to my notice could not tell me.

Best wishes for Cranmer.[3] But you have chosen a more difficult subject than mine.

Yours sincerely,
[T. S. Eliot]

1 – Revd John Crocker (1900–84) was from 1933 chaplain for Episcopal students at Princeton.

2 – Williams responded to TSE's enquiry of 4 Sept.: 'Miss [Vera] Fraser has certainly done a great deal of collation for me at the British Museum, and as far as I have found she has been extremely accurate. We know that she is acquainted with several European languages, and I know that she has a secret acquaintance with the Best. I have not actually tried her on the Italian Renaissance but I should be perfectly prepared to send her a book in the expectation of her producing something reasonably good. As an immoral addition to this, I know she needs money very badly.'

3 – Williams disclosed that he was to be writing on Thomas Cranmer for the Canterbury Festival 1936 [*Thomas Cranmer of Canterbury*] – 'you had a better spectacle!'

12 September 1935   315 East 68th Street,
                                     New York City

My dear Tom:

I have been reading with much enjoyment the issues of *Time and Tide* containing the many-sided controversy which you engaged in last winter, to which you referred briefly in one of your letters. I wish that the 'Readers' Pages' of American periodicals more often contained such lively debates. At the same time, however, such debates usually reveal the vices of most people in debate: their tendency to seize on petty and immaterial points, and to aim rather at making their opponents look the fool than to meet the issue. In this instance, it seems to me, a passage from your preface to *After Strange Gods* is apropos: 'In our time, controversy seems to me, on really fundamental matters, to be futile. It can only usefully be practical where there is common understanding.' With this I agree heartily, provided that by common understanding you do not mean common belief. This particular controversy reminds me of a form of entertainment known as a 'battle royal', which I understand is popular in the Navy and in negro athletic clubs. This is a contest in which a number of pugilists, the more the merrier I suppose, are fitted out with boxing gloves, blindfolded, and turned loose in the ring. Every man's hand is against every other's, and the one left standing at the last is the winner. There is this difference between this kind of spectacle and that afforded by your combatants: that the latter seem to me at too long range to do any effective damage, and most of their blows whistle through the air.

I think that part of the trouble is your practice of discussing abstractly matters which seem to me to require concrete treatment. In one place you take your opponents to task for talking about Liberty in the abstract; whereas your preceding article was largely devoted to discussing, without any apparent difficulty, War in the abstract. I do not have the trouble that some of these correspondents do in getting your ideas about war; at least I think that I understand that you are not willing to utter a sweeping condemnation of war, there being conceivably some wars which are either good or necessary. You don't define such wars, but I should guess that you might endorse a religious war, provided it had none of the disgraceful features which marked the Crusades; or (as I myself should) a war of defense, if it were simon-pure defense and the only alternative to extinction. I also understand that you believe that war is the result of economic causes, and that these causes should be removed; though you doubt that by reorganisation of the social or economic or financial system war can be rendered permanently obsolete.

You seem to have trouble, however, with Liberty in the abstract and with Peace in the abstract. To me, Mr Milne's definition of peace as 'non-war' seems adequate. At a guess, which may not be allowable, I should say that you do not regard as peace a state of affairs in which an under-cover economic war is going on; but that would certainly be putting words in your mouth. I do think that you might have made yourself a good deal clearer to your readers. Sometimes you remind me of a gentleman in full evening dress and white gloves attempting to put something right with the kitchen plumbing without soiling his attire. You are hampered by the fact that, whatever you may want to say, your public expects it to be a worthy permanent addition to the world's literature.

I fear it is largely this, and a certain manner of speaking, which has drawn the fire of so many antagonists. Miss West seems to be the most annoyed, and the violence of her attack suggests that her bile is the accumulation of a number of years. I think that her aim is often poor, but (whether, as one correspondent declares, it is in 'the worst possible taste' to mention what seems to me a mild jibe compared with those that British statesmen have to endure) the legend of the 'Great White Literary Spirit' does exist. It dates a long way back, and my belief is that it arose from a sort of stage-fright in your early career. The T. S. Eliot of those days, as I believe, was a figure created in their own image by the *arbitres elegantiae* of the literary press (perhaps, as we say nowadays, a 'wish-fulfilment' of theirs.) He was a character created for you, a role in which you were cast, and which you felt you had to play like the very devil to meet the expectations of your audience. It is, I think, a rather dreadful character, almost as bad as Wells's caricature of it (which, I dare say, only made it go better with the gallery.) I can trace well back in your writings, however, back to your preface to the 1928 edition of *The Sacred Wood*, your uneasiness in the role and your anxiety to be done with it. I can cite at least a dozen pages in your works to that effect which no critic, so far as I know, has taken the pains to notice; a typical example, I think, of the confirmed habit of critics of wearing side-blinders.

This character is so endeared to the critics, however, and his mannerisms so popular with the gallery, that they constantly clamor for a return engagement. Among such mannerisms is, for instance, a way of confessing ignorance of what your opponent means, which somehow conveys the idea that this is due to failure of intelligence on his part rather than your own. This always, to me, suggests weakness; it is too like that kind of fling that a certain type of woman (and I dare say man too) makes when worsted: 'I'm sure I don't know what you mean!' Another of these habits is illustrated in this series of articles in *Time and Tide*, in your penultimate advice to your readers: 'We do need to think a great deal harder and more patiently,' etc. I do not see how you can fail to observe for yourself how like this is to the tone of a schoolmaster dismissing his class at the end of term-time. (Having said which, I pray to be delivered from the fault of using the same tone in this letter!)

But these considerations would not have moved me to write at length. What has roused me is your announcement, or what looks like an announcement, that you are a sceptic. I might be in greater doubt about this but that these articles of yours in *Time and Tide* appear to bear out the supposition that you are a sceptic. I do not, of course, mean a disbeliever or an agnostic. Back in the attic of my memory there lies the name of a certain Pyrrho, a Greek philosopher, I think, who believed in perpetual suspense of judgment, and practised what he preached till he became a victim of something like aboulia.[1] Your scepticism is manifest in your constant worry over terminology: What is Liberty? What is Work? What is Peace? you ask; and will not stay for an answer. Nor can you reach any conclusion: 'We need to think about the relation of one thing and another, and to be a little clearer about our standards of moral value'.

> Do I dare
> Disturb the universe?
> In a minute there is time
> For decisions and revisions which a minute shall reverse.

All roads lead to the overwhelming question 'If one is going to theorise about liberty, then one must go on from political and economic liberty to moral liberty. And one cannot stop short of theology'. 'The Church today offers the last asylum for the sceptic.' *La sua volontate e nostra pace.* (Incidentally, your *Dante* (F & F) spells this '*voluntade*'; my Italian dictionary gives only '*volontà*'; the Dent edition of *Dante* – your copy – has '*volontate*'.)

This revelation, if revelation it is, is exceedingly interesting to me and no doubt equally interesting to a great many people who would like to know the path which has led you to the Church. I can understand this state of mind, being no stranger to the agonies of indecision or to the mental torture

---

1 – *Abulia*: 'Loss or impairment of the ability to act, make decisions, or initiate physical or mental activity, as a symptom of mental illness or injury to the brain; (*gen.*) absence of will power, indecisiveness; an instance of this' (*OED*). See *L1*, 6 Nov. 1921: 'My nerves are a very mild affair, due . . . to an aboulie and emotional derangement which has been a lifelong affliction' (cited in *OED* from *TWL Facs.*, xxii).

of losing one's way in the pathless forests of philosophical speculation. At the same time, I must say (and I am certainly not alone in this) that the problems of epistemology and ontology and eschatology do not seem to me to have the same immediacy or reality that they seem (judging from the above) to have for you. (And while I am about it, I should like to register a complaint against the philosophers for appropriating to other uses this word 'reality', to which I think the common man has a prior right: for him, quite naturally, it serves to denote the objects of sense. In exchange they have given him the denigratory word 'appearance', reserving 'reality' for all the conflicting fancies of that notoriously fallible instrument, the philosophical mind.)

It is difficult for me to view philosophical scepticism as an acute form of distress, such as could drive any one to desperation and cause him to put his beliefs in trust, so to speak, for sheer relief from doubt and vacillation. I can take my philosophy or leave it, as they say of liquor, and hope that in some future state of human society, no doubt extremely remote, men may attain the omniscience essential for solving such problems.

It interests me that you define the sceptic as 'the man who suspects the origins of his own beliefs, as well as those of others; who is most suspicious of those which are most passionately held; who is still more relentless towards his own beliefs than towards those of others; who suspects other people's motives because he has learned the deceitfulness of his own.' That, I think, is a narrower definition than the common one; but it serves to show the nature of your own scepticism, I should judge, all the better. It is rather a suspicious nature. In the next sentence to the above, you take Voltaire to task and throw doubt on his motives for questioning the Christian Faith. I wish that you had taken the space to present evidence of Voltaire's intellectual dishonesty. I have read at least one life of Voltaire, but I should have to do a good deal more reading, I fear, to discover what are the false motives which you have in mind.

To me, I must say, this challenging of other people's motives suggests that perhaps you (as indeed you say you do) question your own. I am not sure whether it is your past motives alone that you question, or your present motives also; I mean your motives for embracing the Church. (It is hard to see how your doubts, if they included doubts of religion itself, could have brought you to the Church). But that you may also have questioned your present motives, is suggested to me by a certain part of *Murder in the Cathedral*. This is the part where the Fourth Tempter appears. He is evidently a most subtle tempter, doing credit, I think, to your powers of psychological penetration. His entrance is unexpected, even by

Becket, who has anticipated the other three. The Tempter offers the bait of spiritual power, glory after death, pilgrims adoring his glittering shrine, bending the knee; he also pictures the dreadfulness of being forgotten, of being 'de-bunked' by future critics. His advice is to go ahead and become a martyr, because it is the only thing he (Becket) can do anyway, and as a martyr he will 'rule from the tomb'. 'Your thoughts (unworthy motives) have more power than kings to compel you.' Replies Thomas:

> The last temptation is the greatest treason:
> To do the right deed for the wrong reason.

These passages are very fine, and display, I think, your peculiar genius for impregnating intellectual concepts (though not necessarily conclusive ones) with intense emotional value. The feeling is genuine and personal, and it is this quality which when present (in *The Rock* it seems to me not always present) elevates your poetry above the merely good poetry of your contemporaries.

People commonly speak as if motives were always single; whereas they are usually multiple; and often nearly as obscure to oneself as to others. But a great many secondary motives can be classified under the primary motive of wishing to appear well in the eyes of others. In this respect our actions are regulated almost as straitly by public opinion as by legal coercion. The more prominent a man is, therefore, and the more he fills the public eye, the less free he is. Kings are not free. The President of this Republic is not free. He cannot, like the humblest citizen, take his ease in his inn, shoot off his mouth, and curse Congress to his heart's content. He has to 'watch his step.'

You have lived nearly half your life in a society as plagued with tabus as an African tribe, as narrowly regimented by its own standards as a fascist or communist community is by its laws. I refer to Bloomsbury and not to English society in general. It is a small stage, a 'little theatre', but with an enormous gallery, containing a large American element. You have to be as sensitive to the changing moods of this audience and as quick to meet them as an actor is to change his 'stuff' when a 'line' does not get over. You lead, but (like all but the very greatest leaders, rare in history) you have to lead in the direction in which you sense that your followers want to go. You can, to be sure, create a vogue for Dryden or Donne, or a distaste for Shelley; but I have some doubts whether (given your particular audience) you could arouse a new enthusiasm for Shelley or an active antipathy to Donne or Dryden. You are by no means free. I doubt that you are free to express without caution your opinions of the work of James Joyce or Gertrude Stein. (Nor, conversely, are they, as to your work.)

I have already remarked that in the beginning, I believe, the critics determined your role for you. It is curious that these critics, so timid and so subservient to authority, are at the same time so despotic. I firmly believe that it is the rise of the present-day type of reviewer, the supercilious sciolist, that is the cause of the 'fearful progress in self-consciousness' of which Maritain speaks in a quotation which you make in one of your Harvard lectures. I am not sure that Maritain intends the same kind of self-consciousness that I do; I think perhaps he means the kind evidenced in *oeuvres raisonnées*; I mean a kind of stage-fright, together with a phobia of the obvious, the stale and the sentimental. But I can see both kinds in Picasso and in *The Waste Land* and in Stravinsky's *Sacre du Printemps*. Since the critics have this same phobia, it must be due to some power mightier than they. This must be a sort of aesthetic Zeitgeist, and how in the beginning he was created I doubt if anyone can tell.

The Waste Land has been called the perfect expression of the Zeitgeist, but those who so characterise it, I think, refer to the *Weltzeitgeist*; whereas *The Waste Land* is, I think, an expression of the literary *Zeitgeist*. It is a literary poem for literary people. Its lamentation and despair are the lamentation and despair of the poet (and less specifically, the painter, the sculptor and the musician). The land which is waste is the field of the arts. It is waste because our predecessors have exhausted its fertility, have exploited it so prodigally that the modern poet or artist, like Jeeter Lester on his ancestral tobacco farm, has been robbed of his patrimony. Only the verminous critic finds sustenance there. No ordinary rain is needed, but a veritable flood, to coat the ground with new loam. All this agony, however, now appears to have been premature; for an enormous market sprang up for prickly pear and cactus.

This Zeitgeist has a twin sister, and her name is Fashion. Though it was not she who actually inspired the writing of *The Waste Land*, I think (and she seems to have some resemblance to a Poltergeist) I can see her fingerprints on it in spots. In the Sweeney period I suspect that she was (and it is perhaps unimportant which sense of the word one takes) your mistress. You dabbled then in some not wholly convincing diabolism (even then a trifle *passé*), and surrealism (on the lady's inside tip.) But later (though the wench is not dead, and still flirts with you) you entered into the bonds of holy matrimony with the Church. And Fashion – not a bad jade at heart – gave her blessing.

It was a fashionable wedding, and the publicity was immense. It had the sensational elements of the perfect news story. SCION OF OLD NEW ENGLAND FAMILY DECLARES ROYALIST SYMPATHIES!

DESCENDANT OF A HUNDRED UNITARIANS GOES ROMISH; THUNDERS DENUNCIATION OF PARENTAL CREED! APOSTLE OF STRANGENESS AVOWS CLASSICISM! EXTRA! EXTRA! GREATEST PARADOX OF THE CENTURY! Contemporary writers gnashed their teeth. They were scooped.

It is possible that you had no prescience of the effect of this announcement, and were as innocent as the young Lindbergh who thoughtfully provided himself with letters of introduction before his flight to Paris. You have said, 'I now see the danger of suggesting to outsiders that the Faith is a political principle or a literary fashion, and the sum of all a dramatic posture.' But if you were wary of dramatic posture how came you to address to the clergy of Boston, a city saturated with associations of your ancestors, immediate and distant, what seems to me in all truth a fanatically intolerant and shocking tirade? (I refer to the unexpurgated version of it, not that which you gave the *Christian Register*, though I am told by the editor of that paper that he asked you for the original.[1]) I cannot agree with the magnanimous and charitable editor in his editorial that (in this instance) 'Mr Eliot has stood for learning and good taste'. I cannot agree that one's supposed duty to one's church absolves one from the ordinary decencies; furthermore, even the Roman Church approves the injunction, 'Honor thy father and mother.'

Nor can I understand a neophyte upbraiding an audience of Anglican clergy, born and bred in their faith, many of them no doubt venerable, for their laxity in neglecting to expel not only backsliders, but those who 'have not yet slid far enough forward.' The only reason that I can see, why conduct of this kind does not arouse resentment, is that most people expect poets to be eccentric and like them that way.

I dare say we can credit to Fate and not design the brilliant idea which occurred to the English churchmen of obtaining, in a drive for funds, the services of a celebrated poet who was widely known as a brand plucked from the hotbed of Unitarianism. But the idea could not have been improved upon by the most astute American publicity manager. And the best of it was that the ensuing publicity was good for both; it was a square deal. But if you feared misunderstanding of your motives, you were not less than a martyr to their cause.

1–TSE, 'The Modern Dilemma', *The Christian Register* (Boston) 102 (19 Oct. 1933), 675–6; repr. in *The Complete Prose of T. S. Eliot*, vol. 4: *English Lion, 1930–1933*, ed. Jason Harding and Ronald Schuchard (2015), 810–16. This was a substantially revised version of an unpublished address entitled 'Two Masters', given on 3 Apr. 1933 to the Boston Association of Unitarian Ministers in King's Chapel.

It is, indeed, 'fatally easy, under the conditions of the modern world, for a writer of genius to conceive of himself as a Messiah.' And I am not without a certain admiration for a type of courage which it seems to me you displayed in making the addresses which I have just criticised. It is, perhaps, testimony to your sincerity; and certainly no one can say that you have not been industrious in perfecting yourself in Catholic lore. I am almost disposed to believe that it was some form of 'possession' which enabled you to make the Boston address. I do not remember being surprised when I first learned that you had a genius for poetry. But my intimate knowledge of you during the first half of your life (surely a period when a personality is truly revealed, without any subsequent crust of accretions) gave me no evidence whatever of any latent tendency in you toward 'possession', either messianic or demonic.

The step toward the Church was (any question of motive aside) such a superbly fitting gesture that I can honestly understand the compulsion you were under to take it. For it is quite in line with the best hagiological* traditions that the monstrous sinner, the author of 'The 'Potamus' and 'Mr Eliot's Sunday Morning Service' should, passing through the travail of the soul (this of course is the popular interpretation; yours, I believe is that it was 'only the relief of a personal and wholly insignificant grouse against life') of *The Waste Land*, arrive, barefoot, in sackcloth and penitent, at the foot of the Cross. The tableau is, I must say, perfect.

Unlike a certain character in one of your poems, you cannot declare 'I have not made this show purposelessly'. I believe that you have an irresistible, instinctive, more or less unconscious talent for publicity, but your exercise of it is purposeless. I cannot of course say that of Mr Shaw, who has the same talent; he knows perfectly well what he is up to; he knows that an ounce of provocative nonsense is worth a pound of obvious wisdom. But I should like to cite some examples of statements from you that have a high publicity value:

'I think that the modern world suffers from two disasters, which together are enough to undermine our civilisation: the decay of the study of Latin and Greek in colleges and universities, and the dissolution of the monasteries. It is imperative that the next generation shall see to the restoration of the monastic life in society, especially that of the more contemplative orders.'

* And the literary traditions of the late Victorian aesthetic movement. Vide biographies of Swinburne and Pater. Dante of course is a case in point in a different age.

'This (a quotation from Lawrence) speaks to me of that at which I have long aimed, in writing poetry: to write poetry which should be essentially poetry, with nothing poetic about it, poetry standing naked in its bare bones, poetry so transparent that we see not the poetry, but that which we are meant to see through the poetry, poetry so transparent that in reading it we are intent on what the poem points at and not the poetry, this seems to me to be the thing to try for.'

I should also include, but that it is too long, your comparison of some lines of Cowley's with a parody of them in Dryden's *MacFlecknoe*, to the disadvantage of the former. Your enthusiastic sponsorship of Dryden's flippant philippic, with its dull catalogue of nonentities and its hard-hammering couplets, seems to me one of the most startling events in literary history.

I should also include your cryptic notes to *The Waste Land*, and some of the epigraphs to your shorter poems. This same tendency of yours – a kind of elfin mischievousness – is apparent also in the *Time and Tide* imbroglio. You just can't help it.

I am afraid that I have shown some heat in the foregoing remarks. But you must be a salamander by now, and from your placidity during the *Time and Tide* mêlée I am encouraged to hope that you will be equally patient with me.

I can perceive a certain plausibility in the notion that, like Don Quixote, who stuffed his brain with legends of chivalry until an irrepressible desire overcame him to emulate the deeds of his heroes, you, by saturating yourself in Dante and Aquinas and the Schoolmen, have achieved, owing to your strong imaginative powers, a decided empathy in their interests. But the most that you could acquire in this way, I should think, would be merely a belief that you believed, which might not stand the garish glare of day. However, that degree of belief may be all that is necessary, if reinforced by other impulses. Perhaps you felt that you ought not to be writing religious poetry and drawing your inspiration from religious literature without something by way of amends. You owe indeed a great debt to the Church writers and to the Bible; I do not know of any poet who has captured so magnificently the macabre and gloomy grandeur of the religious outlook of the early Fathers. To repay this debt would be in keeping with your action in becoming a British citizen (of which I thoroughly approve). This action, too (joining the Church) would prove you free of the 'pious insincerity' which you attribute to most writers of devotional verse. The concern which you display over the question of discrepancy between poetic and religious belief, particularly in the case of Dante, indicates an attitude something like this.

In passing, I think you would be interested in a book, *Chroniques de ma Vie*, by Stravinsky (Edit. Denoel & Steele, Paris, 1935), the first volume of which has just appeared. I have not the book, of course, but an article about it from the *New York Times*. According to this clipping, Stravinsky is indignant at 'the principle of placing a *spectacle d'art* on the same plane as the symbolical and sacred act that constitutes a religious service.' He adds, says the article, that one cannot imagine a critical attitude (such as is essential for the creative artist) on the part of a devout worshipper in the divine service. Can any one be surprised, he exclaims, at this confusion of spiritual values in an age in which the layman must have his cult and drag in the church to justify his art? I should think that Stravinsky might have trouble in reconciling this stand with a just appreciation of the great religious painters.

I do not know, however, enough about the lives of these painters to tell me whether they were believers or ungodly. (I dare say Leonardo was an agnostic). But it seems to me that religious art may quite well be the work of an unbeliever, and indeed, be the better for the fact of the freer critical point of view thus possible. I do not know at what exact point your poetry can be separated into periods of belief and unbelief, but I do think that there is in *The Rock*, and also in *Murder in the Cathedral* less of a peculiarly stirring intensity than in *Ash Wednesday* and *The Hollow Men*. Perhaps, however, this only bears out your contention that 'we have, whether we know it or not, a prejudice against beatitude as material for poetry.'[1]

If you feel this concern over the question of your sincerity in writing religious poetry from an outside viewpoint, I do not understand why you are not also concerned about the inclusion of your blasphemous poems (and they certainly are blasphemous, despite your fallacious – I think – reasoning that one cannot blaspheme unless one believes) in your collected poems. But perhaps you will delete these when the present edition is sold out.

And if you are worrying about inconsistency, I might remind you that while you were publishing *The Rock*, and damning silly folk who use their Sundays for golf and tennis, you were simultaneously (qua publisher) publishing a work advertising on its jacket that it offers the

---

1 – See too HWE to Alida Monro, 10 July 1935: 'I find Tom's "Murder" less exciting than his earlier (pre-Rock) work, and for my part hope that he will not harp too long in that key. In fact, I hope that he will have a violent reaction from it and that his final works will reveal a lot of stuff which I am sure is still in his well-furnished and interesting mind. But not too much preaching' (BL Add MS 83366).

reader the largest aggregation of Lesbians, homosexuals, and sadists ever assembled between the covers of one book. Shortly followed by another which a New York columnist (who never before or since, to the best of my knowledge, has mentioned a book) bestirred himself to protest against as the all-time low, to date, in literary nudism. (To be quite fair, however, I should add that I doubt if the decision to publish those books was referred to your department of the firm.)

It is a point of interest to me, at just what date your views of religion changed from the attitude taken in your blasphemous poems. (I have some doubts as to whether these poems fairly reflect your actual personal attitude at the time). I feel pretty sure that you were not a convert in 1921, remembering your enthusiasm at that time for *The Golden Bough*. I feel equally sure, for other reasons, that you were a convert in 1926. Between these two dates you wrote *The Waste Land*.

I have here your copy of the Dent edition of Dante's *Divine Comedy*, and I find extremely interesting the passages which you have scored with pencil throughout the three volumes. I have erased none of these nor have I ever made any similar marks on these pages myself. I do not know at what date you acquired these volumes, but in the *Purgatorio* is your name written in Mother's hand. It looks, therefore, as if the books were given you at a time when you did not have much spending money of your own. On the other hand, the pencil lines (and such a line has, I think, a calligraphic character) would suggest that you were then of college age. Your own autograph is not in any of the books.

I do not think you took these books with you when you went to Europe after you left Harvard. (You went twice, I think). They came from the box of your books which was first stored in the St Louis house and later (after I had sent you a list and you had designated those you wanted shipped to England) in the Cambridge house. I do not think you have seen them since your final trip abroad, which, I think, was in 1914.

These markings may be of interest to you, so I have made a catalogue of them:

INFERNO. Canto II, lines 1–3, page 14. (I will abbreviate this to II:1–3:14. Only the even-numbered pages, the Italian, are marked).
III:1–10:26
III:56, 57, 60:30 (These lines *under*scored; otherwise I mean scoring at the side. When scored on two sides, implying more emphasis, I will specify.
Line 56 is quoted by you in *The Waste Land*.
XV:16–21:158. (Line 29 is underscored; it is the simile of the tailor

threading his needle which you comment on somewhere in your works) <Dante essay>

XV:121–124:164 ('those who run for the green cloth', quoted by you, where I cannot find offhand). <Dante essay>

XVI:130–136:176 (Diver simile)

(Parenthetically I note that, rather to my surprise, XX:40–42:216, is not marked. It refers to Tiresias)

PURGATORIO. X:121-127:124.

XVI:85–96:196. (Lines 94–96 scored both sides)

XVII:91–139:208

XVIII:19–40:216

   " 43–45:218"

   " 49–75:218 (Lines 67-69 scored both sides)

XXV:40–109:314–318 (Very faint side scoring)

   " 136–139:318

XXVI:133–136:330 (The passage 133–148 contains the verse of Arnaut Daniel mentioned by you in your essay, p.40)

   " 148:330

PARADISO. III:70–87:30 (Includes 'la sua volontate'; this stanza scored both sides)

IV:41–42:38

   " 124–132:44

VI:133–142:68

IX:103:108

XII:28–32:144

XXIII:1–3:280

XXVI:28–30:316

The most interesting of these passages, from the present point of view, is III:85–87:30 – *la sua volontate e nostra pace*. But there are others which might indicate religious leanings at that early date in your life; they are: X:121–127:124; XVI:85–96:196; XVIII:67–69:218; III:70–87:30; and IV:124–132:44. The first three of these are from the *Purgatorio*, the last two from the *Paradiso*.

Only you yourself know whether it was the poetry or the beliefs in these passages which then moved you. This period, of course, was prior to the ''Potamus' period, in fact, before you had published any poetry at all. I am disposed to think that in part, at least, the religious feeling did appeal to you at that time.

Dr Paul Elmer More, in a review in the *Saturday Review of Books*, has suggested that you suffer from a split personality, which explains to him the discrepancy between your professed allegiance to the classical traditions and your obvious departures from them.

The term 'split personality' is like a lot of other terms which have passed over from psychoanalysis into common speech, and which impart a scientific air to the discussion of human traits of which everyone has been aware for centuries. Dr More of course does not regard your case as pathological; he merely intends, I think, to underscore the idea ordinarily conveyed by the word 'inconsistency'.

Inconsistency is certainly not an abnormal or unusual failing. It is one of the commonest of the human mind. Everyone knows persons who at times make quite astute comments on the behaviour of others, but who surprisingly lack the 'giftie' as regards themselves. The separation of the creative and the critical faculties in the human mind is generally recognised, but not diagnosed as schizophrenia. Corollary to this is the dualism (which may be false, scientifically) between imagination and reason.

Mr I. A. Richards has performed, in my opinion, a highly important service in establishing the dichotomy between 'scientific beliefs' and 'emotive beliefs', which seems to me to parallel the dualism just above mentioned. (This book, so forbiddingly entitled *Principles of Literary Criticism*, might, with the license allowed to the writers of jacket blurbs, fairly be called 'epoch-making' in criticism. It is the still small voice of intelligence which is always, unhappily, so difficult to hear amid the hubbub of Clive Bells and Burton Rascoes and lady 'literary editors' doubling as society reporters.) He has also, I think, made it clear that terms like 'belief' are not, as commonly assumed, verbal instruments of precision. There are kinds of belief, and there are degrees of belief, a whole spectrum of belief. The notion that a person either believes, or does not believe, betrays by its own example the crude mental processes of people who 'believe' it. The range of mental states intended to be covered by the use of the word 'belief' is infinite.

I have been told, incidentally, that Mr Richards twice approached you with the specific intention of discussing with you your beliefs, but was each time overcome by (I judge) a sort of paralysis of embarrassment. I take his example as justifying me in the same attempt.

I think that Mr Richards puts the matter as well as it can be put, when he says: 'In the pre-scientific era, the devout adherent to the Catholic account of the world, for example, found a sufficient basis for nearly all his main attitudes in what he took to be the scientific truth. It would be fairer to say that the difference between ascertained fact and acceptable fiction did not obtrude itself to him. Today this is changed, and if he believes such an account, he does not do so, if intelligent, without considerable difficulty or without a fairly persistent strain.'

Let us observe first how you meet this strain in the simpler case of the discrepancy between your classic ideals and your modernist practice which so bothers Dr More. This claim of traditionalism is the common stock of the modernists in all the arts; it is in keeping with the modernist love of paradox, and serves to baffle simple minds and provoke them to outcry, which is all grist to the modernist mill. It is done, simply, with what (by analogy to the 'rubber dollar' of which we have heard much lately) might be called 'rubber terminology'. The term unity, nowadays, is one of these rubber words; hence we read of the peculiar type of unity exhibited by Joyce's *Ulysses* (granting his Aristotelian unities of time and place, and the highly dubious unity achieved by stretching his story over the framework of the *Odyssey*) which allows him to interpolate long-winded heavy parodies to display his versatility. The same observation is true in the case of *The Waste Land* and Auden's *Orators*. I do not intend by this any detraction from any of these works.

This tendency to 'rubber thinking', it seems to me, is one of the most significant aspects of the modern world. Nowadays we have 'rubber debts', 'rubber consciences', 'rubber philosophy' (relativity), and 'rubber physics'. All our standards are of rubber; hence chaos. In this respect it would be strange if you, who as a poet are expected to do so, should fail to mirror the Weltzeitgeist.

I dare say that at this point you may remark to yourself that there is indeed some truth in this, and that the only thing left in the world which is not rubber is the Rock, which is our refuge. My reply to this is that the Christian Fathers made an enormous use of rubber terms and concepts, which came to them from Greece and Egypt and Persia and from the banks of the Indus, where, it is now shown by objects of glyptic art, Yoga was practised by the pre-Aryan Indians over five thousand years ago.

These concepts of caoutchouc, from every corner of the then known world, inconsistent and inharmonious as they were, were all throughly mixed in the colossal cauldron of Alexandria whence, indirectly, the early Fathers drew sustenance. The fact is generally ignored that this brew included a good deal of barbarous idolatry, or else it is contended that this has been sifted out. Dean Inge, however, acknowledges that the Church owes a larger debt to Greece than to Jerusalem. This you doubtless know, since you say, 'I believe that the Catholic Church, with its inheritance from Greece and Israel, is still, as it always has been, the great repository of wisdom.'

(Here, parenthetically, I am going to indulge myself in the kind of sniping which is the delight of high-brows, and point out to you that Judah, not Israel, was the stronghold of Jehovah. Of the fifteen kings of Israel, all fifteen did that which was wrong in the sight of the Lord – i.e., worshipped Baal; but of the twenty kings of Judah, though eleven fell into paganism, nine upheld the Hebrew religion. And Judah lasted a century and a quarter longer than Israel.)

De religione non est disputandum. I have no desire to enter a conflict in which the Catholic strategy is to lead the enemy into the Dismal Swamp of ancient and mediaeval literature and then bombard him with musty Latin tomes which he has to admit he has not read. I fear I should play a feeble Satan to your Michael.

I do desire, however, to ask two questions: 1. how you reconcile the theory of divine revelation with your knowledge of ancient history; and 2. how you manage to confound faith in God with faith, not in God, but in certain parties, groups, or combinations of men who have undertaken throughout history to demand faith in themselves. The latter question, I admit, is some four hundred years old, but not, I think, yet answered satisfactorily.

I must say, that if I were not aware of the distinction which Richards has lucidly shown between two kinds of belief – one which is subjected every day to verification, and another which exists luxuriously in vacuo – I should be much more distressed than I am about your concerns. The wide gulf between the two kinds of belief is well shown by the fact that you – holding your beliefs – have done nothing at all to rescue the members of your own family, for whom I know that you have the greatest affection, from their peril, which, if I understand plain English, is regarded by the Catholic Church as infinitely more serious than mortal peril. This is a literal way of putting it, and a Catholic might regard it as too crass to require a reply. But I have observed with some trepidation a tendency on your part – due, I think, to the unfortunate effects of mixing a Puritan conscience with Catholic doctrine – to act in a somewhat more literal manner than do more sophisticated Catholics who know their way around. Such a Catholic as the latter, I think, would not be offended at such inquiries as I have addressed to you in this letter; and I hope you will not be.

The greater part of what I have put into this letter might, I think, be addressed to any and all Catholics, not yourself alone; and the strictures I have made in many cases are those which I would make against a large body of persons, I might even almost say against the human race, or rather the modern world. One must divide human epochs at some point of time, and it may be that I belong to the past epoch and you to the present. There is, it is true, a good deal that I deplore about the present epoch; but I do not mean to heap its sins on your head. Even the Church, which is built on a Rock, though it can still fight to the death over points of the Creed, must be complaisant with its flock, must assimilate itself to the world it finds itself in. If you can cause the Church to bestir itself against the rising tide of chauvinism, cynicism, and nihilism in morals, and in behalf of the preservation of certain standards of conduct which, it seems to me, ought to be regarded as of permanent worth and not subject to change of fashion, I shall shout my head off in approval.

I do not think that I can summarise so rambling a letter. But I think that your motives are far more complex than you know, and that it is impossible to unscramble them and isolate the effective ones from those which are merely concomitant. I am in the dark about the seriousness of your philosophical scepticism. I do think that you are one of the most unfree of men and that you live in a society grounded in artifice, accustomed to artificial thinking and having an artificially high opinion of itself. Bloomsbury seems to me like a small room crowded with people, a room with all the windows closed, and all the people talking at once and smoking cigarettes endlessly. In such a room one becomes unaware that the atmosphere is close. It is only if one steps out into the cold air and returns that one can judge. I also think that the blushful hippocrene of the literary press which is so freely handed around is a bit heady and likely to make one say and do foolish things. The habit of hyperbole is universal, and so unrestrained that it would be excessive if applied to the great masters of all time. I hope that you may attain to the *bonhomie* and *aplomb* of the Aga Khan, who, despite the fact that millions of his subjects pay out of their meagre means large sums for small vials of the water he bathes in, and despite the fact that his horses win all the races in England, seems to be very popular.

Unreal City! I do not think that you will find peace in Bloomsbury. I think you will find it here. I am not urging you to return permanently, but occasionally. You may not, perhaps, find it stimulating, but for that reason you will be able to rest. Here you are always welcome. And here – provided your Bloomsbury does not follow you – you are intellectually free.

Affectionately,
Henry

TO *Messrs Macmillan & Co.*   TS BL (Macmillan Archive)

13 September 1935   Faber & Faber Ltd

Dear Sirs,

I understand from Mr C. M. Grieve (Hugh MacDiarmid)[1] that he has already communicated with you about his long poem 'Mature Art', which he is offering for publication. I therefore send on herewith the manuscript, which he gave me the opportunity of examining. I should like to say that it seems to me a remarkable work, which well deserves to be published, and I for one shall be very happy if you think favourably of it. I should willingly have recommended it for publication to my own firm, but as you see, it is a book of considerable length, and with our other commitments for volumes of verse we did not feel prepared at this moment to extend our expenses in this particular field.

Yours faithfully,
T. S. Eliot

TO *Margery Fry*   CC

17 September 1935   [Faber & Faber Ltd]

Dear Miss Fry,

I hope that the lapse of time since you wrote to me on the 23rd August has not been inconvenient. It was necessary before we could come to a decision about Roger Fry's *Mallarmé* that we should have an estimate made of the approximate cost of the book. When this was done we deliberated the matter carefully, and regretfully decided that we could not see our way to publication. We are convinced, of course, that this is a book which ought to be published, but we cannot see how it could be published except at a loss. In the first place the public for a translation of Mallarmé would, I think, differ from the public for ordinary French translations in that it would concern chiefly people who already knew Mallarmé in

1–Christopher Murray Grieve (1892–1978): pseud. Hugh MacDiarmid – poet, journalist, critic, cultural activist, self-styled 'Anglophobe', Scottish Nationalist and Communist; founder member of the Scottish National Party, 1928; founder of the Scottish Centre of PEN. His works include *A Drunk Man Looks at the Thistle* (1926), *To Circumjack Cencrastus* (1930), *'First Hymn to Lenin' and Other Poems* (1931), *Hugh MacDiarmid: Complete Poems, 1920–1976* (2 vols, 1978). See further Alan Bold, *MacDiarmid, Christopher Murray Grieve: A Critical Biography* (1988); *The Letters of Hugh MacDiarmid*, ed. A. Bold (1984); and *Dear Grieve: Letters to Hugh MacDiarmid (C. M. Grieve)*, sel. and ed. John Manson (2011).

French, and were really interested in deciphering his meaning. It would certainly be a very much smaller public than Roger commanded for his own original work.

The publication of this book would be a labour of piety, therefore, and we feel that it is more suitable for such a firm as Chatto and Windus, who have, I think, published more of his writings than we have, or for the Hogarth Press. We happen to be committed to the publication of a large number of books in the near future, and we feel that we simply cannot afford to treat ourselves to the distinction which the publication of this book would undoubtedly give. For myself, I hope very much indeed that the book may be published.[1]

As you said in your letter of the 23rd August, I hesitate to send the book back to you until I know where you are. If you are out of England when this letter reaches you, will you kindly let me know where you wish the book sent?

Yours sincerely,

[T. S. Eliot]

TO *Henry Eliot*   TS Houghton

17 September 1935   Faber & Faber Ltd

My dear Brother,

There are several really more important subjects I must write to you about, but I must write this note at once to introduce to you my dear friend Major Bonamy Dobree (pronounced Doabry) Royal Artillery (retired) and late of Mendham Priory, Norfolk, who is coming to New York, sailing on the 20th, to lecture under the Colston Leigh agency. You do not need to bother to look him up; I told him that unless he had every minute in New York planned out for him, to ring you up and introduce himself. I think you will like him, and I thought that you might arrange for relatives to put him up in several centres, as you did for Alida. He is one of my closest friends. John Hayward has just written a column about him for his London letter to the New York *Sun*.[2] What a man needs when he is doing a lecture tour like that, is sympathetic hosts who will not rush

---

1 – Stéphane Mallarmé, *Poems*, trans. Roger Fry, was published by Chatto & Windus (1936).
2 – JDH wrote of Bonamy Dobrée: 'A companionable man like Addison, a lover of good conversation, good company and good cheer' (New York *Sun*, 7 Sept. 1934).

him too much and give him time to sleep, and also give him roast beef instead of chicken.[1]

The shorter I cut this the more likely I am to write in a few days. I enjoy and appreciate your letters, though such a bad correspondent myself.

> With love to both,
> Affectionately your brother
> Tom

TO *Michael Roberts*

TS Berg

19 September 1935   Faber & Faber Ltd

Dear Roberts,

As your typescript has just come back after having been cast off, I am returning it to you at once. I hope that any changes you have to make will not affect the length. According to the estimate the book will run to 384 pages. Some of the Committee were inclined to think that this was too long, but on second thoughts it was decided not to ask you to omit anything. We were guided partly by the stimulus of competition. Ian Parson's [*sic*] book is to be sold at 5s., and I rather infer from the advertisement in Chatto's catalogue that it will be a much slighter book than yours.[2] We expect to bring your book out early, so the sooner it goes to press the better. It should precede Yeats's Oxford Book, and I do not fear serious competition from the latter.[3] The existence of these two other anthologies, however, makes it desirable that our book should be a bulky one, and I think we are giving very good value for the money. Of course it will take us a considerable time to get our money back, but we are

---

1–HWE would write on 14 Dec. 1935: 'Major Dobrée sailed today and we feel quite a sense of regret at his departure. He is a most charming person and a "parfait gentil knight" (am I quoting correctly, and from what?), essentially thoughtful and courteous and punctilious. He came faithfully with us on a day of many engagements prior to sailing, and went a great distance to see the Porters in Hubbard Woods, and called on Theodora in Baltimore between aeroplane flights. He also saw Ada and Shef. We feel really much attached to him.

'And there were also the Cobden-Sandersons . . . who were so affected by a fancied physical resemblance between me and you that the measure of their cordiality I felt at once to be the measure of their affection for you. Your friends are very devoted to you, and in a manner that is quite touching.'

2–*The Progress of Poetry: An Anthology of Verse from Hardy to the Present Day*, ed. Ian Parsons (1936).

3–*The Oxford Book of Modern Verse 1892–1935*, ed. W. B. Yeats, was to appear in Dec. 1936.

counting on a long run. Incidently, I have all confidence that your book will succeed because it will be the best.

Yours ever,
T. S. Eliot

TO *Stephen Spender*TS Northwestern

19 September 1935   Faber & Faber Ltd

Dear Stephen,

In reply to your letter of September 12th I have brought up before the Committee your query about our proportion of your American royalties.[1] We are perfectly willing with your new book of stories to reduce our proportion to 10 per cent as you ask, and I will see that this alteration is made in the agreement.

At the same time I ought to say on our own behalf that although the difference between 50 per cent and 10 per cent makes it look as if we had been extortionate, this is not the case. Our practice is quite in accordance with publishing custom in the case of a book of poems by a new author. Your first book had to be regarded, like any first book of poems, as a highly speculative venture. One never has any means of knowing what poetry is going to sell and what is not. We were quite prepared to lose money on your book, but at the same time we felt that in anything so speculative we were entitled to recoup possible losses out of American sales to this extent. Now, however, your reputation is such as to put matters on a different footing.

Yours affectionately,
Tom

1 – 'I wonder whether, when you make the contract for my new book, could I either have a separate contract with my American publisher or a different arrangement through Faber? For I notice that Faber takes 50% of my royalties from Random House, and surely this is excessive, since an agent only takes 10%, and here the London publisher is only acting as an agent?'

TO *E. P. Gough*[1]   CC

19 September 1935   [Faber & Faber Ltd]

Dear Mr Gough,

I must apologise for my delay in answering your kind letter of the 9th, and hope you will have understood that I was meanwhile turning the matter over in my mind.[2] In principle I should be delighted to be able to offer you a play for the Tewkesbury Festival, but the position is this. I intend to get to work on a new play as soon as I can, but I shall not have the time even to elaborate the subject matter until December, and you would want to know a good deal about the play even after you were confiding enough to accept it before seeing the finished text. Furthermore, I am not confident that I should be able to finish another play in time for production in July. I do not feel that I can bind myself down to do it because I should not like to run the risk either of failing you or of not satisfying myself, and I found also that the strain of working against time last winter was extremely fatiguing. I feel that whatever I do next I ought to take rather more time over. So far as your next season is concerned, therefore, I feel regretfully that I must say no, but I wish to express my general willingness to have any such work of mine produced at Tewkesbury when it is ready. I wish very much in view of the urgency of your needs in connection with the tower and foundations of the Abbey that I could assist you immediately in this task of advertising them, but I feel that it is impossible. I look forward to the prospect of being able to offer you something for the third Festival, which I hope will take place in 1937.

I enjoyed very much having tea with you and Mrs Gough, and I appreciated the advantage of going over the Abbey under your tutelage. I hope that we may have further excuse for communication and meeting before the problems of 1937 can be discussed.[3]

Yours sincerely,
[T. S. Eliot]

1 – The Revd E. P. Gough: Vicar and Rural Dean of Tewkesbury Abbey.
2 – 'I think I ought to follow up our conversation & try to tell you how wonderful it would be if we felt there was a hope of your writing the Festival play for next July.'
3 – Gough responded (n.d.): 'I had hoped indeed for 1936 *but* if we have the hope of 1937 it would be wonderful . . .'

FROM *Vivien Eliot* TO *Mary Hutchinson*   MS Texas

19 September 1935   68 Clarence Gate Gardens, N.W.1.

Dear Mary,

You once gave me a string bag & a string belt, for which I have a great attachment. The belt has been lost in Selfridge's. Could you tell me where you got it? So that I can get one like it.

I do hope you are well, & that I shall *see you soon.*

With love from
Vivienne Haigh Eliot

TO *Martin Turnell*   CC

20 September 1935   [Faber & Faber Ltd]

Dear Mr Turnell,

Thank you for your two letters of the 12th instant, and for your courtesy in sending me a galley of your review of *Murder in the Cathedral.*[1] ccI cannot see anything in the review that could give offence to anybody. It is curious that you take approximately the opposite point of view to the reviewer in *Blackfriars*, who judged the play to be a good play but bad poetry.[2]

Thank you for giving me Wall's address, and for your advice about Bloy.[3] The fact that Wall has reviewed the same book in the *Colosseum* is something of a draw-back, and I think I will wait in the hope that the

---

1 – 'Mr Eliot and the Church of England', *The Colosseum* 2: 7 (Sept. 1935), 219–21. 'Mr Eliot's new play was written to be acted . . . Like all Mr Eliot's works, this play has great merits, but in so far as it succeeds it is hardly as a dramatic poem. The character of St Thomas is competent, but in spite of the purity and virility of the language it obviously depends too much on the actor . . . Dramatic or not, this play shows a grasp of St Thomas's significance which is altogether unique. Mr Eliot has seen the real issue. He sees . . . that St Thomas effectually prevented the appearance of anything resembling the present State-Church for over three hundred years. St Thomas was, in fact, the great champion of ultramontanism – the champion of spiritual freedom against the encroachment of the civil power . . . Mr Eliot's irony is superb . . . but does it not, after all, recoil upon himself?'
2 – W. H. Shewring, untitled review of *MiC*, *Blackfriars* 14: 186 (Sept. 1935), 709–12. 'As a play, this seems to me a success . . . The verse of the play has been praised as being of Mr Eliot's best. I agree that the style is more consistent than in his earlier work . . . But I have never felt that Mr Eliot is a positive poet of importance, nor do I feel so now.'
3 – Turnell recommended (12 Sept.) TSE to ask Bernard Wall, editor of the *Colosseum*, to review the book on Léon Bloy. Not reviewed.

name of some other suitable reviewer will occur to me. But I should like
to have Wall reviewing in the *Criterion* as well as yourself.

Yours sincerely,
[T. S. Eliot]

TO *Michael Sayers*[1]   cc

20 September 1935   [*The Criterion*]

Dear Mr Sayers,

   About the matter of a Theatre Chronicle which you suggest,[2] I shall
have to reply in much the same terms as I did recently to another writer
who suggested a Chronicle in his own field. At present I have normally
four regular Chronicles in each number, and if I have any more that
section of the Quarterly will get out of proportion. It is difficult enough
to squeeze everything in at present, with so many possible books to be
reviewed and so many people wanting to review them. But I think I
could at the appropriate moment use an article reviewing the dramatic
season as Heppenstall reviewed the Ballet in our current number. I am
afraid there would not be room for this in December in any case, and an
article appearing then would have to be written in advance of some of
the interesting productions. Amongst other things I do want to have the
forthcoming season of the Group Theatre adequately dealt with. Would
you be interested in doing such an article for the March or else for the
June number?[3]

Yours sincerely,
[T. S. Eliot]

1–Michael Sayers (1911–2010), Dublin-born writer of Jewish-Lithuanian ancestry, had
been taught French at Trinity College, Dublin, by Samuel Beckett. In the 1930s he was
drama critic of *NEW* and for a while shared a flat in Kilburn, London, with George Orwell.
Some of his stories were included in *Best British Short Stories*, ed. Edward O'Brien. In 1936
he left London for New York, where he worked as dramaturge for the designer and producer
Norman Bel Geddes. During WW2 his interests pursued a pro-communist direction, for
which he was blacklisted by the House Un-American Activities Committee (having enjoyed
success as a writer for NBC Television). In later years he wrote plays for the BBC, and
contributed episodes to TV series including *Robin Hood* and *Ivanhoe*. He worked too on
the screenplay of *Casino Royale* (1967).

2–Sayers wrote ('Sept.') to suggest a theatre chronicle.

3–'A Year in Theatre', C. 15 (Apr. 1936), 648–62, was unsparing in its criticism of *MiC*:
'One of the more intelligent critics described Mr Eliot's play as a "Christian tragedy". I think
this is a misnomer. The only really tragic figure in the Christian mythology, it seems to me,
is the Devil.

TO *Luigi Berti*[1]   Princeton

20 September 1935   [Faber & Faber Ltd]

My dear Mr Berti,

I must apologise for my delay in answering your letter of August. I am flattered that you should wish to translate some of my poems into Italian, and have no objection in principle. In such cases I know the market value as well as anybody, and naturally expect no profit out of translations. All I should ask would be this, that you should let me know which of my poems you wish to translate in your volume, and that this list should have my approval. Secondly, I should like to have merely *pour la bonne règle* an agreement with your publishers which gave me a small royalty after the sale of a larger number of copies than they are likely to sell.[2]

Yours very sincerely,

[T. S. Eliot]

'But Mr Eliot has undoubtedly produced a specimen of Heroic Drama – and that is a kind of drama impossible to atheists and sceptics. There is a terrible *injustice* at the heart of Mr Eliot's play which gives Thomas the appearance of a tragic protagonist. Indeed, one might say, if Mr Eliot were not a Christian his play would seem to us an outrage . . . Thomas à Becket is exhibited by Mr Eliot (possibly I should say, Mr Eliot is exhibited by Thomas à Becket), and personally I find him a bit of a bore. I think the audience agree with me, for I notice that they rouse themselves for the first time during the performance of this piece upon the entrance of the Shavian knights. Thomas himself is a bore most of the time, a perfect bore in his way, a finished and polished and consummate bore, but a bore all the same like any *objet d'art* without a history, without a definite temporal and spiritual locale. True enough, the sort of psychic catch-as-catch-can Mr Eliot indulges him in is superbly well done in superb verse. The psychological conflict between egoism and faith is always of some interest; but one cannot help feeling that today it ranks among the minor conflicts unless it is stated in contemporary terms, and it is difficult to believe that Mr Eliot's faith supplies these terms.

'My comments on *Murder in the Cathedral* have been perhaps unnecessarily (as it may seem) personal; but a certain desiccated pressure emanates from the poetry that forces one to a personal issue. It is impossible to treat the play adequately on its merits as theatre alone. It is too incisive, too original, too mordant. It is a challenge, and it must be so recognised. In thought, anecdote and language it repudiates almost all the popular values, in life and theatre, of our time. It may occasion a revolution in popular thought and theatre through subsequent imitations, and by its direct influence similar to that brought about by the comedies of Shaw. Or it may go down to the popular limbo as one of the curiosities of a moribund theatre.'

1 – Luigi Berti (1904–64), Italian writer, poet, novelist, and prolific translator.
2 – See *Poesie*, trans. Luigi Berti (1941).

TO *A. Desmond Hawkins*   TS Desmond Hawkins

20 September 1935   Faber & Faber Ltd

Dear Hawkins,

I have been dilatory in answering your letter of the 4th.[1] I presume that you have received *The Arts Today*, which was ordered for you, and which according to Porteus is a very good book indeed.

Maritain, by the way, is coming over here at the end of October to give a couple of lectures. I did not know that he had a new book out, but I have received from him new editions of two old ones, which perhaps is what you mean.

I shall drop you another line in a week or two to suggest lunch. I know the Marquis of Granby and its indifferent sherry quite well, and should be glad to drop in on your group there when it can be found, but not, if I may, when Nina Hamnett is to be there.[2]

> With all best wishes,
> Yours,
> T. S. Eliot

TO *Marianne Moore*   TS Rosenbach Foundation

20 September 1935   Faber & Faber Ltd

Dear Miss Moore,

Thank you for your letter of September 6th.[3] You are one of the strangest children I have ever had anything to do with. Why should you

---

1 – Hawkins repeated his request to review *The Arts Today*, and went on: 'I've just heard from Maritain. He has sent me his new book, I notice in it some comments on *After Strange Gods*.' (E. W. F. Tomlin reviewed *Freedom in the Modern World*, by Jacques Maritain, in C. 15 [Oct. 1935], 130–3.

2 – 'I've been with Dylan Thomas and Nina Hamnett this morning. She's a queer survival, isn't she? So expert in the commonplaces of popular sin, a ghostly bohemian who still mutters "Aldous Huxley" & waits for a pricking of ears in the audience. Very odd. Dylan has been working hard in Ireland apparently, & is now recuperating at the bar counter.' He concluded by inviting TSE to visit his cottage in Radlett in Hertfordshire one weekend, or else: 'sometimes there is a midday drinking party at the Marquis of Granby, in Charlotte St. – Dylan, Porteus, Barker & one or two others. Do you ever sit at those sorts of tables?' Nina Hamnett (1890–1956), artist and writer, bohemian and bibber, studied art in London and Paris and made a name for herself in the artistic communities of both cities; however, from the 1920s she became best known for her carousing in Fitzrovia, where she knew everyone from Augustus John to Dylan Thomas. While her tales were entertaining, her carry-ons were tiresome. See Hamnett, *Laughing Torso* (1951); Denise Hooker, *Nina Hamnett: Queen of Bohemia* (1986).

3 – 'I received from Faber & Faber in August for the sale of my book, two pound, seventeen shillings, tenpence. From the first I had hoped there would be a profit that I could transfer

---

send me a cheque for 15 dollars? Is it not probable that you can spend £2. 17. 10d., which is your own money, just as well as I can spend it? Why on earth should you want to transfer any profits to me? I am almost speechless at meeting with such an absence of avarice in any human being, and can do no more than return the cheque with the hope that the book will eventually reap the harvest it deserves.

I am glad to have a review of Wallace Stevens' book from you, and I shall use it in my next number. Thank you very much.[1] I think your tentative scheme for your small book is a very good one, and I am reading 'Jamestown' with much interest.[2]

Yours sincerely,
T. S. Eliot

P.S. *I* can't lay out your money for you unless you come to London.

TO *I. A. Richards*   TS Magdalene

24 September 1935   Faber & Faber Ltd

Dear Richards,

I am glad to know that you are back. I had been thinking of you especially in the last few days, wondering when you would return, and meaning to ask you to have me down during this term, as the last meeting was so unsatisfactory. I am very sorry about the scarlet fever.[3] It is not so bad in itself, but is apt to leave a weakness somewhere or other, which

---

to you, and would immediately have sent to you Faber & Faber's cheque but that I had not heard from you in a long time and did not wish to be insistent, or intrude if you were ill or away. The bank has collected – to be exact *is* collecting – approximately fifteen dollars; I should much rather have returned the Faber & Faber cheque but I hope you will accept the one I enclose as suggestive of my wish that it were a thing to make you actually rich.'

1–Moore on Wallace Stevens, *Ideas of Order*: C. 15 (Jan. 1936), 307–9.
2–Moore asked TSE to approve the order of a small new sequence, as follows:

'THE OLD DOMINION
    I
JAMESTOWN
    II
BIRD-WITTED
    III
HALF DEITY
PIGEONS
THE PANGOLIN
using as title for all although it comes last, The Pangolin?'
3–IAR wrote on 19 Sept. that no sooner had they returned from the Alps than Dorothy 'went down with scarlet-fever'.

must be looked after – in my case, in the throat. I hope it won't take her in the ears: my father and brother went nearly stone deaf. Give her my sympathy & solicitude. Is the first or second weekend in November possible? I haven't engaged any weekends after the immediate one, which includes my birthday, but I have put all my speaking engagements into October and November, especially October, and that means weekend work. But I think that I could manage either of those two, and had rather come when there wasn't a feast, because

> slept both boy and beast,
> Tired with the pomp of that [*sc.* their] Osirian feast[1]

We might not have so much opportunity for talking. I am grateful for the new edition of *Science & Poetry* and shall read it in the train, collating it with the first edition, on the journey down to Gloucestershire for this weekend: and am properly overawed by your inscription.[2] I should like to hear from you about *Murder*,[3] but am still more anxious to discuss the state of contemporary poetry. Mathiessen need hardly be mentioned.[4] He is such a nice fellow, and his book was so depressing to me: I suppose he wrote it for his pupils: but should he have pupils? I cannot remember what I meant about methods of teaching pupils to read. I am sure that

---

1 – Shelley, 'The Witch of Atlas', ll. 511–12.

2 – IAR wrote of the second edn, revised and enlarged, of *Science and Poetry* (1935), which he posted to TSE: 'It may amuse you to glance at some of the changes – they go deeper I think than the quantity of them would suggest . . .' He wrote in the book: 'Submitted for further correction to T. S. Eliot and in grateful acknowledgment of former corrections, by I. A. Richards since, as Confucius said, "What the superior man requires, is just that in his words there may be nothing incorrect." Analects XIII. iii, 7.' But IAR added a further inscription on the facing page which is what overawed TSE: 'Then Ezekiel said: "The philosophy of the East taught the first principles of human perception: some nations held one principle for the origin, and some another: we of Israel taught that the Poetic Genius (as you now call it) was the first principle and all the others merely derivative, which was the cause of our despising the Priests and Philosophers of other countries, and prophesying that all Gods would at last be proved to originate in ours & to be the tributaries of the Poetic Genius; it was this that our great poet, King David, desired so fervently & invokes so pathetic'ly, saying by this he conquers enemies and governs kingdoms; and we so loved our God, that we cursed in his name all the deities of surrounding nations, and asserted that they had rebelled: from these opinions the vulgar came to believe that all nations would at last be subject to the jews."

'"This," said he, "like all firm perswasions is come to pass; for all nations believe the jews' god and worship the jews's god, and what greater subjection can be?"

'I heard this with some wonder, & I must confess my own conviction.'

3 – 'I'd . . . like to talk about Murder in the Cathedral. Reading it was 50 times better to me than seeing it – for reasons connected, to me interestingly, with the differences between poetry (verse) and prose. And there were other things that I felt were very curious about the effect of it as acted.'

4 – 'Matthiessen's book I haven't got through. Sorry to say it depresses me.'

you have a great deal to do in a *very short time*: because your generation of English dons are people who were educated in other triposes: and the next generation will be men who have excelled in the English tripos – so you have got to make a better discipline of it if it is to make good dons – and I don't think much of any of your colleagues – and as for you, your two best pupils are too disreputable to get the jobs – so what is going to happen?[1] I enclose two more *Landscapes* (these are obviously *not* Words for Music): are they too different in method to go together?[2]

Yours ever

T. S. E.

FROM *Vivien Eliot*   MS Bodleian

25 September 1935   Hotel Constance, 23 & 24
                                     Lancaster Gate, London W.2

Dearest Tom,

This is to wish you very very many happy returns of your birthday, tomorrow. I enclose cheque for £1. Dear boy, I wish you every good thing in this life and for all eternity. *Can't* you let me have another *address except 24, Russell Square*, Faber & Faber?[3]

With love –

Your wife –

V. H. Eliot –

Buy yourself some *socks* at *Marshall & Snelgrove. V. H. E.*

1 – TSE has written 'forgive impertinence' in the margin against 'I cannot remember [. . .] going to happen?'
2 – See John Constable in IAR, *Selected Letters*, 90 note 2: 'One of these poems appears to have been *Burnt Norton*, or probably drafts of parts of it, while [IAR] to Eliot, 29 Sept. 1935, indicates that the other was 'Rannoch, by Glencoe'. The composition of both poems is closely associated with that of *Murder in the Cathedral* (which he had completed earlier in the year), Eliot clipping the manuscript of 'Rannoch, by Glencoe' to a sheaf of notes and drafts for the play.' For an account of these notes [Houghton], see Lyndall Gordon, *Eliot's New Life*, App. 1.
3 – VHE recorded in her diary: 'My cheque for Tom's birthday present, with a very private letter, & card, was returned, *opened*, without a word. So I went to the *Police* in Marylebone Lane, & showed them. They said as I had no *evidence* that Tom was not at 24 Russell Square on Friday, they could not do anything.'
On 17 Sept. she had noted: 'Three years since my Tom left England. The bleeding wound never heals, never eases. I just slowly grope my way through Limbo, sometimes accelerated by a kind of artificial fury, which rages for a time, *during* which I can perform great tasks, & after which I am utterly spent & dry & sick. I think I feel more & more as *Tom* used to feel, & I suppose still does.'

[Envelope addressed as follows]
> *Private* & *Confidential.*
> *Encl.*
> *DO <u>NOT</u> <u>FORWARD</u>.*
> Thomas Stearns Eliot Esq. A. M. *Litt. D. Columb*:
> Editor, *The Criterion* –
> *Director,*
> Messrs Faber & Faber
> – Publishers –
> 24 Russell Square –
> Bloomsbury –
> London w.c.1

TO *M. Wetherall* CC

25 September 1935   [*The Criterion*]

Dear Sir,

Thank you for letting me see the enclosed translation from Franz Kafka.[1] It seems to me too slight to be suitable for the *Criterion*, but I should be willing to consider other pieces.

Yours very truly,
[T. S. Eliot]

TO *Walter de la Mare* CC

26 September 1935   [Faber & Faber Ltd]

Dear de la Mare,

I should be glad if you could let me have your fourth and last payment on account of George Barker as soon as convenient. He has written to me to say that they only have 10s., so I have asked the Bank Manager to pay him immediately, debiting my own account. As before, you can send the cheque either to me or preferably to the Manager, Lloyds Bank Limited, 45 New Oxford Street.

1–Wetherall wrote from Eton College, 20 Sept.: 'I am sending you the translation of one of the 14 small, and as yet unpublished stories from the literary remains of Franz Kafka which will shortly appear as the fifth volume of his collected works in the Schocken Verlag. I was encouraged to do so by my friend Geoffrey Grigson who, however, has not seen this particular piece.'

I should be glad if you had any suggestions to make about what is to be done for Barker for the future. He will certainly need assistance, as I imagine he gets very little reviewing to do, and is hardly qualified to earn his living in this way. His book of poems, although it has received strong praise from several critics, has sold very badly indeed, and I don't expect *Janus* to do any better. We have given him small advances on both of these books, which we can at best expect to recoup after some years. I can try to get some of the same and other benefactors to undertake subscriptions for another year, but one would prefer to find some way of setting him on his own feet.[1]

Yours sincerely,

[T. S. Eliot]

TO *W. B. Yeats*   CC

26 September 1935   [Faber & Faber Ltd]

Dear Yeats,

I have your letter of the 23rd, including the telegram from Lady Gerald.[2] I have not been able to return the typescript at once because I only got it back yesterday from having the estimate made by a firm of printers, and the Chairman was very anxious to look at it at once. I have explained to him that you need it urgently to make your selections, and he has promised to have it posted to you tomorrow. I am glad to hear that you like George Barker so well.

Yours ever,

[T. S. Eliot]

1–De la Mare responded, 27 Sept.: 'I suppose it is impossible for G. B. to attempt to write anything that would be likely to appeal to a wider audience than either the poems or *Janus* – work I mean merely intended to keep the pot boiling? If that *is* out of the question, I can see no alternative but for him to try to get a job of some kind. In fact in his case I feel myself that this is by far the best alternative. But is this practicable?'
2–Lady Gerald Wellesley cabled Yeats, 19 Sept. 1935: 'letter and preface just received delighted I authorize fader [*sc.* faber] give you my selected poems.' Yeats consequently wrote to TSE, 23 Sept.: 'Please send me the copy for Lady Gerald Wellesley's Selected Poems I gave you. I enclose her telegram of authorization. I want to select from it for my anthology. In my anthology, by the by, I shall give much of George Barker.'

28 September 1935

A *Valedictory*[1]
Forbidding Mourning: to the Lady of the House

To Mrs John Carroll Perkins,
Stamford House,
Chipping Campden, Glos.
28. ix. 35.

In springtime, when the year was new,
The morning grass was fresh with dew;
In autumn's season of regret
The morning flowers are moister yet

1–The TS draft of these verses, corrected in TSE's hand – it had been laid into a book donated to the Salvation Army – was purchased by Donald Gallup in 1961 from the Seven Gables Bookshop, New York. TSE wrote to Gallup, 15 Sept. 1961: 'I remember composing a set of occasional verses for Mrs Perkins. She and her husband had rented a house in Campden, Gloucestershire, for several summers, and they were just leaving I think, in 1939 [*sc.* 1935], after the outbreak of war, to return to the United States. Mrs Perkins was a very keen gardener, and very much enjoyed the garden of the lady whose tenants they were. They never returned to England. After the war Dr Perkins died and Mrs Perkins went blind.

'I don't remember whether there was any holograph copy of those verses or not. I should think it quite likely that the verses in possession of the Bodleian Library were as near as to the original draft as there was. But I cannot think why Mrs Perkins sent them to the Bodleian, or what reason there was for imposing any prohibition on their inspection. I would like to see a copy of them myself.' He added in a holograph postscript: 'Perhaps she never sent them to the Bodleian! But I covet a copy for Valerie's collection!'

Gallup, who met Emily Hale in 1937, at some point asked her about the poem, as he related in *Pigeons on the Granite*, 114–16: 'She told me that her aunt had offered "a manuscript" of the poem to the Bodleian on condition that there be no publicity about the gift until both she and Tom were dead. I suspected that the poem had been composed on the typewriter, and that what Mrs Perkins had offered – and given? – the Bodleian was almost certainly a fair copy in longhand. I wrote to the Bodleian for confirmation of my theory, but received no answer. That fall in England my work on the Ezra Pound bibliography took me to Oxford where I was able to repeat my question in person to the Keeper of Western Manuscripts at the library. He apologized for failing to acknowledge my letter, but explained that, although he remembered very well Mrs Perkins's visit and that she had shown him the Eliot poem, he simply could not recall whether she had left it with him; and no record of the gift could be found.

'I eventually determined through a member of the Bodleian manuscript cataloguing staff that Mrs Perkins had indeed made a gift of the poem and that it was a fair copy. It was hidden away so carefully that it was not finally located until both Mrs Perkins and Tom were dead. As for the first, typed copy, she apparently placed it in one of her Eliot books and they, after her death, were given with the rest of her library to the Salvation Army.'

When now the tardy rose appears,
It sparkles, not with dew, but tears;
Its head is bent with patient grief;
There runs a shudder through the leaf.
The violas and hollyhocks
Have now put off their coloured frocks.
The zinnia and marigold
Shall go to join beneath the mould
The tulip and the daffodil.
But on the wall their quivers still
A tear within the lonely eye
Of Clematis Jackmanii.
The myosotis blue proclaim
With colour shrill, their English name;[1]
And still the robin tries to sing
And cheat the winter into spring.

—

O long procession, happy flowers,
That passed through spring and summer hours,
Eager to blossom, and to try
To win approval, and to die.
With grateful knowledge, that they grew
To greet the eyes of one who knew
Their ways and needs in every kind,
And when to prune, and when to bind

D. S. Porter, an assistant at the Dept of Western MSS, Bodleian Library, wrote to EVE, 11 Aug. 1965: 'It was given to us in 1954 by Mrs Perkins herself. At that time she told us that Mr Eliot had stipulated that it was not to be published during his life, but perhaps in some collected edition after his death.'

The TS draft had concluded with this couplet (Omitted from the fair copy):

In conclusion, I wish to express my grateful thanks

For your patient attention, and ~~endurance of~~ forebearance with my pranks.

Gallup told John Bodley, 24 Aug. 1999: 'I am continuing my long-drawn-out attempt to establish the relationship between my original typescript draft and the fair (manuscript) copy of the poem that Tom prepared for Mrs Perkins. It took me several years . . . to determine that Mrs Perkins had given that version to the Bodleian and then to establish that it *was* a "fair copy". Only this spring I asked a friend who happened to be in Oxford to compare (a Xerox of) my typescript with the Bodleian's manuscript, but the library refused to allow this. Instead Mrs Clapinson very kindly offered to make the comparison for me. I had the result from her just before I left . . . (and was relieved to learn that Tom had *not* copied the final two lines).'

See further *The Poems of T. S. Eliot*, ed. Ricks and McCue, I, 292–3, 1195–7.

1 – Against this line, in the longer TS version, TSE has written by hand 'forget-me-not'.

And when to cut and when to move,
With tender skill inspired by love.

—

O happy flowers, that have gone
Quietly, to oblivion,
And with your beauty have repaid
The hand that trimmed, and trained, and sprayed.
O happy stems, that not resent
The winter's long imprisonment;
O happy roots, that live beneath
The calm impertinence of death.
When the revolving year shall bring
The sweet deception of the spring,
Dare you put on your gaudy jerkins,
Unsupervised by Mrs Perkins?

—

We often think that man alone
Remembers. in the singing bone.
'Green earth forgets':[1] but I surmise
That gardens have long memories;
Like houses, have familiar ghosts
Of dear and hospitable hosts.
Laughter and happiness and grief
Revive within the budding leaf.
Houses remember; since you came,
Nothing in Campden is the same.
Objects inanimate will yearn
Inaudibly, for your return,
And human wishes shall be full
Of aspirations audible,
Which, ratified from hour to hour,
Possess, we hope, magnetic power.

T. S. Eliot

---

1 – George Meredith, 'France, December 1870'.

Dear Mrs Perkins,

Instead of waiting the statutory twenty-four hours I am writing at once, lest I should lose you after your departure, and also because it is imperative. I have to thank you again, for a perfect weekend – if one can call four nights a 'weekend': I should like to thank you severally for the happiest birthday party I have had since I was a boy – and for introducing me to the music of the 'Yeomen of the Guard'; and for the general and usual gracious hospitality. And although it is hardly appropriate to thank you for it, for my happiness in your own celebration of Saturday night.

But still more than for the past few days, I want now to thank you for all your kindness and sweetness to me during the past two summers. This is not a feeling to which I want to put many words: let me compress it as much as possible by saying that I had come to feel 'at home' at Campden in a way in which I had not felt at home for some twenty-one years, anywhere.

Looking forward to seeing you all in Rosary Gardens,

Yours very gratefully,
Tom Eliot

TO *Ashley Dukes*[1]   CC

1 October 1935   [Faber & Faber Ltd]

Dear Mr Dukes,

Thank you for your letter of the 30th.[2] I should of course be delighted in principle to have *Murder in the Cathedral* performed, especially with Robert Speaight in the leading part, but I have certain doubts. These concern the chorus. The rest of the play is simple enough to produce, and with Speaight as St Thomas, and if possible Martin Browne as the Fourth Tempter I should have all confidence. If Miss Fogerty can provide the girls and thinks that they can be properly trained in the time left I am quite satisfied. But I wonder whether the Mercury stage can accommodate the number for which the choruses were originally written – ten or twelve as we had at Canterbury – as if they had to be recited by a skeleton chorus of two or three I think that the effect would be much impaired. I should like to be assured of the choral arrangements before giving my consent.

Yours very sincerely,

[T. S. Eliot]

1–Ashley Dukes (1885–1959), theatre manager, playwright, critic, translator, adapter, author. Educated in Manchester and Munich, Dukes started out as theatre critic for *New Age*, *Vanity Fair*, and other journals; he was co-editor and contributor to *Theatre Arts Monthly*, 1926–42; and from 1941 he served on the first panel of the Council for the Encouragement of Music and the Arts (later the Arts Council). In 1933, with a royalty of £10,000 from his play *The Man with a Load of Mischief* (1924), he established – with his wife Marie Rambert, dancer, teacher, and founder of the Ballet Rambert (she studied with Nijinksy and Karsavina, joined Diaghileff's ballet corps, and trained Frederick Ashton and other great figures) – the tiny Mercury Theatre in Notting Hill, London, which (with support from WBY and TSE) became in 1933 a poet's theatre. *MiC*, the first hit – the production ran for 255 performances, and transferred to the West End – was followed by works by Auden and Isherwood (including *The Dog Beneath the Skin*, 1935), Ronald Duncan, Anne Ridler, and Norman Nicolson. (The Mercury Theatre features in the movie *The Red Shoes*, 1948.) See Dukes, *The Scene is Changed* (autobiography, 1942); and TSE, *The Times*, 7 May 1959: 'I should like to add a note to your excellent obituary notice of Mr Ashley Dukes. It was Mr Dukes who, after seeing a performance of *Murder in the Cathedral* at the Canterbury Festival for which it was written, saw that the play had further possibilities, and brought the whole production to London. Owing to his enterprise a play designed for a special occasion and for a very brief run, came to the notice of the general public.'
2–Dukes wrote from the Mercury Theatre, 2 Ladbroke Road, Notting Hill Gate: 'With your consent I should like to produce "Murder in the Cathedral" in this theatre on or about October 29th. I have already discussed the matter with Robert Speaight, who . . . agrees to play the part. I have also written to Martin Browne, who is coming to see me on Wednesday.' Dukes, whose production was to open on All Saints Day, restored the cuts made at Canterbury. He willingly became a tithe-payer, giving the receipts of every tenth performance to the Canterbury Cathedral fabric fund.

2 October 1935   *The Criterion*

Dear Richards,

I find the discussion on page 65 and thereabouts a little confusing.[1] Of course you have to put everything into a very compressed form, but if you could have had another page or two at this point one would like to have some statement as to the differences of *true* and *false* in relation to judgements and pseudo-judgements respectively. I take it that what you mean by a pseudo-judgement is quite different in nature from an ordinary false judgement. That is to say a scientific judgement which happens not to correspond with the facts. The question then arises in what way true and false can be applied in pseudo-judgements. I presume that anyone making a pseudo-judgement has the alternative of one or more other pseudo-judgements which he rejects because they seem to him false. Furthermore, are all pseudo-judgements of the same kind?[2]

I think that points like these matter because *Science and Poetry* is going to remain an essay of capital importance for a long time. It will be read, as it has been read, by a good many people who have not the energy

---

1–IAR in *Science and Poetry* (2nd edn, 1935), 65: 'A pseudo-statement is a form of words which is justified entirely by its effect in releasing or organizing our impulses and attitudes (due regard being had for the better or worse organizations of these *inter se*); a statement, on the other hand, is justified by its truth, *i.e.*, its correspondence, in a highly technical sense, with the fact to which it points.' TSE questioned, in a handwritten note at the foot of the page of the copy that IAR had sent to him, simply: 'Is "pseudo" here equivalent to false?'

2–IAR replied (4 Nov.): 'I would have written before but page 65 of *Science and Poetry* stood in the way. I see that, with the first line of the bottom paragraph, it does still tend to equate pseudo-statements with *false* judgements, which is very misleading. A Pseudo-Statement, for me, is something utterly different in function, powers, status, nature, order of being, etc. from any scientific, or other verifiable, statement, true or false. One way of bringing out the differences might be to say that a statement has ideally one ascertainable limited meaning, and is, for science, defective if it is ambiguous; while a Pseudo-Statement normally has inexhaustible meanings. But that only shifts the difficulty over to "meaning". Another way would be to say that a Pseudo-Statement expresses or invites the contemplation of the whole mind but a statement is a departmental matter. I don't know that these help much, though. They so much need expanding themselves. The sense of *true* and *false* for statements and Pseudo-Statements are, I hold, so different that they cannot be fairly talked of with the same terms. All the analogies have to be severely restricted. For Pseudo-Statements *true* means something near *troth* (O.E.D. 1 and 2). Certainly Pseudo-Statements conflict and have to be accepted or rejected accordingly: but whereas we all know how to find out what a statement says, we don't know (in any similar way) how to find out what Pseudo-Statements offer to us (not *say*: they don't say anything in any sense in which statements do). Or rather, with Pseudo-Statements, the process of finding out is a process of experimental growth and is the same as acceptance or rejection, as the case may be' (*Selected Letters*, 95–6).

to go on to your other books; and for others it will be, as it has been, the introduction to your other work. I have read the second edition with much interest in the changes, and there are a few points I shall want to ask you about. I have also read it with a more mature mind than when I last read it two years ago. I will leave these until I see you on the 2nd November. <*But* I have just heard from some people whose baby I am to god-father, that they want the christening on that Sunday. I said I would find out whether the following weekend would suit you as well or not.>

Yours ever,
T. S. E.

TO *Polly Tandy*

TS BL

2 October 1935   Faber & Faber Ltd

Dear Pollytandy,

Your husband will have apprised you that the pull-over, or Fair Isle jerkin, fits.[1] At least he should have done; but as he evinced a malicious desire to pretend that it was slightly too big for me (the most malignant could not pretend that it was obviously too big for me), which arose manifestly out of envy for my vast size and superior development by the Sandow System, he may have carried home a false report, in fact it would be just like him and I am sure he has done so; consequently I hasten to correct it and say that it is the jumper I mean just a Snug Fit. I would add that the wool is of an exceeding softness most pleasant to touch; that the pattern does equal justice to your skill with the knitting needle and to your good taste, and that I am proud to possess this article of wearing apparell [*sic*], and more than touched by the loving care etc. Also it is most useful. At this point I am tempted to quote Tennyson

---

1 – Polly Tandy had knitted a sweater for TSE's birthday. She wrote to him on 25 Sept.:

'Greetings on your birthday from Pollitandy and Sweet Kate.

'"Ho," you says, "that's the name of the cheeild". No I tells you that is what the cheeild is called cos we're waiting for her godfather to exercise his veto. That's wot.

'She aint pretty but she is good.

'And now *I* am sunk without trace as your Pull-over still has half a sleeve to be knitted and all my minions running over Middlesex and Surrey can't procure me just that ONE ounce of wool necessary to complete it. Otherwise the garment would have been with you on the proper day. As it is the parcel will be posted maybe on Thursday & reach you the next day. Please I *did* try and I did not expect to be confined to my bed until I had seen the job through.

'I find the greatest difficulty in writing in bed so I hope you can read this.

'Do come quite soon to Hogarth Cottage and inspect the last arrival & latest inmate.

'With our united love / Pollitandy.'

Man for the field and woman for the hearth;
Man for the sword and for the knitting needle she;
Man with the head and woman with the heart;
Man to command and woman to obey;
All else confusion.[1]

But we get confusion whichever way, seemingly. I have altered Tennyson's colons to semi-colons, which improves this already improving passage. What I meant to say was that I look forward to taking the field on Saturday in this jumper, with a view to making a good impression on Anthea Margaret Crane,[2] so will close yrs. gratefully

Tp

[On the back of the envelope]

Anthea Margaret Crane
Should know how to come out of the Rain
I'm inclined to suppose
She's a fine Norman nose
And a highly exceptional BRAIN.

---

1 – Tennyson, 'The Princess', V. 427–31:
   Man for the field and woman for the hearth:
   Man for the sword and for the needle she:
   Man with the head and woman with the heart:
   Man to command and woman to obey;
   All else confusion.
2 – The Tandys' third child, Anthea (b. 1935), to whom TSE had become godfather.
   TSE took a lively interest in the healthy development of the child, and seems to have expected the parents to send him bulletins on the baby's growth: the likes of the following:
   'We regret to announce a gain of three ounces (3 oz) only this week in Miss Anthea Margaret Crane Tandy's weight.
   'We cannot assign any physical reason for this small increase and deduce that there must be some mental or psychological cause which may account for it. It is possible that the effort of participating in her godfather's centenary (even 53 years hence [i.e. 1988] may even now be a matter of weight to the child. It is suggested that a half-centenary (3 years hence) may be a solace to the said godfather and by reason of the tender years of the child the organisation of the celebration (at the above address only) may safely be left in the hands of the undersigned, Geoffrey Tandy / Polly Tandy.'
   'We are glad to report that Miss Anthea Margaret Crane Tandy has gained 5¼ oz this week making her total weight 11lbs 8oz. We regret that she should have suffered during the week with slight nasal catarrh which we observed did not impair her nose-breathing. On no occasion was the mouth found open. / Geoffrey Tandy P.A. / Polly Tandy M.A.M.A.'
   And on 12 Dec. 1935:
   'It is with much gratification that we announce a gain of 7½ oz in Miss Anthea Margaret Crane Tandy's weight this week. This gain makes a total of 12lbs 2½oz.

2 October 1935   Faber & Faber Ltd

Dear Ez

Now look Here, les get round to that problem of Selected essays again, and a very pretty little problem it is too. Touching the most recent fasces or faeces you just sent, that it is very fruity little bit in the HOOT.[1] I am pleased to observe, podesta, that your views on education are fundamentally cognate to my own, though yr. approach be from another angle etc. and yr. technique of approach shots different, but I have tried to tell them in their own language or something like that if things go on as they do go on then Eventu'lly there will be nothing to do but EVACUATE the universities. BUT strikes me a little extra elbow grease on your estemmed [*sic*] article wouldnt do any harm and might well repay the efoord: meaning, that it might be alittle longer (it is no whit, not a jot or doit, too *strong*) and a few remarks dropped in to insist that this is not NOT just a local American problem BUT that the CRISIS of Education is worldwide. Thats what blighters wont see that its all one system really and a Bad one, and that besides Local problems there is something etc. and that Eng. better take warning from America as well as from Herself. etc.

I cant see the Paris letters etc. embalmed to this extent. Excellent excellent at the time, but not book material. (Incidentally aint you changed some of your views since then? Proust dont seem as important as he did, and not so much came out of those hopeful years in Paris after all. And aint you found out yet that Lytton Strachey wrote Damb bad English? dead as the T.L.S. and nothing much there to putresce; just mustiness). Well now we got ~~four~~ five thats some progress made: Howson Bowson and Jowson from the Criterion, Active Anthology Prelude, and enlarged and energised HOOT. Well, my next job is to re-read how to read, I spose, God damb it you will be expectin your publishers to write your stuff for you You.

What you got to say about Waley? Sounds a good idea, only point is that I have a long paper by a Chink, so long its awkward all about translations and saying yrs. are the best which has got to be printed some

---

'In every other direction, health and intelligence, there seems good progress.'

TSE was a conscientiously committed godparent, never forgetting a birthday or Christmas; and he was equally kind to the siblings of the godchildren. Richard Tandy wrote to him one Christmas: 'Dear Possum / Thank you very much for all the railway gear. They are all lovely.'

1-'Abject and Utter Farce', *Harkness Hoot* 2 (Nov. 1933), 6–14.

time and they dont want to collide. Any other ideas? I aint got room till MARCH retenez bien le date.

Did you mean Butch. can provide me loan me the back numbers of N.E.W. Because if not Ill have to read them there. Ill ask Mairet about that. I dont keep mine because I havent got room for possessions and riches, only a few clothes and writing materials etc

I should think some remarks about orthology might go in.

TP

TO *A. L. Rowse* TS Exeter

2 October 1935 *The Criterion*

My dear Rowse,

I have been waiting for an opportunity, which I hope may come soon, of wrestling with your long letter at length and properly.[1] It is not a question of argument so much as of trying to make clear what I mean. Meanwhile I wanted to say that I am glad you liked Bernard Walke's book, and if you

---

1 – ALR had written (26 Aug.): 'Thank you kindly for the trouble you took in writing at length in answer to my letter. It was very considerate and kind of you, for perhaps my letter was not worth the bother to you. And I quite agree with your main contention about your politics: it wouldn't be wise for you to attach yourself either to one party or another, and I certainly didn't expect you to come down on the side of Socialism.

'My point was rather a more curious one: it is odd how your poetic sympathies – and especially since you have taken to the Church – very strongly in places are identified with reactionary politics. Take the Archbishop's Sermon for example: it is much the same point as came up in your "Time & Tide" controversy. Where you say that Christ says "My peace I give unto you" and then, if I remember rightly, you connect that text with "Not as the world gives, give I unto you", to suggest that what Christ meant by peace was not the same thing as the world means by it: you certainly there open the doors to the reactionaries. It reminded me when I read it of Reichsbischof Müller's sermon on Christmas Day 1933 on the text "Peace on earth to men of good will", explaining that when Christ said "Peace on earth", he did not mean "No More War".

'Now, I shd say that when Christ said "Peace", he meant by it what ordinary people took him to mean, and that he looked to a time when wars would have ceased between men. And certainly it is what he has been taken to mean by generations of Christian believers through the ages; that is what has attracted countless men, weary of the conflicts of the secular world, to the Christian Faith.

'It is a fraud when you or Reichsbischof Müller tells them that Christ meant no such thing as they mean by Peace, or what historic Christianity has given them to understand he meant . . .

'What I was trying to say was that I wondered you didn't avail yourself of the spiritual resources available to you, in the way of sympathy with the sufferings of simple people: that wd. bring you more into sympathy with the people whom I believe to be right. Perhaps you do, a little, in the choruses of the Women of Canterbury.

care to write a short note about it for the *Criterion* I should be delighted. He seems to me a real man.[1]

I liked your letter in *The Times* yesterday.[2]

Yours ever,
T. S. Eliot

TO *W. T. Symons*[3]   CC

2 October 1935   [Faber & Faber Ltd]

Dear Symons,

Thank you very much for your letter of the 27th September, and for your invitation to attend the next meeting of the Chandos Group.[4] I should very much have liked to come, especially as it promises to be an important meeting. But unfortunately I have to speak at a meeting in Lincoln on the morning of the 17th, which means going down there on the afternoon or evening of the day before, so I shall be unable to come. I hope you will invite me again later.

With many regrets,
Yours sincerely,
[T. S. Eliot]

'I have recently read a wonderful book, in its way: the Memoirs of the parish priest of St Hilary, here in Cornwall: Fr Bernard Walke's "Twenty Years at St Hilary". Do read it – it is so moving a record of a life lived for his people, for the most part of them ungrateful, and filled with just this Franciscan quality.'

1 – ALR responded (9 Oct.): 'That's very like you; and I intended rather to elicit that. But as you know, for me the real man and the saint stand in antithesis to each other: the saint being at the same time rather more, and rather less than, a man.' Bernard Walke (1874–1941), Anglican priest based in Cornwall. *Twenty Years at St Hilary* (1935) was not in fact reviewed by ALR.

2 – ALR wrote to *The Times*, 1 Nov. 1935, 10, to regret the tendency of individuals going abroad to consult foreign dictators for their opinions on matters of high moment in the UK and then coming home to constitute themselves the spokesmen for those opinions.

3 – W. T. Symons was editor of *Purpose* and a director of C. W. Daniel, London publishers.

4 – The Chandos Group was collating and publishing the replies to its questionnaire on Social Credit; and on 16 Oct. the group was due to discuss the international situation. The Chandos Group, named after the restaurant on St Martin's Lane, London, where this discussion group convened – it included Mairet, Reckitt and Demant – had been set up in 1926 with the purpose of establishing 'certain absolute and eternal principles of true sociology': that is, a Christian sociology. See ch. 9: 'Money and the Just Price: Chandos', in John S. Peart-Binns and Giles Heron, *Rebel and Sage: A Biography of Tom Heron, 1890–1983* (2001); Jason Harding, *The Criterion* (2002), 191–2.

TO *Cyril Lakin*[1]

3 October 1935   [Faber & Faber Ltd]

Dear Mr Lakin,

I have your letter of the 2nd and can talk for 20 minutes for you on Monday, November 18th.[2] Would 3 o'clock be too early, as I have a meeting to attend at 4? I should like to know what you want me to talk about.[3]

Yours faithfully,

[T. S. Eliot]

TO *Henry Bamford Parkes*[4]

3 October 1935   [Faber & Faber Ltd]

Dear Mr Parkes,

I have read your manuscript *The Puritan Tradition* with much interest. The fact that it is rather a different book from what I expected does not in the least diminish my personal interest, but it does affect my view of the book as a publisher. What you have written is a very interesting history of the change and decay of Christianity in America during the history of the country, but I am afraid that it is not a book which could have much appeal in this country. The subject certainly gives the opportunity for reflection and generalisation, but I am afraid that these would have to be

1 – Cyril Lakin, literary editor of the *Sunday Times*, 1933–45.

2 – 'You have probably seen the announcement of the third "Sunday Times" Book Exhibition which is to be held this year at Dorland Hall, Lower Regent Street, s.w., from November 4th to November 18th.

'One of the most popular features of these Exhibitions has been the daily series of short Talks given by well known people, and these . . . will be repeated this year. The Sub-Committee of Publishers, which has been making the arrangements, would very much like you to give one of these Talks (they take about 20 minutes) at the forthcoming Exhibition, and if you would care to do it I should like to suggest, as a date and time, Monday, November 18th, at 3.30 p.m.'

3 – Lakin replied, 31 Oct.: 'The Committee suggests as a subject for you "Contemporary Poetry".'

4 – Henry Bamford Parkes (1904–72), born in Sheffield, England, was an author and professor of history at New York University. His works include *Jonathan Edwards, the Fiery Puritan* (1930) and *A History of Mexico* (1938).

done in a different way for the local public here. I am returning the manuscript according to your instructions to Mr D. G. White.

> With best wishes,
> Yours sincerely,
> [T. S. Eliot]

TO *Ashley Dukes*

3 October 1935   [Faber & Faber Ltd]

Dear Mr Dukes,

Thank you for your letter of the 2nd.[1] That sounds all right. If, as you say, Robert Speaight is to take the leading part, and Miss Fogerty is to undertake the chorus, and Martin Browne is to help, I have no objection to your going ahead on the basis which you indicate in this letter. I assume that the terms you propose are for a run at the Mercury Theatre only, and that if the play had the fortune to be transferred to a West End theatre the terms would be revised and we would have a contract drawn up. I do not think, however, that *Murder in the Cathedral* is likely to enjoy so much success as that.

> Yours sincerely,
> [T. S. Eliot]

1–Dukes wrote: 'Within two hours of receiving your letter I was able to see Martin Browne and Miss Fogerty, both of whom have been most helpful. Miss Fogerty came to see the stage, and told me she would like to undertake the play with a chorus of nine or ten. The chorus leader from Canterbury is available . . . Meanwhile Martin Browne has seen Speaight again.' He added formally that the Mercury theatre 'pays a royalty of five per cent on its gross weekly receipts.'

See further Dukes's reminiscences in *Fogie*, 166–7: 'Those of us who went to see the opening in Canterbury were quite unprepared for the immense impact of the play in its stylised production, nowhere more apparent than in the formal handling of the chorus. No doubt there were touches of preciosity here and there, visible signs of the art-and-craft spirit in costume and decoration; but the uniform presentation of the "Women of Canterbury" was a bold and successful stroke. The best of acting or miming in a realistic sense could never have made "the poor" – as these women describe themselves – harmonise with the style and background as a whole. The Chorus with their clear and cultivated voices were a sublimation of the substance of Eliot's poetry: they were the subject – then and later on – of a few jibes at the "young ladies of Kensington"; but this never caused them the slightest anxiety about the integrity of their work. The critics signally failed to observe the subtleties of their distribution of speaking parts, or the beauty of their choral speaking as a whole. These qualities were due in very great measure to Elsie Fogerty's inspiration. And it may be noted that a Chorus of this character does not preserve its standards unaided; yet, when the

3 October 1935   Faber & Faber Ltd

Dear Jeanie,

I want at least to make a punctual, if brief reply to your surprise letter of September 14th.[1] I had no reason to suppose that you knew when my birthday was, but there it is. I won't swear that it actually arrived on the 26th, but I don't know that it didn't, because I went down to Campden that afternoon, and found your letter waiting on my return on Monday morning. I had, of course, a perfectly delightful birthday party. Mrs P. is (almost too consciously, malice would say) the perfect hostess – on Friday the *Yeomen of the Guard* at the Stratford Theatre; on Saturday evening a dinner arranged by Emily with great care in *her* honour – healths and tasteful speeches from and to the servants, and an Occasional Poem by myself which seemed to go down well. (I have steadily tried to make a good impression on Mrs P., both for my own sake and thinking that I might be more useful if she thought well of me.) I wish that we might have that dinner in Paris on the 27th October.

I would gladly put up with the presence of the Perkins's in London permanently, for the sake of liberating E., but the devil of it is that King's Chapel, Boston, is having its tercentenary early in the spring, and Dr P. is living for that, so they are certain to go back. I should be glad to get them over again, if they can be made to move again once they have got to Boston. I do think that some place like Campden is ideal for them – a place with an olde worlde atmosphere stinking of death. The main thing at the moment is for E. to get a job, almost any sort of job anywhere, when she gets back.

I hope you are getting on well with your young pupils. Nobody ever instructed me in the art of 'approaching the slower minds', and I started as a schoolmaster at a time when I was pretty well a nervous wreck anyway, so naturally I did not like it. But you ought to be in a college job. It is odd, but I found teaching French to children more difficult than any other subject. For instance, although I could usually get any irregular verb right when I was using it in a sentence, I had never got them by heart in paradigms, or whatever they are called, and I think my pupils sometimes thought that I was an imposter.

---

play came to the Mercury Theatre the Chorus exchanged parts freely and almost nightly. I [think] this is sufficient proof that Elsie Fogerty was not only an inspired teacher, but a good "show-woman" and woman of the theatre.'
1 – Not traced.

Our Maritain is coming over to lecture, this month, and I have to take the chair for him. Emily is now in Oxford looking after Mrs Hale, of course. I look forward to having her in London for a time (they will be near neighbours) with mixed feelings. The exasperation of looking on at a situation about which I can do nothing has made me want at times to rush out into the garden and pull up all the prize dahlias and whatnots.

Your Panama postcard, by the way, has compelled the admiration of connoisseurs. E.g. Mr W. H. Auden was admiring it only last night. Have you any good local ones ('Did you ever hear Pike's Peak?' and that sort of thing.)

When is *your* birthday, by the way? I have a feeling that I did know and have forgotten.

Yours

Tom

TO *Virginia Woolf*   TS Berg

3 October 1935   Faber & Faber Ltd

My dear Virginia,

Either you will think that I ought to have written before[1] – or else you will think I am an obsequious follower of antiquated fashions to write at all – I am sure I am wrong one way or another – only I depend upon you not to mix me up with Logan and the Henry James gang – I have just had to read some of his complimentary letters to Mary Anderson (Mme. Novarro of Broadway Worcs.) what heavy gallantry it is yet going through the paces of something good in its kind. But I lead a distracted

---

1 – TSE had visited Monks House, 21–3 Sept. VW noted: 'he is more masterly; tells a story like one who has the right; is broader & bonier & more wild eyed – long almond shaped eyes – that he means to write modern verse plays: that he is self confident although going up Charleston Lane in the dark last night (Lottie advancing in her red jacket) he told me that he has no self confidence: Joyce has; but Joyce is interminably bored with everything. What can he do when he's finished this book? Perhaps thats why he procrastinates. We dined at Charleston . . . We walked. Long silences. Bruce Richmond brooded over the week end. *His* week end: his rotund country gentleman ways: port hock bedroom candles; & telling little stories. Tom likes going there; is magisterially accepting new experiences. Likes, more than we do, respectability. Went to service at 8 on Sunday: a wet morning, & he hea[r]d one old woman say to another – in the churchyard, "And she was lying in bed wih a still born child beside her." But he did his duty. A very nice man, Tom: I'm very fond of Tom, & at last not knocked off my perch by him. That is, not as I was when he came here & I writing Jacob's Room. Now he cant much disturb The Years, though he makes me feel that I want to write a play' (*Diary* 4, 343–4).

life – night before last I spent the evening coiled up in a corner of the wings of the Westminster Theatre, crushed by a crowd of sweating young people in bathing costumes lent by Jantzen Ltd of Isleworth, and last night setting off fireworks to amuse Auden and Hayward, and on Saturday I have to inspect a god-daughter, and next week open the Lincoln Diocesan Conference discussion of Sunday Observance, and today I had a young lady to tea named Vera who is a friend of Mirsky and wants to convert me she *said* she could only stay ten minutes and she said when she did leave would I come to lunch with her next week because she has lots of money at the moment and also she knows where to lunch: I do not understand these Russian women she admits to having the *charme slave*[1]; and tomorrow a young negro named Harrison[2] is coming to see me. All this to explain my being distracted so that I do not know my right hand from my left: however, I did enjoy staying with you very much indeed, and even the whirl of gaity [*sic*] was delightful, and I am grateful: besides, last weekend I was in Gloucestershire and ran away from a Bull down a hill into some blackberry bushes. Will you come to Tea or may I come to Tea after your return. Do read the Duke of Portland's reminiscences of Turf & Field, they are amazing. As Clive would say, Je vous assure, chère Madame, de ma consideration la plus que parfaite; so will close,

Yours very gratefully,

Tom

P.S. For Leonard. How we make decisions in the T.U.C.: [cutting]

'Mr Berridge (London) said that the executive seemed to be hypnotised by the employers' federation, and the employers' argument that consolidation could only be brought about if it did not increase production costs.

It was decided to reaffirm the principle of consolidation.

The conference adjourned until today.'

No news of my cousin, Apra [*sic*] Behn.

Perhaps she won't come.

---

1 – *charme slave*: Slavonic charm.
2 – W. E. Harrison, a former student of Babbitt's: given an introduction to TSE by Matthiessen.

TO *Cyril E. Hudson*   CC

8 October 1935   [Faber & Faber Ltd]

Dear Hudson,

Thank you for your letter of the 4th.[1] I am pleased that you should think of me in connection with the Pageant that you have in mind, but I am afraid it is not really my business. I have had several suggestions of this nature which I have declined. Pageant-making is not my business to begin with, and I want to save what time I have of my own for the writing of plays, and for my next I do not want to be bound down to any specifications. I think that Martin Browne is the man you want.

I shall be writing to you about the public letter in a day or two. Meanwhile I am sending you a copy of Eric Gill's new book, with the suggestion that if it appeals to you I should be glad to have a review of it from you for the *Criterion*.[2]

Yours sincerely,
[T. S. Eliot]

TO *John Garrett*   CC

8 October 1935   [*The Criterion*]

Dear Mr Garrett,

I am ordering for you the book mentioned in your letter of 7th, but if it is not yet published it is hardly likely to be in time for you to review it for the December number.

I am glad that you liked J. M. Reeves's review.[3] He is a Cambridge man of about your own generation I should think, and, if I remember rightly, is teaching in a school near London. Etiquette forbids giving addresses, but why don't you write to him, care of the *Criterion*?

1–Hudson invited TSE to write a 'pageant-chronicle' showing 'the concern of the Church with education – i.e. with Truth – down the ages: beginning, perhaps, with a class of catechumens in Rome or Corinth in the first century, and ending up with a Church Tutorial Class or a priest of the Oxford Mission to Calcutta discussing the attributes of God with a group of Brahmins! . . . I am sure such a pageant might be of great propaganda value, as well as – if you wrote it – of great dramatic force.'
2–Hudson on Eric Gill, *Work and Leisure*: C. 15 (Jan. 1936), 352–3.
3–J. M. Reeves on *The Poet's Tongue: An Anthology*, ed. W. H. Auden and John Garrett: C. 15 (Oct. 1935), 118–21.

I am pleased to hear your favourable impression of Tomlin's progress.[1] I do think that his writing has improved, though I think it will be all the better when he has been some time away from the atmosphere of the Modern Greats School.

With best wishes,
Yours sincerely,
[T. S. Eliot]

TO *A. L. Rowse*

8 October 1935   *The Criterion*

My dear Rowse,

Thanks for your letter.[2] If you hadn't already done Walke for the *Spectator* I should have said that a review might do more good coming from you than from me.[3] As it is, I shall try to do something myself. As for your suggestion that Bernard Walke was something like a saint, I should say that if he was a real saint he must also have been, as I said, a real man. I should think that the greater comprehended the less.

Yours,
T. S. E.

1 – 'I heard Tomlin give a paper the other night on Psycho-Analysis, and it struck me that he has made great intellectual strides of late. Certainly his academic reverse though unfortunate seems to have cast him down not at all.'

2 – ALR wrote (3 Oct.) that he had already written on Walke for the *Spectator*. 'I merely thought, if you have read it – it is so moving & true a book – that it wd do so much more good if *you* mentioned it, either in your Chronicle or in a Note.

'It struck me at once on reading your note: Now Bernard Walke is not at all my idea of a man. He's my idea of a saint.'

3 – Bernard Walke (1874–1941): see *Twenty Years at St Hilary* (1935).

TO *Reginald Miller*   TS Bodleian

8 October 1935   *The Criterion*

Dear Doctor Miller,

I have your letter of October 6th,[1] and I am sure that you will understand that I cannot deal with such a communication without consulting my solicitors. I am forwarding it to them, and will write to you as soon as I have their reply, unless they inform me that they are writing to you direct.

With best wishes,
Yours very sincerely,
T. S. Eliot

FROM *Reginald Miller* TO *Vivien Eliot*   TS Bodleian

9 October 1935   110 Harley Street, W.1

Dear Mrs Eliot,

I have written to Mr Eliot on the subject of his settling my account, and have today a letter from his solicitor to say that he very much regrets that he cannot advise Mr Eliot to undertake the payment of my fee. I have also a note from Mr Eliot that he has asked his solicitor to deal with the question.

I think that there can be no doubt that Mr Eliot has been made aware by my letter that you were greatly upset by the action taken in July, and I understand from your letter to me that you thought he ought to know this. So I hope that this will be some help to you.[2]

Yours sincerely,
Reginald Miller

1 – Miller's letter not traced. VHE had instructed him to apply to TSE for payment of a bill of £9 that she owed to the doctor. See next letter.

2 – Dr Miller wrote to VHE again on 18 Oct. 1935: 'I send you, as you request, the letter which I received from Mr Eliot. He did not write again as his solicitors wrote direct to me.

'It is, as you say, amply clear to me that unless you settle my account no one else will. But on the other hand, should opportunity at any time arise to get yourself reimbursed, the mere fact that you had paid my account would not, I think, prejudice your claim. I will, of course, send you a formal receipt.'

VHE finally paid her bill on 27 Oct. 1935; and on the same day she wrote to the Manager, District Bank: 'Will you be so kind as to, acting on my behalf, pay to Doctor Reginald Miller, the sum of nine guineas. *I protest against his action in refusing to allow me to see my husband.*' (VHE had endeavoured to get Dr Miller to arrange for TSE to be present in his consulting rooms when she came to pay the invoice. On 25 Oct. Miller flatly refused to do so; and he told her that he thought it 'hardly gracious' for her to delay any longer in paying his bill.)

TO *E. Martin Browne*   cc

9 October 1935   [*The Criterion*]

My dear Martin Browne,

I am glad to hear from you, because I have been wanting to see you about this business.[1] I am afraid that you are right about the opening of Act II. I will send you a copy of the chorus which I wrote and suppressed, but I am not sure that you will think it suitable. I am perfectly ready to write a new one, but the time is very short for rehearsals anyway. Can we meet as soon as possible? I have lunch and dinner engagements tomorrow, but I shall be here all the afternoon, or I am free for lunch or dinner or the afternoon on Monday.

Yours in haste,
[T. S. Eliot]

TO *Mary Hutchinson*   TS Texas

9 October 1935   *The Criterion*

Dear Mary,

Thank you very much for your letter and cheque.[2] In the circumstances I had not been expecting to hear from you for some time. I did see about Jack's illness in *The Times*, and wondered whether to ring up or not, and finally, as I thought it sounded very serious indeed, decided that I had better wait until I could find out from someone else. I am sorry now that I did not telephone. I spoke to Ted Kauffer on the telephone yesterday

---

1–Browne had written ('Wednesday'): 'First, I'm exceedingly glad we are to do "Murder in the Cathedral" [at the Mercury Theatre, London], & hope you'll pleased with cast & result. I should like to meet you very soon if I could to discuss the exact version, etc. But there's one problem I send for your thought. The interval must come after the sermon. I have no choir, & think that in those circumstances the Priests' ceremonial will not be a success. You did draft a chorus to begin Part II. Is it possible that it could be so far finished as to be used? Nothing very long is necessary, but I feel definitely that the Chorus should open the Part in a theatrical version, don't you?'

2–MH had written (? on 10 Oct.): 'Please forgive me for not sending Barker's cheque before. I have been very anxious about Jack having seen three specialists including Lord Dawson of Penn!! and two doctors. They are now all agreed that there is nothing serious the matter. He has had an attack of "auricular vertigo" and they are taking this opportunity, when they have him imprisoned, to "overhaul him". They advise one months cure in a Castle in Wales.

'I have been anxious because doctors manners are dreadful and one's own ignorance equally terrifying. You never inquired after your old friend! Yours affectionately Mary Hutchinson.'

and he was more reassuring. I am very sorry that you have had such a bad time, and also that I shall not, I suppose, be able to see Jack until his return. Is there any chance, however, of seeing you in the interim?

Do please convey my sympathy to Jack. Apologetically and affectionately,

Tom

TO *Michael Roberts*

TS Berg

10 October 1935   Faber & Faber Ltd

Dear Roberts,

In connection with the Chatto and Windus anthology[1] my secretary wrote to you a few days ago for information about the Chatto authors whose work you are using. I note that they are four in number, Rosenberg, Owen, Quennell, and Empson. To complete my knowledge in order to negotiate with Chattos about the fees they are to pay us for using work of our authors would you please let me know what is the special arrangement that you are making with Mrs Owen. I know that you told me that you were paying her somewhat more than the flat rate. I quite approve of this, but the point is that whatever higher rates we are paying her are relevant to what we shall ask Chattos on behalf of our authors.

I have received several poems of yours which look good, but which I have not yet had time to study.[2]

And I should like to ask if Mrs Roberts would ever be interested in reviewing poetry for the *Criterion*.[3]

Yours ever,

T. S. Eliot

1–Roberts hoped (11 Sept.) that F&F would 'make an effort after all' to get his anthology 'out by Christmas'. 'You will have seen that Chattos announce theirs for the Autumn.'

2–Roberts wrote further (23 Oct.): 'I was pleased that you thought the poems I sent you recently might be worth a second reading: unfortunately I sent "In Time of Peace" to [Derek] Verschoyle [at *The Spectator*] by mistake, and he has had it set up. The others, of course, I have not sent out, and there is no hurry about them whatever.'

3–Roberts answered (14 Oct.): 'Janet tells me that she would be very pleased indeed to review poetry for the *Criterion*.' Janet Adam Smith would write a number of reviews for C.

12 October 1935

8, Clarence Gate Gardens,
London, N.W.1.
and
c/o British Union of Fascists
National HQ. 1 Sanctuary
Buildings, Great Smith Street,
Westminster, London, s.w.1

Dear Tom,

Congratulations on your play, 'Sweeney Agonistes'.[1] Those who have eyes, let them see. And those who have ears, let them hear . . . . . . It is like Kipling's 'The Man Who Was', if there is such a story, or am *I* making it up?[2] I hope you can get this produced again and for a longer run. The first part needs padding.[3]

(Signed) V. H. Eliot

Four letters were forwarded to you c/o the *Box Office, Westminster Theatre*.

1–In October, *SA* was staged for fifteen public performances, in a double bill with WHA's *The Dance of Death*, at the Westminster Theatre. Rupert Doone included this producer's note in the programme: 'My production is concerned with morals as well as aesthetics. I have sought to criticise the conventionalities of modern behaviour with its empty code and heartiness – immoral but never immoral enough – decaying, but so long in dying. I see Sweeney himself as a modern Orestes (the only three-dimensional character in the play). The rest are conventionalised conventional characters – the Eumenides or Bogies of Sweeney's persecution. RD.'

GCF noted in his diary, 3 Oct.: 'To the Westminster Theatre, with E., after dinner, to see Sweeney Agonistes & Dance of Death, put on by that Auden crowd. Monstrous perversion of Sweeney Agonistes – as TSE admitted afterwards. I put it on record, that he wanted no masks; that the tempo is meant to be quick; that the other characters are not meant to gibber like ghosts, nor to sit like a row of dummies; &, in short, that as produced it was unrecognizable by the author! The D. of D. I enjoyed as a revue, without bothering about its tedious & silly message. The last scene was cheapened on the stage, & made very tedious & ineffective.'

2–Kipling, 'The Man Who Was', *Life's Handicap: Being Stories of Mine Own People* (1891; repr. London: Macmillan & Co., 1964), 97–116.

3–VHE's diary, Weds., 2 Oct. 1935: 'There was a performance of Sweeney Agonistes at 6.30. . . . The theatre was very empty. I sat in the front row of the stalls. *Close up*, it was a *terrible* ordeal. How I contrived not to faint I do not know. The absolute horror of the thing. And the awful Homicidal Maniac walking down from the stage, right on top of me, & *seeming* to be *telling me* his hideous, *plausible, perishing wheeze*. A terrible little man, in *spectacles*, with an earnest manner, & a tale *to tell indeed*. A sort of composite character of *Algy, young Stephens,* & the child "Raggy" [her nephew]. What a marvellous brain Tom has. And quite a *pinch* of Jack Culpin in it, as there was in the character of the *Social Agitator* in his *Pageant The Rock*.

TO *Stephen Spender*   MS Northwestern

Saturday [?12] October [1935]   Faber & Faber Ltd

Dear Stephen

I have got to produce a catalogue blurb of your stories by Wednesday –
Could you let me have at once some information about them – how many
– their relation to each other – and anything you think it might be useful
to say. I think I have read two of them?[1]

'Of course I can take these things calmly, & I am well warned & *fore-armed*, thanks to
my great big bad boy Tom, who, being such a unique & rumbustious creature, & coming
from such strange environments, has made me a woman among thousands, a sort of super-
being. He is a Prophet.' On 9 Oct.: 'At 8.45 I went in a taxi to The Westminster Theatre
again. The play Sweeney Agonistes touches me very much. But of course no-one wld. see
how pitiful it is, but me.' And on 11 Oct. she attended for a third time, accompanied by her
friend Louie Purdon.

(Louie Purdon was a cousin of Basil Saunders, who wrote to Lyndall Gordon, 18 Aug.
1993: 'One of Louie's stories, as told to me, was of going with "Mrs Eliot" to a performance
of Sweeney Agonistes. Viv had chosen to go in the uniform of the British Union of Fascists.
They were hissed by the audience as they walked down the aisle to their front seats. This was
embarrassing but Louie recounted it as funny.

'Louie was a somewhat earnest spinster but she had plenty of humour. She needed it
in her work with the certified. She said "I didn't understand the play. It was all about
birth, copulation and death. My only consolation is that at the time I did not know what
copulation was' (cited in Gordon, *Imperfect Life*, 304).

'Always when Tom is producing anything,' VHE remarked in her diary, 'there is a great
Moon. He is a *Moon-Child*.'

1 – Spender responded from Brussels on 15 Oct.: 'I hope this reply will not come too late for
you . . . The book will be ready at latest by Nov. 15th . . . The book will be called The Dead
Island, and will be of about 50,000 words. The title story is the longest & most important
story I have written, and is in two sections, in the first of which a situation is built up: the
second part is a series of rather violent and dramatic variations, one of which is written in
verse. There are only two characters: a man and a woman. This is a story I have always
wanted to write – about an inebriate who parks himself on someone, wanting to be "saved":
the whole problem of people who want to be "saved" by others and the kind of moral
blackmail that involves has always fascinated me. The point about the woman in this story is
that she refuses to "save" him; but that she is a person with a "past", and that his behaviour
shows her something about personal relationships which in a way "saves" her.

'I don't think this is what you want. Here is something more in the nature of a blurb: "These
short stories The Dead Island, The Burning Cactus, The Third and a Half International, The
Strange Death & By the Lake, are neither anecdotes nor incidents. Each story attempts
rather to create a legend. A particular situation is revealed, and developed in such a way that
a comparison of moral interests is achieved."

'I don't know whether this is very clear. The point is that my stories simply match types
of moral behaviour against one another, as one might match several colours. That puts it
best of all.'

(He added, 'I have sketched out my first play now & feel that I can start it as soon as we
get away [to Portugal].')

I have been very busy lately, but hope to see you soon.

Affectionately,

Tom

TO *Gabriel Hebert*

15 October 1935   [Faber & Faber Ltd]

Dear Father Gabriel,

Thank you for your letter of October 11th.[1] I return the card from Norman Hester. This is very good news indeed. The number of copies of *Liturgy and Society* sold up to Monday was 693, 36 copies having been sold during the week ending October 9th, and 9 since that date. I think that we shall eventually have to reprint.

I am interested to hear that it is possible that the Chichester conference may come off so soon.[2] I look forward to the 28th, but I am afraid that it will be quite impossible for me to come on Sunday. I wish that I could do so, but my baptism is outside of London, and there would not be time to get to Kings Cross by 4.55.

Yours very sincerely,

[T. S. Eliot]

TSE's draft blurb (1935) for *The Dead Island* reads: 'This volume contains five stories: *The Dead Island, The Burning Cactus, The Third and a Half International, The Strange Death*, and *By the Lake*. The author says of them: "these are neither anecdotes nor incidents. Each story attempts rather to create a legend. A particular situation is revealed, and developed in such a way that a comparison of moral interests is achieved." The reader will infer that this is not a mere collection of short stories – the title story is indeed a long story – and that the book is no by-product of Mr Spender's activity, but will occupy an important place in the development of his creative work.' The volume was ultimately to be published as *The Burning Cactus* (1936).

1 – 'I asked the Secretary of the CR at Mirfield to send you a copy of their Quarterly Paper, in case you had not seen their excellent review of my book. Also, as the enclosed postcard will testify, we got a puff at the Church Congress. I would be very grateful if you could let me know some time how many copies have sold to date.'

2 – 'There is quite a probability that the "Chichester Conference" may come off in the first week of January: only, the Bishop unfortunately is shutting up his beautiful house for the 3 winter months, and the Conference if it meets will have to be at Hayward's Heath . . .

'We shall expect you on Monday Oct. 28. Or, better still, could you possibly catch the 4.55 train at King's Cross on Sunday after the baby has been baptized?'

TO *Hugh Gordon Porteus*   TS Beinecke

15 October 1935   *The Criterion*

Dear Porteus,

I am glad that you will take the poetry books. I shall have them left
ready for you on Thursday, together with *Men Without Art*, as I shall be
out of town that day.[1]

I should be glad if your wife would review something for the *Criterion*,
but I am afraid I must ask for another suggestion.[2] For one thing, I prefer
in general not to review Faber books in the *Criterion* unless they are
obviously books which it is necessary that we should review, and for other
reasons I think it would be wiser not to review this book at all.

Yours ever,

T. S. Eliot

---

1 – Porteus was due to deliver to RdlM the corrected proofs of his 'Chinese pamphlet'. He had
lent his copy of WL's *Men Without Art* (1934) to TSE. WL, in his chap. III – 'T. S. Eliot: The
Pseudo-Believer' – took TSE (the 'Pseudoist') to task on a number of fronts. 'Mr Eliot – who
as critic and poet may be regarded as the outcome of Ezra on the technical side . . . teaches a
mechanism, a little automatically; for it is evident that the good Ezra hypnotizes him, as well
as laying him under a deep obligation . . . [I. A. Richards] has been responsible for giving
definition to Mr Eliot's critical impulses, and bringing into a glaring prominence the essential
muddle-headedness of this strange classicist and "revolutionary" poet – this odd "cultural"
humanist and true believer. Mr Eliot stands for the maximum of *depersonalization*, and Mr
Richards for the maximum of *disbelief* or suspension of judgement . . . [W]hat I think may
be said is that in a great deal of his literary criticism Mr Eliot has . . . tended to confuse
scientific values with art values' (75). 'The "classical" panache and all the rest of it, that is
in the nature of a disguise . . . [Mr Eliot] exhibited himself as "a royalist" to an indignant
whig public – he called them a lot of naughty whigs and wagged his finger – and supplied
just so much of that comedy as was welcome to brighten up the scene, but not a scrap more
than was safe and comfortable' (77). 'Mr Eliot, according to my notion, is insincere: he has
allowed himself to be robbed of his personality, such as it is, and he is condemned to an
unreal position.' And of TSE's 'uneasy' relations with Herbert Read: 'Mr Eliot, as skipper of
the *Criterion*, has the air of glancing a little sardonically askance at this first mate, as though
he had got on board while he wasn't looking, and was not quite a sufficiently orthodox
seaman to be entrusted with the navigation of such a ship – as indeed he is not . . . the man
. . . if the *Criterion* is to fly the royal ensign, and steer accoring to classical canons.'
    According to Porteus, TSE, who seemed to be apprehensive about buying a copy of WL's
book for himself, borrowed one from Porteus (Ackroyd, 220). Porteus wrote, in 'Some
Notes on a few letters from T. S. E. to H. G. P.': 'He returned my loan gravely over dinner a
few days later, and told me of his decision to "wind up" the *Criterion*.'
2 – Porteus reported on 13 Oct. that his wife wished to review Edith Sitwell's *Queen Victoria*.
Mrs Porteus – Benka Bartek – wrote again on 29 Oct. to ask to review either Herbert
Read's novel *The Green Man* or Margaret Mead's *Sex and Temperament in Three Primitive
Societies*. See Bartek on Mead: C. 15 (Apr. 1936), 565–7.

15 October 1935   [Faber & Faber Ltd]

Dear Mr Williamson,

I have your letter about Robert Waller, and although you say there is no need I am anxious to reply.[1] He called to see me a few days ago, just before going to stay at Horsham with the friend whose London address you give, and told me in his rapid voluble way substantially the same story that you repeat, and a good deal more too. He said that he would like to go to see John MacMurray, for whom he has a very strong admiration, and I encouraged him to do so, as I think MacMurray might have a good influence upon him. I have written to MacMurray about him. Meanwhile I have been racking my brains to think of something for him. What he really needs is a small job, of course, which would enable him to live apart from his family, and I think if he could bring himself to take a job in the country, if one were to be found, it would be healthier for him. But it is not easy to get jobs in general, and you will agree, I am sure, that one cannot recommend unconditionally a young man of such instability. What one wants is to find somebody who could supply a small job, to whom it would be possible to explain the whole situation frankly.

Yours ever sincerely,

[T. S. Eliot]

---

1 – Ross Williamson wrote (n.d.): 'This needs no reply to me: but, since our conversation about Waller in the train going to Kelham, I'm sure you won't mind my writing.

'I've just had a letter from him which is very disturbing. "For the last fortnight I have held myself in check and tried to put up with my condition, but I can't stand it any longer. I am quite certain another week will bring me either a nervous breakdown or a fit of physical violence against my parents. All day long my head burns like fire and my heart beats too rapidly [. . .] My people are allowing me 5/- a week, which doesn't pay my fare to town twice a week: so I just wander for miles about the streets of Croydon and Streatham holding in check impulses to commit a theft [. . .] I can't write a line: with an immense amount I want to finish. I've lost all confidence in myself for the first time that I can remember. Even this letter is hurting my head, driving a hazy pain into the middle of it." And much more.

'Unfortunately I can't help him: I've nowhere to ask him to stay and my own financial position at the moment consists of nothing but an overdraft! And anyhow, money – except that it would enable him to get away – wouldn't really solve "the problem": especially as a gift.

'It occurred to me that, if Faber might eventually publish him, a small advance – £10 – would do the trick: restore his confidence and enable him to get to Germany (where he wants to go) for a little. This is impertinent, but you will forgive it. But if you would just see him, it would mean a lot.'

TO *W. B. Yeats*

CC

16 October 1935   [Faber & Faber Ltd]

My dear Yeats,

I must apologise for my delay in reporting to you on Lady Gerald Wellesley's poems.[1] Several of the Committee had read the poems before they were returned to you, and liked them as much as I had, but our considered opinion is that this is not a book which we need to do. The publication of poetry has to be considered as a public duty rather than a commercial undertaking, inasmuch as it usually means a loss, and except in very few cases it means at least not getting our money back for a considerable time. We feel that Lady Gerald's book is one which any really good publisher would be glad to have, and that therefore it ought to be taken by one of the better firms that do not publish as much poetry as we do. Your name and introduction alone should ensure this. We are influenced, though not decisively, by the fact that it is not a type of poetry generally associated with our house. This consideration would not be conclusive in itself if we thought that Lady Gerald would have any difficulty in getting the volume published, but I should think that Macmillan or any publisher of their standing ought to be glad to have it.[2]

I will write separately to Lady Gerald.

Yours ever,
[T. S. Eliot]

1–For Wellesley, see next letter. See Schuchard, *The Last Minstrels*, 364: 'Eliot now lunched frequently with Yeats to discuss the Poets' Theatre . . . Yeats read Wellesley's poems to Eliot and boldly proposed that he publish them at his firm.'
2–Yeats wrote to Wellesley, 20 Oct. 1935: 'I have just been given Faber and Faber's letter about your book . . . Of course bringing your book to Faber and Faber was very definitely sending the wooden horse into Troy. T. S. Eliot was I know in favour of its acceptance; I would like to see him about it. I think the reason which he gives in his letter, which I enclose, is probably quite sincere. They are concentrating on a certain type of poetry. This winter they are about to bring out a volume of MacNeice, an extreme radical; your book might interfere' (*Letters on Poetry from W. B. Yeats to Dorothy Wellesley* [1940], 39).

804   TSE at forty-seven

TO *Dorothy Wellesley*[1]

16 October 1935   [Faber & Faber Ltd]

Dear Lady Gerald,

Although the other members of the Committee who read your poems liked them as much as I did, we have come to the conclusion that it would be as well if some other firm published them. We are the more strongly influenced to this decision, indeed, by our appreciation of their value, because we feel that both on their own merits, and with the aid of Yeats's introduction, they form a volume which many other publishers would be happy to have. We are not very much influenced by the obvious fact that they belong to a somewhat different category from that of our other poets, but rather by the fact that we have no particular wish to add to our poetry list at present. If no other publisher of the highest class would consider taking your poems I should look at the matter very differently. In that very unlikely contingency I should of course be glad to take the matter up again.[2]

Yours very sincerely,
[T. S. Eliot]

TO *John Macmurray*[3]

16 October 1935   [Faber & Faber Ltd]

Dear MacMurray,

I hope that you will not mind my having given some encouragement to a young man to come and see you. I do not know whether you will remember him. His name is Robert Waller, and he was a pupil of yours

1–Dorothy Wellesley, Duchess of Wellington (1889–1956) – known as Lady Gerald Wellesley (she had married the 7th Duke of Wellington in 1914 but they were separated without divorce in 1922) – socialite, author, poet, editor; close friend of W. B. Yeats, who admired and published her work in the *Oxford Book of English Verse*; editor of the Hogarth Living Poets series.

2–Yeats to Wellesley, 24 Oct. 1935: 'Do not be depressed about the Faber refusal. I find they are bringing out an anthology and I gather from various indications that it will be ultra-radical, its contents having been all approved by Robert Graves and Laura Riding' (*Letters on Poetry*, 40).

3–John Macmurray, MC (1891–1976), Scottish philosopher, educated at Glasgow and Oxford, served in WW1 as a lieutenant in the Cameron Highlanders; Grote Professor of the Philosophy of Mind and Logic, London University, 1928–44. In 'An Exhortation' (Dec. 1937) – light verses addressed to Charles Williams – TSE was to invoke 'the nonconformist virtues of prophetic John Macmurray': see *Poems*, ed. Ricks and McCue, II, 179–80.

at London University for several terms. He will tell you his story himself. It is a story of a very unhappy and sordid life with his parents in a South London suburb, complicated by very poor health and by a very bad heredity. The point is that even if you can make no practical suggestions for his future, he has a tremendous admiration for your work, and your advice and counsel would mean a great deal to him, and influence him in the right directions.

His writing is philosophical and critical, and he also composes a good deal of verse. I feel that he has a lot of unusual ability, although nothing he has shown me yet seemed ripe enough for publication. He works by fits and starts and in a feverish sort of way is very fluent. What he needs at the moment is some very small job which will make it possible for him to live away from his family and have the leisure to develop. Living at home seems to have the worst effect on his health. Then he is always falling in love with somebody or other, which he no doubt will tell you about too, and generally he needs having his head packed in ice. I have heard, for instance, of a small job which may be going in a small country town to assist a local seedsman in his shop. I haven't mentioned this to him yet as I do not know whether it is still open. The trouble is that he is not altogether stable, and I do not know whether he would fit into such a place. If you do see him when he writes to you, I shall be grateful if you will let me have your impressions.[1]

Yours sincerely,
[T. S. Eliot]

TO *The Treasurer, Westminster Theatre* CC

18 October 1935 [Faber & Faber Ltd]

Received with thanks the sum of £8 6s., for the royalty of 2% on the fortnight's takings at The Westminster Theatre during the performance of *Sweeney Agonistes.*[2]

Signed: [T. S. Eliot]

£8 6s. od.

---

1 – Macmurray responded on 22 Oct. that he had not 'seen [Waller] or heard from him yet'. 'I have always thought that there was good stuff in him if he could reach some kind of emotional stability in himself.'
2 – The total box office takings for the double bill (*SA* with Auden's *The Dance of Death*) for two weeks (fifteen performances) amounted to £415.

TO *Roger Hinks*[1]

18 October 1935   [Faber & Faber Ltd]

My dear Hinks,

Frau Gundolf is quite right to wish to be accurate.[2] I should think that *wüst* was the better word of the two. The exact equivalent in French is *gaste, La Gaste Lande*. And if there is any equivalent of the French account of the story in medieval German that would have [been] the right word to use. In any case it is not land which has been laid waste, nor is it merely a *terrain vague*.[3] It is a land which has been subjected to a particular curse of sterility. That is the best that I can do for her.

Yours ever,

[T. S. Eliot]

TO *John Cournos*

22 October 1935   [*The Criterion*]

Dear John,

I have just received your letter of the 9th this morning, which is rather slow going, and have written off to Matthiessen at once about Alfred

---

1 – Roger Hinks (1903–63) – son of Arthur Hinks (Secretary of the Royal Astronomical Society and Gresham Lecturer in Astronomy) – was educated at Trinity College, Cambridge, and at the British School in Rome. From 1926 to 1939 he was Assistant Keeper in the Department of Greek and Roman Antiquities, British Museum, from which he resigned in consequence of a scandal caused by his arrangements for deep-cleaning the Elgin Marbles. He later worked at the Warburg Institute, at the British Legation in Stockholm, and for the British Council (Rome, The Netherlands, Greece, Paris). His writings include *Carolingian Art* (1935), *Myth and Allegory in Ancient Art* (1939) and *Caravaggio: His Life – His Legend – His Works* (1953). See also 'Roger Hinks', *Burlington Magazine* 105: 4738 (Sept. 1964), 423–34; and *The Gymnasium of the Mind: The Journals of Roger Hinks, 1933–1963*, ed. John Goldsmith (1984).
2 – Hinks wrote, 16 Oct. 1935: 'Yesterday I saw Frau Gundolf, the widow of the historian; and she asked me in what exact sense you used the word "waste" in the title of the "Waste Land". She wanted to know whether to translate the title *Das wüste Land* or *Das öde Land*: the difference being that *wüst* means land in which nothing ever could grow, and *öde* land in which, as a matter of fact, nothing does grow. I told her that you had probably not wished to particularize to that extent; but this did not satisfy her exact German soul, and so I undertook to ask you this question, which – I must confess – seems to me rather a trifling one.'
3 – See Jules Laforgue, '*Compleinte sur certains ennuis*', l. 19: '*ce terrain vague*'. Cf. TSE's 'Vers pour la foulque', in *Noctes Binanianae* (1939), l. 22: 'Un terrain vague et désolé' (*Poems*, Ricks and McCue, II, 229–30).

Satterthwaite.[1] I am afraid he won't get it by the 27th, but I hope that it will be in time to do some good. I hope he may get the scholarship and that I may see something of him here. It would be good if his presence might bring you and Mrs Cournos back to England.

Yours ever,

[T. S. E.]

TO *F. O. Matthiessen* CC

22 October 1935 [Faber & Faber Ltd]

Dear Matty,

I have just had a letter from John Cournos, whom I have known for a good many years, and who has always provided the *Criterion* with its Russian Chronicle, about his step-son Alfred Satterthwaite. It appears that the lad is applying for a scholarship of some foundation in which you are in a position of authority. He asks me to put in a word for the boy, which I gladly do, although my knowledge of him is very meagre. I met him when spending the night with the Cournos's in New Haven and liked him. I have also seen one or two things of his which gave me the impression of some literary ability, and I am afraid that is all I know.

Your book seems to have been earning commendations here, except from the critics in whose eyes the subject-matter is enough to damn it. It is impossible for me to regard such a book objectively. All I can say is that I hope that much of what you say is true. By the way, that is a good point about Rose La Touche. Was that pure inspiration, or did we ever mention the subject in conversation?[2]

1–'My stepson, Alfred Satterthwaite ... is about to apply at Harvard for a Rhodes scholarship or some form of Harvard fellowship. Prof. Matthiessen is the state secretary (or some such position) for the Rhodes ... If you feel that, after your casual glimpse of Alfred in New Haven (you spoke at the time of being impressed by his "humility"!), you can write Matthiessen about him, please do. Alfred is as anxious to get back to England as I am, and this is the only thing that would give him the opportunity. I think I told you that the *New Statesman & Nation* published a story of his which he wrote at 14 (in the Spring of 1931). I also gave you a story by Alfred for consideration by the *Criterion*, which you may have lost ... If you feel you can write something to Matthiessen, I understand it should be in Cambridge by October 27th.'

2–Matthiessen, *The Achievement of T. S. Eliot*: 'One of Ruskin's letters to Susan Beever about Rose La Touche, the little girl with whom he fell in love when himself in middle life, seems very suggestive of some of the material that enters into "A Cooking Egg": "But, Susie, you expect to see your Margaret again, and you will be happy with her in heaven. I wanted my Rosie *here*. In heaven I mean to go and talk to Pythagoras and Socrates and Valerius Publicola. I shan't care a bit for Rosie there, she needn't think it".'

I have just had a note from Ted Spencer saying that he was expecting Bonamy Dobrée to stay with him. In that case I hope you will have met him too.

Yours ever,
[T. S. Eliot]

TO *Neil M. Gunn*[1]   CC

23 October 1935   [Faber & Faber Ltd]

My dear Gunn,

I must apologise for my delay in thanking you for sending me a copy of *Whisky and Scotland* and inscribing it for me.[2] I have, however, kept it on my desk and have taken pleasure in picking it up and reading an essay or a page at a time. It is needless to say that I have considered the time well spent. Thank you very much for sending the book, which I hope will make the impression that you want it to make.

The book reminds me also that I hope we may pay you another visit next spring as delightful as the last one.

With kindest regards to Mrs Gunn,

Yours very sincerely,
[T. S. Eliot]

1–Neil M. Gunn (1891–1973), novelist, worked as a clerk in the Civil Service and as an officer of the Customs and Excise before becoming a full-time writer. FVM told Donald Brace, 28 Dec. 1934: 'It is a desperate occupation trying to get any biographical details from Gunn, or even from [George] Blake about Gunn . . . The man's age is a mystery; his up-bringing I suspect to have been much as described in MORNING TIDE [1931]. If the boy in MORNING TIDE isn't Gunn literally, he is spiritually . . . Whatever his formal training, his real life has always been out-of-doors, fishing, walking the moors, watching the anamiles, and taking a hand in whatever poaching was going on.'

See Gunn, *Selected Letters*, ed. J. B. Pick (1987); F. R. Hart, *Neil M. Gunn: A Highland Life* (1981); C. J. L. Stokoe, *A Bibliography of the Works of Neil M. Gunn* (1987).

2–Gunn wrote on 25 Sept.: 'I try not to apologise for sending you this dubious effort by thinking that the third part contains tolerably accurate notes on the real whisky & that they may act on your memory as a spur to future visits to the Highlands – & to us! For the rest, you may understand the intention, however oddly phrased. The attack in Scotland needs many manners.'

TO *Michael Roberts*   TS Berg

25 October 1935   Faber & Faber Ltd

My dear Roberts,

Thank you for your letter of the 14th, but I am afraid that we need a little more information before we can settle the Chatto and Windus matter.[1] You say that you have promised Mrs Owen £7. 7s. for the poem, but on your list there are seven poems. What we should like to know is what you are paying Mrs Owen for the lot, and at how much higher rate she is being paid than are the other Chatto authors. You see I have not got the books here and therefore do not know how many pages of each are represented. Perhaps you could give me the number of pages of each of the four Chatto authors, and the total amount which you are paying in each case. I am sorry to bother you with this.

For the three poems by Harold Monro also, I should like to know how many pages they cover, and what the normal fee would be.[2] Without this information we do not know how much more Mrs Monro is asking than what is usual.

Yours ever,
T. S. Eliot

1–Roberts (14 Oct.) had imparted thus: 'I have promised to pay Mrs Owen £7. 7. 0 for the poem which we are using: I think that is the only special point about the Chatto authors.'
2–Roberts reported that Mrs Monro was asking '£7. 7. 0 for the three poems by Harold Monro'.

TO *Ronald Bottrall*[1]   TS Texas

25 October 1935   *The Criterion*

Dear Bottrall,

Thank you for your letter of the 10th with the poem which I am taking in slowly.[2]

About the new volume of verse, I have discussed this matter with my Committee and I am strongly inclined to advise you to wait until you have more new material that you want to include. 35 pages is a small book, and is just possible for a first book. But I feel that your second book ought to be more voluminous than that to do you any good. Of course, you will very likely say that this is nonsense, and that a poet ought to be able to publish his verse in volumes of any size whenever they seem to him ready for publication, but what I have in mind is the market for poetry, which has to be dealt with very carefully in order to produce even very modest sales, and the impression on reviewers and the public. I should think, however, that you would have enough new stuff that satisfies you by the end of next year to make up a book of reasonable size. We should of course be interested, and we might discuss the matter again in some months time. I don't know of course how much time your academic work gives you for writing, though I am glad to hear you speak so favourably of the College.

                        Yours ever
                        T. S. Eliot

1 – Ronald Bottrall (1906–89), poet, critic, teacher and administrator, studied at Pembroke College, Cambridge, and taught in Helsinki before spending two years at Princeton University. He was Johore Professor of English at Raffles University, Singapore, 1933–7, and taught for a year at the English Institute, Florence, before serving as British Council representative in Sweden, Rome, Brazil, Greece and finally Japan. At the close of his career he was Head of the Fellowships and Training Branch of the Food and Agricultural Organisation of the United Nations in Rome. His poetry includes *The Loosening* (1931) and *Festivals of Fire* (F&F, 1934).
2 – Not traced.

29 October 1935   [Faber & Faber Ltd]

Dear Mrs Coleman,

I have your very interesting letter about Miss Barnes's book.[2] I admit that the extracts which Mr Muir sent me did not seem to me promising

---

1–Andrew Field, *Djuna: The Formidable Miss Barnes* (1983, 1985), 199–202: 'Emily Coleman [1899–1974] was a Californian who graduated from Wellesley College in 1920, came to Europe with her husband in 1926, and two years later separated from him. She threw herself into slightly more than a decade of various countries and passionate loves, beginning with a wild affair with an Italian and progressing to several poets, chief among them Dylan Thomas . . . When she first went to Europe, [she] worked on the European edition of *The Chicago Tribune*. Then for a while she was the society editor of the Paris *Tribune*. Her poetry appeared in *transition*. When Peggy [Guggenheim] met her in 1928 she was installed at St Tropez as the literary secretary to Emma Goldman . . . Though jealousy and rage were very much a part of Emily's character, generosity was too, and she was, happily, convinced of her own genius as well as Djuna's – *Make it marvellous!!!* she exhorted Djuna as she was finishing writing the novel . . . Difficult Emily Coleman is one of the heroines of this story, because, when Barnes returned from America with her much-rejected manuscript in 1934, Emily turned all of her considerable energy to getting it published in England and – after Edwin Muir had pressed the manuscript on Eliot – literally bearded the poet-editor in his office and made it clear to him that Faber would publish the novel, or else. Barnes would eventually say that Emily had to be given seventy percent of the credit for the novel's making it into print.' Field, 18: 'Eliot called her Little Annie Oakley (because of her manner and because she lived on Oakley Street), and in subsequent years felt that the publication of the novel was the primary achievement of his career at Faber.'

2–Coleman wrote from 7 Oakley Street, London s.w.3, on 26 Oct.: 'Mr Edwin Muir has written you about the manuscript of a book provisionally called "Nightwood", by an American, Miss Djuna Barnes. I believe he has also sent you some excerpts which I made from the book, while it was being retyped. He desires me to see you about this mss., which has been turned down by every publisher in America (by some of them twice, since she has revised it recently). It is some years since she wrote it. I should very much like to have a few words with you about it, when you are free. I can bring the manuscript with me then.

'Miss Barnes is 42 years old, and is well known in the New York intellectual world, having had two previous books published; both of which seem to be quite worthless. <Their verbal talent is almost unbelievable.> But this, which she has taken about five years to write, is very different from her other books. I happened to be in New York while she was revising it; read it, and determined to try to get it published. Of course it is not a book which would have a wide sale – except that (as is known, I believe, even to American publishers) genius seems eventually to make itself known . . .

'What I wish to emphasize now, however, are the faults of the book, and of Miss Barnes' writing. These will not be known from the excerpts. The emotional falseness of her former books is sometimes apparent in the present one. (I naturally did not make any selections from these parts.) This is nothing to the faults of organic structure: there seems to be none. It is strange, to me, that anyone of such great unconscious intelligence should be as wanting in a kind of intellect as the writer of this book seems to be. She has no definite philosophical viewpoint. She cannot furthermore create character. She has no sense of dramatic action; she can only describe people. These faults might not be so apparent had she chosen a more

---

as parts of a novel, and the style struck me as incredibly tortured and tedious.[1] I should doubt whether anyone would have the endurance to

———

modest theme. But the subject of her book is apparently that of dramatic tragedy. It will thus be evident to you that the book is an artistic failure.

'It is on a homosexual theme. From what I have said you would perhaps think the book worthless – as a novel, or whatever it was intended to be. But I think you will agree with me that it contains as extraordinary writing as has been done in our time: that the human truths revealed in it (the light it sheds on the relation of good to evil, *in this life*) make it a document which absolutely must be published.'

Monika Faltejskova, *Djuna Barnes, T. S. Eliot and the Gender Dynamics of Modernism: Tracing 'Nightwood'* (2010), 75: 'Neither Barnes nor Coleman mention any communication with Eliot prior to late 1935, months after Barnes had finished the revised third version of the novel under Coleman's guidance. Coleman arranged 18 pages of excerpts from the book and sent them to the poet Edwin Muir, who was to give them to Eliot.'

Coleman wrote to Barnes, 27 Oct. 1935, of TSE: 'He is terribly critical. He is as you know the greatest literary critic of our age; I think the Sacred Wood and the little one on Dante will go down with the best English criticism that has ever been written. Its a pity the poor man cant write as good poetry. BUT HE DOES KNOW LITERATURE. He recognized [George] Barker and has been supporting him (aided by three other people) for a year. Whether he takes your book or not, he will appreciate whats good in it; and if for whatever reasons he may have he thinks he cannot publish it I know he will not leave it high and dry. He will make some constructive criticisms of the book as can ever possibly be made of it' (Faltejskova, 82–3).

Faltejskova notes too, 87: 'Coleman's introduction of the manuscript to T. S. Eliot was very carefully planned by Coleman in order to ensure Eliot's interest in the novel. In August 1935, Coleman herself chose 16 pages of excerpts of what she believed to be the best parts of the novel, which Marion Bouche, Sir Samuel Hoare's secretary, typed. Coleman arranged for the excerpts to be sent to Edwin Muir . . . In her letter to Barnes of 5 November 1935, Coleman reported that Eliot responded immediately but that his response was negative: "He had seen the excerpts – how thoroughly he had read them I dont know – and had been irritated (as I knew he would be) by the style. (I know his weaknesses). He did not even want to see the manuscript, so certain was he that it would not do as a novel."'

See too *Nightwood: The Original Version and Related Drafts*, ed. Cheryl J. Plumb (1995, 2005).

EVE to Phillip Herring, 29 May 1990: 'Yes, Djuna could be maddening because she distrusted all publishers, including my husband when he was wearing his Faber hat. Nevertheless, he was very fond of her and remained patient, when she was being tiresome. Where he was concerned there was an element of needling in her banter as though she hoped to provoke him.

'Djuna was unique and those who loved her, including myself, accepted her without reservation. New York is not the same since her death.'

1 – Muir had written from St Andrews, Fife, 28 Sept. 1935: 'I have intended for some time to send you the enclosed excerpts from a novel by Djuna Barnes, but I have postponed it because I did not want to bother you. But they seem to me so extraordinary and in parts so beautiful that I feel they are bound to impress you, and if you find no other use for them, it is possible that you may wish to publish some of them in "The Criterion". I do not know Djuna Barnes myself, but these extracts were given to me by a friend of hers and of mine, Mrs Coleman, who is living in London at present. She is so enthusiastic about the book that she has given several months to helping to get it into shape, though she is engaged on a book of her own. She says that she can get nobody to publish the book in America, and she says

read through a novel written in this style. In this respect I must say that it does not seem to compare favourably with the work by Miss Kay Boyle on similar themes. As you put the matter, however, I shall be quite willing to look at the whole manuscript and have it read, and if you think that a few preliminary words would be desirable, would you please ring up my secretary and make an appointment to see me here.[1]

Yours very truly,

[T. S. Eliot]

TO *Michael Roberts*   TS Berg

31 October 1935   Faber & Faber Ltd

Dear Roberts,

Thank you for your information of the 26th, which I think provides all the information I need.[2]

We think that Mrs Monro is asking too much, and that she ought to be satisfied with five guineas. As for Pound and Yeats, I believe that you have already made the special terms with them. I presume that you have allowed for me at the 10s. rate, but you will remember my undertaking to forgo part or the whole of this if necessary.

Yours ever,

T. S. Eliot

---

also that it is rather shapeless; and she would like to call upon you sometime and discuss it: she certainly will not try to conceal any of its defects. I really think that if you read these extracts you will be much struck by them.'

1–Emily Coleman to Djuna Barnes, 20 Jan. 1936: 'His first note (re the excerpts) would have frozen Gibraltar' (cited in Faltejskova, *Djuna Barnes*, 75). TSE later told Barnes (23 July 1945) that Coleman had 'practically forced the book down my throat, I admit I didn't appreciate it at first; and as for editing it, well Morley and I cut out a lot ourselves, and all to the good, I say. It was one of those rare books in which cutting out a lot of stuff perfectly good in itself actually improved the whole. What she told you about what she said to me seems to be perfectly true; and she certainly thought you the greatest genius living, which I won't deny either. She was wrong about the title certainly: *Nightwood* is right.' See further Plumb, xx–xxi.

2–Roberts wrote (26 Oct.): 'I find that I have promised:

Mrs Owen	£7. 7s	altogether, for 8 pages
Mrs Rosenberg	£3. 10s	altogether, for 7 pages
Empson	£4	altogether, for 8 pages
Quennell	£2. 10s	altogether, for 5 pages

'Mrs Monro is asking for £7. 7s. for 6 or 7 pages. For other contributors, except Pound, Yeats, and possibly Lindsay, I have promised ten shillings per page.'

P.S. I congratulate you on your knowledge of the Franco-Italian frontier chain, but hope that it will not be required for military purposes.[1]

TO *Ottoline Morrell*   CC

31 October 1935   [Faber & Faber Ltd]

Dear Ottoline,

I will come in for a short time on Thursday 7th to meet Dame Ethel Smythe, but I am afraid I shall have to leave early as I have to dress for dinner that evening.[2]

Affectionately,

[Tom]

TO *Ian Parsons*   TS Special Collections, Reading University

31 October 1935   Faber & Faber Ltd

Dear Parsons,

I must apologise for the delay in settling our terms for the poets you want for your anthology. I had to get information from Michael Roberts, and as I failed to make clear to him in the first place all that I wanted, several letters were necessary. I have now got the information and put the matter before our Committee, who think that the terms for our authors should be as follows: myself, 30s. a page; Pound, 30s. a page; Auden, 20s. a page; Spender, 20s. a page; MacNeice and Marianne Moore, 10s. a page.

These figures are not of course intended to be an estimate of the relative importance of the poets, but of their relative market value at the moment.

I hope that this will be satisfactory.

Yours ever,

T. S. Eliot

1–Roberts (26 Oct.): 'I suppose we all have some curious and unsuspected ambitions, and I was surprised and delighted yesterday to be invited to do an article for the Alpine Journal, bringing up to date the information about the Franco-Italian frontier chain. It turns out that a rather tricky, guideless climb which I did with Janet last year, was probably a first ascent.'
2–OM's journal, 9 Oct. [1935]: 'I have had visits from T. S. Eliot – who seems very much younger & gayer – but so formal still – *quite nice* – but I feel very "superior" – & slow – His mind is a queer flat mind – no surprises. Not a mind that is pushed along by Passion or ardour – His blood is very cold & fishey – & the Temperature of his brain is as I should imagine *below normal*. It is always queer that he is such a good poet for *I* feel him a Critic

TO *Charles Madge*   TS Madge

31 October 1935   Faber & Faber Ltd

Dear Madge,

I hope that there will be an opening for you in the *Daily Mirror*.[1] I think, as I said, that that is the kind of journalism which is the least ignoble. I am quite willing to have your wife use my name in applying for the post of secretary to the Society for Cultural Relations with Russia. I only hope that the use of my name will not do her more harm than good with such a

---

– not a Poet. He would work conscientiously – but I couldn't imagine him writing with Passion – Yes – I think I *can* really – a lonely cold – Religious Passion – rather queer really.'

On 18 Oct.: 'I had another Tea Party to meet Tom Eliot. Hassall came & Bryan Guinness & Dilys Powell & Charles Williams – C.W. is a dear man [. . .] He said it wasn't for him to say what is good or bad for People. That probably a football match is as good for those who really like it as Shakespeare is to him. This came out of Philip's idea – of good Government which he said ought to be as definite as Control of a big business. [. . .] I thought Tom liked Bryan G. He said his usual enigmatic sentence "So much moral Teaching is so immoral" – I was stupid not to ask him what precisely he meant! [. . .] Tom pressed my hand with both of his affectionately when he left. – It is odd that I *never believe anyone is fond of me* [. . .] I advanced the theory that People are surprised at Hamlet because they judge him for Prince Consort Standard of young men, very correct – Public School & I said I could see that he was very odd. Tom agreed with me & he added that he thought Hamlet's behaviour to Ophelia very natural – I felt he knew all about this from [illegible word] experience – with Vivienne. Tom looks a different creature he seems so much happier – since he left her – I don't think he drinks now.'

On Sun., 20 Oct., OM and her husband went to church at St George's Chapel, Windsor, and OM spotted TSE across the way. 'I was sure – he has odd eyes that show the whites – I have never seen it in anyone else – Then I also spied a very obvious severe mouthed, American Parson [*sic*] next him – After service – we met, & his friend Miss Hales [*sic*], & two other American ladies . . . The dominating efficient Hales *understood* us. We offered Tom a lift back – but we weren't given a choice – "No Tom & I will go by bus" – "The older members of our Party will go with you" – No possibility of refusal, – & so back we had to start with 3 Americans – Oh dear they are monotonous – .'

At a tea party on 24 Oct., OM entertained 'Dr Frankford – the Dutch Archaeologist – Dilys Powell – T. S. Eliot who got on with Dr F very well – but he brought that awful American Woman Miss Hales with him – She is like a Sergeant Major *quite* Intolerable – How *can* Tom take her about everywhere – She has perhaps been a Schoolmistress' (BL).

1 – Madge wrote on 28 Oct.: 'I have . . . been thinking of your very kind offer to speak to Mr Richard Jennings about my need for a job. A mutual friend has just written to him, so this would be an opportune moment.' On 30 Oct.: 'I am most grateful to you for speaking to Richard Jennings about me. I saw him at the *Daily Mirror* this evening. There is nothing immediately in prospect, but he was extremely kind.' And on 3 Dec.: 'I must . . . thank you again for your helping word with the *Mirror*, because it has borne fruit, and I am now in my second week there as a reporter. It has the advantage of thrusting one into centres of interest, and at the same time leaves one with many intervals in which to review books, and get on with ones own work.'

society. But politics apart, I have every confidence that she could fill such a post most satisfactorily.[1]

Yours ever,

T. S. Eliot

TO *The Editor,* The New English Weekly

[published 31 October 1935, 58]   [Faber & Faber Ltd]

'Pacifism'

Sir,

It is an obvious principle of controversial writing that one should direct one's attack at the enemy, and not shower blows indiscriminately upon bystanders, some of whom may be sympathisers. One should know whom one is attacking. One may have several enemies; but when these enemies are not allied, there is nothing to be gained by attacking them at once. I make these remarks with a view to the contribution to your last number by Mr C. H. Norman. I read what he had to say with a good deal of sympathy until I reached the words:-

The organised force of society is one of the most remarkable pieces of bluff which has ever controlled human affairs. Its principle is as false as the supernatural basis of religion.[2]

I think that he ought to have said *that* instead of *which*: but that is not the point. I think that if religion has no 'supernatural basis' it has no basis at all: but that is not the point either. Nor is my point that I object to Mr Norman's attacking the supernatural basis of religion. People who believe in the supernatural basis of religion are used to seeing it attacked; and I feel no annoyance with Mr Norman for attacking it. But Mr Norman's interesting article is not about the supernatural basis of religion; it is about

---

1 – Madge to EVE, 15 May 1983: '[TSE] spoke to his friend Richard Jennings, leader writer on the *Daily Mirror* on my behalf, and as a result I was taken on as a reporter. I stayed on the *Mirror* for 15 months, and learnt a great deal from the experience . . . My "wife's" application for the post of secretary to the SSCR came to nothing in spite of his kindly letting her use his name.' Madge, 'Viewpoint', *TLS*, 14 Dec. 1979: 'After two withdrawn years, 1933–35, during which a daughter was born and a good deal of poetry written, I obtained with the help of T. S. Eliot a job as a reporter on the *Daily Mirror*. This, as he probably foresaw, was a useful education: it taught me not to overvalue my own writing just because it was mine and it brought me into touch with certain kinds of "reality" of which Winchester and Cambridge had left me largely ignorant. My fifteen months on the *Mirror* led on to the beginnings of Mass-Observation . . .'

2 – C. H. Norman, 'Pacifism and the War Mind' (a review of books including A. A. Milne, *Peace With Honour*), *NEW* 8: 2 (24 Oct. 1935), 29–30.

something quite different, and his reference is an irrelevance. When I read the preceding part of his article, I assumed that it had some significance even for those who believe in the supernatural basis of religion. Mr Norman makes it clear that he repudiates such people. I suggest that he is making a mistake, and that he is weakening the expression of a conviction, by reinforcing it with a prejudice.[1]

T. S. Eliot

TO *W. T. Symons*   CC

1 November 1935   [Faber & Faber Ltd]

My dear Symons,

I shall be very glad to join the Chandos Group on November 6th at 7.15, for their discussion on foreign affairs.[2]

Yours sincerely,
[T. S. Eliot]

TO *George Rylands*[3]   TS King's

7 November 1935   *The Criterion*

Dear Rylands,

I must apologise for the delay and apparent gross negligence.[4] I was very busy for a fortnight and since then have been in bed with a cold.

1 – Mairet welcomed this contribution on 29 Oct.: 'The letter to the Editor about Norman is . . . very timely and I sincerely trust it will do him good. I am especially glad when a critic of weight takes up Norman, because he is one of those contributors who are valuable but often wrong.'

2 – The Group was to meet in the Chandos Restaurant to discuss foreign affairs including the question of Collective Security (the issue had been raised in *NEW*, 24 Oct.).

3 – George 'Dadie' Rylands (1902–99), literary scholar and theatre director, was from 1927 a Fellow of King's College, Cambridge. His early publications included *Russet and Taffeta* (verse, 1925), *Poems* (1931), *Words and Poetry* (1928) – all published by LW and VW at the Hogarth Press (for which he had worked for six months in 1924). As director of the Marlowe Society, he became famous above all for his productions of plays by Shakespeare; he taught generations of talented students including Peter Hall, Derek Jacobi and Ian McKellen; and he became chairman of the Arts Theatre in 1946. He was appointed CH in 1987.

4 – Rylands wrote on 23 Oct. to ask after Bernard Blackstone's thesis on George Herbert's imagery: the ts had been sent in May. 'Blackstone would of course like to call and receive a verbal opinion and advice, but if that is a bore or unprofitable, perhaps you would write a brief estimate.'

Bernard Blackstone (b. 1911) later edited *The Ferrar Papers* (1938), and wrote studies of Blake, Keats, and Virginia Woolf.

If your man Blackstone can have patience for a week or two I should prefer to have a talk with him. I have so far read about half of his essay, and I find it highly interesting and probably valuable. If I had not been favourably impressed I should have returned it long ago. While I do not know at present what can be done with this essay, he seemed to me to be a man worth taking trouble over.

With apologies,
Yours sincerely,
T. S. Eliot

TO *Stuart Gilbert*[1]   TS Texas

7 November 1935   Faber & Faber Ltd

Dear Gilbert,

I am writing to you because at present I don't know any other way of finding out anything about Joyce. I don't know whether he is in Paris at present, or if so what is his address, and I don't want to have to get at him through Paul Léon. I should be glad of any information available about his health etc., but more particularly about *Work in Progress*. Is he doing any work at present, and have you any idea how near the book may be to completion? Of course one never can tell with Joyce because he is always revising and rewriting indefinitely, but it would be something to know that he had got within measurable distance of finishing the first draft.

I am sorry to bother you, but I should prize any information you could give me. When are you coming over to London again? I have no idea when I shall have the excuse for coming to Paris.[2]

Yours sincerely,
T. S. Eliot

1–Stuart Gilbert (1883–1969), English literary scholar and translator, was educated at Hertford College, Oxford (first class in Classics), and worked in the Indian Civil Service; and then, following military service, as a judge on the Court of Assizes in Burma. It was only after his retirement in 1925 that he undertook work on Joyce, having admired *Ulysses* while in Burma. After befriending Joyce and others in his Paris circle (including Sylvia Beach and Valery Larbaud), he wrote *James Joyce's 'Ulysses': A Study* (F&F, 1930). He helped JJ with the French translation of *Ulysses*; and in 1957 edited *Letters of James Joyce* (with advice from TSE). In addition, he translated works by Antoine de Saint-Exupéry, Paul Valéry, André Malraux, Jean Cocteau, Albert Camus, Jean-Paul Sartre and Georges Simenon.

2–Gilbert replied on 15 Nov. to say he would be dining with the Joyces the following Tuesday. 'Joyce has not been at all fit this summer; he has been on a regime, as have I, and our conversations have been almost exclusively dyspeptic. I believe he did some months' work in the spring, however, and you have seen, of course, the new chapter published in *Transition*.'

TO *I. A. Richards*   TS Magdalene

7 November 1935   *The Criterion*

Dear Richards,

I shall arrive on Saturday bringing your letter with me, but I am sorry
to say that I can't come down in time for lunch, because I have to be on
duty in this office until 12 o'clock. But if you want to ask anybody to
lunch I could arrive in time for coffee. I will try to catch the 12.15 from
Kings Cross on which I see there is a restaurant car. As that arrives at 1.32
I shan't expect you to meet me, but will take a taxi from the station to 37
Chesterton Road.

I warn you that I have been laid up with a cold for a couple of days, and
I am afraid my brain will not be all that you would wish.[1]

Yours ever,
T. S. E.

TO *A. L. Morton*[2]   cc

8 November 1935   [*The Criterion*]

Dear Morton,

I am rather inclined to the opinion that the last two paragraphs of your
review of the *Political Influence of Queen Victoria* are not in their present

---

1–Richards diary, Sat., 9 Nov. 1935: 'D. said to Eliot she would leave us to discuss one
another's views. Whereupon he said, "I certainly find it easier to discuss almost anyone else's
than my own." – Came in, having lunched at the station on egg! Went out for a walk. At 4
Tillyards & Dorothy Hoare – women sat together giggling & gossiping . . . T. S. E. talking
about Sweeney & Yeats. When they left he told me about his scarlet fever experiences 3
weeks at 21 in infirmary & when he got home he was feeling [ill] & had to be sent back for
4 more walks [*sc.* weeks] After dinner discussed the Lindberghs, climbing, notoriety versus
earlier show what you could do. How to get through being famous[.]'
2–A. L. Morton (1903–87), Marxist historian, began his career as a schoolteacher, including
a spell at A. S. Neill's progressive school, Summerhill. He joined the Communist Party in
the late 1920s, and went to work for the *Daily Worker* – as proprietor, and as a reporter
and sub-editor among other capacities – from 1934 to 1937. Soon afterwards he wrote his
pioneer Marxist study *A People's History of England* (1938), a modern classic which has
gone through many printings since Victor Gollancz published it as a Left Book Club choice.
From 1946 he chaired the Historians' Group of the Communist Party of Great Britain. In
addition to distinguished service in Communist Party activities and Marxist education, he
brought out further books including *The English Utopia* (1952), *The Everlasting Gospel:
A Study in the Sources of William Blake* (1958) and *The World of the Ranters: Religious
Radicalism in the English Revolution* (1970). See *Rebels & Their Causes: Essays in Honour
of A. L. Morton*, ed. Maurice Cornforth (1978); *History and the Imagination: Selected
Writings of A. L. Morton*, ed. Margot Heinemann (1990).

form suitable for the *Criterion*. There is a rather higher degree of editorial responsibility for opinions expressed in reviews than there is for opinions expressed in articles. In general the *Criterion* is open for the statement of political philosophies of quite opposed kinds, but the suggestion in a review that the Crown is necessarily associated with the interests of the middle class alone, with the implication that the use of the Crown is confined to enabling this class to exploit colonial possessions and thus maintain its position at home is a view which I should not care to have expressed in this paper. That the powers of the Crown can be manipulated to such ends is obvious, but that they can serve no other or better purpose seems to me untrue. The suggestion appears to be that social reform is impossible with [?without] ~~reforming~~ abolishing the monarchy, which would otherwise provide insuperable obstruction. I feel that such an opinion is out of place in the *Criterion*, and should like to suggest remodelling the last two paragraphs so as not to convey this impression.[1]

Yours sincerely,

[T. S. Eliot]

TO *Ottoline Morrell*   TS Texas

11 November 1935   *The Criterion*

Dear Ottoline,

I had something in mind to ask you on Thursday afternoon, but of course forgot all about it when the time came. In fact it would be difficult to remember anything of the kind while trying to keep up with Dame Ethel Smythe.[2] What I wanted to ask was whether you knew Reginald

1–Morton responded, 9 Nov.: 'I think it is clear from your letter that some of the formulations in my review were made in a way likely to cause misunderstanding. I had not intended to express any opinion as to the general question of the uses which the Crown might serve, but merely to indicate what, in my opinion, were the ways in which the actual ruling class now in power were using or were likely to use the Crown's authority. I hope the changes that I have made in the last two paragraphs will bring this out more clearly.

'If, however, you prefer to do so, the last two paragraphs of the review may be deleted. The review would lose some of its point, but would still be sufficiently clear. Personally I hope that you will not think this course necessary.' See Morton on Frank Hardie, *The Political Influence of Queen Victoria, 1861–1901*: *C.* 15 (Jan. 1936), 311–13.

2–Dame Ethel Smythe (1857–1944): composer, writer, suffragist.

OM noted in her journal that her party on 7 Nov. was 'primarily for Ethel Smythe to meet T. S. Eliot & De la Mare came – & Hope [Mirrlees], Dilys [Powell], & A tiresome young man Desmond Hawkins [who] monopolised T. S. E. [. . .]. – But T. S. E. is so fishey & cold & never seems moved or interested in anyone specially. [. . .] De la Mare was to me far-far

M'Kenna or whether I am likely to know anyone else who does know him.[1] I want to see him for a few minutes if I can on a small matter of business.

I enjoyed your party very much and I think Ethel Smythe is delightful. I have a special ~~passion~~ regard for merry old ladies and fiery old gentlemen and I should love to add her to my collection as one of its most distinguished items.[2]

Affectionately yours,
Tom

TO *George Clutton*[3]   CC

11 November 1935   [*The Criterion*]

Dear Mr Clutton,

I have read with much interest your essay on Stephan George. The obvious difficulty about it is that it is very much too long for the *Criterion*. Furthermore, for the benefit of most of our readers the quotations would all have to be followed by English translations. I have always found George extremely difficult myself, and one would want the essay to be interesting even to readers with no knowledge of German. And I don't see that there is much that you would care to omit. I am returning it with the suggestion that you should try to place it on some periodical that could print it entire, plus the translations.

Yours sincerely,
[T. S. Eliot]

---

more interesting than Tom. – he is [. . .] more of an artist – more generous – more humorous – queerer in an English way .. I don't know him really inside .. but I feel I know him .. & he has seen Hell .. T. S. E. is far more correct – formal – [?unliberated] the New England Puritan is still in his blood. – He and De la Mare talked together very well, & that pleased me – about acting' (BL).

1–Reginald McKenna (1863–1943): Liberal politician (Home Secretary, 1911–15; Chancellor of the Exchequer, 1915–18); from 1918 Chairman of the Midland Bank.

2–OM replied on 11 Nov. that she knew Reginald McKenna. 'Will the enclosed rather formal testimonial do? The McKennas were friends of Ralph Hodgson's in the old days.' 'I am so glad you like Ethel Smyth. She wrote me an enthusiastic letter about you. You must come & meet her again. She is so remarkable & so very big & generous hearted that I find her very lovable.'

3–George Clutton, Department of Printed Books, British Museum.

TO *Charles Smyth*[1]

12 November 1935   [*The Criterion*]

Dear Smyth,

I have your letter of the 10th, and am trying to get the *Life* of Davidson for you.[2]

I am sorry to hear that you are leaving London, although your present cure has not brought us very many meetings.[3] I should think, however, that you would have had quite enough of the type of parish with which you have been associated, and I hope you will be very happy to be in Cambridge again.

Do remind me again of the Ramsay book when it comes out.[4]

Yours ever,

[T. S. Eliot]

1–Charles Smyth (1903–87): ecclesiastical historian and preacher in the Anglican communion. In 1925 he gained a double first in the History Tripos at Corpus Christi College, Cambridge, winning the Thirlwell Medal and the Gladstone Prize, and was elected to a fellowship of Corpus (R. A. Butler was elected a fellow on the same day). He edited the *Cambridge Review* in 1925, and again in 1940–1. He was ordained deacon in 1929, priest in 1930; and in 1946 he was appointed rector of St Margaret's, Westminster, and canon of Westminster Abbey. (On 28 Apr. 1952 TSE expressed the view, in a letter to Janet Adam Smith, that Smyth should be 'moved up to where he so eminently belongs, an episcopal see'.) Smyth's works include *Cranmer and the Reformation under Edward VI* (1926); *The Art of Preaching (747–1939)* (1940); and a biography of Archbishop Cyril Garbett (1959).

Smyth wrote to EVE, 21 May 1979: 'Your husband was one of the best and kindest friends that I have ever had. – He was also a friend of our Siamese cat, Angus (long since departed this life), who was ordinarily terrified of men (particularly bishops in gaiters!), but took to your husband at sight. I have a treasured copy of the *Book of Practical Cats,* inscribed to "Charles and Violet Smyth, and Angus", by "OP" ... It was under his auspices that I broadcast from BBC Savoy Hill (!) in 1932, which is now an uncommon distinction of which to boast ... He had a great sense of fun.'

2–Smyth wished to review the life of Randall Davidson, Archbishop of Canterbury, by G. K. A. Bell (1935). For unknown reasons, the book was not reviewed.

3–Smyth had spent two years at St Saviour's Church, Walton Street, London S.W.3, and was being posted back to a curacy at St Giles, Cambridge – 'purely pastoral ... but no academic work, apart from teaching once or twice a week in a boy's elementary school'.

4–Smyth recommended Michael Ramsay's *The Gospel and the Catholic Church* – 'which is going to put him at a bound into the front rank of English theologians of today'. Not reviewed.

TO *Bernard Blackstone*[1]   CC

12 November 1935   [Faber & Faber Ltd]

Dear Mr Blackstone,

I have your letter of the 9th, and am returning your typescript which I have had for an unconscienceably [*sic*] long time.[2] I am glad that I did not know before that it was your only copy, as it always gives me the fidgets to have the sole copies of people's works in my hands. I am sorry that I have not had the time to finish it, but I should like to tell you, as I have told Mr Rylands, that I have found it an extremely interesting piece of work, which as far as I know is dealing with territory hitherto quite unexamined. I should be very glad if you would come and talk to me about your work. With a few days warning I can probably manage any Thursday afternoon, and should be glad if you would have tea with me here.

Yours very truly,

[T. S. Eliot]

1–Bernard Blackstone (b. 1911), a research student at Trinity College, Cambridge, was to go on to teach for many years (lecturer/senior lecturer) at University College, Swansea; in South America, Cuba and Turkey; and as Byron Professor of English at Athens University. His works include *The Ferrar Papers* (1938), *English Blake* (1949), *Virginia Woolf: A Commentary* (1949), and *The Consecrated Urn: An Interpretation of Keats in Terms of Growth and Form* (1959). See TSE's reference to the Universities Bureau of the British Empire, 5 July 1939: 'I have known Mr Bernard Blackstone slightly for some years, having helped to examine him at Cambridge in connexion with the degree of Doctor of Philosophy, and I have since kept in touch with him. He strikes me as a serious and earnest young man, and he has made a special study of the early seventeenth century. His labours in this field entitle him to be recognised as an authority on the history of the community of Little Gidding and the Ferrar family. At the time when I examined him, I thought that his scholarship, although precise within the limits of his dissertation, was somewhat lacking in breadth, but he has had the opportunity to enlarge his general knowledge since that time and has certainly widened his interests. He was a careful contributor to the now defunct *Criterion*. I regard him as an able and industrious scholar, though not as possessing a mind of the first order of brilliance, and I can recommend him cordially for the post in question.'
2–Blackstone wrote to remind TSE that he had had the sole typescript of his essay on George Herbert since May; it formed part of his work for the PhD. He offered to fetch the ts in person.

12 November 1935   [Faber & Faber Ltd]

Dear Mr Allott,

I am sorry that I failed to answer your interesting letter of June 20th, but I have read it again and I like a great deal of it very much. I am not agreeing with you about Richards, but I am very happy to know that you are interested in Samuel Johnson.² Will you send me some more poems occasionally?³

As for your three conjectures on the last page,⁴ you may be interested to know: 1) Not only that page but the whole section was written at one sitting, and never altered. 2) The page in question antedates the rest of the poem by some months. 3) What you say seems to be correct.

With apologies for my delay,

Yours sincerely,

[T. S. Eliot]

1–Kenneth Allott (1912–73), poet and critic, worked as a reviewer for the *Morning Post* and with Geoffrey Grigson on *New Verse*; he later taught English at Liverpool University, 1948–73. Publications include the five-vol. *Pelican Book of English Prose* (1956), the bestselling *Penguin Book of Contemporary Verse* (ed., 1950; rev., 1962), and *The Poems of Matthew Arnold* (1965).

2–Allott wrote in praise of *UPUC* – 'which I consider a masterpiece': 'But I have one very urgent bone for picking. For the life of me I cannot understand why you defer so frequently to the excellent Dr Richards. Like Johnson you build a palisade round criticism and spend many half hours reproaching yourself for excursions into the surrounding country, but Johnson said outright "I know I have free will and there's an end on't". A little prejudice is a delightful thing. You refuse to accept a psychological theory of value but you only whisper your refusal . . .'

3–The poems Allott enclosed with his letter included one entitled 'Stalemate'.

4–'I had proposed to take up your challenge about the personal and impersonal bits of your poems. Lacking a copy handy [*sic*] of your poems I suggest one or two things about how they were written.

    1. The piece in The Waste Land about bats and fiddling on hair and violet and twilight etc . . . came out very quickly, was touched up very little and I think was exhilarating to write.

    2. The paragraph in Prufrock "No I am not Hamlet etc . . ." the rhythm was "first" and remained unchanged but not the phrasing.

    3. "Whispers of immortality" irritates you for coming to pieces in your hand with sharp edges in too many directions.'

12 November 1935   *The Criterion*

Dear Mr Heppenstall,

I have your letter of the 9th.[1] I should be sorry to think that you were annoyed by Mairet's having shown me your poem, although I agree that it would have been an advantage if I had known that what I saw was a part of a much longer poem. I did find it as a whole more impressive than anything of yours that I have yet read, and the rhythm in places seemed to me so good that I was all the more ill at ease when it fell below its best. I can't agree with you that the passage from Hamlet employs sibilants in quite the same way as the phrases I underlined. Yours I found difficult to speak aloud. I think that it is partly a question of spacing your distribution, and furthermore in the Hamlet passage the sibilants do have the justification of expressing loathing. About the next passage I could not see the justification for saying 'do chafe'. The extra syllable does seem to me a makeshift. However, we can disagree about that. I should like to see the whole poem when it is ready.

Yours sincerely
T. S. Eliot

1–'Thank you for your annotation. I was surprised when Mairet told me he had sent the fragment to you. I was, in fact, rather displeased. I had thought of sending you all that was done of the poem in which that episode occurs and then decided that you would not want to be troubled in any such way . . . The remark that I find most interesting is that two pairs of lines are too "sibilant". One of them, in its context, has the same justification as Hamlet's

Nay, but to live
In the rank sweat of an enseamed bed,
Stewed in corruption, honeying and making love
Over the nasty sty

(or words to that effect). <There are passages in Racine which would provide precedents, if not justification?> . . . I was rather fond of those particular lines . . . I am also troubled that you did not accept the syntactical poeticism of

So much as the sea's tide do chafe the limbs and the hair.

'It may be wrong. I fancy it must be. But it is not, shall I say, a rhythmical makeshift. It (that is, "do") was intended to let the reader down as lightly as possible into (or puff him up into) the deliberate grand-manner pastiche of the following period, so that he should *not*, as you did, feel inclined to comment "inflated", but should accept the inflation as a necessary shift of mood.'

TO *Virginia Woolf* MS Berg

Tuesday 12 November 1935   Faber & Faber Ltd

Dear Virginia

I have had no news of you since your return, but I trust that you have not been bothered, like myself, with a mild influenza – and having to fill some engagement before one has recovered protracts it. But I have just had a weekend at Cambridge and seen most of the English Faculty, including Miss Welsford;[1] and was kept going by a variety of Boots's nostrums – how many there are.

My cousin has not turned up, and is not likely to until next year – which simplifies the situation. But I should like if I might to bring another American friend to see you (who is not only an admirer but I believe admires your works in the right order – I mean, I always prefer people to like best what I have written most recently, & in that order backwards). Anyway, I have heretofore protected you against Americans who wanted to get at you through me – you have no conception – and this is on my own initiative, as she would never presume to press forward.[2]

Affectly

Tom.

---

1 – Enid Welsford (1891–1981), literary scholar who taught at Newnham College, Cambridge; author of *The Court Masque* (1927), which won the Rose Mary Crawshay Prize 1928, and *The Fool: His Social and Literary History* (1935). See Elsie Duncan-Jones, 'Enid Welsford, 1892–1981', in *Cambridge Women: Twelve Portraits*, ed. E. Shils and C. Blacker (1996), 204–19.

2 – TSE brought Emily Hale to tea with the Woolfs on Tues., 26 Nov. See Gordon, *Imperfect Life*, 310–13, for Hale's account of the party, in a letter of 6 Dec. 1935 to her friend Ruth George (first published in *Virginia Woolf Miscellany* no. 12, Spring 1979). Writing to Ethel Smyth on 26 Nov., VW reported that she found Hale a 'dull impeccable Bostonian lady' (*The Sickle Side of the Moon: The Letters of Virginia Woolf, V: 1932–1935*, ed. Nigel Nicolson [1979], 442).

Writing to Ethel Smyth the next day, 13 Nov., VW referred to TSE as 'that lily livered man. I went to his play [*MiC*] last night, and came away as if I'd been rolling in the ash bin; and someone filled my mouth with the bones of a decaying cat thrown there by a workhouse drab' (ibid., 442). On 16 Nov. VW wrote again to Smyth: 'No, my criticism of the Murder was a violent flare, not to be taken as serious criticism. Though violent flares are always good evidence. The truth is it acts far less well than reads: cant manage the human body: only a soliloquy' (ibid., 443). (In early July 1935 she had felt 'proud', as she wrote to him, to receive an inscribed copy of the play.) To Angelica Bell, 18 [17] Nov: 'We went to see Tom Eliot's play the other night. I think what is wanted is for some actress to make plays in which people are like ourselves only heightened; what is so bad is the complete break between the acting, the words and the scenery. Thus you lose all feeling of harmony' (ibid., 444). To Stephen Spender, 19 Nov.: 'we can discuss the interesting case of the Murder in the Cl. I rather suspect it is human nature that floors him: when its in the flesh' (ibid., 446). And

827

TO *The Editor,* The New English Weekly

[published 14 November 1935, 99] [No address given]

Sir,

The sentences given in Mr Norman's letter, which he says were omitted from his article as printed, do not seem to me to alter the situation in any way.[1] I thought that I made it clear in my own letter that I was not taking exception to Mr Norman's views on the subject of the supernatural basis of religion, but merely pointing out that he was only injuring his own case by airing them in the wrong place. I wrote my letter because I have felt a good deal of sympathy with Mr Norman's political views, and it seemed to me regrettable that he should go out of his way to alienate people of good will. I certainly did not write my letter merely to provide readers like Mr Llewelyn Powys with a pretext for violent affirmations.[2]

Incidently, I wonder whether it is 'generally agreed that no person has ever lived the Christian life according to the precepts of Christ except Christ Himself.' This may be generally agreed amongst some limited number of people, but I should have thought that at least a few of the greater saints had arrived at some approximation toward a Christian life according to the precepts of Christ.

Yours faithfully,
T. S. Eliot

---

to Julian Bell, 1 Dec.: 'We went to see Toms play, the Murder, last week; and I had almost to carry Leonard out, shrieking. What was odd was how much better it reads than acts; the tightness, chillness, deadness and general worship of the decay and skeleton made one near sickness. The truth is when he has live bodies on the stage his words thin out, and no rhetoric will save them' (ibid., 448).

OM noted in her journal in Nov. 1935 that she went to see VW one evening – '& only half enjoyed it – for she denounced T. S. Eliot's play as sadistic [. . .] & as awful. She seemed to think that he had invented the Old fundamental Christian Philosophy' (BL).

1–See letter from Norman, *NEW* 8: 4 (7 Nov. 1935), 80.

2–The novelist Llewellyn Powys (1884–1939) wrote in a letter published in the same issue, 14 Nov. 1935: 'In your issue of October 31st, Mr T. S. Eliot finds fault with Mr C. H. Norman for "showering blows indiscriminately." The sentence to which Mr Eliot took exception reads as follows: "The organized force of society is one of the most remarkable pieces of bluff which has ever controlled human affairs. *Its principle is as false as the supernatural basis of religion.*"

'If, as many of us hold, every religion that has its roots in supernatural assumptions is little better than a pathetic illusion, a pathetic nursery neurosis out of which the passing of the centuries will gradually persuade us, surely a writer may be excused for selecting as a kind of household illustration of "bluff" so singular, romantic, and wilful a conception of the human predicament as is offered to us by magical faiths.'

TO *Polly Tandy*   TS BL

14 November [1935]   Faber & Faber Ltd

Dear Pollytandy,

Well it is sure cheering to see your writing again, and your news is more than tolerable, and I trust the improvement continues since the date of your writing.[1] The great thing to begin with is that the Nose should be a Projection and not a Recession, because after that, once you have the material to work upon, it can be worked up into Roman or Norman by will power, prayer, absent treatment or manipulative surgery, but you cant make bricks without straw or a nose out of a dimple or a silk purse either. My health did not suffer but it has suffered a lot worse since, what with one thing and another, and I took to my bed last week and it still lays heavy on my chest. Now about the Future. What with one thing and another. Thanksgiving Day party at the Morleys, they set great store by. First Week END I see for certain is that of the 15th December, is that too near Yule to suit. Would it might be sooner. Otherwise soon after Xmas. The main thing about a nose is that the bearer should be able to breathe through it, that is where I have always been a sufferer in life's handicap.[2] If she can breathe through her nose, she has a chance; which I wish her, never having had a chance myself. Meanwhile I send compliments and the expression of continued thoughts during the interim to the entire family, especially Maggie, most respectfully

                                        TP.

I should like to enquire particularly after your Health.

1–Tandy wrote on 5 Nov.: 'Honoured Sir / I take up my pen just previous to post time to assure you of the good health and continued improvement of your godchild. We trust that your own health did not suffer from your hurried visit here nor from the consumption of christening cake said to be extremely indigestible.

'Parental opinion may be biassed but we trust that our youngest child's countenance may yet prove to have *some* significance. The nose is undoubtedly prominent but whether Norman or Roman only Time will show. Her engaging smile is intriguing her Papa whom she certainly resembles.

'We are hoping that you may be able to find it possible among your many engagements to spend a week-end here early in December. Will you be so kind as to refer to your pocket book and let us know if and when you would care to come?'

2–See Rudyard Kipling, *Life's Handicap: being stories of Mine Own People* (1891).

TO *Dorothy Richards*   MS Magdalene

Thursday, 14 November 1935   Faber & Faber Ltd

Dear Mrs Richards,

Even if I were so ungrateful as not to write to thank you for the weekend, I should still make a point of writing to thank you for the handsome inscription which renders the book more precious. I might retort, if I had a volume just out, with the Familiar Quotation from *The Princess* (Tennyson): except that I don't ascribe any particular merit to the Valley except that it does not make me dizzy.[1]

Thank you both for the society, and for the intervals between society: also for the Regesan nostrums,[2] which I purchased & have persevered with since my return. I look forward to my next visit. Tell I.A.R. that I am trying to find for him (no! here it is) a photograph which will warn him what to expect at Bryn Mawr.*

Yours sincerely
T. S. Eliot.

*Also, that I did *not* catch the 10.15!

TO *Michael Roberts*   TS Berg

15 November 1935   Faber & Faber Ltd

Dear Roberts,

I am sorry to have to bother you again about the Chatto and Windus business. The point now is that they accede to the terms which I am asking them for our authors, but I think that they are asking rather much for their own. Their terms are as follows: Owen 30s. a page; Empson 20s. a page; Monro, Quennell and H.D. 10s. a page. I was under the impression that you had arranged with Mrs Owen for something like £1 or £1. 1s. a page. It looks like that from the figures you gave me. That seems to me

1 – TSE was referring to *The Princess*, Canto VII, ll. 177–84:
     'Come down, O maid, from yonder mountain height:
     What pleasure lives in height (the shepherd sang)
     In height and cold, the splendour of the hills?
     But cease to move so near the Heavens, and cease
     To glide a sunbeam by the blasted Pine,
     To sit upon the sparkling spire;
     And come, for love is of the valley, come,
     For love is of the valley [. . .]'
2 – The brand of Regesan, marketed by Boots the chemists, included cold and catarrh tablets.

quite adequate, but of course if Chattos choose to hold us up Owen is an author you can't do without. But I feel quite certain that at the moment the market value of Willy Empson should be only 10s. a page, which is all that we are asking for MacNeice and Marianne Moore. Next, I can't see why we are concerned with Chatto at all for Harold Monro. Surely you took the poems out of the posthumous volume published by Mrs Monro herself, and I don't see how Chatto come into it. I notice finally that Rosenberg is not mentioned, but I think he ought to come into the 10s. group. I am writing an interim letter of protest, but I want to keep you in touch on what I am doing, and shall be glad of any advices you have to make.

Many thanks for your wire,[1]

Yours ever,
T. S. Eliot

Yours of the 13th meanwhile arrives, but I send this nevertheless.

TO *Ian Parsons*   TS Special Collections, Reading University

15 November 1935   Faber & Faber Ltd

Dear Parsons,

Thank you for your letter of November 11th.[2] My Committee have considered it, and I should like to raise one or two points. 30s. a page seems to us high for Wilfred Owen, especially as I understand that Michael Roberts came to an agreement with Mrs Owen about the rate of payment. I am writing to Roberts for full particulars, and will write to you again on this point. Second, I can't for the life of me see why Empson should be worth double Louis MacNeice. Their volumes have come out in the same season, they are both equally well-known, and equally not as well-known as they deserve to be, and I think that in the long run MacNeice will have a wider and more popular public than Empson.* Third, you raise for the first time the question of Harold Monro. I assume that Roberts chose the

---

1 – Wire not traced.

2 – Parsons had written: 'Very many thanks for your letter [31 Oct.] with the terms for the poets whom I should like to include in my Anthology. These seem to me very reasonable, and I have accordingly written to [Michael] Roberts suggesting a similar scale for those of our poems which he has chosen for his own book . . . [T]he rates I suggested were:–

Owen	30/- a page
Empson	20/- a page
Monro, Quennell & H. D.	10/- a page

'I hope this will strike you as a fair proposition . . .'

Monro poems – in fact I am sure he did – from the posthumous volume produced by Mrs Monro. One of the poems he has chosen never appeared in any previous volume at all. It seems to me, therefore, that Roberts has been correct in conducting his negotiations with Mrs Monro. Finally, you do not mention Rosenberg, but I assume that he is at the 10s. rate.

I am not quite clear at the moment, but I shall verify this point. I was under the impression that Michael Roberts had been in communication with you and that you had agreed upon terms for at least three authors, Empson, Quennell and Rosenberg. If that is so I don't see why we should be discussing the matter further now. Excuse haste.

Yours ever,
T. S. Eliot

You might come and lunch with me over this, I think.

* It is understood that relative merit does not enter into the merits of this discussion.

TO *Reginald McKenna*[1]   CC

15 November 1935   [Faber & Faber Ltd]

My Dear Sir,

I am enclosing a letter of introduction from our friend Lady Ottoline Morrell, which should identify me sufficiently for my present purpose.

My firm is interested in exploring the possibility of publishing a book on banking somewhat on the lines of that which was written for the Home University Library some years ago by the late Dr Walter Leaf,[2] only of a greater length, and of course more up to date. Your name naturally occurred to me as that of the only banker of similar standing and of greater prestige than Dr Leaf, and if I may say so, I was further induced to approach you by my knowledge that yours have been the only Annual Reports that I have seen by any bank chairman which exhibit a mastery of English prose as well as of finance.

---

1 – Reginald McKenna (1863–1943), banker and Liberal politician, had served as Home Secretary and Chancellor of the Exchequer in the administration of H. H. Asquith.

2 – Walter Leaf (1852–1927), banker and classicist; director of Westminster Bank; co-founder of the International Chamber of Commerce; President of the Institute of Bankers. *Banking* (1926).

I do not suppose for a moment that this suggestion will immediately attract you, but as I am writing to ask whether I might come to see you for a few moments at your convenience, I thought it as well to give you some notice in advance of the nature of my business. I think that if I could discuss the matter with you briefly in conversation I could make the proposal seem better worth your consideration.[1]

Yours faithfully,
[T. S. Eliot]

TO *Colin Kendall*   CC

19 November 1935   [Faber & Faber Ltd]

Dear Mr Kendall,

Thank you for your letter of the 18th enclosing a statement of last week's royalties.[2] I am glad to learn that the attendance is still maintained, and that there is a prospect of still more performances during the Christmas holidays.

Yours sincerely,
[T. S. Eliot]

1 – McKenna replied, 16 Nov.: 'Alas! I was never able to do more than one thing at a time and now with old age upon me I have to confine myself rigidly to my single job. The mere thought of starting to write a book makes me miserable. I have frequent and tiresome interruptions during the day, and when the business of the Bank is done I do not feel equal to a new effort.'

2 – TSE's royalties for *MiC* for the week ending 16 Nov. 1935 were £5. 17s. 3d. (5% of box office receipts of £117. 5s. od.). The Business Manager Colin Kendall reported too that they were going to put on additional performances throughout the Chistmas holidays. For the period 1–30 Nov., TSE received a royalty payment of £25. os. 10d. For the week ending 4 Jan. 1936 (when the production passed its fiftieth performance) the receipts amounted to £180. 18s. 1d.; and for the week ending 11 Jan. 1936 receipts attained their highest point at £194. 11s. od. Box office receipts for the period from the end of 1935 to the week ending 1 Feb. added up to £728. 4s. 1d. (of which TSE received £36. 8s. 2d). There were capacity audiences throughout the run.

TO *Ottoline Morrell*   TS Texas

19 November 1935   *The Criterion*

My dear Ottoline,

Thank you so much for your letter about Barker.[1] I had not thought of
Lady Gerald Wellesley, but I should be very glad if you could approach
her, as I think she is a generous person who might be inclined to give
some support.[2] I will certainly write to Bryan Guinness. I can't do
anything about the Hutchinsons at present because of Jack's illness, and I
understood from Mary that she would be staying with him at his nursing
home in Wales until sometime in December. The Hutchinsons also include
Victor Rothschild, whom I should be rather doubtful of approaching
direct. Bob Trevelyan I have not seen for a good many years, and I don't
know whether he is interested enough in the work of very young men.
I should be glad to come and talk to you privately about these matters,
and of the days you suggest Monday afternoon suits me best. I hope that
5 o'clock will suit you.

With many thanks,
Yours affectionately,
Tom

P.S. I am not so worried about *Janus* because although some people don't
like it at all, I have found others enthusiastic.

TO *A. Desmond Hawkins*   TS Desmond Hawkins

22 November 1935   *The Criterion*

My dear Hawkins,

I am rather ashamed to have your second letter before I had answered
your first, although it does indeed make the answer to the first considerably
easier.[3] I had meanwhile been thinking about it. All that I could do for the

---

1 – OM wrote, 17 Nov.: 'I can write to Siegfried Sassoon & ask if he could give as before
or even a little more. Also I could write to Lady Gerald Wellesley asking her if she could
give him 5/- a week. And I feel sure if you wrote to Bryan Guinness he would continue his
support. I am quite willing to give £6.00 or if the worst came to the worst to make it up
to £10. Could you come & talk it over . . . I wish [Barker's] book *Janus* had been better. It
would make it easier to ask . . . Bob Trevelyan is well off but I see him so seldom now. But
I *could* ask if necessary.'
2 – At OM's behest, on 27 Nov. Dorothy Wellesley sent £13 towards the Barker account.
3 – Hawkins reported in a two-page single-spaced letter (10 Nov.) that he was likely to be a
father 'by next summer'. But he was still in some distress, and asked TSE to put him in touch

moment was to give your name as a possible proof reader to Mr de la Mare, in whose department here such matters fall. Secondly, I have thought of a small suggestion which I hope if you like it will fit in to the other work you will be doing. We used to have a fairly regular fiction chronicle which has fallen into desuetude. Orlo Williams, who used to write it, was at that time reviewing a good many novels elsewhere, and in a position not to miss much of any value. But he has now given up most of his reviewing and has completely lost interest in the criticism of fiction, which is what ought normally to happen to anyone after a few years. Now however little there may be worth recording I still think it would be worth-while to have such a chronicle again twice a year. I say twice a year because I doubt whether there is material enough to justify greater frequency. Would you care to undertake such a chronicle, at any rate for a year or two?

A certain number of novels come in to the *Criterion* as it is, heaven knows why, as almost none of them ever gets mentioned. I dare say you see others in other ways, and probably any novel that we ask for would be sent to us. I really do not want, however, a regular comb-out of the Season's fiction, and I had rather risk overlooking something good than trying to cover the whole ground. What would be more suitable to the *Criterion* is occasional reflections on the state of the novel, with mention of any that were worth mentioning. Naturally you would have to guess at what were likely to be the books worth mentioning, or pick up the information by hearsay. It would be quite pointless to devote any specific attention to the great number of highly competent and insignificant novels that are written, so many of them by women. It is rather the exception that is interesting, and the book which would be neglected or condemned elsewhere. I'd like to know what you think about it.

In spite of the more cheerful tone of your second letter I shall continue to keep the problem in mind, and we will talk about it when we next meet.

I thought *Purpose* promising and Unwin good, and look forward to the January number.[1]

Yours ever,
T. S. Eliot

---

with any work he could possibly tackle. 'I am willing to be told that you can do nothing; but I still cherish a golden belief, which I shall never surrender, that in some way you hold all the keys.'

1 – Hawkins sent TSE (8 Nov.) a copy of the Oct. issue of *Purpose*, highlighting an article by the publisher Stanley Unwin: 'I have an idea that one could work out a useful analogy between his anthropological method and contemporary aesthetic technique.' The Jan. issue was to include contributions by Roberts, Porteus, Dyment, Unwin – '& a very good article on Coleridge by Randall Swingler'.

22 November 1935   Faber & Faber Ltd

Dear Laughlin,

I have your letter without date.[1] Use *Rannoch* (not Glencoe, but near Glencoe) if you like; at any rate, as I have printed it here, that will copyright it in America; but if you do, please use the enclosed also, which has more local interest, and is aimed at showing that I can hold my own as an ornithologist with both ~~the~~ pre- and post-Georgians. I wish I thought you wanted my work because you liked it,* but I am used to people wanting to print work of mine that they don't like merely because I am (as you say) Mr Eliot of Russell Square. I am glad to hear that you are 'working in classics', which I hope means the original languages and not even Loeb.[2]

Yours sincerely,

T. S. Eliot

* Many thanks however for your very kind review in the *N.E.W.*[3]

[Enclosed:]

CAPE ANN.

O quick quick quick, quick hear song-sparrow,
Swamp-sparrow, fox-sparrow, vesper-sparrow
At dawn and dusk. Follow the dance
Of the goldfinch at noon. Leave to chance
The Blackburnian warbler, the shy one. Hail
With shrill whistle the note of the quail, the bob-white
Dodging by baybush. Follow the feet

1 – Laughlin had read the poem by TSE that he called 'Glencoe', published in *NEW*, and asked permission to reprint it in the New York periodical *New Democracy* (of which, at Pound's instigation, Laughlin had become literary editor). 'Concentrating naturally on the young writers, but something from you would "give us class", as they say . . . It would have to be a gift, but perhaps you will want to give it.'
2 – 'I am back at Harvard again, working in classics. It is a long, long way from Rapallo . . .'
3 – Laughlin, 'Mr Eliot on Holy Ground', *NEW* 7: 13 (11 July 1935), 250–1. 'However you want to feel about Mr Eliot's "position", *Murder in the Cathedral* proves that he is still a great master of metric and that he knows how to put together a play . . .

'An examination of the psychological angle provides the clue. Aristotle's criteria call for pity and terror to induce the catharsis. But the fall of A'Becket [*sic*] produces neither: he forsees [*sic*] his doom and declines escape though it is offered – hence no terror; he is obviously ready for death and glad to fulfill his faith – and so no pity. And yet the play's action does release emotion within the observer. Of what kind? The same, I think, as is aroused by a Medieval Mystery or Miracle, one of religious exaltation, of completion of faith. It is clear then that Eliot has attempted a fusion of the Classic and Medieval dramatic formulae.'

Of the walker, the water-thrush. Follow the flight
Of the dancing arrow, the purple martin. Greet
In silence the bullbat. All are delectable. Sweet sweet sweet
But resign this land at the end, resign it
To its true owner, the tough one, the sea-gull.
The palaver is finished.

                    T. S. Eliot

FROM *Vivien Eliot* TO *Mr Broad*   CC Bodleian

22 November 1935   [Constance Hotel, London]

Dear Mr Broad,

I did not reply to your letter with ref. to my shaking the mats over the balcony railings in order to clean them, at my flat, because the whole thing is so absurd. If one lives in a place one must keep it clean or the Sanitary Inspecters [*sic*] would interfere. However, at my Mother's definite request I again left the flat and came here. It is impossible to live at 68, Clarence Gate Gardens, for a woman alone, as I told you.

As my husband has now found me, he acts for me. In future all business correspondence will be sent on to him, and he has full powers. There is no occasion therefore, for any further litigation.

                    I am,
                    Yours sincerely,
                    [V. Haigh-Eliot]
When I say found, I mean that he claimed me in public.[1]

TO *Gwynneth L. Thurburn*[2]   CC

25 November 1935   [Faber & Faber Ltd]

Dear Miss Thurburn,

I have been meaning to write to you and ask if you would let me have a corrected list of the names of the new girls in the chorus.[3] As the ones who

1 – See Vivien Eliot to Messrs James & James, 28 Nov., below.
2 – Gwynneth L. Thurburn: Vice-Principal, Central School of Speech Training and Dramatic Art.
3 – The new Women of Canterbury (as Thurburn informed TSE on 27 Nov.) were Cecilia Colley, Lettice Haffenden, Dorothy Gall, Muriel Judd, Elizabeth Latham, Phoebe Waterfield: each was sent a signed copy of *MiC* on 3 Dec.

were at Canterbury have all had copies of the play from me I should like the new ones to have copies too, and it is never safe to trust the spelling of programmes.

I cannot help wondering at the ability of the chorus to go on night after night, apparently for an indefinite period and in the midst of their work. I don't know how they manage to do it unless some of their other work is remitted because of this. When I wrote the play I never expected that it would be played for more than a week or two at a time.[1]

With all best wishes,
Yours sincerely,
[T. S. Eliot]

TO *Robert Waller*

TS BL

25 November 1935   *The Criterion*

Dear Waller,

I am sorry that you should think that my returning your verse was a matter of simple rejection.[2] I returned them because you wanted them, and because most of it, on account of its length, was unsuitable for the *Criterion* anyway. Also I have had all along a belief that with a better and more extroverted life you would begin to write better than you ever have before.

I am not quite clear what is the element in your poetry which you think shocks my taste. The word may possibly be 'bold', but looks more like

---

1–Marion Cole, in *Fogie*, 167–8: 'It should be stressed here that the original Chorus at Canterbury was composed of Teacher-students – proof of the standard of performance expected of them before they set out to teach. But when it became evident that the play was set for a long run, it was necessary to free these students for their Diploma work. Having made sure that the "Albert Hall" method of dealing with these modern choruses was acceptable to both playwright and producer, Fogie had turned over the maintenance of the Chorus to Gwynneth Thurburn – then Vice-Principal of the School, who . . . was, by that time, responsible for all the Voice-work at the Hall. Thus it became her responsibility gradually to replace the Teacher-students with Stage-students: even these might leave to take other professional engagements, so that *Murder in the Cathedral* claimed constant rehearsals and organisation as the play ran on and on . . .'

EMB: 'It was a great achievement to maintain – as Miss Fogerty's School did – the supply of speakers equipped to take their places in the *Murder* Chorus. One of them reckoned that, between 1935 and 1938, forty-two of her past students were in it altogether' (*Fogie*, 168).

2–Waller wrote (n.d.): 'I'm sorry that none of the verse is any use to you: I had a vague hope that it would be and can't quite analyse the fault that disqualifies it, though being of a humble disposition I feel that there must be one.' He asked TSE to return 'Girl in Exeter Cathedral'.

'bald'.[1] In either case, and especially the former, I think you are rather off the mark. What makes your poetry most difficult to me is an abstractness which tends to monotony. There is very little to keep the reader's visual imagination occupied, and with the lack of this the versification, very interesting as it is, has to undertake more work than it can adequately carry out. Only a tremendous metrical virtuosity and versatility could do it. What I am indicating is really something wider than only visual imagination. Your poetry has a certain underlying sensuality but to me it lacks what is more important, sensuousness. That is why I took out 'Girl in Exeter Cathedral' as an explanation, and that poem unfortunately I can't at present find. I am sure that it is amongst my papers, and that I shall be able to turn it up, but for goodness' sake buy some carbon paper, and don't ever again send an editor a poem without keeping a copy yourself.

I hope that your work is progressing well. Do come and see me when you have formed some definite opinion about the job.

Yours sincerely,
[Posted unsigned]

TO *R. B. Savage*

TS R. B. Savage, SJ

25 November 1935   *The Criterion*

Dear Father Savage,

Thank you very much for your kind letter of November 20th.[2] Your invitation to speak at University College is very tempting, especially as it provides a very respectable pretext for my long contemplated visit to Dublin. In principle I should [be] very glad indeed to come on the terms that you propose. I feel a certain diffidence, however, about speaking in

---

1 – 'I have a feeling, though I may be only excusing my immaturity, that there is a bald element in my poetry that will always shock your taste: something which you are expecting to gradually pass away but which never will. It is me.'

2 – Roland Burke Savage, SJ – a student at the time: a Jesuit scholastic pursuing his university studies – invited TSE to participate in the Inaugural Meeting of the English Literary Society of University College, Dublin, to take place on 22 Jan. 1936 (Burke Savage was the Auditor): they would pay a fee of £25 plus expenses. TSE would be expected in the first instance to speak to the Auditor's Paper, 'Literature at the Irish Crossroads' – of which the 'general trend' would be 'an analysis of the "Celtic Renaissance" movement, and some thoughts on the future development of an "English Literature" in Ireland', said Savage – and they would arrange too for TSE to give, on the following day, a lecture on any literary subject of his own choosing.

response to your own paper. I do not know quite what is involved, and I should be glad if the duties of such a task could be made clear. So far as I can see in advance the date, January 22nd, offers no difficulty.[1]

> With many thanks,
> Yours very truly,
> T. S. Eliot

TO *George Rylands*

TS King's

25 November 1935   *The Criterion*

Dear Rylands,

I am sorry that my letter went to King's College, London, instead of King's College, Cambridge. No innuendo was intended. Blackstone called on me last Thursday, and I formed a very good impression of him. But it is a pity that he has no Greek. Why do people try to go into teaching English without a proper foundation? It is kind of you to ask me down to Cambridge for a weekend. I have not been able to get down as often as I should like, and the next time I come, whenever that is, I have promised to come as the guest of Kenneth Pickthorn.[2] But the prospect of seeing *The Frogs* is exciting, and I should like to hear more about it.

> With many thanks,
> Yours sincerely,
> T. S. Eliot

1–Savage replied (27 Nov.) that TSE had no cause for anxiety. 'The custom in the University societies here is that the Auditor of the Society (usually an undergraduate, as I am . . .) reads a short paper which serves as a foil for subsequent discussion by four or five wiser heads. The rest of the speakers will be Irish; your contribution being the opinion of an experienced critic viewing things from a more detached position. Nominally you will propose the motion "That the Auditor deserves the best thanks of the Society for his Address": but your actual speech would deal more with your opinions of the modern Anglo-Irish school (Mr Yeats etc), with my criticisms of it, with your own views as to its development . . . You will be followed by the three or four other speakers: two University Professors, and a Jesuit Professor of Philosophy . . . You will bring a fresher outlook than we can offer over here. As to the Lecture which I propose you should deliver on the following afternoon you are entirely free as to your choice of subject . . .'

2–Kenneth Pickthorn (1892–1975), historian and politician: see Biographical Register.

FROM *Vivien Eliot* TO *Messrs James & James*   MS Bodleian

28 November 1935   68, Clarence Gate Gardens, N.W.1.

Dear Sirs,

I am sure you will be glad to know that I met my husband in public at the Book Exhibition at Dorland Hall on November 18th., where he gave a very good lecture.

Everything was perfectly all right between us.

I am,

Yours very truly,

[Vivienne Haigh Eliot]

P.S. In short, he turned up, and I turned up, and I took my dog, and my dog pursued him. There was a very large audience and many witnesses.[1]

1 – VHE wrote in her diary, Mon, 18 Nov., about going to the *Sunday Times* Book Exhibition: '. . . to hear little Tom Eliot speak. Richard Church in the chair. Then at last I rushed in, seized his 3 *latest* books *which I have* (there are *more* recent, & much grander books of his than these, I see, however) [on 10 July 1935 she had purchased copies of *The Rock*, *After Strange Gods* and *Murder in the Cathedral*, but it is not known whether they were the books she took with her] I put them in my satchel & seized Polly & started off in the most appalling rain & filth. The traffic was *devillishly* [sic] held up, so that I *had* to get out of the vile bus & take a taxi, & so got to Dorland Hall only just in time. It was crowded. Tearing up the stairs with Polly, the poor dog fell off the side & nearly hanged herself but I rescued her. The crush was terribly [sic] and my heart banged a dance. I saw Bridget O'Donovan. I *pushed* my way into the lecture room, very nearly *fighting. Directly* I got well in, I heard steps behind, turned round, & *there was* Tom, just *behind* me. I turned a face to him of such joy that no-one in that great crowd could have had one moment's doubt. I just said Oh *Tom*, & he seized my hand, & said how do you *do*, in quite a loud voice. He walked straight on to the platform then, & gave a most remarkably *clever*, well-thought-out lecture giving food for weeks of thought. I stood the whole time, holding Polly <u>up</u> high in my arms. Polly was very excited & wild. I kept my eyes on Tom's face the whole time, & I kept nodding my head at him & making encouraging signs. He looked a *little* older, more mature & smart, much thinner & <u>not</u> well or robust or rumbustious at all. No sign of a woman's *care* about him. No cosy evenings with dogs & gramophones I should say. When he had finished, there was a lot of applause. I then pushed my way right up to the platform, still holding Polly. I left her off the lead, & she had the *sense*, in all that crowd, to run up to him, and to run round his feet & *jump up to him*. He did not notice her either. I stood beside him on the platform, with my hands on the table, & I said quietly, will you come back with me? He said I cannot talk to you now. He then signed my three books, & went away with his Richard Church' (Bodleian).
    GCF recorded in his diary, 18 Nov.: 'Book Exhibition – Tom's lecture, very crammed. Vivienne turned up. But no scene, thank God'.
    On 20 Nov., VHE wrote to the Manager of The District Bank to say 'I was then writing to my husband giving him full authority to write cheques in their Bank on my behalf, as I had now been *openly* claimed by him, & as I feel it essential that he should be *all ready* in a position to act on my affairs should anything happen to me. So I thus *re-scinded* the instruction I had written to them from Rueil, Seine et Oise, in 1927. I then wrote to Tom,

TO *Ashley Dukes*   CC

28 November 1935   [Faber & Faber Ltd]

Dear Dukes,

I must apologise for not answering your letter sooner.[1] I should at least have acknowledged it, but I assumed that you would know that I was discussing with friends a subject which is quite unfamiliar to me. The agreement in general seems to me very satisfactory, and there are only one or two minor points that I have to raise. I am all the more inclined to accept your proposal, in that I am sure that you would (as an ordinary agent could not be expected to do) safeguard *Murder in the Cathedral* from falling into the hands of the wrong producers.

My first point is this, that I would rather have an agreement with you personally than with a limited company.

I am quite willing to put all the amateur performances in your hands, here as well as abroad (you don't include performances either in English or in translation in non-English speaking countries, but it would be a convenience to me to include them). But I am not quite clear what would be the position supposing that some other intelligent English producer (assuming his existence) wanted to do a professional production of the play at a time or in a way that would not interfere with any actual production of it by yourself? (It seems to be very unlikely, I must say, that any other lot of people could be got together who could do it even competently).

That is all. No doubt we can settle these points quickly.[2]

Yours sincerely,

[T. S. Eliot]

---

merely saying that I empowered him to sign cheques on the District Bank on my behalf, & explaining *why* . . .' (ibid.)

On Sun., 24 Nov. she went up to Hampstead to explain herself to her mother and aunt: 'I was invited, as I had seen Tom. Of-course they are *furious*, & bewildered, & *utterly confounded –* . . . They are *utterly confounded –* '

Earlier, on 8 Nov. she had gone to a Book Exhibition talk by Bertrand Russell – 'the *real Bertie Russell (Earl Russell)*,' as she identified him – '& heard him speak into the Microphone – I saw Miss O'Donovan at Faber's stall, & a lovely new photograph of MY TOM [by Man Ray] is put up *high* on the left – I now think Miss O'Donovan is *sweet*.'

1 – Dukes proposed on 19 Nov. that the Mercury Theatre should act as TSE's agency for professional performances of *MiC* in the USA and Canada, and also for non-professional performances in English-speaking countries. He proposed a commission of 20% (the same amount as that charged by Samuel French, the chief amateur agent). He also recommended TSE to join the League of British Dramatists (a branch of the Society of Authors), which undertook to examine all contracts for members: Dukes himself was chair of the Committee of the League.

2 – TSE duly signed an agency contract with Dukes on 5 Dec. 1935, for a term of three years.

TO *The Editor,* The Times[1]

[published 29 November 1935]   Faber & Faber Ltd

Stilton Cheese

Sir,

May I be allowed the pleasure of supporting Sir John Squire's manly and spirited defence of Stilton cheese? At the same time I should like to add, before it is too late, a few reflections on the project of a statue.

I do not suggest for a moment that the inventor of Stilton cheese is not worthy of a statue. I only criticise the proposal on the ground of the transitory character of the result. Certainly, all the business of public subscriptions, speeches, broadcasts, the wrangling over designs, the eventual unveiling with a military band, and the excellent photograph in *The Times* – this is all exciting indeed. But once a statue is erected, who in this country ever looks at it? Even the work of Mr Epstein is now so familiar to the common man that he no longer stops to ask what it is all about. In a few years' time the Stiltonian monument would be just another bump in a public place, no more inspected than the rank and file of statesmen, warriors, and poets.

No, Sir, if cheese is to be brought back to its own in England, nothing less is required than the formation of a Society for the Preservation of Ancient Cheeses. There is a great deal of work which such a society, and its members individually, could do. For instance, one of its first efforts should be to come to terms, by every possible persuasion, with the potteries which supply those dishes with three compartments, one for little biscuits, one for pats of butter, and one for little cubes of gorgonzola, so called. The production of these dishes could be stopped by a powerful organization of cheese-eaters. Also troops of members should visit all the hotels and inns in Gloucestershire, demanding Double Gloster. (On two occasions I have had to add the explanation: 'it is a kind of cheese.')

On one other point I disagree with Sir John. I do not think even the finest Stilton can hold the field against the noble Old Cheshire when in prime condition – as it very seldom is. But this is no time for disputes between eaters of English cheese: the situation is too precarious, and we must stick together.

Your obedient servant,
T. S. Eliot

1 – Text taken from *The Times*, 29 Nov. 1935, 15.

TO *Ian Parsons*   TS Special Collections, Reading

1 December 1935   Faber & Faber Ltd

Dear Parsons,

I have your letter of the 23rd, and also more recently a letter from Michael Roberts.[1] First, I am quite ready to agree on your compromise price for Owen. There does not seem to be any other issue except the price of Empson. I still consider that Empson and MacNeice have the same market value. When I spoke of their relative dates of publication I really meant simply their respective reputations by this time, as obviously the date of publication in itself has no importance. I must really stand out for the original price for Empson, but if you prefer to raise the price for MacNeice I will bring the matter up before my Committee that way, and I think we can come to an agreement.

Yours ever,

T. S. Eliot

1–Roberts wrote to Parsons on 22 Nov.: 'Fabers tell me that they think that the market value of Empson is at present only ten shillings a page, which is what they are asking for Marianne Moore and Louis MacNeice. I have seen Empson, and he is still quite willing to accept these terms.

'I am not sure how the fee of £7 7 0 which Mrs Owen was prepared to accept for the Owen poems compares with your figure of 30s per page until I know how the pages work out, but I am prepared to offer the £7 7 0 or £1 1 0 per page, whichever is the greater, and I am sure that I can persuade Fabers to accept this.'

Roberts wrote too to TSE, on the same day: 'I enclose a copy of a note which I have sent to Ian Parsons: I gather from Empson that he knew nothing of these manoeuvres and does not sympathize with them . . . Yeats has written to say that he wishes to be paid only the ten shillings per page, and that he is asking his publishers to agree.'

The next day, 23 Nov., Parsons wrote to TSE: 'I am sorry your Committee think 30s. a page [for the poems by Owen] too high, but as you didnt give me any reasons for their opinion I can only answer that our usual rate for Owen's work is two guineas a poem, and that we have been getting this regularly for Mrs Owen for a good many years now . . . [W]e have found that two guineas is accepted without cavil by the many anthologists who have printed Owen's poems during the past five or six years, and . . . the fact that you yourselves ask 30s. a page for Pound – another poet whom few respectable anthologists would care to pass over – does not suggest that the same rate for Owen is unreasonable. After all, we have now printed 9000 copies of his poems . . . At the same time, Mrs Owen expresses a wish that "Mr M. Roberts should not be unduly upset" and I would therefore suggest a compromise in the form of a payment of ten guineas for the seven poems, which is exactly half way between the seven guineas offered and the 30s. a page that we quoted.'

Parsons argued too that he could not agree with TSE's opinion that MacNeice was as well known as Empson – 'whose poems first started appearing in periodicals as long ago as 1928 and have been included, as you know, in nearly every anthology of "contemporary" verse since. A case in point is Roberts' own previous anthology *New Signatures* in which Empson had six poems, but in which there is no mention of MacNeice. So we feel that 20s. a page is really the right price for him.'

1 December 1935   [Faber & Faber Ltd]

Dear Colonel Butler-Bowdon,

I must apologise for my delay in reporting upon the complete *Margery Kempe*, but the book had to be read by some of my colleagues before I had anything more to say to you about it, and as we make a point of having every manuscript under serious consideration read by as many directors as possible you will understand that the work of the whole Board is very heavy.[2]

I am sorry to inform you that my colleagues do not agree with me about the value and interest of *Margery Kempe*'s narrative and feel that the readers will be confined chiefly to those who have the curiosity to read the original when it is published by the Early English Text Society. They point out that the experiences of Mrs Kempe are not of serious interest to students of mysticism, but are rather of a pathological nature, and that furthermore she has very little of interest to say about the places visited on her pilgrimages. These objections I can't refute. We agree in any case on this general point: that we can never make a success of a book which is supported by only one director.

I have no doubt that you will easily find another firm which will be able to handle the book with more enthusiasm, but for my own part I regret that we are not to have the honour of publishing it.

I am returning the three typescript volumes under separate cover.

Yours very sincerely,

[T. S. Eliot]

1–Col. William Butler-Bowdon (1880–1956), descendant of an old Catholic family, discovered at his home – Southgate House, Clowne, nr. Chesterfield, Derbyshire – the sole surviving copy of a testament by the Norfolk mystic and pilgrim Margery Kempe which was authenticated by Hope Emily Allen (who was already noted for her work on the hermit Richard Rolle). After announcing his find in *The Times* (30 Sept. 1934), Butler-Bowdon published a lightly modernised version of the text in 1936.
2–The complete Margery Kempe had been submitted on 30 Nov.

TO *W. C. Roberts*   CC

2 December 1935   [Faber & Faber Ltd]

Dear Father Roberts,

I find that an engagement to speak at some official ceremony at University College, Dublin, is going to fall on the 22nd of January. I am afraid therefore that I shall be unable to speak for your Save the Children Fund on the 23rd. I hope this is not inconveniencing you too much, but it is still a long way ahead, and when you first wrote you suggested two alternative dates.[1]

With many apologies,
Yours sincerely,
[T. S. Eliot]

TO *G. G. Coulton*[2]   CC

2 December 1935   [Faber & Faber Ltd]

Dear Dr Coulton,

Among the host of letters which have reached me on the subject of cheese I feel compelled to answer yours in order to acknowledge your precedence as the originator of the project for a Society for the Preservation of Ancient Cheeses.[3] If I should again express myself publicly on the subject I shall certainly make due acknowledgement. You will, I am sure, agree, however, that my own project is more comprehensive and ambitious than your own.

1–In the event, TSE was to give his address on behalf of the Save the Children Fund at Holborn Town Hall on 30 Jan. 1936: 'Saving the Future: Mission of the Save the Children Fund: Practical Service at Home and Abroad', *The World's Children: The Official Organ of the Save the Children Fund* 16: 6 (Mar. 1936), 85–7

The Rt Hon. Lord Noel-Buxton, PC, thanked TSE on 31 Jan. 1936; and Edward Fuller, Publicity Secretary of the Fund, notified TSE (12 Mar. 1936) that the meeting had generated £35 – 'the gift of which I feel sure is very largely due to your able advocacy of this work'.

2–George Gordon Coulton, FBA (1858–1947): historian of medieval history and religion; controversialist; anti-Catholic. His many publications include *Life in the Middle Ages* (1910; revised in 4 vols, 1928); *Papal Infallibility* (1922); *In Defence of the Reformation* (1931); *Five Centuries of Religion* (4 vols, 1927–50).

3–See TSE's letter about cheese published in *The Times* on 29 Nov., above.

Coulton wrote, 29 Nov.: 'You may be amused to see that, on one small point, I have to some extent anticipated you. But I must add my heartiest adhesion to your second point – the value of Cheshire at a proper stage of antiquity. This summer there was a piece of 3½ lbs left high & dry at [the cheese shop] opposite Trinity; I bought it when I saw it in Sept, and, supported by one daughter against the rest of the household, produced it daily until the last ½ lb was banished to my cupboard in College, each amber-coloured & tasting like pepper.'

You may have wondered at my omission of the name of Wensleydale. This was deliberate and out of tenderness for the memory of that great cheese. The output of the last few years seems to me to have been distinctly inferior, and I have heard rumours that the Wensleydale industry has fallen into the hands of the Rowntree family.

With many thanks,

Yours very sincerely,

[T. S. Eliot]

TO *Donald Brace* CC

2 December 1935   [Faber & Faber Ltd]

My dear Brace,

I have decided to let Ashley Dukes of the Mercury Theatre here handle the dramatic rights of *Murder in the Cathedral*. It seemed to me desirable to have a specialist to deal with these matters. Ashley Dukes has put on a very successful production of the play here, and he seems to be acquainted with the sort of people in America who would be likely to produce the play properly there.[1] I am arranging an agreement with him, and I dare

---

1 – The Mercury Theatre production, with Speaight (and with EMB as Fourth Tempter and Knight), which opened on 1 Nov. – All Saints' Day – ran for nearly a year (225 performances) before going on tour.

Among those who went to see the production was VHE, who recorded in her diary on Sat., 30 Nov.: 'Took a taxi to the *Mercury Theatre*, in *pouring rain* – & found myself sitting next to Aldous Huxley & Maria. The Play itself is a nightmare of horror, & to sit through it next to Aldous Huxley is the acme of fantastic terror. The little theatre itself was quite full, & all *very* nice people in the audience. It is obviously a *great* success. I daresay Aldous is terribly jealous of Tom, *now*. I remember years ago, when his plays, The World of Light, & This Way To Paradise (both little nightmares, in themselves) were running at the Royalty in Dean Street. Compared to *Tom's* plays, they are quite commonplace. *Tom* is really dashing about in a most sinister fashion. I foresee he will be the big noise as a Playwright. He has got *everything*. Historic sense, *music* in his very blood, *rhythm* & *sound* & *time sense* to an extent which is almost *incredible*. So there was Aldous Huxley, & Maria, & [Sybille] Bedford. I was very wary, remembering that the Huxleys were *in* New York while Tom was there in 1933 – and I have Tom's letters referring to that. I think I shall *leave it to the Huxleys* to *take* the initiative so far as I am concerned, as, indeed I think I may safely leave it now for all those I know or ever have known to take the initiative. And since I have now met Tom in *public*, I am no longer obliged to come forward in any way. I can, in point of *fact*, refuse to negotiate *except* through him.'

According to Carole Seymour-Jones, Sybille Bedford found the encounter 'terrifying': 'Gaunt and swaying, still smelling of ether, her make-up misapplied, half recognising people and half not, Vivienne made such an intense impression on Sybille that she was forced to leave the room and have a brandy' (*Painted Shadow: A Life of Vivienne Eliot* [2001], 538).

say that you will be glad to be relieved of those petty problems of fees for amateur performances. After this all enquiries about either professional or amateur productions should be addressed to Ashley Dukes, The Mercury Theatre, 2 Ladbroke Road, London w.11.

Yours ever,
[T. S. Eliot]

TO *Henry Eliot*

3 December 1935 *The Criterion*

Dear Henry,

I wonder if you could help me to get a Christmas present for Ada, though I am afraid it may give you some trouble. But if you are too busy before Christmas, please attend to it after Christmas – it doesn't matter getting it to her before so much as all that. I gave her four little salt-cellars for her birthday, and I wanted to complete them with four little pepper-casters as soon as possible. I don't think it is possible to *match* them exactly, but they ought to be the suitable *size*. If you have not seen them, you could get Sheff to steal one for you to serve as a pattern (I think she only uses them for parties). I think the draft enclosed for 30 dols. ought to cover it (I am sorry I could not get one payable in Cambridge) but if not please let me know the difference. I bought the salt-cellars at that shop at the Corner of Beacon Street and the street (?? Park Street) that skirts the Common going up hill just as you issue from the subway at Park Street. It is *over* that basement junk shop that used to be Koopman, and the entrance is in Beacon Street. It is Somebody & Somebody, I'm not sure that one of the names is not Partridge, and it has been there for a long time.

On a second visit (26 Dec.), VHE considered the play 'a *stupendous success*'. She mused: 'Dear Tom, how proud I am of him. His cleancut mouth, his fine head, his keen deep hawk like eyes. How often Ottoline used to say to me & *how sadly* – "isn't Tom beautiful, Vivienne, such a *fine* [?mouth], such a grand expression. Such a good *walk*!" Dear Ottoline, however much she neglects me now, I shall always cherish *her* because she so sympathised with Tom. Felt all his *pain*, & knew how he was *hurt* & wounded, & *by whom* . . . Robert Speaight is very *fine* as Becket. Very fine. I do *not* like him, & I did *not* like his behaviour to Tom in 1932. But he is *acting* well now, & may be he will, *one day*, get a *wider* & broader point of view – .'

See too C. B. Mortlock, '"Murder in the Cathedral": T. S. Eliot's Play in London', *Church Times*, 8 Nov. 1935, 529.

I shall be grateful. I have been very pushed lately, but I hope to write a letter tomorrow night.

Affectionately,
Tom

TO *Ian Parsons*

TS Special Collections, Reading

6 December 1935   Faber & Faber Ltd

Dear Parsons,

Thank you for your letter of December 4th.[1] I feel quite exhausted by this continued bartering, and am therefore quite ready to accept your alternative suggestion about Empson and MacNeice for 15s. each way. I haven't looked up the files to see who, if either, profits by this compromise.

Yours ever,
T. S. Eliot

TO *George Barker*

CC

6 December 1935   [Faber & Faber Ltd]

Dear Barker,

I have not yet had time to study your poems and story,[2] but I am writing to tell you that we shall at least be able to continue the fund for you for another year to the extent of £13 a quarter. I have asked the bank to send you that sum on the 15th December, plus a special sum of £5 received from a separate source. It is still possible that there may be one or two more contributions.

With all best wishes,
Yours sincerely,
[T. S. Eliot]

1 – Parsons was 'very glad' they had settled upon a price for Owen. 'With regard to Empson, I still think that you are either under-estimating his market value or over-estimating MacNeice's, but if you are adamant about their being on a par let's make it 15/- a page for both and call it a day.'

2 – Barker submitted on 18 Nov. a short story and two recent poems (one entitled 'Though Lovely & Lonely'); plus 'a piece called Mannikin Mannikin which I wrote last night . . .'

TO *Ottoline Morrell* TS Texas

6 December 1935   *The Criterion*

My dear Ottoline,

Thank you very much for your letter of December 4th,[1] and also for your further note enclosing Mrs Sanger's cheque, which I have sent to the bank. I have also written to Mrs Sanger to thank her.[2]

We now have sufficient to pay Barker a pound a week for another year, and the £5 from Mrs Sanger as an extra contribution for Christmas. I should be glad of course to increase it a little, but I think that another contributor of £13 should be enough. As I said a year ago, I think that unless Barker has an unexpected reason for expenses during the coming year, such as illness of either himself or his wife, it is better not to increase the payments over last year, as we can't expect to continue them for ever. I am again very grateful to you for interesting yourself so much, and taking so much trouble. I am very much engaged until the end of next week, but I hope I may come and see you again after that.

Affectionately yours,
Tom

TO *A. Desmond Hawkins* TS Desmond Hawkins

6 December 1935   *The Criterion*

My dear Hawkins,

I have been thinking over your letter of the 3rd.[3] The difficulty about a roving chronicle amongst so many others which are quarterly is that

---

1 – 'I threw out a hint to Maynard Keynes and lent him Barker's Poems . . . & as you see he offers to give something.

'I feel it is better to accept whatever sum one can catch rather than to ask for a definite sum. People seem to prefer that . . .

'Dora Sanger also promised me £5 but it hasn't appeared yet! I told Bryan G[uinness] that he must not let us down!

'Now I am writing to David Cecil & think of attempting Lord Berners. I hear he has built a "folly" at his Garden in the country so he must be rich! £5 or £6 means so little to them!

'I am so pleased you & the Duke got on so well. I wish I could take you to Welbeck. It would interest you very much. Perhaps in the summer . . .'

2 – Dora Sanger, widow of the economist and barrister Charles Sanger (1871–1930).

3 – 'I think the Fiction Chronicle is an excellent idea . . . I like the suggestion in the way you put it: to be broadly sketched and not "compendious" . . . The type of book I should like to do would cover Barker's *Janus*, Wynyard Browne's *Sheldon's Way*, John Pudney's *And Lastly the Fireworks*, Calder-Marshall's *Dead Centre* and Sean O'Faolain's last book. And then there are people like Gascoyne, Isherwood, Beechcroft and others . . . This has grown, stewing in my mind, into a tentative suggestion that I am unable to keep out of this letter

of finding a name for it. Another difficulty is of finding space for a new chronicle every quarter, as I think that the inclusion of theatre and cinema might call for. However I see no objection to your divagating as much as you like and saying that you have the Editor's encouragement to talk about other kinds of fiction than that represented by the novel. The theatre is certainly fiction, and so for the most part is the film: even if the news-reel cannot be called fiction, it at least serves the purpose of distracting the public mind from important events, or else presenting them in an unimportant way.

I am afraid that one or two of the books which you mention have been already cast out, before the idea of a chronicle occurred to me. If you would send a list of books you would like me to get for review in the March number I will see which ones we can still send for. Meanwhile I have a few here at your disposal which you may or may not want to mention, such as *The Asiatics* and the book by Hargrave, which I hear is very bad. Would you call for them?[1]

Now about the lawyer.[2] I will write privately to the head of the firm, but I am enclosing a line of introduction for you to use in asking for an appointment.

Yours ever,

T. S. Eliot

P.S. Michael Sayers is doing an article on contemporary theatre for the March number which will not be treated as a chronicle but as a body article. In any case I don't want him to do the theatre regularly for us, because there is no point in duplicating the *N.E.W.* Furthermore I had rather have you handle the theatre than anyone else I can think of in subsequent issues.

... To do a roving Chronicle on the three main folk arts – one quarter Cinema, one quarter Theatre, and two quarters Fiction ... I have a mixed interest, perhaps an "historical" anthropological interest, in the stuff of these popular arts. However sluggish, however wholly demotic they become they are not static. They are the only broadly typical art we have the most reliable *mass* evidence ... Your readers should have a rough sense of touch on the world of the Marx Brothers and Noel Coward.'

1–Hawkins on John Hargrave, *Summer Time Ends* ('Any comparison with *Ulysses*, apart from bulk, is immediately laughable') and Prokosch, *The Asiatics*, which he thought 'a profound insult' to the genre ('It is the journal of a travel, which appears to have been pleasantly distorted to gain the advantage of interrelated incident'): 'Fiction Chronicle', *C.* 15 (Apr. 1936), 478–8.

2–'I want to change Billie's name. Can I go to these lawyers you mentioned? I can raise £10 or £12, as long as they don't run me into more than that. The child looks almost a certainty by this time. She is well, and is being very careful ... I shall never worry when she's well again.'

6 December 1935   Faber & Faber Ltd

Dear Roberts,

I ran into Sacheverell Sitwell yesterday at the Chinese Exhibition, and he still professed to have heard nothing from you about the anthology, and complained about his post office. I put the matter to him briefly, and he said to go ahead with the anthology. I think, however, that it would be best to get something from him in writing, so will you, as I asked, send me copies of the important letters for me to forward to him. The anthology will go to press anyway.

I have finally compromised with Parsons about the payments for Owen and Empson. We have agreed to pay each other 15s. a page, the same price for Empson and for MacNeice.

As for the excess of payments over the allowance, apart from those additional items arranged by myself, we will try to iron that out. In any case there is no reason why you should suffer to any considerable extent.[1]

About the publication of the notes of *The Waste Land*. I think it would be very much pleasanter, and it would be a relief to myself, if *The Waste Land* could be published without the notes, which were set up by mistake. De la Mare tells me that this could be managed if you could select some other poem of mine to fill the same number of pages as the notes. It would of course have to be something chronologically later than *The Waste Land*, but you are welcome to chose [sic] anything you like except from *Murder in the Cathedral*. It is really for *you* to decide, *not* for me, whether you prefer another poem to the notes.[2]

Yours ever,
T. S. Eliot

1–Roberts wrote on 2 Dec.: 'If you pay £5 for the Empson poems & £10–10–0 for those by Owen, the cost of the book, in authors' fees, will be £190, including £14 due to yourself.

'As you know, I am willing to sacrifice all or part of the £30 advance which will be due to me on publication in order to help meet this £40 excess over the estimated £150. I am reluctant to accept your offer to give up part of your own fees – which are ridiculously low (Yeats has written to say that he has asked his publishers to accept the rate of 10/- per page, so that the most fierce demands do not always come from the writers of the greatest commercial value) – I should much prefer that Fabers should increase their advance on account of royalties, but if they are unwilling to do this, then anything which you gave up would obviously be a first charge on any subsequent payment of royalties.'

2–Roberts determined on 8 Dec. to print *Marina*, *Ash-Wednesday II*, and *Triumphal March*.

TO *The Editor,* The Church Times

[published 6 December 1935, 641] [No address given]

A Bookshop 'Pro Fide'

Sir,

A primary obstacle to the propagation of the Gospel in the Western world is the widespread ignorance of its essential character on the part of those who who are, or believe themselves to be, hostile to Christianity. There is a fairly continuous output of first-rate literature in defence and explication of the faith, but there is ground for believing that it only reaches those who are disposed to welcome its message in advance. It does not get through to those whose opposition to Christianity is largely the result of their acquaintance with what any informed Christian would recognise to be caricatures of the Gospel and the traditions of the Church.

Such persons will not, without great difficulty, be induced to listen to a properly qualified exponent of the Christian Faith. Still less are they likely to enter an ordinary religious bookshop, even when the existence of such specialised establishments is known to them. In view of such a situation, it is submitted that there is room for a new kind of bookshop, which will have for its primary purpose, not the purveying of devotional or controversial literature for the faithful, but the presentation, in attractive and even provocative form, in the heart of the world's Vanity Fair, of the best contemporary Christian apologetic.

Christ came to call not the righteous but sinners to repentance, and repentance involves a change of mind no less than a change of heart. But 'sinners' cannot be called in accents appropriate to the devout; we have to go into the highways, and by effective persuasion compel men to come in. Such a shop as is here envisaged must be one into which wayfarers will be positively tempted to enter; it must be open to the street; and its wares – of all prices and standards – must be attractively displayed. It will specialise in books, pamphlets and periodicals which state the case for Christianity with authority, and in terms of the spiritual, psychological and sociological issues of today.

During the last twelve months a small interdenominational committee, including Anglican, Roman Catholic and Free Church members, has been meeting to discuss the possibility of launching such an enterprise. This committee has met upon the basis of a dogmatic faith in the Incarnation, being convinced that a merely naturalistic, humanitarian Christology has no message of power for the modern world. It has found no insuperable difficulties in collaborating to forward this project, and is now led to invite the sympathy and assistance of Christian people of every denomination who feel the urgency of securing a better and wider understanding of the basic Christian truths.

The committee is convinced that it would be neither wise nor feasible to manage such a shop itself, and proposes rather to organise in support of a man of business acumen and tact, who would be prepared to enter upon the undertaking in a spirit of Christian vocation. We calculate that the shop could not be securely launched without the assurance of a reserve of £1,000 for each of the first three years. This does not appear to be a prohibitive sum, and the committee is already in a position to guarantee about a quarter of it. We now appeal for promises of sums which may in the aggregate enable us to proceed with confidence to the appointment of the responsible individual aforementioned. It will be a great encouragement to us to hear from any who are in a position to guarantee any proportion of the total required, or can put us in the way of obtaining such guarantees. Such information should be sent to Canon Hudson, Hillingdon, St Albans.

(Signed)   H. R. L. Sheppard

T. S. Eliot

Maurice B. Reckitt

Cyril E. Hudson

FROM *Vivien Eliot* TO *Jack St John Hutchinson*   TS Texas

8 December 1935   68 Clarence Gate Gardens, N.W.1

Dear Jack,[1]

For no reason at all except that it is more normal to see one's friends than not to. But I have got to go and sing somewhere now.

As to Tom's *mind, I am* his mind.[2]

I should like to commend to your notice a little old poem by Ezra Pound called Portrait D'une Femme.

Yours sincerely,

V. H. Eliot

1–VW to Julian Bell, 1 Dec. 1935: 'Jack [Hutchinson] grown pale and thin . . . very cordial; but plagued by Mrs [Vivien] Eliot who has taken to the stage. She wears a black shirt, believes in Mussolini, and accosts Tom just as hes about to lecture on the Future of Poetry before a devout and cultured audience' (*The Sickle Side of the Moon: The Letters of Virginia Woolf* V, ed. Nigel Nicolson [1979], 450). See VHE's letter to James & James, 28 Nov. 1935.
2–On 23 Dec. 1935 VHE sent a Christmas card to OM as from 'Mr and Mrs T. S. Eliot' (Texas).

11 December 1935   Faber & Faber Ltd

Dear Mrs Perkins,

I want to write to you, not only to have some word from me waiting for you as a 'steamer-letter'; but because I have not succeeded in expressing all my gratitude and appreciation of your hospitality to me in Campden and in London. No reception could have been more gracious or given more pleasure. You succeeded (whether you intended so much as that or not) in making me feel that I was almost one of the family. Imagine me (or perhaps Dr Perkins can) on a raw dark drizzling January day at lunch time, at my favourite table below the gloomy portrait of the late Sir Wm. Vernon Harcourt, grumbling at Old Foster the waiter because of the dryness of the Old Cheshire (I am a testy person) but really repining at the loss of a home in Rosary Gardens. It is unusual that people should so completely make furnished houses (and not only a congenially furnished and gardened house like Stamford House, but an antipathetically furnished one like Rosary Gardens) quite their own, while they are in them.

I find it difficult to think of you so appropriately settled in Boston (though this is disloyal of me).

And I can hardly bear to mention my appreciation of your kindness in most recent circumstances: though this is the strongest reason for my writing as I do.

Affectionately yours,
Tom Eliot

TO *Alsina Gwyer*   CC

13 December 1935   [Faber & Faber Ltd]

Dear Lady Gwyer,

It was extremely pleasant to get your letter of December 9th,[1] and I am very sorry that I have been so busy with extraneous matters that I have

1–Alsina Gwyer invited TSE for the following weekend at Swinbrook Cottage, Burford, Oxfordshire. Lady Gwyer (daughter of the philanthropist Sir Henry Burdett) and Sir Maurice (1878–1952) were co-proprietors of the company that had run the joint enterprise of the Scientific Press (launched by Burdett, who had died in 1920), the *Nursing Mirror*, and the general publishing house of Faber & Gwyer. Although the Gwyers were co-owners – Lady Gwyer understandably felt it her duty to be the vigilant trustee of her late father's interests – Maurice Gwyer was a major shareholder but did not serve as a director of the company, and was otherwise fully employed in public service, as Treasury Solicitor.

not had the time to write any letters this week. It would be delightful to come down for a weekend with you, and I hope that you will renew your invitation. Unfortunately I have to go away for this weekend, the first for some time past, to visit a goddaughter. I should like to come at some later date. I am so sorry that I did not let you know at once, and hope that it has not put you out.

With all best wishes,
Yours sincerely,
[T. S. Eliot]

TO *William Empson*

CC

16 December 1935   [*The Criterion*]

Dear Empson,

I should always be glad to publish more articles of yours along the same lines, but we never have contributions by the same author in two numbers in succession, so I couldn't possibly use it before June at the very earliest.[1] If that would do, please let me see it when it is ready. I hope we may meet when you get back from Austria.

Yours sincerely,
[T. S. Eliot]

1–WE wrote ('Sunday' [15 Dec. 1935]): 'I want to ask if you'd be prepared to consider another verbalist article, about the same length, to be called "Statements in Words" or something like that. The main idea is that when you use a word in two senses at once you may assert that the two are connected; it is already like a sentence. The thing can be made to bring in psychology and language theory and the Primitive Mind and heaven knows what, and is getting very clumsy. It would be a convenience to have to boil it down into a clear article, if you think that would be any good for the *Criterion*.

'I am off to Austria next week for a little ski-ing.'

Empson's 'Feelings in Words' was to appear in C. 15 (Jan. 1936), 183–99: Empson had written of that essay, 15 Oct. 1935: 'I tinkered a bit with this when it came back from Richards, and feel quite good about it now, but it may well not be suitable for the Criterion. If it has turned out too long, the paragraphs on *nice* and *so* would come out easily, and the next would begin "This word is" not "These words are".' 'Statements in Words' appeared in C. 16 (Apr. 1937), 452–67.

TO *F. R. Leavis*   TS Texas

16 December 1935   *The Criterion*

Dear Mr Leavis,

I am returning the *Experimental College* with apologies for having kept it so long.[1] I am afraid that I have not been able to find the time to give it a proper reading. I have only read enough to assure myself of its interest and value. Thank you very much for lending it to me.

Thank you for what you say about my Marvell essay.[2] I don't know whether it is one of my best or not, but I am inclined to think that my essays of this kind have more permanent value than the more theoretic ones.

Yours sincerely,
T. S. Eliot

TO *Robert Fitzgerald*[3]   TS Beinecke

16 December 1935   *The Criterion*

Dear Mr Fitzgerald,

I was glad to receive your letter of November 25th after not hearing from you for such a long time. There was no need for you to ask permission

---

1–FRL wrote, 7 Dec.: 'If you can lay hands on that copy of [Alexander] Meiklejohn's *Experimental College* without much bother I wonder if you would send it along? My Professor, Q., has asked several times if he might borrow it, & it seems a pity to baulk his interest. – Not that there's much chance of an experiment being initiated at Cambridge. I wish there might be an English edition.'

2–'P.S. May I say that I have (while reviewing the *Oxford Book of 17th Verse*) recently re-read your Marvell essay with fresh admiration? It seems to me one of your very best things, though (as you'll see if you still look at *Scrutiny*) that I register a marginal query or two. F.R.L.' See 'Andrew Marvell' (1921), in *SE*.

3–Robert Fitzgerald (1910–85), poet, critic, translator of Greek and Latin classics including Euripides, Sophocles and Homer, studied at Harvard, 1929–33, and worked in the 1930s for the *New York Herald Tribune* and *Time*. He was Boylston Professor of Rhetoric and Oratory, Harvard, 1965–81; Consultant in Poetry to the Library of Congress, 1984–5. TSE wrote to Henry Allen Moe, John Simon Guggenheim Memorial Foundation, 22 Dec. 1939: 'Fitzgerald I saw something of during 1932–33 while he was an undergraduate at Harvard . . . [A]t that time I was more interested in the work of Fitzgerald than in that of any other young poet in America . . .'

The Alcestis of Euripides: an English version by Dudley Fitts and Robert Fitzgerald (F&F, 1936) was advertised thus: 'The story of Admetus, and his wife Alcestis who gave her life for his, and his friend Heracles who brought her back to him from the Country of the Dead, is the plot of one of the best known and most moving of the plays of Euripides. This is a translation into modern verse by two of the most interesting of the younger American poets.

to reprint in book form anything published in the *Criterion*, though we always like to have the usual acknowledgement of prior publication.[1] I shall look forward to seeing your poems, and with great interest also to your translation of *Alcestis*.[2] I should be glad to know what you are doing now, and how you like it.

With best wishes,
Yours sincerely,
T. S. Eliot

———

Every age must make its own translations. Our own is a time in which the style of poetry has undergone a radical change, and we need new translations by poets to interpret Greek poetry to us. Readers of this version of the *Alcestis* will find Euripides very much alive. We are glad to have this text to put beside the *Agamemnon* of Louis MacNeice.'

When Fitzgerald applied for Guggenheim support for his translation of the *Odyssey*, TSE wrote: 'I have known Mr Robert Fitzgerald ever since he was a Senior in Harvard College. He is a poet of original merit, who has hitherto produced all too little work of his own. He is a very good Greek scholar – of his scholarship there will no doubt be testimony on better authority than mine; but I speak with some confidence when I say that as a translator of Greek verse into English verse he is quite in the front rank. The publishing firm of which I am a Director (Faber & Faber Ltd) have published in England two of his translations of Greek tragedy – his OEDIPUS and the ALCESTIS which he translated in collaboration with Mr Dudley Fitts. For the project which he has submitted I have not the slightest hesitation in recommending him, and shall look forwards with keen interest to the fruits of his labours. 29 November 1951.'

1 – Fitzgerald reported that 'January Night' had been included in his volume *Poems* without acknowledgement to the *Criterion*: he expected most of the copies to include an addendum. 2 – 'Dudley Fitts and I have finished a verse translation of the Euripides *Alcestis*, which I shall send to you as soon as we have a clean manuscript. Perhaps it is worth publishing. It is better than Aldington's and very far from Murray's. If these are its only merits, however, I hardly think it belongs among the Great Translations!'

TO *Michael Roberts*

TS Berg

16 December 1935   Faber & Faber Ltd

Dear Roberts,

As for whether you use the poem by Eberhart[1] or one by Rickword,[2] that is entirely for you to decide.[3] I don't know Rickword's work, but I doubt if he is any better than Eberhart, and it is probably better to print an indifferent poem by a younger man than an indifferent poem by an older. I dare say I am prejudiced about Eberhart by my personal impression of him. I saw him several times while I was at Harvard two years ago, and thought him very soft and immature.[4]

You may have heard from De la Mare. We agree to your including *Marina, Ash Wednesday II,* and *Triumphal March* in place of the notes.

Yours ever,

T. S. Eliot

1 – Richard Eberhart (1904–2005), American poet and playwright. See *Collected Poems 1930–1960* (1960); *Collected Verse Plays* (1962).

2 – Edgell Rickword (1898–1982), critic and editor. As editor of the *Calendar of Modern Letters,* 1925–7, his criticism set an acknowledged precedent for F. R. Leavis's work in *Scrutiny*. Leavis published in 1933 a selection from the Calendar under the title *Towards Standards of Criticism* (republished with new introduction, 1976). In the 1930s Rickword joined the Communist Party and worked for *Left Review,* which he edited from Jan. 1936 to June 1937; he later edited the Communist periodical *Our Time,* 1944–7. Though well received as a poet in early years, he ceased to write lyric poetry on joining the Communist Party (from which he withdrew after the Soviet invasion of Hungary in 1956). Works include *Invocations to Angels* (poetry, 1928); *Essays and Opinions 1921–1931* (1974). See the memoirs and opinions in 'Edgell Rickword: A Celebration', *PN Review* 6:1 (1979).

3 – Roberts was proposing to substitute, for the notes appended to a poem by Sacheverell Sitwell, a poem by Eberhart entitled 'The Groundhog' (which was to be included in Eberhart's collection *Reading the Spirit,* in 1937). Roberts told TSE on 8 Dec., 'On the other hand, I see his limitations and am willing to be guided by you: a poem by Edgell Rickword would fill the space as well, and fit the age-order as well, too.' Roberts wrote to RdlM, 12 Dec. 1935: 'I haven't heard from Eliot about my suggestion that Eberhart should be put in in place of Sacheverell Sitwell's notes; I expect he's tired of the whole business, as we all are. I wavered for a long time between Eberhart and Rickword. Eliot is rather against Eberhart, who is little known (though I think I'm persuading Chatto to take his poems) and I agree that Rickword deserves a place on historical grounds . . .' RdlM replied, 13 Dec.: 'I spoke to Eliot about the poem by Richard Eberhart and we decided together that it should go in – so may we then leave out the one by Edgell Rickword? That, at any rate, is what I am doing.'

Revised proofs of the whole volume were to be available by Christmas.

4 – Eberhart had written to TSE, 9 Feb. 1935: 'I recall the two or three hours I had with you [during a conversation at Harvard University in 1933] with considerable feeling.'

TO *R. B. Savage*   TS R. B. Savage, SJ

16 December 1935   *The Criterion*

Dear Father Savage,

Thank you for your letter of December 9th.[1] I shall be very pleased to accept your invitation to come to Dublin on the understanding that you let me have a copy of your paper as far ahead as possible, so that I may reply adequately. I am still undecided about the title for the lecture, but I will write later and make suggestions.[2]

Yours very sincerely,
T. S. Eliot

TO *Margerie Fenwick*   CC

16 December 1935   [Faber & Faber Ltd]

Dear Madam,

I return herewith the two letters from your son Michael which you sent me to read.[3] They are very interesting and forward for his years. I am sorry that he thinks that I take an early Greek view of the After Life. I was merely trying to give an impression of hell, or at any rate of one possible hell, and I should be sorry to have him continue to think that my views were epicurean.

Yours very truly,
[T. S. Eliot]

1 – 'I am wondering have you come to a decision about coming to Dublin . . . as I wish to make some arrangements before the Christmas recess.'

2 – The Inaugural Meeting of the English Literary Society, University College, Dublin, 23 Jan. 1936, was to be chaired by Denis J. Coffey, President. Savage's 'Auditor's Address' was entitled 'Literature at the Irish Crossroads' (Houghton). TSE would propose the 'Resolution', 'That the Auditor deserves the best thanks of the Society for his Address'; and was to be seconded by Professor Daniel Corkery.

TSE's untitled seven-page reply to Savage's presentation is at Houghton bMS Am 1691 (28).

3 – Mrs Fenwick attended TSE's talk at the *Sunday Times* Book Exhibition, and coincidentally had soon thereafter received two letters from her son which she forwarded. Michael Fenwick's letters have not been traced, but evidently referred to the powerful chorus in *MiC* opening: 'I have smelt them, the death-bringers, senses are quickened / By subtle forebodings . . .'

TO *Jeffrey Mark*   CC

16 December 1935   [Faber & Faber Ltd]

Dear Mr Mark,

I have your letter of the 11th, about *Analysis of Usury*.[1] This is an awkward situation, and I must ask you to treat what I have to say in confidence. I sent the book for review to someone whom I considered to be well qualified. I am afraid that the reviewer must have been very over-worked at the time. The review when it arrived proved to be very empty of content, indifferently written, and although favourable so far as one could perceive, said very little about the book. It was distinctly below our standard, and would not have been of any help to you. As the review really arrived too late to go into the December number the problem was solved for the moment, but I am still uncertain what to do. It is possible that I may decide to write frankly to the reviewer and explain to him my dissatisfaction with what he has written and give him the opportunity of writing another review.[2]

I quite agree with you about the tendency of monetary reformers to take the easiest course in concentrating their whole attack upon the bankers. I don't think that this is the wisest course in the long run, and I think that they ought to spend more time working out the implications of fundamental principles in other directions.

Yours sincerely,

[T. S. Eliot]

1 – Mark hoped that his book, *The Modern Idolatry, being an Analysis of Usury & the Pathology of Debt*, which had been published by J. M. Dent, might be reviewed soon in the *Criterion*; he wanted the ideas it contained to get over to monetary reformers. 'It seems to me that the latter, in confining their attacks almost solely to the bankers and the "monopoly of credit", are, to some large extent, trying to pass the buck in the matter of rent and interest, and the whole phenomenon of capital debt and unearned income generally.

'The historical ideology of socialism – and the traditional attitude of the Catholic Church in the matter of usury – cannot be ignored in this large way by people or groups of people who affect to be violently concerned about *fundamental changes* in the monetary and economic systems. And I believe my book to be of some importance, not only in that it makes some connection between the socialist and the monetary reformer, but also because it is the only book I know of which gives a specific plan for the abolition of capital debt, rent and interest – as well as details to effect the transference of the issue and control of credit from the banks to governmental authority.'

2 – R. McNair Wilson had been invited on 18 Oct. to write a review of the book.

TO *Kenneth Mackenzie*[1]

16 December 1935   [Faber & Faber Ltd]

My dear Lord Bishop,

Thank you very much for your letter of November 30th.[2] I must apologise for my apparent discourtesy in not replying immediately to thank you, but I found myself exceedingly busy during the first days of this month.

I am very much pleased and reassured by what you say. I am not quite sure who should take the next step, and I shall have a word with Lockhart about it first. I went to see Harris last Thursday, at his nursing home, a week after his operation, and found him full of enthusiasm and courage as ever. I very much doubt whether he will be able to be as active as he hopes. The operation was only partially successful, and he will apparently have to spend the rest of his life in continuous discomfort and frequent pain. He told me that he was unable to take general anaesthetics because of his heart, and that for some obscure reason local anaesthetics have no effect upon him whatever, so that his operations have had to be undergone in a state of full consciousness. In the circumstances I am surprised that he should be as well as he is.

I will write to you again when I have spoken to Lockhart.

I am, my Lord Bishop,
Yours very sincerely,
[T. S. Eliot]

TO *Donald Brace*

17 December 1935   [Faber & Faber Ltd]

Dear Brace,

Morley has handed me your letter of December 4th on account of the third paragraph asking about my copyrights in America.[3] Of the

---

1–The Rt Revd Kenneth Mackenzie (1876–1966), priest, author; Bishop of Brechin (Ordinary of the Scottish Episcopal Diocese of Brechin), 1935–43; author of *The Case for Episcopacy*.

2–Mackenzie wrote on 30 Nov.: 'I do not think you need have any qualms about asking Dr Harris to let me deputize for him. It was always his wish, and indeed I thought that it had been definitely settled at a meeting of the Book Committee in the early part of this year.'

3–C. A. Pearce (Harcourt, Brace & Co.) asked FVM on 14 Sept. 1935: 'I have been drawing up a list of publications for the spring and in it I have included Eliot's COLLECTED POEMS . . . [I]f we are to count on Eliot's poems for the spring, I shall be grateful to have from you poems that are to be added to the volume I think that *Ash Wednesday* was copyrighted by Putnam's in America. At any rate they set it up. But they took it over from a queer bird named Adams who had bought some limited edition press and found he could not make it a success. I will look up the agreements. I do not think that any of the five *Ariel Poems* was published in any periodical in America, but the sixth one, which was never published here, called *Difficulties of a Statesman*, appeared in *Hound and Horn* toward the end of 1932. Then there are a few more unpublished poems to be added, but two short poems, one called *Rannoch* and the other *Cape Anne*, I sent not long ago to young James Laughlin to publish in his paper called *New Democracy* (Eliot House, Cambridge, Mass). If he has not used them yet he ought to do so within the next month or so. There will be four or five poems previously unpublished anywhere which will have to be protected. The difficult case is *Sweeney Agonistes*. I never published this in America myself, but it was pirated by the famous Sam Roth at the time when he was publishing that magazine of his which existed so largely on piracy. I should be glad to know whether anything can be done now to protect the copyright.

I think that this is all there is to be said, except that I will let you know shortly the position about *Ash Wednesday*.

With all best wishes for Christmas,
Yours ever,
[T. S. Eliot]

---

as soon as possible an informative paragraph about it.' FVM replied on 26 Sept.: 'I am hoping for Eliot's Poems in the Spring also. He has been worked pretty hard all summer, and yesterday murmured something about not being able to get the text of the Poems ready until Christmas. I am trying to get him to come to scratch by Thanksgiving Day, and I am going to struggle with a paragraph, which I hope to send you by the next mail.' FVM wrote again on 15 Oct.: 'Here are two blurbs for Eliot's Poems. You will perceive which is which. One was my own effort, the second was Eliot's corrected version. We are using the corrected version. Do as you like.' Pearce responded on 26 Oct.: 'Mr Brace and I believe that we shall want to use the corrected version, though of course we shan't decide for another week or two.'

The published blurb of *Collected Poems 1909–1935* (F&F, 1936) reads with all of TSE's characteristic understatement: 'This volume contains all Mr Eliot's poetry that he wishes to preserve, with the exception of *Murder in the Cathedral*. It includes *Sweeney Agonistes* and the choruses from *The Rock* as well as all the poems in *Poems 1909–1925*.'

TO *G. Hutchinson*   CC

17 December 1935   [Faber & Faber Ltd]

Dear Sir,

I have been recommended to try one of your Old Blue Cheshire Cheeses, and I should be obliged if you would kindly let me have your prices, and let me know whether you could deliver a prime Old Blue Cheshire to me in London. I should have it delivered at my club, and if proved satisfactory I should endeavour to get them to place an order with you.

Yours faithfully,
[T. S. Eliot]

TO *P. Mansell Jones*   CC

17 December 1935   [Faber & Faber Ltd]

Dear Mr Mansell Jones,

I have read your book[1] with much interest and sympathy, and so have two other directors, but I am afraid that we cannot see our way to publishing it. It is an extremely penetrating and well meditated study, and I should be very glad to see it published, but it is a book which must necessarily have a very small sale, and we have already [illegible word] list for next year as many books of such a kind as we feel justified in carrying. When I say 'of such a kind' I mean of course books which add to the distinction of the list, but which will almost certainly represent a loss of money.

I hope that you can find some other publisher to interest himself. I suggest that you might get into touch with Mr Herbert Read, who has a certain influence with Heinemann's.

With many regrets,
Yours very sincerely,
[T. S. Eliot]

1 – Provisionally entitled 'From Montaigne to André Gide – Studies in French Introspection', or else 'The Quest of the Self: French Introspectives from Montaigne to Gide'.

TO *Michael Markoff*[1]

17 December 1935   [*The Criterion*]

Dear Mr Markoff,

I thank you for your letter of November 17th, and am glad to inform you that we have no objection to your using 'Cameras and Naughty Worms'[2] in volume form, provided that acknowledgement is made to the *Criterion*.

I should also be glad to see some of your other stories from time to time. What I am more interested in, however, is your suggestion of putting together the stories and studies to make a book. You have not asked my advice in this matter, but as on the strength of the two stories we have seen, we should be much interested in the possibility of a book by you, I venture to offer my opinion. I think that a book of separate studies of types and of different aspects of life would have a very much better prospect of sale if it could be given some form as a whole, and some continuity, than if the different parts were left unrelated. There is needed either a picture of contemporary Palestine as a whole, or even a tenuous thread of narrative involving yourself as the observer. Anything that looks superficially like a collection of stories is difficult to sell, whereas there is a very steady demand for books which appear to be the record of a single explorer in unknown lands.

The material you have is so unusual, and your treatment of it so individual, that we believe there would be very interesting possibilities in such a book as I suggest, and I should be very glad to discuss the project further with you.

Yours very truly,
[T. S. Eliot]

1 – Markoff had been introduced to Faber & Faber by the poet Wilfrid Gibson, who wrote of his stories, 'When I came to read them . . . they struck me as remarkable work. The author, a young "White" refugee, who has been educated in England, seems to have that half-oriental mystical temperament of the Russian which seems strange to us; and he certainly manages to convey a convincing atmosphere.'
2 – Markoff's 'Chocolates, Saints, Cameras and Naughty Worms [*sic*]', was to be published in C. 15 (Jan. 1936), 210–23.

TO *Leonard P. Moore*   CC

17 December 1935   [Faber & Faber Ltd]

Dear Mr Moore,

The last item in our long drawn out correspondence about Miss Mary
Butts seems to be your letter of May 27th. I have now got hold of a book
by an American author called *Wild Talents*, which I am sending to Miss
Butts in your care.[1] I shall be very much obliged if you will forward it to
her explaining that I think the sort of material in the book is very much
in her line, and that the actual treatment by the author is an obvious
example of how not to do it. If the book suggested to Miss Butts some
work dealing with similar material which interested her we are sure that
she would be able to make a very much better thing of it. I hope that
after seeing the book Miss Butts may be able to make some more hopeful
response than to our rather vague suggestions of the past.

Yours sincerely,
[T. S. Eliot]

TO *John Maynard Keynes*   CC

17 December 1935   [Faber & Faber Ltd]

My dear Keynes,

Thank you very much for your contribution to the Barker fund, which,
in view of your difficulty with his work, which most people share, is
extremely generous.[2] I will admit at least that Barker has a great deal to
learn before he is much older. I propose to ask the bank to add this £5 to
the payment which they will make at the March quarter, because I have

---

1 – *Wild Talents* (1932) by Charles Fort (1874–1932), writer and researcher into the
paranormal.
2 – Keynes sent his contribution on 15 Dec.: 'I couldn't make much of his stuff – I didn't feel
I was meant to – but it looked as if there might be a talent imprisoned somewhere.'
    Keynes to Ottoline Morrell on 1 Dec., of Barker: 'Though I have a feeling that this is
rather good, I can't make much of it. I am afraid that he does not mean us to understand it
fully. But if only he could bring himself to write intelligibly and to have something to tell us,
he might write well and perhaps beautifully.
    'Tell me if you are still collecting a small fund for him. If so, I will send you a modest
contribution.'

had one such contribution to add to the December payment, and I think it is better that his small stipend should be spread out as evenly as possible.

With grateful thanks,
Yours ever,
[T. S. Eliot]

TO *Raphael Demos*[1]   CC

17 December 1935   [Faber & Faber Ltd]

Dear Demos,

Thank you very much for sending me a copy of *Kuklos* including translations of some of my poems. I am very glad indeed to have it, and can of course follow the translation fairly well, but without being able to judge how competent it is. I am afraid that I am a little nettled to find that *The Waste Land* has been translated by someone and published without so much as by your leave, because a Greek friend of mine in California – or rather a friend of Greek race but of Roumanian nationality – has taken a great deal of trouble to translate the same poem, and I was hoping that she would be able to get it placed in some periodical in Athens. And I have meanwhile received two copies of *Ta Nea Grammata* with more translation by somebody else.

I hope that you are flourishing, and that you have written some more poems also. If you have I should like to see them. I hope to be in Cambridge at some time during next year, and look forward to another meal with you at the Olympia.

Yours very sincerely,
[T. S. Eliot]

1 – Raphael Demos (1892–1968), philosopher, reached Harvard from Asia Minor in 1913, and worked as a waiter to pay his doctoral fees. Professor of Philosophy, Harvard, 1919–62; author of *The Philosophy of Plato* (1939). TSE to Horace Kallen, 13 Mar. 1956: 'Actually my closest friends in the Graduate School of Philosophy were Raphael Demos, who is still at Harvard, and George Boas, who went to Johns Hopkins.' TSE told Francis Sweeney, SJ, in 1961: 'He [Demos] was the brightest one of our group.'

18 December 1935   [Faber & Faber Ltd]

My dear Aylward,

I was more than pleased to get your letter of the 28th November, and feel that my communication to *The Times* is more than justified by having evoked such communicativeness after such a long silence. The silence is as much my fault as yours, but you know what a business life is.

You must not think that my taste in cheese is very narrow, or nationalistic. There cannot be too many kinds of cheese, and variety is as important with cheeses as with anything else. I partook yesterday of the best bit of Wensleydale that I have tasted this year, and during the Christmas season, when the rest of the world is in an ill temper as a consequence of popping into Austin Reed's and such-like activities, I hope that you will come to lunch or dinner and partake of a little cheese with me. You mention one cheese which is unknown to me, but a part of the reason for living is the discovery of new cheeses. I have visited Poitiers and its environs but I have never before heard of Chabichou. But there are other excellent French cheeses which you do not mention, Pont l'Evêque for instance, which in prime condition is better than an imperfect Brie. And also Bondon, which has its attractions. You mention the Welsh cheeses, which as you say are not too easy to get, but have you also tasted a good Fressingfield? Double Cottenham I have never tasted. Perhaps it is the rarest of all. There are also the exotic cheeses such as Liptauer and Yet Ost, the delicate Bayerische Beerkäse, which as I remember is a delicious shell-pink. I do not like a month to pass without one good feast of Limburger, which requires the accompaniment of quantities of dark Münchener. And beyond them all rises in gloomy and solitary grandeur the majestic Gammel Ost, the Mount Everest of cheeses, in its brilliant colours of bright orange and emerald green, made of reindeer milk and then stored for years under the beds of the Norwegian farm folk. I have only made one ascent of this cheese, which ended in disaster, but I hope to try again with a better equipped expedition.

Thank you for your information about the Grosvenor at Chester.

But I did not mean to write solely about matters of public interest. I am happy to hear that your affairs have been settled, as I know what a state of uncertainty in such matters can mean. The future does not look

---

1 – James de Vine Aylward (1870–1966), colleague and friend at Lloyds Bank; later author of *The Small-Sword in England, Its History, Its Forms, Its Makers, and Its Masters* (1946).

cheerful, and I shall not try to find lying words to encourage you. Better if we could console each other over a meal at my club. Drop me a line to tell me where to reach you at that season, and I will suggest one of the days following Christmas.

I am sorry to hear of the death of Szilagyi.[1] I always liked him myself, though I don't know how far I would have trusted him. But he had good manners and he was intelligent, both qualities rare in bank managers. He was also appreciative and not without cultivation.

Until I hear from you again, and with cordial Christmas wishes.

Yours ever,

[T. S. E.]

TO *Barbara Burnham*[2]   TS BBC

19 December 1935   *The Criterion*

Dear Miss Burnham,

Thank you for your letter of the 17th and for letting me have such full information about the rehearsals.[3] I had been on the point of writing to you about the cutting, but as I understand from Mr Browne that you are to have one and a half hours for the production I presume very little cutting will be needed, and if Mr Browne is co-operating with you in this work I have every confidence. It does not matter whether Mr Speaight uses for the sermon the Canterbury text or the published text. I think that he had better go on doing what he has been doing at the Mercury Theatre.

I find that I have no written agreement with the B.B.C. beyond a letter from Mr Hamilton Marr offering 30 guineas for the single performance. Should I not have a formal agreement as one does with a series of talks?

1–A. A. Szilagyi was one of the two managers (the other being H. C. Crofton) in the Colonial and Foreign Department of Lloyds Bank.

2–Barbara Burnham: Features and Drama Producer, BBC; known for her adaptations of theatre plays for radio, 1933–45; from 1943 to 1953 she edited and produced plays, before transferring to television in 1953.

3–'[T]he date of the broadcast for "Murder in the Cathedral" is Sunday 5th January at 9.15. I am hoping to do the play as it stands in the published version, with so few cuts that I am leaving these until rehearsal – that's why I haven't sent you a copy, because there is no special copy to send!

'I have been in touch with Mr Martin Browne . . . and he is playing his part of the Fourth Tempter . . . and it will be very nice to have his help here in the Studio. I understand from him that the Sermon, as now spoken by Mr Robert Speaight at the Mercury Theatre, is a little different from the text and I shall make that change accordingly because Mr Speaight speaks that so beautifully that I could not wish to alter it in any way.'

I will try to come to as many rehearsals as possible.[1]

> Yours sincerely,
> T. S. Eliot

FROM *Vivien Eliot* TO *Brigid O'Donovan*   MS Faber

23 December 1935   Written in the Reception and
Writing Rooms of Selfridge & Co,
London, W.1[2]

Dear Miss O'Donovan,
    You asked me to lend you my pencil this afternoon, & you did *not* give it back to me. Please keep it for me. A short red one. I will call tomorrow. It is rather an important pencil.

> Yrs.
> V. H. Eliot.

TO *Tom Faber*   TS Valerie Eliot

25 December 1935   Faber & Faber Ltd

Dear Tom,

> Many thanks for your letter and card which details
> With precision the pleasures of winter in Wales.
> Your snow-man is truly a stout looking yeoman
> Of noble proportions and ample abdomen
> Or abdomen, if you pronounce it like that;
> I also admire both his pipe and his hat.
> And I venture to hope you are still feeling perky,
> After such a huge pudding and such a small turkey.
> The subjoined design, although rude and ungainly,
> Will exhibit our Christmas festivities plainly –
> I mean me and my friend, the Man in White Spats,
> Both buried in Cheese till you can't see our hats.
> And afterwards, see us take our constitutional
> Along Piccadilly, and also Constitution Hill.
> And now as there's danger that I may be froze

---

1 – Burnham wrote on 17 Dec., 'I may need your help with Miss Fogerty and the Chorus!'
2 – The notepaper is printed thus.

From the ends of my fingers to tips of my toes,
I am thinking, dear Thomas, it's time that I close.
So sending my love (or whatever is proper)
To your brother & sister & mommer & popper
Without stopping to think about colons and commas
I will end,

most devotedly yours,
UNCLE THOMAS

TO *Ivor Nicholson*[1]   CC

26 December 1935   [Faber & Faber Ltd]

Dear Mr Nicholson,

I must apologise for having kept for so long the typescript of Mr Colin Still's book, *The Endless Theme*, before writing to you about it. I have only been able to read by snatches the chapters suggested by Mr Still;[2] and since reading them I have had no time to write to you about them until now.

I have read, several years ago, Mr Still's book on *The Tempest*, and therefore, in the time at my disposal, did not look at the second volume of the typescript. I read particularly the three chapters of Volume I that Mr Still mentioned to me.

So far as I can judge from what I have read – but I think I have read enough to be able to judge – this is a very good book: a book of importance whether the author is right or wrong. I think him more right than wrong, myself; but this can never be proved to everyone's satisfaction. The author

---

1 – Ivor Nicholson, Messrs Ivor Nicholson & Watson (publishers).
2 – Still had suggested to TSE (12 Nov.) that he read the chapters entitled 'The World Within', 'The Living Art', and 'Paradise Regained'.

says modestly that it is either very good stuff indeed or sheer fantasy. Readers can be divided in advance into those who will think one way or the other. I understand that the question is: how to market it?

There is, I believe, a large looney public, but I do not know how to reach it, and I have no reason to suppose that you do either. (I am using 'looney' of course in the special sense, not in the general sense in which all publishers depend upon public folly). Furthermore, this queer public has its compartments: the people who fall for the Atlantean theory, cosmic cataclysms etc. will not buy spiritualistic literature, and the spiritualists are distinct from the occultists. If you *could* reach the occultists you might do well with a large edition at a low price. I don't believe you can, and it would be prostitution of a good book. If I were handling the book, I should incline to print it well and price it rather high, aiming at getting a few good reviews rather than an immediate sale, and settle its respectability first. After a year or so I should go out for a cheap edition, not merely a reduction in price, but a cheap edition, whether the first edition sold well or not. But I should begin with it as a high-class anthropology, and make it respectable. You will get some very sneering reviews but if you plant it well you ought to get a few good ones as well. Choose a few people like Denis Saurat and send them complimentary copies. You can tell them that I have expressed great interest, if that is any help. I don't believe Malinowski[1] would be of any use.

All this is without responsibility or prejudice, and you know as well as I do what a gamble publishing is. But this is a book which I should get fun out of publishing, whatever happened. It is a good book, and I should take a long view about its sales.

Yours sincerely,
[T. S. Eliot]

1–Bronisław Malinowski (1884–1944): renowned Polish anthropologist who taught for many years at the London School of Economics. Publications include *Sex and Repression in Savage Society* (1927) and *The Sexual Life of Savages* (1929).

TO *J. H. Oldham*[1]   CC

St Stephen's Day, 26 December 1935   [Faber & Faber Ltd]

My dear Oldham,

I now have three sets of papers: Brunner on the Church, Brunner and Tillich on Man, and Zimmern (is that Alfred?) and Menn. I have not yet tackled Menn; Zimmern seemed to me rather shallow, and not profoundly Christian. I have read most of Brunner on Man, once, and I like it but do not know it well enough to express any views; Tillich I have not reached.[2]

As for Brunner on the Church, I must apologise for not writing about it when I said I would; although I was in a sense free by the middle of the month, I had not allowed for arrears, the amount of time to be spent on Christmas presents for god-children etc. My comments are scrappy; but if I wait to put them in order it will probably be a long time.

I understand that Brunner's paper was meant for local application in Switzerland. Allowing for this, I have still grave misgivings about the possibilities of extreme differences of view.

I am taken aback on p. 3 by his expression 'unpersonal and naturalistic sacramental magic'. I do not find any use of the word 'sacrament' later to indicate that he distinguishes between sacrament (as we use it) and sacramental magic. On p. 5 he says that 'not the act of baptism as such, but only such baptism as is confirmed by an act of repentance and faith on the part of the person baptised and accompanied by a personal confession,

---

1–Joseph ('Joe') Oldham (1874–1969): indefatigable missionary, adviser and organiser for national and international councils and mission boards. Travelling all over the world to confer with missionary educators and colonial administrators, he worked closely with governments and public policy makers. From 1912 to 1927 he was editor of the *International Review of Missions*; and in 1921 became secretary of a new International Missionary Council (IMC) He was also Administrative Director of the International Institute of African Languages and Cultures, 1931–8. From 1934 he was Chair of the Research Committee for the Universal Christian Council for Life and Work, ably preparing the ground for the establishment in 1948 of the World Council of Churches. In 1939 he launched the fortnightly *Christian News Letter*, to which TSE became a faithful contributor, and he set up too an intellectual discussion group called 'The Moot', a think-tank to which TSE contributed. His works include *The World and the Gospel* (1916), *Christianity and the Race Problem* (1924), *The New Christian Adventure* (1929), *White and Black in Africa* (1930), and *New Hope for Africa* (1955). He was appointed CBE in 1951. See further Kathleen Bliss, 'J. H. Oldham, 1874–1969: from "Edinburgh 1910" to the World Council of Churches', in *Mission Legacies*, ed. G. H. Anderson et al. (1994); K. Clements, *Faith on the Frontier: The Life of J. H. Oldham* (1999); *The Moot Papers: Faith, Freedom and Society, 1938–1947*, ed. K. Clements (2010).
2–EVE to Prof. Joon Hak Rhee, 17 Sept. 1996: 'my husband had a high regard for Paul Tillich and his library has the three volumes of *Systematic Theology*, *The Interpretation of History*, and *Biblical Religion and the Search for Ultimate Reality* – the latter book being a gift from the author.'

873

incorporates a man into the Church'. This seems to do away with infant baptism, or to render it provisional to an act of repentance and faith on reaching years of responsibility. I do not know what he means here by 'personal confession', but perhaps the German would make this clear. It obviously does not allude to the use of the sacrament of penance before the baptism of an adult. Again, p. 10, 'it is not being baptised, the opus operatum of the sacrament, that makes men Christians, but only the baptismal promise appropriated in faith'.

The question of The Church seems to me here involved with the question of the meaning of 'sacrament', on which I foresee wide divergence of view.

Brunner's understanding of terms such as 'communion of Saints', and 'Body of Christ' seems to me rationalistic, so that he misses part of the meaning always. Is the German for 'fellowship' *Gesellschaft* or what? Surely 'communion of saints' is a kind of triadic relation, or more than that: a relation of individuals to each other because of their common relation to God – a relation of each to a society because of the relation of God to each individually *and* to their collective consciousness etc.

I object (merely as a choice of metaphorical expression) to the identification of 'love' and 'brotherhood'. As he is defining the Church, he ought to define his other terms too, and the word 'love' not the least.

I think that exception can be taken (p. 4) to his criticism of clericalism. It is surely a travesty to denominate the Church, in the aspect of clericalism, as a *Heilanstalt*. What does he mean by a 'sacramental deposit of salvation ... substantially conceived, and effective independently of faith'. The question of the efficacy of the sacraments independent of faith is a very delicate one, involving again the question of infant baptism; there is also the question of the damnatory efficacy of the sacraments (communion or penance) taken in bad faith.

P. 4 'only where the Word is proclaimed, and indeed only where it is proclaimed truly and in accordance with its Source, does the Church exist'. Who is to decide? Does the Church exist, for instance, in Abyssinia, or among the Nestorians?

P. 4 also, 'theology': this seems to imply a narrow view of the term. P. 5. 'The Church does not exist where men merely preach correctly, but only where men also believe.' This implies an attitude towards 'preaching' and a definition of 'correct preaching' which I suppose is intelligible to a Lutheran. But how is one to decide where men believe and where they do not? One cannot even be quite certain for oneself when one is believing and when one is not. And if we do not decide, then in effect we never know where the Church exists and where it does not.

P. 5. I do not understand his distinction between 'merely correct theology' and 'the proclamation of the Word of God'.

P. 6 and elsewhere suggest that Brunner is unconcerned with the ideal of one visible Church throughout the world. His attitude towards 'secession from the national or state Church'.

P. 10. 'Only he who can say "I know who is my Redeemer", only he who can say that honestly, in heartfelt repentance and heartfelt trust, is a member of Christ's Body and knows himself to be.' But there are degrees of knowledge, and the same proposition (I know who is my Redeemer) may mean a great deal more or less. And who knows how honest he is, or how honest anybody else is? What does 'heartfelt' mean? On these terms, I could never *know* myself to be a member of Christ's Body.

Brunner's use of the terms 'state' and 'national' Churches should not, I think, be applied to the Anglican Church.

His exhortation 'that the Church should itself become a Church again' cannot be accepted by those who believe that the Church is such because of its continuity, so that if it ceased to be the Church it could not of its own power become a Church again. Of course if he meant merely that the Church ought to pull its socks up, the demand would be reasonable.

P. 17 middle. Again a use of the word 'sacrament' which I do not understand. 'There is a sermon where there is a sacrament.'

There are of course a lot of good remarks by the way, such as those about the 'missionary' Church. But apart from these points of detail that I have listed, there is a general question of semantics. The definitions of 'Church' in the N.E.D. leave much to seek, and the historical method, within the limitations of even the largest dictionary, is inadequate. But what a study of the definitions of any important word (such as 'knowledge' or 'love') seems to show is that no one comprehensive definition can be found. The most that can be said is that *all* the meanings of a word are cognate, but that no one definition can be found from which all others can be seen to be derivatives. The life and history of any word is a very queer business. What is wanted is a reconciliation of *all* the meanings of the word 'Church', not a meaning to replace others. You can add to the meaning of a word, but you cannot get rid of previous meanings.

Yours very sincerely,

[T. S. Eliot]

Dear Jeanie,

Before I have written to thank you for your letter of November 16th, I receive your letter of December 16th.[1] At any rate, I shall be thanking you for both before I receive your letter of January 16th. I have had another cold since November 16th, but am now quite well, thank you. I am sorry you had so much trouble in tracking down the boys' school (Fountain), but I almost prayed that you might fail, because what sort of manslaughter a boys' school would make of my lovely murder I shudder to think. There has been a great deal of brouhaha and charivari and potins in New York, and a deal of a muddle, and I am sorry to say that the Murder is to be done to death by Elmer Rice's Blue Eagle barnstormers or unemployed hams for a fortnight (netting me a paltry hundred dollars, less Income tax), which may take the edge off the projected American Tour of the London company (not only somebody blundered, everybody blundered[2]). My memory of trying to teach French cannot produce anything as good as your fried potatoes, but only this for *oeuf à la coque*: 'egg laid by a rooster'. No doubt that has been committed by other peoples' pupils ever since French was taught.

I parted from Mrs Perkins on the best of terms – in fact I am still wondering why she formed such a good opinion of me. I seem to have got onto her right, or sentimental side. But the fact is that Mrs P. is fairly intelligent about Emily's interests except where she herself comes in. She said, for instance, that she thought it would be better for E. to be somewhere else than Boston, because it was so much better for her not to be able to go to see her mother; and she also seemed to understand that it was much better for her to have a job, and preferably the right kind of job. (I like to hear you call her Wendy, but I could not do it myself, because no one else is associated with the name 'Emily' for me but her, and because 'Wendy' conjures up to me that crafty old compatriot of yours James Barrie, about whom I think H. M. Tomlinson said that his saying should be: 'Suffer Jacky Coogan and Shirley Temple to come unto me, for of such is the kingdom of heaven'.) (It was Elizabeth Bergner, in any case, who when asked whether Barrie had written a play for her, replied in an 'awed whisper': 'God wrote it for him').

1–Not traced.
2–Tennyson, 'The Charge of the Light Brigade', l. 12: 'Someone had blundered.'

Still I am not happy about Emily being becalmed in Boston between the Perkins's, and Miss Ware (!) and so near to her mother. And somehow I don't feel that Dr Perkins, that loveable schoolboy, is any too good for her either, intellectually. Emily has such respect for her elder relatives that one dare not do anything about it. If you could inveigle her out west, it would help.

I hope that next year will bring you a more lucrative job – even enabling you to take your holidays in France, as a teacher of that language should. May I meet you in the Luxembourg Gardens early in the summer.

At 11.15, I indite my greetings for the New Year.

Tom

I will look out for a good post card for you, from time to time.

TO *Ruthven Todd* CC

31 December 1935   [*The Criterion*]

Dear Mr Todd,

In reply to your undated letter I think it would be best if you would let me see such of the translations as you have available, so that I may form my own opinion.[1] At the same time it is only fair to say in advance that I think the prospects for a book of this kind would not be bright. Possibly there would be more interest in an anthology of Surrealist poets if there are enough others besides Eluard who are good enough to anthologise. But if you let me have some Eluard poems I will bring the matter up before my Committee. I am sorry to say that I have no acquaintance with Eluard's poetry in French.[2]

I have kept you in mind for possible reviewing since receiving your previous letter.[3]

Yours sincerely,
[T. S. Eliot]

1–Todd (Edinburgh) offered a volume of translations from the work of Paul Eluard on which he was at work. 'I think that Paul Eluard is the best poet in the surrealist movement, (in spite of the fact that I did some of the translations in David Gascoyne's recent book) and I know that Herbert Read agrees with me.'
2–Paul Eluard (1895–1952): poet and surrealist.
3–Todd had recently lost a job and needed some reviewing to keep him going: he had good experience of writing for the *Scottish Bookman* (of which he had been assistant editor), *NEW*, and the *Morning Post*; his poems had been published in outlets including the *Westminster Anthology*; and he knew about subjects including poetry and art, and surrealism.

31 December 1935   Faber & Faber Ltd

Dear Bonamy,

Yes, YES, I shall be delighted to join a family party (Frank Flint, who came in on Christmas Eve, quite alive, and looking healthier and saner than I have seen him for years, having had the booze drained out of him by 9 weeks in hospital, said I pronounce *fambly*, but that it is just a gesture of superiority) on Saturday the 11th for the panto, if you & yr. fambly will join me for lunch somewhere beforehand – if there is a chop-house in London of sufficient dignity to entertain – divine Zenocrate[1] – I mean a Young Lady of the presence of Georgina: perhaps you can make a suggestion. Well.

I am eager to see you, and hope that your digestion has not been ruined and may your Wad of Greenbacks have increased. I have to mention that my fambly in various parts has been much affected by your courtesy to ~~them~~ it: one of them refers to you as a parfit gentil knight, with a query about the spelling. I only regret that you were not able to see under the proper conditions Mrs Sheffield, who, as I have elsewhere remarked, is the most intelligent woman in America barring Marianne Moore.[2]

1–Christopher Marlowe, *Tamburlaine the Great*, Part 2, II. iv.: 'To entertain divine Zenocrate'.

2–Ada Eliot Sheffield (1869–1943): eldest of the seven Eliot children; author of *The Social Case History: Its Construction and Content* (1920) and *Social Insight in Case Situations* (1937). TSE considered her 'a very exceptional woman' – the Mycroft to his Holmes – and 'an authority on Organized Philanthrophy'. FVM informed Helen Gardner, in 1978: 'she and he, when he was a child, had the habit of communicating with each other, as they sat on the steps of their home in St Louis, in lengthy and happy communications by rhythms. Throughout life Tom relied on Ada's understanding.' TSE told JDH, 20 Feb. 1943: 'Being nearly twenty years older than I, and having no children of her own, she came to occupy a quasi-parental relation with me (my mother would be 100 this year!) Also she and I have always had more in common than with the rest of our family. She has far more brains than any of the others, and with my grandfather's organising and executive ability combined a more reflective mind, and a capacity of abstraction, coming from the other side of the family. Without being "masculine" in any way to suggest psychological distortion, she has a capacity for impersonal thought, and for detaching herself from emotion and prejudice, which I have never found in any other member of her sex. So I have always felt a tacit understanding with her, and a more satisfactory relationship, than I have ever found in those of either excitement or friendship with women – in the long run' (King's).

Yours etc. et je vous (pluriel) envoie mes voeux fervents pour la bonne année

T.

P.S. When you next visit me in my eyrie at Russell Sq. I shall be able to show you a photograph of the portrait of the Revd Charles Chauncy D.D., Fellow of Trinity College and Tutor of Hebrew in the University of Cambridge, and second President of Harvard. A Schismatic. Original in the common Room of Dunster, Cambridge (Mass.).[1]

P.S. I am not quite confident that I know how to pronounce C O L N E. It should just not quite rhyme with bone, shouldn't it?

TO *Polly Tandy*   TS BL

31 December 1935   Faber & Faber Ltd

O Pollytandy Pollytandy O[2]:

This is very sad. I do not mean the pest of measles, rougeole etc. so much because I gather that these scourges have afflicted the prospective guests rather than the immediate fambly, no, what I mourn is that I have just promised to go on Saturday the 11th January to the panto with the Dobrée fambly, so I can't help hoping that the projected Party will have to be postponed another week irksome as that will be. If another date is arranged I will come annointed <anointed> with lavender soap till it runs down to the hemb of my garment. What about halibut liver oil for Anthea. Capsules.

dejectedly
Possum

With best wishes for the New Year to the Licensee of the Bell

TO *Donald Brace*   CC

31 December 1935   [Faber & Faber Ltd]

My dear Brace,

I am sending you under separate cover all of the material for the collected volume of verse with the exception of one poem which is

1–Charles Chauncy (1592–1672), nonconformist divine, succeeded Henry Dunster as President of Harvard.
2–Cf. this verse of the ballad *Danny Boy* (1910), by Frederic Weatherley, sung to the tune of the 'Londonderry Air' – 'Oh Danny boy, O Danny boy, I love you so' – adopted by the Irish.

unfinished, and which I will forward if I can finish it within the next fortnight.[1] This poem would come at the end in any case. I am inclosing a copy of *Poems 1909–1925* in order to call attention to a few misprints and one omitted epigraph. I also enclose a copy of *The Rock* marked to show what choruses I want to include. I can't send a printed copy of *Marina* because it is out of print, so I am sending a typed copy instead.

The only question not quite cleared up is that of *Ash Wednesday*, but Morley anticipates no difficulty over this.

I am sorry about the contretemps with Elmer Rice, which is nobody's fault.[2] I fear it may put an end to the prospect of a professional production with the English company, but we must make the best of a bad job.[3]

Yours ever sincerely,

[T. S. Eliot]

---

1 – 'Burnt Norton'.

FVM had written to Brace on 6 Dec. 1935: 'Eliot had hoped to produce the text of the Collected Poems by the end of December; he now swears to have the collection complete by the middle of January; and has cabled you to that effect.'

2 – Brace had reported on 14 Dec. that, in advance of TSE's agreement with Ashley Dukes for licensing performances, Harcourt, Brace had agreed terms with Yale University ($35) and with a number of other out-of-town amateur productions. 'We also have negotiations under way with Elmer Rice, who is Regional Director for New York of the Federal Theatre Project. This is a government relief project, and after some enquiry from friends who are professional producers, we have quoted a fee of $50 a week.' On 18 Dec. he cabled TSE that the Federal Theatre Project had already accepted the terms proposed, and indeed had started preparing their production. Although TSE immediately cabled back, 'THINK NEW YORK PRODUCTION MURDER INADVISABLE AT PRESENT STOP LONDON COMPANY MAY COME OVER STOP DUKES ARRIVING LAFAYETTE JANUARY SIXTEENTH WILL SEE YOU IMMEDIATELY STOP MEANWHILE NO OBJECTION OUTTOWN PERFORMANCES', Brace declared that permission had already been promised to Elmer Rice's organisation, which was for the benefit of unemployed actors. Both Brace and Rice assured TSE that the Federal Theater production could not possibly damage the prospects of a fully professional production in New York City. Dukes reassured TSE in a letter of 30 Dec. that no one had blundered; using a phrase taken from TSE's very play, he added: 'It just happened that Harcourt Brace did the wrong deed for the right reason.' The Federal Theater production of *MiC*, directed by Edward Goodman, would duly open at the Manhattan Theatre in Jan. 1936.

3 – Cf. *The Cocktail Party*:
> EDWARD
> Lavinia, we must make the best of a bad job.
> That is what he means.
> REILLY
> When you find, Mr Chamberlayne,
> The best of a bad job is all any of us make of it –

UPUC, 45: 'in poetry as in life our business is to make the best of a bad job'; *The Family Reunion*: 'The making the best of a bad job.' Cf. *Dry Salvages* V: 'For most of us, this is the aim / Never here to be realised; / Who are only undefeated / Because we have gone on trying . . .'

BIOGRAPHICAL REGISTER

W. H. Auden (1907–73), poet, playwright, librettist, translator, essayist and editor. He was educated at Gresham's School, Holt, Norfolk, and at Christ Church, Oxford, where he co-edited *Oxford Poetry* (1926, 1927), and where his friend Stephen Spender hand-set about thirty copies of his first book, a pamphlet entitled *Poems* (1928). After going down from Oxford with a third-class degree in English in 1928, he visited Belgium and then lived for a year in Berlin. He worked as a tutor in London, 1929–30; then as a schoolmaster at Larchfield Academy Helensburgh, Dunbartonshire, 1930–2; followed by the Downs School, Colwall, Herefordshire, 1932–5. Although Eliot turned down his initial submission of a book of poems in 1927, he would presently accept 'Paid on Both Sides: A Charade' for the *Criterion*; and Eliot went on for the rest of his life to publish all of Auden's books at Faber & Faber: *Poems* (featuring 'Paid on Both Sides' and thirty short poems, 1930); *The Orators* (1932); *Look, Stranger!* (1937); *Spain* (1936); *Another Time* (1940); *New Year Letter* (1941; published in the USA as *The Double Man*); *The Age of Anxiety* (1947); *For the Time Being* (1945); *The Age of Anxiety: A Baroque Eclogue* (1948); *Nones* (1952); *The Shield of Achilles* (1955); *Homage to Clio* (1960); *About the House* (1966). Eliot was happy too to publish Auden's play *The Dance of Death* (1933), which was performed by the Group Theatre in 1934 and 1935; and three further plays written with Christopher Isherwood: *The Dog Beneath the Skin* (1935), which would be performed by the Group Theatre in 1936; *The Ascent of F6* (1936); and *On the Frontier* (1937). In 1935–6 Auden went to work for the General Post Office film unit, writing verse commentaries for two celebrated documentary films, *Coal Face* and *Night Mail*. He collaborated with Louis MacNeice on *Letters from Iceland* (1937); and with Isherwood again on *Journey to a War* (1939). His first libretto was *Paul Bunyan* (performed with music by Benjamin Britten, 1941); and in 1947 he began collaborating with Igor Stravinsky on *The Rake's Progress* (performed in Venice, 1951); and he co-wrote two librettos for Hans Werner Henze. Other works include *The Oxford Book of Light Verse* (1938); *The Enchafed Flood: The Romantic Iconography* *of the Sea* (1951); *The Dyer's Hand* (1963); *Secondary Worlds* (1968). Cyril Connolly, 'Poet and privacy', *Sunday Times*, 18 Aug. 1974 (on T. S. Matthews's *Great Tom: Notes towards the definition of T. S. Eliot*): 'Auden told me that he got on particularly well with Eliot because he knew how to tease him and there were very few people who dared. Great men like to be teased as large predators like to be scratched.' Humphrey Carpenter, *W. H. Auden: A Biography* (1981); Richard Davenport-Hines, *Auden* (1995); Edward Mendelson, *Early Auden* (1981), *Later Auden* (1999); David Collard, 'More worthy than Lark: a television tribute to T. S. Eliot, by W. H. Auden and others', *TLS*, 9 Mar. 2012, 14.

George Barker (1913–91), poet and author. Works include *Poems* (1933), *Calamiterror* (1937), *The True Confession of George Barker* (1950), and *Collected Poems*, ed. Robert Fraser (1987). With support from TSE, he became Professor of English Literature, Tohoku University, Sendai, Japan, 1939–40. His liaison with Elizabeth Smart is memorialised in her novel *By Grand Central Station I Sat Down and Wept* (1945). TSE wrote to the University of Durham (where Barker had applied for a lectureship in English Literature), 14 May 1936: 'He is one of a very small number of younger poets whose work I consider important: I have been concerned with it both as editor and as publisher. His prose, both imaginative and critical, is also of great interest and merit. I believe that he has a wide knowledge of English poetry and some experience of lecturing; and I am sure that he would not fail to make any subject in which he lectured, interesting and stimulating to his pupils.' To H. G. Wayment, British Council, Nov. 1945: 'I have your letter of the 13th November about the application of Mr George Barker for the Byron Chair of English at Athens and the Chair of British History and Institutions at Salonica. I am afraid that I can only speak of Mr Barker in his capacity as a poet, of which, of course, I have a very high opinion. I have known him for some years and find him also a very charming and agreeable person.'

Barker told EVE, 5 Jan. 1965: '[TSE] was kind to me, as he was, I know, to many others. Most of all I think of the constant help he gave to me in matters of circumstance when I was young. If it had not been for him, I would not (to speak too much of myself) have had a chance.' Robert Fraser adds: 'As the years passed, he would weave anecdotes portraying his erstwhile mentor as lounge lizard, footpad, Sweeney, nightbird, Mr Hyde. Eliot, he would grow accustomed to relating, had worn green eye-shadow. He had prowled the back streets of London after hours dressed as a policeman. He had kept a secret *pied à terre* in the Charing Cross

Road, visitors to which were obliged to ask the porter for "the Captain".'
(Fraser's source was Barker himself, 10 Oct. 1981.) See further Barker,
'A Note for T. S. Eliot', *New English Weekly*, 11: 3 (Mar. 1949), 188–92;
Robert Fraser, *The Chameleon Poet: A Life of George Barker* (2001).

Montgomery ('Monty') Belgion (1892–1973), author, was born in Paris of
British parents and grew up with a deep feeling for the language and culture
of France. In 1915–16 he was editor-in-charge of the European edition of
the *New York Herald*; and for the remainder of WW1 he served first in the
Honourable Artillery Company, 1916–18, and then was commissioned
in the Dorsetshire Regiment. Between the wars he worked for the Paris
review *This Quarter* and for newspapers including the *Daily Mail* and
Daily Mirror, and for a while he was an editor for Harcourt, Brace & Co.,
New York. In WW2 he was a captain in the Royal Engineers, and spent
two years in prison camps in Germany. In 1929 Faber & Faber brought
out (on TSE's recommendation) *Our Present Philosophy of Life*. Later
works include *Reading for Profit* (1945) and booklets on H. G. Wells and
David Hume. See further Belgion, 'T. S. Eliot edited "The Criterion"',
Monday World: The magazine of the radical right (Summer 1972), 7–8;
Jason Harding, *'The Criterion': Cultural Politics and Periodical Networks
in Inter-War Britain* (2002), 143–58.

Serge (Sergius) Bolshakoff (1901–90), Russian-born ecumenist; educated
in St Petersburg and in Tartu, Estonia, he lived for a while in France and
then in England, 1928–51, where he resided for his first ten years at the
Anglican Benedictine community of Nashdom, at Burnham in Berkshire.
An oblate rather than a monk, he committed his extraordinary personal
energies to working towards an Anglican–Orthodox rapprochement: he
set up an International Academy of Christian Sociologists: a confraternity
with the object of Christian unity. His publications include *The Christian
Church and the Soviet Union* (1942), *The Foreign Missions of the
Russian Orthodox Church* (1943) and *Russian Mystics* (1976). On 14
Dec. 1933 V. A. Demant asked TSE, in confidence: 'Sergius Bolshakoff
tells me that you are standing in with him over some project to form a
Christian International, and he has for a long time worried me to come
in too. I should be very grateful if you are able to tell me what you really
think about him and his project. I understand him to be an able man
with a most synthetic philosophy, but frequent requests to expound it
have brought only enthusiastic proposal for a strong movement to express
it. So, frankly, I am a little suspicious that he may be little else than an

unconscious charlatan. I am putting it at its strongest, and I shall be glad if you can tell me that you think differently.' TSE seems to have replied to Demant's enquiry in a (now lost) letter dated 15 Dec. – 'I find from other sources', wrote Demant (16 Dec.), 'that Bolshakoff has told a number of people that others have accepted his invitation, including myself, who have declined' – and thereafter TSE tended wisely to hold himself at a distance from Bolshakoff's project.

E. (Elliott) Martin Browne (1900–80), theatre director, read history and theology at Christ Church, Oxford, before working for the British Drama League and the Adult Education Movement; he then went to the USA as Assistant Professor of Speech and Drama at the Carnegie Institute of Technology, Pittsburgh, 1927–30, before being appointed in 1930, by Bishop George Bell, as Director of Religious Drama for the diocese of Chichester. He collaborated with TSE on *The Rock* (to raise funds for London churches), which was produced at Sadler's Wells Theatre, 28 May–9 June 1934; and thereafter he directed all of TSE's plays: see his *The Making of T. S. Eliot's Plays* (1969). He was director of a touring company called the Pilgrim Players, 1939–49; Director of the British Drama League (affording help to amateur productions), 1948–57; and in 1951 he directed the first revival since 1572 of the medieval cycle of York Mystery Plays. He was Visiting Professor of Religious Drama at Union Theological College, New York, 1956–62; Drama Advisor to Coventry Cathedral, 1962–5; and in 1967–8 he directed plays at the Yvonne Arnaud Theatre, Guildford. Appointed CBE in 1952. His first wife was the actress Henzie Raeburn (1901–73).

Marguerite Caetani, née Chapin (1880–1963) – born in New London, Connecticut, she was half-sister to Mrs Katherine Biddle, and a cousin of TSE – was married in 1911 to the composer Roffredo Caetani, 17th Duke of Sermoneta and Prince di Bassiano (a godson of Lizst), whose ancestors included two Popes (one of whom had the distinction of being put in Hell by Dante). A patron of the arts, she founded in Paris the review *Commerce* – the title being taken from a line in St-John Perse's *Anabase* (*'ce pur commerce de mon âme'*) – see Sophie Levie, *La rivista Commerce e il ruolo di Marguerite Caetani nella letteratura europea 1924–1932* (1985); and then, in Rome, *Botteghe oscure*, 1949–60, a biannual review featuring poetry and fiction from many nations – England, Germany, Italy, France, Spain, USA – with contributions published in their original languages. Contributors included André Malraux, Albert Camus, Paul

Valéry, Robert Graves, E. E. Cummings, Marianne Moore. See too a profile of Caetani: 'Patron of the Arts', *The Times*, 21 Jan. 1959.

Alistair (Alfred) Cooke (1908–2004), broadcaster and writer, was brought up in Salford, Lancashire, and read English at Jesus College, Cambridge – where he founded the Mummers, the university's first dramatic group to admit women, and contributed to *Granta,* which in due course he also edited. From Cambridge he went in 1932 to the USA on a Commonwealth Fund fellowship which enabled him to study theatre at Yale and linguistics at Harvard. (He had long nurtured a passion for all things American including jazz music.) During his travels, he interviewed *inter alia* Charlie Chaplin, who hired him as a scriptwriter for a film about Napoleon that was never completed. From the mid-1930s, back in London, he made shift to begin a career with the BBC, while also working for the American network NBC on a London letter that was broadcast to New York every Sunday. In later years he wrote a great deal for the *Manchester Guardian*; and in 1946 he essayed a short series of radio talks entitled *Letter from America* which eventuated in a record run of fifty-eight years. In the 1970s he became ever more famous with a TV series entitled *Alistair Cooke's America* – the accompanying book sold two million copies – and a series on American music. Having taken US citizenship in 1941, he was made honorary KBE in 1973. See Nick Clarke, *Alistair Cooke: The Biography* (1999).

Martin D'Arcy (1888–1976), Jesuit priest and theologian, entered the novitiate in 1906, took a first in Literae Humaniores at Pope's Hall – the Jesuit private hall of Oxford University – and was ordained in 1921. After teaching at Stonyhurst College, in 1925 he undertook doctoral research, first at the Gregorian University in Rome, then at the Jesuit House at Farm Street, London. In 1927 he returned to Campion Hall (successor to Pope's Hall), where he taught philosophy at the university. He was Rector and Master of Campion Hall, 1933–45; Provincial of the British Province of the Jesuits in London, 1945–50. Charismatic and influential as a lecturer, and as an apologist for Roman Catholicism (his prominent converts included Evelyn Waugh), he also wrote studies including *The Nature of Belief* (1931) and *The Mind and Heart of Love* (1945). Lesley Higgins notes: 'Five of his books were reviewed in *The Criterion*, some by Eliot himself; his twenty-two reviews and articles in the latter certainly qualify him as part of what Eliot termed the journal's "definite . . . [and] comprehensive constellation of contributors".' See further H. J. A. Sire,

Father Martin D'Arcy: Philosopher of Christian Love (1997); Richard Harp, 'A conjuror at the Xmas party', *TLS*, 11 Dec. 2009, 13–15.

Christopher Dawson (1889–1970), cultural historian. An independent and erudite scholar of private means (he would inherit estates in Yorkshire on the death of his father in 1933), he taught for a while, part-time, at the University College of Exeter, 1925–33; and, though not a professional academic, was ultimately appointed at the good age of sixty-eight to a chair in Roman Catholic Studies at Harvard, 1958–62. A convert to Roman Catholicism, he devoted much of his research to the idea of religion as the driver of social culture. His works include *Progress and Religion* (1929), *The Making of Europe* (1932), and *Religion and the Rise of Western Culture* (1950); as well as a series entitled *Essays in Order* which he edited from the 1930s for the Catholic publishers Sheed and Ward: his own contributions were *Enquiries into Religion and Culture* (1934), *Medieval Religion* (1934), *The Judgement of Nations* (1943). For TSE he wrote Criterion Miscellany pamphlet no. 13: *Christianity and Sex* (1930). See Christina Scott – Dawson's daughter – *An Historian and His World: A Life of Christopher Dawson 1889–1970* (1984); Bradley H. Birzer, *Sanctifying the World: The Augustinian Life and Mind of Christopher Dawson* (2007); James R. Lothian, *The Making and Unmaking of the English Catholic Intellectual Community, 1910–1950* (2009); Christopher McVey, 'Backgrounds to *The Idea of a Christian Society*: Charles Maurras, Christopher Dawson, and Jacques Maritain', and Benjamin G. Lockerd, 'T. S. Eliot and Christopher Dawson on Religion and Culture', both in *T. S. Eliot and Christian Tradition*, ed. Benjamin G. Lockerd (2014). See too Dawson, 'Mr T. S. Eliot and the Meaning of Culture', *The Month* ns 1: 3 (Mar. 1949), 151–7.

Vigo Auguste Demant (1893–1983) trained as an engineer but embraced a wholly different career when he converted to Anglicanism and became a deacon in 1919, priest in 1920. Following various curacies, he became, while working at St Silas, Kentish Town, London, Director of Research for the Christian Social Council – the Council of Churches in England for Social Questions – 1929–33. As noted in the *ODNB*, he was 'the major theoretician in the Christendom Group of Anglican Catholic thinkers, whose concern was to establish the centrality of what they termed "Christian sociology", an analysis of society fundamentally rooted in a Catholic and incarnational theology'. The group's quarterly, *Christendom*, ran from 1931 to 1950. He was vicar of St John-the-

Divine, Richmond, Surrey, 1933–42; Canon Residentiary, St Paul's Cathedral, 1942–9; and Canon of Christ Church and Regius Professor of Moral and Pastoral Theology, Oxford, 1949–71. Works include *This Unemployment: Disaster or Opportunity?* (1931), *God, Man and Society* (1933), *Christian Polity* (1936) and *The Religious Prospect* (1939). On 8 Aug. 1940 TSE was to write this unsolicited recommendation to Sir Stephen Gaselee (Foreign Office): 'My friend the Reverend V. A. Demant, whom I have been associated with intellectually for some years, has been recommended by the Bishop of Bath and Wells for a vacant canonry at Westminster. Demant is, in my opinion, one of the most brilliant, or perhaps the most brilliant, of the younger theologians in England, and I also consider him thoroughly sound both in theology and politics. His book, *The Religious Prospect,* was one of the very few important books of last year. He is a very conscientious parish priest, with a large straggling parish in Richmond, and if he is to make the most of his gifts and do what he should do for Anglican theology in the future, he ought to be freed from this routine.' Demant remarked at the Requiem Mass for TSE at St Stephen's Church, 17 Feb. 1965: 'The Revd Frank Hillier, to whom Eliot used to go for confession and spiritual direction after the death of Father Philip Bacon [at St Simon's, Kentish Town], writes to me: "Eliot had, along with that full grown stature of mind, a truly child-like heart – the result of his sense of dependence on GOD. And along with it he had the sense of responsibility to GOD for the use of his talents. To his refinedness of character is due the fact that like his poetry he himself was not easily understood – but unbelievers always recognized his faith"' (*St Stephen's Church Magazine,* Apr. 1965, 9).

Bonamy Dobrée (1891–1974), scholar and critic, was Professor of English Literature at Leeds University, 1936–55. After service in the army during WWI (he was twice mentioned in despatches and attained the rank of major), he read English at Christ's College, Cambridge, and taught in London and as a professor of English at the Egyptian University, Cairo, 1925–9. His works include *Restoration Comedy* (1924), *Essays in Biography* (1925), *Restoration Tragedy, 1660–1720* (1929), *Alexander Pope* (1951). On 8 Sept. 1938, TSE would write to George Every, SSM, on the subject of the 'Moot': 'I think [Dobrée] would be worth having . . . He has his nose to the grindstone of the provincial university machine . . . but he is not without perception of the futilities of contemporary education. His mental formation is Liberal, but he has the rare advantage of being a man of breeding, so that his instincts with regard, for instance, to society, the community and the land, are likely to be right. He is also a person of strong, and I imagine hereditary, public spirit.' In Feb. 1963, TSE urged his merits as future editor of Kipling's stories: 'He is far and away the best authority on Kipling . . . I have often discussed Kipling with him, and know that we see eye to eye about the stories. As for Dobrée's general literary achievements, they are very high indeed: his published work is not only very scholarly, but of the highest critical standing, and he writes well . . . If this job is ever done – and I should like to see it done during my lifetime – Dobrée is the man to do it.' See also Jason Harding, *The 'Criterion': Cultural Politics and Periodical Networks in Inter-War Britain* (2002).

Rupert Doone (1903–66), dancer, choreographer, producer, founded the Group Theatre, London, in 1932. See obituary by Tyrone Guthrie and John Moody in *The Times*, 8 Mar. 1966. Browne (*Making*, 38) thought Doone 'one of the most intriguing personalities of the theatre of the 'thirties. He came from a Worcestershire family in humble circumstances but with a background which included a link with the Shakespeares and which accounts for his range of intellectual and artistic interests. Leaving home at sixteen he became, through many struggles and privations, a ballet dancer, and finally rose to the most coveted position in that profession – premier danseur in the Diaghileff company. But only for a few weeks: the great impresario died in the same year, 1929.

'Doone left the ballet to enter a new field: he went to the Festival Theatre, Cambridge, where Tyrone Guthrie was working with Anmer Hall [Alderson Burrell Horne (1863–1953): theatre manager and owner, producer, actor; proprietor of the Westminster Theatre, 1931–46], to learn acting and production. This was typical of his endlessly questing mind; and there, as before in the ballet, he found natural friendship with the most imaginative artists of the day. From a play-reading circle at Cambridge there developed the Group Theatre.

'Within a year the Group has its own rooms on the top floor of a building in Great Newport Street . . . Its purpose was the synthesis of all the elements of theatre – movement, mime, rhythm, speech and design – the "total theatre" of which we have heard so much since then. Doone associated with himself such artists (then hardly known to fame) as Benjamin Britten, Brian Easdaile, John Piper, Henry Moore. The reputation of his seasons rests on the series of original plays he produced between 1934 and 1939, by such writers as W. H. Auden and Christopher Isherwood, Louis MacNeice, Stephen Spender and, to begin with, T. S. Eliot.'

See further Robert Medley, *Drawn from the Life: A Memoir* (1983); Michael J. Sidnell, *Dances of Death: The Group Theatre of London in the Thirties* (1984).

Henry Ware Eliot, Jr (1879–1947), TSE's elder brother, went to school at Smith Academy, and then passed two years at Washington University, St Louis, before progressing to Harvard. At Harvard, he displayed a gift for light verse in *Harvard Celebrities* (1901), illustrated with 'Caricatures and Decorative Drawings' by two fellow undergraduates. After graduating, he spent a year at law school, but subsequently followed a career in printing, publishing and advertising. He attained a partnership in Husband & Thomas (later the Buchen Company), a Chicago advertising agency, from 1917 to 1929, during which time he gave financial assistance to TSE and regularly advised him on investments. He accompanied their mother on her visit to London in the summer of 1921, his first trip away from the USA. In February 1926, he married Theresa Anne Garrett (1884–1981). It was not until late in life that he found his true calling, as a Research Fellow in Near Eastern Archaeology at the Peabody Museum, Harvard, where his principal publication was a discussion of the prehistoric chronology of northern Mesopotamia, together with a description of the pottery from Kudish Saghir (1939): see too his posthumous publication *Excavations in Mesopotamia and Western Iran: Sites of 4000 – 500 B.C.: Graphic Analyses* (1950), prefaced by Lauriston Ward: 'It was a labor of love, of such magnitude as to be practically unique in the annals of archaeology . . . a monument to his scholarship and devotion . . . Eliot had all the qualities of the true scholar, which include modesty as well as ability.' In 1932 he published a detective novel, *The Rumble Murders*, under the pseudonym Mason Deal. He was instrumental in building up the T. S. Eliot collection at Eliot House (Houghton Library). Of slighter build than his brother – who noted his 'Fred Astaire figure' – Henry suffered from deafness owing to scarlet fever as a child, and this may have contributed to his diffidence. It was with his dear brother in mind that TSE wrote: 'The notion of some infinitely gentle / Infinitely suffering thing' ('Preludes' IV).

Vivien Eliot, née Haigh-Wood (1888–1947). Born in Bury, Lancashire, on 28 May 1888, 'Vivy' was brought up in Hampstead from the age of three. After meeting TSE in company with Scofield Thayer in Oxford early in 1915, she and TSE hastened to be married just a few weeks later, on 26 June 1915. (TSE, who was lodging at 35 Greek Street, London, was recorded in the marriage certificate as 'of no occupation'.) She developed close friendships with Mary Hutchinson, Ottoline Morrell and others in TSE's circle. Despite chronic personal and medical difficulties, they remained together until 1933, when TSE resolved to separate from her following his academic year in America. She was never to be reconciled to the separation, became increasingly ill, and in 1938 was confined to a psychiatric hospital, where she died (of 'syncope' and 'cardiovascular degeneration') on 22 January 1947. She is the dedicatee of *Ash-Wednesday* (1930). She published sketches in the *Criterion* (under pseudonyms with the initials 'F. M.'), and collaborated on the *Criterion*. See Michael Karwoski, 'The Bride from Bury', *Lancashire Life*, Mar. 1984, 52–3; Carole Seymour-Jones, *Painted Shadow: The Life of Vivienne Eliot* (2001); Ken Craven, *The Victorian Painter and the Poet's Wife: A biography of the Haigh-Wood Family* (e-book, 2012); Robert Crawford, *Young Eliot: From St Louis to 'The Waste Land'* (2015).

Geoffrey Faber (1889–1961), publisher and poet, was educated at Malvern College and Christ Church, Oxford, where he took a double first in Classical Moderations (1910) and Literae Humaniores (1912). He was called to the Bar by the Inner Temple (1921), though he was never to practise law. In 1919 he was elected a prize fellow of All Souls College, Oxford, which he went on to serve in the capacity of Estates Bursar, 1923–51. Before WW1 – in which he served with the London Regiment (Post Office Rifles), seeing action in France and Belgium – he spent eighteen months as assistant to Humphrey Milford, publisher of Oxford University Press. After the war he passed three years working for Strong & Co., brewers (there was a family connection), before going in for publishing on a full-time basis by joining forces with his All Souls colleague Maurice Gwyer and his wife, Lady Alsina Gwyer, who were trying to run a specialised imprint called the Scientific Press that Lady Gwyer had inherited from her father, Sir Henry Burdett: its weekly journal, the *Nursing Mirror*, was their most successful production. Following protractedly difficult negotiations, in 1925 Faber became chair of their restructured general publishing house, which was provisionally styled Faber & Gwyer. After being introduced by Charles Whibley to TSE, Faber was so impressed by the personality and aptitude of the 37-year-old American that he chose both to take on the running of the *Criterion* and to appoint Eliot to the board of his company (Eliot's *Poems 1909–1925* was one of the first books to be put out by the new imprint, and the firm's first best-seller), which was relocated from Southampton Row to 24 Russell Square. By 1929 both the Gwyers and the *Nursing Mirror* were disposed of to advantage, and the firm took final shape as Faber & Faber, with Richard de la Mare and two additional Americans, Frank Morley and Morley Kennerley, joining the board. Faber chaired the Publishers' Association, 1939–41 – campaigning successfully for the repeal of a wartime tax on books – and helping to set up the National Book League. He was knighted in 1954, and gave up the chairmanship of Faber & Faber in 1960. His publications as poet include *The Buried Stream* (1941), and his works of non-fiction were *Oxford Apostles* (1933), *Jowett* (1957), and an edition of the works of John Gay (1926). In 1920 he married Enid Richards, with whom he had two sons and a daughter.

John Garrett (1902–66), pioneering schoolmaster, read history at Oxford. Head of English at Whitgift School, 1931–5, he was then appointed head-master of a new county secondary school at Raynes Park in Surrey, where he galvanised the curriculum, recruited talented teachers, stimulated imaginations, and invited figures from the arts – including TSE, Benjamin Britten, Louis MacNeice, Stephen Spender – to address the school. By 1942 Raynes Park School was deemed one of the best schools in the UK. He was head of Bristol Grammar School, 1942–60.

Maurice Haigh-Wood (1896–1980): TSE's brother-in-law. He was eight years younger than his sister Vivien, and after attending Ovingdean prep school and Malvern School, trained at Sandhurst Military Academy before receiving his commission on 11 May 1915 as a second lieutenant in the Manchester Regiment. He served in the infantry for the rest of the war, and on regular visits home gave TSE his closest contact with the nightmare of life and death in the trenches. After the war, he found it difficult to get himself established, but became a stockbroker, and he remained friendly with, and respectful towards, TSE even after his separation from Vivien in 1933. In September 1968 he told Robert Sencourt – as he related in a letter to Valerie Eliot (2 Sept. 1968) – 'I had the greatest admiration & love for Tom whom I regarded as my elder brother for fifty years, & I would never think of acting against his wishes.' In 1930 he married a 25-year-old American dancer, Ahmé Hoagland, and they had two children.

Emily Hale (1891–1969) came from a similar Bostonian milieu to the Eliot family. Her father was an architect turned Unitarian preacher who taught at Harvard Divinity School, and her uncle was a music critic for the *Boston Herald*. Eliot met Emily at the home of his cousin Eleanor Hinkley in 1912, and in an unpublished memoir wrote that he fell in love with her before leaving for Europe in 1914. However, after his marriage in 1915, he did not see her again for many years. Although she did not go to college, a fact which handicapped her career, Emily was a passionate theatre-goer, amateur actor and director, and was to forge a career as a drama teacher. In 1921 she took a post as administrator and drama tutor at Milwaukee-Downer College, a private women's school, and later taught at Scripps College, Smith College, Concord Academy, and Abbott Academy. During the 1930s and 1940s, Eliot once again took up his relationship with her, and they saw a lot of one another both in England, where they visited Burnt Norton together in 1934–5, and during his trips to the USA. She half-joked to her students at Scripps, 'Emily Hale speaks only to Eliot, and Eliot speaks only to God.' However, following Vivien's death in 1947, Emily was disappointed that Eliot did not want to marry her, and there was a cooling of their friendship. According to Emily's account (in a letter to a friend, 7 August 1947), Eliot had given her to understand that his love was 'not in the way usual to men less gifted i.e. with complete love through a married relationship': she registered this as an 'abnormal reaction'. However, W. F. Tomlin recounted – this is a report of what he said that Theresa Eliot told him – that HWE had been categorical in his attitude towards the relationship: 'Tom has made one mistake, and if he marries Emily he will make another.' Towards the end of his life Eliot ordered her letters to him to be destroyed, while she deposited his letters to her at Princeton University, where they are sealed until 2020. See Lyndall Gordon, *T. S. Eliot: An Imperfect Life* (1998); Robert Crawford, *Young Eliot: From St Louis to 'The Waste Land'* (2015).

A. Desmond Hawkins (1908–99), novelist, critic and broadcaster, worked in the 1930s as literary editor of the *New English Weekly*, then of the quarterly *Purpose* (where TSE persuaded the owner–editor to allow Hawkins a free hand), and as regular fiction reviewer for the *Criterion*. In 1946 he became Features Producer, BBC West Region, and Head of Programmes in 1955. He founded the BBC Natural History Unit in 1959. Works include *Poetry and Prose of John Donne* (1938), *The BBC Naturalist* (1957), *Hardy the Novelist* (1965), *When I Was* (autobiog., 1989). TSE wrote to the British Council, 31 May 1940: 'I have known Mr. A. Desmond Hawkins for a number of years, ever since he began his literary career, and I have a very high opinion of his ability and of his character. I am happy to regard him as a personal friend, as well as a valued contributor in the past on *The Criterion*, which I edited. He writes admirably both imaginative and critical prose, has keen sensibility and distinguished intelligence, a good knowledge and exceptional critical appreciation of English literature. I believe also that his combination of intellectual gifts, character and personal charm make him very well qualified to fill with success a post in a foreign country.' And to the General Establishment Officer, BBC, 17 Jan. 1942: 'I have no hesitation in recommending Mr Desmond Hawkins. I have known him well for a number of years; he was one of a small number of people whom I most relied on for regular collaboration in *The Criterion*; and I have a high opinion of his intellect and his character. I recommend him warmly.'

John Hayward (1905–65), editor, critic, anthologist, read modern languages at King's College, Cambridge. Despite the early onset of muscular dystrophy, he became a prolific and eminent critic and editor, bringing out in quick succession editions of the works of Rochester, Saint-Évremond, Jonathan Swift, Robert Herrick and Samuel Johnson. Other publications included *Complete Poems and Selected Prose of John Donne* (1929), *Donne* (1950), *T. S. Eliot: Selected Prose* (1953), *The Penguin Book of English Verse* (1958), and *The Oxford Book of Nineteenth Century English Verse* (1964). Celebrated as the learned and acerbic editor of *The Book Collector*, he was made a chevalier of the Légion d'honneur in 1952, a CBE in 1953. Writers including Graham Greene and Stevie Smith valued his editorial counsel; and Paul Valéry invited him to translate his comedy *Mon Faust*. Hayward advised TSE on various essays, poems, and plays including *The Cocktail Party* and *The Confidential Clerk*, and most helpfully of all on *Four Quartets*. See further Helen Gardner, *The Composition of 'Four Quartets'* (1978); John Smart, *Tarantula's Web: John Hayward, T. S. Eliot and Their Circle* (2013).

Mary Hutchinson, née Barnes (1889–1977), a half-cousin of Lytton Strachey, married St John ('Jack') Hutchinson in 1910. A prominent Bloomsbury hostess, she was for several years the acknowledged mistress of the art critic, Clive Bell, and became a close friend of TSE and VHE. TSE published one of her stories ('War') in *The Egoist*, and she later brought out a book of sketches, *Fugitive Pieces* (Hogarth Press, 1927). She wrote a brief unpublished memoir of TSE (Harry Ransom Humanities Research Center). See David Bradshaw, '"Those Extraordinary Parakeets": Clive Bell and Mary Hutchinson', *The Charleston Magazine*: 16 (Autumn/Winter 1997), 5–12; 17 (Spring/Summer 1998), 5–11; James Strachey Barnes, 'My Sister Mary', in *Half a Life* (1933), 87–93; and Nancy Hargrove,

'The Remarkable Relationship of T. S. Eliot and Mary Hutchinson', *Yeats Eliot Review* 28: 3–4 (Fall–Winter 2011), 3–15.

James Joyce (1882–1941), expatriate Irish novelist, playwright and poet. Having lived in Zurich and Trieste, he moved in 1920 to Paris, where he became a focus for expatriate writers including Pound and Stein. In *Blasting and Bombardiering* (1937), Wyndham Lewis recounts his and TSE's first encounter with Joyce there in August 1920 when bringing him a parcel of shoes. Joyce's *A Portrait of the Artist* was serialised in *The Egoist*, and *Ulysses* in the *Little Review* up to 1920. When *Ulysses* first appeared in book form in 1922, the same year as *The Waste Land*, TSE hailed it as 'the most important expression which the present age has found' – 'a book to which we are all indebted, and from which none of us can escape' ('*Ulysses*, Order and Myth', *Dial* 75: 5, Nov. 1923). TSE published in the *Criterion* a number of pieces by and about Joyce, and at Faber – which, as the present volume shows, failed at the crucial moment to secure the rights to *Ulysses* – he was responsible for the publication of *Finnegans Wake* (1939). See further *The Letters of James Joyce*, ed. Stuart Gilbert and Richard Ellmann (3 vols, 1957, 1966); Richard Ellmann, *James Joyce* (2nd edn, 1982); Kevin Birmingham, *The Most Dangerous Book: The Battle for James Joyce's 'Ulysses'* (2014).

F. R. Leavis (1895–1978), literary critic; Fellow of Downing College, Cambridge, 1927–62, Reader from 1959; founding editor of *Scrutiny*, 1932–53. His works include *New Bearings in English Poetry* (1932), *The Great Tradition* (1948), *The Common Pursuit* (1952), and *D. H. Lawrence: Novelist* (1955). See further Ian MacKillop, *F. R. Leavis: A Life in Criticism* (1995).

On 23 July 1942, TSE wrote to Sir Malcolm Robertson, British Council, to recommend a subsidy for *Scrutiny*: 'Some of us are privately not very happy when we see so many emigré periodicals cropping up mostly of dubious ephemeral value – copies are sent to me and I wonder who reads them – while it is such a struggle to keep any serious indigenous magazines alive.' To Desmond McCarthy, 14 Nov. 1947: 'I think that Leavis deserves some encouragement for having carried *Scrutiny* under considerable difficulties; for, with all its limitations and tiresomeness, it is the best academic periodical we have, and indeed almost the only serious periodical of a literary kind that is readable at all. He knows that I regard the establishment of English Schools at Oxford and Cambridge as a great mistake.' To the Revd M. Jarrett-Kerr, CR, 20 Aug. 1951: 'I have been increasingly distressed in the last year or two, to observe that Leavis is abandoning criticism in favour of invective. A great deal of his spleen takes the form of innuendos and sneers at a number of writers in passing. It is all a very great pity.'

Louis MacNeice (1907–63), brought up in Carrickfergus, was educated at Marlborough School and Oxford University. In the 1930s he taught classics at Birmingham University and Bedford College, London; and for twenty years from 1940 he worked for the BBC as writer and producer of radio features and plays. Publications include *Autumn Journal* (1939), *Solstices* (1961), *The Burning Perch* (1963); and – in collaboration with WHA – *Letters from Iceland* (1937). TSE was to write of him on 30 May 1941, to the General Establishment Officer of the BBC: 'Mr MacNeice is extremely well-known both as one of the leading poets of his generation and as a prose writer. I should certainly consider that his abilities are such as to make him a valuable addition to the staff of the British Broadcasting Corporation and very much hope that you will be able to find a place for him. He is, incidentally, a classical scholar of some distinction, and may be regarded as belonging to that rather uncommon type, the well-educated man. He has also a very distinct social charm and likeability.'

TSE wrote in *The Times*, 5 Sept. 1963: 'There is little that I can add to the encomiums of Louis MacNeice which have already appeared in the press, except the expression of my own grief and shock. The grief one must feel at the death of a poet of genius, younger than oneself, and the shock of his unexpected death just as my firm had ready for publication a new volume of his verse [*The Burning Perch*].

'MacNeice was one of several brilliant poets who were up at Oxford at the same time, and whose names were at first always associated, but the difference between whose gifts shows more and more clearly with the lapse of time. MacNeice in particular stands apart. If the term "poet's poet" means a poet whose virtuosity can be fully appreciated only by other poets, it may be applied to MacNeice. But if it were taken to imply that his work cannot be enjoyed by the larger public of poetry readers, the term would be misleading. He had the Irishman's unfailing ear for the music of verse, and he never published a line that is not good reading. I am very proud of having published the first volume he had to offer after coming down from the university.

'As for the radio plays, no other poet, with the exception of the author of *Under Milk Wood,* has written works as haunting as MacNeice.'

F. O. Matthiessen (1902–50), author and academic, graduated Phi Beta Kappa from Yale University in 1923 and was thereafter a Rhodes Scholar at New College, Oxford, before gaining his PhD at Harvard in 1927. After two years at Yale, he taught for twenty-one years in the English department at Harvard, where he specialised in American literature and Shakespeare, becoming Professor of History and Literature in 1942. The first senior tutor at Eliot House (where he befriended TSE in 1932–3), he was a resident tutor from 1933 to 1939. Works include *The Achievement of T. S. Eliot* (1935) and *American Renaissance* (1941). TSE to the Master of Eliot House, 5 Apr. 1950 (following Matthiessen's suicide on 1 Apr. 1950): 'I always thought him a person of a kind of repressed excessive intensity. I think that Matty was, in his way, a very religious man. Perhaps that was part of the trouble – I mean that he had a capacity for religious fanaticism, without the discipline and control of a dogma or a church.' See *F. O. Matthiessen (1902–1950): A Collective Portrait*, ed. Paul M. Sweezy and Leo Huberman (1950); George Abbott White, 'Ideology and Literature: *American Renaissance* and F. O. Matthiessen', in *Literature and Revolution*, ed. George Abbott White and Charles Newman (1972), 430–500; *F. O. Matthiessen: The Critical Achievement*, ed. Giles B. Gunn (1975); Kenneth S. Lynn, 'Teaching: F. O. Matthiessen', *The American Scholar* 46: 1 (Winter 1976–7), 86–93; and Harry Levin, 'The Private Life of F. O. Matthiessen', *New York Review of Books*, 20 July 1978.

Marianne Moore (1887–1972), American poet and critic, contributed to *The Egoist* from 1915. Her first book, *Poems*, was published in London in 1921. She went on to become in 1925 acting editor of *The Dial*, editor 1927–9, and an important and influential modern poet. Eliot found her 'an extremely intelligent person, very shy . . . One of the most observant people I have ever met.' Writing to her on 3 April 1921, he had said her verse interested him 'more than that of anyone now writing in America'. And in Eliot's introduction to her *Selected Poems* (1935), he declared that her 'poems form part of the small body of durable poetry written in our time'. See her review of TSE's *Collected Poems*: '"It Is Not Forbidden to Think"', *The Nation*, 27 May 1936, 680–1: 'The grouping of these poems . . . seems to point to a mental chronology of evolvement and deepening technique. But two tendencies mark them all: the instinct for order and certitude, and "contempt for sham."' See too Moore, 'A Virtuoso of Make-Believe', in *T. S. Eliot: A Symposium*, compiled by Richard March and Tambimittu (1948), 179–80; *Selected Letters of*

Marianne Moore, ed. Bonnie Costello (1998); Linda Leavell, *Holding On Upside Down: The Life and Work of Marianne Moore* (2013).

Paul Elmer More (1864–1937), critic, scholar, philosopher, prolific writer, had grown up in St Louis, Missouri, and attended Washington University before going on to Harvard; at one time he had taught French to TSE's brother Henry. Initially a humanist, by the 1930s he assumed an Anglo-Catholic position not unlike that of TSE (who appreciated the parallels between their spiritual development). See also 'An Anglican Platonist: the Conversion of Paul Elmer More', *TLS*, 30 Oct. 1937, 792. At the outset of his career, More taught classics at Harvard and Bryn Mawr; thereafter he became a journalist, serving as literary editor of *The Independent*, 1901–3, and the *New York Evening Post*, 1903–9, and as editor of *The Nation*, 1909–14, before finally turning to freelance writing and teaching. TSE keenly admired More's many works, in particular *Shelburne Essays* (11 vols, 1904–21), *The Greek Tradition* (5 vols, 1924–31), and *The Demon of the Absolute* (1928); and he took trouble in the 1930s to try to secure a publisher for *Pages from an Oxford Diary* (1937), which More stipulated he would only publish in anonymity.

In 1937, TSE wrote in tribute: 'The place of Paul More's writings in my own life has been of such a kind that I find [it] easiest, and perhaps most effective, to treat it in a kind of autobiographical way. What is significant to me . . . is not simply the conclusions at which he has arrived, but the fact that he arrived there from somewhere else; and not simply that he came from somewhere else, but that he took a particular route . . . If I find an analogy with my own journey, that is perhaps of interest to no one but myself, except in so far as it explains my retrospective appreciation of the *Shelburne Essays*; but my appreciation of the whole work cannot be disengaged from the way in which I arrived at it.

'It was not until my senior year [at Harvard], as a pupil of [Irving] Babbitt's, that More's work was forced on my attention: for one of the obligations of any pupil of Babbitt was to learn a proper respect for "my friend More". But while one was directly exposed to so powerful an influence as Babbitt's, everything that one read was merely a supplement to Babbitt.

'It was not until one or two of the volumes of *The Greek Tradition* had appeared, that More began to have any importance for me. It was possibly Irving Babbitt himself, in a conversation in London, in 1927 or '28, during which I had occasion to indicate the steps I had recently taken, who first made me clearly cognizant of the situation. In the later volumes of *The*

Greek Tradition, and in the acquaintance and friendship subsequently formed, I came to find an auxiliary to my own progress of thought, which no English theologian <at the time> could have given me. The English theologians, born and brought up in surroundings of private belief and public form, and often themselves descended from ecclesiastics, at any rate living mostly in an environment of religious practice, did not seem to me to know enough of the new world of barbarism and infidelity that was forming all about them. The English Church was familiar with the backslider, but it knew nothing of the convert – certainly not of the convert who had come such a long journey. I might almost say that I never met any Christians until after I had made up my mind to become one. It was of the greatest importance, then, to have at hand the work of a man who had come by somewhat the same route, to <almost> the same conclusions, at almost the same time: with a maturity, a weight of scholarship, a discipline of thinking, which I did not, and never shall, possess.

'I had met More only once in earlier years – at a reception given by the Babbitts to which some of Babbitt's pupils had the honor of invitation and that remained only a visual memory. My first meeting with him in London, however, seemed more like the renewal of an old acquaintance than the formation of a new one: More was a St Louisian, and had known my family' (*Princeton Alumni Magazine* 37 [5 Feb. 1937], 373–4).

See Arthur Hazard Dakin, *Paul Elmer More* (1960) – of which TSE wrote on 29 Mar. 1960: 'What the author says about Paul More and myself seems to me very accurate . . . [W]e did see very nearly eye to eye in theological matters' – and David Huisman, '"A Long Journey Afoot": The Pilgrimages toward Orthodoxy of T. S. Eliot and Paul Elmer More', in *T. S. Eliot and Christian Tradition*, ed. Benjamin G. Lockerd (2014), 251–64.

Frank Vigor Morley (1899–1980), son of a distinguished mathematician – his brothers were the writer Christopher, and Felix (editor of *The Washington Post*) – was brought up in the USA before travelling as a Rhodes Scholar to New College, Oxford, where he earned a doctorate in mathematics. After working for a while at the *Times Literary Supplement*, he became London Manager of The Century Company (Publishers) of New York. In 1929 he became a founding director of Faber & Faber, where he would be a close friend of TSE: for some time they shared a top-floor office at Russell Square. Morley would remark that TSE's 'great skill' as a publisher was that he 'had an unerring gift for spotting talent, but he would never fight for people. I used to watch, and know him so well that if he quietly suggested publishing the poetry of Marianne Moore, whom nobody knew, I would take up the cudgels and be the loud hailer' ('The time when Eliot lit the fuse', *Sunday Times*, 8 June 1980).

In 1933 when TSE separated from Vivien, Morley arranged convivial temporary accommodation for him near his farmhouse at Pike's Farm, Lingfield, Surrey. In 1939 Morley moved to the USA, where he became Vice-President of Harcourt Brace and Company (and during the war he served on the National War Labor Board in Washington, DC). In 1947 he returned with his family to England to take up the post of Director at Eyre & Spottiswoode. A large, learned, ebullient figure, he earned the sobriquet 'Whale' – though not merely on account of his corpulence: in his youth he had spent time aboard a whaling ship (he was revolted by the slaughter), and subsequently wrote (with J. S. Hodgson) *Whaling North and South* (1927) – which was reviewed in the *Monthly Criterion* by his friend Herbert Read. His other publications include *Travels in East Anglia* (1923), *River Thames* (1926), *Inversive Geometry* (1933), *My One Contribution to Chess* (1947), *The Great North Road* (1961), *The Long Road West: A Journey in History* (1971), and *Literary Britain* (1980); and contributions in verse (together with Eliot, Geoffrey Faber and John Hayward) to *Noctes Binanianae* (privately printed, 1939).

Morley Kennerley told *The Times* (25 Oct. 1980) that 'one of [Morley's] hobbies was to work out complicated problems for his friends, and for those baffled there were amazing practical jokes. Convivial lunches with interesting people were a joy to him ... He found jobs for many and squeezed me into Fabers where he generously put up with my sharing a corner of his room for some years. I was present all day during his interviews, dictation, visitors and often lunch. How he put up with all this I do not know. His correspondence with Ezra Pound was quite something, and I think he out-Pounded Pound. As his family say, he was a compulsive letter writer and was rarely without a pencil in his hand or pocket.'

In 1939, when Frank Morley was on the point of returning to the USA, Geoffrey Faber wrote of him to the editor of *The Times*: 'Morley is a quite outstanding person ... [His] first obvious quality is that he is a born "mixer", with an extraordinary range of friends in different walks of life. He is a very good talker, though rather fond – like many Americans – of spinning the yarn out. But he never spins without a purpose. As a negotiator he is in a class by himself. His judgment of men and situations is first rate. He knows the personnel of both the English and American publishing and journalistic worlds. As for his mental equipment, he took a doctorate at Oxford with a mathematical thesis. The story is that nobody in Oxford could understand it, and help had to be got from Cambridge. But he is at least as good a man of letters as he is a mathematician.'

On 2 July 1978 Morley wrote to Helen Gardner, of Eliot: 'I loved him, as I think you know, near to the side of idolatry.'

Lady Ottoline Morrell (1873–1938): daughter of Lieutenant-General Arthur Bentinck and half-sister to the Duke of Portland. In 1902 she married Philip Morrell (1870–1941), Liberal MP for South Oxfordshire 1902–18. A patron of the arts, she entertained a notable literary and artistic circle, first at 44 Bedford Square, then at Garsington Manor, near Oxford, where she moved in 1915. She was a lover of Bertrand Russell, who introduced her to TSE, and her friends included Lytton Strachey, D. H. Lawrence, Aldous Huxley, Siegfried Sassoon, the Woolfs, and the Eliots. Her memoirs (ed. by Robert Gathorne-Hardy) appeared as *Ottoline* (1963) and *Ottoline at Garsington* (1974). See Miranda Seymour, *Life on the Grand Scale: Lady Ottoline Morrell* (1992, 1998).

Edwin Muir (1887–1959): Scottish poet, novelist, critic; translator (with his wife Willa) of Franz Kafka. TSE was to write to LW on 22 Aug. 1946: 'I am anxious to do anything I can for Muir because I think highly of his best poetry and I think he has not had enough recognition.' To Eleanor Hinkley, 25 Dec. 1955: 'Edwin is a sweet creature, who never says anything when his wife is present, and only an occasional word when she isn't. An evening alone with him is very fatiguing. But he is a good poet, and I believe, what is even rarer, a literary man of complete integrity. He is not really Scottish, but Orcadian – in other words, pure Scandinavian.' On 1 Jan. 1959, when pressing the claims of Muir upon the Royal Literary Fund, TSE wrote to Alan Pryce-Jones: 'I have a very high opinion indeed of Edwin Muir as a poet, and admire him particularly because his poetry has gone on gaining in strength in later years. And I think that both he and Willa deserve recognition because of their work in translation. It is through them, you remember, that Kafka became known in this country, as they translated, I think, all his novels.' In a tribute: 'Muir's literary criticism had always seemed to me of the best of our time: after I came to know him, I realised that it owed its excellence not only to his power of intellect and acuteness of sensibility, but to those moral qualities which make us remember him, as you say justly, as "in some ways almost a saintly man". It was more recently that I came to regard his poetry as ranking with the best poetry of our time. As a poet he began late; as a poet he was recognised late; but some of his finest work – perhaps his very finest work – was written when he was already over sixty . . . For this late development we are reminded of the later poetry of Yeats; and Muir had to struggle with bad health also: but in the one case as in the other (and Muir is by no means unworthy to be mentioned together with Yeats) we recognise a triumph of the human spirit' (*The Times*, 7 Jan. 1959). Willa Muir commented on TSE's plaudits: 'Eliot, in his desire to present Edwin as an orthodox Christian, overdid, I think, the desolations and the saintliness. Edwin's wine could never be contained in any orthodox creed' (letter to Kathleen Raine, 7 Apr. 1960). TSE to Willa Muir, 9 Aug. 1962: 'I think that Edwin's collected poems will go on being enjoyed by true poetry lovers as long as the poems of any poet in our century.' He would later say of Muir: 'He was a reserved, reticent man . . . Yet his personality made a deep impression upon me, and especially the impression of one very rare and precious quality . . . unmistakable integrity'; and of his poems: 'under the pressure of emotional intensity, and possessed by his vision, he found almost unconsciously the right, the inevitable, way of saying what he wanted to say' ('Edwin Muir: 1887–1959: An Appreciation', *The Listener*, 28 May 1964, 872). Writings include *An Autobiography* (1954); *Selected Poems of Edwin Muir*, with preface by TSE (1966); *Selected Letters of Edwin Muir*, ed. P. H. Butter (1974).

John Middleton Murry (1889–1957): English writer, critic and editor, founded the magazine *Rhythm*, 1911–13, and worked as a reviewer for the *Westminster Gazette*, 1912–14, and the *Times Literary Supplement*, 1914–18, before becoming editor, 1919–21, of the *Athenaeum*, which he turned into a lively cultural forum – in a letter of 2 July 1919, TSE called it 'the best literary weekly in the Anglo-Saxon world'. In his 'London Letter', *Dial* 72 (May 1921), Eliot considered Murry 'genuinely studious to maintain a serious criticism', but he disagreed with his 'particular tastes, as well as his general statements'. After the demise of the *Athenaeum*, Murry went on to edit *The Adelphi*, 1923–48. In 1918, he married Katherine Mansfield (d. 1923). He was friend and biographer of D. H. Lawrence; and as an editor he provided a platform for writers as various as George Santayana, Paul Valéry, D. H. Lawrence, Aldous Huxley, Virginia Woolf, and Eliot. His first notable critical work was *Dostoevsky* (1916); his most influential study, *The Problem of Style* (1922). Though as a Romanticist he was an intellectual opponent of the avowedly 'Classicist' Eliot, Murry offered Eliot in 1919 the post of assistant editor on the *Athenaeum* (which Eliot had to decline); in addition, he recommended him to be Clark lecturer at Cambridge in 1926, and was a steadfast friend to both TSE and his wife

Vivien. Eliot wrote in a reference on 9 Sept. 1945 that Murry was 'one of the most distinguished men of letters of this time, and testimony from a contemporary seems superfluous. Several volumes of literary essays of the highest quality are evidence of his eminence as a critic; and even if one took no account of his original contribution, his conduct of *The Athenaeum*, which he edited from 1919 until its absorption into *The Nation*, should be enough to entitle him to the gratitude of his contemporaries and juniors. His direction of *The Adelphi* should also be recognised. Since he has devoted his attention chiefly to social and religious problems, he has written a number of books which no one who is concerned with the same problems, whether in agreement with him or not, can afford to neglect. I am quite sure that no future student of these matters who wishes to understand this age will be able to ignore them, and that no future student of the literary spirit of this age will be able to ignore Mr Murry's criticism.' He wrote to Murry's widow, 29 May 1957: 'The friendship between John and myself was of a singular quality, such that it was rather different from any other of my friendships. We did not often meet. We disagreed throughout many years on one point after another. But on the other hand, a very warm affection existed between us in spite of differences of view and infrequency of meetings. This affection was not merely, on my part, a feeling of gratitude for the opportunities he had given me early in my career during his editorship of *The Athenaeum*, but was something solid and permanent. He was one of the strangest and most remarkable men I have known, and no less strange and remarkable was the tie of affection between us.' See F. A. Lea, *The Life of John Middleton Murry* (1959); David Goldie, *A Critical Difference: T. S. Eliot and John Middleton Murry in English Literary Criticism, 1919–1928* (1998).

Arthur J. Penty (1875–1937), architect (he was involved in the development of Hampstead Garden Suburb, London) and social critic influenced variously by Ruskin, Carlyle, Matthew Arnold and Edward Carpenter, as well as by G. K. Chesterton and Hilaire Belloc; advocate of guild socialism, anti-modernism and anti-industrialism, agrarian reconstructionism and Anglican socialism. A contributor to periodicals including *The Guildsman, G. K.'s Weekly, The Crusader* and C., his works include *Old Worlds for New* (1917), *A Guildsman's Interpretation of History* (1920) and *Towards a Christian Sociology* (1923). TSE noted in *The Idea of a Christian Society* (1939) that 'modern material organization . . . has produced a world for which Christian social forms are imperfectly adapted'; but there are simplifications of the problem that are 'suspect':

'One is to insist that the only salvation for society is to return to a simpler mode of life, scrapping all the constructions of the modern world that we can bring ourselves to dispense with. This is an extreme statement of the neo-Ruskinian view, which was put forward with much vigour by the late A. J. Penty. When one considers the large amount of determination in social structure, this policy appears Utopian: if such a way of life ever comes to pass, it will be – as may well happen in the long run – from natural causes, and not from the moral will of men' (new edn with intro. by David L. Edwards, 1982).

Kenneth Pickthorn (1892–1975): historian and politician; Fellow of Corpus Christi College, Cambridge, from 1914; Dean, 1919–29; Tutor, 1927–35; President, 1937–44. From 1950 to 1966 he was Conservative MP for a Midlands constituency; an outspoken parliamentarian, critical of cant, he was made a baronet in 1959, Privy Councillor in 1964. His writings include *Some Historical Principles of the Constitution* (1925) and *Early Tudor Government* (2 vols, 1934).

Ezra Pound (1885–1972), American poet and critic, was one of the prime impresarios of the modernist movement in London and Paris, and played a major part in launching Eliot as poet and critic – as well as Joyce, Lewis, and many others. Eliot called on him in Kensington, on 22 Sept. 1914, with an introduction from Conrad Aiken. On 30 Sept. 1914, Pound hailed 'Prufrock' as 'the best poem I have yet had or seen from an American'; and on 3 October called Eliot 'the last intelligent man I've found – a young American . . . worth watching – mind "not primitive"' (*Selected Letters of Ezra Pound*, 40–1). Pound was instrumental in arranging for 'Prufrock' to be published in *Poetry* in 1915, and helped to shape *The Waste Land* (1922), which Eliot dedicated to him as 'il miglior fabbro'. The poets remained in loyal correspondence for the rest of their lives. Having initially dismissed Pound's poetry (to Conrad Aiken, 30 Sept. 1914) as 'well-meaning but touchingly incompetent', Eliot went on to champion his work, writing to Gilbert Seldes (27 Dec. 1922): 'I sincerely consider Ezra Pound the most important living poet in the English language.' He wrote an early critical study, *Ezra Pound: His Metric and Poetry* (1917), and went on, as editor of the *Criterion* and publisher at Faber & Faber, to publish most of Pound's work in the UK, including *Selected Shorter Poems*, *The Cantos* and *Selected Literary Essays*. After his move to Italy in the 1920s, Pound became increasingly sceptical about the direction of TSE's convictions and poetry, but they continued to correspond. TSE wrote to James Laughlin, on the occasion of Pound's seventieth birthday: 'I believe that I have in the past made clear enough my personal debt to Ezra Pound during the years 1915–22. I have also expressed in several ways my opinion of his rank as a poet, as a critic, as impresario of other writers, and as pioneer of metric and poetic language. His 70th birthday is not a moment for qualifying one's praise, but merely for recognition of those services to literature for which he will deserve the gratitude of posterity, and for appreciation of those achievements which even his severest critics must acknowledge' (3 Nov. 1955). TSE told Eaghor G. Kostetsky on 6 Jan. 1960 that the Cantos 'is unquestionably the most remarkable long contemporary poem in the English language'. After TSE's death, Pound said of him: 'His was the true Dantescan voice – not honoured enough, and deserving more than I ever gave him.' See *The Selected Letters of Ezra Pound 1907–1941*, ed. D. D. Paige (1950); Humphrey Carpenter, *A Serious Character* (1988); A. David Moody, *Ezra Pound: Poet: A Portrait of the Man and his Work* I: *The Young Genius 1885–1920* (2007); II: *The Epic Years 1921–1939* (2014); III: *The Tragic Years 1939–1972* (2015).

Mario Praz (1896–1982), scholar of English life and literature; author of *La Carne, la Morte e Il Diavolo nella Letteratura Romantica* (1930: *The Romantic Agony*, 1933). Educated in Bologna, Rome and Florence, he came to England in 1923 to study for the title of *libero docente*. He was Senior Lecturer in Italian, Liverpool University, 1924–32; Professor of Italian Studies, Victoria University of Manchester, 1932–4; Professor of English Language and Literature at the University of Rome, 1934–66. Other works include *Il giardino dei sensi* (1975). In 1952 he was made KBE. In 'An Italian Critic on Donne and Crashaw' (*TLS*, 17 Dec. 1925, 878), TSE hailed Praz's *Secentismo e Marinismo in Inghilterra: John Donne – Richard Crashaw* (1925) as 'indispensable for any student of this period'. In 'A Tribute to Mario Praz', 15 Apr. 1964: 'My first acquaintance with the work of Mario Praz came when, many years ago, the *Times Literary Supplement* sent me for review his *Secentismo e Marinismo in Inghilterra*. I immediately recognized these essays – and especially his masterly study of Crashaw – as among the best that I had ever read in that field. His knowledge of the poetry of that period in four languages – English, Italian, Spanish and Latin – was encyclopaedic, and, fortified by his own judgment and good taste, makes that book essential reading for any student of the English "metaphysical poets" . . . I tender these few words in testimony to my gratitude and admiration, not wishing my name to be absent from the roster of men of letters who, as well as more learned scholars of the period, owe him homage' (*Friendship's Garland: Essays presented to Mario Praz on His Seventieth Birthday*, ed. Vittorio Gabrieli [1966]). See Praz, 'Dante in Inghilterra', *La Cultura*, Jan. 1930, 65–6; 'T. S. Eliot e Dante', *Letteratura* 15 (July 1937), 12–28; 'T. S. Eliot and Dante', *Southern Review* no. 3 (Winter 1937), 525–48; *The Flaming Heart* (1958).

Herbert Read (1893–1968): English poet and literary critic, and one of the most influential art critics of the century. Son of a tenant farmer, Read spent his first years in rural Yorkshire; at sixteen, he went to work as a bank clerk, then studied law and economics at Leeds University; later still, he joined the Civil Service, working first in the Ministry of Labour and then at the Treasury. During his years of service in WW1, he rose to be a captain in the Green Howards, a Yorkshire regiment (his war poems were published in *Naked Warriors*, 1919); and when on leave to receive the Military Cross in 1917, he arranged to dine with TSE at the Monico Restaurant in Piccadilly Circus. This launched a life-long friendship which he was to recall in 'T. S. E. – A Memoir', in *T. S. Eliot: The Man and his Work*, ed. Allen Tate (1966). Within the year, he had also become acquainted with the Sitwells, Ezra Pound, Wyndham Lewis, Richard Aldington and Ford Madox Ford. He co-founded the journal *Art & Letters*, 1917–20, and wrote essays too for A. R. Orage, editor of the *New Age*. In 1922 he was appointed a curator in the department of ceramics and glass at the Victoria and Albert Museum; and in later years he was to work for the publishers Routledge & Kegan Paul, and as editor of the *Burlington Magazine*, 1933–9.

By 1923 he was writing for the *Criterion*: he was to become one of Eliot's regular leading contributors and a reliable ally and adviser. In 1924 he edited T. E. Hulme's posthumous *Speculations*. His later works include *Art Now* (1933); the introduction to the catalogue of the International Surrealist Exhibition held at the New Burlington Galleries, London, 1936; *Art and Society* (1937); *Education through Art* (1943); and *A Concise History of Modern Painting* (1959). In 1947 he founded (with Roland Penrose) the Institute of Contemporary Art; and in 1953 he was knighted for services to literature. Eliot, he was to recall (perhaps only half in jest), was 'rather like a gloomy priest presiding over my affections and spontaneity'. According to Stephen Spender in 1966, Eliot said 'of the anarchism of his friend Herbert Read, whom he loved and esteemed very highly: "Sometimes when I read Herbert's inflammatory pamphlets I have the impression that I am reading the pronouncements of an old-fashioned nineteenth-century liberal"' ('Remembering Eliot', *The Thirties and After* [1978], 251). Joseph Chiari recalled TSE saying of Read: 'Ah, there is old Herbie, again; he can't resist anything new!'

See further Herbert Read, 'Eliot, The Leader', *Yorkshire Post*, 5 Jan. 1965; James King, *The Last Modern: A Life of Herbert Read* (1990); *Herbert Read Reassessed*, ed. by D. Goodway (1998). Jason Harding (*'The Criterion': Cultural Politics and Periodical Networks in Inter-War Britain* [2002]) calculates that Read wrote 68 book reviews, 4 articles, and 5 poems for the *Criterion*.

I. A. Richards (1893–1979): theorist of literature, education and communication studies. At Cambridge University he studied history but switched to moral sciences, graduating from Magdalene College, where in 1922 he was appointed College Lecturer in English and Moral Sciences. A vigorous, spell-binding lecturer, he was to the fore in the advancement of the English Tripos. His early writings – *The Foundations of Aesthetics* (with C. K. Ogden and James Wood, 1922), *The Meaning of Meaning* (also with Ogden, 1923), *Principles of Literary Criticism* (1924), *Science and Poetry* (1926), *Practical Criticism: A Study of Literary Judgment* (1929) – are foundational texts in modern English literary studies. After teaching at National Tsing Hua University in Peking, 1929–30, he repaired for the remainder of his career to Harvard University, where he was made a university professor in 1944. His other works include *Basic in Teaching: East and West* (1935), *Mencius on the Mind* (1932), *Coleridge on Imagination* (1934), *The Philosophy of Rhetoric* (1936), *Interpretation in Teaching* (1938), and *Speculative Instruments* (1955), as well as translations from Plato and Homer. He was appointed Companion of Honour in 1963, and awarded the Emerson–Thoreau medal of the American Academy of Arts and Sciences, 1970. Out of the teaching term, he enjoyed with his wife Dorothea (1894–1986) an adventurous life of travel and mountain-climbing. See *Selected Letters of I. A. Richards, CH*, ed. John Constable (1990); John Constable, 'I. A. Richards, T. S. Eliot, and the Poetry of Belief', *Essays in Criticism* (July 1990), 222–43; *I. A. Richards and his Critics*, ed. John Constable – vol. 10 of *I. A. Richards: Selected Works 1919–1938* (2001) – John Paul Russo, *I. A. Richards: His Life and Work* (1989).

Bruce Richmond (1871–1964), literary editor, was educated at Winchester and New College, Oxford, and called to the Bar in 1897. However, he never practised as a barrister; instead, George Buckle, editor of *The Times*, appointed him an assistant editor in 1899, and in 1902 he assumed the editorship of the fledgling *Times Literary Supplement*, which he commanded for thirty-five years. During this period, the 'Lit. Sup.' established itself as the premier academic and critical periodical in Britain. He was knighted in 1935. See 'Sir Bruce Richmond' (obit.), *The Times*, 2 Oct. 1964. TSE, who was introduced to Richmond by Richard Aldington in 1919, enthused to his mother that year that writing the leading article for the *TLS* was the highest honour 'in the critical world of literature'. In a tribute, he recalled Richmond's 'bird-like alertness of eye, body and mind ... It was from Bruce Richmond that I learnt editorial standards ... I learnt from him that it is the business of an editor to know his contributors personally, to keep in touch with them and to make suggestions to them. I tried [at the *Criterion*] to form a nucleus of writers (some of them, indeed, recruited from *The Times Literary Supplement*, and introduced to me by Richmond) on whom I could depend, differing from each other in many things, but not in love of literature and seriousness of purpose ... It is a final tribute to Richmond's genius as an editor that some of his troupe of regular contributors (I am thinking of myself as well as of others) produced some of their most distinguished critical essays as leaders for the *Literary Supplement* ... Good literary criticism requires good editors as well as good critics. And Bruce Richmond was a great editor' ('Bruce Lyttelton Richmond', *TLS*, 13 Jan. 1961, 17).

Michael Roberts (1902–48), critic, editor, poet, was educated at King's College, London (where he read chemistry), and at Trinity College, Cambridge (mathematics). In the 1930s he worked as a schoolmaster, in London and at the Royal Grammar School, Newcastle upon Tyne. He married the author and journalist Janet Adam Smith in 1935; they had four children. After WW2, during which he worked for the BBC European Service, he became Principal of the Church of England training college of St Mark and St John, Chelsea, London. He edited the watershed anthologies *New Signatures* (1932) and *New Country* (1933); and *The Faber Book of Modern Verse* (1936). Other works include *The Modern Mind* (1937), *T. E. Hulme* (1938), *The Recovery of the West* (1941). See *A Portrait of Michael Roberts*, ed. T. W. Eason and R. Hamilton (1949); Jason Harding, *'The Criterion': Cultural Politics and Periodical Networks in Inter-War Britain* (2002).

TSE wrote after Roberts's death: 'His scientific bent and training were supplemented and corrected by a philosophic cast of mind; by critical abilities of a very high order; and by an imaginative gift which expressed itself in poetry of a meditative type. Such a combination of powers is unusual; and among men of letters of his generation it was unique. His first notoriety was due to the volume *New Signatures,* a presentation of the poetry which was beginning to attract attention in the late nineteen-twenties; a book which seemed to promise him the place of expositor and interpreter of the poetry of his generation. This book was followed in 1934 by *Critique of Poetry,* a collection of essays ranging between literary criticism, aesthetics and philosophy; then by *The Modern Mind,* a more coherent and profound examination of the age; by a study of T. E. Hulme, which remains the essential piece of bibliography for a man who occupied for his generation something like the place to which Roberts was entitled for his own; and finally, in 1941, by *The Recovery of the West,* an important essay in moral and sociological criticism . . . A little earlier . . . appeared *Orion Marches,* which contains, I think, some of the best of his poems.' Elsewhere TSE noted too: 'He would have made an admirable editor of a review of ideas: indeed, had the *Criterion* continued, he was the only man junior to myself of whom I could think for the editorship' ('Introduction', *A Portrait of Michael Roberts,* x–xii; 'Views and Reviews: Michael Roberts', *The New English Weekly* 34 [13 Jan. 1949], 164).

Janet Adam Smith wrote to TSE, Good Friday 1949 (following MR's death): 'I told Michael, after I had seen you in September, that you had said "I love Michael." He came back to it more than once – "I had not known he had felt that."'

A. L. Rowse (1903–97), Cornish historian, was educated at Christ Church, Oxford, and elected a Prize Fellow of All Souls in 1925. He was a lecturer at Merton College, 1927–30, and taught also at the London School of Economics. His books include *Sir Richard Grenville of the Revenge* (1937), *William Shakespeare: A Biography* (1963), *Simon Forman: Sex and Society in Shakespeare's Age* (1974), *All Souls in My Time* (1993), and poetry gathered up in *A Life* (1981). Though he failed in 1952 to be elected Warden of All Souls, he was elected a Fellow of the British Academy in 1958 and made a Companion of Honour in 1997. See Richard Ollard, *A Man of Contradictions: A Life of A. L. Rowse* (1999), and *The Diaries of A. L. Rowse* (ed. Ollard, 2003). TSE, who for a while knew him as 'Al', wrote to Geoffrey Curtis, 1 May 1944: 'Rowse is an old friend of mine, and a very touching person: the suppressed Catholic and the rather less suppressed Tory (with a real respect for Good Families), the miner's son and the All Souls Fellow, the minor poet and the would-be politician, the proletarian myth and the will-to-power, are always at odds in a scholarly retiring mind and a frail body. He is also very patronising, and one likes it.' Rowse for his part saluted Eliot as 'nursing father to us all', and he dedicated *The Expansion of Elizabethan England* (1955) to 'T. S. Eliot who gave me my first introduction to the world of letters'. See Rowse, *All Souls In My Time* (1993); *The Diaries of A. L. Rowse*, ed. Richard Ollard (2003); Ollard, *A Man of Contradictions: A Life of A. L. Rowse* (1999).

Robert Esmonde Gordon George – Robert Sencourt (1890–1969): critic, historian, biographer. Born in New Zealand, he was educated in Tamaki and at St John's College, Oxford. By 1929 – perhaps to avoid confusion with Professor George Gordon (President of Magdalen College, Oxford) – he was to take the name of Robert Sencourt. He taught in India and Portugal before serving as Vice-Dean of the Faculty of Arts and Professor of English Literature, University of Egypt, 1933–6. The *Times* obituarist noted that he was 'born an Anglican [but] was converted to Roman Catholicism which alone could inspire him with the spiritual dimension of the life of grace . . . [He] was the most fervent and devout of religious men, with the same personal mysticism which makes his life of St John of the Cross a joy to read. Never fearing to speak his mind in religious matters, even when (as often) his view ran counter to the church's, he was intolerant of any form of ecclesiastical cant or humbug.' His books include *Carmelite and Poet: St John of the Cross* (1943), biographies of George Meredith, the Empress Eugénie, Napoleon III, and Edward VIII, and the posthumous *T. S. Eliot: A Memoir*, ed. Donald Adamson (1971). EVE to Russell Kirk, 15 May 1973: 'Sencourt's memoir is, to put it mildly, unfortunate, and leaves a nasty taste. As you say, the whole background is both strange and malicious. He had nothing whatsoever to do with Tom's conversion – this long, slow process had come to fruition before they met.' See too Sencourt, 'T. S. Eliot: His Religion', *PAX: A Benedictine Review*, no. 312 (Spring 1965), 15–19.

Charles Arthur Siepmann (1899–1985), radio producer and educator, was awarded the Military Cross in WW1. He joined the BBC in 1927, and became Director of Talks, 1932–5; Regional Relations, 1935–6; Programme Planning, 1936–9. He was University Lecturer, Harvard, 1939–42; worked for the Office of War Information, 1942–5; and was Professor of Education, New York University, 1946–67. Works include *Radio's Second Chance* (1946), *Radio, Television and Society* (1950),

TV and Our School Crisis (1959). See Richard J. Meyer, 'Charles A. Siepmann and Educational Broadcasting', *Educational Technology Research and Development* 12: 4 (Winter 1964), 413–30. TSE told HWE in March 1937: 'In spite of his name he is in all appearance a perfectly English person, and was educated at Rugby and Oxford. I think his father or grandfather was German. Siepmann is an extremely serious, not to say solemn, young man, of about 36, who has been in the British Broadcasting Corporation longer than anyone I have ever heard of except Sir John Reith himself . . . [H]is political sympathies are rather liberal and left. He is a very nice fellow, although somewhat humourless.'

Stephen Spender (1909–95), poet and critic, won a rapid reputation with his first collection *Poems* (F&F, 1933), following an appearance in Michael Roberts's anthology *New Signatures* (1932). He cultivated friendships with some of the foremost younger writers of the period, including W. H. Auden, Christopher Isherwood, John Lehmann, and J. R. Ackerley. For a brief while in the 1930s he joined the Communist Party and went to Spain to serve the Republican cause. With Cyril Connolly he set up the magazine *Horizon* in 1940. In the post-war years he was to be a visiting professor at a number of American universities, and he undertook trips on behalf of the British Society for Cultural Freedom, the Congress for Cultural Freedom, and PEN. He served too as poetry consultant to the Library of Congress, 1965–6. For fourteen years from 1953 he was co-editor of the magazine *Encounter*, which – as it was ultimately proven – was from the start the beneficiary of funding from the CIA.

Other works include *The Destructive Element* (1935), *Forward from Liberalism* (1937), *World within World* (autobiography, 1951), *Collected Poems* (1955), *The Struggle of the Modern* (1963), *The Thirties and After* (1978), *New Selected Journals 1939–1995*, ed. Lara Feigel and John Sutherland with Natasha Spender (2012), and *The Temple* (novel, 1989). See too John Sutherland, *Stephen Spender: The Authorized Biography* (2004). He was instrumental in setting up *Index on Censorship* in 1971, and was Professor of English at University College, London, 1970–5. He was elected Companion of Literature by the Royal Society of Literature (1977), and knighted in 1983.

Walter F. Tomlin (1914–88): writer and administrator. Educated at Brasenose College, Oxford, he joined the British Council and served in Iraq, Turkey and France; also in Japan. Anglo-Catholic in religion, he wrote a study of Simone Weil; a book on R. G. Collingwood; and he edited volumes on Wyndham Lewis, Arnold Toynbee and Dickens. He was President of the Dickens Fellowship, 1987–8, and served on the executive committee of international PEN. His memoir *T. S. Eliot: A Friendship* appeared in 1988. TSE was to write to Ashley Sampson, 31 May 1937: 'A young man as yet unknown to the public, and of whose abilities I have a high opinion, is E. W. F. Tomlin.' To W. E. Salt, Director of Extra-Mural Studies, Univ. of Bristol, 25 May 1939: 'I have known him for a number of years, indeed before he even went up to Oxford, and have always regarded him as a young man of very unusual promise . . . I consider him a young man of quite exceptional abilities, as well as of character and seriousness of purpose.'

Leonard Woolf (1880–1969): writer and publisher; husband of Virginia Woolf. A friend of Lytton Strachey and J. M. Keynes at Cambridge, he played a central part in the Bloomsbury Group. He wrote a number of novels, including *The Village and the Jungle* (1913), and political studies including *Imperialism and Civilization* (1928). As founder-editor, with Virginia Woolf, of the Hogarth Press, he published TSE's *Poems* (1919) and *The Waste Land* (1923). In 1923 he became literary editor of *The Nation & Athenaeum* (after TSE had turned the post down), commissioning reviews from him, and he remained a firm friend. See *An Autobiography* (2 vols, 1980); *Letters of Leonard Woolf*, ed. Frederic Spotts (1990); Victoria Glendinning, *Leonard Woolf: A Life* (2006).

Virginia Woolf (1882–1941), novelist, essayist and critic, was author of *Jacob's Room* (1922), *Mrs Dalloway* (1925), and *To the Lighthouse* (1927); *A Room of One's Own* (1928), a classic of feminist criticism; and *The Common Reader* (1925). Daughter of the biographer and editor Leslie Stephen (1832–1904), she married Leonard Woolf in 1912, published her first novel *The Voyage Out* in 1915, and founded the Hogarth Press with her husband in 1917. The Hogarth Press published TSE's *Poems* (1919), *The Waste Land* (1923), and *Homage to John Dryden* (1923). TSE published in the *Criterion* Woolf's essays and talks including 'Kew Gardens', 'Character in Fiction', and 'On Being Ill'. Woolf became a friend and correspondent; her diaries and letters give first-hand accounts of him. Woolf wrote to her sister Vanessa Bell, 22 July 1936: 'I had a visit, long ago, from Tom Eliot, whom I love, or could have loved, had we both been in the prime and not in the sere; how necessary do you think copulation is to friendship? At what point does "love" become sexual?' (*Letters*, vol. 6). Eliot wrote in 1941 that Woolf 'was the centre, not merely of an esoteric group, but of the literary life of London. Her position was due to a concurrence of qualities and circumstances which never happened before, and which I do not think will ever happen again. It maintained the dignified and admirable tradition of Victorian upper middle-class culture – a situation in which the artist was neither the servant of the exalted patron, the parasite of the plutocrat, nor the entertainer of the mob – a situation in which the producer and the consumer of art were on an equal footing, and that neither the highest nor the lowest.' To Enid Faber, 27 Apr. 1941: 'she was a personal friend who seemed to me (mutatis considerably mutandis) like a member of my own family; and I miss her dreadfully, but I don't see her exactly as her relatives see her, and my admiration for the ideas of her milieu – now rather old-fashioned – is decidedly qualified.' See further Hermione Lee, *Virginia Woolf* (1996).

William Butler Yeats (1865–1939): Irish poet and playwright; Nobel Laureate. According to TSE, he was 'one of those few whose history is the history of their own time, who are part of the consciousness of an age' (*On Poetry and Poets*). TSE met Yeats soon after his arrival in London, but despite their mutual admiration of Pound, they had little contact until 1922, when TSE told Ottoline Morrell that Yeats was 'one of the very small number of people with whom one can talk profitably of poetry'. In his review of *Per Amica Silentia Lunae*, TSE said 'One is never weary of the voice, though the accents are strange' ('A Foreign Mind', *Athenaeum*, 4 July 1919). He was keen to publish Yeats in the *Criterion*: see 'A Biographical Fragment', in *Criterion* 1 (July 1923), 'The Cat and the Moon', 2 (July 1924), 'The Tower', 5 (June 1927). Yeats was instinctively opposed to TSE's work, but he discussed it at length in his Introduction to the *Oxford Book of Modern Verse* (1936), and declared after the publication of *The Waste Land* that he found it 'very beautiful' (Jan. 1923). Valerie Eliot told Francis Warner, 21 Sept. 1966: 'There is very little correspondence between the two poets in my files and, curiously enough, in more than fifteen years I only heard my husband speak of Yeats occasionally and he said that no particular meeting remained in his mind. They had, of course, met many times – and there was the vicarious association when Pound was acting as the Irishman's secretary – but it was a formal friendship, due partly, perhaps, to the difference of age.' See further Michael Butler Yeats, 'Eliot and Yeats: A Personal View', in *The Placing of T. S. Eliot,* ed. Jewel Spears Brooker (1991), 169–84; Roy Foster, *Yeats: A Life*: I *The Apprentice Mage* (1997), II *The Arch-Poet* (2003).

INDEX OF CORRESPONDENTS
AND RECIPIENTS

Butler-Bowdon, William, 845

Caetani, Marguerite, 410, 678
Cambridge University Press: The Secretary, 511
Carpenter, S. C., 181
Carter, Barbara Barclay, 431
Case, Lilian M., 167
Cecil, Lord David, 111
Cerf, Bennett A. (from FVM), 299
Chambers, F. W., 570
Champvans de Farémont, le Marquis de, 79
Charteris, Evan, 88
Cheetham, Eric, 34
Church Times, The: The Editor, 45, 348, 730, 853
Clifford, Derek Phit, 109, 142
Clutton, George, 822
Cobden-Sanderson, Sally, 334, 336
Cockerell, Sydney, 649
Codrington, Kenneth de Burgh, 42, 321
Coffey, Brian, 215, 268
Coia, Emilio, 626
Coleman, Emily Holmes, 811
Cooke, Alistair, 43, 134, 149, 517, 583
Cory, Daniel, 328
Coulton, G. G., 846
Cournos, John, 5, 807
Crofton, H. C., 141, 650
Cullis, Michael F., 599
Culpin, Jan (from Erica Wright), 360
Curtis, Geoffrey, 311, 703, 707
Curtius, E. R., 196
Cyriax, J. H., 577

Daniells, J. Roy, 72
D'Arcy, M. C., 514; (from Erica Wright), 360
Dark, Sidney, 702
Davies, Charles, 470
Davies, Hugh Sykes see Sykes Davies, Hugh
Davies, Idris, 85
Dawson, Christopher, 97, 114, 178, 264, 290, 294, 653, 723
de la Mare, Walter, 235, 240, 392, 396, 480, 486, 776
Demos, Raphael, 867
Devlin, Denis, 88
Dickson, George, 743
Dismorr, Jessica, 627
District Bank (from VHE), 461

Dobrée, Bonamy, 94, 123, 127, 153, 161, 176, 180, 262, 379, 385, 657, 677, 878
Dobrée, Valentine, 75
Doone, Rupert, 67, 198, 282, 376, 564, 701
du Bos, Charles, 201
Duff, Audrey, 330
Dukes, Ashley, 782, 790, 842
Duncan-Jones, Revd A. S., 465

Earp, T. W., 204, 217, 631
Eliot, Revd Frederick May, 455, 611
Eliot, Henry Ware, Jr (TSE's elder brother), 28, 75, 199, 242, 457, 510, 531, 578, 592, 765, 848
Eliot, Vivien (from Geoffrey Faber), 29; (from Bird & Bird), 360; (from Allen & Hanbury's), 453; (from Reginald Miller), 694, 796
Elisséeff, S., 635
Elliott, G. R., 691
Empson, William, 102, 554, 732, 856
Every, George, 500
Ewart, Gavin, 138, 418

Faber, Enid, 324, 709
Faber, Geoffrey, 297, 427, 462, 467, 571, 704, 720; (from VHE), 573
Faber, Tom, 870
Fenwick, Margerie, 860
Ferro, António, 644
Fitzgerald, F. Scott, 31, 218
Fitzgerald, Robert, 857
Flanagan, Hallie, 64, 78, 115, 271
Flint, F. S., 330
Fogerty, Elsie, 386, 590, 639
Ford, Alexander Langridge, 332
Ford, Ford Madox, 146
Forwood, Muriel, 403
Fry, Margery, 727, 764

Garrett, John, 158, 197, 351, 371, 481, 675, 794
Gascoyne, David, 336, 625
Gaye, Phoebe Fenwick, 161
George, R. E. Gordon, see Robert Sencourt
Gilbert, Stuart, 819
Gill, Eric, 199
Gilliam, Laurence, 314
Gough, E. P., 768
Graham, Gerald, 319
Greenwood, Ormerod, 120, 129, 304

GENERAL INDEX

play for Group Theatre, 282n, 496; and John Pudney, 306n; royalties, 374; cockney dialect, 401; flies to Copenhagen, 447; theatre season, 459, 475, 508, 523, 564, 580, 590; Macleod on poetic drama of, 494n; TSE sends Prokosch printed poems to, 546; portrait photograph, 547; in *Faber Book of Modern Verse*, 555n; politics, 559; and R. J. G. Johnson's pamphlet on theatre, 574n; Heppenstall offers to review, 612; TSE describes to VW, 666n; on radio comment on *MiC*, 668; arrangement with Curtis Brown over *The Dog Beneath the Skin*, 669n; Jennings on, 735n; admires Jeanette McPherrin's postcard, 792; *The Dance of Death*, 51–2, 64n, 67, 78, 87, 91, 116, 187n, 269–70, 283, 530n, 616, 660n, 661, 799n, 806n; *The Dog Beneath the Skin* (earlier *The Chase* and *Where is Francis?*; with Isherwood), 304n, 374–5, 476, 502n, 524n, 547, 551n, 616, 642n, 652, 669n, 713, 782n; 'Five Early Poems' (ed. Ed Mendelson), 261n; *The Orators*, 51, 154, 260, 261n, 269, 761; *Poems*, 154n, 269n; *The Poet's Tongue: An Anthology* (ed. with John Garrett), 794n; *Two Poems*, 546n
Aylward, James de Vine, 650, **868n**
Azam, Eugène, 280n

Babington, Margaret: on fees for Canterbury Festival works, 404n, 405n; as steward of Friends of Canterbury Cathedral, 496n; and costumes for *MiC*, 498n, 520, 530n; on title of *MiC*, 526n, 571n; and Group Theatre production of *MiC*, 590; and E. M. Browne, 612n, 613; IAR and, 669; finds seat for Schiff for *MiC*, 682n
Badger, The (Downs School magazine), 270
Balzac, Honoré de, 618
Barber, Cesar Lombardi ('Joe'), **553n**
Barker, Ernest, **522n**, 529
Barker, George, **882–3**; TSE campaigns for financial help, 211n, 235, 240, 257, 281, 286, 387–8, 392–4, 486, 776–7, 797n, 834, 849–50, 866; invited to review for *Criterion*, 212; writer's block, 258; birth of child, 396; TSE publishes poems, 407–9; OM praises, 445; gives up child for adoption, 481; sends long poem to

TSE, 561; visit to Capri, 561; poems sent to SS, 567; Heppenstall reviews, 603–4, 611; TSE recommends to Siepmann, 639; Roberts on, 698n; TSE asks Bridson to review, 740; in *Oxford Book of Modern Verse*, 777n; submits story and poems to TSE, 849; *The Bacchant*, 190–1, 211, 212n, 471, 486; *Documents of a Death*, 471, 486; 'Elegy Anticipating Death', 91; 'Elegy' ('Count them as they cluster'), 396n, 407n, 409n; *Janus*, 740, 834; 'The Multiple Figure', 394n; 'Narcissus I, II, III', 407; *Poems*, 190–1, 211, 212n; 'Though Lovely and Lonely', 849n
Barker, Miss (F&F secretary), 343n
Barlow Lectures (University of London), 581n
Barnes, Djuna: *Nightwood*, 811–13
Barrie, James Matthew, 876; *Dear Brutus*, 362n
Barrington-Ward, Robert, **123n**, 127
Bartek, Zenka *see* Porteus, Zenka
Barth, Karl, **312n**
Bartlett, Vernon, 289
Basic English, 523n
Bath, 709
Baudelaire, Charles, 575, 722
Baylis, Lilian, 120n, **260n**, 435n, 727n
Bazin, René: *Vie de Charles de Foucauld*, 648
Beach, Sylvia, 819n
Beachcroft, T. O., **6n**; reviews Basil Willey, 85; TSE describes to IAR, 135; sends stories to TSE, 559–60; *The Man Who Spoke to Lenin*, 559
Becket, St Thomas, 359n, 387, 523, 544, 569n, 670n, 769n, 771n
Beckett, Samuel, 186, 215n, 382n
Bedford, Sybille, 847n
Behan, Beatrice, 382n
Belgion, Montgomery, 72, 488, 733, **883**
Bell, Angelica, 827n
Bell, Bernard Iddings *see* Iddings Bell, Canon Bernard
Bell, Clive, 617n, 618
Bell, George, Bishop of Chichester (earlier Dean of Canterbury), **226n**; postpones Chichester conference, 239; TSE refers Perkinses and Emily Hale to, 354; and Laurence Irving in Masefield's *Coming of Christ*, 359n; wishes TSE to write play for Canterbury Festival, 404n; and Hebert's

Liturgy and Society, 442; appoints
Margaret Babington steward of Friends
of Canterbury Cathedral, 496n; praises
MiC, 689; *Life of Randall Davidson*, 823
Bell, Henrietta, 689n
Bell, Julian, 138n, 673n, 828n, 854n
Belloc, Hilaire, 435n
Benckendorff, Count Djon, 358n
Bennett, Arnold, 381n, 586n
Benson, Sir Frank, 260
Benson, Stella, 441n
Berder, Germaine, 140
Berdiev: controversy with Hecker, 295
Bergson, Henri, 183; *La Pensée et la
Mouvant*, 333
Berkeley, George, Bishop of Cloyne, 677
Berlin, Sir Isaiah, 150n, **679n**
Berner, Gerald Tyrwhitt-Wilson, 14th
Baron, 850n
Berry, Revd S. M., 437n
Berti, Luigi, **771n**
Bethell, S. L.: TSE recommends to Bowdoin
College, Maine, 221n; 'Suggestions
towards a Theory of Value', 488
Bevan, Freda, 35n, 37n
Bhagavad-Geeta, 365
'Bible as Literature, The' (lecture), 259
Biddle, Nicholas, 20
Bina Gardens, London, 609n
Binyon, Laurence, 23n, 380, **449n**, 472n,
492, 528n, 587; translates *Divine
Comedy*, 449, 597; *Boadicea*, 591n; *The
Young King*, 359n, 404n, 405n
Bird & Bird, Messrs (solicitors): telegraphic
address, 94n; issues writ for possession
of goods to VHE, 338–40, 360, 399; TSE
settles account with, 340n; recovers TSE's
possessions, 505, 696n
Bird, Ernest: sends account to TSE, 69;
and TSE's disposal of effects, 93, 235,
252; advises TSE on rental and dealings
with VHE, 188, 216, 251–2, 287, 323;
on difficulty of serving writ on VHE,
340n; on responsibility for expenses of
separation agreement, 413; and James
& James account to TSE, 468–9, 492;
advises TSE on will, 469–70, 493
Bird, William, 100n
Birrell, Augustus, 621n
Birrell, Francis, 349, 395, 446, 448
Blacker, Perry, 723
Blackfriars (magazine), 769

'Blackshirts, The', 45, 71n
Blackstone, Bernard, 818, **824n**, 840
Blackwell, Basil, 463n
Blake, Ellie, 642n
Blake, George, **411n**, 614n, 642
Blake, William, 605
Blomfield, Charles James, Bishop of
London, 677
Bloomsbury Group, 752, 763
Blunden, Edmund, 207–8, **228n**, 280, 463n
Blunt, Wilfrid, 21n
Boas, George, 867n
Bodley Head (publishing house), 12n
Bodley, John, 16n, 372n, 779n
Boggust, W. H.: 'Dave Hadley's Last Fight',
559n
Bolliger, Aurelia *see* Hodgson, Aurelia
Bolshakoff, Serge (Sergius), 883–4; on
Catholic Church and fascism, 61n; TSE
gives Dawson's address to, 61, 97, 264;
organises Christian academy, 83, 290,
294n, 295n, 313, 653–4; and Japanese
fascists, 654
Boothroyd, B. J., 303n
Boriswood (publishing house), 6n, 550
Bosanquet, Theodora, 344n
Bottomley, Gordon, 197; 'The Acts of St
Peter', 62n
Bottrall, Ronald, 810n; TSE seeks IAR's
view of, 69, 74n; poems sent to Bridson,
335; omitted from *Faber Book of Modern
Verse*, 556n; Bridson supports, 740; TSE
advises on new volume of verse, 810;
Festivals of Fire, 74n; 'Preamble to a
Great Adventure', 555
Bouche, Marion, 812n
Bourne, Cardinal Francis Alphonsus, 570n
Bowen, Elizabeth (Mrs Alan Cameron),
131n, 138n, **177n**
Bowen, Esther 'Stella', **687n**
Bowra, (Sir) C. Maurice, 81n, **118n**
Box, Revd Hubert S., 443
Boyle, James Le B., **597n**
Boyle, Kay, **586n**, 813
Brace, Donald, **152n**; publishes Pareto,
152; TSE sends copies of *The Rock* to,
213, 257n; and title of *The Rock*, 305;
on HR's *Poems*, 306; visits Gunns at
Inverness, 614n; letter from FVM on
S. I. Hsiung's works, 638n; letter from
FVM on performance of *MiC*, 669n; and
FVM's difficulty in getting biographical

188n, 251–2, 260; Jan Culpin reports on, 189n; and W. L. Janes, 189n; attends performance of *The Rock*, 200n; birthday, 200; irrationality, 200n, 326n; moves from Clarence Gate flat, 205, 241, 837; attends Sadler's Wells meeting, 259n; TSE meets at Sadler's Wells, 260n; on visit of Theodora Eliot Smith and Margaret Dawes Eliot to England, 262n; sees bust of TSE, 285n; brother asked to intervene with over Clarence Gate property, 287; on TSE's 46th birthday, 326, 327n; Bird & Bird issue writ against for possession of goods, 338–42, 360, 399; befriended by Hope Mirrlees, 355n; and settlement of Separation Agreement, 413; claims own books, 427; TSE's weekly allowance to, 444–5; complains of being unwell, 451, 461, 540; overuses Faivres' Cachets (medication), 453; finances, 458; claims books stolen from flat, 461n; complains to bank of not being able to see TSE, 461; and TSE's will, 469, 580; and recovery of TSE's possessions from flat, 505–6; membership of British Union of Fascists, 515n; increased income after mother's death, 531; reclaims books and magazines, 570; requests TSE advertise *Criterion* in programme for Queen Charlotte Hospital appeal, 591; letter to Janes, 658; attempts to let flat, 659; plans visit to Paris, 684; Dr Reginald Miller attempts to call on, 694–5; complains of Clarence Gate Gardens flat, 705–6; visits Oxford, 705n; told of TSE's living in Kensington, 710n; protests to James & James over entry to flat, 719; copies letter from Father Pierre Jean de Menasce, 726n; asks to be present at brother Maurice's meetings with TSE, 732, 742; on Church's effect on TSE, 741; enquires of Mary Hutchinson about lost string belt, 769; sends greetings and cheque for TSE's birthday, 775; congratulates TSE on *Sweeney Agonistes*, 799; meets TSE at Dorland Hall lecture, 841; sees Mercury Theatre production of *MiC*, 847n; Seymour-Jones on, 847n; harasses Jack Hutchinson, 854; complains to Brigid O'Donovan about unreturned borrowed pencil, 870; 'On the Eve', 381n

Eliot, Walter Graeme: *Genealogy of the Eliot Family*, 243
Eliot, Revd William Greenleaf, 23n, 242n, 505
Elisséeff, S., **635n**
Ellerman, Annie Winifred *see* Bryher
Elliot, Walter Elliot, **96n**, 97, 110, 264
Elliott, G. R., **691n**; visit to England, 691; 'The Altar Among Emblems', 691n
Ellmann, Richard, 427n
Eluard, Paul, 877
Emck, John, 223
Emerson, Ralph Waldo, 169
Emperor's Gate, London, 69n
Empson, William, 102n; on encounters with TSE, 102n; TSE praises intellect, 132; poem published in *Criterion*, 554; introduces TSE to Sampson, 732; published by Chatto, 798; and payment to Chatto for publishing poems, 830–2, 844, 849, 852; submits verbalist articles to *Criterion*, 856
Enciclopedia Italiana, 46
English Verse Speaking Association, 386–7, 450, 471–2
Epstein, Jacob, 843
Euripides: *Alcestis* (transl. Dudley Fitts and Robert Fitzgerald), 857n
Evelyn, John, 124, 128
Everitt, Raymond, 134
Every, George, 373n, 500n, 527n, 629n
Ewart, Gavin, 138n; 'Ode on a Distant Prospect of Eton College', 418
Ezra Pound: His Metric and Poetry, 355
'Ezra Pound II', 586n

Faber Book of Modern Verse (ed. Michael Roberts), 533n, 555, 562, 573, 584, 596, 630, 687–8, 697–8, 721–2, 734, 766, 798, 830–1, 852
Faber, Enid (Geoffrey's wife), 30, 31n, **324n**, 705
Faber and Faber (publishers): and publication of *Ulysses*, 15–17; and publication of George Barker's *Bacchant*, 191n; takes over the Porpoise Press, 411n; TSE's shares in, 469; VHE visits hoping to see TSE, 684–6; share of SS's royalties, 767; WBY proposes Dorothy Wellesley's poems for publication, 803
Faber, Geoffrey (Cust), 890–1; and publication of *Ulysses*, 16n; intervenes

Fry, Margery, **727n**; and Roger Fry's
  Mallarmé, 764
Fry, Roger, 131n, 200n, 727, 764–5
Frye, Northrop, 228n, 246n
'Fugitives' (US literary circle), 738n
Fulham Skilled Apprenticeship Committee,
  330n
Fuller, Edward, 846n

Gall, Dorothy, 837n
Gallup, Donald C., 168n, 382n, 778n
Gardner, Helen: on TSE at Kelham, 629n;
  told of Ada Sheffield as child, 878n
Garrett, John, **158n**, 891; asks TSE to
  contribute to *REP*, 197n; sends copy
  of *REP* to TSE, 351; reviews Pudney's
  Open the Sky, 371; TSE asks for review
  of WBY as dramatist, 481; TSE asks to
  review WHA play, 551; takes schoolboys
  to *MiC*, 675; co-edits *The Poet's Tongue*
  with WHA, 794
Garrick Club, 359
Garrigou-Lagrange, Réginald, 733
Gascoyne, David, 156, **336n**, 625, 698n,
  850, 877n
Gatti, Commander Attilio, 595n
Gautier, Théophile, 722
Gaye, Phoebe Fenwick, **161n**
Gelre, Hank van, 599n
George, R. E. Gordon (Robert Sencourt),
  908–9; on TSE's religious practices, 37n;
  invites TSE to lecture in Cairo, 48, 377n,
  378; on Muriel Forwood, 403n; in Cairo,
  419
George, Ruth, 827n
George, Stefan, 559, 822
Georgian Anthology (ed. Edward Marsh),
  607
Germany: Nazism in, 515n
Gerontion, 195n, 279n; record, 485n
Gesell, Silvio, 713; *The Natural Economic
  Order*, 584
Gide, André, 438n, 526n
Gielgud, Val, 306, 741
Gilbert, Stuart, 598n, **819n**
Gilbert and Sullivan: *Yeomen of the Guard*,
  791
Gilbert, Tacon, 68n
Gill, Eric, 95n, **199n**, 251; *Work and
  Leisure*, 794
Gilliam, Laurence, 306–7, **314n**, 724n, 741
Giraudoux, Jean: *Racine*, 598

Girodias, Maurice (born Kahane), 662n
Goddard, Mr Justice Rayner, 339n, 360
Goethe, Johann Wolfgang von, 567n, 673
Goffin, R. C., 729n
Goldman, Emma, 811
Gollancz, Victor, 119n, 402
Goodman, Edward, 880n
Goodman, Julian, 389
Goodman, Victor, 389n
Goodman, William B., 328n
Gordon, James, Bishop of Jarrow, 519, 541
Gordon, Lyndall, 239n, 800n; *T. S. Eliot:
  An Imperfect Life*, 69n
Gordon, R. K. (ed.): *The Story of Troilus*,
  335
Gore, Charles, Bishop of Oxford, 473,
  648n, 704n
Gorky, Maxim, 358n
Gosse, Sylvia, 217n
Gough, Revd E. P., **768n**
Gourmont, Rémy de, 53, 349, 722
Graham, Emily, 319n
Graham, Gerald, **319n**
Granville-Barker, Harley, 198
Graves, Robert, 555n, 698n, 804n
Gray, Thomas, 132, 163n
Greene, Graham, 423n
Greene, O'Dwyer, 644
Greenleaf, Revd Daniel, 137, 242n
Greenslet, Ferris, 318n
Greenwood, Ormerod, **120n**, 126, 304
Gregory, Horace, 7n, **253n**
Gregory, T. S., **256n**; loses position in
  Methodist church, 468, 474; TSE helps
  find employment, 493, 522, 534; finds
  work, 514; recommended to Verschoyle,
  529; TSE gives address to Bruce
  Richmond, 534; proposes book on five
  18th-century men, 548; *The Unfinished
  Universe*, 297, 474n, 529, 534,548
Grenville Place, South Kensington, 69
Grenville, Sir Richard, 679
Grierson, Herbert John Clifford, 659n
Grieve, Christopher Murray (Hugh
  MacDiarmid), **764n**; 'Mature Art', 764
Griffin, J., 435n
Grigson, Geoffrey, **173n**; TSE praises, 13,
  40; Edith Sitwell accused of plagiarising,
  41n, 422n; and sale of TSE's collected
  poems, 54n; on Hugh Ross Williamson,
  344n; letter from Dylan Thomas, 372n;
  criticises Day Lewis, 552; birth of child,

568; and G. M. Hopkins, 568; reviews MacNeice poems, 715; suggests number of *New Verse* on poets and the theatre, 735

Group Theatre: produces WHA's *Dance of Death*, 67n; TSE supports, 120, 126; and production of *Sweeney Agonistes*, 198, 375, 388, 735; Dartington Hall's interest in, 282n; TSE gives talk for, 304n; premises, 371n; and Mercury Theatre season, 496, 770; proposed for first production of *MiC*, 509n; performs in Westminster Theatre, 701n; produces WHA's *Dog Beneath the Skin*, 713; as subject of critical article, 735

Grune, Karl, 709n

Guggenheim, Peggy, 586n, 811n

Guinness, Alec, 648n

Guinness, Bryan, 126–7, 393, 395, 435n, 445, 815n, 834, 850n

Gundolf, Frau, 807

Gunn, Jessie (Daisy), **614n**

Gunn, Neil M., 412n, 614n, 642, 809n; *Whisky and Scotland*, 809

'Gus: The Theatre Cat', 234n

Guthrie, Tyrone, 78, 135n, 564n

Gutteridge, Bernard, 560n

Gwyer, Alsina, Lady, 855

Gwyer, Sir Maurice, 855n

Gwynn, Denis, 518

Haecker, Theodor, 295

Haffenden, Lettice, 495n, 498, 509, 520, 837n

Haigh-Wood, Maurice (VHE's brother), 891–2; TSE asks to intervene in disputes with VHE, 287, 322–3; 39th birthday, 322n; and TSE's writ against VHE for possession of goods, 338, 341n; finances, 458; on attempts to seize papers from VHE's flat, 696n; VHE asks to be present at meetings with TSE, 732, 742; on Church's effect on TSE, 741

Haigh-Wood, Ruth Esther (VHE's mother), 531

Haigh-Wood, 'Raggy' (Maurice's son), 743, 799n

Hale, Emily, **891–2**; cared for by Perkinses, 202n; visit to England, 238, 713; visits Chichester, 354, 356n; birthday, 356n; visits OM, 357n, 388, 815n; friendship with Jeanette McPherrin, 410–11, 414n;

594, 615, 623, 657, 726; in London, 623; relations with aunt Irene Hale, 647–8, 656; and Margaret Thorp, 729; Gallup meets, 778n; relations with Perkinses, 791, 876; in Oxford, 792; visits Woolfs with TSE, 827n

Hale, Irene (Mrs Philip Hale, née Baumgras; 'Victor Rene'), 647–8, **656n**, 792

Halifax, Edward Frederick Lindley Wood, 1st Earl of, 648n

Hall, Anmer, 701n

Hall, Donald, 358n

Hamilton, Hamish (publisher), 651n

Hamlin, Mary P., 305n

Hamnett, Nina, 772

Hampden, John, **693n**

Hamsa, Bhagwan Shri: *The Holy Mountain* (Intro. by WBY), 59, 160, 192n, 333, 363n

Hanley, James, **352n**, 586; 'A Changed Man', 352, 494; 'Stoker Haslett', 352

Harcourt, Alfred, 152n

Harcourt, Brace and Co. (US publishers), 652, 880

Harding, Denys W., **634n**

Hardy, Thomas, 81n, 246n, 617

Hargrave, John: *Summer Time Ends*, 851

Harper & Brothers (US publishers), 213n

Harris, Revd Charles, 176n, 406–7, **413n**, 462–3, 862

Harrison, G. B., 487, 534

Harrison, Ruth, **575n**; *Approach to French Poetry*, 575

Harrison, W. E., 793

Harrisson, Tom, 384n

Hart, Captain Basil Liddell, 463n

Harvard Advocate, 23, 63, 597n

Harvard College Class of 1910: 25th Anniversary Report (1935): biography of TSE, 433–6

Haskell, Arnold Lionel: *Balletomania*, 611

Hassall, Christopher, 815n

Hastings, Donald, 177, 180; offers sculpted portrait head to TSE, 285

Hastings, Michael, 341n

Hattersley, C. Marshall, 225, 263

Hauptmann, Richard, 532

Häusermann, Hans W., **370n**; 'T. S. Eliot's religiöse Entwicklung', 370, 381

Hawkins, A. Desmond, **892–3**; TSE praises Elizabeth Bowen to, 177n; divorce,

250; on Dylan Thomas registering as conscientious objector, 343n; and *New English Weekly*, 440; reviews Marianne Moore's *Collected Poems*, 551, 557; on EP, 557n; reviews *The Arts Today*, 772; visits OM, 821n; impending fatherhood, 834n, 850n; TSE suggests contributing Fiction Chronicle to *Criterion*, 834–5, 850; 'The Poet in the Theatre', 223

Hawthorne, Nathaniel, 618

Hayward, John Davy, **893**; and OM's view of TSE, 81n; physical handicap, 166; and Theodore Spencer's visit, 166; on modifications to *The Rock*, 233n; TSE visits, 286; on Emily Hale, 356n; friendship with Richard Jennings, 369n; Kauffer tells of George Barker's financial troubles, 387; plans visit to Birrell, 448; and TSE's prospective move to flat in Bina Gardens, 609n; entertains Reads, 666n; on Charles Williams's anthology, 690; Charles Williams acknowledges in *New Book of English Verse*, 729n; Empson proposes calling on, 732n; writes on Dobrée, 765; TSE praises Ada Sheffield to, 878n

H.D. *see* Doolittle, Hilda

Heard, Gerald, **60n**, 358n, 395, 482, 666

Hebert, Fr Arthur Gabriel, **47n**, 177, 354, 454, 629; *Liturgy and Society* (earlier *The Foundations of the City*), 89–90, 373, 416n, 442, 589, 801

Hegel, G. W. F., 428

Heinemann (publishers), 612, 864

Hemingway, Ernest, 218n, 278, 586n; *Farewell to Arms*, 31n

Henderson, J. F., 11, 12n

Henry II, King of England, 452

Heppenstall, Rayner, **539n**; TSE sends Barker's poems to, 539; reviews Barker's poem, 603–4, 611; wishes to become ballet critic, 612; reviews ballet in *Criterion*, 770; Mairet shows poem fragment to TSE, 826; *Middleton Murry: A Study in Excellent Normality*, 539n; 'The Year in Ballet', 551n

Herbert, George, 135n, 818n, 824n

Herring, Phillip, 812n

Hester, Norman, 38n, 501

Hibbert Journal, 293, 296

Higginson, G. F., 399n, 505n

Higham, David, 134n, **183n**, 699

Hiler, Hilaire, 101

Hinkley, Eleanor Holmes: *Aphra Behn* (play), 623n

Hinkley, Susan Heywood (née Stearns; TSE's aunt), **196n**, 205, 578, 655, 713

Hinks, Roger, 101, 122, 176, 807n

Hitler, Adolf: assassination attempt on, 227n; rise to power, 515n

Hoare, Dorothy, 820n

Hobson, Enid, **711n**

Hobson, J. A., 436n

Hodder & Stoughton (publishers), 373

Hodgson, Aurelia (née Bolliger), **124n**, 462

Hodgson, Ralph, 124n, 125, 294n, **365n**, 621n

Hogarth Press, 170, 582, 765, 818n

Hogg, Quintin (Baron Hailsham of St Marylebone), **350n**

Hölderlin, Friedrich, 545, 559, 567, 615n

Hollow Men, The, 195, 279n, 465n, 466n, 757; record, 485n

Holst, Gustav, 226n

Hood, Revd A. F., 407

Hopkins, Gerard (of OUP), 425n

Hopkins, Gerard Manley (poet), 425, 502, 558, 562, 568, 687–8

Horgan, Paul, 343n

Horwell, H. W.: *A Dictionary of Modern American Usage*, 657n

Hoskyns, Sir Edwin and Francis Noel Davey: *The Riddle of the New Testament*, 373n

Hound & Horn (magazine), 54n, 296, 863

House, Humphry, **425n**, 568n

Howard League for Penal Reform, 727n

Howson, Revd Vincent, **233n**, 234n

Hsiung, S. I. (Hsiung Shih-I, or Xiong Shiyi), **638n**; *The Dream of the Western Chambers*, 638; *Lady Precious Stream*, 638

Hudson, Revd Cyril E., **397n**, 436, 794, 854

Hudson, G. F., 452, 499

Hudson, Stephen *see* Schiff, Sydney

Hulme, T. E., 72, 171, 273–4, 355

Hunter, Leslie, Archdeacon of Northumberland (later Bishop of Sheffield), 95

Hutchinson, Jack St John, 286, 797, 834, 854

Hutchinson, Jeremy and Mary, 260n

Hutchinson, Mary (née Barnes), **893**;

sends handkerchiefs to TSE, 3; TSE hopes to win support for Group Theatre from, 126, 129; TSE entertains, 131n; and TSE's campaign to raise money for Barker, 281, 285–6, 393–4, 797n, 834; serves on Executive Committee of Sadler's Wells Society, 435n; VHE enquires about lost string belt, 769; and Jack's illness, 797, 834

Huxley, Aldous, 110n; and Donald Main, 103n; signs joint letter to *Times*, 110–12, 121, 134, 162; TSE sends greetings to, 126; praises Pareto, 152, 162; contributes to *Time and Tide*, 161n; TSE corresponds with, 177; ALR attacks, 319–20, 349, 383; TSE's views on, 319–21; interest in spiritualism, 482, 490; on wars in Central America, 503; VHE sees at Mercury Theatre production of *MiC*, 847n; *Beyond the Mexique Bay*, 504n

Huxley, Sir Julian, 110n

Huxley, Maria, 376n; informs Mary Hutchinson about birth of Barbara Rothschild's daughter, 329; TSE invites to dine and attend *Sweeney Agonistes*, 376; at Dartington, 500; unable to keep engagement with TSE, 500n; sees Mercury Theatre production of *MiC*, 847n

Hyndman, Tony, 34n, 50

'Hysteria', 426n

Iddings Bell, Canon Bernard, 213n, 327, **346n**, 665, 700; 'The Decay of Intelligence in America', 346; 'Is Anglo-Catholicism Conquering?', 730–1

Idea of a Christian Society, 499n

'In Memoriam Marie Lloyd', 381n

'In Sincerity and Earnestness: New Britain As I See It', 272n

Inge, William Ralph, Dean of St Paul's, 174, 437n, 761

International Academy of Christian Sociologists, 83n

International Missionary Council, 665

International Students House, London, 398n

'Interpretation of Primitive Ritual, The', 550n

Iovetz-Tereshchenko, Nicholas Mikhailovich, **581n**, 613n, 640–1; *Friendship-Love in Adolescence*, 582n, 624, 625n

Iremonger, Revd F. A., **724n**, 741n

irony: TSE on functions of, 280n

Irvine, Lyn, 266

Irving, Sir Henry, 359n

Irving, Laurence, **359n**, 387, 404n, 511, 520, 526

Isaacs, Jack, 388n, 634n

Isherwood, Christopher, **524n**; collaborates with WHA in writing plays, 447n, 524, 642, 782n

Israel (ancient), 761–2

Italy: politics in, 179

Jacks, L. P., 244n, 363, 429

Jackson, Andrew, 618

Jacobs, Helen, 183n, 266

James & James (solicitors): sends accounts to TSE, 69, 413, 426, 468–9, 492; and TSE's dealings with VHE, 189; and TSE's income tax, 291, 484; TSE cancels power of attorney, 444; returns articles to VHE, 696; VHE protests to, 719

James, Alfred E., 14n, 216n, 251, 287, 705, 719

James, Francis, 722

James, Henry, 53, 54n, 218n, 310, 615n, 616n, 617–18, 619n; *The Altar of the Dead*, 618; *The Friends of the Friends*, 618; *The Ivory Tower* (unfinished), 746; *The Sense of the Past*, 106

Jameson, Storm, 95n

Janes, William Leonard, 188n, **189n**, 216, 322, 323n, 327n, 341n, 658n

Jefferson, Thomas, 20

Jennings, Humphrey, 58, 70n, 132–3, 163, 735n

Jennings, Richard, 40, 369n, 816n

Jessner, Leopold, 431n

Jews: TSE's attitude to, 155n, 635n, 641n

Jewsbury, Geraldine, 169

John of the Cross, St, 233

John, K.: 'The Grand Inquisitor', 76n

John Quill Ltd (agents), 289n

Johnson, Alvin, 284n

Johnson, Hewlett, Dean of Canterbury, 111, 123n, 134

Johnson, Jack, 739

Johnson, John, 375n

Johnson, R. J. G., **574n**

Johnson, Samuel, 825

Johnston, Denis: *The Moon in the Yellow River*, 329

475, 496, 510n, 523, 564n, 590, 782, 790, 842n, 847
Merril, Stuart, 52
Merriman, Roger Bigelow, 76
Mew, Charlotte, 607, 628
Migne, Jacques-Paul, 174
Miles, Hamish, 111, 121, 123n, 134
Miller, Alastair W. R., 325n; sends poems and play fragment to TSE, 325–6, 463; *The Man of Gingerbread*, 463n; 'Towards a Blessing', 605
Miller, Henry, 432n; writes on D. H. Lawrence, 432, 598, 662; *Black Spring*, 632n, 633, 663; *The Rosy Crucifixion*, 663n; *Tropic of Cancer*, 585, 598–9, 632, 662, 716n
Miller, John, 359n
Miller, Dr Reginald, 694n; attempts to call on VHE, 694–5; sends account for VHE's treatment, 796
Milne, A. A.: dispute with TSE on war and death, 476n, 477–80, 499, 503–4, 536, 749; anthologised, 606; *Peace with Honour*, 449n, 477n, 503n, 817n
Milner, Sir William, 291
Milton, John, 587
'Miner's Dream of Home, The' (song), 447
Mirfield: House of the Resurrection, 704
Mirrlees, Emily Lina (Moncrieff; 'Mappie'), 637n
Mirrlees, Hope, 355n, 368n, 401n, 483n, 490n, 527n, 662, 821n
Mirsky, Dmitri S., 51n, 793; reads WHA's *Orators*, 51
Mitchell, Sir Chalmers, 595
Mitrinovic, Dimitrije ('Mita'), 237, 379
Mockel, Albert, 347
'Modern Dilemma, The', 754n
Modern Monthly, 51–2
Moe, Henry Allen, 7n, 857n
Molesworth, Charles: *Marianne Moore: A Literary Life*, 8n
Molière (Jean Baptiste Poquelin), 575
Money in Industry, 739
Monologue, The (magazine), 66n
Monro, Alida (née Klementaski), 24n; visit to USA, 24–6, 76, 166; sells stock, 266; teetotalism, 477; takes tea with TSE and VW, 569n; and *For Your Delight* (anthology), 606–7, 628; supports Charlotte Mew, 607n; letter from HWE on *MiC*, 757; and payment for Harold's

published poems, 810, 814, 831–2
Monro, Harold: marriage to Alida, 24n; poems anthologised, 810, 830–2
Monro, Saw, Messrs, 17
Monroe, Harriet, 82n; declines EP's Canto 37, 72n, 82, 84, 157n
Montague, A. J., 435
Monteith, Charles, 606n
Montespan, Françoise Athénaïs, Marquise de, 576n
Moore, Henry, 67n
Moore, Marianne, 896; reviews EP's *Cantos*, 7; TSE proposes publishing selected poems, 8, 54, 56, 78, 81, 122, 151, 166–7, 204; TSE introduces Alida Monro to, 25; FVM meets in New York, 78, 122, 151; refuses to review William Carlos Williams, 97; meets EP, 121; requests TSE write Preface to *Selected Poems*, 151, 204n; sends poems to TSE, 151; reviews William Carlos Williams's poems, 194; TSE sends EP's poems to, 204; TSE writes introduction to, 256–7, 332, 464; TSE discusses with EP, 281; TSE sends proofs to, 332; thanks TSE for comments on poetry, 362n; reviewed by Hawkins, 551, 557; TSE publishes, 587; enquires about order of poems, 714; sends money to TSE, 772–3; reviews Wallace Stevens, 773; in *Faber Book of Modern Verse*, 831; payments for poems, 844n; TSE praises intelligence, 878; *Collected Poems* (1951), 248n; *Complete Poems* (1967), 248n; *Observations*, 78; *Poems* (1921), 249n; *Selected Poems*, 151n, 244, 247–50, 256
Moore, Merrill, 738n
Moore, T. Sturge, 253n, 277n
More, Leonard P.: and Mary Butts, 865
More, Paul Elmer, 896–8; on *The Waste Land* and *Ash Wednesday*, 144n, 145; praises *After Strange Gods*, 244; George Every reviews, 500; and D'Arcy's trip to America, 514; asked to review Temple's *Gifford Lectures*, 553; TSE defends against Geoffrey Curtis's criticism, 707; TSE recommends F. T. Prince to, 747; on TSE's split personality, 759–61; *Anglicanism* (ed. with F. L. Cross), 106n 454; *The Greek Tradition*, 312; *The Sceptical Approach to Religion*, 247n, 417n

Morgan, Charles, 388n, **554n**
Morley, Christopher, **29n**
Morley, Donald, 200, 269n, 560n, 813n
Morley, Frank V., **898–9**; and publication
of Joyce's *Ulysses*, 11, 12n, 15; and
writing of EP's *Cantos*, 19n; visit to
USA, 29, 32, 55, 72, 76, 78, 113, 122;
reads Hyndman's work, 50; and WHA's
Orators, 51; on sale of TSE's collected
poems, 54n; reads Iovetz-Tereshchenko's
book, 61; and payment for EP's *Cantos*,
101; returns from USA, 127; and
publication of Pareto, 152n; on reprint of
SS's poems, 154n; and TSE's meeting with
BD, 161; and publication of Marianne
Moore's poems, 166n, 167; on David
Higham, 183n; TSE gives budgerigars to,
184; and proposed US publication of *The
Rock*, 213n; agrees to lunch with Earp,
217; TSE stays with in Lingfield, 234; and
Thorold's book on Hulme, 273; meets
Roosevelt, 282n; on Philip Jordan's story,
290n; and Marianne Moore's proofs, 292;
resets Crossword clues, 294n; admires
Saroyan, 299–300; favours J. W. Scott's
proposals for book on Homecraft system,
303; SS writes to on *Vienna* poem, 310n;
and F. S. Flint, 330; on Douglasite theory,
347; on Porpoise Press, 412n; declines
Wallace Stevens's *Harmonium*, 420;
declines Joseph Gordon Macleod's plays,
423n; expertise on gammel-ost, 457n;
and title of *MiC*, 526n, 571n; helps found
Society of Translators, 579; and *Faber
Book of Modern Verse*, 596; introduces
Crawley to F&F, 606n; discourages SS's
proposed book on Henry James, 615n; on
S. I. Hsiung's works, 638n; in Scotland,
642n; praises Henry Miller's *Tropic of
Cancer*, 663n; on production of *MiC* at
Canterbury, 669n; on Prokosch's move to
Chatto, 693n; changes arrangement for
TSE's visit, 704n; on difficulty in getting
biographical information from Neil
Gunn, 809; and TSE's *Collected Poems
1909–1936*, 863n, 880n; on TSE and Ada
Sheffield as children, 878n
Morley, Oliver: sends napkin ring to TSE,
423
Morrell, Lady Ottoline, **899–900**; views on
TSE, 80n, 81n, 131n, 814n, 821n; Doone
hopes for support from, 107; TSE visits,

131, 277n, 814, 821; on Hugh Walpole,
275n; meets and dislikes Emily Hale,
356n, 357n; introduces Ralph Hodgson
and TSE, 365n; attends performance of
Sweeney Agonistes, 376, 388n, 401n;
invites TSE and Emily Hale to visit,
388; helps in campaign to raise money
for George Barker, 395, 834, 850; likes
Barker's poems, 445; visit to India, 445;
visits VW, 828n; on TSE's appearance,
848n; and Keynes's view of George
Barker's poems, 866n
Morrell, Philip, 815n
Morrell, Roy, 246n
Morris, William: *The Hollow Land*, 467
Mortimer, Raymond, 401n
Morton, A. L., **820n**
Mosley, Sir Oswald, 45n, 46n, 84, 100,
128, 164n, 272n, 515, 565
Moynihan, Father, 455, 611
'Mr Eliot's Sunday Morning Service', 755
Muir, Edwin, **900–1**; reviews TSE's *After
Strange Gods*, 94, 104, 115, 246; signs
joint letter to *Times*, 111n, 121, 123n,
134; and George Barker's poems, 190;
introduces Broch to TSE, 284, 655; on
Broch's printing TSE's Joyce lecture,
315n; SS proposes as collaborator in
translating Hölderlin, 545n, 546, 567;
TSE gives testimonial for Edinburgh
University post, 659; and Djuna Barnes's
Nightwood, 811, 812n, 813n; 'Variations
on a Time Theme', 173
Mullard, Revd George, 243n
Müller, Reichsbischof Ludwig, 680, 787n
Mullin, Pat, 358
Murder in the Cathedral: Bishop Bell
proposes, 227n, 404n; chorus, 386n,
530n, 579, 670n, 790, 838; publication,
389–90; Irving and, 404–6; HWE on,
451–2, 757; costumes, 498n, 509, 511,
520, 525; Browne produces, 509, 511,
520–1, 526, 530, 541–3, 545n, 571,
578–9, 589–90, 612, 657n, 670n, 676,
701; Mercury Theatre production, 510,
797, 847n; title, 523, 526, 530n, 531,
538, 571–2, 579, 627; writing, 523, 532,
579, 700; Browne on presenting, 541–3,
589; Robert Speaight plays Becket in,
554n, 670n, 676n, 702n; and Group
Theatre, 590; acting edition, 612n;
performed at Canterbury, 650, 668–9,

675n, 676, 682–3; prospective London production, 656; reception, 656n, 668–9, 671–3, 680n, 682n, 689, 769n, 770n, 836n; VW dislikes, 673n, 827n; Bishop Bell supports, 700; Browne plays Fourth Tempter in, 702n, 782, 847n, 869n; broadcast version, 711, 713, 718, 724, 741, 869; WBY admires, 744n; Martin Turnell reviews, 769; TSE asks IAR for view on, 774; royalties, 833n; Mercury Theatre act as agency for, 842, 847; in USA, 876, 880n
Murray, Gilbert, 472n, 528n
Murry, John Middleton, 901–2; TSE disagrees with, 44; *William Blake*, 480–1
Mussolini, Benito, 46, 179
Mussorgsky, Modest: *Boris Godunov* (opera), 728
'Mysterious Mr Eliot, The' (BBC TV programme), 239n

Nashdom, Abbot of, 653n
National Book League, 683
Naughton, John: 'Arm in arm with a literary legend', 15n
Neill, A. S., 270n, 820n
Neilson, Francis, 700n
Neuburg, Kathleen, 372n; sends Dylan Thomas poems to TSE, 372
Neuburg, Victor, 372n
Neville (publicist), 233–4
Nevinson, Henry Wood, 368
New Adelphi (journal; earlier *Adelphi*), 13, 85, 229n
New Age (journal), 385
New Britain (magazine), 272, 380, 385
New Church Union, 406
New Democracy (New York magazine), 836n, 863
New Directions in Prose and Poetry (annual anthologies), 345n
New English Weekly, The: TSE's religious dispute with EP in, 91–3, 148, 173–4; TSE subscribes to, 96; TSE criticises theological ideas, 129–30; TSE replies to EP's review of *The Use of Poetry and the Use of Criticism*, 230–2; and Mitrinovic, 379–80; and Orage's death, 379–80, 385; Mairet edits, 424n, 489, 787; editorial committee, 440; TSE acts as adviser, 459; Heppenstall enquires about books sent to, 539n; and TSE's differences with Reckitt,

540–1; TSE praises, 620; TSE proposes Marianne Moore poem for, 714–15; TSE discards back numbers, 787; C. H. Norman writes in, 816–17, 828
New Republic (journal), 317
New Statesman (journal), 76, 224, 348, 421–2
New Verse (journal), 121, 173, 735n
New York: *MiC* production, 880n
New Yorker, The (magazine), 356
Newbolt, Sir Henry, 235n
Newman, Cardinal John Henry, 81n, 89, 171
Newton, Stella Mary, **671n**
Nicholson, Ivor: and Still's *The Endless Theme*, 871
Nickerson, Hoffman: 'War, Democracy and Peace', 680
Nicolson, Norman, 782n
Niebuhr, Reinhold: *Reflections on the End of an Era*, 264n
Nin, Anaïs, 432n
Noble, Mrs (biographer of Geraldine Jewsbury), 169
Noel-Buxton, Noel Edward, 1st Baron, 846n
Norman, C. H., 817, 828
Norman, Charles, 26n
Norman, Montagu, 162
Nott, Stanley, 530, 587, 664

Obey, André, 107n
Observer (newspaper), 148
O'Casey, Sean, 161n; *Within the Gates*, 74
O'Conor, Norreys Jephson: *Godes Peace and the Queenes*, 679
O'Dea, James: *The Subway Express*, 448n
Odle, John Elsden, 180, 379
O'Donovan, Brigid, 613n, 672n, 685n, 841, 842n, 870; 'The Love Song of T. S. Eliot's Secretary', 423n, 686n
Ogden, C. K., **523n**
Oldham, J. H. ('Joe'), 227n, 437n, 501n, 566, 665, **873n**
Oliphant, Laurence, 313
Oliver, F. S.: death, 219
Olivier, Laurence, 386n
Olshausen, George G., 663n
Olympia Press, 662n
O'Neill, Eugene, 43n, 77, 134
'On the Eve', 381n
Orage, A. R., **108n**; and EP's Cantos, 84;

Pottinger, David T., 485
Pound, Dorothy, 720
Pound, Ezra, 903–4; Harriet Monroe
declines Canto, 72n, 82, 157–8; reviews
and criticises TSE's *After Strange Gods* in
New English Weekly, 91–3, 104, 147–9,
173–5; and BD's letter to *The Times*, 95n;
political views, 100; on TSE's Virginian
lectures, 104; complains to Orage of TSE,
109n; payments for, 122n, 596, 814; and
comparison of *Cantos* with *The Waste
Land*, 144; TSE publishes *Selected Poems*,
151; TSE suggests collected edition of
juvenilia, 172; on Basil Bunting, 194n;
TSE sends poems to Marianne Moore,
204; TSE requests title for essays, 214;
reviews TSE's *The Use of Poetry and
the Use of Criticism*, 230n; TSE's 1917
pamphlet on, 255; TSE praises as critic,
265n; TSE writes blurb for published
essays, 271n; supports Douglasite
theory, 331n, 348; misspells Quincy,
338; knowledge of Chinese questioned,
362; Edith Sitwell on, 400; Noh plays,
423n, 630; TSE wishes to discuss wih
Mairet, 425; and *New English Weekly*,
429; and title of *IX Cantos*, 430; letter in
Criterion, 452; TSE writes introductions
for, 464; favours Basic English, 489;
believes libelled in caption to photograph,
513n; TSE warns against Mosley, 516n;
WHA dislikes poems, 546–7; Cantos
reviewed in *Criterion*, 551, 557; in
Faber Book of Modern Verse, 555n,
573n, 596, 630, 722; Hawkins criticises,
557n; SS praises Cantos, 567; protests
at fee for *Faber Book* inclusion, 573–4;
reviews Henry Miller's *Tropic of Cancer*,
585n, 598–9; H. M. Wade writes on,
653; edits Ideogramic series, 664; and
French poets, 722; and Symbolists,
734n; on education, 786; and Laughlin's
editorship of *New Democracy*, 836n;
ABC of Reading, 21n, 185n, 272;
'Canto 36', 475n; 'Debabelization and
Ogden', 489n; *A Draft of XXX Cantos*,
7n, 19n; 'Ecclesiastical History, or the
Work Always Falls on Papa', 232n;
Eleven New Cantos: XXXI–XLI, 19n;
'Hell', 39; *Homage to Sextus Propertius*,
18–19, 40, 49, 65, 72, 335, 587, 596;
Hugh Selwyn Mauberley, 418, 574n,

596; 'Ignite! Ignite!', 23, 63; 'In the
Wounds (Memoriam A. R. Orage)', 391n;
'Jefferson and/or Mussolini', 18, 20, 721,
738; 'Leaving out Economics', 585n;
Make It New, 19n, 237, 265n, 271,
345n, 346, 362, 588, 616n; *Personae*, 49;
'Portrait d'une Femme', 854; *Quia Pauper
Amavi*, 49, 55, 65; *Select Essays*, 65, 72,
84, 237, 786; *Selected Poems*, 247–8,
256; *Selected Prose 1909–1965*, 232n;
'A Study of French Poets', 52n
Pound, Homer Louis (Ezra's father), 588n,
713
Powell, Dilys (Mrs Payne), 131, 292, 815n,
821n
Powys, Llewellyn, 828
Practical Cats, 206n
Prayer Book: proposed Child's Companion
to, 444, 463
Praz, Mario, 904; enquires about
publication of TSE's Clark lectures, 670
Preston, Raymond, 239n
Price, Nancy, 675
Priestley, J. B., 95n
Prince, Frank Templeton, 533, **746n**;
'Epistle to a Patron', 746; 'Tshaka', 746
Principles of Modern Heresy, The, 645n
'Pro Fide' bookshop: proposed, 436–7
Prokosch, Frederic, **526n**; prints poems,
51n, 526–7, 546; TSE confesses ignorance
of, 546; submits poems to TSE, 605,
651n; published by Chatto, 672n, 692;
The Asiatics, 605n, 649, 692n, 851;
'Going Southward', 527n
Proudhon, Pierre Joseph, 585n
Pudney, John, 187n, **306n**, 481; 'Joseph'
(play), 306, 371; *Open the Sky*, 371
Purdon, Louie, 341n, 800n
Purohit Swami, Shri, 192, 292, 296n,
363n; *Stories of Indian Mysticism*, 364–5
Purpose: A Quarterly Magazine, 558, 835
Purtcher-Wydenbruck, Countess Nora, 46n
Pushkin, Alexander Sergeyevich, 743–4
Putnam's (US publishers), 863

Quadragesimo Anno, 175
Queen Charlotte Hospital rebuilding fund,
591
Quennell, Peter, 798, 830, 832

Racine, Jean, 280, 587, 598, 618, 826n
Radcliffe, Philip, **654n**

Radcliffe (publisher), 122
Radio Times: photograph of 'Uncle Tom', 467n
Raeburn, Henzie *see* Browne, Henzie
Rahere (d. 1144), 62
Raine, Kathleen, 726n
Raleigh, Lucy, Lady, **665n**, 666n, 6570n
Rambert, Marie, 782
Ramsay, Michael: *The Gospel and the Catholic Church*, 823n
Randall, (Sir) Alec W. G., **105n**, 485n
Random House (publishers), 317, 534
'Rannoch, by Glencoe', 775n, 836n, 863
Ransom, John Crowe, 698n, 738n
Rapallo, 588
Ray, Cyril, **402n**, 570
Ray, Man, **513n**, 842n
Raymond, Harold, **683n**
Raynes Park School, Surrey, 158n
Read, Bill, 343n
Read, Herbert, **905–6**; TSE asks for help in selecting poems, 67–8; on *After Strange Gods*, 70–1; drafts and signs joint letter to *Times*, 111, 121, 123n, 134; proposed to read Brandler's *Hoere Israel*, 119n; on George Barker's poems, 150, 190; TSE gives address to Thorold, 171; Horace Gregory meets, 253n; dress, 263; reviews Wildman's translation of Cocteau, 316n; unacqainted with T. E. Hulme, 355; Häusermann asks about authorship of 'On the Eve', 381n; Edith Sitwell accused of copying, 422n; TSE sends Frank Prince poem to, 533; reviewed in *Criterion*, 551; and Coia's caricature of TSE, 626; admires *Tropic of Cancer*, 663; Hayward entertains, 666n; in *Faber Book of Modern Verse*, 687–8, 698; edits *Burlington Magazine*, 717; Miller wishes to meet, 717n; TSE's relations with, 802n; TSE refers P. Mansell Jones to, 864; *End of the War*, 91; *Essential Communism*, 712; *Poems*, 306
Read, Ludo (Mrs Herbert Read), 666n
Real Presence (in sacrament), 455, 472–3
Reckitt, Maurice, 83, 98, **309n**, 407, 424n, 501, 540–1, 565, 654, 788n
Red Shoes, The (film), 496n, 782n
Redfern, Revd Lawrence, 244n
Redgrave, Michael, 649n
Reed, Revd D. V., 44n
Rees, Dr J. R., 613, 641

Rees, Sir Richard: edits *Adelphi*, 85
Reeves, J. M., 794
Régnier, Henri de, 52
'Religion without Humanism', 212n
'Religious Drama and the Church', 159n, 351n
REP (magazine), 158, 159n, 197n, 351, 700n
Rhondda, Margaret Haig Thomas, Viscountess, 161n, 503, 504n
Rice, Elmer, 876, 880
Rice, Virginia, 304–5
Richards, Audrey, 720
Richards, Dorothy (née Pilley), **41n**; entertains TSE, 86, 830; on TSE's speaking of verse, 195n; TSE praises book, 667; scarlet fever, 773n; *Climbing Days*, 627, 667n
Richards, I. A., **906**; marriage to Dorothy, 41n; helps Jennings find museum job, 68–9, 70; opinion of Bottrall, 69, 74; signs joint letter to *Times*, 111n, 121, 123, 123n, 134; recommends Jennings's book on Gray, 163n; theory of values, 221n; TSE recommends Manning to, 224; EP alludes to, 231n, 232, 440; reviews Snyder's book on Coleridge's *Treatise on Methods*, 280n; on *The Rock*, 280n; invites TSE to Pepys Feast, 523; and completion of *MiC*, 627; attends *MiC* at Canterbury, 669; HWE on, 760, 762; on pseudo-statements, 783; influence on TSE, 802n; TSE visits, 819–20; Allott criticises, 825; *Basic Rules of Reason*, 13; *Coleridge on Imagination*, 135, 163, 523; *Principles of Literary Criticism*, 760; *Science and Poetry*, 774, 783
Richmond, Bruce Lyttelton, 246, 522, **534n**, 792n, **906–7**
Ricketts, Charles, 226n
Rickword, Edgell, 698n, **859n**
Riding, Laura, 698n, 804n
Ridler, Anne, 556n, 686n, 782n
Rilke, Rainer Maria, 186n, 559
Rimbaud, Arthur, 722
Ritchie, Ken, 369n
ritual: and belief, 550
Roberts, Adam, 1889n
Roberts, Jack: *The wonderful adventures of Ludo: the little green duck*, 607n
Roberts, Michael, **907–8**; marriage to Janet Adam Smith, 168n, 533n; submits essay